CQ

2018
ALMANAC

115TH CONGRESS
2ND SESSION

VOLUME LXXIV

CQ Roll Call
1201 Pennsylvania Avenue, NW
Washington, D.C. 20004

A FiscalNote business

TABLE OF CONTENTS

CONGRESS
& ITS MEMBERS

Members of the 115th Congress, Second Session and

As of Dec. 10, 2018

REPRESENTATIVES
R 236, D 197
Vacancies: 2
(Florida 6, West Virginia 3)

— A —

Abraham, Ralph, R-La. (5)
Adams, Alma, D-N.C. (12)
Aderholt, Robert B., R-Ala. (4)
Aguilar, Pete, D-Calif. (31)
Allen, Rick W., R-Ga. (12)
Amash, Justin, R-Mich. (3)
Amodei, Mark, R-Nev. (2)
Arrington, Jodey C., R-Texas (19)

— B —

Babin, Brian, R-Texas (36)
Bacon, Don, R-Neb. (2)
Balderson, Troy, R-Ohio (12)
Banks, Jim, R-Ind. (3)
Barletta, Lou, R-Pa. (11)
Barr, Andy, R-Ky. (6)
Barragán, Nanette, D-Calif. (44)
Barton, Joe L., R-Texas (6)
Bass, Karen, D-Calif. (37)
Beatty, Joyce, D-Ohio (3)
Bera, Ami, D-Calif. (7)
Bergman, Jack, R-Mich. (1)
Beyer, Donald S. Jr., D-Va. (8)
Biggs, Andy, R-Ariz. (5)
Bilirakis, Gus, R-Fla. (12)
Bishop, Mike, R-Mich. (8)
Bishop, Rob, R-Utah (1)
Bishop, Sanford D. Jr., D-Ga. (2)
Black, Diane, R-Tenn. (6)
Blackburn, Marsha, R-Tenn. (7)
Blum, Rod, R-Iowa (1)
Blumenauer, Earl, D-Ore. (3)
Blunt Rochester, Lisa, D-Del. AL
Bonamici, Suzanne, D-Ore. (1)
Bost, Mike, R-Ill. (12)
Boyle, Brendan F., D-Pa. (13)
Brady, Kevin, R-Texas (8)
Brady, Robert A., D-Pa. (1)
Brat, Dave, R-Va. (7)
Brooks, Mo, R-Ala. (5)
Brooks, Susan W., R-Ind. (5)
Brown, Anthony G., D-Md. (4)
Brownley, Julia, D-Calif. (26)
Buchanan, Vern, R-Fla. (16)
Buck, Ken, R-Colo. (4)
Bucshon, Larry, R-Ind. (8)
Budd, Ted, R-N.C. (13)
Burgess, Michael C., R-Texas (26)
Bustos, Cheri, D-Ill. (17)
Butterfield, G.K., D-N.C. (1)
Byrne, Bradley, R-Ala. (1)

— C —

Calvert, Ken, R-Calif. (42)
Capuano, Michael E., D-Mass. (7)
Carbajal, Salud, D-Calif. (24)
Cárdenas, Tony, D-Calif. (29)
Carson, André, D-Ind. (7)
Carter, Earl L. "Buddy," R-Ga. (1)
Carter, John, R-Texas (31)
Cartwright, Matt, D-Pa. (17)
Castor, Kathy, D-Fla. (14)
Castro, Joaquin, D-Texas (20)
Chabot, Steve, R-Ohio (1)
Cheney, Liz, R-Wyo. AL
Chu, Judy, D-Calif. (27)
Cicilline, David, D-R.I. (1)
Clark, Katherine M., D-Mass. (5)
Clarke, Yvette D., D-N.Y. (9)
Clay, William Lacy, D-Mo. (1)
Cleaver, Emanuel II, D-Mo. (5)
Cloud, Michael, R-Texas (27)
Clyburn, James E., D-S.C. (6)
Coffman, Mike, R-Colo. (6)
Cohen, Steve, D-Tenn. (9)
Cole, Tom, R-Okla. (4)
Collins, Chris, R-N.Y. (27)
Collins, Doug, R-Ga. (9)
Comer, James R., R-Ky. (1)
Comstock, Barbara, R-Va. (10)
Conaway, K. Michael, R-Texas (11)
Connolly, Gerald E., D-Va. (11)
Cook, Paul, R-Calif. (8)

Cooper, Jim, D-Tenn. (5)
Correa, Lou, D-Calif. (46)
Costa, Jim, D-Calif. (16)
Costello, Ryan A., R-Pa. (6)
Courtney, Joe, D-Conn. (2)
Cramer, Kevin, R-N.D. AL
Crawford, Rick, R-Ark. (1)
Crist, Charlie, D-Fla. (13)
Crowley, Joseph, D-N.Y. (14)
Cuellar, Henry, D-Texas (28)
Culberson, John, R-Texas (7)
Cummings, Elijah E., D-Md. (7)
Curbelo, Carlos, R-Fla. (26)
Curtis, John, R-Utah (3)

— D —

Davidson, Warren, R-Ohio (8)
Davis, Danny K., D-Ill. (7)
Davis, Rodney, R-Ill. (13)
Davis, Susan A., D-Calif. (53)
DeFazio, Peter A., D-Ore. (4)
DeGette, Diana, D-Colo. (1)
Delaney, John, D-Md. (6)
DeLauro, Rosa, D-Conn. (3)
DelBene, Suzan, D-Wash. (1)
Demings, Val B., D-Fla. (10)
Denham, Jeff, R-Calif. (10)
DeSaulnier, Mark, D-Calif. (11)
DesJarlais, Scott, R-Tenn. (4)
Deutch, Ted, D-Fla. (22)
Diaz-Balart, Mario, R-Fla. (25)
Dingell, Debbie, D-Mich. (12)
Doggett, Lloyd, D-Texas (35)
Donovan, Dan, R-N.Y. (11)
Doyle, Mike, D-Pa. (14)
Duffy, Sean P., R-Wis. (7)
Duncan, Jeff, R-S.C. (3)
Duncan, John J. Jr., R-Tenn. (2)
Dunn, Neal, R-Fla. (2)

— E, F —

Ellison, Keith, D-Minn. (5)
Emmer, Tom, R-Minn. (6)
Engel, Eliot L., D-N.Y. (16)
Eshoo, Anna G., D-Calif. (18)
Espaillat, Adriano, D-N.Y. (13)
Estes, Ron, R-Kan. (4)
Esty, Elizabeth, D-Conn. (5)
Evans, Dwight, D-Pa. (2)
Faso, John J., R-N.Y. (19)
Ferguson, Drew, R-Ga. (3)
Fitzpatrick, Brian, R-Pa. (8)
Fleischmann, Chuck, R-Tenn. (3)
Flores, Bill, R-Texas (17)
Fortenberry, Jeff, R-Neb. (1)
Foster, Bill, D-Ill. (11)
Foxx, Virginia, R-N.C. (5)
Frankel, Lois, D-Fla. (21)
Frelinghuysen, Rodney, R-N.J. (11)
Fudge, Marcia L., D-Ohio (11)

— G —

Gabbard, Tulsi, D-Hawaii (2)
Gaetz, Matt, R-Fla. (1)
Gallagher, Mike, R-Wis. (8)
Gallego, Ruben, D-Ariz. (7)
Garamendi, John, D-Calif. (3)
Garrett, Tom, R-Va. (5)
Gianforte, Greg, R-Mont. AL
Gibbs, Bob, R-Ohio (7)
Gohmert, Louie, R-Texas (1)
Gomez, Jimmy, D-Calif. (34)
Gonzalez, Vicente, D-Texas (15)
Goodlatte, Robert W., R-Va. (6)
Gosar, Paul, R-Ariz. (4)
Gottheimer, Josh, D-N.J. (5)
Gowdy, Trey, R-S.C. (4)
Granger, Kay, R-Texas (12)
Graves, Garret, R-La. (6)
Graves, Sam, R-Mo. (6)
Graves, Tom, R-Ga. (14)
Green, Al, D-Texas (9)
Green, Gene, D-Texas (29)
Griffith, Morgan, R-Va. (9)
Grijalva, Raúl M., D-Ariz. (3)
Grothman, Glenn, R-Wis. (6)
Guthrie, Brett, R-Ky. (2)
Gutiérrez, Luis V., D-Ill. (4)

— H —

Hanabusa, Colleen, D-Hawaii (1)
Handel, Karen, R-Ga. (6)
Harper, Gregg, R-Miss. (3)
Harris, Andy, R-Md. (1)
Hartzler, Vicky, R-Mo. (4)
Hastings, Alcee L., D-Fla. (20)
Heck, Denny, D-Wash. (10)
Hensarling, Jeb, R-Texas (5)
Hern, Kevin, R-Okla. (1)
Herrera Beutler, Jaime, R-Wash. (3)
Hice, Jody B., R-Ga. (10)
Higgins, Brian, D-N.Y. (26)
Higgins, Clay, R-La. (3)
Hill, French, R-Ark. (2)
Himes, Jim, D-Conn. (4)
Holding, George, R-N.C. (2)
Hollingsworth, Trey, R-Ind. (9)
Hoyer, Steny H., D-Md. (5)
Hudson, Richard, R-N.C. (8)
Huffman, Jared, D-Calif. (2)
Huizenga, Bill, R-Mich. (2)
Hultgren, Randy, R-Ill. (14)
Hunter, Duncan, R-Calif. (50)
Hurd, Will, R-Texas (23)

— I, J —

Issa, Darrell, R-Calif. (49)
Jackson Lee, Sheila, D-Texas (18)
Jayapal, Pramila, D-Wash. (7)
Jeffries, Hakeem, D-N.Y. (8)
Jenkins, Lynn, R-Kan. (2)
Johnson, Bill, R-Ohio (6)
Johnson, Eddie Bernice, D-Texas (30)
Johnson, Hank, D-Ga. (4)
Johnson, Mike, R-La. (4)
Johnson, Sam, R-Texas (3)
Jones, Brenda, D-Mich. (13)
Jones, Walter B., R-N.C. (3)
Jordan, Jim, R-Ohio (4)
Joyce, David, R-Ohio (14)

— K —

Kaptur, Marcy, D-Ohio (9)
Katko, John, R-N.Y. (24)
Keating, William, D-Mass. (9)
Kelly, Mike, R-Pa. (3)
Kelly, Robin, D-Ill. (2)
Kelly, Trent, R-Miss. (1)
Kennedy, Joseph P. III, D-Mass. (4)
Khanna, Ro, D-Calif. (17)
Kihuen, Ruben, D-Nev. (4)
Kildee, Dan, D-Mich. (5)
Kilmer, Derek, D-Wash. (6)
Kind, Ron, D-Wis. (3)
King, Peter T., R-N.Y. (2)
King, Steve, R-Iowa (4)
Kinzinger, Adam, R-Ill. (16)
Knight, Steve, R-Calif. (25)
Krishnamoorthi, Raja, D-Ill. (8)
Kuster, Ann McLane, D-N.H. (2)
Kustoff, David, R-Tenn. (8)

— L —

Labrador, Raúl R., R-Idaho (1)
LaHood, Darin, R-Ill (18)
LaMalfa, Doug, R-Calif. (1)
Lamb, Conor, D-Pa. (18)
Lamborn, Doug, R-Colo. (5)
Lance, Leonard, R-N.J. (7)
Langevin, Jim, D-R.I. (2)
Larsen, Rick, D-Wash. (2)
Larson, John B., D-Conn. (1)
Latta, Bob, R-Ohio (5)
Lawrence, Brenda, D-Mich. (14)
Lawson, Al, D-Fla. (5)
Lee, Barbara, D-Calif. (13)
Lesko, Debbie, R-Ariz. (8)
Levin, Sander M., D-Mich. (9)
Lewis, Jason, R-Minn. (2)
Lewis, John, D-Ga. (5)
Lieu, Ted, D-Calif. (33)
Lipinski, Daniel, D-Ill. (3)
LoBiondo, Frank A., R-N.J. (2)
Loebsack, Dave, D-Iowa (2)
Lofgren, Zoe, D-Calif. (19)
Long, Billy, R-Mo. (7)
Loudermilk, Barry, R-Ga. (11)
Love, Mia, R-Utah (4)
Lowenthal, Alan, D-Calif. (47)
Lowey, Nita M., D-N.Y. (17)
Lucas, Frank D., R-Okla. (3)
Luetkemeyer, Blaine, R-Mo. (3)

Luján, Ben Ray, D-N.M. (3)
Lujan Grisham, Michelle, D-N.M. (1)
Lynch, Stephen F., D-Mass. (8)

— M —

MacArthur, Tom, R-N.J. (3)
Maloney, Carolyn B., D-N.Y. (12)
Maloney, Sean Patrick, D-N.Y. (18)
Marchant, Kenny, R-Texas (24)
Marino, Tom, R-Pa. (10)
Marshall, Roger, R-Kan. (1)
Massie, Thomas, R-Ky. (4)
Mast, Brian, R-Fla. (18)
Matsui, Doris, D-Calif. (6)
McCarthy, Kevin, R-Calif. (23)
McCaul, Michael, R-Texas (10)
McClintock, Tom, R-Calif. (4)
McCollum, Betty, D-Minn. (4)
McEachin, A. Donald, D-Va. (4)
McGovern, Jim, D-Mass. (2)
McHenry, Patrick T., R-N.C. (10)
McKinley, David B., R-W.Va. (1)
McMorris Rodgers, Cathy, R-Wa. (5)
McNerney, Jerry, D-Calif. (9)
McSally, Martha, R-Ariz. (2)
Meadows, Mark, R-N.C. (11)
Meeks, Gregory W., D-N.Y. (5)
Meng, Grace, D-N.Y. (6)
Messer, Luke, R-Ind. (6)
Mitchell, Paul, R-Mich. (10)
Moolenaar, John, R-Mich. (4)
Mooney, Alex X., R-W.Va. (2)
Moore, Gwen, D-Wis. (4)
Morelle, Joseph D., D-N.Y. (25)
Moulton, Seth, D-Mass. (6)
Mullin, Markwayne, R-Okla. (2)
Murphy, Stephanie, D-Fla. (7)

— N, O —

Nadler, Jerrold, D-N.Y. (10)
Napolitano, Grace F., D-Calif. (32)
Neal, Richard E., D-Mass. (1)
Newhouse, Dan, R-Wash. (4)
Noem, Kristi, R-S.D. AL
Nolan, Rick, D-Minn. (8)
Norcross, Donald, D-N.J. (1)
Norman, Ralph, R-S.C. (5)
Nunes, Devin, R-Calif. (22)
O'Halleran, Tom, D-Ariz. (1)
O'Rourke, Beto, D-Texas (16)
Olson, Pete, R-Texas (22)

— P —

Palazzo, Steven M., R-Miss. (4)
Pallone, Frank Jr., D-N.J. (6)
Palmer, Gary, R-Ala. (6)
Panetta, Jimmy, D-Calif. (20)
Pascrell, Bill Jr., D-N.J. (9)
Paulsen, Erik, R-Minn. (3)
Payne, Donald M. Jr., D-N.J. (10)
Pearce, Steve, R-N.M. (2)
Pelosi, Nancy, D-Calif. (12)
Perlmutter, Ed, D-Colo. (7)
Perry, Scott, R-Pa. (4)
Peters, Scott, D-Calif. (52)
Peterson, Collin C., D-Minn. (7)
Pingree, Chellie, D-Maine (1)
Pittenger, Robert, R-N.C. (9)
Pocan, Mark, D-Wis. (2)
Poe, Ted, R-Texas (2)
Poliquin, Bruce, R-Maine (2)
Polis, Jared, D-Colo. (2)
Posey, Bill, R-Fla. (8)
Price, David E., D-N.C. (4)

— Q, R —

Quigley, Mike, D-Ill. (5)
Raskin, Jamie, D-Md. (8)
Ratcliffe, John, R-Texas (4)
Reed, Tom, R-N.Y. (23)
Reichert, Dave, R-Wash. (8)
Renacci, James B., R-Ohio (16)
Rice, Kathleen, D-N.Y. (4)
Rice, Tom, R-S.C. (7)
Richmond, Cedric L., D-La. (2)
Roby, Martha, R-Ala. (2)
Roe, Phil, R-Tenn. (1)
Rogers, Harold, R-Ky. (5)
Rogers, Mike D., R-Ala. (3)
Rohrabacher, Dana, R-Calif. (48)
Rokita, Todd, R-Ind. (4)

Governors, Supreme Court and Executive Branch

Rooney, Francis, R-Fla. (19)
Rooney, Tom, R-Fla. (17)
Rosen, Jacky, D-Nev. (3)
Ros-Lehtinen, Ileana, R-Fla. (27)
Roskam, Peter, R-Ill. (6)
Ross, Dennis A., R-Fla. (15)
Rothfus, Keith, R-Pa. (12)
Rouzer, David, R-N.C. (7)
Roybal-Allard, Lucille, D-Calif. (40)
Royce, Ed, R-Calif. (39)
Ruiz, Raul, D-Calif. (36)
Ruppersberger, C.A. Dutch, D-Md. (2)
Rush, Bobby L., D-Ill. (1)
Russell, Steve, R-Okla. (5)
Rutherford, John, R-Fla. (4)
Ryan, Paul D., R-Wis. (1)
Ryan, Tim, D-Ohio (13)

— S —

Sánchez, Linda T., D-Calif. (38)
Sanford, Mark, R-S.C. (1)
Sarbanes, John, D-Md. (3)
Scalise, Steve, R-La. (1)
Scanlon, Mary Gay, D-Pa. (7)
Schakowsky, Jan, D-Ill. (9)
Schiff, Adam B., D-Calif. (28)
Schneider, Brad, D-Ill. (10)
Schrader, Kurt, D-Ore. (5)
Schweikert, David, R-Ariz. (6)
Scott, Austin, R-Ga. (8)
Scott, David, D-Ga. (13)
Scott, Robert C., D-Va. (3)
Sensenbrenner, Jim, R-Wis. (5)
Serrano, José E., D-N.Y. (15)
Sessions, Pete, R-Texas (32)
Sewell, Terri A., D-Ala. (7)
Shea-Porter, Carol, D-N.H. (1)
Sherman, Brad, D-Calif. (30)
Shimkus, John, R-Ill. (15)
Shuster, Bill, R-Pa. (9)
Simpson, Mike, R-Idaho (2)
Sinema, Kyrsten, D-Ariz. (9)
Sires, Albio, D-N.J. (8)
Smith, Adam, D-Wash. (9)
Smith, Adrian, R-Neb. (3)
Smith, Christopher H., R-N.J. (4)
Smith, Jason, R-Mo. (8)
Smith, Lamar, R-Texas (21)
Smucker, Lloyd K., R-Pa. (16)
Soto, Darren, D-Fla. (9)
Speier, Jackie, D-Calif. (14)
Stefanik, Elise, R-N.Y. (21)
Stewart, Chris, R-Utah (2)
Stivers, Steve, R-Ohio (15)
Suozzi, Tom, D-N.Y. (3)
Swalwell, Eric, D-Calif. (15)

— T —

Takano, Mark, D-Calif. (41)
Taylor, Scott, R-Va. (2)
Tenney, Claudia, R-N.Y. (22)
Thompson, Bennie, D-Miss. (2)
Thompson, Glenn 'GT', R-Pa. (5)
Thompson, Mike, D-Calif. (5)
Thornberry, Mac, R-Texas (13)
Tipton, Scott, R-Colo. (3)
Titus, Dina, D-Nev. (1)
Tonko, Paul, D-N.Y. (20)
Torres, Norma J., D-Calif. (35)
Trott, Dave, R-Mich. (11)
Tsongas, Niki, D-Mass. (3)
Turner, Michael R., R-Ohio (10)

— U, V —

Upton, Fred, R-Mich. (6)
Valadao, David, R-Calif. (21)
Vargas, Juan C., D-Calif. (51)
Veasey, Marc, D-Texas (33)
Vela, Filemon, D-Texas (34)
Velázquez, Nydia M., D-N.Y. (7)
Visclosky, Peter J., D-Ind. (1)

— W —

Wagner, Ann, R-Mo. (2)
Walberg, Tim, R-Mich. (7)
Walden, Greg, R-Ore. (2)
Walker, Mark, R-N.C. (6)
Walorski, Jackie, R-Ind. (2)
Walters, Mimi, R-Calif. (45)
Walz, Tim, D-Minn. (1)
Wasserman Schultz, Debbie, D-Fla. (23)

Waters, Maxine, D-Calif. (43)
Watson Coleman, Bonnie, D-N.J. (12)
Weber, Randy, R-Texas (14)
Webster, Daniel, R-Fla. (11)
Welch, Peter, D-Vt. AL
Wenstrup, Brad, R-Ohio (2)
Westerman, Bruce, R-Ark. (4)
Wild, Susan, D-Pa. (15)
Williams, Roger, R-Texas (25)
Wilson, Frederica S., D-Fla. (24)
Wilson, Joe, R-S.C. (2)
Wittman, Rob, R-Va. (1)
Womack, Steve, R-Ark. (3)
Woodall, Rob, R-Ga. (7)

— X, Y, Z —

Yarmuth, John, D-Ky. (3)
Yoder, Kevin, R-Kan. (3)
Yoho, Ted, R-Fla. (3)
Young, David, R-Iowa (3)
Young, Don, R-Alaska AL
Zeldin, Lee, R-N.Y. (1)

DELEGATES
D 3, R 2, I 1

Bordallo, Madeleine Z., D-Guam
González-Colón, Jenniffer, R-P.R.
Norton, Eleanor Holmes, D-D.C.
Plaskett, Stacey, D-V.I.
Radewagen, Aumua Amata Coleman, R-A.S.
Sablan, Gregorio Kilili Camacho, I-N. Marianas

SENATORS
R 51, D 47, I 2

Alexander, Lamar, R-Tenn.
Baldwin, Tammy, D-Wis.
Barrasso, John, R-Wyo.
Bennet, Michael, D-Colo.
Blumenthal, Richard, D-Conn.
Blunt, Roy, R-Mo.
Booker, Cory, D-N.J.
Boozman, John, R-Ark.
Brown, Sherrod, D-Ohio
Burr, Richard M., R-N.C.
Cantwell, Maria, D-Wash.
Capito, Shelley Moore, R-W.Va.
Cardin, Benjamin L., D-Md.
Carper, Thomas R., D-Del.
Casey, Bob, D-Pa.
Cassidy, Bill, R-La.
Collins, Susan, R-Maine
Coons, Chris, D-Del.
Corker, Bob, R-Tenn.
Cornyn, John, R-Texas
Cortez Masto, Catherine, D-Nev.
Cotton, Tom, R-Ark.
Crapo, Michael D., R-Idaho
Cruz, Ted, R-Texas
Daines, Steve, R-Mont.
Donnelly, Joe, D-Ind.
Duckworth, Tammy, D-Ill.
Durbin, Richard J., D-Ill.
Enzi, Michael B., R-Wyo.
Ernst, Joni, R-Iowa
Feinstein, Dianne, D-Calif.
Fischer, Deb, R-Neb.
Flake, Jeff, R-Ariz.
Gardner, Cory, R-Colo.
Gillibrand, Kirsten, D-N.Y.
Graham, Lindsey, R-S.C.
Grassley, Charles E., R-Iowa
Harris, Kamala, D-Calif.
Hassan, Maggie, D-N.H.
Hatch, Orrin G., R-Utah
Heinrich, Martin, D-N.M.
Heitkamp, Heidi, D-N.D.
Heller, Dean, R-Nev.
Hirono, Mazie K., D-Hawaii
Hoeven, John, R-N.D.
Hyde-Smith, Cindy, R-Miss.
Inhofe, James M., R-Okla.
Isakson, Johnny, R-Ga.
Johnson, Ron, R-Wis.
Jones, Doug, D-Ala.
Kaine, Tim, D-Va.
Kennedy, John, R-La.
King, Angus, I-Maine
Klobuchar, Amy, D-Minn.

Kyl, Jon, R-Ariz.
Lankford, James, R-Okla.
Leahy, Patrick J., D-Vt.
Lee, Mike, R-Utah
Manchin, Joe III, D-W.Va.
Markey, Edward J., D-Mass.
McCaskill, Claire, D-Mo.
McConnell, Mitch, R-Ky.
Menendez, Robert, D-N.J.
Merkley, Jeff, D-Ore.
Moran, Jerry, R-Kan.
Murkowski, Lisa, R-Alaska
Murphy, Christopher S., D-Conn.
Murray, Patty, D-Wash.
Nelson, Bill, D-Fla.
Paul, Rand, R-Ky.
Perdue, David, R-Ga.
Peters, Gary, D-Mich.
Portman, Rob, R-Ohio
Reed, Jack, D-R.I.
Risch, Jim, R-Idaho
Roberts, Pat, R-Kan.
Rounds, Mike, R-S.D.
Rubio, Marco, R-Fla.
Sanders, Bernie, I-Vt.
Sasse, Ben, R-Neb.
Schatz, Brian, D-Hawaii
Schumer, Charles E., D-N.Y.
Scott, Tim, R-S.C.
Shaheen, Jeanne, D-N.H.
Shelby, Richard C., R-Ala.
Smith, Tina, D-Minn.
Stabenow, Debbie, D-Mich.
Sullivan, Dan, R-Alaska
Tester, Jon, D-Mont.
Thune, John, R-S.D.
Tillis, Thom, R-N.C.
Toomey, Patrick J., R-Pa.
Udall, Tom, D-N.M.
Van Hollen, Chris, D-Md.
Warner, Mark, D-Va.
Warren, Elizabeth, D-Mass.
Whitehouse, Sheldon, D-R.I.
Wicker, Roger, R-Miss.
Wyden, Ron, D-Ore.
Young, Todd, R-Ind.

GOVERNORS
R 33, D 16, I 1

Ala. — Kay Ivey, R
Alaska — Bill Walker, I
Ariz. — Doug Ducey, R
Ark. — Asa Hutchinson, R
Calif. — Jerry Brown, D
Colo. — John W. Hickenlooper, D
Conn. — Dannel P. Malloy, D
Del. — John Carney, D
Fla. — Rick Scott, R
Ga. — Nathan Deal, R
Hawaii — David Ige, D
Idaho — C.L. "Butch" Otter, R
Ill. — Bruce Rauner, R
Ind. — Eric Holcomb, R
Iowa — Kim Reynolds, R
Kan. — Jeff Colyer, R
Ky. — Matt Bevin, R
La. — John Bel Edwards, D
Maine — Paul R. LePage, R
Md. — Larry Hogan, R
Mass. — Charlie Baker, R
Mich. — Rick Snyder, R
Minn. — Mark Dayton, D
Miss. — Phil Bryant, R
Mo. — Michael L. Parson, R
Mont. — Steve Bullock, D
Neb. — Pete Ricketts, R
Nev. — Brian Sandoval, R
N.H. — Chris Sununu, R
N.J. — Phil Murphy, D
N.M. — Susana Martinez, R
N.Y. — Andrew M. Cuomo, D
N.C. — Roy Cooper, D
N.D. — Doug Burgum, R
Ohio — John R. Kasich, R
Okla. — Mary Fallin, R
Ore. — Kate Brown, D
Pa. — Tom Wolf, D
R.I. — Gina Raimondo, D
S.C. — Henry McMaster, R
S.D. — Dennis Daugaard, R
Tenn. — Bill Haslam, R
Texas — Greg Abbott, R

Utah — Gary R. Herbert, R
Vt. — Phil Scott, R
Va. — Ralph S. Northam, D
Wash. — Jay Inslee, D
W.Va. — Jim Justice, R
Wis. — Scott Walker, R
Wyo. — Matt Mead, R

SUPREME COURT

John G. Roberts Jr. — Md., Chief Justice
Samuel A. Alito Jr. — N.J.
Stephen G. Breyer — Mass.
Ruth Bader Ginsburg — N.Y.
Neil M. Gorsuch — Colo,
Elena Kagan — N.Y.
Brett M. Kavanaugh — Md.
Sonia Sotomayor — N.Y.
Clarence Thomas — Ga.

EXECUTIVE BRANCH

President — Donald Trump
Vice President — Mike Pence

DEPARTMENT SECRETARIES

Agriculture
  Sonny Perdue
Attorney General
  Matthew Whitaker (Acting)
Commerce
  Wilbur Ross
Defense
  James Mattis
Education
  Betsy DeVos
Energy
  Rick Perry
Health and Human Services
  Alex Azar
Homeland Security
  Kirstjen Nielsen
Housing and Urban Development
  Ben Carson
Interior
  Ryan Zinke
Labor
  Alexander Acosta
State
  Mike Pompeo
Transportation
  Elaine Chao
Treasury
  Steven Mnuchin
Veterans Affairs
  Robert Wilkie

OTHER EXECUTIVE BRANCH OFFICERS

CIA Director
  Gina Haspel
Director of National Intelligence
  Dan Coats
Joint Chiefs of Staff Chairman
  Gen. Joseph F. Dunford Jr.
Office of Management and Budget Director
  Mick Mulvaney
U.S. Trade Representative
  Robert Lighthizer
EPA Administrator
  Andrew Wheeler (Acting)
U.N. Ambassador
  Nikki Haley
White House Chief of Staff
  John F. Kelly
Assistant to the President for National Security Affairs
  John Bolton
National Economic Council Director
  Larry Kudlow

Glossary of Congressional Terms

Act — The term for legislation once it has passed both chambers of Congress and has been signed by the president or passed over his veto, thus becoming law. Also used in parliamentary terminology for a bill that has been passed by one house and engrossed. (Also see engrossed bill.)

Adjournment sine die — Adjournment without a fixed day for reconvening; literally, "adjournment without a day." Usually used to connote the final adjournment of a session of Congress. A session can continue until noon Jan. 3 of the following year, when, under the 20th Amendment to the Constitution, it automatically terminates. Both chambers must agree to a concurrent resolution for either chamber to adjourn for more than three days.

Adjournment to a day certain — Adjournment under a motion or resolution that fixes the next time of meeting. Under the Constitution, neither chamber can adjourn for more than three days without the concurrence of the other. A session of Congress is not ended by adjournment to a day certain.

Amendment — A proposal by a member of Congress to alter the language, provisions or stipulations in a bill or in another amendment. An amendment usually is printed, debated and voted upon in the same manner as a bill.

Amendment in the nature of a substitute — Usually an amendment that seeks to replace the entire text of a bill by striking out everything after the enacting clause and inserting a new version of the bill. An amendment in the nature of a substitute can also refer to an amendment that replaces a large portion of the text of a bill.

Appeal — A member's challenge of a ruling or decision made by the presiding officer of the chamber. A senator can appeal to members of the Senate to override the decision. If carried by a majority vote, the appeal nullifies the presiding officer's ruling. In the House, the decision of the speaker traditionally has been final; seldom are there successful appeals to the members to reverse the speaker's stand. To appeal a ruling is considered an attack on the speaker.

Appropriations bill — A bill that gives legal authority to spend or obligate money from the Treasury. The Constitution disallows money to be drawn from the Treasury "but in Consequence of Appropriations made by Law."

By congressional custom, an appropriations bill originates in the House. It is not supposed to be considered by the full House or Senate until a related measure authorizing the spending is enacted. An appropriations bill grants the actual budget authority approved by the authorization bill, though not necessarily the full amount permissible under the authorization.

If the 12 regular appropriations bills are not enacted by the start of the fiscal year, Congress must pass a stopgap spending bill or the departments and agencies covered by the unfinished bills must shut down.

About half of all budget authority, notably that for Social Security and interest on the federal debt, does not require annual appropriations; those programs exist under permanent appropriations. (Also see authorization bill, budget authority, budget process and supplemental appropriations bill.)

Authorization bill — Basic, substantive legislation that establishes or continues the legal operation of a federal program or agency either indefinitely or for a specific period of time, or which sanctions a particular type of obligation or expenditure. Under the rules of both chambers, appropriations for a program or agency may not be considered until the program has been authorized, although this requirement is often waived. An authorization sets the maximum amount that may be appropriated to a program or agency, although sometimes it merely authorizes "such sums as may be necessary." (Also see backdoor spending authority.)

Backdoor spending authority — Budget authority provided in legislation outside the normal appropriations process. The most common forms of backdoor spending are borrowing authority, contract authority, entitlements and loan guarantees that commit the government to payments of principal and interest on loans made by banks or other private lenders. Loan guarantees result in actual outlays only when there is a default by the borrower.

In some cases, such as interest on the public debt, a permanent appropriation is provided that becomes available without further action by Congress.

Bills — Most legislative proposals before Congress are in the form of bills and are designated according to the chamber in which they originate — HR in the House of Representatives or S in the Senate — and by a number assigned in the order in which they are introduced during the two-year period of a congressional term.

"Public bills" address general questions and become public laws if they are cleared by Congress and signed by the president. "Private bills" deal with individual matters, such as claims against the government, immigration and naturalization cases, or land titles, and become private laws if cleared and signed. (Also see private bill, resolution.)

Bills introduced — In both the House and Senate, any number of members may join in introducing a single bill or resolution. The first member listed is the sponsor of the bill, and all subsequent members listed are co-sponsors.

Many bills are committee bills and are introduced under the name of the chairman of the committee or subcommittee. All appropriations bills fall into this category. A committee frequently holds hearings on a number of related bills and may agree to one of them or to an entirely new bill. (Also see clean bill.)

Bills referred — After a bill is introduced, it is referred to the committee or committees that have jurisdiction over the subject with which

the bill is concerned. Under the standing rules of the House and Senate, bills are referred by the speaker in the House and by the presiding officer in the Senate. In practice, the House and Senate parliamentarians act for these officials and refer the vast majority of bills. (Also see discharge a committee.)

Borrowing authority — Statutory authority that permits a federal agency to incur obligations and make payments for specified purposes with borrowed money.

Budget — The document sent to Congress by the president early each year estimating government revenue and expenditures for the ensuing fiscal year.

Budget Act — The common name for the Congressional Budget and Impoundment Control Act of 1974, which established the current budget process and created the Congressional Budget Office. The act also put limits on presidential authority to spend appropriated money. It has undergone several major revisions since 1974. (Also see budget process.)

Budget authority — Authority for federal agencies to enter into obligations that result in immediate or future outlays. The basic forms of budget authority are appropriations, contract authority and borrowing authority. Budget authority may be classified by (1) the period of availability (one-year, multiple-year or without a time limitation), (2) the timing of congressional action (current or permanent) or (3) the manner of determining the amount available (definite or indefinite). (Also see appropriations bill, outlays.)

Budget process — The annual budget process was created by the Congressional Budget and Impoundment Control Act of 1974, with a timetable that was modified in 1990. Under the law, the president must submit his proposed budget by the first Monday in February. Congress is supposed to complete an annual budget resolution by April 15, setting guidelines for congressional action on spending and tax measures. (Also see "cut-as-you-go" rules.)

Budget resolution — A concurrent resolution that is adopted by both chambers of Congress and sets a strict ceiling on discretionary budget authority, along with nonbinding recommendations about how the spending should be allocated. The budget resolution may also contain "reconciliation instructions" requiring authorizing and tax-writing committees to propose changes in existing law to meet deficit reduction goals. If more than one committee is involved, the Budget Committee in each chamber bundles those proposals, without change, into a reconciliation bill and sends it to the floor. The budget resolution is a congressional document and is not sent to the president. (Also see reconciliation.)

By request — A phrase used when a senator or representative introduces a bill at the request of an executive agency or private organization but does not necessarily endorse the legislation.

Calendar — An agenda or list of business awaiting possible action by each chamber. The House uses four legislative calendars. They are the Discharge, House, Private and Union calendars. (Also see individual calendar listings.)

In the Senate, all legislative matters reported from committee go on one calendar. They are listed there in the order in which committees report them or the Senate places them on the calendar, but they may be called up out of order by the majority leader, either by obtaining unanimous consent of the Senate or by a motion to call up a bill. The Senate also has one non-legislative calendar, which is used for treaties and nominations. (Also see Executive Calendar.)

Call of the calendar — Senate bills that are not brought up for debate by a motion, unanimous consent or a unanimous consent agreement are brought before the Senate for action when the calendar listing them is "called." Bills must be called in the order listed. Measures considered by this method usually are noncontroversial, and debate on the bill and any proposed amendments is limited to five minutes for each senator.

Chamber — The meeting place for the membership of either the House or the Senate; also the membership of the House or Senate meeting as such.

Chief administrative officer — An elected officer of the House who, under House rules, has operational and functional responsibility for matters assigned by the House Administration Committee. The office of the chief administrative officer was established under a 1995 change to House rules and replaced the office of director of non-legislative and financial services.

Clean bill — Frequently after a committee has finished a major revision of a bill, one of the committee members, usually the chairman, will assemble the changes and what is left of the original bill into a new measure and introduce it as a "clean bill." The revised measure, which is given a new number, is referred back to the committee, which reports it to the floor for consideration. This often is a time saver, as committee-recommended changes in a clean bill do not have to be considered and voted on by the chamber. Reporting a clean bill also protects committee amendments that could be subject to points of order concerning germaneness.

Clerk of the House — An officer of the House of Representatives who supervises its records and legislative business.

Cloture — The process by which a filibuster can be ended in the Senate other than by unanimous consent. A motion for cloture can apply to any measure before the Senate, including a proposal to change the chamber's rules. To end a filibuster, the cloture motion must obtain the votes of three-fifths of the entire Senate membership (60 if there are no vacancies), except when the filibuster is against a proposal to amend the standing rules of the Senate; then a two-thirds vote of senators present and voting is required.

Under a ruling by the president of the Senate in November 2013 that was upheld by a narrow voting majority of the chamber, the interpretation of the cloture rule was changed as applied to executive branch nominees subject to confirmation and to lower-court judges. Following the reinterpretation, cloture could be imposed on nominees (except for those named to the Supreme Court) by a simple majority vote. The rule was changed again in 2017 to include Supreme Court nominees.

The cloture request is put to a roll call vote one hour after the Senate meets on the second day following introduction of the motion. If approved, cloture limits each senator to one hour of debate. The bill or amendment in question comes to a final vote after 30 hours of consideration, including debate time and the time it takes to conduct roll calls, quorum calls and other procedural motions. (Also see filibuster.)

Committee — A division of the House or Senate that prepares legislation for action by the parent chamber or makes investigations as directed by the parent chamber.

There are several types of committees. Most standing committees are divided into subcommittees, which study legislation, hold hearings and report bills, with or without amendments, to the full committee. Only the full committee can report legislation for action by the House or Senate. (Also see standing, oversight, and select or special committees.)

Committee of the Whole — The working title of what is formally "The Committee of the Whole House [of Representatives] on the State of the Union." The membership is composed of all House members sitting as a committee. Any 100 members who are present on the floor of the chamber to consider legislation constitute a quorum of the committee.

Technically, the Committee of the Whole considers only bills directly or indirectly appropriating money, authorizing appropriations, or involving taxes or charges on the public. Because the Committee of the Whole need number only 100 representatives, a quorum is more readily attained and legislative business is expedited. Before 1971, members' positions were not individually recorded on votes taken in the Committee of the Whole. Periodically, delegates from the District of Columbia and several U.S. territories have been permitted to vote in the Committee of the Whole. A rules change adopted at the beginning of the 112th Congress, removed the permission for delegates to vote. (Also see delegate.)

When the full House resolves itself into the Committee of the Whole, it replaces the speaker with a "chairman." A measure is debated and amendments may be proposed, with votes on amendments as needed. (Also see five-minute rule.)

When the committee completes its work on the measure, it dissolves itself by "rising." The speaker returns, and the chairman of the Committee of the Whole reports to the House that the committee's work has been completed. At this time, members may demand a roll call vote on any amendment adopted in the Committee of the Whole. The final vote is on passage of the legislation.

Committee veto — A requirement added to a few statutes directing that certain policy directives by an executive department or agency be reviewed by certain congressional committees before they are implemented. Under common practice, the government department or agency and the committees involved are expected to reach a consensus before the directives are carried out.

Concurrent resolution — A concurrent resolution, designated H Con Res or S Con Res, must be adopted by both chambers to have effect, but it is not sent to the president for approval and, therefore, does not have the force of law. A concurrent resolution, for example, is used to fix the time for adjournment of a Congress. It is also used to express the sense of Congress on a foreign policy or domestic issue. The annual budget resolution is a concurrent resolution.

Conference — A meeting between designated representatives of the House and the Senate to reconcile differences between the two chambers on provisions of a bill. House conferees are appointed by the speaker; Senate conferees are appointed by the presiding officer of the Senate.

A majority of the conferees for each chamber must agree on a compromise, reflected in a "conference report," before the final bill can go back to both chambers for approval. When the conference report goes to the floor, it is difficult to amend. If it is not approved by both chambers, the bill may go back to conference under certain situations, or a new conference may be convened. Many rules and informal practices govern the conduct of conference committees.

Bills that are passed by both chambers do not have to be sent to conference. Either chamber may "concur" with the other's amendments, completing action on the legislation, or they may further amend the measure and send it back to the other chamber. Sometimes leaders of the committees of jurisdiction work out an informal compromise instead of having a formal conference. (Also see custody of the papers.)

Confirmations — (See nominations.)

Congressional Record — The daily printed account of proceedings in both the House and Senate chambers, showing substantially verbatim debate and statements and a record of floor action. Highlights of legislative and committee action are given in a Daily Digest section of the Record, and members are entitled to have their extraneous remarks printed in an appendix known as "Extension of Remarks." Members may edit and revise remarks made on the floor during debate.

The Congressional Record provides a way to distinguish remarks spoken on the floor of the House and Senate from undelivered speeches. In the Senate, all speeches, articles and other matter that members insert in the Record without actually reading them on the floor are set off by large black dots, or bullets. However, a loophole allows a member to avoid the bulleting if he or she delivers any portion of the speech in person. In the House, undelivered speeches and other material are printed in a distinctive typeface. The record is also available in electronic form. (Also see Journal.)

Congressional terms of office — Terms normally begin on Jan. 3 of the year following a general election. Terms are two years for representatives and six years for senators. Representatives elected in special elections are sworn in for the remainder of a term. Under most state laws, a person may be appointed to fill a Senate vacancy and serve until a successor is elected; the successor serves until the end of the term applying to the vacant seat.

Continuing resolution — Typically, but not always, a joint resolution, cleared by Congress and signed by the president, is used to

provide new budget authority for federal agencies and programs whose regular appropriations bills have not been enacted. Also known as CRs or continuing appropriations, continuing resolutions are used to keep agencies operating when, as often happens, Congress does not finish the regular appropriations process by the Oct. 1 start of a new fiscal year.

The CR usually specifies a maximum rate at which an agency may incur obligations, based on the rate of the prior year, the president's budget request, or an appropriations bill passed by either or both chambers of Congress but not yet enacted. A CR can be a short-term measure that finances programs temporarily until the regular appropriations bill is enacted, or it can carry spending for the balance of the fiscal year in lieu of regular appropriations bills.

Contract authority — Budget authority contained in an authorization bill that permits the federal government to enter into contracts or other obligations for future payments from money not yet appropriated by Congress. The assumption is that money will be provided in a subsequent appropriations act. (Also see budget authority.)

Correcting recorded votes — Rules prohibit members from changing their votes after the result has been announced. Occasionally, however, a member may announce hours, days or months after a vote has been taken that he or she was "incorrectly recorded." In the Senate, a request to change one's vote almost always receives unanimous consent, as long as it does not change the outcome. In the House, members are prohibited from changing votes if they were tallied by the electronic voting system.

Co-sponsor — (See bills introduced.)

Current services estimates — Estimated budget authority and outlays for federal programs and operations for the forthcoming fiscal year based on continuation of existing levels of service without policy changes but with adjustments for inflation and for demographic changes that affect programs. These estimates, accompanied by the underlying economic and policy assumptions upon which they are based, are transmitted by the president to Congress when the budget is submitted.

Custody of the papers — To reconcile differences between the House and Senate versions of a bill, a conference may be arranged. The chamber with "custody of the papers" — the engrossed bill, engrossed amendments, messages of transmittal — is the only body empowered to request the conference. By custom, the chamber that asks for a conference is the last to act on the conference report.

Custody of the papers sometimes is manipulated to ensure that a particular chamber acts either first or last on the conference report. (Also see conference.)

'Cut-as-you-go' rules — House rules for the 112th Congress made it out of order to consider any legislation, including conference reports, that has the net effect of increasing mandatory spending. The restriction applies to the current year and the following five years, as well as the current year and the following 10 years.

The previous rule, known as "pay as you go," made it out of order to consider legislation, including conference reports, that contained tax provisions or new or expanded entitlement spending that had the net effect of increasing the deficit or reducing the surplus.

Deferral — Executive branch action to defer, or delay, the spending of appropriated money. The 1974 Congressional Budget and Impoundment Control Act requires a special message from the president to Congress reporting a proposed deferral of spending. Deferrals may not extend beyond the end of the fiscal year in which the message is transmitted. A federal district court in 1986 struck down the president's authority to defer spending for policy reasons; the ruling was upheld by a federal appeals court in 1987. Congress can prohibit proposed deferrals by clearing a law doing so; most often, cancellations of proposed deferrals are included in appropriations bills. (Also see rescission.)

Delegate — A nonvoting official representing the District of Columbia, Guam, American Samoa, the U.S. Virgin Islands, the Northern Mariana Islands or Puerto Rico in the House. The first five serve two-year terms. Puerto Rico's nonvoting representative is known as a resident commissioner and serves a four-year term. Delegates may not vote in the full House but are permitted to vote in committees and can introduce and co-sponsor legislation. Periodically, delegates have been permitted to vote in the Committee of the Whole House, where some legislative business is conducted. That permission was eliminated by a House rules change at the beginning of the 112th Congress. (See also Committee of the Whole.)

Dilatory motion — A motion made for the purpose of killing time and preventing action on a bill or amendment. House rules outlaw dilatory motions, but enforcement is largely within the discretion of the speaker or chairman of the Committee of the Whole. The Senate does not have a rule barring dilatory motions except under cloture.

Discharge a committee — Occasionally, attempts are made to relieve a committee of jurisdiction over a bill that is before it. This is attempted more often in the House than in the Senate, and the procedure rarely is successful.

In the House, if a committee does not report a bill within 30 days after the measure is referred to it, any member may file a discharge motion. Once offered, the motion is treated as a petition needing the signatures of a majority of members (218 if there are no vacancies). After the required signatures have been obtained, there is a delay of seven days.

Afterward, on the second and fourth Mondays of each month, except during the last six days of a session, any member who has signed the petition must be recognized, if he or she so desires, to move that the committee be discharged. Debate on the motion to discharge is limited to 20 minutes. If the motion is approved, consideration of the bill becomes a matter of high privilege.

If a resolution to consider a bill is held up in the Rules Committee for more than seven legislative days, any member may enter a motion to discharge the committee. The motion is handled like any other discharge petition in the House. Occasionally, to expedite noncontroversial legislative business, a committee is discharged by unanimous

consent of the House, and a petition is not required. In 1993, the signatures on pending discharge petitions — previously kept secret — were made a matter of public record. (For Senate procedure, see discharge resolution.)

Discharge Calendar — The House calendar to which motions to discharge committees are referred when they have the required number of signatures (218) and are awaiting floor action. (Also see calendar.)

Discharge petition — (See discharge a committee.)

Discharge resolution — In the Senate, a special motion that any senator may introduce to relieve a committee from consideration of a bill before it. The resolution can be called up for Senate approval or disapproval in the same manner as any other Senate business. (For House procedure, see discharge a committee.)

Discretionary spending — Budget authority provided through appropriations bills in amounts determined annually by Congress. In recent years, Congress has established caps on discretionary spending that are enforced through points of order that must be waived to permit action to exceed the cap, or by automatic spending cuts called a sequester. (Also see mandatory spending, sequester.)

Direct spending — (See mandatory spending.)

Division of a question for voting — A practice that is more common in the Senate but also used in the House whereby a member may demand a division of an amendment or a motion for purposes of voting. When the amendment or motion lends itself to such a division, the individual parts are voted on separately.

Emergency spending — Spending that the president and Congress have designated as an emergency requirement. Emergency spending is not subject to limits on discretionary spending set in the budget resolution or to cut-as-you-go rules, which require offsets. The designation is intended for unanticipated items that are not included in the budget for a fiscal year, such as spending to respond to disasters. However, most of the appropriations for the wars in Iraq and Afghanistan have been designated as emergency spending or, more recently, as overseas contingency operations not subject to discretionary spending limits.

Enacting clause — Key phrase in bills beginning, "Be it enacted by the Senate and House of Representatives." A successful motion to strike it from legislation kills the measure.

Engrossed bill — The copy of a bill as passed by one chamber, with the text as amended by floor action and certified by the clerk of the House or the secretary of the Senate.

Enrolled bill — The final copy of a bill that has been passed in identical form by both chambers. It is certified by an officer of the chamber of origin (clerk of the House or secretary of the Senate) and then sent on for the signatures of the House speaker, the Senate president pro tempore and the president of the United States. An enrolled bill is printed on parchment.

Entitlement — A program that guarantees payments to anyone who meets the eligibility criteria set in law. Examples include Social Security, Medicare, Medicaid and food stamps. (Also see mandatory spending.)

Executive Calendar — A nonlegislative calendar in the Senate that lists presidential documents such as treaties and nominations. (Also see calendar.)

Executive document — A document, usually a treaty, sent to the Senate by the president for consideration or approval. Executive documents are referred to committee in the same manner as other measures. Unlike legislative documents, treaties do not die at the end of a Congress but remain "live" proposals until acted on by the Senate or withdrawn by the president.

Executive session — A meeting of a Senate or House committee (or occasionally of either chamber) that only its members may attend. Witnesses regularly appear at committee meetings in executive session — for example, Defense Department officials during presentations of classified defense information. Other members of Congress may be invited, but the public and news media are not allowed to attend.

Filibuster — A time-delaying tactic associated with the Senate and used by a minority in an effort to prevent a vote on a bill, amendment, motion or nomination that probably would prevail if voted upon directly. The most common method is to take advantage of the Senate's rules permitting unlimited debate, but other forms of parliamentary maneuvering may be used. The chamber can vote to invoke cloture to end a filibuster, but that generally requires a majority of 60 votes, and in some cases two-thirds of the chamber. In November 2013, the Senate reinterpreted its cloture rule as it applies to executive branch nominations and lower federal court judges (other than those for the Supreme Court). A simple majority was then all that was required to cut off debate on non-Supreme Court nominations and end a filibuster. In 2017, the Senate voted to apply this rule to Supreme Court nominations as well. (Also see cloture.) The stricter rules of the House make filibusters more difficult, but delaying tactics are employed occasionally through various procedural devices allowed by House rules.

Fiscal year — Financial operations of the government are carried out in a 12-month fiscal year, beginning Oct. 1 and ending Sept. 30. The fiscal year carries the date of the calendar year in which it ends. (From fiscal 1844 to fiscal 1976, the fiscal year began July 1 and ended the following June 30.)

Five-minute rule — A debate-limiting rule of the House that is invoked when the House sits as the Committee of the Whole. Under the rule, a member offering an amendment and a member opposing it are each allowed to speak for five minutes. Debate is then closed. In practice, amendments regularly are debated for more than 10 minutes, with members gaining the floor by offering pro forma amendments or obtaining unanimous consent to speak longer than five minutes. (Also see Committee of the Whole, hour rule, strike out the last word.)

Floor manager — A member who has the task of steering legislation through floor debate and amendment to a final vote in the House

or the Senate. Floor managers usually are chairmen or ranking members of the committee that reported the bill. Managers are responsible for apportioning the debate time granted to supporters of the bill. The ranking minority member of the committee normally apportions time for the minority party's participation in the debate.

Frank — A member's facsimile signature, which is used on envelopes in lieu of stamps for the member's official outgoing mail. The "franking privilege" is the right to send mail postage-free.

Germane — Pertaining to the subject matter of the measure at hand. All House amendments must be germane to the bill being considered. The Senate requires that amendments be germane when they are proposed to general appropriations bills or to bills being considered once cloture has been invoked or, frequently, when the Senate is proceeding under a unanimous consent agreement placing a time limit on consideration of a bill. The 1974 Budget Act also requires that amendments to concurrent budget resolutions be germane.

In the House, floor debate must be germane, and the first three hours of debate each day in the Senate must be germane to the pending business. (Also see cloture.)

Gramm-Rudman Deficit Reduction Act — (See sequester.)

Grandfather clause — A provision that exempts people or other entities already engaged in an activity from new rules or legislation affecting that activity.

Hearings — Committee sessions for taking testimony from witnesses. At hearings on legislation, witnesses usually include specialists, government officials, and spokesmen for individuals or entities affected by the bill or bills under study. Hearings related to special investigations bring forth a variety of witnesses. Committees sometimes use their subpoena power to summon reluctant witnesses. The public and news media may attend open hearings but are barred from closed, or "executive," hearings. The vast majority of hearings are open to the public. (Also see executive session.)

Hold-harmless clause — A provision added to legislation to ensure that recipients of federal money do not receive less in a future year than they did in the current year if a new formula for allocating money authorized in the legislation would result in a reduction to the recipients. This clause has been used most often to soften the impact of sudden reductions in federal grants.

Hopper — A box on the House clerk's desk into which members deposit bills and resolutions to introduce them.

Hour rule — A provision in the rules of the House that permits one hour of debate time for each member on amendments debated in the House of Representatives sitting as the House. Therefore, the House normally amends bills while sitting as the Committee of the Whole, where the five-minute rule on amendments operates.

House as in the Committee of the Whole — A procedure that can be used to expedite consideration of certain measures such as continuing resolutions and, when there is debate, private bills. The pro-

cedure can be invoked only with the unanimous consent of the House or a rule from the Rules Committee and has procedural elements of both the House sitting as the House of Representatives, such as the speaker presiding and the previous question motion being in order, and the House sitting as the Committee of the Whole, with the five-minute rule being in order. (Also see Committee of the Whole.)

House Calendar — A listing for action by the House of public bills and resolutions that do not directly or indirectly appropriate money or raise revenue. (Also see calendar.)

Immunity — The constitutional privilege of members of Congress to make verbal statements on the floor and in committee for which they cannot be sued or arrested for slander or libel. Also, freedom from arrest while traveling to or from sessions of Congress or on official business. Members in this status may be arrested only for treason, felonies or a breach of the peace, as defined by congressional manuals.

Joint committee — A committee composed of a specified number of members of both the House and Senate. A joint committee may be investigative or research-oriented, an example of the latter being the Joint Economic Committee. Others have housekeeping duties; examples include the joint committees on Printing and the Library of Congress. In 2011, Congress convened a Joint Select Committee on Deficit Reduction and charged it with proposing $1.2 trillion in budget savings. The committee did not agree on a plan, and it disbanded in November 2011.

Joint resolution — Like a bill, a joint resolution, designated H J Res or S J Res, requires the approval of both chambers and generally the signature of the president and has the force of law if approved. In most cases, there is no practical difference between a bill and a joint resolution. A joint resolution generally is used to address a limited matter such as a single appropriation.

Joint resolutions also are used to propose amendments to the Constitution. In that case, they require a two-thirds majority in both chambers. They do not require a presidential signature, but they must be ratified by three-fourths of the states to become a part of the Constitution. (Also see concurrent resolution, resolution.)

Journal — The official record of the proceedings of the House and Senate. The Journal records the actions taken in each chamber, but, unlike the Congressional Record, it does not include the substantially verbatim report of speeches, debates, statements and the like.

Law — An act of Congress that has been signed by the president or passed, over his veto, by Congress. Public bills, when signed, become public laws and are cited by the letters PL and a hyphenated number. The number before the hyphen corresponds to the Congress, and the one or more digits after the hyphen refer to the numerical sequence in which the president signed the bills during that Congress. Private bills, when signed, become private laws. (Also see bills, private bill.)

Legislative day — The "day" extending from the time either chamber meets after an adjournment until the time it next adjourns. Because the House normally adjourns from day to day, legislative days and calendar days usually coincide. But in the Senate, a legislative day

may, and frequently does, extend over several calendar days. (Also see recess.)

Line-item veto— Presidential authority to strike individual items from appropriations bills, which presidents since Ulysses S. Grant have sought. Congress gave the president a form of the power in 1996 (PL 104-130), but this "enhanced rescission authority" was struck down by the Supreme Court in 1998 as unconstitutional because it allowed the president to change laws on his own.

Loan guarantees — Loans to third parties for which the federal government guarantees the repayment of principal or interest, in whole or in part, to the lender in the event of default.

Lobby— A group seeking to influence the passage or defeat of legislation. Originally the term referred to people frequenting the lobbies or corridors of legislative chambers to speak to lawmakers.

The definition of a lobby and the activity of lobbying is a matter of differing interpretation. By some definitions, lobbying is limited to direct attempts to influence lawmakers through personal interviews and persuasion. Under other definitions, lobbying includes attempts at indirect, or grass-roots, influence, such as persuading members of a group to write or visit their district's representative and state's senators or attempting to create a climate of opinion favorable to a desired legislative goal.

The right to attempt to influence legislation is based on the First Amendment to the Constitution, which says Congress shall make no law abridging the right of the people "to petition the government for a redress of grievances."

Majority leader— The floor leader for the majority party in each chamber. In the Senate, in consultation with the minority leader, the majority leader directs the legislative schedule for the chamber. This person is also the party's spokesman and chief strategist. In the House, the majority leader is second to the speaker in the majority party's leadership and serves as the party's legislative strategist. (Also see speaker, whip.)

Mandatory spending — Budget authority and outlays often provided under laws other than appropriations acts, although some mandatory spending is provided by annual appropriations (as is all discretionary spending). Mandatory spending, also known as direct spending, covers entitlements and payment of interest on the public debt. (Also see discretionary spending, entitlement.)

Manual — The official handbook in each chamber prescribing in detail its organization, procedures and operations.

Marking up a bill — Going through the contents of a piece of legislation in committee or subcommittee to, for example, consider the provisions, act on amendments to provisions and proposed revisions to the language, and insert new sections and phraseology. If the bill is extensively amended, the committee's version may be introduced as a separate (or "clean") bill, with a new number, before being considered by the full House or Senate. (Also see clean bill.)

Minority leader— The floor leader for the minority party in each chamber.

Morning hour — The time set aside at the beginning of each legislative day for the consideration of regular, routine business. The "hour" is of indefinite duration in the House, where it is rarely used. In the Senate, it is the first two hours of a session following an adjournment, as distinguished from a recess. The morning hour can be terminated earlier if the morning business has been completed.

Business includes such matters as messages from the president, communications from the heads of departments, messages from the House, the presentation of petitions, reports of standing and select committees, and the introduction of bills and resolutions.

During the first hour of the morning hour in the Senate, no motion to proceed to the consideration of any bill on the calendar is in order except by unanimous consent. During the second hour, motions can be made but must be decided without debate. Senate committees may meet while the Senate conducts the morning hour.

Motion— In the House or Senate chamber, a request by a member to institute any one of a wide array of parliamentary actions. He or she "moves" for a certain procedure, such as the consideration of a measure. The precedence of motions, and whether they are debatable, is set forth in the House and Senate rules.

Nominations — Presidential appointments to office subject to Senate confirmation. Although most nominations win quick Senate approval, some are controversial and become the topic of hearings and debate. Sometimes senators object to appointees for patronage reasons — for example, when a nomination to a local federal job is made without consulting the senators of the state concerned. In some situations a senator may object that the nominee is "personally obnoxious" to him. Usually other senators join in blocking such appointments out of courtesy to their colleagues. In recent years, executive branch and judicial nominations have been blocked by filibusters. As a result, the Senate in November 2013 changed its interpretation of the cloture rule used to end filibusters. (Also see cloture, filibuster, senatorial courtesy.)

One-minute speeches — Addresses by House members at the beginning of a legislative day. The speeches may cover any subject but are limited to one minute's duration.

Outlays— Actual spending that flows from the liquidation of budget authority. Outlays associated with appropriations bills and other legislation are estimates of future spending made by the Congressional Budget Office and the White House's Office of Management and Budget. The CBO's estimates govern bills for the purpose of congressional floor debate, while the OMB's numbers govern when it comes to determining whether legislation exceeds spending caps.

Outlays in a given fiscal year may result from budget authority provided in the current year or in previous years. (Also see budget authority, budget process.)

Override a veto — If the president vetoes a bill and sends it back to Congress with his objections, Congress may try to override his veto

and enact the bill into law. Neither chamber is required to attempt to override a veto. The override of a veto requires a recorded vote with a two-thirds majority of those present and voting in each chamber. The question put to each chamber is: "Shall the bill pass, the objections of the president to the contrary notwithstanding?" (Also see pocket veto, veto.)

Oversight committee — A congressional committee or designated subcommittee that is charged with general oversight of one or more federal agencies' programs and activities. Usually, the oversight panel for a particular agency is also the authorizing committee for that agency's programs and operations.

Pair — A voluntary, informal arrangement that two lawmakers, usually on opposite sides of an issue, make on recorded votes. In many cases, the result is to subtract a vote from each side with no effect on the outcome.

Pairs are not authorized in the rules of either chamber, are not counted in tabulating the final result and have no official standing. However, paired members are identified in the Congressional Record, along with their positions on such votes, if known. A member who expects to be absent for a vote can pair with a member who plans to vote, with the latter agreeing to withhold his or her vote.

There are three types of pairs:

(1) A live pair involves a member who is present for a vote and another who is absent. The member in attendance votes and then withdraws the vote, announcing that he or she has a live pair with colleague "X" and stating how the two members would have voted, one in favor, the other opposed. A live pair may affect the outcome of a closely contested vote, since it subtracts one "yea" or one "nay" from the final tally. A live pair may cover one or several specific issues.

(2) A general pair, widely used in the House, does not entail any arrangement between two members and does not affect the vote. Members who expect to be absent notify the clerk that they wish to make a general pair. Each member then is paired with another desiring a pair, and their names are listed in the Congressional Record. The member may or may not be paired with another taking the opposite position, and no indication of how the members would have voted is given.

(3) A specific pair is similar to a general pair, except that the opposing stands of the two members are identified and printed in the Congressional Record.

Petition — A request or plea sent to one or both chambers from an organization or private citizens group seeking support for particular legislation or favorable consideration of a matter not yet receiving congressional attention. Petitions are referred to appropriate committees. In the House, a petition signed by a majority of members (218) can discharge a bill from a committee. (Also see discharge a committee.)

Pocket veto — The act of the president in withholding his approval of a bill after Congress has adjourned. When Congress is in session, a bill becomes law without the president's signature if he does not act upon it within 10 days, excluding Sundays, from the time he receives

it. But if Congress adjourns sine die within that 10-day period, the bill, if unsigned, will die even if the president does not formally veto it.

The Supreme Court in 1986 agreed to decide whether the president could pocket veto a bill during recesses and between sessions of the same Congress or only between Congresses. The justices in 1987 declared the case moot, however, because the bill in question was invalid once the case reached the court. The House has treated pocket vetoes between sessions as regular vetoes. (Also see adjournment sine die, veto.)

Point of order — An objection raised by a member that the chamber is departing from rules governing its conduct of business. The objector cites the rule violated, with the chairman sustaining his or her objection if correctly made. The chairman restores order by suspending proceedings of the chamber until it conforms to the prescribed "order of business."

Both chambers have procedures for overcoming a point of order, either by vote or — as is most common in the House — by including language in the rule for floor consideration that waives a point of order against a given bill. (Also see rules.)

President of the Senate — Under the Constitution, the vice president of the United States presides over the Senate. In his absence, the president pro tempore, or a senator designated by the president pro tempore, presides over the chamber.

President pro tempore — The chief officer of the Senate in the absence of the vice president — literally, but loosely, the president for a time. The president pro tempore is elected by his fellow senators. Recent practice has been to elect the senator of the majority party with the longest period of continuous service. The president pro tempore is third in the line of presidential succession, after the vice president and the speaker of the House.

Previous question — A motion for the previous question, when carried, has the effect of cutting off further debate, preventing the offering of further amendments and forcing a vote on the pending matter. In the House, a motion for the previous question is not permitted in the Committee of the Whole, unless a rule governing debate provides otherwise. The motion for the previous question is not in order in the Senate.

Printed amendment — Some House rules guarantee five minutes of floor debate in support and five minutes in opposition, and no other debate time, on amendments printed in the Congressional Record at least one day prior to the amendment's consideration in the Committee of the Whole.

In the Senate, while amendments may be submitted for printing, they have no parliamentary standing or status. An amendment submitted for printing in the Senate, however, may be called up by any senator.

Private bill — A bill dealing with individual matters, such as claims against the government, immigration or land titles. If two members officially object to consideration of a private bill that is before the

chamber, it is recommitted to committee. The backers still have recourse, however. The measure can be put into an omnibus claims bill — several private bills rolled into one. As with any bill, no part of an omnibus claims bill may be deleted without a vote. When the private bill goes back to the House floor in this form, it can be deleted from the omnibus bill only by majority vote.

Private Calendar — The House calendar for private bills. The Private Calendar must be called on the first Tuesday of each month, and the speaker may call it on the third Tuesday of each month, as well. (Also see calendar, private bill.)

Privileged questions — The order in which bills, motions and other legislative measures are considered on the floor of the Senate and House is governed by strict priorities. A motion to table, for instance, is more privileged than a motion to recommit. Thus, if a member moves to recommit a bill to committee for further consideration, another member can supersede the first action by moving to table it, and a vote will occur on the motion to table (or kill) before the motion to recommit. A motion to adjourn is considered "of the highest privilege" and must be considered before virtually any other motion.

Pro forma amendment — (See strike out the last word.)

Pro forma session — A meeting of the House and Senate during which no legislative business is conducted. The sessions are held to satisfy a provision of the Constitution that prohibits either chamber from adjourning for more than three days without the permission of the other chamber. When the House or Senate recesses or adjourns for more than three days, both chambers adopt concurrent resolutions providing for the recess or adjournment. Also, the Senate sometimes holds pro forma sessions during recess periods to prevent the president from making recess appointments.

Public laws — (See law.)

Questions of privilege — These are matters affecting members of Congress individually or collectively. Matters affecting the rights, safety, dignity and integrity of proceedings of the House or Senate as a whole are questions of privilege in both chambers.

Questions involving individual members are called questions of "personal privilege." A member rising to ask a question of personal privilege is given precedence over almost all other proceedings. For instance, if a member feels that he or she has been improperly impugned in comments by another member, he or she can immediately demand to be heard on the floor on a question of personal privilege. An annotation in the House rules points out that the privilege rests primarily on the Constitution, which gives members a conditional immunity from arrest and an unconditional freedom to speak in the House.

In 1993, the House changed its rules to allow the speaker to delay for two legislative days the floor consideration of a resolution raising a question of the privileges of the House unless it is offered by the majority leader or minority leader.

Quorum — The number of members whose presence is necessary for the transaction of business. In the Senate and House, it is a majority of the membership. In the Committee of the Whole, a quorum is 100. If a point of order is made that a quorum is not present, the only business that is in order is either a motion to adjourn or a motion to direct the sergeant at arms to request the attendance of absentees. In practice, however, both chambers conduct much of their business without a quorum present. (Also see Committee of the Whole.)

Quorum call — Procedures used in the House and Senate to establish that a quorum is present. In the House, quorum calls are usually conducted using the electronic voting system, and no roll call is recorded. In the Senate, quorum calls are usually conducted by calling the roll of senators. The House and Senate conduct annual quorum calls at the beginning of each session of Congress. The Senate also uses quorum calls when no senators are speaking on the floor.

Reading of bills — Traditional parliamentary procedure required bills to be read three times before they were passed. This custom is of little modern significance. Normally a bill is considered to have its first reading when it is introduced and printed, by title, in the Congressional Record. In the House, a bill's second reading comes when floor consideration begins. (The actual reading of a bill is most likely to occur at this point if at all.) The second reading in the Senate is supposed to occur on the legislative day after the measure is introduced, but before it is referred to committee. The third reading (again, usually by title) takes place when floor action has been completed on amendments.

Recess — A recess, as distinguished from adjournment, does not end a legislative day and, therefore, does not interrupt unfinished business. The House usually adjourns from day to day. The Senate often recesses, thus meeting on the same legislative day for several calendar days or even weeks at a time. The rules in each chamber set forth certain matters to be taken up and disposed of at the beginning of each legislative day.

Recognition — The power of recognition of a member is lodged in the speaker of the House and the presiding officer of the Senate. The presiding officer names the member to speak first when two or more members simultaneously request recognition. The order of recognition is governed by precedents and tradition for many situations. In the Senate, for instance, the majority leader has the right to be recognized first.

Recommit — A motion to return a bill or joint resolution to committee after the measure has been debated on the floor. In the House, the right to offer a motion to recommit is guaranteed to the minority leader or someone he or she designates, and there must be an opponent.

Under a 2009 House rules change, a motion to recommit with instructions must direct a committee to report the bill back "forthwith" — that is, immediately. Previously, the motion could include the term "promptly," which did not require that the bill be returned to the floor and instead required full committee action.

Reconciliation — The 1974 Budget Act created a reconciliation procedure for bringing existing tax and spending laws into conformity with ceilings set in the congressional budget resolution. Under the procedure, the budget resolution sets specific deficit reduction targets and instructs tax-writing and authorizing committees to propose changes in existing law to meet those targets. If more than one committee is

involved, the Budget committees consolidate the recommendations, without change, into an omnibus reconciliation bill, which then must be considered and approved by both chambers of Congress.

Special rules in the Senate limit debate on a reconciliation bill to 20 hours and bar extraneous or nongermane amendments. (Also see budget resolution, sequester.)

Reconsider a vote — Until it is disposed of, a motion to reconsider the vote by which an action was taken has the effect of putting the action in abeyance. In the Senate, the motion can be made only by a member who voted on the prevailing side of the original question or by a member who did not vote at all. In the House, it can be made only by a member on the prevailing side.

A common practice in the Senate after close votes on an issue is a motion to reconsider, followed by a motion to table the motion to reconsider. On this motion to table, senators vote as they voted on the original question, which allows the motion to table to prevail, assuming there are no switches. That closes the matter, and further motions to reconsider are not entertained.

In the House, as a routine precaution, a motion to reconsider usually is made every time a measure is passed. Such a motion almost always is tabled immediately, thus shutting off the possibility of future reconsideration except by unanimous consent.

Motions to reconsider must be entered in the Senate within the next two days the Senate is in session after the original vote has been taken. In the House, they must be entered either on the same day or the next succeeding day that the House is in session. Sometimes on a close vote, a member — in the Senate, often the majority leader — will switch his or her vote to be eligible to offer a motion to reconsider.

Recorded vote — A vote upon which each member's stand is individually made known. In the Senate, this is accomplished through a roll call of the entire membership, to which each senator on the floor must answer "yea," "nay" or "present." Since January 1973, the House has used an electronic voting system for recorded votes, including "yea" and "nay" votes formerly taken by a call of the roll.

When not required by the Constitution, a recorded vote can be obtained on questions in the House on the demand of one-fifth (44 members) of a quorum or one-fourth (25) of a quorum in the Committee of the Whole. Recorded votes are required in the House for appropriations, budget and tax bills. (Also see "yeas" and "nays.")

Report — Both a verb and a noun as a congressional term. A committee that has been examining a bill referred to it by the parent chamber "reports" its findings and recommendations to the chamber when it completes consideration and returns the measure. The process is called "reporting" a bill. In some cases, a bill is reported without a written report.

A "report" is the document setting forth the committee's explanation of its action. Senate and House reports are numbered separately and are designated S Rept or H Rept. When a committee report is not unanimous, the dissenting committee members may file a statement

of their views, called minority or dissenting views and referred to as a minority report. Members in disagreement with some provisions of a bill may file additional or supplementary views. Sometimes a bill or resolution is reported without a committee recommendation.

Legislative committees occasionally submit adverse reports. However, when a committee is opposed to a bill, it usually does not report the bill at all. Some laws require that committee reports — favorable or adverse — be filed.

Rescission — Cancellation of budget authority that was previously appropriated but has not yet been spent.

Resolution — A "simple" resolution, designated H Res or S Res, deals with matters entirely within the prerogatives of a single chamber. It requires neither adoption by the other chamber nor approval by the president, and it does not have the force of law. Most resolutions deal with the rules or procedures of one chamber. They are also used to express the sentiments of a single chamber, such as condolences to the family of a deceased member, or to comment on foreign policy or executive business. A simple resolution is the vehicle for a "rule" from the House Rules Committee. (Also see concurrent and joint resolutions, rules.)

Rider — An amendment, usually not germane, that its sponsor hopes to get through more easily by including it in other legislation. A rider becomes law if the bill to which it is attached is enacted. Amendments providing legislative directives in appropriations bills are examples of riders, although technically legislation is barred from appropriations bills.

The House, unlike the Senate, has a strict germaneness rule; thus, riders usually are Senate devices to get legislation enacted quickly or to bypass lengthy House consideration and, possibly, opposition.

Rules — Each chamber has a body of rules and precedents that govern the conduct of business. These rules deal with issues such as duties of officers, the order of business, admission to the floor, parliamentary procedures on handling amendments and voting, and jurisdictions of committees.

The House re-adopts its rules, usually with some changes, at the beginning of each Congress. Senate rules carry over from one Congress to the next.

In the House, a rule may also be a resolution reported by the Rules Committee to govern the handling of a particular bill on the floor. The committee may report a rule, also called a special order, in the form of a simple resolution. If the House adopts the resolution, the temporary rule becomes as valid as any standing rule and lapses only after action has been completed on the measure to which it pertains.

The rule sets the time limit on general debate. It also may waive points of order against provisions of the bill in question, such as nongermane language, or against certain amendments expected on the floor. It may even forbid all amendments or all amendments except those proposed by the legislative committee that handled the bill. In this instance, it is known as a "closed" rule, as opposed to an "open"

rule, which puts no limitation on floor amendments, thus leaving the bill open to alteration by the adoption of germane amendments. (Also see point of order.)

Secretary of the Senate — Chief administrative officer of the Senate, responsible for overseeing the duties of Senate employees, educating Senate pages, administering oaths, overseeing the registration of lobbyists and handling other tasks necessary for the continuing operation of the Senate. (Also see Clerk of the House.)

Select or special committee — A committee set up for a special purpose and, usually, for a limited time by resolution of either the House or Senate. Most special committees are investigative and lack legislative authority: Legislation is not referred to them, and they cannot report bills to their parent chambers. Each chamber has a Select Committee on Intelligence.

Senatorial courtesy — A general practice with no written rule — sometimes referred to as "the courtesy of the Senate" — applied to consideration of executive nominations. Generally, it means nominees from a state are not to be confirmed unless they have been approved by the senators of the president's party of that state, with other senators following their colleagues' lead in the attitude they take toward consideration of such nominations. (Also see nominations.)

Sequester — Automatic percentage spending cuts for all discretionary spending and some mandatory spending, with exceptions. Under the 1985 Gramm-Rudman anti-deficit law, modified in 1987, a year-end, across-the-board sequester was triggered if the deficit exceeded a preset maximum. The Budget Control Act of 2011 required a $1.2 billion sequester, spread equally over nine years, after a joint deficit reduction committee was unable to agree on savings. For fiscal 2014 and after, the sequester resulted in lower discretionary spending caps and a second across-the-board sequester to enforce those caps. In December 2013, the caps were adjusted higher and the sequester was extended beyond fiscal 2021 for certain spending.

Sine die — (See adjournment sine die.)

Speaker — The presiding officer of the House of Representatives, selected by the majority party's caucus and formally elected by the whole House. While both parties nominate candidates, choice by the majority party is tantamount to election. The speaker is second in the line of presidential succession, after the vice president.

Special session — A session of Congress after it has adjourned sine die, completing its regular session. Special sessions are convened by the president.

Spending authority — The 1974 Budget Act defines spending authority as borrowing authority, contract authority and entitlement authority for which budget authority is not provided in advance by appropriations acts.

Sponsor — (See bills introduced.)

Standing committees — Committees that are permanently established by House and Senate rules. The standing committees are

legislative committees: Legislation may be referred to them, and they may report bills and resolutions to their parent chambers.

Standing vote — A nonrecorded vote used in both the House and Senate. (A standing vote is also called a division vote.) Members in favor of a proposal stand and are counted by the presiding officer. Then members opposed stand and are counted. There is no record of how individual members voted.

Statutes at large — A chronological arrangement of the laws enacted in each session of Congress. Though indexed, the laws are not arranged by subject matter, and there is no indication of how they changed previously enacted laws. (Also see law, U.S. Code.)

Strike from the Record — A member of the House who is offended by remarks made on the House floor may move that the offending words be "taken down" for the speaker's cognizance and then expunged from the debate as published in the Congressional Record.

Strike out the last word — A motion whereby a House member is entitled to speak for five minutes on an amendment then being debated by the chamber. A member gains recognition from the chair by moving to "strike out the last word" of the amendment or section of the bill under consideration. The motion is pro forma, requires no vote and does not change the amendment being debated. (Also see five-minute rule.)

Substitute — A motion, amendment or entire bill introduced in place of the pending legislative business. Adoption of the substitute supplants the original text. The substitute may also be amended. (Also see amendment in the nature of a substitute.)

Supplemental appropriations bill — Legislation appropriating money after the regular annual appropriations bill for a federal department or agency has been enacted. In the past, supplemental appropriations bills often arrived about halfway through the fiscal year to pay for urgent needs, such as relief from natural disasters, that Congress and the president did not anticipate (or may not have wanted to finance).

Suspend the rules — A time-saving procedure for passing bills in the House. The wording of the motion, which may be made by any member recognized by the speaker, is "I move to suspend the rules and pass the bill." A favorable vote by two-thirds of those present is required for passage. Debate is limited to 40 minutes, and no amendments from the floor are permitted.

If a two-thirds favorable vote is not attained, the bill may be considered later under regular procedures. The suspension procedure is in order every Monday, Tuesday and Wednesday, and it is intended to be reserved for noncontroversial bills. It also may be used to concur in Senate amendments, adopt conference reports and agree to resolutions.

Table a bill — Motions to table, or to "lay on the table," are used to block or kill amendments or other parliamentary questions. When approved, a tabling motion is considered the final disposition of that issue. One of the most widely used parliamentary procedures, the motion to table is not debatable, and adoption requires a simple majority vote.

In the Senate, however, different language sometimes is used. The motion may be worded to let a bill "lie on the table," perhaps for subsequent "picking up." This motion is more flexible, keeping the bill pending for later action, if desired. Tabling motions on amendments are effective debate-ending devices in the Senate.

Treaties — Executive proposals — in the form of resolutions of ratification — that must be submitted to the Senate for approval by two-thirds of the senators present. Treaties are normally sent to the Foreign Relations Committee for scrutiny before the Senate takes action. Foreign Relations has jurisdiction over all treaties, regardless of the subject matter. Treaties are read three times and debated on the floor in much the same manner as legislative proposals. After approval by the Senate, treaties are formally ratified by the president.

Trust funds — Money collected and used by the federal government for carrying out specific purposes and programs according to terms of a trust agreement or statute such as the Social Security and unemployment compensation trust funds. Such funds are administered by the government in a fiduciary capacity and are not available for the general purposes of the government.

Unanimous consent — A procedure used to expedite floor action. Proceedings of the House or Senate and action on legislation often take place upon the unanimous consent of the chamber, whether or not a rule of the chamber is being violated. It is frequently used in a routine fashion, such as by a senator requesting the unanimous consent of the Senate to have specified members of his or her staff present on the floor during debate on a specific amendment. A single member's objection blocks a unanimous consent request.

Unanimous consent agreement — A device used in the Senate to expedite legislation. Much of the Senate's legislative business, dealing with both minor and controversial issues, is conducted through unanimous consent or unanimous consent agreements. On major legislation, such agreements usually are printed and transmitted to all senators before floor debate. Once agreed to, they are binding on all members unless the Senate, by unanimous consent, agrees to modify them. An agreement may list the order in which various bills are to be considered; specify the length of time for debate on bills and contested amendments and when they are to be voted upon; and, frequently, require that all amendments introduced be germane to the bill under consideration.

In this regard, unanimous consent agreements are similar to the "rules" issued by the House Rules Committee for bills pending in the House. The House rarely sets conditions for floor debate under unanimous consent.

Union Calendar — Bills that directly or indirectly appropriate money or raise revenue are placed on this House calendar according to the date they are reported from committee. (Also see calendar.)

U.S. Code — A consolidation and codification of the general and permanent laws of the United States arranged by subject under 50 titles, the first six dealing with general or political subjects, and the other 44 alphabetically arranged from agriculture to war. The U.S. Code is updated annually, and a new set of bound volumes is published

every six years. (Also see law, statutes at large.)

Veto — Disapproval by the president of a bill or joint resolution (other than one proposing an amendment to the Constitution). When Congress is in session, the president must veto a bill within 10 days, excluding Sundays, after he has received it; otherwise, it becomes law without his signature. When the president vetoes a bill, he returns it to the chamber of origin along with a message stating his objections. (Also see pocket veto, override a veto.)

Voice vote — In either the House or Senate, members answer "aye" or "no" in chorus, and the presiding officer decides the result. The term is also used loosely to indicate action by unanimous consent or without objection. (Also see "yeas" and "nays.")

Whip — In effect, the assistant majority or minority leader, in either the House or Senate. His or her job is to help marshal votes in support of party strategy and legislation.

Without objection — Used in lieu of a vote on noncontroversial motions, amendments or bills that may be passed in either chamber if no member voices an objection.

"Yeas" and "nays" — The Constitution requires that "yea" and "nay" votes be taken and recorded when requested by one-fifth of the members present. In the House, the speaker determines whether one-fifth of the members present requested a vote. In the Senate, practice requires only 11 members. The Constitution requires the yeas and nays on a veto override attempt. (Also see recorded vote.)

Yielding — When a member has been recognized to speak, no other member may speak unless he or she obtains permission from the member recognized. This permission is called yielding and usually is requested in the form, "Will the gentleman (or gentlelady) yield to me?" While this activity occasionally is seen in the Senate, the Senate has no rule or practice to parcel out time. In the House, the floor manager of a bill usually apportions debate time by yielding specific amounts of time to members who have requested it. ■

Vote Studies

Moderation Unrewarded

Centrists crossed the aisle more often in 2018, but voters still cast them out of office

By JONATHAN MILLER

After Democrats and Republicans reached record highs sticking together by party on congressional votes in 2017, those numbers nose-dived in 2018 as lawmakers worked across the aisle on high-profile legislation, including a rewrite of the Dodd-Frank financial law, a package dealing with the opioid crisis, spending bills and an overhaul of the country's criminal justice laws.

CQ's annual vote study shows that in the House the total number of party unity votes — defined as those with each party's majority on opposing sides — fell from 76 percent of the total votes taken in the House in 2017, a record, to 59 percent in 2018. That latter figure is the lowest since 2010, the most recent year of unified Democratic control of Congress. Election years typically have fewer votes and 2018 was no exception — the total number of votes taken in the House, 498, was the lowest since 2002.

In the Senate, the decline was even more dramatic — the total number of unity votes dropped 19 points from the year before — from 68.9 percent of all votes taken down to just under half of all votes — 49.6 percent. That marks the second-lowest figure since 2002.

Republican Sen. John Cornyn of Texas seemingly predicted such an occurrence. He told CQ last year that he thought 2018 would be different because "the margin is thinner, and thankfully there are a number of things we agree on." He noted a desire among lawmakers to work on overhauls to financial regulation and criminal justice, two big-ticket items that got signed into law in 2018 with bipartisan support.

Molly E. Reynolds, a fellow at the Brookings Institution, agrees, saying that in 2017, "We saw the Senate controlled by the Republicans using a lot of its agenda to pursue things on which they didn't need Democrats." These votes were generally in three distinct buckets: nominations, Congressional Review Act resolutions striking down Obama-era regulations, and the budget reconciliation process for a successful overhaul of the tax code and a failed attempt at repealing the Affordable Care Act. None of those votes were subject to the 60-vote filibuster threshold, and nearly all Republicans and Democrats held together on many of these votes, upping their unity scores.

In 2018, things changed, as is typical of unified congressional control in an election year, says Reynolds, as lawmakers seek to show voters they can govern. A host of must-pass bills needed bipartisan support to get through Congress, including a reauthorization of the Federal Aviation Administration, the farm bill and a water infrastructure bill.

"In year two we still see a fair amount of nomination-related votes, but there's many more things that the Senate was considering in the second year that it needed 60 votes to get done," she says.

Still, the 2018 election succeeded in wiping out a large swath of moderates on both sides of the aisle — those members who most often crossed their party on such votes — making it an open question just how much legislating will get done in the next two years.

The early results for 2019 suggest that unity scores will return to their 2017 levels: Most legislation that has moved in the Democratic-controlled House has broken along partisan lines. The Republican-controlled Senate has been a tad more bipartisan. And if history is any guide, a divided Congress during the last two years of a president's first term usually means a sharp dive in enacted laws.

The likelihood, say observers, is that Democrats in the House will pass partisan bills they campaigned on, such as an ethics and campaign finance bill (HR 1) that has no prospect in the Senate.

Even in this barren environment, there are some opportunities to work on meaningful legislation, Reynolds notes. Two high-profile chairmen in Congress have already talked about ways to combat high prescription drug prices: GOP Sen. Charles E. Grassley of Iowa, the Finance Commit-

tee chairman, and Democratic Rep. Frank Pallone Jr. of New Jersey, the House Energy and Commerce chairman. Already, hearings have been held in both chambers on the matter. Republican allies of President Donald Trump say the president is serious about working on a solution in a bipartisan way. Still, says Reynolds: "I'm not terribly optimistic."

In addition, Trump's trade policies will continue to come under scrutiny. Grassley has been a vocal opponent of administration-imposed tariffs on aluminum and steel, as has the new chairman of the House Ways and Means Committee, Democrat Richard E. Neal of Massachusetts.

Congress will also need to make a decision on Trump's renegotiated North American Free Trade Agreement.

The chances for any overhaul to immigration are small following Trump's emergency declaration on building the wall along the southern border.

Despite the fall in total unity votes, both Democrats and Republicans maintained fealty to their parties overall in 2018. In the House, Republicans stuck with their party an average of 91 percent of the time on such votes and Democrats did 89 percent of the time, both slightly down from 2017, but still hovering around historic highs.

The Republican position prevailed on 92.1 percent of the 269 House votes that split majorities of the two parties. Such a feat can be largely attributed to tight control by party leaders on how legislation reaches the floor: In the 115th Congress, the number of bills that reached the floor without any chance for amendment — so-called closed rules — broke the previous record of 83 set four years ago.

In the Senate, Republicans worked with a narrower majority in 2018, as Democrat Doug Jones of Alabama won a special election to serve out the remainder of Republican Jeff Sessions' term, and Republican John McCain of Arizona was away from Congress the entire year until his death in August. The result was a 50-49 split and a decline in wins for Republicans on party unity votes — from 89.7 in 2017 to 79.4 in 2018 on 136 votes.

Still, even with that decline, the win percentage for Republicans was the second-highest since 2005. The figure was bolstered by Vice President Mike Pence, who was brought in to break ties in the Senate seven times, up from six times in 2017.

Fewer Votes, Fights

A year after the parties opposed each other more than ever in both chambers, 2018 was less contentious. In the House, the parties opposed each other at the lowest frequency since 2010. In the Senate, the two parties split on fewer than half of the votes, down from more than 2/3 of roll calls in 2017.

Frequency of party unity votes:

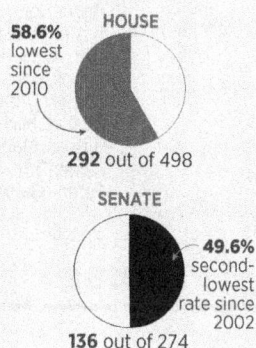

HOUSE
58.6% lowest since 2010
292 out of 498

SENATE
49.6% second-lowest rate since 2002
136 out of 274

AVERAGE FOR BOTH CHAMBERS: 55.4%

How often the majority won:

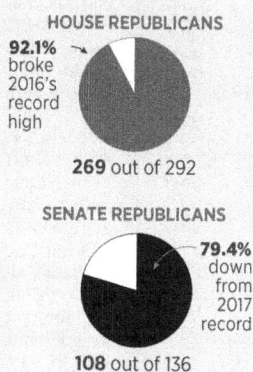

HOUSE REPUBLICANS
92.1% broke 2016's record high
269 out of 292

SENATE REPUBLICANS
79.4% down from 2017 record
108 out of 136

AVERAGE FOR BOTH CHAMBERS: 88.1%

Average chamber party unity scores:

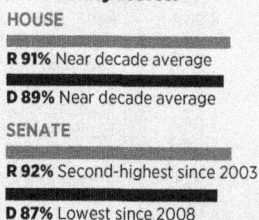

HOUSE
R 91% Near decade average
D 89% Near decade average

SENATE
R 92% Second-highest since 2003
D 87% Lowest since 2008

In the Senate, five Democrats had perfect unity scores, all but one of them either declared or potential 2020 presidential aspirants: Cory Booker of New Jersey, Kirsten Gillibrand of New York, Jeff Merkley of Oregon and Elizabeth Warren of Massachusetts. Edward J. Markey of Massachusetts was the exception.

Those senators will be closely watched on votes this year. They will be working on a dual track to court primary votes in what is proving to be an already crowded race for the Democratic nomination, while needing to move must-pass legislation like spending bills and an impending debt ceiling hike. In 2017, Gillibrand made an early decision to oppose nearly every nomination to Trump's Cabinet, and she continued that opposition in 2018, helping push her unity score to a perfect 100 percent.

Reynolds sees these Democratic senators playing a crucial role in 2019, and foresees Majority Leader Mitch McConnell scheduling a host of potentially tough votes. Already, he has begun making them walk the plank on a bill (S 311) scheduled for a vote Feb. 25 that would require that babies born during a botched abortion be given the same care as any other human. He is also planning to hold a vote on the so-called Green New Deal, a Democratic proposal dealing with climate change and economics.

"McConnell wants to get those senators on record," says Reynolds, the Brookings scholar. "That could cut both ways. There are some senators who are running for president who are eager to register their support for something like that. I think there are other ones who are a little more nervous."

The statistics compiled by CQ show that both Democrats and Republicans shed lawmakers in the 2018 election who most often crossed over to vote with the other party on votes.

In the Senate, a group of red-state Democrats often joined with Republicans on votes for federal judges and the rewrite of the Dodd-Frank bill.

But of the top six Democrats who broke from their party the most in 2018, four are no longer in Congress, having been defeated by a Republican challenger: Heidi Heitkamp of North Dakota, Joe Donnelly of Indiana, Claire McCaskill of Missouri and Bill Nelson of Florida.

The only two of that group who remain are Joe Manchin III of West Virginia and

Leading Scorers: Party Unity

Support shows those who, in 2018, voted most often with a majority of their party against a majority of the other party.
Opposition shows those who voted most often against his position. Absences do not count.
Members with identical scores are listed alphabetically.

SENATE

SUPPORT

Democrats		Republicans	
Booker, Cory	100.0%	Cochran, Thad	100.0%
Gillibrand, Kirsten	100.0	Kyl, Jon	100.0
Markey, Edward J.	100.0	Cotton, Tom	99.3
Merkley, Jeff	100.0	Sasse, Ben	99.3
Warren, Elizabeth	100.0	Inhofe, James M.	99.2
Harris, Kamala	99.3	Barrasso, John	98.5
Brown, Sherrod	98.5	Blunt, Roy	98.5
Smith, Tina	98.5	Enzi, Michael B.	98.5
Blumenthal, Richard	98.5	Thune, John	98.5
Durbin, Richard J.	98.5	Perdue, David	98.5
Hirono, Mazie K.	98.5	Fischer, Deb	98.5
Murray, Patty	98.5		

OPPOSITION

Democrats		Republicans	
Manchin, Joe III	53.3%	Paul, Rand	17.4%
Heitkamp, Heidi	46.0	Collins, Susan	16.9
Donnelly, Joe	45.5	Murkowski, Lisa	15.9
Jones, Doug	37.3	Flake, Jeff	12.3
McCaskill, Claire	33.3	Lee, Mike	11.9
Nelson, Bill	29.6	Moran, Jerry	11.4
Tester, Jon	25.2		
Shaheen, Jeanne	21.1		
Warner, Mark	20.7		
Coons, Chris	19.7		
Carper, Thomas R.	17.8		
Bennet, Michael	17.0		
Hassan, Maggie	16.5		
Kaine, Tim	14.7		
Peters, Gary	11.8		

HOUSE

SUPPORT

Democrats		Republicans	
Capuano, Michael E.	100.0%	Balderson, Troy	100.0%
Crowley, Joseph	100.0	Bridenstine, Jim	100.0
Jones, Brenda	100.0	Dent, Charlie	100.0
Morelle, Joseph D.	100.0	Guthrie, Brett	100.0
Wild, Susan	100.0	Scalise, Steve	100.0
McGovern, Jim	99.7	Tiberi, Pat	100.0
Sanchez, Linda T.	99.6	Wagner, Ann	99.7
Schakowsky, Jan	99.3	Arrington, Jodey C.	99.6
Levin, Sander M.	99.3	Johnson, Sam	99.6
Espaillat, Adriano	99.3	Kustoff, David	99.6
Watson Coleman, Bonnie	99.3	Walters, Mimi	99.6
Price, David E.	99.3	Hensarling, Jeb	99.3
Velazquez, Nydia M.	99.3	Estes, Ron	99.3
Lewis, John	99.2	Chabot, Steve	99.0
Roybal-Allard, Lucille	99.0	Byrne, Bradley	99.0
Jayapal, Pramila	99.0	Abraham, Ralph	99.0
Maloney, Carolyn B.	99.0	McCarthy, Kevin	99.0
Gomez, Jimmy	98.9	Luetkemeyer, Blaine	98.9
Brady, Robert A.	98.9	Olson, Pete	98.9
Grijalva, Raul M.	98.9	Lesko, Debbie	98.9
Gutierrez, Luis V.	98.8	Collins, Doug	98.9
Serrano, Jose E.	98.6	Higgins, Clay	98.9
Clarke, Yvette D.	98.6	Messer, Luke	98.8
Fudge, Marcia L.	98.6	Handel, Karen	98.6
Hastings, Alcee L.	98.5	Banks, Jim	98.6
Neal, Richard E.	98.5	Bucshon, Larry	98.6
Thompson, Bennie	98.5	Westerman, Bruce	98.6
Bass, Karen	98.4	Sessions, Pete	98.6
Pallone, Frank Jr.	98.3	Mullin, Markwayne	98.6
Raskin, Jamie	98.3	Walker, Mark	98.6
Green, Al	98.3	Curtis, John	98.6
Sarbanes, John	98.3	Goodlatte, Robert W.	98.6
Lee, Barbara	98.2	Allen, Rick W.	98.6
Rush, Bobby L.	98.0	Dunn, Neal	98.6
		Smucker, Lloyd K.	98.3
		Nunes, Devin	98.3
		Gibbs, Bob	98.3
		McCaul, Michael	98.3
		Ross, Dennis A.	98.2
		Aderholt, Robert B.	98.2
		Hultgren, Randy	98.2
		Brady, Kevin	98.2
		Smith, Lamar	98.2
		Gowdy, Trey	98.1

OPPOSITION

Democrats		Republicans	
Sinema, Kyrsten	30.8%	Amash, Justin	31.7
Cuellar, Henry	28.8	Fitzpatrick, Brian	25.2
Peterson, Collin C.	28.0	Ros-Lehtinen, Ileana	23.3
Gottheimer, Josh	24.7	Massie, Thomas	21.7
Murphy, Stephanie	24.1	Lance, Leonard	20.2
Schneider, Brad	23.9	LoBiondo, Frank A.	19.0
Lamb, Conor	23.6	Sanford, Mark	17.5
Costa, Jim	22.3	Curbelo, Carlos	16.7
Cooper, Jim	19.7	Smith, Christopher H.	15.9
O'Halleran, Tom	19.5	Costello, Ryan A.	15.2
Gonzalez, Vicente	16.7	Katko, John	14.4
Peters, Scott	14.4	Faso, John J.	14.1
Correa, Lou	14.4	Upton, Fred	13.6
Suozzi, Tom	14.3	Stefanik, Elise	13.4
Scott, David	14.2	Biggs, Andy	13.1
Lipinski, Daniel	14.0	Paulsen, Erik	13.1
Schrader, Kurt	14.0	Mast, Brian	12.0
Bustos, Cheri	13.8	Brooks, Mo	11.5
Ruppersberger, C.A. Dutch	13.8	MacArthur, Tom	11.4
Vela, Filemon	13.0	Roskam, Peter	11.0
Bishop, Sanford D. Jr.	12.9	Gaetz, Matt	10.9
Kuster, Ann McLane	12.6	Gohmert, Louie	10.8
Rosen, Jacky	12.5	Blum, Rod	10.7
Lujan Grisham, Michelle	12.1	Duncan, John J. Jr.	10.4
Himes, Jim	12.1	King, Peter T.	10.3
Scanlon, Mary Gay	11.8	Coffman, Mike	10.3
Lawson, Al	11.4	Reed, Tom	10.2
Kind, Ron	11.4		
Perlmutter, Ed	11.4		
Bera, Ami	11.3		
O'Rourke, Beto	11.1		
Rice, Kathleen	10.8		
Polis, Jared	10.8		
Loebsack, Dave	10.5		
Garamendi, John	10.4		
Heck, Denny	10.3		
Jones, Walter B.	42.3%		

Party Unity Votes

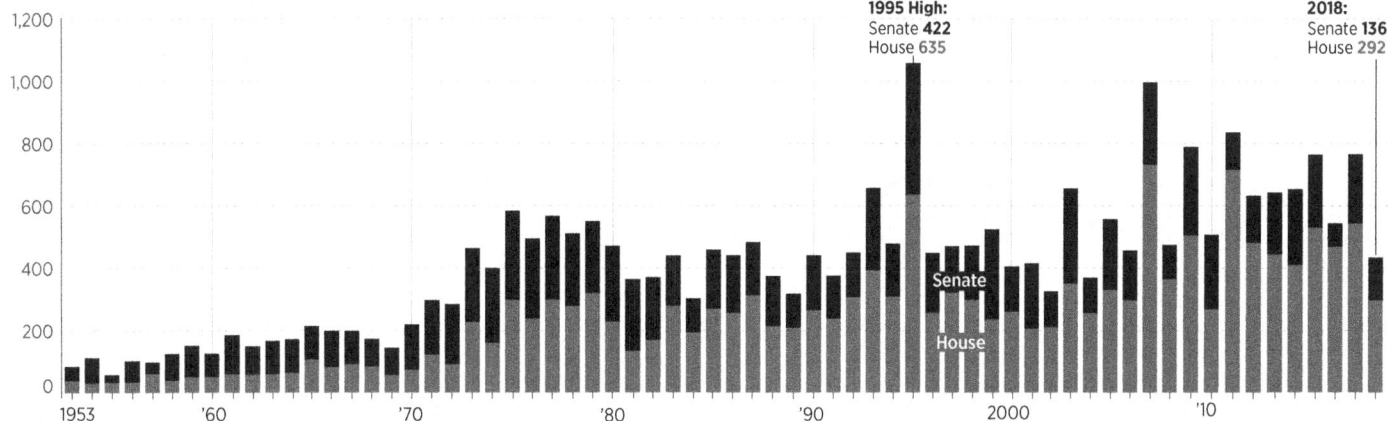

1995 High:
Senate **422**
House **635**

2018:
Senate **136**
House 292

Senate

House

HOUSE

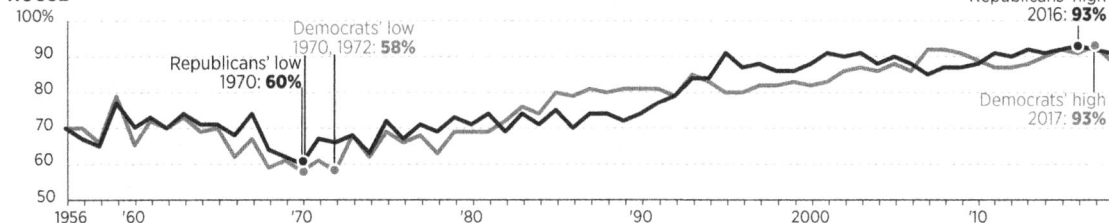

Republicans' high
2016: **93%**

Democrats' low
1970, 1972: **58%**

Republicans' low
1970: **60%**

Democrats' high
2017: **93%**

In both the House and Senate, Republicans voted together at higher rates than their Democratic counterparts on votes that split the two parties.

SENATE

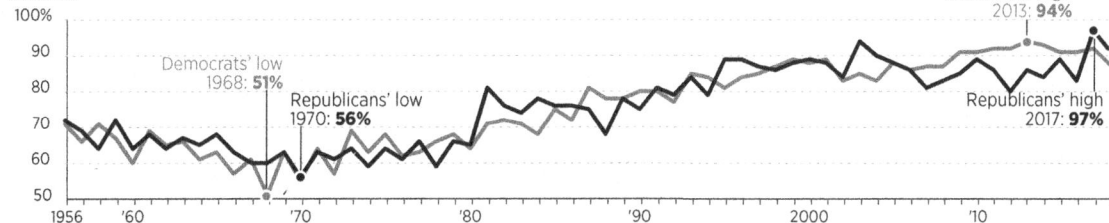

Democrats' high
2013: **94%**

Democrats' low
1968: **51%**

Republicans' low
1970: **56%**

Republicans' high
2017: **97%**

This solidarity, combined with their majority status, led to them winning 88 percent of these votes.

Doug Jones of Alabama. Jones, who is up for election to a full six-year term in 2020, has already cast votes that Republicans are poised to use against him for re-election, including a "no" in September in the confirmation of Supreme Court Justice Brett M. Kavanaugh. The Alabama GOP was quick to say that Jones' vote "betrays our state."

In the House, it was Republican moderates who got wiped out: Of the top 11 Republicans crossing over to vote with the other party the most in 2018, seven are no longer in Congress. Three lost re-election: Leonard Lance of New Jersey, Mark Sanford of South Carolina and Carlos Curbelo of Florida. Three retired: Ileana Ros-Lehtinen of Florida, Frank A. LoBiondo of New Jersey and Ryan A. Costello of Pennsylvania. The one who broke with his party the most, Walter B. Jones of North Carolina, died in February.

The other four from that group who remain in Congress are Justin Amash of Michigan, Brian Fitzpatrick of Pennsylvania, Thomas Massie of Kentucky and Christopher H. Smith of New Jersey.

"Certainly centrists get squeezed out when there's a wave," says Curbelo, a moderate Republican from Florida who introduced a carbon tax bill in 2018 but lost his re-election bid in 2018. He questions whether the two-party system is viable anymore.

"The two-party system is yielding a lot of leaders who don't see the incentive to compromise, don't see the incentive to negotiate and actually solve the nation's problems," he said. "On the contrary, they like to leave the challenges unsolved. That way they can exploit them come campaign season."

While it's true that Republican moderates got the axe in 2018, many Democratic moderates held on, including the top 10 who broke with the party the most on unity votes: Kyrsten Sinema of Arizona, who won

her election bid for Senate; Henry Cuellar of Texas; Collin C. Peterson of Minnesota; Josh Gottheimer of New Jersey; Stephanie Murphy of Florida; Brad Schneider of Illinois; Conor Lamb of Pennsylvania; Jim Costa of California; Jim Cooper of Tennessee; and Tom O'Halleran of Arizona.

A number of names on that list, like Murphy, O'Halleran and Peterson, were targeted by Republicans in 2018, but they survived nevertheless. The first list released by the National Republican Congressional Committee earlier this month includes all three again this year, and 52 others, the majority freshman.

In a release targeting the Democrats, the NRCC made it clear how they are going to go after them in 2020, by holding "these targeted members accountable for the radical policies being pushed by the socialist Democrats in their party." ■

History: Party Unity

The table below on the left shows how frequently a majority of Democrats aligned against a majority of Republicans. The average scores in the other columns for each chamber are computed including absences.

YEAR	Frequency of Unity Votes		House Average Scores		Senate Average Scores	
	HOUSE	SENATE	DEMOCRATS	REPUBLICANS	DEMOCRATS	REPUBLICANS
2018	58.6%	49.6%	89%	91%	87%	92%
2017	76.0	68.9	93	92	92	97
2016	73.4	46.0	91	93	91	83
2015	75.1	69.3	92	92	91	89
2014	72.6	66.7	90	91	93	84
2013	68.6	69.8	88	92	94	86
2012	72.8	59.8	87	90	92	80
2011	75.8	51.1	87	91	92	86
2010	40.0	78.6	89	88	91	89
2009	50.9	72.0	91	87	91	85
2008	53.3	51.6	92	87	87	83
2007	62.0	60.2	92	85	87	81
2006	54.5	57.3	86	88	86	86
2005	49.0	62.6	88	90	88	88
2004	47.0	52.3	86	88	83	90
2003	51.7	66.7	87	91	85	94
2002	43.3	45.5	86	90	83	84
2001	40.2	55.3	83	91	89	88
2000	43.2	48.7	82	88	88	89
1999	47.3	62.8	83	86	89	88
1998	55.5	55.7	82	86	87	86
1997	50.4	50.3	82	88	85	87
1996	56.4	62.4	80	87	84	89
1995	73.2	68.8	80	91	81	89
1994	61.8	51.7	83	84	84	79
1993	65.5	67.1	85	84	85	84
1992	64.5	53.0	79	79	77	79
1991	55.1	49.3	81	77	80	81
1990	49.1	54.3	81	74	80	75
1989	56.3	35.3	81	72	78	78
1988	47.0	42.5	80	74	78	68
1987	63.7	40.7	81	74	81	75
1986	56.5	52.3	79	70	72	76
1985	61.0	49.6	80	75	75	76
1984	47.1	40.0	74	71	68	78
1983	55.6	43.7	76	74	71	74
1982	36.4	43.4	72	69	72	76
1981	37.4	47.8	69	74	71	81
1980	37.6	45.8	69	71	64	65
1979	47.3	46.7	69	73	68	66
1978	33.2	45.2	63	69	66	59
1977	42.2	42.4	68	71	63	66
1976	35.9	37.2	66	67	62	61
1975	48.4	47.8	69	72	68	64
1974	29.4	44.3	62	63	63	59
1973	41.8	39.9	68	68	69	64
1972	27.1	36.5	58	66	57	61
1971	37.8	41.6	61	67	64	63
1970	27.1	35.2	58	60	55	56
1969	31.1	36.3	61	62	63	63
1968	35.2	32.0	59	64	51	60
1967	36.3	34.6	67	74	61	60
1966	41.5	50.2	62	68	57	63
1965	52.2	41.9	70	71	63	68
1964	54.9	35.7	69	71	61	65
1963	48.7	47.2	73	74	66	67
1962	46.0	41.1	70	70	65	64
1961	50.0	62.3	72	73	69	68
1960	52.7	36.7	65	70	60	64
1959	55.2	47.9	79	77	67	72
1958	39.8	43.5	66	65	71	64
1957	59.0	35.5	70	67	66	69
1956	43.8	53.1	70	70	71	72

Tallying Party Unity Votes

In the House in 2018, the two parties aligned against each other on 292 of 498 roll call votes, or 58.6 percent of the time — down 17.4 percentage points from 2017. In the Senate, the parties opposed each other on 136 of 274 roll calls, or 49.6 percent of the time. That's down from last year's 68.9 percent, the second-lowest rate since 2002. A list of roll-call votes that pitted majorities of the two parties against each other is available upon request from CQ Roll Call.

Calculations of average scores by chamber and party are based on all eligible "yea" or "nay" votes, whether or not all members participated. Under this methodology, average support and opposition scores are reduced when members choose not to vote. Party and chamber averages are not strictly comparable to individual member scores. (Complete member scores, pp. 45-47)

Also, in the member score tables, Sens. Angus King, I-Maine, and Bernie Sanders, I-Vt., were treated as if they were Democrats when calculating their support and opposition scores. They do not, however, qualify to be listed among the party's leaders in any category.

Background: Party Unity

Roll-call votes used for the party unity study are all those on which a majority of Democrats opposed a majority of Republicans. Support indicates the percentage of the time that members voted in agreement with their party on such party unity votes. The tables below also show the number of party unity votes on which each party was victorious and the number of instances in which either party voted unanimously.

AVERAGE PARTY UNITY SCORE BY CHAMBERS

		SUPPORT	
		2017	**2018**
HOUSE	Democrats	93%	89%
	Republicans	92	91
SENATE	Democrats	92	87
	Republicans	97	92
CONGRESS	Democrats	93	89
	Republicans	93	91

Average scores for chamber and party are calculated based on all party unity votes for which members were eligible. A member's failure to vote lowers the score for the group.

VICTORIES IN PARTY UNITY VOTES

	HOUSE		SENATE		CONGRESS	
YEAR	Democrats	Republicans	Democrats	Republicans	Democrats	Republicans
2018	23	269	28	108	51	337
2017	51	488	23	201	74	689
2016	40	416	53	22	93	438
2015	68	460	93	142	161	602
2014	55	353	224	20	279	373
2013	50	389	171	32	221	421
2012	67	411	103	47	170	458
2011	82	634	87	33	169	667
2010	236	28	196	39	432	67
2009	473	29	264	22	737	51
2008	342	25	60	51	402	76
2007	658	72	179	87	837	159
2006	59	236	53	107	112	343
2005	50	278	47	182	97	460
2004	42	213	28	85	70	298
2003	39	310	56	250	95	560
2002	39	170	42	73	81	243
2001	27	177	95	115	122	292
2000	77	182	31	114	108	296
1999	58	177	77	211	135	388
1998	80	216	61	114	141	330
1997	58	261	46	104	104	365
1996	48	208	59	132	107	340

UNANIMOUS VOTING ON UNITY VOTES

	HOUSE		SENATE		CONGRESS	
YEAR	Democrats	Republicans	Democrats	Republicans	Democrats	Republicans
2018	117	91	50	92	167	183
2017	242	176	125	160	367	336
2016	109	118	24	11	133	129
2015	174	177	96	77	270	254
2014	92	159	180	76	272	235
2013	97	152	106	62	203	214
2012	40	99	60	19	100	118
2011	76	209	55	31	131	240
2010	10	91	67	106	77	197
2009	29	144	79	74	108	218
2008	66	96	30	19	96	115
2007	170	177	102	35	272	212
2006	70	62	34	30	104	92
2005	82	91	69	59	151	150
2004	70	77	3	31	73	108
2003	94	109	32	130	126	239
2002	37	54	12	23	49	77
2001	1	66	37	55	38	121
2000	1	67	52	19	53	86
1999	11	59	100	63	111	122
1998	8	42	46	33	54	75
1997	11	63	35	38	46	101
1996	10	32	35	47	45	79

Trump's Last Hurrah

The president's winning streak continued in 2018, but Democratic control of the House spells its end

By **JOHN T. BENNETT**

Riding Republican majorities in both chambers last year, President Donald Trump put up strong numbers for the second consecutive year in getting support for his nominees and legislation he backed, winning 93.4 percent of the time, according to data compiled for CQ's annual vote study of presidential support.

That's among the highest for any chief executive since CQ began tracking the data in 1954, during the Eisenhower administration — third to be exact. But it is down 5 percentage points from Trump's record-high level of support during his first year in office, when Congress supported his positions 98.7 percent of the time.

Trump's 2017 figure set a bicameral record, besting President Barack Obama's 96.7 percent success rate in 2009. Obama, like Trump, benefited from two years of his party controlling both chambers of Congress before losing the House majority.

More than state or district or other factors shaping an election cycle, what matters most in predicting how members will vote when a president has taken a position in America's current hyper-partisan era is whether the lawmaker and president belong to the same party. So with a Democratic House newly installed for the 116th Congress, Trump's winning pattern might abruptly become a thing of the past.

Though the 45th president's support figure dipped last year, it was nearly 6 percentage points higher than the previous Republican president's highest score: George W. Bush ended 2002 with an 87.8 percent success rate.

Despite periodic criticism last year from GOP lawmakers — and signs of their support cracking since the recent partial government shutdown — they again were reluctant to cast or even hold votes that appeared likely to fail, especially ones that might anger Trump and his conservative base. The fear of being targeted by a Trump-backed primary challenger with farther-right leanings has been perhaps the president's most effective tool in winning and retaining his party's support.

Of course, the luxury of Republican control of both chambers primed the pump for all Trump's 2018 winning. One longtime Capitol Hill observer and analyst chalks up much of the success to a combination of factors: members eager to keep leadership happy, and Republican leaders seeing few reasons to buck Trump.

"Given how leadership in both the House and Senate seemed reluctant to challenge the president … that has definitely been a major factor," says G. William Hoagland, an aide to then-Senate Majority Leader Bill Frist in the mid-2000s. The votes of Republican members, he says, "do reflect the strength of their conservative convictions, which while not totally in sync with President Trump, nonetheless requires them to hold the line."

The recent Washington drama that culminated with Trump supporting a border security spending agreement to avert a government shutdown illustrated that. As the president and his staff reviewed the legislation — and whether to trigger another partial shutdown — Senate Republican leaders were reluctant to bring the bill to the floor if passing it would anger Trump. "We'd like to know it's a bill the president's going to sign," Senate Majority Whip John Thune, the South Dakota Republican, told reporters Feb. 14, just hours before Trump signaled his support.

The voting data shows Trump again last year enjoyed overwhelming support from his own party.

GOP senators voted with Trump 93 percent of the time, down slightly from his 96 percent rate in 2017. House Republicans stuck with the president's stated positions 89 percent of the time, down from 93 percent during his first year.

House Democrats backed Trump-supported positions 31 percent of the time last year, on average, almost twice as often as in 2017. They opposed his stances 66 percent of the time, a considerable drop from 83 percent in 2017, which was second only to their opposition to George W. Bush during his second-to-last year in office (90 percent in 2007). (The figures do not add up to 100 percent because representatives missed some of the votes.)

As they did in the president's first year, Senate Democrats supported his stated positions an average of 37 percent of the time. They opposed him 60 percent of the time, down from 62 percent in 2017.

Within the GOP, even some of Trump's sharpest detractors have found it difficult to resist him much.

Former Senate Foreign Relations Chairman Bob Corker of Tennessee, who retired in January, and Sen. Tim Scott of South Carolina both have sharply criticized Trump — the former for the president's foreign policy moves and the latter for his racially-tinged rhetoric.

Scott last year blocked a vote on Trump's nomination of Thomas Farr to a federal judgeship in North Carolina over allegations of racism. The nomination expired with the last Congress, but White House officials want to revive it.

According to a McClatchy report, Scott expressed frustration with Trump's insistence. "Why they have chosen to expend so much energy on this particular nomination I do not know, but what I do know is they have not spent anywhere near as much time on true racial reconciliation efforts ... or working to move our party together towards a stronger, more unified future," he said.

Likewise, Corker hasn't pulled punches over Trump's trade disputes with allies and rivals alike.

"The United States just seems to wake up and there doesn't seem to be any rhyme or reason to what we're doing — it's kind of a ready, fire and aim," he told reporters in September.

Yet, despite their sometimes deep frustrations with the president, Scott and Corker in 2018 rarely split with him. On issues where Trump stated his view, Scott voted with the president 99 percent of the time, and Corker 97 percent.

In short, even for the two sometimes-Trump critics, party came first.

Other factors also helped Trump's numbers. Senate rules changes eliminating the 60-vote threshold for judicial and executive nominees — which, by definition, arrive with a clear presidential position — meant the White House didn't need Democrats' approval. Though Democrats used rules to slow consideration of a long list of nominees, there was virtually no chance Republicans would fail to confirm them.

Trump had a perfect score last year on nominations that made it to the Senate floor, with all 91 votes ending in confirmations for executive and judicial branch nominees.

Subtract those confirmation votes, and the rate of success plunges. Trump only took a position on 8.7 percent of other Senate votes. Of those 16 votes, he won nine and lost seven, just over 56 percent.

Trump campaigned as a once-in-a-generation real estate mogul whose negotiating skills and experience would help him set a new tone of collaboration in Washington. But his alleged deal-making savvy already is being tested since control of Congress is now divided with a Democratic-run House, which immediately united to stand up to him on his demands for border wall funding. And he faces tough hurdles in attempts to repeat the bipartisan successes of 2018.

Guide to the Vote Studies

CQ has analyzed voting patterns of members of Congress since 1945. The three current studies — presidential support, party unity and voting participation — have been conducted in a consistent manner since 1954.

Selecting votes CQ bases its vote studies on all floor votes for which senators and House members were asked to vote "yea" or "nay." In 2018, there were 498 such roll-call votes in the House and 274 in the Senate. The House total excludes two quorum calls in 2018.

The House total counts all votes on procedural matters, including votes to approve the journal.

The presidential support and party unity studies are based on a set of votes selected according to the criteria detailed on pages 33 and 38.

Individual scores Member scores are based only on the votes each actually cast. This makes individual support and opposition scores total 100 percent. The same method is used to identify the leading scorers on pages 26-27 and 34.

Overall scores To be consistent with previous years, calculations of average scores by chamber and party are based on all eligible votes, whether or not all members cast a "yea" or "nay." The lack of participation by lawmakers in a roll call vote reduces chamber and party average support and opposition scores.

Rounding Scores in the tables that follow are rounded to the nearest percentage point. Scores for the presidential and party support leaders are reported to one decimal point in order to rank them more precisely.

— Statistical research by Ryan Kelly

Fewer Presidential-Position Votes Makes for High Support Scores

President Donald Trump took a position on less than 18 percent of the votes recorded in Congress last year, and many of those were confirmation votes on his nominees. On other Senate votes, Trump only took a position 8.7 percent of the time. Of those 16 votes, he won nine and lost seven.

Percentage of Presidential Support Votes, for Congress as a whole;
the year highlighted is president's second year in office

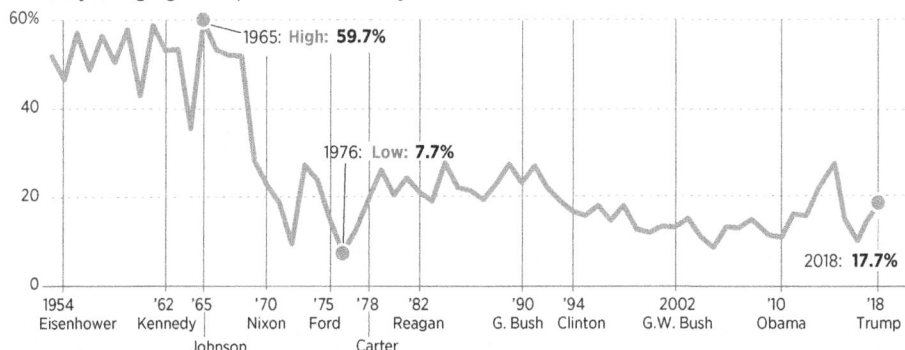

1965: High: **59.7%**
1976: Low: **7.7%**
2018: **17.7%**

1954 Eisenhower | '62 Kennedy | '65 | '70 Nixon | '75 Ford | '78 | '82 Reagan | '90 G. Bush | '94 Clinton | 2002 G.W. Bush | '10 Obama | '18 Trump
Johnson | Carter

Leading Scorers: Presidential Support

Support shows those who, in 2018, voted most often for President Donald Trump's position when it was clearly known. **Opposition** shows those who voted most often against his position. Absences do not count.
Members with identical scores are listen alphabetically.

SENATE

SUPPORT

Democrats		Republicans	
Manchin, Joe III	72.4%	Alexander, Lamar	100.0%
Heitkamp, Heidi	69.5	Capito, Shelley Moore	100.0
Donnelly, Joe	67.9	Cochran, Thad	100.0
Jones, Doug	62.9	Cornyn, John	100.0
McCaskill, Claire	59.4	Hatch, Orrin G.	100.0
Nelson, Bill	58.9	Hyde-Smith, Cindy	100.0
Tester, Jon	55.1	Kyl, Jon	100.0
Warner, Mark	49.1	Roberts, Pat	100.0
Hassan, Maggie	47.6	Shelby, Richard C.	100.0
Shaheen, Jeanne	47.6	Wicker, Roger	100.0
Coons, Chris	46.5	Hoeven, John	99.1
Bennet, Michael	46.2	McConnell, Mitch	99.1
Carper, Thomas R.	45.8	Portman, Rob	99.1
Kaine, Tim	44.9	Young, Todd	99.1
Klobuchar, Amy	43.0	Boozman, John	99.1
Murphy, Christopher S.	42.5	Scott, Tim	99.0
Leahy, Patrick J.	42.0	Blunt, Roy	99.0
Casey, Bob	40.6	Isakson, Johnny	99.0
		Perdue, David	99.0
		Tillis, Thom	99.0
		Toomey, Patrick J.	99.0
		Graham, Lindsey	99.0

OPPOSITION

Democrats		Republicans	
Booker, Cory	82.4%	Paul, Rand	14.7%
Gillibrand, Kirsten	82.1	Flake, Jeff	9.7
Merkley, Jeff	81.9	Lee, Mike	8.7
Warren, Elizabeth	81.3	Daines, Steve	5.7
Markey, Edward J.	81.1	Collins, Susan	5.6
Harris, Kamala	79.2	Cruz, Ted	4.3
Wyden, Ron	73.8	Murkowski, Lisa	4.1
Menendez, Robert	71.7	Sullivan, Dan	3.9
Stabenow, Debbie	70.8	Kennedy, John	3.8
Blumenthal, Richard	70.5	Sasse, Ben	3.8
Hirono, Mazie K.	70.1	Enzi, Michael B.	3.7
		Heller, Dean	3.1

HOUSE

SUPPORT

Democrats

Cuellar, Henry	76.7%
Gottheimer, Josh	76.7
Peterson, Collin C.	76.7
Sinema, Kyrsten	76.7
Murphy, Stephanie	73.3
O'Halleran, Tom	70.0
Bera, Ami	66.7
Lamb, Conor	66.7
Kuster, Ann McLane	65.5
Schneider, Brad	65.5
Rosen, Jacky	63.3
Bishop, Sanford D. Jr.	62.1
Carbajal, Salud	59.3
Costa, Jim	58.6
Rice, Kathleen	58.6
Bustos, Cheri	56.7
Cooper, Jim	56.7
Correa, Lou	56.7
Lawson, Al	56.7
Maloney, Sean Patrick	55.6
Lipinski, Daniel	55.2
Brownley, Julia	53.3
Crist, Charlie	53.3
Loebsack, Dave	53.3
Ruiz, Raul	53.3
Delaney, John	51.7
Garamendi, John	50.0
Peters, Scott	50.0

Republicans (100%)

Amodei, Mark	Marino, Tom
Bacon, Don	Marshall, Roger
Balderson, Tony	McCarthy, Kevin
Barr, Andy	McCaul, Michael
Bilirakis, Gus	McHenry, Patrick
Bishop, Mike	McSally, Martha
Bost, Mike	Messer, Luke
Brady, Kevin	Mitchell, Paul
Bridenstine, Jim	Moolenaar, John
Brooks, Susan W.	Nunes, Devin
Bucshon, Larry	Paulsen, Erik
Calvert, Ken	Pittenger, Robert
Cloud, Michael	Poliquin, Bruce
Cole, Tom	Rogers, Harold
Collins, Chris	Rooney, Tom
Collins, Doug	Rooney, Francis
Conaway, K. Michael	Ross, Dennis A.
Cramer, Kevin	Royce, Ed
Dent, Charlie	Rutherford, John
Dunn, Neal	Scalise, Steve
Flores, Bill	Scott, Austin
Gibbs, Bob	Shimkus, John
Goodlatte, Robert W.	Shuster, Bill
Guthrie, Brett	Simpson, Mike
Handel, Karen	Stivers, Steve
Hartzler, Vicky	Thornberry, Mac
Hill, French	Tiberi, Pat
Huizenga, Bill	Trott, Dave
Hultgren, Randy	Valadao, David
Jenkins, Lynn	Wagner, Ann
Johnson, Bill	Walberg, Tim
Joyce, David	Walden, Greg
Kinzinger, Adam	Walters, Mimi
Knight, Steve	Wenstrup, Brad
Lucas, Frank D.	Wilson, Joe
Luetkemeyer, Blaine	Womack, Steve

OPPOSITION

Democrats

Ellison, Keith	93.8%
Watson Coleman, Bonnie	93.3
Lee, Barbara	92.9
Chu, Judy	90.0
Clarke, Yvette D.	90.0
Grijalva, Raul M.	90.0
Johnson, Hank	90.0
Schakowsky, Jan	90.0
Velazquez, Nydia M.	90.0
Lewis, John	89.7
Moore, Gwen	89.7
DeSaulnier, Mark	89.3
Espaillat, Adriano	86.7
Jayapal, Pramila	86.7
Lowenthal, Alan	86.7
McGovern, Jim	86.7
Napolitano, Grace F.	86.7
Pocan, Mark	86.7
Raskin, Jamie	86.7
Davis, Danny K.	85.2

Republicans

Jones, Walter B.	85.0%
Amash, Justin	63.3
Massie, Thomas	56.7
Sanford, Mark	46.7
Labrador, Raul R.	41.7
Biggs, Andy	40.0
McClintock, Tom	37.9
Duncan, John J. Jr.	34.5
Farenthold, Blake	33.3
Garrett, Tom	33.3
Gosar, Paul	31.0
Gaetz, Matt	30.0
Rohrabacher, Dana	30.0
Gohmert, Louie	28.6
Ros-Lehtinen, Ileana	27.6
Brooks, Mo	23.3
Jordan, Jim	23.3
Mooney, Alex X.	23.3
Buck, Ken	20.7
Perry, Scott	20.7
Brat, Dave	20.0
Budd, Ted	20.0
Davidson, Warren	20.0
Graves, Garret	20.0
Harris, Andy	20.0
Loudermilk, Barry	20.0
Meadows, Mark	20.0
Rothfus, Keith	20.0
Sensenbrenner, Jim	20.0

2018 Votes: Presidential Position

These were the 30 House and 107 Senate roll-call votes in 2018 on which the president took a clear position. A victory is a vote on which the president's position prevailed.

TOTAL CONGRESS SUCCESS	
Victories	128
Defeats	9
Total	137
Success rate	**93.4%**

HOUSE SUCCESS

Victories	28
Defeats	2
Total	30
Success rate	**93.3%**

SENATE SUCCESS

Victories	100
Defeats	7
Total	107
Success rate	**93.5%**

Defense and Foreign Policy

VOTE NUMBER	DESCRIPTION
3 Victories	
49	Appropriations
313	Appropriations
326	Intelligence programs

Domestic Policy

VOTE NUMBER	DESCRIPTION
21 Victories	
14	Surveillance programs
16	Surveillance programs
33	Appropriations
60	Appropriations
69	Appropriations
80	Disability programs
106	Education policy
127	Appropriations
171	Consumer regulation
214	Health care policy
238	Water projects
243	Appropriations
265	Drug policy
268	Drug policy
276	Drug policy
278	Health care policy
284	Farm programs
288	Drug policy
372	Health care policy
376	Health care policy
377	Health care policy
2 Defeats	
205	Farm programs
297	Immigration policy

Economic Policy and Trade

VOTE NUMBER	DESCRIPTION
4 Victories	
216	Financial regulation
411	Tax policy
412	Tax policy
414	Tax policy

Defense and Foreign Policy

VOTE NUMBER	DESCRIPTION
2 Defeats	
29	Appropriations
266	Military deployment

Domestic Policy

VOTE NUMBER	DESCRIPTION
8 Victories	
12	Surveillance programs
31	Appropriations
63	Appropriations
76	Consumer regulation
106	Veterans affairs
210	Drug policy
226	Health care policy
274	Appropriations
5 Defeats	
14	Appropriations
25	Abortion rights
36	Immigration policy
97	Telecommunications regulation
134	Appropriations

Economic Policy and Trade

VOTE NUMBER	DESCRIPTION
1 Victory	
54	Financial regulation

Nominations

VOTE NUMBER	DESCRIPTION
91 Victories	
1	John C. Rood
3	William C. Campbell, Jr.
5	Thomas Lee Robinson Parker
7	Michael Lawrence Brown
9	Walter David Counts, III
19	Jerome H. Powell
21	Alex Michael Azar II
23	Samuel Dale Brownback
24	R. D. James
27	David Ryan Stras
28	Andrei Iancu
38	Elizabeth L. Branch
40	Russell Vought
42	A. Marvin Quattlebaum, Jr.
46	Karen Gren Scholer
47	Tilman Eugene Self III
49	Terry A. Doughty
56	Kevin K. McAleenan
65	Claria Horn Boom
67	John F. Ring
69	Patrick Pizzella
71	Andrew Wheeler
72	John W. Broomes
73	Rebecca Grady Jennings
79	Carlos G. Muniz
80	James Bridenstine
82	Stuart Kyle Duncan
84	Mike Pompeo
85	Richard Grenell
87	Kurt D. Engelhardt
89	Michael B. Brennan
92	Michael Y. Scudder
93	Amy J. St. Eve
94	Joel M. Carson III
95	John B. Nalbandian
98	Mitchell Zais
101	Gina Haspel
103	Dana Baiocco
105	Brian D. Montgomery
109	Jelena McWilliams
111	James Randolph Evans
113	Robert Earl Wier
115	Fernando Rodriguez, Jr.
117	Annemarie Carney Axon
118	Kenneth L. Marcus
145	Mark Jeremy Bennett
152	Brian Allen Benczkowski
154	Paul C. Ney, Jr.
155	Scott Stump
156	James Blew
158	Randal Quarles
160	Andrew S. Oldham
161	Ryan Wesley Bounds
163	Robert L. Wilkie
174	Britt Cagle Grant
183	A. Marvin Quattlebaum, Jr.
185	Julius Ness Richardson
195	Lynn A. Johnson
197	Richard Clarida
198	Joseph H. Hunt
199	Isabel Marie Keenan Patelunas
200	Charles Barnes Goodwin
202	Elad L. Roisman
203	Dominic W. Lanza
204	Charles J. Williams
206	Charles P. Rettig
213	Jackie Wolcott
215	Peter A. Feldman
217	Peter A. Feldman
218	Lisa Porter
223	Brett M. Kavanaugh
228	Jeffrey Bossert Clark
230	Eric S. Dreiband
231	David James Porter
232	Ryan Douglas Nelson
233	Richard J. Sullivan
234	William M. Ray II
235	Liles Clifton Burke
236	Michael Joseph Juneau
237	Mark Saalfield Norris, Sr.
238	Eli Jeremy Richardson
239	Thomas S. Kleeh
244	Michelle Bowman
246	Stephen Alexander Vaden
248	Karen Dunn Kelley
249	Thomas Alvin Farr
254	Bernard L. McNamee
255	Kathleen Laura Kraninger
257	Justin George Muzinich
258	Jonathan A. Kobes
272	Joseph Maguire

Despite Trump's claims of being a master negotiator, he failed to score a single major bipartisan legislative victory in his first year. "The one thing the guy has never done is try to expand his base or his support," said one Republican pollster.

Last year, however, he signed several sweeping bills that had support from both parties, including a criminal justice overhaul, opioid legislation, the farm bill and changes affecting veterans' care. He highlighted those successes in his Feb. 5 State of the Union address. "Now is the time for bipartisan action. Believe it or not, we have already proven that it is possible," he told a joint session of Congress. "As we have seen, when we are united, we can make astonishing strides for our country."

But his third address to a joint session was a microcosm of his presidency. For all his talk of bipartisanship in the first half of the speech, he quickly turned on Democrats with repeated digs, further alienating them with hard-line rhetoric about illegal immigration and a lengthy pitch for his proposed southern border wall.

From Speaker Nancy Pelosi of California and Senate Minority Leader Charles E. Schumer of New York to rank-and-file members, Democrats have shown few signs so far of keeping Trump's vote support figures at such high levels.

Following the president's State of the Union address, Rep. Alexandria Ocasio-Cortez, the New York Democrat, described the evening as "an unsettling night for our country."

"The president failed to offer any plan, any vision at all, for our future," she tweeted. "We're flying without a pilot. And I'm not here to comfort anyone about that fact."

If Trump wants to strike deals on major legislation, like an infrastructure overhaul or lowering prescription drug prices, Democrats claim they are willing to work with him. That potential cooperation would bolster his voting support score.

Following a Jan. 28 phone call with the president, Pelosi said they discussed issues they could work on together, including infrastructure.

"So I look forward to moving forward on that," she said.

So far in 2019, however, efforts that might lead Democrats to vote with Trump have yet to materialize.

If the president wants to pass major leg-

Lending Support

Whether he was pushing his administration's agenda or merely endorsing the efforts of congressional Republicans, President Donald Trump got his way nearly every time he made his position known.

Share of votes on which the president took a clear position:

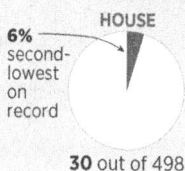

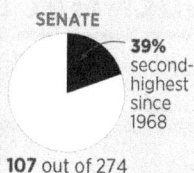

HOUSE

6% second-lowest on record

30 out of 498

SENATE

39% second-highest since 1968

107 out of 274

AVERAGE FOR BOTH CHAMBERS:
17.7%

How often the president won:

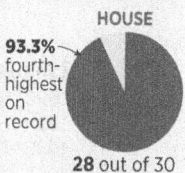

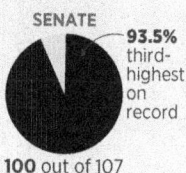

HOUSE

93.3% fourth-highest on record

28 out of 30

SENATE

93.5% third-highest on record

100 out of 107

AVERAGE FOR BOTH CHAMBERS:
93.4%

Average chamber presidential support scores:

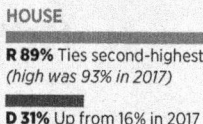

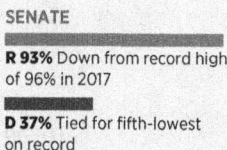

HOUSE

R 89% Ties second-highest (high was 93% in 2017)

D 31% Up from 16% in 2017

SENATE

R 93% Down from record high of 96% in 2017

D 37% Tied for fifth-lowest on record

islation in 2019 and 2020 in preparation for his expected bid for a second term, he will need the support of large numbers of House Democrats and at least a handful of their party's caucus in the Senate, where legislation still requires 60 votes to end debate.

History suggests Trump's average likely will plummet this year. For instance, Obama's support score dipped from 85.8 percent in 2011 with Democratic control on the Hill to 57 percent the next year after a GOP tidal wave gave that party control of the House. After Bush lost both chambers in 2006, his support score fell from 80 percent to 47.7 percent.

For Trump to avoid a similar fate, top Democrats have signaled he will need to focus less on placating his conservative base and more on finding ways to attract Democratic support.

The morning after Trump's State of the Union address, House Majority Leader Steny H. Hoyer panned the president's approach and message. "It reminded me more of his political rallies than the State of the Union," the Maryland Democrat said.

And one former White House official predicted Trump will struggle to get Democrats' support in numbers large enough to pass legislation and keep his scores high.

"When he perceives things are looking bad for him, he lashes out and his base loves it," Elaine Kamarck, a former Clinton White House official now with the Brookings Institution, said recently. "But Democrats don't, and he's only alienating independents. He doesn't do a thing to try to expand that base, which is all he seems to care about."

But the president himself blames Democratic leaders for his struggles so far with the party. As he wrangled over a border security spending deal with Democrats this month, Trump tweeted: "I don't think the Dems on the Border Committee are being allowed by their leaders to make a deal."

Regardless of the reasons or the president's attempts to explain them away, he is faced with a new reality that will likely alter the winning he has become accustomed to under a GOP-controlled Congress. ∎

Ryan Kelly, Lindsey McPherson and Jason Dick contributed to this report.

Background: Presidential Support

CQ editors select presidential support votes each year based on clear statements by the president or authorized spokesmen. Success scores show how often the president prevailed. Average scores for each chamber are lowered by absences.

PRESIDENTIAL SUCCESS BY ISSUES

	Defense/Foreign Policy		Defense		Economic Affairs		Overall	
	2018	2017	2018	2017	2018	2017	2018	2017
House	100.0%	100.0%	91.3%	100.0%	100.0%	100.0%	93.3%	100.0%
Senate	0.0	--	61.5	88.2	100.0	100.0	93.5	98.7
Congress	60.0	100.0	80.6	100.0	100.0	0	93.4	98.7

Economic affairs includes votes on taxes, trade, omnibus and some supplemental spending bills that cover both domestic and foreign policy programs. Confirmation votes in the Senate are included only in the chamber's overall scores.

AVERAGE PRESIDENTIAL SUPPORT SCORES

	House		Senate	
	Democrats	Republicans	Democrats	Republicans
Eisenhower				
1954	44%	71%	38%	73%
1955	53	60	56	72
1956	52	72	39	72
1957	49	54	51	69
1958	44	67	44	67
1959	40	68	38	72
1960	44	59	43	66
Kennedy				
1961	73	37	65	36
1962	72	42	63	39
1963	72	32	63	44
Johnson				
1964	74	38	61	45
1965	74	41	64	48
1966	63	37	57	43
1967	69	46	61	53
1968	64	51	48	47
Nixon				
1969	48	57	47	66
1970	53	66	45	60
1971	47	72	40	64
1972	47	64	44	66
1973	35	62	37	61
1974	46	65	39	57
Ford				
1974	41	51	39	55
1975	38	63	47	68
1976	32	63	39	62
Carter				
1977	63	42	70	52
1978	60	36	66	41
1979	64	34	68	47
1980	63	40	62	45
Reagan				
1981	42	68	49	80
1982	39	64	43	74
1983	28	70	42	73
1984	34	60	41	76

	House		Senate	
	Democrats	Republicans	Democrats	Republicans
1985	30	67	35	75
1986	25	65	37	78
1987	24	62	36	64
1988	25	57	47	68
G. Bush				
1989	36	69	55	82
1990	25	63	38	70
1991	34	72	41	83
1992	25	71	32	73
Clinton				
1993	77	39	87	29
1994	75	47	86	42
1995	75	22	81	29
1996	74	38	83	37
1997	71	30	85	60
1998	74	26	82	41
1999	73	23	84	34
2000	73	27	89	46
G.W. Bush				
2001	31	86	66	94
2002	32	82	71	89
2003	26	89	48	94
2004	30	80	60	91
2005	24	81	38	86
2006	31	85	51	85
2007	7	72	37	78
2008	16	64	34	70
Obama				
2009	90	26	92	50
2010	84	29	94	41
2011	80	22	92	53
2012	77	17	93	47
2013	83	12	96	40
2014	81	12	95	55
2015	86	11	87	53
2016	88	8	86	49
Trump				
2017	16	93	37	96
2018	31	89	37	93

Standing By Their Man

In both years of his first term, President Donald Trump enjoyed record support from Congress on bills where he took a clear position. He received the highest second-year support of any president going back to Eisenhower. One reason for the high scores, though, is Trump took a stance on fewer bills than most of his predecessors.

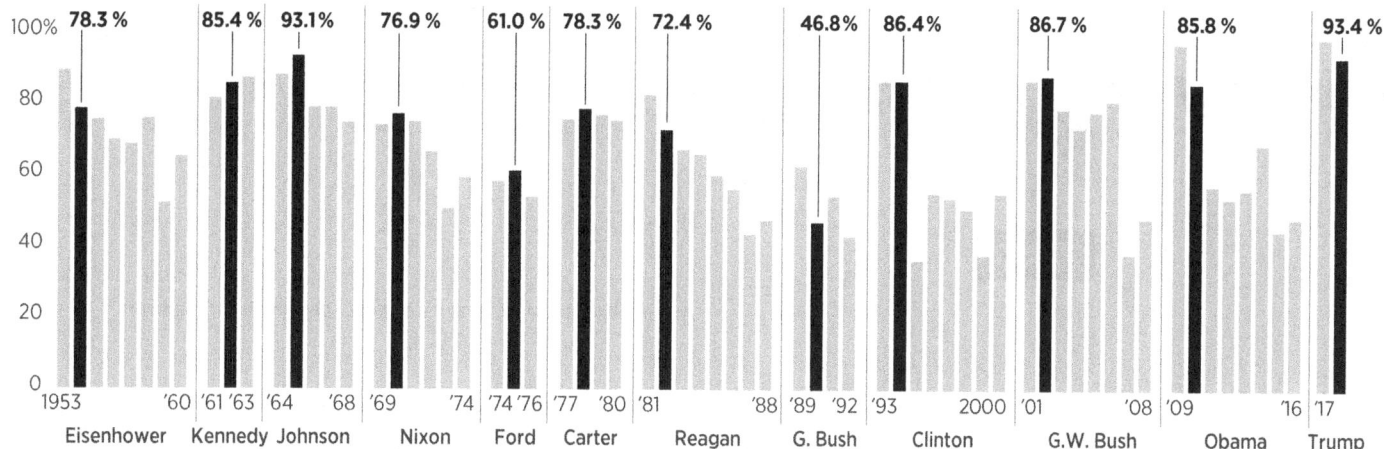

Some Excused Absences

Running for other office, retirement and illness: Congress hits lowest participation rate in a decade

By RYAN KELLY

Leaders of Congress are adept at scheduling votes when members will be available to cast them —avoiding weekends, keeping to short work days and making sure members get days off.

That helps avoid voting participation low points, such as 1970 — when lawmakers cast votes only 79 percent of the time and fewer than a quarter had a 90 percent showing or higher.

Even so, last year members of Congress across both chambers weighed in to vote 94.3 percent of the time, a 10-year low that was dragged down by absences in the House.

Lawmakers in the House produced a 93.9 percent rate of vote participation. While that's higher than any of the first 31 years of CQ's vote study (1954-1984), it was the lowest for the chamber since 1992, and that was despite relatively modest demands — the number of actual roll call votes (498) was the lowest since 2002. The vote performance can be attributed to members taking time off for election year campaigning, as well as a large number of retirements — 31 members of the House announced they were leaving, the highest total since 1996, when 34 retired.

The Senate did not feature such a drop-off in participation. The average participation rate there was 96.8 percent on the 274 "yea" or "nay" votes cast in the session, the Senate's highest election-year participation rate since 2006.

Average voting participation rate *by chamber*

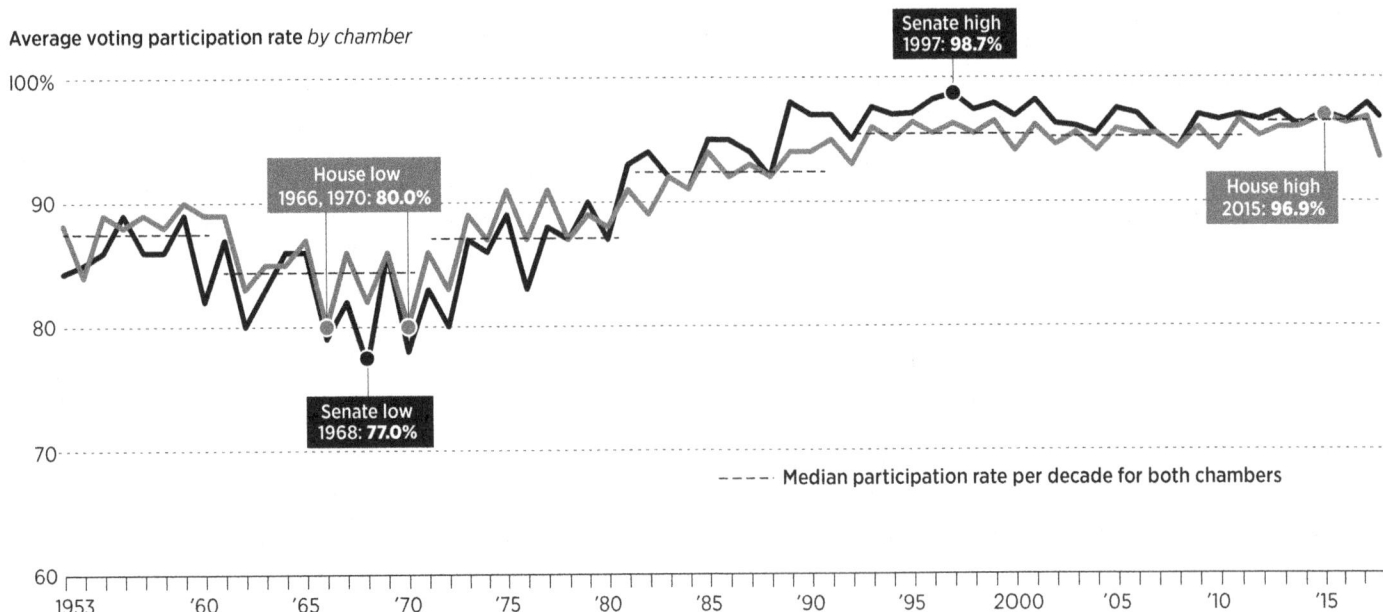

Senate high
1997: **98.7%**

House low
1966, 1970: **80.0%**

House high
2015: **96.9%**

Senate low
1968: **77.0%**

- - - - Median participation rate per decade for both chambers

1953   '60   '65   '70   '75   '80   '85   '90   '95   2000   '05   '10   '15

12 Members Cast Fewer than 70% of Eligible Votes

Sen. John McCain | 0%
R-Ariz.
Illness

Rep. Tim Walz | 30%
D-Minn.
Running for governor

Rep. Diane Black | 47%
R-Tenn.
Running for governor

Rep. Keith Ellison | 61%
D-Minn.
Running for AG

Rep. Walter B. Jones | 65%
R-N.C.
Illness

Rep. Kristi Noem | 66%
R-S.D.
Running for governor

Rep. Marsha Blackburn | 66%
R-Tenn.
Running for Senate

Rep. Elijah E. Cummings | 67%
D-Md.
Illness

Rep. Colleen Hanabusa | 68%
D-Hawaii
Running for governor

Rep. Jared Polis | 68%
D-Colo.
Running for governor

Rep. Luis V. Gutiérrez | 69%
D-Ill.
Retired

Rep. Jackie Speier | 69%
D-Calif.
Medical

Twelve members of Congress cast votes on fewer than 70 percent of the floor votes for which they were eligible.

Of those, 11 were in the House. Five representatives — Minnesota's Tim Walz, Tennessee's Diane Black, South Dakota's Kristi Noem, Hawaii's Colleen Hanabusa and Colorado's Jared Polis — missed votes as they mounted runs for governorships. Minnesota's Keith Ellison and Tennessee's Marsha Blackburn spent their time successfully running for state attorney general and the Senate, respectively. Illinois' Luis V. Gutiérrez missed 31 percent of his eligible votes after announcing his retirement in late 2017. The remaining three — North Carolina's Walter B. Jones, Maryland's Elijah E. Cummings and California's Jackie Speier — were

dealing with personal health issues. Jones died earlier this month after being sworn in from his home in Farmville, N.C., to serve his 12th term in the House.

The total does not include Speaker Paul D. Ryan, who continued the tradition of speakers casting votes only when they want to send a message, or when it really matters. Ryan cast just a dozen votes in his final year in office, and just 33 since being elected speaker in October 2015. He retired last year after serving 10 terms.

On the Senate side, John McCain was the only senator to miss more than 30 percent of votes. He left Washington in December 2017 to battle brain cancer and succumbed to the disease in late August without casting a vote in 2018.

On the plus side, 25 members of Congress — 14 senators and 11 representatives — weighed in on every floor vote offered. Despite undergoing outpatient surgery over a March weekend, Republican Charles E. Grassley, the 85-year-old from Iowa, extended his record streak to more than 25 years without missing a vote. "It's pretty important for me to be able to quantify that I'm on the job, and I don't know how else to do that when the Senate's in session except not to miss a vote," Grassley says. Trailing 1,440 votes behind Grassley, Maine Republican Susan Collins continued her perfect record of attendance since taking office in 1997. ■

History: Voting Participation

These tables show the number of roll-call votes in each chamber and in Congress as a whole since 1954, as well as the frequency with which lawmakers on average cast "yea" or "nay" votes. Participation in floor votes has hovered around 96 percent over the past two decades.

YEAR	House ROLL CALL VOTES	House RATE	Senate ROLL CALL VOTES	Senate RATE	Congress as a Whole ROLL CALL VOTES	Congress as a Whole RATE
2018	498	93.9%	274	96.8%	772	94.3%
2017	708	96.4	325	97.9	1033	96.5
2016	621	95.3	163	95.6	784	95.4
2015	702	96.9	339	97.2	1,041	96.9
2014	562	95.6	366	95.6	928	95.6
2013	640	96.0	291	97.2	931	96.1
2012	657	95.3	251	96.6	908	95.4
2011	945	96.6	235	97.0	1,180	96.6
2010	660	94.2	299	96.6	959	94.4
2009	987	96.0	397	97.0	1,384	96.1
2008	688	94.3	215	94.3	903	94.3
2007	1,177	95.5	442	95.0	1,619	95.4
2006	541	95.5	279	97.1	820	95.7
2005	669	95.9	366	97.4	1,035	96.1
2004	543	94.1	216	95.5	759	94.2
2003	675	95.6	459	96.1	1,134	95.7
2002	483	94.6	253	96.3	736	94.8
2001	507	96.2	380	98.2	887	96.5
2000	600	94.1	298	96.9	898	94.4
1999	609	96.5	374	97.9	983	96.6
1998	533	95.5	314	97.4	847	95.7
1997	633	96.3	298	98.7	931	96.5
1996	454	95.5	306	98.2	760	95.8
1995	867	96.4	613	97.1	1,480	96.5
1994	497	95.0	329	97.0	826	95.0
1993	597	96.0	395	97.6	992	96.0
1992	473	93.0	270	95.0	743	93.4
1991	428	95.0	280	97.0	708	95.0
1990	536	94.0	326	97.0	862	95.0
1989	368	94.0	312	98.0	680	95.0
1988	451	92.0	379	92.0	830	92.0
1987	488	93.0	420	94.0	908	93.0
1986	451	92.0	354	95.0	805	93.0
1985	439	94.0	381	95.0	820	94.0
1984	408	91.0	275	91.0	683	91.0
1983	498	92.0	371	92.0	869	92.0
1982	459	89.0	465	94.0	924	90.0
1981	353	91.0	483	93.0	836	92.0
1980	604	88.0	531	87.0	1,135	87.0
1979	672	89.0	497	90.0	1,169	89.0
1978	834	87.0	516	87.0	1,350	87.0
1977	706	91.0	635	88.0	1,341	90.0
1976	661	87.0	688	83.0	1,349	86.0
1975	612	91.0	602	89.0	1,214	91.0
1974	537	87.0	544	86.0	1,081	87.0
1973	541	89.0	594	87.0	1,135	89.0
1972	329	83.0	532	80.0	861	82.0
1971	320	86.0	423	83.0	743	85.0
1970	266	80.0	418	78.0	684	79.0
1969	177	86.0	245	86.0	422	86.0
1968	233	82.0	281	77.0	514	80.0
1967	245	86.0	315	82.0	560	85.0
1966	193	80.0	235	79.0	428	79.0
1965	201	87.0	258	86.0	459	87.0
1964	113	85.0	305	86.0	418	85.0
1963	119	85.0	229	83.0	348	84.0
1962	124	83.0	224	80.0	348	82.0
1961	116	89.0	204	87.0	320	88.0
1960	93	89.0	207	82.0	300	87.0
1959	87	90.0	215	89.0	302	89.0
1958	93	88.0	200	86.0	293	87.0
1957	100	89.0	107	86.0	207	88.0
1956	73	88.0	130	89.0	203	88.0
1955	76	89.0	87	86.0	163	88.0
1954	76	84.0	171	85.0	247	84.0

Perfect Attendance

The count of those who never missed a roll-call vote fell in the House from 14 members in 2017 to 11 members in 2018. The number of senators who cast a "yea" or a "nay" on every recorded vote ticked up one, to 14 members.

HOUSE

Democrats

Bera, Ami	Calif.
Soto, Darren	Fla.

Republicans

Bacon, Don	Neb.
Fleischmann, Chuck	Tenn.
Guthrie, Brett	Ky.
Lance, Leonard	N.J.
Latta, Bob	Ohio
Walberg, Tim	Ill.
Walorski, Jackie	Ind.
Womack, Steve	Ark.
Young, David	Iowa

SENATE

Democrats

Cantwell, Maria	Wash.
Kaine, Tim	Va.
Reed, Jack	R.I.
Smith, Tina	Minn.
Van Hollen, Chris	Md.
Warren, Elizabeth	Mass.

Independent

King, Angus	Maine

Republicans

Barrasso, John	Wyo.
Collins, Susan	Maine
Enzi, Michael B.	Wyo.
Ernst, Joni	Iowa
Grassley, Charles E.	Iowa
McConnell, Mitch	Ky.
Thune, John	S.D.

In the Senate: 2018

1. Presidential Support

Percentage of recorded votes cast in 2018 on which President Donald Trump took a position and on which the senator voted "yea" or "nay" in agreement with the president's position. Failure to vote does not lower an individual's score.

2. Party Unity

Percentage of recorded votes cast in 2018 on which a senator voted "yea" or "nay" in agreement with a majority of his or her party. (Party unity votes are those in which a majority of voting Democrats opposed a majority of voting Republicans.) Percentages are based on votes cast; this failure to vote does not lower a member's score.

3. Participation

Percentage of recorded votes cast in 2018 on which a senator was eligible and present, and voted "yea" or "nay." There were a total of 274 such recorded votes.

Sen. Cindy Hyde-Smith, R-Miss., was sworn in on April 8, 2018, to fill the seat vacated by the April 1 resignation of Sen. Thad Cochran, R-Miss. The last vote Cochran was eligible for was Vote 63. The first vote Hyde-Smith was eligible for was Vote 64.

Sen. Jon Kyl, R-Ariz., was sworn in on Sept. 5, 2018, to fill the seat vacated by the Aug. 25 death of Sen. John McCain, R-Ariz. The last vote McCain was eligible for was Vote 193. The first vote Kyl was eligible for was Vote 203.

KEY	**Republicans**	Democrats	*Independent*

	PRES 1	UNI 2	VOTE 3
ALABAMA			
Shelby	100	96	99
Jones	63	63	98
ALASKA			
Murkowski	96	84	96
Sullivan	96	97	97
ARIZONA			
McCain	--	--	0
Kyl	100	100	99
Flake	90	88	86
ARKANSAS			
Boozman	99	98	99
Cotton	98	99	99
CALIFORNIA			
Feinstein	31	96	96
Harris	21	99	99
COLORADO			
Bennet	46	83	99
Gardner	97	96	99
CONNECTICUT			
Blumenthal	30	99	99
Murphy	42	92	99
DELAWARE			
Carper	46	82	99
Coons	47	80	95
FLORIDA			
Rubio	99	97	92
Nelson	59	70	89
GEORGIA			
Isakson	99	96	95
Perdue	99	99	98
HAWAII			
Schatz	31	96	97
Hirono	30	98	98
IDAHO			
Crapo	97	98	99
Risch	97	98	99
ILLINOIS			
Durbin	31	99	97
Duckworth	35	97	73
INDIANA			
Young	99	93	99
Donnelly	68	54	99
IOWA			
Grassley	98	95	100
Ernst	98	97	100
KANSAS			
Roberts	100	94	99
Moran	97	89	95
KENTUCKY			
McConnell	99	96	100
Paul	85	83	97
LOUISIANA			
Cassidy	98	94	98
Kennedy	96	96	99
MAINE			
Collins	94	83	100
King	51	76	100
MARYLAND			
Cardin	40	96	98
Van Hollen	37	97	100
MASSACHUSETTS			
Warren	19	100	100
Markey	19	100	99
MICHIGAN			
Stabenow	29	92	99
Peters	36	88	99
MINNESOTA			
Klobuchar	43	93	99
Smith	37	99	100
MISSISSIPPI			
Wicker	100	96	99
Cochran	100	100	98
Hyde-Smith	100	95	97
MISSOURI			
Blunt	99	99	98
McCaskill	59	67	99

	PRES 1	UNI 2	VOTE 3
MONTANA			
Tester	55	75	99
Daines	94	92	99
NEBRASKA			
Fischer	98	99	99
Sasse	96	99	99
NEVADA			
Cortez Masto	36	93	99
Heller	97	95	93
NEW HAMPSHIRE			
Shaheen	48	79	94
Hassan	48	83	99
NEW JERSEY			
Menendez	28	98	99
Booker	18	100	95
NEW MEXICO			
Udall	31	98	99
Heinrich	31	98	92
NEW YORK			
Schumer	34	98	99
Gillibrand	18	100	99
NORTH CAROLINA			
Burr	97	97	95
Tillis	99	97	92
NORTH DAKOTA			
Hoeven	99	96	99
Heitkamp	69	54	94
OHIO			
Brown	30	99	99
Portman	99	96	99
OKLAHOMA			
Inhofe	98	99	96
Lankford	97	97	99
OREGON			
Wyden	26	98	99
Merkley	18	100	98
PENNSYLVANIA			
Casey	41	90	99
Toomey	99	98	93
RHODE ISLAND			
Reed	39	92	100
Whitehouse	36	94	99
SOUTH CAROLINA			
Graham	99	93	92
Scott	99	98	99
SOUTH DAKOTA			
Thune	98	99	100
Rounds	98	98	97
TENNESSEE			
Alexander	100	92	95
Corker	97	95	92
TEXAS			
Cornyn	100	98	99
Cruz	96	97	91
UTAH			
Lee	91	88	97
Hatch	100	94	99
VERMONT			
Leahy	42	90	96
Sanders	15	100	98
VIRGINIA			
Warner	49	79	99
Kaine	45	85	100
WASHINGTON			
Murray	34	98	95
Cantwell	33	98	100
WEST VIRGINIA			
Manchin	72	47	99
Capito	100	97	99
WISCONSIN			
Johnson	98	97	99
Baldwin	39	94	99
WYOMING			
Enzi	96	99	100
Barrasso	97	99	100

In the House: 2018

1. Presidential Support

Percentage of recorded votes cast in 2018 on which President Donald Trump took a position and on which the senator voted "yea" or "nay" in agreement with the president's position. Failure to vote does not lower an individual's score.

2. Party Unity

Percentage of recorded votes cast in 2018 on which a member voted "yea" or "nay" in agreement with a majority of his or her party. (Party unity votes are those in which a majority of voting Democrats opposed a majority of voting Republicans.) Percentages are based on votes cast; this failure to vote does not lower a member's score.

3. Participation

Percentage of recorded votes cast in 2018 on which a member was eligible and present, and voted "yea" or "nay." There were a total of 498 such recorded votes. Quorum calls, although they are included in the House list of recorded roll calls, are not counted as votes because lawmakers are asked only to respond "present."

Rep. Debbie Lesko, R-Ariz., was sworn in on May 7, 2018, to fill the seat vacated by the Dec. 8, 2017 resignation of Rep. Trent Franks, R-Ariz. The first vote Lesko was eligible for was Vote 168.

Rep. Ron DeSantis, R-Fla., resigned on Sept. 10, 2018. The last vote DeSantis was eligible for was Vote 393.

Rep. Brenda Jones, D-Mich., was sworn in on Nov. 29, 2018, to fill the seat vacated by the Dec. 5, 2017 resignation of Rep. John Conyers, D-Mich. The first vote Jones was eligible for was Vote 423.

Rep. Joseph D. Morelle, D-N.Y., was sworn in on Nov. 13, 2018, to fill the seat vacated by the Mar. 16, 2018 death of Rep. Louise M. Slaughter, D-N.Y. The last vote Slaughter was eligible for was Vote 114. The first vote Morelle was eligible for was Vote 417.

Rep. Troy Balderson, R-Ohio, was sworn in on Sept. 5, 2018, to fill the seat vacated by the Jan. 15, 2018 resignation of Rep. Pat Tiberi, R-Ohio. The last vote Tiberi was eligible for was Vote 17. The first vote Balderson was eligible for was Vote 385.

Rep. Kevin Hern, R-Okla., was sworn in on Nov. 13, 2018, to fill the seat vacated by the Apr. 23, 2018 resignation of Rep. Jim Bridenstine, R-Okla. The last vote Bridenstine was eligible for was Vote 147. The first vote Hern was eligible for was Vote 417.

Rep. Conor Lamb, D-Pa., was sworn in on Mar. 13, 2018, to fill the seat vacated by the Oct. 21, 2017 resignation of Rep. Tim Murphy, R-Pa. The first vote Lamb was eligible for was Vote 139.

Rep. Mary Gay Scanlon, D-Pa., was sworn in on Nov. 6, 2018, to fill the seat vacated by the Apr. 27, 2018 resignation of Rep. Patrick Meehan, R-Pa. The last vote Meehan was eligible for was Vote 166. The first vote Scanlon was eligible for was Vote 417.

Rep. Susan Wild, D-Pa., was sworn in on Nov. 6, 2018, to fill the seat vacated by the May 12, 2018 resignation of Rep. Charlie Dent, R-Pa. The last vote Dent was eligible for was Vote 175. The first vote Wild was eligible for was Vote 422.

Rep. Michael Cloud, R-Texas, was sworn in on June 30, 2018, to fill the seat vacated by the Apr. 6, 2018 resignation of Rep. Blake Farenthold, R-Texas. The last vote Farenthold was eligible for was Vote 129. The first vote Cloud was eligible for was Vote 315.

Rep. Evan Jenkins, R-W.Va., resigned on Sept. 30, 2018. The last vote Jenkins was eligible for was Vote 410.

	PRES 1	UNI 2	VOTE 3
ALABAMA			
1 **Byrne**	97	99	99
2 **Roby**	97	97	93
3 **Rogers**	97	92	99
4 **Aderholt**	96	98	96
5 **Brooks**	77	88	98
6 **Palmer**	90	97	99
7 Sewell	48	92	90
ALASKA			
AL **Young**	90	90	96
ARIZONA			
1 O'Halleran	70	80	98
2 **McSally**	100	93	94
3 Grijalva	10	99	92
4 **Gosar**	69	91	96
5 **Biggs**	60	87	99
6 **Schweikert**	87	97	99
7 Gallego	23	97	98
8 **Lesko**	95	99	99
9 Sinema	77	69	85
ARKANSAS			
1 **Crawford**	97	96	95
2 **Hill**	100	94	99
3 **Womack**	100	98	100
4 **Westerman**	90	99	99
CALIFORNIA			
1 **LaMalfa**	93	98	98
2 Huffman	19	94	95
3 Garamendi	50	90	93
4 **McClintock**	62	96	99
5 Thompson	30	97	99
6 Matsui	20	97	99
7 Bera	67	89	100
8 **Cook**	97	98	99
9 McNerney	22	93	92
10 **Denham**	97	91	85
11 DeSaulnier	11	95	97
12 Pelosi	31	95	92
13 Lee	7	98	97
14 Speier	24	92	69
15 Swalwell	33	97	89
16 Costa	59	78	87
17 Khanna	17	98	99
18 Eshoo	27	94	87
19 Lofgren	17	96	95
20 Panetta	43	91	99
21 **Valadao**	100	92	98
22 **Nunes**	100	98	97
23 **McCarthy**	100	99	98
24 Carbajal	59	91	94
25 **Knight**	100	94	96
26 Brownley	53	94	97
27 Chu	10	94	97
28 Schiff	33	97	99
29 Cardenas	25	96	86
30 Sherman	24	92	97
31 Aguilar	47	90	98
32 Napolitano	13	96	96
33 Lieu	32	96	93
34 Gomez	17	99	96
35 Torres	47	96	97
36 Ruiz	53	92	99
37 Bass	16	98	87
38 Sanchez	21	99	96
39 **Royce**	100	98	97
40 Roybal-Allard	17	99	98
41 Takano	17	95	99
42 **Calvert**	100	97	99
43 Waters	17	95	94
44 Barragan	27	97	98
45 **Walters**	100	99	84
46 Correa	57	86	99
47 Lowenthal	13	98	86
48 **Rohrabacher**	70	91	91
49 **Issa**	93	98	81
50 **Hunter**	97	95	95
51 Vargas	24	97	94
52 Peters	50	86	97
53 Davis	27	93	99
COLORADO			
1 DeGette	17	94	95
2 Polis	24	89	68
3 **Tipton**	97	93	98
4 **Buck**	79	93	95
5 **Lamborn**	93	98	98
6 **Coffman**	97	90	99
7 Perlmutter	32	89	93

	PRES 1	UNI 2	VOTE 3
CONNECTICUT			
1 Larson	38	94	97
2 Courtney	36	95	97
3 DeLauro	33	95	95
4 Himes	45	88	99
5 Esty	37	97	99
DELAWARE			
AL Blunt Rochester	46	91	98
FLORIDA			
1 **Gaetz**	70	89	90
2 **Dunn**	100	99	97
3 **Yoho**	83	94	95
4 **Rutherford**	100	95	99
5 Lawson	57	89	99
6 **DeSantis**	93	94	84
7 Murphy	73	76	98
8 **Posey**	83	95	96
9 Soto	30	98	100
10 Demings	30	94	99
11 **Webster**	82	97	90
12 **Bilirakis**	100	97	96
13 Crist	53	90	99
14 Castor	33	97	95
15 **Ross**	100	98	84
16 **Buchanan**	93	92	92
17 **Rooney, T.**	100	96	77
18 **Mast**	90	88	99
19 **Rooney, F.**	100	96	90
20 Hastings	27	99	86
21 Frankel	33	94	93
22 Deutch	34	94	96
23 Wasserman Schultz	31	94	97
24 Wilson	24	95	76
25 **Diaz-Balart**	93	92	98
26 **Curbelo**	86	83	95
27 **Ros-Lehtinen**	72	77	92
GEORGIA			
1 **Carter**	97	95	99
2 Bishop	62	87	95
3 **Ferguson**	97	97	99
4 Johnson	10	95	97
5 Lewis	10	99	89
6 **Handel**	100	99	99
7 **Woodall**	97	94	99
8 **Scott, A.**	100	98	97
9 **Collins**	100	99	94
10 **Hice**	83	93	98
11 **Loudermilk**	80	98	98
12 **Allen**	93	99	97
13 Scott, D.	40	86	87
14 **Graves**	97	94	98
HAWAII			
1 Hanabusa	29	93	68
2 Gabbard	34	94	90
IDAHO			
1 **Labrador**	58	94	78
2 **Simpson**	100	96	92
ILLINOIS			
1 Rush	17	98	85
2 Kelly	20	97	95
3 Lipinski	55	86	90
4 Gutierrez	15	99	69
5 Quigley	32	95	98
6 **Roskam**	93	89	89
7 Davis, D.	15	96	79
8 Krishnamoorthi	37	94	99
9 Schakowsky	10	99	99
10 Schneider	66	76	97
11 Foster	37	91	96
12 **Bost**	100	92	99
13 **Davis, R.**	97	96	99
14 **Hultgren**	100	98	88
15 **Shimkus**	100	96	99
16 **Kinzinger**	100	92	94
17 Bustos	57	86	99
18 **LaHood**	93	95	99
INDIANA			
1 Visclosky	37	97	97
2 **Walorski**	97	97	100
3 **Banks**	97	99	99
4 **Rokita**	85	94	93
5 **Brooks**	100	97	98
6 **Messer**	100	99	83
7 Carson	21	96	96
8 **Bucshon**	100	99	99
9 **Hollingsworth**	87	95	99

Column headers for all tables: PRES (1) · UNI (2) · VOTE (3)

IOWA

	PRES 1	UNI 2	VOTE 3
1 Blum	85	89	89
2 Loebsack	53	90	97
3 Young	97	97	100
4 King	87	95	98

KANSAS

	PRES 1	UNI 2	VOTE 3
1 Marshall	100	95	99
2 Jenkins	100	95	82
3 Yoder	82	93	97
4 Estes	97	99	98

KENTUCKY

	PRES 1	UNI 2	VOTE 3
1 Comer	87	96	99
2 Guthrie	100	100	100
3 Yarmuth	23	94	95
4 Massie	43	78	98
5 Rogers	100	97	84
6 Barr	100	98	98

LOUISIANA

	PRES 1	UNI 2	VOTE 3
1 Scalise	100	100	83
2 Richmond	23	97	87
3 Higgins	96	99	95
4 Johnson	86	98	97
5 Abraham	93	99	97
6 Graves	80	93	97

MAINE

	PRES 1	UNI 2	VOTE 3
1 Pingree	28	96	94
2 Poliquin	100	90	99

MARYLAND

	PRES 1	UNI 2	VOTE 3
1 Harris	80	95	98
2 Ruppersberger	40	86	97
3 Sarbanes	23	98	98
4 Brown	31	93	92
5 Hoyer	30	98	92
6 Delaney	52	92	96
7 Cummings	25	97	67
8 Raskin	13	98	99

MASSACHUSETTS

	PRES 1	UNI 2	VOTE 3
1 Neal	28	99	94
2 McGovern	13	99	99
3 Tsongas	24	95	81
4 Kennedy	17	94	93
5 Clark	20	98	99
6 Moulton	32	92	94
7 Capuano	17	100	85
8 Lynch	41	95	95
9 Keating	40	96	81

MICHIGAN

	PRES 1	UNI 2	VOTE 3
1 Bergman	97	91	98
2 Huizenga	100	97	97
3 Amash	37	68	99
4 Moolenaar	100	97	99
5 Kildee	27	93	99
6 Upton	90	86	96
7 Walberg	100	96	100
8 Bishop	100	95	90
9 Levin	23	99	99
10 Mitchell	100	96	99
11 Trott	100	97	83
12 Dingell	27	95	98
13 Jones	0	100	100
14 Lawrence	27	96	99

MINNESOTA

	PRES 1	UNI 2	VOTE 3
1 Walz	25	93	30
2 Lewis	82	97	94
3 Paulsen	100	87	97
4 McCollum	24	92	98
5 Ellison	6	94	61
6 Emmer	82	93	98
7 Peterson	77	72	90
8 Nolan	40	94	81

MISSISSIPPI

	PRES 1	UNI 2	VOTE 3
1 Kelly	90	97	99
2 Thompson	25	98	82
3 Harper	96	97	93
4 Palazzo	96	97	89

MISSOURI

	PRES 1	UNI 2	VOTE 3
1 Clay	24	95	92
2 Wagner	100	99	99
3 Luetkemeyer	100	99	97
4 Hartzler	100	97	96
5 Cleaver	27	97	94
6 Graves	96	92	95
7 Long	90	98	94
8 Smith	89	98	97

MONTANA

	PRES 1	UNI 2	VOTE 3
AL Gianforte	90	98	99

NEBRASKA

	PRES 1	UNI 2	VOTE 3
1 Fortenberry	97	92	98
2 Bacon	100	97	100
3 Smith	93	98	98

NEVADA

	PRES 1	UNI 2	VOTE 3
1 Titus	21	93	94
2 Amodei	100	96	96
4 Kihuen	20	97	99
SB Rosen	63	88	85

NEW HAMPSHIRE

	PRES 1	UNI 2	VOTE 3
1 Shea-Porter	33	92	78
2 Kuster	66	87	93

NEW JERSEY

	PRES 1	UNI 2	VOTE 3
1 Norcross	31	96	97
2 LoBiondo	90	81	98
3 MacArthur	97	89	99
4 Smith	87	84	99
5 Gottheimer	77	75	97
6 Pallone	17	98	99
7 Lance	83	80	100
8 Sires	33	98	93
9 Pascrell	28	96	98
10 Payne	18	98	93
11 Frelinghuysen	86	94	96
12 Watson Coleman	7	99	98

NEW MEXICO

	PRES 1	UNI 2	VOTE 3
1 Lujan Grisham	41	88	76
2 Pearce	85	93	85
3 Lujan	20	93	99

NEW YORK

	PRES 1	UNI 2	VOTE 3
1 Zeldin	83	92	94
2 King	90	90	94
3 Suozzi	48	86	94
4 Rice	59	89	88
5 Meeks	30	93	95
6 Meng	24	97	97
7 Velazquez	10	99	96
8 Jeffries	21	97	97
9 Clarke	10	99	97
10 Nadler	20	94	99
11 Donovan	97	91	95
12 Maloney, C.	20	99	97
13 Espaillat	13	99	99
14 Crowley	19	100	81
15 Serrano	17	99	99
16 Engel	20	95	94
17 Lowey	28	97	98
18 Maloney, S.	56	91	93
19 Faso	97	86	99
20 Tonko	38	97	96
21 Stefanik	93	87	94
22 Tenney	97	92	99
23 Reed	93	90	98
24 Katko	86	86	95
25 Morelle	--	100	99
25 Slaughter	29	93	83
26 Higgins	33	95	97
27 Collins	100	97	99

NORTH CAROLINA

	PRES 1	UNI 2	VOTE 3
1 Butterfield	30	95	90
2 Holding	90	95	96
3 Jones	15	58	65
4 Price	27	99	94
5 Foxx	93	93	99
6 Walker	90	99	97
7 Rouzer	90	95	97
8 Hudson	93	95	95
9 Pittenger	100	96	86
10 McHenry	100	97	94
11 Meadows	80	96	98
12 Adams	30	98	94
13 Budd	80	98	99

NORTH DAKOTA

	PRES 1	UNI 2	VOTE 3
SA Cramer	100	98	84

OHIO

	PRES 1	UNI 2	VOTE 3
1 Chabot	97	99	99
2 Wenstrup	100	97	97
3 Beatty	27	94	90
4 Jordan	77	92	99
5 Latta	93	96	100
6 Johnson	100	94	98
7 Gibbs	100	98	99
8 Davidson	80	96	99
9 Kaptur	33	92	97
10 Turner	97	91	94
11 Fudge	30	99	94
11 Tiberi	100	100	100
12 Balderson	100	100	99
13 Ryan	30	95	97
14 Joyce	100	92	97
15 Stivers	100	93	92
16 Renacci	93	93	88

OKLAHOMA

	PRES 1	UNI 2	VOTE 3
1 Hern	--	94	100
1 Bridenstine	100	100	72
2 Mullin	93	99	99
3 Lucas	100	98	99
4 Cole	100	96	98
5 Russell	93	96	90

OREGON

	PRES 1	UNI 2	VOTE 3
1 Bonamici	27	94	99
2 Walden	100	96	99
3 Blumenauer	21	93	90
4 DeFazio	19	97	93
5 Schrader	43	86	98

PENNSYLVANIA

	PRES 1	UNI 2	VOTE 3
1 Fitzpatrick	87	75	99
1 Brady	27	99	84
2 Boyle	31	96	89
3 Evans	30	95	99
4 Costello	97	85	94
7 Scanlon	--	88	99
7 Meehan	100	92	95
8 Cartwright	40	91	98
9 Shuster	100	96	74
10 Perry	79	91	99
11 Smucker	90	98	99
11 Barletta	93	96	83
12 Rothfus	80	98	99
12 Marino	100	97	98
15 Thompson	97	93	98
15 Dent	100	100	98
15 Wild	--	100	87
16 Kelly	93	95	99
17 Lamb	67	76	99
18 Doyle	30	98	97

RHODE ISLAND

	PRES 1	UNI 2	VOTE 3
1 Cicilline	27	95	97
2 Langevin	40	97	98

SOUTH CAROLINA

	PRES 1	UNI 2	VOTE 3
1 Sanford	53	83	96
2 Wilson	100	98	98
3 Duncan	83	94	87
4 Gowdy	97	98	78
5 Norman	83	98	96
6 Clyburn	30	98	97
7 Rice	90	98	96

SOUTH DAKOTA

	PRES 1	UNI 2	VOTE 3
AL Noem	88	97	66

TENNESSEE

	PRES 1	UNI 2	VOTE 3
1 Roe	93	97	99
2 Duncan	66	90	97
3 Fleischmann	97	97	100
4 DesJarlais	90	98	96
5 Cooper	57	80	99
6 Black	88	98	47
7 Blackburn	87	95	66
8 Kustoff	97	99	95
9 Cohen	20	95	98

TEXAS

	PRES 1	UNI 2	VOTE 3
1 Gohmert	71	89	93
2 Poe	86	93	85
3 Johnson, S.	97	99	91
4 Ratcliffe	90	95	85
5 Hensarling	97	99	99
6 Barton	90	97	92
7 Culberson	97	97	95
8 Brady	100	98	94
9 Green, A.	23	98	98
10 McCaul	100	98	99
11 Conaway	100	94	99
12 Granger	97	97	97
13 Thornberry	100	97	96
14 Weber	87	95	98
15 Gonzalez	47	83	96
16 O'Rourke	41	89	97
17 Flores	100	95	96
18 Jackson Lee	20	97	97
19 Arrington	97	99	95
20 Castro	23	95	99
21 Smith	97	98	92
22 Olson	97	99	94
23 Hurd	93	91	98
24 Marchant	96	97	92
25 Williams	86	98	99
26 Burgess	90	94	98
27 Cloud	100	98	100
27 Farenthold	67	93	98
28 Cuellar	77	71	98
29 Green, G.	38	91	91
30 Johnson, E.	32	96	90
31 Carter	96	96	94
32 Sessions	97	99	98
33 Veasey	34	94	98
34 Vela	43	87	87
35 Doggett	17	94	97
36 Babin	93	97	98

UTAH

	PRES 1	UNI 2	VOTE 3
1 Bishop	93	98	98
2 Stewart	97	98	98
3 Curtis	93	99	98
4 Love	97	94	86

VERMONT

	PRES 1	UNI 2	VOTE 3
AL Welch	23	94	99

VIRGINIA

	PRES 1	UNI 2	VOTE 3
1 Wittman	90	94	99
2 Taylor	97	94	90
3 Scott	30	94	98
4 McEachin	30	94	97
5 Garrett	67	92	96
6 Goodlatte	100	99	96
7 Brat	80	96	98
8 Beyer	30	95	91
9 Griffith	86	94	99
10 Comstock	97	95	88
11 Connolly	33	95	99

WASHINGTON

	PRES 1	UNI 2	VOTE 3
1 DelBene	30	92	99
2 Larsen	33	93	97
3 Herrera Beutler	90	91	98
4 Newhouse	93	96	98
5 McMorris Rodgers	93	97	99
6 Kilmer	43	94	99
7 Jayapal	13	99	98
8 Reichert	97	92	96
9 Smith	18	94	96
10 Heck	33	90	99

WEST VIRGINIA

	PRES 1	UNI 2	VOTE 3
1 McKinley	97	91	99
2 Mooney	77	96	98
3 Jenkins	96	91	79

WISCONSIN

	PRES 1	UNI 2	VOTE 3
1 Ryan	89	91	2
2 Pocan	13	95	98
3 Kind	39	89	81
4 Moore	10	94	92
5 Sensenbrenner	80	95	97
6 Grothman	93	97	96
7 Duffy	96	97	97
8 Gallagher	97	93	98

WYOMING

	PRES 1	UNI 2	VOTE 3
AL Cheney	96	96	91

KEY VOTES

Key Senate and House Votes in 2018

The oldest of CQ Roll Call's annual studies, Key Votes is a selection of the major votes for both House and Senate for the past year. Editors choose the single vote on each issue that best presents a member's stance or that determined the year's legistative outcome. Charts of how each member voted on this list can be found at cq.com.

Attributes of a Key Vote

Since its 1945 founding, CQ Roll Call has selected a series of key votes in Congress on major issues of the year.

A vote is judged to be key by the extent to which it represents:
    a matter of major controversy.
    a matter of presidential or political power.
    a matter of potentially great impact on the nation and the lives of Americans.

For each group of related votes on an issue in each chamber, one key vote is usually chosen — one that, in the opinion of CQ Roll Call editors, was most important in determining the outcome of the issue for the year or best reflected the views of individual lawmakers on that issue.

SENATE VOTES

11   FISA Amendments Reauthorization

Motion to invoke cloture to concur in the House amendment to the bill (S 139) that would reauthorize for six years, through 2023, the Foreign Intelligence Surveillance Act, which governs electronic surveillance of foreign terrorism suspects. Agreed to 60-38 (R 41-8; D 18-29; I 1-1) on Jan. 16, 2018.

The run-up to the Senate's January vote reauthorizing the Foreign Intelligence Surveillance Act had much the same flavor as the last congressional debate on the broad powers Congress authorized after the Sept. 11, 2001, attacks to monitor communications in an effort to uncover terrorist plots.

There was plenty of skepticism, colored by the 2013 revelations of National Security Agency whistleblower Edward Snowden that revealed the government was scooping up more information about regular Americans than Congress had expected when it granted the powers.

So it was surprising when the Senate invoked cloture and then passed, with relative ease, an extension of the powers without doing much to curtail them.

The powers in question, in section 702 of the Foreign Intelligence Surveillance Act, permit the National Security Agency to listen to phone calls involving suspected terrorists and read emails mentioning their names, all without a warrant. Before Snowden, the power was thought to apply only to calls and emails involving foreigners, but Snowden revealed that the agency has, in fact, monitored Americans' communications in some instances — when they are communicating with foreigners, for instance, or when their emails are routed through servers overseas.

Three years earlier, Congress embarked on a similar reauthori-

zation debate over provisions in the 2001 Patriot Act that permitted the NSA to collect data, but not the content, of Americans' phone calls, specifically the numbers called and the duration of the calls. Then, over Senate Majority Leader Mitch McConnell's objections, senators passed a bill rescinding the NSA's power, requiring it to subpoena call data from the phone companies.

But in the intervening three years, the dynamics on surveillance shifted. While in 2015 President Barack Obama supported civil libertarians in Congress eager to curtail domestic surveillance, in 2018 President Donald Trump pushed for a permanent reauthorization of the existing law. Instances of domestic terrorism both in the United States and Europe had given security hawks talking points. When the vote came, Republican senators weren't united, but far more of them were willing to give Trump what he wanted than to stick with the surveillance skeptics in their caucus.

35   Immigration Overhaul

Motion to invoke cloture on a bill (HR 2579) to appropriate $25 billion from fiscal 2019-27 for border security purposes, such as physical barriers, technology and facilities. It would prohibit deportation of recipients of the Deferred Action for Childhood Arrivals immigration program if they meet certain qualifications, and reduce the cap on family-sponsored immigrant visas. It would require the Homeland Security Department to prioritize enforcement of immigration activities for aliens that have committed felonies or misdemeanors, and those who are unlawfully present in the United States and arrived after June 30, 2018. Rejected 54-45 (R 8-42; D 44-3; I 2-0) on Feb. 15, 2018.

This was the closest the Senate came to meeting President Donald Trump's demand for $25 billion to strengthen border security, but the administration itself scuttled the deal by refusing to go along with a path to citizenship for the so-called Dreamers, about 1.8 million immigrants brought to the United States illegally as children.

The bipartisan bill crafted by Mike Rounds, a South Dakota Republican, and Angus King, an independent from Maine, garnered 54 votes — six short of the 60 needed to advance — with eight Republicans in support despite Trump's opposition. That was more than went along with the bill the president favored: providing $25 billion for the border wall and giving Dreamers an eventual path to citizenship, but also setting strict limits on legal immigration and ending a visa lottery aimed at increasing diversity. That bill, sponsored by Iowa Republican Charles E. Grassley, received only 39 "yes" votes.

Two other bipartisan proposals, including one by Arizona Republican John McCain and Delaware Democrat Chris Coons, also failed to get over the 60-vote hurdle to invoke cloture, leaving the Senate in a deadlock over immigration policy that would continue for the rest of the year.

The measures were spawned by Trump's decision in Septem-

ber 2017 to phase out the Deferred Action for Childhood Arrivals program instituted by President Barack Obama to protect Dreamers from deportation. The end of DACA had been delayed by federal court orders, but program supporters wanted to give its 800,000 enrollees and others who might be eligible more permanent status as U.S. residents.

Trump attempted to leverage the Dreamers to secure funding for the border wall he promised during his campaign. But when offered $25 billion for "physical barriers, technology and facilities" at the southern border in return for a 10- to 12-year path to citizenship for the Dreamers and continuation of the visa lottery, the administration balked.

Just before the vote on the Rounds/King bill, Trump tweeted a statement from the Department of Homeland Security saying it "would effectively make the United States a sanctuary nation where ignoring the rule of law is encouraged."

In retrospect, it may have been Trump's last chance to get what he wanted for the border. As the 115th Congress came to a close in December, the president refused to back a continuing resolution that included no money for the wall, forcing a record-long, 35-day shutdown of numerous government agencies. The shutdown ended in February when Congress, with Democrats now in control of the House, approved funding for the rest of fiscal 2019 with only $1.6 billion for border security enhancements.

52   Dodd-Frank Partial Repeal

Motion to invoke cloture on the bill (S 2155) that would apply the more stringent bank regulation provisions of the 2010 financial overhaul to banks with $250 billion in assets, instead of those with at least $50 billion in assets. Agreed to 67-31 (R 50-0; D 16-30, I 1-1) on March 14, 2018.

The Senate led the way in repealing sections of the 2010 Dodd-Frank financial regulatory law that was Congress' response to the 2008 financial crisis.

Banking, Housing and Urban Affairs Chairman Michael D. Crapo forged the deal with moderate Democrats, several of whom faced re-election in 2018. The bill freed all but the nation's largest banks from strict federal oversight.

The bill also freed small and mid-sized banks from the "stress tests" established by the Dodd-Frank law, which tasked regulators with assuring that banks had the capital to weather recessions. It also reduced the number of financial institutions considered "systemically important" and therefore subject to tough scrutiny of their books. And it exempted smaller banks from having to reveal information about their lending practices.

The banks had argued that the rules were excessively burdensome.

Crapo laid the groundwork in 2017, winning over several Democratic co-sponsors, including Joe Donnelly of Indiana, Heidi Heitkamp of North Dakota, Jon Tester of Montana, Joe Manchin III of West Virginia and Claire McCaskill of Missouri, all of whom were in tough 2018 re-election races.

When he brought the bill before his committee in December, the panel approved it on a bipartisan 16-7 vote. When it went to the Senate floor in March, most Democrats voted "no," but a united Republican caucus was joined by plenty of dissenters in the Democratic ranks. It marked a major victory for President Donald Trump in his effort to scale back regulations imposed during the presidency of his predecessor, Barack Obama.

76   Auto Loan Rule

Passage of the joint resolution (SJ Res 57) that would nullify and disapprove of a Consumer Financial Protection Bureau rule that provides guidance to third parties that offer indirect financing for automobile loans. Passed 51-47 (R 50-0; D 1-45; I 0-2) on April 18, 2018.

For years now a small but devoted band of conservatives has argued that Congress could strike down decades-old regulations — if only it would act.

Using a tool known as the Congressional Review Act, which allows Congress to disapprove recently finalized rules, they have argued that thousands of regulations, including guidance documents, could also be wiped out by Congress due to what amounts to an administrative hiccup — the failure to file paperwork with Congress and the Government Accountability Office.

In April 2018, the Senate took the unprecedented step of eliminating a 2013 guidance document from the Consumer Financial Protection Bureau that sought to prevent discriminatory practices among auto lenders who had been accused of charging minorities higher interest rates. Patrick J. Toomey, a Pennsylvania Republican, called the regulation, which has led to fines in the tens of millions, a "back-door effort to regulate auto loans."

An agency rule that is struck down using the CRA cannot be resubmitted in the future if it is "substantially the same" as the old one. In 2017, Congress struck down 15 recently finalized rules.

Under normal circumstances, the CRA applies only to recently finalized rules; Congress has 60 legislative days to take action to disapprove. But in the case of the auto-lending regulation, the CFPB did not notify Congress and the GAO, which, under the law, would open up the door for Congress to act. Toomey also asked the Government Accountability Office to look at whether the CFPB's auto-lending guidance could also be treated as a rule under the CRA. The GAO's answer? Yes.

Critics argue that expanding the use of the CRA to old rules opens a "Pandora's box" for the legislative system. Regulations dating back to 1996 could now be subject to the CRA.

221   Opioid Abuse

Motion to concur on a bill (HR 6) to expand Medicare and Medicaid to cover medication-assisted treatment for substance use disorder and would place new requirements on states regarding Medicaid drug review and utilization requirements. It would appropriate $15 million annually from fiscal 2019-23 to support public health laboratories to detect synthetic opioids. It would allow Medicaid patients with opioid use or cocaine use disorders to stay up to 30 days per year in certain treatment facilities with more than 16 beds. Passed, clearing it for the president, 98-1 (R 49-1; D 47-0; I 2-0) on Oct. 3, 2018.

A near-unanimous vote in the Senate capped a months-long effort to develop a multi-pronged response to the nation's opioid crisis, which the National Institute on Drug Abuse says is causing an average of 130 overdose deaths every day.

The 98-1 tally, with Utah Republican Sen. Mike Lee as the lone dissenter, sent the package approved earlier by the House to the White House. President Donald Trump signed it into law on Oct. 24.

The measure includes new programs for prevention, treatment, research and enforcement of regulations for distributing prescription drugs. For instance, it funds research to find a nonaddictive painkiller and increases support for state monitoring programs to prevent abuse.

"We're not pretending that a single act here can fix the problem," said Health, Education, Labor and Pensions Chairman Lamar Alexander, a Tennessee Republican who worked with House Energy and Commerce Chairman Greg Walden, an Oregon Republican, to develop the legislation over much of the year. "We want to do everything that we can do to provide tools to parents and patients and doctors and nurses and communities and governors, anyone we can, to fight this crisis."

Alexander said the bill supplements the approximately $8.5 billion Congress appropriated in 2018 to battle the opioid crisis.

222   Kavanaugh

Motion to invoke cloture on the nomination of Brett M. Kavanaugh of Maryland to be an Associate Justice of the Supreme Court of the United States, agreed to 51-49 (R 50-1; D 1-46; I 0-2) on Oct. 5, 2018.

The bitter and divisive confirmation process for Justice Brett M. Kavanaugh reached a fever pitch when the full Senate voted on his appointment for the first time.

President Donald Trump sought to put a second conservative on the Supreme Court in as many years, with Kavanaugh expected to solidify the Supreme Court's conservative tilt for decades on issues such as access to abortion and LGBT rights. Majority Leader Mitch McConnell said the push was key to his Senate legacy.

At first, the confirmation battle raged over that ideological balance. Then, a decades-old sexual assault allegation against Kavanaugh from Christine Blasey Ford forced a dramatic Judiciary Committee hearing, one that Saturday Night Live parodied and that added questions about Kavanaugh's judicial temperament and the truthfulness of his Senate testimony.

The full Senate was supposed to vote a week earlier than it did. But Jeff Flake of Arizona and other Republicans forced a limited, one-week supplemental FBI background investigation that ultimately answered few questions. Protesters confronted senators and prompted extra security measures as pressure mounted on the few undecided senators.

Lisa Murkowski of Alaska was the only Republican for whom the lingering questions warranted a vote against Kavanaugh. Sen. Joe Manchin III of West Virginia was the only Democrat to vote for Kavanaugh. The 51-49 vote to move to the final confirmation vote reflected a divided Senate and a divided country.

Senators said the fight energized voters on both sides and they spoke of how Ford's allegations awoke something in their constituents, who shared stories of being sexually assaulted. The Senate voted 50-48 to confirm Kavanaugh the next day, and he heard his first case as a justice three days later.

226   Short-Term Health Insurance

Passage of a resolution (SJ Res 63) to nullify and disapprove of a rule from the departments of Treasury, Labor, and Health and Human Services that would expand the duration of short-term health insurance plans. Rejected 50-50 (R 1-50; D 47-0; I 2-0) on Oct. 10, 2018.

Democrats fell just one vote short in a bid to overturn a Trump administration rule allowing expansion of short-term health insurance plans, but they were successful in putting Republicans on the record for supporting what some call "junk insurance" without several of the guarantees provided in the 2010 health care overhaul.

All 49 Democrats and independents in the Senate supported the measure and were joined by Maine Republican Susan Collins to make it an unsuccessful tie vote. "Short-term limited duration plans do not provide protections for enrollees who suffer from pre-existing conditions," Collins said in a statement after the vote. "As I have often emphasized, it is essential that individuals who suffer from pre-existing conditions are covered."

Republicans argued that short-term plans do not block people with pre-existing conditions from obtaining insurance, but instead offer a way for people who can't afford plans under the 2010 law to get coverage.

"This resolution has nothing to do with pre-existing conditions," said Lamar Alexander, the Tennessee Republican who chairs the Health, Education, Labor and Pensions Committee. "It doesn't change one single word of the Affordable Care Act, which guarantees that if you have a pre-existing condition, you have a right to buy Obamacare and you can't be charged more because of it."

The vote was largely a chance for Democrats, heading into the midterm elections, to put Republicans on the record on the administration's August final rule to expand the length of time consumers can maintain a short-term health insurance plan. The plans are not required to meet all of the regulations under the 2010 health care law, and under the August rule are required to disclose that.

266   Yemen

Passage of the joint resolution (S J Res 54) that would direct the president to remove U.S. armed forces from hostilities in or affecting the Republic of Yemen, except forces engaged in operations directed at al-Qaida or associated forces. Passed 56-41 (R 7-41; D 47-0; I 2-0) on Dec. 13, 2018.

Not since 1973 has the Senate invoked the War Powers Act to debate and pass a joint resolution ordering the executive branch to cease military operations.

The vote was ultimately symbolic as House Republican leaders in the last Congress used a procedural move to block a similar resolution from receiving a floor vote.

Nonetheless, the Senate vote was historic for marking a rare congressional rebuke of the U.S. military, for its watershed potential in paving the way for similar future votes under the act and for its implications for U.S. relations with Saudi Arabia, which is leading the military campaign in Yemen.

The resolution from independent Bernie Sanders of Vermont and Republican Mike Lee of Utah explicitly permitted the continuance of military operations in Yemen targeted against al-Qaida. It defined prohibited military activities to include in-flight fueling for non-U.S. aircraft conducting missions over Yemen.

The vote was also consequential for being an exception to the traditional Republican-versus-Democratic voting structure that characterized so many Senate votes in the 115th Congress. Seven Republicans voted with all 49 Democrats to end military operations in Yemen. The measure required a simple majority for

passage.

An even greater number of Republicans (14) voted in late November with all Democrats, 63-37, on a motion to discharge the joint resolution from the Foreign Relations Committee, paving the way for floor votes on the measure.

That was a result of significant GOP sentiment that a public debate on why the United States was providing military support to Saudi Arabia — despite its worsening human rights record — was worth having, regardless of the ultimate vote outcome.

In the days prior to the vote on passage, the Trump administration dispatched to Capitol Hill Cabinet officials including Secretary of State Mike Pompeo, then-Defense Secretary James Mattis and later CIA Director Gina Haspel to argue against the resolution.

But senators were frustrated with the lack of detail they received in the classified briefings and were particularly angered by an initial administration decision to keep Haspel from briefing senators.

The CIA was reported to have concluded that Saudi Crown Prince Mohammed bin Salman was behind the October assassination of a prominent dissident Saudi journalist — a conclusion not accepted by the White House. Jamal Khashoggi's death, while not directly related to the Yemen war, unleashed bipartisan criticism of the administration's handling of relations with the Gulf kingdom.

271 Criminal Justice Overhaul

Motion to concur with a bill (S 756) to reduce federally incarcerated individuals through changes in sentencing laws. The bill would seek to do so, in part, by allowing judges more flexibility when handing down sentences below the mandatory minimum for nonviolent drug offenders. It would also establish programs to provide support for prisoners returning to society in an attempt to reduce rates of recidivation. Approved 87-12 (R 38-12; D 47-0; I 2-0) on Dec. 18, 2018.

Though it was overshadowed by a looming government shutdown, passage of a criminal-justice overhaul was one of the biggest successes of the 115th Congress.

The legislation approved by the Senate in an 87-12 vote was years in the making and came at the end of a Congress mired in gridlock over immigration policy, federal spending and other major issues. The House would pass the measure two days later and President Donald Trump signed it into law on Dec. 21 — the same day he forced a partial government shutdown by refusing to sign a stop-gap spending bill that did not include funding for a wall along the U.S.-Mexico border.

Among its many provisions, the bill aims to lower the number of federal inmates through changes in some sentencing laws and through better support for prisoners returning to society so they don't commit new crimes and return to prison. It gives judges more freedom to hand down sentences below the mandatory minimum for nonviolent drug offenders and reduces mandatory minimums associated with the three-strikes law for habitual offenders.

It would also eliminate a provision that prosecutors used to "stack" firearm charges for long sentences for first-time offenders. And it makes retroactive a 2010 law that reduced the sentencing disparity between crack and powder cocaine.

On the prison side, the bill creates more job training and drug treatment for inmates, among other changes. It increases direct spending by $346 million over the next 10 years, according to the Congressional Budget Office.

The legislation also prohibits the shackling of pregnant inmates and the use of solitary confinement for juveniles in almost all cases.

Judiciary Chairman Charles E. Grassley, an Iowa Republican who co-wrote the bill, said before the vote that it had support across the political spectrum. "I don't know whether we've had legislation like this before the United States Senate where you put together such a diverse group of people and organizations supporting the bill," he said.

HOUSE VOTES

16 FISA Reauthorization

Passage of a bill (S 139) that would reauthorize for six years, through 2023, the Foreign Intelligence Surveillance Act, which governs electronic surveillance of foreign terrorism suspects. Passed 256-164 (R 191-45; D 65-119) on Jan. 11, 2018.

Much as they had in 2015, civil libertarians in the House GOP targeted the sunset of the Foreign Intelligence Surveillance Act as a prime opportunity to roll back powers granted to intelligence agencies after the Sept. 11, 2001, attacks. The revelations, in 2013, by former National Security Agency contractor Edward Snowden, had bolstered their case by shining light on the fact that the communications of regular Americans were getting caught up in the dragnet. Three years earlier, the libertarians had successfully scuttled the National Security Agency's collection of data on Americans' phone calls — the numbers called and duration but not content — and they followed the same game plan in 2017, convincing the bipartisan leadership of the Judiciary Committee to back the effort. The panel moved legislation late in the year to add a new warrant requirement and oversight of the NSA's use of section 702 of the Foreign Intelligence Surveillance Act. That section has allowed the agency to, in some situations, read the emails and listen to phone calls involving Americans, in the search for terrorist suspects.

The committee approved the measure on a bipartisan basis, but then it stalled. In 2015, House Republicans had joined forces with civil liberties advocates in the Democratic Party, with the blessing of then-President Barack Obama.

In the interim, however, terrorist attacks in the United States and in Europe had bolstered the position of security hawks. And whereas Obama backed the civil libertarians, President Donald Trump made it clear he preferred a permanent reauthorization of the expiring powers, without the warrant requirement or oversight. For Republicans eager to help their president, he was persuasive. When the House voted in January, it was on a Senate measure that gave Trump a clean reauthorization. The libertarians could claim a minor victory in that it was not permanent and they will have another opportunity to debate domestic surveillance in 2023.

35   Trump Impeachment

Motion to table (kill) the resolution (H Res 705) that would impeach President Donald Trump for high crimes and misdemeanors, and would provide that the resolution's articles of impeachment be exhibited to the Senate. Motion agreed to 355-66 (R 234-0; D 121-66) on Jan. 19, 2018.

Just one month after forcing a vote on a failed impeachment resolution, liberal Democrats were at it again in January, and this time, they found more support for their efforts — but nowhere near enough to pass the resolution.

Al Green, a Texas Democrat, was able to prevail in getting a vote on the resolution that highlighted Trump's "bigoted statements" and other actions, including a travel ban on citizens from majority-

Muslim counties, his ambivalence about white nationalists who rallied in Charlottesville, Va., and his reported comments about people from "shithole countries" like Haiti.

In December 2017, 58 Democrats voted for a similar impeachment measure. This time around, 66 did so — over a third of the caucus — including moderate lawmakers like David Scott of Georgia. Three other Democrats voted "present." Republicans were unanimous in their opposition.

Some vulnerable Democrats complained that the vote would put them in a tough position, especially in an election year: Cheri Bustos, who represents an Illinois district carried by Trump in 2016, said she was "disappointed" in the vote, calling it "self-inflicted damage."

171   Auto Loan Rule

Passage of the joint resolution (S J Res 57) that would nullify and disapprove of a Consumer Financial Protection Bureau rule that provides guidance to third parties that offer indirect financing for automobile loans. Passed 234-175 (R 223-1; D 11-174) on May 8, 2018.

In 2018, Congress took the unprecedented step of eliminating a 2013 guidance document from the Consumer Financial Protection Bureau that sought to prevent discriminatory practices among auto lenders who had been accused of charging minorities higher interest rates. Critics had decried the regulation as a "back-door effort" to regulate auto loans.

Under normal circumstances, the CRA applies only to recently finalized rules and Congress has 60 legislative days to take action to disapprove. An agency rule that Congress has struck down using the CRA cannot be resubmitted in the future if it is "substantially the same" as the old one. In 2017, Congress struck down 15 recently finalized rules, a watershed after having utilized it only once before.

In the case of the auto-lending regulation, the CFPB did not notify Congress and the GAO, which under the law opened the door for Congress to act. The Government Accountability Office said the guidance could be treated as a rule under the CRA.

In April, the Senate passed the measure; just a few weeks later, the House took it up. Only one Republican voted "no" — Ileana Ros-Lehtinen of Florida. Eleven Democrats, all of them part of the fiscally conservative Blue Dog Coalition, joined with Republicans, and after the president's signature later that month, the measure became law.

189   Veterans Health Care

Passage of a bill (S 2372) to consolidate programs that allow veterans to seek medical care outside of the VA into a new singular entity, the Veterans Community Care Program. The bill would continue the current VA Choice Program for one year, and would authorize an additional $5.2 billion for the costs of providing non-VA medical care through the old program and for transitioning to the new one. Passed 347-70 (R 231-0; D 116-70) on May 16, 2018.

Faced with expiration of the popular Veterans Choice program at the end of May, the House voted overwhelmingly to both extend and expand opportunities for veterans to seek health care outside of facilities run by the Department of Veterans Affairs.

The 347-70 vote provided another $5.2 billion for the Choice program, which began in 2014 in the wake of a national scandal about the quality of VA care. Designed as a temporary solution to the problems, the program allows veterans to seek care outside of the VA if they live more than 40 miles from a VA facility or have to wait more than 30 days for an appointment.

But the House, after months of negotiations with the Senate, went further toward privatization of veterans' health care by creating a permanent entity within the VA called the Veterans Community Care Program to consolidate other initiatives providing care for veterans outside of the VA network.

The bill also would establish a commission, similar to the Pentagon's Base Realignment and Closure process, to review proposals from the VA to close existing facilities. Opponents argue the expansion of private care could weaken the VA's existing operations, so negotiators added authorization of funds to recruit more VA doctors to garner support for the bill. As a result, the measure was widely supported by Democrats and veterans' groups.

Movement on an overhaul of private care programs was a politically thorny issue for Congress and the Veterans' Affairs committees that are known for bipartisan deal-making.

But the changes were largely forced by the VA's 2014 scandal when patients were found to have died while waiting for care — some of whom were kept on wait lists outside of the formal patient scheduling system in an attempt to conceal long wait times for appointments.

216   Bank Regulations

Passage of a bill (S 2155) that would apply the more stringent bank regulation provisions of the 2010 financial overhaul to banks with $250 billion in assets, instead of those with at least $50 billion in assets. Passed, clearing it for the president, 258-159 (R 225-1; D 33-158) on May 22, 2018.

The House, in 2017, had led the way in using the 1995 Congressional Review Act to rescind regulations imposed toward the end of President Barack Obama's presidency. But the financial rules imposed by the 2010 Dodd-Frank law, aimed at preventing another recession of the magnitude of that of 2007-09, were too long in force to be vulnerable to that line of attack. The review act requires that rules be relatively recent in order to trigger its expedited procedures for repeal.

To go after Dodd-Frank rules imposing "stress tests" on small and mid-sized banks and transparency requirements on smaller lenders, the Senate would have to lead. When Senate Banking, Housing and Urban Affairs Chairman Michael D. Crapo, the Idaho Republican, forged a bipartisan deal to scale back Dodd-

Frank, it was only a matter of time before the House followed.

After the Senate passed Crapo's bill in March on a bipartisan basis, the House moved quickly. The vast majority of Democrats voted "no," an indication of the different political dynamics facing representatives, where Democrats were ascendant, and senators, where several Democrats from states that President Donald Trump had won in 2016 were up for re-election. Still, with a united GOP caucus, the rollback of Dodd-Frank rules passed with ease.

297   DACA and Border Security

Passage of a bill (HR 6136) to appropriate $23.4 billion for various border security activities. Included would be $16.6 billion for a "border wall system," which would be available from fiscal 2019-27, and $6.8 billion for border security investments, which would be available from fiscal 2019-23. It would provide those with Deferred Action for Childhood Arrivals status a six-year renewable contingent non-immigrant legal status and would allow them to apply for a green card after five years, providing a path to citizenship. It would modify legal immigration by ending the diversity visa program and reallocating those visas to other classifications. The bill would require that undocumented immigrants who are charged with a misdemeanor offense for improper entry into the United States be detained with their minor children. Rejected 121-301 (R 121-112; D 0-189) on June 27, 2018.

A last-ditch attempt to put billions of dollars into border security as requested by President Donald Trump failed miserably in June when a "compromise" immigration bill won only 121 Republican votes and none from Democrats.

The package crafted by the GOP's moderate and conservative wings proposed to crack down on both legal and illegal immigration with $23.6 billion in investments, including a wall along the southern border, while offering a path to citizenship for so-called Dreamers, immigrants brought to the United States illegally as children who had been protected from deportation by the Deferred Action for Childhood Arrivals program started by President Barack Obama in 2014.

But the DACA provisions in the bill turned out to be its downfall. Conservatives supported Trump's plan to phase out the program and believed their base would punish them in the midterm elections if they went against the president. Democrats, who overwhelmingly support the Dreamers, did not want them be used as bargaining chips to secure funding for Trump's border wall.

"Protecting Dreamers stands on its own merit," House Minority Leader Nancy Pelosi, a California Democrat, had tweeted earlier in the month. Most Democrats also opposed new limits on legal immigration and ending the visa lottery.

After the bill's defeat, Republicans acknowledged there would be no immigration overhaul unless the two parties developed legislation both could support.

"I think it's important to recognize that it's going to take a bipartisan bill that both addresses border security as well as a permanent fix for Dreamers," said California's Jeff Denham, who had worked with fellow Republican Carlos Curbelo of Florida throughout the spring gathering signatures to force votes on just such a measure, without success.

"I'm really troubled," said Fred Upton, a Michigan Republican and one of the moderates who supported the doomed bill. "I don't know what Plan B is going to be."

In fact, there would be no Plan B for the remainder of 2018.

When Congress moved at the end of the year to fund the rest of fiscal 2019 without money for a border wall, Trump said he would not sign the legislation and part of the government was shutdown for a record 35 days.

306   Justice Department Subpoenas

Adoption of the resolution (H Res 970) that would insist that the Justice Department fully comply with the document requests and subpoenas issued by the Intelligence and Judiciary committees with regard to potential violations of the Foreign Intelligence Surveillance Act by Justice Department personnel and related matters, by Friday, July 6, 2018. Adopted 226-183 (R 226-0; D 0-183) on June 28, 2018.

Ever since the probes began into Russian interference in the 2016 election, Republicans in Congress have run something of a rear guard action: subpoenaing information on the investigation, threatening the FBI and Justice Department when they don't get what they want and requesting the launch of a second special counsel investigation to prove what they believe to be a plot against President Donald Trump.

On the same day Deputy Attorney General Rod Rosenstein went to Capitol Hill to testify about all this, the House voted on a resolution calling for the release of documents from the Justice Department related to the Russia investigation and Hillary Clinton's email server use.

During his testimony before the Judiciary Committee, Rosenstein, who oversees the investigation conducted by Special Counsel Robert S. Mueller III, told Republican Jim Jordan of Ohio: "I am not keeping any information from Congress." Jordan, a Trump ally, retorted: "In a few minutes, Mr. Rosenstein, I think the House of Representatives is going to say something different."

And the House did, with the vote playing out entirely along partisan lines.

For months, Republicans had been seeking information on Foreign Intelligence Surveillance Act (FISA) warrants used to surveil the Trump campaign and administration, specifically as it related to former Trump campaign aide Carter Page. They believe that the FISA warrant to surveil Page should not have been approved because it came from what they consider a dubious source — the dossier compiled by former British spy Christopher Steele. In May, the Judiciary Committee issued a subpoena to produce the information. Numerous Republicans, including Judiciary Chairman Robert W. Goodlatte and Intelligence Chairman Devin Nunes, complained that the FBI and Justice were not complying with their requests.

A month later, Jordan led a group of Republicans seeking the impeachment of Rosenstein, but that effort went nowhere as Speaker Paul D. Ryan said he preferred a less confrontational approach to getting fuller compliance. In September, however, following calls from Republican lawmakers, Trump took the extraordinary step of declassifying documents related to the Russia probe, including Page's FISA warrant.

337   Border Law Enforcement

Motion to adopt a resolution (H Res 990) that would express continued support for U.S. Immigration and Customs Enforcement and all government entities tasked with law enforcement duties on or near the nation's borders. It would also denounce calls to abolish ICE. Approved 244-35 (R 226-1; D 18-34) on July 18, 2018.

Amid an uproar over the Trump administration's policy of separating families who illegally entered the United States at the southern border, some Democrats publicly called for abolishing Immigration and Customs Enforcement, the arm of the Department of Homeland Security charged with border security.

Republicans blasted the idea as a call for open borders and decided to force Democrats in the House to take a stand on the issue by putting a resolution of support for ICE on the floor in mid-July.

Majority Whip Steve Scalise, a Louisiana Republican, told Roll Call before the vote that Democrats who did not vote "yes" would have a hard time explaining their stance headed into the midterm elections.

"Voting 'present' means that they're not willing to stand up for our men and women who sacrifice their lives to keep America safe," Scalise said. "It's a clear vote."

But most Democrats did exactly what Scalise predicted and voted "present" as party leaders had suggested. In the 244-35 vote to approve the resolution, 18 Democrats voted to back ICE and 34 opposed the resolution (along with Republican Justin Amash of Michigan), while 133 voted "present."

"This isn't about whether you support ICE or not," Minority Leader Nancy Pelosi said in a floor speech. "I'm going to vote present on it because they'll use it politically," the California Democrat added, noting members should vote how they wish but understand the vote is just about making a political point.

Republican leaders had originally planned to bring up a bill by Progressive Caucus members that would have terminated ICE after enactment of a more humane immigration enforcement system, but the authors of the bill said Democrats would have unanimously opposed it in protest to the GOP's political ploy.

Majority Leader Kevin McCarthy said in a floor speech that he offered Democrats a vote on their bill and they said they'd vote against it. The California Republican accused the minority of wanting the glory of introducing a bill to appease the far left, but noted, "They didn't have the guts to accept the consequences."

415   Opioid Abuse Prevention and Health Programs

Motion to adopt a resolution (H Res 1099) to modify Medicare and Medicaid and a variety of other health programs in relation to opioid abuse. It would expand both Medicare and Medicaid to cover medication-assisted treatment for substance use disorder and would place new requirements on states regarding Medicaid drug review and utilization requirements. It would appropriate $15 million annually, from fiscal 2019-23, to support public health laboratories to detect synthetic opioids. Approved 393-8 (R 215-8; D 178-0) on Sept. 28, 2018.

The overwhelming vote for a bill addressing the nation's opioid crisis culminated months of negotiations between the House and Senate. The consensus legislation, approved 393-8, includes new programs for prevention, treatment, research and enforcement in the use of prescription painkillers.

A few days before the House vote, negotiators from the two chambers came together on final revisions after the Congressional Budget Office estimated the bill would increase the deficit by $44 million over the next 10 years.

The new plan added two offsets to help pay for the bill.

One would require the makers of expensive biotech drugs and their potential generic competitors to inform the Federal Trade Commission if they have a financial deal that would delay the introduction of a copycat drug. The policy could result in savings if it results in biologic drugs facing competition from cheaper biosimilars more quickly.

The final agreement would also allow Medicaid funding for individuals to seek treatment at an inpatient substance abuse facility with more than 16 beds. Current law limits Medicaid reimbursement to facilities with fewer beds, though states are able to apply for waivers to bypass the regulation. CBO estimates that offset would save $32 million over 10 years.

Overall the bill would make a number of changes to Medicare and Medicaid to cover treatments for substance-abuse disorders. It would also help prevent illicit opioids from being shipped to the United States through international mail, provide grants to a variety of substance abuse prevention programs, and increase research on non-addictive painkillers.

432   Yemen Resolution

Adoption of the rule (H Res 1176) that would provide for floor consideration of the conference report to accompany the farm bill. The rule would also waive Section 7 of the War Powers Act for a concurrent resolution related to hostilities in Yemen. Passed 206-203 (R 202-18; D 5-185) on Dec. 12, 2018.

Republican leaders acted pre-emptively and used the rules process to prevent a likely floor vote on a Yemen resolution under the War Powers Act that was poised to pass the Senate.

The War Powers Act permits lawmakers to force a floor vote on a joint resolution directing the Pentagon to cease military operations not explicitly authorized by Congress. Republican House leaders were aware the Senate was about to pass a resolution (S J Res 54) ordering the Defense Department to end its mid-air refueling assistance to the Saudi-led coalition fighting in Yemen.

Amid bipartisan rancor from rank-and-file lawmakers over a number of Saudi human rights violations, Republican leadership was concerned the joint resolution might clear the House if allowed a floor vote. That could have set up a potentially embarrassing veto showdown with President Donald Trump, who was insistent on protecting his relationship with Saudi Arabia's ruler, Crown Prince Mohammed bin Salman.

In an effort to prevent such an outcome, GOP leaders during a Dec. 11 Rules Committee markup attached an amendment to the rule for consideration of the conference report for the must-pass 2018 farm bill. The amendment prevented for the remainder of the 115th Congress a vote on any privileged resolution regarding Yemen filed under the auspices of the War Powers Act.

Democrats opposed the rules maneuver, but they lacked the votes to stop it.

"This is one of the worst humanitarian crises in the world," said the Rules Committee's then-ranking Democrat, Jim McGovern of Massachusetts, describing the situation in Yemen, where Saudi Arabia is leading a military campaign. "We should not be shutting off the privileges of the House in terms of the War Powers Resolution."

The actual vote backing the resolution to pass the farm bill

was razor thin, 206-203. However, the closeness of the vote was attributed to two factors: frustration on the part of some Republicans with the price tag of the farm bill, and an eagerness on the part of the five Democrats who voted for the measure to finally clear the agriculture legislation for the president's signature.

448 Criminal Justice Overhaul

Motion to approve a bill (S 756) to reduce numbers of federally incarcerated individuals through changes in sentencing laws. The bill would seek to do so, in part, by allowing judges more flexibility when handing down sentences below the mandatory minimum for nonviolent drug offenders. It would also establish programs to provide support for prisoners returning to society in an attempt to reduce rates of recidivation. Approved 358-36 (R 182-36; D 176-0) on Dec. 20, 2018.

After years of debate, the House wrapped up its 2018 session by approving a sweeping criminal justice overhaul and sending it to President Donald Trump for his promised signature. The House passed the bill 358-36 in a year-end rush.

The measure (S 756) united a diverse group of odd bedfellows, including Republican Robert W. Goodlatte of Virginia, who led negotiations on the bill as chairman of the Judiciary Committee, and liberals such as New York Democrat Hakeem Jeffries.

Among other provisions, the bill aims to lower the number of federal inmates through changes in some sentencing laws and through better support for prisoners returning to society so they don't commit new crimes and return to prison.

The bill's main provisions include modest changes to sentencing. It gives judges more freedom to hand down sentences below the mandatory minimum for nonviolent drug offenders, and it reduces mandatory minimums associated with the three-strikes law.

It eliminates a provision that prosecutors used to "stack" firearm charges for long sentences for first-time offenders. And it makes retroactive a 2010 law that reduced the sentencing disparity between crack and powder cocaine.

On the prison side, the bill creates more job training and drug treatment for inmates, among other changes. It increases direct spending by $346 million over the next 10 years, according to the Congressional Budget Office.

The action in Congress, and eventually by the White House, does not affect state prisons directly, which is where the majority of the country's incarcerated people are held. Many of the provisions were modeled after initiatives in state prison systems that were successful in reducing costs and improving outcomes in the criminal justice system.

472 Continuing Resolution

Passage of a bill (HR 695) to fund the government through Feb. 8, 2019. It would also authorize $5.7 billion for construction of a border wall on the U.S.-Mexico border, as well as an estimated $7.8 billion in emergency disaster relief funding. Passed 217-185 (R 217-8; D 0-177) on Dec. 20, 2018.

Everyone thought Congress was out the door for the holidays after the Senate passed a continuing resolution by voice vote Dec. 19, thus sending it over to the House for approval. But Trump, after taking flak from right-wing commentators for capitulating on getting less money than he wanted for a border wall, said he wouldn't sign it.

The House instead passed this continuing resolution that included $5.7 billion for the wall, Trump's desired amount, but a non-starter in the Senate. The result was a partial government shutdown that lasted a record 35 days.

Eight Republicans — a mix of fiscal hard-liners and moderates — joined Democrats in voting against the bill.

Trump had at least some reason to be irritated — after all, he had made building a wall along the southern border with Mexico the cornerstone of his 2016 campaign. Republicans had repeatedly warned him that shutting down the government in October over wall funding would be problematic during an election year, so the matter of Department of Homeland Security funding, along with six other spending bills, was punted to December.

The grim irony for Congress is that the most successful appropriations process in 20 years ended in calamity. Early on, following a deal to raise discretionary budget caps, appropriators hit on a strategy to package spending bills into so-called minibuses. Doing so forestalled "poison-pill" provisions that had tripped up spending bills in the past. In total, lawmakers passed five spending bills, which funded 75 percent of the government. ■

TEXTS

Trump High on Heroes in State of the Union Address

Following is the CQ transcript of President Donald Trump's state of the union address, delivered Jan. 30, 2018 in the chamber of the United States House of Representatives.

Mr. Speaker, Mr, Vice President, Members of Congress, first lady of the United States, and my fellow Americans, less than one year has passed since I first stood at this podium in this majestic chamber to speak on behalf of the American people and to address their concerns, their hopes and their dreams.

That night, our new Administration had already taken very swift action. A new tide of optimism was already sweeping across our land.

Each day since, we have gone forward with a clear vision and a righteous mission: to make America great again for all Americans.

Over the last year, we have made incredible progress and achieved extraordinary success. We have faced challenges we expected and others we could never have imagined. We have shared in the heights of victory and the pains of hardship. We have endured floods and fires and storms. But through it all, we have seen the beauty of America's soul and the steel in America's spine.

AMERICAN HEROES

Each test has forged new American heroes to remind us who we are and show us what we can be. We saw the volunteers of the Cajun Navy, racing to the rescue with their fishing boats to save people in the aftermath of a totally devastating hurricane.

We saw strangers shielding strangers from a hail of gunfire on the Las Vegas strip. We heard tales of Americans, like Coast Guard Petty Officer Ashlee Leppert, who is here tonight in the gallery with Melania.

Ashlee was aboard one of the first helicopters on the scene in Houston during the Hurricane Harvey. Through 18 hours of wind and rain, Ashlee braved live power lines and deep water to help save more than 40 lives.

Ashlee, we all thank you. Thank you very much.

We heard about Americans like firefighter David Dahlberg. He's here with us, also. David faced down walls of flame to rescue almost 60 children trapped at a California summer camp threatened by those devastating wildfires.

To everyone still recovering in Texas, Florida, Louisiana, Puerto Rico, and the Virgin Islands, everywhere, we are with you, we love you, and we always will pull through together always.

Thank you to David and the brave people of California. Thank you very much, David. Great job.

Some trials over the past year touched this chamber very personally. With us tonight is one of the toughest people ever to serve in this House, a guy who took a bullet, almost died, and was back to work three-and-a-half months later, the legend from Louisiana, Congressman Steve Scalise.

I think they like you, Steve.

We're incredibly grateful for the heroic efforts of the Capitol Police officers, the Alexandria Police, and the doctors, nurses, and paramedics who saved his life and the lives of many others, some in this room. In the aftermath—yes. Yes.

In the aftermath of that terrible shooting, we came together, not as Republicans or Democrats, but as representatives of the people. But it is not enough to come together only in times of tragedy. Tonight, I call upon all of us to set aside our differences, to seek out common ground, and to summon the unity we need to deliver for the people. This is really the key. These are the people we were elected to serve.

Thank you.

Over the last year, the world has seen what we always knew: that no people on Earth are so fearless, or daring, or determined as Americans. If there is a mountain, we climb it. If there's a frontier, we cross it. If there's a challenge, we tame it. If there's an opportunity, we seize it.

So let's begin tonight by recognizing that the state of our union is strong because our people are strong.

And together we are building a safe, strong, and proud America.

THE ECONOMY

Since the election, we have created 2.4 million new jobs, including...

...including 200,000 new jobs in manufacturing alone. Tremendous number.

After years and years of wage stagnation, we are finally seeing rising wages.

Unemployment claims have hit a 45-year low.

And something I'm very proud of, African-American unemployment stands at the lowest rate ever recorded.

And Hispanic-American unemployment has also reached the lowest levels in history.

Small-business confidence is at an all-time high. The stock market has smashed one record after another, gaining $8 trillion and more in value in just this short period of time. The great news...

The great news for Americans, 401K, retirement, pension, and college savings accounts have gone through the roof.

And just as I promised the American people from this podium 11 months ago, we enacted the biggest tax cuts and reforms in American history.

Our massive tax cuts provide tremendous relief for the middle class and small business.

To lower tax rates for hardworking Americans, we nearly doubled the standard deduction for everyone.

Now the first $24,000 earned by a married couple is completely tax-free.

We also doubled the child tax credit.

A typical family of four making $75,000 will see their tax bill reduced by $2,000, slashing their tax bill in half.

In April, this will be the last time you will ever file under the old and very broken system, and millions of Americans will have more take-home pay starting next month. A lot more.

We eliminated an especially cruel tax that fell mostly on Americans making less than $50,000 a year, forcing them to pay tremendous penalties simply because they couldn't afford government-ordered health plans. We repealed the core of the disastrous Obamacare. The individual mandate is now gone.

We slashed the business tax rate from 35 percent all the way down

to 21 percent, so American companies can compete and win against anyone else anywhere in the world.

These changes alone are estimated to increase average family income by more than $4,000. A lot of money.

Small businesses have also received a massive tax cut and can now deduct 20 percent of their business income.

Here tonight are Steve Staub and Sandy Keplinger of Staub Manufacturing, a small beautiful business in Ohio. They've just finished the best year in their 20-year history.

Because of tax reform, they are handing out raises, hiring an additional 14 people, and expanding into the building next door. Good feeling.

One of Staub's employees, Corey Adams, is also with us tonight. Corey is an all-American worker. He supported himself through high school, lost his job during the 2008 recession, and was later hired by Staub, where he trained to become a welder. Like many hardworking Americans, Corey plans to invest his tax cut raise into his new home and his two daughters' education. Corey, please stand.

And he's a great welder.

I was told that by the man that owns that company that's doing so well, so congratulations, Corey.

Since we passed tax cuts, roughly 3 million workers have already gotten tax cut bonuses, many of them thousands and thousands of dollars per worker. And it's getting more every month, every week. Apple has just announced it plans to invest a total of $350 billion in America and hire another 20,000 workers.

And just a little while ago, ExxonMobil announced a $50 billion investment in the United States. Just a little while ago.

This, in fact, is our new American moment. There has never been a better time to start living the American dream.

So to every citizen watching at home tonight, no matter where you've been or where you've come from, this is your time. If you work hard, if you believe in yourself, if you believe in America, then you can dream anything, you can be anything, and together, we can achieve absolutely anything.

Tonight, I want to talk about what kind of future we are going to have and what kind of a nation we are going to be. All of us, together, as one team, one people, and one American family can do anything. We all share the same home, the same heart, the same destiny, and the same great American flag.

Together, we are rediscovering the American way. In America, we know that faith and family, not government and bureaucracy, are the center of American life.

The motto is "in God we trust."

And we celebrate our police, our military, and our amazing veterans as heroes who deserve our total and unwavering support.

Here tonight is Preston Sharp, a 12-year-old boy from Redding, California, who noticed that veterans' graves were not marked with flags on Veterans Day. He decided all by himself to change that and started a movement that has now placed 40,000 flags at the graves of our great heroes.

Preston, a job well done.

Young patriots like Preston teach all of us about our civic duty as Americans. And I met Preston a little while ago, and he is something very special, that I can tell you. Great future. Thank you very much for all you've done, Preston. Thank you very much.

Preston's reverence for those who have served our nation reminds us why we salute our flag, why we put our hands on our hearts for the Pledge of Allegiance, and why we proudly stand for the national anthem.

Americans love their country. And they deserve a government that shows them the same love and loyalty in return. For the last year, we have sought to restore the bonds of trust between our citizens and their government.

Working with the Senate, we are appointing judges who will interpret the Constitution as written, including a great new Supreme Court justice and more circuit court judges than any new administration in the history of our country.

We are totally defending our Second Amendment and have taken historic actions to protect religious liberty.

And we are serving our brave veterans, including giving our veterans choice in their health care decisions.

Last year, Congress also passed, and I signed, the landmark V.A. Accountability Act.

Since its passage, my administration has already removed more than 1,500 V.A. employees who failed to give our veterans the care they deserve, and we are hiring talented people who love our vets as much as we do.

And I will not stop until our veterans are properly taken care of, which has been my promise to them from the very beginning of this great journey.

All Americans deserve accountability and respect, and that's what we are giving to our wonderful heroes, our veterans. Thank you.

So tonight, I call on Congress to empower every cabinet secretary with the authority to reward good workers and to remove federal employees who undermine the public trust or fail the American people.

In our drive to make Washington accountable, we have eliminated more regulations in our first year than any administration in the history of our country.

We have ended the war on American energy, and we have ended the war on beautiful clean coal.

We are now very proudly an exporter of energy to the world.

In Detroit, I halted government mandates that crippled America's great, beautiful autoworkers so that we can get Motor City revving its engines again. And that's what's happening.

Many car companies are now building and expanding plants in the United States, something we haven't seen for decades. Chrysler is moving a major plant from Mexico to Michigan. Toyota and Mazda are opening up a plant in Alabama, a big one. And we haven't seen this in a long time. It's all coming back.

Very soon, auto plants and other plants will be opening up all over our country. This is all news Americans are totally unaccustomed to hearing. For many years, companies and jobs were only leaving us. But now they are roaring back, they're coming back. They want to be where the action is.

They want to be in the United States of America. That's where they want to be.

Exciting progress is happening every single day. To speed access to breakthrough cures and affordable generic drugs, last year the FDA approved more new and generic drugs and medical devices than ever before in our country's history.

We also believe that patients with terminal conditions and terminal illness should have access to experimental treatment immediately that could potentially save their lives.

People who are terminally ill should not have to go from country to country to seek a cure. I want to give them a chance right here at home. It's time for Congress to give these wonderful, incredible Americans the right to try.

One of my greatest priorities is to reduce the price of prescription drugs.

In many other countries, these drugs cost far less than what we pay in the United States. And it's very, very unfair. That is why I have directed my administration to make fixing the injustice of high drug prices one of my top priorities for the year.

And prices will come down substantially. Watch.

America has also finally turned the page on decades of unfair trade deals that sacrificed our prosperity and shipped away our companies, our jobs, and our wealth. Our nation has lost its wealth, but we're getting it back so fast. The era of economic surrender is totally over.

From now on, we expect trading relationships to be fair and, very importantly, reciprocal.

We will work to fix bad trade deals and negotiate new ones. And they'll be good ones, but they'll be fair.

And we will protect American workers and American intellectual property through strong enforcement of our trade rules.

As we rebuild our industries, it is also time to rebuild our crumbling infrastructure.

America is a nation of builders. We built the Empire State Building in just one year. Isn't it a disgrace that it can now take 10 years just to get a minor permit approved for the building of a simple road?

I am asking both parties to come together to give us safe, fast, reliable, and modern infrastructure that our economy needs and our people deserve.

Tonight I'm calling on Congress to produce a bill that generates at least $1.5 trillion for the new infrastructure investment that our country so desperately needs.

Every federal dollar should be leveraged by partnering with state and local governments and, where appropriate, tapping into private sector investment to permanently fix the infrastructure deficit. And we can do it.

Any bill must also streamline the permitting and approval process, getting it down to no more than two years, and perhaps even one.

Together, we can reclaim our great building heritage.

We will build gleaming new roads, bridges, highways, railways, and waterways all across our land. And we will do it with American heart, American hands, and American grit.

We want every American to know the dignity of a hard day's work. We want every child to be safe in their home at night. And we want every citizen to be proud of this land that we all love so much. We can lift our citizens from welfare to work, from dependence to independence, and from poverty to prosperity. As...

As tax cuts create new jobs, let's invest in workforce development and let's invest in job training, which we need so badly.

Let's open great vocational schools so our future workers can learn a craft and realize their full potential. And let's support working families by supporting paid family leave.

As America regains its strength, opportunity must be extended to all citizens. That is why this year we will embark on reforming our prisons to help former inmates who have served their time get a second chance at life.

Struggling communities, especially immigrant communities, will

also be helped by immigration policies that focus on the best interests of American workers and American families.

THE HOMELAND

For decades, open borders have allowed drugs and gangs to pour into our most vulnerable communities. They've allowed millions of low-wage workers to compete for jobs and wages against the poorest Americans. Most tragically, they have caused the loss of many innocent lives.

Here tonight are two fathers and two mothers: Evelyn Rodriguez, Freddy Cuevas, Elizabeth Alvarado, and Robert Mickens. Their two teenage daughters — Kayla Cuevas and Nisa Mickens — were close friends on Long Island.

But in September 2016, on the eve of Nisa's 16th birthday, such a happy time it should have been, neither of them came home. These two precious girls were brutally murdered while walking together in their hometown. Six members of the savage MS-13 gang have been charged with Kayla and Nisa's murders. Many of these gang members took advantage of glaring loopholes in our laws to enter the country as illegal unaccompanied alien minors and wound up in Kayla and Nisa's high school.

Evelyn, Elizabeth, Freddy, and Robert, tonight, everyone in this chamber is praying for you. Everyone in America is grieving for you.

Please stand. Thank you very much.

I want you to know that 320 million hearts are right now breaking for you. We love you. Thank you.

While we cannot imagine the depths of that kind of sorrow, we can make sure that other families never have to endure this kind of pain.

Tonight, I am calling on Congress to finally close the deadly loopholes that have allowed MS-13, and other criminal gangs, to break into our country. We have proposed new legislation that will fix our immigration laws, and support our ICE and Border Patrol agents — these are great people, these are great, great people that work so hard in the midst of such danger — so that this can never happen again.

The United States is a compassionate nation. We are proud that we do more than any other country anywhere in the world to help the needy, the struggling, and the underprivileged all over the world. But as president of the United States, my highest loyalty, my greatest compassion, my constant concern is for America's children, America's struggling workers, and America's forgotten communities. I want our youth to grow up to achieve great things. I want our poor to have their chance to rise.

So tonight, I am extending an open hand to work with members of both parties — Democrats and Republicans — to protect our citizens of every background, color, religion, and creed.

My duty, and the sacred duty of every elected official in this chamber, is to defend Americans, to protect their safety, their families, their communities, and their right to the American dream. Because Americans are dreamers, too.

Here tonight is one leader in the effort to defend our country, Homeland Security Investigations Special Agent Celestino Martinez. He goes by DJ. And CJ. He said call me either one. So we'll call you CJ.

Served 15 years in the Air Force before becoming an ICE agent and spending the last 15 years fighting gang violence and getting dangerous criminals off of our streets. Tough job. At one point, MS-13 leaders ordered CJ's murder, and they wanted it to happen quickly. But he did not cave to threats or to fear. Last May, he commanded an operation to

track down gang members on Long Island. His team has arrested nearly 400, including more than 220 MS-13 gang members.

And I have to tell you what the Border Patrol and ICE have done. We have sent thousands and thousands and thousands of MS-13 horrible people out of this country or into our prisons. So I just want to congratulate you, CJ. You're a brave guy. Thank you very much.

And I asked CJ, what's the secret? He said, "We're just tougher than they are." And I like that answer.

Now let's get Congress to send you — and all of the people in this great chamber have to do it, we have no choice — CJ, we're going to send you reinforcements and we're going to send them to you quickly. It's what you need.

Over the next few weeks, the House and Senate will be voting on an immigration reform package. In recent months, my administration has met extensively with both Democrats and Republicans to craft a bipartisan approach to immigration reform. Based on these discussions, we presented Congress with a detailed proposal that should be supported by both parties as a fair compromise, one where nobody gets everything they want, but where our country gets the critical reforms it needs and must have.

Here are the four pillars of our plan. The first pillar of our framework generously offers a path to citizenship for 1.8 million illegal immigrants who were brought here by their parents at a young age. That covers almost three times more people than the previous administration covered.

Under our plan, those who meet education and work requirements, and show good moral character, will be able to become full citizens of the United States over a 12-year period.

The second pillar fully secures the border.

That means building a great wall on the southern border, and it means hiring more heroes like CJ to keep our communities safe.

Crucially, our plan closes the terrible loopholes exploited by criminals and terrorists to enter our country, and it finally ends the horrible and dangerous practice of catch and release.

The third pillar ends the visa lottery, a program that randomly hands out green cards without any regard for skill, merit, or the safety of American people.

It's time to begin moving toward a merit-based immigration system, one that admits people who are skilled, who want to work, who will contribute to our society, and who will love and respect our country.

The fourth and final pillar protects the nuclear family by ending chain migration.

Under the current broken system, a single immigrant can bring in virtually unlimited numbers of distant relatives.

Under our plan, we focus on the immediate family by limiting sponsorships to spouses and minor children.

This vital reform is necessary, not just for our economy, but for our security and for the future of America.

In recent weeks, two terrorist attacks in New York were made possible by the visa lottery and chain migration. In the age of terrorism, these programs present risks we can just no longer afford. It's time to reform...

... these outdated immigration rules and finally bring our immigration system into the 21st century.

These four pillars represent a down-the-middle compromise and one that will create a safe, modern, and lawful immigration system.

For over 30 years, Washington has tried and failed to solve this problem. This Congress can be the one that finally makes it happen.

Most importantly, these four pillars will produce legislation that fulfills my ironclad pledge to sign a bill that puts America first.

So let's come together, set politics aside, and finally get the job done.

OPIOIDS

These reforms will also support our response to the terrible crisis of opioid and drug addiction. Never before has it been like it is now. It is terrible. We have to do something about it.

In 2016, we lost 64,000 Americans to drug overdoses, 174 deaths per day, seven per hour. We must get much tougher on drug dealers and pushers if we are going to succeed in stopping this scourge.

My administration is committed to fighting the drug epidemic and helping get treatment for those in need, for those who have been so terribly hurt. The struggle will be long and it will be difficult, but as Americans always do, in the end, we will succeed, we will prevail.

As we have seen tonight, the most difficult challenges bring out the best in America. We see a vivid expression of this truth in the story of the Holets family of New Mexico. Ryan Holets is 27 years old, an officer with the Albuquerque Police Department. He's here tonight with his wife, Rebecca.

Thank you, Ryan.

Last year, Ryan was on duty when he saw a pregnant, homeless woman preparing to inject heroin. When Ryan told her she was going to harm her unborn child, she began to weep. She told him she didn't know where to turn, but badly wanted a safe home for her baby.

In that moment, Ryan said he felt God speak to him: "You will do it because you can." He heard those words. He took out a picture of his wife and their four kids. Then he went home to tell his wife, Rebecca. In an instant, she agreed to adopt. The Holets named their new daughter Hope.

Ryan and Rebecca, you embody the goodness of our nation. Thank you.

Thank you, Ryan and Rebecca.

MILITARY

As we rebuild America's strength and confidence at home, we are also restoring our strength and standing abroad.

Around the world, we face rogue regimes, terrorist groups, and rivals like China and Russia that challenge our interests, our economy, and our values. In confronting these horrible dangers, we know that weakness is the surest path to conflict, and unmatched power is the surest means to our true and great defense.

For this reason, I am asking Congress to end the dangerous defense sequester and fully fund our great military.

As part of our defense, we must modernize and rebuild our nuclear arsenal, hopefully never having to use it, but making it so strong and so powerful that it will deter any acts of aggression by any other nation or anyone else.

Perhaps some day in the future there will be a magical moment when the countries of the world will get together to eliminate their nuclear weapons. Unfortunately, we are not there yet, sadly.

Last year, I also pledged that we would work with our allies to extinguish ISIS from the face of the Earth. One year later, I am proud to report that the coalition to defeat ISIS has liberated very close to 100 percent of the territory just recently held by these killers in Iraq and in Syria and in other locations, as well.

But there is much more work to be done. We will continue our fight until ISIS is defeated.

Army Staff Sergeant Justin Peck is here tonight. Near Raqqa last

November, Justin and his comrade, Chief Petty Officer Kenton Stacy, were on a mission to clear buildings that ISIS had rigged with explosive so that civilians could return to that city, hopefully soon and hopefully safely.

Clearing the second floor of a vital hospital, Kenton Stacy was severely wounded by an explosion. Immediately, Justin bounded into the booby-trapped and unbelievably dangerous and unsafe building and found Kenton, but in very, very bad shape. He applied pressure to the wound and inserted a tube to reopen an airway.

He then performed CPR for 20 straight minutes during the ground transport and maintained artificial respiration through two-and-a-half hours and through emergency surgery.

Kenton Stacy would have died if it were not for Justin's selfless love for his fellow warrior. Tonight, Kenton is recovering in Texas. Raqqa is liberated. And Justin is wearing his new Bronze Star, with a V for Valor.

Staff Sergeant Peck: All of America salutes you.

Terrorists who do things like place bombs in civilian hospitals are evil. When possible, we have no choice but to annihilate them. When necessary, we must be able to detain and question them. But we must be clear: Terrorists are not merely criminals. They are unlawful enemy combatants.

And when captured overseas, they should be treated like the terrorists they are. In the past, we have foolishly released hundreds of dangerous terrorists, only to meet them again on the battlefield, including the ISIS leader, al-Baghdadi, who we captured, who we had, who we released.

So today, I am keeping another promise. I just signed prior to walking in an order directing Secretary Mattis — who is doing a great job, thank you...

... to re-examine our military detention policy and to keep open the detention facilities in Guantanamo Bay.

I am asking Congress to ensure that in the fight against ISIS and Al Qaida we continue to have all necessary power to detain terrorists, wherever we chase them down, wherever we find them. And in many cases, for them it will now be Guantanamo Bay.

At the same time, as of a few months ago, our warriors in Afghanistan have new rules of engagement.

Along with their heroic Afghan partners, our military is no longer undermined by artificial timelines, and we no longer tell our enemies our plans.

Last month, I also took an action endorsed unanimously by the U.S. Senate just months before. I recognized Jerusalem as the capital of Israel.

Shortly afterwards, dozens of countries voted in the United Nations General Assembly against America's sovereign right to make this decision. In 2016, American taxpayers generously sent those same countries more than $20 billion in aid. That is why tonight I am asking Congress to pass legislation to help ensure American foreign assistance dollars always serve American interests and only go to friends of America, not enemies of America.

As we strengthen friendships all around the world, we are also restoring clarity about our adversaries. When the people of Iran rose up against the crimes of their corrupt dictatorship, I did not stay silent. America stands with the people of Iran in their courageous struggle for freedom.

I am asking Congress to address the fundamental flaws in the ter-rible Iran nuclear deal. My administration has also imposed tough sanctions on the communist and socialist dictatorships in Cuba and Venezuela.

NORTH KOREA

But no regime has oppressed its own citizens more totally or brutally than the cruel dictatorship in North Korea. North Korea's reckless pursuit of nuclear missiles could very soon threaten our homeland. We are waging a campaign of maximum pressure to prevent that from ever happening.

Past experience has taught us that complacency and concessions only invite aggression and provocation. I will not repeat the mistakes of past administrations that got us into this very dangerous position.

We need only look at the depraved character of the North Korean regime to understand the nature of the nuclear threat it could pose to America and to our allies.

Otto Warmbier was a hardworking student at the University of Virginia. And a great student, he was. On his way to study abroad in Asia, Otto joined a tour to North Korea. At its conclusion, this wonderful young man was arrested and charged with crimes against the state.

After a shameful trial, the dictatorship sentenced Otto to 15 years of hard labor, before returning him to America last June, horribly injured and on the verge of death. He passed away just days after his return.

Otto's wonderful parents, Fred and Cindy Warmbier, are here with us tonight, along with Otto's brother and sister, Austin and Greta. Please.

Incredible people. You are powerful witnesses to a menace that threatens our world, and your strength truly inspires us all. Thank you very much. Thank you.

Tonight we pledge to honor Otto's memory with total American resolve. Thank you. Finally...

... we are joined by one more witness to the ominous nature of this regime. His name is Mr. Ji Seong-ho.

In 1996, Seong-ho was a starving boy in North Korea. One day, he tried to steal coal from a railroad car to barter for a few scraps of food, which were very hard to get. In the process, he passed out on the train tracks, exhausted from hunger. He woke up as a train ran over his limbs. He then endured multiple amputations without anything to dull the pain or the hurt.

His brother and sister gave what little food they had to help him recover and ate dirt themselves, permanently stunting their own growth. Later, he was tortured by North Korean authorities after returning from a brief visit to China. His tormentors wanted to know if he'd met any Christians. He had, and he resolved after that to be free.

Seong-ho traveled thousands of miles on crutches all across China and Southeast Asia to freedom. Most of his family followed. His father was caught trying to escape and was tortured to death. Today he lives in Seoul, where he rescues other defectors, and broadcasts into North Korea what the regime fears most: the truth.

Today he has a new leg, but Seong-ho, I understand you still keep those old crutches as a reminder of how far you've come. Your great sacrifice is an inspiration to us all. Please. Thank you.

Seong-ho's story is a testament to the yearning of every human soul to live in freedom.

It was that same yearning for freedom that nearly 250 years ago gave birth to a special place called America. It was a small cluster of colonies caught between a great ocean and a vast wilderness. It was home to an

incredible people with a revolutionary idea, that they could rule themselves, that they could chart their own destiny, and that, together, they could light up the entire world.

That is what our country has always been about. That is what Americans have always stood for, always strived for, and always done.

Atop the dome of this Capitol stands the Statue of Freedom. She stands tall and dignified among the monuments to our ancestors who fought and lived and died to protect her. Monuments to Washington and Jefferson, and Lincoln and King. Memorials to the heroes of Yorktown and Saratoga, to young Americans who shed their blood on the shores of Normandy and the fields beyond. And others who went down in the waters of the Pacific and the skies all over Asia.

And freedom stands tall over one more monument: this one. This Capitol. This living monument. This is the monument to the American people.

We're a people whose heroes live not only in the past, but all around us, defending hope, pride, and defending the American way. They work in every trade. They sacrifice to raise a family. They care for our children at home. They defend our flag abroad. And they are strong moms and brave kids. They are firefighters and police officers and border agents, medics and Marines. But above all else, they are Americans. And this Capitol, this city, this Nation belongs entirely to them.

Our task is to respect them, to listen to them, to serve them, to protect them, and to always be worthy of them. Americans fill the world with art and music. They push the bounds of science and discovery. And they forever remind us of what we should never, ever forget: The people dreamed this country. The people built this country. And it's the people who are making America great again.

As long as we are proud of who we are and what we are fighting for, there is nothing we cannot achieve. As long as we have confidence in our values, faith in our citizens, and trust in our God, we will never fail.

Our families will thrive. Our people will prosper. And our nation will forever be safe and strong and proud and mighty and free. Thank you, and God bless America. Good night. ■

Rep. Joe Kennedy Responds

Thank you. Good evening, ladies and gentlemen. It is an absolute privilege to join you all tonight.

We are here in Fall River, Massachusetts, a proud American city...

An American city built by immigrants.

From textiles to robots, this is a place that knows how to make great things.

The students who are with us here this evening in the auto tech program at Diman Regional Technical School carry on that rich legacy.

Like many American hometowns, Fall River has faced its share of storms. But the people here are tough. They fight for each other. They pull for their city. It is a fitting place to gather as our nation reflects on the state of our union.

FALL RIVER FEAR

This is a difficult task. Many have spent the last year anxious, angry, afraid. We all feel the fractured fault lines across our country. We hear the voices of Americans who are forgotten and feel forsaken.

We see an economy that makes stocks soar, investor portfolios bulge, and corporate profits climb, but fails to give workers their fair share of the reward. A government that struggles to keep itself open. Russia knee-deep in our democracy. An all-out war on environmental protection. A Justice Department rolling back civil rights by the day. Hatred and supremacy proudly marching in our streets. Bullets tearing through our classrooms, concerts, and congregations, targeting our safest, sacred places.

And this nagging, sinking feeling, no matter your political beliefs, that this is not right. This is not who we are.

Folks, it would be easy to dismiss this past year as chaos. Partisanship. As politics. But it's far, far bigger than that. This administration isn't just targeting the laws that protect us; they are targeting the very idea that we are all worthy of protection.

For them, dignity isn't something you're born with but something you measure, by your net worth, your celebrity, your headlines, your crowd size, not to mention the gender of your spouse, the country of your birth, the color of your skin, the God of your prayers.

Their record is a rebuke to our highest American ideal, the belief that we are all worthy, that we are all equal, that we all count, in the eyes of our law and our leaders, our God and our government. That is the American promise.

But today, ladies and gentlemen, today that promise is being broken by an administration that callously appraises our worthiness and decides who makes the cut and who can be bargained away. They are turning American life into a zero-sum game, where for one to win, another must lose, where we can guarantee America's safety if we slash our safety net, where we can extend health care in Mississippi if we gut it in Massachusetts, we can cut taxes for corporations today if we raise them on families tomorrow, where we can take care of sick kids if we sacrifice Dreamers.

We are bombarded with one false choice after another: coal miners or single moms, rural communities or inner cities, the coast or the heartland. As if the mechanic in Pittsburgh, a teacher in Tulsa, and a daycare worker in Birmingham are bitter rivals rather than mutual casualties of a system forcefully rigged towards those at the top.

As if the parent who lies awake terrified that their transgender son or daughter will be beaten and bullied at school is any more or less legitimate than a parent whose heart is shattered by a daughter in the grips of an opioid addiction.

NO CHOICE TO BE MADE

So here is the answer that Democrats offer tonight: We choose both.

We fight — we fight for both. Because the greatest, strongest, richest nation in the world shouldn't have to leave anyone behind.

We choose — we choose a better deal for all who call our country home. We choose a living wage, and paid leave, and affordable child care your family needs to survive. We choose pensions that are solvent, trade pacts that are fair, roads and bridges that won't rust away, a good education that you can afford.

We choose a health care system that offers you mercy, whether you suffer from cancer or depression or addiction. We choose an economy strong enough to boast record stock prices and brave enough to admit that top CEOs making 300 times their average worker is not right.

We choose Fall River. We choose the thousands of American communities whose roads aren't paved with power or privilege, but with an honest effort, with good faith, and the resolve to build something better for your kids.

That—that is our story. It began the day our founding fathers and mothers set sail for a new world, fleeing oppression and intolerance. It continued with every word of our independence, the audacity to declare that all men are created equal, an imperfect promise for a nation struggling to become a more perfect union.

It grew with every suffragette's step, every Freedom Rider's voice, and every weary soul we welcomed to our shores.

DREAMERS

And to all the Dreamers out there watching tonight, let me be absolutely clear: Ustedes son parte de nuestra historia. Vamos a luchar...

Vamos a luchar por ustedes y no nos vamos alejar. You are part of our story. We will fight for you. And we will not walk away.

America, we carry that story on our shoulders. You swarmed to Washington last year to ensure that no parent has to worry if they can afford to save their child's life. You've proudly marched together last weekend — thousands deep — on the streets of Las Vegas and Philadelphia and Nashville.

You sat high atop your mom's shoulders and held a sign that read, "Build a wall and my generation will tear it down."

You bravely say, "Me, too." You steadfastly say, "Black lives matter." You wade through flood waters, battle hurricanes, brave wildfires and mudslides to save a stranger. You battle your own, quiet battles every single day.

You drag your weary bodies to that extra shift so that your families won't feel the sting of scarcity. You leave loved ones at home to defend our country overseas or patrol our neighborhoods at night. You serve. You rescue. You help. You heal. That — more than any law or leader, debate or disagreement — that is what drives us towards progress.

Bullies may land a punch. They may leave a mark. But they have never — not once in the history of our United States — managed to match the strength and spirit of a people united in defense of their future. Politicians...

Politicians can be cheered for the promises they make. Our country will be judged by the promises we keep.

That is the measure of our character. That is who we are. Out of many, one.

Ladies and gentlemen, have faith. Have faith. The state of our union is hopeful, resilient, and enduring.

God bless you. God bless your families. And may God bless the United States of America. Thank you. ■

PUBLIC LAWS

Laws Enacted in the Second Session Of the 115th Congress

■ **PL 115-98** (HR4661) Reauthorize the United States Fire Administration, the Assistance to Firefighters Grants program, the Fire Prevention and Safety Grants program, and the Staffing for Adequate Fire and Emergency Response grant program, and for other purposes. *Jan. 3, 2018.*

■ **PL 115-99** (S1536) Designate a human trafficking prevention coordinator and to expand the scope of activities authorized under the Federal Motor Carrier Safety Administration's outreach and education program to include human trafficking prevention activities, and for other purposes. *Jan. 3, 2018.*

■ **PL 115-100** (S2273) Extend the period during which vessels that are shorter than 79 feet in length and fishing vessels are not required to have a permit for discharges incidental to the normal operation of the vessel. *Jan. 3, 2018.*

■ **PL 115-101** (HR560) Amend the Delaware Water Gap National Recreation Area Improvement Act to provide access to certain vehicles serving residents of municipalities adjacent to the Delaware Water Gap National Recreation Area, and for other purposes. *Jan. 8, 2018.*

■ **PL 115-102** (HR1242) Establish the 400 Years of African-American History Commission, and for other purposes. *Jan. 8, 2018.*

■ **PL 115-103** (HR1306) Provide for the conveyance of certain Federal land in the State of Oregon, and for other purposes. *Jan. 8, 2018.*

■ **PL 115-104** (HR1927) Amend title 54, United States Code, to establish within the National Park Service the African American Civil Rights Network, and for other purposes. *Jan. 8, 2018.*

■ **PL 115-105** (S1393) Streamline the process by which active duty military, reservists, and veterans receive commercial driver's licenses. *Jan. 8, 2018.*

■ **PL 115-106** (S1532) Disqualify from operating a commercial motor vehicle for life an individual who uses a commercial motor vehicle in committing a felony involving human trafficking. *Jan. 8, 2018.*

■ **PL 115-107** (S1766) Reauthorize the SAFER Act of 2013, and for other purposes. *Jan. 8, 2018.*

■ **PL 115-108** (HR267) Redesignate the Martin Luther King, Junior, National Historic Site in the State of Georgia, and for other purposes. *Jan. 8, 2018.*

■ **PL 115-109** (HR381) Designate a mountain in the John Muir Wilderness of the Sierra National Forest as "Sky Point" *Jan. 10, 2018.*

■ **PL 115-110** (HR699) Amend the Omnibus Public Land Management Act of 2009 to modify provisions relating to certain land exchanges in the Mt. Hood Wilderness in the State of Oregon. *Jan. 10, 2018.*

■ **PL 115-111** (HR863) Facilitate the addition of park administration at the Coltsville National Historical Park, and for other purposes. *Jan. 10, 2018.*

■ **PL 115-112** (HR2142) Improve the ability of U.S. Customs and Border Protection to interdict fentanyl, other synthetic opioids, and other narcotics and psychoactive substances that are illegally imported into the United States, and for other purposes. *Jan. 10, 2018.*

■ **PL 115-113** (HR2228) Provide support for law enforcement agency efforts to protect the mental health and well-being of law enforcement officers, and for other purposes. *Jan. 10, 2018.*

■ **PL 115-114** (HR2331) Require a new or updated Federal website that is intended for use by the public to be mobile friendly, and for other purposes. *Jan. 10, 2018.*

■ **PL 115-115** (HR518) Amend the Energy Policy and Conservation Act to exclude power supply circuits, drivers, and devices designed to be connected to, and power, light-emitting diodes or organic light-emitting diodes providing illumination from energy conservation standards for external power supplies, and for other purposes. *Jan. 12, 2018.*

■ **PL 115-116** (HR954) Remove the use restrictions on certain land transferred to Rockingham County, Virginia, and for other purposes. *Jan. 12, 2018.*

■ **PL 115-117** (HR2611) Modify the boundary of the Little Rock Central High School National Historic Site, and for other purposes. *Jan. 12, 2018.*

■ **PL 115-118** (S139) Implement the use of Rapid DNA instruments to inform decisions about pretrial release or detention and their conditions, to solve and prevent violent crimes and other crimes, to exonerate the innocent, to prevent DNA analysis backlogs, and for other purposes. *Jan. 19, 2018.*

■ **PL 115-119** (HR3759) Provide for the establishment and maintenance of a Family Caregiving Strategy, and for other purposes. *Jan. 22, 2018.*

■ **PL 115-120** (HR195) Further continuing appropriations for the fiscal year ending September 30, 2018, and for other purposes. *Jan. 22, 2018.*

■ **PL 115-121** (HR984) Extend Federal recognition to the Chickahominy Indian Tribe, the Chickahominy Indian Tribe-Eastern Division, the Upper Mattaponi Tribe, the Rappahannock Tribe, Inc., the Monacan Indian Nation, and the Nansemond Indian Tribe. *Jan. 29, 2018.*

■ **PL 115-122** (S117) Designate a mountain peak in the State of Montana as "Alex Diekmann Peak." *Jan. 31, 2018.*

■ **PL 115-123** (HR1892) Amend title 4, United States Code, to provide for the flying of the flag at half-staff in the event of the death of a first responder in the line of duty. *Feb. 9, 2018.*

■ **PL 115-124** (HR1301) Appropriations for the Department of Defense for the fiscal year ending September 30, 2017, and for other purposes. *Feb. 9, 2018.*

■ **PL 115-125** (HR4708) Amend the Homeland Security Act of 2002 to require the Secretary of Homeland Security to issue Department of Homeland Security-wide guidance and develop training programs as part of the Department of Homeland Security Blue Campaign, and for other purposes. *Feb. 14, 2018.*

■ **PL 115-126** (S534) Prevent the sexual abuse of minors and amateur athletes by requiring the prompt reporting of sexual abuse to law enforcement authorities, and for other purposes. *Feb. 14, 2018.*

■ **PL 115-127** (HR582) Amend the Communications Act of 1934 to require multi-line telephone systems to have a configuration that permits users to directly initiate a call to 9-1-1 without dialing any additional digit, code, prefix, or post-fix, and for other purposes. *Feb. 16, 2018.*

■ **PL 115-128** (S1438) Redesignate the Jefferson National Expansion Memorial in the State of Missouri as the "Gateway Arch National Park." *Feb. 22, 2018.*

■ **PL 115-129** (S96) Amend the Communications Act of 1934 to ensure the integrity of voice communications and to prevent unjust or unreasonable discrimination among areas of the United States in the delivery of such communications. *Feb. 26, 2018.*

■ **PL 115-130** (HR1725) Direct the Secretary of Veterans Affairs to submit certain reports relating to medical evidence submitted in support of claims for benefits under the laws administered by the Secretary. *March 9, 2018.*

■ **PL 115-131** (HR3122) Protect individuals who are eligible for increased pension under laws administered by the Secretary of Veterans Affairs on the basis of need of regular aid and attendance from dishonest, predatory, or otherwise unlawful practices, and for other purposes. *March 9, 2018.*

■ **PL 115-132** (HR4533) Designate the health care system of the Department of Veterans Affairs in Lexington, Kentucky, as the "Lexington VA Health Care System" and to make certain other designations. *March 9, 2018.*

■ **PL 115-133** (HR294) Designate the facility of the United States Postal Service located at 2700 Cullen Boulevard in Pearland, Texas, as the "Endy Ekpanya Post Office Building." *March 16, 2018.*

■ **PL 115-134** (HR452) Designate the facility of the United States Postal Service located at 324 West Saint Louis Street in Pacific, Missouri, as the "Specialist Jeffrey L. White, Jr. Post Office." *March 16, 2018.*

■ **PL 115-135** (HR535) Encourage visits between the United States and Taiwan at all levels, and for other purposes." *March 16, 2018.*

■ **PL 115-136** (HR3656) Amend title 38, United State Code, to provide for a consistent eligibility date for provision of Department of Veterans Affairs memorial headstones and markers for eligible spouses and dependent children of veterans whose remains are unavailable. *March 16, 2018.*

■ **PL 115-137** (S831) Designate the facility of the United States Postal Service located at 120 West Pike Street in Canonsburg, Pennsylvania, as the "Police Officer Scott Bashioum Post Office Building." *March 16, 2018.*

■ **PL 115-138** (HR1208) Designate the facility of the United States Postal Service located at 9155 Schaefer Road, Converse, Texas, as the "Converse Veterans Post Office Building." *March 16, 2018.*

■ **PL 115-139** (HR1858) Designate the facility of the United States Postal Service located at 4514 Williamson Trail in Liberty, Pennsylvania, as the "Staff Sergeant Ryan Scott Ostrom Post Office." *March 20, 2018.*

■ **PL 115-140** (HR1988) Designate the facility of the United States Postal Service located at 1730 18th Street in Bakersfield, California, as the "Merle Haggard Post Office Building." *March 20, 2018.*

■ **PL 115-141** (HR1625) To amend the State Department Basic Authorities Act of 1956 to include severe forms of trafficking in persons within the definition of transnational organized crime for purposes of the rewards program of the Department of State, and for other purposes. *March 23, 2018.*

■ **PL 115-142** (HR2254) Designate the facility of the United States Postal Service located at 2635 Napa Street in Vallejo, California, as the "Janet Capello Post Office Building." *March 23, 2018.*

■ **PL 115-143** (HR2302) Designate the facility of the United States Postal Service located at 259 Nassau Street, Suite 2 in Princeton, New Jersey, as the "Dr. John F. Nash, Jr. Post Office." *March 23, 2018.*

■ **PL 115-144** (HR2464) Designate the facility of the United States Postal Service located at 25 New Chardon Street Lobby in Boston, Massachusetts, as the "John Fitzgerald Kennedy Post Office." *March 23, 2018.*

■ **PL 115-145** (HR2672) Designate the facility of the United States Postal Service located at 520 Carter Street in Fairview, Illinois, as the "Sgt. Douglas J. Riney Post Office." *March 23, 2018.*

■ **PL 115-146** (HR2815) Designate the facility of the United States Postal Service located at 30 East Somerset Street in Raritan, New Jersey, as the "Sergeant John Basilone Post Office." *March 23, 2018.*

■ **PL 115-147** (HR2873) Designate the facility of the United States Postal Service located at 207 Glenside Avenue in Wyncote, Pennsylvania, as the "Staff Sergeant Peter Taub Post Office Building." *March 23, 2018.*

■ **PL 115-148** (HR3109),Designate the facility of the United States Postal Service located at 1114 North 2nd Street in Chillicothe, Illinois, as the "Sr. Chief Ryan Owens Post Office Building." *March 23, 2018.*

■ **PL 115-149** (HR3369), Designate the facility of the United States Postal Service located at 225 North Main Street in Spring Lake, North Carolina, as the "Howard B. Pate, Jr. Post Office." *March 23, 2018.*

■ **PL 115-150** (HR3638), Designate the facility of the United States Postal Service located at 1100 Kings Road in Jacksonville, Florida, as the "Rutledge Pearson Post Office Building." *March 23, 2018.*

■ **PL 115-151** (HR3655) Designate the facility of the United States Postal Service located at 1300 Main Street in Belmar, New Jersey, as the "Dr. Walter S. McAfee Post Office Building." *March 23, 2018.*

■ **PL 115-152** (HR3821) Designate the facility of the United States Postal Service located at 430 Main Street in Clermont, Georgia, as the "Zach T. Addington Post Office." *March 23, 2018.*

■ **PL 115-153** (HR3893) Designate the facility of the United States Postal Service located at 100 Mathe Avenue in Interlachen, Florida, as the "Robert H. Jenkins, Jr. Post Office" *March 23, 2018.*

■ **PL 115-154**,(HR4042) Designate the facility of the United States Postal Service located at 1415 West Oak Street, in Kissimmee, Florida, as the "Borinqueneers Post Office Building." *March 23, 2018.*

■ **PL 115-155** (HR4285) Designate the facility of the United States Postal Service located at 123 Bridgeton Pike in Mullica Hill, New Jersey, as the "James C. 'Billy' Johnson Post Office Building." *March 23, 2018.*

■ **PL 115-156** (HR1177) Direct the Secretary of Agriculture to release on behalf of the United States the condition that certain lands conveyed to the City of Old Town, Maine, be used for a municipal airport, and for other purposes. *March 26, 2018.*

■ **PL 115-157** (HR2154) Rename the Red River Valley Agricultural Research Center in Fargo, North Dakota, as the Edward T. Schafer Agricultural Research Center. *March 27, 2018.*

■ **PL 115-158** (S188) Prohibit the use of Federal funds for the costs of painting portraits of officers and employees of the Federal Government. *March 27, 2018.*

■ **PL 115-159** (S324) Amend title 38, United States Code, to improve the provision of adult day health care services for veterans. *March 27, 2018.*

■ **PL 115-160** (HR3731) Provide overtime pay for employees of the United States Secret Service, and for other purposes. *April 3, 2018.*

■ **PL 115-161** (S2030) Deem the compliance date for amended energy conservation standards for ceiling light kits to be January 21, 2020, and for other purposes. *April 3, 2018.*

■ **PL 115-162** (S2040) Designate the facility of the United States Postal Service located at 621 Kansas Avenue in Atchison, Kansas, as the "Amelia Earhart Post Office Building." *April 3, 2018.*

■ **PL 115-163** (HR4851) Establish the Kennedy-King National Commemorative Site in the State of Indiana, and for other purposes. *April 4, 2018.*

■ **PL 115-164** (HR1865) Amend the Communications Act of 1934 to clarify that section 230 of such Act does not prohibit the enforcement against providers and users of interactive computer services of Federal and State criminal and civil law relating to sexual exploitation of children or sex trafficking, and for other purposes. *April 11, 2018.*

■ **PL 115-165** (HR4547) Amend titles II, VIII, and XVI of the Social Security Act to improve and strengthen the representative payment program. *April 13, 2018.*

■ **PL 115-166** (S772) Amend the PROTECT Act to make Indian tribes eligible for AMBER Alert grants. *April 13, 2018.*

■ **PL 115-167** (HR3445) Enhance the transparency and accelerate the impact of programs under the African Growth and Opportunity Act and the Millennium Challenge Corporation, and for other purposes. *April 23, 2018.*

■ **PL 115-168** (HR3979) Amend the Fish and Wildlife Act of 1956 to reauthorize the volunteer services, community partnership, and refuge education programs of the National Wildlife Refuge System, and for other purposes. *April 23, 2018.*

■ **PL 115-169** (S167) Designate a National Memorial to Fallen Educators at the National Teachers Hall of Fame in Emporia, Kansas. *April 23, 2018.*

■ **PL 115-170** (HR4300) Authorize Pacific Historic Parks to establish a commemorative display to honor members of the United States Armed Forces who served in the Pacific Theater of World War II, and for other purposes. *May 7, 2018.*

■ **PL 115-171** (S447) Require reporting on acts of certain foreign countries on Holocaust era assets and related issues. *May 9, 2018.*

■ **PL 115-172** (SJRES57) Providing for congressional disapproval under chapter 8 of title 5, United States Code, of the rule submitted by Bureau of Consumer Financial Protection relating to "Indirect Auto Lending and Compliance with the Equal Credit Opportunity Act." *May 21, 2018.*

■ **PL 115-173** (HR3210) Require the Director of the National Background Investigations Bureau to submit a report on the backlog of personnel security clearance investigations, and for other purposes. *May 22, 2018.*

■ **PL 115-174** (S2155) Promote economic growth, provide tailored regulatory relief, and enhance consumer protections, and

for other purposes. *May 24, 2018.*

■ **PL 115-175** (S35) Transfer administrative jurisdiction over certain Bureau of Land Management land from the Secretary of the Interior to the Secretary of Veterans Affairs for inclusion in the Black Hills National Cemetery, and for other purposes. *May 25, 2018.*

■ **PL 115-176** (S204) Authorize the use of unapproved medical products by patients diagnosed with a terminal illness in accordance with State law, and for other purposes. *May 30, 2018.*

■ **PL 115-177** (HR3562) Amend title 38, United States Code, to authorize the Secretary of Veterans Affairs to furnish assistance for adaptations of residences of veterans in rehabilitation programs under chapter 31 of such title, and for other purposes. *June 1, 2018.*

■ **PL 115-178** (HR4009) Authorize the Board of Regents of the Smithsonian Institution to plan, design, and construct a central parking facility on National Zoological Park property in the District of Columbia. *June 1, 2018.*

■ **PL 115-179** (S1285) Allow the Confederated Tribes of Coos, Lower Umpqua, and Siuslaw Indians, the Confederated Tribes of the Grand Ronde Community of Oregon, the Confederated Tribes of Siletz Indians of Oregon, the Confederated Tribes of Warm Springs, and the Cow Creek Band of Umpqua Tribe of Indians to lease or transfer certain lands. *June 1, 2018.*

■ **PL 115-180** (S292) Maximize discovery, and accelerate development and availability, of promising childhood cancer treatments, and for other purposes. *June 5, 2018.*

■ **PL 115-181** (S1282) Redesignate certain clinics of the Department of Veterans Affairs located in Montana. *June 5, 2018.*

■ **PL 115-182** (S2372) Amend title 38, United States Code, to provide outer burial receptacles for remains buried in National Parks, and for other purposes. *June 6, 2018.*

■ **PL 115-183** (HR3663) Designate the medical center of the Department of Veterans Affairs in Huntington, West Virginia, as the "Hershel "Woody" Williams VA Medical Center." *June 15, 2018.*

■ **PL 115-184** (HR4910) Amend title 38, United States Code, to provide outer burial receptacles for remains buried in National Parks, and for other purposes. *June 15, 2018.*

■ **PL 115-185** (HR3249) Authorize the Project Safe Neighborhoods Grant Program, and for other purposes. *June 18, 2018.*

■ **PL 115-186** (HR1900) Designate the Veterans Memorial and Museum in Columbus, Ohio, as the National Veterans Memorial and Museum, and for other purposes. *June 21, 2018.*

■ **PL 115-187** (HR2333) Amend the Small Business Investment Act of 1958 to increase the amount of leverage made available to small business investment companies. *June 21, 2018.*

■ **PL 115-188** (HR2772) Amend title 38, United States Code, to provide for requirements relating to the reassignment of Department of Veterans Affairs senior executive employees.

June 21, 2018.

■ **PL 115-189** (HR4743) Amend the Small Business Act to strengthen the Office of Credit Risk Management within the Small Business Administration, and for other purposes. *June 21, 2018.*

■ **PL 115-190** (HR1397) Authorize, direct, facilitate, and expedite the transfer of administrative jurisdiction of certain Federal land, and for other purposes. *June 22, 2018.*

■ **PL 115-191** (HR1719) Authorize the Secretary of the Interior to acquire approximately 44 acres of land in Martinez, California, and for other purposes. *June 22, 2018.*

■ **PL 115-192** (S1869) Reauthorize and rename the position of Whistleblower Ombudsman to be the Whistleblower Protection Coordinator. *June 25, 2018.*

■ **PL 115-193** (S2246) Designate the health care center of the Department of Veterans Affairs in Tallahassee, Florida, as the "Sergeant Ernest I. "Boots" Thomas VA Clinic," and for other purposes. *June 25, 2018.*

■ **PL 115-194** (HR931) Require the Secretary of Health and Human Services to develop a voluntary registry to collect data on cancer incidence among firefighters. *July 7, 2018.*

■ **PL 115-195** (HR2229) Amend title 5, United States Code, to provide authority for judicial review of certain Merit Systems Protection Board decisions relating to whistleblowers, and for other purposes. *July 7, 2018.*

■ **PL 115-196** (S1091) Establish a Federal Advisory Council to Support Grandparents Raising Grandchildren. *July 7, 2018.*

■ **PL 115-197** (HR770) Require the Secretary of the Treasury to mint coins in recognition of American innovation and significant innovation and pioneering efforts of individuals or groups from each of the 50 States, the District of Columbia, and the United States territories, to promote the importance of innovation in the United States, the District of Columbia, and the United States territories, and for other purposes. *July 20, 2018.*

■ **PL 115-198** (HR2061) Reauthorize the North Korean Human Rights Act of 2004, and for other purposes. *July 20, 2018.*

■ **PL 115-199** (SJRES60) Providing for the reappointment of Barbara M. Barrett as a citizen regent of the Board of Regents of the Smithsonian Institution. *July 20, 2018.*

■ **PL 115-200** (HR219) Correct the Swan Lake hydroelectric project survey boundary and to provide for the conveyance of the remaining tract of land within the corrected survey boundary to the State of Alaska. *July 20, 2018.*

■ **PL 115-201** (HR220) Authorize the expansion of an existing hydroelectric project, and for other purposes. *July 20, 2018.*

■ **PL 115-202** (HR446) Extend the deadline for commencement of construction of a hydroelectric project. *July 23, 2018.*

■ **PL 115-203** (HR447) Extend the deadline for commencement of construction of a hydroelectric project. *July 23, 2018.*

■ **PL 115-204** (HR951) Extend the deadline for commencement of construction of a hydroelectric project. *July 23, 2018.*

■ **PL 115-205** (HR2122) Reinstate and extend the deadline for commencement of construction of a hydroelectric project involving Jennings Randolph Dam. *July 23, 2018.*

■ **PL 115-206** (HR2292) Extend a project of the Federal Energy Regulatory Commission involving the Cannonsville Dam. *July 23, 2018.*

■ **PL 115-207** (HR1496) Designate the facility of the United States Postal Service located at 3585 South Vermont Avenue in Los Angeles, California, as the "Marvin Gaye Post Office." *July 7, 2018.*

■ **PL 115-208** (HR2673) Designate the facility of the United States Postal Service located at 514 Broadway Street in Pekin, Illinois, as the "Lance Corporal Jordan S. Bastean Post Office." *July 24, 2018.*

■ **PL 115-209** (HR3183) Designate the facility of the United States Postal Service located at 13683 James Madison Highway in Palmyra, Virginia, as the "U.S. Navy Seaman Dakota Kyle Rigsby Post Office." *July 24, 2018.*

■ **PL 115-210** (HR4301) Designate the facility of the United States Postal Service located at 201 Tom Hall Street in Fort Mill, South Carolina, as the "J. Elliott Williams Post Office Building." *July 24, 2018.*

■ **PL 115-211** (HR4406) Designate the facility of the United States Postal Service located at 99 Macombs Place in New York, New York, as the "Tuskegee Airmen Post Office Building," *July 24, 2018.*

■ **PL 115-212** (HR4463) Designate the facility of the United States Postal Service located at 6 Doyers Street in New York, New York, as the "Mabel Lee Memorial Post Office." *July 24, 2018.*

■ **PL 115-213** (HR4574) Designate the facility of the United States Postal Service located at 108 West Schick Road in Bloomingdale, Illinois, as the "Bloomingdale Veterans Memorial Post Office Building." *July 24, 2018.*

■ **PL 115-214** (HR4646) Designate the facility of the United States Postal Service located at 1900 Corporate Drive in Birmingham, Alabama, as the "Lance Corporal Thomas E. Rivers, Jr. Post Office Building." *July 24, 2018.*

■ **PL 115-215** (HR4685) Designate the facility of the United States Postal Service located at 515 Hope Street in Bristol, Rhode Island, as the "First Sergeant P. Andrew McKenna Jr. Post Office." *July 24, 2018.*

■ **PL 115-216** (HR4722) Designate the facility of the United States Postal Service located at 111 Market Street in Saugerties, New York, as the "Maurice D. Hinchey Post Office Building." *July 24, 2018.*

■ **PL 115-217** (HR4840) Designate the facility of the United States Postal Service located at 567 East Franklin Street in Oviedo, Florida, as the "Sergeant First Class Alwyn Crendall Cashe Post Office Building." *July 24, 2018.*

■ **PL 115-218** (HR5956) Incentivize the hiring of United States workers in the Commonwealth of the Northern Mariana Islands, and for other purposes. *July 24, 2018.*

■ **PL 115-219** (S490) Reinstate and extend the deadline for commencement of construction of a hydroelectric project involving the Gibson Dam. *July 27, 2018.*

■ **PL 115-220** (S931) Designate the facility of the United States Postal Service located at 4910 Brighton Boulevard in Denver, Colorado, as the "George Sakato Post Office." *July 27, 2018.*

■ **PL 115-221** (S2734) Designate the Federal building and United States courthouse located at 1300 Victoria Street in Laredo, Texas, as the "George P. Kazen Federal Building and United States Courthouse." *July 27, 2018.*

■ **PL 115-222** (HR6042) Amend title XIX of the Social Security Act to delay the reduction in Federal medical assistance percentage for Medicaid personal care services furnished without an electronic visit verification system, and for other purposes. *July 30, 2018.*

■ **PL 115-223** (S2692) Designate the facility of the United States Postal Service located at 4558 Broadway in New York, New York, as the "Stanley Michels Post Office Building." *July 30, 2018.*

■ **PL 115-224** (HR2353) Reauthorize the Carl D. Perkins Career and Technical Education Act of 2006. *July 31, 2018.*

■ **PL 115-225** (S1182) Extend the National Flood Insurance Program, and for other purposes. *July 31, 2018.*

■ **PL 115-226** (S2245) Include New Zealand in the list of foreign states whose nationals are eligible for admission into the United States as E-1 and E-2 nonimmigrants if United States nationals are treated similarly by the Government of New Zealand. *Aug 1, 2018.*

■ **PL 115-227** (S2850) Amend the White Mountain Apache Tribe Water Rights Quantification Act of 2010 to clarify the use of amounts in the WMAT Settlement Fund. *Aug 1, 2018.*

■ **PL 115-228** (HR4528) Make technical amendments to certain marine fish conservation statutes, and for other purposes. *Aug 1, 2018.*

■ **PL 115-229** (HR4645) Amend the Wild and Scenic Rivers Act to designate certain segments of East Rosebud Creek in Carbon County, Montana, as components of the Wild and Scenic Rivers System. *Aug 2, 2018.*

■ **PL 115-230** (HR5729) Restrict the department in which the Coast Guard is operating from implementing any rule requiring the use of biometric readers for biometric transportation security cards until after submission to Congress of the results of an assessment of the effectiveness of the transportation security card program. *Aug 2, 2018.*

■ **PL 115-231** (S2779) Amend the Zimbabwe Democracy and Economic Recovery Act of 2001. *Aug 8, 2018.*

■ **PL 115-232** (HR5515) Authorize appropriations for fiscal year 2019 for military activities of the Department of Defense and for military construction, to prescribe military personnel strengths for such fiscal year, and for other purposes. *Aug 13, 2018.*

■ **PL 115-233** (HR2345) Require the Federal Communications Commission to study the feasibility of designating a simple, easy-to-remember dialing code to be used for a national suicide prevention and mental health crisis hotline system. *Aug 14, 2018.*

■ **PL 115-234** (HR5554) Amend the Federal Food, Drug, and Cosmetic Act to reauthorize user fee programs relating to new animal drugs and generic new animal drugs. *Aug 14, 2018.*

■ **PL 115-235** (HR6414) Amend title 23, United States Code, to extend the deadline for promulgation of regulations under the tribal transportation self-governance program. *Aug 14, 2018.*

■ **PL 115-236** (S770) Require the Director of the National Institute of Standards and Technology to disseminate resources to help reduce small business cybersecurity risks, and for other purposes. *Aug 14, 2018.*

■ **PL 115-237** (S717) Promote pro bono legal services as a critical way in which to empower survivors of domestic violence. *Sept 4, 2018.*

■ **PL 115-238** (S899) Amend title 38, United States Code, to ensure that the requirements that new Federal employees who are veterans with service-connected disabilities are provided leave for purposes of undergoing medical treatment for such disabilities apply to certain employees of the Veterans Health Administration, and for other purposes. *Sept 7, 2018.*

■ **PL 115-239** (HR4318) Amend the Harmonized Tariff Schedule of the United States to modify temporarily certain rates of duty. *Sept 13, 2018.*

■ **PL 115-240** (HR2147) Require the Secretary of Veterans Affairs to hire additional Veterans Justice Outreach Specialists to provide treatment court services to justice-involved veterans, and for other purposes. *Sept 17, 2018.*

■ **PL 115-241** (HR5385) Amend the Public Health Service Act to reauthorize the program of payments to children's hospitals that operate graduate medical education programs, and for other purposes. *Sept 18, 2018.*

■ **PL 115-242** (HR5772) Designate the J. Marvin Jones Federal Building and Courthouse in Amarillo, Texas, as the "J. Marvin Jones Federal Building and Mary Lou Robinson United States Courthouse." *Sept 18, 2018.*

■ **PL 115-243** (HR6124) Amend title II of the Social Security Act to authorize voluntary agreements for coverage of Indian tribal council members, and for other purposes. *Sept 20, 2018.*

■ **PL 115-244** (HR5895) Appropriations for energy and water development and related agencies for the fiscal year ending September 30, 2019, and for other purposes. *Sept 21, 2018.*

■ **PL 115-245** (HR6157) Appropriations for the Department of Defense for the fiscal year ending September 30, 2019, and for other purposes. *Sept 28, 2018.*

■ **PL 115-246** (HR589) Establish Department of Energy policy for science and energy research and development programs, and reform National Laboratory management and technology transfer programs, and for other purposes. *Sept 28, 2018.*

■ **PL 115-247** (HR1109) Amend section 203 of the Federal Power Act. *Sept 28, 2018.*

■ **PL 115-248** (S97) Enable civilian research and development of advanced nuclear energy technologies by private and public institutions, to expand theoretical and practical knowledge of nuclear physics, chemistry, and materials science, and for other purposes. *Sept 28, 2018.*

■ **PL 115-249** (S994) Amend title 18, United States Code, to provide for the protection of community centers with religious affiliation, and for other purposes. *Sept 28, 2018.*

■ **PL 115-250** (HR6897) Extend the authorizations of Federal aviation programs, to extend the funding and expenditure authority of the Airport and Airway Trust Fund, and for other purposes. *Sept 29, 2018.*

■ **PL 115-251** (S3479) Amend title 38, United States Code, to extend certain expiring provisions of law administered by the Secretary of Veterans Affairs, and for other purposes. *Sept 29, 2018.*

■ **PL 115-252** (HR698) Require a land conveyance involving the Elkhorn Ranch and the White River National Forest in the State of Colorado, and for other purposes. *Oct 3, 2018.*

■ **PL 115-253** (S2946) Amend title 18, United States Code, to clarify the meaning of the terms "act of war" and "blocked asset," and for other purposes. *Oct 3, 2018.*

■ **PL 115-254** (HR302) Provide protections for certain sports medicine professionals who provide certain medical services in a secondary State. *Oct 5, 2018.*

■ **PL 115-255** (HR46) Authorize the Secretary of the Interior to conduct a special resource study of Fort Ontario in the State of New York. *Oct 9, 2018.*

■ **PL 115-256** (HR2259) Amend the Peace Corps Act to expand services and benefits for volunteers, and for other purposes. *Oct 9, 2018.*

■ **PL 115-257** (HR4854) Amend the DNA Analysis Backlog Elimination Act of 2000 to provide additional resources to State and local prosecutors, and for other purposes. *Oct 9, 2018.*

■ **PL 115-258** (HR4958) Increase, effective as of December 1, 2018, the rates of compensation for veterans with service-connected disabilities and the rates of dependency and indemnity compensation for the survivors of certain disabled veterans, and for other purposes. *Oct 9, 2018.*

■ **PL 115-259** (S791) Amend the Small Business Act to expand intellectual property education and training for small businesses, and for other purposes. *Oct 9, 2018.*

■ **PL 115-260** (S1668) Rename a waterway in the State of New York as the "Joseph Sanford Jr. Channel." *Oct 9, 2018.*

■ **PL 115-261** (S2559) Amend title 17, United States Code, to implement the Marrakesh Treaty, and for other purposes. *Oct 9, 2018.*

■ **PL 115-262** (S2553) Amend title XVIII of the Social Security Act to prohibit health plans and pharmacy benefit managers from restricting pharmacies from informing individuals regarding the prices for certain drugs and biologicals. *Oct 10, 2018.*

■ **PL 115-263** (S2554) Ensure that health insurance issuers and group health plans do not prohibit pharmacy providers from providing certain information to enrollees. *Oct 10, 2018.*

■ **PL 115-264** (HR1551) Amend the Internal Revenue Code of 1986 to modify the credit for production from advanced nuclear power facilities. *Oct 11, 2018.*

■ **PL 115-265** (S3508) Reauthorize and amend the Marine Debris Act to promote international action to reduce marine debris, and for other purposes. *Oct 11, 2018.*

■ **PL 115-266** (S2269) Reauthorize the Global Food Security Act of 2016 for 5 additional years. *Oct 11, 2018.*

■ **PL 115-267** (S3354) Amend the Missing Children's Assistance Act, and for other purposes. *Oct 11, 2018.*

■ **PL 115-268** (S3509) Reauthorize the Congressional Award Act. *Oct 11, 2018.*

■ **PL 115-269** (HR4921) Require the Surface Board of Transportation to implement certain recommendations of the Inspector General of the Department of Transportation. *Oct 16, 2018.*

■ **PL 115-270** (S3021) Provide for improvements to the rivers and harbors of the United States, to provide for the conservation and development of water and related resources, to provide for water pollution control activities, and for other purposes. *Oct 23, 2018.*

■ **PL 115-271** (HR6) Provide for opioid use disorder prevention, recovery, and treatment, and for other purposes. *Oct 24, 2018.*

■ **PL 115-272** (S1595) Amend the Hizballah International Financing Prevention Act of 2015 to impose additional sanctions with respect to Hizballah, and for other purposes. *Oct 25, 2018.*

■ **PL 115-273** (HR6758) Direct the Under Secretary of Commerce for Intellectual Property and Director of the United States Patent and Trademark Office, in consultation with the Administrator of the Small Business Administration, to study and provide recommendations to promote the participation of women and minorities in entrepreneurship activities and the patent system, to extend by 8 years the Patent and Trademark Office's authority to set the amounts for the fees it charges, and for other purposes. *Oct 31, 2018.*

■ **PL 115-274** (HR6896) Provide for the continued performance of the functions of the United States Parole Commission, and for other purposes. *Oct 31, 2018.*

■ **PL 115-275** (HR1037) Authorize the National Emergency Medical Services Memorial Foundation to establish a commemorative work in the District of Columbia and its environs, and for other purposes. *Nov 3, 2018.*

■ **PL 115-276** (HR3834) Provide that members of public safety agencies who died of 9/11-related health conditions are eligible for the Presidential 9/11 Heroes Medal of Valor, and for other purposes. *Nov 3, 2018.*

■ **PL 115-277** (HR6870) Rename the Stop Trading on Congressional Knowledge Act of 2012 in honor of Representative Louise McIntosh Slaughter. *Nov 3, 2018.*

■ **PL 115-278** (HR3359) Amend the Homeland Security Act of 2002 to authorize the Cybersecurity and Infrastructure Security Agency of the Department of Homeland Security, and for other purposes. *Nov 16, 2018.*

■ **PL 115-279** (HR2615) Authorize the exchange of certain land located in Gulf Islands National Seashore, Jackson County, Mississippi, between the National Park Service and the Veterans of Foreign Wars, and for other purposes. *Nov 20, 2018.*

■ **PL 115-280** (S3554) Extend the effective date for the sunset for collateral requirements for Small Business Administration disaster loans. *Nov 29, 2018.*

■ **PL 115-281** (HR7187) Extend the National Flood Insurance Program until December 7, 2018. *Dec 1, 2018.*

■ **PL 115-282** (S140) Amend the White Mountain Apache Tribe Water Rights Quantification Act of 2010 to clarify the use of amounts in the WMAT Settlement Fund. *Dec 4, 2018.*

■ **PL 115-283** (HR606) Designate the facility of the United States Postal Service located at 1025 Nevin Avenue in Richmond, California, as the "Harold D. McCraw, Sr. Post Office Building." *Dec 6, 2018.*

■ **PL 115-284** (HR1209) Designate the facility of the United States Postal Service located at 901 N. Francisco Avenue, Mission, Texas, as the "Mission Veterans Post Office Building." *Dec 6, 2018.*

■ **PL 115-285** (HR2979) Designate the facility of the United States Postal Service located at 390 West 5th Street in San Bernardino, California, as the "Jack H. Brown Post Office Building." *Dec 6, 2018.*

■ **PL 115-286** (HR3230) Designate the facility of the United States Postal Service located at 915 Center Avenue in Payette, Idaho, as the "Harmon Killebrew Post Office Building." *Dec 6, 2018.*

■ **PL 115-287** (HR4890) Designate the facility of the United States Postal Service located at 9801 Apollo Drive in Upper Marlboro, Maryland, as the "Wayne K. Curry Post Office Building." *Dec 6, 2018.*

■ **PL 115-288** (HR4913) Designate the facility of the United States Postal Service located at 816 East Salisbury Parkway in Salisbury, Maryland, as the "Sgt. Maj. Wardell B. Turner Post Office Building." *Dec 6, 2018.*

■ **PL 115-289** (HR4946) Designate the facility of the United States Postal Service located at 1075 North Tustin Street in Orange, California, as the "Specialist Trevor A. Win'E Post Office." *Dec 6, 2018.*

■ **PL 115-290** (HR4960) Designate the facility of the United States Postal Service located at 511 East Walnut Street in Columbia, Missouri, as the "Spc. Sterling William Wyatt Post Office Building." *Dec 6, 2018.*

■ **PL 115-291** (HR5349) Designate the facility of the United States Postal Service located at 1320 Autumn Avenue in Memphis, Tennessee, as the "Judge Russell B. Sugarmon Post Office Building." *Dec 6, 2018.*

■ **PL 115-292** (HR5504) Designate the facility of the United States Postal Service located at 4801 West Van Giesen Street in West Richland, Washington, as the "Sergeant Dietrich Schmieman Post Office Building." *Dec 6, 2018.*

■ **PL 115-293** (HR5737) Designate the facility of the United States Postal Service located at 108 West D Street in Alpha, Illinois, as the "Captain Joshua E. Steele Post Office." *Dec 6, 2018.*

■ **PL 115-294** (HR5784) Designate the facility of the United States Postal Service located at 2650 North Doctor Martin Luther King Drive in Milwaukee, Wisconsin, as the "Vel R. Phillips Post Office Building." *Dec 6, 2018.*

■ **PL 115-295** (HR5868) Designate the facility of the United States Postal Service located at 530 Claremont Avenue in Ashland, Ohio, as the "Bill Harris Post Office." *Dec 6, 2018.*

■ **PL 115-296** (HR5935) Designate the facility of the United States Postal Service located at 1355 North Meridian Road in Harristown, Illinois, as the "Logan S. Palmer Post Office." *Dec 6, 2018.*

■ **PL 115-297** (HR6116) Designate the facility of the United States Postal Service located at 362 North Ross Street in Beaverton, Michigan, as the "Colonel Alfred Asch Post Office." *Dec 6, 2018.*

■ **PL 115-298** (HJRES143) Making further continuing appropriations for fiscal year 2019, and for other purposes. *Dec 7, 2018.*

■ **PL 115-299** (S2152) Amend title 18, United States Code, to provide for assistance for victims of child pornography, and for other purposes. *Dec 7, 2018.*

■ **PL 115-300** (HR390) Provide emergency relief for victims of genocide, crimes against humanity, and war crimes in Iraq and Syria, for accountability for perpetrators of these crimes, and for other purposes. *Dec 11, 2018.*

■ **PL 115-301** (HR1074) Repeal the Act entitled "An Act to confer jurisdiction on the State of Iowa over offenses committed by or against Indians on the Sac and Fox Indian Reservation." *Dec 11, 2018.*

■ **PL 115-302** (HR2422) The Public Health Service Act to improve essential oral health care for low-income and other underserved individuals by breaking down barriers to care, and for other purposes. *Dec 11, 2018.*

■ **PL 115-303** (HR4254) Amend the National Science Foundation Authorization Act of 2002 to strengthen the aerospace workforce pipeline by the promotion of Robert Noyce Teacher Scholarship Program and National Aeronautics and Space Administration internship and fellowship opportunities to women, and for other purposes. *Dec 11, 2018.*

■ **PL 115-304** (HR5317) Repeal section 2141 of the Revised Statutes to remove the prohibition on certain alcohol manufacturing on Indian lands. *Dec 11, 2018.*

■ **PL 115-305** (HR6651) Extend certain authorities relating to United Sates efforts to combat HIV/AIDS, tuberculosis, and malaria globally, and for other purposes. *Dec 11, 2018.*

■ **PL 115-306** (S440) Establish a procedure for the conveyance of certain Federal property around the Dickinson Reservoir in the State of North Dakota. *Dec 11, 2018.*

■ **PL 115-307** (S1768) Reauthorize and amend the National Earthquake Hazards Reduction Program, and for other purposes. *Dec 11, 2018.*

■ **PL 115-308** (S2074) Establish a procedure for the conveyance of certain Federal property around the Jamestown Reservoir in the State of North Dakota, and for other purposes. *Dec 11, 2018.*

■ **PL 115-309** (S3389) Redesignate a facility of the National Aeronautics and Space Administration. *Dec 11, 2018.*

■ **PL 115-310** (HR754) Award the Congressional Gold Medal to Anwar Sadat in recognition of his heroic achievements and courageous contributions to peace in the Middle East. *Dec 13, 2018.*

■ **PL 115-311** (HR1207) Designate the facility of the United States Postal Service located at 306 River Street in Tilden, Texas, as the "Tilden Veterans Post Office." *Dec 13, 2018.*

■ **PL 115-312** (S2377) Designate the Federal building and United States courthouse located at 200 West 2nd Street in Dayton, Ohio, as the "Walter H. Rice Federal Building and United States Courthouse." *Dec 13, 2018.*

■ **PL 115-313** (S3414) Designate the facility of the United States Postal Service located at 20 Ferry Road in Saunderstown, Rhode Island, as the "Captain Matthew J. August Post Office." *Dec 13, 2018.*

■ **PL 115-314** (S3442) Designate the facility of the United States Postal Service located at 105 Duff Street in Macon, Missouri, as the "Arla W. Harrell Post Office." *Dec 13, 2018.*

■ **PL 115-315** (HR3946) Name the Department of Veterans Affairs community-based outpatient clinic in Statesboro, Georgia, the "Ray Hendrix Veterans Clinic." *Dec 14, 2018.*

■ **PL 115-316** (HR4407) Designate the facility of the United States Postal Service located at 3s101 Rockwell Street in Warrenville, Illinois, as the "Corporal Jeffery Allen Williams Post Office Building." *Dec 14, 2018.*

■ **PL 115-317** (HR5238) Designate the facility of the United States Postal Service located at 1234 Saint Johns Place in Brooklyn, New York, as the "Major Robert Odell Owens Post Office." *Dec 14, 2018.*

■ **PL 115-318** (S3209) Designate the facility of the United States Postal Service located at 413 Washington Avenue in Belleville, New Jersey, as the "Private Henry Svehla Post Office Building." *Dec 14, 2018.*

■ **PL 115-319** (S3237) Designate the facility of the United States Postal Service located at 120 12th Street Lobby in Columbus, Georgia, as the "Richard W. Williams Chapter of the Triple Nickles (555th P.I.A.) Post Office." *Dec 14, 2018.*

■ **PL 115-320** (HR315) Amend the Public Health Service Act to distribute maternity care health professionals to health professional shortage areas identified as in need of maternity care health services. *Dec 17, 2018.*

■ **PL 115-321** (HR1417) Amend the National Law Enforcement Museum Act to allow the Museum to acquire, receive, possess, collect, ship, transport, import, and display firearms, and for other purposes. *Dec 17, 2018.*

■ **PL 115-322** (HR1861) Award a Congressional Gold Medal in honor of Lawrence Eugene "Larry" Doby in recognition of his achievements and contributions to American major league athletics, civil rights, and the Armed Forces during World War II. *Dec 17, 2018.*

■ **PL 115-323** (HR3398) Amend the Real ID Act of 2005 to permit Freely Associated States to meet identification requirements under such Act, and for other purposes. *Dec 17, 2018.*

■ **PL 115-324** (HR6330) Amend the Small Business Act to modify the method for prescribing size standards for business concerns. *Dec 17, 2018.*

■ **PL 115-325** (S245) Amend the Indian Tribal Energy Development and Self Determination Act of 2005, and for other purposes. *Dec 18, 2018.*

■ **PL 115-326** (S825) Provide for the conveyance of certain property to the Southeast Alaska Regional Health Consortium located in Sitka, Alaska, and for other purposes. *Dec 18, 2018.*

■ **PL 115-327** (S2465) Amend the Public Health Service Act to reauthorize a sickle cell disease prevention and treatment demonstration program and to provide for sickle cell disease research, surveillance, prevention, and treatment. *Dec 18, 2018.*

■ **PL 115-328** (S3029) Revise and extend the Prematurity Research Expansion and Education for Mothers who deliver Infants Early Act (PREEMIE Act). *Dec 18, 2018.*

■ **PL 115-329** (S3119) Allow for the taking of sea lions on the Columbia River and its tributaries to protect endangered and threatened species of salmon and other nonlisted fish species. *Dec 18, 2018.*

■ **PL 115-330** (HR1872) Promote access for United States officials, journalists, and other citizens to Tibetan areas of the People's Republic of China, and for other purposes. *Dec 19, 2018.*

■ **PL 115-331** (HR2454) Direct the Secretary of Homeland Security to establish a data framework to provide access for appropriate personnel to law enforcement and other information of the Department, and for other purposes. *Dec 19, 2018.*

■ **PL 115-332** (HR3996) Amend title 28, United States Code, to permit other courts to transfer certain cases to United States Tax Court. *Dec 19, 2018.*

■ **PL 115-333** (HR4111) Amend the Small Business Investment Act of 1958 to improve the number of small business investment companies in underlicensed States, and for other purposes. *Dec 19, 2018.*

■ **PL 115-334** (HR2) Provide for the reform and continuation of agricultural and other programs of the Department of Agriculture through fiscal year 2023, and for other purposes. *Dec 20, 2018.*

■ **PL 115-335** (HR1918) Oppose loans at international financial institutions for the Government of Nicaragua unless the Government of Nicaragua is taking effective steps to hold free, fair, and transparent elections, and for other purposes. *Dec 20, 2018.*

■ **PL 115-336** (HR5759) Improve executive agency digital services, and for other purposes. *Dec 20, 2018.*

■ **PL 115-337** (S1050) Award a Congressional Gold Medal, collectively, to the Chinese-American Veterans of World War II, in recognition of their dedicated service during World War II. *Dec 20, 2018.*

■ **PL 115-338** (S2101) Award a Congressional Gold Medal, collectively, to the crew of the U.S.S. Indianapolis, in recognition of their perseverance, bravery, and service to the United States. *Dec 20, 2018.*

■ **PL 115-339** (HR1162) Direct the Secretary of Veterans Affairs to carry out a pilot program to provide access to magnetic EEG/EKG-guided resonance therapy to veterans. *Dec 21, 2018.*

■ **PL 115-340** (HR1210) Designate the facility of the United States Postal Service located at 122 W. Goodwin Street, Pleasanton, Texas, as the "Pleasanton Veterans Post Office." *Dec 21, 2018.*

■ **PL 115-341** (HR1211) Designate the facility of the United States Postal Service located at 400 N. Main Street, Encinal, Texas, as the "Encinal Veterans Post Office." *Dec 21, 2018.*

■ **PL 115-342** (HR1222) Amend the Public Health Service Act to coordinate Federal congenital heart disease research efforts and to improve public education and awareness of congenital heart disease, and for other purposes. *Dec 21, 2018.*

■ **PL 115-343** (HR1235) Require the Secretary of the Treasury to mint coins in recognition of the 60th Anniversary of the Naismith Memorial Basketball Hall of Fame. *Dec 21, 2018.*

■ **PL 115-344** (HR1318) Support States in their work to save and sustain the health of mothers during pregnancy, childbirth, and in the postpartum period, to eliminate disparities in maternal health outcomes for pregnancy-related and pregnancy-associated deaths, to identify solutions to improve health care quality and health outcomes for mothers, and for other purposes. *Dec 21, 2018.*

■ **PL 115-345** (HR1733) Direct the Secretary of Energy to review and update a report on the energy and environmental benefits of the re-refining of used lubricating oil. *Dec 21, 2018.*

■ **PL 115-346** (HR1850) Designate the facility of the United States Postal Service located at 907 Fourth Avenue in Lake Odessa, Michigan, as the "Donna Sauers Besko Post Office." *Dec 21, 2018.*

■ **PL 115-347** (HR3184) Designate the facility of the United States Postal Service located at 180 McCormick Road in Charlottesville, Virginia, as the "Captain Humayun Khan Post Office." *Dec 21, 2018.*

■ **PL 115-348** (HR3342) To impose sanctions on foreign persons that are responsible for gross violations of internationally recognized human rights by reason of the use by Hizballah of civilians as human shields, and for other purposes. *Dec 21, 2018.*

■ **PL 115-349** (HR3383) Designate the flood control project in Sedgwick County, Kansas, commonly known as the Wichita-Valley Center Flood Control Project, as the "M.S. 'Mitch' Mitchell Floodway." *Dec 21, 2018.*

■ **PL 115-350** (HR4032) Confirm undocumented Federal rights-of-way or easements on the Gila River Indian Reservation, clarify the northern boundary of the Gila River Indian Community's Reservation, to take certain land located in Maricopa County and Pinal County, Arizona, into trust for the benefit of the Gila River Indian Community, and for other purposes. *Dec 21, 2018.*

■ **PL 115-351** (HR4326) Designate the facility of the United States Postal Service located at 1211 Towanda Avenue in Bloomington, Illinois, as the "Sgt. Josh Rodgers Post Office." *Dec 21, 2018.*

■ **PL 115-352** (HR4431) Amend title 5, United States Code, to provide for interest payments by agencies in the case of administrative error in processing certain annuity deposits for prior military service. *Dec 21, 2018.*

■ **PL 115-353** (HR4819) Promote inclusive economic growth through conservation and biodiversity programs that facilitate transboundary cooperation, improve natural resource management, and build local capacity to protect and preserve threatened wildlife species in the greater Okavango River Basin of southern Africa. *Dec 21, 2018.*

■ **PL 115-354** (HR5205) Designate the facility of the United States Postal Service located at 701 6th Street in Hawthorne, Nevada, as the "Sergeant Kenneth Eric Bostic Post Office." *Dec 21, 2018.*

■ **PL 115-355** (HR5395) Designate the facility of the United States Postal Service located at 116 Main Street in Dansville, New York, as the "Staff Sergeant Alexandria Gleason-Morrow Post Office Building." *Dec 21, 2018.*

■ **PL 115-356** (HR5412) Designate the facility of the United States Postal Service located at 25 2nd Avenue in Brentwood, New York, as the "Army Specialist Jose L. Ruiz Post Office Building." *Dec 21, 2018.*

■ **PL 115-357** (HR5475) Designate the facility of the United States Postal Service located at 108 North Macon Street in Bevier, Missouri, as the "SO2 Navy SEAL Adam Olin Smith Post Office." *Dec 21, 2018.*

■ **PL 115-358** (HR5787) Amend the Coastal Barrier Resources Act to give effect to more accurate maps of units of the John H. Chafee Coastal Barrier Resources System that were produced by digital mapping of such units, and for other purposes. *Dec 21, 2018.*

■ **PL 115-359** (HR5791) Designate the facility of the United States Postal Service located at 9609 South University Boulevard in Highlands Ranch, Colorado, as the "Deputy Sheriff Zackari Spurlock Parrish, III, Post Office Building." *Dec 21, 2018.*

■ **PL 115-360** (HR5792) Designate the facility of the United States Postal Service located at 90 North 4th Avenue in Brighton, Colorado, as the "Deputy Sheriff Heath McDonald Gumm Post Office." *Dec 21, 2018.*

■ **PL 115-361** (HR5923) Direct the Secretary of Agriculture to exchange certain public lands in Ouachita National Forest, and for other purposes. *Dec 21, 2018.*

■ **PL 115-362** (HR6020) Designate the facility of the United States Postal Service located at 325 South Michigan Avenue in Howell, Michigan, as the "Sergeant Donald Burgett Post Office Building." *Dec 21, 2018.*

■ **PL 115-363** (HR6059) Designate the facility of the United States Postal Service located at 51 Willow Street in Lynn, Massachusetts, as the "Thomas P. Costin, Jr. Post Office Building." *Dec 21, 2018.*

■ **PL 115-364** (HR6160) Amend title 5, United States Code, to clarify the sources of the authority to issue regulations regarding certifications and other criteria applicable to legislative branch employees under Wounded Warriors Federal Leave Act. *Dec 21, 2018.*

■ **PL 115-365** (HR6167) Designate the facility of the United States Postal Service located at 5707 South Cass Avenue in Westmont, Illinois, as the "James William Robinson Jr. Memorial Post Office Building." *Dec 21, 2018.*

■ **PL 115-366** (HR6216) Designate the facility of the United States Postal Service located at 3025 Woodgate Road in Montrose, Colorado, as the "Sergeant David Kinterknecht Post Office." *Dec 21, 2018.*

■ **PL 115-367** (HR6217) Designate the facility of the United States Postal Service located at 241 N 4th Street in Grand Junction, Colorado, as the "Deputy Sheriff Derek Geer Post Office Building." *Dec 21, 2018.*

■ **PL 115-368** (HR6227) Provide for a coordinated Federal program to accelerate quantum research and development for the economic and national security of the United States. *Dec 21, 2018.*

■ **PL 115-369** (HR6335) Designate the facility of the United States Postal Service located at 322 Main Street in Oakville, Connecticut, as the "Veterans Memorial Post Office." *Dec 21, 2018.*

■ **PL 115-370** (HR6347) Adjust the real estate appraisal thresholds under the 7(a) program to bring them into line with the thresholds used by the Federal banking regulators, and for other purposes. *Dec 21, 2018.*

■ **PL 115-371** (HR6348) Adjust the real estate appraisal thresholds under the section 504 program to bring them into line with the thresholds used by the Federal banking regulators, and for other purposes. *Dec 21, 2018.*

■ **PL 115-372** (HR6400) Require the Secretary of Homeland Security to conduct a threat and operational analysis of ports of entry, and for other purposes. *Dec 21, 2018.*

■ **PL 115-373** (HR6405) Designate the facility of the United States Postal Service located at 2801 Mitchell Road in Ceres, California, as the "Lance Corporal Juana Navarro Arellano Post Office Building." *Dec 21, 2018.*

■ **PL 115-374** (HR6428) Designate the facility of the United States Postal Service located at 332 Ramapo Valley Road in Oakland, New Jersey, as the "Frank Leone Post Office." *Dec 21, 2018.*

■ **PL 115-375** (HR6513) Designate the facility of the United States Postal Service located at 1110 West Market Street in Athens, Alabama, as the "Judge James E. Horton, Jr. Post Office Building." *Dec 21, 2018.*

■ **PL 115-376** (HR6591) Designate the facility of the United States Postal Service located at 501 South Kirkman Road in Orlando, Florida, as the "Napoleon 'Nap' Ford Post Office Building." *Dec 21, 2018.*

■ **PL 115-377** (HR6615) Reauthorize the Traumatic Brain Injury program. *Dec 21, 2018.*

■ **PL 115-378** (HR6621) Designate the facility of the United States Postal Service located at 530 East Main Street in Johnson City, Tennessee, as the "Major Homer L. Pease Post Office." *Dec 21, 2018.*

■ **PL 115-379** (HR6628) Designate the facility of the United States Postal Service located at 4301 Northeast 4th Street in Renton, Washington, as the "James Marshall 'Jimi' Hendrix Post Office Building." *Dec 21, 2018.*

■ **PL 115-380** (HR6655) Designate the facility of the United States Postal Service located at 44160 State Highway 299 East Suite 1 in McArthur, California, as the "Janet Lucille Oilar Post Office." *Dec 21, 2018.*

■ **PL 115-381** (HR6780) Designate the facility of the United States Postal Service located at 7521 Paula Drive in Tampa, Florida, as the "Major Andreas O'Keeffe Post Office Building." *Dec 21, 2018.*

■ **PL 115-382** (HR6831) Designate the facility of the United States Postal Service located at 35 West Main Street in Frisco, Colorado, as the "Patrick E. Mahany, Jr., Post Office Building." *Dec 21, 2018.*

■ **PL 115-383** (HR6893) Amend the Overtime Pay for Protective Services Act of 2016 to extend the Secret Service overtime pay exception through 2019, and for other purposes. *Dec 21, 2018.*

■ **PL 115-384** (HR6930) Designate the facility of the United States Postal Service located at 10 Miller Street in Plattsburgh, New York, as the "Ross Bouyea Post Office Building." *Dec 21, 2018.*

■ **PL 115-385** (HR6964) Reauthorize and improve the Juvenile Justice and Delinquency Prevention Act of 1974, and for other purposes. *Dec 21, 2018.*

■ **PL 115-386** (HR7120) Amend the Federal Election Campaign Act of 1971 to extend through 2023 the authority of the Federal Election Commission to impose civil money penalties on the basis of a schedule of penalties established and published by the Commission. *Dec 21, 2018.*

■ **PL 115-387** (HR7213) Amend the Homeland Security Act of 2002 to establish the Countering Weapons of Mass Destruction Office, and for other purposes. *Dec 21, 2018.*

■ **PL 115-388** (HR7230) Designate the facility of the United States Postal Service located at 226 West Main Street in Lake City, South Carolina, as the "Postmaster Frazier B. Baker Post Office." *Dec 21, 2018.*

■ **PL 115-389** (HR7243) Amend Public Law 115-217 to change the address of the postal facility designated by such Public Law in honor of Sergeant First Class Alwyn Crendall Cashe, and for other purposes. *Dec 21, 2018.*

■ **PL 115-390** (HR7327) Require the Secretary of Homeland Security to establish a security vulnerability disclosure policy, to establish a bug bounty program for the Department of Homeland Security, to amend title 41, United States Code, to provide for Federal acquisition supply chain security, and for other purposes. *Dec 21, 2018.*

■ **PL 115-391** (S756) Reauthorize and amend the Marine Debris Act to promote international action to reduce marine debris, and for other purposes. *Dec 21, 2018.*

■ **PL 115-392** (S1311) Provide assistance in abolishing human trafficking in the United States. *Dec 21, 2018.*

■ **PL 115-393** (S1312) Prioritize the fight against human trafficking in the United States. *Dec 21, 2018.*

■ **PL 115-394** (S2511) Require the Under Secretary of Commerce for Oceans and Atmosphere to carry out a program on coordinating the assessment and acquisition by the National Oceanic and Atmospheric Administration of unmanned maritime systems, to make available to the public data collected by the Administration using such systems, and for other purposes. *Dec 21, 2018.*

■ **PL 115-395** (S3170) Amend title 18, United States Code, to make certain changes to the reporting requirement of certain service providers regarding child sexual exploitation visual depictions, and for other purposes. *Dec 21, 2018.*

■ **PL 115-396** (S3628) Reauthorize the National Flood Insurance Program. *Dec 21, 2018.*

■ **PL 115-397** (S3749) Amend the Congressional Accountability Act of 1995 to reform the procedures provided under such Act for the initiation, review, and resolution of claims alleging that employing offices of the legislative branch have violated the rights and protections provided to their employees under such Act, including protections against sexual harassment, and for other purposes. *Dec 21, 2018.*

■ **PL 115-398** (HR767) Establish the Stop, Observe, Ask, and Respond to Health and Wellness Training pilot program to address human trafficking in the health care system. *Dec 31, 2018.*

■ **PL 115-399** (HR2606) Amend the Act of August 4, 1947, (commonly known as the Stigler Act) with respect to restrictions applicable to Indians of the Five Civilized Tribes of Oklahoma, and for other purposes. *Dec 31, 2018.*

■ **PL 115-400** (HR4227) Require the Secretary of Homeland Security to examine what actions the Department of Homeland Security is undertaking to combat the threat of vehicular terrorism, and for other purposes. *Dec 31, 2018.*

■ **PL 115-401** (HR5075) Encourage, enhance, and integrate Ashanti Alert plans throughout the United States and for other purposes. *Dec 31, 2018.*

■ **PL 115-402** (HR5509) Direct the National Science Foundation to provide grants for research about STEM education approaches and the STEM-related workforce, and for other purposes. *Dec 31, 2018.*

■ **PL 115-403** (S7) Amend title 51, United States Code, to extend the authority of the National Aeronautics and Space Administration to enter into leases of non-excess property of the Administration. *Dec 31, 2018.*

■ **PL 115-404** (S943) Direct the Secretary of the Interior to conduct an accurate comprehensive student count for the purposes of calculating formula allocations for programs under the Johnson-O'Malley Act, and for other purposes. *Dec 31, 2018.*

■ **PL 115-405** (S1520) Expand recreational fishing opportunities through enhanced marine fishery conservation and management, and for other purposes. *Dec 31, 2018.*

■ **PL 115-406** (S2076) Amend the Public Health Service Act to authorize the expansion of activities related to Alzheimer's disease, cognitive decline, and brain health under the Alzheimer's Disease and Healthy Aging Program, and for other purposes. *Dec 31, 2018.*

■ **PL 115-407** (S2248) Amend title 38, United States Code, to authorize the Secretary of Veterans Affairs to provide certain burial benefits for spouses and children of veterans who are buried in tribal cemeteries, and for other purposes. *Dec 31, 2018.*

■ **PL 115-408** (S2278) Amend the Public Health Service Act to provide grants to improve health care in rural areas. *Dec 31, 2018.*

■ **PL 115-409** (S2736) Develop a long-term strategic vision and a comprehensive, multifaceted, and principled United States policy for the Indo-Pacific region, and for other purposes. *Dec 31, 2018.*

■ **PL 115-410** (S3530) Reauthorize the Museum and Library Services Act. *Dec 31, 2018.*

■ **PL 115-411** (HR1660) Direct the Administrator of the United States Agency for International Development to submit to Congress a report on the development and use of global health innovations in the programs, projects, and activities of the Agency. *Jan 3, 2019.*

■ **PL 115-412** (HR3460) Designate the United States courthouse located at 323 East Chapel Hill Street in Durham, North Carolina, as the "John Hervey Wheeler United States Courthouse." *Jan 3, 2019.*

■ **PL 115-413** (HR6287) Provide competitive grants for the operation, security, and maintenance of certain memorials to victims of the terrorist attacks of September 11, 2001. *Jan 3, 2019.*

■ **PL 115-414** (S2276) Require agencies to submit reports on outstanding recommendations in the annual budget justification submitted to Congress. *Jan 3, 2019.*

■ **PL 115-415** (S2652) Award a Congressional Gold Medal to Stephen Michael Gleason. *Jan 3, 2019.*

■ **PL 115-416** (S2679) Provide access to and manage the distribution of excess or surplus property to veteran-owned small businesses. *Jan 3, 2019.*

■ **PL 115-417** (S2765) Amend the Investment Advisers Act of 1940 to exempt investment advisers who solely advise certain rural business investment companies, and for other purposes. *Jan 3, 2019.*

■ **PL 115-418** (S2896) Require disclosure by lobbyists of convictions for bribery, extortion, embezzlement, illegal kickbacks, tax evasion, fraud, conflicts of interest, making false statements, perjury, or money laundering. *Jan 3, 2019.*

■ **PL 115-419** (S3031) Amend chapter 5 of title 40, United States Code, to improve the management of Federal personal property. *Jan 3, 2019.*

■ **PL 115-420** (S3367) Amend certain transportation-related

reporting requirements to improve congressional oversight, reduce reporting burdens, and promote transparency, and for other purposes. *Jan 3, 2019.*

■ **PL 115-421** (S3444) Designate the community-based outpatient clinic of the Department of Veterans Affairs in Lake Charles, Louisiana, as the "Douglas Fournet Department of Veterans Affairs Clinic." *Jan 3, 2019.*

■ **PL 115-422** (S3777) Require the Secretary of Veterans Affairs to establish a tiger team dedicated to addressing the difficulties encountered by the Department of Veterans Affairs in carrying out section 3313 of title 38 United States Code, after the enactment of sections 107 and 501 of the Harry W. Colmery Veterans Educational Assistance Act of 2017. *Jan 3, 2019.*

■ **PL 115-423** (S2200) Reauthorize the National Integrated Drought Information System, and for other purposes. *Jan 7, 2019.*

■ **PL 115-424** (S2961) Reauthorize subtitle A of the Victims of Child Abuse Act of 1990. *Jan 7, 2019.*

■ **PL 115-425** (HR2200) Reauthorize the Trafficking Victims Protection Act of 2000, and for other purposes. *Jan 8, 2019.*

■ **PL 115-426** (S3191) Provide for the expeditious disclosure of records related to civil rights cold cases, and for other purposes. *Jan 8, 2019.*

■ **PL 115-427** (S1862) Amend the Trafficking Victims Protection Act of 2000 to modify the criteria for determining whether countries are meeting the minimum standards for the elimination of human trafficking, and for other purposes. *Jan 9, 2019.*

■ **PL 115-428** (S3247) Improve programs and activities relating to women's entrepreneurship and economic empowerment that are carried out by the United States Agency for International Development, and for other purposes. *Jan 9, 2019.*

■ **PL 115-429** (HR4689) Authorize early repayment of obligations to the Bureau of Reclamation within the Northport Irrigation District in the State of Nebraska. *Jan 10, 2019.*

■ **PL 115-430** (HR5636) Designate additions to the Flatside Wilderness on the Ouachita National Forest, and for other purposes. *Jan 10, 2019.*

■ **PL 115-431** (HR6602) Reauthorize the New Jersey Coastal Heritage Trail Route, and for other purposes. *Jan 10, 2019.*

■ **PL 115-432** (S3456) Redesignate Hobe Sound National Wildlife Refuge as the Nathaniel P. Reed Hobe Sound National Wildlife Refuge, and for other purposes. *Jan 10, 2019.*

■ **PL 115-433** (S3661) Provide for a program of the Department of Defense to commemorate the 75th anniversary of World War II. *Jan 10, 2019.*

■ **PL 115-434** (HR672) Require continued and enhanced annual reporting to Congress in the Annual Report on International Religious Freedom on anti-Semitic incidents in Europe, the safety and security of European Jewish communities, and the efforts of the United States to partner with European governments, the European Union, and civil society groups, to combat anti-Semitism, and for other purposes. *Jan 14, 2019.*

■ **PL 115-435** (HR4174) Amend titles 5 and 44, United States Code, to require Federal evaluation activities, improve Federal data management, and for other purposes. *Jan 14, 2019.*

■ **PL 115-436** (HR7279) Amend the Federal Water Pollution Control Act to provide for an integrated planning process, to promote green infrastructure, and for other purposes. *Jan 14, 2019.*

■ **PL 115-437** (HR7318) Amend the Federal Assets Sale and Transfer Act of 2016 to ensure that the Public Buildings Reform Board has adequate time to carry out the responsibilities of the Board, and for other purposes. *Jan 14, 2019.*

■ **PL 115-438** (HR7319) Amend the Federal Assets Sale and Transfer Act of 2016 to provide flexibility with respect to the leaseback of certain Federal real property, and for other purposes. *Jan 14, 2019.*

■ **PL 115-439** (S512) Modernize the regulation of nuclear energy. *Jan 14, 2019.*

■ **PL 115-440** (S1023) Reauthorize the Tropical Forest Conservation Act of 1998 through fiscal year 2021, and for other purposes. *Jan 14, 2019.*

■ **PL 115-441** (S1158) Help prevent acts of genocide and other atrocity crimes, which threaten national and international security, by enhancing United States Government capacities to prevent, mitigate, and respond to such crises. *Jan 14, 2019.*

■ **PL 115-442** (S1580) Enhance the transparency, improve the coordination, and intensify the impact of assistance to support access to primary and secondary education for displaced children and persons, including women and girls, and for other purposes. *Jan 14, 2019.*

CQ

HOUSE ROLL CALL VOTES

House Roll Call Index by Subject

EXECUTIVE BRANCH

FINANCIAL SERVICES

FOREIGN POLICY

GOVERNMENT OPERATIONS

VETERANS

WELFARE & HOUSING

House Roll Call Index by Bill Number

VOTE NUMBER

1. QUORUM CALL/CALL OF THE HOUSE. Quorum was present. Jan. 8, 2018.

2. HRES676. IRANIAN HUMAN RIGHTS AND CIVIL LIBERTIES VIOLATIONS/PASSAGE. Ros-Lehtinen R-Fla, motion to suspend the rules and agree to the resolution that would condemn the human rights abuses occurring in Iran, demand that the Iranian regime abide by international obligations with respect to human rights and civil liberties and encourage the administration to expedite the licensing of communications technology to Iran to improve the ability of the Iranian people to speak freely. Motion agreed to 415-2: R 233-2; D 182-0. Jan. 9, 2018.

3. HR4564. THREAT ASSESSMENT OF TERRORIST FOREIGN FIGHTERS/ PASSAGE. Higgins R-La., motion to suspend the rules and pass the bill that would require the Department of Homeland Security, in coordination with the State Department and the National Intelligence director, to conduct a threat assessment of current foreign terrorist fighter travel and activity trends. In addition, the bill would specify that the report must include countries of origin, travel destinations, means of travel, an analysis of any country or region with a significant increase in foreign terrorist fighter activity, and an analysis of foreign terrorist fighter travel trends in and out of Iraq and Syria. Motion agreed to 413-0: R 235-0; D 178-0. Jan. 9, 2018.

4. HR4581. ADVANCED PASSENGER INFORMATION COUNTERTERRORISM SCREENING/PASSAGE. Fitzpatrick R-Pa., motion to suspend the rules and pass the bill that would direct the Department of Homeland Security to develop best practices for utilizing advanced passenger information and passenger name record data for counterterrorism screening and vetting operations. In addition, the bill would direct DHS to share best practices with Visa Waiver Program countries, and to provide assistance to those countries in implementing such best practices. Motion agreed to 415-1: R 234-1; D 181-0. Jan. 9, 2018.

5. PROCEDURAL MOTION/MOTION TO ADJOURN. Espaillat D-N.Y., motion to adjourn. Motion rejected 51-331: R 0-215; D 51-116. Jan. 10, 2018.

6. PROCEDURAL MOTION/MOTION TO ADJOURN. Gutierrez D-Ill., motion to adjourn. Motion rejected 54-311: R 0-216; D 54-95. Jan. 10, 2018.

7. PROCEDURAL MOTION/MOTION TO ADJOURN. Grijalva D-Ariz., motion to adjourn. Motion rejected 62-324: R 1-213; D 61-111. Jan. 10, 2018.

		2	3	4	5	6	7
ALABAMA							
1	**Byrne**	Y	Y	Y	N	N	N
2	**Roby**	Y	Y	Y	N	N	N
3	**Rogers**	Y	Y	Y	N	N	N
4	**Aderholt**	Y	Y	Y	N	N	N
5	**Brooks**	Y	Y	Y	N	N	N
6	**Palmer**	Y	Y	Y	N	N	N
7	Sewell	Y	Y	Y	Y	Y	N
ALASKA							
AL	**Young**	Y	Y	Y	?	N	?
ARIZONA							
1	O'Halleran	Y	Y	Y	N	N	N
2	**McSally**	Y	Y	Y	N	N	N
3	Grijalva	Y	?	Y	Y	Y	Y
4	**Gosar**	Y	Y	Y	?	N	N
5	**Biggs**	Y	Y	Y	N	N	N
6	**Schweikert**	Y	Y	Y	N	N	N
7	Gallego	Y	Y	Y	Y	Y	Y
8	Sinema	Y	Y	Y	N	?	N
ARKANSAS							
1	**Crawford**	Y	Y	Y	N	N	N
2	**Hill**	Y	Y	Y	N	N	N
3	**Womack**	Y	Y	Y	N	N	N
4	**Westerman**	Y	Y	Y	N	N	N
CALIFORNIA							
1	**LaMalfa**	Y	Y	Y	N	N	N
2	Huffman	Y	Y	Y	Y	Y	Y
3	Garamendi	Y	Y	?	N	N	?
4	**McClintock**	Y	Y	Y	N	N	N
5	Thompson	Y	Y	Y	N	N	N
6	Matsui	Y	Y	Y	N	N	N
7	Bera	Y	Y	Y	N	N	N
8	**Cook**	Y	Y	Y	N	N	?
9	McNerney	?	?	?	?	?	?
10	**Denham**	Y	Y	Y	?	?	?
11	DeSaulnier	Y	Y	Y	N	N	N
12	Pelosi	Y	Y	Y	Y	Y	Y
13	Lee	Y	Y	Y	Y	Y	Y
14	Speier	Y	?	Y	N	N	N
15	Swalwell	Y	Y	Y	N	N	N
16	Costa	Y	Y	Y	N	N	N
17	Khanna	Y	Y	Y	Y	Y	Y
18	Eshoo	Y	Y	Y	N	N	N
19	Lofgren	Y	Y	Y	N	N	N
20	Panetta	Y	Y	Y	N	N	N
21	**Valadao**	Y	Y	Y	N	N	N
22	**Nunes**	Y	Y	Y	N	N	N
23	**McCarthy**	Y	Y	Y	N	N	N
24	Carbajal	Y	Y	Y	N	N	N
25	**Knight**	Y	Y	Y	N	N	N
26	Brownley	Y	Y	Y	N	N	N
27	Chu	Y	Y	Y	N	N	N
28	Schiff	Y	Y	Y	N	N	N
29	Cardenas	Y	Y	Y	N	N	N
30	Sherman	Y	Y	Y	N	N	N
31	Aguilar	Y	Y	Y	N	N	N
32	Napolitano	Y	Y	Y	Y	Y	Y
33	Lieu	Y	Y	Y	N	N	N
34	Gomez	Y	Y	Y	Y	Y	Y
35	Torres	Y	Y	Y	N	N	N
36	Ruiz	Y	Y	Y	N	N	N
37	Bass	Y	Y	Y	?	?	Y
38	Sánchez, Linda	Y	Y	Y	Y	Y	?
39	**Royce**	Y	Y	Y	N	N	N
40	Roybal-Allard	Y	Y	Y	N	N	N
41	Takano	Y	Y	Y	Y	Y	Y
42	**Calvert**	Y	Y	Y	N	?	N
43	Waters	Y	Y	Y	Y	Y	Y
44	Barragan	Y	Y	Y	N	N	N
45	**Walters**	Y	Y	Y	N	N	N
46	Correa	Y	Y	Y	Y	Y	Y
47	Lowenthal	Y	Y	Y	N	N	N
48	**Rohrabacher**	Y	Y	Y	N	N	N
49	**Issa**	Y	Y	Y	N	N	N
50	**Hunter**	Y	Y	Y	N	N	N
51	Vargas	Y	Y	Y	N	N	N
52	Peters	Y	Y	Y	N	N	N
53	Davis	Y	Y	Y	N	N	?%

		2	3	4	5	6	7
COLORADO							
1	DeGette	Y	Y	Y	N	N	N
2	Polis	Y	Y	Y	N	N	N
3	**Tipton**	Y	Y	Y	N	N	N
4	**Buck**	Y	Y	Y	N	N	N
5	**Lamborn**	Y	Y	Y	N	N	N
6	**Coffman**	Y	Y	Y	N	N	N
7	Perlmutter	Y	?	Y	N	N	N
CONNECTICUT							
1	Larson	Y	Y	Y	?	?	?
2	Courtney	Y	Y	Y	Y	Y	Y
3	DeLauro	Y	Y	Y	N	?	N
4	Himes	Y	Y	Y	N	N	?
5	Esty	Y	Y	Y	N	N	N
DELAWARE							
AL	Blunt Rochester	Y	Y	Y	N	?	N
FLORIDA							
1	**Gaetz**	Y	Y	Y	N	?	?
2	**Dunn**	Y	Y	Y	N	N	N
3	**Yoho**	Y	Y	Y	N	N	N
4	**Rutherford**	Y	Y	Y	N	N	N
5	Lawson	Y	Y	Y	N	?	N
6	**DeSantis**	Y	Y	Y	N	?	?
7	Murphy	Y	Y	Y	N	N	N
8	**Posey**	Y	Y	Y	?	N	?
9	Soto	Y	Y	Y	N	N	N
10	Demings	Y	Y	Y	N	?	N
11	**Webster**	Y	Y	Y	N	N	N
12	**Bilirakis**	Y	Y	Y	N	N	N
13	Crist	Y	Y	Y	N	N	N
14	Castor	Y	?	Y	Y	Y	Y
15	**Ross**	Y	Y	Y	N	N	N
16	**Buchanan**	Y	Y	Y	N	N	N
17	**Rooney, T.**	Y	Y	Y	?	?	?
18	**Mast**	Y	Y	Y	?	?	?
19	**Rooney, F.**	Y	Y	Y	N	N	N
20	Hastings	Y	Y	Y	Y	Y	Y
21	Frankel	Y	Y	Y	N	N	N
22	Deutch	Y	Y	Y	N	N	N
23	Wasserman Schultz	Y	Y	Y	N	N	Y
24	Wilson	+	+	+	+	+	+
25	**Diaz-Balart**	Y	Y	Y	N	N	N
26	**Curbelo**	Y	Y	Y	N	N	N
27	**Ros-Lehtinen**	Y	Y	Y	N	N	N
GEORGIA							
1	**Carter**	Y	Y	Y	N	N	N
2	Bishop	+	+	+	N	?	N
3	**Ferguson**	Y	Y	Y	N	N	N
4	Johnson	Y	Y	Y	Y	?	Y
5	Lewis	Y	Y	Y	?	?	Y
6	**Handel**	Y	Y	Y	N	N	N
7	**Woodall**	Y	Y	Y	N	N	N
8	**Scott, A.**	Y	Y	Y	N	N	N
9	**Collins**	Y	Y	Y	N	N	N
10	**Hice**	Y	Y	Y	N	N	N
11	**Loudermilk**	Y	Y	Y	N	N	N
12	**Allen**	Y	Y	Y	N	N	N
13	Scott, D.	Y	Y	Y	N	?	?
14	**Graves**	Y	Y	Y	N	N	N
HAWAII							
1	Hanabusa	?	?	?	?	?	?
2	Gabbard	Y	Y	Y	?	?	?
IDAHO							
1	**Labrador**	Y	Y	Y	N	N	N
2	**Simpson**	Y	Y	Y	N	N	N
ILLINOIS							
1	Rush	Y	Y	Y	N	?	N
2	Kelly	Y	Y	Y	?	?	Y
3	Lipinski	Y	Y	Y	N	N	N
4	Gutierrez	Y	Y	Y	Y	Y	Y
5	Quigley	Y	Y	Y	N	?	?
6	**Roskam**	Y	Y	Y	N	N	?
7	Davis, D.	Y	Y	Y	?	?	N
8	Krishnamoorthi	Y	Y	Y	N	N	N
9	Schakowsky	Y	Y	Y	Y	Y	?
10	Schneider	Y	Y	Y	N	N	N
11	Foster	+	+	+	N	N	N
12	**Bost**	Y	Y	Y	N	N	N
13	**Davis, R.**	Y	Y	Y	N	N	N

KEY   **Republicans**   Democrats   *Independents*

Y Voted for (yea)	X Paired against	C Voted "present" to avoid possible conflict of interest
# Paired for	– Announced against	
+ Announced for	P Voted "present"	? Did not vote or otherwise make a position known
N Voted against (nay)		

	2	3	4	5	6	7
14 **Hultgren**	Y	Y	Y	N	N	N
15 **Shimkus**	Y	Y	Y	N	N	N
16 **Kinzinger**	Y	Y	Y	N	N	N
17 Bustos	Y	Y	Y	N	N	N
18 **LaHood**	Y	Y	Y	N	N	N
INDIANA						
1 Visclosky	Y	Y	Y	N	N	N
2 **Walorski**	Y	Y	Y	N	N	N
3 **Banks**	Y	Y	Y	N	N	N
4 **Rokita**	Y	Y	Y	N	N	N
5 **Brooks**	Y	Y	Y	N	N	N
6 **Messer**	Y	Y	Y	?	?	?
7 Carson	Y	Y	Y	N	?	N
8 **Bucshon**	Y	Y	Y	N	N	N
9 **Hollingsworth**	Y	Y	Y	?	N	N
IOWA						
1 **Blum**	Y	Y	Y	N	N	?
2 Loebsack	Y	Y	Y	N	N	N
3 **Young**	Y	Y	Y	N	N	N
4 **King**	Y	Y	Y	N	N	N
KANSAS						
1 **Marshall**	Y	Y	Y	N	N	N
2 **Jenkins**	Y	Y	Y	N	N	N
3 **Yoder**	Y	Y	Y	N	N	N
4 **Estes**	Y	Y	Y	N	N	N
KENTUCKY						
1 **Comer**	Y	Y	Y	?	N	N
2 **Guthrie**	Y	Y	Y	N	N	N
3 Yarmuth	Y	Y	Y	N	N	N
4 **Massie**	N	Y	Y	N	N	N
5 **Rogers**	Y	Y	Y	N	N	N
6 **Barr**	Y	Y	Y	N	N	N
LOUISIANA						
1 **Scalise**	+	+	+	–	–	–
2 Richmond	Y	Y	Y	Y	?	Y
3 **Higgins**	Y	Y	Y	N	N	N
4 **Johnson**	Y	Y	Y	N	N	N
5 **Abraham**	Y	Y	Y	N	N	N
6 **Graves**	Y	Y	Y	N	N	N
MAINE						
1 Pingree	?	?	?	N	N	N
2 **Poliquin**	Y	Y	Y	N	N	N
MARYLAND						
1 **Harris**	Y	Y	Y	?	N	N
2 Ruppersberger	Y	Y	Y	N	N	N
3 Sarbanes	Y	Y	Y	Y	Y	Y
4 Brown	Y	Y	Y	N	?	N
5 Hoyer	Y	Y	Y	N	N	N
6 Delaney	Y	Y	Y	N	N	N
7 Cummings	?	?	?	?	?	?
8 Raskin	Y	Y	Y	N	N	N
MASSACHUSETTS						
1 Neal	Y	Y	Y	N	N	N
2 McGovern	Y	Y	Y	Y	Y	Y
3 Tsongas	Y	Y	Y	?	Y	Y
4 Kennedy	Y	Y	Y	N	N	N
5 Clark	Y	Y	Y	N	N	N
6 Moulton	Y	Y	Y	N	N	N
7 Capuano	Y	Y	Y	Y	Y	Y
8 Lynch	Y	Y	Y	?	N	N
9 Keating	Y	Y	Y	N	N	N
MICHIGAN						
1 **Bergman**	Y	Y	Y	N	N	N
2 **Huizenga**	Y	Y	Y	N	N	N
3 *Amash*	Y	Y	N	N	N	N
4 **Moolenaar**	Y	Y	Y	N	N	N
5 Kildee	Y	Y	Y	N	N	N
6 **Upton**	Y	Y	Y	N	N	N
7 **Walberg**	Y	Y	Y	N	N	N
8 **Bishop**	Y	Y	Y	N	N	N
9 Levin	Y	Y	Y	N	N	N
10 **Mitchell**	Y	Y	Y	N	N	N
11 **Trott**	Y	Y	Y	N	?	N
12 Dingell	Y	Y	Y	N	N	N
14 Lawrence	Y	Y	Y	N	Y	N
MINNESOTA						
1 Walz	?	?	?	?	?	N
2 **Lewis**	Y	Y	Y	N	N	N
3 **Paulsen**	Y	Y	Y	N	N	N
4 McCollum	Y	Y	Y	N	N	N%

	2	3	4	5	6	7
5 Ellison	Y	Y	Y	Y	Y	Y
6 **Emmer**	Y	Y	Y	N	N	N
7 Peterson	Y	Y	Y	N	N	N
8 Nolan	Y	Y	Y	N	N	N
MISSISSIPPI						
1 **Kelly**	Y	Y	Y	N	N	N
2 Thompson	Y	Y	Y	Y	Y	Y
3 **Harper**	Y	Y	Y	N	N	N
4 **Palazzo**	Y	Y	Y	N	N	N
MISSOURI						
1 Clay	Y	Y	Y	N	N	N
2 **Wagner**	Y	Y	Y	?	N	?
3 **Luetkemeyer**	Y	Y	Y	N	N	N
4 **Hartzler**	Y	Y	Y	N	N	N
5 Cleaver	Y	Y	Y	?	?	Y
6 **Graves**	Y	Y	Y	N	N	N
7 **Long**	Y	Y	Y	N	N	N
8 **Smith**	Y	Y	Y	N	N	N
MONTANA						
AL **Gianforte**	Y	Y	Y	N	N	N
NEBRASKA						
1 **Fortenberry**	Y	Y	Y	N	N	N
2 **Bacon**	Y	Y	Y	N	N	N
3 **Smith**	Y	Y	Y	N	N	N
NEVADA						
1 Titus	Y	Y	Y	N	N	N
2 **Amodei**	Y	Y	Y	N	N	N
3 Rosen	Y	Y	Y	Y	Y	Y
4 Kihuen	Y	Y	Y	N	Y	Y
NEW HAMPSHIRE						
1 Shea-Porter	Y	Y	Y	Y	Y	Y
2 Kuster	Y	Y	Y	N	N	N
NEW JERSEY						
1 Norcross	Y	Y	Y	Y	Y	Y
2 **LoBiondo**	Y	Y	Y	N	N	N
3 **MacArthur**	Y	Y	Y	N	N	N
4 **Smith**	Y	Y	Y	N	N	N
5 Gottheimer	Y	Y	Y	N	N	N
6 Pallone	Y	Y	Y	Y	Y	Y
7 **Lance**	Y	Y	Y	N	N	N
8 Sires	Y	Y	Y	N	N	N
9 Pascrell	Y	Y	Y	N	?	N
10 Payne	Y	Y	Y	?	?	Y
11 **Frelinghuysen**	Y	Y	Y	N	N	N
12 Watson Coleman	Y	Y	Y	?	Y	Y
NEW MEXICO						
1 Lujan Grisham	Y	Y	Y	N	N	N
2 **Pearce**	Y	Y	Y	N	N	N
3 Luján	Y	Y	Y	N	N	N
NEW YORK						
1 **Zeldin**	Y	Y	Y	N	N	N
2 **King**	Y	Y	Y	N	N	N
3 Suozzi	Y	Y	Y	Y	Y	Y
4 Rice	Y	Y	Y	Y	Y	Y
5 Meeks	Y	Y	Y	?	?	Y
6 Meng	Y	Y	Y	Y	Y	Y
7 Velázquez	Y	Y	Y	Y	Y	Y
8 Jeffries	Y	Y	Y	Y	N	N
9 Clarke	Y	Y	Y	Y	?	Y
10 Nadler	Y	Y	Y	Y	Y	Y
11 **Donovan**	Y	Y	Y	N	N	N
12 Maloney, C.	Y	Y	Y	N	Y	Y
13 Espaillat	Y	Y	Y	Y	Y	Y
14 Crowley	Y	Y	Y	Y	Y	Y
15 Serrano	Y	Y	Y	Y	Y	Y
16 Engel	Y	Y	Y	Y	Y	Y
17 Lowey	Y	Y	Y	N	Y	Y
18 Maloney, S.P.	Y	Y	Y	N	N	N
19 **Faso**	Y	Y	Y	N	N	N
20 Tonko	Y	Y	Y	Y	Y	Y
21 **Stefanik**	Y	Y	Y	N	?	N
22 **Tenney**	Y	Y	Y	N	N	N
23 **Reed**	Y	Y	Y	N	N	N
24 **Katko**	Y	Y	Y	N	N	N
25 Slaughter	Y	Y	Y	Y	Y	Y
26 Higgins	Y	Y	Y	?	?	?
27 **Collins**	Y	Y	Y	N	N	N
NORTH CAROLINA						
1 Butterfield	Y	Y	Y	?	?	?
2 **Holding**	Y	Y	Y	N	N	N
3 **Jones**	N	Y	Y	N	N	N
4 Price	Y	Y	Y	N	N	N

	2	3	4	5	6	7
5 **Foxx**	Y	Y	Y	N	N	N
6 **Walker**	Y	Y	Y	?	N	N
7 **Rouzer**	Y	Y	Y	N	N	N
8 **Hudson**	Y	Y	Y	N	N	N
9 **Pittenger**	Y	Y	Y	N	N	N
9 Vacant						
10 **McHenry**	Y	Y	Y	?	?	?
11 **Meadows**	Y	Y	Y	N	N	N
12 Adams	+	+	+	+	+	+
13 **Budd**	Y	Y	Y	N	N	N
NORTH DAKOTA						
AL **Cramer**	Y	Y	Y	N	N	N
OHIO						
1 **Chabot**	Y	Y	Y	N	N	N
2 **Wenstrup**	Y	Y	Y	N	N	N
3 Beatty	Y	Y	Y	N	?	N
4 **Jordan**	Y	Y	Y	N	?	N
5 **Latta**	Y	Y	Y	N	N	N
6 **Johnson**	Y	Y	Y	N	N	N
7 **Gibbs**	Y	Y	Y	N	N	N
8 **Davidson**	Y	Y	Y	N	N	N
9 Kaptur	Y	Y	Y	N	Y	N
10 **Turner**	Y	Y	Y	–	–	–
11 Fudge	Y	Y	Y	?	?	Y
12 **Tiberi**	Y	Y	Y	N	N	Y
13 Ryan	Y	Y	Y	N	N	N
14 **Joyce**	Y	Y	Y	N	N	N
15 **Stivers**	Y	Y	Y	N	N	N
16 **Renacci**	+	+	+	?	?	?
OKLAHOMA						
1 **Bridenstine**	Y	Y	Y	N	N	N
2 **Mullin**	Y	Y	Y	N	N	N
3 **Lucas**	Y	Y	Y	?	N	N
4 **Cole**	Y	Y	Y	N	N	N
5 **Russell**	Y	Y	Y	?	?	?
OREGON						
1 Bonamici	Y	Y	Y	Y	Y	Y
2 **Walden**	Y	Y	Y	N	?	N
3 Blumenauer	Y	Y	Y	N	N	N
4 DeFazio	Y	Y	Y	?	?	Y
5 Schrader	Y	Y	Y	N	N	?
PENNSYLVANIA						
1 Brady	Y	Y	Y	Y	Y	Y
2 Evans	Y	Y	Y	N	N	N
3 **Kelly**	Y	Y	Y	N	N	N
4 **Perry**	Y	Y	Y	N	N	N
5 **Thompson**	Y	Y	Y	N	N	N
6 **Costello**	Y	Y	Y	N	N	N
7 **Meehan**	Y	Y	Y	N	N	N
8 **Fitzpatrick**	Y	Y	Y	N	N	N
9 **Shuster**	Y	Y	Y	N	?	?
10 **Marino**	Y	Y	Y	N	N	N
11 **Barletta**	Y	Y	Y	N	N	?
12 **Rothfus**	Y	Y	Y	N	N	N
13 Boyle	Y	Y	Y	N	?	N
14 Doyle	Y	Y	Y	Y	Y	Y
15 **Dent**	Y	Y	Y	?	?	?
16 **Smucker**	Y	Y	Y	N	N	N
17 Cartwright	Y	Y	Y	N	N	N
RHODE ISLAND						
1 Cicilline	Y	Y	Y	N	N	N
2 Langevin	Y	Y	Y	N	?	?
SOUTH CAROLINA						
1 **Sanford**	Y	Y	Y	N	N	N
2 **Wilson**	Y	Y	Y	N	N	N
3 **Duncan**	Y	Y	Y	N	N	N
4 **Gowdy**	Y	Y	Y	N	N	N
5 **Norman**	Y	Y	Y	N	N	N
6 Clyburn	Y	Y	Y	N	?	N
7 **Rice**	Y	Y	Y	N	N	N
SOUTH DAKOTA						
AL **Noem**	Y	Y	Y	N	N	N
TENNESSEE						
1 **Roe**	Y	Y	Y	N	N	N
2 **Duncan**	Y	Y	Y	N	N	N
3 **Fleischmann**	Y	Y	Y	N	N	N
4 **DesJarlais**	Y	Y	Y	N	N	N
5 Cooper	Y	Y	Y	N	N	N
6 **Black**	Y	Y	Y	N	N	N
7 **Blackburn**	?	?	?	N	N	N
8 **Kustoff**	Y	Y	Y	N	N	N
9 Cohen	Y	Y	Y	N	N	N

	2	3	4	5	6	7
TEXAS						
1 **Gohmert**	Y	Y	Y	N	N	N
2 **Poe**	Y	Y	Y	N	N	N
3 **Johnson, S.**	Y	Y	Y	N	N	N
4 **Ratcliffe**	Y	Y	Y	N	N	N
5 **Hensarling**	Y	Y	Y	N	N	N
6 **Barton**	Y	Y	Y	N	N	N
7 **Culberson**	Y	Y	Y	–	N	N
8 **Brady**	Y	Y	Y	N	?	N
9 Green, A.	Y	Y	Y	Y	Y	Y
10 **McCaul**	Y	Y	Y	N	N	N
11 **Conaway**	Y	Y	Y	–	N	N
12 **Granger**	Y	Y	Y	?	?	?
13 **Thornberry**	Y	Y	Y	N	N	N
14 **Weber**	Y	Y	Y	N	N	N
15 Gonzalez	Y	Y	Y	Y	Y	N
16 O'Rourke	Y	Y	Y	N	N	N
17 **Flores**	Y	Y	Y	N	N	N
18 Jackson Lee	Y	Y	Y	Y	?	Y
19 **Arrington**	Y	Y	Y	N	N	N
20 Castro	Y	Y	Y	Y	Y	Y
21 **Smith**	Y	Y	Y	N	N	N
22 **Olson**	Y	Y	Y	N	N	N
23 **Hurd**	Y	Y	Y	N	N	N
24 **Marchant**	Y	Y	Y	N	N	N
25 **Williams**	Y	Y	Y	N	N	N
26 **Burgess**	Y	Y	Y	N	N	?
27 **Farenthold**	Y	Y	Y	N	N	N
28 Cuellar	Y	Y	Y	N	N	N
29 Green, G.	+	+	+	N	N	N
30 Johnson, E.B.	Y	Y	Y	Y	Y	Y
31 **Carter**	Y	Y	Y	N	N	N
32 **Sessions**	Y	Y	Y	N	N	N
33 Veasey	Y	Y	Y	N	N	N
34 Vela	Y	Y	Y	N	N	N
35 Doggett	Y	Y	Y	?	?	?
36 **Babin**	Y	Y	Y	N	N	N
UTAH						
1 **Bishop**	Y	Y	Y	N	N	N
2 **Stewart**	Y	Y	Y	N	?	N
3 **Curtis**	Y	Y	Y	N	N	N
4 **Love**	Y	Y	Y	N	N	N
VERMONT						
AL Welch	Y	Y	Y	N	N	Y
VIRGINIA						
1 **Wittman**	Y	Y	Y	N	N	N
2 **Taylor**	Y	Y	Y	N	?	N
3 Scott	Y	Y	Y	N	?	N
4 McEachin	Y	Y	Y	N	N	N
5 **Garrett**	Y	Y	Y	N	N	N
6 **Goodlatte**	Y	Y	Y	N	N	N
7 **Brat**	Y	Y	Y	N	N	N
8 Beyer	Y	Y	Y	N	?	N
9 **Griffith**	Y	Y	Y	N	N	N
10 **Comstock**	Y	Y	Y	N	N	N
11 Connolly	Y	Y	Y	N	N	N
WASHINGTON						
1 DelBene	Y	Y	Y	N	N	N
2 Larsen	Y	Y	Y	?	?	?
3 **Herrera Beutler**	Y	Y	Y	N	N	?
4 **Newhouse**	Y	Y	Y	N	N	N
5 **McMorris Rodgers**	Y	Y	Y	N	N	N
6 Kilmer	Y	Y	Y	N	N	N
7 Jayapal	Y	Y	Y	Y	Y	Y
8 **Reichert**	Y	Y	Y	N	N	N
9 Smith	Y	Y	Y	N	N	N
10 Heck	Y	Y	Y	N	N	N
WEST VIRGINIA						
1 **McKinley**	Y	Y	Y	N	N	N
2 **Mooney**	Y	Y	Y	N	N	N
3 **Jenkins**	Y	Y	Y	?	?	?
WISCONSIN						
1 **Ryan**						
2 Pocan	Y	Y	Y	?	Y	Y
3 Kind	+	+	+	?	?	?
4 Moore	Y	Y	Y	Y	Y	Y
5 **Sensenbrenner**	Y	Y	Y	N	N	N
6 **Grothman**	Y	Y	Y	N	N	N
7 **Duffy**	Y	Y	Y	N	N	N
8 **Gallagher**	Y	Y	Y	N	N	N
WYOMING						
AL **Cheney**	Y	Y	Y	N	N	N

VOTE NUMBER

8. S139. FISA AMENDMENTS REAUTHORIZATION/RULE. Adoption of the rule (H Res 682) that would provide for House floor consideration of the bill (S 139) that would reauthorize Title VII of the Foreign Intelligence Surveillance Act through Dec. 31, 2023, and would require the development of procedures for searching the Section 702 database that protect the Fourth Amendment rights of U.S. citizens. Adopted 233-181: R 231-2; D 2-179. Jan. 10, 2018.

9. HRES681. TRIBAL LANDS AND LABOR RELATIONS/PREVIOUS QUESTION. Cole, R-Okla., motion to order the previous question (thus ending debate and the possibility of amendment) on the rule (H Res 681) that would provide for House floor consideration of the bill (S 140) that would amend the White Mountain Apache Tribe Water Rights Quantification Act of 2010 to clarify the use of amounts in the WMAT Settlement Fund. Motion agreed to 234-181: R 234-0; D 0-181. Jan. 10, 2018.

10. HRES681. TRIBAL LANDS AND LABOR RELATIONS/RULE. Adoption of the rule (H Res 681) that would provide for House floor consideration of the bill (S 140) that would provide for House floor consideration of the bill that would amend the White Mountain Apache Tribe Water Rights Quantification Act of 2010 to clarify the use of amounts in the WMAT Settlement Fund. Adopted 227-181: R 227-0; D 0-181. Jan. 10, 2018.

11. S140. TRIBAL LANDS AND LABOR RELATIONS/PASSAGE. Passage of the bill that would amend the White Mountain Apache Tribe Water Rights Quantification Act of 2010 to specify that settlement funds may be used for the planning, design, and construction of the tribe's rural water system. In addition, the bill would also amend the National Labor Relations Act to exclude Native American tribes and any institutions or enterprises owned or operated by a Native American tribe from being defined as employers under the NLRA. The bill further includes provisions that would aid specific tribes with development and land issues. Passed 239-173: R 216-15; D 23-158. Jan. 10, 2018.

12. HR4567. HOMELAND SECURITY OVERSEAS ACTIVITIES/PASSAGE. Katko R-N.Y., motion to suspend the rules and pass the bill that would require the Department of Homeland Security to report to Congress on the department's activities that are conducted outside of the United States, and on the effectiveness of such activities. Motion agreed to 415-0: R 232-0; D 183-0. Jan. 10, 2018.

13. PROCEDURAL MOTION/JOURNAL. Approval of the House Journal of Jan. 9, 2018. Approved 231-178: R 146-85; D 85-93. Jan. 10, 2018.

Member	8	9	10	11	12	13
ALABAMA						
1 Byrne	Y	Y	Y	Y	Y	Y
2 Roby	Y	Y	Y	Y	Y	Y
3 Rogers	Y	Y	Y	Y	Y	N
4 Aderholt	Y	Y	Y	Y	Y	Y
5 Brooks	Y	Y	Y	Y	Y	N
6 Palmer	Y	Y	Y	Y	Y	N
7 Sewell	N	N	N	Y	Y	N
ALASKA						
AL Young	Y	Y	Y	Y	Y	N
ARIZONA						
1 O'Halleran	N	N	N	Y	Y	N
2 McSally	Y	Y	Y	Y	Y	N
3 Grijalva	N	N	N	N	Y	?
4 Gosar	Y	Y	Y	Y	Y	Y
5 Biggs	Y	Y	Y	Y	Y	Y
6 Schweikert	Y	Y	Y	Y	Y	Y
7 Gallego	N	N	N	N	Y	N
9 Sinema	N	N	N	N	Y	N
ARKANSAS						
1 Crawford	Y	Y	Y	Y	Y	Y
2 Hill	Y	Y	Y	Y	Y	N
3 Womack	Y	Y	Y	Y	Y	Y
4 Westerman	Y	Y	Y	Y	Y	Y
CALIFORNIA						
1 LaMalfa	Y	Y	Y	Y	Y	Y
2 Huffman	N	N	N	N	Y	Y
3 Garamendi	N	N	N	N	Y	Y
4 McClintock	Y	Y	Y	Y	Y	Y
5 Thompson	N	N	N	N	Y	N
6 Matsui	N	N	N	N	Y	N
7 Bera	N	N	N	N	Y	N
8 Cook	Y	Y	Y	Y	Y	Y
9 McNerney	?	?	?	?	?	?
10 Denham	Y	Y	Y	Y	Y	N
11 DeSaulnier	-	-	-	-	-	+
12 Pelosi	N	N	N	N	Y	?
13 Lee	N	N	N	N	Y	N
14 Speier	N	N	N	N	Y	N
15 Swalwell	N	N	N	N	Y	N
16 Costa	N	N	N	N	Y	N
17 Khanna	N	N	N	N	Y	N
18 Eshoo	N	N	N	N	Y	N
19 Lofgren	N	N	N	N	Y	N
20 Panetta	N	N	N	N	Y	Y
21 Valadao	Y	Y	Y	Y	Y	N
22 Nunes	Y	Y	Y	Y	Y	Y
23 McCarthy	Y	Y	Y	Y	Y	Y
24 Carbajal	-	-	-	?	+	?
25 Knight	Y	Y	Y	Y	Y	N
26 Brownley	N	N	N	N	Y	N
27 Chu	N	N	N	N	Y	N
28 Schiff	N	N	N	N	Y	N
29 Cardenas	N	N	N	Y	Y	N
30 Sherman	N	N	N	N	Y	Y
31 Aguilar	N	N	N	Y	Y	Y
32 Napolitano	N	N	N	N	Y	N
33 Lieu	N	N	N	N	Y	N
34 Gomez	N	N	N	N	Y	N
35 Torres	N	N	N	N	Y	N
36 Ruiz	N	N	N	Y	Y	N
37 Bass	N	N	N	N	Y	N
38 Sánchez, Linda	N	N	N	N	Y	N
39 Royce	Y	Y	Y	Y	Y	Y
40 Roybal-Allard	N	N	N	N	Y	N
41 Takano	N	N	N	N	Y	N
42 Calvert	Y	Y	Y	Y	Y	Y
43 Waters	N	N	N	N	Y	Y
44 Barragan	N	N	N	N	Y	N
45 Walters	Y	Y	?	Y	Y	Y
46 Correa	N	N	N	N	Y	N
47 Lowenthal	N	N	N	N	Y	Y
48 Rohrabacher	Y	Y	Y	Y	Y	N
49 Issa	Y	Y	Y	Y	Y	Y
50 Hunter	Y	Y	Y	Y	Y	N
51 Vargas	N	N	N	N	Y	N
52 Peters	N	N	N	N	Y	Y
53 Davis	N	N	N	N	Y	Y

Member	8	9	10	11	12	13
COLORADO						
1 DeGette	N	N	N	N	Y	Y
2 Polis	N	N	N	N	Y	Y
3 Tipton	Y	Y	Y	Y	Y	N
4 Buck	Y	Y	Y	Y	Y	N
5 Lamborn	Y	Y	Y	Y	Y	Y
6 Coffman	Y	Y	Y	Y	Y	N
7 Perlmutter	N	N	N	N	Y	Y
CONNECTICUT						
1 Larson	N	N	N	N	Y	N
2 Courtney	N	N	N	N	Y	N
3 DeLauro	N	N	N	N	Y	Y
4 Himes	N	N	N	N	Y	Y
5 Esty	N	N	N	N	Y	N
DELAWARE						
AL Blunt Rochester	N	N	N	N	Y	Y
FLORIDA						
1 Gaetz	Y	Y	Y	?	?	?
2 Dunn	Y	Y	Y	Y	Y	Y
3 Yoho	Y	Y	Y	Y	Y	Y
4 Rutherford	Y	Y	Y	Y	Y	Y
5 Lawson	N	N	N	N	Y	Y
6 DeSantis	Y	Y	Y	Y	Y	N
7 Murphy	Y	N	N	N	Y	N
8 Posey	Y	Y	Y	Y	Y	Y
9 Soto	N	N	N	N	Y	N
10 Demings	N	N	N	N	Y	N
11 Webster	Y	Y	Y	Y	Y	Y
12 Bilirakis	Y	Y	Y	Y	Y	Y
13 Crist	N	N	N	N	Y	N
14 Castor	N	N	N	N	Y	N
15 Ross	Y	Y	Y	Y	Y	Y
16 Buchanan	Y	Y	Y	Y	Y	Y
17 Rooney, T.	Y	Y	Y	Y	Y	Y
18 Mast	Y	Y	Y	Y	Y	N
19 Rooney, F.	Y	Y	Y	Y	Y	Y
20 Hastings	N	N	N	N	Y	N
21 Frankel	N	N	N	N	Y	Y
22 Deutch	N	N	N	Y	Y	Y
23 Wasserman Schultz	N	N	N	N	Y	Y
24 Wilson	-	-	-	-	+	-
25 Diaz-Balart	Y	Y	Y	Y	Y	N
26 Curbelo	Y	Y	Y	Y	Y	N
27 Ros-Lehtinen	Y	Y	Y	N	Y	N
GEORGIA						
1 Carter	Y	Y	Y	Y	Y	N
2 Bishop	N	N	N	N	Y	N
3 Ferguson	Y	Y	Y	Y	Y	Y
4 Johnson	N	N	N	N	Y	N
5 Lewis	N	N	N	N	Y	N
6 Handel	Y	Y	Y	Y	Y	N
7 Woodall	Y	Y	Y	Y	Y	N
8 Scott, A.	Y	Y	Y	Y	Y	N
9 Collins	Y	Y	Y	Y	Y	Y
10 Hice	Y	Y	Y	Y	Y	Y
11 Loudermilk	Y	Y	Y	Y	Y	Y
12 Allen	Y	Y	Y	Y	Y	Y
13 Scott, D.	N	N	N	?	Y	Y
14 Graves	Y	Y	Y	Y	Y	N
HAWAII						
1 Hanabusa	?	?	?	?	?	?
2 Gabbard	?	?	?	?	?	?
IDAHO						
1 Labrador	Y	Y	Y	Y	Y	Y
2 Simpson	Y	Y	Y	Y	Y	Y
ILLINOIS						
1 Rush	N	N	N	N	Y	?
2 Kelly	N	N	N	N	Y	N
3 Lipinski	N	N	N	N	Y	Y
4 Gutierrez	N	-	-	N	Y	N
5 Quigley	N	N	N	N	Y	N
6 Roskam	Y	Y	Y	Y	Y	N
7 Davis, D.	N	N	N	N	Y	Y
8 Krishnamoorthi	N	N	N	N	Y	N
9 Schakowsky	N	N	N	N	Y	N
10 Schneider	Y	N	N	N	Y	Y
11 Foster	N	N	N	N	Y	Y
12 Bost	Y	Y	Y	N	Y	N
13 Davis, R.	Y	Y	Y	N	Y	N

	8	9	10	11	12	13
14 **Hultgren**	Y	Y	Y	Y	Y	Y
15 **Shimkus**	Y	Y	Y	Y	Y	Y
16 **Kinzinger**	Y	Y	Y	N	Y	N
17 Bustos	N	N	N	N	Y	Y
18 **LaHood**	Y	Y	Y	Y	Y	N
INDIANA						
1 Visclosky	N	N	N	N	Y	N
2 **Walorski**	Y	Y	Y	Y	Y	Y
3 **Banks**	Y	Y	Y	Y	Y	Y
4 **Rokita**	Y	Y	Y	Y	Y	N
5 **Brooks**	Y	Y	?	?	Y	Y
6 **Messer**	Y	Y	Y	Y	Y	Y
7 Carson	N	N	N	N	Y	N
8 **Bucshon**	Y	Y	Y	Y	Y	Y
9 **Hollingsworth**	Y	Y	Y	Y	Y	Y
IOWA						
1 **Blum**	Y	Y	Y	Y	Y	N
2 Loebsack	N	N	N	N	Y	N
3 **Young**	Y	Y	Y	Y	Y	Y
4 **King**	Y	Y	+	Y	Y	Y
KANSAS						
1 **Marshall**	Y	Y	Y	Y	Y	Y
2 **Jenkins**	Y	Y	Y	Y	Y	N
3 **Yoder**	Y	Y	Y	Y	Y	N
4 **Estes**	Y	Y	Y	Y	Y	Y
KENTUCKY						
1 **Comer**	Y	Y	Y	Y	Y	Y
2 **Guthrie**	Y	Y	Y	Y	Y	Y
3 Yarmuth	N	?	?	?	Y	Y
4 **Massie**	N	Y	Y	Y	Y	Y
5 **Rogers**	Y	Y	Y	Y	Y	Y
6 **Barr**	Y	Y	?	Y	Y	Y
LOUISIANA						
1 **Scalise**	+	+	+	+	+	+
2 Richmond	N	N	N	N	Y	N
3 **Higgins**	Y	Y	Y	Y	Y	Y
4 **Johnson**	Y	Y	Y	Y	Y	Y
5 **Abraham**	Y	Y	Y	Y	Y	Y
6 **Graves**	Y	Y	Y	Y	Y	N
MAINE						
1 Pingree	N	N	N	N	Y	Y
2 **Poliquin**	Y	Y	Y	Y	Y	N
MARYLAND						
1 **Harris**	Y	Y	Y	Y	Y	Y
2 Ruppersberger	N	N	N	N	Y	Y
3 Sarbanes	N	N	N	N	Y	N
4 Brown	N	N	N	N	Y	Y
5 Hoyer	N	N	N	N	Y	N
6 Delaney	N	N	N	N	Y	N
7 Cummings	?	?	?	?	?	?
8 Raskin	N	N	N	N	Y	N
MASSACHUSETTS						
1 Neal	N	N	N	N	Y	N
2 McGovern	N	N	N	N	Y	N
3 Tsongas	N	N	N	N	Y	Y
4 Kennedy	N	N	N	N	Y	Y
5 Clark	N	N	N	N	Y	Y
6 Moulton	N	N	N	N	Y	Y
7 Capuano	N	N	N	N	Y	N
8 Lynch	N	N	N	N	Y	N
9 Keating	?	N	N	N	Y	N
MICHIGAN						
1 **Bergman**	Y	Y	Y	Y	Y	N
2 **Huizenga**	Y	Y	Y	Y	Y	N
3 *Amash*	Y	Y	Y	Y	Y	N
4 **Moolenaar**	Y	Y	Y	Y	Y	Y
5 Kildee	N	N	N	Y	Y	Y
6 **Upton**	Y	Y	Y	Y	Y	N
7 **Walberg**	Y	Y	Y	Y	Y	N
8 **Bishop**	Y	Y	Y	Y	Y	N
9 Levin	N	N	N	N	Y	N
10 **Mitchell**	Y	Y	Y	Y	Y	N
11 **Trott**	Y	Y	Y	Y	Y	Y
12 Dingell	N	N	N	N	Y	Y
14 Lawrence	N	N	N	N	Y	Y
MINNESOTA						
1 Walz	N	N	N	Y	Y	Y
2 **Lewis**	Y	Y	Y	Y	Y	Y
3 **Paulsen**	Y	Y	Y	Y	Y	N
4 McCollum	N	N	N	Y	Y	Y
5 Ellison	N	N	N	N	Y	Y
6 **Emmer**	Y	Y	Y	Y	Y	N
7 Peterson	N	N	N	Y	Y	N
8 Nolan	?	?	?	?	?	?
MISSISSIPPI						
1 **Kelly**	Y	Y	Y	Y	Y	Y
2 Thompson	N	N	N	N	Y	N
3 **Harper**	Y	Y	Y	Y	Y	Y
4 **Palazzo**	Y	Y	Y	Y	Y	Y
MISSOURI						
1 Clay	N	N	N	N	Y	Y
2 **Wagner**	Y	Y	Y	Y	Y	Y
3 **Luetkemeyer**	Y	Y	Y	Y	Y	Y
4 **Hartzler**	Y	Y	Y	Y	Y	Y
5 Cleaver	N	N	N	N	Y	N
6 **Graves**	Y	Y	Y	Y	Y	N
7 **Long**	Y	Y	Y	Y	Y	Y
8 **Smith**	Y	Y	Y	Y	Y	Y
MONTANA						
AL **Gianforte**	Y	Y	Y	Y	Y	Y
NEBRASKA						
1 **Fortenberry**	Y	Y	Y	Y	Y	Y
2 **Bacon**	Y	Y	Y	Y	Y	Y
3 **Smith**	Y	Y	Y	Y	Y	Y
NEVADA						
1 Titus	N	N	N	N	Y	Y
2 **Amodei**	Y	Y	Y	Y	Y	Y
3 Rosen	N	N	N	N	Y	N
4 Kihuen	N	N	N	N	Y	N
NEW HAMPSHIRE						
1 Shea-Porter	N	N	N	N	Y	Y
2 Kuster	N	N	N	N	Y	Y
NEW JERSEY						
1 Norcross	N	N	N	N	Y	N
2 **LoBiondo**	Y	Y	Y	N	Y	N
3 **MacArthur**	Y	Y	Y	N	Y	N
4 **Smith**	Y	Y	Y	N	Y	Y
5 Gottheimer	N	N	N	N	Y	N
6 Pallone	N	N	N	N	Y	N
7 **Lance**	Y	Y	Y	N	Y	N
8 Sires	N	N	N	N	Y	N
9 Pascrell	N	N	N	N	Y	Y
10 Payne	N	N	N	N	Y	N
11 **Frelinghuysen**	Y	Y	?	Y	Y	Y
12 Watson Coleman	N	N	N	N	Y	N
NEW MEXICO						
1 Lujan Grisham	N	N	N	Y	Y	Y
2 **Pearce**	Y	Y	Y	Y	Y	N
3 Luján	N	N	N	Y	Y	N
NEW YORK						
1 **Zeldin**	Y	Y	Y	Y	Y	N
2 **King**	Y	Y	Y	N	Y	Y
3 Suozzi	N	N	N	N	Y	N
4 Rice	N	N	N	N	Y	N
5 Meeks	N	N	N	Y	Y	Y
6 Meng	N	N	N	N	Y	Y
7 Velázquez	N	N	N	N	Y	N
8 Jeffries	N	N	N	N	Y	N
9 Clarke	N	N	N	N	Y	Y
10 Nadler	N	N	N	N	Y	Y
11 **Donovan**	Y	Y	Y	N	Y	Y
12 Maloney, C.	N	N	N	N	Y	N
13 Espaillat	N	N	N	N	Y	N
14 Crowley	N	N	N	N	Y	N
15 Serrano	N	N	N	N	Y	Y
16 Engel	N	N	N	N	Y	Y
17 Lowey	N	N	N	N	Y	N
18 Maloney, S.P.	N	N	N	N	Y	N
19 **Faso**	Y	Y	Y	Y	Y	N
20 Tonko	N	N	N	N	Y	P
21 **Stefanik**	Y	Y	Y	Y	Y	Y
22 **Tenney**	Y	Y	Y	Y	Y	N
23 **Reed**	Y	Y	Y	Y	Y	N
24 **Katko**	Y	Y	Y	N	Y	N
25 Slaughter	N	N	N	N	Y	N
26 Higgins	N	N	N	N	Y	N
27 **Collins**	Y	Y	Y	Y	Y	Y
NORTH CAROLINA						
1 Butterfield	N	N	N	N	Y	?
2 **Holding**	Y	Y	Y	Y	Y	N
3 **Jones**	N	Y	Y	Y	Y	N
4 Price	N	N	N	N	Y	N
5 **Foxx**	Y	Y	Y	Y	Y	N
6 **Walker**	Y	Y	Y	Y	Y	Y
7 **Rouzer**	Y	Y	Y	Y	Y	N
8 **Hudson**	Y	Y	Y	Y	Y	N
9 **Pittenger**	Y	Y	Y	Y	Y	N
9 **Vacant**						
10 **McHenry**	?	?	?	?	?	?
11 **Meadows**	Y	Y	Y	Y	Y	Y
12 Adams	–	–	–	–	+	+
13 **Budd**	Y	Y	Y	Y	Y	Y
NORTH DAKOTA						
AL **Cramer**	Y	Y	Y	Y	Y	Y
OHIO						
1 **Chabot**	Y	Y	Y	Y	Y	Y
2 **Wenstrup**	Y	Y	Y	Y	Y	Y
3 Beatty	N	N	N	N	Y	Y
4 **Jordan**	Y	Y	Y	Y	Y	N
5 **Latta**	Y	Y	Y	Y	Y	N
6 **Johnson**	Y	Y	Y	Y	Y	N
7 **Gibbs**	Y	Y	Y	Y	Y	Y
8 **Davidson**	Y	Y	Y	Y	Y	Y
9 Kaptur	N	N	N	N	Y	Y
10 **Turner**	+	+	+	+	+	+
11 Fudge	N	N	N	N	Y	N
12 **Tiberi**	Y	Y	Y	Y	Y	Y
13 Ryan	N	N	N	N	Y	N
14 **Joyce**	Y	Y	Y	N	Y	Y
15 **Stivers**	Y	Y	Y	Y	Y	N
16 **Renacci**	Y	Y	Y	Y	Y	N
OKLAHOMA						
1 **Bridenstine**	Y	Y	Y	Y	Y	Y
2 **Mullin**	Y	Y	Y	Y	Y	Y
3 **Lucas**	Y	Y	Y	Y	Y	Y
4 **Cole**	Y	Y	Y	Y	Y	Y
5 **Russell**	Y	Y	Y	Y	Y	Y
OREGON						
1 Bonamici	N	N	N	N	Y	Y
2 **Walden**	Y	Y	Y	Y	Y	Y
3 Blumenauer	N	N	N	N	Y	Y
4 DeFazio	N	N	N	N	Y	N
5 Schrader	N	N	N	Y	Y	N
PENNSYLVANIA						
1 Brady	N	N	N	N	Y	N
2 Evans	N	N	N	N	Y	Y
3 **Kelly**	Y	Y	Y	Y	Y	Y
4 **Perry**	Y	Y	Y	Y	Y	N
5 **Thompson**	Y	Y	Y	Y	Y	N
6 **Costello**	Y	Y	Y	N	Y	N
7 **Meehan**	Y	Y	Y	Y	Y	Y
8 **Fitzpatrick**	Y	Y	Y	N	Y	N
9 **Shuster**	Y	Y	Y	?	?	?
10 **Marino**	Y	Y	Y	Y	Y	Y
11 **Barletta**	Y	Y	Y	Y	Y	Y
12 **Rothfus**	Y	Y	Y	Y	Y	Y
13 Boyle	N	N	N	N	Y	N
14 Doyle	N	N	N	N	Y	N
15 **Dent**	Y	Y	Y	Y	Y	Y
16 **Smucker**	Y	Y	Y	Y	Y	Y
17 Cartwright	N	N	N	N	Y	Y
RHODE ISLAND						
1 Cicilline	?	N	N	N	Y	Y
2 Langevin	N	N	N	N	Y	Y
SOUTH CAROLINA						
1 **Sanford**	Y	Y	Y	Y	Y	Y
2 **Wilson**	Y	Y	Y	Y	Y	Y
3 **Duncan**	Y	Y	Y	Y	Y	Y
4 **Gowdy**	Y	Y	Y	Y	Y	N
5 **Norman**	Y	Y	Y	Y	Y	Y
6 Clyburn	N	N	N	N	Y	N
7 **Rice**	Y	Y	Y	Y	Y	N
SOUTH DAKOTA						
AL **Noem**	Y	Y	Y	Y	Y	Y
TENNESSEE						
1 **Roe**	Y	Y	Y	Y	Y	Y
2 **Duncan**	Y	Y	Y	Y	Y	Y
3 **Fleischmann**	Y	Y	Y	Y	Y	Y
4 **DesJarlais**	Y	Y	Y	Y	Y	Y
5 Cooper	N	N	N	N	Y	Y
6 **Black**	Y	Y	Y	Y	Y	Y
7 **Blackburn**	Y	Y	Y	Y	Y	Y
8 **Kustoff**	Y	Y	Y	Y	Y	Y
9 Cohen	N	N	N	N	Y	N
TEXAS						
1 **Gohmert**	Y	Y	Y	Y	Y	N
2 **Poe**	?	Y	Y	Y	Y	Y
3 **Johnson, S.**	Y	Y	?	Y	Y	Y
4 **Ratcliffe**	Y	Y	Y	Y	Y	N
5 **Hensarling**	Y	Y	Y	Y	Y	Y
6 **Barton**	Y	Y	Y	Y	Y	N
7 **Culberson**	Y	Y	Y	Y	Y	N
8 **Brady**	Y	Y	Y	Y	Y	Y
9 Green, A.	N	N	N	N	Y	N
10 **McCaul**	Y	Y	Y	Y	Y	Y
11 **Conaway**	Y	Y	Y	Y	Y	Y
12 **Granger**	Y	Y	Y	Y	Y	Y
13 **Thornberry**	Y	Y	Y	Y	Y	Y
14 **Weber**	Y	Y	Y	Y	Y	Y
15 Gonzalez	N	N	N	N	Y	Y
16 O'Rourke	N	N	N	N	Y	Y
17 **Flores**	Y	Y	Y	Y	Y	N
18 Jackson Lee	N	N	N	N	Y	Y
19 **Arrington**	Y	Y	Y	Y	Y	Y
20 Castro	N	N	N	N	Y	Y
21 **Smith**	Y	Y	Y	Y	Y	Y
22 **Olson**	Y	Y	Y	Y	Y	Y
23 **Hurd**	Y	Y	Y	Y	Y	N
24 **Marchant**	Y	Y	Y	Y	Y	Y
25 **Williams**	Y	Y	Y	Y	Y	Y
26 **Burgess**	Y	Y	Y	Y	Y	N
27 **Farenthold**	Y	Y	Y	Y	Y	N
28 Cuellar	N	N	N	Y	Y	Y
29 Green, G.	N	N	N	N	Y	N
30 Johnson, E.B.	N	N	N	N	Y	Y
31 **Carter**	Y	Y	Y	Y	Y	Y
32 **Sessions**	Y	Y	Y	Y	Y	Y
33 Veasey	N	N	N	N	Y	N
34 Vela	N	N	N	Y	Y	N
35 Doggett	N	N	N	N	Y	Y
36 **Babin**	Y	Y	Y	Y	Y	Y
UTAH						
1 **Bishop**	Y	Y	Y	Y	Y	Y
2 **Stewart**	Y	Y	Y	Y	Y	Y
3 **Curtis**	Y	Y	Y	Y	Y	Y
4 **Love**	Y	Y	Y	Y	Y	Y
VERMONT						
AL Welch	N	N	N	N	Y	N
VIRGINIA						
1 **Wittman**	Y	Y	Y	Y	Y	N
2 **Taylor**	Y	Y	Y	Y	Y	Y
3 Scott	N	N	N	N	Y	Y
4 McEachin	N	N	N	N	Y	Y
5 **Garrett**	Y	Y	?	Y	Y	Y
6 **Goodlatte**	Y	Y	Y	Y	Y	?
7 **Brat**	Y	Y	Y	Y	Y	Y
8 Beyer	N	N	N	Y	Y	N
9 **Griffith**	Y	Y	Y	Y	Y	Y
10 **Comstock**	Y	Y	Y	Y	Y	Y
11 Connolly	N	N	N	N	Y	N
WASHINGTON						
1 DelBene	N	N	N	Y	Y	Y
2 Larsen	N	N	N	N	Y	Y
3 **Herrera Beutler**	Y	Y	Y	Y	Y	N
4 **Newhouse**	Y	Y	Y	Y	Y	Y
5 **McMorris Rodgers**	Y	Y	Y	Y	Y	Y
6 Kilmer	N	N	N	Y	Y	N
7 Jayapal	N	N	N	N	Y	N
8 **Reichert**	Y	Y	Y	Y	Y	Y
9 Smith	N	N	N	N	Y	Y
10 Heck	N	N	N	Y	Y	Y
WEST VIRGINIA						
1 **McKinley**	Y	Y	Y	N	Y	N
2 **Mooney**	Y	Y	Y	Y	Y	Y
3 **Jenkins**	?	?	?	+	+	?
WISCONSIN						
1 **Ryan**						
2 Pocan	N	N	N	N	Y	Y
3 Kind	?	?	?	+	?	?
4 Moore	N	N	N	Y	Y	Y
5 **Sensenbrenner**	Y	Y	Y	Y	Y	N
6 **Grothman**	Y	Y	Y	Y	Y	Y
7 **Duffy**	Y	Y	Y	Y	Y	Y
8 **Gallagher**	Y	Y	Y	Y	Y	N
WYOMING						
AL **Cheney**	Y	Y	Y	Y	Y	Y

ⅠⅠⅠ HOUSE VOTES

VOTE NUMBER

14. S139. FISA AMENDMENTS REAUTHORIZATION/SECTION 702 SEARCH WARRANT REQUIREMENT. Amash R-Mich., amendment that would end NSA collection of communications data that is neither to nor from an approved foreign target, but rather communications "about" a foreign target entirely between American citizens. It would prohibit the FBI and intelligence agencies from searching the Section 702 database for information on U.S. citizens without first obtaining a warrant, except in certain circumstances. The amendment would end the so-called "reverse targeting" practice, in which an American communicating with a foreign target is also subject to surveillance, and would modify oversight of and appointments to the Foreign Intelligence Surveillance Court. Rejected in Committee of the Whole 183-233: R 58-178; D 125-55. Jan. 11, 2018.

15. S139. FISA AMENDMENTS REAUTHORIZATION/RECOMMIT. Himes D-Conn., motion to recommit the bill to the House Intelligence Committee with instructions to report it back immediately with an amendment that would include additional requirements related to obtaining warrants in order to query information incidentally collected on U.S. citizens. Motion rejected 189-227: R 6-227; D 183-0. Jan. 11, 2018.

16. S139. FISA AMENDMENTS REAUTHORIZATION/PASSAGE. Passage of the bill that would reauthorize for six years, through 2023, the Foreign Intelligence Surveillance Act, which governs electronic surveillance of foreign terrorism suspects. The bill would reauthorize Section 702 surveillance authorities on foreign targets, and would require the development of procedures for searching the Section 702 database that would protect the Fourth Amendment rights of U.S. citizens. The bill would prohibit the FBI from accessing information without an order from the secret FISA court in certain cases. The measure would increase penalties for the unauthorized removal of classified documents or information. Passed 256-164: R 191-45; D 65-119. Jan. 11, 2018.

17. HR4578. NATIONAL TARGETING CENTER DISMANTLING TERRORIST NETWORKS/PASSAGE. Estes R-Kan., motion to suspend the rules and pass the bill that would authorize the United States Customs and Border Protection's National Targeting Center to collaborate with federal, state, local, tribal and international organizations to further efforts to disrupt and dismantle foreign terrorist networks and address related border security matters. Motion agreed to 410-2: R 228-2; D 182-0. Jan. 11, 2018.

18. HR4318. TEMPORARY DUTY AND TARIFF SUSPENSIONS/PASSAGE. Bishop, R-Mich., motion to suspend the rules and pass the bill that would suspend duties and tariffs on 1,662 products that have no domestic production. Most of the products that would receive temporary suspensions of U.S. duties would be complex chemicals used by U.S. manufacturers, and the other products would include various household items. Motion agreed to 402-0: R 222-0; D 180-0. Jan. 16, 2018.

19. S117. ALEX DIEKMANN PEAK/PASSAGE. Gianforte, R-Mont., motion to suspend the rules and pass the bill that would designate an unnamed peak in the Lee Metcalf Wilderness in Montana as the "Alex Diekmann Peak." Motion agreed to 400-3: R 219-3; D 181-0. Jan. 16, 2018"

	14	15	16	17	18	19
ALABAMA						
1 **Byrne**	N	N	Y	Y	Y	Y
2 **Roby**	N	N	Y	Y	Y	Y
3 **Rogers**	N	N	Y	Y	Y	Y
4 **Aderholt**	N	N	Y	?	Y	Y
5 **Brooks**	Y	N	Y	Y	Y	Y
6 **Palmer**	N	N	Y	Y	Y	Y
7 Sewell	N	Y	Y	Y	Y	Y
ALASKA						
AL **Young**	Y	N	Y	Y	?	?
ARIZONA						
1 O'Halleran	N	Y	Y	Y	Y	Y
2 **McSally**	N	N	Y	Y	Y	Y
3 Grijalva	Y	Y	N	Y	Y	Y
4 **Gosar**	Y	N	N	Y	Y	Y
5 **Biggs**	Y	N	N	Y	Y	N
6 **Schweikert**	Y	N	Y	Y	Y	Y
7 Gallego	Y	Y	N	Y	Y	Y
9 Sinema	N	Y	Y	Y	Y	Y
ARKANSAS						
1 **Crawford**	N	N	Y	Y	Y	Y
2 **Hill**	N	N	Y	Y	Y	Y
3 **Womack**	N	N	Y	Y	Y	Y
4 **Westerman**	N	N	Y	Y	Y	Y
CALIFORNIA						
1 **LaMalfa**	N	N	Y	Y	Y	Y
2 Huffman	+	Y	N	Y	Y	Y
3 Garamendi	Y	Y	Y	Y	Y	Y
4 **McClintock**	Y	N	N	Y	Y	Y
5 Thompson	N	Y	Y	Y	Y	Y
6 Matsui	Y	Y	N	Y	Y	Y
7 Bera	N	Y	Y	Y	Y	Y
8 **Cook**	N	N	Y	Y	Y	Y
9 McNerney	?	?	?	?	Y	Y
10 **Denham**	N	N	Y	Y	Y	Y
11 DeSaulnier	+	+	–	+	Y	Y
12 Pelosi	N	Y	Y	Y	Y	Y
13 Lee	Y	Y	N	Y	Y	Y
14 Speier	Y	Y	N	Y	Y	Y
15 Swalwell	N	Y	Y	Y	Y	Y
16 Costa	N	Y	Y	Y	Y	Y
17 Khanna	Y	Y	N	Y	Y	Y
18 Eshoo	Y	Y	N	Y	Y	Y
19 Lofgren	Y	Y	N	Y	Y	Y
20 Panetta	N	Y	Y	Y	Y	Y
21 **Valadao**	N	N	Y	Y	Y	Y
22 **Nunes**	N	N	Y	Y	Y	Y
23 **McCarthy**	N	N	Y	Y	Y	Y
24 Carbajal	+	+	–	+	Y	Y
25 **Knight**	N	N	Y	Y	Y	Y
26 Brownley	N	Y	Y	Y	Y	Y
27 Chu	Y	Y	N	Y	Y	Y
28 Schiff	N	Y	Y	Y	Y	Y
29 Cardenas	?	Y	N	Y	Y	Y
30 Sherman	Y	Y	N	Y	Y	Y
31 Aguilar	N	Y	Y	Y	Y	Y
32 Napolitano	Y	Y	N	Y	Y	Y
33 Lieu	Y	Y	N	Y	Y	Y
34 Gomez	Y	Y	N	Y	Y	Y
35 Torres	N	Y	Y	Y	Y	Y
36 Ruiz	N	Y	Y	Y	Y	Y
37 Bass	Y	Y	N	Y	Y	Y
38 Sánchez, Linda	Y	Y	N	Y	Y	Y
39 **Royce**	N	N	Y	Y	Y	Y
40 Roybal-Allard	Y	Y	N	Y	Y	Y
41 Takano	Y	Y	N	Y	Y	Y
42 **Calvert**	N	N	Y	?	Y	Y
43 Waters	Y	Y	N	Y	Y	Y
44 Barragan	Y	Y	N	Y	Y	Y
45 **Walters**	N	N	Y	Y	Y	Y
46 Correa	Y	Y	N	Y	Y	Y
47 Lowenthal	Y	Y	N	Y	Y	Y
48 **Rohrabacher**	Y	N	N	Y	?	?
49 **Issa**	Y	N	Y	Y	?	?
50 **Hunter**	N	N	Y	Y	?	?
51 Vargas	Y	Y	N	Y	Y	Y
52 Peters	N	Y	Y	Y	Y	Y
53 Davis	Y	Y	N	Y	Y	Y

	14	15	16	17	18	19
COLORADO						
1 DeGette	Y	Y	N	Y	Y	Y
2 Polis	Y	Y	N	Y	Y	Y
3 **Tipton**	N	N	Y	Y	Y	Y
4 **Buck**	N	N	N	Y	Y	Y
5 **Lamborn**	Y	N	Y	Y	Y	Y
6 **Coffman**	N	N	Y	Y	Y	Y
7 Perlmutter	Y	Y	Y	Y	Y	Y
CONNECTICUT						
1 Larson	Y	Y	N	Y	Y	Y
2 Courtney	Y	Y	N	Y	Y	Y
3 DeLauro	Y	Y	N	Y	Y	Y
4 Himes	N	Y	N	Y	Y	Y
5 Esty	N	Y	N	Y	Y	Y
DELAWARE						
AL **Blunt**						
Rochester	N	Y	Y	Y	Y	Y
FLORIDA						
1 **Gaetz**	N	N	Y	Y	Y	Y
2 **Dunn**	N	N	Y	Y	Y	Y
3 **Yoho**	Y	N	N	Y	Y	Y
4 **Rutherford**	N	N	Y	Y	Y	Y
5 Lawson	N	Y	Y	Y	Y	Y
6 **DeSantis**	N	N	Y	Y	Y	Y
7 Murphy	N	Y	Y	Y	Y	Y
8 **Posey**	Y	N	N	Y	Y	Y
9 Soto	Y	Y	N	Y	Y	Y
10 Demings	N	Y	Y	Y	Y	Y
11 **Webster**	Y	N	N	Y	?	?
12 **Bilirakis**	N	N	Y	Y	Y	Y
13 Crist	Y	Y	Y	Y	Y	Y
14 Castor	N	Y	Y	Y	Y	Y
15 **Ross**	N	N	Y	Y	Y	Y
16 **Buchanan**	N	N	Y	?	Y	Y
17 **Rooney, T.**	N	N	Y	?	Y	Y
18 **Mast**	Y	N	Y	Y	Y	Y
19 **Rooney, F.**	N	N	Y	Y	?	?
20 Hastings	Y	Y	N	Y	Y	Y
21 Frankel	N	Y	Y	Y	Y	Y
22 Deutch	Y	Y	Y	Y	Y	Y
23 Wasserman						
Schultz	N	Y	Y	Y	Y	Y
24 Wilson	+	+	–	+	?	?
25 **Diaz-Balart**	N	N	Y	Y	Y	Y
26 **Curbelo**	N	N	Y	Y	Y	Y
27 **Ros-Lehtinen**	N	N	Y	Y	Y	Y
GEORGIA						
1 **Carter**	N	N	Y	Y	Y	Y
2 Bishop	N	Y	Y	Y	Y	Y
3 **Ferguson**	N	N	Y	Y	Y	Y
4 Johnson	Y	Y	N	Y	Y	Y
5 Lewis	Y	Y	N	Y	Y	Y
6 **Handel**	N	N	Y	Y	Y	Y
7 **Woodall**	Y	N	Y	Y	Y	Y
8 **Scott, A.**	N	N	Y	Y	Y	Y
9 **Collins**	N	N	Y	Y	Y	Y
10 **Hice**	Y	N	Y	Y	Y	Y
11 **Loudermilk**	Y	N	N	Y	Y	Y
12 **Allen**	N	N	Y	Y	Y	Y
13 Scott, D.	Y	Y	Y	Y	Y	Y
14 **Graves**	N	N	Y	Y	Y	Y
HAWAII						
1 Hanabusa	?	?	?	?	Y	Y
2 Gabbard	Y	Y	N	Y	Y	Y
IDAHO						
1 **Labrador**	Y	N	N	Y	Y	Y
2 **Simpson**	N	N	Y	Y	Y	Y
ILLINOIS						
1 Rush	?	Y	N	Y	Y	Y
2 Kelly	Y	Y	N	Y	Y	Y
3 Lipinski	N	Y	Y	Y	Y	Y
4 Gutierrez	Y	Y	N	Y	+	+
5 Quigley	N	Y	Y	Y	Y	Y
6 **Roskam**	N	N	Y	Y	Y	Y
7 Davis, D.	Y	Y	N	Y	Y	Y
8 Krishnamoorthi	Y	Y	Y	Y	Y	Y
9 Schakowsky	Y	Y	N	Y	Y	Y
10 Schneider	N	Y	Y	Y	?	?
11 Foster	Y	Y	Y	Y	Y	Y
12 **Bost**	N	N	Y	Y	Y	Y
13 **Davis, R.**	Y	N	Y	Y	Y	Y

KEY	Republicans	Democrats	*Independents*	
Y Voted for (yea)		**X** Paired against		**C** Voted "present" to avoid possible conflict of interest
# Paired for		**–** Announced against		
+ Announced for		**P** Voted "present"		**?** Did not vote or otherwise make a position known
N Voted against (nay)				

	14	15	16	17	18	19
14 **Hultgren**	N	N	Y	Y	Y	Y
15 **Shimkus**	N	N	Y	Y	Y	Y
16 **Kinzinger**	N	N	Y	Y	Y	Y
17 Bustos	N	Y	Y	Y	Y	Y
18 **LaHood**	N	N	Y	Y	Y	Y
INDIANA						
1 Visclosky	N	Y	N	Y	Y	Y
2 **Walorski**	N	N	Y	Y	Y	Y
3 **Banks**	N	N	Y	Y	Y	Y
4 **Rokita**	Y	N	Y	Y	Y	Y
5 **Brooks**	N	N	Y	Y	Y	Y
6 **Messer**	N	N	Y	Y	Y	Y
7 Carson	Y	Y	Y	Y	Y	Y
8 **Bucshon**	N	N	Y	Y	Y	Y
9 **Hollingsworth**	N	N	Y	Y	Y	Y
IOWA						
1 **Blum**	Y	N	N	Y	Y	Y
2 Loebsack	N	Y	Y	Y	Y	Y
3 **Young**	N	N	Y	Y	Y	Y
4 **King**	N	N	Y	Y	Y	Y
KANSAS						
1 **Marshall**	N	N	Y	Y	Y	Y
2 **Jenkins**	N	N	Y	Y	Y	Y
3 **Yoder**	Y	N	N	Y	Y	Y
4 **Estes**	N	N	Y	Y	Y	Y
KENTUCKY						
1 **Comer**	Y	N	Y	Y	Y	Y
2 **Guthrie**	N	N	Y	Y	Y	Y
3 Yarmuth	Y	Y	N	Y	Y	Y
4 **Massie**	Y	Y	N	N	Y	N
5 **Rogers**	N	N	Y	Y	Y	Y
6 **Barr**	N	N	Y	Y	Y	Y
LOUISIANA						
1 **Scalise**	–	–	+	+	+	+
2 Richmond	Y	Y	N	Y	Y	Y
3 **Higgins**	N	N	Y	Y	Y	Y
4 **Johnson**	Y	N	Y	Y	?	?
5 **Abraham**	Y	N	N	Y	Y	Y
6 **Graves**	Y	N	N	Y	Y	Y
MAINE						
1 Pingree	Y	Y	N	Y	Y	Y
2 **Poliquin**	N	N	Y	Y	Y	Y
MARYLAND						
1 **Harris**	Y	N	N	Y	Y	Y
2 Ruppersberger	N	Y	Y	Y	Y	Y
3 Sarbanes	Y	Y	N	Y	Y	Y
4 Brown	N	Y	Y	Y	Y	Y
5 Hoyer	N	Y	Y	Y	Y	Y
6 Delaney	N	Y	Y	Y	Y	Y
7 Cummings	?	?	?	?	?	?
8 Raskin	Y	Y	N	Y	Y	Y
MASSACHUSETTS						
1 Neal	Y	Y	N	Y	Y	Y
2 McGovern	Y	Y	N	Y	Y	Y
3 Tsongas	Y	Y	N	Y	?	?
4 Kennedy	Y	Y	N	Y	Y	Y
5 Clark	Y	Y	N	Y	Y	Y
6 Moulton	Y	Y	Y	Y	Y	Y
7 Capuano	Y	Y	N	Y	Y	Y
8 Lynch	Y	Y	N	Y	Y	Y
9 Keating	Y	Y	Y	Y	Y	Y
MICHIGAN						
1 **Bergman**	N	N	Y	Y	Y	Y
2 **Huizenga**	N	N	Y	Y	Y	Y
3 *Amash*	Y	Y	N	N	Y	N
4 **Moolenaar**	N	N	Y	Y	Y	Y
5 Kildee	Y	Y	N	Y	Y	Y
6 **Upton**	N	N	Y	Y	Y	Y
7 **Walberg**	N	N	Y	Y	Y	Y
8 **Bishop**	N	N	Y	Y	Y	Y
9 Levin	Y	Y	N	Y	Y	Y
10 **Mitchell**	N	N	Y	Y	Y	Y
11 **Trott**	N	N	Y	Y	Y	Y
12 Dingell	Y	Y	N	Y	Y	Y
14 Lawrence	Y	Y	N	Y	Y	Y
MINNESOTA						
1 Walz	Y	Y	N	Y	Y	Y
2 **Lewis**	Y	N	N	Y	Y	Y
3 **Paulsen**	N	N	Y	Y	Y	Y
4 McCollum	Y	Y	N	Y	Y	Y

	14	15	16	17	18	19
5 Ellison	Y	Y	N	Y	Y	Y
6 **Emmer**	Y	N	N	Y	Y	Y
7 Peterson	N	Y	Y	Y	?	?
8 Nolan	+	+	–	+	Y	Y
MISSISSIPPI						
1 **Kelly**	Y	N	Y	Y	Y	Y
2 Thompson	Y	Y	N	Y	Y	Y
3 **Harper**	N	N	Y	Y	Y	Y
4 **Palazzo**	N	N	Y	Y	Y	Y
MISSOURI						
1 Clay	Y	Y	N	Y	Y	Y
2 **Wagner**	N	N	Y	Y	Y	Y
3 **Luetkemeyer**	N	N	Y	Y	Y	Y
4 **Hartzler**	N	N	Y	Y	Y	Y
5 Cleaver	Y	Y	N	Y	Y	Y
6 **Graves**	N	N	Y	Y	Y	Y
7 **Long**	N	N	Y	Y	Y	Y
8 **Smith**	N	N	Y	Y	Y	Y
MONTANA						
AL **Gianforte**	Y	N	Y	Y	Y	Y
NEBRASKA						
1 **Fortenberry**	N	N	Y	Y	Y	Y
2 **Bacon**	N	N	Y	Y	Y	Y
3 **Smith**	N	N	Y	Y	Y	Y
NEVADA						
1 Titus	Y	Y	N	Y	+	+
2 **Amodei**	N	N	Y	Y	Y	Y
3 Rosen	N	Y	Y	Y	Y	Y
4 Kihuen	Y	Y	N	Y	Y	Y
NEW HAMPSHIRE						
1 Shea-Porter	Y	Y	N	Y	Y	Y
2 Kuster	N	Y	Y	Y	Y	Y
NEW JERSEY						
1 Norcross	N	Y	Y	Y	Y	Y
2 **LoBiondo**	N	N	Y	Y	Y	Y
3 **MacArthur**	N	N	Y	Y	Y	Y
4 **Smith**	N	N	Y	Y	Y	Y
5 Gottheimer	N	Y	Y	Y	Y	Y
6 Pallone	Y	Y	N	Y	Y	Y
7 **Lance**	N	N	Y	Y	Y	Y
8 Sires	N	Y	Y	Y	Y	Y
9 Pascrell	?	Y	N	Y	Y	Y
10 Payne	Y	?	N	Y	Y	Y
11 **Frelinghuysen**	N	N	Y	Y	Y	Y
12 Watson Coleman	Y	Y	N	Y	Y	Y
NEW MEXICO						
1 Lujan Grisham	Y	Y	Y	Y	Y	Y
2 **Pearce**	Y	N	N	Y	Y	Y
3 Luján	Y	Y	N	Y	Y	Y
NEW YORK						
1 **Zeldin**	Y	N	Y	Y	Y	Y
2 **King**	N	N	Y	Y	Y	Y
3 Suozzi	N	Y	Y	Y	Y	Y
4 Rice	N	Y	Y	Y	Y	Y
5 Meeks	Y	Y	Y	Y	Y	Y
6 Meng	Y	Y	N	Y	Y	Y
7 Velázquez	Y	Y	N	Y	Y	Y
8 Jeffries	Y	Y	N	Y	Y	Y
9 Clarke	Y	Y	N	Y	Y	Y
10 Nadler	Y	Y	N	Y	Y	Y
11 **Donovan**	N	N	Y	Y	Y	Y
12 Maloney, C.	Y	Y	N	Y	Y	Y
13 Espaillat	Y	Y	N	Y	Y	Y
14 Crowley	Y	Y	N	Y	Y	Y
15 Serrano	Y	Y	N	Y	Y	Y
16 Engel	Y	Y	N	Y	Y	Y
17 Lowey	N	Y	Y	Y	Y	Y
18 Maloney, S.P.	N	Y	Y	Y	Y	Y
19 **Faso**	N	N	Y	Y	Y	Y
20 Tonko	Y	Y	N	Y	Y	Y
21 **Stefanik**	N	N	Y	Y	+	+
22 **Tenney**	N	N	Y	Y	Y	Y
23 **Reed**	N	N	Y	Y	Y	Y
24 **Katko**	N	N	Y	Y	Y	Y
25 Slaughter	Y	Y	Y	Y	Y	Y
26 Higgins	N	Y	Y	Y	Y	Y
27 **Collins**	N	N	Y	Y	Y	Y
NORTH CAROLINA						
1 Butterfield	Y	Y	N	Y	?	?
2 **Holding**	N	N	Y	Y	Y	Y
3 **Jones**	Y	Y	N	Y	Y	Y
4 Price	Y	Y	N	Y	Y	Y

	14	15	16	17	18	19
5 **Foxx**	N	N	Y	Y	Y	Y
6 **Walker**	N	N	Y	Y	Y	Y
7 **Rouzer**	N	N	Y	Y	Y	Y
8 **Hudson**	N	N	Y	Y	Y	Y
9 **Pittenger**	N	N	Y	Y	Y	Y
9 **Vacant**						
10 **McHenry**	?	?	?	?	Y	Y
11 **Meadows**	Y	N	N	Y	Y	Y
12 Adams	+	+	–	+	Y	Y
13 **Budd**	Y	N	N	Y	Y	Y
NORTH DAKOTA						
AL **Cramer**	N	N	Y	Y	Y	Y
OHIO						
1 **Chabot**	N	N	Y	Y	Y	Y
2 **Wenstrup**	N	N	Y	Y	Y	Y
3 Beatty	Y	Y	N	Y	Y	Y
4 **Jordan**	Y	N	N	Y	Y	Y
5 **Latta**	N	N	Y	Y	Y	Y
6 **Johnson**	N	N	Y	Y	Y	Y
7 **Gibbs**	N	N	Y	Y	Y	Y
8 **Davidson**	Y	N	N	Y	Y	Y
9 Kaptur	N	Y	N	Y	Y	Y
10 **Turner**	N	N	Y	Y	Y	Y
11 Fudge	Y	Y	N	Y	Y	Y
13 Ryan	Y	Y	N	Y	+	Y
14 **Joyce**	N	N	Y	Y	Y	Y
15 **Stivers**	N	N	Y	Y	Y	Y
16 **Renacci**	N	N	Y	Y	?	?
OKLAHOMA						
1 **Bridenstine**	N	N	Y	Y	Y	Y
2 **Mullin**	N	N	Y	Y	Y	Y
3 **Lucas**	N	N	Y	Y	Y	Y
4 **Cole**	N	N	Y	Y	Y	Y
5 **Russell**	N	N	Y	Y	Y	Y
OREGON						
1 Bonamici	Y	Y	N	Y	Y	Y
2 **Walden**	N	N	Y	Y	Y	Y
3 Blumenauer	Y	Y	N	Y	Y	Y
4 DeFazio	Y	Y	N	Y	Y	Y
5 Schrader	Y	Y	N	Y	Y	Y
PENNSYLVANIA						
1 Brady	Y	Y	N	Y	Y	Y
2 Evans	Y	Y	N	Y	Y	Y
3 **Kelly**	N	N	Y	Y	Y	Y
4 **Perry**	Y	N	N	Y	Y	Y
5 **Thompson**	N	N	Y	Y	Y	Y
6 **Costello**	N	N	Y	Y	Y	Y
7 **Meehan**	N	N	Y	Y	Y	Y
8 **Fitzpatrick**	N	N	Y	Y	Y	Y
9 **Shuster**	N	N	Y	Y	Y	Y
10 **Marino**	N	N	Y	Y	Y	Y
11 **Barletta**	N	N	Y	Y	Y	Y
12 **Rothfus**	N	N	Y	Y	Y	Y
13 Boyle	Y	Y	Y	Y	Y	Y
14 Doyle	Y	Y	N	Y	Y	Y
15 **Dent**	N	N	Y	Y	Y	Y
16 **Smucker**	N	N	Y	Y	Y	Y
17 Cartwright	N	Y	Y	Y	Y	Y
RHODE ISLAND						
1 Cicilline	Y	Y	N	Y	Y	Y
2 Langevin	N	Y	Y	Y	Y	Y
SOUTH CAROLINA						
1 **Sanford**	Y	N	N	Y	Y	Y
2 **Wilson**	N	N	Y	Y	Y	Y
3 **Duncan**	Y	N	N	Y	Y	Y
4 **Gowdy**	N	N	Y	Y	Y	Y
5 **Norman**	Y	N	N	Y	Y	Y
6 Clyburn	Y	Y	Y	Y	Y	Y
7 **Rice**	N	N	Y	Y	Y	Y
SOUTH DAKOTA						
AL **Noem**	N	N	Y	Y	?	?
TENNESSEE						
1 **Roe**	N	N	N	Y	Y	Y
2 **Duncan**	Y	Y	N	Y	Y	Y
3 **Fleischmann**	N	N	Y	Y	Y	Y
4 **DesJarlais**	Y	N	Y	Y	Y	Y
5 Cooper	N	Y	Y	Y	Y	Y
6 **Black**	N	N	N	Y	Y	Y
7 **Blackburn**	N	N	N	Y	Y	Y
8 **Kustoff**	N	N	Y	Y	Y	Y
9 Cohen	Y	Y	N	Y	Y	Y

	14	15	16	17	18	19
TEXAS						
1 **Gohmert**	Y	Y	N	Y	Y	Y
2 **Poe**	Y	N	N	Y	?	?
3 **Johnson, S.**	N	N	Y	Y	Y	Y
4 **Ratcliffe**	N	N	Y	Y	Y	Y
5 **Hensarling**	N	N	Y	Y	Y	Y
6 **Barton**	Y	Y	Y	Y	Y	Y
7 **Culberson**	N	N	Y	Y	+	+
8 **Brady**	N	N	Y	Y	+	+
9 Green, A.	Y	Y	N	Y	Y	Y
10 **McCaul**	N	N	Y	Y	Y	?
11 **Conaway**	N	N	Y	Y	Y	Y
12 **Granger**	N	N	Y	Y	Y	Y
13 **Thornberry**	N	N	Y	Y	Y	Y
14 **Weber**	Y	N	N	Y	Y	Y
15 Gonzalez	Y	Y	N	?	Y	Y
16 O'Rourke	Y	Y	N	Y	Y	Y
17 **Flores**	N	N	Y	Y	Y	Y
18 Jackson Lee	Y	Y	N	Y	Y	Y
19 **Arrington**	N	N	Y	Y	Y	Y
20 Castro	N	Y	N	Y	Y	Y
21 **Smith**	N	N	Y	Y	Y	Y
22 **Olson**	N	N	Y	Y	Y	Y
23 **Hurd**	N	N	Y	Y	Y	Y
24 **Marchant**	N	N	Y	Y	Y	Y
25 **Williams**	N	N	N	Y	Y	Y
26 **Burgess**	Y	N	N	Y	Y	Y
27 **Farenthold**	Y	N	N	Y	Y	Y
28 Cuellar	N	Y	Y	Y	+	+
29 Green, G.	Y	Y	N	?	+	+
30 Johnson, E.B.	Y	Y	N	Y	Y	Y
31 **Carter**	N	N	Y	Y	Y	Y
32 **Sessions**	N	N	Y	Y	Y	Y
33 Veasey	Y	Y	Y	Y	Y	Y
34 Vela	Y	Y	N	Y	?	?
35 Doggett	Y	Y	N	Y	Y	Y
36 **Babin**	?	?	?	?	Y	Y
UTAH						
1 **Bishop**	N	N	N	Y	Y	Y
2 **Stewart**	N	N	Y	Y	Y	Y
3 **Curtis**	N	N	Y	Y	Y	Y
4 **Love**	N	N	Y	Y	Y	Y
VERMONT						
AL Welch	Y	Y	N	Y	Y	Y
VIRGINIA						
1 **Wittman**	Y	N	Y	Y	Y	Y
2 **Taylor**	N	N	Y	Y	Y	Y
3 Scott	Y	Y	N	Y	Y	Y
4 McEachin	N	Y	Y	Y	Y	Y
5 **Garrett**	Y	?	N	Y	Y	Y
6 **Goodlatte**	N	N	Y	Y	Y	Y
7 **Brat**	Y	N	N	Y	Y	Y
8 Beyer	Y	Y	N	Y	Y	Y
9 **Griffith**	Y	?	N	Y	Y	Y
10 **Comstock**	N	N	Y	Y	Y	Y
11 Connolly	Y	Y	N	Y	Y	Y
WASHINGTON						
1 DelBene	Y	Y	N	Y	Y	Y
2 Larsen	Y	Y	N	Y	Y	Y
3 **Herrera Beutler**	Y	N	N	Y	Y	Y
4 **Newhouse**	N	N	Y	Y	Y	Y
5 **McMorris Rodgers**	Y	N	Y	Y	Y	Y
6 Kilmer	N	Y	N	Y	Y	Y
7 Jayapal	Y	Y	N	Y	Y	Y
8 **Reichert**	N	N	Y	Y	Y	Y
9 Smith	Y	Y	N	Y	Y	Y
10 Heck	N	Y	N	Y	Y	Y
WEST VIRGINIA						
1 **McKinley**	N	N	Y	Y	Y	Y
2 **Mooney**	Y	N	N	Y	Y	Y
3 **Jenkins**	N	N	Y	Y	+	Y
WISCONSIN						
1 **Ryan**	N		Y			
2 Pocan	Y	Y	N	Y	Y	Y
3 Kind	?	?	?	?	+	+
4 Moore	Y	Y	N	Y	Y	Y
5 **Sensenbrenner**	Y	N	N	Y	Y	Y
6 **Grothman**	N	N	Y	?	Y	Y
7 **Duffy**	N	N	N	Y	Y	Y
8 **Gallagher**	N	N	Y	Y	Y	Y
WYOMING						
AL **Cheney**	N	N	Y	Y	Y	Y

VOTE NUMBER

20. HRES693. MORTGAGE RECORDS DISCLOSURE AND WORLD BANK CONTRIBUTION/PREVIOUS QUESTION. Buck, R-Colo., motion to order the previous question (thus ending debate and the possibility for amendment) on the rule (H Res 693) that would provide for consideration of the bill (HR 2954) that would exempt some depository institutions from certain mortgage records disclosure requirements and would provide for consideration of the bill (HR 3326) that would authorize $3.29 billion for the United States' contribution to the World Bank's International Development Association. Motion agreed to 230-187: R 230-0; D 0-187. Jan. 17, 2018.

21. HR3326. MORTGAGE RECORDS DISCLOSURE AND WORLD BANK CONTRIBUTION/RULE. Adoption of the rule (H Res 693) that would provide for House floor consideration for the bill (HR 2954) that would exempt some depository institutions from certain mortgage records disclosure requirements. It would provide for consideration of the bill (HR 3326) that would authorize $3.29 billion for the United States' contribution to the World Bank's International Development Association for fiscal 2018 through fiscal 2020, but would, for fiscal 2018 through fiscal 2023, withhold up to 30 percent of authorized funding to the bank until the Treasury secretary reports to Congress that the World Bank is undertaking certain changes. Adopted 228-188: R 228-0; D 0-188. Jan. 17, 2018.

22. HR4258. LOW-INCOME FAMILY ASSISTANCE EXPANSION/PASSAGE. Duffy, R-Wis., motion to suspend the rules and pass the bill that would permanently expand HUD's Family Self-Sufficiency Program, which funds coordinators to help build partnerships with employers and assist low-income families in obtaining jobs and supportive services, to the project-based Section 8 housing assistance program. It would allow property owners that participate in Section 8 programs to enter into agreements with local public housing authorities to utilize their self-sufficiency programs or create their own programs. Motion agreed to 412-5: R 224-5; D 188-0. Jan. 17, 2018.

23. HR3326. WORLD BANK CONTRIBUTION/HUMAN TRAFFICKING. Connolly, D-Va., amendment that would require that the Treasury Department include in its report on the World Bank any actions intended to ensure that foreign domestic workers employed by a diplomat or staff of the bank are informed of their rights and protections in relation to anti-human trafficking laws. Adopted 420-0: R 231-0; D 189-0. Jan. 17, 2018.

24. HR3326. WORLD BANK CONTRIBUTION/PASSAGE. Passage of the bill, as amended, that would authorize $3.29 billion for the U.S. contribution to the World Bank's International Development Association for fiscal 2018 through fiscal 2020. It would require that, for fiscal 2018 through fiscal 2023, 15 percent of funds authorized to the World Bank be withheld until it the Treasury secretary reports that the bank is prioritizing poverty reduction and capable project management. An additional 15 percent would be withheld, for fiscal 2018 through fiscal 2023, until the Treasury secretary reports that the bank's policies emphasize support for secure property rights and due process of law, and that the bank is strengthening its projects' ability to undermine violent extremism. Passed 237-184: R 216-16; D 21-168. Jan. 17, 2018.

25. HR4279. CLOSED-END INVESTMENT COMPANIES/PASSAGE. Duffy, R-Wis., motion to suspend the rules and pass the bill that would extend reduced Securities and Exchange Commission filing and proxy requirements for issuing securities that apply to "well-known seasoned issuers," to registered closed-end investment companies and would require the SEC to propose a rule related to such expansion. Motion agreed to 418-2: R 230-1; D 188-1. Jan. 17, 2018.

		20	21	22	23	24	25
ALABAMA							
1	**Byrne**	Y	Y	Y	Y	Y	Y
2	**Roby**	Y	Y	Y	Y	Y	Y
3	**Rogers**	Y	Y	Y	Y	Y	Y
4	**Aderholt**	Y	Y	Y	Y	Y	Y
5	**Brooks**	Y	Y	N	Y	N	Y
6	**Palmer**	Y	Y	Y	Y	Y	Y
7	Sewell	N	N	Y	Y	N	Y
ALASKA							
AL	**Young**	Y	Y	Y	Y	Y	Y
ARIZONA							
1	O'Halleran	N	N	Y	Y	Y	Y
2	**McSally**	Y	Y	Y	Y	Y	Y
3	Grijalva	N	N	Y	Y	N	Y
4	**Gosar**	Y	Y	Y	Y	Y	Y
5	**Biggs**	Y	Y	N	Y	N	Y
6	**Schweikert**	Y	Y	Y	Y	Y	Y
7	Gallego	N	N	Y	Y	N	Y
9	Sinema	N	N	Y	Y	Y	Y
ARKANSAS							
1	**Crawford**	Y	Y	Y	Y	Y	Y
2	**Hill**	Y	Y	Y	Y	Y	Y
3	**Womack**	Y	Y	Y	Y	Y	Y
4	**Westerman**	Y	Y	Y	Y	Y	Y
CALIFORNIA							
1	**LaMalfa**	Y	?	Y	Y	Y	Y
2	Huffman	N	N	Y	Y	N	Y
3	Garamendi	N	N	Y	Y	Y	Y
4	**McClintock**	Y	Y	Y	Y	N	Y
5	Thompson	N	N	Y	Y	N	Y
6	Matsui	N	N	Y	Y	N	Y
7	Bera	N	N	Y	Y	N	Y
8	**Cook**	Y	Y	Y	Y	Y	Y
9	McNerney	N	N	Y	Y	N	Y
10	**Denham**	Y	Y	Y	Y	Y	Y
11	DeSaulnier	N	N	Y	Y	N	Y
12	Pelosi	N	N	Y	Y	N	Y
13	Lee	N	N	Y	Y	N	Y
14	Speier	N	N	Y	Y	N	Y
15	Swalwell	N	N	Y	Y	N	Y
16	Costa	N	N	Y	Y	Y	Y
17	Khanna	N	N	Y	Y	N	Y
18	Eshoo	N	N	Y	Y	N	Y
19	Lofgren	N	N	Y	Y	N	Y
20	Panetta	N	N	Y	Y	N	Y
21	**Valadao**	Y	Y	Y	Y	Y	Y
22	**Nunes**	Y	Y	Y	Y	Y	Y
23	**McCarthy**	Y	Y	Y	Y	Y	Y
24	Carbajal	N	N	Y	Y	N	Y
25	**Knight**	Y	Y	Y	Y	Y	Y
26	Brownley	N	N	Y	Y	N	Y
27	Chu	N	N	Y	Y	N	Y
28	Schiff	N	N	Y	Y	N	Y
29	Cardenas	N	N	Y	Y	N	Y
30	Sherman	N	N	Y	Y	Y	Y
31	Aguilar	N	N	Y	Y	N	Y
32	Napolitano	N	N	Y	Y	N	Y
33	Lieu	N	N	Y	Y	N	Y
34	Gomez	N	N	Y	Y	N	Y
35	Torres	N	N	Y	Y	N	Y
36	Ruiz	N	N	Y	Y	N	Y
37	Bass	N	N	Y	Y	N	Y
38	Sánchez, Linda	N	N	Y	Y	N	Y
39	**Royce**	Y	Y	Y	Y	Y	Y
40	Roybal-Allard	N	N	Y	Y	N	Y
41	Takano	N	N	Y	Y	N	Y
42	**Calvert**	Y	Y	Y	Y	Y	Y
43	Waters	N	N	Y	Y	N	Y
44	Barragan	N	N	Y	Y	N	Y
45	**Walters**	Y	Y	Y	Y	Y	Y
46	Correa	N	N	Y	Y	Y	Y
47	Lowenthal	N	N	Y	Y	N	Y
48	**Rohrabacher**	Y	Y	Y	Y	Y	Y
49	**Issa**	Y	Y	Y	Y	Y	Y
50	**Hunter**	Y	Y	Y	Y	Y	Y
51	Vargas	N	N	Y	Y	N	Y
52	Peters	N	N	Y	Y	Y	Y
53	Davis	N	N	Y	Y	N	Y

		20	21	22	23	24	25
COLORADO							
1	**DeGette**	N	N	Y	Y	N	Y
2	Polis	N	N	Y	Y	Y	Y
3	Tipton	Y	Y	Y	Y	Y	Y
4	**Buck**	Y	Y	Y	Y	Y	Y
5	**Lamborn**	Y	Y	Y	Y	Y	Y
6	**Coffman**	Y	Y	Y	Y	Y	Y
7	Perlmutter	N	N	Y	Y	N	Y
CONNECTICUT							
1	Larson	N	N	Y	Y	N	Y
2	Courtney	N	N	Y	Y	N	Y
3	DeLauro	N	N	Y	Y	N	Y
4	Himes	N	N	Y	Y	N	Y
5	Esty	N	N	Y	Y	N	Y
DELAWARE							
AL	Blunt Rochester	N	N	Y	Y	N	Y
FLORIDA							
1	**Gaetz**	Y	?	?	Y	N	Y
2	**Dunn**	Y	Y	Y	Y	Y	Y
3	**Yoho**	Y	Y	Y	Y	Y	Y
4	**Rutherford**	Y	Y	Y	Y	Y	Y
5	Lawson	N	N	Y	Y	Y	Y
6	**DeSantis**	Y	Y	Y	Y	Y	Y
7	Murphy	N	N	Y	Y	N	Y
8	**Posey**	Y	Y	Y	Y	Y	Y
9	Soto	N	N	Y	Y	N	Y
10	Demings	N	N	Y	Y	N	Y
11	**Webster**	Y	Y	Y	Y	Y	Y
12	**Bilirakis**	Y	Y	Y	Y	Y	Y
13	Crist	N	N	Y	Y	N	Y
14	Castor	N	N	Y	Y	N	Y
15	**Ross**	Y	Y	Y	Y	Y	Y
16	**Buchanan**	Y	Y	Y	Y	Y	Y
17	**Rooney, T.**	Y	Y	Y	Y	Y	?
18	**Mast**	Y	Y	Y	Y	Y	Y
19	**Rooney, F.**	Y	Y	Y	Y	Y	Y
20	Hastings	N	N	Y	Y	N	Y
21	Frankel	N	N	Y	Y	N	Y
22	Deutch	N	N	Y	Y	N	Y
23	Wasserman Schultz	N	N	Y	Y	N	Y
24	Wilson	N	N	Y	Y	N	Y
25	**Diaz-Balart**	Y	Y	Y	Y	Y	Y
26	**Curbelo**	Y	Y	Y	Y	Y	Y
27	**Ros-Lehtinen**	Y	Y	Y	Y	Y	Y
GEORGIA							
1	**Carter**	Y	Y	Y	Y	Y	Y
2	Bishop	N	N	Y	Y	N	Y
3	**Ferguson**	Y	Y	Y	Y	Y	Y
4	Johnson	N	N	Y	Y	N	Y
5	Lewis	?	?	?	?	?	?
6	**Handel**	Y	Y	Y	Y	Y	Y
7	**Woodall**	Y	Y	Y	Y	Y	Y
8	**Scott, A.**	Y	Y	Y	Y	Y	Y
9	**Collins**	Y	Y	Y	Y	Y	Y
10	**Hice**	Y	Y	Y	Y	Y	Y
11	**Loudermilk**	Y	Y	Y	?	Y	Y
12	**Allen**	Y	Y	Y	Y	Y	Y
13	Scott, D.	N	N	Y	Y	N	Y
14	**Graves**	Y	Y	Y	Y	Y	Y
HAWAII							
1	Hanabusa	N	N	Y	Y	N	Y
2	Gabbard	N	N	Y	Y	N	Y
IDAHO							
1	**Labrador**	Y	Y	Y	Y	N	Y
2	**Simpson**	Y	Y	Y	Y	Y	Y
ILLINOIS							
1	Rush	?	N	Y	Y	N	Y
2	Kelly	N	N	Y	Y	N	Y
3	Lipinski	N	N	Y	Y	Y	Y
4	Gutierrez	N	N	Y	Y	N	Y
5	Quigley	N	N	Y	Y	N	Y
6	**Roskam**	Y	Y	Y	Y	Y	Y
7	Davis, D.	N	N	Y	Y	N	Y
8	Krishnamoorthi	N	N	Y	Y	N	Y
9	Schakowsky	N	N	Y	Y	N	Y
10	Schneider	?	?	?	Y	Y	Y
11	Foster	N	N	Y	Y	N	Y
12	**Bost**	Y	Y	Y	Y	Y	Y
13	**Davis, R.**	Y	Y	Y	Y	Y	Y

	20	21	22	23	24	25
14 **Hultgren**	Y	Y	Y	Y	Y	Y
15 **Shimkus**	Y	Y	Y	Y	Y	Y
16 **Kinzinger**	Y	Y	Y	Y	Y	Y
17 **Bustos**	N	N	Y	Y	N	Y
18 **LaHood**	Y	Y	Y	Y	Y	Y
INDIANA						
1 Visclosky	N	N	Y	Y	N	Y
2 **Walorski**	Y	Y	Y	Y	Y	Y
3 **Banks**	Y	Y	Y	Y	Y	Y
4 **Rokita**	Y	Y	Y	Y	Y	Y
5 **Brooks**	Y	Y	Y	Y	Y	Y
6 **Messer**	Y	Y	Y	Y	Y	Y
7 Carson	N	N	Y	Y	Y	Y
8 **Bucshon**	Y	Y	Y	Y	Y	Y
9 **Hollingsworth**	Y	Y	Y	Y	Y	Y
IOWA						
1 **Blum**	Y	Y	Y	Y	Y	Y
2 Loebsack	N	N	Y	Y	N	Y
3 **Young**	Y	Y	Y	Y	Y	Y
4 **King**	Y	+	Y	Y	Y	Y
KANSAS						
1 **Marshall**	Y	Y	Y	Y	Y	Y
2 **Jenkins**	Y	Y	Y	Y	Y	Y
3 **Yoder**	Y	Y	Y	Y	Y	Y
4 **Estes**	Y	Y	Y	Y	Y	Y
KENTUCKY						
1 **Comer**	Y	Y	Y	Y	Y	Y
2 **Guthrie**	Y	Y	Y	Y	Y	Y
3 Yarmuth	N	N	Y	Y	N	Y
4 **Massie**	Y	Y	N	Y	N	Y
5 **Rogers**	Y	Y	Y	Y	Y	Y
6 **Barr**	Y	Y	Y	Y	Y	Y
LOUISIANA						
1 **Scalise**	+	+	+	+	+	+
2 Richmond	N	N	Y	Y	N	Y
3 **Higgins**	Y	Y	Y	Y	Y	Y
4 **Johnson**	Y	Y	Y	Y	Y	Y
5 **Abraham**	Y	Y	Y	Y	Y	Y
6 **Graves**	Y	Y	Y	Y	Y	Y
MAINE						
1 Pingree	N	N	Y	Y	N	Y
2 Poliquin	Y	Y	Y	Y	Y	Y
MARYLAND						
1 **Harris**	Y	Y	Y	Y	N	Y
2 Ruppersberger	N	N	Y	Y	N	Y
3 Sarbanes	N	N	Y	Y	N	Y
4 Brown	N	N	Y	Y	N	Y
5 Hoyer	N	N	Y	Y	N	Y
6 Delaney	N	N	Y	Y	N	Y
7 Cummings	?	?	?	?	?	?
8 Raskin	N	N	Y	Y	N	Y
MASSACHUSETTS						
1 Neal	N	N	Y	Y	N	Y
2 McGovern	N	N	Y	Y	N	Y
3 Tsongas	N	N	Y	Y	N	Y
4 Kennedy	N	N	Y	Y	N	Y
5 Clark	N	N	Y	Y	N	Y
6 Moulton	N	N	Y	Y	N	Y
7 Capuano	N	N	Y	Y	N	Y
8 Lynch	N	N	Y	Y	N	N
9 Keating	N	N	Y	Y	N	Y
MICHIGAN						
1 **Bergman**	Y	Y	Y	Y	Y	Y
2 **Huizenga**	Y	Y	Y	Y	Y	Y
3 *Amash*	Y	Y	N	Y	N	Y
4 **Moolenaar**	Y	Y	Y	Y	Y	Y
5 Kildee	N	N	Y	Y	N	Y
6 **Upton**	Y	Y	Y	Y	Y	Y
7 **Walberg**	Y	Y	Y	Y	Y	Y
8 **Bishop**	Y	Y	Y	Y	Y	Y
9 Levin	N	N	Y	Y	N	Y
10 **Mitchell**	Y	Y	Y	Y	Y	Y
11 **Trott**	Y	Y	Y	Y	Y	Y
12 Dingell	N	N	Y	Y	N	Y
14 Lawrence	N	N	Y	Y	N	Y
MINNESOTA						
1 Walz	N	N	Y	Y	N	Y
2 **Lewis**	Y	Y	Y	Y	Y	Y
3 **Paulsen**	Y	Y	Y	Y	Y	Y
4 McCollum	N	N	Y	Y	N	Y

	20	21	22	23	24	25
5 Ellison	N	N	Y	Y	N	Y
6 **Emmer**	Y	Y	Y	Y	Y	Y
7 Peterson	N	N	Y	Y	Y	Y
8 Nolan	N	N	Y	Y	N	Y
MISSISSIPPI						
1 **Kelly**	Y	Y	Y	Y	Y	Y
2 Thompson	N	N	Y	Y	N	Y
3 **Harper**	Y	Y	Y	Y	Y	Y
4 **Palazzo**	Y	Y	Y	Y	Y	Y
MISSOURI						
1 Clay	N	N	Y	Y	N	Y
2 **Wagner**	Y	Y	Y	Y	Y	Y
3 **Luetkemeyer**	Y	Y	Y	Y	Y	Y
4 **Hartzler**	Y	Y	Y	Y	Y	Y
5 Cleaver	N	N	Y	Y	N	Y
6 **Graves**	Y	Y	Y	Y	Y	Y
7 **Long**	+	+	+	+	+	+
8 **Smith**	Y	Y	Y	Y	Y	Y
MONTANA						
AL **Gianforte**	Y	Y	Y	Y	Y	Y
NEBRASKA						
1 **Fortenberry**	Y	Y	Y	Y	Y	Y
2 **Bacon**	Y	Y	Y	Y	Y	Y
3 **Smith**	Y	Y	Y	Y	Y	Y
NEVADA						
1 Titus	N	N	Y	Y	N	Y
2 **Amodei**	?	?	?	Y	Y	Y
3 Rosen	N	N	Y	Y	Y	Y
4 Kihuen	N	N	Y	Y	N	Y
NEW HAMPSHIRE						
1 Shea-Porter	N	N	Y	Y	N	Y
2 Kuster	N	N	Y	Y	N	Y
NEW JERSEY						
1 Norcross	N	N	Y	Y	N	Y
2 **LoBiondo**	Y	Y	Y	Y	Y	Y
3 **MacArthur**	Y	Y	Y	Y	Y	Y
4 **Smith**	Y	Y	Y	Y	Y	Y
5 Gottheimer	N	N	Y	Y	Y	Y
6 Pallone	N	N	Y	Y	N	Y
7 **Lance**	Y	Y	Y	Y	Y	Y
8 Sires	N	N	Y	Y	N	Y
9 Pascrell	N	N	Y	Y	N	Y
10 Payne	N	N	Y	Y	N	Y
11 **Frelinghuysen**	Y	Y	Y	Y	Y	Y
12 Watson Coleman	N	N	Y	Y	N	Y
NEW MEXICO						
1 Lujan Grisham	N	N	Y	Y	N	Y
2 **Pearce**	Y	Y	Y	Y	Y	Y
3 Luján	N	N	Y	Y	N	Y
NEW YORK						
1 **Zeldin**	Y	Y	Y	Y	Y	Y
2 **King**	Y	Y	Y	Y	Y	Y
3 Suozzi	N	N	Y	Y	Y	Y
4 Rice	N	N	Y	Y	N	Y
5 Meeks	N	N	Y	Y	N	Y
6 Meng	N	N	Y	Y	N	Y
7 Velázquez	N	N	Y	Y	N	Y
8 Jeffries	N	N	Y	Y	N	Y
9 Clarke	N	N	Y	Y	N	Y
10 Nadler	N	N	Y	Y	N	Y
11 **Donovan**	Y	Y	Y	Y	Y	Y
12 Maloney, C.	N	N	Y	Y	N	Y
13 Espaillat	N	N	Y	Y	N	Y
14 Crowley	N	N	Y	Y	N	Y
15 Serrano	N	N	Y	Y	N	Y
16 Engel	N	N	Y	Y	N	Y
17 Lowey	N	N	Y	Y	N	Y
18 Maloney, S.P.	N	N	Y	Y	Y	Y
19 **Faso**	Y	Y	Y	Y	Y	Y
20 Tonko	N	N	Y	Y	N	Y
21 **Stefanik**	Y	Y	Y	Y	Y	Y
22 **Tenney**	Y	Y	Y	Y	Y	Y
23 **Reed**	Y	Y	Y	Y	Y	Y
24 **Katko**	Y	Y	Y	Y	Y	Y
25 Slaughter	N	N	Y	Y	N	Y
26 Higgins	N	N	Y	Y	N	Y
27 **Collins**	Y	Y	Y	Y	Y	Y
NORTH CAROLINA						
1 Butterfield	N	N	Y	Y	N	Y
2 **Holding**	Y	Y	Y	Y	Y	Y
3 **Jones**	Y	Y	N	Y	N	N
4 Price	N	N	Y	Y	N	Y

	20	21	22	23	24	25
5 **Foxx**	Y	Y	Y	Y	Y	Y
6 **Walker**	Y	Y	Y	Y	Y	Y
7 **Rouzer**	Y	Y	Y	Y	Y	Y
8 **Hudson**	Y	Y	Y	Y	Y	Y
9 **Pittenger**	Y	Y	Y	Y	Y	Y
9 **Vacant**						
10 **McHenry**	Y	Y	Y	Y	Y	Y
11 **Meadows**	Y	Y	Y	Y	Y	Y
12 Adams	N	N	Y	Y	N	Y
13 **Budd**	Y	Y	Y	Y	Y	Y
NORTH DAKOTA						
AL **Cramer**	Y	Y	Y	Y	Y	Y
OHIO						
1 **Chabot**	Y	Y	Y	Y	Y	Y
2 **Wenstrup**	Y	Y	Y	Y	Y	Y
3 Beatty	N	N	Y	Y	N	Y
4 **Jordan**	Y	Y	Y	Y	N	Y
5 **Latta**	Y	Y	Y	Y	Y	Y
6 **Johnson**	Y	Y	Y	Y	Y	Y
7 **Gibbs**	Y	Y	Y	Y	Y	Y
8 **Davidson**	Y	Y	Y	Y	Y	Y
9 Kaptur	N	N	Y	Y	N	Y
10 **Turner**	Y	Y	Y	Y	Y	Y
11 Fudge	N	N	Y	Y	N	Y
12 **Vacant**						
13 Ryan	N	N	Y	Y	N	Y
14 **Joyce**	Y	Y	Y	Y	Y	Y
15 **Stivers**	Y	Y	Y	Y	Y	Y
16 **Renacci**	Y	Y	Y	Y	Y	Y
OKLAHOMA						
1 **Bridenstine**	Y	Y	Y	Y	Y	Y
2 **Mullin**	Y	Y	Y	Y	Y	Y
3 **Lucas**	Y	Y	Y	Y	Y	Y
4 **Cole**	Y	Y	Y	Y	Y	Y
5 **Russell**	Y	Y	Y	Y	Y	Y
OREGON						
1 Bonamici	N	N	Y	Y	N	Y
2 **Walden**	Y	Y	Y	Y	Y	Y
3 Blumenauer	N	N	Y	Y	N	Y
4 DeFazio	N	N	Y	Y	N	Y
5 Schrader	N	N	Y	Y	Y	Y
PENNSYLVANIA						
1 Brady	N	N	Y	Y	N	Y
2 Evans	N	N	Y	Y	N	Y
3 **Kelly**	Y	Y	Y	Y	Y	Y
4 **Perry**	Y	Y	Y	Y	N	Y
5 **Thompson**	Y	Y	Y	Y	Y	Y
6 **Costello**	Y	Y	Y	Y	Y	Y
7 **Meehan**	Y	Y	Y	Y	Y	Y
8 **Fitzpatrick**	Y	Y	Y	Y	Y	Y
9 **Shuster**	Y	Y	Y	Y	Y	Y
10 **Marino**	Y	Y	Y	Y	Y	Y
11 **Barletta**	?	Y	Y	Y	Y	Y
12 **Rothfus**	Y	Y	Y	Y	Y	Y
13 Boyle	N	N	Y	Y	N	Y
14 Doyle	N	N	Y	Y	N	Y
15 **Dent**	Y	Y	Y	Y	Y	Y
16 **Smucker**	Y	Y	Y	Y	Y	Y
17 Cartwright	N	N	Y	Y	N	Y
RHODE ISLAND						
1 Cicilline	N	N	Y	Y	N	Y
2 Langevin	N	N	Y	Y	N	Y
SOUTH CAROLINA						
1 **Sanford**	Y	Y	Y	Y	N	Y
2 **Wilson**	Y	Y	Y	Y	Y	Y
3 **Duncan**	Y	Y	Y	Y	Y	Y
4 **Gowdy**	Y	Y	Y	Y	Y	Y
5 **Norman**	Y	Y	Y	Y	Y	Y
6 Clyburn	N	N	Y	Y	N	Y
7 **Rice**	Y	Y	Y	Y	Y	Y
SOUTH DAKOTA						
AL **Noem**	?	?	?	?	?	?
TENNESSEE						
1 **Roe**	Y	Y	Y	Y	Y	Y
2 **Duncan**	Y	Y	Y	Y	N	Y
3 **Fleischmann**	Y	Y	Y	Y	Y	Y
4 **DesJarlais**	Y	Y	Y	Y	Y	Y
5 Cooper	N	N	Y	Y	N	Y
6 **Black**	Y	Y	Y	Y	Y	Y
7 **Blackburn**	Y	Y	Y	Y	Y	Y
8 **Kustoff**	Y	Y	Y	Y	Y	Y
9 Cohen	N	N	Y	Y	N	Y

	20	21	22	23	24	25
TEXAS						
1 **Gohmert**	Y	Y	Y	Y	N	Y
2 **Poe**	?	?	?	?	?	?
3 **Johnson, S.**	Y	Y	Y	Y	Y	Y
4 **Ratcliffe**	Y	Y	Y	Y	Y	Y
5 **Hensarling**	Y	Y	Y	Y	Y	Y
6 **Barton**	Y	Y	Y	Y	Y	Y
7 **Culberson**	Y	Y	Y	Y	Y	Y
8 **Brady**	+	+	+	+	+	+
9 Green, A.	N	N	Y	Y	N	Y
10 **McCaul**	Y	Y	Y	Y	Y	Y
11 **Conaway**	Y	Y	Y	Y	Y	Y
12 **Granger**	Y	Y	Y	Y	Y	Y
13 **Thornberry**	Y	Y	Y	Y	Y	Y
14 **Weber**	Y	Y	Y	Y	Y	Y
15 Gonzalez	N	N	Y	Y	Y	Y
16 O'Rourke	N	N	Y	Y	N	Y
17 **Flores**	Y	Y	Y	Y	Y	Y
18 Jackson Lee	N	N	Y	Y	N	Y
19 **Arrington**	Y	Y	Y	Y	Y	Y
20 Castro	N	N	Y	Y	N	Y
21 **Smith**	Y	Y	?	Y	Y	Y
22 **Olson**	Y	Y	Y	Y	Y	Y
23 **Hurd**	Y	Y	Y	Y	Y	Y
24 **Marchant**	Y	Y	Y	Y	N	Y
25 **Williams**	Y	Y	Y	Y	Y	Y
26 **Burgess**	Y	Y	Y	Y	Y	Y
27 **Farenthold**	Y	Y	Y	Y	Y	Y
28 Cuellar	N	N	Y	Y	Y	Y
29 Green, G.	N	N	Y	Y	N	Y
30 Johnson, E.B.	N	N	Y	Y	N	Y
31 **Carter**	Y	Y	Y	Y	Y	Y
32 **Sessions**	Y	Y	Y	Y	Y	Y
33 Veasey	N	N	Y	Y	N	Y
34 Vela	?	?	?	?	?	?
35 Doggett	N	N	Y	Y	N	Y
36 **Babin**	Y	Y	Y	Y	Y	Y
UTAH						
1 **Bishop**	Y	Y	Y	Y	Y	Y
2 **Stewart**	Y	Y	Y	Y	Y	Y
3 **Curtis**	Y	Y	Y	Y	Y	Y
4 **Love**	Y	Y	Y	Y	Y	Y
VERMONT						
AL Welch	N	N	Y	Y	N	Y
VIRGINIA						
1 **Wittman**	Y	Y	Y	Y	Y	Y
2 **Taylor**	Y	Y	Y	Y	Y	Y
3 Scott	N	N	Y	Y	N	Y
4 McEachin	N	N	Y	Y	N	Y
5 **Garrett**	Y	Y	Y	Y	Y	Y
6 **Goodlatte**	Y	Y	Y	Y	Y	Y
7 **Brat**	Y	Y	Y	Y	Y	Y
8 Beyer	N	N	Y	Y	N	Y
9 **Griffith**	Y	Y	Y	Y	Y	Y
10 **Comstock**	Y	Y	Y	Y	Y	Y
11 Connolly	N	N	Y	Y	N	Y
WASHINGTON						
1 DelBene	N	N	Y	Y	N	Y
2 Larsen	N	N	Y	Y	N	Y
3 **Herrera Beutler**	Y	Y	Y	Y	Y	Y
4 **Newhouse**	Y	Y	Y	Y	Y	Y
5 **McMorris Rodgers**	Y	Y	Y	Y	Y	Y
6 Kilmer	N	N	Y	Y	N	Y
7 Jayapal	N	N	Y	Y	N	Y
8 **Reichert**	Y	Y	Y	Y	Y	Y
9 Smith	N	N	Y	Y	N	Y
10 Heck	N	N	Y	Y	N	Y
WEST VIRGINIA						
1 **McKinley**	Y	Y	Y	Y	Y	Y
2 **Mooney**	Y	Y	Y	Y	Y	Y
3 **Jenkins**	Y	Y	Y	Y	Y	Y
WISCONSIN						
1 **Ryan**						
2 Pocan	N	N	Y	Y	N	Y
3 Kind	?	?	?	?	?	?
4 Moore	N	N	Y	Y	N	Y
5 **Sensenbrenner**	Y	Y	Y	Y	Y	Y
6 **Grothman**	Y	Y	Y	Y	Y	Y
7 **Duffy**	Y	Y	Y	Y	Y	Y
8 **Gallagher**	Y	Y	Y	Y	Y	Y
WYOMING						
AL **Cheney**	Y	Y	Y	Y	Y	Y

VOTE NUMBER

26. PROCEDURAL MOTION/JOURNAL. Approval of the House Journal of Jan. 16, 2018. Approved 225-185: R 143-86; D 82-99. Jan. 17, 2018.

27. HRES696. SHORT-TERM FISCAL 2018 CONTINUING APPROPRIATIONS AND CHIP FUNDING/PREVIOUS QUESTION. Cole, R-Texas, motion to order the previous question (thus ending debate and the possibility for amendment) on the rule (H Res 696) that would provide for House floor consideration of the Senate amendment to the bill (HR 195) that is the expected legislative vehicle for an extension of the current continuing resolution through Feb. 16, 2018, and funding for the Children's Health Insurance Program through fiscal 2023. Motion agreed to 229-191: R 229-0; D 0-191. Jan. 18, 2018.

28. HR195. SHORT-TERM FISCAL 2018 CONTINUING APPROPRIATIONS AND CHIP FUNDING/RULE. Adoption of the rule (H Res 696) that would provide for House floor consideration of the Senate amendment to the bill (HR 195) that is the expected legislative vehicle for an extension of the current continuing resolution through Feb. 16, 2018, and funding for the Children's Health Insurance Program through fiscal 2023. It would waive, through the legislative day of January 20, 2018, the two-thirds vote requirement to consider legislation on the same day it is reported from the House Rules Committee and would also provide for motions to suspend the rules through the legislative day of January 20, 2018. Adopted 226-194: R 226-3; D 0-191. Jan. 18, 2018.

29. HRES694. ABORTION PROVISIONS/PREVIOUS QUESTION. Cheney, R-Wyo., motion to order the previous question on the rule (thus ending debate and the possibility for amendment) on the rule (H Res 694) that would provide for House floor consideration of the bill (HR 4712) that would require health care practitioners to give the same level of care to an infant born alive during an abortion procedure as they would give to any other infant born at the same gestational age, and would set criminal fines and penalties for not doing so. Motion agreed to 229-190: R 229-0; D 0-190. Jan. 18, 2018.

30. HRES694. ABORTION PROVISIONS/RULE. Adoption of the rule (H Res 694) that would provide for House floor consideration of the bill (HR 4712) that would require health care practitioners to give the same level of care to an infant born alive during an abortion procedure as they would give to any other infant born at the same gestational age, and would set criminal fines and penalties for not doing so. Adopted 228-189: R 226-1; D 2-188. Jan. 18, 2018.

31. HR2954. MORTGAGE RECORDS DISCLOSURE/RECOMMIT. Ellison, D-Minn., motion to recommit the bill to the House Financial Services Committee with instructions to report it back immediately with an amendment that would require a depository institution utilizing the bill's exemptions to annually attest that the institution is in compliance with all relevant federal fair lending laws and attest that its employees have completed anti-discrimination training. Motion rejected 191-236: R 1-234; D 190-2. Jan. 18, 2018.

	26	27	28	29	30	31
ALABAMA						
1 **Byrne**	Y	Y	Y	Y	Y	N
2 **Roby**	Y	Y	Y	Y	Y	N
3 **Rogers**	N	Y	Y	Y	Y	N
4 **Aderholt**	Y	Y	Y	Y	Y	N
5 **Brooks**	N	Y	Y	Y	Y	N
6 **Palmer**	Y	Y	Y	Y	Y	N
7 Sewell	N	N	N	N	N	Y
ALASKA						
AL **Young**	N	Y	Y	Y	Y	N
ARIZONA						
1 O'Halleran	N	N	N	N	N	Y
2 **McSally**	N	Y	Y	Y	Y	N
3 Grijalva	N	N	N	N	N	Y
4 **Gosar**	Y	Y	Y	Y	?	N
5 **Biggs**	N	Y	Y	Y	Y	N
6 **Schweikert**	Y	Y	Y	Y	Y	N
7 Gallego	N	N	N	N	N	Y
9 Sinema	N	N	N	N	N	Y
ARKANSAS						
1 **Crawford**	N	Y	Y	Y	Y	N
2 **Hill**	N	Y	Y	Y	Y	N
3 **Womack**	Y	Y	Y	Y	Y	N
4 **Westerman**	Y	Y	Y	Y	Y	N
CALIFORNIA						
1 **LaMalfa**	Y	Y	Y	Y	Y	N
2 Huffman	Y	N	N	N	N	Y
3 Garamendi	Y	N	N	N	N	Y
4 **McClintock**	Y	Y	Y	Y	Y	N
5 Thompson	N	N	N	N	N	Y
6 Matsui	N	N	N	N	N	Y
7 Bera	N	N	N	N	N	Y
8 **Cook**	Y	Y	Y	Y	Y	N
9 McNerney	Y	N	N	N	N	Y
10 **Denham**	N	Y	Y	Y	Y	N
11 DeSaulnier	Y	N	N	N	N	Y
12 Pelosi	Y	N	N	N	N	Y
13 Lee	N	N	N	N	N	Y
14 Speier	Y	N	N	N	N	Y
15 Swalwell	N	N	N	N	N	Y
16 Costa	N	N	N	N	N	Y
17 Khanna	N	N	N	N	N	Y
18 Eshoo	Y	N	N	N	N	Y
19 Lofgren	N	N	N	N	N	Y
20 Panetta	Y	N	N	N	N	Y
21 **Valadao**	N	Y	Y	Y	Y	N
22 **Nunes**	Y	Y	Y	Y	Y	N
23 **McCarthy**	Y	Y	Y	Y	Y	N
24 Carbajal	N	N	N	N	N	Y
25 **Knight**	Y	Y	Y	Y	Y	N
26 Brownley	N	N	N	N	N	Y
27 Chu	Y	N	N	N	N	Y
28 Schiff	Y	N	N	N	N	Y
29 Cardenas	N	N	N	N	N	Y
30 Sherman	Y	N	N	N	N	Y
31 Aguilar	Y	N	N	N	N	Y
32 Napolitano	Y	N	N	N	N	Y
33 Lieu	N	N	N	N	N	Y
34 Gomez	N	N	N	N	N	Y
35 Torres	Y	N	N	N	N	Y
36 Ruiz	N	N	N	N	N	Y
37 Bass	N	N	N	N	N	Y
38 Sánchez, Linda	N	N	N	N	N	Y
39 **Royce**	Y	Y	Y	Y	Y	N
40 Roybal-Allard	?	N	N	N	N	Y
41 Takano	?	N	N	N	N	Y
42 **Calvert**	Y	Y	Y	Y	Y	N
43 Waters	Y	N	N	N	N	Y
44 Barragan	N	N	N	N	N	Y
45 **Walters**	Y	Y	Y	Y	Y	N
46 Correa	N	N	N	N	N	Y
47 Lowenthal	N	N	N	N	N	Y
48 **Rohrabacher**	Y	Y	Y	Y	Y	N
49 **Issa**	Y	Y	Y	Y	Y	N
50 **Hunter**	Y	Y	Y	Y	Y	N
51 Vargas	N	N	N	N	N	Y
52 Peters	N	N	N	N	N	Y
53 Davis	Y	N	N	N	N	Y

	26	27	28	29	30	31
COLORADO						
1 DeGette	Y	N	N	N	N	Y
2 Polis	Y	N	N	N	N	Y
3 **Tipton**	N	Y	Y	Y	Y	N
4 **Buck**	N	Y	Y	Y	Y	N
5 **Lamborn**	Y	Y	Y	Y	Y	N
6 **Coffman**	N	Y	Y	Y	Y	N
7 Perlmutter	Y	N	N	N	N	Y
CONNECTICUT						
1 Larson	N	N	N	N	N	Y
2 Courtney	Y	N	N	N	N	Y
3 DeLauro	Y	N	N	N	N	Y
4 Himes	Y	N	N	N	N	Y
5 Esty	N	N	N	N	N	Y
DELAWARE						
AL Blunt Rochester	Y	N	N	N	N	Y
FLORIDA						
1 **Gaetz**	N	Y	Y	Y	Y	N
2 **Dunn**	?	Y	Y	Y	Y	N
3 **Yoho**	Y	Y	Y	Y	Y	N
4 **Rutherford**	Y	Y	Y	Y	Y	N
5 Lawson	N	N	N	N	N	Y
6 **DeSantis**	N	Y	Y	Y	Y	N
7 Murphy	Y	N	N	N	N	Y
8 **Posey**	Y	Y	Y	Y	Y	N
9 Soto	N	N	N	N	N	Y
10 Demings	Y	N	N	N	N	Y
11 **Webster**	Y	Y	Y	Y	Y	N
12 **Bilirakis**	Y	Y	Y	Y	Y	N
13 Crist	N	N	N	N	N	Y
14 Castor	N	N	N	N	N	Y
15 **Ross**	Y	Y	Y	Y	Y	N
16 **Buchanan**	Y	Y	Y	Y	Y	N
17 **Rooney, T.**	?	Y	Y	Y	Y	N
18 **Mast**	N	Y	Y	Y	Y	N
19 **Rooney, F.**	Y	Y	Y	Y	Y	N
20 Hastings	N	N	N	N	N	Y
21 Frankel	Y	N	N	N	N	Y
22 Deutch	Y	N	N	N	N	Y
23 Wasserman Schultz	Y	N	N	N	N	Y
24 Wilson	Y	N	N	N	N	Y
25 **Diaz-Balart**	Y	Y	Y	Y	Y	N
26 **Curbelo**	N	Y	Y	Y	Y	N
27 **Ros-Lehtinen**	N	Y	Y	Y	Y	N
GEORGIA						
1 **Carter**	N	Y	Y	Y	Y	N
2 Bishop	N	N	N	N	N	Y
3 **Ferguson**	Y	Y	Y	Y	Y	N
4 Johnson	Y	N	N	N	N	Y
5 Lewis	?	N	N	N	N	Y
6 **Handel**	Y	Y	Y	Y	Y	N
7 **Woodall**	N	Y	Y	Y	Y	N
8 **Scott, A.**	Y	Y	Y	Y	Y	N
9 **Collins**	Y	Y	Y	Y	Y	N
10 **Hice**	N	Y	Y	Y	Y	N
11 **Loudermilk**	Y	Y	Y	Y	Y	N
12 **Allen**	Y	Y	Y	Y	Y	N
13 Scott, D.	Y	N	N	N	N	Y
14 **Graves**	N	Y	Y	Y	Y	N
HAWAII						
1 Hanabusa	N	N	N	N	N	Y
2 Gabbard	Y	N	N	N	N	Y
IDAHO						
1 **Labrador**	Y	Y	Y	Y	Y	N
2 **Simpson**	Y	Y	Y	Y	Y	N
ILLINOIS						
1 Rush	N	N	N	N	N	Y
2 Kelly	Y	N	N	N	N	Y
3 Lipinski	Y	N	N	N	Y	Y
4 Gutierrez	N	N	N	N	N	Y
5 Quigley	Y	N	N	N	N	Y
6 **Roskam**	N	Y	Y	Y	Y	N
7 Davis, D.	N	N	N	N	N	Y
8 Krishnamoorthi	N	N	N	N	N	Y
9 Schakowsky	N	N	N	N	N	Y
10 Schneider	N	N	N	N	N	Y
11 Foster	Y	N	N	N	N	Y
12 **Bost**	N	Y	Y	Y	Y	N
13 **Davis, R.**	Y	Y	Y	Y	Y	N

	26	27	28	29	30	31
14 **Hultgren**	Y	Y	Y	Y	Y	N
15 **Shimkus**	Y	Y	Y	Y	Y	N
16 **Kinzinger**	N	Y	Y	Y	Y	N
17 Bustos	Y	N	N	N	N	Y
18 **LaHood**	N	Y	Y	Y	Y	N
INDIANA						
1 Visclosky	N	N	N	N	N	Y
2 **Walorski**	Y	Y	Y	Y	Y	N
3 **Banks**	Y	Y	Y	Y	Y	N
4 **Rokita**	N	Y	Y	Y	Y	N
5 **Brooks**	Y	Y	Y	Y	Y	N
6 **Messer**	Y	Y	Y	Y	Y	N
7 Carson	Y	N	N	N	N	Y
8 **Bucshon**	Y	Y	Y	Y	Y	N
9 **Hollingsworth**	Y	Y	Y	Y	Y	N
IOWA						
1 **Blum**	N	Y	Y	Y	Y	N
2 Loebsack	N	N	N	N	N	Y
3 **Young**	Y	Y	Y	Y	Y	N
4 **King**	Y	Y	Y	Y	N	N
KANSAS						
1 **Marshall**	N	Y	Y	Y	Y	N
2 **Jenkins**	N	Y	Y	Y	Y	N
3 **Yoder**	N	Y	Y	Y	Y	N
4 **Estes**	Y	Y	Y	Y	Y	N
KENTUCKY						
1 **Comer**	Y	Y	Y	Y	Y	N
2 **Guthrie**	Y	Y	Y	Y	Y	N
3 Yarmuth	Y	N	N	N	N	Y
4 **Massie**	Y	Y	N	Y	Y	N
5 **Rogers**	Y	Y	Y	Y	Y	N
6 **Barr**	Y	Y	Y	Y	Y	N
LOUISIANA						
1 **Scalise**	+	+	+	+	+	–
2 Richmond	N	N	N	N	N	Y
3 **Higgins**	Y	Y	Y	Y	Y	N
4 **Johnson**	Y	Y	Y	Y	Y	N
5 **Abraham**	Y	Y	Y	Y	Y	N
6 **Graves**	N	Y	Y	Y	Y	N
MAINE						
1 Pingree	?	N	N	N	N	Y
2 Poliquin	N	Y	Y	Y	Y	N
MARYLAND						
1 **Harris**	Y	Y	Y	Y	Y	N
2 Ruppersberger	Y	N	N	N	N	Y
3 Sarbanes	N	N	N	N	N	Y
4 Brown	Y	N	N	N	N	Y
5 Hoyer	?	N	N	N	N	Y
6 Delaney	N	N	N	N	N	Y
7 Cummings	?	?	?	?	?	?
8 Raskin	N	N	N	N	N	Y
MASSACHUSETTS						
1 Neal	N	N	N	N	N	Y
2 McGovern	N	N	N	N	N	Y
3 Tsongas	?	N	N	N	N	Y
4 Kennedy	Y	N	N	N	N	Y
5 Clark	N	N	N	N	N	Y
6 Moulton	Y	N	N	N	N	Y
7 Capuano	N	N	N	N	N	Y
8 Lynch	N	N	N	N	N	Y
9 Keating	N	N	N	N	N	Y
MICHIGAN						
1 **Bergman**	N	Y	Y	Y	Y	N
2 **Huizenga**	Y	Y	Y	Y	Y	N
3 *Amash*	N	Y	N	Y	Y	N
4 **Moolenaar**	Y	Y	Y	Y	Y	N
5 Kildee	Y	N	N	N	N	Y
6 Upton	N	Y	Y	Y	Y	N
7 Walberg	N	Y	Y	Y	Y	N
8 Bishop	N	Y	Y	Y	Y	N
9 Levin	N	N	N	N	N	Y
10 Mitchell	Y	Y	Y	Y	Y	N
11 Trott	Y	Y	Y	Y	Y	N
12 Dingell	Y	N	N	N	N	Y
14 Lawrence	N	N	N	N	N	Y
MINNESOTA						
1 Walz	Y	N	N	N	N	Y
2 **Lewis**	Y	Y	Y	Y	Y	N
3 **Paulsen**	N	Y	Y	Y	Y	N
4 **McCollum**	+	N	N	N	N	Y
5 Ellison	Y	N	N	N	N	Y
6 **Emmer**	N	Y	Y	Y	Y	N
7 Peterson	N	N	N	N	Y	Y
8 Nolan	N	N	N	N	N	Y
MISSISSIPPI						
1 **Kelly**	Y	Y	Y	Y	Y	N
2 Thompson	N	N	N	N	N	Y
3 **Harper**	Y	Y	Y	Y	Y	N
4 Palazzo	N	Y	Y	Y	Y	N
MISSOURI						
1 Clay	Y	N	N	N	N	Y
2 **Wagner**	Y	Y	Y	Y	Y	N
3 **Luetkemeyer**	Y	Y	Y	Y	Y	N
4 **Hartzler**	Y	Y	Y	Y	Y	N
5 Cleaver	N	N	N	N	N	Y
6 **Graves**	N	Y	Y	Y	Y	N
7 **Long**	+	Y	Y	Y	Y	N
8 **Smith**	N	Y	Y	Y	Y	N
MONTANA						
AL **Gianforte**	Y	Y	Y	Y	Y	N
NEBRASKA						
1 **Fortenberry**	Y	Y	Y	Y	Y	N
2 **Bacon**	Y	Y	Y	Y	Y	N
3 **Smith**	Y	Y	Y	Y	Y	N
NEVADA						
1 Titus	Y	N	N	N	N	Y
2 **Amodei**	Y	Y	Y	Y	Y	N
3 Rosen	N	N	N	N	N	Y
4 Kihuen	N	N	N	N	N	Y
NEW HAMPSHIRE						
1 Shea-Porter	Y	N	N	N	N	Y
2 Kuster	Y	N	N	N	N	Y
NEW JERSEY						
1 Norcross	N	N	N	N	N	Y
2 **LoBiondo**	N	Y	Y	Y	Y	N
3 **MacArthur**	N	Y	Y	Y	Y	N
4 **Smith**	Y	Y	Y	Y	Y	N
5 Gottheimer	N	N	N	N	N	Y
6 Pallone	N	N	N	N	N	Y
7 **Lance**	N	Y	Y	Y	Y	N
8 Sires	N	N	N	N	N	Y
9 Pascrell	N	N	N	N	N	Y
10 Payne	N	N	N	N	N	Y
11 **Frelinghuysen**	Y	Y	Y	Y	Y	N
12 Watson Coleman	N	N	N	N	N	Y
NEW MEXICO						
1 Lujan Grisham	Y	N	N	N	N	Y
2 **Pearce**	N	Y	Y	Y	Y	N
3 Luján	Y	N	N	N	N	Y
NEW YORK						
1 **Zeldin**	N	Y	Y	Y	Y	N
2 **King**	Y	Y	Y	Y	Y	N
3 Suozzi	N	N	N	N	N	Y
4 Rice	N	N	N	N	N	Y
5 Meeks	N	N	N	N	N	Y
6 Meng	Y	N	N	N	N	Y
7 Velázquez	N	N	N	N	N	Y
8 Jeffries	Y	N	N	N	N	Y
9 Clarke	N	N	N	N	N	Y
10 Nadler	Y	N	N	N	N	Y
11 **Donovan**	Y	Y	Y	Y	Y	N
12 Maloney, C.	N	N	N	N	N	Y
13 Espaillat	N	N	N	N	N	Y
14 Crowley	N	N	N	N	N	Y
15 Serrano	Y	N	N	N	N	Y
16 Engel	Y	N	N	N	N	Y
17 Lowey	N	N	N	N	N	N
18 Maloney, S.P.	N	N	N	N	N	Y
19 **Faso**	N	Y	Y	Y	Y	N
20 Tonko	P	N	N	N	N	Y
21 **Stefanik**	Y	Y	Y	Y	Y	N
22 **Tenney**	N	Y	Y	Y	Y	N
23 **Reed**	N	Y	Y	Y	Y	N
24 **Katko**	N	Y	Y	Y	Y	N
25 Slaughter	N	N	N	N	N	Y
26 Higgins	N	N	N	N	N	Y
27 **Collins**	Y	Y	Y	Y	Y	N
NORTH CAROLINA						
1 Butterfield	Y	N	N	N	N	Y
2 **Holding**	N	Y	Y	Y	Y	N
3 **Jones**	N	Y	N	Y	Y	Y
4 Price	N	N	N	N	N	Y
5 **Foxx**	N	Y	Y	Y	Y	N
6 **Walker**	Y	Y	Y	Y	Y	N
7 **Rouzer**	N	Y	Y	Y	Y	N
8 **Hudson**	N	Y	Y	Y	Y	N
9 **Pittenger**	N	Y	Y	Y	Y	N
9 **Vacant**						
10 **McHenry**	Y	Y	Y	Y	Y	N
11 **Meadows**	Y	Y	Y	Y	Y	N
12 Adams	N	N	N	N	N	Y
13 **Budd**	Y	Y	Y	Y	Y	N
NORTH DAKOTA						
AL **Cramer**	Y	Y	Y	Y	Y	N
OHIO						
1 **Chabot**	Y	Y	Y	Y	Y	N
2 **Wenstrup**	N	Y	Y	Y	Y	N
3 Beatty	Y	N	N	N	N	Y
4 **Jordan**	N	Y	Y	Y	Y	N
5 **Latta**	N	Y	Y	Y	Y	N
6 **Johnson**	N	Y	Y	Y	Y	N
7 **Gibbs**	Y	Y	Y	Y	Y	N
8 **Davidson**	Y	Y	Y	Y	Y	N
9 Kaptur	Y	N	N	N	N	Y
10 **Turner**	N	Y	Y	Y	Y	N
11 Fudge	N	N	N	N	N	Y
12 **Vacant**						
13 Ryan	N	N	N	N	N	Y
14 **Joyce**	Y	Y	Y	Y	Y	N
15 **Stivers**	N	Y	Y	Y	Y	N
16 **Renacci**	N	Y	Y	Y	Y	N
OKLAHOMA						
1 **Bridenstine**	Y	Y	Y	Y	Y	N
2 **Mullin**	Y	Y	Y	Y	Y	N
3 **Lucas**	Y	Y	Y	Y	Y	N
4 **Cole**	Y	Y	Y	Y	Y	N
5 **Russell**	Y	Y	Y	Y	Y	N
OREGON						
1 Bonamici	Y	N	N	N	?	Y
2 **Walden**	Y	Y	Y	Y	Y	N
3 Blumenauer	Y	N	N	N	N	Y
4 DeFazio	N	N	N	N	N	Y
5 Schrader	N	N	N	N	N	Y
PENNSYLVANIA						
1 Brady	N	N	N	N	N	Y
2 Evans	Y	N	N	N	N	Y
3 **Kelly**	Y	?	?	?	?	N
4 **Perry**	N	Y	Y	Y	Y	N
5 **Thompson**	N	?	?	?	?	N
6 **Costello**	N	Y	Y	Y	Y	N
7 **Meehan**	N	+	+	+	+	N
8 **Fitzpatrick**	N	Y	Y	Y	Y	N
9 **Shuster**	Y	?	?	?	?	N
10 **Marino**	Y	Y	Y	Y	Y	N
11 **Barletta**	Y	?	?	?	?	N
12 **Rothfus**	Y	?	?	?	?	N
13 Boyle	N	N	N	N	N	Y
14 Doyle	N	N	N	N	N	Y
15 **Dent**	Y	Y	Y	Y	Y	N
16 **Smucker**	Y	Y	Y	Y	Y	N
17 Cartwright	Y	N	N	N	N	Y
RHODE ISLAND						
1 Cicilline	Y	N	N	N	N	Y
2 Langevin	N	N	N	N	N	Y
SOUTH CAROLINA						
1 **Sanford**	Y	Y	Y	Y	Y	N
2 **Wilson**	Y	Y	Y	Y	Y	N
3 **Duncan**	Y	Y	Y	Y	Y	N
4 **Gowdy**	Y	Y	Y	Y	Y	N
5 **Norman**	Y	Y	Y	Y	?	N
6 Clyburn	N	N	N	N	N	Y
7 **Rice**	Y	Y	Y	Y	Y	N
SOUTH DAKOTA						
AL **Noem**	?	?	?	?	?	?
TENNESSEE						
1 **Roe**	Y	Y	Y	Y	Y	N
2 **Duncan**	Y	Y	Y	Y	Y	N
3 **Fleischmann**	Y	Y	Y	Y	Y	N
4 **DesJarlais**	Y	Y	Y	Y	Y	N
5 Cooper	Y	N	N	N	N	Y
6 **Black**	Y	Y	Y	Y	Y	N
7 **Blackburn**	N	Y	Y	Y	Y	N
8 **Kustoff**	Y	Y	Y	Y	Y	N
9 Cohen	N	N	N	N	N	Y
TEXAS						
1 **Gohmert**	N	Y	Y	Y	Y	N
2 **Poe**	?	Y	Y	Y	Y	N
3 **Johnson, S.**	Y	Y	Y	Y	Y	N
4 **Ratcliffe**	N	Y	Y	Y	Y	N
5 **Hensarling**	Y	Y	Y	Y	Y	N
6 **Barton**	Y	Y	Y	Y	Y	N
7 **Culberson**	N	Y	Y	Y	Y	N
8 **Brady**	+	Y	Y	Y	Y	N
9 Green, A.	N	N	N	N	N	Y
10 **McCaul**	Y	Y	Y	Y	Y	N
11 **Conaway**	N	Y	Y	Y	Y	N
12 **Granger**	Y	Y	Y	Y	Y	N
13 **Thornberry**	Y	Y	Y	Y	Y	N
14 **Weber**	Y	Y	Y	Y	Y	N
15 Gonzalez	Y	N	N	N	N	N
16 O'Rourke	Y	N	N	N	N	Y
17 **Flores**	N	Y	Y	Y	Y	N
18 Jackson Lee	N	N	N	N	N	Y
19 **Arrington**	Y	Y	Y	Y	Y	N
20 Castro	?	N	N	N	N	Y
21 **Smith**	Y	Y	Y	Y	Y	N
22 **Olson**	Y	Y	Y	Y	Y	N
23 **Hurd**	N	Y	Y	Y	Y	N
24 **Marchant**	N	Y	Y	Y	Y	N
25 **Williams**	Y	Y	Y	Y	Y	N
26 **Burgess**	N	Y	Y	Y	Y	N
27 **Farenthold**	Y	Y	Y	Y	Y	N
28 Cuellar	Y	N	N	N	N	Y
29 Green, G.	N	N	N	N	N	Y
30 Johnson, E.B.	N	N	N	N	N	Y
31 **Carter**	Y	Y	Y	Y	Y	N
32 **Sessions**	Y	Y	Y	Y	Y	N
33 Veasey	N	N	N	N	N	Y
34 Vela	?	N	N	N	N	Y
35 Doggett	Y	N	N	N	N	Y
36 **Babin**	N	Y	Y	Y	Y	N
UTAH						
1 **Bishop**	Y	Y	Y	Y	Y	N
2 **Stewart**	Y	Y	Y	Y	Y	N
3 **Curtis**	N	Y	Y	Y	Y	N
4 **Love**	Y	Y	Y	Y	Y	N
VERMONT						
AL Welch	Y	N	N	N	N	Y
VIRGINIA						
1 **Wittman**	N	Y	Y	Y	Y	N
2 **Taylor**	Y	Y	Y	Y	Y	N
3 Scott	Y	N	N	N	N	Y
4 McEachin	Y	N	N	N	N	Y
5 **Garrett**	Y	Y	Y	Y	Y	N
6 **Goodlatte**	Y	Y	Y	Y	Y	N
7 **Brat**	Y	Y	Y	Y	Y	N
8 Beyer	N	N	N	+	N	Y
9 **Griffith**	Y	Y	Y	Y	Y	N
10 **Comstock**	Y	Y	Y	Y	Y	N
11 Connolly	N	N	N	N	N	Y
WASHINGTON						
1 DelBene	Y	N	N	N	N	Y
2 Larsen	Y	N	N	N	N	Y
3 **Herrera Beutler**	N	Y	Y	Y	Y	N
4 **Newhouse**	Y	Y	Y	Y	Y	N
5 **McMorris Rodgers**	Y	Y	Y	Y	Y	N
6 Kilmer	N	N	N	N	N	Y
7 Jayapal	N	N	N	N	N	Y
8 **Reichert**	?	Y	Y	Y	Y	N
9 Smith	Y	N	N	N	N	Y
10 Heck	Y	N	N	N	N	Y
WEST VIRGINIA						
1 **McKinley**	N	Y	Y	Y	Y	N
2 **Mooney**	Y	Y	Y	Y	Y	N
3 **Jenkins**	N	Y	Y	Y	Y	N
WISCONSIN						
1 **Ryan**						
2 Pocan	Y	N	N	N	N	Y
3 Kind	?	?	?	?	?	Y
4 Moore	Y	N	N	N	N	Y
5 **Sensenbrenner**	Y	Y	Y	Y	Y	N
6 **Grothman**	Y	Y	Y	Y	Y	N
7 **Duffy**	Y	Y	Y	Y	Y	N
8 **Gallagher**	N	Y	Y	Y	Y	N
WYOMING						
AL **Cheney**	N	Y	Y	Y	Y	N

VOTE NUMBER

32. HR2954. MORTGAGE RECORDS DISCLOSURE/PASSAGE. Passage of the bill that would exempt a depository institution from certain reporting and record-keeping requirements that seek specific information on loans if a depository institution originated a limited number of closed-end mortgage loans or open-end lines of credit in in each of the two preceding calendar years. Passed 243-184: R 234-1; D 9-183. Jan. 18, 2018.

33. HR195. SHORT-TERM FISCAL 2018 CONTINUING APPROPRIATIONS AND CHIP FUNDING/MOTION TO CONCUR. Frelinghuysen, R-N.J., motion to concur in the Senate amendment to the bill with an amendment that would provide funding for federal government operations and services at current levels through Feb. 16, 2018, at an annualized rate of $1.23 trillion for federal departments and agencies covered by the 12 unfinished fiscal 2018 spending bills, of which an annualized rate of $621.5 billion would be designated for defense and an annualized rate of $511 billion for nondefense discretionary spending. The measure would fund the state Children's Health and Insurance Programs at $21.5 billion annually starting in fiscal 2018 and would gradually increase the funding annually through fiscal 2023. It would suspend or delay three health-related taxes enacted as part of the 2010 health care overhaul. It would allow the ballistic missile defense funding included in the last short-term funding bill to be used for certain related intelligence activities. Additionally, it would prohibit the Government Publishing Office from providing a free printed copy of the Federal Register to any member of Congress or other U.S. government office unless a specific issue or a subscription was requested by the member or office. Motion agreed to 230-197: R 224-11; D 6-186. Jan. 18, 2018.

34. HR1660. GLOBAL HEALTH RESEARCH/PASSAGE. Royce, R-Calif., motion to suspend the rules and pass the bill that would require the United States Agency for International Development to submit a report to Congress clarifying its health research and development goals, as well as the development and use of global health innovations in the agency's programs, projects and activities. Motion agreed to 423-3: R 231-3; D 192-0. Jan. 18, 2018.

35. HRES705. ARTICLES OF IMPEACHMENT/MOTION TO TABLE. McCarthy, R-Calif., motion to table (kill) the resolution that would impeach President Donald Trump for high misdemeanors, and would provide that the resolution's articles of impeachment be exhibited to the Senate. Motion agreed to 355-66: R 234-0; D 121-66. Jan. 19, 2018.

36. HR4712. ABORTION PROVISIONS/PASSAGE. Passage of the bill that would require health care practitioners to provide care to an infant born alive during a failed abortion that is equivalent to the care they would provide to any other infant born at the same gestational age. It would impose criminal fines, and penalties of up to five years in prison, for failure to do so, and would provide for a patient in such circumstances to file a lawsuit against the health care provider for certain monetary and punitive damages. The bill would require hospital and clinic practitioners and employees to report any knowledge of failures to provide such care to the appropriate state or federal law enforcement agency, and would permit prosecution of individuals who fail to do so. Passed 241-183: R 235-0; D 6-183. Jan. 19, 2018.

37. PROCEDURAL MOTION/MOTION TO ADJOURN. Hoyer, D-Md., motion to adjourn. Motion rejected 1-418: R 1-231; D 0-187. Jan. 19, 2018.

		32	33	34	35	36	37
ALABAMA							
1	Byrne	Y	Y	Y	Y	Y	N
2	Roby	Y	Y	Y	Y	Y	N
3	Rogers	Y	Y	Y	Y	Y	N
4	Aderholt	Y	Y	Y	Y	Y	N
5	Brooks	Y	Y	Y	Y	Y	N
6	Palmer	Y	Y	Y	Y	Y	N
7	Sewell	N	N	Y	Y	N	N
ALASKA							
AL	Young	Y	Y	Y	Y	Y	N
ARIZONA							
1	O'Halleran	N	N	Y	Y	N	N
2	McSally	Y	Y	Y	Y	Y	N
3	Grijalva	N	N	Y	N	N	?
4	Gosar	Y	N	Y	Y	Y	N
5	Biggs	Y	N	Y	Y	Y	N
6	Schweikert	Y	Y	Y	Y	Y	N
7	Gallego	N	N	Y	Y	N	N
8	Franks						
9	Sinema	N	N	Y	Y	N	N
ARKANSAS							
1	Crawford	Y	Y	Y	Y	Y	N
2	Hill	Y	Y	Y	Y	Y	N
3	Womack	Y	Y	Y	Y	Y	N
4	Westerman	Y	Y	Y	Y	Y	N
CALIFORNIA							
1	LaMalfa	Y	Y	Y	Y	Y	N
2	Huffman	N	N	Y	N	N	N
3	Garamendi	N	N	Y	N	N	N
4	McClintock	Y	Y	Y	Y	Y	N
5	Thompson	N	N	Y	Y	N	N
6	Matsui	N	N	Y	Y	N	N
7	Bera	N	N	Y	Y	N	N
8	Cook	Y	Y	Y	Y	Y	N
9	McNerney	N	N	Y	N	N	N
10	Denham	Y	Y	Y	Y	Y	N
11	DeSaulnier	N	N	Y	N	N	N
12	Pelosi	N	N	Y	Y	N	N
13	Lee	N	N	Y	N	N	N
14	Speier	N	N	Y	Y	N	N
15	Swalwell	N	N	Y	Y	N	N
16	Costa	N	Y	Y	Y	N	N
17	Khanna	N	N	Y	N	N	N
18	Eshoo	N	N	Y	N	N	N
19	Lofgren	N	N	Y	N	N	N
20	Panetta	N	N	Y	Y	N	N
21	Valadao	Y	Y	Y	Y	Y	N
22	Nunes	Y	Y	Y	Y	Y	N
23	McCarthy	Y	Y	Y	Y	Y	N
24	Carbajal	N	Y	Y	Y	N	N
25	Knight	Y	Y	Y	Y	Y	N
26	Brownley	N	N	Y	Y	N	N
27	Chu	N	N	Y	Y	N	N
28	Schiff	N	N	Y	Y	N	N
29	Cardenas	N	N	Y	Y	N	N
30	Sherman	N	N	Y	N	N	N
31	Aguilar	N	N	Y	Y	N	N
32	Napolitano	N	N	Y	N	N	N
33	Lieu	N	N	Y	N	N	N
34	Gomez	N	N	Y	N	N	N
35	Torres	N	N	Y	Y	N	N
36	Ruiz	N	N	Y	Y	N	N
37	Bass	N	N	Y	N	?	?
38	Sánchez, Linda	N	N	Y	Y	N	N
39	Royce	Y	Y	Y	Y	Y	N
40	Roybal-Allard	N	N	Y	Y	N	N
41	Takano	N	N	Y	Y	N	N
42	Calvert	Y	Y	Y	Y	Y	N
43	Waters	N	N	Y	N	N	N
44	Barragan	N	N	Y	N	N	N
45	Walters	Y	Y	Y	Y	Y	N
46	Correa	Y	N	Y	Y	N	N
47	Lowenthal	N	N	Y	N	N	N
48	Rohrabacher	Y	Y	Y	Y	Y	N
49	Issa	Y	Y	Y	Y	Y	?
50	Hunter	Y	Y	Y	Y	Y	N
51	Vargas	N	N	Y	N	N	N
52	Peters	N	N	Y	Y	N	N
53	Davis	N	N	Y	Y	N	N

		32	33	34	35	36	37
COLORADO							
1	DeGette	N	N	Y	Y	N	N
2	Polis	N	N	Y	N	N	N
3	Tipton	Y	Y	Y	Y	Y	N
4	Buck	Y	Y	Y	Y	Y	N
5	Lamborn	Y	Y	Y	Y	Y	N
6	Coffman	Y	Y	Y	Y	Y	N
7	Perlmutter	Y	N	Y	Y	N	N
CONNECTICUT							
1	Larson	N	N	Y	Y	N	N
2	Courtney	N	N	Y	Y	N	N
3	DeLauro	N	N	Y	Y	N	N
4	Himes	N	N	Y	Y	N	N
5	Esty	N	N	Y	Y	N	N
DELAWARE							
AL	Blunt Rochester	N	N	Y	Y	N	N
FLORIDA							
1	Gaetz	Y	N	Y	Y	Y	N
2	Dunn	Y	Y	Y	Y	Y	N
3	Yoho	Y	Y	Y	Y	Y	N
4	Rutherford	Y	Y	Y	Y	Y	N
5	Lawson	N	N	Y	Y	N	N
6	DeSantis	Y	Y	Y	Y	Y	N
7	Murphy	N	N	Y	Y	N	N
8	Posey	Y	Y	Y	Y	Y	N
9	Soto	N	N	Y	Y	N	N
10	Demings	N	N	Y	Y	N	N
11	Webster	Y	Y	Y	Y	Y	N
12	Bilirakis	Y	Y	Y	Y	Y	N
13	Crist	N	N	Y	Y	N	N
14	Castor	N	N	Y	Y	N	N
15	Ross	Y	Y	Y	Y	Y	N
16	Buchanan	Y	Y	Y	Y	Y	N
17	Rooney, T.	Y	Y	Y	Y	Y	N
18	Mast	Y	Y	Y	Y	Y	N
19	Rooney, F.	Y	Y	Y	Y	Y	N
20	Hastings	N	N	Y	N	N	N
21	Frankel	N	N	Y	N	N	N
22	Deutch	N	N	Y	Y	N	N
23	Wasserman Schultz	N	N	Y	Y	N	N
24	Wilson	N	N	Y	N	N	N
25	Diaz-Balart	Y	Y	Y	Y	Y	N
26	Curbelo	Y	Y	Y	Y	Y	N
27	Ros-Lehtinen	Y	N	Y	Y	Y	N
GEORGIA							
1	Carter	Y	Y	Y	Y	Y	N
2	Bishop	N	N	Y	Y	N	N
3	Ferguson	Y	Y	Y	Y	Y	N
4	Johnson	N	N	Y	Y	N	N
5	Lewis	N	N	Y	N	N	N
6	Handel	Y	Y	Y	Y	Y	N
7	Woodall	Y	Y	Y	Y	Y	N
8	Scott, A.	Y	Y	Y	Y	Y	N
9	Collins	Y	Y	Y	Y	Y	N
10	Hice	Y	Y	Y	Y	Y	N
11	Loudermilk	Y	Y	Y	Y	Y	N
12	Allen	Y	Y	Y	Y	Y	N
13	Scott, D.	Y	N	Y	N	N	N
14	Graves	Y	Y	Y	Y	Y	N
HAWAII							
1	Hanabusa	N	N	Y	Y	N	N
2	Gabbard	N	N	Y	Y	N	N
IDAHO							
1	Labrador	Y	Y	Y	Y	Y	N
2	Simpson	Y	Y	Y	Y	Y	N
ILLINOIS							
1	Rush	N	N	Y	N	N	N
2	Kelly	N	N	Y	N	N	N
3	Lipinski	N	N	Y	Y	Y	N
4	Gutierrez	N	N	Y	N	N	N
5	Quigley	N	N	Y	Y	N	N
6	Roskam	Y	Y	Y	Y	Y	N
7	Davis, D.	N	N	Y	?	?	?
8	Krishnamoorthi	N	N	Y	Y	N	N
9	Schakowsky	N	N	Y	N	N	N
10	Schneider	Y	N	Y	Y	N	N
11	Foster	N	N	Y	Y	N	N
12	Bost	Y	Y	Y	Y	Y	N
13	Davis, R.	Y	Y	Y	Y	Y	N

	32	33	34	35	36	37
14 **Hultgren**	Y	Y	Y	Y	Y	N
15 **Shimkus**	Y	Y	Y	Y	Y	N
16 **Kinzinger**	Y	Y	Y	Y	Y	N
17 Bustos	N	N	Y	Y	N	N
18 **LaHood**	Y	Y	Y	Y	Y	N
INDIANA						
1 Visclosky	N	N	Y	Y	N	N
2 **Walorski**	Y	Y	Y	Y	Y	N
3 **Banks**	Y	Y	Y	Y	Y	N
4 **Rokita**	Y	Y	Y	Y	Y	N
5 **Brooks**	Y	Y	Y	Y	Y	N
6 **Messer**	Y	Y	Y	Y	Y	N
7 Carson	N	N	Y	N	N	N
8 **Bucshon**	Y	Y	Y	Y	Y	N
9 **Hollingsworth**	Y	N	Y	Y	Y	N
IOWA						
1 **Blum**	Y	Y	Y	Y	Y	N
2 Loebsack	N	N	Y	Y	N	N
3 **Young**	Y	Y	Y	Y	Y	N
4 **King**	Y	Y	Y	Y	Y	N
KANSAS						
1 **Marshall**	Y	Y	Y	Y	Y	N
2 **Jenkins**	Y	Y	Y	Y	Y	N
3 **Yoder**	Y	Y	Y	Y	Y	N
4 **Estes**	Y	Y	Y	Y	Y	N
KENTUCKY						
1 **Comer**	Y	Y	Y	Y	Y	N
2 **Guthrie**	Y	Y	Y	Y	Y	N
3 Yarmuth	N	N	Y	Y	N	N
4 **Massie**	Y	N	Y	Y	Y	Y
5 **Rogers**	Y	Y	Y	Y	Y	N
6 **Barr**	Y	Y	Y	Y	Y	N
LOUISIANA						
1 **Scalise**	+	+	+	+	+	–
2 Richmond	N	N	Y	N	N	N
3 **Higgins**	Y	Y	Y	Y	Y	N
4 **Johnson**	Y	Y	Y	Y	Y	N
5 **Abraham**	Y	Y	Y	Y	Y	N
6 **Graves**	Y	Y	Y	Y	Y	N
MAINE						
1 Pingree	N	N	Y	N	N	N
2 Poliquin	Y	Y	Y	Y	Y	N
MARYLAND						
1 **Harris**	Y	Y	Y	Y	Y	N
2 Ruppersberger	N	N	Y	Y	N	N
3 Sarbanes	N	N	Y	Y	N	N
4 Brown	N	N	Y	Y	N	N
5 Hoyer	N	N	Y	Y	N	N
6 Delaney	N	N	Y	Y	N	N
7 Cummings	?	?	?	?	?	?
8 Raskin	N	N	Y	N	N	N
MASSACHUSETTS						
1 Neal	N	N	Y	Y	N	N
2 McGovern	N	N	Y	N	N	N
3 Tsongas	N	N	Y	Y	N	N
4 Kennedy	N	N	Y	Y	N	N
5 Clark	N	N	Y	N	N	N
6 Moulton	N	N	Y	N	N	N
7 Capuano	N	N	Y	N	N	N
8 Lynch	N	N	Y	Y	N	N
9 Keating	N	N	Y	Y	N	N
MICHIGAN						
1 **Bergman**	Y	Y	Y	Y	Y	N
2 **Huizenga**	Y	Y	Y	Y	Y	N
3 *Amash*	Y	N	N	Y	Y	N
4 **Moolenaar**	Y	Y	Y	Y	Y	N
5 Kildee	N	N	Y	Y	N	N
6 Upton	Y	Y	Y	Y	Y	N
7 Walberg	Y	Y	Y	Y	Y	N
8 Bishop	Y	Y	Y	Y	Y	N
9 Levin	N	N	Y	Y	N	N
10 Mitchell	Y	Y	Y	Y	Y	N
11 Trott	Y	Y	Y	Y	Y	N
12 Dingell	N	N	Y	Y	N	N
14 Lawrence	N	N	Y	N	N	N
MINNESOTA						
1 Walz	N	N	Y	N	Y	N
2 **Lewis**	Y	Y	Y	Y	Y	N
3 **Paulsen**	Y	Y	Y	Y	Y	N
4 **McCollum**	N	N	Y	N	N	N

	32	33	34	35	36	37
5 Ellison	N	N	Y	N	N	N
6 **Emmer**	Y	Y	Y	Y	Y	N
7 Peterson	N	Y	Y	Y	Y	N
8 Nolan	N	N	Y	Y	N	N
MISSISSIPPI						
1 **Kelly**	Y	Y	Y	Y	Y	N
2 Thompson	N	N	Y	N	N	N
3 **Harper**	Y	Y	Y	Y	Y	N
4 Palazzo	Y	Y	Y	Y	Y	N
MISSOURI						
1 Clay	N	N	Y	N	N	N
2 **Wagner**	Y	Y	Y	Y	Y	N
3 **Luetkemeyer**	Y	Y	Y	Y	Y	N
4 **Hartzler**	Y	Y	Y	Y	Y	N
5 Cleaver	N	N	Y	Y	N	N
6 **Graves**	Y	Y	Y	Y	Y	N
7 **Long**	Y	Y	Y	Y	Y	N
8 **Smith**	Y	Y	Y	Y	Y	N
MONTANA						
AL **Gianforte**	Y	Y	Y	Y	Y	N
NEBRASKA						
1 **Fortenberry**	Y	Y	Y	Y	Y	N
2 **Bacon**	Y	Y	Y	Y	Y	N
3 **Smith**	Y	Y	Y	Y	Y	N
NEVADA						
1 Titus	N	N	Y	N	N	N
2 **Amodei**	Y	Y	Y	Y	Y	N
3 Rosen	N	N	Y	Y	N	N
4 Kihuen	N	N	Y	Y	N	N
NEW HAMPSHIRE						
1 Shea-Porter	N	N	Y	P	N	N
2 Kuster	N	N	Y	Y	N	N
NEW JERSEY						
1 Norcross	N	N	Y	N	N	N
2 **LoBiondo**	Y	Y	Y	Y	Y	N
3 **MacArthur**	Y	Y	Y	Y	Y	N
4 **Smith**	Y	Y	Y	Y	Y	N
5 Gottheimer	N	Y	Y	Y	N	N
6 Pallone	N	N	Y	N	N	N
7 **Lance**	Y	Y	Y	Y	Y	N
8 Sires	N	N	Y	Y	N	N
9 Pascrell	N	N	Y	N	N	N
10 Payne	N	N	Y	N	N	N
11 **Frelinghuysen**	Y	Y	Y	Y	Y	N
12 Watson Coleman	N	N	Y	N	N	N
NEW MEXICO						
1 Lujan Grisham	N	N	Y	Y	N	N
2 **Pearce**	Y	Y	Y	Y	Y	N
3 Luján	N	N	Y	Y	N	N
NEW YORK						
1 **Zeldin**	Y	Y	Y	Y	Y	N
2 **King**	Y	Y	Y	Y	Y	N
3 Suozzi	N	N	Y	Y	N	N
4 Rice	N	N	Y	Y	N	N
5 Meeks	N	N	Y	Y	N	N
6 Meng	N	N	Y	Y	N	N
7 Velázquez	N	N	Y	N	N	N
8 Jeffries	N	N	Y	N	N	N
9 Clarke	N	N	Y	N	N	N
10 Nadler	N	N	Y	Y	N	N
11 **Donovan**	Y	Y	Y	Y	Y	N
12 Maloney, C.	N	N	Y	Y	N	N
13 Espaillat	N	N	Y	N	N	N
14 Crowley	N	N	Y	Y	N	N
15 Serrano	N	N	Y	N	N	N
16 Engel	N	N	Y	N	N	N
17 Lowey	N	N	Y	Y	N	N
18 Maloney, S.P.	N	N	Y	Y	N	N
19 **Faso**	Y	Y	Y	Y	Y	N
20 Tonko	N	N	Y	Y	N	N
21 **Stefanik**	Y	Y	Y	Y	Y	N
22 **Tenney**	Y	Y	Y	Y	Y	N
23 **Reed**	Y	Y	Y	Y	Y	N
24 **Katko**	Y	Y	Y	Y	Y	N
25 Slaughter	N	N	Y	Y	N	N
26 Higgins	N	N	Y	N	N	N
27 **Collins**	Y	Y	Y	Y	Y	N
NORTH CAROLINA						
1 Butterfield	N	N	Y	N	N	N
2 **Holding**	Y	Y	Y	Y	Y	N
3 **Jones**	N	N	N	Y	Y	N
4 Price	N	N	Y	Y	N	N

	32	33	34	35	36	37
5 **Foxx**	Y	Y	Y	Y	Y	N
6 **Walker**	Y	Y	Y	Y	Y	N
7 **Rouzer**	Y	Y	Y	Y	Y	N
8 **Hudson**	Y	Y	Y	Y	Y	N
9 **Pittenger**	Y	Y	Y	Y	Y	N
9 **Vacant**						
10 **McHenry**	Y	Y	Y	Y	Y	N
11 **Meadows**	Y	Y	Y	Y	Y	N
12 Adams	N	N	Y	N	N	N
13 **Budd**	Y	Y	Y	Y	Y	N
NORTH DAKOTA						
AL **Cramer**	Y	Y	Y	Y	Y	N
OHIO						
1 **Chabot**	Y	Y	Y	Y	Y	N
2 **Wenstrup**	Y	Y	Y	Y	Y	N
3 Beatty	N	N	Y	N	N	N
4 **Jordan**	Y	Y	Y	Y	Y	N
5 **Latta**	Y	Y	Y	Y	Y	N
6 **Johnson**	Y	Y	Y	Y	Y	N
7 **Gibbs**	Y	Y	Y	Y	Y	N
8 **Davidson**	Y	Y	Y	Y	Y	N
9 Kaptur	N	N	Y	Y	N	N
10 **Turner**	Y	Y	Y	Y	Y	N
11 Fudge	N	N	Y	?	?	?
12 **Vacant**						
13 Ryan	N	N	Y	Y	N	N
14 **Joyce**	Y	Y	Y	Y	Y	?
15 **Stivers**	Y	Y	Y	Y	Y	N
16 **Renacci**	Y	Y	?	Y	Y	N
OKLAHOMA						
1 **Bridenstine**	Y	?	Y	Y	Y	N
2 **Mullin**	Y	Y	Y	Y	Y	N
3 **Lucas**	Y	Y	Y	Y	Y	N
4 **Cole**	Y	Y	Y	Y	Y	N
5 **Russell**	Y	Y	Y	Y	Y	N
OREGON						
1 Bonamici	N	N	Y	Y	N	N
2 **Walden**	Y	Y	Y	Y	Y	N
3 Blumenauer	N	N	Y	Y	N	N
4 DeFazio	N	N	Y	Y	N	N
5 Schrader	Y	N	Y	Y	N	N
PENNSYLVANIA						
1 Brady	N	N	Y	N	N	N
2 Evans	N	N	Y	N	N	P
3 **Kelly**	Y	Y	Y	Y	Y	N
4 **Perry**	Y	Y	Y	Y	Y	N
5 **Thompson**	Y	Y	Y	Y	Y	N
6 **Costello**	Y	Y	Y	Y	Y	N
7 **Meehan**	Y	Y	Y	Y	Y	N
8 **Fitzpatrick**	Y	Y	Y	Y	Y	N
9 **Shuster**	Y	Y	Y	Y	Y	N
10 **Marino**	Y	Y	Y	Y	Y	N
11 **Barletta**	Y	Y	Y	Y	Y	N
12 **Rothfus**	Y	Y	Y	Y	Y	N
13 Boyle	N	N	Y	Y	N	N
14 Doyle	N	N	Y	Y	N	N
15 **Dent**	Y	Y	Y	Y	Y	N
16 **Smucker**	Y	Y	Y	Y	Y	N
17 Cartwright	Y	N	Y	Y	Y	N
RHODE ISLAND						
1 Cicilline	N	N	Y	Y	N	N
2 Langevin	N	N	Y	Y	N	N
SOUTH CAROLINA						
1 **Sanford**	Y	Y	Y	Y	Y	N
2 **Wilson**	Y	Y	Y	Y	Y	N
3 **Duncan**	Y	Y	Y	Y	Y	N
4 **Gowdy**	Y	Y	Y	Y	Y	N
5 **Norman**	Y	Y	Y	Y	Y	N
6 Clyburn	N	N	Y	Y	N	N
7 **Rice**	Y	Y	Y	Y	Y	N
SOUTH DAKOTA						
AL **Noem**	?	?	?	Y	Y	N
TENNESSEE						
1 **Roe**	Y	Y	Y	Y	Y	N
2 **Duncan**	Y	Y	Y	Y	Y	N
3 **Fleischmann**	Y	Y	Y	Y	Y	N
4 **DesJarlais**	Y	Y	Y	Y	Y	N
5 Cooper	Y	N	Y	Y	N	N
6 **Black**	Y	Y	Y	Y	Y	N
7 **Blackburn**	Y	Y	Y	Y	Y	N
8 **Kustoff**	Y	Y	Y	Y	Y	N
9 Cohen	N	N	Y	N	N	N

	32	33	34	35	36	37
TEXAS						
1 **Gohmert**	Y	Y	N	Y	Y	N
2 **Poe**	Y	Y	Y	Y	Y	N
3 **Johnson, S.**	Y	Y	Y	Y	Y	N
4 **Ratcliffe**	Y	Y	Y	Y	Y	N
5 **Hensarling**	Y	Y	Y	Y	Y	N
6 **Barton**	Y	Y	Y	Y	Y	N
7 **Culberson**	Y	Y	Y	Y	Y	N
8 **Brady**	Y	Y	Y	Y	Y	N
9 Green, A.	N	N	Y	N	N	N
10 **McCaul**	Y	Y	Y	Y	Y	N
11 **Conaway**	Y	Y	Y	Y	Y	N
12 **Granger**	Y	Y	Y	Y	Y	N
13 **Thornberry**	Y	Y	Y	Y	Y	N
14 **Weber**	Y	Y	Y	Y	Y	N
15 Gonzalez	N	Y	Y	Y	N	N
16 O'Rourke	N	N	Y	Y	N	N
17 **Flores**	Y	Y	Y	Y	Y	N
18 Jackson Lee	N	N	Y	N	N	N
19 **Arrington**	Y	Y	Y	?	Y	N
20 Castro	N	N	Y	P	N	N
21 **Smith**	Y	Y	Y	Y	Y	N
22 **Olson**	Y	Y	Y	Y	Y	N
23 **Hurd**	Y	Y	Y	Y	Y	N
24 **Marchant**	Y	Y	Y	Y	Y	N
25 **Williams**	Y	Y	Y	Y	Y	N
26 **Burgess**	Y	Y	Y	Y	Y	N
27 **Farenthold**	Y	Y	Y	Y	Y	N
28 Cuellar	Y	Y	Y	Y	Y	N
29 Green, G.	N	N	Y	Y	N	N
30 Johnson, E.B.	N	N	Y	N	N	N
31 **Carter**	Y	Y	Y	Y	Y	N
32 **Sessions**	Y	Y	Y	Y	Y	N
33 Veasey	N	N	Y	P	N	N
34 Vela	N	N	Y	N	N	N
35 Doggett	N	N	Y	N	N	N
36 **Babin**	Y	Y	Y	Y	Y	N
UTAH						
1 **Bishop**	Y	Y	Y	Y	Y	N
2 **Stewart**	Y	Y	Y	Y	Y	N
3 **Curtis**	Y	Y	Y	Y	Y	N
4 **Love**	Y	Y	Y	Y	Y	N
VERMONT						
AL Welch	N	N	Y	Y	N	N
VIRGINIA						
1 **Wittman**	Y	N	Y	Y	Y	N
2 **Taylor**	Y	Y	Y	Y	Y	N
3 Scott	N	N	Y	Y	N	N
4 McEachin	N	N	Y	Y	N	N
5 **Garrett**	Y	Y	Y	Y	Y	N
6 **Goodlatte**	Y	Y	Y	Y	Y	N
7 **Brat**	Y	Y	Y	Y	Y	N
8 Beyer	N	N	Y	Y	N	N
9 **Griffith**	Y	Y	Y	Y	Y	N
10 **Comstock**	Y	Y	Y	Y	Y	N
11 Connolly	N	N	Y	Y	N	N
WASHINGTON						
1 DelBene	N	N	Y	Y	N	N
2 Larsen	N	N	Y	Y	N	N
3 **Herrera Beutler**	Y	Y	Y	Y	Y	N
4 **Newhouse**	Y	Y	Y	Y	Y	N
5 **McMorris Rodgers**	Y	Y	Y	Y	Y	N
6 Kilmer	N	N	Y	Y	N	N
7 Jayapal	N	N	Y	N	N	N
8 **Reichert**	Y	Y	Y	?	?	?
9 Smith	N	N	Y	Y	N	N
10 Heck	N	N	Y	Y	N	N
WEST VIRGINIA						
1 **McKinley**	Y	Y	Y	Y	Y	N
2 **Mooney**	Y	N	Y	Y	Y	N
3 **Jenkins**	Y	Y	Y	Y	Y	?
WISCONSIN						
1 **Ryan**	Y					
2 Pocan	N	N	Y	N	N	N
3 Kind	Y	N	Y	Y	N	N
4 Moore	N	N	Y	N	N	N
5 **Sensenbrenner**	Y	Y	Y	Y	Y	N
6 **Grothman**	Y	Y	Y	Y	Y	N
7 **Duffy**	Y	Y	Y	Y	Y	N
8 **Gallagher**	Y	Y	Y	Y	Y	N
WYOMING						
AL **Cheney**	Y	Y	Y	Y	Y	N

VOTE NUMBER

38. PROCEDURAL MOTION/CALL OF THE HOUSE. Guthrie, R-Ky., motion to order a call of the House. Motion agreed to 224-150: R 205-0; D 19-150. Jan. 20, 2018.

39. QUORUM CALL/CALL OF THE HOUSE. Quorum was present 0-0: R 0-0; D 0-0. Jan. 20, 2018.

40. VIOLATION OF THE DECORUM OF THE HOUSE/MOTION TO TABLE. Cole, R-Okla., motion to table (kill) the appeal of the ruling of a chair that a Byrne, R-Ala., floor chart does not violate the decorum of the House. Motion agreed to 224-173: R 218-0; D 6-173. Jan. 20, 2018.

41. HRES708. SAME DAY CONSIDERATION AUTHORITY/PREVIOUS QUESTION. Session, R-Texas, motion to order the previous question on the rule (thus ending debate and the possibility for amendment) on the rule (H Res 708) that would waive, through the legislative day of January 29, 2018, the two-thirds vote requirement to consider legislation on the same day it is reported from the House Rules Committee. The rule would also provide for motions to suspend the rules through the calendar day of January 28, 2018. Motion agreed to 224-180: R 224-0; D 0-180. Jan. 20, 2018.

42. HRES708. SAME DAY CONSIDERATION AUTHORITY/RULE. Adoption of the rule (H Res 708) that would waive, through the legislative day of January 29, 2018, the two-thirds vote requirement to consider legislation on the same day it is reported from the House Rules Committee. The rule would also provide for motions to suspend the rules through the calendar day of January 28, 2018. Adopted 235-170: R 222-1; D 13-169. Jan. 20, 2018.

43. PROCEDURAL MOTION/CHANGE CONVENING TIME. Session, R-Texas, motion to change the time that the House would convene for legislative business on Sunday, Jan. 21 to 2 p.m. Motion agreed to 394-0: R 219-0; D 175-0. Jan. 20, 2018.

	38	39	40	41	42	43
ALABAMA						
1 **Byrne**	Y	P	Y	Y	Y	Y
2 **Roby**	Y	P	Y	Y	Y	Y
3 **Rogers**	Y	P	Y	Y	Y	Y
4 **Aderholt**	Y	P	Y	Y	Y	Y
5 **Brooks**	Y	P	Y	Y	Y	Y
6 **Palmer**	Y	P	Y	Y	Y	Y
7 Sewell	N	P	N	N	N	Y
ALASKA						
AL **Young**	?	?	Y	Y	Y	Y
ARIZONA						
1 O'Halleran	?	?	?	?	?	?
2 **McSally**	Y	P	Y	Y	Y	Y
3 **Grijalva**	?	?	N	N	N	Y
4 **Gosar**	Y	P	Y	Y	Y	Y
5 **Biggs**	Y	P	Y	Y	Y	Y
6 **Schweikert**	?	?	Y	Y	Y	Y
7 Gallego	N	P	N	N	N	Y
9 Sinema	Y	P	Y	N	Y	Y
ARKANSAS						
1 **Crawford**	Y	P	Y	Y	Y	Y
2 **Hill**	Y	P	Y	Y	Y	Y
3 **Womack**	Y	P	Y	Y	Y	Y
4 **Westerman**	Y	P	Y	Y	Y	Y
CALIFORNIA						
1 **LaMalfa**	Y	P	Y	Y	Y	Y
2 Huffman	N	P	N	N	N	Y
3 Garamendi	Y	?	N	N	N	Y
4 **McClintock**	Y	P	Y	Y	Y	Y
5 Thompson	N	P	N	N	N	Y
6 Matsui	N	P	N	N	N	Y
7 Bera	Y	P	N	N	Y	Y
8 **Cook**	Y	P	Y	Y	Y	Y
9 McNerney	N	P	N	N	N	?
10 **Denham**	Y	P	Y	Y	Y	Y
11 DeSaulnier	N	P	N	N	N	Y
12 Pelosi	N	P	N	N	N	Y
13 Lee	N	P	N	N	N	Y
14 Speier	N	P	N	N	N	Y
15 Swalwell	N	P	N	N	N	Y
16 Costa	N	P	N	N	N	Y
17 Khanna	N	P	N	N	N	Y
18 Eshoo	N	P	N	N	N	Y
19 Lofgren	P	P	N	N	N	Y
20 Panetta	N	P	N	N	Y	Y
21 **Valadao**	Y	P	Y	Y	Y	Y
22 **Nunes**	Y	P	Y	Y	Y	Y
23 **McCarthy**	Y	P	Y	Y	Y	Y
24 Carbajal	Y	P	N	N	Y	Y
25 **Knight**	Y	P	Y	Y	Y	Y
26 Brownley	N	P	N	N	N	Y
27 Chu	N	?	N	N	N	?
28 Schiff	N	P	N	N	N	Y
29 Cardenas	N	P	N	N	N	Y
30 Sherman	N	P	N	N	N	Y
31 Aguilar	N	P	N	N	N	Y
32 Napolitano	N	P	N	N	N	Y
33 Lieu	P	P	P	N	N	Y
34 Gomez	N	P	N	N	N	Y
35 Torres	N	P	N	N	N	Y
36 Ruiz	Y	P	N	N	N	Y
37 Bass	N	P	N	N	N	Y
38 Sánchez, Linda	N	P	N	N	N	Y
39 **Royce**	Y	P	Y	Y	Y	Y
40 Roybal-Allard	N	P	N	N	N	Y
41 Takano	N	P	N	N	N	Y
42 **Calvert**	Y	P	Y	Y	Y	Y
43 Waters	?	?	N	N	N	?
44 Barragan	N	P	N	N	N	Y
45 **Walters**	Y	P	Y	Y	Y	Y
46 Correa	Y	?	N	N	Y	Y
47 Lowenthal	N	P	N	N	N	Y
48 **Rohrabacher**	Y	P	Y	Y	Y	Y
49 **Issa**	Y	P	Y	Y	Y	Y
50 **Hunter**	Y	P	Y	Y	Y	Y
51 Vargas	?	?	?	?	?	?
52 Peters	N	P	N	N	Y	Y
53 Davis	N	P	N	N	N	Y

	38	39	40	41	42	43
COLORADO						
1 DeGette	N	P	N	N	N	Y
2 Polis	Y	P	N	N	N	Y
3 **Tipton**	Y	P	Y	Y	Y	Y
4 **Buck**	?	?	?	?	?	?
5 **Lamborn**	Y	P	Y	Y	Y	Y
6 **Coffman**	Y	P	Y	Y	Y	Y
7 Perlmutter	N	P	N	N	N	Y
CONNECTICUT						
1 Larson	N	P	N	N	N	Y
2 Courtney	N	P	N	N	N	Y
3 DeLauro	N	P	N	N	N	Y
4 Himes	N	?	N	N	N	Y
5 Esty	N	P	N	N	N	Y
DELAWARE						
AL Blunt Rochester	N	P	N	N	N	Y
FLORIDA						
1 **Gaetz**	Y	P	Y	Y	Y	Y
2 **Dunn**	?	?	Y	Y	Y	?
3 **Yoho**	+	?	+	Y	Y	Y
4 **Rutherford**	Y	P	Y	Y	Y	Y
5 Lawson	N	P	N	N	N	Y
6 **DeSantis**	?	?	?	?	?	?
7 Murphy	Y	P	N	N	N	Y
8 **Posey**	?	?	Y	Y	Y	Y
9 Soto	N	P	N	N	N	Y
10 Demings	N	P	N	N	N	Y
11 **Webster**	?	?	Y	Y	Y	Y
12 **Bilirakis**	Y	P	Y	Y	Y	Y
13 Crist	N	P	N	N	N	Y
14 Castor	?	?	N	N	N	?
15 **Ross**	Y	P	Y	Y	Y	Y
16 **Buchanan**	Y	P	Y	Y	Y	Y
17 **Rooney, T.**	Y	P	Y	Y	Y	Y
18 **Mast**	Y	P	Y	Y	Y	Y
19 **Rooney, F.**	?	?	Y	Y	Y	Y
20 Hastings	N	P	N	N	N	Y
21 Frankel	N	P	N	N	N	Y
22 Deutch	N	P	N	N	N	Y
23 Wasserman Schultz	N	P	N	N	N	Y
24 Wilson	N	P	N	N	N	Y
25 **Diaz-Balart**	Y	P	Y	Y	Y	Y
26 **Curbelo**	?	?	Y	Y	Y	Y
27 **Ros-Lehtinen**	Y	P	Y	Y	Y	Y
GEORGIA						
1 **Carter**	Y	P	Y	Y	Y	Y
2 Bishop	N	P	N	N	N	Y
3 **Ferguson**	Y	P	Y	Y	Y	Y
4 Johnson	N	P	?	N	N	Y
5 Lewis	?	?	N	N	N	Y
6 **Handel**	Y	P	Y	Y	Y	Y
7 **Woodall**	Y	P	Y	Y	Y	Y
8 **Scott, A.**	Y	P	Y	Y	Y	Y
9 **Collins**	Y	P	Y	Y	Y	Y
10 **Hice**	Y	P	Y	Y	Y	Y
11 **Loudermilk**	Y	P	Y	Y	Y	Y
12 **Allen**	Y	P	Y	Y	Y	Y
13 Scott, D.	N	P	N	N	N	Y
14 **Graves**	Y	P	Y	Y	Y	Y
HAWAII						
1 Hanabusa	N	P	N	?	N	Y
2 Gabbard	N	P	N	N	Y	Y
IDAHO						
1 **Labrador**	Y	P	Y	Y	Y	Y
2 **Simpson**	?	?	Y	Y	Y	Y
ILLINOIS						
1 Rush	N	P	N	N	N	Y
2 Kelly	N	P	N	N	N	Y
3 Lipinski	N	P	N	N	N	Y
4 Gutierrez	P	P	N	N	N	?
5 Quigley	N	P	N	N	N	Y
6 **Roskam**	Y	P	?	Y	Y	Y
7 Davis, D.	?	?	?	?	?	?
8 Krishnamoorthi	N	P	N	N	N	Y
9 Schakowsky	N	P	N	N	N	Y
10 Schneider	Y	P	N	N	N	Y
11 Foster	N	P	N	?	N	Y
12 **Bost**	Y	P	Y	Y	Y	Y
13 **Davis, R.**	Y	P	Y	Y	Y	Y

KEY   **Republicans**   Democrats   *Independents*

Y Voted for (yea)	X Paired against	C Voted "present" to avoid possible conflict of interest
# Paired for	– Announced against	
+ Announced for	P Voted "present"	? Did not vote or otherwise make a position known
N Voted against (nay)		

	38	39	40	41	42	43
14 **Hultgren**	Y	P	Y	Y	Y	Y
15 **Shimkus**	Y	P	Y	Y	Y	Y
16 **Kinzinger**	Y	P	Y	Y	Y	Y
17 Bustos	N	P	N	N	N	Y
18 **LaHood**	Y	P	Y	Y	Y	Y
INDIANA						
1 Visclosky	N	P	N	N	N	Y
2 **Walorski**	Y	P	Y	Y	Y	Y
3 **Banks**	Y	P	Y	Y	Y	Y
4 **Rokita**	Y	P	Y	Y	Y	Y
5 **Brooks**	Y	P	Y	Y	Y	Y
6 **Messer**	Y	?	Y	Y	Y	Y
7 Carson	N	P	?	N	N	Y
8 **Bucshon**	Y	P	Y	Y	Y	Y
9 **Hollingsworth**	Y	P	Y	Y	Y	Y
IOWA						
1 **Blum**	Y	P	Y	Y	Y	Y
2 Loebsack	Y	P	N	N	Y	?
3 **Young**	Y	P	Y	Y	Y	Y
4 **King**	Y	P	Y	Y	Y	Y
KANSAS						
1 **Marshall**	Y	P	Y	Y	Y	Y
2 **Jenkins**	+	?	Y	Y	Y	Y
3 **Yoder**	Y	P	Y	Y	Y	Y
4 **Estes**	Y	P	Y	Y	Y	Y
KENTUCKY						
1 **Comer**	Y	P	Y	Y	Y	Y
2 **Guthrie**	Y	P	Y	Y	Y	Y
3 Yarmuth	N	P	N	N	N	Y
4 **Massie**	?	?	?	?	?	?
5 **Rogers**	Y	P	Y	Y	Y	Y
6 **Barr**	Y	P	Y	Y	Y	Y
LOUISIANA						
1 **Scalise**	+	?	+	+	+	+
2 Richmond	N	P	N	N	N	Y
3 **Higgins**	Y	P	Y	Y	Y	Y
4 **Johnson**	Y	P	Y	Y	Y	Y
5 **Abraham**	?	?	?	?	?	?
6 **Graves**	Y	P	Y	Y	Y	Y
MAINE						
1 Pingree	N	P	N	N	N	Y
2 **Poliquin**	Y	P	Y	Y	Y	Y
MARYLAND						
1 **Harris**	Y	P	Y	Y	Y	Y
2 Ruppersberger	?	?	N	N	N	Y
3 Sarbanes	N	P	N	N	N	Y
4 Brown	N	P	N	N	N	Y
5 Hoyer	N	P	N	N	N	Y
6 Delaney	N	P	N	N	N	Y
7 Cummings	?	?	?	?	?	?
8 Raskin	N	P	Y	N	N	Y
MASSACHUSETTS						
1 Neal	N	P	N	N	N	Y
2 McGovern	P	P	Y	N	N	Y
3 Tsongas	N	P	N	N	N	Y
4 Kennedy	N	P	N	N	N	Y
5 Clark	N	P	N	N	N	?
6 Moulton	N	P	N	N	N	Y
7 Capuano	N	P	N	N	N	Y
8 Lynch	N	P	N	N	N	Y
9 Keating	N	P	N	N	N	Y
MICHIGAN						
1 **Bergman**	Y	P	Y	Y	Y	Y
2 **Huizenga**	Y	P	Y	Y	Y	Y
3 *Amash*	Y	P	Y	Y	N	Y
4 **Moolenaar**	Y	P	Y	Y	Y	Y
5 Kildee	Y	P	N	N	N	Y
6 **Upton**	Y	P	Y	Y	Y	Y
7 **Walberg**	Y	P	Y	Y	Y	Y
8 **Bishop**	Y	P	Y	Y	Y	Y
9 Levin	N	P	N	N	N	Y
10 **Mitchell**	Y	P	Y	Y	Y	Y
11 **Trott**	Y	P	Y	Y	Y	Y
12 Dingell	N	P	N	N	N	Y
14 Lawrence	N	P	N	N	N	Y
MINNESOTA						
1 Walz	N	P	N	N	N	Y
2 **Lewis**	Y	P	Y	Y	Y	Y
3 **Paulsen**	Y	P	Y	Y	Y	Y
4 McCollum	N	P	Y	N	N	Y

	38	39	40	41	42	43
5 Ellison	P	P	N	N	N	Y
6 **Emmer**	Y	P	Y	Y	Y	Y
7 Peterson	Y	P	N	N	N	Y
8 Nolan	N	?	N	N	N	Y
MISSISSIPPI						
1 **Kelly**	?	?	?	Y	Y	Y
2 Thompson	N	P	N	N	N	Y
3 **Harper**	Y	P	Y	Y	Y	Y
4 Palazzo	Y	P	?	Y	Y	Y
MISSOURI						
1 Clay	?	?	?	?	?	?
2 **Wagner**	Y	P	Y	Y	Y	Y
3 **Luetkemeyer**	Y	P	Y	Y	Y	Y
4 **Hartzler**	Y	P	Y	Y	Y	Y
5 Cleaver	P	P	N	N	N	Y
6 **Graves**	Y	P	Y	Y	Y	Y
7 **Long**	Y	P	Y	Y	Y	?
8 **Smith**	Y	P	Y	Y	Y	Y
MONTANA						
AL **Gianforte**	Y	P	Y	Y	Y	Y
NEBRASKA						
1 **Fortenberry**	Y	P	Y	Y	Y	Y
2 **Bacon**	Y	P	Y	Y	Y	Y
3 **Smith**	Y	P	Y	Y	Y	Y
NEVADA						
1 Titus	N	P	N	N	N	Y
2 **Amodei**	?	?	Y	Y	Y	Y
3 Rosen	N	P	N	N	Y	Y
4 Kihuen	N	P	N	N	N	Y
NEW HAMPSHIRE						
1 Shea-Porter	Y	P	N	N	N	Y
2 Kuster	N	P	N	N	N	Y
NEW JERSEY						
1 Norcross	N	P	N	N	N	Y
2 **LoBiondo**	Y	P	Y	Y	Y	Y
3 **MacArthur**	Y	P	Y	Y	Y	Y
4 **Smith**	Y	P	Y	Y	Y	Y
5 Gottheimer	Y	P	N	N	Y	Y
6 Pallone	N	P	N	N	N	Y
7 **Lance**	Y	P	Y	Y	Y	Y
8 Sires	N	P	N	N	N	Y
9 Pascrell	N	P	N	N	N	Y
10 Payne	N	P	N	N	N	Y
11 **Frelinghuysen**	Y	P	Y	Y	Y	Y
12 Watson Coleman	N	P	N	N	N	Y
NEW MEXICO						
1 Lujan Grisham	N	P	N	N	–	Y
2 **Pearce**	?	?	Y	Y	Y	Y
3 Luján	N	P	N	N	N	Y
NEW YORK						
1 **Zeldin**	Y	P	Y	Y	Y	Y
2 **King**	?	?	Y	Y	Y	Y
3 Suozzi	N	P	N	N	N	Y
4 Rice	N	P	N	N	Y	Y
5 Meeks	N	P	N	N	N	Y
6 Meng	P	P	N	N	N	Y
7 Velázquez	N	?	N	N	N	Y
8 Jeffries	?	?	?	?	?	Y
9 Clarke	N	P	N	N	N	Y
10 Nadler	N	P	N	N	N	Y
11 **Donovan**	Y	P	Y	Y	Y	Y
12 Maloney, C.	N	P	N	N	N	Y
13 Espaillat	P	P	N	N	N	Y
14 Crowley	N	P	N	N	N	Y
15 Serrano	N	P	N	N	N	Y
16 Engel	N	P	N	N	N	Y
17 Lowey	N	P	N	N	N	Y
18 Maloney, S.P.	N	P	N	N	N	Y
19 **Faso**	Y	P	Y	Y	Y	Y
20 Tonko	N	P	N	N	N	Y
21 **Stefanik**	Y	P	Y	Y	Y	Y
22 **Tenney**	Y	P	Y	Y	Y	Y
23 **Reed**	Y	P	Y	Y	Y	Y
24 **Katko**	Y	P	Y	Y	Y	Y
25 Slaughter	N	P	N	N	N	Y
26 Higgins	?	?	?	?	?	?
27 **Collins**	Y	P	Y	Y	Y	Y
NORTH CAROLINA						
1 Butterfield	N	P	N	N	N	Y
2 **Holding**	Y	P	Y	Y	Y	Y
3 **Jones**	?	?	?	?	?	?
4 Price	N	P	N	N	N	Y

	38	39	40	41	42	43
5 **Foxx**	Y	P	Y	Y	Y	Y
6 **Walker**	Y	P	Y	Y	Y	?
7 **Rouzer**	Y	P	Y	Y	Y	Y
8 **Hudson**	Y	P	Y	Y	Y	Y
9 **Pittenger**	Y	P	Y	Y	Y	Y
9 **Vacant**						
10 **McHenry**	Y	P	Y	Y	Y	Y
11 **Meadows**	Y	P	Y	Y	Y	Y
12 Adams	N	P	N	N	N	Y
13 **Budd**	Y	P	Y	Y	Y	Y
NORTH DAKOTA						
AL **Cramer**	Y	P	Y	Y	Y	Y
OHIO						
1 **Chabot**	Y	P	Y	Y	Y	Y
2 **Wenstrup**	Y	P	Y	Y	Y	Y
3 Beatty	N	P	N	N	N	Y
4 **Jordan**	Y	P	Y	Y	Y	Y
5 **Latta**	Y	P	Y	Y	Y	Y
6 **Johnson**	Y	P	Y	Y	Y	Y
7 **Gibbs**	Y	P	Y	Y	Y	Y
8 **Davidson**	Y	P	Y	Y	Y	Y
9 Kaptur	P	P	N	N	N	Y
10 **Turner**	Y	P	Y	Y	Y	Y
11 Fudge	N	P	N	N	N	Y
12 **Vacant**						
13 Ryan	N	P	N	N	N	Y
14 **Joyce**	Y	P	Y	Y	Y	Y
15 **Stivers**	Y	P	Y	Y	Y	Y
16 **Renacci**	Y	P	Y	Y	Y	Y
OKLAHOMA						
1 **Bridenstine**	?	?	?	?	?	?
2 **Mullin**	Y	P	Y	Y	Y	Y
3 **Lucas**	Y	P	Y	Y	Y	Y
4 **Cole**	Y	P	Y	Y	Y	Y
5 **Russell**	?	?	?	?	Y	Y
OREGON						
1 Bonamici	N	P	N	N	N	Y
2 **Walden**	Y	P	Y	Y	Y	Y
3 Blumenauer	N	P	N	N	N	Y
4 DeFazio	N	P	N	?	N	Y
5 Schrader	Y	P	N	N	N	Y
PENNSYLVANIA						
1 Brady	N	P	N	N	N	Y
2 Evans	N	P	N	N	N	Y
3 **Kelly**	Y	P	Y	Y	Y	Y
4 **Perry**	?	?	Y	Y	Y	Y
5 **Thompson**	Y	P	Y	Y	Y	Y
6 **Costello**	Y	P	Y	Y	Y	Y
7 **Meehan**	?	?	?	?	?	?
8 **Fitzpatrick**	Y	P	Y	Y	Y	Y
9 **Shuster**	Y	P	?	Y	Y	Y
10 **Marino**	Y	P	Y	Y	Y	Y
11 **Barletta**	Y	P	Y	Y	Y	Y
12 **Rothfus**	Y	P	Y	Y	Y	Y
13 Boyle	N	P	?	?	?	?
14 Doyle	N	P	N	N	N	Y
15 **Dent**	Y	P	Y	Y	Y	Y
16 **Smucker**	Y	P	Y	Y	Y	Y
17 Cartwright	N	P	N	N	N	Y
RHODE ISLAND						
1 Cicilline	N	P	Y	N	N	Y
2 Langevin	N	P	N	N	N	Y
SOUTH CAROLINA						
1 **Sanford**	Y	P	Y	Y	Y	Y
2 **Wilson**	Y	P	Y	Y	Y	Y
3 **Duncan**	Y	P	Y	Y	Y	Y
4 **Gowdy**	Y	P	Y	Y	Y	?
5 **Norman**	Y	P	Y	Y	Y	Y
6 Clyburn	N	P	N	N	N	Y
7 **Rice**	Y	P	Y	Y	Y	Y
SOUTH DAKOTA						
AL **Noem**	Y	P	Y	Y	Y	Y
TENNESSEE						
1 **Roe**	Y	P	Y	Y	Y	Y
2 **Duncan**	?	?	Y	Y	Y	Y
3 **Fleischmann**	Y	P	Y	Y	Y	Y
4 **DesJarlais**	Y	P	Y	Y	Y	Y
5 Cooper	Y	P	N	N	N	Y
6 **Black**	Y	P	Y	Y	Y	Y
7 **Blackburn**	?	?	Y	Y	Y	Y
8 **Kustoff**	Y	P	Y	Y	Y	Y
9 Cohen	P	P	P	N	N	Y

	38	39	40	41	42	43
TEXAS						
1 **Gohmert**	?	?	?	Y	Y	Y
2 **Poe**	Y	P	Y	Y	Y	Y
3 **Johnson, S.**	?	?	?	?	?	?
4 **Ratcliffe**	Y	P	Y	Y	Y	Y
5 **Hensarling**	Y	P	Y	Y	Y	Y
6 **Barton**	?	?	?	?	?	?
7 **Culberson**	Y	P	Y	Y	Y	Y
8 **Brady**	Y	P	Y	Y	Y	Y
9 Green, A.	N	P	N	N	N	Y
10 **McCaul**	Y	P	Y	Y	Y	Y
11 **Conaway**	Y	P	Y	Y	Y	Y
12 **Granger**	?	?	?	?	?	?
13 **Thornberry**	Y	P	Y	Y	Y	Y
14 **Weber**	Y	P	Y	Y	Y	Y
15 Gonzalez	N	P	N	N	N	Y
16 O'Rourke	Y	P	N	N	N	Y
17 **Flores**	Y	P	Y	Y	Y	Y
18 Jackson Lee	N	P	N	N	N	Y
19 **Arrington**	Y	P	Y	Y	Y	Y
20 Castro	N	P	N	N	N	Y
21 **Smith**	Y	P	Y	Y	Y	Y
22 **Olson**	Y	P	Y	Y	Y	Y
23 **Hurd**	Y	P	Y	Y	Y	Y
24 **Marchant**	Y	P	Y	Y	Y	Y
25 **Williams**	Y	P	Y	Y	Y	Y
26 **Burgess**	Y	P	Y	Y	Y	Y
27 **Farenthold**	Y	P	Y	Y	Y	Y
28 Cuellar	Y	P	N	N	N	Y
29 Green, G.	?	?	?	?	?	?
30 Johnson, E.B.	?	?	?	?	?	?
31 **Carter**	Y	P	Y	Y	Y	Y
32 **Sessions**	Y	P	Y	Y	Y	Y
33 Veasey	N	P	N	N	N	Y
34 Vela	N	P	N	N	N	Y
35 Doggett	N	P	Y	N	N	Y
36 **Babin**	Y	P	Y	Y	Y	Y
UTAH						
1 **Bishop**	Y	P	Y	Y	Y	Y
2 **Stewart**	Y	P	Y	Y	Y	Y
3 **Curtis**	Y	P	Y	Y	Y	Y
4 **Love**	Y	P	Y	Y	Y	Y
VERMONT						
AL Welch	N	?	N	N	N	?
VIRGINIA						
1 **Wittman**	Y	P	Y	Y	Y	Y
2 **Taylor**	Y	P	Y	Y	Y	Y
3 Scott	N	P	N	N	N	Y
4 McEachin	N	P	N	N	N	Y
5 **Garrett**	Y	P	Y	Y	?	Y
6 **Goodlatte**	Y	P	Y	Y	Y	Y
7 **Brat**	Y	P	Y	Y	Y	Y
8 Beyer	N	P	N	N	N	Y
9 **Griffith**	Y	P	Y	Y	Y	Y
10 **Comstock**	Y	P	Y	Y	Y	Y
11 Connolly	N	P	N	N	N	Y
WASHINGTON						
1 DelBene	N	P	N	N	N	Y
2 Larsen	N	P	N	N	N	Y
3 **Herrera Beutler**	Y	P	Y	Y	Y	Y
4 **Newhouse**	Y	P	Y	Y	Y	Y
5 **McMorris Rodgers**	Y	P	Y	Y	Y	Y
6 Kilmer	N	P	N	N	N	Y
7 Jayapal	N	P	N	N	N	Y
8 **Reichert**	?	?	?	?	?	?
9 Smith	N	P	N	N	N	Y
10 Heck	N	P	N	N	N	Y
WEST VIRGINIA						
1 **McKinley**	Y	P	Y	Y	Y	Y
2 **Mooney**	?	P	Y	Y	Y	Y
3 **Jenkins**	Y	P	Y	Y	Y	?
WISCONSIN						
1 **Ryan**						
2 Pocan	N	P	N	N	N	Y
3 Kind	Y	P	N	N	N	Y
4 Moore	N	P	N	N	N	Y
5 **Sensenbrenner**	Y	P	Y	Y	Y	Y
6 **Grothman**	Y	P	Y	Y	?	?
7 **Duffy**	Y	P	Y	Y	Y	Y
8 **Gallagher**	Y	P	Y	Y	Y	Y
WYOMING						
AL **Cheney**	Y	P	Y	Y	Y	Y

VOTE NUMBER

44. HR195. SHORT-TERM FISCAL 2018 CONTINUING APPROPRIATIONS AND CHIP FUNDING/MOTION TO CONCUR. McCarthy, R-Calif., motion to concur in the Senate amendment to the House amendment to the Senate amendment to the bill that would provide funding for federal government operations and services at current levels through Feb. 8, 2018. The measure would fund the state Children's Health and Insurance Programs at $21.5 billion annually starting in fiscal 2018 and would gradually increase the funding annually through fiscal 2023. It would suspend or delay three health-related taxes enacted as part of the 2010 health care overhaul. It would allow the ballistic missile defense funding included in the last short-term funding bill to be used for certain related intelligence activities. Additionally, it would prohibit the Government Publishing Office from providing a free printed copy of the Federal Register to any member of Congress or other U.S. government office unless a specific issue or a subscription was requested by the member or office. Motion agreed to 266-150: R 221-6; D 45-144. Jan. 22, 2018.

45. S534. ABUSE IN SPORTS/PASSAGE. Poe, R-Texas, motion to suspend the rules and pass the bill that would require adults authorized to interact with minor amateur athletes to report any suspected incidents of child abuse, including sexual abuse, to the sport's governing body, and would set criminal penalties for failure to report such suspected incidents. It would establish the United States Center for Safe Sport as an independent organization with jurisdiction over the United States Olympic Committee and all paralympic sports organizations, in relation to safeguarding amateur athletes against abuse in sports. Motion agreed to 406-3: R 225-3; D 181-0. Jan. 29, 2018.

46. HR1457. ONLINE FINANCIAL SERVICES IDENTIFICATION/PASSAGE. Tipton, R-Colo., motion to suspend the rules and pass the bill that would allow financial institutions to record an individual's personal information from a scan, copy, or image of an individual's driver's license or personal identification card when an individual uses an online service to request a financial product or service. Motion agreed to 397-8: R 219-8; D 178-0. Jan. 29, 2018.

47. HR695. FISCAL 2018 DEFENSE APPROPRIATIONS/PREVIOUS QUESTION. Cheney, R-Wyo., motion to order the previous question (thus ending debate and possibility of amendment) on the rule (H Res 714) that would provide for House floor consideration of the Senate amendment to the bill (HR 695) that is the expected legislative vehicle for a measure that would provide $659.2 billion in discretionary funding for the Defense Department in fiscal 2018. Motion agreed to 232-187: R 232-0; D 0-187. Jan. 30, 2018.

48. HRES714. FISCAL 2018 DEFENSE APPROPRIATIONS/RULE. Adoption of the rule (H Res 714) that would provide for House floor consideration of the Senate amendment to the bill (HR 695) that is the expected legislative vehicle for a measure that would provide $659.2 billion in discretionary funding for the Defense Department in fiscal 2018. Adopted 236-183: R 231-2; D 5-181. Jan. 30, 2018.

49. HR695. FISCAL 2018 DEFENSE APPROPRIATIONS/MOTION TO CONCUR. Granger, R-Texas, motion to concur in Senate amendment to the bill with an amendment that would provide $659.2 billion in discretionary funding for the Defense Department in fiscal 2018. The total would include $584 billion in base Defense Department funding subject to spending caps. It also would include $75.1 billion in overseas contingency operations funding, $1.2 billion of which would be for additional U.S. troops in Afghanistan. The bill would provide approximately $191.7 billion for operations and maintenance and $138.2 billion for military personnel, including a 2.4 percent pay raise. It also would provide $34.3 billion for defense health programs. The measure would prohibit use of funds to construct or modify potential facilities in the United States to house Guantanamo Bay detainees. It would also make permanent a pilot program that allows volunteer groups to obtain criminal history background checks on prospective employees through a fingerprint check using state and federal records, which are the original provisions of the bill. Motion agreed to 250-166: R 227-4; D 23-162. Jan. 30, 2018.

	44	45	46	47	48	49
ALABAMA						
1 Byrne	Y	Y	Y	Y	Y	Y
2 Roby	Y	Y	Y	Y	Y	Y
3 Rogers	Y	Y	Y	Y	Y	Y
4 Aderholt	Y	Y	Y	Y	Y	Y
5 Brooks	Y	Y	Y	Y	Y	Y
6 Palmer	Y	Y	Y	Y	Y	Y
7 Sewell	Y	Y	Y	N	N	N
ALASKA						
AL Young	Y	Y	Y	Y	Y	Y
ARIZONA						
1 O'Halleran	Y	Y	Y	N	N	N
2 McSally	Y	Y	Y	Y	Y	Y
3 Grijalva	N	Y	N	N	N	N
4 Gosar	N	Y	Y	Y	Y	Y
5 Biggs	N	Y	Y	Y	Y	Y
6 Schweikert	Y	Y	Y	Y	Y	Y
7 Gallego	N	?	?	N	N	N
9 Sinema	Y	Y	Y	N	Y	Y
ARKANSAS						
1 Crawford	Y	Y	Y	Y	Y	Y
2 Hill	Y	Y	Y	Y	Y	Y
3 Womack	Y	Y	Y	Y	Y	Y
4 Westerman	Y	Y	Y	Y	Y	Y
CALIFORNIA						
1 LaMalfa	Y	Y	Y	Y	Y	Y
2 Huffman	N	Y	N	N	N	N
3 Garamendi	Y	Y	Y	N	N	Y
4 McClintock	Y	?	?	?	?	?
5 Thompson	N	Y	N	N	N	N
6 Matsui	N	Y	N	N	N	N
7 Bera	Y	Y	Y	N	N	Y
8 Cook	Y	Y	Y	Y	Y	Y
9 McNerney	N	?	?	N	N	N
10 Denham	Y	Y	Y	Y	Y	Y
11 DeSaulnier	N	Y	N	N	N	N
12 Pelosi	N	Y	N	N	N	N
13 Lee	N	Y	N	N	N	N
14 Speier	N	Y	N	N	N	N
15 Swalwell	N	Y	N	N	N	N
16 Costa	Y	Y	Y	N	N	N
17 Khanna	N	Y	N	N	N	N
18 Eshoo	N	Y	N	N	N	N
19 Lofgren	N	Y	N	N	N	N
20 Panetta	N	Y	N	N	N	N
21 Valadao	+	Y	Y	Y	Y	Y
22 Nunes	Y	Y	Y	Y	Y	Y
23 McCarthy	Y	Y	Y	Y	Y	Y
24 Carbajal	N	Y	Y	N	N	Y
25 Knight	Y	Y	Y	Y	Y	Y
26 Brownley	N	Y	?	N	N	Y
27 Chu	N	Y	Y	N	N	N
28 Schiff	N	Y	Y	N	N	N
29 Cardenas	N	?	?	?	?	?
30 Sherman	N	Y	Y	N	N	N
31 Aguilar	N	Y	N	N	N	N
32 Napolitano	N	Y	N	N	N	N
33 Lieu	N	Y	N	N	N	N
34 Gomez	N	Y	N	N	N	N
35 Torres	N	Y	N	N	N	N
36 Ruiz	Y	Y	Y	N	N	Y
37 Bass	N	?	?	N	N	N
38 Sánchez, Linda	N	Y	Y	N	N	N
39 Royce	Y	Y	Y	Y	Y	Y
40 Roybal-Allard	N	Y	N	N	N	N
41 Takano	N	Y	N	N	N	N
42 Calvert	Y	Y	Y	Y	Y	Y
43 Waters	N	Y	N	N	N	N
44 Barragan	N	Y	N	N	N	N
45 Walters	Y	Y	Y	Y	Y	Y
46 Correa	N	Y	N	N	N	N
47 Lowenthal	N	Y	Y	N	N	N
48 Rohrabacher	Y	Y	Y	Y	Y	Y
49 Issa	Y	Y	?	Y	Y	?
50 Hunter	Y	Y	Y	Y	Y	Y
51 Vargas	N	Y	Y	N	N	N
52 Peters	N	Y	Y	N	N	Y
53 Davis	N	Y	Y	N	N	N

	44	45	46	47	48	49
COLORADO						
1 DeGette	N	Y	Y	N	N	N
2 Polis	N	Y	Y	N	N	N
3 Tipton	Y	Y	Y	Y	Y	Y
4 Buck	Y	Y	Y	Y	Y	Y
5 Lamborn	Y	Y	Y	Y	Y	Y
6 Coffman	Y	Y	Y	Y	Y	Y
7 Perlmutter	Y	Y	Y	N	N	N
CONNECTICUT						
1 Larson	Y	Y	Y	N	N	N
2 Courtney	Y	?	?	–	–	–
3 DeLauro	N	Y	N	N	N	N
4 Himes	N	Y	Y	N	N	N
5 Esty	N	Y	Y	N	N	N
DELAWARE						
AL Blunt Rochester	N	Y	Y	N	N	?
FLORIDA						
1 Gaetz	Y	Y	Y	Y	Y	Y
2 Dunn	Y	Y	Y	Y	Y	Y
3 Yoho	Y	Y	Y	Y	Y	Y
4 Rutherford	Y	Y	Y	Y	Y	Y
5 Lawson	Y	Y	Y	N	N	N
6 DeSantis	Y	Y	Y	Y	Y	Y
7 Murphy	Y	Y	Y	N	Y	Y
8 Posey	Y	Y	Y	Y	Y	Y
9 Soto	N	Y	Y	N	N	N
10 Demings	N	Y	Y	N	N	N
11 Webster	Y	Y	Y	Y	Y	Y
12 Bilirakis	Y	Y	Y	Y	Y	Y
13 Crist	Y	Y	Y	N	Y	N
14 Castor	N	Y	Y	N	N	N
15 Ross	Y	Y	Y	Y	Y	Y
16 Buchanan	Y	Y	Y	Y	Y	Y
17 Rooney, T.	Y	Y	Y	Y	Y	Y
18 Mast	Y	Y	Y	Y	Y	Y
19 Rooney, F.	Y	Y	Y	Y	Y	Y
20 Hastings	N	Y	Y	N	N	N
21 Frankel	N	Y	Y	N	N	N
22 Deutch	N	Y	Y	N	N	N
23 Wasserman Schultz	N	Y	Y	N	N	N
24 Wilson	N	Y	Y	N	N	?
25 Diaz-Balart	Y	Y	Y	Y	Y	Y
26 Curbelo	Y	?	?	?	Y	Y
27 Ros-Lehtinen	N	Y	Y	Y	Y	Y
GEORGIA						
1 Carter	Y	Y	Y	Y	Y	Y
2 Bishop	Y	Y	Y	N	N	Y
3 Ferguson	Y	Y	Y	Y	Y	Y
4 Johnson	N	Y	Y	N	N	N
5 Lewis	N	Y	Y	N	N	N
6 Handel	Y	Y	Y	Y	Y	Y
7 Woodall	Y	Y	Y	Y	Y	Y
8 Scott, A.	Y	Y	Y	Y	Y	Y
9 Collins	Y	Y	Y	Y	Y	Y
10 Hice	Y	Y	Y	Y	Y	Y
11 Loudermilk	Y	Y	Y	Y	Y	Y
12 Allen	Y	Y	Y	Y	Y	Y
13 Scott, D.	Y	Y	Y	N	N	N
14 Graves	Y	Y	Y	Y	Y	Y
HAWAII						
1 Hanabusa	Y	Y	Y	N	N	N
2 Gabbard	N	Y	N	N	N	N
IDAHO						
1 Labrador	Y	Y	N	Y	Y	Y
2 Simpson	Y	Y	Y	Y	Y	Y
ILLINOIS						
1 Rush	N	Y	Y	N	N	N
2 Kelly	N	?	?	N	N	N
3 Lipinski	Y	Y	Y	N	N	N
4 Gutierrez	N	?	?	N	N	N
5 Quigley	N	Y	Y	N	N	N
6 Roskam	Y	Y	Y	Y	Y	Y
7 Davis, D.	N	Y	Y	N	N	N
8 Krishnamoorthi	N	Y	Y	N	N	N
9 Schakowsky	N	Y	N	N	N	N
10 Schneider	Y	Y	Y	N	Y	N
11 Foster	N	Y	Y	N	N	N
12 Bost	Y	Y	Y	Y	Y	Y
13 Davis, R.	Y	Y	Y	Y	Y	Y

	44	45	46	47	48	49
14 **Hultgren**	Y	Y	Y	Y	Y	Y
15 **Shimkus**	Y	Y	Y	Y	Y	Y
16 **Kinzinger**	Y	Y	Y	Y	Y	Y
17 Bustos	Y	Y	Y	N	N	Y
18 **LaHood**	Y	Y	Y	Y	Y	Y
INDIANA						
1 Visclosky	N	Y	Y	N	N	N
2 **Walorski**	Y	Y	Y	Y	Y	Y
3 **Banks**	Y	Y	Y	Y	Y	Y
4 **Rokita**	Y	Y	Y	Y	Y	Y
5 **Brooks**	Y	Y	Y	Y	Y	Y
6 **Messer**	Y	Y	Y	Y	Y	Y
7 Carson	–	Y	Y	N	N	N
8 **Bucshon**	Y	Y	Y	Y	Y	Y
9 **Hollingsworth**	Y	Y	Y	Y	Y	Y
IOWA						
1 **Blum**	Y	Y	Y	Y	Y	Y
2 Loebsack	Y	Y	Y	N	N	Y
3 **Young**	Y	Y	Y	Y	Y	Y
4 **King**	Y	Y	Y	Y	Y	Y
KANSAS						
1 **Marshall**	Y	Y	Y	Y	Y	Y
2 **Jenkins**	Y	?	?	Y	Y	Y
3 **Yoder**	Y	Y	Y	Y	Y	Y
4 **Estes**	Y	+	Y	Y	Y	Y
KENTUCKY						
1 **Comer**	Y	Y	Y	Y	Y	Y
2 **Guthrie**	Y	Y	Y	Y	Y	Y
3 Yarmuth	N	Y	Y	N	N	N
4 **Massie**	N	N	N	Y	N	N
5 **Rogers**	Y	Y	Y	Y	Y	Y
6 **Barr**	Y	Y	Y	Y	Y	Y
LOUISIANA						
1 **Scalise**	Y	Y	Y	Y	Y	Y
2 Richmond	N	Y	Y	N	N	N
3 **Higgins**	Y	Y	Y	Y	Y	Y
4 **Johnson**	Y	Y	Y	Y	Y	Y
5 **Abraham**	Y	Y	Y	Y	Y	Y
6 **Graves**	Y	Y	Y	Y	Y	Y
MAINE						
1 Pingree	N	Y	Y	N	N	N
2 **Poliquin**	Y	Y	Y	Y	Y	Y
MARYLAND						
1 **Harris**	Y	Y	Y	Y	Y	Y
2 Ruppersberger	Y	Y	Y	N	N	N
3 Sarbanes	N	Y	Y	N	N	N
4 Brown	N	Y	Y	N	N	N
5 Hoyer	N	Y	Y	N	N	N
6 Delaney	Y	Y	Y	N	N	N
7 Cummings	?	?	?	?	?	?
8 Raskin	N	Y	Y	N	N	N
MASSACHUSETTS						
1 Neal	N	Y	Y	N	N	N
2 McGovern	N	Y	Y	N	N	N
3 Tsongas	N	Y	Y	N	N	N
4 Kennedy	N	?	?	?	?	?
5 Clark	N	Y	Y	N	N	N
6 Moulton	N	Y	Y	N	N	N
7 Capuano	N	Y	Y	N	N	N
8 Lynch	Y	Y	Y	N	N	N
9 Keating	Y	Y	Y	N	N	N
MICHIGAN						
1 **Bergman**	Y	Y	Y	Y	Y	Y
2 **Huizenga**	Y	Y	Y	Y	Y	Y
3 *Amash*	N	N	N	Y	N	N
4 **Moolenaar**	Y	Y	Y	Y	Y	Y
5 Kildee	N	Y	Y	N	N	N
6 Upton	Y	Y	Y	Y	Y	Y
7 Walberg	Y	Y	Y	Y	Y	Y
8 Bishop	Y	Y	Y	Y	Y	Y
9 Levin	N	Y	Y	N	N	N
10 Mitchell	Y	Y	Y	Y	Y	Y
11 Trott	Y	Y	Y	Y	Y	Y
12 Dingell	N	Y	Y	N	N	N
14 Lawrence	N	Y	Y	N	N	N
MINNESOTA						
1 Walz	N	Y	Y	N	N	N
2 **Lewis**	Y	Y	Y	Y	Y	Y
3 **Paulsen**	Y	Y	Y	Y	Y	Y
4 **McCollum**	N	Y	Y	N	N	N

	44	45	46	47	48	49
5 Ellison	N	Y	Y	N	N	N
6 **Emmer**	Y	Y	Y	Y	Y	Y
7 Peterson	Y	Y	Y	N	N	Y
8 Nolan	Y	Y	Y	N	N	N
MISSISSIPPI						
1 **Kelly**	Y	Y	Y	Y	Y	Y
2 Thompson	N	Y	Y	N	N	N
3 **Harper**	Y	Y	Y	Y	Y	Y
4 Palazzo	Y	Y	Y	Y	Y	Y
MISSOURI						
1 Clay	N	Y	Y	N	N	N
2 **Wagner**	Y	Y	Y	Y	Y	Y
3 **Luetkemeyer**	Y	Y	Y	+	+	+
4 **Hartzler**	Y	Y	Y	Y	Y	Y
5 Cleaver	N	Y	Y	N	N	N
6 **Graves**	Y	Y	Y	Y	Y	Y
7 **Long**	Y	Y	Y	Y	Y	Y
8 **Smith**	Y	Y	Y	Y	Y	Y
MONTANA						
AL **Gianforte**	Y	Y	Y	Y	Y	Y
NEBRASKA						
1 **Fortenberry**	Y	Y	Y	Y	Y	Y
2 **Bacon**	Y	Y	Y	Y	Y	Y
3 **Smith**	Y	Y	Y	Y	Y	Y
NEVADA						
1 Titus	N	Y	Y	N	N	N
2 **Amodei**	?	Y	Y	Y	Y	Y
3 Rosen	N	Y	Y	N	N	Y
4 Kihuen	N	Y	Y	N	N	N
NEW HAMPSHIRE						
1 Shea-Porter	N	Y	Y	N	N	N
2 Kuster	Y	Y	Y	N	N	Y
NEW JERSEY						
1 Norcross	N	Y	Y	N	N	N
2 **LoBiondo**	Y	Y	Y	Y	Y	Y
3 **MacArthur**	Y	Y	Y	Y	Y	Y
4 **Smith**	Y	Y	Y	Y	Y	Y
5 Gottheimer	Y	Y	Y	N	Y	Y
6 Pallone	N	Y	Y	N	N	N
7 **Lance**	Y	Y	Y	Y	Y	Y
8 Sires	N	Y	Y	N	N	N
9 Pascrell	N	Y	Y	N	N	N
10 Payne	N	Y	Y	N	N	N
11 **Frelinghuysen**	Y	Y	Y	Y	Y	Y
12 Watson Coleman	N	Y	Y	N	N	N
NEW MEXICO						
1 Lujan Grisham	N	Y	Y	N	N	Y
2 **Pearce**	Y	Y	Y	?	?	Y
3 Luján	N	Y	Y	N	N	N
NEW YORK						
1 **Zeldin**	Y	Y	Y	Y	Y	Y
2 **King**	Y	Y	Y	Y	Y	Y
3 Suozzi	N	Y	Y	N	N	N
4 Rice	Y	Y	Y	N	N	N
5 Meeks	N	Y	Y	N	N	N
6 Meng	N	Y	Y	N	N	N
7 Velázquez	N	Y	Y	N	N	N
8 Jeffries	N	Y	Y	N	N	N
9 Clarke	N	Y	Y	N	N	N
10 Nadler	N	Y	Y	N	N	N
11 **Donovan**	Y	Y	Y	Y	Y	Y
12 Maloney, C.	N	Y	Y	N	N	N
13 Espaillat	N	Y	Y	N	N	N
14 Crowley	N	Y	Y	N	N	N
15 Serrano	N	Y	Y	N	N	N
16 Engel	N	Y	Y	N	N	N
17 Lowey	N	Y	Y	N	N	N
18 Maloney, S.P.	N	Y	Y	N	N	Y
19 **Faso**	Y	Y	Y	Y	Y	Y
20 Tonko	N	Y	Y	N	N	N
21 **Stefanik**	Y	Y	Y	Y	Y	Y
22 **Tenney**	Y	Y	Y	?	?	Y
23 **Reed**	Y	Y	Y	Y	Y	Y
24 **Katko**	Y	Y	Y	Y	Y	Y
25 Slaughter	Y	Y	Y	N	N	N
26 Higgins	N	Y	Y	N	N	N
27 **Collins**	Y	Y	Y	Y	Y	Y
NORTH CAROLINA						
1 Butterfield	N	Y	Y	N	N	N
2 **Holding**	Y	Y	Y	Y	Y	Y
3 **Jones**	?	Y	Y	Y	Y	?
4 Price	N	Y	Y	N	N	N

	44	45	46	47	48	49
5 **Foxx**	Y	Y	Y	Y	Y	Y
6 **Walker**	Y	Y	Y	Y	Y	Y
7 **Rouzer**	Y	Y	Y	Y	Y	Y
8 **Hudson**	Y	Y	Y	Y	Y	Y
9 **Pittenger**	Y	Y	Y	Y	Y	Y
9 **Vacant**						
10 **McHenry**	Y	Y	Y	Y	Y	Y
11 **Meadows**	Y	Y	Y	Y	Y	Y
12 Adams	N	Y	Y	N	N	N
13 **Budd**	Y	Y	Y	Y	Y	Y
NORTH DAKOTA						
AL **Cramer**	Y	Y	Y	Y	Y	Y
OHIO						
1 **Chabot**	Y	Y	Y	Y	Y	Y
2 **Wenstrup**	Y	Y	Y	Y	Y	Y
3 Beatty	N	Y	Y	N	N	N
4 **Jordan**	Y	Y	Y	Y	Y	Y
5 **Latta**	Y	Y	Y	Y	Y	Y
6 **Johnson**	+	Y	Y	Y	Y	Y
7 **Gibbs**	Y	Y	Y	Y	Y	Y
8 **Davidson**	Y	Y	Y	Y	Y	Y
9 Kaptur	Y	Y	Y	N	N	N
10 **Turner**	Y	?	?	Y	Y	Y
11 Fudge	N	Y	Y	N	N	N
12 **Vacant**						
13 Ryan	N	Y	Y	N	N	N
14 **Joyce**	Y	Y	Y	Y	Y	Y
15 **Stivers**	Y	Y	Y	Y	Y	Y
16 **Renacci**	Y	+	+	Y	Y	Y
OKLAHOMA						
1 **Bridenstine**	?	Y	Y	Y	Y	Y
2 **Mullin**	Y	Y	Y	Y	Y	Y
3 **Lucas**	Y	Y	Y	Y	Y	Y
4 **Cole**	Y	Y	Y	Y	Y	Y
5 **Russell**	Y	+	+	Y	Y	Y
OREGON						
1 Bonamici	N	Y	Y	N	N	N
2 **Walden**	Y	Y	Y	Y	Y	Y
3 Blumenauer	N	?	?	–	–	–
4 DeFazio	N	Y	Y	N	N	N
5 Schrader	N	Y	Y	N	N	N
PENNSYLVANIA						
1 Brady	N	Y	Y	N	N	N
2 Evans	N	Y	Y	N	N	N
3 **Kelly**	Y	Y	Y	Y	Y	Y
4 **Perry**	Y	Y	Y	Y	Y	Y
5 **Thompson**	Y	Y	Y	Y	Y	Y
6 **Costello**	Y	Y	Y	Y	Y	Y
7 **Meehan**	Y	Y	Y	Y	Y	Y
8 **Fitzpatrick**	Y	Y	Y	Y	Y	Y
9 **Shuster**	Y	Y	Y	Y	Y	Y
10 **Marino**	Y	Y	Y	Y	Y	Y
11 **Barletta**	Y	Y	Y	Y	Y	Y
12 **Rothfus**	Y	Y	Y	Y	Y	Y
13 Boyle	N	Y	Y	N	N	N
14 Doyle	Y	Y	Y	N	N	N
15 **Dent**	Y	Y	Y	Y	Y	Y
16 **Smucker**	Y	Y	Y	Y	Y	Y
17 Cartwright	Y	Y	Y	N	N	N
RHODE ISLAND						
1 Cicilline	N	Y	Y	N	N	N
2 Langevin	Y	Y	Y	N	N	N
SOUTH CAROLINA						
1 **Sanford**	Y	N	N	Y	Y	N
2 **Wilson**	Y	Y	Y	Y	Y	Y
3 **Duncan**	Y	Y	Y	Y	Y	Y
4 **Gowdy**	Y	Y	Y	Y	Y	Y
5 **Norman**	Y	Y	Y	Y	Y	Y
6 Clyburn	N	Y	Y	N	N	N
7 **Rice**	Y	Y	Y	Y	Y	Y
SOUTH DAKOTA						
AL **Noem**	Y	Y	Y	Y	Y	Y
TENNESSEE						
1 **Roe**	Y	Y	Y	Y	Y	Y
2 **Duncan**	Y	Y	Y	Y	Y	N
3 **Fleischmann**	Y	Y	Y	Y	Y	Y
4 **DesJarlais**	Y	?	?	Y	Y	Y
5 Cooper	Y	Y	Y	N	N	Y
6 **Black**	Y	Y	N	Y	Y	Y
7 **Blackburn**	Y	Y	?	Y	Y	?
8 **Kustoff**	Y	Y	Y	Y	Y	Y
9 Cohen	Y	Y	Y	N	N	N

	44	45	46	47	48	49
TEXAS						
1 **Gohmert**	Y	Y	Y	Y	Y	Y
2 **Poe**	Y	Y	Y	Y	Y	?
3 **Johnson, S.**	Y	Y	Y	Y	Y	Y
4 **Ratcliffe**	Y	Y	Y	Y	Y	Y
5 **Hensarling**	Y	Y	Y	Y	Y	Y
6 **Barton**	?	?	?	Y	Y	Y
7 **Culberson**	Y	Y	Y	Y	Y	Y
8 **Brady**	Y	Y	Y	Y	Y	Y
9 Green, A.	N	Y	Y	N	N	N
10 **McCaul**	Y	Y	Y	Y	Y	Y
11 **Conaway**	Y	Y	Y	Y	Y	Y
12 **Granger**	?	Y	Y	Y	Y	Y
13 **Thornberry**	Y	Y	Y	Y	Y	Y
14 **Weber**	Y	Y	Y	Y	Y	Y
15 Gonzalez	Y	Y	Y	N	N	N
16 O'Rourke	N	Y	Y	N	N	Y
17 **Flores**	Y	Y	Y	Y	Y	Y
18 Jackson Lee	N	Y	Y	N	N	N
19 **Arrington**	Y	Y	Y	Y	Y	Y
20 Castro	N	Y	?	N	N	N
21 **Smith**	Y	Y	Y	Y	Y	Y
22 **Olson**	Y	Y	Y	Y	Y	Y
23 **Hurd**	Y	Y	Y	Y	Y	Y
24 **Marchant**	Y	Y	Y	Y	Y	Y
25 **Williams**	Y	Y	Y	Y	Y	Y
26 **Burgess**	+	Y	N	Y	Y	Y
27 **Farenthold**	Y	Y	Y	Y	Y	Y
28 Cuellar	Y	Y	Y	N	N	N
29 Green, G.	?	Y	Y	N	N	N
30 Johnson, E.B.	?	?	?	?	?	?
31 **Carter**	Y	Y	Y	Y	Y	Y
32 **Sessions**	Y	Y	Y	Y	Y	Y
33 Veasey	N	Y	Y	N	N	Y
34 Vela	N	Y	Y	N	N	N
35 Doggett	N	Y	Y	N	N	N
36 **Babin**	Y	Y	Y	Y	Y	Y
UTAH						
1 **Bishop**	Y	Y	Y	Y	Y	Y
2 **Stewart**	Y	Y	Y	Y	Y	Y
3 **Curtis**	Y	Y	Y	Y	Y	Y
4 **Love**	Y	Y	Y	Y	Y	Y
VERMONT						
AL Welch	N	Y	Y	N	?	N
VIRGINIA						
1 **Wittman**	Y	Y	Y	Y	Y	Y
2 **Taylor**	Y	Y	Y	Y	Y	Y
3 Scott	Y	Y	Y	N	N	N
4 McEachin	N	Y	Y	N	N	N
5 **Garrett**	+	Y	Y	Y	Y	Y
6 **Goodlatte**	Y	Y	Y	Y	Y	Y
7 **Brat**	Y	Y	Y	Y	Y	Y
8 Beyer	N	Y	Y	N	N	N
9 **Griffith**	Y	Y	N	Y	Y	Y
10 **Comstock**	Y	Y	Y	Y	Y	Y
11 Connolly	Y	Y	Y	N	N	N
WASHINGTON						
1 DelBene	Y	Y	Y	N	N	N
2 Larsen	N	Y	Y	N	N	N
3 **Herrera Beutler**	+	Y	Y	Y	Y	Y
4 **Newhouse**	Y	Y	Y	Y	Y	Y
5 **McMorris Rodgers**	Y	Y	Y	Y	Y	Y
6 Kilmer	Y	Y	Y	N	N	N
7 Jayapal	N	Y	Y	N	N	N
8 **Reichert**	Y	Y	Y	Y	Y	Y
9 Smith	N	Y	Y	N	N	N
10 Heck	Y	Y	?	N	N	N
WEST VIRGINIA						
1 **McKinley**	Y	Y	Y	Y	Y	Y
2 **Mooney**	N	Y	Y	Y	Y	Y
3 **Jenkins**	Y	Y	Y	Y	Y	Y
WISCONSIN						
1 **Ryan**						
2 Pocan	N	?	?	N	N	N
3 Kind	N	Y	Y	N	N	N
4 Moore	N	Y	Y	N	N	N
5 **Sensenbrenner**	Y	Y	Y	Y	Y	Y
6 **Grothman**	Y	Y	N	Y	Y	Y
7 **Duffy**	Y	Y	Y	Y	Y	Y
8 **Gallagher**	Y	Y	Y	Y	Y	Y
WYOMING						
AL **Cheney**	Y	Y	Y	Y	Y	Y

VOTE NUMBER

50. HR4292. LIVING WILL REGULATIONS/PASSAGE. Tipton, R-Colo., motion to suspend the rules and pass the bill that would require large financial institutions to submit living will resolutions to federal regulators every two years and would require federal regulators to publicly disclose the assessment framework they use to review the adequacy of resolution plans. Motion agreed to 414-0: R 231-0; D 183-0. Jan. 30, 2018.

51. HR4547. SOCIAL SECURITY REPRESENTATIVE PAYEES/PASSAGE. Brady, R-Texas, motion to suspend the rules and pass the bill that would make the monitoring and selection process for the Social Security Administration's representative payee program more stringent, including preventing those convicted of certain felonious actions from serving as representative payees. It would eliminate the requirement that certain family members serving as representative payees file annual reports. Motion agreed to 396-0: R 225-0; D 171-0. Feb. 5, 2018.

52. PROCEDURAL MOTION/JOURNAL. Approval of the House Journal of Feb. 2, 2018. Approved 232-159: R 145-78; D 87-81. Feb. 5, 2018.

53. HRES726. MEMBER CONDUCT/MOTION TO TABLE. Buck, R-Colo., motion to table (kill) a resolution related to comments made by Rep. Gosar, R-Ariz., on Jan. 30, 2018, and their compliance with the Code of Official Conduct for the House. Motion agreed to 231-187: R 231-0; D 0-187. Feb. 6, 2018.

54. HR4771. FOOD LABELING, MORTGAGE FEES AND SMALL BANK ASSET THRESHOLDS/PREVIOUS QUESTION. Buck, R-Colo., motion to order the previous question (thus ending debate and possibility of amendment) on the rule (H Res 725) that would provide for House floor consideration of the bill (HR 772) that would require the Food and Drug Administration to make various modifications to its menu labeling rules, would provide for consideration of the bill (HR 1153) that would exclude certain fees from limits on points and fees imposed on qualified mortgages, and would provide for consideration of the bill (HR 4771) that would require the Board of Governors of the Federal Reserve System to raise the consolidated asset threshold for certain banks. Motion agreed to 231-188: R 231-1; D 0-187. Feb. 6, 2018.

55. HR1153. FOOD LABELING, MORTGAGE FEES AND SMALL BANK ASSET THRESHOLDS/RULE. Adoption of the rule that would provide for House floor consideration of the bill (HR 772) that would require the Food and Drug Administration to make various modifications to its menu labeling rules, would provide for consideration of the bill (HR 1153) that would exclude certain fees from limits on points and fees imposed on qualified mortgages, and would provide for consideration of the bill (HR 4771) that would require the Board of Governors of the Federal Reserve System to raise the consolidated asset threshold for certain banks. It would waive, through the legislative day of Feb. 9, 2018, the two-thirds vote requirement to consider legislation on the same day it is reported from the House Rules Committee and would also provide for motions to suspend the rules through the legislative day of Feb. 8 or Feb. 9, 2018. Adopted 231-186: R 229-2; D 2-184. Feb. 6, 2018.

	50	51	52	53	54	55
ALABAMA						
1 Byrne	Y	Y	Y	Y	Y	Y
2 Roby	Y	Y	Y	Y	Y	Y
3 Rogers	Y	Y	N	Y	Y	Y
4 Aderholt	Y	Y	Y	Y	Y	Y
5 Brooks	Y	Y	N	Y	Y	Y
6 Palmer	Y	Y	N	Y	Y	Y
7 Sewell	Y	Y	N	N	N	N
ALASKA						
AL Young	Y	Y	N	?	Y	Y
ARIZONA						
1 O'Halleran	Y	Y	N	N	N	N
2 McSally	Y	Y	N	Y	Y	Y
3 Grijalva	Y	Y	N	N	N	N
4 Gosar	Y	Y	N	Y	Y	Y
5 Biggs	Y	Y	N	Y	Y	Y
6 Schweikert	Y	Y	Y	Y	Y	Y
7 Gallego	Y	Y	N	N	N	N
9 Sinema	Y	Y	N	N	N	Y
ARKANSAS						
1 Crawford	Y	Y	Y	Y	Y	Y
2 Hill	Y	Y	N	Y	Y	Y
3 Womack	Y	Y	Y	Y	Y	Y
4 Westerman	Y	Y	Y	Y	Y	Y
CALIFORNIA						
1 LaMalfa	Y	Y	Y	Y	Y	Y
2 Huffman	Y	Y	N	N	N	N
3 Garamendi	Y	Y	Y	N	N	N
4 McClintock	?	Y	Y	Y	Y	Y
5 Thompson	Y	Y	N	N	N	N
6 Matsui	Y	Y	N	N	N	N
7 Bera	Y	Y	N	N	N	N
8 Cook	Y	Y	Y	Y	Y	Y
9 McNerney	Y	Y	N	N	N	N
10 Denham	+	Y	N	Y	N	Y
11 DeSaulnier	Y	Y	Y	N	N	N
12 Pelosi	Y	Y	N	N	N	N
13 Lee	Y	?	?	N	N	N
14 Speier	Y	Y	N	N	N	N
15 Swalwell	Y	Y	Y	N	N	N
16 Costa	Y	Y	N	N	N	N
17 Khanna	Y	Y	N	N	N	N
18 Eshoo	Y	Y	N	N	N	N
19 Lofgren	Y	Y	N	N	N	N
20 Panetta	Y	Y	Y	N	N	N
21 Valadao	Y	Y	N	Y	Y	Y
22 Nunes	Y	Y	Y	Y	Y	Y
23 McCarthy	Y	Y	Y	Y	Y	Y
24 Carbajal	Y	Y	N	N	N	N
25 Knight	Y	Y	N	Y	Y	Y
26 Brownley	?	Y	N	N	N	N
27 Chu	Y	Y	Y	N	N	?
28 Schiff	Y	Y	Y	N	N	N
29 Cardenas	?	Y	N	N	N	N
30 Sherman	Y	Y	Y	N	N	N
31 Aguilar	Y	Y	N	N	N	N
32 Napolitano	Y	Y	N	N	N	N
33 Lieu	Y	Y	N	N	N	N
34 Gomez	Y	Y	N	N	N	N
35 Torres	Y	Y	Y	N	N	N
36 Ruiz	Y	Y	N	N	N	N
37 Bass	Y	Y	N	N	N	N
38 Sánchez, Linda	Y	Y	N	N	N	N
39 Royce	Y	Y	Y	Y	Y	Y
40 Roybal-Allard	Y	Y	N	N	N	N
41 Takano	Y	Y	N	N	N	N
42 Calvert	Y	Y	Y	Y	Y	Y
43 Waters	Y	Y	N	N	N	N
44 Barragan	Y	Y	N	N	N	N
45 Walters	Y	Y	Y	Y	Y	Y
46 Correa	Y	Y	N	N	N	N
47 Lowenthal	Y	Y	N	N	N	N
48 Rohrabacher	Y	Y	Y	Y	Y	Y
49 Issa	?	Y	Y	Y	Y	Y
50 Hunter	Y	Y	Y	Y	Y	Y
51 Vargas	Y	?	?	N	N	N
52 Peters	Y	Y	Y	N	N	N
53 Davis	Y	Y	Y	N	N	N

	50	51	52	53	54	55
COLORADO						
1 DeGette	Y	Y	Y	N	N	N
2 Polis	Y	Y	Y	N	N	N
3 Tipton	Y	Y	N	Y	Y	Y
4 Buck	Y	Y	N	Y	Y	Y
5 Lamborn	Y	Y	Y	Y	Y	Y
6 Coffman	Y	Y	Y	Y	Y	Y
7 Perlmutter	Y	Y	N	N	N	N
CONNECTICUT						
1 Larson	Y	Y	N	N	N	N
2 Courtney	+	Y	N	N	N	N
3 DeLauro	Y	Y	N	N	N	N
4 Himes	Y	Y	N	N	N	N
5 Esty	Y	Y	N	N	N	N
DELAWARE						
AL Blunt Rochester	Y	Y	Y	N	N	N
FLORIDA						
1 Gaetz	Y	Y	N	Y	Y	Y
2 Dunn	Y	Y	Y	Y	Y	Y
3 Yoho	Y	Y	Y	Y	Y	Y
4 Rutherford	Y	Y	Y	Y	Y	Y
5 Lawson	Y	Y	N	N	N	N
6 DeSantis	Y	Y	N	Y	Y	Y
7 Murphy	Y	Y	N	N	N	N
8 Posey	Y	Y	N	N	N	N
9 Soto	Y	Y	N	N	N	N
10 Demings	Y	Y	N	N	N	N
11 Webster	Y	Y	Y	Y	Y	Y
12 Bilirakis	Y	Y	Y	Y	Y	Y
13 Crist	Y	Y	N	N	N	N
14 Castor	Y	Y	N	N	N	N
15 Ross	Y	Y	Y	Y	Y	Y
16 Buchanan	Y	Y	Y	Y	Y	Y
17 Rooney, T.	Y	Y	Y	?	?	?
18 Mast	Y	Y	N	Y	Y	Y
19 Rooney, F.	Y	Y	Y	Y	Y	Y
20 Hastings	Y	Y	N	N	N	N
21 Frankel	Y	Y	N	N	N	N
22 Deutch	Y	Y	N	N	N	N
23 Wasserman Schultz	Y	Y	N	N	N	N
24 Wilson	?	?	?	?	?	?
25 Diaz-Balart	Y	Y	N	Y	Y	Y
26 Curbelo	Y	Y	Y	Y	Y	Y
27 Ros-Lehtinen	Y	Y	N	Y	Y	Y
GEORGIA						
1 Carter	Y	Y	N	Y	Y	Y
2 Bishop	Y	Y	N	N	N	N
3 Ferguson	Y	Y	Y	Y	Y	Y
4 Johnson	Y	Y	Y	N	N	N
5 Lewis	Y	Y	N	N	N	N
6 Handel	Y	Y	Y	Y	Y	Y
7 Woodall	Y	Y	N	Y	Y	Y
8 Scott, A.	Y	Y	Y	Y	Y	Y
9 Collins	Y	Y	Y	Y	Y	Y
10 Hice	Y	Y	N	Y	Y	Y
11 Loudermilk	Y	Y	Y	Y	Y	Y
12 Allen	Y	Y	Y	Y	Y	Y
13 Scott, D.	?	Y	Y	N	N	N
14 Graves	Y	Y	N	Y	Y	Y
HAWAII						
1 Hanabusa	Y	Y	Y	N	N	N
2 Gabbard	Y	Y	Y	N	N	N
IDAHO						
1 Labrador	Y	?	?	Y	Y	Y
2 Simpson	Y	Y	Y	Y	Y	Y
ILLINOIS						
1 Rush	Y	?	?	N	N	N
2 Kelly	?	Y	Y	N	N	N
3 Lipinski	Y	Y	Y	N	N	N
4 Gutierrez	Y	+	-	-	-	-
5 Quigley	Y	Y	Y	N	N	N
6 Roskam	Y	Y	N	Y	Y	Y
7 Davis, D.	Y	?	?	N	N	N
8 Krishnamoorthi	Y	Y	Y	N	N	N
9 Schakowsky	Y	Y	N	N	N	N
10 Schneider	Y	Y	Y	N	N	N
11 Foster	Y	Y	N	N	N	N
12 Bost	Y	Y	N	Y	Y	Y
13 Davis, R.	Y	Y	Y	Y	Y	Y

KEY	Republicans	Democrats	Independents
Y Voted for (yea)	**X** Paired against	**C** Voted "present" to avoid possible conflict of interest
# Paired for	**–** Announced against	
+ Announced for	**P** Voted "present"	**?** Did not vote or otherwise make a position known
N Voted against (nay)		

	50	51	52	53	54	55
14 **Hultgren**	Y	Y	Y	Y	Y	Y
15 **Shimkus**	Y	Y	Y	Y	Y	Y
16 **Kinzinger**	Y	Y	N	Y	Y	Y
17 Bustos	Y	Y	Y	N	N	N
18 **LaHood**	Y	Y	N	Y	Y	Y
INDIANA						
1 Visclosky	Y	Y	N	N	N	N
2 **Walorski**	Y	Y	Y	Y	Y	Y
3 **Banks**	Y	Y	Y	Y	Y	Y
4 **Rokita**	Y	Y	Y	Y	Y	Y
5 **Brooks**	Y	Y	Y	Y	Y	Y
6 **Messer**	Y	Y	?	Y	Y	Y
7 Carson	Y	Y	N	N	N	N
8 **Bucshon**	Y	Y	Y	Y	Y	Y
9 **Hollingsworth**	Y	Y	Y	Y	Y	Y
IOWA						
1 **Blum**	Y	?	?	Y	Y	Y
2 Loebsack	Y	Y	N	N	N	N
3 **Young**	Y	Y	Y	Y	Y	Y
4 **King**	Y	Y	Y	Y	Y	Y
KANSAS						
1 **Marshall**	Y	Y	Y	Y	Y	Y
2 **Jenkins**	Y	Y	N	Y	Y	Y
3 **Yoder**	Y	Y	N	Y	Y	Y
4 **Estes**	Y	Y	Y	Y	Y	Y
KENTUCKY						
1 **Comer**	Y	Y	Y	Y	Y	Y
2 **Guthrie**	Y	Y	Y	Y	Y	Y
3 Yarmuth	Y	?	?	N	N	N
4 **Massie**	Y	Y	Y	Y	N	N
5 **Rogers**	Y	Y	Y	Y	Y	Y
6 **Barr**	Y	Y	Y	Y	Y	Y
LOUISIANA						
1 **Scalise**	Y	Y	Y	Y	Y	Y
2 Richmond	Y	Y	N	N	N	N
3 **Higgins**	Y	Y	Y	Y	Y	Y
4 **Johnson**	Y	?	?	?	?	?
5 **Abraham**	Y	Y	Y	Y	Y	Y
6 **Graves**	Y	Y	N	Y	Y	Y
MAINE						
1 Pingree	Y	Y	Y	N	N	N
2 Poliquin	Y	Y	N	Y	Y	Y
MARYLAND						
1 **Harris**	Y	Y	Y	Y	Y	Y
2 Ruppersberger	Y	Y	Y	N	N	N
3 Sarbanes	Y	Y	N	N	N	N
4 Brown	Y	Y	Y	N	N	N
5 Hoyer	Y	Y	Y	N	N	N
6 Delaney	Y	Y	N	N	N	N
7 Cummings	?	?	?	?	?	?
8 Raskin	Y	Y	N	N	N	N
MASSACHUSETTS						
1 Neal	Y	Y	N	N	N	N
2 McGovern	Y	Y	N	N	N	N
3 Tsongas	Y	Y	?	N	N	N
4 Kennedy	?	Y	Y	N	N	N
5 Clark	Y	Y	N	N	N	N
6 Moulton	Y	Y	Y	N	N	N
7 Capuano	Y	Y	Y	N	N	N
8 Lynch	Y	Y	Y	N	N	N
9 Keating	Y	Y	N	N	N	N
MICHIGAN						
1 **Bergman**	Y	Y	N	Y	Y	Y
2 **Huizenga**	Y	Y	N	Y	Y	Y
3 *Amash*	Y	Y	N	Y	Y	N
4 **Moolenaar**	Y	Y	Y	Y	Y	Y
5 Kildee	Y	Y	Y	N	N	N
6 Upton	Y	Y	N	Y	Y	Y
7 Walberg	Y	Y	Y	Y	Y	Y
8 Bishop	Y	Y	N	Y	Y	Y
9 Levin	Y	Y	N	N	N	N
10 Mitchell	Y	Y	Y	Y	Y	Y
11 Trott	Y	Y	Y	Y	Y	Y
12 Dingell	Y	?	?	N	N	N
14 Lawrence	Y	Y	Y	N	N	N
MINNESOTA						
1 Walz	Y	+	?	?	?	?
2 **Lewis**	Y	Y	Y	Y	Y	Y
3 **Paulsen**	Y	Y	N	Y	Y	Y
4 **McCollum**	Y	Y	Y	N	N	N

	50	51	52	53	54	55
5 Ellison	Y	Y	Y	N	N	N
6 **Emmer**	Y	Y	N	Y	Y	Y
7 Peterson	Y	Y	N	N	N	N
8 Nolan	Y	?	?	N	N	N
MISSISSIPPI						
1 **Kelly**	Y	Y	Y	Y	Y	Y
2 Thompson	Y	Y	N	N	N	N
3 **Harper**	Y	Y	Y	Y	Y	Y
4 Palazzo	Y	?	?	?	?	?
MISSOURI						
1 Clay	Y	?	?	?	?	?
2 **Wagner**	Y	Y	Y	Y	Y	Y
3 **Luetkemeyer**	+	Y	Y	Y	Y	Y
4 **Hartzler**	Y	Y	Y	Y	Y	Y
5 Cleaver	Y	Y	Y	N	N	N
6 **Graves**	Y	Y	N	Y	Y	Y
7 **Long**	Y	Y	Y	Y	Y	Y
8 **Smith**	Y	Y	Y	Y	Y	Y
MONTANA						
AL **Gianforte**	Y	Y	Y	Y	Y	Y
NEBRASKA						
1 **Fortenberry**	Y	Y	Y	Y	Y	Y
2 **Bacon**	Y	Y	Y	Y	Y	Y
3 **Smith**	Y	Y	Y	Y	Y	Y
NEVADA						
1 Titus	Y	Y	Y	N	N	N
2 **Amodei**	Y	Y	Y	Y	Y	Y
3 Rosen	Y	+	–	N	N	N
4 Kihuen	Y	Y	N	N	N	N
NEW HAMPSHIRE						
1 Shea-Porter	Y	Y	Y	N	N	N
2 Kuster	Y	Y	Y	N	N	N
NEW JERSEY						
1 Norcross	Y	Y	N	N	N	N
2 **LoBiondo**	Y	Y	N	Y	Y	Y
3 **MacArthur**	Y	Y	N	Y	Y	?
4 **Smith**	Y	Y	Y	Y	Y	Y
5 Gottheimer	Y	Y	N	N	N	Y
6 Pallone	Y	Y	N	N	N	N
7 **Lance**	Y	Y	N	Y	Y	Y
8 Sires	Y	?	?	N	N	N
9 Pascrell	Y	Y	Y	N	N	N
10 Payne	Y	Y	N	N	N	N
11 **Frelinghuysen**	Y	Y	Y	Y	Y	Y
12 Watson Coleman	Y	Y	N	N	N	N
NEW MEXICO						
1 Lujan Grisham	Y	Y	Y	N	N	N
2 **Pearce**	Y	?	?	?	?	?
3 Luján	Y	Y	Y	N	N	N
NEW YORK						
1 **Zeldin**	Y	Y	N	Y	Y	Y
2 **King**	Y	Y	Y	Y	Y	Y
3 Suozzi	Y	Y	N	N	N	N
4 Rice	Y	Y	Y	N	N	N
5 Meeks	Y	?	?	N	N	N
6 Meng	Y	?	?	N	N	N
7 Velázquez	Y	Y	N	N	N	N
8 Jeffries	Y	Y	Y	N	N	N
9 Clarke	Y	Y	N	N	N	N
10 Nadler	Y	Y	Y	N	N	N
11 **Donovan**	Y	Y	Y	Y	Y	Y
12 Maloney, C.	Y	Y	Y	N	N	N
13 Espaillat	Y	Y	N	N	N	N
14 Crowley	Y	Y	N	N	N	N
15 Serrano	Y	Y	N	N	N	N
16 Engel	Y	?	?	N	N	N
17 Lowey	Y	Y	Y	N	N	N
18 Maloney, S.P.	Y	Y	N	N	N	N
19 **Faso**	Y	Y	N	Y	Y	Y
20 Tonko	Y	Y	P	N	N	N
21 **Stefanik**	Y	Y	Y	Y	Y	Y
22 **Tenney**	Y	Y	N	Y	Y	Y
23 **Reed**	Y	Y	N	Y	Y	Y
24 **Katko**	Y	Y	N	Y	Y	Y
25 Slaughter	Y	Y	N	N	N	N
26 Higgins	Y	Y	Y	N	N	N
27 **Collins**	Y	Y	Y	Y	Y	Y
NORTH CAROLINA						
1 Butterfield	Y	Y	Y	N	N	N
2 **Holding**	Y	Y	N	Y	Y	Y
3 **Jones**	?	Y	N	Y	Y	Y
4 Price	Y	Y	N	N	N	N

	50	51	52	53	54	55
5 **Foxx**	Y	Y	N	Y	Y	Y
6 **Walker**	Y	Y	Y	Y	Y	Y
7 **Rouzer**	Y	Y	N	Y	Y	Y
8 **Hudson**	Y	Y	N	Y	Y	Y
9 **Pittenger**	Y	Y	N	Y	Y	Y
9 **Vacant**						
10 **McHenry**	Y	Y	Y	Y	Y	Y
11 **Meadows**	Y	Y	Y	Y	Y	Y
12 Adams	Y	Y	N	N	N	N
13 **Budd**	Y	Y	Y	Y	Y	Y
NORTH DAKOTA						
AL **Cramer**	Y	Y	Y	Y	Y	Y
OHIO						
1 **Chabot**	Y	Y	Y	Y	Y	Y
2 **Wenstrup**	Y	Y	Y	Y	Y	Y
3 Beatty	Y	Y	N	N	N	N
4 **Jordan**	Y	Y	N	Y	Y	Y
5 **Latta**	Y	Y	N	Y	Y	Y
6 **Johnson**	Y	?	?	Y	Y	Y
7 **Gibbs**	Y	Y	N	Y	Y	Y
8 **Davidson**	Y	Y	Y	Y	Y	Y
9 Kaptur	Y	?	?	N	N	N
10 **Turner**	Y	Y	N	Y	Y	Y
11 Fudge	Y	Y	N	N	N	N
12 **Vacant**						
13 Ryan	Y	Y	N	N	N	N
14 **Joyce**	Y	Y	Y	Y	Y	Y
15 **Stivers**	Y	Y	N	Y	Y	Y
16 **Renacci**	Y	Y	N	Y	Y	Y
OKLAHOMA						
1 **Bridenstine**	Y	Y	Y	?	?	?
2 **Mullin**	Y	Y	Y	Y	Y	Y
3 **Lucas**	Y	Y	Y	Y	Y	Y
4 **Cole**	Y	+	+	Y	Y	Y
5 **Russell**	Y	Y	Y	Y	Y	Y
OREGON						
1 Bonamici	Y	Y	Y	N	N	N
2 **Walden**	Y	Y	Y	Y	Y	Y
3 Blumenauer	+	Y	Y	N	N	N
4 DeFazio	Y	Y	N	N	N	N
5 Schrader	Y	Y	N	N	N	N
PENNSYLVANIA						
1 Brady	Y	Y	N	N	N	N
2 Evans	Y	Y	N	N	N	N
3 **Kelly**	Y	Y	Y	Y	Y	Y
4 **Perry**	Y	Y	N	Y	Y	Y
5 **Thompson**	Y	Y	N	Y	Y	Y
6 **Costello**	Y	Y	N	Y	Y	Y
7 **Meehan**	Y	Y	N	Y	Y	Y
8 **Fitzpatrick**	Y	Y	N	Y	Y	Y
9 **Shuster**	Y	?	?	Y	Y	Y
10 **Marino**	Y	Y	Y	Y	Y	Y
11 **Barletta**	Y	Y	Y	Y	Y	Y
12 **Rothfus**	Y	Y	Y	Y	Y	Y
13 Boyle	Y	Y	N	N	N	N
14 Doyle	Y	Y	N	N	N	N
15 **Dent**	Y	Y	Y	Y	Y	Y
16 **Smucker**	Y	Y	Y	Y	Y	Y
17 Cartwright	Y	Y	Y	N	N	N
RHODE ISLAND						
1 Cicilline	Y	Y	Y	N	N	N
2 Langevin	Y	Y	N	N	N	N
SOUTH CAROLINA						
1 **Sanford**	Y	Y	Y	Y	Y	Y
2 **Wilson**	Y	Y	Y	Y	Y	Y
3 **Duncan**	Y	Y	Y	Y	Y	Y
4 **Gowdy**	Y	Y	Y	Y	Y	Y
5 **Norman**	Y	Y	Y	Y	Y	Y
6 Clyburn	Y	Y	Y	N	N	N
7 **Rice**	Y	Y	Y	Y	Y	Y
SOUTH DAKOTA						
AL **Noem**	Y	Y	Y	Y	Y	Y
TENNESSEE						
1 **Roe**	Y	Y	Y	Y	Y	Y
2 **Duncan**	Y	?	?	Y	Y	Y
3 **Fleischmann**	Y	Y	Y	Y	Y	Y
4 **DesJarlais**	Y	Y	Y	Y	Y	Y
5 Cooper	Y	Y	Y	N	N	N
6 **Black**	Y	+	?	Y	Y	Y
7 **Blackburn**	?	Y	N	Y	Y	Y
8 **Kustoff**	Y	Y	Y	Y	Y	Y
9 Cohen	Y	+	–	N	N	N

	50	51	52	53	54	55
TEXAS						
1 **Gohmert**	Y	Y	N	Y	Y	Y
2 **Poe**	Y	Y	N	Y	Y	Y
3 **Johnson, S.**	Y	Y	Y	Y	Y	Y
4 **Ratcliffe**	Y	Y	N	Y	Y	Y
5 **Hensarling**	Y	Y	Y	Y	Y	Y
6 **Barton**	Y	Y	Y	Y	Y	Y
7 **Culberson**	Y	Y	Y	Y	Y	Y
8 **Brady**	Y	Y	Y	Y	Y	Y
9 Green, A.	Y	Y	N	N	N	N
10 **McCaul**	Y	Y	Y	Y	Y	Y
11 **Conaway**	Y	Y	N	Y	Y	Y
12 **Granger**	Y	Y	Y	Y	Y	Y
13 **Thornberry**	Y	Y	Y	Y	Y	Y
14 **Weber**	Y	Y	N	Y	Y	Y
15 Gonzalez	Y	+	–	N	N	N
16 O'Rourke	Y	+	+	N	N	N
17 **Flores**	Y	Y	N	Y	Y	Y
18 Jackson Lee	Y	Y	N	N	N	N
19 **Arrington**	Y	Y	Y	Y	Y	Y
20 Castro	Y	Y	Y	N	N	N
21 **Smith**	Y	Y	Y	Y	Y	Y
22 **Olson**	Y	Y	Y	Y	Y	Y
23 **Hurd**	Y	Y	N	Y	Y	Y
24 **Marchant**	Y	Y	Y	Y	Y	Y
25 **Williams**	Y	Y	Y	Y	Y	Y
26 **Burgess**	Y	Y	?	Y	Y	Y
27 **Farenthold**	Y	Y	N	Y	Y	Y
28 Cuellar	Y	Y	N	N	N	N
29 Green, G.	Y	Y	N	N	N	N
30 Johnson, E.B.	?	Y	Y	N	N	N
31 **Carter**	Y	Y	Y	Y	Y	Y
32 **Sessions**	Y	Y	Y	Y	Y	Y
33 Veasey	Y	Y	Y	N	N	N
34 Vela	Y	Y	Y	N	N	N
35 Doggett	Y	Y	Y	N	N	N
36 **Babin**	Y	Y	Y	Y	Y	Y
UTAH						
1 **Bishop**	Y	Y	Y	Y	Y	Y
2 **Stewart**	Y	Y	Y	Y	Y	Y
3 **Curtis**	Y	Y	Y	Y	Y	Y
4 **Love**	Y	Y	Y	Y	Y	Y
VERMONT						
AL Welch	Y	Y	Y	N	N	N
VIRGINIA						
1 **Wittman**	Y	Y	Y	Y	Y	Y
2 **Taylor**	Y	Y	N	Y	Y	Y
3 Scott	Y	Y	Y	N	N	N
4 McEachin	Y	?	?	N	N	N
5 **Garrett**	Y	Y	N	Y	Y	Y
6 **Goodlatte**	Y	Y	Y	Y	Y	Y
7 **Brat**	Y	Y	Y	Y	Y	Y
8 Beyer	Y	Y	N	–	–	–
9 **Griffith**	Y	Y	Y	Y	Y	Y
10 **Comstock**	Y	Y	Y	Y	Y	Y
11 Connolly	Y	Y	N	N	N	N
WASHINGTON						
1 DelBene	Y	Y	Y	N	N	N
2 Larsen	Y	Y	?	N	N	N
3 **Herrera Beutler**	Y	Y	N	Y	Y	Y
4 **Newhouse**	Y	Y	Y	Y	Y	Y
5 **McMorris Rodgers**	Y	Y	Y	Y	Y	Y
6 Kilmer	Y	Y	N	N	N	N
7 Jayapal	Y	Y	N	N	N	N
8 **Reichert**	Y	Y	Y	Y	Y	Y
9 Smith	Y	Y	Y	N	N	N
10 Heck	Y	Y	Y	N	N	N
WEST VIRGINIA						
1 **McKinley**	Y	Y	N	Y	Y	Y
2 **Mooney**	Y	Y	Y	Y	Y	Y
3 **Jenkins**	Y	+	?	Y	Y	Y
WISCONSIN						
1 **Ryan**						
2 Pocan	Y	Y	Y	N	N	N
3 Kind	Y	Y	N	N	N	N
4 Moore	Y	Y	N	N	N	N
5 **Sensenbrenner**	Y	Y	Y	Y	Y	Y
6 **Grothman**	Y	Y	Y	Y	Y	Y
7 **Duffy**	Y	+	–	Y	Y	Y
8 **Gallagher**	Y	Y	N	Y	Y	Y
WYOMING						
AL **Cheney**	Y	Y	Y	Y	Y	Y

VOTE NUMBER

56. HR772. FOOD LABELING REQUIREMENTS/PASSAGE. Passage of the bill that would modify the Food and Drug Administration's menu labeling regulations to allow nutritional information to be provided online, as opposed to on a menu board, and would allow restaurants and other food establishments to determine the serving size for which nutritional information would be posted. It would prohibit states from enacting laws regarding the disclosure of nutritional information that are different from the federal law. It would prohibit the FDA from enforcing compliance with menu labeling regulations for 90 days after a violation is discovered. Passed 266-157: R 234-1; D 32-156. Feb. 6, 2018.

57. INTELLIGENCE COMMITTEE MEMO/MOTION TO TABLE. McCarthy, R-Calif., motion to table (kill) the Pelosi, D-Calif., motion to appeal the ruling of the Chair that the Pelosi resolution related to a memo released by the House Intelligence Committee on Feb. 2, 2018, does not constitute a question of the privileges of the House. Motion agreed to 236-190: R 236-0; D 0-190. Feb. 6, 2018.

58. HRES727. FISCAL 2018 ONGOING APPROPRIATIONS PACKAGE/ PREVIOUS QUESTION. Sessions, R-Texas, motion to order the previous question (thus ending debate and possibility of amendment) on the rule (H Res 727) that would provide for House floor consideration of a Senate amendment to the bill (HR 1892) that is the expected legislative vehicle for an extension of the current continuing resolution through March 23, 2018. It would also provide $659.2 billion in discretionary funding for the Defense Department in fiscal 2018 and would fund community health centers through fiscal 2019. Motion agreed to 235-189: R 235-0; D 0 189. Feb. 6, 2018.

59. HRES727. FISCAL 2018 ONGOING APPROPRIATIONS PACKAGE/ RULE. Adoption of the rule (H Res 727) that would provide for House floor consideration of a Senate amendment to the bill (HR 1892) that is the expected legislative vehicle for an extension of the current continuing resolution through March 23, 2018. It would provide $659.2 billion in discretionary funding for the Defense Department in fiscal 2018 and would provide $3.6 billion annually for community health centers for fiscal 2018 and fiscal 2019. Adopted 236-188: R 232-3; D 4-185. Feb. 6, 2018.

60. HR1892. FISCAL 2018 ONGOING APPROPRIATIONS PACKAGE/ MOTION TO CONCUR. Frelinghuysen, R-N.J., motion to concur in the Senate amendment to the bill with an amendment that would provide for an extension of the current continuing resolution through March 23, 2018. The measure would provide for $659.2 billion in discretionary funding for the Defense Department through fiscal 2018 and would provide $3.6 billion annually for community health centers through fiscal 2019. It would also eliminate the cap on various Medicare payments and would extend funding for rural hospitals that see large numbers of Medicare patients. Motion agreed to 245-182: R 228-8; D 17-174. Feb. 6, 2018.

61. HR3851. WAR CRIMES INFORMATION REWARDS/PASSAGE. Royce, R-Calif., motion to suspend the rules and pass the bill that would allow the secretary of State to make additional individuals eligible for rewards under the department's War Crimes Rewards Program. Individuals would be eligible if they provide information that leads to the arrest or conviction of foreign nationals who have committed genocide or war crimes as defined by an international tribunal, U.S. law, or the laws of another nation. Motion agreed to 407-0: R 224-0; D 183-0. Feb. 7, 2018.

	56	57	58	59	60	61
ALABAMA						
1 **Byrne**	Y	Y	Y	Y	Y	Y
2 **Roby**	Y	Y	Y	Y	Y	Y
3 **Rogers**	?	Y	Y	Y	Y	Y
4 **Aderholt**	Y	Y	Y	Y	Y	Y
5 **Brooks**	Y	Y	Y	Y	Y	Y
6 **Palmer**	Y	Y	Y	Y	Y	Y
7 Sewell	N	N	N	N	N	Y
ALASKA						
AL **Young**	Y	Y	Y	Y	Y	Y
ARIZONA						
1 O'Halleran	Y	N	N	N	Y	Y
2 **McSally**	Y	Y	Y	Y	Y	Y
3 Grijalva	N	N	N	N	N	Y
4 **Gosar**	Y	Y	Y	Y	Y	Y
5 **Biggs**	Y	Y	Y	Y	Y	Y
6 **Schweikert**	Y	Y	Y	Y	Y	Y
7 Gallego	N	N	N	N	N	Y
9 Sinema	Y	N	N	Y	Y	+
ARKANSAS						
1 **Crawford**	Y	Y	Y	Y	Y	Y
2 **Hill**	Y	Y	Y	Y	Y	Y
3 **Womack**	Y	Y	Y	Y	Y	Y
4 **Westerman**	Y	Y	Y	Y	Y	
CALIFORNIA						
1 **LaMalfa**	Y	Y	Y	Y	Y	Y
2 Huffman	N	N	N	N	N	Y
3 Garamendi	N	N	N	N	Y	Y
4 **McClintock**	Y	Y	Y	Y	Y	Y
5 Thompson	Y	N	N	N	N	Y
6 Matsui	Y	N	N	N	N	Y
7 Bera	N	N	N	N	N	Y
8 **Cook**	Y	Y	Y	Y	Y	Y
9 McNerney	N	N	N	N	N	Y
10 **Denham**	Y	Y	Y	Y	Y	Y
11 DeSaulnier	N	N	N	N	N	Y
12 Pelosi	N	N	N	N	N	Y
13 Lee	N	N	N	N	N	Y
14 Speier	N	N	N	N	N	Y
15 Swalwell	N	N	N	N	N	Y
16 Costa	Y	N	N	N	Y	Y
17 Khanna	N	N	N	N	N	Y
18 Eshoo	N	N	N	N	N	Y
19 Lofgren	N	N	N	N	N	Y
20 Panetta	N	N	N	N	N	
21 **Valadao**	Y	Y	Y	Y	Y	Y
22 **Nunes**	Y	Y	Y	Y	Y	Y
23 **McCarthy**	Y	Y	Y	Y	Y	Y
24 Carbajal	N	N	N	N	Y	Y
25 **Knight**	Y	Y	Y	Y	Y	Y
26 Brownley	N	N	N	N	N	Y
27 Chu	N	N	N	N	N	Y
28 Schiff	N	N	N	N	N	Y
29 Cardenas	N	N	N	N	N	Y
30 Sherman	N	N	N	N	N	Y
31 Aguilar	Y	N	N	N	N	Y
32 Napolitano	N	N	N	N	N	Y
33 Lieu	N	N	N	N	N	Y
34 Gomez	N	N	N	N	N	Y
35 Torres	N	N	N	N	N	Y
36 Ruiz	N	N	N	N	Y	Y
37 Bass	N	N	N	N	N	Y
38 Sánchez, Linda	N	N	N	N	N	Y
39 **Royce**	Y	Y	Y	Y	Y	Y
40 Roybal-Allard	N	N	N	N	N	Y
41 Takano	N	N	N	N	N	Y
42 **Calvert**	Y	Y	Y	Y	Y	Y
43 Waters	N	N	N	N	N	Y
44 Barragan	N	N	N	N	N	?
45 **Walters**	Y	Y	Y	Y	Y	Y
46 Correa	Y	N	N	N	N	Y
47 Lowenthal	N	N	N	N	N	Y
48 **Rohrabacher**	Y	Y	Y	Y	Y	Y
49 **Issa**	Y	Y	Y	Y	Y	Y
50 **Hunter**	Y	Y	Y	Y	Y	Y
51 Vargas	N	N	N	N	N	Y
52 Peters	N	N	N	N	N	Y
53 Davis	N	N	N	N	N	Y

	56	57	58	59	60	61
COLORADO						
1 DeGette	N	N	N	N	N	Y
2 Polis	N	N	N	N	N	Y
3 **Tipton**	Y	Y	Y	Y	Y	Y
4 **Buck**	Y	Y	Y	Y	Y	Y
5 **Lamborn**	Y	Y	Y	Y	Y	Y
6 **Coffman**	Y	Y	Y	Y	Y	Y
7 Perlmutter	N	N	N	N	N	Y
CONNECTICUT						
1 Larson	N	N	N	N	N	Y
2 Courtney	N	N	N	N	N	Y
3 DeLauro	N	N	N	N	N	Y
4 Himes	N	N	N	N	N	Y
5 Esty	N	N	N	N	N	Y
DELAWARE						
AL Blunt Rochester	N	N	N	N	N	Y
FLORIDA						
1 **Gaetz**	Y	Y	Y	Y	Y	Y
2 **Dunn**	Y	Y	Y	Y	Y	Y
3 **Yoho**	Y	Y	Y	Y	Y	Y
4 **Rutherford**	Y	Y	Y	Y	Y	Y
5 Lawson	N	N	N	N	Y	Y
6 **DeSantis**	Y	Y	Y	Y	Y	?
7 Murphy	Y	N	N	N	N	Y
8 **Posey**	Y	Y	Y	Y	Y	Y
9 Soto	N	N	N	N	N	Y
10 Demings	Y	N	N	N	N	+
11 **Webster**	Y	Y	Y	Y	Y	Y
12 **Bilirakis**	Y	Y	Y	Y	Y	Y
13 Crist	N	N	N	N	N	?
14 Castor	N	N	N	N	N	Y
15 **Ross**	Y	Y	Y	Y	Y	Y
16 **Buchanan**	Y	Y	Y	Y	Y	Y
17 Rooney, T.	Y	Y	Y	Y	Y	Y
18 **Mast**	Y	Y	Y	Y	Y	Y
19 **Rooney, F.**	Y	Y	Y	Y	Y	Y
20 Hastings	N	N	N	N	N	Y
21 Frankel	N	N	N	N	N	Y
22 Deutch	N	N	N	N	N	Y
23 Wasserman Schultz	N	N	N	N	N	Y
24 Wilson	N	N	N	N	N	Y
25 **Diaz-Balart**	Y	Y	Y	Y	Y	Y
26 **Curbelo**	Y	Y	Y	Y	Y	Y
27 **Ros-Lehtinen**	Y	Y	Y	Y	N	Y
GEORGIA						
1 **Carter**	Y	Y	Y	Y	Y	Y
2 Bishop	N	N	N	N	Y	Y
3 **Ferguson**	Y	Y	Y	Y	Y	Y
4 Johnson	N	N	N	?	N	Y
5 Lewis	N	N	N	N	N	?
6 **Handel**	Y	Y	Y	Y	Y	Y
7 **Woodall**	Y	Y	Y	Y	Y	Y
8 **Scott, A.**	Y	Y	Y	Y	Y	Y
9 **Collins**	Y	Y	Y	Y	Y	Y
10 **Hice**	Y	Y	Y	Y	Y	Y
11 **Loudermilk**	Y	Y	Y	Y	Y	Y
12 **Allen**	Y	Y	Y	Y	Y	Y
13 Scott, D.	Y	N	N	N	N	Y
14 **Graves**	Y	Y	Y	Y	Y	Y
HAWAII						
1 Hanabusa	Y	N	N	N	N	Y
2 Gabbard	N	N	N	N	N	Y
IDAHO						
1 **Labrador**	Y	Y	Y	Y	N	Y
2 **Simpson**	Y	Y	Y	Y	Y	Y
ILLINOIS						
1 Rush	N	N	N	N	N	Y
2 Kelly	N	N	N	N	N	Y
3 Lipinski	Y	N	N	N	N	Y
4 Gutierrez	N	N	N	N	N	Y
5 Quigley	N	N	N	N	N	Y
6 **Roskam**	Y	Y	Y	Y	Y	Y
7 Davis, D.	N	N	N	N	N	Y
8 Krishnamoorthi	N	N	N	N	N	Y
9 Schakowsky	N	N	N	N	N	Y
10 Schneider	Y	N	N	N	N	Y
11 Foster	N	N	N	N	N	Y
12 **Bost**	Y	Y	Y	Y	Y	Y
13 **Davis, R.**	Y	Y	Y	Y	Y	Y

	56	57	58	59	60	61
14 **Hultgren**	Y	Y	Y	Y	Y	?
15 **Shimkus**	Y	Y	Y	Y	Y	Y
16 **Kinzinger**	Y	Y	Y	Y	Y	Y
17 Bustos	Y	N	N	N	Y	Y
18 **LaHood**	Y	Y	Y	Y	Y	Y
INDIANA						
1 Visclosky	N	N	N	N	N	Y
2 **Walorski**	Y	Y	Y	Y	Y	Y
3 **Banks**	Y	Y	Y	Y	Y	Y
4 **Rokita**	Y	Y	Y	Y	Y	Y
5 **Brooks**	Y	Y	Y	Y	Y	Y
6 **Messer**	Y	Y	Y	Y	Y	Y
7 Carson	N	N	N	N	N	Y
8 **Bucshon**	Y	Y	Y	Y	Y	Y
9 **Hollingsworth**	Y	Y	Y	Y	Y	Y
IOWA						
1 **Blum**	Y	Y	Y	Y	Y	Y
2 Loebsack	N	N	N	N	Y	Y
3 **Young**	Y	Y	Y	Y	Y	Y
4 **King**	Y	Y	Y	Y	Y	Y
KANSAS						
1 **Marshall**	Y	Y	Y	Y	Y	Y
2 **Jenkins**	Y	Y	Y	Y	Y	Y
3 **Yoder**	Y	Y	Y	Y	Y	Y
4 **Estes**	Y	Y	Y	Y	Y	Y
KENTUCKY						
1 **Comer**	Y	Y	Y	Y	Y	Y
2 **Guthrie**	Y	Y	Y	Y	Y	Y
3 Yarmuth	P	N	N	N	N	Y
4 **Massie**	N	Y	Y	N	N	Y
5 **Rogers**	Y	Y	Y	Y	Y	Y
6 **Barr**	Y	Y	Y	Y	Y	Y
LOUISIANA						
1 **Scalise**	Y	Y	Y	Y	Y	Y
2 Richmond	N	N	N	N	N	Y
3 **Higgins**	Y	Y	Y	Y	Y	Y
4 **Johnson**	Y	Y	Y	Y	Y	Y
5 **Abraham**	Y	Y	Y	Y	Y	Y
6 **Graves**	Y	Y	Y	Y	Y	Y
MAINE						
1 Pingree	N	N	N	N	N	Y
2 **Poliquin**	Y	Y	Y	Y	Y	Y
MARYLAND						
1 **Harris**	Y	Y	Y	Y	Y	?
2 Ruppersberger	Y	N	N	N	N	Y
3 Sarbanes	N	N	N	N	N	Y
4 Brown	N	N	N	N	N	Y
5 Hoyer	N	N	N	N	N	Y
6 Delaney	N	N	N	N	N	Y
7 Cummings	?	?	?	?	?	?
8 Raskin	N	N	N	N	N	Y
MASSACHUSETTS						
1 Neal	Y	N	N	N	N	Y
2 McGovern	N	N	N	N	N	Y
3 Tsongas	N	N	N	N	N	Y
4 Kennedy	Y	N	N	N	N	Y
5 Clark	N	N	N	N	N	Y
6 Moulton	N	N	N	N	N	+
7 Capuano	N	N	N	N	N	Y
8 Lynch	N	N	N	N	N	?
9 Keating	Y	N	N	N	N	Y
MICHIGAN						
1 **Bergman**	Y	Y	Y	Y	Y	Y
2 **Huizenga**	Y	Y	Y	Y	Y	Y
3 *Amash*	Y	Y	Y	N	N	Y
4 **Moolenaar**	Y	Y	Y	Y	Y	Y
5 Kildee	N	N	N	N	N	Y
6 **Upton**	Y	Y	Y	Y	Y	Y
7 **Walberg**	Y	Y	Y	Y	Y	Y
8 **Bishop**	Y	Y	Y	Y	Y	Y
9 Levin	N	N	N	N	N	Y
10 **Mitchell**	Y	Y	Y	Y	Y	Y
11 **Trott**	Y	Y	Y	Y	Y	?
12 Dingell	Y	N	N	N	N	Y
14 Lawrence	N	N	N	N	N	Y
MINNESOTA						
1 Walz	+	–	?	?	–	+
2 **Lewis**	Y	Y	Y	Y	Y	Y
3 **Paulsen**	Y	Y	Y	Y	Y	Y
4 McCollum	N	N	N	N	N	Y

	56	57	58	59	60	61
5 Ellison	N	N	N	N	N	Y
6 **Emmer**	Y	Y	Y	Y	Y	Y
7 Peterson	N	N	N	N	Y	Y
8 Nolan	N	N	N	N	N	Y
MISSISSIPPI						
1 **Kelly**	Y	Y	Y	Y	Y	Y
2 Thompson	N	N	N	N	N	Y
3 **Harper**	Y	Y	Y	Y	Y	Y
4 Palazzo	Y	Y	Y	Y	Y	Y
MISSOURI						
1 Clay	?	N	N	N	N	Y
2 **Wagner**	Y	Y	Y	Y	Y	Y
3 **Luetkemeyer**	Y	Y	Y	Y	Y	Y
4 **Hartzler**	Y	Y	Y	Y	Y	+
5 Cleaver	N	N	N	N	N	Y
6 **Graves**	Y	Y	Y	Y	Y	Y
7 **Long**	Y	Y	Y	Y	Y	?
8 **Smith**	Y	Y	Y	Y	Y	Y
MONTANA						
AL **Gianforte**	Y	Y	Y	Y	Y	Y
NEBRASKA						
1 **Fortenberry**	Y	Y	Y	Y	Y	Y
2 **Bacon**	Y	Y	Y	Y	Y	Y
3 **Smith**	Y	Y	Y	Y	Y	Y
NEVADA						
1 Titus	N	N	N	N	N	Y
2 **Amodei**	Y	Y	Y	Y	Y	Y
3 Rosen	N	N	N	N	N	Y
4 Kihuen	N	N	N	N	N	Y
NEW HAMPSHIRE						
1 Shea-Porter	N	N	N	N	N	Y
2 Kuster	N	N	N	N	N	Y
NEW JERSEY						
1 Norcross	N	N	N	N	N	Y
2 **LoBiondo**	Y	Y	Y	Y	Y	Y
3 **MacArthur**	Y	Y	Y	Y	Y	Y
4 **Smith**	Y	Y	Y	Y	Y	Y
5 Gottheimer	Y	N	N	Y	Y	Y
6 Pallone	N	N	N	N	N	Y
7 **Lance**	Y	Y	Y	Y	Y	Y
8 Sires	Y	N	N	N	N	Y
9 Pascrell	N	N	?	N	N	Y
10 Payne	N	N	N	N	N	Y
11 **Frelinghuysen**	Y	Y	Y	Y	Y	Y
12 Watson Coleman	N	N	N	N	N	Y
NEW MEXICO						
1 Lujan Grisham	N	N	N	N	N	Y
2 **Pearce**	Y	Y	Y	Y	Y	Y
3 Luján	N	N	N	N	N	Y
NEW YORK						
1 **Zeldin**	Y	Y	Y	Y	Y	Y
2 **King**	Y	Y	Y	Y	Y	Y
3 Suozzi	N	N	N	N	N	Y
4 Rice	N	N	N	N	N	Y
5 Meeks	N	N	N	N	N	Y
6 Meng	N	N	N	N	N	Y
7 Velázquez	N	N	N	N	N	Y
8 Jeffries	N	N	N	N	N	Y
9 Clarke	N	N	N	N	N	Y
10 Nadler	N	N	N	N	N	Y
11 **Donovan**	Y	Y	Y	Y	Y	Y
12 Maloney, C.	N	N	N	N	N	Y
13 Espaillat	N	N	N	N	N	Y
14 Crowley	N	N	N	N	N	Y
15 Serrano	N	N	N	N	N	Y
16 Engel	N	N	N	N	N	Y
17 Lowey	N	N	N	N	N	Y
18 Maloney, S.P.	N	N	N	N	N	Y
19 **Faso**	Y	Y	Y	Y	Y	Y
20 Tonko	Y	N	N	N	N	Y
21 **Stefanik**	Y	Y	Y	Y	Y	Y
22 **Tenney**	Y	Y	Y	Y	Y	Y
23 **Reed**	Y	Y	Y	Y	Y	Y
24 **Katko**	Y	Y	Y	Y	Y	?
25 Slaughter	N	N	N	N	N	Y
26 Higgins	N	N	N	N	N	Y
27 **Collins**	Y	Y	Y	Y	Y	Y
NORTH CAROLINA						
1 Butterfield	Y	N	N	N	N	Y
2 **Holding**	Y	Y	Y	Y	Y	Y
3 **Jones**	Y	Y	Y	N	N	?
4 Price	N	N	N	N	N	Y

	56	57	58	59	60	61
5 **Foxx**	Y	Y	Y	Y	Y	Y
6 **Walker**	Y	Y	Y	Y	Y	?
7 **Rouzer**	Y	Y	Y	Y	Y	+
8 **Hudson**	Y	Y	Y	Y	Y	Y
9 **Pittenger**	Y	Y	Y	Y	Y	Y
9 Vacant						
10 **McHenry**	Y	Y	Y	Y	Y	Y
11 **Meadows**	Y	Y	Y	Y	Y	Y
12 Adams	N	N	N	N	N	Y
13 **Budd**	Y	Y	Y	Y	Y	Y
NORTH DAKOTA						
AL **Cramer**	Y	Y	Y	Y	Y	Y
OHIO						
1 **Chabot**	Y	Y	Y	Y	Y	Y
2 **Wenstrup**	Y	Y	Y	Y	Y	Y
3 Beatty	N	N	N	N	N	Y
4 **Jordan**	Y	Y	Y	Y	Y	Y
5 **Latta**	Y	Y	Y	Y	Y	Y
6 **Johnson**	Y	Y	Y	Y	Y	Y
7 **Gibbs**	Y	Y	Y	Y	Y	Y
8 **Davidson**	Y	Y	Y	Y	Y	Y
9 Kaptur	N	N	N	N	N	Y
10 **Turner**	Y	Y	Y	Y	Y	Y
11 Fudge	N	N	N	N	N	Y
12 **Vacant**						
13 Ryan	N	N	N	N	N	Y
14 **Joyce**	Y	Y	Y	Y	Y	Y
15 **Stivers**	Y	Y	Y	Y	Y	Y
16 **Renacci**	Y	Y	Y	Y	Y	Y
OKLAHOMA						
1 **Bridenstine**	Y	Y	Y	Y	?	?
2 **Mullin**	Y	Y	Y	Y	Y	Y
3 **Lucas**	Y	Y	Y	Y	Y	Y
4 **Cole**	Y	Y	Y	Y	Y	Y
5 **Russell**	Y	Y	Y	Y	Y	Y
OREGON						
1 Bonamici	N	N	N	N	N	Y
2 **Walden**	Y	Y	Y	Y	Y	Y
3 Blumenauer	N	N	N	N	N	Y
4 DeFazio	Y	N	N	N	N	Y
5 Schrader	N	N	N	N	N	Y
PENNSYLVANIA						
1 Brady	N	N	N	N	N	?
2 Evans	N	N	N	N	N	Y
3 **Kelly**	Y	Y	Y	Y	Y	Y
4 **Perry**	Y	Y	Y	Y	Y	Y
5 **Thompson**	Y	Y	Y	Y	Y	Y
6 **Costello**	Y	Y	Y	Y	Y	Y
7 **Meehan**	Y	Y	Y	Y	Y	Y
8 **Fitzpatrick**	Y	Y	Y	Y	Y	Y
9 **Shuster**	?	?	?	?	Y	?
10 **Marino**	Y	Y	Y	Y	Y	Y
11 **Barletta**	Y	Y	Y	Y	Y	Y
12 **Rothfus**	Y	Y	Y	Y	Y	Y
13 Boyle	N	N	N	N	N	Y
14 Doyle	Y	N	N	N	N	Y
15 **Dent**	Y	Y	Y	Y	Y	Y
16 **Smucker**	Y	Y	Y	Y	Y	Y
17 Cartwright	N	N	N	N	N	Y
RHODE ISLAND						
1 Cicilline	N	N	N	N	N	Y
2 Langevin	N	N	N	N	N	Y
SOUTH CAROLINA						
1 **Sanford**	Y	Y	Y	Y	N	Y
2 **Wilson**	Y	Y	Y	Y	Y	Y
3 **Duncan**	Y	Y	Y	Y	Y	Y
4 **Gowdy**	Y	Y	Y	Y	Y	?
5 **Norman**	Y	Y	Y	Y	Y	Y
6 Clyburn	N	N	N	N	N	Y
7 **Rice**	Y	Y	Y	Y	Y	Y
SOUTH DAKOTA						
AL **Noem**	Y	Y	Y	Y	Y	Y
TENNESSEE						
1 **Roe**	Y	Y	Y	Y	Y	Y
2 **Duncan**	Y	Y	Y	Y	N	Y
3 **Fleischmann**	Y	Y	Y	Y	Y	Y
4 **DesJarlais**	Y	Y	Y	Y	Y	Y
5 Cooper	N	N	N	N	Y	Y
6 **Black**	Y	Y	Y	Y	Y	Y
7 **Blackburn**	Y	Y	?	?	Y	Y
8 **Kustoff**	Y	Y	Y	Y	Y	Y
9 Cohen	N	N	N	N	N	Y

	56	57	58	59	60	61
TEXAS						
1 **Gohmert**	Y	Y	Y	Y	Y	Y
2 **Poe**	Y	Y	Y	Y	Y	Y
3 **Johnson, S.**	Y	Y	Y	Y	Y	Y
4 **Ratcliffe**	Y	Y	Y	Y	Y	Y
5 **Hensarling**	Y	Y	Y	Y	Y	Y
6 **Barton**	Y	Y	Y	Y	Y	Y
7 **Culberson**	Y	Y	Y	Y	Y	Y
8 **Brady**	Y	Y	Y	Y	Y	Y
9 Green, A.	N	N	N	N	N	Y
10 **McCaul**	Y	Y	Y	Y	Y	Y
11 **Conaway**	Y	Y	Y	Y	Y	Y
12 **Granger**	Y	Y	Y	Y	Y	Y
13 **Thornberry**	Y	Y	Y	Y	Y	Y
14 **Weber**	Y	Y	Y	Y	Y	Y
15 Gonzalez	Y	N	N	N	N	Y
16 O'Rourke	N	N	N	N	N	Y
17 **Flores**	Y	Y	Y	Y	Y	Y
18 Jackson Lee	N	N	N	N	N	Y
19 **Arrington**	Y	Y	Y	Y	Y	Y
20 Castro	N	N	N	N	N	Y
21 **Smith**	Y	Y	Y	Y	Y	Y
22 **Olson**	Y	Y	Y	Y	Y	Y
23 **Hurd**	Y	Y	Y	Y	Y	Y
24 **Marchant**	Y	Y	Y	Y	Y	Y
25 **Williams**	Y	Y	Y	Y	Y	Y
26 **Burgess**	Y	Y	Y	Y	Y	Y
27 **Farenthold**	Y	Y	Y	Y	Y	Y
28 Cuellar	Y	N	N	N	N	Y
29 Green, G.	N	N	N	N	N	Y
30 Johnson, E.B.	N	N	N	N	N	Y
31 **Carter**	Y	Y	Y	Y	Y	Y
32 **Sessions**	Y	Y	Y	Y	Y	Y
33 Veasey	N	N	N	N	N	Y
34 Vela	Y	N	N	N	Y	Y
35 Doggett	N	N	N	N	N	Y
36 **Babin**	Y	Y	Y	Y	Y	Y
UTAH						
1 **Bishop**	Y	Y	Y	Y	Y	Y
2 **Stewart**	Y	Y	Y	Y	Y	Y
3 **Curtis**	Y	Y	Y	Y	Y	Y
4 **Love**	Y	Y	Y	Y	Y	Y
VERMONT						
AL Welch	Y	N	N	N	N	Y
VIRGINIA						
1 **Wittman**	Y	Y	Y	Y	Y	Y
2 **Taylor**	Y	Y	Y	Y	Y	Y
3 Scott	N	N	N	N	N	Y
4 McEachin	N	N	N	N	N	Y
5 **Garrett**	Y	Y	Y	Y	Y	Y
6 **Goodlatte**	Y	Y	Y	Y	Y	Y
7 **Brat**	Y	Y	Y	Y	Y	Y
8 Beyer	–	–	–	–	N	Y
9 **Griffith**	Y	Y	Y	Y	Y	Y
10 **Comstock**	Y	Y	Y	Y	Y	Y
11 Connolly	N	N	N	N	N	Y
WASHINGTON						
1 DelBene	N	N	N	N	N	Y
2 Larsen	N	N	N	N	N	Y
3 **Herrera Beutler**	Y	Y	Y	Y	Y	Y
4 **Newhouse**	Y	Y	Y	Y	Y	Y
5 **McMorris Rodgers**	Y	Y	Y	Y	Y	Y
6 Kilmer	N	N	N	N	N	Y
7 Jayapal	N	N	N	N	N	Y
8 **Reichert**	Y	Y	Y	Y	Y	Y
9 Smith	N	N	N	N	N	Y
10 Heck	N	N	N	N	N	Y
WEST VIRGINIA						
1 **McKinley**	Y	Y	Y	Y	Y	Y
2 **Mooney**	Y	Y	Y	Y	Y	Y
3 **Jenkins**	Y	Y	Y	Y	Y	Y
WISCONSIN						
1 **Ryan**						
2 Pocan	N	N	N	N	N	Y
3 Kind	Y	N	N	N	N	Y
4 Moore	N	N	N	N	N	Y
5 **Sensenbrenner**	Y	Y	Y	Y	Y	Y
6 **Grothman**	Y	Y	Y	Y	Y	Y
7 **Duffy**	Y	Y	Y	Y	Y	Y
8 **Gallagher**	Y	Y	Y	Y	Y	Y
WYOMING						
AL **Cheney**	Y	Y	Y	Y	Y	Y

VOTE NUMBER

62. HR1997. UKRANIAN CYBERSECURITY/PASSAGE. Royce, R-Calif., motion to suspend the rules and pass the bill that would require the State Department to report to Congress on US and NATO efforts to strengthen cybersecurity in Ukraine and on new areas for bilateral collaboration. It would also express the sense of Congress that the department should support Ukraine's efforts to improve its cybersecurity as well as its ability to respond to Russian supported disinformation and propaganda efforts through social media and other outlets. Motion agreed to 404-3: R 220-3; D 184-0. Feb. 7, 2018.

63. PROCEDURAL MOTION/JOURNAL. Approval of the House Journal of Feb. 6, 2018. Approved 210-185: R 130-89; D 80-96. Feb. 7, 2018.

64. HR1153. QUALIFIED MORTGAGE REGULATIONS/PASSAGE. Passage of the bill that would exclude insurance paid at closing into escrow, as well as fees paid for related services to lender-affiliated companies, from the three percent cap on points and fees imposed on qualified mortgages by modifying the definition of "points and fees." Passed 280-131: R 228-0; D 52-131. Feb. 8, 2018.

65. PROCEDURAL MOTION/JOURNAL. Approval of the House Journal of Feb. 7, 2018. Approved 208-194: R 128-96; D 80-98. Feb. 8, 2018.

66. HR4771. SMALL BANK ASSET LIMIT/PASSAGE. Passage of the bill that would require the Federal Reserve Board to increase, from $1 billion to $3 billion, the asset limit for banks and holding companies exempt from certain leverage and risk based capital requirements and therefore allowed to have higher debt levels than larger institutions. Passed 280-139: R 230-0; D 50-139. Feb. 8, 2018.

67. HRES734. FISCAL 2018 ONGOING APPROPRIATIONS PACKAGE/ PREVIOUS QUESTION. Session, R-Texas, motion to order the previous question (thus ending debate and possibility of amendment) on the rule (H Res 734) that would provide for House floor consideration of the Senate amendment to the House amendment to the Senate amendment to the bill (HR 1892) that would provide funding for federal government operations and services at current levels through March 23, 2018. Motion agreed to 224-186: R 224-0; D 0-186. Feb. 9, 2018.

		62	63	64	65	66	67
ALABAMA							
1	Byrne	Y	Y	Y	Y	Y	Y
2	Roby	Y	Y	Y	Y	Y	Y
3	Rogers	Y	N	Y	N	Y	Y
4	Aderholt	Y	Y	Y	Y	Y	Y
5	Brooks	Y	N	Y	N	Y	Y
6	Palmer	Y	Y	Y	N	Y	Y
7	Sewell	Y	N	N	N	Y	N
ALASKA							
AL	Young	Y	N	Y	N	Y	Y
ARIZONA							
1	O'Halleran	Y	N	Y	N	Y	N
2	McSally	Y	N	Y	N	Y	Y
3	Grijalva	Y	N	N	N	N	N
4	Gosar	Y	N	Y	N	Y	?
5	Biggs	Y	?	Y	N	Y	Y
6	Schweikert	Y	Y	Y	N	Y	Y
7	Gallego	Y	N	N	N	N	N
9	Sinema	+	–	Y	N	Y	N
ARKANSAS							
1	Crawford	Y	Y	Y	Y	Y	Y
2	Hill	Y	N	Y	N	Y	Y
3	Womack	Y	Y	Y	Y	Y	Y
4	Westerman	Y	Y	Y	N	Y	Y
CALIFORNIA							
1	LaMalfa	Y	Y	Y	N	Y	Y
2	Huffman	Y	N	N	Y	N	N
3	Garamendi	Y	P	N	N	N	N
4	McClintock	Y	Y	Y	Y	Y	Y
5	Thompson	Y	N	N	N	N	N
6	Matsui	Y	N	N	N	N	N
7	Bera	Y	N	N	N	Y	N
8	Cook	Y	Y	Y	Y	Y	Y
9	McNerney	Y	Y	Y	Y	Y	N
10	Denham	Y	N	Y	N	Y	Y
11	DeSaulnier	Y	N	N	N	N	N
12	Pelosi	Y	Y	N	Y	N	N
13	Lee	Y	N	N	N	N	N
14	Speier	Y	N	Y	N	Y	N
15	Swalwell	Y	N	Y	N	Y	N
16	Costa	Y	N	Y	N	Y	N
17	Khanna	Y	N	N	Y	N	N
18	Eshoo	Y	N	Y	N	Y	N
19	Lofgren	Y	N	Y	N	Y	N
20	Panetta	Y	Y	N	Y	Y	N
21	Valadao	Y	N	Y	N	Y	Y
22	Nunes	Y	Y	Y	Y	Y	Y
23	McCarthy	Y	Y	Y	Y	Y	Y
24	Carbajal	Y	N	Y	N	Y	N
25	Knight	Y	N	Y	N	Y	Y
26	Brownley	Y	N	N	N	N	N
27	Chu	Y	?	N	Y	N	N
28	Schiff	Y	N	N	N	N	N
29	Cardenas	Y	N	N	Y	N	N
30	Sherman	Y	Y	Y	Y	Y	N
31	Aguilar	Y	N	Y	Y	N	N
32	Napolitano	Y	Y	N	N	N	N
33	Lieu	Y	N	N	N	N	N
34	Gomez	Y	N	N	N	N	N
35	Torres	Y	N	N	N	Y	N
36	Ruiz	Y	N	Y	N	Y	N
37	Bass	Y	N	N	N	N	N
38	Sánchez, Linda	Y	?	N	N	N	N
39	Royce	Y	Y	Y	Y	Y	Y
40	Roybal-Allard	Y	N	N	Y	N	N
41	Takano	Y	N	N	Y	N	N
42	Calvert	Y	Y	Y	Y	Y	Y
43	Waters	Y	Y	N	Y	N	N
44	Barragan	?	?	?	?	?	N
45	Walters	Y	Y	Y	Y	Y	Y
46	Correa	Y	N	Y	N	Y	N
47	Lowenthal	Y	N	N	N	N	N
48	Rohrabacher	Y	Y	Y	N	Y	Y
49	Issa	Y	Y	Y	Y	Y	Y
50	Hunter	Y	Y	Y	Y	Y	Y
51	Vargas	Y	N	N	N	N	N
52	Peters	Y	Y	Y	N	Y	N
53	Davis	Y	N	Y	N	Y	?

		62	63	64	65	66	67
COLORADO							
1	DeGette	Y	N	Y	N	Y	N
2	Polis	Y	Y	N	?	N	N
3	Tipton	Y	N	Y	N	Y	Y
4	Buck	Y	N	Y	N	Y	Y
5	Lamborn	Y	Y	Y	Y	Y	Y
6	Coffman	Y	N	Y	N	Y	Y
7	Perlmutter	Y	Y	Y	N	N	N
CONNECTICUT							
1	Larson	Y	N	N	?	N	N
2	Courtney	Y	Y	N	?	N	N
3	DeLauro	Y	Y	N	Y	N	N
4	Himes	Y	Y	N	Y	Y	N
5	Esty	Y	N	N	N	Y	N
DELAWARE							
AL	Blunt Rochester	Y	Y	N	N	Y	N
FLORIDA							
1	Gaetz	Y	N	Y	N	Y	Y
2	Dunn	Y	Y	Y	Y	Y	Y
3	Yoho	Y	N	Y	N	Y	+
4	Rutherford	Y	N	Y	Y	Y	Y
5	Lawson	Y	Y	Y	N	Y	N
6	DeSantis	?	?	Y	N	Y	Y
7	Murphy	Y	Y	Y	Y	Y	N
8	Posey	Y	N	Y	Y	Y	Y
9	Soto	Y	N	Y	N	Y	N
10	Demings	+	+	N	Y	N	N
11	Webster	Y	Y	Y	Y	Y	Y
12	Bilirakis	Y	Y	Y	Y	Y	Y
13	Crist	?	?	N	N	Y	N
14	Castor	Y	N	N	N	N	N
15	Ross	Y	Y	Y	Y	Y	Y
16	Buchanan	Y	Y	Y	Y	Y	Y
17	Rooney, T.	Y	Y	Y	Y	Y	Y
18	Mast	Y	N	Y	N	Y	Y
19	Rooney, F.	Y	Y	Y	Y	?	Y
20	Hastings	Y	Y	–	?	–	
21	Frankel	Y	Y	–	?	–	N
22	Deutch	Y	Y	N	Y	N	N
23	Wasserman Schultz	Y	Y	N	Y	Y	N
24	Wilson	Y	Y	N	?	N	N
25	Diaz-Balart	Y	N	Y	N	Y	Y
26	Curbelo	Y	Y	Y	N	Y	Y
27	Ros-Lehtinen	Y	N	Y	N	Y	Y
GEORGIA							
1	Carter	Y	N	Y	Y	Y	Y
2	Bishop	Y	N	Y	N	Y	N
3	Ferguson	Y	Y	Y	N	Y	Y
4	Johnson	Y	Y	?	Y	N	?
5	Lewis	?	?	N	N	N	?
6	Handel	Y	Y	Y	Y	Y	Y
7	Woodall	Y	N	Y	N	Y	Y
8	Scott, A.	Y	Y	Y	Y	Y	Y
9	Collins	Y	Y	Y	Y	Y	Y
10	Hice	Y	N	Y	N	Y	Y
11	Loudermilk	Y	Y	Y	N	Y	Y
12	Allen	Y	Y	Y	Y	Y	Y
13	Scott, D.	Y	N	Y	Y	Y	N
14	Graves	Y	N	Y	N	Y	Y
HAWAII							
1	Hanabusa	Y	N	Y	N	Y	N
2	Gabbard	Y	Y	N	Y	N	N
IDAHO							
1	Labrador	Y	Y	Y	N	Y	Y
2	Simpson	Y	Y	Y	Y	Y	Y
ILLINOIS							
1	Rush	Y	N	N	N	N	N
2	Kelly	Y	Y	N	Y	N	N
3	Lipinski	Y	Y	Y	Y	Y	N
4	Gutierrez	Y	N	N	N	N	N
5	Quigley	Y	Y	Y	Y	N	N
6	Roskam	Y	N	Y	N	Y	Y
7	Davis, D.	Y	Y	N	Y	N	N
8	Krishnamoorthi	Y	Y	Y	N	N	N
9	Schakowsky	Y	N	N	N	N	N
10	Schneider	Y	Y	Y	Y	Y	N
11	Foster	Y	Y	Y	Y	N	N
12	Bost	Y	N	Y	N	Y	Y
13	Davis, R.	Y	N	Y	Y	Y	Y

KEY	**Republicans**	Democrats	*Independents*
Y Voted for (yea)		X Paired against	C Voted "present" to avoid possible conflict of interest
# Paired for		– Announced against	
+ Announced for		P Voted "present"	? Did not vote or otherwise make a position known
N Voted against (nay)			

	62	63	64	65	66	67
14 **Hultgren**	?	?	Y	Y	Y	Y
15 **Shimkus**	Y	Y	Y	Y	Y	Y
16 **Kinzinger**	Y	N	Y	N	Y	Y
17 Bustos	Y	Y	Y	Y	Y	N
18 **LaHood**	Y	N	Y	Y	Y	?
INDIANA						
1 Visclosky	Y	N	–	–	N	N
2 **Walorski**	Y	Y	Y	Y	Y	Y
3 **Banks**	Y	Y	Y	Y	Y	Y
4 **Rokita**	Y	N	Y	N	Y	Y
5 **Brooks**	Y	Y	Y	Y	Y	Y
6 **Messer**	Y	N	Y	Y	Y	Y
7 Carson	Y	N	N	N	N	N
8 **Bucshon**	Y	?	Y	Y	Y	Y
9 **Hollingsworth**	Y	Y	Y	Y	Y	Y
IOWA						
1 **Blum**	Y	N	Y	N	Y	+
2 Loebsack	Y	N	Y	N	Y	N
3 **Young**	Y	Y	Y	Y	Y	Y
4 **King**	Y	Y	Y	Y	Y	Y
KANSAS						
1 **Marshall**	Y	Y	Y	N	Y	Y
2 **Jenkins**	Y	N	Y	N	Y	Y
3 **Yoder**	Y	N	Y	N	Y	Y
4 **Estes**	Y	Y	Y	Y	Y	Y
KENTUCKY						
1 **Comer**	Y	N	Y	N	Y	Y
2 **Guthrie**	Y	Y	Y	Y	Y	Y
3 Yarmuth	Y	Y	?	Y	N	N
4 **Massie**	N	N	Y	Y	Y	Y
5 **Rogers**	Y	Y	Y	Y	Y	Y
6 **Barr**	Y	Y	Y	Y	Y	Y
LOUISIANA						
1 **Scalise**	Y	Y	Y	Y	Y	Y
2 Richmond	Y	Y	N	N	N	N
3 **Higgins**	Y	Y	Y	Y	Y	Y
4 **Johnson**	Y	Y	Y	Y	Y	Y
5 **Abraham**	Y	Y	Y	Y	Y	Y
6 **Graves**	Y	N	+	–	Y	Y
MAINE						
1 Pingree	Y	Y	N	Y	N	N
2 Poliquin	Y	N	Y	N	Y	Y
MARYLAND						
1 **Harris**	?	?	Y	Y	Y	Y
2 Ruppersberger	Y	Y	Y	Y	Y	N
3 Sarbanes	Y	N	N	N	N	N
4 Brown	Y	Y	N	Y	N	N
5 Hoyer	Y	N	N	N	N	N
6 Delaney	Y	N	Y	N	Y	N
7 Cummings	?	?	?	?	?	?
8 Raskin	Y	N	N	N	N	N
MASSACHUSETTS						
1 Neal	Y	N	N	Y	N	N
2 McGovern	Y	N	N	N	N	N
3 Tsongas	Y	Y	N	Y	N	N
4 Kennedy	Y	Y	N	Y	N	N
5 Clark	Y	N	N	N	N	N
6 Moulton	+	+	?	?	?	N
7 Capuano	Y	N	N	N	N	N
8 Lynch	Y	N	N	N	N	N
9 Keating	Y	N	N	N	N	N
MICHIGAN						
1 **Bergman**	Y	N	Y	N	Y	Y
2 **Huizenga**	Y	N	Y	?	Y	Y
3 *Amash*	N	N	Y	N	Y	Y
4 **Moolenaar**	Y	Y	Y	Y	Y	Y
5 Kildee	Y	Y	Y	Y	N	N
6 Upton	Y	N	Y	N	Y	Y
7 Walberg	Y	N	Y	N	Y	Y
8 Bishop	Y	N	Y	N	Y	Y
9 Levin	Y	N	N	N	N	N
10 Mitchell	Y	Y	Y	N	Y	Y
11 Trott	?	?	?	?	?	Y
12 Dingell	Y	Y	Y	Y	N	N
14 Lawrence	Y	Y	Y	Y	N	N
MINNESOTA						
1 Walz	+	?	–	?	N	N
2 **Lewis**	Y	Y	Y	Y	Y	Y
3 **Paulsen**	Y	N	Y	N	Y	Y
4 **McCollum**	Y	Y	Y	Y	N	N
5 Ellison	Y	Y	N	N	N	N
6 **Emmer**	Y	Y	Y	Y	Y	Y
7 Peterson	Y	?	Y	N	Y	N
8 Nolan	Y	N	Y	N	Y	N
MISSISSIPPI						
1 **Kelly**	Y	Y	Y	N	Y	Y
2 Thompson	Y	N	N	N	N	N
3 **Harper**	Y	Y	Y	Y	Y	Y
4 Palazzo	Y	N	Y	Y	Y	?
MISSOURI						
1 Clay	Y	Y	N	Y	N	N
2 **Wagner**	Y	Y	Y	Y	Y	Y
3 **Luetkemeyer**	Y	Y	Y	Y	Y	Y
4 **Hartzler**	+	+	Y	Y	Y	Y
5 Cleaver	Y	P	N	P	N	N
6 **Graves**	Y	N	Y	N	Y	Y
7 **Long**	?	?	Y	Y	Y	Y
8 **Smith**	Y	Y	Y	Y	Y	Y
MONTANA						
AL **Gianforte**	Y	Y	Y	Y	Y	Y
NEBRASKA						
1 **Fortenberry**	Y	Y	Y	Y	Y	Y
2 **Bacon**	Y	Y	Y	Y	Y	Y
3 **Smith**	Y	Y	Y	Y	Y	Y
NEVADA						
1 Titus	Y	Y	Y	Y	N	N
2 **Amodei**	Y	Y	Y	Y	Y	Y
3 Rosen	Y	N	Y	N	N	N
4 Kihuen	Y	N	Y	N	Y	N
NEW HAMPSHIRE						
1 Shea-Porter	Y	Y	N	Y	Y	N
2 Kuster	Y	Y	N	Y	Y	N
NEW JERSEY						
1 Norcross	Y	N	N	N	N	N
2 **LoBiondo**	Y	N	Y	N	Y	Y
3 **MacArthur**	Y	N	Y	N	Y	Y
4 **Smith**	Y	Y	Y	Y	Y	Y
5 Gottheimer	Y	N	Y	N	Y	N
6 Pallone	Y	N	N	N	N	N
7 **Lance**	Y	N	Y	N	Y	Y
8 Sires	Y	N	N	N	N	N
9 Pascrell	Y	Y	N	N	N	N
10 Payne	Y	N	N	?	N	N
11 **Frelinghuysen**	Y	Y	Y	Y	Y	Y
12 Watson Coleman	Y	N	N	N	Y	N
NEW MEXICO						
1 Lujan Grisham	Y	Y	N	Y	N	N
2 **Pearce**	Y	N	Y	Y	Y	Y
3 Luján	Y	Y	N	Y	N	N
NEW YORK						
1 **Zeldin**	Y	N	Y	N	Y	Y
2 **King**	Y	Y	Y	Y	Y	Y
3 Suozzi	Y	N	Y	N	Y	N
4 Rice	Y	?	Y	N	Y	N
5 Meeks	Y	N	Y	Y	Y	N
6 Meng	Y	Y	N	Y	N	N
7 Velázquez	Y	N	N	N	N	N
8 Jeffries	Y	N	N	Y	N	N
9 Clarke	Y	N	N	N	N	N
10 Nadler	Y	Y	N	Y	N	N
11 **Donovan**	Y	Y	Y	Y	Y	Y
12 Maloney, C.	Y	N	N	Y	N	N
13 Espaillat	Y	N	N	N	N	N
14 Crowley	Y	N	N	N	N	N
15 Serrano	Y	N	N	N	N	N
16 Engel	Y	Y	N	Y	N	N
17 Lowey	Y	Y	N	N	N	N
18 Maloney, S.P.	Y	N	Y	N	N	N
19 **Faso**	Y	N	Y	N	Y	Y
20 Tonko	Y	P	N	P	N	N
21 **Stefanik**	Y	Y	Y	Y	Y	Y
22 **Tenney**	Y	N	Y	N	Y	Y
23 **Reed**	Y	N	Y	N	Y	Y
24 **Katko**	?	?	Y	?	Y	Y
25 Slaughter	Y	N	N	N	N	N
26 Higgins	Y	Y	Y	N	N	N
27 **Collins**	Y	Y	Y	Y	Y	Y
NORTH CAROLINA						
1 Butterfield	Y	Y	N	Y	N	N
2 **Holding**	Y	N	Y	N	Y	Y
3 **Jones**	?	?	?	?	?	?
4 Price	Y	N	N	N	N	N
5 **Foxx**	Y	N	Y	N	Y	Y
6 **Walker**	?	?	Y	N	Y	Y
7 **Rouzer**	+	+	Y	N	Y	Y
8 **Hudson**	Y	N	+	–	Y	+
9 **Pittenger**	Y	N	Y	N	Y	Y
9 **Vacant**						
10 **McHenry**	Y	Y	Y	Y	Y	Y
11 **Meadows**	Y	Y	Y	Y	Y	Y
12 Adams	Y	N	N	Y	N	N
13 **Budd**	Y	Y	Y	Y	Y	Y
NORTH DAKOTA						
AL **Cramer**	Y	Y	Y	Y	Y	Y
OHIO						
1 **Chabot**	Y	Y	Y	Y	Y	Y
2 **Wenstrup**	Y	Y	Y	Y	Y	Y
3 Beatty	Y	Y	Y	Y	Y	N
4 **Jordan**	Y	N	Y	N	Y	Y
5 **Latta**	Y	N	Y	N	Y	Y
6 **Johnson**	Y	N	Y	N	Y	Y
7 **Gibbs**	Y	N	Y	N	Y	Y
8 **Davidson**	Y	Y	Y	N	Y	Y
9 Kaptur	Y	Y	N	Y	N	?
10 **Turner**	Y	N	Y	N	Y	+
11 Fudge	Y	N	N	N	N	N
12 **Vacant**						
13 Ryan	Y	N	N	N	N	N
14 **Joyce**	Y	Y	Y	N	Y	Y
15 **Stivers**	Y	N	Y	N	Y	Y
16 **Renacci**	Y	N	Y	N	Y	?
OKLAHOMA						
1 Bridenstine	?	?	?	?	?	?
2 **Mullin**	Y	Y	Y	Y	Y	Y
3 **Lucas**	Y	Y	Y	Y	Y	Y
4 **Cole**	Y	Y	Y	Y	Y	Y
5 **Russell**	Y	Y	Y	Y	Y	Y
OREGON						
1 Bonamici	Y	Y	N	Y	N	N
2 **Walden**	Y	Y	Y	Y	Y	Y
3 Blumenauer	Y	Y	N	Y	N	N
4 DeFazio	Y	N	N	N	N	–
5 Schrader	Y	N	Y	N	N	N
PENNSYLVANIA						
1 Brady	?	?	N	N	N	N
2 Evans	Y	Y	N	Y	N	N
3 **Kelly**	Y	Y	Y	N	Y	Y
4 **Perry**	Y	N	Y	N	Y	Y
5 **Thompson**	Y	N	Y	N	Y	Y
6 **Costello**	Y	N	Y	Y	Y	Y
7 **Meehan**	Y	N	Y	N	Y	Y
8 **Fitzpatrick**	Y	N	Y	N	Y	+
9 **Shuster**	?	?	?	?	?	Y
10 **Marino**	Y	Y	Y	Y	Y	Y
11 **Barletta**	Y	Y	Y	Y	Y	Y
12 **Rothfus**	Y	Y	Y	Y	Y	Y
13 Boyle	Y	Y	Y	N	N	N
14 Doyle	Y	N	Y	N	N	N
15 **Dent**	Y	Y	Y	Y	Y	Y
16 **Smucker**	Y	Y	Y	Y	Y	Y
17 Cartwright	Y	Y	Y	Y	N	?
RHODE ISLAND						
1 Cicilline	Y	Y	N	N	N	N
2 Langevin	Y	N	–	N	N	N
SOUTH CAROLINA						
1 **Sanford**	Y	Y	Y	N	Y	Y
2 **Wilson**	Y	Y	Y	Y	Y	Y
3 **Duncan**	Y	N	Y	N	Y	Y
4 **Gowdy**	?	?	?	?	Y	Y
5 **Norman**	Y	Y	Y	Y	Y	Y
6 Clyburn	Y	N	N	N	N	N
7 **Rice**	Y	Y	Y	N	Y	Y
SOUTH DAKOTA						
AL **Noem**	Y	Y	Y	N	Y	Y
TENNESSEE						
1 **Roe**	Y	Y	Y	Y	Y	Y
2 **Duncan**	N	Y	Y	Y	Y	Y
3 **Fleischmann**	Y	Y	Y	Y	Y	Y
4 **DesJarlais**	Y	Y	Y	Y	Y	Y
5 Cooper	Y	Y	Y	Y	Y	N
6 **Black**	?	?	?	?	?	?
7 **Blackburn**	Y	N	Y	N	Y	Y
8 **Kustoff**	Y	Y	Y	Y	Y	Y
9 Cohen	Y	N	N	Y	N	N
TEXAS						
1 **Gohmert**	Y	N	?	?	Y	Y
2 **Poe**	Y	N	Y	N	Y	Y
3 **Johnson, S.**	Y	Y	Y	Y	Y	Y
4 **Ratcliffe**	Y	?	Y	N	?	Y
5 **Hensarling**	Y	Y	Y	Y	Y	Y
6 **Barton**	Y	Y	Y	Y	Y	Y
7 **Culberson**	Y	?	Y	Y	Y	Y
8 **Brady**	Y	Y	Y	N	Y	Y
9 Green, A.	Y	N	N	N	N	N
10 **McCaul**	Y	Y	Y	Y	Y	Y
11 **Conaway**	Y	Y	Y	N	Y	Y
12 **Granger**	Y	Y	Y	Y	Y	Y
13 **Thornberry**	Y	Y	Y	Y	Y	Y
14 **Weber**	Y	N	Y	Y	Y	Y
15 Gonzalez	Y	Y	Y	N	Y	N
16 O'Rourke	Y	Y	N	Y	Y	N
17 **Flores**	Y	N	Y	Y	Y	Y
18 Jackson Lee	Y	N	N	N	N	N
19 **Arrington**	Y	Y	Y	Y	Y	Y
20 Castro	Y	Y	N	Y	N	N
21 **Smith**	Y	Y	Y	Y	Y	Y
22 **Olson**	Y	Y	Y	Y	Y	Y
23 **Hurd**	Y	N	Y	?	Y	Y
24 **Marchant**	Y	N	Y	?	Y	Y
25 **Williams**	Y	Y	Y	Y	Y	Y
26 **Burgess**	Y	N	Y	Y	Y	Y
27 **Farenthold**	Y	N	Y	N	Y	Y
28 Cuellar	Y	Y	Y	Y	Y	N
29 Green, G.	Y	N	–	–	Y	N
30 Johnson, E.B.	Y	N	N	N	N	N
31 **Carter**	Y	Y	Y	Y	Y	Y
32 **Sessions**	Y	Y	Y	Y	Y	Y
33 Veasey	Y	N	N	N	N	N
34 Vela	Y	N	Y	Y	Y	N
35 Doggett	Y	Y	N	N	N	N
36 **Babin**	Y	Y	Y	Y	Y	Y
UTAH						
1 **Bishop**	Y	Y	Y	Y	Y	?
2 **Stewart**	Y	Y	Y	Y	Y	Y
3 **Curtis**	Y	Y	Y	Y	Y	Y
4 **Love**	Y	N	Y	N	Y	Y
VERMONT						
AL Welch	Y	Y	N	Y	N	N
VIRGINIA						
1 **Wittman**	Y	N	Y	N	Y	Y
2 **Taylor**	Y	Y	Y	N	Y	Y
3 Scott	Y	Y	N	Y	Y	N
4 McEachin	Y	Y	N	Y	N	N
5 **Garrett**	Y	Y	Y	N	Y	Y
6 **Goodlatte**	Y	Y	Y	Y	Y	Y
7 **Brat**	Y	Y	Y	N	Y	Y
8 Beyer	Y	N	N	N	N	N
9 **Griffith**	Y	Y	Y	N	Y	Y
10 **Comstock**	Y	Y	Y	Y	Y	Y
11 Connolly	Y	N	Y	N	Y	N
WASHINGTON						
1 DelBene	Y	Y	N	Y	N	N
2 Larsen	Y	?	N	Y	N	N
3 **Herrera Beutler**	Y	N	Y	N	Y	Y
4 **Newhouse**	Y	Y	Y	Y	Y	Y
5 **McMorris Rodgers**	Y	Y	Y	Y	Y	Y
6 Kilmer	Y	N	N	N	N	N
7 Jayapal	Y	N	N	N	N	N
8 **Reichert**	Y	N	Y	Y	Y	Y
9 Smith	Y	Y	N	Y	N	N
10 Heck	Y	Y	Y	Y	N	N
WEST VIRGINIA						
1 **McKinley**	Y	N	Y	N	Y	Y
2 **Mooney**	Y	Y	Y	Y	Y	Y
3 **Jenkins**	Y	N	Y	N	Y	Y
WISCONSIN						
1 **Ryan**						
2 Pocan	Y	Y	N	?	N	N
3 Kind	Y	N	Y	N	Y	N
4 Moore	Y	Y	N	Y	N	N
5 **Sensenbrenner**	Y	Y	Y	Y	Y	Y
6 **Grothman**	Y	N	Y	N	Y	Y
7 **Duffy**	Y	N	Y	Y	Y	Y
8 **Gallagher**	Y	N	Y	N	Y	Y
WYOMING						
AL **Cheney**	Y	Y	Y	Y	Y	Y

VOTE NUMBER

68. HR1892. FISCAL 2018 ONGOING APPROPRIATIONS PACKAGE/RULE.
Adoption of the rule (H Res 734) that would provide for House floor consideration of the Senate amendment to the House amendment to the Senate amendment to the bill (HR 1892) that is the expected legislative vehicle for an extension of the current continuing resolution through March 23, 2018. Adopted 224-193: R 221-7; D 3-186. Feb. 9, 2018.

69. HR1892. FISCAL 2018 ONGOING APPROPRIATIONS PACKAGE/MOTION TO CONCUR. Frelinghuysen, R-N.J., motion to concur in the Senate amendment to the House amendment to the Senate amendment to the bill that would provide funding for federal government operations and services at current levels through March 23, 2018. The bill would increase defense spending caps to $629 billion for fiscal 2018 and $647 billion for fiscal 2019, and would increase non-defense spending caps by $63 billion in fiscal 2018 and $68 billion in fiscal 2019. It would suspend the debt ceiling through March 1, 2019, and would provide $89.3 billion in emergency supplemental funding. (Truncated, visit cq.com for more.) Motion agreed to 240-186: R 167-67; D 73-119. Feb. 9, 2018.

70. HR4533. LEXINGTON VA HEALTH CARE SYSTEM/PASSAGE. Roe, R-Tenn., motion to suspend the rules and pass the bill that would designate the health care system of the Veterans Affairs Department in Lexington, Kentucky, as the "Lexington VA Health Care System." It would also rename the VA facility at 2250 Leestown Road, Lexington, Ky., as "Franklin R. Sousley Campus" and the VA facility at 1101 Veterans Drive, Lexington, Ky., as "Troy Bowling Campus." Motion agreed to 402-0: R 220-0; D 182-0. Feb. 13, 2018.

71. HR4979. GENERALIZED SYSTEM OF PREFERENCES PROGRAM EXTENSION/ PASSAGE. Reichert, R-Wash., motion to suspend the rules and pass the bill that would extend, through Dec. 31, 2020, the Generalized System of Preferences program, managed by the U.S. Trade Representative. The bill would also make the preferences retroactive to the program's 2017 expiration date. Motion agreed to 400-2: R 217-2; D 183-0. Feb. 13, 2018.

72. HR3299. ADA INFRACTION NOTIFICATION, FINANCIAL INSTITUTION ASSESSMENT REQUIREMENTS AND INTEREST RATE REGULATION/ PREVIOUS QUESTION. Collins, Doug, R-Ga., motion to order the previous question (thus ending debate and possibility of amendment) on the rule (H Res 736) that would provide for House floor consideration of the bill (HR 3299) that would amend the Home Owners' Loan Act, the Federal Credit Union Act, and the Federal Deposit Insurance Act to codify the "valid-when-made" doctrine, which requires that the rate of interest of certain loans remain unchanged after sale, assignment or transfer of the loans; would provide for consideration of the bill (HR 3978) that would makes changes to certain market trading, financial institution and systemic safety and soundness, and mortgage lending regulations; and would provide for consideration of the bill (HR 620) that would change certain notification requirements for plaintiffs before they can file a lawsuit under the Americans for Disabilities Act against a business or other establishment for failing to accommodate the disabled. The rule would also provide for proceedings during the period from Feb. 16 and Feb. 23, 2018. Motion agreed to 228-187: R 228-0; D 0-187. Feb. 14, 2018.

73. HR620. ADA INFRACTION NOTIFICATION, FINANCIAL INSTITUTION ASSESSMENT REQUIREMENTS AND INTEREST RATE REGULATION/ RULE. Adoption of the rule that would provide for House floor consideration of the bill (HR 3299) that would amend the Home Owners' Loan Act, the Federal Credit Union Act, and the Federal Deposit Insurance Act to codify the "valid-when-made" doctrine, which requires that the rate of interest of certain loans remain unchanged after sale, assignment or transfer of the loans; would provide for consideration of the bill (HR 3978) that would makes changes to certain market trading, financial institution and systemic safety and soundness, and mortgage lending regulations; and would provide for consideration of the bill (HR 620) that would change certain notification requirements for plaintiffs before they can file a lawsuit under the Americans for Disabilities Act against a business or other establishment for failing to accommodate the disabled. The rule would also provide for proceedings during the period from Feb. 16 and Feb. 23, 2018. Adopted 227-187: R 227-0; D 0-187. Feb. 14, 2018.

	68	69	70	71	72	73
ALABAMA						
1 Byrne	Y	Y	?	?	?	?
2 Roby	Y	Y	Y	Y	Y	Y
3 Rogers	Y	Y	Y	Y	Y	Y
4 Aderholt	Y	Y	Y	Y	Y	Y
5 Brooks	Y	N	Y	Y	Y	Y
6 Palmer	Y	N	Y	Y	Y	Y
7 Sewell	N	Y	Y	Y	N	N
ALASKA						
AL Young	Y	Y	Y	Y	Y	Y
ARIZONA						
1 O'Halleran	N	Y	Y	Y	N	N
2 McSally	Y	Y	Y	Y	Y	Y
3 Grijalva	N	N	Y	Y	N	N
4 Gosar	?	N	Y	Y	Y	Y
5 Biggs	N	N	Y	Y	Y	Y
6 Schweikert	Y	N	Y	Y	Y	Y
7 Gallego	N	N	Y	Y	N	N
9 Sinema	Y	Y	Y	Y	N	N
ARKANSAS						
1 Crawford	Y	Y	Y	Y	Y	Y
2 Hill	Y	Y	Y	Y	Y	Y
3 Womack	Y	Y	Y	Y	Y	Y
4 Westerman	Y	N	Y	Y	Y	Y
CALIFORNIA						
1 LaMalfa	Y	Y	Y	Y	Y	Y
2 Huffman	N	Y	Y	Y	N	N
3 Garamendi	N	Y	Y	Y	N	N
4 McClintock	Y	N	Y	Y	Y	Y
5 Thompson	N	Y	Y	Y	N	N
6 Matsui	N	N	Y	Y	N	N
7 Bera	N	Y	Y	Y	N	N
8 Cook	Y	Y	Y	Y	Y	Y
9 McNerney	N	Y	Y	Y	N	N
10 Denham	Y	Y	+	+	+	+
11 DeSaulnier	N	N	Y	Y	N	N
12 Pelosi	N	N	Y	Y	N	N
13 Lee	N	N	Y	Y	N	N
14 Speier	N	N	Y	Y	N	N
15 Swalwell	N	N	Y	Y	N	N
16 Costa	N	Y	?	?	?	?
17 Khanna	N	N	Y	Y	N	N
18 Eshoo	N	N	Y	Y	N	N
19 Lofgren	N	N	Y	Y	N	N
20 Panetta	N	N	Y	Y	N	N
21 Valadao	Y	Y	?	?	Y	Y
22 Nunes	Y	Y	+	+	Y	Y
23 McCarthy	Y	Y	Y	Y	Y	Y
24 Carbajal	N	Y	Y	Y	N	N
25 Knight	Y	Y	Y	Y	Y	Y
26 Brownley	N	N	Y	Y	N	N
27 Chu	N	N	Y	Y	N	N
28 Schiff	N	N	Y	Y	N	N
29 Cardenas	N	N	Y	Y	N	N
30 Sherman	N	N	Y	Y	N	N
31 Aguilar	N	N	Y	Y	N	N
32 Napolitano	N	N	Y	Y	N	N
33 Lieu	N	N	Y	Y	N	N
34 Gomez	N	N	Y	Y	N	N
35 Torres	N	N	Y	Y	N	N
36 Ruiz	N	Y	Y	Y	N	N
37 Bass	N	N	?	?	?	?
38 Sánchez, Linda	N	N	Y	Y	N	N
39 Royce	Y	Y	Y	Y	Y	Y
40 Roybal-Allard	N	N	Y	Y	N	N
41 Takano	N	N	Y	Y	N	N
42 Calvert	Y	Y	Y	Y	Y	Y
43 Waters	N	N	Y	Y	N	N
44 Barragan	N	N	Y	Y	N	N
45 Walters	Y	Y	Y	Y	Y	Y
46 Correa	N	N	Y	Y	N	N
47 Lowenthal	N	N	Y	Y	N	N
48 Rohrabacher	Y	N	?	?	Y	Y
49 Issa	Y	Y	?	Y	Y	Y
50 Hunter	Y	Y	Y	N	Y	Y
51 Vargas	N	N	?	?	N	N
52 Peters	N	N	Y	Y	N	N
53 Davis	?	N	Y	Y	N	N

	68	69	70	71	72	73
COLORADO						
1 DeGette	N	N	Y	Y	N	N
2 Polis	N	N	Y	Y	N	N
3 Tipton	Y	Y	Y	Y	Y	Y
4 Buck	Y	N	Y	Y	Y	Y
5 Lamborn	Y	Y	Y	Y	Y	Y
6 Coffman	Y	Y	Y	Y	Y	Y
7 Perlmutter	N	N	Y	Y	N	N
CONNECTICUT						
1 Larson	N	Y	Y	Y	N	N
2 Courtney	N	Y	Y	Y	N	N
3 DeLauro	N	Y	Y	Y	N	N
4 Himes	N	Y	Y	Y	N	N
5 Esty	N	Y	Y	Y	N	N
DELAWARE						
AL Blunt Rochester	N	Y	?	?	N	N
FLORIDA						
1 Gaetz	Y	N	?	?	Y	Y
2 Dunn	Y	Y	Y	Y	Y	Y
3 Yoho	+	N	Y	Y	Y	Y
4 Rutherford	Y	Y	Y	Y	Y	Y
5 Lawson	N	Y	Y	Y	N	N
6 DeSantis	Y	Y	Y	Y	Y	Y
7 Murphy	Y	Y	Y	Y	N	N
8 Posey	N	N	?	?	?	?
9 Soto	N	Y	Y	Y	N	N
10 Demings	N	N	Y	Y	N	N
11 Webster	Y	N	Y	Y	Y	Y
12 Bilirakis	Y	Y	Y	Y	Y	Y
13 Crist	N	Y	Y	Y	N	N
14 Castor	N	Y	Y	Y	N	N
15 Ross	Y	Y	Y	Y	Y	Y
16 Buchanan	Y	Y	?	Y	Y	Y
17 Rooney, T.	Y	Y	Y	Y	Y	Y
18 Mast	Y	Y	Y	Y	Y	Y
19 Rooney, F.	Y	Y	Y	Y	Y	Y
20 Hastings	N	N	Y	Y	N	N
21 Frankel	N	N	?	?	N	N
22 Deutch	N	Y	Y	Y	N	N
23 Wasserman Schultz	N	N	Y	Y	N	N
24 Wilson	N	N	Y	Y	N	N
25 Diaz-Balart	Y	Y	Y	Y	Y	Y
26 Curbelo	Y	Y	Y	Y	Y	Y
27 Ros-Lehtinen	Y	N	Y	Y	Y	Y
GEORGIA						
1 Carter	Y	Y	Y	Y	Y	Y
2 Bishop	N	Y	Y	Y	N	N
3 Ferguson	Y	Y	Y	Y	Y	Y
4 Johnson	N	N	Y	Y	N	N
5 Lewis	N	N	Y	Y	N	N
6 Handel	Y	Y	Y	Y	Y	Y
7 Woodall	Y	Y	Y	Y	Y	Y
8 Scott, A.	Y	Y	Y	Y	Y	Y
9 Collins	Y	Y	Y	Y	Y	Y
10 Hice	Y	N	Y	Y	Y	Y
11 Loudermilk	Y	Y	Y	Y	Y	Y
12 Allen	Y	Y	Y	Y	Y	Y
13 Scott, D.	N	Y	Y	Y	N	N
14 Graves	Y	Y	Y	Y	Y	Y
HAWAII						
1 Hanabusa	N	Y	Y	Y	N	N
2 Gabbard	N	N	Y	Y	N	N
IDAHO						
1 Labrador	Y	N	Y	Y	Y	Y
2 Simpson	Y	Y	Y	Y	Y	Y
ILLINOIS						
1 Rush	N	N	Y	Y	N	N
2 Kelly	N	N	Y	Y	N	N
3 Lipinski	N	N	Y	Y	N	N
4 Gutierrez	N	N	+	+	–	–
5 Quigley	N	N	Y	Y	N	N
6 Roskam	Y	Y	Y	Y	Y	Y
7 Davis, D.	N	N	Y	Y	N	N
8 Krishnamoorthi	N	N	Y	Y	N	N
9 Schakowsky	N	N	Y	Y	N	N
10 Schneider	Y	Y	Y	Y	N	N
11 Foster	N	Y	Y	Y	N	N
12 Bost	Y	Y	Y	Y	Y	Y
13 Davis, R.	Y	Y	Y	Y	Y	Y

KEY   **Republicans**   Democrats   *Independents*

Y	Voted for (yea)
#	Paired for
+	Announced for
N	Voted against (nay)
X	Paired against
–	Announced against
P	Voted "present"
C	Voted "present" to avoid possible conflict of interest
?	Did not vote or otherwise make a position known

	68	69	70	71	72	73
14 **Hultgren**	Y	Y	Y	Y	Y	Y
15 **Shimkus**	Y	Y	Y	Y	Y	Y
16 **Kinzinger**	Y	Y	Y	Y	Y	Y
17 Bustos	N	Y	Y	Y	N	N
18 **LaHood**	Y	Y	Y	Y	Y	Y
INDIANA						
1 Visclosky	N	Y	Y	Y	N	N
2 **Walorski**	Y	Y	Y	Y	Y	Y
3 **Banks**	Y	Y	Y	Y	Y	Y
4 **Rokita**	Y	N	Y	Y	Y	?
5 **Brooks**	Y	Y	Y	Y	Y	Y
6 **Messer**	Y	Y	?	?	Y	Y
7 Carson	N	N	Y	Y	N	N
8 **Bucshon**	Y	Y	Y	Y	Y	Y
9 **Hollingsworth**	Y	N	Y	Y	Y	Y
IOWA						
1 **Blum**	+	–	Y	Y	Y	Y
2 Loebsack	N	Y	Y	Y	N	N
3 **Young**	Y	Y	Y	Y	Y	Y
4 **King**	Y	N	Y	Y	Y	Y
KANSAS						
1 **Marshall**	Y	Y	Y	Y	Y	Y
2 **Jenkins**	Y	Y	Y	Y	Y	Y
3 **Yoder**	Y	N	Y	Y	Y	Y
4 **Estes**	Y	Y	Y	Y	Y	Y
KENTUCKY						
1 **Comer**	Y	N	Y	Y	Y	Y
2 **Guthrie**	Y	Y	Y	Y	Y	Y
3 Yarmuth	N	Y	Y	Y	N	N
4 **Massie**	N	N	Y	Y	Y	Y
5 **Rogers**	Y	Y	+	+	+	+
6 **Barr**	Y	Y	Y	Y	?	Y
LOUISIANA						
1 **Scalise**	Y	Y	Y	Y	Y	Y
2 Richmond	N	N	Y	Y	N	N
3 **Higgins**	Y	Y	Y	Y	Y	Y
4 **Johnson**	Y	N	Y	Y	Y	Y
5 **Abraham**	Y	Y	Y	Y	Y	Y
6 **Graves**	Y	N	Y	Y	Y	Y
MAINE						
1 Pingree	N	N	Y	Y	N	N
2 **Poliquin**	Y	Y	Y	Y	Y	Y
MARYLAND						
1 **Harris**	Y	N	Y	Y	Y	Y
2 Ruppersberger	N	Y	Y	Y	N	N
3 Sarbanes	N	N	Y	Y	N	N
4 Brown	N	N	Y	Y	N	N
5 Hoyer	N	N	Y	Y	N	N
6 Delaney	N	N	Y	Y	N	N
7 Cummings	?	?	?	?	?	?
8 Raskin	N	N	Y	Y	N	N
MASSACHUSETTS						
1 Neal	N	N	Y	Y	N	N
2 McGovern	N	N	Y	Y	N	N
3 Tsongas	N	Y	Y	Y	N	N
4 Kennedy	N	N	Y	Y	N	N
5 Clark	N	N	Y	Y	N	N
6 Moulton	N	N	Y	Y	N	N
7 Capuano	N	N	Y	Y	N	N
8 Lynch	N	Y	Y	Y	N	N
9 Keating	N	Y	Y	Y	N	N
MICHIGAN						
1 **Bergman**	Y	Y	Y	Y	Y	Y
2 **Huizenga**	Y	Y	Y	Y	Y	Y
3 *Amash*	N	N	Y	N	Y	Y
4 **Moolenaar**	Y	Y	Y	Y	Y	Y
5 Kildee	N	N	Y	Y	N	N
6 Upton	Y	Y	Y	Y	Y	Y
7 Walberg	Y	Y	Y	Y	Y	Y
8 Bishop	Y	Y	Y	Y	Y	Y
9 Levin	N	N	Y	Y	N	N
10 Mitchell	Y	Y	Y	Y	Y	Y
11 Trott	Y	Y	Y	Y	Y	Y
12 Dingell	N	N	Y	Y	N	N
14 Lawrence	N	Y	Y	Y	N	N
MINNESOTA						
1 Walz	N	N	Y	Y	N	N
2 **Lewis**	Y	N	Y	Y	Y	Y
3 **Paulsen**	Y	Y	Y	Y	Y	Y
4 **McCollum**	N	Y	Y	Y	N	N

	68	69	70	71	72	73
5 Ellison	N	N	Y	Y	N	N
6 **Emmer**	Y	N	Y	Y	Y	Y
7 Peterson	N	N	Y	Y	N	N
8 Nolan	N	Y	Y	Y	N	N
MISSISSIPPI						
1 **Kelly**	Y	Y	Y	Y	Y	Y
2 Thompson	N	Y	Y	Y	N	N
3 **Harper**	Y	Y	Y	Y	Y	Y
4 Palazzo	?	Y	Y	Y	Y	Y
MISSOURI						
1 Clay	N	N	Y	Y	N	N
2 **Wagner**	Y	Y	Y	Y	Y	Y
3 **Luetkemeyer**	Y	Y	Y	Y	Y	Y
4 **Hartzler**	Y	Y	Y	Y	Y	Y
5 Cleaver	N	N	Y	Y	N	N
6 **Graves**	Y	Y	Y	Y	Y	Y
7 **Long**	Y	N	Y	Y	Y	Y
8 **Smith**	Y	N	Y	Y	Y	Y
MONTANA						
AL **Gianforte**	Y	N	Y	Y	Y	Y
NEBRASKA						
1 **Fortenberry**	Y	Y	Y	Y	Y	Y
2 **Bacon**	Y	Y	Y	Y	Y	Y
3 **Smith**	Y	N	Y	Y	Y	Y
NEVADA						
1 Titus	N	N	+	+	N	N
2 **Amodei**	Y	Y	Y	Y	Y	Y
3 Rosen	N	Y	Y	Y	N	N
4 Kihuen	N	N	Y	Y	N	N
NEW HAMPSHIRE						
1 Shea-Porter	N	Y	Y	Y	N	N
2 Kuster	N	Y	Y	Y	N	N
NEW JERSEY						
1 Norcross	N	N	Y	Y	N	N
2 **LoBiondo**	Y	Y	Y	Y	Y	?
3 **MacArthur**	Y	Y	Y	Y	Y	Y
4 **Smith**	Y	Y	Y	Y	Y	Y
5 Gottheimer	N	Y	Y	Y	N	N
6 Pallone	N	N	Y	Y	N	N
7 **Lance**	Y	Y	Y	Y	Y	Y
8 Sires	N	N	Y	Y	N	N
9 Pascrell	N	Y	Y	Y	N	N
10 Payne	N	N	Y	Y	N	N
11 **Frelinghuysen**	Y	Y	Y	Y	Y	Y
12 Watson Coleman	N	N	Y	Y	–	–
NEW MEXICO						
1 Lujan Grisham	N	N	Y	Y	N	N
2 **Pearce**	Y	N	?	?	?	?
3 Luján	N	N	Y	Y	N	N
NEW YORK						
1 **Zeldin**	Y	N	Y	Y	Y	Y
2 **King**	Y	Y	Y	Y	Y	Y
3 Suozzi	N	N	Y	Y	N	N
4 Rice	N	Y	Y	Y	N	N
5 Meeks	N	N	Y	Y	N	N
6 Meng	N	N	Y	Y	N	N
7 Velázquez	N	N	Y	Y	N	N
8 Jeffries	N	N	Y	Y	N	N
9 Clarke	N	N	Y	Y	N	N
10 Nadler	N	N	Y	Y	N	N
11 **Donovan**	Y	Y	Y	Y	Y	Y
12 Maloney, C.	N	N	Y	Y	N	N
13 Espaillat	N	N	Y	Y	N	N
14 Crowley	N	N	Y	Y	N	N
15 Serrano	N	N	Y	Y	N	N
16 Engel	N	N	Y	Y	N	N
17 Lowey	N	N	Y	Y	N	N
18 Maloney, S.P.	N	N	Y	Y	N	N
19 **Faso**	Y	Y	Y	Y	Y	Y
20 Tonko	N	Y	Y	Y	N	N
21 **Stefanik**	Y	Y	Y	Y	Y	Y
22 **Tenney**	Y	Y	Y	Y	Y	Y
23 **Reed**	Y	N	Y	Y	Y	Y
24 **Katko**	Y	Y	Y	Y	Y	Y
25 Slaughter	N	Y	Y	Y	N	N
26 Higgins	N	Y	Y	Y	N	N
27 **Collins**	Y	Y	Y	Y	Y	Y
NORTH CAROLINA						
1 Butterfield	N	Y	Y	Y	N	N
2 **Holding**	Y	N	Y	Y	Y	Y
3 **Jones**	?	?	Y	Y	Y	Y
4 Price	N	N	Y	Y	N	N

	68	69	70	71	72	73
5 **Foxx**	Y	N	Y	Y	Y	Y
6 **Walker**	Y	N	Y	Y	Y	Y
7 **Rouzer**	Y	N	Y	Y	Y	Y
8 **Hudson**	Y	N	Y	Y	Y	Y
9 **Pittenger**	Y	Y	Y	Y	Y	Y
9 **Vacant**						
10 **McHenry**	Y	Y	Y	Y	Y	Y
11 **Meadows**	N	N	Y	Y	Y	Y
12 Adams	N	N	Y	Y	N	N
13 **Budd**	Y	N	Y	Y	Y	Y
NORTH DAKOTA						
AL **Cramer**	Y	Y	Y	Y	Y	Y
OHIO						
1 **Chabot**	Y	N	Y	Y	Y	Y
2 **Wenstrup**	Y	Y	Y	Y	Y	Y
3 Beatty	N	Y	Y	Y	N	N
4 **Jordan**	N	N	Y	Y	Y	Y
5 **Latta**	Y	Y	Y	Y	Y	Y
6 **Johnson**	Y	Y	Y	Y	Y	Y
7 **Gibbs**	Y	Y	Y	Y	Y	Y
8 **Davidson**	Y	N	Y	Y	Y	Y
9 Kaptur	?	Y	Y	Y	N	N
10 **Turner**	+	Y	Y	Y	Y	Y
11 Fudge	N	Y	Y	Y	N	N
12 **Vacant**						
13 Ryan	N	Y	Y	Y	N	N
14 **Joyce**	Y	Y	Y	Y	Y	Y
15 **Stivers**	Y	Y	?	?	?	?
16 **Renacci**	Y	N	Y	Y	Y	Y
OKLAHOMA						
1 **Bridenstine**	?	?	Y	Y	Y	Y
2 **Mullin**	Y	Y	Y	Y	Y	Y
3 **Lucas**	Y	Y	Y	Y	Y	Y
4 **Cole**	Y	Y	Y	Y	Y	Y
5 **Russell**	Y	Y	Y	Y	Y	Y
OREGON						
1 Bonamici	N	N	Y	Y	N	N
2 **Walden**	Y	Y	Y	Y	Y	Y
3 Blumenauer	N	N	+	+	N	N
4 DeFazio	–	N	Y	Y	N	N
5 Schrader	N	N	Y	Y	N	N
PENNSYLVANIA						
1 Brady	N	N	Y	Y	N	N
2 Evans	N	Y	Y	Y	N	N
3 **Kelly**	Y	Y	Y	Y	Y	Y
4 **Perry**	N	N	Y	Y	+	Y
5 **Thompson**	Y	Y	Y	Y	Y	Y
6 **Costello**	Y	Y	Y	Y	Y	Y
7 **Meehan**	Y	Y	Y	Y	Y	Y
8 **Fitzpatrick**	Y	Y	Y	Y	Y	Y
9 **Shuster**	Y	Y	Y	Y	Y	Y
10 **Marino**	Y	Y	Y	Y	Y	Y
11 **Barletta**	Y	Y	Y	Y	Y	Y
12 **Rothfus**	Y	N	Y	Y	Y	Y
13 Boyle	N	N	Y	Y	?	?
14 Doyle	N	Y	Y	Y	N	N
15 **Dent**	Y	Y	Y	Y	Y	Y
16 **Smucker**	Y	N	Y	Y	Y	Y
17 Cartwright	N	Y	Y	Y	N	N
RHODE ISLAND						
1 Cicilline	N	N	Y	Y	N	N
2 Langevin	N	Y	Y	Y	N	N
SOUTH CAROLINA						
1 **Sanford**	Y	N	Y	Y	Y	Y
2 **Wilson**	Y	Y	Y	Y	Y	Y
3 **Duncan**	Y	N	?	?	?	?
4 **Gowdy**	Y	Y	Y	Y	Y	Y
5 **Norman**	Y	N	Y	Y	Y	Y
6 Clyburn	N	N	Y	Y	N	N
7 **Rice**	Y	N	Y	Y	Y	Y
SOUTH DAKOTA						
AL **Noem**	Y	N	Y	Y	Y	Y
TENNESSEE						
1 **Roe**	Y	Y	Y	Y	Y	Y
2 **Duncan**	Y	N	Y	Y	Y	Y
3 **Fleischmann**	Y	Y	Y	Y	Y	Y
4 **DesJarlais**	Y	Y	Y	Y	Y	Y
5 Cooper	N	N	Y	Y	N	N
6 **Black**	?	–	?	?	Y	Y
7 **Blackburn**	Y	Y	Y	Y	Y	Y
8 **Kustoff**	Y	Y	Y	Y	Y	Y
9 Cohen	N	Y	Y	Y	N	N

	68	69	70	71	72	73
TEXAS						
1 **Gohmert**	Y	N	Y	Y	Y	Y
2 **Poe**	Y	Y	Y	Y	Y	Y
3 **Johnson, S.**	Y	Y	Y	Y	Y	Y
4 **Ratcliffe**	Y	N	Y	Y	Y	Y
5 **Hensarling**	Y	N	Y	Y	Y	Y
6 **Barton**	Y	N	Y	Y	Y	Y
7 **Culberson**	Y	Y	Y	Y	Y	Y
8 **Brady**	Y	Y	Y	Y	Y	Y
9 Green, A.	N	Y	Y	Y	N	N
10 **McCaul**	Y	Y	Y	Y	Y	Y
11 **Conaway**	Y	Y	Y	Y	Y	Y
12 **Granger**	Y	Y	Y	Y	Y	Y
13 **Thornberry**	Y	Y	Y	Y	Y	Y
14 **Weber**	Y	Y	Y	Y	Y	Y
15 Gonzalez	N	Y	+	Y	N	N
16 O'Rourke	N	Y	+	+	N	N
17 **Flores**	Y	Y	?	?	Y	Y
18 Jackson Lee	N	Y	Y	Y	N	N
19 **Arrington**	Y	Y	Y	Y	Y	Y
20 Castro	N	N	Y	Y	N	N
21 **Smith**	Y	Y	Y	Y	Y	Y
22 **Olson**	Y	Y	Y	Y	Y	Y
23 **Hurd**	Y	Y	Y	Y	Y	Y
24 **Marchant**	Y	Y	Y	Y	Y	Y
25 **Williams**	Y	Y	Y	Y	Y	Y
26 **Burgess**	Y	Y	Y	Y	Y	Y
27 **Farenthold**	Y	Y	Y	Y	Y	Y
28 Cuellar	N	Y	Y	Y	N	N
29 Green, G.	N	Y	Y	Y	N	N
30 Johnson, E.B.	N	Y	Y	Y	N	N
31 **Carter**	Y	Y	?	?	Y	?
32 **Sessions**	Y	Y	?	?	Y	Y
33 Veasey	N	N	Y	Y	N	N
34 Vela	N	Y	Y	Y	N	N
35 Doggett	N	N	Y	Y	N	N
36 **Babin**	Y	Y	Y	Y	Y	Y
UTAH						
1 **Bishop**	?	Y	Y	Y	Y	Y
2 **Stewart**	Y	Y	Y	Y	Y	Y
3 **Curtis**	Y	N	Y	Y	Y	Y
4 **Love**	Y	Y	Y	Y	Y	Y
VERMONT						
AL Welch	N	Y	Y	Y	N	N
VIRGINIA						
1 **Wittman**	Y	Y	Y	Y	Y	Y
2 **Taylor**	Y	Y	Y	Y	Y	Y
3 Scott	N	Y	Y	Y	N	N
4 McEachin	N	N	Y	Y	N	N
5 **Garrett**	Y	N	Y	Y	Y	Y
6 **Goodlatte**	Y	Y	Y	Y	Y	Y
7 **Brat**	Y	N	Y	Y	Y	Y
8 Beyer	N	N	Y	Y	N	N
9 **Griffith**	Y	N	Y	Y	Y	Y
10 **Comstock**	Y	Y	Y	Y	Y	Y
11 Connolly	N	Y	Y	Y	N	N
WASHINGTON						
1 DelBene	N	Y	Y	Y	N	N
2 Larsen	N	Y	Y	Y	N	N
3 **Herrera Beutler**	Y	N	Y	Y	Y	Y
4 **Newhouse**	Y	N	Y	Y	Y	Y
5 **McMorris Rodgers**	Y	Y	Y	Y	Y	Y
6 Kilmer	N	Y	Y	Y	N	N
7 Jayapal	N	N	Y	Y	N	N
8 **Reichert**	Y	Y	Y	Y	Y	Y
9 Smith	N	N	Y	Y	N	N
10 Heck	N	Y	Y	Y	N	N
WEST VIRGINIA						
1 **McKinley**	Y	Y	Y	Y	Y	Y
2 **Mooney**	Y	N	Y	Y	Y	Y
3 **Jenkins**	Y	Y	Y	Y	Y	Y
WISCONSIN						
1 **Ryan**		Y				
2 Pocan	N	N	Y	Y	N	N
3 Kind	N	N	Y	Y	N	N
4 Moore	N	N	Y	Y	N	N
5 **Sensenbrenner**	Y	N	Y	Y	Y	Y
6 **Grothman**	Y	Y	Y	Y	Y	Y
7 **Duffy**	Y	Y	Y	Y	Y	Y
8 **Gallagher**	Y	Y	Y	Y	Y	Y
WYOMING						
AL **Cheney**	Y	Y	Y	Y	Y	Y

VOTE NUMBER

74. HR3542. HAMAS HUMAN SHIELD SANCTIONS/PASSAGE. Wilson, R-S.C., motion to suspend the rules and pass the bill that would direct the president to impose sanctions, including freezing of bank accounts and property in the United States, and the revocation or denial of visas, against members of Hamas who are responsible for ordering or directing the use of human shields. The measure would also call on the president to direct the U.S. ambassador to the United Nations to secure support for a resolution that would impose multilateral sanctions against Hamas for the use of human shields to protect combatants and military objects from attack. Motion agreed to 415-0: R 228-0; D 187-0. Feb. 14, 2018.

75. HRES129. RECOVERING MISSING AND UNACCOUNTED-FOR U.S. PERSONNEL WORLDWIDE/PASSAGE. Wilson, R-S.C., motion to suspend the rules and agree to the resolution that would call upon the Defense POW/MIA Accounting Agency and other elements of the Defense Department, as well as other federal agencies and all foreign governments, to intensify efforts to investigate, recover, identify and as fully as possible account for all missing and unaccounted-for U.S. personnel worldwide. Motion agreed to 411-0: R 227-0; D 184-0. Feb. 14, 2018.

76. HR3978. FINANCIAL INSTITUTION ASSESSMENT REQUIREMENTS/ RECOMMIT. Capuano D-Mass., motion to recommit the bill to the House Financial Services committee with instructions to report back immediately with an amendment that would extend the current policy requiring executive officer incentive-based compensation be clawed-back in a case where the issuer is required to prepare an accounting restatement due to noncompliance with any reporting requirements under securities laws. Motion rejected 189-228: R 2-228; D 187-0. Feb. 14, 2018.

77. HR3978. FINANCIAL INSTITUTION ASSESSMENT REQUIREMENTS/ PASSAGE. Passage of the bill that would modify regulations related to financial services, including exempting from state regulations all securities that qualify for trading in any registered national market system, the listing standards of which have been approved by the Securities and Exchange Commission. It would also prohibit the SEC, unless it has issued a subpoena, from compelling a person to produce or furnish source code for automated trading to the agency, including algorithmic trading source code. It would exempt, for an additional five years, emerging growth companies from the requirement that an independent auditor attest to management's assessment of the company's internal controls over financial reporting. It would require the Financial Stability Oversight Council to consider the appropriateness of imposing heightened prudential standards as opposed to other forms of regulation to mitigate identified risks to the U.S. financial stability when determining whether to subject a U.S. or a foreign nonbank financial company to supervision by the Federal Reserve. In addition, the bill would modify the mortgage disclosure requirements that must be provided by a lender to borrowers by allowing the disclosure to include a discounted rate that a title insurance company may provide to borrowers if they were to simultaneously purchase both a lenders and owners title insurance policy. (Truncated, visit cq.com for more.) Passed 271-145: R 228-1; D 43-144. Feb. 14, 2018.

78. HR3299. INTEREST RATE REGULATION/PASSAGE. Passage of the bill that would amend the Home Owners' Loan Act, the Federal Credit Union Act, and the Federal Deposit Insurance Act to codify the "valid-when-made" doctrine, which requires that the rate of interest of certain loans remain unchanged after sale, assignment or transfer of the loans. Passed 245-171: R 229-1; D 16-170. Feb. 14, 2018.

79. HR620. ADA INFRACTION NOTIFICATION/WRITTEN NOTIFICATION REQUIREMENT. Langevin D-R.I., amendment that would remove the bill's requirement that a person who claims discrimination must first provide written notice that allows 60 days for an owner to acknowledge receipt of the complaint and 120 days to demonstrate substantial progress in removing the barrier before legal action may be pursued. Rejected in Committee of the Whole 188-226: R 15-215; D 173-11. Feb. 15, 2018.

	74	75	76	77	78	79
ALABAMA						
1 **Byrne**	?	?	N	Y	Y	N
2 **Roby**	Y	Y	N	Y	Y	N
3 **Rogers**	Y	Y	N	Y	Y	N
4 **Aderholt**	Y	Y	N	Y	Y	N
5 **Brooks**	Y	Y	N	Y	Y	N
6 **Palmer**	Y	Y	N	Y	Y	N
7 Sewell	Y	Y	Y	Y	N	Y
ALASKA						
AL **Young**	Y	Y	N	Y	Y	N
ARIZONA						
1 O'Halleran	Y	Y	Y	Y	N	Y
2 **McSally**	Y	Y	N	Y	Y	N
3 Grijalva	Y	Y	Y	N	N	Y
4 **Gosar**	Y	Y	N	Y	Y	N
5 **Biggs**	Y	Y	N	Y	Y	N
6 **Schweikert**	Y	Y	N	Y	Y	N
7 Gallego	Y	Y	Y	N	N	Y
9 Sinema	Y	Y	Y	Y	Y	N
ARKANSAS						
1 **Crawford**	Y	Y	N	Y	Y	N
2 **Hill**	Y	Y	N	Y	Y	N
3 **Womack**	Y	Y	N	Y	Y	N
4 **Westerman**	Y	Y	N	Y	Y	N
CALIFORNIA						
1 **LaMalfa**	Y	Y	N	Y	Y	N
2 Huffman	Y	Y	Y	N	N	Y
3 Garamendi	Y	Y	Y	N	N	Y
4 **McClintock**	Y	Y	N	Y	Y	N
5 Thompson	Y	Y	Y	N	N	Y
6 Matsui	Y	Y	Y	N	N	Y
7 Bera	Y	Y	Y	Y	N	N
8 **Cook**	Y	Y	N	Y	Y	N
9 McNerney	Y	Y	Y	N	N	Y
10 **Denham**	+	+	N	Y	Y	N
11 DeSaulnier	Y	Y	Y	N	N	Y
12 Pelosi	Y	Y	Y	N	N	Y
13 Lee	Y	Y	Y	N	N	Y
14 Speier	Y	Y	Y	N	N	N
15 Swalwell	Y	Y	Y	N	N	Y
16 Costa	?	?	?	?	?	?
17 Khanna	Y	Y	Y	N	N	Y
18 Eshoo	Y	Y	Y	N	N	Y
19 Lofgren	Y	Y	Y	N	N	Y
20 Panetta	Y	Y	Y	N	N	Y
21 **Valadao**	Y	Y	N	Y	Y	N
22 **Nunes**	Y	Y	N	Y	Y	N
23 **McCarthy**	Y	Y	N	Y	Y	N
24 Carbajal	Y	Y	Y	N	N	Y
25 **Knight**	Y	Y	N	Y	Y	N
26 Brownley	Y	Y	Y	N	N	Y
27 Chu	Y	Y	Y	N	N	Y
28 Schiff	Y	Y	Y	N	N	Y
29 Cardenas	Y	Y	Y	N	Y	Y
30 Sherman	Y	Y	Y	Y	N	Y
31 Aguilar	Y	Y	Y	Y	N	Y
32 Napolitano	Y	Y	Y	Y	N	Y
33 Lieu	Y	Y	Y	N	N	Y
34 Gomez	Y	Y	Y	N	N	Y
35 Torres	Y	Y	Y	N	N	N
36 Ruiz	Y	Y	Y	N	N	Y
37 Bass	?	?	?	?	?	?
38 Sánchez, Linda	Y	Y	Y	N	N	Y
39 **Royce**	Y	Y	N	Y	Y	N
40 Roybal-Allard	Y	Y	Y	N	N	Y
41 Takano	Y	Y	Y	N	N	Y
42 **Calvert**	Y	Y	N	Y	Y	N
43 Waters	Y	Y	Y	N	N	Y
44 Barragan	Y	Y	Y	N	N	Y
45 **Walters**	Y	Y	N	Y	Y	N
46 Correa	Y	Y	Y	Y	Y	N
47 **Lowenthal**	Y	Y	Y	N	N	Y
48 **Rohrabacher**	Y	Y	N	Y	Y	N
49 **Issa**	Y	Y	N	Y	Y	N
50 **Hunter**	Y	Y	N	Y	Y	N
51 Vargas	Y	Y	Y	N	N	Y
52 Peters	Y	Y	Y	Y	N	N
53 Davis	Y	Y	Y	N	N	Y

	74	75	76	77	78	79
COLORADO						
1 DeGette	Y	Y	Y	N	N	Y
2 Polis	Y	Y	Y	Y	N	Y
3 **Tipton**	Y	Y	N	Y	Y	N
4 **Buck**	Y	Y	N	Y	Y	N
5 **Lamborn**	Y	Y	N	Y	Y	N
6 **Coffman**	Y	Y	N	Y	Y	N
7 Perlmutter	Y	Y	Y	N	N	Y
CONNECTICUT						
1 Larson	Y	Y	Y	N	N	Y
2 Courtney	Y	Y	Y	N	N	?
3 DeLauro	Y	Y	Y	N	N	Y
4 Himes	Y	Y	Y	N	Y	Y
5 Esty	Y	Y	Y	N	N	Y
DELAWARE						
AL Blunt Rochester	Y	Y	Y	N	N	Y
FLORIDA						
1 **Gaetz**	Y	Y	N	Y	Y	?
2 **Dunn**	Y	Y	N	Y	Y	N
3 **Yoho**	Y	Y	N	Y	Y	N
4 **Rutherford**	Y	Y	N	Y	Y	N
5 Lawson	Y	Y	Y	N	N	Y
6 **DeSantis**	Y	Y	N	Y	Y	N
7 Murphy	Y	Y	Y	Y	Y	Y
8 **Posey**	?	?	?	?	?	N
9 Soto	Y	Y	Y	N	N	Y
10 Demings	Y	Y	Y	N	N	Y
11 **Webster**	Y	Y	N	Y	Y	N
12 **Bilirakis**	Y	Y	N	Y	Y	N
13 Crist	Y	Y	Y	N	N	Y
14 Castor	Y	Y	Y	N	N	Y
15 **Ross**	Y	Y	N	Y	Y	N
16 **Buchanan**	Y	Y	N	Y	Y	N
17 **Rooney, T.**	Y	Y	N	Y	Y	N
18 **Mast**	Y	Y	N	Y	Y	N
19 **Rooney, F.**	Y	Y	N	Y	Y	N
20 Hastings	Y	Y	Y	N	Y	Y
21 Frankel	Y	Y	Y	N	N	Y
22 Deutch	Y	Y	Y	N	N	?
23 Wasserman Schultz	Y	Y	Y	N	N	?
24 Wilson	Y	Y	Y	N	N	Y
25 **Diaz-Balart**	Y	Y	N	Y	Y	N
26 **Curbelo**	Y	Y	N	Y	Y	N
27 **Ros-Lehtinen**	Y	Y	N	Y	Y	Y
GEORGIA						
1 **Carter**	Y	Y	N	Y	Y	N
2 Bishop	Y	Y	Y	N	N	?
3 **Ferguson**	Y	Y	Y	N	Y	N
4 Johnson	Y	Y	Y	N	?	?
5 Lewis	Y	Y	Y	N	N	Y
6 **Handel**	Y	Y	N	Y	Y	N
7 **Woodall**	Y	Y	N	Y	Y	N
8 **Scott, A.**	Y	Y	N	Y	Y	N
9 **Collins**	Y	Y	N	Y	Y	N
10 **Hice**	Y	Y	N	Y	Y	N
11 **Loudermilk**	Y	Y	N	Y	Y	N
12 **Allen**	Y	Y	N	Y	Y	N
13 **Scott, D.**	Y	Y	Y	Y	Y	Y
14 **Graves**	Y	Y	N	Y	Y	N
HAWAII						
1 Hanabusa	Y	Y	Y	N	N	Y
2 Gabbard	Y	Y	Y	N	N	Y
IDAHO						
1 **Labrador**	Y	Y	N	Y	Y	N
2 **Simpson**	Y	Y	N	Y	Y	N
ILLINOIS						
1 Rush	Y	Y	Y	N	N	Y
2 Kelly	Y	Y	Y	N	N	Y
3 Lipinski	Y	Y	Y	Y	N	Y
4 Gutierrez	+	+	+	–	–	+
5 Quigley	Y	Y	Y	N	N	Y
6 **Roskam**	Y	Y	N	Y	Y	N
7 Davis, D.	Y	Y	Y	N	N	Y
8 Krishnamoorthi	Y	Y	Y	N	N	Y
9 Schakowsky	Y	Y	Y	N	N	Y
10 Schneider	Y	Y	Y	Y	Y	Y
11 Foster	Y	Y	Y	Y	N	N
12 **Bost**	Y	Y	N	Y	Y	N
13 **Davis, R.**	Y	Y	N	Y	Y	N

	74	75	76	77	78	79
14 **Hultgren**	Y	Y	N	Y	Y	N
15 **Shimkus**	Y	Y	N	Y	Y	N
16 **Kinzinger**	Y	Y	N	Y	Y	N
17 Bustos	Y	Y	Y	Y	N	Y
18 **LaHood**	Y	Y	N	Y	Y	N
INDIANA						
1 Visclosky	Y	Y	Y	N	N	Y
2 **Walorski**	Y	Y	N	Y	Y	N
3 **Banks**	Y	Y	N	Y	Y	N
4 **Rokita**	Y	Y	N	Y	Y	N
5 **Brooks**	Y	Y	N	Y	Y	N
6 **Messer**	Y	Y	N	Y	Y	N
7 Carson	Y	Y	Y	N	N	Y
8 **Bucshon**	Y	Y	N	Y	Y	N
9 **Hollingsworth**	Y	Y	N	Y	Y	N
IOWA						
1 **Blum**	Y	Y	Y	Y	Y	N
2 Loebsack	Y	Y	Y	Y	N	Y
3 **Young**	Y	Y	N	Y	Y	N
4 **King**	Y	Y	N	Y	Y	N
KANSAS						
1 **Marshall**	Y	Y	N	Y	Y	N
2 **Jenkins**	Y	Y	N	Y	Y	N
3 **Yoder**	Y	Y	N	Y	Y	Y
4 **Estes**	Y	Y	N	Y	Y	N
KENTUCKY						
1 **Comer**	Y	Y	N	Y	Y	N
2 **Guthrie**	Y	Y	N	Y	Y	N
3 Yarmuth	Y	?	Y	N	N	Y
4 **Massie**	Y	Y	N	Y	Y	N
5 **Rogers**	+	+	–	+	+	–
6 **Barr**	Y	Y	N	Y	Y	N
LOUISIANA						
1 **Scalise**	Y	Y	N	+	+	N
2 Richmond	Y	Y	Y	N	N	Y
3 **Higgins**	Y	Y	N	Y	Y	N
4 **Johnson**	Y	Y	N	Y	Y	N
5 **Abraham**	Y	Y	N	Y	Y	N
6 **Graves**	Y	?	N	Y	Y	N
MAINE						
1 Pingree	Y	Y	Y	N	N	Y
2 **Poliquin**	Y	Y	N	Y	Y	N
MARYLAND						
1 **Harris**	Y	Y	N	Y	Y	N
2 Ruppersberger	Y	Y	Y	Y	N	Y
3 Sarbanes	Y	Y	Y	N	N	Y
4 Brown	Y	Y	Y	N	N	Y
5 Hoyer	Y	Y	Y	N	N	Y
6 Delaney	Y	Y	Y	Y	N	Y
7 Cummings	?	?	?	?	?	?
8 Raskin	Y	Y	Y	N	N	Y
MASSACHUSETTS						
1 Neal	Y	Y	Y	N	N	Y
2 McGovern	Y	Y	Y	N	N	Y
3 Tsongas	Y	Y	Y	N	N	Y
4 Kennedy	Y	Y	Y	N	N	Y
5 Clark	Y	Y	Y	N	N	Y
6 Moulton	Y	Y	Y	N	N	Y
7 Capuano	Y	Y	Y	N	N	Y
8 Lynch	Y	Y	Y	N	N	Y
9 Keating	Y	Y	Y	N	N	Y
MICHIGAN						
1 **Bergman**	Y	Y	N	Y	Y	N
2 **Huizenga**	Y	Y	N	Y	Y	N
3 *Amash*	Y	Y	N	Y	Y	N
4 **Moolenaar**	Y	Y	N	Y	Y	N
5 Kildee	Y	Y	Y	N	N	Y
6 Upton	Y	Y	N	Y	Y	Y
7 Walberg	Y	Y	N	Y	Y	N
8 Bishop	Y	Y	N	Y	Y	N
9 Levin	Y	Y	Y	N	N	Y
10 Mitchell	Y	Y	N	Y	Y	N
11 Trott	Y	Y	N	Y	Y	N
12 Dingell	Y	Y	Y	N	N	Y
14 Lawrence	Y	Y	Y	N	N	Y
MINNESOTA						
1 Walz	Y	Y	Y	N	N	Y
2 **Lewis**	Y	Y	N	Y	Y	N
3 **Paulsen**	Y	Y	N	Y	Y	N
4 **McCollum**	Y	Y	Y	N	N	Y

	74	75	76	77	78	79
5 Ellison	Y	Y	Y	N	N	Y
6 **Emmer**	Y	Y	N	Y	Y	N
7 Peterson	Y	Y	Y	Y	Y	Y
8 Nolan	Y	Y	Y	N	N	Y
MISSISSIPPI						
1 **Kelly**	Y	Y	N	Y	Y	N
2 Thompson	Y	Y	Y	N	N	Y
3 **Harper**	Y	Y	N	Y	Y	Y
4 Palazzo	Y	Y	N	Y	Y	N
MISSOURI						
1 Clay	Y	Y	Y	N	N	Y
2 **Wagner**	Y	Y	N	Y	Y	N
3 **Luetkemeyer**	Y	Y	N	Y	Y	N
4 **Hartzler**	Y	Y	N	Y	Y	N
5 Cleaver	Y	Y	Y	N	N	Y
6 **Graves**	Y	Y	N	Y	Y	N
7 **Long**	Y	Y	N	Y	Y	N
8 **Smith**	Y	Y	N	Y	Y	N
MONTANA						
AL **Gianforte**	Y	Y	N	Y	Y	N
NEBRASKA						
1 **Fortenberry**	Y	Y	N	Y	Y	N
2 **Bacon**	Y	Y	N	Y	Y	N
3 **Smith**	Y	Y	N	Y	Y	N
NEVADA						
1 Titus	Y	Y	Y	N	N	Y
2 **Amodei**	Y	Y	N	Y	Y	N
3 Rosen	Y	Y	Y	N	N	Y
4 Kihuen	Y	Y	Y	Y	N	Y
NEW HAMPSHIRE						
1 Shea-Porter	Y	Y	Y	N	N	Y
2 Kuster	Y	Y	Y	Y	N	Y
NEW JERSEY						
1 Norcross	Y	Y	Y	N	N	Y
2 **LoBiondo**	?	?	?	?	?	?
3 **MacArthur**	Y	Y	N	Y	Y	N
4 **Smith**	Y	Y	N	Y	Y	Y
5 Gottheimer	Y	Y	Y	Y	Y	Y
6 Pallone	Y	Y	Y	N	N	Y
7 **Lance**	Y	Y	N	Y	Y	Y
8 Sires	Y	Y	Y	N	N	Y
9 Pascrell	Y	Y	Y	N	N	Y
10 Payne	Y	Y	Y	N	N	Y
11 **Frelinghuysen**	Y	Y	N	Y	Y	Y
12 Watson Coleman	+	+	+	–	–	Y
NEW MEXICO						
1 Lujan Grisham	Y	Y	Y	N	N	Y
2 **Pearce**	?	?	?	?	?	?
3 Luján	Y	Y	Y	N	N	Y
NEW YORK						
1 **Zeldin**	Y	Y	N	Y	Y	N
2 **King**	Y	Y	N	Y	Y	Y
3 Suozzi	Y	Y	Y	Y	Y	Y
4 Rice	Y	Y	Y	Y	N	N
5 Meeks	Y	Y	Y	Y	Y	Y
6 Meng	Y	Y	Y	N	N	Y
7 Velázquez	Y	?	Y	N	N	Y
8 Jeffries	Y	Y	Y	N	N	Y
9 Clarke	Y	Y	Y	N	N	Y
10 Nadler	Y	Y	Y	N	N	Y
11 **Donovan**	Y	Y	N	Y	Y	N
12 Maloney, C.	Y	Y	Y	N	N	Y
13 Espaillat	Y	Y	Y	N	N	Y
14 Crowley	Y	Y	Y	N	N	Y
15 Serrano	Y	Y	Y	N	N	Y
16 Engel	Y	Y	Y	N	N	Y
17 Lowey	Y	Y	Y	N	N	Y
18 Maloney, S.P.	Y	Y	Y	Y	N	Y
19 **Faso**	Y	Y	N	Y	Y	N
20 Tonko	Y	Y	Y	N	N	Y
21 **Stefanik**	Y	Y	N	Y	Y	N
22 **Tenney**	Y	Y	?	Y	Y	N
23 **Reed**	Y	Y	N	Y	Y	N
24 **Katko**	Y	Y	N	Y	Y	Y
25 Slaughter	Y	Y	Y	N	N	Y
26 Higgins	Y	Y	Y	N	N	Y
27 **Collins**	Y	Y	N	Y	Y	N
NORTH CAROLINA						
1 Butterfield	Y	Y	Y	N	N	Y
2 **Holding**	Y	Y	N	Y	Y	N
3 **Jones**	Y	Y	Y	N	N	N
4 Price	Y	Y	Y	N	N	Y

	74	75	76	77	78	79
5 **Foxx**	Y	Y	N	Y	Y	N
6 **Walker**	Y	Y	N	Y	Y	N
7 **Rouzer**	Y	Y	N	Y	Y	N
8 **Hudson**	Y	Y	N	Y	Y	N
9 **Pittenger**	Y	Y	N	Y	Y	N
9 **Vacant**						
10 **McHenry**	Y	Y	N	Y	Y	N
11 **Meadows**	Y	Y	N	Y	Y	N
12 Adams	Y	Y	Y	N	N	Y
13 **Budd**	Y	Y	N	Y	Y	N
NORTH DAKOTA						
AL **Cramer**	Y	Y	N	Y	Y	N
OHIO						
1 **Chabot**	Y	Y	N	Y	Y	N
2 **Wenstrup**	Y	Y	N	Y	Y	N
3 Beatty	Y	Y	Y	N	N	Y
4 **Jordan**	Y	Y	N	Y	Y	N
5 **Latta**	Y	Y	N	Y	Y	N
6 **Johnson**	Y	Y	N	Y	Y	N
7 **Gibbs**	Y	Y	N	Y	Y	N
8 **Davidson**	Y	Y	N	Y	Y	N
9 Kaptur	Y	Y	Y	N	N	Y
10 **Turner**	Y	Y	N	Y	Y	?
11 Fudge	Y	Y	Y	N	N	Y
12 **Vacant**						
13 Ryan	Y	Y	Y	N	N	Y
14 **Joyce**	?	Y	N	Y	Y	N
15 **Stivers**	?	?	?	?	?	N
16 **Renacci**	Y	Y	N	Y	Y	N
OKLAHOMA						
1 **Bridenstine**	Y	Y	N	Y	Y	N
2 **Mullin**	Y	Y	N	Y	Y	N
3 **Lucas**	Y	Y	N	Y	Y	N
4 **Cole**	Y	Y	N	Y	Y	N
5 **Russell**	Y	Y	N	Y	Y	N
OREGON						
1 Bonamici	Y	Y	Y	N	N	Y
2 **Walden**	Y	Y	N	Y	Y	N
3 Blumenauer	Y	Y	Y	N	N	Y
4 DeFazio	Y	Y	Y	N	N	Y
5 Schrader	Y	Y	Y	Y	N	N
PENNSYLVANIA						
1 Brady	Y	Y	Y	N	N	Y
2 Evans	Y	Y	Y	N	N	Y
3 **Kelly**	Y	Y	N	Y	Y	N
4 **Perry**	Y	Y	N	Y	Y	N
5 **Thompson**	Y	Y	N	Y	Y	Y
6 **Costello**	Y	Y	N	Y	Y	Y
7 **Meehan**	Y	Y	N	Y	Y	N
8 **Fitzpatrick**	Y	Y	N	Y	Y	Y
9 **Shuster**	Y	Y	N	Y	Y	N
10 **Marino**	Y	Y	N	Y	Y	N
11 **Barletta**	Y	Y	N	Y	Y	N
12 **Rothfus**	Y	Y	N	Y	Y	N
13 Boyle	?	?	?	?	?	Y
14 Doyle	Y	Y	Y	N	N	Y
15 **Dent**	Y	Y	N	Y	Y	N
16 **Smucker**	Y	Y	N	Y	Y	N
17 Cartwright	Y	Y	Y	N	N	Y
RHODE ISLAND						
1 Cicilline	Y	Y	Y	N	N	Y
2 Langevin	Y	Y	Y	N	N	Y
SOUTH CAROLINA						
1 **Sanford**	Y	Y	N	Y	Y	N
2 **Wilson**	Y	Y	N	Y	Y	N
3 **Duncan**	?	?	?	?	?	?
4 **Gowdy**	Y	Y	N	Y	Y	N
5 **Norman**	Y	Y	N	Y	Y	N
6 Clyburn	Y	Y	Y	N	N	Y
7 **Rice**	Y	Y	N	Y	Y	N
SOUTH DAKOTA						
AL **Noem**	Y	Y	N	Y	Y	N
TENNESSEE						
1 **Roe**	Y	Y	N	Y	Y	N
2 **Duncan**	Y	Y	N	Y	Y	N
3 **Fleischmann**	Y	Y	N	Y	Y	N
4 **DesJarlais**	Y	Y	N	Y	Y	N
5 Cooper	Y	Y	Y	Y	N	N
6 **Black**	Y	Y	N	Y	Y	N
7 **Blackburn**	Y	Y	N	Y	Y	N
8 **Kustoff**	Y	Y	N	Y	Y	N
9 Cohen	Y	Y	Y	N	N	Y

	74	75	76	77	78	79
TEXAS						
1 **Gohmert**	Y	Y	N	Y	Y	N
2 **Poe**	Y	Y	N	Y	Y	N
3 **Johnson, S.**	Y	Y	N	Y	Y	N
4 **Ratcliffe**	Y	Y	N	Y	Y	N
5 **Hensarling**	Y	Y	N	Y	Y	N
6 **Barton**	Y	Y	N	Y	Y	N
7 **Culberson**	Y	Y	N	Y	Y	N
8 **Brady**	Y	Y	N	Y	Y	N
9 Green, A.	Y	Y	Y	N	N	Y
10 McCaul	Y	Y	N	Y	Y	N
11 **Conaway**	Y	Y	N	Y	Y	N
12 **Granger**	Y	Y	N	Y	Y	N
13 **Thornberry**	Y	Y	N	Y	Y	N
14 **Weber**	Y	Y	N	Y	Y	N
15 Gonzalez	Y	Y	Y	Y	N	Y
16 O'Rourke	Y	Y	Y	Y	N	Y
17 **Flores**	Y	Y	N	Y	Y	N
18 Jackson Lee	Y	Y	Y	N	N	Y
19 **Arrington**	Y	Y	N	Y	Y	N
20 Castro	Y	Y	Y	N	N	Y
21 **Smith**	Y	Y	N	Y	Y	N
22 **Olson**	Y	Y	N	Y	Y	N
23 **Hurd**	Y	Y	N	Y	Y	N
24 **Marchant**	Y	Y	N	Y	Y	N
25 **Williams**	Y	Y	N	Y	Y	N
26 **Burgess**	Y	Y	N	Y	Y	N
27 **Farenthold**	Y	Y	N	Y	Y	N
28 Cuellar	Y	Y	Y	Y	Y	N
29 Green, G.	Y	Y	Y	N	Y	Y
30 Johnson, E.B.	Y	Y	Y	N	N	Y
31 **Carter**	Y	Y	N	Y	Y	N
32 **Sessions**	Y	Y	N	Y	Y	N
33 Veasey	Y	Y	Y	Y	N	Y
34 Vela	Y	Y	Y	Y	N	Y
35 Doggett	Y	Y	Y	N	N	Y
36 **Babin**	Y	?	N	Y	Y	N
UTAH						
1 **Bishop**	Y	Y	N	Y	Y	N
2 **Stewart**	Y	Y	N	Y	Y	N
3 **Curtis**	Y	Y	N	Y	Y	N
4 **Love**	Y	Y	N	Y	Y	N
VERMONT						
AL Welch	Y	Y	Y	N	N	Y
VIRGINIA						
1 **Wittman**	Y	Y	N	Y	Y	N
2 **Taylor**	Y	Y	N	Y	Y	N
3 Scott	Y	Y	Y	N	N	Y
4 McEachin	Y	Y	Y	N	N	Y
5 **Garrett**	Y	Y	N	Y	Y	N
6 **Goodlatte**	Y	Y	N	Y	Y	N
7 **Brat**	Y	Y	N	Y	Y	N
8 Beyer	Y	Y	Y	Y	N	Y
9 **Griffith**	Y	Y	N	Y	Y	N
10 **Comstock**	Y	Y	N	Y	Y	Y
11 Connolly	Y	Y	Y	N	N	Y
WASHINGTON						
1 DelBene	Y	Y	Y	Y	N	Y
2 Larsen	Y	Y	Y	Y	N	Y
3 **Herrera Beutler**	Y	Y	N	Y	Y	N
4 **Newhouse**	Y	Y	N	Y	Y	N
5 **McMorris Rodgers**	Y	Y	N	Y	Y	N
6 Kilmer	Y	Y	Y	Y	N	Y
7 Jayapal	Y	?	Y	N	N	Y
8 **Reichert**	Y	Y	N	Y	Y	Y
9 Smith	Y	Y	Y	N	N	Y
10 Heck	Y	Y	Y	Y	Y	Y
WEST VIRGINIA						
1 **McKinley**	Y	Y	N	Y	Y	N
2 **Mooney**	Y	Y	N	Y	Y	N
3 **Jenkins**	Y	Y	N	Y	Y	N
WISCONSIN						
1 **Ryan**						
2 Pocan	Y	Y	Y	N	N	Y
3 Kind	Y	Y	Y	Y	Y	Y
4 Moore	Y	Y	Y	N	Y	Y
5 **Sensenbrenner**	Y	Y	N	Y	Y	Y
6 **Grothman**	Y	Y	N	?	Y	N
7 **Duffy**	Y	Y	N	Y	Y	N
8 **Gallagher**	Y	Y	N	Y	Y	N
WYOMING						
AL **Cheney**	Y	Y	N	Y	Y	?

VOTE NUMBER

80. HR620. ADA INFRACTION NOTIFICATION/PASSAGE. Passage of the bill that would require individuals to verbally request the removal of an architectural barrier and provide written notice to give an establishment sufficient time to correct the infraction before filing a lawsuit under the Americans for Disabilities Act. It would also require the Justice Department to establish a program that would provide educational and training grants for professionals to provide guidance to state and local governments and property owners on the required public accommodations. Passed 225-192: R 213-19; D 12-173. Feb. 15, 2018.

81. HR1222. CONGENITAL HEART DISEASE RESEARCH/PASSAGE. Burgess, R-Texas, motion to suspend the rules and pass the bill that would authorize $4 million annually, through fiscal 2022, for the Health and Human Services Department to conduct a national study of congenital heart diseases and to increase awareness of congenital heart diseases. Motion agreed to 394-7: R 217-7; D 177-0. Feb. 26, 2018.

82. HR2422. DENTAL HEALTH PROGRAMS/PASSAGE. Burgess, R-Texas, motion to suspend the rules and pass the bill that would authorize $14 million annually, through fiscal 2022 for the Health Resources and Services Administration's dental health grant program and would allow funds to be used to provide comprehensive dental care to the elderly, children and individuals with disabilities. It would also authorize $18 million annually, through fiscal 2022, for existing water fluoridation and school tooth sealant programs and a new Centers for Disease Control program to improve oral health education. Motion agreed to 387-13: R 209-13; D 178-0. Feb. 26, 2018.

83. GUN REGULATIONS/MOTION TO TABLE. Burgess, R-Texas, motion to table (kill) the Thompson, D-Calif., motion to appeal the ruling of the Chair that the Thompson resolution related to the consideration of legislation related to gun regulations does not constitute a question of the privileges of the House. Motion agreed to 228-184: R 228-0; D 0-184. Feb. 27, 2018.

84. HRES748. WEBSITES FACILITATING SEX TRAFFICKING/PREVIOUS QUESTION. Collins, R-Ga., motion to order the previous question (thus ending debate and possibility of amendment) on the rule (H Res 748) that would provide for House floor consideration of the bill (HR 1865) that would explicitly make the use or operation of a website to promote or facilitate prostitution a federal crime. Motion agreed to 228-184: R 228-0; D 0-184. Feb. 27, 2018.

85. HR1865. WEBSITES FACILITATING SEX TRAFFICKING/RULE. Adoption of the rule (H Res 748) that would provide for consideration of the bill (HR 1865) that would make the use or operation of a website to promote or facilitate prostitution a federal crime. It would allow states to prosecute such conduct under state law, regardless of the immunity provisions in the 1996 Communications Decency Act, as long as the state's laws mirror federal prohibitions. Adopted 235-175: R 226-0; D 9-175. Feb. 27, 2018.

	80	81	82	83	84	85
ALABAMA						
1 **Byrne**	Y	Y	Y	Y	Y	Y
2 **Roby**	Y	Y	Y	Y	Y	Y
3 **Rogers**	Y	Y	Y	Y	Y	Y
4 **Aderholt**	Y	Y	Y	Y	Y	Y
5 **Brooks**	Y	N	N	Y	Y	Y
6 **Palmer**	Y	Y	Y	Y	Y	Y
7 Sewell	N	Y	Y	N	N	N
ALASKA						
AL **Young**	N	Y	Y	Y	Y	Y
ARIZONA						
1 O'Halleran	N	Y	Y	N	N	Y
2 **McSally**	Y	Y	Y	Y	Y	Y
3 Grijalva	N	Y	?	N	N	N
4 **Gosar**	Y	Y	Y	Y	Y	Y
5 **Biggs**	Y	N	N	Y	Y	Y
6 **Schweikert**	Y	Y	Y	Y	Y	Y
7 Gallego	N	Y	N	N	N	N
9 Sinema	N	Y	Y	N	N	Y
ARKANSAS						
1 **Crawford**	Y	Y	Y	Y	Y	Y
2 **Hill**	Y	Y	Y	Y	Y	Y
3 **Womack**	Y	Y	Y	Y	Y	Y
4 **Westerman**	Y	Y	Y	Y	Y	Y
CALIFORNIA						
1 **LaMalfa**	Y	Y	Y	Y	Y	Y
2 Huffman	N	Y	N	N	N	N
3 Garamendi	N	Y	Y	N	N	N
4 **McClintock**	Y	Y	N	Y	Y	Y
5 Thompson	N	Y	Y	N	N	N
6 Matsui	N	Y	N	N	N	N
7 Bera	Y	Y	Y	N	N	N
8 **Cook**	Y	Y	Y	Y	Y	Y
9 McNerney	N	Y	N	N	N	N
10 **Denham**	Y	Y	Y	Y	Y	Y
11 DeSaulnier	N	Y	N	N	N	N
12 Pelosi	N	Y	N	N	N	N
13 Lee	N	Y	N	N	N	N
14 Speier	Y	?	?	?	?	?
15 Swalwell	N	Y	N	N	N	N
16 Costa	?	Y	N	N	N	N
17 Khanna	N	Y	N	N	N	N
18 Eshoo	N	Y	N	N	N	N
19 Lofgren	N	Y	N	N	N	N
20 Panetta	N	Y	N	N	N	N
21 **Valadao**	Y	Y	Y	Y	Y	Y
22 **Nunes**	Y	Y	Y	Y	Y	Y
23 **McCarthy**	Y	Y	Y	Y	Y	Y
24 Carbajal	N	Y	N	N	N	N
25 **Knight**	Y	Y	Y	Y	Y	Y
26 Brownley	N	Y	N	N	N	N
27 Chu	N	Y	N	N	N	?
28 Schiff	N	Y	N	N	N	N
29 Cardenas	N	Y	N	N	N	N
30 Sherman	N	Y	N	N	N	N
31 Aguilar	Y	Y	N	N	N	N
32 Napolitano	N	Y	N	N	N	N
33 Lieu	N	Y	N	N	N	N
34 Gomez	N	Y	N	N	N	N
35 Torres	Y	Y	Y	–	–	–
36 Ruiz	N	Y	N	N	N	N
37 Bass	?	Y	N	N	N	N
38 Sánchez, Linda	N	Y	N	N	N	N
39 **Royce**	Y	Y	Y	Y	Y	Y
40 Roybal-Allard	N	Y	N	N	N	N
41 Takano	N	Y	N	N	N	N
42 **Calvert**	Y	Y	Y	Y	Y	Y
43 Waters	N	Y	N	N	N	N
44 Barragan	N	Y	N	N	N	N
45 **Walters**	Y	Y	Y	Y	Y	Y
46 Correa	Y	Y	Y	N	N	N
47 Lowenthal	N	Y	N	N	N	N
48 **Rohrabacher**	Y	Y	Y	Y	Y	Y
49 **Issa**	Y	Y	?	Y	Y	Y
50 **Hunter**	Y	Y	Y	Y	Y	Y
51 Vargas	N	?	?	N	N	N
52 Peters	Y	Y	Y	N	N	N
53 Davis	N	Y	Y	N	–	N

	80	81	82	83	84	85
COLORADO						
1 DeGette	N	Y	N	N	N	N
2 Polis	N	Y	N	N	N	N
3 **Tipton**	Y	Y	Y	Y	Y	Y
4 **Buck**	Y	Y	N	Y	Y	Y
5 **Lamborn**	Y	Y	Y	Y	Y	Y
6 **Coffman**	Y	Y	Y	Y	Y	Y
7 Perlmutter	N	Y	N	N	N	N
CONNECTICUT						
1 Larson	N	Y	N	N	N	N
2 Courtney	–	Y	Y	N	N	N
3 DeLauro	N	Y	N	N	N	N
4 Himes	N	Y	N	N	N	N
5 Esty	N	Y	N	N	N	N
DELAWARE						
AL Blunt Rochester	N	Y	Y	N	N	N
FLORIDA						
1 **Gaetz**	Y	Y	N	Y	Y	Y
2 **Dunn**	Y	Y	Y	Y	Y	Y
3 **Yoho**	Y	Y	Y	Y	Y	Y
4 **Rutherford**	Y	Y	Y	Y	Y	Y
5 Lawson	N	Y	N	N	N	N
6 **DeSantis**	Y	Y	Y	Y	Y	Y
7 Murphy	N	Y	N	N	N	N
8 **Posey**	Y	Y	Y	Y	Y	Y
9 Soto	N	Y	N	N	N	N
10 Demings	N	Y	N	N	N	N
11 **Webster**	Y	Y	Y	Y	Y	Y
12 **Bilirakis**	Y	Y	Y	Y	Y	Y
13 Crist	N	Y	N	N	N	Y
14 Castor	N	Y	N	N	N	N
15 **Ross**	Y	Y	Y	Y	Y	Y
16 **Buchanan**	Y	Y	Y	Y	Y	Y
17 **Rooney, T.**	Y	Y	Y	Y	Y	Y
18 **Mast**	Y	Y	Y	Y	Y	Y
19 **Rooney, F.**	Y	?	?	Y	Y	Y
20 Hastings	N	Y	N	N	N	N
21 Frankel	N	Y	N	N	N	N
22 Deutch	?	Y	Y	N	N	N
23 Wasserman Schultz	?	Y	Y	N	N	N
24 Wilson	N	Y	N	N	N	N
25 **Diaz-Balart**	N	Y	Y	Y	Y	Y
26 **Curbelo**	Y	Y	Y	Y	Y	Y
27 **Ros-Lehtinen**	Y	Y	Y	Y	Y	Y
GEORGIA						
1 **Carter**	Y	Y	Y	Y	Y	Y
2 Bishop	?	Y	Y	N	N	N
3 **Ferguson**	Y	Y	Y	Y	Y	Y
4 Johnson	N	Y	N	N	N	N
5 Lewis	N	Y	N	N	N	N
6 **Handel**	Y	Y	Y	Y	Y	Y
7 **Woodall**	Y	Y	Y	Y	Y	Y
8 **Scott, A.**	Y	Y	Y	Y	Y	Y
9 **Collins**	Y	Y	Y	Y	Y	Y
10 **Hice**	Y	Y	Y	Y	Y	Y
11 **Loudermilk**	Y	Y	Y	Y	Y	Y
12 **Allen**	Y	Y	Y	Y	Y	Y
13 Scott, D.	N	Y	Y	N	N	N
14 **Graves**	Y	Y	Y	Y	Y	Y
HAWAII						
1 Hanabusa	N	Y	N	N	N	N
2 Gabbard	N	Y	Y	N	N	N
IDAHO						
1 **Labrador**	Y	Y	Y	Y	Y	Y
2 **Simpson**	Y	Y	Y	Y	Y	Y
ILLINOIS						
1 Rush	N	?	?	N	N	N
2 Kelly	N	Y	N	N	N	N
3 Lipinski	N	Y	N	N	N	N
4 Gutierrez	–	Y	Y	N	N	N
5 Quigley	N	Y	N	N	N	N
6 **Roskam**	N	Y	Y	Y	Y	?
7 Davis, D.	N	Y	N	N	N	N
8 Krishnamoorthi	N	Y	N	N	N	N
9 Schakowsky	N	Y	N	N	N	N
10 Schneider	N	Y	N	N	N	N
11 Foster	Y	Y	N	N	N	N
12 **Bost**	Y	Y	Y	Y	Y	Y
13 **Davis, R.**	Y	Y	Y	Y	Y	Y

KEY

Republicans	Democrats	Independents
Y Voted for (yea)	X Paired against	C Voted "present" to avoid possible conflict of interest
# Paired for	– Announced against	
+ Announced for	P Voted "present"	? Did not vote or otherwise make a position known
N Voted against (nay)		

	80	81	82	83	84	85
14 **Hultgren**	Y	Y	Y	Y	Y	Y
15 **Shimkus**	Y	Y	Y	Y	Y	Y
16 **Kinzinger**	Y	Y	Y	Y	Y	Y
17 Bustos	N	Y	Y	N	N	N
18 **LaHood**	Y	Y	Y	Y	Y	Y
INDIANA						
1 Visclosky	N	Y	Y	N	N	N
2 **Walorski**	Y	Y	Y	Y	Y	Y
3 **Banks**	Y	Y	Y	Y	Y	Y
4 **Rokita**	Y	Y	Y	Y	Y	Y
5 **Brooks**	Y	Y	Y	Y	Y	Y
6 **Messer**	Y	Y	Y	Y	Y	Y
7 Carson	N	Y	Y	N	N	N
8 **Bucshon**	Y	Y	Y	Y	Y	Y
9 **Hollingsworth**	Y	Y	Y	Y	Y	Y
IOWA						
1 **Blum**	Y	Y	Y	Y	Y	Y
2 Loebsack	N	Y	Y	N	N	N
3 **Young**	N	Y	Y	Y	Y	Y
4 **King**	Y	Y	Y	Y	Y	Y
KANSAS						
1 **Marshall**	Y	Y	Y	Y	Y	Y
2 **Jenkins**	Y	Y	Y	Y	Y	Y
3 **Yoder**	N	Y	Y	Y	Y	Y
4 **Estes**	Y	Y	Y	Y	Y	Y
KENTUCKY						
1 **Comer**	Y	Y	Y	Y	Y	Y
2 **Guthrie**	Y	Y	Y	Y	Y	Y
3 Yarmuth	N	Y	Y	N	N	N
4 **Massie**	Y	N	N	Y	Y	Y
5 **Rogers**	+	Y	Y	Y	Y	Y
6 **Barr**	Y	Y	Y	Y	Y	Y
LOUISIANA						
1 **Scalise**	Y	Y	Y	Y	Y	Y
2 Richmond	N	Y	Y	N	N	N
3 **Higgins**	Y	Y	Y	Y	Y	Y
4 **Johnson**	Y	Y	Y	Y	Y	?
5 **Abraham**	Y	Y	Y	Y	Y	Y
6 **Graves**	Y	Y	?	Y	Y	Y
MAINE						
1 Pingree	N	Y	Y	N	N	N
2 Poliquin	Y	Y	Y	Y	Y	Y
MARYLAND						
1 **Harris**	Y	Y	Y	Y	Y	Y
2 Ruppersberger	N	Y	Y	N	N	N
3 Sarbanes	N	Y	Y	N	N	N
4 Brown	N	Y	Y	N	N	N
5 Hoyer	N	Y	Y	N	N	N
6 Delaney	N	Y	Y	N	N	N
7 Cummings	?	?	?	?	?	?
8 Raskin	N	Y	Y	N	N	N
MASSACHUSETTS						
1 Neal	N	?	?	N	N	N
2 McGovern	N	?	?	N	N	N
3 Tsongas	N	Y	Y	N	N	N
4 Kennedy	N	?	?	N	N	N
5 Clark	N	Y	Y	N	N	N
6 Moulton	N	Y	Y	N	N	N
7 Capuano	N	Y	Y	N	N	N
8 Lynch	N	Y	Y	N	N	N
9 Keating	N	Y	Y	N	N	N
MICHIGAN						
1 **Bergman**	Y	Y	Y	+	+	+
2 **Huizenga**	Y	+	+	+	+	+
3 *Amash*	Y	N	N	Y	Y	Y
4 **Moolenaar**	Y	Y	Y	Y	Y	Y
5 Kildee	N	Y	Y	N	N	N
6 Upton	Y	Y	Y	Y	Y	Y
7 Walberg	Y	Y	Y	Y	Y	Y
8 Bishop	Y	Y	Y	Y	Y	Y
9 Levin	N	Y	Y	N	N	N
10 Mitchell	Y	Y	Y	Y	Y	Y
11 Trott	Y	?	?	?	?	?
12 Dingell	N	Y	Y	N	N	N
14 Lawrence	N	Y	Y	N	N	N
MINNESOTA						
1 Walz	N	Y	Y	?	?	?
2 **Lewis**	Y	Y	Y	Y	Y	Y
3 **Paulsen**	Y	Y	Y	Y	Y	Y
4 **McCollum**	N	Y	Y	N	N	N

	80	81	82	83	84	85
5 Ellison	N	Y	Y	N	N	N
6 **Emmer**	Y	Y	Y	Y	Y	Y
7 Peterson	Y	Y	Y	N	N	N
8 Nolan	N	?	?	N	N	N
MISSISSIPPI						
1 **Kelly**	Y	Y	Y	Y	Y	Y
2 Thompson	N	Y	Y	N	N	N
3 **Harper**	N	Y	Y	Y	Y	Y
4 Palazzo	Y	Y	Y	Y	Y	Y
MISSOURI						
1 Clay	N	Y	Y	N	N	N
2 **Wagner**	Y	Y	Y	Y	Y	Y
3 **Luetkemeyer**	Y	Y	Y	Y	Y	Y
4 **Hartzler**	Y	Y	Y	Y	Y	Y
5 Cleaver	N	+	+	–	–	–
6 **Graves**	Y	+	+	+	+	+
7 **Long**	Y	+	+	+	+	+
8 **Smith**	Y	Y	Y	Y	Y	Y
MONTANA						
AL **Gianforte**	Y	Y	Y	Y	Y	Y
NEBRASKA						
1 **Fortenberry**	N	Y	Y	Y	Y	Y
2 **Bacon**	Y	Y	Y	Y	Y	Y
3 **Smith**	Y	Y	Y	Y	Y	Y
NEVADA						
1 Titus	N	Y	Y	N	N	N
2 **Amodei**	Y	Y	Y	Y	Y	Y
3 Rosen	N	Y	Y	N	N	N
4 Kihuen	N	Y	Y	N	N	N
NEW HAMPSHIRE						
1 Shea-Porter	N	Y	Y	N	N	N
2 Kuster	N	Y	Y	N	N	N
NEW JERSEY						
1 Norcross	N	Y	Y	N	N	N
2 **LoBiondo**	?	Y	Y	Y	Y	Y
3 **MacArthur**	Y	Y	Y	Y	Y	Y
4 **Smith**	N	Y	Y	Y	Y	Y
5 Gottheimer	N	Y	Y	N	N	Y
6 Pallone	N	Y	Y	N	N	N
7 **Lance**	N	Y	Y	Y	Y	Y
8 Sires	N	Y	Y	N	N	N
9 Pascrell	N	Y	Y	N	N	N
10 Payne	N	+	+	–	–	–
11 **Frelinghuysen**	N	Y	Y	Y	Y	Y
12 Watson Coleman	N	Y	Y	N	N	N
NEW MEXICO						
1 Lujan Grisham	N	Y	Y	N	N	N
2 **Pearce**	?	?	?	?	?	?
3 Luján	N	Y	Y	N	N	N
NEW YORK						
1 **Zeldin**	Y	Y	Y	Y	Y	Y
2 **King**	Y	Y	Y	Y	Y	Y
3 Suozzi	N	Y	Y	N	N	N
4 Rice	Y	Y	Y	N	N	N
5 Meeks	N	Y	Y	N	N	N
6 Meng	N	Y	Y	N	N	N
7 Velázquez	N	Y	Y	–	N	N
8 Jeffries	N	Y	Y	N	N	N
9 Clarke	N	Y	Y	N	N	N
10 Nadler	N	Y	Y	N	N	N
11 **Donovan**	Y	Y	Y	Y	Y	Y
12 Maloney, C.	N	?	Y	N	N	N
13 Espaillat	N	Y	Y	N	N	N
14 Crowley	N	Y	Y	N	N	N
15 Serrano	N	Y	Y	N	N	N
16 Engel	N	?	?	?	?	?
17 Lowey	N	Y	Y	N	N	N
18 Maloney, S.P.	N	Y	Y	N	N	N
19 **Faso**	Y	Y	Y	Y	Y	Y
20 Tonko	N	Y	Y	N	N	N
21 **Stefanik**	Y	Y	Y	Y	Y	Y
22 **Tenney**	Y	Y	Y	Y	Y	Y
23 **Reed**	Y	Y	Y	Y	Y	Y
24 **Katko**	N	Y	Y	Y	Y	Y
25 Slaughter	N	Y	Y	N	N	Y
26 Higgins	N	Y	Y	N	N	N
27 **Collins**	Y	Y	Y	Y	Y	Y
NORTH CAROLINA						
1 Butterfield	N	Y	Y	N	N	N
2 **Holding**	Y	Y	Y	Y	Y	Y
3 **Jones**	Y	N	N	Y	Y	Y
4 Price	N	Y	Y	N	N	N

	80	81	82	83	84	85
5 **Foxx**	Y	Y	Y	Y	Y	Y
6 **Walker**	Y	Y	Y	Y	Y	Y
7 **Rouzer**	Y	Y	Y	Y	Y	Y
8 **Hudson**	Y	Y	Y	Y	Y	Y
9 **Pittenger**	Y	Y	Y	Y	Y	Y
9 **Vacant**						
10 **McHenry**	Y	Y	Y	Y	Y	Y
11 **Meadows**	Y	Y	Y	Y	Y	Y
12 Adams	N	Y	Y	N	N	N
13 **Budd**	Y	Y	Y	Y	Y	Y
NORTH DAKOTA						
AL **Cramer**	Y	?	?	?	?	?
OHIO						
1 **Chabot**	Y	Y	Y	Y	Y	Y
2 **Wenstrup**	Y	Y	Y	Y	Y	Y
3 Beatty	N	Y	Y	N	N	N
4 **Jordan**	Y	Y	Y	Y	Y	Y
5 **Latta**	Y	Y	Y	Y	Y	Y
6 **Johnson**	Y	Y	Y	Y	Y	Y
7 **Gibbs**	Y	Y	Y	Y	Y	Y
8 **Davidson**	Y	Y	N	Y	Y	Y
9 Kaptur	N	Y	Y	N	N	N
10 **Turner**	Y	Y	Y	Y	Y	Y
11 Fudge	N	Y	Y	N	N	N
12 **Vacant**						
13 Ryan	N	Y	Y	N	N	N
14 **Joyce**	Y	Y	Y	Y	Y	Y
15 **Stivers**	Y	Y	Y	Y	Y	Y
16 **Renacci**	Y	Y	Y	Y	Y	Y
OKLAHOMA						
1 **Bridenstine**	Y	Y	Y	Y	Y	Y
2 **Mullin**	Y	Y	Y	Y	Y	Y
3 **Lucas**	Y	Y	Y	Y	Y	Y
4 **Cole**	Y	Y	Y	Y	Y	Y
5 **Russell**	Y	Y	Y	Y	Y	Y
OREGON						
1 Bonamici	N	Y	Y	N	N	N
2 **Walden**	Y	Y	Y	Y	Y	Y
3 Blumenauer	N	Y	Y	N	N	N
4 DeFazio	N	Y	Y	N	N	N
5 Schrader	Y	Y	Y	N	N	N
PENNSYLVANIA						
1 Brady	N	?	?	N	N	N
2 Evans	N	Y	Y	N	N	N
3 **Kelly**	Y	Y	Y	Y	Y	Y
4 **Perry**	Y	Y	Y	Y	Y	Y
5 **Thompson**	N	Y	Y	Y	Y	Y
6 **Costello**	N	Y	Y	Y	Y	Y
7 **Meehan**	Y	Y	Y	Y	Y	Y
8 **Fitzpatrick**	N	Y	Y	Y	Y	Y
9 **Shuster**	Y	?	?	Y	Y	Y
10 **Marino**	Y	Y	Y	Y	Y	Y
11 **Barletta**	N	?	?	Y	Y	Y
12 **Rothfus**	Y	Y	Y	Y	Y	Y
13 Boyle	N	Y	Y	N	N	N
14 Doyle	N	Y	Y	N	N	N
15 **Dent**	Y	Y	Y	Y	Y	Y
16 **Smucker**	Y	Y	Y	Y	Y	Y
17 Cartwright	N	Y	Y	N	N	N
RHODE ISLAND						
1 Cicilline	N	?	Y	N	N	N
2 Langevin	N	Y	Y	N	N	N
SOUTH CAROLINA						
1 **Sanford**	Y	N	N	Y	Y	Y
2 **Wilson**	Y	Y	Y	Y	Y	Y
3 **Duncan**	?	Y	Y	Y	Y	Y
4 **Gowdy**	Y	Y	Y	Y	Y	Y
5 **Norman**	Y	Y	Y	Y	Y	Y
6 Clyburn	N	Y	Y	N	N	N
7 **Rice**	Y	Y	Y	Y	Y	Y
SOUTH DAKOTA						
AL **Noem**	Y	?	?	Y	Y	Y
TENNESSEE						
1 **Roe**	Y	Y	Y	Y	Y	Y
2 **Duncan**	Y	Y	Y	Y	Y	Y
3 **Fleischmann**	Y	Y	Y	Y	Y	Y
4 **DesJarlais**	Y	Y	Y	Y	Y	Y
5 Cooper	Y	Y	Y	N	N	N
6 **Black**	Y	?	?	?	?	?
7 **Blackburn**	Y	Y	Y	Y	Y	Y
8 **Kustoff**	Y	Y	Y	Y	Y	Y
9 Cohen	N	Y	Y	N	N	N

	80	81	82	83	84	85
TEXAS						
1 **Gohmert**	Y	Y	N	Y	Y	Y
2 **Poe**	Y	Y	Y	Y	Y	Y
3 **Johnson, S.**	Y	Y	Y	Y	Y	Y
4 **Ratcliffe**	Y	Y	Y	Y	Y	Y
5 **Hensarling**	Y	Y	Y	Y	Y	Y
6 **Barton**	Y	Y	Y	Y	Y	Y
7 **Culberson**	Y	Y	Y	Y	Y	Y
8 **Brady**	Y	Y	Y	Y	Y	Y
9 Green, A.	N	Y	Y	N	N	N
10 **McCaul**	Y	Y	Y	Y	Y	Y
11 **Conaway**	Y	Y	Y	Y	Y	Y
12 **Granger**	Y	Y	Y	Y	Y	Y
13 **Thornberry**	Y	Y	Y	Y	Y	Y
14 **Weber**	Y	Y	Y	Y	Y	Y
15 Gonzalez	N	Y	Y	N	N	N
16 O'Rourke	N	Y	Y	N	N	N
17 **Flores**	Y	Y	Y	Y	Y	Y
18 Jackson Lee	N	Y	Y	N	N	N
19 **Arrington**	Y	Y	Y	Y	Y	Y
20 Castro	N	Y	Y	N	N	N
21 **Smith**	Y	Y	Y	Y	Y	Y
22 **Olson**	Y	Y	Y	Y	Y	Y
23 **Hurd**	Y	Y	Y	Y	Y	Y
24 **Marchant**	Y	Y	Y	Y	Y	Y
25 **Williams**	Y	Y	Y	Y	Y	Y
26 **Burgess**	Y	Y	Y	Y	Y	Y
27 **Farenthold**	Y	Y	N	Y	Y	Y
28 Cuellar	Y	Y	Y	N	N	N
29 Green, G.	N	Y	Y	N	N	N
30 Johnson, E.B.	N	Y	Y	N	N	N
31 **Carter**	Y	?	?	?	?	?
32 **Sessions**	Y	Y	Y	Y	Y	Y
33 Veasey	N	Y	Y	N	N	N
34 Vela	N	Y	Y	N	N	N
35 Doggett	N	?	?	N	N	N
36 **Babin**	Y	Y	Y	Y	Y	Y
UTAH						
1 **Bishop**	Y	Y	Y	Y	Y	Y
2 **Stewart**	Y	Y	Y	Y	Y	Y
3 **Curtis**	Y	Y	Y	Y	Y	Y
4 **Love**	Y	Y	Y	Y	Y	Y
VERMONT						
AL Welch	N	Y	Y	N	N	N
VIRGINIA						
1 **Wittman**	Y	Y	Y	Y	Y	Y
2 **Taylor**	Y	Y	Y	Y	Y	Y
3 Scott	N	Y	Y	N	N	N
4 McEachin	N	Y	Y	N	N	N
5 **Garrett**	Y	Y	N	Y	Y	Y
6 **Goodlatte**	Y	Y	Y	Y	Y	Y
7 **Brat**	Y	Y	Y	Y	Y	Y
8 Beyer	N	Y	Y	N	N	N
9 **Griffith**	Y	Y	Y	Y	Y	Y
10 **Comstock**	N	Y	Y	Y	Y	Y
11 Connolly	N	Y	Y	N	N	Y
WASHINGTON						
1 DelBene	N	Y	Y	N	N	N
2 Larsen	N	Y	Y	N	N	N
3 **Herrera Beutler**	Y	Y	Y	Y	Y	Y
4 **Newhouse**	Y	Y	Y	Y	Y	Y
5 **McMorris Rodgers**	N	Y	Y	Y	Y	Y
6 Kilmer	N	Y	Y	N	N	N
7 Jayapal	N	Y	Y	N	N	N
8 **Reichert**	N	Y	Y	Y	Y	Y
9 Smith	N	+	+	–	–	–
10 Heck	N	Y	Y	N	N	N
WEST VIRGINIA						
1 **McKinley**	Y	Y	Y	Y	Y	Y
2 **Mooney**	Y	N	Y	Y	Y	Y
3 **Jenkins**	Y	Y	Y	Y	Y	Y
WISCONSIN						
1 **Ryan**						
2 Pocan	N	Y	Y	N	N	N
3 Kind	N	Y	Y	N	N	N
4 Moore	N	Y	Y	N	N	N
5 **Sensenbrenner**	N	Y	Y	Y	Y	Y
6 **Grothman**	Y	Y	Y	Y	Y	Y
7 **Duffy**	Y	+	+	Y	Y	Y
8 **Gallagher**	Y	Y	Y	Y	Y	Y
WYOMING						
AL **Cheney**	?	Y	Y	Y	Y	Y

VOTE NUMBER

86. HRES747. OPERATIONAL RISK CAPITAL REQUIREMENTS AND FEDERAL FINANCIAL REGULATOR REVIEWS/PREVIOUS QUESTION. Buck, R-Colo., motion to order the previous question (thus ending debate and possibility of amendment) on the rule (H Res 747) that would provide for House floor consideration of the bill (HR 4296) that would require federal banking regulators to base operational risk capital requirements imposed on certain financial institutions on the bank's current activities and businesses, as opposed to past experiences and losses, and would provide for House floor consideration of the bill (HR 4607) that would modify the cycle for federal financial regulators to review rules under the Economic Growth and Regulatory Paperwork Reduction Act of 1996. Motion agreed to 227-185: R 227-0; D 0-185. Feb. 27, 2018"

87. HR4607. OPERATIONAL RISK CAPITAL REQUIREMENTS AND FEDERAL FINANCIAL REGULATOR REVIEWS/RULE. Adoption of the rule (H Res 747) that would provide for House floor consideration of the bill (HR 4296) that would require federal banking regulators to base operational risk capital requirements imposed on certain financial institutions on the bank's current activities and businesses, as opposed to past experiences and losses, and would provide for House floor consideration of the bill (HR 4607) that would modify the cycle for federal financial regulators to review rules under the Economic Growth and Regulatory Paperwork Reduction Act of 1996 from once every 10 years to once every seven years. Adopted 230-177: R 226-0; D 4-177. Feb. 27, 2018.

88. HR4296. OPERATIONAL RISK CAPITAL REQUIREMENTS/RECOMMIT. Waters, D-Calif., motion to recommit the bill to the House Financial Services Committee with instructions to report it back immediately with an amendment that would exempt any global systemically important bank holding company or any subsidiary that has "engaged in a pattern or practice of unsafe or unsound banking practices" from the bill's provisions. Motion rejected 185-228: R 2-228; D 183-0. Feb. 27, 2018.

89. HR4296. OPERATIONAL RISK CAPITAL REQUIREMENTS/PASSAGE. Passage of the bill that would require federal banking regulators to base operational risk capital requirements imposed on certain financial institutions on the bank's current activities and businesses, as opposed to past experiences and losses. It would also allow for regulators to adjust capital risk requirements based on other operational risk mitigation factors. Passed 245-169: R 226-3; D 19-166. Feb. 27, 2018.

90. HR1865. WEBSITES FACILITATING SEX TRAFFICKING/CLARIFICATION OF LIMITS ON PROSECUTION. Walters, R-Calif., amendment that would clarify that nothing in the bill should be interpreted as limiting the civil and criminal prosecution of websites that knowingly facilitate online sex trafficking and would explicitly state that a state attorney general may bring civil prosecution against such websites for the purpose of obtaining relief for victims in the state. Adopted in Committee of the Whole 308-107: R 169-61; D 139-46. Feb. 27, 2018.

91. HR1865. WEBSITES FACILITATING SEX TRAFFICKING/PASSAGE. Passage of the bill that would explicitly make the use or operation of a website to promote or facilitate prostitution a federal crime. It would allow states to prosecute such conduct under state law, regardless of the immunity provisions in the 1996 Communications Decency Act, as long as the state's laws mirror federal prohibitions, and would allow victims of such sex trafficking or prostitution to recover civil damages from the website operator. Passed 388-25: R 214-14; D 174-11. Feb. 27, 2018.

	86	87	88	89	90	91
ALABAMA						
1 Byrne	Y	Y	N	Y	Y	Y
2 Roby	Y	Y	N	Y	Y	Y
3 Rogers	Y	Y	N	Y	Y	Y
4 Aderholt	Y	Y	N	Y	Y	Y
5 Brooks	Y	Y	N	Y	N	Y
6 Palmer	Y	Y	N	Y	N	Y
7 Sewell	N	N	Y	N	Y	Y
ALASKA						
AL Young	Y	Y	N	Y	Y	Y
ARIZONA						
1 O'Halleran	N	N	Y	Y	Y	Y
2 McSally	Y	Y	N	Y	Y	Y
3 Grijalva	N	N	Y	N	Y	Y
4 Gosar	Y	Y	N	Y	N	N
5 Biggs	Y	Y	N	Y	N	N
6 Schweikert	Y	Y	N	Y	N	Y
7 Gallego	N	N	Y	N	Y	Y
9 Sinema	N	Y	Y	Y	Y	Y
ARKANSAS						
1 Crawford	Y	Y	N	Y	Y	Y
2 Hill	Y	Y	N	Y	Y	Y
3 Womack	Y	Y	N	Y	Y	Y
4 Westerman	Y	Y	N	Y	Y	Y
CALIFORNIA						
1 LaMalfa	Y	Y	N	Y	N	Y
2 Huffman	N	N	Y	N	N	N
3 Garamendi	N	N	Y	N	Y	Y
4 McClintock	Y	Y	N	Y	N	N
5 Thompson	N	N	Y	N	Y	Y
6 Matsui	N	N	Y	N	Y	Y
7 Bera	N	N	Y	N	Y	Y
8 Cook	Y	Y	N	Y	Y	Y
9 McNerney	N	N	Y	N	N	Y
10 Denham	Y	Y	N	Y	Y	Y
11 DeSaulnier	N	N	Y	N	N	N
12 Pelosi	N	N	Y	N	Y	Y
13 Lee	N	N	Y	N	N	N
14 Speier	?	?	?	?	?	?
15 Swalwell	N	N	Y	N	Y	Y
16 Costa	N	Y	Y	Y	Y	Y
17 Khanna	N	N	Y	N	N	N
18 Eshoo	N	N	Y	N	N	N
19 Lofgren	N	N	Y	N	N	N
20 Panetta	N	N	Y	N	Y	Y
21 Valadao	Y	Y	N	Y	Y	Y
22 Nunes	Y	Y	N	Y	Y	Y
23 McCarthy	Y	Y	N	Y	Y	Y
24 Carbajal	N	N	Y	N	Y	Y
25 Knight	Y	Y	N	Y	Y	Y
26 Brownley	N	N	Y	N	Y	Y
27 Chu	N	N	Y	N	Y	Y
28 Schiff	N	N	Y	N	Y	Y
29 Cardenas	N	N	Y	N	Y	Y
30 Sherman	N	N	Y	N	Y	Y
31 Aguilar	N	N	Y	N	Y	Y
32 Napolitano	N	N	Y	N	N	Y
33 Lieu	N	N	Y	N	N	Y
34 Gomez	N	N	Y	N	N	Y
35 Torres	–	–	?	?	?	?
36 Ruiz	N	N	Y	N	Y	Y
37 Bass	N	N	Y	N	N	Y
38 Sánchez, Linda	N	N	Y	N	Y	Y
39 Royce	Y	Y	N	Y	Y	Y
40 Roybal-Allard	N	N	Y	N	Y	Y
41 Takano	N	N	Y	N	N	N
42 Calvert	Y	Y	N	Y	Y	Y
43 Waters	N	N	Y	N	Y	Y
44 Barragan	N	N	Y	N	Y	Y
45 Walters	Y	Y	N	Y	Y	Y
46 Correa	N	N	Y	Y	Y	Y
47 Lowenthal	N	N	Y	N	N	Y
48 Rohrabacher	Y	Y	N	Y	N	N
49 Issa	Y	Y	N	Y	Y	Y
50 Hunter	Y	Y	N	Y	Y	Y
51 Vargas	N	N	Y	N	Y	Y
52 Peters	N	N	Y	N	Y	Y
53 Davis	N	N	Y	N	Y	Y

	86	87	88	89	90	91
COLORADO						
1 DeGette	N	N	Y	N	Y	Y
2 Polis	N	N	Y	Y	Y	Y
3 Tipton	Y	Y	N	Y	Y	Y
4 Buck	Y	Y	N	Y	N	Y
5 Lamborn	Y	Y	N	Y	Y	Y
6 Coffman	Y	Y	N	Y	Y	Y
7 Perlmutter	N	N	Y	N	Y	Y
CONNECTICUT						
1 Larson	N	N	Y	N	Y	Y
2 Courtney	N	N	Y	N	Y	Y
3 DeLauro	N	N	Y	N	Y	Y
4 Himes	N	N	Y	N	Y	Y
5 Esty	N	N	Y	N	Y	Y
DELAWARE						
AL Blunt Rochester	N	N	Y	N	Y	Y
FLORIDA						
1 Gaetz	Y	Y	N	Y	N	N
2 Dunn	Y	Y	N	Y	Y	Y
3 Yoho	Y	Y	N	Y	Y	Y
4 Rutherford	Y	Y	N	Y	Y	Y
5 Lawson	N	N	Y	N	Y	Y
6 DeSantis	Y	Y	N	Y	Y	Y
7 Murphy	N	N	Y	Y	Y	Y
8 Posey	Y	Y	N	Y	Y	Y
9 Soto	N	N	Y	N	Y	Y
10 Demings	N	N	Y	N	Y	Y
11 Webster	Y	Y	N	Y	Y	Y
12 Bilirakis	Y	Y	N	Y	Y	Y
13 Crist	N	N	Y	N	Y	Y
14 Castor	N	N	Y	N	Y	Y
15 Ross	Y	Y	N	Y	Y	Y
16 Buchanan	Y	Y	N	Y	Y	Y
17 Rooney, T.	Y	Y	N	Y	Y	Y
18 Mast	Y	Y	N	Y	Y	Y
19 Rooney, F.	Y	Y	N	Y	N	Y
20 Hastings	N	N	Y	N	Y	Y
21 Frankel	N	N	Y	N	Y	Y
22 Deutch	N	N	Y	N	Y	Y
23 Wasserman Schultz	N	N	Y	N	Y	Y
24 Wilson	N	N	+	N	N	Y
25 Diaz-Balart	Y	Y	N	Y	Y	Y
26 Curbelo	Y	Y	N	+	Y	Y
27 Ros-Lehtinen	Y	Y	N	Y	Y	Y
GEORGIA						
1 Carter	Y	Y	N	Y	Y	Y
2 Bishop	N	N	Y	N	Y	Y
3 Ferguson	Y	Y	N	Y	N	Y
4 Johnson	N	N	Y	N	Y	Y
5 Lewis	N	N	Y	N	Y	Y
6 Handel	Y	Y	N	Y	Y	Y
7 Woodall	Y	Y	N	Y	Y	Y
8 Scott, A.	Y	Y	N	Y	N	Y
9 Collins	Y	Y	N	Y	Y	Y
10 Hice	Y	Y	N	Y	N	Y
11 Loudermilk	Y	Y	N	Y	N	Y
12 Allen	+	Y	N	Y	Y	Y
13 Scott, D.	N	N	Y	Y	Y	Y
14 Graves	Y	Y	N	Y	N	Y
HAWAII						
1 Hanabusa	N	N	Y	N	Y	Y
2 Gabbard	N	N	Y	N	N	Y
IDAHO						
1 Labrador	Y	Y	N	Y	N	N
2 Simpson	Y	Y	N	Y	Y	?
ILLINOIS						
1 Rush	N	N	Y	N	N	Y
2 Kelly	N	N	Y	N	N	Y
3 Lipinski	N	N	Y	N	Y	Y
4 Gutierrez	N	N	Y	N	Y	Y
5 Quigley	N	N	Y	N	Y	Y
6 Roskam	Y	Y	N	Y	Y	Y
7 Davis, D.	N	N	Y	N	N	Y
8 Krishnamoorthi	N	N	Y	N	Y	Y
9 Schakowsky	N	N	Y	N	Y	Y
10 Schneider	N	Y	Y	Y	Y	Y
11 Foster	N	N	Y	N	N	Y
12 Bost	Y	Y	N	Y	Y	Y
13 Davis, R.	Y	Y	N	Y	Y	Y

KEY	Republicans	Democrats	Independents
Y Voted for (yea)		**X** Paired against	**C** Voted "present" to avoid possible conflict of interest
# Paired for		**–** Announced against	
+ Announced for		**P** Voted "present"	**?** Did not vote or otherwise make a position known
N Voted against (nay)			

	86	87	88	89	90	91
14 **Hultgren**	Y	Y	N	Y	Y	Y
15 **Shimkus**	Y	Y	N	Y	Y	Y
16 **Kinzinger**	Y	Y	N	Y	Y	Y
17 Bustos	N	N	Y	N	Y	Y
18 **LaHood**	Y	Y	N	Y	Y	Y
INDIANA						
1 Visclosky	N	N	Y	N	Y	Y
2 **Walorski**	Y	Y	N	Y	Y	Y
3 **Banks**	Y	Y	N	Y	N	Y
4 **Rokita**	Y	Y	N	Y	N	Y
5 **Brooks**	Y	Y	N	Y	Y	Y
6 **Messer**	Y	Y	N	Y	Y	Y
7 Carson	N	N	Y	Y	N	Y
8 **Bucshon**	Y	Y	N	Y	Y	Y
9 **Hollingsworth**	Y	Y	N	Y	Y	Y
IOWA						
1 **Blum**	Y	Y	N	Y	N	Y
2 Loebsack	N	N	Y	N	Y	Y
3 **Young**	Y	Y	N	Y	N	Y
4 **King**	Y	Y	N	Y	N	Y
KANSAS						
1 **Marshall**	Y	Y	N	Y	Y	Y
2 **Jenkins**	Y	Y	N	Y	Y	Y
3 **Yoder**	Y	Y	N	Y	Y	Y
4 **Estes**	Y	Y	N	Y	Y	Y
KENTUCKY						
1 **Comer**	Y	Y	N	Y	N	Y
2 **Guthrie**	Y	Y	N	Y	Y	Y
3 Yarmuth	N	N	Y	N	Y	Y
4 **Massie**	Y	Y	N	Y	N	N
5 **Rogers**	Y	Y	N	Y	Y	Y
6 **Barr**	Y	Y	N	Y	Y	Y
LOUISIANA						
1 **Scalise**	Y	Y	N	Y	Y	Y
2 Richmond	N	N	Y	N	N	Y
3 **Higgins**	Y	Y	N	Y	Y	Y
4 **Johnson**	Y	Y	N	Y	N	Y
5 **Abraham**	Y	Y	N	Y	Y	Y
6 **Graves**	Y	Y	N	Y	Y	Y
MAINE						
1 Pingree	N	?	Y	N	Y	Y
2 Poliquin	Y	Y	N	Y	Y	Y
MARYLAND						
1 **Harris**	Y	Y	N	Y	N	Y
2 Ruppersberger	N	N	Y	Y	Y	Y
3 Sarbanes	N	N	Y	N	Y	Y
4 Brown	N	N	Y	N	Y	Y
5 Hoyer	N	N	Y	N	Y	Y
6 Delaney	N	N	Y	Y	Y	Y
7 Cummings	?	?	?	?	?	?
8 Raskin	N	N	Y	N	N	Y
MASSACHUSETTS						
1 Neal	N	N	Y	N	Y	Y
2 McGovern	N	N	Y	N	N	Y
3 Tsongas	N	N	Y	N	N	Y
4 Kennedy	N	N	Y	N	N	Y
5 Clark	N	N	Y	N	N	Y
6 Moulton	N	N	Y	N	Y	Y
7 Capuano	N	N	Y	N	N	Y
8 Lynch	N	N	Y	N	N	Y
9 Keating	N	N	Y	N	Y	Y
MICHIGAN						
1 **Bergman**	+	+	N	Y	N	Y
2 **Huizenga**	+	+	–	+	+	+
3 *Amash*	Y	Y	N	Y	N	N
4 **Moolenaar**	Y	Y	N	Y	Y	Y
5 Kildee	N	N	Y	N	N	Y
6 Upton	Y	Y	N	Y	Y	Y
7 Walberg	Y	Y	N	Y	Y	Y
8 Bishop	Y	Y	N	Y	Y	Y
9 Levin	N	N	Y	N	Y	Y
10 Mitchell	Y	Y	N	Y	Y	Y
11 Trott	?	?	?	?	?	?
12 Dingell	N	N	Y	N	Y	Y
14 Lawrence	N	N	Y	N	Y	Y
MINNESOTA						
1 Walz	?	?	?	–	?	+
2 **Lewis**	Y	Y	N	Y	N	Y
3 **Paulsen**	Y	Y	N	Y	Y	Y
4 **McCollum**	N	N	Y	N	Y	Y

	86	87	88	89	90	91
5 Ellison	N	N	Y	N	Y	Y
6 **Emmer**	Y	Y	N	Y	N	Y
7 Peterson	N	N	Y	Y	Y	Y
8 Nolan	N	N	Y	N	N	Y
MISSISSIPPI						
1 **Kelly**	Y	Y	N	Y	N	Y
2 Thompson	N	N	Y	N	Y	Y
3 **Harper**	Y	Y	N	Y	Y	Y
4 Palazzo	Y	Y	N	Y	N	Y
MISSOURI						
1 Clay	N	N	Y	N	N	Y
2 **Wagner**	Y	Y	N	Y	Y	Y
3 **Luetkemeyer**	Y	Y	N	Y	Y	Y
4 **Hartzler**	Y	Y	N	Y	Y	Y
5 Cleaver	–	–	+	–	+	+
6 **Graves**	+	+	N	Y	Y	Y
7 **Long**	+	+	–	+	+	+
8 **Smith**	Y	Y	N	Y	Y	Y
MONTANA						
AL **Gianforte**	Y	Y	N	Y	Y	Y
NEBRASKA						
1 **Fortenberry**	Y	Y	N	Y	Y	Y
2 **Bacon**	Y	Y	N	Y	N	Y
3 **Smith**	Y	Y	N	Y	Y	+
NEVADA						
1 Titus	N	N	Y	N	N	Y
2 **Amodei**	Y	Y	N	Y	Y	Y
3 Rosen	N	N	Y	N	Y	Y
4 Kihuen	N	N	Y	N	Y	Y
NEW HAMPSHIRE						
1 Shea-Porter	N	N	Y	N	Y	Y
2 Kuster	N	N	Y	N	Y	Y
NEW JERSEY						
1 Norcross	N	N	Y	N	Y	Y
2 **LoBiondo**	Y	Y	N	Y	Y	Y
3 **MacArthur**	Y	Y	N	Y	Y	Y
4 **Smith**	Y	Y	N	Y	Y	Y
5 Gottheimer	N	Y	Y	Y	Y	Y
6 Pallone	N	N	Y	N	Y	Y
7 **Lance**	Y	Y	N	Y	Y	Y
8 Sires	N	N	Y	N	Y	Y
9 Pascrell	N	N	Y	N	Y	Y
10 Payne	–	–	+	–	–	+
11 **Frelinghuysen**	Y	Y	N	Y	Y	Y
12 Watson Coleman	N	N	Y	N	N	N
NEW MEXICO						
1 Lujan Grisham	N	N	Y	N	Y	Y
2 **Pearce**	?	?	?	?	?	?
3 Luján	N	N	Y	N	Y	Y
NEW YORK						
1 **Zeldin**	Y	Y	N	Y	Y	Y
2 **King**	Y	Y	N	Y	Y	Y
3 Suozzi	N	N	Y	Y	Y	Y
4 Rice	N	?	Y	Y	Y	Y
5 Meeks	N	N	Y	Y	Y	Y
6 Meng	N	N	Y	N	Y	Y
7 Velázquez	N	N	+	N	Y	Y
8 Jeffries	N	N	Y	N	N	Y
9 Clarke	N	N	Y	N	N	Y
10 Nadler	N	N	Y	N	Y	Y
11 **Donovan**	Y	Y	N	Y	Y	Y
12 Maloney, C.	N	N	Y	N	Y	Y
13 Espaillat	N	N	Y	N	Y	Y
14 Crowley	N	N	Y	N	Y	Y
15 Serrano	N	N	Y	N	Y	Y
16 Engel	?	?	?	?	?	?
17 Lowey	N	N	Y	N	Y	Y
18 Maloney, S.P.	N	N	Y	N	Y	Y
19 **Faso**	Y	Y	N	Y	Y	Y
20 Tonko	N	N	Y	N	Y	Y
21 **Stefanik**	Y	Y	N	Y	Y	Y
22 **Tenney**	Y	Y	N	Y	Y	Y
23 **Reed**	Y	Y	N	Y	Y	Y
24 **Katko**	Y	Y	N	Y	Y	Y
25 Slaughter	N	N	Y	N	Y	Y
26 Higgins	N	N	Y	N	N	Y
27 **Collins**	Y	Y	N	Y	Y	Y
NORTH CAROLINA						
1 Butterfield	N	N	Y	N	Y	Y
2 **Holding**	Y	Y	N	Y	Y	Y
3 **Jones**	Y	?	Y	N	N	N
4 Price	N	N	Y	N	Y	Y

	86	87	88	89	90	91
5 **Foxx**	Y	Y	N	Y	N	Y
6 **Walker**	Y	Y	N	Y	N	Y
7 **Rouzer**	Y	Y	N	Y	N	Y
8 **Hudson**	Y	Y	N	Y	N	Y
9 **Pittenger**	Y	Y	N	Y	Y	Y
9 **Vacant**						
10 **McHenry**	Y	Y	N	Y	Y	Y
11 **Meadows**	Y	Y	N	Y	N	Y
12 Adams	N	N	Y	N	Y	Y
13 **Budd**	Y	Y	N	Y	Y	Y
NORTH DAKOTA						
AL **Cramer**	?	?	?	?	?	?
OHIO						
1 **Chabot**	Y	Y	N	Y	Y	Y
2 **Wenstrup**	Y	Y	N	Y	Y	Y
3 Beatty	N	N	Y	N	Y	Y
4 **Jordan**	Y	Y	N	Y	N	Y
5 **Latta**	Y	Y	N	Y	Y	Y
6 **Johnson**	Y	Y	N	Y	Y	Y
7 **Gibbs**	Y	Y	N	Y	Y	Y
8 **Davidson**	Y	Y	N	Y	N	N
9 Kaptur	N	N	Y	N	Y	Y
10 Turner	Y	Y	N	Y	Y	Y
11 Fudge	N	N	Y	N	N	Y
12 **Vacant**						
13 Ryan	N	N	Y	N	Y	Y
14 **Joyce**	Y	Y	N	Y	Y	Y
15 **Stivers**	Y	Y	N	Y	Y	Y
16 **Renacci**	Y	Y	N	Y	Y	Y
OKLAHOMA						
1 **Bridenstine**	Y	Y	N	Y	N	Y
2 **Mullin**	Y	Y	N	Y	Y	Y
3 **Lucas**	Y	Y	N	Y	Y	Y
4 **Cole**	Y	Y	N	Y	Y	Y
5 **Russell**	Y	Y	N	Y	Y	Y
OREGON						
1 Bonamici	N	N	Y	N	N	Y
2 **Walden**	Y	Y	N	Y	Y	Y
3 Blumenauer	N	?	Y	N	Y	Y
4 DeFazio	N	N	Y	N	Y	Y
5 Schrader	N	N	Y	Y	Y	Y
PENNSYLVANIA						
1 Brady	N	N	Y	N	N	Y
2 Evans	N	N	Y	N	Y	Y
3 **Kelly**	Y	Y	N	Y	Y	Y
4 **Perry**	Y	Y	N	Y	N	Y
5 **Thompson**	Y	Y	N	Y	Y	Y
6 **Costello**	Y	Y	N	Y	Y	Y
7 **Meehan**	Y	Y	N	Y	Y	Y
8 **Fitzpatrick**	Y	Y	N	Y	Y	Y
9 **Shuster**	Y	?	N	Y	Y	Y
10 **Marino**	Y	Y	N	Y	Y	Y
11 **Barletta**	Y	Y	N	Y	Y	Y
12 **Rothfus**	Y	Y	N	Y	Y	Y
13 Boyle	N	N	Y	N	Y	Y
14 Doyle	N	N	Y	N	Y	Y
15 **Dent**	Y	Y	N	Y	Y	Y
16 **Smucker**	Y	Y	N	Y	Y	Y
17 **Cartwright**	N	N	Y	N	Y	Y
RHODE ISLAND						
1 Cicilline	N	N	Y	N	Y	Y
2 Langevin	N	N	Y	N	Y	Y
SOUTH CAROLINA						
1 **Sanford**	Y	Y	N	N	N	N
2 **Wilson**	Y	Y	N	Y	Y	Y
3 **Duncan**	Y	Y	N	Y	N	N
4 **Gowdy**	Y	Y	N	Y	Y	Y
5 **Norman**	Y	Y	N	Y	Y	Y
6 Clyburn	N	N	Y	N	Y	Y
7 **Rice**	Y	Y	N	Y	Y	Y
SOUTH DAKOTA						
AL **Noem**	Y	Y	N	Y	Y	Y
TENNESSEE						
1 **Roe**	Y	Y	N	Y	Y	Y
2 **Duncan**	Y	Y	Y	N	N	Y
3 **Fleischmann**	Y	Y	N	Y	Y	Y
4 **DesJarlais**	Y	Y	N	Y	N	Y
5 Cooper	N	N	Y	N	Y	Y
6 **Black**	?	?	?	?	?	?
7 **Blackburn**	Y	Y	N	Y	Y	Y
8 **Kustoff**	Y	Y	N	Y	N	Y
9 Cohen	N	N	Y	N	Y	Y

	86	87	88	89	90	91
TEXAS						
1 **Gohmert**	Y	Y	N	Y	N	Y
2 **Poe**	Y	Y	N	Y	Y	Y
3 **Johnson, S.**	Y	Y	N	Y	Y	Y
4 **Ratcliffe**	Y	Y	N	Y	N	Y
5 **Hensarling**	Y	Y	N	Y	Y	Y
6 **Barton**	Y	Y	N	Y	Y	Y
7 **Culberson**	Y	Y	N	Y	Y	Y
8 **Brady**	Y	Y	N	Y	Y	Y
9 Green, A.	N	N	Y	N	Y	Y
10 **McCaul**	Y	Y	N	Y	Y	Y
11 **Conaway**	Y	Y	N	Y	Y	Y
12 **Granger**	Y	Y	N	Y	Y	Y
13 **Thornberry**	Y	Y	N	Y	Y	Y
14 **Weber**	Y	Y	N	Y	N	Y
15 Gonzalez	N	N	Y	N	Y	Y
16 O'Rourke	N	N	Y	N	N	Y
17 **Flores**	Y	Y	N	Y	Y	Y
18 Jackson Lee	N	N	Y	N	Y	Y
19 **Arrington**	Y	Y	N	Y	Y	Y
20 Castro	N	N	Y	N	Y	Y
21 **Smith**	Y	Y	N	Y	Y	Y
22 **Olson**	Y	Y	N	Y	Y	Y
23 **Hurd**	Y	Y	N	Y	Y	Y
24 **Marchant**	Y	Y	N	Y	Y	Y
25 **Williams**	Y	Y	N	Y	N	N
26 **Burgess**	Y	Y	N	Y	Y	Y
27 **Farenthold**	Y	Y	N	Y	N	Y
28 Cuellar	N	N	Y	Y	Y	Y
29 Green, G.	N	N	Y	N	Y	Y
30 Johnson, E.B.	N	N	Y	N	Y	Y
31 **Carter**	?	?	?	?	?	?
32 **Sessions**	Y	Y	N	Y	Y	Y
33 Veasey	N	N	Y	Y	Y	Y
34 Vela	N	N	Y	N	Y	Y
35 Doggett	N	N	Y	N	Y	Y
36 **Babin**	Y	Y	N	Y	N	Y
UTAH						
1 **Bishop**	Y	Y	N	Y	Y	Y
2 **Stewart**	Y	Y	N	Y	Y	Y
3 **Curtis**	Y	Y	N	Y	Y	Y
4 **Love**	Y	Y	N	Y	Y	Y
VERMONT						
AL Welch	N	?	Y	N	Y	Y
VIRGINIA						
1 **Wittman**	Y	Y	N	Y	N	Y
2 **Taylor**	Y	Y	N	Y	Y	Y
3 Scott	N	N	Y	N	N	N
4 McEachin	N	N	Y	N	Y	Y
5 **Garrett**	Y	Y	N	Y	N	Y
6 **Goodlatte**	Y	Y	N	Y	N	Y
7 **Brat**	Y	Y	N	Y	N	Y
8 Beyer	N	N	Y	N	N	N
9 **Griffith**	Y	Y	N	Y	N	N
10 **Comstock**	Y	Y	N	Y	Y	Y
11 Connolly	N	N	Y	N	Y	Y
WASHINGTON						
1 DelBene	N	N	Y	N	N	Y
2 Larsen	N	N	Y	N	Y	Y
3 **Herrera Beutler**	Y	Y	N	Y	Y	Y
4 **Newhouse**	Y	Y	N	Y	Y	Y
5 **McMorris Rodgers**	Y	Y	N	Y	Y	Y
6 Kilmer	N	N	Y	N	Y	Y
7 Jayapal	N	N	Y	N	N	N
8 **Reichert**	Y	Y	N	Y	Y	Y
9 Smith	–	–	+	–	–	–
10 Heck	N	N	Y	N	N	Y
WEST VIRGINIA						
1 **McKinley**	Y	Y	N	Y	Y	Y
2 **Mooney**	Y	Y	N	Y	Y	Y
3 **Jenkins**	Y	Y	N	Y	Y	Y
WISCONSIN						
1 **Ryan**						
2 Pocan	N	N	Y	N	N	Y
3 Kind	N	N	Y	N	Y	Y
4 Moore	N	N	Y	N	N	Y
5 **Sensenbrenner**	Y	Y	N	Y	Y	Y
6 **Grothman**	Y	Y	N	Y	N	Y
7 **Duffy**	Y	Y	N	Y	Y	Y
8 **Gallagher**	Y	Y	N	Y	Y	Y
WYOMING						
AL **Cheney**	Y	Y	N	Y	Y	Y

VOTE NUMBER

92. HR3183. DAKOTA KYLE RIGSBY POST OFFICE/PASSAGE. Palmer, R-Ala., motion to suspend the rules and pass the bill that would designate the postal facility at 13683 James Madison Highway in Palmyra, Va., as the "U.S. Navy Seaman Dakota Kyle Rigsby Post Office." Motion agreed to 389-0: R 225-0; D 164-0. March 5, 2018.

93. HR4406. TUSKEGEE AIRMAN POST OFFICE/PASSAGE. Palmer, R-Ala., motion to suspend the rules and pass the bill that would designate the postal facility at 99 Macombs Pl. in New York, N.Y., as the "Tuskegee Airman Post Office Building." Motion agreed to 387-0: R 223-0; D 164-0. March 5, 2018.

94. HR4607. FINANCIAL REGULATION REVIEW PROCESS/RECOMMIT. Clark, D-Mass., motion to recommit the bill to the House Financial Services Committee with instructions to report it back immediately with an amendment that would prohibit a federal financial regulator from including certain rules in its review under the Economic Growth and Regulatory Paperwork Reduction Act of 1996 if such rules were issued or made at the "request of and for the personal gain of" the president, the president's family members, or senior executive branch officials who are required to file annual financial disclosure forms. Motion rejected 182-228: R 2-227; D 180-1. March 6, 2018.

95. HR4607. FINANCIAL REGULATION REVIEW PROCESS/PASSAGE. Passage of the bill that would modify the cycle for federal financial regulators to review rules under the Economic Growth and Regulatory Paperwork Reduction Act of 1996 from once every 10 years to once every seven years. It would require agencies conducting such reviews to seek to tailor existing regulations to limit regulatory compliance impacts, costs, liability risks and other burdens, and would expand the agencies' scope of rules under review to include those that impose requirements on individuals or companies that offer consumer financial products or services. Passed 264-143: R 226-0; D 38-143. March 6, 2018.

96. HR1119. POWER PLANT EMISSIONS STANDARDS AND KILN REGULATIONS/PREVIOUS QUESTION. Cheney, R-Wyo., motion to order the previous question (thus ending debate and possibility of amendment) on the rule (H Res 762) that would provide for consideration of the bill (HR 1119) that would subject an electricity-generating power plant that can get at least 75 percent of its energy from coal mining byproduct to the original emissions standards as set in the Environmental Protection Agency's Cross-State Air Pollution Rule, rather than the lowered emissions standards currently set through 2020, and would provide for consideration of the bill (HR 1917) that would suspend certain Environmental Protection Agency rules issued Oct. 26, 2015 and Dec. 4, 2015 setting new emissions standards for hazardous air pollutants from kilns and other facilities that manufacture brick and structural clay products or clay ceramics. Motion agreed to 229-183: R 229-0; D 0-183. March 7, 2018.

97. HRES762. POWER PLANT EMISSIONS STANDARDS AND KILN REGULATIONS/RULE. Adoption of the rule (H Res 762) that would provide for consideration of the bill (HR 1119) that would subject an electricity-generating power plant that can get at least 75 percent of its energy from coal mining byproduct to the original emissions standards as set in the Environmental Protection Agency's Cross-State Air Pollution Rule, rather than the lowered emissions standards currently set through 2020, and would provide for consideration of the bill (HR 1917) that would suspend certain Environmental Protection Agency rules issued Oct. 26, 2015 and Dec. 4, 2015 setting new emissions standards for hazardous air pollutants from kilns and other facilities that manufacture brick and structural clay products or clay ceramics. Adopted 227-185: R 227-0; D 0-185. March 7, 2018.

	92	93	94	95	96	97
ALABAMA						
1 **Byrne**	Y	Y	N	Y	Y	Y
2 **Roby**	Y	Y	N	Y	Y	Y
3 **Rogers**	Y	Y	N	Y	Y	Y
4 **Aderholt**	Y	Y	N	Y	Y	Y
5 **Brooks**	Y	Y	N	Y	Y	Y
6 **Palmer**	Y	Y	N	Y	Y	Y
7 Sewell	Y	Y	Y	Y	N	N
ALASKA						
AL **Young**	Y	Y	N	Y	Y	Y
ARIZONA						
1 O'Halleran	Y	Y	Y	Y	N	N
2 **McSally**	Y	Y	N	Y	Y	Y
3 Grijalva	?	?	Y	N	N	N
4 **Gosar**	Y	Y	N	Y	Y	Y
5 **Biggs**	Y	Y	N	Y	Y	Y
6 **Schweikert**	Y	Y	N	Y	Y	Y
7 Gallego	Y	Y	Y	N	N	N
9 Sinema	Y	Y	Y	Y	N	N
ARKANSAS						
1 **Crawford**	Y	Y	N	Y	Y	Y
2 **Hill**	Y	Y	N	Y	Y	Y
3 **Womack**	Y	Y	N	Y	Y	Y
4 **Westerman**	Y	Y	N	Y	Y	Y
CALIFORNIA						
1 **LaMalfa**	Y	Y	N	Y	Y	Y
2 Huffman	Y	Y	Y	N	N	N
3 Garamendi	Y	Y	Y	N	N	N
4 **McClintock**	Y	Y	N	Y	Y	Y
5 Thompson	Y	Y	Y	N	N	N
6 Matsui	Y	Y	Y	N	N	N
7 Bera	Y	Y	Y	Y	N	N
8 **Cook**	Y	Y	N	Y	Y	Y
9 McNerney	Y	Y	Y	N	N	N
10 **Denham**	Y	Y	N	Y	Y	Y
11 DeSaulnier	Y	Y	Y	N	N	N
12 Pelosi	Y	Y	Y	N	N	N
13 Lee	Y	Y	Y	N	N	N
14 Speier	Y	Y	Y	N	N	N
15 Swalwell	Y	Y	Y	N	N	N
16 Costa	Y	Y	Y	Y	N	N
17 Khanna	Y	Y	Y	N	N	N
18 Eshoo	Y	Y	Y	N	N	N
19 Lofgren	Y	Y	Y	N	N	N
20 Panetta	Y	Y	Y	N	N	N
21 **Valadao**	Y	Y	N	Y	Y	Y
22 **Nunes**	Y	Y	N	Y	Y	Y
23 **McCarthy**	Y	Y	N	Y	Y	Y
24 Carbajal	Y	Y	Y	Y	N	N
25 **Knight**	Y	Y	N	Y	Y	Y
26 Brownley	Y	Y	Y	N	N	N
27 Chu	Y	Y	Y	N	N	N
28 Schiff	Y	Y	Y	N	N	N
29 Cardenas	Y	Y	Y	N	N	N
30 Sherman	Y	Y	Y	N	N	N
31 Aguilar	Y	Y	Y	Y	N	N
32 Napolitano	Y	Y	Y	N	N	N
33 Lieu	Y	Y	?	?	?	?
34 Gomez	Y	Y	Y	N	N	N
35 Torres	Y	Y	Y	N	N	N
36 Ruiz	Y	Y	Y	N	N	N
37 Bass	Y	Y	Y	N	N	N
38 Sánchez, Linda	Y	Y	Y	N	N	N
39 **Royce**	Y	Y	N	Y	Y	Y
40 Roybal-Allard	Y	Y	Y	N	N	N
41 Takano	Y	Y	Y	N	N	N
42 **Calvert**	Y	Y	N	Y	Y	Y
43 Waters	Y	Y	Y	N	?	N
44 Barragan	Y	Y	Y	N	N	N
45 **Walters**	Y	Y	N	Y	Y	Y
46 Correa	Y	Y	Y	Y	N	N
47 Lowenthal	Y	Y	Y	N	N	N
48 **Rohrabacher**	?	?	N	Y	Y	Y
49 **Issa**	Y	?	Y	N	Y	Y
50 **Hunter**	Y	Y	N	Y	Y	Y
51 Vargas	Y	Y	Y	N	N	N
52 Peters	?	?	Y	N	N	N
53 Davis	Y	Y	Y	N	N	N

	92	93	94	95	96	97
COLORADO						
1 DeGette	Y	Y	Y	N	N	N
2 Polis	?	?	+	–	–	?
3 **Tipton**	Y	Y	N	Y	Y	Y
4 **Buck**	Y	Y	N	Y	Y	Y
5 **Lamborn**	Y	Y	N	Y	Y	Y
6 **Coffman**	Y	Y	N	Y	Y	Y
7 Perlmutter	?	?	Y	Y	N	N
CONNECTICUT						
1 Larson	Y	Y	Y	N	N	N
2 Courtney	Y	Y	Y	N	N	N
3 DeLauro	Y	Y	Y	N	N	N
4 Himes	Y	Y	Y	Y	N	N
5 Esty	Y	Y	Y	Y	N	N
DELAWARE						
AL Blunt Rochester	Y	Y	Y	Y	N	N
FLORIDA						
1 **Gaetz**	Y	Y	N	Y	Y	Y
2 **Dunn**	Y	Y	N	Y	Y	Y
3 **Yoho**	Y	Y	N	Y	Y	Y
4 **Rutherford**	Y	Y	N	Y	Y	Y
5 Lawson	Y	Y	Y	N	N	N
6 **DeSantis**	Y	Y	N	Y	Y	Y
7 Murphy	Y	Y	Y	Y	N	N
8 **Posey**	Y	Y	N	Y	Y	Y
9 Soto	Y	Y	Y	N	N	N
10 Demings	Y	Y	Y	N	N	N
11 **Webster**	Y	Y	N	Y	Y	Y
12 **Bilirakis**	Y	Y	N	Y	Y	Y
13 Crist	Y	Y	Y	N	N	N
14 Castor	Y	Y	Y	N	N	N
15 **Ross**	Y	Y	N	Y	Y	Y
16 **Buchanan**	Y	Y	N	Y	Y	Y
17 **Rooney, T.**	Y	Y	N	Y	Y	Y
18 **Mast**	Y	Y	N	Y	Y	Y
19 **Rooney, F.**	Y	Y	N	Y	Y	Y
20 Hastings	Y	Y	Y	N	N	N
21 Frankel	Y	Y	Y	N	N	N
22 Deutch	?	?	Y	N	N	N
23 Wasserman Schultz	Y	Y	Y	N	N	N
24 Wilson	Y	Y	Y	N	?	N
25 **Diaz-Balart**	Y	Y	N	Y	Y	Y
26 **Curbelo**	Y	Y	+	Y	Y	Y
27 **Ros-Lehtinen**	Y	Y	N	Y	Y	Y
GEORGIA						
1 **Carter**	Y	Y	N	Y	Y	Y
2 Bishop	Y	Y	Y	Y	N	N
3 **Ferguson**	Y	Y	N	Y	Y	Y
4 Johnson	Y	Y	Y	N	N	N
5 Lewis	Y	Y	Y	N	N	N
6 **Handel**	Y	Y	N	Y	Y	Y
7 **Woodall**	Y	Y	N	Y	Y	Y
8 **Scott, A.**	Y	Y	N	Y	Y	Y
9 **Collins**	Y	Y	N	Y	Y	Y
10 **Hice**	Y	Y	N	Y	?	?
11 **Loudermilk**	Y	Y	N	Y	Y	Y
12 **Allen**	Y	Y	N	Y	Y	Y
13 Scott, D.	Y	Y	Y	Y	N	N
14 **Graves**	Y	Y	N	Y	Y	Y
HAWAII						
1 Hanabusa	Y	Y	Y	N	N	N
2 Gabbard	?	?	Y	N	N	?
IDAHO						
1 **Labrador**	?	?	N	Y	Y	Y
2 **Simpson**	Y	Y	N	Y	Y	Y
ILLINOIS						
1 Rush	?	?	Y	N	N	N
2 Kelly	Y	Y	Y	N	N	N
3 Lipinski	Y	Y	Y	N	N	N
4 Gutierrez	+	+	Y	N	N	N
5 Quigley	Y	Y	Y	N	N	N
6 **Roskam**	Y	Y	N	Y	Y	Y
7 Davis, D.	?	?	Y	N	N	N
8 Krishnamoorthi	Y	Y	Y	N	N	N
9 Schakowsky	Y	Y	Y	N	N	N
10 Schneider	Y	Y	Y	Y	N	N
11 Foster	Y	Y	Y	N	N	N
12 **Bost**	Y	Y	N	Y	Y	Y
13 **Davis, R.**	Y	Y	N	Y	Y	Y

KEY	**Republicans**	Democrats	*Independents*		
Y	Voted for (yea)	**X**	Paired against	**C**	Voted "present" to avoid possible conflict of interest
#	Paired for	**–**	Announced against		
+	Announced for	**P**	Voted "present"	**?**	Did not vote or otherwise make a position known
N	Voted against (nay)				

	92	93	94	95	96	97
14 **Hultgren**	Y	Y	N	Y	Y	Y
15 **Shimkus**	Y	Y	N	Y	Y	Y
16 **Kinzinger**	Y	Y	N	Y	Y	Y
17 Bustos	Y	Y	Y	Y	N	N
18 **LaHood**	Y	?	N	Y	Y	Y
INDIANA						
1 Visclosky	Y	Y	Y	N	N	N
2 **Walorski**	Y	Y	N	Y	Y	Y
3 **Banks**	Y	Y	N	Y	Y	Y
4 **Rokita**	Y	Y	N	Y	Y	Y
5 **Brooks**	Y	Y	N	Y	Y	Y
6 **Messer**	Y	Y	N	Y	Y	Y
7 Carson	Y	Y	Y	N	N	N
8 **Bucshon**	Y	Y	N	Y	Y	Y
9 **Hollingsworth**	Y	Y	N	Y	Y	?
IOWA						
1 **Blum**	Y	Y	Y	Y	Y	Y
2 Loebsack	Y	Y	Y	Y	N	N
3 **Young**	Y	Y	N	Y	Y	Y
4 **King**	Y	Y	N	Y	Y	Y
KANSAS						
1 **Marshall**	Y	Y	N	Y	Y	Y
2 **Jenkins**	Y	Y	N	Y	Y	Y
3 **Yoder**	Y	Y	N	Y	Y	Y
4 **Estes**	Y	Y	N	Y	Y	Y
KENTUCKY						
1 **Comer**	Y	Y	N	Y	Y	Y
2 **Guthrie**	Y	Y	N	Y	Y	Y
3 Yarmuth	Y	Y	Y	N	N	N
4 **Massie**	Y	Y	N	Y	Y	Y
5 **Rogers**	Y	Y	N	Y	Y	Y
6 **Barr**	Y	Y	N	Y	?	?
LOUISIANA						
1 **Scalise**	Y	Y	–	+	Y	Y
2 Richmond	Y	Y	Y	N	N	N
3 **Higgins**	Y	Y	N	Y	Y	Y
4 **Johnson**	?	?	N	Y	Y	Y
5 **Abraham**	Y	Y	N	Y	Y	Y
6 **Graves**	Y	Y	N	Y	Y	Y
MAINE						
1 Pingree	?	?	Y	N	N	N
2 Poliquin	Y	Y	N	Y	Y	Y
MARYLAND						
1 **Harris**	Y	Y	N	Y	Y	Y
2 Ruppersberger	Y	Y	Y	Y	N	N
3 Sarbanes	Y	Y	Y	N	N	N
4 Brown	Y	Y	Y	N	N	N
5 Hoyer	Y	Y	Y	N	N	N
6 Delaney	Y	Y	Y	Y	N	N
7 Cummings	?	?	?	?	?	?
8 Raskin	Y	Y	Y	N	N	N
MASSACHUSETTS						
1 Neal	?	?	Y	N	N	N
2 McGovern	Y	Y	Y	N	N	N
3 Tsongas	?	?	Y	N	N	N
4 **Kennedy**	Y	Y	Y	N	N	N
5 Clark	Y	Y	Y	N	N	N
6 Moulton	Y	Y	Y	Y	N	N
7 Capuano	Y	Y	Y	N	N	N
8 Lynch	Y	Y	Y	N	N	N
9 Keating	Y	Y	Y	N	N	N
MICHIGAN						
1 **Bergman**	Y	Y	N	Y	Y	Y
2 **Huizenga**	Y	Y	N	Y	Y	Y
3 *Amash*	Y	Y	N	Y	Y	Y
4 **Moolenaar**	Y	Y	N	Y	Y	Y
5 Kildee	Y	Y	Y	N	N	N
6 Upton	Y	Y	N	Y	Y	Y
7 Walberg	Y	Y	N	Y	Y	Y
8 Bishop	Y	Y	N	Y	Y	Y
9 Levin	Y	Y	Y	N	N	N
10 Mitchell	Y	Y	N	Y	Y	Y
11 Trott	Y	Y	N	Y	Y	Y
12 Dingell	Y	Y	Y	N	N	N
14 Lawrence	Y	Y	Y	N	N	N
MINNESOTA						
1 Walz	?	?	?	–	N	N
2 **Lewis**	Y	Y	N	Y	Y	Y
3 **Paulsen**	Y	Y	N	Y	Y	Y
4 **McCollum**	Y	Y	Y	N	N	N

	92	93	94	95	96	97
5 Ellison	Y	Y	Y	N	N	N
6 **Emmer**	Y	Y	N	Y	Y	Y
7 Peterson	Y	Y	N	Y	N	N
8 Nolan	?	?	?	?	?	?
MISSISSIPPI						
1 **Kelly**	Y	Y	N	Y	Y	Y
2 Thompson	Y	Y	Y	N	N	N
3 **Harper**	Y	Y	N	Y	Y	Y
4 Palazzo	Y	Y	N	Y	Y	?
MISSOURI						
1 Clay	Y	Y	Y	N	N	N
2 **Wagner**	Y	Y	N	Y	Y	Y
3 **Luetkemeyer**	Y	Y	N	Y	Y	Y
4 **Hartzler**	Y	Y	N	Y	Y	Y
5 Cleaver	Y	Y	+	–	N	N
6 **Graves**	Y	Y	N	Y	Y	Y
7 **Long**	Y	Y	N	Y	Y	Y
8 **Smith**	Y	Y	N	Y	Y	Y
MONTANA						
AL **Gianforte**	Y	Y	N	Y	Y	Y
NEBRASKA						
1 **Fortenberry**	Y	Y	N	Y	Y	Y
2 **Bacon**	Y	Y	N	Y	Y	Y
3 **Smith**	Y	Y	N	Y	Y	Y
NEVADA						
1 Titus	Y	Y	Y	N	N	N
2 **Amodei**	Y	Y	N	Y	Y	Y
3 Rosen	?	?	Y	Y	N	N
4 Kihuen	Y	Y	Y	N	N	N
NEW HAMPSHIRE						
1 Shea-Porter	?	?	?	?	?	?
2 Kuster	Y	Y	Y	Y	N	N
NEW JERSEY						
1 Norcross	Y	Y	Y	N	N	N
2 **LoBiondo**	Y	Y	N	Y	Y	Y
3 **MacArthur**	Y	Y	N	Y	Y	Y
4 **Smith**	Y	Y	N	Y	Y	Y
5 Gottheimer	Y	Y	Y	Y	N	N
6 Pallone	Y	Y	Y	N	N	N
7 **Lance**	Y	Y	N	Y	Y	Y
8 Sires	Y	Y	Y	N	N	N
9 Pascrell	Y	Y	Y	N	N	N
10 Payne	Y	Y	Y	N	N	N
11 **Frelinghuysen**	Y	Y	N	Y	Y	Y
12 Watson Coleman	Y	Y	Y	N	N	N
NEW MEXICO						
1 Lujan Grisham	Y	Y	Y	Y	N	N
2 **Pearce**	?	?	?	?	?	?
3 Luján	Y	Y	Y	N	N	N
NEW YORK						
1 **Zeldin**	Y	Y	N	Y	Y	Y
2 **King**	Y	Y	N	Y	Y	Y
3 Suozzi	Y	Y	Y	Y	N	N
4 Rice	?	?	Y	Y	N	N
5 Meeks	Y	Y	Y	N	?	N
6 Meng	Y	Y	Y	N	N	N
7 Velázquez	Y	Y	Y	N	N	N
8 Jeffries	Y	Y	Y	N	N	N
9 Clarke	Y	Y	Y	N	N	N
10 Nadler	Y	Y	Y	N	N	N
11 **Donovan**	Y	Y	N	Y	Y	Y
12 Maloney, C.	Y	Y	Y	N	N	N
13 Espaillat	Y	Y	Y	N	N	N
14 Crowley	Y	Y	Y	N	N	N
15 Serrano	Y	Y	Y	N	N	N
16 Engel	Y	Y	Y	N	N	N
17 Lowey	Y	Y	Y	N	N	N
18 Maloney, S.P.	Y	Y	Y	Y	N	N
19 **Faso**	Y	Y	N	Y	Y	Y
20 Tonko	Y	Y	Y	N	N	N
21 **Stefanik**	Y	Y	N	Y	Y	Y
22 **Tenney**	Y	Y	N	Y	Y	Y
23 **Reed**	Y	Y	N	Y	Y	Y
24 **Katko**	Y	Y	N	Y	Y	Y
25 Slaughter	Y	Y	Y	N	?	?
26 Higgins	Y	Y	Y	N	N	N
27 **Collins**	Y	Y	N	Y	Y	Y
NORTH CAROLINA						
1 Butterfield	Y	Y	Y	N	N	N
2 **Holding**	Y	Y	N	Y	Y	Y
3 **Jones**	Y	Y	Y	Y	Y	Y
4 Price	Y	Y	Y	N	N	N

	92	93	94	95	96	97
5 **Foxx**	Y	Y	N	Y	Y	Y
6 **Walker**	Y	Y	N	Y	Y	Y
7 **Rouzer**	Y	Y	N	Y	Y	Y
8 **Hudson**	Y	Y	N	Y	Y	Y
9 **Pittenger**	Y	Y	N	Y	Y	Y
9 **Vacant**						
10 **McHenry**	Y	Y	N	Y	Y	Y
11 **Meadows**	Y	Y	N	Y	Y	Y
12 Adams	Y	Y	Y	N	N	N
13 **Budd**	Y	Y	N	Y	Y	Y
NORTH DAKOTA						
AL **Cramer**	?	?	?	?	?	?
OHIO						
1 **Chabot**	Y	Y	N	Y	Y	Y
2 **Wenstrup**	Y	Y	N	Y	Y	Y
3 Beatty	Y	Y	Y	N	N	N
4 **Jordan**	Y	Y	N	Y	Y	Y
5 **Latta**	Y	Y	N	Y	Y	Y
6 **Johnson**	Y	Y	N	Y	Y	Y
7 **Gibbs**	Y	Y	N	Y	Y	Y
8 **Davidson**	Y	Y	N	Y	Y	Y
9 Kaptur	Y	Y	Y	N	N	N
10 **Turner**	Y	Y	N	Y	Y	Y
11 Fudge	Y	Y	Y	N	N	N
12 Vacant						
13 Ryan	Y	Y	Y	N	N	N
14 **Joyce**	Y	Y	N	Y	Y	Y
15 **Stivers**	Y	Y	?	?	?	?
16 **Renacci**	+	+	N	Y	Y	Y
OKLAHOMA						
1 **Bridenstine**	Y	Y	N	Y	Y	Y
2 **Mullin**	Y	Y	N	Y	Y	Y
3 **Lucas**	Y	Y	N	Y	Y	Y
4 **Cole**	Y	Y	N	Y	Y	Y
5 **Russell**	Y	Y	N	Y	Y	Y
OREGON						
1 Bonamici	Y	Y	Y	N	N	N
2 **Walden**	Y	Y	N	Y	Y	Y
3 Blumenauer	+	+	Y	N	N	N
4 DeFazio	+	+	+	–	N	N
5 Schrader	Y	Y	Y	Y	N	N
PENNSYLVANIA						
1 Brady	?	?	Y	N	N	N
2 Evans	Y	Y	Y	N	N	N
3 **Kelly**	Y	Y	N	Y	Y	Y
4 **Perry**	Y	Y	N	Y	Y	Y
5 **Thompson**	Y	Y	N	Y	Y	Y
6 **Costello**	Y	Y	N	Y	Y	Y
7 **Meehan**	Y	Y	N	Y	Y	Y
8 **Fitzpatrick**	Y	Y	N	Y	Y	Y
9 **Shuster**	Y	Y	N	Y	?	?
10 **Marino**	Y	Y	N	Y	Y	Y
11 **Barletta**	Y	Y	N	Y	Y	Y
12 **Rothfus**	Y	Y	N	Y	Y	Y
13 Boyle	Y	Y	Y	N	N	N
14 Doyle	Y	Y	Y	N	N	N
15 **Dent**	Y	Y	N	Y	Y	Y
16 **Smucker**	Y	Y	N	Y	Y	Y
17 Cartwright	Y	Y	Y	N	N	N
RHODE ISLAND						
1 Cicilline	Y	Y	Y	N	N	N
2 Langevin	Y	Y	Y	N	N	N
SOUTH CAROLINA						
1 **Sanford**	Y	Y	N	Y	Y	Y
2 **Wilson**	Y	Y	N	Y	Y	Y
3 **Duncan**	Y	Y	N	Y	Y	Y
4 **Gowdy**	Y	Y	N	Y	Y	Y
5 **Norman**	Y	Y	N	Y	Y	Y
6 Clyburn	?	?	Y	N	N	N
7 **Rice**	Y	Y	N	Y	Y	Y
SOUTH DAKOTA						
AL **Noem**	Y	Y	N	Y	Y	Y
TENNESSEE						
1 **Roe**	Y	Y	N	Y	Y	Y
2 **Duncan**	Y	Y	N	Y	Y	Y
3 **Fleischmann**	Y	Y	N	Y	Y	Y
4 **DesJarlais**	Y	Y	N	Y	Y	Y
5 Cooper	Y	Y	Y	Y	N	N
6 **Black**	?	?	N	?	Y	Y
7 **Blackburn**	Y	Y	N	Y	Y	Y
8 **Kustoff**	Y	Y	N	Y	Y	Y
9 Cohen	Y	Y	Y	N	N	N

	92	93	94	95	96	97
TEXAS						
1 **Gohmert**	Y	Y	?	?	Y	Y
2 **Poe**	Y	Y	N	?	?	?
3 **Johnson, S.**	Y	Y	N	Y	Y	Y
4 **Ratcliffe**	Y	Y	N	Y	Y	Y
5 **Hensarling**	Y	Y	N	Y	Y	Y
6 **Barton**	Y	Y	N	Y	Y	Y
7 **Culberson**	Y	Y	N	Y	Y	Y
8 **Brady**	Y	Y	N	Y	Y	Y
9 Green, A.	Y	Y	Y	N	N	N
10 **McCaul**	Y	Y	N	Y	Y	Y
11 **Conaway**	Y	Y	N	Y	Y	Y
12 **Granger**	Y	Y	N	Y	Y	Y
13 **Thornberry**	Y	Y	N	Y	Y	Y
14 **Weber**	Y	Y	N	Y	Y	Y
15 Gonzalez	Y	Y	Y	Y	N	N
16 O'Rourke	Y	Y	Y	N	N	N
17 **Flores**	Y	Y	N	Y	Y	Y
18 Jackson Lee	+	+	+	–	N	N
19 **Arrington**	Y	Y	N	Y	Y	Y
20 Castro	Y	Y	Y	N	N	N
21 **Smith**	Y	Y	N	Y	?	?
22 **Olson**	+	+	–	+	Y	Y
23 **Hurd**	Y	Y	N	Y	Y	Y
24 **Marchant**	?	?	?	?	Y	Y
25 **Williams**	Y	Y	N	Y	Y	Y
26 **Burgess**	Y	Y	?	?	Y	Y
27 **Farenthold**	Y	Y	N	Y	Y	Y
28 Cuellar	Y	Y	Y	Y	N	N
29 Green, G.	+	+	+	–	N	N
30 Johnson, E.B.	?	?	?	?	?	?
31 **Carter**	?	?	N	Y	Y	Y
32 **Sessions**	Y	Y	N	Y	Y	Y
33 Veasey	?	?	?	?	N	N
34 Vela	?	?	Y	Y	N	N
35 Doggett	Y	Y	Y	N	N	N
36 **Babin**	Y	Y	N	Y	Y	Y
UTAH						
1 **Bishop**	Y	Y	N	Y	Y	Y
2 **Stewart**	Y	Y	N	Y	Y	Y
3 **Curtis**	Y	Y	N	Y	Y	Y
4 **Love**	Y	Y	N	Y	Y	Y
VERMONT						
AL **Welch**	Y	Y	Y	N	N	N
VIRGINIA						
1 **Wittman**	Y	Y	N	Y	Y	Y
2 **Taylor**	Y	Y	N	Y	Y	Y
3 Scott	Y	Y	Y	N	N	N
4 McEachin	Y	Y	Y	N	N	N
5 **Garrett**	Y	Y	N	Y	Y	Y
6 **Goodlatte**	Y	Y	N	Y	Y	Y
7 **Brat**	Y	Y	N	Y	Y	Y
8 Beyer	Y	Y	Y	N	N	N
9 **Griffith**	Y	Y	N	Y	Y	Y
10 **Comstock**	Y	Y	N	Y	Y	Y
11 Connolly	Y	Y	Y	N	N	N
WASHINGTON						
1 DelBene	Y	Y	Y	N	N	N
2 Larsen	Y	Y	Y	N	N	N
3 **Herrera Beutler**	Y	Y	N	Y	Y	Y
4 **Newhouse**	Y	Y	N	Y	Y	Y
5 **McMorris Rodgers**	Y	Y	N	Y	Y	Y
6 Kilmer	Y	Y	Y	Y	N	N
7 Jayapal	Y	Y	Y	N	N	N
8 **Reichert**	Y	Y	N	Y	Y	Y
9 Smith	Y	Y	Y	N	N	N
10 Heck	Y	Y	Y	Y	N	N
WEST VIRGINIA						
1 **McKinley**	Y	Y	N	Y	Y	Y
2 **Mooney**	Y	Y	N	Y	Y	Y
3 **Jenkins**	?	?	N	Y	Y	Y
WISCONSIN						
1 **Ryan**						
2 Pocan	Y	Y	Y	N	N	N
3 Kind	?	?	Y	Y	N	N
4 Moore	+	+	Y	N	N	N
5 **Sensenbrenner**	Y	Y	N	Y	Y	Y
6 **Grothman**	Y	Y	N	Y	Y	Y
7 **Duffy**	+	+	N	Y	Y	Y
8 **Gallagher**	Y	Y	N	Y	Y	Y
WYOMING						
AL **Cheney**	Y	Y	N	Y	Y	Y

VOTE NUMBER

98. HR1917. SUSPENDING KILN EMISSION STANDARDS/RECOMMIT.
Castor, D-Fla., motion to recommit the bill to the House Energy and Commerce Committee with instructions to report it back immediately with an amendment that would clarify that nothing in the bill would authorize the administrator of the Environmental Protection Agency to charter a flight, or travel by any air accommodation above coach class, in order to make certain changes to rules and guidance documents for the purpose of implementing the bill's provision regarding standards for residential wood heaters. Motion rejected 186-227: R 2-227; D 184-0. March 7, 2018.

99. HR1917. SUSPENDING KILN EMISSION STANDARDS/PASSAGE.
Passage of the bill that would suspend the Environmental Protection Agency's rules issued Oct. 26, 2015 and Dec. 4, 2015 regarding emissions standards for hazardous air pollutants from kilns and other facilities that manufacture brick and structural clay products or clay ceramics until all judicial reviews of such rules are completed. It would also delay implementation of an agency rule setting performance standards for new residential wood heaters until May 15, 2023. Passed 234-180: R 228-1; D 6-179. March 7, 2018.

100. HR1119. POWER PLANT EMISSIONS STANDARDS/RECOMMIT. Kildee, D-Mich., motion to recommit the bill to the House Energy and Commerce Committee with instructions to report it back immediately with an amendment that would prohibit the bill's provisions from applying to any coal-refuse-burning electricity-generating facility that produces air pollution known to cause certain risks to human health, including potential harm to brain development or increase in risk of cancer, or increases mercury deposition to lakes, rivers and other water sources. Motion rejected 181-225: R 1-225; D 180-0. March 8, 2018.

101. HR1119. POWER PLANT EMISSIONS STANDARDS/PASSAGE. Passage of the bill that would subject an electricity-generating unit that can get at least 75 percent of its energy from coal mining byproduct to the original emissions standards as set in the Environmental Protection Agency's Cross-State Air Pollution Rule (CSAPR), rather than the lowered emissions totals currently set through 2020. It would not allow for unused emissions to be transferred to other entities, but would allow for unused emissions to be added to future compliance periods. The bill would also alter standards under which an electricity-generating unit could meet the Clear Air Act's (PL-91-604) Mercury and Air Toxics Standards Rule through meeting requirements for either sulfur dioxide or hydrogen chloride, but not for both. Passed 215-189: R 210-14; D 5-175. March 8, 2018.

102. HR5247. EXPERIMENTAL DRUGS FOR TERMINAL ILLNESS/PASSAGE.
Walden, R-Ore., motion to suspend the rules and pass the bill that would allow eligible patients to seek access to drugs through the manufacturer, that have not yet been cleared by the Food and Drug Administration. The measure specifies that a patient must be diagnosed with a disease or condition from which they are likely to die within a matter of months, or one that causes significant irreversible morbidity likely to lead to severely premature death, and that any drugs they may try must have completed phase one clinical trials, have not been approved or licensed for any use and are currently under an active FDA application or are undergoing clinical trials. Motion rejected 259-140: R 227-2; D 32-138. March 13, 2018.

103. HR4465. ENDANGERED SPECIES PROTECTION COOPERATIVE PROGRAM FUNDING/PASSAGE. Curtis, R-Utah, motion to suspend the rules and pass the bill that would reauthorize, through Sept. 30, 2023, the Energy Department's Western Area Power Administration to use funds paid by users of the electricity it generates for the existing cooperative programs that assist in the recovery of four endangered species of native fish. Motion agreed to 392-6: R 222-6; D 170-0. March 13, 2018.

	98	99	100	101	102	103
ALABAMA						
1 Byrne	N	Y	N	Y	Y	Y
2 Roby	N	Y	N	Y	Y	Y
3 Rogers	N	Y	N	Y	Y	Y
4 Aderholt	N	Y	N	Y	Y	Y
5 Brooks	N	Y	N	Y	Y	Y
6 Palmer	N	Y	N	Y	Y	Y
7 Sewell	Y	Y	Y	N	N	Y
ALASKA						
AL Young	N	Y	N	Y	Y	Y
ARIZONA						
1 O'Halleran	Y	N	Y	N	Y	Y
2 McSally	N	Y	N	Y	Y	Y
3 Grijalva	Y	N	Y	N	N	Y
4 Gosar	N	Y	N	Y	Y	Y
5 Biggs	N	Y	N	Y	Y	Y
6 Schweikert	N	Y	N	Y	Y	Y
7 Gallego	Y	N	Y	N	N	Y
9 Sinema	Y	Y	Y	N	Y	Y
ARKANSAS						
1 Crawford	N	Y	?	?	Y	Y
2 Hill	N	Y	N	Y	Y	Y
3 Womack	N	Y	N	Y	Y	Y
4 Westerman	N	Y	N	Y	Y	Y
CALIFORNIA						
1 LaMalfa	N	Y	N	Y	Y	Y
2 Huffman	Y	N	Y	N	N	Y
3 Garamendi	Y	N	?	?	N	Y
4 McClintock	N	Y	N	Y	Y	N
5 Thompson	Y	N	Y	N	N	Y
6 Matsui	Y	N	Y	N	N	Y
7 Bera	Y	N	Y	N	N	Y
8 Cook	N	Y	N	Y	Y	Y
9 McNerney	Y	N	Y	N	N	Y
10 Denham	N	Y	N	Y	Y	Y
11 DeSaulnier	Y	N	Y	N	N	Y
12 Pelosi	Y	N	Y	N	N	Y
13 Lee	Y	N	Y	N	N	Y
14 Speier	Y	N	Y	N	N	Y
15 Swalwell	Y	N	Y	N	N	Y
16 Costa	Y	N	Y	N	Y	Y
17 Khanna	Y	N	Y	N	N	Y
18 Eshoo	Y	N	Y	N	N	Y
19 Lofgren	Y	N	Y	N	Y	Y
20 Panetta	Y	N	Y	N	N	Y
21 Valadao	N	Y	N	Y	Y	Y
22 Nunes	N	Y	N	Y	Y	Y
23 McCarthy	N	Y	N	Y	Y	Y
24 Carbajal	Y	N	Y	N	Y	Y
25 Knight	N	Y	N	Y	Y	Y
26 Brownley	Y	N	Y	N	N	Y
27 Chu	Y	N	Y	N	N	Y
28 Schiff	Y	N	Y	N	N	Y
29 Cardenas	?	?	?	?	N	Y
30 Sherman	Y	N	Y	N	N	Y
31 Aguilar	Y	N	Y	N	N	Y
32 Napolitano	Y	N	Y	N	N	Y
33 Lieu	?	?	?	?	?	?
34 Gomez	Y	N	Y	N	N	Y
35 Torres	Y	N	Y	N	N	Y
36 Ruiz	Y	N	Y	N	N	Y
37 Bass	Y	N	?	?	N	Y
38 Sánchez, Linda	Y	N	Y	N	N	Y
39 Royce	N	Y	N	Y	Y	Y
40 Roybal-Allard	Y	N	Y	N	N	Y
41 Takano	Y	N	Y	N	N	Y
42 Calvert	N	Y	N	Y	Y	Y
43 Waters	Y	N	Y	N	N	Y
44 Barragan	Y	N	Y	N	N	Y
45 Walters	N	Y	N	Y	Y	Y
46 Correa	Y	N	Y	N	Y	Y
47 Lowenthal	Y	N	Y	N	N	?
48 Rohrabacher	N	Y	N	Y	?	?
49 Issa	N	Y	N	Y	?	?
50 Hunter	N	Y	N	Y	?	?
51 Vargas	Y	N	Y	N	?	?
52 Peters	Y	N	Y	N	N	Y
53 Davis	Y	N	Y	N	N	Y

	98	99	100	101	102	103
COLORADO						
1 DeGette	Y	N	Y	N	N	Y
2 Polis	+	–	+	–	Y	Y
3 Tipton	N	Y	N	Y	Y	Y
4 Buck	N	Y	N	Y	Y	Y
5 Lamborn	N	Y	N	Y	Y	Y
6 Coffman	N	Y	N	Y	Y	Y
7 Perlmutter	Y	N	Y	N	Y	Y
CONNECTICUT						
1 Larson	Y	N	Y	N	N	Y
2 Courtney	Y	N	Y	N	N	Y
3 DeLauro	Y	N	+	–	N	Y
4 Himes	Y	N	Y	N	N	Y
5 Esty	Y	N	Y	N	N	Y
DELAWARE						
AL Blunt Rochester	Y	N	Y	N	N	Y
FLORIDA						
1 Gaetz	N	Y	?	?	Y	Y
2 Dunn	N	Y	N	Y	Y	Y
3 Yoho	N	Y	N	Y	Y	Y
4 Rutherford	N	Y	N	Y	Y	Y
5 Lawson	Y	N	Y	N	Y	Y
6 DeSantis	N	Y	N	Y	?	?
7 Murphy	Y	N	Y	N	N	Y
8 Posey	N	Y	N	Y	Y	Y
9 Soto	Y	N	Y	N	N	Y
10 Demings	Y	N	Y	N	N	Y
11 Webster	N	Y	N	Y	Y	Y
12 Bilirakis	N	Y	N	Y	Y	Y
13 Crist	Y	N	Y	N	Y	Y
14 Castor	Y	N	Y	N	N	Y
15 Ross	N	Y	N	Y	Y	Y
16 Buchanan	N	Y	N	Y	Y	Y
17 Rooney, T.	N	Y	N	Y	Y	Y
18 Mast	N	Y	N	N	Y	Y
19 Rooney, F.	N	Y	N	Y	Y	Y
20 Hastings	Y	N	Y	N	N	Y
21 Frankel	Y	N	Y	N	N	Y
22 Deutch	Y	N	Y	N	N	Y
23 Wasserman Schultz	Y	N	Y	N	N	Y
24 Wilson	Y	N	Y	N	?	?
25 Diaz-Balart	N	Y	N	Y	Y	Y
26 Curbelo	N	Y	N	Y	Y	Y
27 Ros-Lehtinen	N	Y	N	N	?	?
GEORGIA						
1 Carter	N	Y	N	Y	Y	Y
2 Bishop	Y	Y	Y	Y	Y	Y
3 Ferguson	N	Y	N	Y	Y	Y
4 Johnson	Y	N	Y	N	N	Y
5 Lewis	Y	N	Y	N	N	Y
6 Handel	N	Y	N	Y	Y	Y
7 Woodall	N	Y	N	Y	Y	Y
8 Scott, A.	N	Y	N	Y	Y	Y
9 Collins	N	Y	N	Y	Y	Y
10 Hice	?	?	N	Y	Y	Y
11 Loudermilk	N	Y	N	Y	Y	Y
12 Allen	N	Y	N	Y	Y	N
13 Scott, D.	Y	N	Y	N	?	?
14 Graves	N	Y	N	Y	Y	Y
HAWAII						
1 Hanabusa	Y	N	Y	N	Y	Y
2 Gabbard	Y	N	?	?	N	Y
IDAHO						
1 Labrador	N	Y	N	Y	Y	Y
2 Simpson	N	Y	N	Y	?	?
ILLINOIS						
1 Rush	Y	N	Y	N	?	?
2 Kelly	Y	N	Y	N	N	Y
3 Lipinski	Y	N	Y	N	N	Y
4 Gutierrez	Y	N	Y	N	–	–
5 Quigley	Y	N	Y	N	N	Y
6 Roskam	N	Y	N	Y	Y	Y
7 Davis, D.	Y	N	Y	N	?	?
8 Krishnamoorthi	Y	N	Y	N	N	Y
9 Schakowsky	Y	N	Y	N	N	Y
10 Schneider	Y	N	Y	N	N	Y
11 Foster	Y	N	Y	N	N	Y
12 Bost	N	Y	N	Y	Y	Y
13 Davis, R.	N	Y	N	Y	Y	Y

	98	99	100	101	102	103
14 **Hultgren**	N	Y	N	Y	Y	Y
15 **Shimkus**	N	Y	N	Y	Y	Y
16 **Kinzinger**	N	Y	N	Y	Y	Y
17 Bustos	Y	N	Y	N	N	Y
18 **LaHood**	N	Y	N	Y	Y	Y
INDIANA						
1 Visclosky	Y	N	Y	N	N	Y
2 **Walorski**	N	Y	N	Y	Y	Y
3 **Banks**	N	Y	N	Y	Y	Y
4 **Rokita**	N	Y	N	Y	Y	Y
5 **Brooks**	N	Y	N	Y	Y	Y
6 **Messer**	N	Y	?	?	Y	Y
7 Carson	Y	N	Y	Y	N	Y
8 **Bucshon**	N	Y	N	Y	Y	Y
9 **Hollingsworth**	N	Y	N	Y	Y	Y
IOWA						
1 **Blum**	Y	Y	N	Y	Y	Y
2 Loebsack	Y	N	Y	N	Y	Y
3 **Young**	N	Y	N	Y	Y	Y
4 **King**	N	Y	N	Y	Y	Y
KANSAS						
1 **Marshall**	N	Y	N	Y	Y	Y
2 **Jenkins**	N	Y	N	Y	Y	Y
3 **Yoder**	N	Y	N	Y	Y	Y
4 **Estes**	N	Y	N	Y	Y	Y
KENTUCKY						
1 **Comer**	N	Y	N	Y	Y	Y
2 **Guthrie**	N	Y	N	Y	Y	Y
3 Yarmuth	Y	N	Y	N	?	?
4 **Massie**	N	Y	N	Y	Y	N
5 **Rogers**	N	Y	N	Y	Y	Y
6 **Barr**	?	?	N	Y	Y	Y
LOUISIANA						
1 **Scalise**	–	+	N	Y	Y	Y
2 Richmond	Y	N	?	?	Y	Y
3 **Higgins**	N	Y	N	Y	Y	Y
4 **Johnson**	N	Y	N	Y	Y	Y
5 **Abraham**	N	Y	N	Y	Y	Y
6 **Graves**	N	Y	N	Y	Y	Y
MAINE						
1 Pingree	Y	P	Y	N	N	Y
2 **Poliquin**	N	Y	N	N	Y	Y
MARYLAND						
1 **Harris**	N	Y	N	Y	Y	Y
2 Ruppersberger	Y	N	Y	N	N	Y
3 Sarbanes	Y	N	Y	N	N	Y
4 Brown	Y	N	Y	N	Y	Y
5 Hoyer	Y	N	Y	N	N	Y
6 Delaney	Y	N	Y	N	Y	Y
7 Cummings	?	?	?	?	?	?
8 Raskin	Y	N	Y	N	N	Y
MASSACHUSETTS						
1 Neal	Y	N	Y	N	N	Y
2 McGovern	Y	N	Y	N	N	Y
3 Tsongas	Y	N	Y	N	?	?
4 Kennedy	Y	N	Y	N	?	?
5 Clark	Y	N	Y	N	N	Y
6 Moulton	Y	N	Y	N	N	Y
7 Capuano	?	N	Y	N	?	?
8 Lynch	Y	N	Y	N	?	?
9 Keating	Y	N	Y	N	?	?
MICHIGAN						
1 **Bergman**	N	Y	N	Y	Y	Y
2 **Huizenga**	N	Y	N	Y	Y	Y
3 *Amash*	N	Y	N	N	Y	N
4 **Moolenaar**	N	Y	N	Y	Y	Y
5 Kildee	Y	N	Y	N	N	Y
6 **Upton**	N	Y	N	Y	Y	Y
7 **Walberg**	N	Y	N	Y	Y	Y
8 **Bishop**	N	Y	N	Y	Y	Y
9 Levin	Y	N	Y	N	N	Y
10 **Mitchell**	N	Y	N	Y	Y	Y
11 **Trott**	N	Y	N	Y	Y	Y
12 Dingell	Y	N	Y	N	N	Y
14 Lawrence	Y	N	Y	N	N	Y
MINNESOTA						
1 Walz	Y	N	?	–	N	Y
2 **Lewis**	N	Y	N	Y	Y	Y
3 **Paulsen**	N	Y	N	Y	N	Y
4 McCollum	Y	N	Y	N	N	Y

	98	99	100	101	102	103
5 Ellison	Y	N	Y	N	N	Y
6 **Emmer**	N	Y	N	Y	Y	Y
7 Peterson	Y	Y	Y	Y	Y	Y
8 Nolan	?	?	?	?	N	Y
MISSISSIPPI						
1 **Kelly**	N	Y	N	Y	Y	Y
2 Thompson	Y	N	Y	N	N	Y
3 **Harper**	N	Y	N	Y	Y	Y
4 **Palazzo**	N	Y	N	Y	Y	Y
MISSOURI						
1 Clay	Y	N	Y	N	N	Y
2 **Wagner**	N	Y	N	Y	Y	Y
3 **Luetkemeyer**	N	Y	N	Y	+	+
4 **Hartzler**	N	Y	N	Y	Y	Y
5 Cleaver	Y	N	Y	N	N	Y
6 **Graves**	N	Y	N	Y	Y	Y
7 **Long**	N	Y	N	Y	Y	Y
8 **Smith**	N	Y	N	Y	Y	Y
MONTANA						
AL **Gianforte**	N	Y	N	Y	Y	Y
NEBRASKA						
1 **Fortenberry**	N	Y	N	Y	Y	Y
2 **Bacon**	N	Y	N	Y	Y	Y
3 **Smith**	N	Y	N	Y	Y	Y
NEVADA						
1 Titus	Y	N	Y	N	N	Y
2 **Amodei**	N	Y	N	Y	Y	Y
3 Rosen	Y	N	Y	N	Y	Y
4 Kihuen	Y	N	Y	N	N	Y
NEW HAMPSHIRE						
1 Shea-Porter	?	?	?	?	N	Y
2 Kuster	Y	N	Y	N	N	Y
NEW JERSEY						
1 Norcross	Y	N	Y	N	?	?
2 **LoBiondo**	N	Y	N	N	Y	Y
3 **MacArthur**	N	Y	N	Y	Y	Y
4 **Smith**	N	Y	N	N	Y	Y
5 Gottheimer	Y	N	Y	N	Y	Y
6 Pallone	Y	N	Y	N	N	Y
7 **Lance**	N	Y	N	N	Y	Y
8 Sires	Y	N	Y	N	N	Y
9 Pascrell	Y	N	Y	N	N	Y
10 Payne	Y	N	Y	N	N	Y
11 **Frelinghuysen**	N	Y	N	Y	Y	Y
12 Watson Coleman	Y	N	Y	N	N	Y
NEW MEXICO						
1 Lujan Grisham	Y	N	Y	N	Y	Y
2 **Pearce**	?	?	?	?	Y	Y
3 Luján	Y	N	Y	N	N	Y
NEW YORK						
1 **Zeldin**	N	Y	N	Y	Y	Y
2 **King**	N	Y	N	Y	Y	Y
3 Suozzi	Y	N	Y	N	Y	Y
4 Rice	Y	N	Y	N	?	?
5 Meeks	?	N	Y	N	N	Y
6 Meng	Y	N	Y	N	N	Y
7 Velázquez	Y	N	Y	N	–	+
8 Jeffries	Y	N	Y	N	N	Y
9 Clarke	Y	N	Y	N	N	Y
10 Nadler	Y	N	Y	N	N	Y
11 **Donovan**	N	Y	N	Y	Y	Y
12 Maloney, C.	Y	N	Y	N	N	Y
13 Espaillat	Y	N	Y	N	N	Y
14 Crowley	Y	N	Y	N	–	+
15 Serrano	Y	N	Y	N	N	Y
16 Engel	Y	N	Y	N	N	Y
17 Lowey	Y	N	Y	N	N	Y
18 Maloney, S.P.	Y	N	Y	N	Y	Y
19 **Faso**	N	Y	N	N	Y	Y
20 Tonko	Y	N	Y	N	N	Y
21 **Stefanik**	N	Y	N	N	Y	Y
22 **Tenney**	N	Y	N	Y	Y	Y
23 **Reed**	N	Y	N	N	?	?
24 **Katko**	N	Y	N	Y	Y	Y
25 Slaughter	?	?	?	?	?	?
26 Higgins	Y	N	Y	N	N	Y
27 **Collins**	N	Y	N	Y	Y	Y
NORTH CAROLINA						
1 Butterfield	Y	N	Y	N	N	Y
2 **Holding**	N	Y	N	Y	Y	Y
3 **Jones**	Y	Y	Y	Y	Y	Y
4 Price	Y	N	Y	N	N	Y

	98	99	100	101	102	103
5 **Foxx**	N	Y	N	Y	Y	Y
6 **Walker**	N	Y	N	Y	Y	Y
7 **Rouzer**	N	Y	N	Y	Y	Y
8 **Hudson**	N	Y	–	+	Y	Y
9 **Pittenger**	N	Y	N	Y	Y	Y
9 **Vacant**						
10 **McHenry**	N	Y	N	Y	Y	Y
11 **Meadows**	N	Y	N	Y	Y	Y
12 Adams	Y	N	Y	N	N	Y
13 **Budd**	N	Y	N	Y	Y	Y
NORTH DAKOTA						
AL **Cramer**	?	?	?	?	Y	Y
OHIO						
1 **Chabot**	N	Y	N	Y	Y	Y
2 **Wenstrup**	N	Y	N	Y	Y	Y
3 Beatty	Y	N	Y	N	N	Y
4 **Jordan**	N	Y	N	Y	Y	Y
5 **Latta**	N	Y	N	Y	Y	Y
6 **Johnson**	N	Y	N	Y	Y	Y
7 **Gibbs**	N	Y	N	Y	Y	Y
8 **Davidson**	N	Y	N	Y	Y	Y
9 Kaptur	Y	N	Y	N	N	Y
10 **Turner**	N	Y	N	Y	Y	Y
11 Fudge	Y	N	Y	N	N	Y
12 **Vacant**						
13 Ryan	Y	N	Y	N	N	Y
14 **Joyce**	N	Y	N	Y	Y	Y
15 **Stivers**	N	Y	N	Y	Y	Y
16 **Renacci**	N	Y	N	Y	Y	Y
OKLAHOMA						
1 **Bridenstine**	?	?	?	?	Y	Y
2 **Mullin**	N	Y	N	Y	Y	Y
3 **Lucas**	N	Y	N	?	Y	Y
4 **Cole**	N	Y	N	Y	Y	Y
5 **Russell**	N	Y	N	Y	Y	Y
OREGON						
1 Bonamici	Y	N	Y	N	N	Y
2 **Walden**	N	Y	N	Y	Y	Y
3 Blumenauer	Y	N	Y	N	N	Y
4 DeFazio	Y	Y	Y	N	–	+
5 Schrader	Y	N	Y	N	N	Y
PENNSYLVANIA						
1 Brady	Y	N	Y	N	?	?
2 Evans	Y	N	Y	N	Y	Y
3 **Kelly**	N	Y	N	Y	Y	Y
4 **Perry**	N	Y	N	Y	Y	Y
5 **Thompson**	N	Y	N	Y	Y	Y
6 **Costello**	N	Y	?	?	Y	Y
7 **Meehan**	N	Y	N	Y	N	Y
8 **Fitzpatrick**	N	N	N	N	Y	Y
9 **Shuster**	N	Y	N	Y	Y	Y
10 **Marino**	N	Y	N	Y	Y	Y
11 **Barletta**	N	Y	N	Y	Y	Y
12 **Rothfus**	N	Y	N	Y	Y	Y
13 Boyle	Y	N	Y	N	N	Y
14 Doyle	Y	N	Y	N	?	?
15 **Dent**	N	Y	N	Y	Y	Y
16 **Smucker**	N	Y	N	Y	Y	Y
17 Cartwright	Y	N	Y	N	N	Y
RHODE ISLAND						
1 Cicilline	Y	N	Y	N	N	Y
2 Langevin	Y	N	Y	N	+	+
SOUTH CAROLINA						
1 **Sanford**	N	Y	N	N	Y	N
2 **Wilson**	N	Y	N	Y	Y	Y
3 **Duncan**	N	Y	N	Y	Y	Y
4 **Gowdy**	N	Y	N	Y	Y	Y
5 **Norman**	N	Y	N	Y	Y	Y
6 Clyburn	Y	N	Y	N	N	Y
7 **Rice**	N	Y	N	?	Y	N
SOUTH DAKOTA						
AL **Noem**	N	Y	N	Y	Y	Y
TENNESSEE						
1 **Roe**	N	Y	N	Y	Y	Y
2 **Duncan**	N	Y	N	Y	Y	Y
3 **Fleischmann**	N	Y	N	Y	Y	Y
4 **DesJarlais**	N	Y	N	Y	Y	Y
5 Cooper	Y	N	Y	N	Y	Y
6 **Black**	N	Y	?	?	Y	Y
7 **Blackburn**	N	Y	N	Y	Y	Y
8 **Kustoff**	N	Y	N	Y	Y	Y
9 Cohen	Y	N	Y	N	Y	Y

	98	99	100	101	102	103
TEXAS						
1 **Gohmert**	N	Y	N	Y	Y	Y
2 **Poe**	?	?	?	?	Y	Y
3 **Johnson, S.**	N	Y	N	Y	Y	Y
4 **Ratcliffe**	N	Y	N	Y	Y	Y
5 **Hensarling**	N	Y	N	Y	Y	Y
6 **Barton**	N	Y	N	Y	Y	Y
7 **Culberson**	N	Y	N	Y	Y	Y
8 **Brady**	N	Y	N	Y	Y	Y
9 Green, A.	Y	N	Y	N	N	Y
10 **McCaul**	N	Y	N	Y	Y	Y
11 **Conaway**	N	Y	N	Y	Y	Y
12 **Granger**	N	Y	N	Y	Y	Y
13 **Thornberry**	N	Y	N	Y	Y	Y
14 **Weber**	N	Y	N	Y	Y	Y
15 Gonzalez	Y	N	Y	Y	N	Y
16 O'Rourke	Y	N	Y	N	Y	Y
17 **Flores**	N	Y	N	Y	Y	Y
18 Jackson Lee	Y	N	Y	N	N	Y
19 **Arrington**	N	Y	N	Y	Y	Y
20 Castro	Y	N	Y	N	N	Y
21 **Smith**	?	?	?	?	Y	Y
22 **Olson**	N	Y	N	Y	Y	Y
23 **Hurd**	N	Y	N	Y	Y	Y
24 **Marchant**	N	Y	N	Y	Y	?
25 **Williams**	N	Y	N	Y	Y	Y
26 **Burgess**	N	Y	N	Y	Y	Y
27 **Farenthold**	N	Y	N	Y	Y	Y
28 Cuellar	Y	Y	Y	Y	Y	Y
29 Green, G.	Y	N	Y	N	N	Y
30 Johnson, E.B.	Y	N	Y	N	N	Y
31 **Carter**	N	Y	N	Y	Y	Y
32 **Sessions**	N	Y	N	Y	Y	Y
33 Veasey	Y	N	Y	N	Y	Y
34 Vela	Y	N	Y	N	N	Y
35 Doggett	Y	N	Y	N	N	Y
36 **Babin**	N	Y	N	Y	Y	Y
UTAH						
1 **Bishop**	N	Y	N	Y	Y	Y
2 **Stewart**	N	Y	N	Y	Y	Y
3 **Curtis**	N	Y	N	Y	Y	Y
4 **Love**	N	Y	N	Y	Y	Y
VERMONT						
AL Welch	Y	N	Y	N	N	Y
VIRGINIA						
1 **Wittman**	N	Y	N	Y	Y	Y
2 **Taylor**	N	Y	N	Y	Y	Y
3 Scott	Y	N	Y	N	N	Y
4 McEachin	Y	N	Y	N	N	Y
5 **Garrett**	N	Y	N	Y	Y	Y
6 **Goodlatte**	N	Y	N	Y	Y	Y
7 **Brat**	N	Y	N	Y	Y	Y
8 Beyer	Y	N	Y	N	N	Y
9 **Griffith**	N	Y	N	Y	Y	Y
10 **Comstock**	N	Y	N	Y	Y	Y
11 Connolly	Y	N	Y	N	N	Y
WASHINGTON						
1 DelBene	Y	N	Y	N	N	Y
2 Larsen	Y	N	Y	N	N	Y
3 **Herrera Beutler**	N	Y	N	Y	Y	Y
4 **Newhouse**	N	Y	N	Y	Y	Y
5 **McMorris Rodgers**	N	Y	N	Y	Y	Y
6 Kilmer	Y	N	Y	N	N	Y
7 Jayapal	Y	N	Y	N	N	Y
8 **Reichert**	N	Y	N	Y	Y	Y
9 Smith	Y	N	Y	N	N	Y
10 Heck	Y	N	Y	N	N	Y
WEST VIRGINIA						
1 **McKinley**	N	Y	N	Y	Y	Y
2 **Mooney**	N	Y	N	Y	Y	Y
3 **Jenkins**	N	Y	N	Y	Y	Y
WISCONSIN						
1 **Ryan**						
2 Pocan	Y	N	Y	N	N	Y
3 Kind	Y	N	Y	N	Y	Y
4 Moore	Y	N	Y	N	N	Y
5 **Sensenbrenner**	N	Y	N	Y	Y	Y
6 **Grothman**	N	Y	N	Y	Y	Y
7 **Duffy**	N	Y	N	Y	Y	Y
8 **Gallagher**	N	Y	N	Y	Y	Y
WYOMING						
AL **Cheney**	N	Y	N	Y	Y	Y

VOTE NUMBER

104. HR1116. BANKING REGULATION LIMITATIONS/PREVIOUS QUESTION. Buck, R-Colo., motion to order the previous question (thus ending debate and possibility of amendment) on the rule (H Res 773) that would provide for consideration of the Financial Institutions Examination Fairness and Reform Act (HR 4545), the Taking Account of Institutions with Low Operation Risk (TAILOR) Act (HR 1116), and the Regulation A+ Improvement Act (HR 4263). Motion agreed to 234-183: R 234-0; D 0-183. March 14, 2018.

105. HR4545. BANKING REGULATION LIMITATIONS/RULE. Adoption of the rule (H Res 773) that would provide for consideration of the Financial Institutions Examination Fairness and Reform Act (HR 4545), the Taking Account of Institutions with Low Operation Risk (TAILOR) Act (HR 1116), and the Regulation A+ Improvement Act (HR 4263). Adopted 235-182: R 232-0; D 3-182. March 14, 2018.

106. HR4909. SCHOOL VIOLENCE PREVENTION/PASSAGE. Goodlatte, R-Va., motion to suspend the rules and pass the bill that would authorize $75 million a year through fiscal 2028 for the Secure Our Schools grant program and would revise it to more explicitly focus the program on preventing student violence. It would modify the program's mission to improve school security through evidence-based training and technical assistance to prevent violence. It would also expand the eligible uses for the grant to include help for state and local governments to provide training to prevent student violence, development and operation of anonymous reporting systems for threats of school violence, and the development and operation of school threat assessment intervention teams. Motion agreed to 407-10: R 229-5; D 178-5. March 14, 2018.

107. HR1116. BUSINESS MODEL-SHAPED FINANCIAL REGULATIONS/ RECOMMIT. Connolly D-Va., motion to recommit the bill to the House Financial Services Committee with instructions to report it back immediately with an amendment that would prevent changes in financial regulations in the bill from being made at the request of, or for the personal gain of, the president, a member of his family, or other senior Executive Branch official. Motion rejected 182-232: R 1-232; D 181-0. March 14, 2018.

108. HR1116. BUSINESS MODEL-SHAPED FINANCIAL REGULATIONS/ PASSAGE. Passage of the bill that would require federal financial regulators to tailor their rules and regulations on covered institutions in a manner that would take into account the risk profile and business models of the different types and classes of financial institutions. It would also require a review of all regulations adopted during the seven years prior to the introduction date of this bill and would revise as appropriate any that do not meet the bill's requirements. Passed 247-169: R 231-1; D 16-168. March 14, 2018.

109. HR4263. SECURITIES REGULATIONS FOR NEW BUSINESSES/ RECOMMIT. Beatty D-Ohio motion to recommit the bill to the House Financial Services Committee with instructions to report it back immediately with an amendment that would eliminate the increase in the maximum amount of securities that a company that could offer in a 12-month period without registering with the Securities and Exchange Commission. The amendment would also require the SEC to review and revise regulations. Motion rejected 182-235: R 2-231; D 180-4. March 15, 2018.

	104	105	106	107	108	109
ALABAMA						
1 Byrne	Y	Y	Y	N	Y	N
2 Roby	Y	Y	Y	N	Y	N
3 Rogers	Y	Y	Y	N	Y	N
4 Aderholt	Y	Y	Y	N	Y	N
5 Brooks	Y	Y	Y	N	Y	N
6 Palmer	Y	Y	Y	N	Y	N
7 Sewell	N	N	Y	Y	N	Y
ALASKA						
AL Young	Y	Y	Y	N	Y	N
ARIZONA						
1 O'Halleran	N	N	Y	Y	Y	Y
2 McSally	Y	Y	Y	N	Y	N
3 Grijalva	N	N	Y	Y	N	Y
4 Gosar	Y	Y	Y	N	Y	N
5 Biggs	Y	Y	Y	N	Y	N
6 Schweikert	Y	Y	Y	N	Y	N
7 Gallego	N	N	Y	Y	N	Y
9 Sinema	N	N	Y	Y	N	N
ARKANSAS						
1 Crawford	Y	Y	Y	N	Y	N
2 Hill	Y	Y	Y	N	Y	N
3 Womack	Y	Y	Y	N	Y	N
4 Westerman	Y	Y	Y	N	Y	N
CALIFORNIA						
1 LaMalfa	Y	Y	Y	N	Y	N
2 Huffman	N	N	Y	Y	N	Y
3 Garamendi	N	N	Y	Y	N	Y
4 McClintock	Y	Y	Y	N	Y	N
5 Thompson	N	N	Y	Y	N	Y
6 Matsui	N	N	Y	Y	N	Y
7 Bera	N	N	Y	Y	N	Y
8 Cook	Y	Y	Y	N	Y	N
9 McNerney	N	N	Y	Y	N	Y
10 Denham	Y	Y	Y	N	Y	N
11 DeSaulnier	N	N	Y	Y	N	Y
12 Pelosi	?	N	Y	Y	N	Y
13 Lee	N	N	N	Y	N	Y
14 Speier	N	N	Y	?	N	Y
15 Swalwell	N	N	Y	Y	N	Y
16 Costa	N	N	Y	Y	Y	+
17 Khanna	N	N	Y	Y	N	Y
18 Eshoo	N	N	Y	Y	N	Y
19 Lofgren	N	N	Y	Y	N	Y
20 Panetta	N	N	Y	Y	N	Y
21 Valadao	Y	Y	Y	N	Y	N
22 Nunes	Y	Y	Y	N	Y	N
23 McCarthy	Y	Y	Y	N	Y	N
24 Carbajal	N	N	Y	Y	N	Y
25 Knight	Y	Y	Y	N	Y	N
26 Brownley	N	N	Y	Y	N	Y
27 Chu	N	N	Y	Y	N	Y
28 Schiff	N	N	Y	Y	N	Y
29 Cardenas	N	N	N	?	N	Y
30 Sherman	N	N	Y	Y	N	Y
31 Aguilar	N	N	Y	Y	N	Y
32 Napolitano	N	N	Y	Y	N	Y
33 Lieu	?	?	?	?	?	Y
34 Gomez	N	N	Y	Y	N	Y
35 Torres	N	N	Y	Y	N	Y
36 Ruiz	N	N	Y	Y	N	Y
37 Bass	N	N	?	Y	N	Y
38 Sánchez, Linda	N	N	Y	Y	N	Y
39 Royce	Y	Y	Y	N	Y	N
40 Roybal-Allard	N	N	Y	Y	N	Y
41 Takano	N	N	Y	Y	N	Y
42 Calvert	Y	Y	Y	N	Y	N
43 Waters	N	N	Y	Y	N	Y
44 Barragan	N	N	Y	Y	N	Y
45 Walters	Y	Y	Y	N	Y	N
46 Correa	N	N	Y	Y	Y	Y
47 Lowenthal	N	N	Y	Y	N	Y
48 Rohrabacher	Y	Y	Y	N	Y	N
49 Issa	Y	Y	Y	N	Y	N
50 Hunter	Y	Y	Y	N	Y	N
51 Vargas	N	N	Y	Y	N	Y
52 Peters	N	N	Y	Y	N	Y
53 Davis	N	N	Y	Y	N	Y

	104	105	106	107	108	109
COLORADO						
1 DeGette	N	N	Y	Y	N	Y
2 Polis	N	N	Y	Y	N	Y
3 Tipton	Y	Y	Y	N	Y	N
4 Buck	Y	Y	Y	N	Y	N
5 Lamborn	Y	Y	Y	N	Y	N
6 Coffman	Y	Y	Y	N	Y	N
7 Perlmutter	N	N	Y	Y	N	Y
CONNECTICUT						
1 Larson	N	N	Y	Y	N	Y
2 Courtney	N	N	Y	Y	N	Y
3 DeLauro	N	N	Y	Y	N	Y
4 Himes	N	N	Y	Y	N	Y
5 Esty	N	N	Y	Y	N	Y
DELAWARE						
AL Blunt Rochester	N	N	Y	Y	N	Y
FLORIDA						
1 Gaetz	Y	Y	Y	N	Y	N
2 Dunn	Y	Y	Y	N	Y	N
3 Yoho	Y	Y	Y	N	Y	N
4 Rutherford	Y	Y	Y	N	Y	N
5 Lawson	N	N	Y	Y	N	Y
6 DeSantis	Y	Y	Y	N	Y	N
7 Murphy	N	Y	Y	Y	Y	Y
8 Posey	Y	Y	Y	N	Y	N
9 Soto	N	N	Y	Y	N	Y
10 Demings	N	N	Y	Y	N	Y
11 Webster	Y	Y	Y	N	Y	N
12 Bilirakis	Y	Y	Y	N	Y	N
13 Crist	N	N	Y	Y	N	Y
14 Castor	N	N	Y	Y	N	Y
15 Ross	Y	Y	Y	N	Y	N
16 Buchanan	Y	Y	Y	N	Y	N
17 Rooney, T.	Y	Y	Y	N	Y	N
18 Mast	Y	Y	Y	N	Y	N
19 Rooney, F.	Y	Y	Y	?	?	N
20 Hastings	N	N	Y	Y	N	Y
21 Frankel	–	N	Y	Y	N	Y
22 Deutch	N	N	Y	Y	N	Y
23 Wasserman Schultz	N	N	Y	Y	N	Y
24 Wilson	–	–	+	+	–	?
25 Diaz-Balart	Y	Y	Y	N	Y	N
26 Curbelo	Y	Y	Y	N	Y	N
27 Ros-Lehtinen	?	?	?	?	?	?
GEORGIA						
1 Carter	Y	Y	Y	N	Y	N
2 Bishop	N	N	Y	Y	N	Y
3 Ferguson	Y	Y	Y	N	Y	N
4 Johnson	N	N	N	Y	N	Y
5 Lewis	N	N	Y	Y	N	Y
6 Handel	Y	Y	Y	N	Y	N
7 Woodall	Y	Y	Y	N	Y	N
8 Scott, A.	Y	Y	Y	N	Y	N
9 Collins	Y	Y	Y	N	Y	N
10 Hice	Y	Y	Y	N	Y	N
11 Loudermilk	Y	Y	Y	N	Y	?
12 Allen	Y	?	Y	N	Y	N
13 Scott, D.	N	N	Y	Y	N	Y
14 Graves	Y	Y	Y	N	Y	N
HAWAII						
1 Hanabusa	N	N	Y	Y	N	Y
2 Gabbard	N	N	Y	Y	N	Y
IDAHO						
1 Labrador	Y	Y	Y	N	Y	N
2 Simpson	Y	Y	Y	N	Y	N
ILLINOIS						
1 Rush	N	N	?	Y	N	Y
2 Kelly	N	N	Y	Y	N	Y
3 Lipinski	N	N	Y	?	?	?
4 Gutierrez	N	N	Y	Y	N	Y
5 Quigley	N	N	Y	Y	N	Y
6 Roskam	Y	Y	Y	N	Y	N
7 Davis, D.	?	?	?	?	?	?
8 Krishnamoorthi	N	N	Y	Y	N	Y
9 Schakowsky	N	N	Y	Y	N	Y
10 Schneider	N	N	Y	Y	Y	Y
11 Foster	N	N	Y	Y	N	Y
12 Bost	Y	Y	Y	N	Y	N
13 Davis, R.	Y	Y	Y	N	Y	N

	104	105	106	107	108	109
14 **Hultgren**	Y	Y	Y	N	Y	N
15 **Shimkus**	Y	Y	Y	N	Y	N
16 **Kinzinger**	Y	Y	Y	N	Y	N
17 Bustos	N	N	Y	Y	N	Y
18 **LaHood**	Y	Y	Y	N	Y	N
INDIANA						
1 Visclosky	N	N	Y	Y	N	Y
2 **Walorski**	Y	Y	Y	N	Y	N
3 **Banks**	Y	Y	Y	N	Y	N
4 **Rokita**	Y	Y	Y	N	Y	N
5 **Brooks**	Y	Y	Y	N	Y	N
6 **Messer**	Y	Y	Y	N	Y	N
7 Carson	N	N	?	Y	N	Y
8 **Bucshon**	Y	Y	Y	N	Y	N
9 **Hollingsworth**	Y	Y	Y	N	Y	N
IOWA						
1 **Blum**	Y	Y	Y	N	Y	N
2 Loebsack	N	N	Y	Y	Y	Y
3 **Young**	Y	Y	Y	N	Y	N
4 **King**	Y	Y	Y	N	Y	N
KANSAS						
1 **Marshall**	Y	Y	Y	N	Y	N
2 **Jenkins**	Y	Y	Y	N	Y	N
3 **Yoder**	Y	Y	Y	N	Y	N
4 **Estes**	Y	Y	Y	N	Y	N
KENTUCKY						
1 **Comer**	Y	Y	Y	N	Y	N
2 **Guthrie**	Y	Y	Y	N	Y	N
3 Yarmuth	N	N	Y	Y	N	Y
4 **Massie**	Y	Y	N	N	Y	N
5 **Rogers**	Y	Y	Y	N	Y	N
6 **Barr**	Y	Y	Y	N	Y	N
LOUISIANA						
1 **Scalise**	Y	Y	Y	N	Y	N
2 Richmond	N	N	Y	Y	N	Y
3 **Higgins**	Y	Y	Y	N	Y	N
4 **Johnson**	Y	Y	Y	N	Y	N
5 **Abraham**	Y	Y	Y	N	Y	N
6 **Graves**	Y	Y	Y	N	Y	N
MAINE						
1 Pingree	N	N	Y	Y	N	Y
2 **Poliquin**	Y	Y	Y	N	Y	N
MARYLAND						
1 **Harris**	Y	Y	Y	N	Y	N
2 Ruppersberger	N	N	Y	Y	N	Y
3 Sarbanes	N	N	Y	Y	N	Y
4 Brown	N	N	Y	Y	N	Y
5 Hoyer	N	N	Y	Y	N	Y
6 Delaney	N	N	Y	Y	N	Y
7 Cummings	?	?	?	?	?	?
8 Raskin	N	N	Y	Y	N	Y
MASSACHUSETTS						
1 Neal	N	N	Y	Y	N	Y
2 McGovern	N	N	Y	Y	N	Y
3 Tsongas	?	?	?	?	?	Y
4 Kennedy	?	?	Y	Y	N	Y
5 Clark	N	N	Y	Y	N	Y
6 Moulton	N	N	Y	Y	N	Y
7 Capuano	N	N	Y	Y	N	Y
8 Lynch	N	N	Y	Y	N	Y
9 Keating	N	N	Y	Y	N	Y
MICHIGAN						
1 **Bergman**	Y	Y	Y	N	Y	N
2 **Huizenga**	Y	Y	Y	N	Y	N
3 *Amash*	Y	Y	N	N	Y	N
4 **Moolenaar**	Y	Y	Y	N	Y	N
5 Kildee	N	N	Y	Y	N	Y
6 **Upton**	Y	Y	Y	N	Y	N
7 **Walberg**	Y	Y	Y	N	Y	N
8 **Bishop**	Y	Y	Y	N	Y	N
9 Levin	N	N	Y	Y	N	Y
10 **Mitchell**	Y	Y	Y	N	Y	N
11 **Trott**	Y	Y	Y	N	Y	N
12 Dingell	N	N	Y	Y	N	Y
14 Lawrence	N	N	Y	Y	N	Y
MINNESOTA						
1 Walz	N	N	Y	?	?	?
2 **Lewis**	Y	Y	Y	N	Y	N
3 **Paulsen**	Y	Y	Y	N	Y	N
4 McCollum	N	N	Y	Y	N	Y

	104	105	106	107	108	109
5 Ellison	N	N	Y	Y	N	?
6 **Emmer**	Y	Y	Y	N	Y	N
7 Peterson	N	N	Y	Y	Y	N
8 Nolan	N	N	N	Y	N	Y
MISSISSIPPI						
1 **Kelly**	Y	Y	Y	N	Y	N
2 Thompson	N	N	Y	Y	N	Y
3 **Harper**	Y	Y	Y	N	Y	N
4 **Palazzo**	Y	Y	Y	N	Y	N
MISSOURI						
1 Clay	N	N	Y	Y	N	Y
2 **Wagner**	Y	Y	Y	N	Y	N
3 **Luetkemeyer**	Y	Y	Y	N	Y	N
4 **Hartzler**	Y	Y	Y	N	Y	N
5 Cleaver	N	N	Y	Y	N	Y
6 **Graves**	Y	+	Y	N	Y	N
7 **Long**	Y	Y	Y	N	Y	N
8 **Smith**	?	?	?	?	?	N
MONTANA						
AL **Gianforte**	Y	Y	Y	N	Y	N
NEBRASKA						
1 **Fortenberry**	Y	Y	Y	N	Y	N
2 **Bacon**	Y	Y	Y	N	Y	N
3 **Smith**	Y	Y	Y	N	Y	N
NEVADA						
1 Titus	N	N	Y	Y	N	Y
2 **Amodei**	Y	Y	Y	N	Y	N
3 Rosen	N	N	Y	Y	N	N
4 Kihuen	N	N	Y	Y	N	Y
NEW HAMPSHIRE						
1 Shea-Porter	N	N	Y	Y	N	Y
2 Kuster	N	N	Y	Y	N	Y
NEW JERSEY						
1 Norcross	N	N	Y	Y	N	Y
2 **LoBiondo**	Y	Y	Y	N	Y	N
3 **MacArthur**	Y	Y	Y	N	Y	N
4 **Smith**	Y	Y	Y	N	Y	N
5 Gottheimer	N	Y	Y	Y	Y	Y
6 Pallone	N	N	Y	Y	N	Y
7 **Lance**	Y	Y	Y	N	Y	N
8 Sires	N	N	Y	Y	N	Y
9 Pascrell	N	N	Y	Y	N	Y
10 Payne	N	N	Y	Y	N	Y
11 **Frelinghuysen**	Y	Y	Y	N	Y	N
12 Watson Coleman	N	N	N	Y	N	Y
NEW MEXICO						
1 Lujan Grisham	N	N	Y	Y	N	Y
2 **Pearce**	Y	Y	Y	N	Y	N
3 Luján	N	N	Y	Y	N	Y
NEW YORK						
1 **Zeldin**	Y	Y	Y	N	Y	N
2 **King**	Y	Y	Y	N	Y	N
3 Suozzi	N	N	Y	Y	Y	Y
4 Rice	?	?	?	?	?	?
5 Meeks	N	N	Y	Y	N	Y
6 Meng	N	N	Y	Y	N	Y
7 Velázquez	N	N	Y	Y	N	Y
8 Jeffries	N	N	Y	Y	N	Y
9 Clarke	N	N	Y	Y	N	Y
10 Nadler	N	N	Y	Y	N	Y
11 **Donovan**	Y	Y	Y	N	Y	N
12 Maloney, C.	N	N	Y	Y	N	Y
13 Espaillat	N	N	Y	Y	N	Y
14 Crowley	N	N	Y	Y	N	Y
15 Serrano	N	N	Y	Y	N	Y
16 Engel	N	N	Y	Y	N	Y
17 Lowey	N	N	Y	Y	N	Y
18 Maloney, S.P.	N	N	Y	Y	Y	Y
19 **Faso**	Y	Y	Y	N	Y	N
20 Tonko	N	N	Y	Y	N	Y
21 **Stefanik**	Y	Y	Y	N	Y	N
22 **Tenney**	Y	Y	Y	N	Y	N
23 **Reed**	Y	Y	Y	N	Y	N
24 **Katko**	+	+	+	–	+	–
25 Slaughter	?	?	?	?	?	?
26 Higgins	N	N	Y	Y	N	Y
27 **Collins**	Y	Y	Y	N	Y	N
NORTH CAROLINA						
1 Butterfield	N	N	Y	Y	N	Y
2 **Holding**	Y	Y	Y	N	Y	N
3 **Jones**	Y	Y	N	N	Y	Y
4 Price	N	N	Y	Y	N	Y

	104	105	106	107	108	109
5 **Foxx**	Y	Y	Y	N	Y	N
6 **Walker**	Y	Y	Y	N	Y	N
7 **Rouzer**	Y	Y	Y	N	Y	N
8 **Hudson**	Y	Y	Y	N	Y	N
9 **Pittenger**	Y	Y	Y	N	Y	N
9 **Vacant**						
10 **McHenry**	Y	Y	Y	N	Y	N
11 **Meadows**	Y	Y	Y	N	Y	N
12 Adams	N	N	Y	Y	N	Y
13 **Budd**	Y	Y	Y	N	Y	N
NORTH DAKOTA						
AL **Cramer**	Y	Y	Y	N	Y	N
OHIO						
1 **Chabot**	Y	Y	Y	N	Y	N
2 **Wenstrup**	Y	Y	Y	N	Y	N
3 Beatty	N	N	Y	Y	N	Y
4 **Jordan**	Y	Y	N	N	Y	N
5 **Latta**	Y	Y	Y	N	Y	N
6 **Johnson**	Y	Y	Y	N	Y	N
7 **Gibbs**	Y	Y	Y	N	Y	N
8 **Davidson**	Y	Y	Y	N	Y	N
9 Kaptur	N	N	Y	Y	N	Y
10 **Turner**	Y	Y	Y	N	Y	N
11 Fudge	N	N	Y	Y	N	Y
12 **Vacant**						
13 Ryan	N	N	Y	Y	N	Y
14 **Joyce**	Y	Y	Y	N	Y	N
15 **Stivers**	Y	Y	Y	N	Y	N
16 **Renacci**	Y	Y	Y	N	Y	N
OKLAHOMA						
1 **Bridenstine**	Y	Y	Y	N	Y	N
2 **Mullin**	Y	Y	Y	N	Y	N
3 **Lucas**	Y	Y	Y	N	Y	N
4 **Cole**	Y	Y	Y	N	Y	N
5 **Russell**	Y	Y	Y	N	Y	N
OREGON						
1 Bonamici	N	N	Y	Y	N	Y
2 **Walden**	Y	Y	Y	N	Y	N
3 Blumenauer	N	N	Y	Y	N	Y
4 DeFazio	N	N	Y	Y	N	Y
5 Schrader	N	N	Y	Y	N	Y
PENNSYLVANIA						
1 Brady	N	N	Y	Y	N	Y
2 Evans	N	N	Y	Y	N	Y
3 **Kelly**	Y	Y	Y	N	Y	N
4 **Perry**	Y	Y	Y	N	Y	N
5 **Thompson**	Y	Y	Y	N	Y	N
6 **Costello**	Y	Y	Y	N	Y	N
7 **Meehan**	Y	Y	Y	N	Y	N
8 **Fitzpatrick**	Y	Y	Y	N	Y	N
9 **Shuster**	Y	Y	Y	N	Y	N
10 **Marino**	Y	Y	Y	N	Y	N
11 **Barletta**	Y	Y	Y	N	Y	N
12 **Rothfus**	Y	Y	Y	N	Y	N
13 Boyle	N	N	Y	Y	N	Y
14 Doyle	N	N	Y	Y	N	Y
15 **Dent**	Y	Y	Y	N	Y	N
16 **Smucker**	Y	Y	Y	N	Y	N
17 Cartwright	N	N	Y	Y	N	Y
RHODE ISLAND						
1 Cicilline	N	N	Y	Y	N	Y
2 Langevin	N	N	Y	Y	N	Y
SOUTH CAROLINA						
1 **Sanford**	Y	Y	N	N	Y	N
2 **Wilson**	Y	Y	Y	N	Y	N
3 **Duncan**	Y	Y	Y	N	Y	N
4 **Gowdy**	Y	Y	Y	N	Y	N
5 **Norman**	Y	Y	Y	N	Y	N
6 Clyburn	N	N	Y	Y	N	Y
7 **Rice**	Y	Y	Y	N	Y	N
SOUTH DAKOTA						
AL **Noem**	Y	Y	Y	N	Y	N
TENNESSEE						
1 **Roe**	Y	Y	Y	N	Y	N
2 **Duncan**	Y	Y	Y	N	Y	Y
3 **Fleischmann**	Y	Y	Y	N	Y	N
4 **DesJarlais**	Y	Y	Y	N	Y	N
5 Cooper	N	N	Y	Y	Y	Y
6 **Black**	Y	Y	Y	N	Y	N
7 **Blackburn**	Y	Y	Y	N	Y	N
8 **Kustoff**	Y	Y	Y	N	Y	N
9 Cohen	N	N	Y	Y	N	Y

	104	105	106	107	108	109
TEXAS						
1 **Gohmert**	Y	Y	Y	N	Y	N
2 **Poe**	Y	Y	Y	N	Y	N
3 **Johnson, S.**	Y	Y	Y	N	Y	N
4 **Ratcliffe**	Y	Y	Y	N	Y	N
5 **Hensarling**	Y	Y	Y	N	Y	N
6 **Barton**	Y	Y	Y	N	Y	N
7 **Culberson**	Y	Y	Y	N	Y	N
8 **Brady**	Y	Y	Y	N	Y	N
9 Green, A.	N	N	Y	Y	N	Y
10 **McCaul**	Y	Y	Y	N	Y	N
11 **Conaway**	Y	Y	Y	N	Y	N
12 **Granger**	Y	Y	Y	N	Y	N
13 **Thornberry**	Y	Y	Y	N	Y	N
14 **Weber**	Y	Y	Y	N	Y	N
15 Gonzalez	N	N	Y	Y	Y	N
16 O'Rourke	N	N	Y	Y	N	Y
17 **Flores**	Y	Y	Y	N	Y	N
18 Jackson Lee	N	N	Y	Y	N	Y
19 **Arrington**	Y	Y	Y	N	Y	N
20 Castro	N	N	Y	Y	N	Y
21 **Smith**	Y	Y	Y	N	Y	N
22 **Olson**	Y	Y	Y	N	?	N
23 **Hurd**	Y	Y	Y	N	Y	N
24 **Marchant**	Y	Y	Y	N	Y	N
25 **Williams**	Y	Y	Y	N	Y	N
26 **Burgess**	Y	Y	Y	N	Y	N
27 **Farenthold**	Y	Y	Y	N	Y	N
28 Cuellar	N	N	Y	Y	Y	Y
29 Green, G.	N	N	Y	Y	N	Y
30 Johnson, E.B.	N	N	Y	Y	N	Y
31 **Carter**	Y	Y	Y	N	Y	?
32 **Sessions**	Y	Y	Y	N	Y	N
33 Veasey	N	N	Y	Y	N	Y
34 Vela	N	N	Y	Y	Y	Y
35 Doggett	N	N	Y	Y	N	Y
36 **Babin**	Y	Y	Y	N	Y	N
UTAH						
1 **Bishop**	Y	Y	Y	N	Y	N
2 **Stewart**	Y	Y	Y	N	Y	N
3 **Curtis**	Y	Y	Y	N	Y	N
4 **Love**	Y	Y	Y	N	Y	N
VERMONT						
AL Welch	N	N	Y	Y	N	Y
VIRGINIA						
1 **Wittman**	Y	Y	Y	N	Y	N
2 **Taylor**	Y	Y	Y	N	Y	N
3 Scott	N	N	Y	Y	N	Y
4 McEachin	N	N	Y	Y	N	Y
5 **Garrett**	Y	Y	Y	N	Y	N
6 **Goodlatte**	Y	Y	Y	N	Y	N
7 **Brat**	Y	Y	Y	N	Y	N
8 Beyer	N	N	Y	Y	N	Y
9 **Griffith**	Y	Y	Y	N	Y	N
10 **Comstock**	Y	Y	Y	N	Y	N
11 Connolly	N	N	Y	Y	N	Y
WASHINGTON						
1 DelBene	N	N	Y	Y	N	Y
2 Larsen	N	N	Y	Y	N	Y
3 **Herrera Beutler**	Y	Y	Y	N	Y	N
4 **Newhouse**	Y	Y	Y	N	Y	N
5 **McMorris Rodgers**	Y	Y	Y	N	Y	N
6 Kilmer	N	N	Y	Y	N	Y
7 Jayapal	N	N	Y	Y	N	Y
8 **Reichert**	Y	Y	Y	N	Y	N
9 Smith	N	N	Y	Y	N	Y
10 Heck	N	N	Y	Y	Y	Y
WEST VIRGINIA						
1 **McKinley**	Y	Y	Y	N	Y	N
2 **Mooney**	Y	Y	Y	N	Y	N
3 **Jenkins**	Y	Y	Y	N	Y	N
WISCONSIN						
1 **Ryan**						
2 Pocan	N	N	Y	Y	N	Y
3 Kind	N	N	Y	Y	N	Y
4 Moore	N	N	Y	+	N	Y
5 **Sensenbrenner**	Y	Y	Y	N	Y	N
6 **Grothman**	Y	Y	Y	N	Y	N
7 **Duffy**	Y	Y	Y	N	Y	N
8 **Gallagher**	Y	Y	Y	N	Y	N
WYOMING						
AL **Cheney**	Y	Y	Y	N	Y	N

VOTE NUMBER

110. HR4263. SECURITIES REGULATIONS FOR NEW BUSINESSES/ PASSAGE. Passage of the bill that would immediately increase, from $50 million to $75 million, the maximum amount of securities certain companies could offer in a 12-month period without full Securities and Exchange Commission registration or without having to meet state registration and qualification requirements. The bill would also require that the maximum threshold be adjusted for inflation every two years, rounded to the nearest $10,000. Passed 246-170: R 232-1; D 14-169. March 15, 2018.

111. HR4545. FINANCIAL INSTITUTION APPEALS/APPEALS PROCESS LIMITATION. Waters, D-Calif., amendment that would limit the appeals process specified in the bill such that it would only apply to banks and credit unions with less than $10 billion in assets. Rejected in Committee of the Whole 184-233: R 1-232; D 183-1. March 15, 2018.

112. HR4545. FINANCIAL INSTITUTION APPEALS/PASSAGE. Passage of the bill that would create an Office of Independent Examination Review within the Federal Financial Institutions Examination Council, which would hear appeals by financial institutions regarding reports by banking regulatory agencies. The bill would prohibit federal banking regulators from retaliating against a financial institution for exercising its appellate rights. It would also include nondepository institutions subject to supervision by the Consumer Financial Protection Bureau under the law's definition of financial institutions, and would require the CFPB to establish its own independent intra-agency appellate process to consider appeals of its actions. Passed 283-133: R 231-1; D 52-132. March 15, 2018.

113. HRES780. NONBANK FINANCIAL REGULATIONS AND FEDERAL RESERVE PROCEDURES/PREVIOUS QUESTIONS. Buck, R-Colo., motion to order the previous question (thus ending debate and possibility of amendment) on the rule (H Res 780) that would provide for consideration of the bill (HR 4061) that would require the Financial Stability Oversight Council to consider alternative regulatory strategies for nonbank financial institutions, and would provide for consideration of the bill (HR 4293) regarding frequency and procedures for the Federal Reserve's so-called "stress testing" of banks. Motion agreed to 232-182: R 232-0; D 0-182. March 15, 2018.

114. HR4061. NONBANK FINANCIAL REGULATIONS AND FEDERAL RESERVE PROCEDURES/RULE. Adoption of the rule (H Res 780) that would provide for consideration of the bill (HR 4061) that would require the Financial Stability Oversight Council to consider alternative regulatory strategies for nonbank financial institutions, and would provide for consideration of the bill (HR 4293) regarding frequency and procedures for the Federal Reserve's so-called "stress testing" of banks. Adopted 235-177: R 230-0; D 5-177. March 15, 2018.

115. HR835. FLORISSANT FOSSIL BEDS NATIONAL MONUMENT BOUNDARY/PASSAGE. Lamborn, R-Colo., motion to suspend the rules and pass the bill that would increase, from 6,000 to 6,300 acres, the maximum amount of land to be included in the Florissant Fossil Beds National Monument in Colorado, and provides for updates to the official map of the monument. Motion agreed to 385-3: R 220-3; D 165-0. March 19, 2018.

	110	111	112	113	114	115
ALABAMA						
1 Byrne	Y	N	Y	Y	Y	Y
2 Roby	Y	N	Y	Y	Y	Y
3 Rogers	Y	N	Y	Y	Y	Y
4 Aderholt	Y	N	Y	Y	Y	Y
5 Brooks	Y	N	Y	Y	Y	Y
6 Palmer	Y	N	Y	Y	Y	Y
7 Sewell	N	Y	Y	N	N	Y
ALASKA						
AL Young	Y	N	Y	Y	Y	Y
ARIZONA						
1 O'Halleran	N	Y	Y	N	N	Y
2 McSally	Y	N	Y	Y	Y	Y
3 Grijalva	N	Y	N	N	N	Y
4 Gosar	Y	N	Y	Y	Y	?
5 Biggs	Y	N	Y	Y	Y	N
6 Schweikert	Y	N	Y	Y	Y	Y
7 Gallego	N	Y	N	N	N	Y
9 Sinema	Y	Y	Y	N	Y	Y
ARKANSAS						
1 Crawford	Y	N	Y	Y	Y	Y
2 Hill	Y	N	Y	Y	Y	Y
3 Womack	Y	N	Y	Y	Y	Y
4 Westerman	Y	N	Y	Y	Y	Y
CALIFORNIA						
1 LaMalfa	Y	N	Y	Y	Y	Y
2 Huffman	N	Y	N	N	N	Y
3 Garamendi	Y	Y	N	N	N	Y
4 McClintock	Y	N	Y	Y	Y	Y
5 Thompson	N	Y	N	N	N	+
6 Matsui	N	Y	N	N	N	Y
7 Bera	N	Y	Y	N	N	Y
8 Cook	Y	N	Y	Y	Y	Y
9 McNerney	N	Y	N	N	N	Y
10 Denham	Y	N	Y	Y	Y	Y
11 DeSaulnier	N	Y	N	N	N	Y
12 Pelosi	N	Y	N	N	N	?
13 Lee	N	Y	N	N	N	Y
14 Speier	?	Y	N	N	N	Y
15 Swalwell	N	Y	N	N	N	Y
16 Costa	+	+	+	–	–	Y
17 Khanna	N	Y	N	N	N	Y
18 Eshoo	Y	Y	N	N	N	+
19 Lofgren	N	Y	N	N	N	Y
20 Panetta	N	Y	Y	N	N	Y
21 Valadao	Y	N	Y	Y	Y	Y
22 Nunes	Y	N	Y	Y	Y	Y
23 McCarthy	Y	N	Y	Y	Y	Y
24 Carbajal	N	Y	N	N	N	Y
25 Knight	Y	N	Y	Y	Y	Y
26 Brownley	N	Y	N	N	N	Y
27 Chu	N	Y	N	N	N	?
28 Schiff	N	Y	N	N	N	Y
29 Cardenas	N	Y	N	N	N	Y
30 Sherman	N	Y	N	N	N	Y
31 Aguilar	N	Y	Y	N	N	Y
32 Napolitano	N	Y	N	N	N	Y
33 Lieu	N	Y	N	N	N	Y
34 Gomez	N	Y	N	N	N	?
35 Torres	N	Y	N	N	N	Y
36 Ruiz	N	Y	N	N	N	Y
37 Bass	N	Y	N	N	N	Y
38 Sánchez, Linda	N	Y	N	N	N	Y
39 Royce	Y	N	Y	Y	Y	Y
40 Roybal-Allard	N	Y	N	N	N	Y
41 Takano	N	Y	N	N	N	Y
42 Calvert	Y	N	Y	Y	Y	Y
43 Waters	N	Y	N	N	N	Y
44 Barragan	N	Y	N	N	N	Y
45 Walters	Y	N	Y	Y	Y	Y
46 Correa	Y	Y	Y	N	Y	Y
47 Lowenthal	N	Y	N	N	N	Y
48 Rohrabacher	Y	N	Y	Y	Y	Y
49 Issa	Y	N	Y	Y	Y	Y
50 Hunter	Y	N	Y	Y	Y	Y
51 Vargas	N	Y	Y	N	N	?
52 Peters	Y	Y	Y	N	N	Y
53 Davis	N	Y	N	N	N	Y
COLORADO						
1 DeGette	N	Y	N	N	N	Y
2 Polis	Y	Y	N	N	N	Y
3 Tipton	Y	N	Y	Y	Y	Y
4 Buck	Y	N	Y	Y	Y	Y
5 Lamborn	Y	N	Y	Y	Y	Y
6 Coffman	Y	N	Y	Y	Y	Y
7 Perlmutter	Y	Y	Y	N	N	Y
CONNECTICUT						
1 Larson	N	Y	N	N	N	Y
2 Courtney	N	Y	N	N	N	Y
3 DeLauro	N	Y	N	N	N	Y
4 Himes	N	Y	N	N	N	Y
5 Esty	N	Y	Y	N	N	Y
DELAWARE						
AL Blunt Rochester	N	Y	Y	N	N	Y
FLORIDA						
1 Gaetz	Y	N	Y	Y	Y	Y
2 Dunn	Y	N	Y	Y	Y	Y
3 Yoho	Y	N	Y	Y	Y	Y
4 Rutherford	Y	N	Y	Y	Y	Y
5 Lawson	N	Y	N	N	N	Y
6 DeSantis	Y	N	Y	Y	Y	Y
7 Murphy	N	Y	N	N	N	?
8 Posey	Y	N	Y	Y	Y	Y
9 Soto	N	Y	N	N	N	Y
10 Demings	N	Y	N	N	N	Y
11 Webster	Y	N	Y	Y	Y	Y
12 Bilirakis	Y	N	Y	Y	Y	Y
13 Crist	N	Y	N	N	N	Y
14 Castor	N	Y	N	N	N	Y
15 Ross	Y	N	?	Y	Y	Y
16 Buchanan	Y	N	Y	Y	Y	Y
17 Rooney, T.	Y	Y	Y	Y	Y	Y
18 Mast	Y	N	Y	Y	Y	Y
19 Rooney, F.	Y	N	Y	Y	Y	Y
20 Hastings	N	Y	N	N	N	Y
21 Frankel	N	Y	N	N	N	Y
22 Deutch	N	Y	N	N	N	Y
23 Wasserman Schultz	N	Y	N	N	N	Y
24 Wilson	?	?	?	?	?	Y
25 Diaz-Balart	Y	N	Y	Y	Y	Y
26 Curbelo	Y	N	Y	?	Y	Y
27 Ros-Lehtinen	?	?	?	?	?	Y
GEORGIA						
1 Carter	Y	N	Y	Y	Y	Y
2 Bishop	N	Y	N	N	N	Y
3 Ferguson	Y	N	Y	Y	Y	Y
4 Johnson	N	Y	N	N	N	Y
5 Lewis	N	Y	N	N	N	Y
6 Handel	Y	N	Y	Y	Y	Y
7 Woodall	Y	N	Y	Y	Y	Y
8 Scott, A.	Y	N	Y	Y	Y	Y
9 Collins	Y	N	Y	Y	Y	Y
10 Hice	Y	N	Y	Y	Y	Y
11 Loudermilk	Y	N	Y	Y	Y	Y
12 Allen	Y	N	Y	Y	Y	Y
13 Scott, D.	N	Y	N	N	N	Y
14 Graves	Y	N	Y	Y	Y	Y
HAWAII						
1 Hanabusa	N	Y	Y	N	N	Y
2 Gabbard	N	Y	N	N	N	Y
IDAHO						
1 Labrador	Y	N	Y	Y	Y	?
2 Simpson	Y	N	Y	Y	Y	Y
ILLINOIS						
1 Rush	N	Y	N	N	N	?
2 Kelly	N	Y	N	N	N	?
3 Lipinski	?	?	?	?	?	?
4 Gutierrez	N	Y	N	N	N	+
5 Quigley	N	Y	N	N	N	Y
6 Roskam	Y	N	Y	Y	Y	Y
7 Davis, D.	?	?	?	?	?	?
8 Krishnamoorthi	N	Y	Y	N	N	Y
9 Schakowsky	N	Y	N	N	N	Y
10 Schneider	Y	Y	Y	N	Y	Y
11 Foster	N	Y	Y	N	N	Y
12 Bost	Y	N	Y	Y	Y	Y
13 Davis, R.	Y	N	Y	Y	Y	Y

	110	111	112	113	114	115
14 **Hultgren**	Y	N	Y	Y	Y	Y
15 **Shimkus**	Y	N	Y	Y	Y	Y
16 **Kinzinger**	Y	N	Y	Y	Y	Y
17 Bustos	N	Y	Y	N	N	Y
18 **LaHood**	Y	N	Y	Y	Y	Y
INDIANA						
1 Visclosky	N	Y	N	N	N	Y
2 **Walorski**	Y	N	Y	Y	Y	Y
3 **Banks**	Y	N	Y	Y	Y	Y
4 **Rokita**	Y	N	Y	Y	Y	Y
5 **Brooks**	Y	N	Y	Y	Y	Y
6 **Messer**	Y	N	Y	Y	Y	?
7 Carson	N	Y	N	N	N	Y
8 **Bucshon**	Y	N	Y	Y	Y	Y
9 **Hollingsworth**	Y	N	Y	Y	Y	Y
IOWA						
1 **Blum**	Y	N	Y	Y	Y	Y
2 Loebsack	N	Y	Y	N	N	Y
3 **Young**	Y	N	Y	Y	Y	Y
4 **King**	Y	N	Y	Y	Y	Y
KANSAS						
1 **Marshall**	Y	N	Y	Y	Y	Y
2 **Jenkins**	Y	N	Y	Y	Y	Y
3 **Yoder**	Y	N	Y	Y	Y	Y
4 **Estes**	Y	N	Y	Y	Y	Y
KENTUCKY						
1 **Comer**	Y	N	Y	Y	Y	Y
2 **Guthrie**	Y	N	Y	Y	Y	Y
3 Yarmuth	N	Y	N	N	N	Y
4 **Massie**	Y	N	Y	Y	Y	N
5 **Rogers**	Y	N	Y	Y	Y	Y
6 **Barr**	Y	N	Y	Y	Y	Y
LOUISIANA						
1 **Scalise**	+	–	+	+	+	Y
2 Richmond	N	Y	N	N	N	?
3 **Higgins**	Y	N	Y	Y	Y	Y
4 **Johnson**	Y	N	Y	Y	Y	Y
5 **Abraham**	Y	N	Y	Y	Y	Y
6 **Graves**	Y	N	Y	Y	Y	Y
MAINE						
1 Pingree	N	Y	N	N	N	?
2 **Poliquin**	Y	N	Y	Y	Y	Y
MARYLAND						
1 **Harris**	Y	N	Y	Y	Y	Y
2 Ruppersberger	N	Y	Y	N	N	Y
3 Sarbanes	N	Y	N	N	N	Y
4 Brown	N	Y	N	N	N	Y
5 Hoyer	N	Y	N	N	N	Y
6 Delaney	N	Y	Y	N	N	Y
7 Cummings	?	?	?	?	?	?
8 Raskin	N	Y	N	N	N	Y
MASSACHUSETTS						
1 Neal	N	Y	N	N	N	Y
2 McGovern	N	Y	N	N	N	Y
3 Tsongas	N	Y	N	N	N	?
4 Kennedy	N	Y	N	N	N	Y
5 Clark	N	Y	N	N	N	Y
6 Moulton	N	Y	N	N	N	Y
7 Capuano	N	Y	N	N	N	+
8 Lynch	N	Y	N	N	N	Y
9 Keating	N	Y	N	N	N	Y
MICHIGAN						
1 **Bergman**	Y	N	Y	Y	Y	Y
2 **Huizenga**	Y	N	Y	Y	Y	Y
3 *Amash*	Y	N	Y	Y	Y	N
4 **Moolenaar**	Y	N	Y	Y	Y	Y
5 Kildee	N	Y	N	N	N	Y
6 **Upton**	Y	N	Y	Y	Y	Y
7 **Walberg**	Y	N	Y	Y	Y	Y
8 **Bishop**	Y	N	Y	Y	Y	Y
9 Levin	N	Y	N	N	N	Y
10 **Mitchell**	Y	N	Y	Y	Y	Y
11 **Trott**	Y	N	Y	Y	Y	Y
12 Dingell	N	Y	N	N	N	Y
14 Lawrence	N	Y	N	N	N	Y
MINNESOTA						
1 Walz	?	?	?	?	?	?
2 **Lewis**	Y	N	Y	Y	Y	Y
3 **Paulsen**	Y	N	Y	Y	Y	Y
4 McCollum	N	Y	N	N	N	Y

	110	111	112	113	114	115
5 Ellison	?	?	?	?	?	?
6 **Emmer**	Y	N	Y	Y	Y	Y
7 Peterson	Y	Y	Y	N	N	Y
8 Nolan	N	Y	N	?	?	Y
MISSISSIPPI						
1 **Kelly**	Y	N	Y	Y	Y	Y
2 Thompson	N	Y	N	N	N	Y
3 **Harper**	Y	N	Y	Y	Y	Y
4 **Palazzo**	Y	N	Y	Y	Y	Y
MISSOURI						
1 Clay	N	Y	N	N	N	Y
2 **Wagner**	Y	N	Y	Y	Y	Y
3 **Luetkemeyer**	Y	N	Y	Y	Y	Y
4 **Hartzler**	Y	N	Y	Y	Y	Y
5 Cleaver	N	Y	N	N	N	Y
6 **Graves**	Y	N	Y	Y	Y	Y
7 **Long**	Y	N	Y	Y	Y	Y
8 **Smith**	Y	N	Y	Y	Y	Y
MONTANA						
AL **Gianforte**	Y	N	Y	Y	Y	Y
NEBRASKA						
1 **Fortenberry**	Y	N	Y	Y	Y	Y
2 **Bacon**	Y	N	Y	Y	Y	Y
3 **Smith**	Y	N	Y	Y	Y	Y
NEVADA						
1 Titus	N	Y	N	N	N	Y
2 **Amodei**	Y	N	Y	Y	Y	Y
3 Rosen	Y	Y	Y	N	N	Y
4 Kihuen	N	Y	Y	N	N	Y
NEW HAMPSHIRE						
1 Shea-Porter	N	Y	N	N	N	Y
2 Kuster	N	Y	Y	N	N	Y
NEW JERSEY						
1 Norcross	N	Y	N	N	N	Y
2 **LoBiondo**	Y	N	Y	Y	Y	Y
3 **MacArthur**	Y	N	Y	Y	Y	Y
4 **Smith**	Y	N	Y	Y	Y	Y
5 Gottheimer	Y	Y	Y	N	Y	Y
6 Pallone	N	Y	N	N	N	Y
7 **Lance**	Y	N	Y	Y	Y	Y
8 Sires	N	Y	N	N	N	?
9 Pascrell	N	Y	N	N	N	Y
10 Payne	N	Y	N	N	N	Y
11 **Frelinghuysen**	Y	N	Y	Y	Y	Y
12 Watson Coleman	N	Y	N	N	N	Y
NEW MEXICO						
1 Lujan Grisham	N	Y	Y	N	N	Y
2 **Pearce**	Y	N	Y	Y	Y	Y
3 Luján	N	Y	N	N	N	Y
NEW YORK						
1 **Zeldin**	Y	N	Y	Y	Y	Y
2 **King**	Y	N	Y	Y	Y	?
3 Suozzi	Y	Y	Y	N	Y	Y
4 Rice	?	?	?	?	?	?
5 Meeks	N	Y	Y	N	N	?
6 Meng	N	Y	N	N	N	Y
7 Velázquez	N	Y	N	N	N	Y
8 Jeffries	N	Y	N	N	N	Y
9 Clarke	N	Y	N	N	N	Y
10 Nadler	N	Y	N	N	N	Y
11 **Donovan**	Y	N	Y	Y	Y	Y
12 **Maloney, C.**	N	Y	Y	N	N	Y
13 Espaillat	N	Y	N	N	N	Y
14 Crowley	N	Y	N	N	N	Y
15 Serrano	N	Y	N	N	N	Y
16 Engel	N	Y	N	N	N	Y
17 Lowey	N	Y	N	N	N	Y
18 Maloney, S.P.	Y	Y	Y	N	N	Y
19 **Faso**	Y	N	Y	Y	Y	Y
20 Tonko	N	Y	N	N	N	Y
21 **Stefanik**	Y	N	Y	Y	Y	Y
22 **Tenney**	Y	N	Y	Y	Y	Y
23 **Reed**	Y	N	Y	Y	Y	Y
24 **Katko**	+	–	+	+	+	?
26 Higgins	N	Y	N	N	N	Y
27 **Collins**	Y	N	Y	Y	Y	Y
NORTH CAROLINA						
1 Butterfield	N	Y	N	N	N	?
2 **Holding**	Y	N	Y	Y	Y	Y
3 **Jones**	N	N	N	Y	Y	?
4 Price	N	Y	N	N	N	Y

	110	111	112	113	114	115
5 **Foxx**	Y	N	Y	Y	Y	Y
6 **Walker**	Y	N	Y	Y	Y	Y
7 **Rouzer**	Y	N	Y	Y	Y	Y
8 **Hudson**	Y	N	Y	Y	Y	Y
9 **Pittenger**	Y	N	Y	Y	Y	Y
9 **Vacant**						
10 **McHenry**	Y	N	Y	Y	Y	Y
11 **Meadows**	Y	N	Y	Y	Y	Y
12 Adams	N	Y	N	N	N	Y
13 **Budd**	Y	N	Y	Y	Y	Y
NORTH DAKOTA						
AL **Cramer**	Y	N	Y	Y	Y	Y
OHIO						
1 **Chabot**	Y	N	Y	Y	Y	Y
2 **Wenstrup**	Y	N	Y	Y	Y	Y
3 Beatty	N	Y	N	N	N	+
4 **Jordan**	Y	N	Y	Y	Y	Y
5 **Latta**	Y	N	Y	Y	Y	Y
6 **Johnson**	Y	N	Y	Y	Y	Y
7 **Gibbs**	Y	N	Y	Y	Y	Y
8 **Davidson**	Y	N	Y	Y	Y	Y
9 Kaptur	N	Y	N	N	N	Y
10 **Turner**	Y	N	Y	Y	Y	Y
11 Fudge	N	Y	N	N	N	Y
12 **Vacant**						
13 Ryan	N	Y	N	N	N	Y
14 **Joyce**	Y	N	Y	Y	?	Y
15 **Stivers**	Y	N	Y	Y	Y	Y
16 **Renacci**	Y	N	Y	Y	Y	Y
OKLAHOMA						
1 **Bridenstine**	Y	N	Y	Y	Y	Y
2 **Mullin**	Y	N	Y	Y	Y	Y
3 **Lucas**	Y	N	Y	Y	Y	Y
4 **Cole**	Y	N	Y	Y	Y	Y
5 **Russell**	Y	N	Y	Y	Y	Y
OREGON						
1 Bonamici	N	Y	N	N	N	Y
2 **Walden**	Y	N	Y	Y	Y	Y
3 Blumenauer	N	Y	N	N	N	Y
4 DeFazio	N	Y	N	N	N	Y
5 Schrader	N	Y	Y	N	N	Y
PENNSYLVANIA						
1 Brady	N	Y	N	N	N	?
2 Evans	N	Y	N	N	N	Y
3 **Kelly**	Y	N	Y	Y	Y	Y
4 **Perry**	Y	N	Y	Y	Y	Y
5 **Thompson**	Y	N	Y	Y	Y	Y
6 **Costello**	Y	N	Y	Y	Y	Y
7 **Meehan**	Y	N	Y	Y	Y	Y
8 **Fitzpatrick**	Y	N	Y	Y	Y	Y
9 **Shuster**	Y	N	Y	Y	Y	Y
10 **Marino**	Y	N	Y	Y	Y	Y
11 **Barletta**	Y	N	Y	Y	Y	Y
12 **Rothfus**	Y	N	Y	Y	Y	Y
13 Boyle	N	Y	N	N	N	Y
14 Doyle	N	Y	N	N	N	Y
15 **Dent**	Y	N	Y	Y	Y	Y
16 **Smucker**	Y	N	Y	Y	Y	Y
17 Cartwright	N	Y	N	N	?	Y
RHODE ISLAND						
1 Cicilline	N	Y	N	N	N	Y
2 Langevin	N	Y	N	N	N	Y
SOUTH CAROLINA						
1 **Sanford**	Y	N	Y	Y	Y	Y
2 **Wilson**	Y	N	Y	Y	Y	Y
3 **Duncan**	Y	N	Y	Y	Y	?
4 **Gowdy**	Y	N	Y	Y	Y	Y
5 **Norman**	Y	N	Y	Y	Y	Y
6 Clyburn	N	Y	N	N	N	Y
7 **Rice**	Y	N	Y	Y	Y	Y
SOUTH DAKOTA						
AL **Noem**	Y	N	Y	Y	Y	Y
TENNESSEE						
1 **Roe**	Y	N	Y	Y	Y	Y
2 **Duncan**	Y	N	Y	Y	Y	Y
3 **Fleischmann**	Y	N	Y	Y	Y	Y
4 **DesJarlais**	Y	N	Y	Y	Y	Y
5 Cooper	N	Y	Y	N	N	Y
6 **Black**	Y	N	Y	Y	Y	?
7 **Blackburn**	Y	N	Y	Y	Y	?
8 **Kustoff**	Y	N	Y	Y	Y	Y
9 Cohen	N	Y	N	N	N	Y

	110	111	112	113	114	115
TEXAS						
1 **Gohmert**	Y	N	Y	Y	Y	Y
2 **Poe**	Y	N	Y	Y	Y	?
3 **Johnson, S.**	Y	N	Y	Y	Y	Y
4 **Ratcliffe**	Y	N	Y	Y	Y	Y
5 **Hensarling**	Y	N	Y	Y	Y	Y
6 **Barton**	Y	N	Y	Y	Y	Y
7 **Culberson**	Y	N	Y	Y	Y	Y
8 **Brady**	Y	N	Y	Y	Y	Y
9 Green, A.	N	Y	N	N	N	Y
10 **McCaul**	Y	N	Y	Y	Y	Y
11 **Conaway**	Y	N	Y	Y	Y	Y
12 **Granger**	Y	N	Y	Y	Y	Y
13 **Thornberry**	Y	N	Y	Y	Y	Y
14 **Weber**	Y	N	Y	Y	Y	Y
15 Gonzalez	N	Y	N	N	N	Y
16 O'Rourke	N	Y	Y	N	N	Y
17 **Flores**	Y	N	Y	Y	Y	Y
18 Jackson Lee	N	Y	N	N	N	+
19 **Arrington**	Y	N	Y	Y	Y	Y
20 Castro	N	Y	N	N	N	Y
21 **Smith**	Y	N	Y	Y	Y	Y
22 **Olson**	Y	N	Y	Y	Y	Y
23 **Hurd**	Y	N	Y	Y	Y	Y
24 **Marchant**	Y	N	Y	Y	Y	?
25 **Williams**	Y	N	Y	Y	Y	Y
26 **Burgess**	Y	N	Y	Y	Y	Y
27 **Farenthold**	Y	N	Y	Y	Y	?
28 Cuellar	Y	N	Y	N	N	Y
29 Green, G.	N	Y	N	N	N	Y
30 Johnson, E.B.	N	Y	Y	N	N	Y
31 **Carter**	?	?	?	?	?	Y
32 **Sessions**	Y	N	Y	Y	Y	Y
33 Veasey	N	Y	Y	N	N	Y
34 Vela	N	Y	Y	N	N	Y
35 Doggett	N	Y	N	N	N	Y
36 **Babin**	Y	N	Y	Y	Y	Y
UTAH						
1 **Bishop**	Y	N	Y	Y	Y	Y
2 **Stewart**	Y	N	Y	Y	Y	Y
3 **Curtis**	Y	N	Y	Y	Y	Y
4 **Love**	Y	N	Y	Y	Y	Y
VERMONT						
AL Welch	N	Y	N	–	N	Y
VIRGINIA						
1 **Wittman**	Y	N	Y	Y	Y	Y
2 **Taylor**	Y	N	Y	Y	Y	Y
3 Scott	N	Y	N	N	N	Y
4 McEachin	N	Y	N	N	N	Y
5 **Garrett**	Y	N	Y	Y	Y	Y
6 **Goodlatte**	Y	N	Y	Y	Y	Y
7 **Brat**	Y	N	Y	Y	Y	Y
8 Beyer	N	Y	Y	N	N	Y
9 **Griffith**	Y	N	Y	Y	Y	Y
10 **Comstock**	Y	N	Y	Y	Y	Y
11 Connolly	N	Y	Y	N	N	Y
WASHINGTON						
1 DelBene	N	Y	Y	N	N	Y
2 Larsen	N	Y	N	N	N	Y
3 **Herrera Beutler**	Y	N	Y	Y	Y	Y
4 **Newhouse**	Y	N	Y	Y	Y	Y
5 **McMorris Rodgers**	Y	N	Y	Y	Y	Y
6 Kilmer	N	Y	Y	N	N	Y
7 Jayapal	N	Y	N	N	N	Y
8 **Reichert**	Y	N	Y	?	?	Y
9 Smith	N	Y	N	N	N	Y
10 Heck	N	Y	Y	N	N	Y
WEST VIRGINIA						
1 **McKinley**	Y	N	Y	Y	Y	Y
2 **Mooney**	Y	N	Y	Y	Y	?
3 **Jenkins**	Y	N	Y	Y	Y	?
WISCONSIN						
1 **Ryan**						
2 Pocan	N	Y	N	N	N	Y
3 Kind	N	Y	N	N	N	Y
4 Moore	N	Y	Y	N	N	?
5 **Sensenbrenner**	Y	N	Y	Y	Y	Y
6 **Grothman**	Y	N	Y	Y	Y	Y
7 **Duffy**	Y	N	Y	Y	Y	Y
8 **Gallagher**	Y	N	Y	Y	Y	Y
WYOMING						
AL **Cheney**	Y	N	Y	Y	Y	Y

VOTE NUMBER

116. HR4851. KENNEDY-KING COMMEMORATIVE SITE/PASSAGE.
Lamborn, R-Colo., motion to suspend the rules and pass the bill that would designate the Landmark for Peace Memorial in Martin Luther King, Jr. Park in Indianapolis, Ind. as the Kennedy-King National Commemorative Site. Motion agreed to 391-0: R 222-0; D 169-0. March 19, 2018.

117. HR5247. STRESS TESTING REQUIREMENTS AND EXPERIMENTAL DRUGS/PREVIOUS QUESTION. Burgess, R-Texas, motion to order the previous question (thus ending debate and possibility of amendment) on the rule (H Res 787) that would provide for consideration of the bill (HR 4566) that would exempt certain financial institutions from stress-testing regulations, and would provide for consideration of the bill (HR 5247) that would allow eligible patients to try experimental drugs that have not yet been fully cleared by the Food and Drug Administration. The rule would also waive, through the legislative day of March 23, 2018, the two-thirds vote requirement to consider legislation on the same day it is reported from the House Rules Committee and would also provide for motions to suspend the rules through the legislative day of March 23, 2018. The rule would also extend the Holman Rule standing order provided in H Res 5 through the end of the 115th Congress. Motion agreed to 233-181: R 233-0; D 0-181. March 20, 2018.

118. HR4566. STRESS TESTING REQUIREMENTS AND EXPERIMENTAL DRUGS/RULE. Adoption of the rule (H Res 787) that would provide for consideration of the bill (HR 4566) that would exempt certain financial institutions from stress-testing regulations, and would provide for consideration of the bill (HR 5247) that would allow eligible patients to try experimental drugs that have not yet been fully cleared by the Food and Drug Administration. The rule would also waive, through the legislative day of March 23, 2018, the two-thirds vote requirement to consider legislation on the same day it is reported from the House Rules Committee and would also provide for motions to suspend the rules through the legislative day of March 23, 2018. The rule would also extend the Holman Rule standing order provided in H Res 5 through the end of the 115th Congress. Adopted 225-183: R 225-3; D 0-180. March 20, 2018.

119. HR4566. STRESS TESTING REQUIREMENT REGULATIONS/PASSAGE.
Passage of the bill that would exempt nonbank financial institutions that have not been designated as systemically important from requirements that they conduct annual financial stress tests. It would also allow the Securities and Exchange Commission and the Commodity Futures Trading Commission to issue regulations for financial companies that have assets totaling more than $10 billion. Passed 395-19: R 233-0; D 162-19. March 20, 2018"

120. HR5247. EXPERIMENTAL DRUGS FOR TERMINAL ILLNESS/RECOMMIT. Pallone, D-N.J., motion to recommit the bill to the House Energy and Commerce Committee with instructions to report it back immediately with an amendment that would require the Food and Drug Administration to issue guidance on how to expand access to products currently under review. It would also provide liability protections for drug manufacturers, physicians, clinical investigators and hospitals when they are involved in offering a product under expanded access. Motion rejected 182-233: R 1-232; D 181-1. March 21, 2018.

121. HR5247. EXPERIMENTAL DRUGS FOR TERMINAL ILLNESS/PASSAGE.
Passage of the bill that would allow eligible patients to seek access to drugs, through drug manufacturers, that have not yet been cleared by the Food and Drug Administration. The measure specifies that, in order to be eligible, a patient must be diagnosed with a disease or condition from which they are likely to die within a matter of months, or one that causes significant irreversible morbidity likely to lead to a severely premature death. The bill specifies that any such drugs that patients could try would need to have completed phase-one clinical trials, not have been approved or licensed for any use, and would need to currently be under an active FDA application or undergoing clinical trials. Passed 267-149: R 232-2; D 35-147. March 21, 2018.

	116	117	118	119	120	121
ALABAMA						
1 **Byrne**	Y	Y	Y	Y	N	Y
2 **Roby**	Y	Y	Y	Y	N	Y
3 **Rogers**	Y	Y	Y	Y	N	Y
4 **Aderholt**	Y	Y	Y	Y	N	Y
5 **Brooks**	Y	Y	Y	Y	N	Y
6 **Palmer**	Y	Y	Y	Y	N	Y
7 Sewell	Y	N	N	Y	Y	N
ALASKA						
AL **Young**	Y	Y	Y	Y	N	Y
ARIZONA						
1 O'Halleran	Y	N	N	Y	Y	Y
2 **McSally**	Y	Y	?	?	N	Y
3 Grijalva	Y	N	N	N	Y	N
4 **Gosar**	?	Y	Y	Y	N	Y
5 **Biggs**	Y	Y	Y	Y	N	Y
6 **Schweikert**	Y	Y	Y	Y	N	Y
7 Gallego	Y	N	N	Y	Y	N
9 Sinema	Y	N	N	Y	Y	Y
ARKANSAS						
1 **Crawford**	Y	Y	Y	Y	N	Y
2 **Hill**	Y	Y	Y	Y	N	Y
3 **Womack**	Y	Y	Y	Y	N	Y
4 **Westerman**	Y	Y	Y	Y	N	Y
CALIFORNIA						
1 **LaMalfa**	Y	Y	Y	Y	N	Y
2 Huffman	Y	N	N	Y	Y	N
3 Garamendi	Y	N	N	Y	Y	N
4 **McClintock**	Y	Y	Y	Y	N	Y
5 Thompson	+	–	–	+	Y	N
6 Matsui	Y	N	N	Y	Y	N
7 Bera	Y	N	N	Y	Y	N
8 **Cook**	Y	Y	Y	Y	N	Y
9 McNerney	Y	N	N	Y	Y	N
10 **Denham**	Y	Y	Y	Y	N	Y
11 DeSaulnier	Y	N	N	N	Y	N
12 Pelosi	?	N	N	Y	Y	N
13 Lee	Y	N	N	N	Y	N
14 Speier	Y	N	N	N	Y	N
15 Swalwell	Y	N	N	Y	Y	N
16 Costa	Y	N	N	Y	Y	Y
17 Khanna	Y	N	N	N	Y	N
18 Eshoo	+	N	N	Y	Y	N
19 Lofgren	Y	N	N	Y	Y	Y
20 Panetta	Y	N	N	Y	Y	N
21 **Valadao**	Y	Y	Y	Y	N	Y
22 **Nunes**	Y	Y	Y	Y	N	Y
23 **McCarthy**	Y	Y	Y	Y	N	Y
24 Carbajal	Y	N	N	Y	Y	N
25 **Knight**	Y	Y	Y	Y	N	Y
26 Brownley	Y	N	N	Y	Y	N
27 Chu	?	?	?	?	Y	N
28 Schiff	Y	N	N	Y	Y	N
29 Cardenas	Y	N	N	Y	Y	N
30 Sherman	Y	N	N	Y	Y	N
31 Aguilar	Y	N	N	Y	Y	N
32 Napolitano	Y	N	N	Y	Y	N
33 Lieu	Y	N	N	Y	Y	Y
34 Gomez	?	N	N	Y	Y	N
35 Torres	Y	N	N	Y	Y	N
36 Ruiz	Y	N	N	Y	Y	N
37 Bass	Y	N	N	Y	Y	N
38 Sánchez, Linda	Y	N	N	N	Y	N
39 **Royce**	Y	Y	Y	Y	N	Y
40 Roybal-Allard	Y	N	N	Y	Y	N
41 Takano	Y	N	N	Y	Y	N
42 **Calvert**	Y	Y	Y	Y	N	Y
43 Waters	Y	N	N	Y	?	?
44 Barragan	Y	N	N	Y	Y	Y
45 **Walters**	Y	Y	Y	Y	N	Y
46 Correa	Y	N	N	Y	Y	Y
47 Lowenthal	Y	N	N	Y	Y	N
48 **Rohrabacher**	Y	Y	Y	Y	N	Y
49 **Issa**	?	Y	Y	Y	N	Y
50 **Hunter**	Y	Y	Y	Y	N	Y
51 Vargas	?	N	N	Y	Y	N
52 Peters	Y	N	N	Y	Y	N
53 Davis	Y	N	N	Y	Y	N

	116	117	118	119	120	121
COLORADO						
1 DeGette	Y	N	N	Y	Y	N
2 Polis	Y	N	N	Y	Y	Y
3 **Tipton**	Y	Y	Y	Y	N	Y
4 **Buck**	Y	Y	Y	Y	N	Y
5 **Lamborn**	Y	Y	Y	Y	N	Y
6 **Coffman**	Y	Y	Y	Y	N	Y
7 Perlmutter	Y	N	N	Y	Y	Y
CONNECTICUT						
1 Larson	Y	N	N	Y	Y	Y
2 Courtney	Y	N	N	Y	Y	N
3 DeLauro	Y	N	N	Y	Y	N
4 Himes	Y	N	N	Y	Y	Y
5 Esty	Y	N	N	Y	Y	N
DELAWARE						
AL Blunt Rochester	Y	N	N	Y	Y	N
FLORIDA						
1 **Gaetz**	Y	Y	Y	Y	N	Y
2 **Dunn**	Y	Y	Y	Y	N	Y
3 **Yoho**	Y	Y	Y	Y	N	Y
4 **Rutherford**	Y	Y	Y	Y	N	Y
5 Lawson	Y	N	N	Y	Y	N
6 **DeSantis**	Y	Y	Y	Y	N	Y
7 Murphy	?	N	N	Y	Y	N
8 **Posey**	Y	Y	Y	Y	N	Y
9 Soto	Y	N	N	Y	Y	N
10 Demings	Y	N	N	Y	Y	N
11 **Webster**	Y	Y	Y	Y	N	Y
12 **Bilirakis**	Y	Y	Y	Y	N	Y
13 Crist	Y	N	N	Y	Y	Y
14 Castor	Y	N	N	Y	Y	N
15 **Ross**	Y	Y	Y	Y	N	Y
16 **Buchanan**	Y	Y	Y	Y	N	Y
17 **Rooney, T.**	Y	Y	Y	Y	N	Y
18 **Mast**	Y	Y	Y	Y	N	Y
19 **Rooney, F.**	Y	Y	Y	Y	?	?
20 Hastings	Y	N	N	Y	Y	N
21 Frankel	Y	N	N	Y	Y	N
22 Deutch	Y	N	N	Y	Y	N
23 Wasserman Schultz	Y	N	N	Y	Y	N
24 Wilson	Y	N	N	Y	Y	N
25 **Diaz-Balart**	Y	Y	?	Y	N	Y
26 **Curbelo**	Y	Y	Y	Y	N	Y
27 **Ros-Lehtinen**	Y	Y	Y	Y	N	Y
GEORGIA						
1 **Carter**	Y	Y	Y	Y	N	Y
2 Bishop	Y	N	N	Y	Y	Y
3 **Ferguson**	Y	Y	Y	Y	N	Y
4 Johnson	Y	N	N	N	Y	N
5 Lewis	Y	N	N	Y	Y	N
6 **Handel**	Y	Y	Y	Y	N	Y
7 **Woodall**	Y	Y	Y	Y	N	Y
8 **Scott, A.**	Y	Y	Y	Y	N	Y
9 **Collins**	Y	Y	Y	Y	N	Y
10 **Hice**	Y	Y	Y	Y	N	Y
11 **Loudermilk**	Y	Y	Y	Y	N	Y
12 **Allen**	Y	Y	Y	Y	N	Y
13 Scott, D.	Y	N	N	Y	Y	N
14 **Graves**	Y	Y	Y	Y	N	Y
HAWAII						
1 Hanabusa	Y	N	N	Y	Y	Y
2 Gabbard	Y	N	N	Y	Y	N
IDAHO						
1 **Labrador**	?	Y	Y	Y	N	Y
2 **Simpson**	Y	Y	Y	Y	N	Y
ILLINOIS						
1 Rush	?	?	?	?	?	?
2 Kelly	?	?	?	?	?	?
3 Lipinski	?	?	?	?	Y	N
4 Gutierrez	+	N	N	N	Y	N
5 Quigley	Y	N	N	Y	Y	N
6 **Roskam**	Y	Y	Y	Y	N	Y
7 Davis, D.	?	?	?	?	?	?
8 Krishnamoorthi	Y	N	N	Y	Y	N
9 Schakowsky	Y	N	N	N	Y	N
10 Schneider	Y	N	N	Y	Y	Y
11 Foster	Y	N	N	Y	Y	N
12 **Bost**	Y	Y	Y	Y	N	Y
13 **Davis, R.**	Y	Y	Y	Y	N	Y

	116	117	118	119	120	121
14 **Hultgren**	Y	Y	Y	Y	N	Y
15 **Shimkus**	Y	Y	Y	Y	Y	Y
16 **Kinzinger**	Y	Y	Y	Y	N	Y
17 Bustos	Y	N	N	Y	Y	N
18 **LaHood**	Y	Y	Y	Y	N	Y
INDIANA						
1 Visclosky	Y	N	N	N	Y	N
2 **Walorski**	Y	Y	Y	Y	N	Y
3 **Banks**	Y	Y	Y	Y	N	Y
4 **Rokita**	Y	Y	Y	Y	N	Y
5 **Brooks**	Y	Y	Y	Y	N	Y
6 **Messer**	?	Y	Y	Y	N	Y
7 Carson	Y	N	N	Y	Y	Y
8 **Bucshon**	Y	Y	Y	Y	N	Y
9 **Hollingsworth**	Y	Y	Y	Y	N	Y
IOWA						
1 **Blum**	Y	Y	Y	Y	N	Y
2 Loebsack	Y	N	N	Y	Y	Y
3 **Young**	Y	Y	Y	Y	N	Y
4 **King**	Y	Y	Y	Y	N	Y
KANSAS						
1 **Marshall**	Y	Y	Y	Y	N	Y
2 **Jenkins**	Y	Y	Y	Y	N	Y
3 **Yoder**	Y	Y	Y	Y	N	Y
4 **Estes**	Y	Y	Y	Y	N	Y
KENTUCKY						
1 **Comer**	Y	Y	Y	Y	N	Y
2 **Guthrie**	Y	Y	Y	Y	N	Y
3 Yarmuth	Y	N	N	Y	Y	N
4 **Massie**	Y	Y	N	Y	N	Y
5 **Rogers**	Y	Y	Y	Y	N	Y
6 **Barr**	Y	Y	Y	Y	N	Y
LOUISIANA						
1 **Scalise**	Y	Y	Y	Y	N	Y
2 Richmond	?	N	N	Y	Y	N
3 **Higgins**	Y	Y	Y	Y	N	Y
4 **Johnson**	Y	Y	Y	Y	N	Y
5 **Abraham**	Y	Y	Y	Y	N	Y
6 **Graves**	Y	Y	Y	Y	N	Y
MAINE						
1 Pingree	?	?	?	?	?	?
2 **Poliquin**	Y	Y	Y	Y	N	Y
MARYLAND						
1 **Harris**	Y	Y	Y	Y	N	Y
2 Ruppersberger	Y	N	N	Y	Y	N
3 Sarbanes	Y	N	N	N	?	?
4 Brown	Y	N	N	Y	Y	Y
5 Hoyer	Y	?	?	?	Y	N
6 Delaney	Y	N	N	Y	Y	N
7 Cummings	?	?	?	?	?	?
8 Raskin	Y	N	N	Y	Y	N
MASSACHUSETTS						
1 Neal	Y	N	N	Y	Y	N
2 McGovern	Y	N	N	Y	Y	N
3 Tsongas	?	N	N	Y	Y	Y
4 Kennedy	Y	N	N	Y	Y	N
5 Clark	Y	N	N	N	Y	N
6 Moulton	Y	N	N	Y	Y	N
7 Capuano	+	N	N	Y	Y	N
8 Lynch	Y	N	N	Y	Y	Y
9 Keating	Y	N	N	Y	Y	N
MICHIGAN						
1 **Bergman**	Y	Y	Y	Y	N	Y
2 **Huizenga**	Y	Y	Y	Y	N	Y
3 *Amash*	Y	Y	N	Y	N	Y
4 **Moolenaar**	Y	Y	Y	Y	N	Y
5 Kildee	Y	N	N	Y	Y	N
6 **Upton**	Y	Y	Y	Y	N	Y
7 **Walberg**	Y	Y	Y	Y	N	Y
8 **Bishop**	Y	Y	Y	Y	N	Y
9 Levin	Y	N	N	Y	Y	N
10 **Mitchell**	Y	Y	Y	Y	N	Y
11 **Trott**	Y	Y	Y	Y	N	Y
12 Dingell	Y	N	N	Y	Y	N
14 Lawrence	Y	N	N	Y	Y	N
MINNESOTA						
1 Walz	?	?	?	?	?	?
2 **Lewis**	Y	Y	Y	Y	N	Y
3 **Paulsen**	Y	Y	Y	Y	N	N
4 McCollum	Y	N	N	Y	Y	N

	116	117	118	119	120	121
5 Ellison	Y	N	N	N	Y	N
6 **Emmer**	Y	Y	Y	Y	N	Y
7 Peterson	Y	N	N	Y	N	Y
8 Nolan	Y	N	N	Y	Y	N
MISSISSIPPI						
1 **Kelly**	Y	Y	Y	Y	N	Y
2 Thompson	Y	N	N	Y	Y	N
3 **Harper**	Y	Y	Y	Y	N	Y
4 **Palazzo**	Y	Y	Y	Y	N	Y
MISSOURI						
1 Clay	Y	N	N	Y	?	?
2 **Wagner**	Y	Y	Y	Y	N	Y
3 **Luetkemeyer**	Y	Y	Y	Y	N	Y
4 **Hartzler**	Y	Y	Y	Y	N	Y
5 Cleaver	Y	N	N	Y	Y	N
6 **Graves**	Y	Y	Y	Y	N	Y
7 **Long**	Y	Y	Y	Y	N	Y
8 **Smith**	Y	Y	Y	Y	N	Y
MONTANA						
AL **Gianforte**	Y	Y	Y	Y	N	Y
NEBRASKA						
1 **Fortenberry**	Y	Y	Y	Y	N	Y
2 **Bacon**	Y	Y	Y	Y	N	Y
3 **Smith**	Y	Y	Y	Y	N	Y
NEVADA						
1 Titus	Y	N	N	Y	Y	N
2 **Amodei**	Y	Y	Y	Y	N	Y
3 Rosen	Y	N	N	Y	Y	Y
4 Kihuen	Y	N	N	Y	Y	N
NEW HAMPSHIRE						
1 Shea-Porter	Y	N	N	Y	Y	N
2 Kuster	Y	N	N	Y	Y	N
NEW JERSEY						
1 Norcross	Y	N	N	Y	Y	N
2 **LoBiondo**	Y	Y	Y	Y	N	Y
3 **MacArthur**	Y	Y	Y	Y	N	Y
4 **Smith**	Y	Y	Y	Y	N	Y
5 Gottheimer	Y	N	N	Y	Y	Y
6 Pallone	Y	N	N	Y	Y	N
7 **Lance**	Y	Y	Y	Y	N	Y
8 Sires	?	N	N	Y	Y	N
9 Pascrell	Y	N	N	Y	Y	N
10 Payne	Y	N	N	Y	Y	N
11 **Frelinghuysen**	Y	Y	Y	Y	N	Y
12 Watson Coleman	Y	N	N	Y	Y	N
NEW MEXICO						
1 Lujan Grisham	Y	N	N	Y	Y	Y
2 **Pearce**	Y	Y	Y	Y	N	Y
3 Luján	Y	N	N	Y	Y	N
NEW YORK						
1 **Zeldin**	Y	Y	Y	Y	N	Y
2 **King**	?	Y	Y	Y	N	Y
3 Suozzi	Y	N	N	Y	Y	Y
4 Rice	?	N	N	Y	Y	N
5 Meeks	Y	N	N	Y	Y	N
6 Meng	Y	N	N	Y	Y	N
7 Velázquez	Y	N	N	Y	Y	N
8 Jeffries	Y	N	N	Y	Y	N
9 Clarke	Y	N	N	Y	Y	N
10 Nadler	Y	N	N	Y	Y	N
11 **Donovan**	Y	Y	Y	Y	N	Y
12 Maloney, C.	Y	N	N	Y	Y	N
13 Espaillat	Y	N	N	N	Y	N
14 Crowley	Y	N	N	Y	Y	N
15 Serrano	Y	N	N	N	Y	N
16 Engel	Y	N	N	Y	Y	N
17 Lowey	Y	N	N	Y	Y	N
18 Maloney, S.P.	Y	N	N	Y	Y	Y
19 **Faso**	Y	Y	Y	Y	N	Y
20 Tonko	Y	N	N	Y	Y	N
21 **Stefanik**	Y	Y	Y	Y	N	Y
22 **Tenney**	Y	Y	Y	Y	N	Y
23 **Reed**	Y	Y	Y	Y	N	Y
24 **Katko**	?	Y	Y	Y	N	Y
25 **Vacant**						
26 Higgins	Y	N	N	Y	Y	N
27 **Collins**	Y	Y	Y	Y	N	Y
NORTH CAROLINA						
1 Butterfield	?	N	N	Y	Y	N
2 **Holding**	Y	Y	Y	Y	N	Y
3 **Jones**	?	?	?	?	?	?
4 Price	Y	N	N	Y	Y	N

	116	117	118	119	120	121
5 **Foxx**	Y	Y	Y	Y	N	Y
6 **Walker**	Y	Y	Y	Y	N	Y
7 **Rouzer**	Y	Y	Y	Y	N	Y
8 **Hudson**	Y	Y	Y	Y	N	Y
9 **Pittenger**	Y	Y	Y	Y	N	Y
9 **Vacant**						
10 **McHenry**	Y	Y	Y	Y	N	Y
11 **Meadows**	Y	Y	?	Y	N	Y
12 Adams	Y	N	N	Y	Y	N
13 **Budd**	Y	Y	Y	Y	N	Y
NORTH DAKOTA						
AL **Cramer**	Y	Y	Y	Y	?	?
OHIO						
1 **Chabot**	Y	Y	Y	Y	N	Y
2 **Wenstrup**	Y	Y	Y	Y	N	Y
3 Beatty	Y	N	N	Y	Y	N
4 **Jordan**	Y	Y	Y	Y	N	Y
5 **Latta**	Y	Y	Y	Y	N	Y
6 **Johnson**	Y	Y	Y	Y	N	Y
7 **Gibbs**	Y	Y	Y	Y	N	Y
8 **Davidson**	Y	Y	Y	Y	N	Y
9 Kaptur	Y	N	N	Y	Y	N
10 **Turner**	Y	Y	Y	Y	N	Y
11 Fudge	Y	N	N	Y	Y	N
12 **Vacant**						
13 Ryan	Y	N	N	Y	Y	N
14 **Joyce**	Y	Y	Y	Y	N	Y
15 **Stivers**	Y	Y	Y	Y	N	Y
16 **Renacci**	Y	Y	Y	Y	N	Y
OKLAHOMA						
1 **Bridenstine**	Y	Y	Y	Y	N	Y
2 **Mullin**	Y	Y	Y	Y	N	Y
3 **Lucas**	Y	Y	Y	Y	N	Y
4 **Cole**	Y	Y	Y	Y	N	Y
5 **Russell**	Y	Y	Y	Y	N	Y
OREGON						
1 Bonamici	Y	N	N	Y	Y	N
2 **Walden**	Y	Y	Y	Y	N	Y
3 Blumenauer	Y	N	N	Y	Y	N
4 DeFazio	Y	N	N	Y	+	-
5 Schrader	Y	N	N	Y	Y	N
PENNSYLVANIA						
1 Brady	?	N	N	Y	Y	N
2 Evans	Y	N	N	Y	Y	N
3 **Kelly**	Y	Y	Y	Y	N	Y
4 **Perry**	Y	Y	Y	Y	N	Y
5 **Thompson**	Y	Y	Y	Y	N	Y
6 **Costello**	Y	Y	Y	Y	N	Y
7 **Meehan**	Y	Y	Y	Y	N	N
8 **Fitzpatrick**	Y	Y	Y	Y	N	Y
9 **Shuster**	Y	Y	Y	Y	?	Y
10 **Marino**	Y	Y	Y	Y	N	Y
11 **Barletta**	Y	?	?	?	N	Y
12 **Rothfus**	Y	Y	Y	Y	N	Y
13 Boyle	Y	N	N	N	Y	N
14 Doyle	Y	N	N	Y	Y	N
15 **Dent**	Y	Y	Y	Y	N	Y
16 **Smucker**	Y	Y	Y	Y	N	Y
17 Cartwright	Y	N	N	Y	Y	N
RHODE ISLAND						
1 Cicilline	Y	N	N	Y	Y	N
2 Langevin	Y	N	N	Y	Y	N
SOUTH CAROLINA						
1 **Sanford**	Y	Y	Y	Y	N	Y
2 **Wilson**	Y	Y	Y	Y	N	Y
3 **Duncan**	?	Y	Y	Y	N	Y
4 **Gowdy**	Y	Y	Y	Y	N	Y
5 **Norman**	Y	Y	Y	Y	N	Y
6 Clyburn	Y	N	N	Y	Y	N
7 Rice	Y	Y	Y	Y	N	Y
SOUTH DAKOTA						
AL **Noem**	Y	Y	Y	Y	N	Y
TENNESSEE						
1 **Roe**	Y	Y	Y	Y	N	Y
2 **Duncan**	Y	Y	Y	Y	N	Y
3 **Fleischmann**	Y	Y	Y	Y	N	Y
4 **DesJarlais**	Y	Y	Y	Y	N	Y
5 Cooper	Y	N	N	Y	Y	Y
6 **Black**	?	?	?	?	N	Y
7 **Blackburn**	?	Y	Y	Y	N	Y
8 **Kustoff**	Y	Y	Y	Y	N	Y
9 Cohen	Y	N	N	Y	Y	Y

	116	117	118	119	120	121
TEXAS						
1 **Gohmert**	Y	Y	Y	Y	N	Y
2 **Poe**	?	Y	Y	Y	N	Y
3 **Johnson, S.**	Y	Y	Y	Y	N	Y
4 **Ratcliffe**	Y	Y	Y	Y	N	Y
5 **Hensarling**	Y	Y	Y	Y	N	Y
6 **Barton**	Y	Y	Y	Y	N	Y
7 **Culberson**	Y	Y	Y	Y	N	Y
8 **Brady**	Y	Y	Y	Y	N	Y
9 Green, A.	Y	N	N	Y	Y	N
10 **McCaul**	Y	Y	?	Y	N	Y
11 **Conaway**	Y	Y	Y	Y	N	Y
12 **Granger**	Y	Y	Y	Y	N	Y
13 **Thornberry**	Y	Y	Y	Y	N	Y
14 **Weber**	Y	Y	Y	Y	N	Y
15 Gonzalez	Y	N	N	Y	Y	N
16 O'Rourke	Y	N	N	Y	Y	Y
17 **Flores**	Y	Y	Y	Y	N	Y
18 Jackson Lee	Y	N	N	Y	Y	N
19 **Arrington**	Y	Y	?	Y	N	Y
20 Castro	Y	N	N	Y	Y	Y
21 **Smith**	Y	Y	Y	Y	N	Y
22 **Olson**	Y	Y	Y	Y	N	Y
23 **Hurd**	Y	Y	Y	Y	N	Y
24 **Marchant**	?	Y	Y	Y	N	Y
25 **Williams**	Y	Y	Y	Y	N	Y
26 **Burgess**	Y	Y	Y	Y	N	Y
27 **Farenthold**	?	Y	Y	Y	N	Y
28 Cuellar	Y	N	N	Y	Y	Y
29 Green, G.	Y	N	N	Y	Y	N
30 Johnson, E.B.	Y	?	?	?	Y	N
31 **Carter**	Y	Y	Y	Y	N	Y
32 **Sessions**	Y	Y	Y	Y	N	Y
33 Veasey	Y	N	N	Y	Y	Y
34 Vela	Y	N	?	Y	Y	N
35 Doggett	Y	N	N	Y	Y	N
36 **Babin**	Y	Y	Y	Y	N	Y
UTAH						
1 **Bishop**	Y	Y	Y	Y	N	Y
2 **Stewart**	Y	Y	Y	Y	N	Y
3 **Curtis**	Y	Y	Y	Y	N	Y
4 **Love**	Y	Y	Y	Y	N	Y
VERMONT						
AL Welch	Y	N	N	Y	Y	N
VIRGINIA						
1 **Wittman**	Y	Y	Y	Y	N	Y
2 **Taylor**	Y	Y	Y	Y	N	Y
3 Scott	Y	N	N	Y	Y	N
4 McEachin	Y	N	N	Y	Y	N
5 **Garrett**	Y	Y	Y	Y	N	Y
6 **Goodlatte**	Y	Y	Y	Y	N	Y
7 **Brat**	Y	Y	Y	Y	N	Y
8 Beyer	Y	N	N	Y	Y	N
9 **Griffith**	Y	Y	Y	Y	N	Y
10 **Comstock**	Y	Y	N	Y	N	Y
11 Connolly	Y	N	N	Y	Y	N
WASHINGTON						
1 DelBene	Y	N	N	Y	Y	N
2 Larsen	Y	N	N	Y	Y	N
3 **Herrera Beutler**	Y	Y	Y	Y	N	Y
4 **Newhouse**	Y	Y	Y	Y	N	Y
5 **McMorris Rodgers**	Y	Y	Y	Y	N	Y
6 Kilmer	Y	N	N	Y	Y	N
7 Jayapal	Y	N	N	N	Y	N
8 **Reichert**	Y	Y	Y	Y	N	Y
9 Smith	Y	N	N	Y	Y	N
10 Heck	Y	N	N	Y	Y	N
WEST VIRGINIA						
1 **McKinley**	Y	Y	Y	Y	N	Y
2 **Mooney**	?	?	?	Y	N	Y
3 **Jenkins**	?	Y	Y	Y	N	Y
WISCONSIN						
1 **Ryan**						
2 Pocan	Y	N	N	N	Y	N
3 Kind	Y	N	N	Y	Y	Y
4 Moore	?	N	N	Y	Y	N
5 **Sensenbrenner**	Y	Y	Y	Y	N	Y
6 **Grothman**	Y	Y	Y	Y	N	Y
7 **Duffy**	Y	Y	Y	Y	N	Y
8 **Gallagher**	Y	Y	Y	Y	N	Y
WYOMING						
AL **Cheney**	Y	Y	Y	Y	N	Y

VOTE NUMBER

122. PROCEDURAL MOTION/JOURNAL. Approval of the House Journal of March 20, 2018. Approved 216-192: R 136-96; D 80-96. March 21, 2018.

123. HR1625. FISCAL 2018 OMNIBUS APPROPRIATIONS/PREVIOUS QUESTION. Sessions, R-Texas, motion to order the previous question (thus ending debate and possibility of amendment) on the rule (H Res 796) that would provide for House floor consideration for the Senate amendment to HR 1625, the legislative vehicle for the fiscal 2018 omnibus appropriations package. Motion agreed to 233-186: R 233-0; D 0-186. March 22, 2018.

124. HR1625. FISCAL 2018 OMNIBUS APPROPRIATIONS/RULE. Adoption of the rule (H Res 796) that would provide for consideration for the Senate amendment to HR 1625, the legislative vehicle for the fiscal 2018 omnibus appropriations package. Adopted 211-207: R 210-25; D 1-182. March 22, 2018.

125. HR4227. MANAGING VEHICULAR TERRORIST THREATS/PASSAGE. Estes, R-Kan., motion to suspend the rules and pass the bill that would direct the Secretary of the Department of Homeland Security to examine how the department is managing the threat of vehicular terrorism and to develop a strategy to work with first responders and the private sector to improve the prevention, mitigation and response to such treats. Motion agreed to 417-2: R 232-2; D 185-0. March 22, 2018.

126. HR5131. TRANSPORTATION SECURITY REVIEW/PASSAGE. Bacon, R-Neb., motion to suspend the rules and pass the bill that would require the Department of Homeland Security to conduct a broad, strategic review, and report on transportation security programs including personnel training, research and development, and best practices. Motion agreed to 409-5: R 228-5; D 181-0. March 22, 2018.

127. HR1625. FISCAL 2018 OMNIBUS APPROPRIATIONS/MOTION TO CONCUR. Frelinghuysen, R-N.J., motion to concur in the Senate amendment to the bill with a further amendment that would provide roughly $1.3 trillion in funding for federal government operations and services through Sept. 30, 2018. The measure would provide a total of $654.6 billion in additional funding to the Defense Department, including $589.5 billion in discretionary funding and $65.2 billion in funding for the Overseas Contingency Operations account. It would provide $98.7 billion to the Health and Human Services Department, including $5.1 billion to the Food and Drug Administration and $5.5 billion to the Indian Health Service. It would provide $3.4 billion to the Substance Abuse and Mental Health Services Administration for substance abuse block grants, and would provide roughly $3.7 billion to the National Institutes of Health, including an additional $500 million for research into opioid addiction. It would provide $47.7 billion to the Homeland Security Department, including $1.6 billion for the purpose of bolstering security measures on the U.S.-Mexico border, including the construction of new fencing along sections of the border, and would provide $7.1 billion for Immigration and Customs Enforcement operations and enforcement. The measure includes provisions from multiple bills related to school safety and firearms regulations, including a bill (S 2135) that would require the Department of Justice to certify that appropriate records have been submitted to the National Instant Criminal Background Check System by federal agencies and state governments with respect to individuals who are not eligible to purchase firearms. The measure includes language from the bill (S 2495) that would authorize $75 million a year through fiscal 2028 for the Secure Our Schools grant program and would revise it to more explicitly focus the program on preventing student violence. Motion agreed to 256-167: R 145-90; D 111-77. March 22, 2018.

	122	123	124	125	126	127
ALABAMA						
1 **Byrne**	Y	Y	Y	Y	Y	Y
2 **Roby**	Y	Y	Y	Y	Y	Y
3 **Rogers**	N	Y	Y	Y	Y	Y
4 **Aderholt**	Y	Y	Y	Y	Y	Y
5 **Brooks**	N	Y	N	Y	Y	N
6 **Palmer**	Y	Y	Y	Y	Y	N
7 Sewell	N	N	N	Y	Y	Y
ALASKA						
AL **Young**	N	Y	Y	Y	Y	Y
ARIZONA						
1 O'Halleran	N	N	N	Y	Y	Y
2 **McSally**	N	Y	Y	Y	Y	Y
3 Grijalva	?	N	N	Y	N	N
4 **Gosar**	N	Y	N	Y	N	N
5 **Biggs**	N	Y	N	Y	N	N
6 **Schweikert**	Y	Y	Y	Y	Y	N
7 Gallego	N	N	N	Y	Y	N
9 Sinema	N	N	Y	Y	Y	Y
ARKANSAS						
1 **Crawford**	N	Y	Y	Y	Y	Y
2 **Hill**	Y	Y	Y	Y	Y	Y
3 **Womack**	Y	Y	Y	Y	Y	Y
4 **Westerman**	Y	Y	Y	Y	Y	N
CALIFORNIA						
1 **LaMalfa**	Y	Y	Y	Y	N	Y
2 Huffman	Y	N	N	Y	Y	N
3 Garamendi	Y	N	N	Y	Y	Y
4 **McClintock**	Y	Y	Y	Y	Y	N
5 Thompson	N	N	N	Y	Y	N
6 Matsui	Y	N	N	Y	Y	N
7 Bera	N	N	N	Y	Y	N
8 **Cook**	Y	Y	Y	Y	Y	N
9 McNerney	N	Y	Y	Y	Y	N
10 **Denham**	N	Y	Y	Y	Y	N
11 DeSaulnier	Y	N	N	Y	?	N
12 Pelosi	Y	N	N	Y	Y	N
13 Lee	N	N	N	Y	Y	N
14 Speier	Y	N	N	Y	Y	N
15 Swalwell	N	N	N	Y	Y	N
16 Costa	N	N	N	Y	Y	Y
17 Khanna	Y	N	N	Y	Y	N
18 Eshoo	Y	N	N	Y	Y	Y
19 Lofgren	Y	N	N	Y	Y	N
20 Panetta	N	N	N	Y	Y	N
21 **Valadao**	N	Y	Y	Y	Y	Y
22 **Nunes**	Y	Y	Y	Y	Y	Y
23 **McCarthy**	Y	Y	Y	Y	Y	Y
24 Carbajal	N	N	N	Y	Y	Y
25 **Knight**	N	Y	Y	Y	Y	Y
26 Brownley	N	N	N	Y	Y	Y
27 Chu	Y	N	N	Y	Y	N
28 Schiff	Y	N	N	Y	Y	N
29 Cardenas	N	N	N	Y	Y	N
30 Sherman	Y	N	N	Y	Y	Y
31 Aguilar	Y	N	N	Y	?	N
32 Napolitano	Y	N	N	Y	Y	N
33 Lieu	N	N	N	Y	Y	N
34 Gomez	N	N	N	Y	Y	N
35 Torres	N	N	N	Y	Y	N
36 Ruiz	N	N	N	Y	Y	Y
37 Bass	Y	N	N	Y	Y	N
38 Sánchez, Linda	N	N	N	Y	Y	N
39 **Royce**	Y	Y	Y	Y	Y	Y
40 Roybal-Allard	N	N	N	Y	Y	N
41 Takano	N	N	N	Y	Y	N
42 **Calvert**	Y	Y	Y	Y	Y	Y
43 Waters	?	N	N	Y	Y	N
44 Barragan	N	N	N	Y	Y	N
45 **Walters**	Y	Y	Y	Y	Y	Y
46 Correa	N	N	N	Y	Y	N
47 Lowenthal	N	N	N	Y	Y	N
48 **Rohrabacher**	Y	Y	Y	Y	Y	N
49 **Issa**	Y	Y	Y	Y	?	Y
50 **Hunter**	Y	Y	Y	Y	Y	Y
51 Vargas	N	N	N	Y	Y	N
52 Peters	Y	N	N	Y	Y	N
53 Davis	Y	N	N	Y	Y	Y

	122	123	124	125	126	127
COLORADO						
1 DeGette	Y	N	N	Y	Y	N
2 Polis	Y	N	N	Y	Y	N
3 **Tipton**	N	Y	Y	Y	Y	Y
4 **Buck**	Y	Y	Y	Y	Y	Y
5 **Lamborn**	Y	Y	Y	Y	Y	Y
6 **Coffman**	N	Y	Y	Y	Y	N
7 Perlmutter	Y	N	N	Y	Y	Y
CONNECTICUT						
1 Larson	Y	N	N	Y	Y	Y
2 Courtney	N	N	N	Y	Y	Y
3 DeLauro	Y	N	N	Y	Y	Y
4 Himes	Y	N	N	Y	Y	Y
5 Esty	N	N	N	Y	Y	Y
DELAWARE						
AL Blunt Rochester	Y	N	N	Y	Y	Y
FLORIDA						
1 **Gaetz**	N	Y	Y	Y	Y	N
2 **Dunn**	Y	Y	Y	Y	Y	Y
3 **Yoho**	N	Y	Y	Y	Y	N
4 **Rutherford**	Y	Y	Y	Y	Y	Y
5 Lawson	N	N	N	Y	Y	Y
6 **DeSantis**	N	Y	Y	Y	Y	N
7 Murphy	Y	N	?	Y	Y	Y
8 **Posey**	N	Y	N	Y	Y	N
9 Soto	N	N	N	Y	Y	N
10 Demings	Y	N	N	Y	Y	Y
11 **Webster**	Y	Y	N	Y	Y	N
12 **Bilirakis**	Y	Y	Y	Y	Y	Y
13 Crist	N	N	N	Y	Y	Y
14 Castor	N	N	N	Y	Y	Y
15 **Ross**	Y	Y	Y	Y	Y	Y
16 **Buchanan**	Y	Y	Y	Y	Y	Y
17 **Rooney, T.**	Y	Y	Y	Y	Y	Y
18 **Mast**	N	Y	Y	Y	Y	N
19 **Rooney, F.**	?	Y	Y	Y	Y	Y
20 Hastings	N	N	N	Y	Y	Y
21 Frankel	Y	N	N	Y	Y	Y
22 Deutch	Y	N	N	Y	?	Y
23 Wasserman Schultz	Y	N	N	Y	Y	Y
24 Wilson	N	?	N	?	Y	Y
25 **Diaz-Balart**	Y	Y	Y	Y	Y	Y
26 **Curbelo**	N	Y	Y	Y	Y	N
27 **Ros-Lehtinen**	N	Y	Y	Y	Y	N
GEORGIA						
1 **Carter**	Y	Y	Y	Y	Y	Y
2 Bishop	N	N	N	Y	Y	Y
3 **Ferguson**	Y	Y	Y	Y	Y	Y
4 Johnson	N	N	?	Y	Y	Y
5 Lewis	N	N	N	Y	?	N
6 **Handel**	Y	Y	Y	Y	Y	Y
7 **Woodall**	N	Y	Y	Y	Y	Y
8 **Scott, A.**	Y	Y	Y	Y	Y	Y
9 **Collins**	Y	Y	Y	Y	Y	Y
10 Hice	N	Y	N	Y	Y	N
11 **Loudermilk**	Y	Y	Y	Y	Y	N
12 **Allen**	N	Y	Y	Y	Y	N
13 Scott, D.	Y	N	N	Y	?	Y
14 **Graves**	N	Y	Y	Y	Y	Y
HAWAII						
1 Hanabusa	N	N	N	Y	Y	Y
2 Gabbard	Y	N	N	Y	Y	Y
IDAHO						
1 **Labrador**	Y	Y	N	Y	N	N
2 **Simpson**	Y	Y	Y	Y	Y	Y
ILLINOIS						
1 Rush	?	N	N	Y	?	N
2 Kelly	?	N	N	Y	Y	N
3 Lipinski	Y	N	N	Y	Y	Y
4 Gutierrez	N	N	N	Y	Y	N
5 Quigley	N	N	N	Y	Y	Y
6 **Roskam**	N	Y	Y	Y	Y	Y
7 Davis, D.	?	?	?	?	?	?
8 Krishnamoorthi	Y	N	N	Y	Y	N
9 Schakowsky	N	N	N	Y	Y	N
10 Schneider	Y	N	N	Y	Y	Y
11 Foster	Y	N	N	Y	Y	Y
12 **Bost**	N	Y	Y	Y	Y	Y
13 **Davis, R.**	Y	Y	Y	Y	Y	Y

KEY	Republicans	Democrats	Independents
Y Voted for (yea)		X Paired against	C Voted "present" to avoid possible conflict of interest
# Paired for		– Announced against	
+ Announced for		P Voted "present"	? Did not vote or otherwise make a position known
N Voted against (nay)			

	122	123	124	125	126	127
14 **Hultgren**	Y	Y	Y	Y	Y	Y
15 **Shimkus**	N	Y	Y	Y	Y	Y
16 **Kinzinger**	N	Y	Y	Y	Y	Y
17 Bustos	Y	N	N	Y	Y	Y
18 **LaHood**	N	Y	Y	Y	Y	N
INDIANA						
1 Visclosky	N	N	N	Y	Y	Y
2 **Walorski**	Y	Y	Y	Y	Y	Y
3 **Banks**	Y	Y	Y	Y	Y	Y
4 **Rokita**	N	Y	Y	Y	Y	N
5 **Brooks**	Y	Y	Y	Y	Y	Y
6 **Messer**	N	Y	Y	Y	Y	Y
7 Carson	Y	N	N	Y	Y	Y
8 **Bucshon**	Y	Y	Y	Y	Y	Y
9 **Hollingsworth**	Y	Y	Y	Y	Y	N
IOWA						
1 **Blum**	Y	Y	N	Y	Y	N
2 Loebsack	N	N	N	Y	Y	Y
3 **Young**	Y	Y	Y	Y	Y	Y
4 **King**	Y	Y	Y	Y	Y	N
KANSAS						
1 **Marshall**	N	Y	Y	Y	Y	Y
2 **Jenkins**	N	Y	Y	Y	Y	Y
3 **Yoder**	N	Y	Y	Y	Y	Y
4 **Estes**	Y	Y	Y	Y	Y	Y
KENTUCKY						
1 **Comer**	Y	Y	Y	Y	Y	N
2 **Guthrie**	Y	Y	Y	Y	Y	Y
3 Yarmuth	Y	N	N	Y	Y	N
4 **Massie**	Y	Y	N	N	N	N
5 **Rogers**	Y	Y	Y	Y	Y	Y
6 **Barr**	Y	Y	Y	Y	Y	Y
LOUISIANA						
1 **Scalise**	Y	Y	Y	Y	Y	Y
2 Richmond	N	N	N	Y	Y	Y
3 **Higgins**	Y	Y	Y	Y	Y	N
4 **Johnson**	Y	Y	Y	Y	Y	N
5 **Abraham**	Y	Y	Y	Y	Y	N
6 **Graves**	N	Y	Y	Y	Y	N
MAINE						
1 Pingree	?	?	?	?	?	?
2 **Poliquin**	N	Y	Y	Y	Y	Y
MARYLAND						
1 **Harris**	Y	Y	N	Y	Y	N
2 Ruppersberger	Y	N	N	Y	Y	Y
3 Sarbanes	?	N	N	Y	Y	Y
4 Brown	Y	N	N	Y	Y	Y
5 Hoyer	Y	N	N	Y	Y	N
6 Delaney	N	N	N	Y	Y	Y
7 Cummings	?	?	?	?	?	?
8 Raskin	N	N	N	Y	Y	N
MASSACHUSETTS						
1 Neal	N	N	N	Y	Y	Y
2 McGovern	N	N	N	Y	Y	N
3 Tsongas	Y	N	N	Y	Y	Y
4 Kennedy	Y	N	N	Y	Y	N
5 Clark	Y	N	N	Y	Y	N
6 Moulton	Y	N	N	Y	Y	Y
7 Capuano	N	N	N	Y	Y	N
8 Lynch	N	N	N	Y	Y	Y
9 Keating	N	N	N	Y	Y	Y
MICHIGAN						
1 **Bergman**	N	Y	Y	Y	Y	N
2 **Huizenga**	N	Y	Y	Y	Y	N
3 *Amash*	N	Y	N	N	N	N
4 **Moolenaar**	Y	Y	Y	Y	Y	Y
5 Kildee	Y	N	N	Y	Y	Y
6 **Upton**	N	Y	Y	Y	Y	Y
7 **Walberg**	N	Y	Y	Y	Y	Y
8 **Bishop**	N	Y	Y	Y	Y	Y
9 Levin	N	N	N	Y	Y	Y
10 **Mitchell**	Y	Y	Y	Y	Y	Y
11 **Trott**	Y	Y	Y	Y	Y	Y
12 Dingell	Y	N	N	Y	Y	Y
14 Lawrence	Y	N	N	Y	Y	Y
MINNESOTA						
1 Walz	?	?	?	?	?	?
2 **Lewis**	Y	Y	Y	Y	Y	N
3 **Paulsen**	N	Y	Y	Y	Y	Y
4 McCollum	Y	N	N	Y	Y	Y
5 Ellison	Y	N	N	Y	Y	N
6 **Emmer**	N	Y	Y	Y	Y	N
7 Peterson	N	N	N	Y	Y	N
8 Nolan	N	N	N	Y	Y	N
MISSISSIPPI						
1 **Kelly**	Y	Y	Y	Y	Y	N
2 Thompson	N	N	N	Y	Y	Y
3 **Harper**	Y	Y	Y	Y	Y	Y
4 **Palazzo**	N	Y	Y	Y	Y	Y
MISSOURI						
1 Clay	?	N	N	Y	Y	Y
2 **Wagner**	Y	Y	Y	Y	Y	Y
3 **Luetkemeyer**	Y	Y	Y	Y	Y	Y
4 **Hartzler**	Y	Y	Y	Y	Y	Y
5 Cleaver	P	N	N	Y	Y	Y
6 **Graves**	N	Y	Y	Y	Y	Y
7 **Long**	Y	Y	Y	Y	Y	N
8 **Smith**	Y	Y	Y	Y	Y	N
MONTANA						
AL **Gianforte**	Y	Y	Y	Y	Y	N
NEBRASKA						
1 **Fortenberry**	Y	Y	Y	Y	Y	Y
2 **Bacon**	Y	Y	Y	Y	Y	Y
3 **Smith**	Y	Y	Y	Y	Y	Y
NEVADA						
1 Titus	Y	N	N	Y	Y	N
2 **Amodei**	Y	?	Y	Y	Y	Y
3 Rosen	N	N	N	Y	Y	Y
4 Kihuen	N	N	N	Y	Y	N
NEW HAMPSHIRE						
1 Shea-Porter	Y	N	N	Y	Y	Y
2 Kuster	?	N	N	Y	Y	Y
NEW JERSEY						
1 Norcross	N	N	N	Y	Y	N
2 **LoBiondo**	N	Y	Y	Y	Y	Y
3 **MacArthur**	N	Y	Y	Y	Y	Y
4 **Smith**	Y	Y	Y	Y	Y	Y
5 Gottheimer	N	N	?	Y	Y	Y
6 Pallone	N	N	N	Y	Y	N
7 **Lance**	N	Y	Y	Y	Y	Y
8 Sires	N	N	N	Y	Y	Y
9 Pascrell	Y	N	N	Y	Y	Y
10 Payne	N	N	N	Y	Y	Y
11 **Frelinghuysen**	Y	Y	Y	Y	Y	Y
12 Watson Coleman	N	N	N	Y	Y	N
NEW MEXICO						
1 Lujan Grisham	Y	N	N	Y	Y	N
2 **Pearce**	N	Y	N	Y	Y	N
3 Luján	Y	N	N	Y	Y	N
NEW YORK						
1 **Zeldin**	N	Y	Y	Y	Y	N
2 **King**	Y	Y	Y	Y	Y	Y
3 Suozzi	N	N	N	Y	Y	N
4 Rice	?	N	N	Y	Y	Y
5 Meeks	N	N	N	Y	Y	Y
6 Meng	Y	N	N	Y	Y	Y
7 Velázquez	N	N	N	Y	Y	N
8 Jeffries	N	N	N	Y	Y	Y
9 Clarke	N	–	N	Y	Y	N
10 Nadler	Y	N	N	Y	Y	Y
11 **Donovan**	Y	Y	Y	Y	Y	Y
12 Maloney, C.	N	N	N	Y	Y	N
13 Espaillat	N	N	N	Y	Y	N
14 Crowley	N	N	N	Y	Y	N
15 Serrano	N	N	N	Y	Y	N
16 Engel	Y	N	N	Y	Y	N
17 Lowey	N	N	N	Y	Y	Y
18 Maloney, S.P.	N	N	N	Y	Y	N
19 **Faso**	N	Y	Y	Y	Y	Y
20 Tonko	P	N	N	Y	Y	Y
21 **Stefanik**	Y	Y	Y	Y	Y	Y
22 **Tenney**	N	Y	Y	Y	Y	Y
23 **Reed**	N	Y	Y	Y	Y	N
24 **Katko**	N	Y	Y	Y	Y	Y
25 **Vacant**						
26 Higgins	Y	N	N	Y	Y	Y
27 **Collins**	Y	Y	Y	Y	Y	Y
NORTH CAROLINA						
1 Butterfield	Y	N	N	?	Y	Y
2 **Holding**	N	Y	Y	Y	Y	N
3 **Jones**	?	?	?	?	?	?
4 Price	N	N	N	Y	Y	Y
5 **Foxx**	N	Y	Y	Y	Y	Y
6 **Walker**	Y	Y	Y	Y	Y	N
7 **Rouzer**	N	Y	Y	Y	Y	N
8 **Hudson**	N	Y	Y	Y	Y	Y
9 **Pittenger**	N	Y	Y	Y	Y	Y
9 **Vacant**						
10 **McHenry**	Y	Y	Y	Y	Y	Y
11 **Meadows**	?	Y	N	Y	Y	N
12 Adams	Y	N	N	Y	Y	Y
13 **Budd**	Y	Y	Y	Y	Y	N
NORTH DAKOTA						
AL **Cramer**	?	?	?	?	?	?
OHIO						
1 **Chabot**	Y	Y	Y	Y	Y	Y
2 **Wenstrup**	Y	Y	Y	Y	Y	Y
3 Beatty	Y	N	N	Y	Y	Y
4 **Jordan**	N	Y	N	Y	Y	N
5 **Latta**	N	Y	Y	Y	Y	N
6 **Johnson**	N	Y	Y	Y	Y	Y
7 **Gibbs**	Y	Y	Y	Y	Y	Y
8 **Davidson**	N	Y	N	Y	Y	N
9 Kaptur	Y	N	N	Y	Y	Y
10 **Turner**	N	Y	Y	Y	Y	Y
11 Fudge	N	N	N	Y	Y	Y
12 **Vacant**						
13 Ryan	N	N	N	Y	Y	Y
14 **Joyce**	N	Y	Y	Y	Y	Y
15 **Stivers**	N	Y	Y	Y	Y	Y
16 **Renacci**	N	Y	Y	Y	Y	N
OKLAHOMA						
1 **Bridenstine**	Y	?	?	?	?	?
2 **Mullin**	Y	Y	Y	Y	Y	N
3 **Lucas**	Y	Y	Y	Y	Y	Y
4 **Cole**	Y	Y	Y	Y	Y	Y
5 **Russell**	Y	Y	Y	Y	Y	N
OREGON						
1 Bonamici	Y	N	N	Y	Y	Y
2 **Walden**	Y	Y	Y	Y	Y	Y
3 Blumenauer	Y	N	–	Y	Y	N
4 DeFazio	?	N	N	Y	Y	Y
5 Schrader	N	N	?	Y	Y	Y
PENNSYLVANIA						
1 Brady	N	N	N	Y	Y	Y
2 Evans	N	N	N	Y	Y	Y
3 **Kelly**	Y	Y	Y	Y	Y	N
4 **Perry**	N	Y	N	Y	Y	N
5 **Thompson**	N	Y	Y	Y	Y	Y
6 **Costello**	N	Y	Y	Y	Y	Y
7 **Meehan**	N	Y	Y	Y	Y	Y
8 **Fitzpatrick**	N	Y	Y	Y	Y	Y
9 **Shuster**	Y	Y	Y	Y	Y	Y
10 **Marino**	Y	Y	Y	Y	Y	Y
11 **Barletta**	Y	Y	Y	Y	Y	Y
12 **Rothfus**	Y	Y	Y	Y	Y	N
13 Boyle	N	N	N	Y	Y	N
14 Doyle	N	N	N	Y	Y	Y
15 **Dent**	Y	Y	Y	Y	Y	Y
16 **Smucker**	Y	Y	Y	Y	Y	N
17 Cartwright	Y	N	N	Y	?	Y
RHODE ISLAND						
1 Cicilline	Y	N	N	Y	Y	Y
2 Langevin	N	N	N	Y	Y	Y
SOUTH CAROLINA						
1 **Sanford**	N	Y	N	Y	Y	N
2 **Wilson**	Y	Y	Y	Y	Y	Y
3 **Duncan**	N	Y	Y	Y	Y	N
4 **Gowdy**	Y	Y	Y	Y	Y	Y
5 **Norman**	Y	Y	N	Y	N	N
6 Clyburn	?	N	N	Y	Y	Y
7 **Rice**	Y	Y	Y	Y	Y	N
SOUTH DAKOTA						
AL **Noem**	N	Y	Y	Y	Y	N
TENNESSEE						
1 **Roe**	Y	Y	Y	Y	Y	Y
2 **Duncan**	Y	Y	N	Y	N	N
3 **Fleischmann**	Y	Y	Y	Y	Y	Y
4 **DesJarlais**	Y	Y	Y	Y	Y	N
5 Cooper	Y	N	N	Y	Y	Y
6 **Black**	Y	Y	Y	Y	Y	N
7 **Blackburn**	Y	Y	Y	Y	Y	N
8 **Kustoff**	Y	Y	Y	Y	Y	Y
9 Cohen	Y	N	N	Y	Y	N
TEXAS						
1 **Gohmert**	N	Y	N	Y	Y	N
2 **Poe**	N	Y	Y	Y	Y	N
3 **Johnson, S.**	Y	Y	Y	Y	Y	Y
4 **Ratcliffe**	N	Y	Y	Y	Y	N
5 **Hensarling**	Y	Y	Y	Y	Y	Y
6 **Barton**	N	Y	Y	Y	Y	N
7 **Culberson**	Y	Y	Y	Y	Y	Y
8 **Brady**	Y	Y	Y	Y	Y	Y
9 Green, A.	N	N	N	Y	Y	Y
10 **McCaul**	Y	Y	Y	Y	Y	Y
11 **Conaway**	N	Y	Y	Y	Y	Y
12 **Granger**	Y	Y	Y	Y	Y	Y
13 **Thornberry**	Y	Y	Y	Y	Y	Y
14 **Weber**	N	Y	N	Y	Y	N
15 Gonzalez	Y	N	N	Y	Y	N
16 O'Rourke	Y	N	N	Y	Y	Y
17 **Flores**	N	Y	Y	Y	Y	Y
18 Jackson Lee	N	N	N	Y	Y	N
19 **Arrington**	Y	Y	Y	Y	Y	Y
20 Castro	Y	N	N	Y	Y	N
21 **Smith**	Y	Y	Y	Y	Y	Y
22 **Olson**	Y	Y	Y	Y	Y	Y
23 **Hurd**	N	Y	Y	Y	Y	Y
24 **Marchant**	N	Y	Y	Y	Y	Y
25 **Williams**	Y	Y	Y	Y	Y	N
26 **Burgess**	N	Y	Y	Y	Y	Y
27 **Farenthold**	N	Y	Y	Y	Y	N
28 Cuellar	Y	N	N	Y	Y	Y
29 Green, G.	N	N	N	Y	Y	Y
30 Johnson, E.B.	N	N	N	Y	Y	Y
31 **Carter**	Y	Y	Y	Y	Y	Y
32 **Sessions**	Y	Y	Y	Y	Y	Y
33 Veasey	N	N	N	Y	Y	N
34 Vela	N	N	N	Y	Y	N
35 Doggett	Y	N	N	Y	Y	N
36 **Babin**	N	Y	Y	Y	Y	N
UTAH						
1 **Bishop**	Y	Y	Y	Y	Y	N
2 **Stewart**	Y	Y	Y	Y	Y	N
3 **Curtis**	Y	Y	Y	Y	Y	N
4 **Love**	N	Y	Y	Y	Y	N
VERMONT						
AL Welch	Y	N	N	Y	Y	Y
VIRGINIA						
1 **Wittman**	N	Y	Y	Y	Y	Y
2 **Taylor**	N	Y	Y	Y	Y	Y
3 Scott	N	N	N	Y	Y	Y
4 McEachin	N	N	N	Y	Y	Y
5 **Garrett**	N	Y	N	Y	Y	N
6 **Goodlatte**	Y	Y	Y	Y	Y	Y
7 **Brat**	Y	Y	Y	Y	Y	N
8 Beyer	N	N	N	Y	Y	Y
9 **Griffith**	Y	Y	N	Y	Y	N
10 **Comstock**	Y	Y	Y	Y	Y	Y
11 Connolly	N	N	N	Y	Y	Y
WASHINGTON						
1 DelBene	Y	N	N	Y	Y	Y
2 Larsen	Y	N	N	Y	Y	Y
3 **Herrera Beutler**	N	Y	Y	Y	Y	Y
4 **Newhouse**	Y	Y	Y	Y	Y	N
5 **McMorris Rodgers**	Y	Y	Y	Y	Y	Y
6 Kilmer	N	N	N	Y	Y	Y
7 Jayapal	N	N	N	Y	?	N
8 **Reichert**	?	Y	Y	Y	Y	Y
9 Smith	Y	N	N	Y	Y	N
10 Heck	Y	N	N	Y	Y	Y
WEST VIRGINIA						
1 **McKinley**	N	Y	Y	Y	Y	Y
2 **Mooney**	Y	Y	N	Y	Y	N
3 **Jenkins**	N	Y	Y	Y	Y	Y
WISCONSIN						
1 **Ryan**			Y			Y
2 Pocan	Y	N	N	Y	Y	N
3 Kind	N	N	N	Y	Y	N
4 Moore	N	N	N	Y	Y	N
5 **Sensenbrenner**	Y	Y	Y	Y	Y	N
6 **Grothman**	Y	Y	Y	Y	Y	N
7 **Duffy**	Y	Y	Y	Y	Y	Y
8 **Gallagher**	N	Y	Y	Y	Y	Y
WYOMING						
AL **Cheney**	Y	Y	Y	Y	Y	Y

VOTE NUMBER

128. HR4467. AVIATION SECURITY STRATEGIES/PASSAGE. Bacon, R-Neb., motion to suspend the rules and pass the bill that would require the Federal Air Marshal Service, administered by the Transportation Security Administration, to use risk-based strategies when allocating resources between international and domestic flight coverage. Motion agreed to 408-0: R 230-0; D 178-0. March 22, 2018.

129. HR5089. FUSION CENTER PERSONNEL ASSIGNMENT PROTOCOLS/ PASSAGE. Bacon, R-Neb., motion to suspend the rules and pass the bill that would prioritize the assignment of Department of Homeland Security personnel to state and local fusion centers that have assets deemed to be high in risk. It would also allow DHS to develop training programs through the Federal Law Enforcement Training Centers to better prepare law enforcement agencies to manage terrorist threats and others. Motion agreed to 397-1: R 221-1; D 176-0. March 22, 2018.

130. HR2219. MONEY LAUNDERING FOR HUMAN TRAFFICKING/PASSAGE. Royce, R-Calif., motion to suspend the rules and pass the bill that would add the secretary of the Treasury as a member of the president's Interagency Task Force To Monitor and Combat Trafficking and would require the task force and the Financial Institutions Examination Council to review and report on ways to curb money laundering related to human trafficking. Motion agreed to 408-2: R 226-2; D 182-0. April 10, 2018.

131. HR4203. INCREASING PENALTY FOR STALKING MINORS/PASSAGE. Goodlatte, R-Va., motion to suspend the rules and pass the bill that would increase, by five years, the maximum penalty for individuals convicted of stalking minors. Motion agreed to 409-2: R 226-2; D 183-0. April 10, 2018.

132. PROCEDURAL MOTION/JOURNAL. Approval of the House Journal of April 10, 2018. Approved 231-166: R 135-85; D 96-81. April 10, 2018.

133. HR4790. VOLCKER RULE REGULATION AND EXEMPTION/PREVIOUS QUESTION. Buck, R-Colo., motion to order the previous question (thus ending debate and possibility of amendment) on the rule (H Res 811) that would provide for consideration of the bill (HR 4790) regarding "Volcker Rule" regulation and exemptions thereto, and providing for the speaker to entertain motions to suspend the rules on April 12, 2018, relating to the joint resolution (H J Res 2) that would propose a balanced budget amendment to the U.S. Constitution. Motion agreed to 231-186: R 231-1; D 0-185. April 11, 2018.

	128	129	130	131	132	133
ALABAMA						
1 **Byrne**	Y	Y	Y	Y	Y	Y
2 **Roby**	Y	Y	Y	Y	Y	Y
3 **Rogers**	Y	Y	Y	Y	N	Y
4 **Aderholt**	Y	Y	Y	Y	Y	Y
5 **Brooks**	Y	Y	Y	Y	N	Y
6 **Palmer**	Y	Y	Y	Y	N	Y
7 Sewell	Y	Y	Y	Y	N	N
ALASKA						
AL **Young**	Y	Y	Y	Y	N	Y
ARIZONA						
1 O'Halleran	Y	Y	Y	Y	N	N
2 **McSally**	Y	Y	Y	Y	N	Y
3 Grijalva	Y	Y	Y	?	N	N
4 **Gosar**	Y	Y	Y	N	?	?
5 **Biggs**	Y	Y	Y	Y	N	Y
6 **Schweikert**	Y	Y	Y	Y	Y	Y
7 Gallego	Y	Y	Y	Y	N	N
9 Sinema	Y	Y	Y	Y	N	N
ARKANSAS						
1 **Crawford**	Y	Y	Y	Y	?	Y
2 **Hill**	Y	Y	Y	Y	N	Y
3 **Womack**	Y	Y	Y	Y	Y	Y
4 **Westerman**	Y	Y	Y	Y	Y	Y
CALIFORNIA						
1 **LaMalfa**	Y	Y	Y	Y	Y	N
2 Huffman	Y	Y	Y	Y	N	N
3 Garamendi	Y	Y	Y	Y	Y	N
4 **McClintock**	Y	Y	Y	Y	Y	Y
5 Thompson	Y	Y	Y	N	N	N
6 Matsui	Y	Y	Y	Y	N	N
7 Bera	Y	Y	Y	N	N	N
8 **Cook**	Y	Y	Y	Y	Y	Y
9 McNerney	Y	Y	Y	Y	N	N
10 **Denham**	Y	Y	Y	N	Y	N
11 DeSaulnier	Y	Y	Y	Y	Y	N
12 Pelosi	?	?	Y	Y	Y	N
13 Lee	Y	Y	Y	N	N	N
14 Speier	Y	Y	Y	Y	N	N
15 Swalwell	Y	Y	Y	Y	N	N
16 Costa	Y	Y	Y	Y	N	N
17 Khanna	Y	Y	Y	Y	N	N
18 Eshoo	Y	Y	Y	Y	N	N
19 Lofgren	Y	Y	Y	Y	N	N
20 Panetta	Y	Y	Y	Y	N	N
21 **Valadao**	Y	Y	Y	Y	N	Y
22 **Nunes**	Y	Y	Y	Y	Y	Y
23 **McCarthy**	Y	Y	Y	Y	Y	Y
24 Carbajal	Y	Y	Y	Y	N	N
25 **Knight**	Y	Y	Y	Y	N	Y
26 Brownley	Y	Y	Y	Y	N	N
27 Chu	Y	Y	Y	Y	Y	N
28 Schiff	Y	Y	Y	Y	N	?
29 Cardenas	Y	Y	Y	N	?	?
30 Sherman	Y	Y	Y	Y	Y	N
31 Aguilar	Y	Y	Y	Y	Y	N
32 Napolitano	Y	Y	Y	Y	Y	N
33 Lieu	Y	Y	Y	N	N	N
34 Gomez	Y	Y	Y	Y	N	N
35 Torres	Y	Y	Y	Y	Y	N
36 Ruiz	Y	Y	Y	Y	Y	N
37 Bass	Y	Y	Y	N	N	N
38 Sánchez, Linda	Y	Y	Y	Y	N	N
39 **Royce**	Y	Y	Y	Y	Y	Y
40 Roybal-Allard	Y	Y	Y	N	N	N
41 Takano	Y	Y	Y	Y	N	N
42 **Calvert**	Y	Y	Y	Y	?	Y
43 Waters	Y	Y	Y	Y	Y	N
44 Barragan	Y	Y	Y	Y	N	N
45 **Walters**	Y	Y	Y	Y	Y	Y
46 Correa	Y	Y	Y	Y	N	N
47 Lowenthal	Y	Y	Y	Y	Y	N
48 **Rohrabacher**	Y	Y	?	?	?	Y
49 **Issa**	Y	Y	?	?	?	?
50 **Hunter**	Y	Y	Y	Y	Y	Y
51 Vargas	Y	Y	Y	N	N	N
52 Peters	Y	Y	Y	Y	N	N
53 Davis	Y	Y	Y	Y	Y	N

	128	129	130	131	132	133
COLORADO						
1 DeGette	Y	Y	Y	Y	Y	N
2 Polis	Y	?	Y	Y	Y	N
3 **Tipton**	Y	Y	Y	Y	N	Y
4 **Buck**	Y	Y	Y	N	Y	Y
5 **Lamborn**	Y	Y	Y	Y	Y	Y
6 **Coffman**	Y	Y	Y	N	Y	Y
7 Perlmutter	Y	Y	Y	Y	?	N
CONNECTICUT						
1 Larson	Y	Y	Y	Y	Y	N
2 Courtney	Y	Y	Y	Y	N	N
3 DeLauro	Y	Y	Y	Y	Y	N
4 Himes	Y	Y	Y	Y	Y	N
5 Esty	Y	Y	Y	Y	Y	N
DELAWARE						
AL **Blunt**						
Rochester	Y	Y	Y	Y	N	N
FLORIDA						
1 **Gaetz**	Y	Y	Y	Y	N	Y
2 **Dunn**	Y	Y	Y	Y	Y	Y
3 **Yoho**	Y	Y	Y	Y	N	Y
4 **Rutherford**	Y	Y	Y	Y	N	Y
5 Lawson	Y	Y	Y	Y	N	N
6 **DeSantis**	Y	Y	Y	Y	Y	Y
7 Murphy	?	?	Y	Y	N	N
8 **Posey**	Y	Y	Y	Y	Y	Y
9 Soto	Y	Y	Y	Y	N	N
10 Demings	Y	?	Y	Y	N	N
11 **Webster**	?	?	Y	Y	Y	Y
12 **Bilirakis**	Y	Y	Y	Y	Y	Y
13 Crist	Y	Y	Y	Y	N	N
14 Castor	Y	Y	Y	Y	N	?
15 **Ross**	?	?	Y	Y	Y	Y
16 **Buchanan**	Y	Y	Y	Y	Y	Y
17 **Rooney, T.**	Y	Y	Y	Y	Y	Y
18 **Mast**	Y	Y	Y	N	Y	Y
19 **Rooney, F.**	Y	Y	?	?	?	Y
20 Hastings	Y	Y	Y	N	N	N
21 Frankel	Y	Y	?	?	?	?
22 Deutch	Y	Y	Y	Y	Y	N
23 Wasserman						
Schultz	?	?	Y	Y	Y	N
24 Wilson	Y	Y	+	+	–	N
25 **Diaz-Balart**	Y	Y	Y	Y	N	Y
26 **Curbelo**	Y	Y	Y	Y	N	Y
27 **Ros-Lehtinen**	Y	Y	Y	Y	N	Y
GEORGIA						
1 **Carter**	Y	Y	Y	Y	N	Y
2 Bishop	?	Y	Y	Y	Y	?
3 **Ferguson**	Y	Y	Y	Y	Y	Y
4 Johnson	Y	Y	Y	Y	Y	N
5 Lewis	Y	Y	Y	N	N	N
6 **Handel**	Y	Y	Y	Y	Y	Y
7 **Woodall**	Y	Y	Y	Y	N	Y
8 **Scott, A.**	Y	Y	Y	Y	Y	Y
9 **Collins**	?	?	Y	Y	Y	N
10 **Hice**	Y	Y	Y	N	Y	Y
11 **Loudermilk**	Y	Y	Y	Y	?	Y
12 **Allen**	Y	Y	Y	Y	Y	Y
13 Scott, D.	Y	Y	Y	Y	N	N
14 **Graves**	Y	Y	Y	Y	N	Y
HAWAII						
1 Hanabusa	Y	Y	Y	Y	Y	N
2 Gabbard	Y	Y	Y	Y	Y	N
IDAHO						
1 **Labrador**	Y	Y	?	?	?	Y
2 **Simpson**	Y	Y	?	?	?	?
ILLINOIS						
1 Rush	Y	Y	Y	N	N	N
2 Kelly	Y	Y	Y	Y	N	N
3 Lipinski	?	Y	Y	Y	N	N
4 Gutierrez	?	Y	+	+	–	N
5 Quigley	Y	Y	Y	N	N	N
6 **Roskam**	Y	Y	Y	N	Y	Y
7 Davis, D.	?	?	Y	Y	Y	N
8 Krishnamoorthi	Y	Y	Y	Y	Y	N
9 Schakowsky	Y	Y	Y	Y	?	N
10 Schneider	Y	Y	Y	Y	Y	N
11 Foster	Y	Y	Y	Y	Y	N
12 **Bost**	Y	Y	Y	Y	N	Y
13 **Davis, R.**	Y	Y	Y	Y	Y	Y

	128	129	130	131	132	133
14 **Hultgren**	Y	Y	Y	Y	Y	Y
15 **Shimkus**	Y	Y	Y	Y	Y	Y
16 **Kinzinger**	Y	Y	Y	Y	N	Y
17 Bustos	Y	Y	Y	Y	Y	N
18 **LaHood**	Y	Y	Y	Y	Y	Y
INDIANA						
1 Visclosky	Y	Y	Y	Y	N	N
2 **Walorski**	Y	Y	Y	Y	Y	Y
3 **Banks**	Y	Y	Y	Y	Y	Y
4 **Rokita**	Y	Y	Y	Y	N	Y
5 **Brooks**	Y	Y	Y	Y	Y	Y
6 **Messer**	Y	Y	Y	Y	Y	Y
7 Carson	Y	Y	Y	Y	Y	N
8 **Bucshon**	Y	Y	Y	Y	Y	Y
9 **Hollingsworth**	Y	Y	Y	Y	Y	Y
IOWA						
1 **Blum**	Y	Y	Y	Y	N	Y
2 Loebsack	Y	Y	Y	Y	N	N
3 **Young**	Y	Y	Y	Y	Y	Y
4 **King**	Y	Y	Y	Y	Y	Y
KANSAS						
1 **Marshall**	Y	Y	Y	Y	Y	Y
2 **Jenkins**	Y	Y	Y	Y	N	Y
3 **Yoder**	Y	Y	Y	Y	N	Y
4 **Estes**	Y	Y	Y	Y	Y	Y
KENTUCKY						
1 **Comer**	Y	Y	Y	Y	Y	Y
2 **Guthrie**	Y	Y	Y	Y	Y	Y
3 Yarmuth	Y	Y	Y	Y	?	N
4 **Massie**	Y	?	N	N	N	Y
5 **Rogers**	Y	Y	Y	Y	Y	Y
6 **Barr**	Y	Y	Y	Y	N	Y
LOUISIANA						
1 **Scalise**	Y	Y	Y	Y	Y	Y
2 Richmond	Y	Y	Y	Y	N	N
3 **Higgins**	Y	?	Y	Y	Y	Y
4 **Johnson**	Y	Y	Y	Y	Y	Y
5 **Abraham**	Y	Y	Y	Y	Y	Y
6 **Graves**	Y	Y	Y	Y	N	Y
MAINE						
1 Pingree	?	?	Y	Y	Y	N
2 **Poliquin**	Y	Y	Y	Y	N	Y
MARYLAND						
1 **Harris**	Y	Y	Y	Y	Y	Y
2 Ruppersberger	Y	Y	Y	Y	Y	N
3 Sarbanes	Y	Y	Y	Y	N	N
4 Brown	Y	Y	Y	Y	Y	N
5 Hoyer	Y	Y	Y	Y	N	N
6 Delaney	Y	Y	Y	Y	N	N
7 Cummings	?	?	Y	Y	Y	N
8 Raskin	Y	?	Y	Y	Y	N
MASSACHUSETTS						
1 Neal	Y	Y	Y	Y	Y	N
2 McGovern	Y	Y	Y	Y	N	N
3 Tsongas	Y	Y	Y	Y	Y	N
4 Kennedy	Y	Y	Y	Y	Y	N
5 Clark	Y	Y	Y	Y	N	N
6 Moulton	Y	Y	Y	Y	Y	N
7 Capuano	Y	Y	Y	Y	N	N
8 Lynch	Y	Y	Y	Y	N	N
9 Keating	Y	Y	Y	Y	N	N
MICHIGAN						
1 **Bergman**	Y	Y	Y	Y	N	Y
2 **Huizenga**	Y	Y	Y	Y	Y	Y
3 *Amash*	Y	N	N	N	N	Y
4 **Moolenaar**	Y	Y	Y	Y	Y	Y
5 Kildee	Y	Y	Y	Y	Y	N
6 **Upton**	Y	Y	Y	Y	N	Y
7 **Walberg**	Y	Y	Y	Y	N	Y
8 **Bishop**	Y	Y	Y	Y	N	Y
9 Levin	Y	Y	Y	Y	N	N
10 **Mitchell**	Y	Y	Y	Y	Y	Y
11 **Trott**	Y	Y	Y	Y	Y	Y
12 Dingell	Y	Y	Y	Y	Y	N
14 Lawrence	Y	Y	Y	Y	N	N
MINNESOTA						
1 Walz	?	?	?	?	?	?
2 **Lewis**	Y	Y	Y	Y	Y	Y
3 **Paulsen**	Y	Y	Y	Y	N	Y
4 McCollum	Y	Y	Y	Y	Y	N

	128	129	130	131	132	133
5 Ellison	Y	Y	Y	Y	Y	N
6 **Emmer**	Y	Y	Y	Y	N	Y
7 Peterson	Y	Y	Y	Y	Y	N
8 Nolan	Y	Y	Y	Y	N	N
MISSISSIPPI						
1 **Kelly**	Y	Y	Y	Y	Y	Y
2 Thompson	Y	Y	Y	Y	N	N
3 **Harper**	Y	Y	Y	Y	Y	Y
4 **Palazzo**	?	?	Y	Y	N	Y
MISSOURI						
1 Clay	Y	Y	Y	Y	Y	N
2 **Wagner**	Y	Y	Y	Y	Y	Y
3 **Luetkemeyer**	Y	Y	Y	Y	Y	Y
4 **Hartzler**	Y	Y	Y	Y	N	Y
5 Cleaver	Y	Y	Y	Y	N	N
6 **Graves**	Y	Y	Y	Y	N	Y
7 **Long**	Y	Y	Y	Y	Y	Y
8 **Smith**	Y	Y	Y	Y	Y	Y
MONTANA						
AL **Gianforte**	Y	Y	Y	Y	Y	Y
NEBRASKA						
1 **Fortenberry**	Y	Y	Y	Y	Y	Y
2 **Bacon**	Y	Y	Y	Y	Y	Y
3 **Smith**	Y	Y	Y	Y	Y	Y
NEVADA						
1 Titus	Y	Y	Y	Y	Y	N
2 **Amodei**	Y	Y	Y	Y	Y	Y
3 Rosen	Y	Y	Y	Y	N	N
4 Kihuen	Y	Y	Y	Y	N	N
NEW HAMPSHIRE						
1 Shea-Porter	Y	Y	?	?	?	?
2 Kuster	Y	Y	Y	Y	Y	N
NEW JERSEY						
1 Norcross	Y	Y	Y	Y	Y	N
2 **LoBiondo**	Y	Y	Y	Y	N	Y
3 **MacArthur**	Y	Y	Y	Y	N	Y
4 **Smith**	Y	Y	Y	Y	Y	Y
5 Gottheimer	Y	Y	Y	Y	N	N
6 Pallone	Y	Y	Y	Y	N	N
7 **Lance**	Y	Y	Y	Y	N	Y
8 Sires	Y	Y	Y	Y	Y	N
9 Pascrell	Y	Y	Y	Y	Y	N
10 Payne	Y	Y	Y	Y	N	N
11 **Frelinghuysen**	Y	Y	Y	Y	Y	Y
12 Watson Coleman	Y	Y	Y	Y	N	N
NEW MEXICO						
1 Lujan Grisham	Y	Y	+	+	+	N
2 **Pearce**	Y	Y	Y	Y	N	Y
3 Luján	Y	Y	Y	Y	Y	N
NEW YORK						
1 **Zeldin**	Y	Y	Y	Y	N	Y
2 **King**	Y	Y	Y	Y	Y	Y
3 Suozzi	Y	Y	Y	Y	N	N
4 Rice	Y	?	Y	Y	N	N
5 Meeks	Y	Y	Y	Y	Y	N
6 Meng	Y	Y	Y	Y	Y	N
7 Velázquez	Y	Y	Y	Y	N	N
8 Jeffries	Y	Y	Y	Y	N	N
9 Clarke	Y	Y	Y	Y	N	N
10 Nadler	Y	Y	Y	Y	Y	N
11 **Donovan**	Y	Y	Y	Y	Y	Y
12 Maloney, C.	Y	Y	Y	Y	N	N
13 Espaillat	?	?	Y	Y	N	N
14 Crowley	Y	Y	Y	Y	Y	N
15 Serrano	Y	Y	Y	Y	N	N
16 Engel	Y	Y	Y	Y	Y	N
17 Lowey	Y	Y	Y	Y	Y	N
18 Maloney, S.P.	Y	Y	Y	Y	N	N
19 **Faso**	Y	Y	Y	Y	N	Y
20 Tonko	Y	Y	Y	Y	P	N
21 **Stefanik**	Y	Y	Y	Y	Y	Y
22 **Tenney**	Y	Y	Y	Y	Y	Y
23 **Reed**	Y	Y	Y	Y	Y	Y
24 **Katko**	Y	Y	Y	Y	N	Y
25 **Vacant**						
26 Higgins	Y	Y	Y	Y	Y	N
27 **Collins**	Y	Y	Y	Y	Y	Y
NORTH CAROLINA						
1 Butterfield	Y	Y	Y	Y	Y	N
2 **Holding**	Y	Y	Y	Y	?	Y
3 **Jones**	?	?	Y	Y	Y	N
4 Price	Y	Y	Y	Y	N	N

	128	129	130	131	132	133
5 **Foxx**	Y	Y	Y	Y	N	Y
6 **Walker**	Y	Y	Y	Y	Y	Y
7 **Rouzer**	Y	?	Y	Y	N	Y
8 **Hudson**	Y	Y	Y	Y	N	Y
9 **Pittenger**	Y	Y	Y	Y	Y	Y
9 **Vacant**						
10 **McHenry**	Y	?	Y	Y	Y	Y
11 **Meadows**	Y	Y	Y	Y	Y	Y
12 Adams	?	?	Y	Y	Y	N
13 **Budd**	Y	Y	Y	Y	Y	Y
NORTH DAKOTA						
AL **Cramer**	?	?	Y	Y	Y	Y
OHIO						
1 **Chabot**	Y	Y	Y	Y	Y	Y
2 **Wenstrup**	Y	Y	Y	Y	Y	Y
3 Beatty	Y	Y	Y	Y	N	N
4 **Jordan**	Y	Y	Y	Y	N	Y
5 **Latta**	Y	Y	Y	Y	Y	Y
6 **Johnson**	Y	Y	Y	Y	N	Y
7 **Gibbs**	Y	Y	Y	Y	N	Y
8 **Davidson**	Y	Y	Y	Y	Y	Y
9 Kaptur	Y	Y	Y	Y	Y	N
10 **Turner**	Y	Y	Y	Y	N	Y
11 Fudge	Y	Y	Y	Y	N	N
12 **Vacant**						
13 Ryan	Y	Y	Y	Y	N	N
14 **Joyce**	Y	Y	Y	Y	N	Y
15 **Stivers**	Y	Y	Y	Y	N	Y
16 **Renacci**	Y	Y	Y	Y	N	Y
OKLAHOMA						
1 **Bridenstine**	?	?	Y	Y	Y	Y
2 **Mullin**	Y	Y	Y	Y	Y	Y
3 **Lucas**	Y	Y	Y	Y	Y	Y
4 **Cole**	Y	Y	Y	Y	Y	Y
5 **Russell**	Y	Y	Y	Y	?	Y
OREGON						
1 Bonamici	Y	Y	Y	Y	Y	N
2 **Walden**	Y	Y	Y	Y	Y	Y
3 Blumenauer	+	Y	+	+	+	N
4 DeFazio	Y	?	Y	Y	Y	N
5 Schrader	Y	Y	Y	Y	N	N
PENNSYLVANIA						
1 Brady	Y	Y	?	?	?	N
2 Evans	Y	Y	Y	Y	Y	N
3 **Kelly**	Y	Y	Y	Y	Y	Y
4 **Perry**	Y	Y	Y	Y	N	Y
5 **Thompson**	Y	Y	Y	Y	N	Y
6 **Costello**	Y	Y	Y	Y	Y	Y
7 **Meehan**	Y	Y	Y	Y	N	Y
8 **Fitzpatrick**	Y	Y	Y	Y	N	Y
9 **Shuster**	Y	?	Y	Y	?	Y
10 **Marino**	Y	Y	Y	Y	Y	Y
11 **Barletta**	Y	Y	Y	Y	Y	Y
12 **Rothfus**	Y	Y	Y	Y	Y	Y
13 Boyle	Y	Y	Y	Y	N	N
14 Doyle	Y	Y	Y	Y	N	N
15 **Dent**	Y	Y	Y	Y	Y	Y
16 **Smucker**	Y	Y	Y	Y	Y	Y
17 Cartwright	Y	Y	Y	Y	Y	N
RHODE ISLAND						
1 Cicilline	Y	Y	Y	Y	Y	N
2 Langevin	Y	Y	Y	Y	Y	N
SOUTH CAROLINA						
1 **Sanford**	Y	Y	Y	Y	N	Y
2 **Wilson**	Y	Y	Y	Y	Y	Y
3 **Duncan**	Y	Y	Y	Y	N	Y
4 **Gowdy**	Y	Y	?	?	?	Y
5 **Norman**	Y	Y	Y	Y	Y	Y
6 Clyburn	Y	Y	Y	Y	Y	N
7 **Rice**	Y	Y	Y	Y	N	Y
SOUTH DAKOTA						
AL **Noem**	Y	Y	Y	Y	Y	Y
TENNESSEE						
1 **Roe**	Y	Y	Y	Y	N	Y
2 **Duncan**	Y	Y	Y	Y	Y	Y
3 **Fleischmann**	Y	Y	Y	Y	Y	Y
4 **DesJarlais**	Y	Y	Y	Y	?	Y
5 Cooper	Y	Y	Y	Y	Y	N
6 **Black**	Y	Y	Y	Y	Y	+
7 **Blackburn**	Y	Y	Y	Y	N	Y
8 **Kustoff**	Y	Y	Y	Y	Y	Y
9 Cohen	Y	Y	Y	Y	Y	N

	128	129	130	131	132	133
TEXAS						
1 **Gohmert**	Y	Y	Y	Y	N	Y
2 **Poe**	Y	?	Y	Y	N	Y
3 Johnson, S.	Y	Y	Y	Y	Y	Y
4 **Ratcliffe**	Y	Y	Y	Y	N	Y
5 **Hensarling**	Y	Y	Y	Y	Y	Y
6 **Barton**	Y	Y	Y	Y	Y	Y
7 **Culberson**	Y	Y	Y	Y	Y	Y
8 **Brady**	Y	Y	Y	Y	Y	Y
9 Green, A.	Y	Y	Y	Y	N	N
10 **McCaul**	Y	Y	Y	Y	Y	Y
11 **Conaway**	Y	Y	Y	Y	N	Y
12 **Granger**	Y	Y	Y	Y	Y	Y
13 **Thornberry**	Y	Y	Y	Y	Y	Y
14 **Weber**	Y	Y	Y	Y	Y	Y
15 Gonzalez	Y	Y	Y	Y	N	N
16 O'Rourke	?	?	Y	Y	Y	N
17 **Flores**	Y	Y	Y	Y	N	Y
18 Jackson Lee	Y	Y	Y	Y	N	N
19 **Arrington**	Y	Y	Y	Y	Y	Y
20 Castro	Y	Y	Y	Y	Y	N
21 **Smith**	Y	Y	Y	Y	Y	Y
22 **Olson**	Y	Y	Y	Y	Y	Y
23 **Hurd**	Y	Y	Y	Y	N	Y
24 **Marchant**	Y	Y	Y	Y	?	Y
25 **Williams**	Y	Y	Y	Y	Y	Y
26 **Burgess**	Y	Y	Y	Y	N	Y
28 Cuellar	Y	Y	Y	Y	N	N
29 Green, G.	Y	Y	Y	Y	N	N
30 Johnson, E.B.	Y	Y	Y	Y	Y	N
31 **Carter**	Y	Y	Y	Y	Y	Y
32 **Sessions**	Y	Y	Y	Y	Y	Y
33 Veasey	Y	Y	Y	Y	N	N
34 Vela	Y	?	Y	Y	N	N
35 Doggett	Y	Y	Y	Y	?	N
36 **Babin**	Y	Y	Y	Y	Y	Y
UTAH						
1 **Bishop**	Y	Y	Y	Y	Y	Y
2 **Stewart**	Y	Y	Y	Y	Y	Y
3 **Curtis**	Y	Y	Y	Y	Y	Y
4 **Love**	Y	Y	Y	Y	Y	Y
VERMONT						
AL Welch	Y	Y	Y	Y	Y	N
VIRGINIA						
1 **Wittman**	Y	Y	Y	Y	Y	Y
2 **Taylor**	Y	Y	Y	Y	N	Y
3 Scott	Y	Y	Y	Y	Y	N
4 McEachin	Y	Y	Y	Y	Y	N
5 **Garrett**	Y	Y	Y	Y	N	Y
6 **Goodlatte**	Y	Y	Y	Y	Y	Y
7 **Brat**	Y	Y	Y	Y	Y	Y
8 Beyer	Y	Y	Y	Y	Y	N
9 **Griffith**	Y	Y	Y	Y	Y	Y
10 **Comstock**	Y	?	Y	Y	Y	Y
11 Connolly	Y	Y	Y	Y	N	N
WASHINGTON						
1 DelBene	Y	Y	Y	Y	Y	N
2 Larsen	Y	Y	Y	Y	Y	N
3 **Herrera Beutler**	Y	Y	+	+	+	Y
4 **Newhouse**	Y	Y	Y	Y	Y	Y
5 **McMorris Rodgers**	Y	?	Y	Y	Y	Y
6 Kilmer	Y	Y	Y	Y	N	N
7 Jayapal	Y	Y	+	Y	N	N
8 **Reichert**	Y	Y	Y	Y	N	Y
9 Smith	Y	Y	Y	Y	Y	N
10 Heck	Y	Y	Y	Y	Y	N
WEST VIRGINIA						
1 **McKinley**	Y	Y	Y	Y	N	Y
2 **Mooney**	Y	Y	Y	Y	Y	Y
3 **Jenkins**	Y	Y	+	+	+	Y
WISCONSIN						
1 **Ryan**						
2 Pocan	Y	Y	Y	Y	Y	N
3 Kind	Y	Y	Y	Y	N	N
4 Moore	Y	Y	+	+	+	–
5 **Sensenbrenner**	Y	Y	Y	Y	Y	Y
6 **Grothman**	Y	Y	Y	Y	N	Y
7 **Duffy**	Y	Y	Y	Y	Y	Y
8 **Gallagher**	Y	Y	Y	Y	N	Y
WYOMING						
AL **Cheney**	Y	Y	Y	Y	Y	Y

⦀ HOUSE VOTES

VOTE NUMBER

134. HRES811. VOLCKER RULE REGULATION AND EXEMPTION/RULE. Adoption of the rule (H Res 811) that would provide for consideration of the bill (HR 4790) regarding "Volcker Rule" regulation and exemptions thereto, and providing for the speaker to entertain motions to suspend the rules on April 12, 2018, relating to the joint resolution (H J Res 2) that would propose a balanced budget amendment to the U.S. Constitution. Adopted 230-184: R 229-0; D 1-184. April 11, 2018.

135. HR4061. FINANCIAL STABILITY OVERSIGHT COUNCIL REGULATION/ PASSAGE. Passage of the bill that would change the process that the Financial Stability Oversight Council (FSOC) would use to designate a nonbank financial institution as systemically important. It would require the FSOC to consider if other means of regulation would be sufficient before making its designation, and would require that the council be available to meet with the financial institution under review throughout the process. Passed 297-121: R 231-1; D 66-120. April 11, 2018.

136. HR4293. FINANCIAL STRESS TEST PROCEDURES/RECOMMIT. Waters, D-Calif., motion to recommit the bill to the House Financial Services Committee with instructions to report it back immediately with an amendment that would require global systematically important banks that have engaged in a pattern of unsafe banking practices to adhere to more stringent and frequent oversight by the Federal Reserve. Motion rejected 188-231: R 2-231; D 186-0. April 11, 2018.

137. HR4293. FINANCIAL STRESS TEST PROCEDURES/PASSAGE. Passage of the bill that would reduce certain conditions and the frequency of the Federal Reserve's stress testing of financial institutions. It would also prohibit the Fed from objecting to a company's capital plan on the basis of qualitative deficiencies in the company's capital planning process when conducting a Comprehensive Capital Analysis and Review test. Passed 245-174: R 232-1; D 13-173. April 11, 2018.

138. HJRES2. BALANCED BUDGET AMENDMENT/PASSAGE. Goodlatte, R-Va., motion to suspend the rules and pass the joint resolution that would propose a constitutional amendment that would require the U.S. government to operate under a balanced budget each year, beginning five years after ratification. Under the proposal, three-fifths of the entire House and Senate would be required to approve deficit spending or an increase in the public debt limit, but a simple majority would be sufficient to waive the requirement in times of congressionally declared war or in the face of a serious military threat. Motion rejected 233-184: R 226-6; D 7-178. April 12, 2018.

139. HR4790. VOLCKER RULE REGULATION AUTHORITY/PASSAGE. Passage of the bill that would grant the Federal Reserve sole rulemaking authority with respect to Section 619 of the 2010 financial regulatory overhaul, the so-called "Volcker Rule." The rule restricts financial institutions that are insured by the Federal Deposit Insurance Corporation from using their own funds for proprietary trading. The bill would also exempt community banks from the rule, provided that the banks have less than $10 billion in total consolidated assets and have trading and liability assets totaling less than five percent of total consolidated assets. Passed 300-104: R 222-1; D 78-103. April 13, 2018.

	134	135	136	137	138	139
ALABAMA						
1 Byrne	Y	Y	N	Y	Y	Y
2 Roby	Y	Y	N	Y	Y	Y
3 Rogers	Y	Y	N	Y	Y	Y
4 Aderholt	Y	Y	N	Y	Y	Y
5 Brooks	Y	Y	N	Y	Y	Y
6 Palmer	Y	Y	N	Y	Y	Y
7 Sewell	N	Y	Y	N	N	?
ALASKA						
AL Young	Y	Y	N	Y	Y	Y
ARIZONA						
1 O'Halleran	N	Y	Y	Y	N	Y
2 McSally	Y	Y	N	Y	Y	Y
3 Grijalva	N	N	Y	N	N	N
4 Gosar	?	Y	N	Y	N	?
5 Biggs	Y	Y	N	Y	N	Y
6 Schweikert	Y	Y	N	Y	Y	Y
7 Gallego	N	N	Y	N	N	N
9 Sinema	Y	Y	Y	Y	Y	Y
ARKANSAS						
1 Crawford	Y	Y	N	Y	Y	Y
2 Hill	Y	Y	N	Y	Y	Y
3 Womack	Y	Y	N	Y	Y	Y
4 Westerman	Y	Y	N	Y	Y	Y
CALIFORNIA						
1 LaMalfa	Y	Y	N	Y	Y	Y
2 Huffman	N	N	Y	N	N	N
3 Garamendi	N	N	Y	N	N	N
4 McClintock	Y	Y	N	Y	Y	Y
5 Thompson	N	Y	Y	N	N	N
6 Matsui	N	N	Y	N	N	N
7 Bera	N	Y	Y	N	N	Y
8 Cook	Y	Y	N	Y	Y	Y
9 McNerney	N	N	Y	N	N	N
10 Denham	Y	Y	N	Y	Y	Y
11 DeSaulnier	N	N	Y	N	N	N
12 Pelosi	N	N	Y	N	N	N
13 Lee	N	N	Y	N	N	N
14 Speier	N	N	Y	N	N	N
15 Swalwell	N	N	Y	N	N	N
16 Costa	N	Y	Y	Y	Y	N
17 Khanna	N	N	Y	N	N	N
18 Eshoo	N	N	Y	N	N	N
19 Lofgren	N	N	Y	N	N	N
20 Panetta	N	N	Y	N	N	Y
21 Valadao	Y	Y	N	Y	Y	Y
22 Nunes	Y	Y	N	Y	Y	Y
23 McCarthy	Y	Y	N	Y	Y	Y
24 Carbajal	N	Y	Y	N	N	Y
25 Knight	Y	Y	N	Y	Y	Y
26 Brownley	N	Y	Y	N	N	Y
27 Chu	N	N	Y	N	N	N
28 Schiff	N	N	Y	N	N	N
29 Cardenas	N	Y	Y	N	N	Y
30 Sherman	N	Y	Y	N	N	N
31 Aguilar	N	Y	Y	N	N	Y
32 Napolitano	N	N	Y	N	N	N
33 Lieu	N	N	Y	N	N	N
34 Gomez	N	N	Y	N	N	N
35 Torres	N	N	Y	N	N	N
36 Ruiz	N	Y	Y	N	N	N
37 Bass	N	N	Y	N	N	?
38 Sánchez, Linda	N	N	Y	N	N	N
39 Royce	Y	Y	N	Y	Y	Y
40 Roybal-Allard	N	N	Y	N	N	N
41 Takano	N	N	Y	N	N	?
42 Calvert	Y	Y	N	Y	Y	Y
43 Waters	N	N	Y	N	N	N
44 Barragan	N	N	Y	N	N	Y
45 Walters	Y	Y	N	Y	Y	Y
46 Correa	N	Y	Y	Y	N	Y
47 Lowenthal	N	N	?	N	N	N
48 Rohrabacher	?	Y	N	Y	Y	Y
49 Issa	?	Y	N	Y	Y	Y
50 Hunter	Y	Y	N	Y	Y	Y
51 Vargas	N	Y	Y	N	N	Y
52 Peters	?	Y	Y	N	N	Y
53 Davis	N	Y	Y	N	N	Y

	134	135	136	137	138	139
COLORADO						
1 DeGette	N	N	Y	N	N	N
2 Polis	N	N	Y	N	N	N
3 Tipton	Y	Y	N	Y	?	?
4 Buck	Y	Y	N	Y	?	?
5 Lamborn	Y	Y	N	Y	Y	Y
6 Coffman	Y	Y	N	Y	Y	Y
7 Perlmutter	N	Y	Y	N	N	N
CONNECTICUT						
1 Larson	N	N	Y	N	N	N
2 Courtney	N	N	Y	N	N	N
3 DeLauro	N	N	Y	N	N	N
4 Himes	N	Y	Y	N	N	Y
5 Esty	N	Y	Y	N	N	Y
DELAWARE						
AL Blunt Rochester	N	Y	Y	N	N	Y
FLORIDA						
1 Gaetz	Y	Y	N	Y	Y	Y
2 Dunn	Y	Y	N	Y	Y	Y
3 Yoho	Y	Y	N	Y	Y	Y
4 Rutherford	Y	Y	N	Y	Y	Y
5 Lawson	N	Y	Y	N	N	Y
6 DeSantis	Y	Y	N	Y	Y	Y
7 Murphy	N	Y	Y	N	N	Y
8 Posey	Y	Y	N	Y	Y	Y
9 Soto	N	N	Y	N	N	N
10 Demings	N	N	Y	N	N	N
11 Webster	Y	Y	N	Y	Y	Y
12 Bilirakis	Y	Y	N	Y	Y	Y
13 Crist	N	Y	Y	N	N	N
14 Castor	?	N	Y	N	N	N
15 Ross	Y	Y	N	Y	Y	Y
16 Buchanan	Y	Y	N	Y	Y	?
17 Rooney, T.	Y	?	?	?	Y	Y
18 Mast	Y	Y	N	Y	Y	Y
19 Rooney, F.	Y	Y	N	Y	Y	Y
20 Hastings	N	N	Y	N	N	N
21 Frankel	?	?	?	?	?	?
22 Deutch	N	N	Y	N	N	N
23 Wasserman Schultz	N	N	Y	N	N	N
24 Wilson	N	–	Y	N	N	Y
25 Diaz-Balart	Y	Y	N	Y	Y	Y
26 Curbelo	Y	Y	N	Y	N	Y
27 Ros-Lehtinen	Y	Y	N	Y	Y	Y
GEORGIA						
1 Carter	Y	Y	N	Y	Y	Y
2 Bishop	?	?	?	?	?	?
3 Ferguson	Y	Y	N	Y	Y	Y
4 Johnson	N	N	Y	N	N	N
5 Lewis	N	N	Y	N	N	N
6 Handel	Y	Y	N	Y	Y	Y
7 Woodall	Y	Y	N	Y	Y	Y
8 Scott, A.	Y	Y	N	Y	Y	Y
9 Collins	Y	Y	N	Y	Y	Y
10 Hice	Y	Y	N	Y	Y	Y
11 Loudermilk	Y	Y	N	Y	Y	Y
12 Allen	Y	Y	N	Y	Y	Y
13 Scott, D.	N	Y	Y	Y	?	+
14 Graves	Y	Y	N	Y	Y	Y
HAWAII						
1 Hanabusa	N	Y	Y	N	N	Y
2 Gabbard	N	N	Y	N	N	N
IDAHO						
1 Labrador	Y	Y	N	Y	Y	Y
2 Simpson	?	?	?	?	+	+
ILLINOIS						
1 Rush	N	N	Y	N	N	N
2 Kelly	N	N	Y	N	N	Y
3 Lipinski	N	Y	Y	N	N	N
4 Gutierrez	N	N	Y	N	N	N
5 Quigley	N	Y	Y	N	N	Y
6 Roskam	Y	Y	N	Y	Y	Y
7 Davis, D.	N	N	Y	N	N	N
8 Krishnamoorthi	N	N	Y	N	N	N
9 Schakowsky	N	N	Y	N	N	N
10 Schneider	N	Y	Y	N	N	Y
11 Foster	N	Y	Y	N	N	Y
12 Bost	Y	Y	N	Y	Y	Y
13 Davis, R.	Y	Y	N	Y	Y	Y

	134	135	136	137	138	139
14 **Hultgren**	Y	Y	N	Y	Y	Y
15 **Shimkus**	Y	Y	N	Y	Y	Y
16 **Kinzinger**	Y	Y	N	Y	Y	Y
17 Bustos	N	Y	Y	N	N	?
18 **LaHood**	Y	Y	N	Y	Y	Y
INDIANA						
1 Visclosky	N	N	Y	N	N	N
2 **Walorski**	Y	Y	N	Y	Y	Y
3 **Banks**	Y	Y	N	Y	Y	Y
4 **Rokita**	Y	Y	N	Y	Y	Y
5 **Brooks**	Y	Y	N	Y	Y	Y
6 **Messer**	Y	Y	N	Y	Y	Y
7 Carson	N	N	Y	N	N	N
8 **Bucshon**	Y	Y	N	Y	Y	Y
9 **Hollingsworth**	Y	Y	N	Y	Y	Y
IOWA						
1 **Blum**	Y	Y	N	Y	Y	Y
2 Loebsack	N	Y	Y	N	N	Y
3 **Young**	Y	Y	N	Y	Y	Y
4 **King**	Y	Y	N	Y	Y	Y
KANSAS						
1 **Marshall**	Y	Y	N	Y	Y	Y
2 **Jenkins**	Y	Y	N	Y	Y	Y
3 **Yoder**	Y	Y	N	Y	Y	Y
4 **Estes**	Y	Y	N	Y	Y	Y
KENTUCKY						
1 **Comer**	Y	Y	N	Y	Y	Y
2 **Guthrie**	Y	Y	N	Y	Y	Y
3 Yarmuth	N	N	Y	N	N	N
4 **Massie**	Y	Y	N	Y	N	?
5 **Rogers**	Y	Y	N	Y	Y	Y
6 **Barr**	Y	Y	N	Y	Y	Y
LOUISIANA						
1 **Scalise**	Y	+	–	+	Y	Y
2 Richmond	N	N	Y	N	N	Y
3 **Higgins**	Y	Y	N	Y	Y	Y
4 **Johnson**	Y	Y	N	Y	Y	+
5 **Abraham**	Y	Y	N	Y	Y	Y
6 **Graves**	Y	Y	N	Y	Y	Y
MAINE						
1 Pingree	N	N	Y	N	N	N
2 **Poliquin**	Y	Y	N	Y	Y	Y
MARYLAND						
1 **Harris**	Y	Y	N	Y	Y	Y
2 Ruppersberger	N	Y	Y	N	N	Y
3 Sarbanes	N	N	Y	N	N	N
4 Brown	N	Y	Y	N	N	Y
5 Hoyer	N	N	Y	N	N	Y
6 Delaney	N	Y	Y	N	N	Y
7 Cummings	N	N	Y	N	?	N
8 Raskin	N	N	Y	N	N	N
MASSACHUSETTS						
1 Neal	N	Y	Y	N	N	N
2 McGovern	N	N	Y	N	N	N
3 Tsongas	N	N	Y	N	N	N
4 Kennedy	N	Y	Y	N	N	N
5 Clark	N	Y	Y	N	N	N
6 Moulton	N	Y	Y	N	N	Y
7 Capuano	N	N	Y	N	N	N
8 Lynch	N	N	Y	N	N	N
9 Keating	N	Y	Y	N	N	N
MICHIGAN						
1 **Bergman**	Y	Y	N	Y	Y	Y
2 **Huizenga**	Y	Y	N	Y	Y	Y
3 *Amash*	Y	Y	N	Y	N	Y
4 **Moolenaar**	Y	Y	N	Y	Y	Y
5 Kildee	N	N	Y	N	N	N
6 **Upton**	Y	Y	N	Y	Y	Y
7 **Walberg**	Y	Y	N	Y	Y	Y
8 **Bishop**	Y	Y	N	Y	Y	Y
9 Levin	N	N	Y	N	N	N
10 **Mitchell**	Y	Y	N	Y	Y	Y
11 **Trott**	Y	Y	N	Y	Y	Y
12 Dingell	N	N	Y	N	N	?
14 Lawrence	N	N	Y	N	N	Y
MINNESOTA						
1 Walz	?	?	?	?	?	?
2 **Lewis**	Y	Y	N	Y	Y	Y
3 **Paulsen**	Y	Y	N	Y	Y	Y
4 McCollum	N	N	Y	N	N	N

	134	135	136	137	138	139
5 Ellison	N	N	Y	N	N	N
6 **Emmer**	Y	Y	N	Y	Y	Y
7 Peterson	N	Y	Y	Y	Y	Y
8 Nolan	N	N	Y	?	N	N
MISSISSIPPI						
1 **Kelly**	Y	Y	N	Y	Y	Y
2 Thompson	N	N	Y	N	N	Y
3 **Harper**	Y	Y	N	Y	Y	Y
4 **Palazzo**	Y	Y	N	Y	Y	Y
MISSOURI						
1 Clay	N	N	Y	N	N	Y
2 **Wagner**	Y	Y	N	Y	Y	Y
3 **Luetkemeyer**	Y	Y	N	Y	Y	Y
4 **Hartzler**	Y	Y	N	Y	Y	Y
5 Cleaver	N	N	Y	N	N	Y
6 **Graves**	Y	Y	N	Y	Y	Y
7 **Long**	Y	Y	N	Y	Y	Y
8 **Smith**	Y	Y	N	Y	Y	Y
MONTANA						
AL **Gianforte**	Y	Y	N	Y	Y	Y
NEBRASKA						
1 **Fortenberry**	Y	Y	N	Y	Y	Y
2 **Bacon**	Y	Y	N	Y	Y	Y
3 **Smith**	Y	Y	N	Y	Y	Y
NEVADA						
1 Titus	N	N	Y	N	N	N
2 **Amodei**	Y	Y	N	Y	Y	Y
3 Rosen	N	N	Y	N	N	Y
4 Kihuen	N	Y	Y	N	N	N
NEW HAMPSHIRE						
1 Shea-Porter	?	?	?	?	?	?
2 Kuster	N	Y	Y	N	N	Y
NEW JERSEY						
1 Norcross	N	Y	Y	N	N	N
2 **LoBiondo**	Y	Y	N	Y	Y	Y
3 **MacArthur**	Y	Y	N	Y	Y	Y
4 **Smith**	Y	Y	N	Y	Y	Y
5 Gottheimer	N	Y	Y	Y	Y	Y
6 Pallone	N	N	Y	N	N	N
7 **Lance**	Y	Y	N	Y	Y	Y
8 Sires	N	N	Y	N	N	N
9 Pascrell	N	N	Y	N	N	N
10 Payne	N	Y	Y	N	N	N
11 **Frelinghuysen**	Y	Y	N	Y	Y	Y
12 Watson Coleman	N	N	Y	N	N	N
NEW MEXICO						
1 Lujan Grisham	N	Y	Y	N	N	Y
2 **Pearce**	Y	Y	N	Y	Y	Y
3 Luján	N	N	Y	N	N	N
NEW YORK						
1 **Zeldin**	Y	Y	N	Y	Y	Y
2 **King**	Y	Y	N	Y	Y	Y
3 Suozzi	N	Y	Y	Y	N	Y
4 Rice	N	Y	Y	N	N	Y
5 Meeks	N	Y	Y	N	N	Y
6 Meng	N	Y	Y	N	N	Y
7 Velázquez	N	N	Y	N	N	N
8 Jeffries	N	N	Y	N	N	Y
9 Clarke	N	N	Y	N	N	Y
10 Nadler	N	N	Y	N	N	N
11 **Donovan**	Y	Y	N	Y	Y	Y
12 Maloney, C.	N	N	Y	N	N	N
13 Espaillat	N	N	Y	N	N	N
14 Crowley	N	N	Y	N	N	N
15 Serrano	N	N	Y	N	N	N
16 Engel	N	N	Y	N	N	N
17 Lowey	N	N	Y	N	N	N
18 Maloney, S.P.	N	Y	Y	N	N	Y
19 **Faso**	Y	Y	N	Y	Y	Y
20 Tonko	N	N	Y	N	N	N
21 **Stefanik**	Y	Y	N	Y	Y	Y
22 **Tenney**	Y	Y	N	Y	Y	Y
23 **Reed**	Y	Y	N	Y	Y	Y
24 **Katko**	Y	Y	N	Y	Y	Y
25 Vacant						
26 Higgins	N	N	Y	N	N	N
27 **Collins**	Y	Y	N	Y	Y	Y
NORTH CAROLINA						
1 Butterfield	N	N	Y	N	N	Y
2 **Holding**	Y	Y	N	Y	Y	Y
3 **Jones**	Y	N	N	Y	N	N
4 Price	N	N	Y	N	N	N

	134	135	136	137	138	139
5 **Foxx**	Y	Y	N	Y	Y	Y
6 **Walker**	Y	Y	N	Y	Y	?
7 **Rouzer**	Y	Y	N	Y	Y	Y
8 **Hudson**	+	Y	N	Y	Y	Y
9 **Pittenger**	Y	Y	N	Y	Y	Y
9 Vacant						
10 **McHenry**	Y	Y	N	Y	Y	Y
11 **Meadows**	Y	Y	N	Y	Y	Y
12 Adams	N	N	Y	N	N	Y
13 **Budd**	Y	Y	N	Y	Y	Y
NORTH DAKOTA						
AL **Cramer**	Y	?	N	Y	Y	Y
OHIO						
1 **Chabot**	Y	Y	N	Y	Y	Y
2 **Wenstrup**	Y	Y	N	Y	Y	Y
3 Beatty	N	Y	Y	Y	N	Y
4 **Jordan**	Y	Y	N	Y	Y	Y
5 **Latta**	Y	Y	N	Y	Y	Y
6 **Johnson**	Y	Y	N	Y	Y	Y
7 **Gibbs**	Y	Y	N	Y	Y	Y
8 **Davidson**	Y	Y	N	Y	Y	Y
9 Kaptur	N	N	Y	N	N	N
10 **Turner**	Y	Y	N	Y	Y	Y
11 Fudge	N	N	Y	N	N	Y
12 **Vacant**						
13 Ryan	N	N	Y	N	N	Y
14 **Joyce**	Y	Y	N	Y	Y	Y
15 **Stivers**	Y	Y	N	Y	Y	Y
16 **Renacci**	Y	Y	N	Y	Y	Y
OKLAHOMA						
1 **Bridenstine**	Y	Y	N	Y	Y	?
2 **Mullin**	Y	Y	N	Y	Y	Y
3 **Lucas**	Y	Y	N	Y	Y	Y
4 **Cole**	Y	Y	N	Y	Y	Y
5 **Russell**	Y	Y	N	Y	Y	Y
OREGON						
1 Bonamici	N	N	Y	N	N	N
2 **Walden**	?	Y	N	Y	Y	Y
3 Blumenauer	N	N	Y	N	N	N
4 DeFazio	N	N	Y	N	N	N
5 Schrader	N	Y	Y	N	N	N
PENNSYLVANIA						
1 Brady	N	N	Y	N	N	?
2 Evans	N	N	Y	N	N	Y
3 **Kelly**	Y	Y	N	Y	Y	Y
4 **Perry**	Y	Y	N	Y	Y	Y
5 **Thompson**	Y	Y	N	Y	Y	Y
6 **Costello**	Y	Y	N	Y	Y	Y
7 **Meehan**	Y	Y	N	Y	Y	Y
8 **Fitzpatrick**	Y	Y	N	Y	Y	Y
9 **Shuster**	Y	Y	N	Y	Y	Y
10 **Marino**	Y	Y	N	Y	Y	Y
11 **Barletta**	Y	Y	N	Y	Y	Y
12 **Rothfus**	Y	Y	N	Y	Y	Y
13 Boyle	N	Y	Y	N	N	Y
14 Doyle	N	N	Y	N	N	N
15 **Dent**	Y	Y	N	Y	Y	Y
16 **Smucker**	Y	Y	N	Y	Y	Y
17 Cartwright	N	N	Y	N	N	N
RHODE ISLAND						
1 Cicilline	N	N	Y	N	N	N
2 Langevin	N	N	Y	N	N	N
SOUTH CAROLINA						
1 **Sanford**	Y	Y	N	Y	Y	Y
2 **Wilson**	Y	Y	N	Y	Y	Y
3 **Duncan**	Y	Y	N	Y	Y	Y
4 **Gowdy**	Y	Y	N	Y	Y	Y
5 **Norman**	Y	Y	N	Y	Y	Y
6 Clyburn	N	N	Y	N	N	Y
7 **Rice**	Y	Y	N	Y	?	?
SOUTH DAKOTA						
AL **Noem**	Y	Y	N	Y	Y	?
TENNESSEE						
1 **Roe**	Y	Y	N	Y	Y	Y
2 **Duncan**	Y	Y	N	Y	Y	Y
3 **Fleischmann**	Y	Y	N	Y	Y	Y
4 **DesJarlais**	Y	Y	N	Y	Y	Y
5 Cooper	N	Y	Y	N	Y	Y
6 **Black**	Y	Y	N	Y	Y	Y
7 **Blackburn**	Y	Y	N	Y	Y	Y
8 **Kustoff**	Y	Y	N	Y	Y	Y
9 Cohen	N	N	Y	Y	N	N

	134	135	136	137	138	139
TEXAS						
1 **Gohmert**	Y	Y	N	Y	N	Y
2 **Poe**	Y	Y	N	Y	Y	Y
3 **Johnson, S.**	Y	Y	N	Y	Y	Y
4 **Ratcliffe**	Y	Y	N	Y	Y	Y
5 **Hensarling**	Y	Y	N	Y	Y	Y
6 **Barton**	Y	Y	N	Y	Y	Y
7 **Culberson**	Y	Y	N	Y	Y	Y
8 **Brady**	?	Y	N	Y	Y	Y
9 Green, A.	N	N	Y	N	N	N
10 **McCaul**	Y	Y	N	Y	Y	Y
11 **Conaway**	Y	Y	N	Y	Y	Y
12 **Granger**	Y	Y	N	Y	Y	Y
13 **Thornberry**	Y	Y	N	Y	Y	Y
14 **Weber**	Y	Y	N	Y	Y	Y
15 Gonzalez	N	Y	Y	N	N	Y
16 O'Rourke	N	N	Y	N	N	Y
17 **Flores**	Y	Y	N	Y	Y	Y
18 Jackson Lee	N	N	Y	N	N	Y
19 **Arrington**	Y	Y	N	Y	Y	Y
20 Castro	N	N	Y	N	N	N
21 **Smith**	Y	Y	N	Y	Y	?
22 **Olson**	Y	Y	N	Y	Y	Y
23 **Hurd**	Y	Y	N	Y	Y	Y
24 **Marchant**	Y	Y	N	Y	Y	Y
25 **Williams**	Y	Y	N	Y	Y	Y
26 **Burgess**	Y	Y	N	Y	Y	Y
28 Cuellar	N	Y	Y	Y	Y	Y
29 Green, G.	N	N	Y	N	N	Y
30 Johnson, E.B.	N	N	Y	N	N	Y
31 **Carter**	Y	Y	N	Y	Y	Y
32 **Sessions**	Y	Y	N	Y	Y	Y
33 Veasey	N	Y	Y	N	N	Y
34 Vela	N	Y	Y	N	N	Y
35 Doggett	N	N	Y	N	N	N
36 **Babin**	Y	Y	N	Y	Y	Y
UTAH						
1 **Bishop**	Y	Y	N	Y	Y	Y
2 **Stewart**	Y	Y	N	Y	Y	Y
3 **Curtis**	Y	Y	N	Y	Y	Y
4 **Love**	Y	Y	N	Y	Y	Y
VERMONT						
AL Welch	N	N	Y	N	N	N
VIRGINIA						
1 **Wittman**	Y	Y	N	Y	Y	Y
2 **Taylor**	Y	Y	N	Y	Y	Y
3 Scott	N	N	Y	N	N	N
4 McEachin	N	Y	Y	N	N	Y
5 **Garrett**	Y	Y	N	Y	Y	Y
6 **Goodlatte**	Y	Y	N	Y	Y	Y
7 **Brat**	Y	Y	N	Y	Y	Y
8 Beyer	N	Y	Y	N	N	Y
9 **Griffith**	Y	Y	N	Y	Y	Y
10 **Comstock**	Y	Y	N	Y	Y	Y
11 Connolly	N	N	Y	N	N	Y
WASHINGTON						
1 DelBene	N	Y	Y	N	N	Y
2 Larsen	N	Y	Y	N	N	Y
3 **Herrera Beutler**	Y	Y	N	Y	Y	Y
4 **Newhouse**	Y	Y	N	Y	Y	Y
5 **McMorris Rodgers**	Y	Y	N	Y	Y	Y
6 Kilmer	N	Y	Y	N	N	Y
7 Jayapal	N	N	Y	N	N	N
8 **Reichert**	Y	Y	N	Y	Y	Y
9 Smith	N	N	Y	N	N	N
10 Heck	N	Y	Y	N	N	Y
WEST VIRGINIA						
1 **McKinley**	Y	Y	N	Y	Y	Y
2 **Mooney**	Y	Y	N	Y	Y	Y
3 **Jenkins**	Y	Y	N	Y	Y	+
WISCONSIN						
1 **Ryan**						
2 Pocan	N	N	Y	N	N	N
3 Kind	N	Y	Y	N	Y	Y
4 Moore	–	–	+	–	–	?
5 **Sensenbrenner**	Y	Y	N	Y	Y	Y
6 **Grothman**	Y	Y	N	Y	Y	Y
7 **Duffy**	Y	Y	N	Y	Y	Y
8 **Gallagher**	Y	Y	N	Y	Y	Y
WYOMING						
AL **Cheney**	Y	Y	N	Y	Y	Y

VOTE NUMBER

140. HR146. LAND FOR CHEROKEE INDIANS/PASSAGE. McClintock, R-Calif., motion to suspend the rules and pass the bill that would place into trust five parcels of federal land in Monroe County, Tenn., currently managed by the Tennessee Valley Authority, for use by the Eastern Band of Cherokee Indians. Motion agreed to 383-2: R 215-2; D 168-0. April 16, 2018.

141. S167. FALLEN EDUCATORS MEMORIAL DESIGNATION/PASSAGE. McClintock, R-Calif., motion to suspend the rules and pass the bill that would designate a memorial located at the National Teachers Hall of Fame in Emporia, Kan., as the "National memorial to Fallen Educators." Motion agreed to 384-1: R 216-1; D 168-0. April 16, 2018.

142. HR5192. IDENTITY VERIFICATION DATABASE/PASSAGE. Passage of the bill that would require that the Commissioner of the Social Security Administration establish and maintain a database, which permitted entities such as financial institutions could use to verify the identity of individuals seeking financial services. The bill would allow for financial institutions and their affiliates to query the database only when performing credit checks under the Fair Credit Reporting Act, or pursuant to the written or electronic consent of an individual seeking financial services. Passed 420-1: R 230-1; D 190-0. April 17, 2018.

143. HR5445. IRS PROCEDURES, STRUCTURE AND INFORMATION SECURITY/PREVIOUS QUESTION. Newhouse, R-Wash., motion to order the previous question (thus ending debate and possibility of amendment) on the rule (H Res 831) that would provide for consideration of the bill (HR 5444) that would require a number of structural and procedural changes at the IRS, including changes to customer service priorities and enforcement rules, and would also provide for consideration of the bill (HR 5445) that would update and expand the information technology infrastructure of the IRS. Motion agreed to 226-189: R 226-1; D 0-188. April 18, 2018.

144. HR5445. IRS PROCEDURES, STRUCTURE AND INFORMATION SECURITY/RULE. Adoption of the rule (H Res 831) provide for consideration of the bill (HR 5444) that would require a number of structural and procedural changes at the IRS, including changes to customer service priorities and enforcement rules, and would also provide for consideration of the bill (HR 5445) that would update and expand the information technology infrastructure of the IRS. Adopted 239-177: R 227-2; D 12-175. April 18, 2018.

145. HR5445. IRS INFORMATION TECHNOLOGY MODERNIZATION/ PASSAGE. Passage of the bill that would require the IRS to develop protections for taxpayer information against cybersecurity threats and identity theft. The bill would require the IRS to expand the use of the electronic filing system and information technology infrastructure so that more taxpayers can file taxes and interact with the IRS online. The bill would also create a Chief Information Officer position to lead the modernization efforts of the IRS. Passed 414-3: R 225-3; D 189-0. April 18, 2018.

	140	141	142	143	144	145
ALABAMA						
1 Byrne	Y	Y	Y	Y	Y	Y
2 Roby	Y	Y	Y	Y	Y	Y
3 Rogers	Y	Y	Y	Y	Y	Y
4 Aderholt	Y	Y	Y	Y	Y	Y
5 Brooks	Y	Y	Y	?	?	Y
6 Palmer	Y	Y	Y	Y	Y	Y
7 Sewell	Y	Y	Y	N	N	Y
ALASKA						
AL Young	Y	Y	Y	Y	Y	Y
ARIZONA						
1 O'Halleran	Y	Y	Y	N	Y	Y
2 McSally	?	?	Y	Y	Y	Y
3 Grijalva	Y	Y	Y	N	N	Y
4 Gosar	Y	Y	Y	Y	Y	Y
5 Biggs	Y	Y	Y	Y	Y	Y
6 Schweikert	Y	Y	Y	Y	Y	Y
7 Gallego	Y	Y	Y	N	N	Y
8 Franks						
9 Sinema	Y	Y	Y	N	Y	Y
ARKANSAS						
1 Crawford	Y	Y	Y	Y	Y	Y
2 Hill	Y	Y	Y	Y	Y	Y
3 Womack	Y	Y	Y	Y	Y	Y
4 Westerman	Y	Y	Y	Y	Y	Y
CALIFORNIA						
1 LaMalfa	Y	Y	Y	Y	Y	Y
2 Huffman	Y	Y	Y	N	N	Y
3 Garamendi	Y	Y	Y	N	N	?
4 McClintock	Y	Y	Y	Y	Y	Y
5 Thompson	Y	Y	Y	N	N	Y
6 Matsui	Y	Y	Y	N	N	Y
7 Bera	Y	Y	Y	N	N	Y
8 Cook	Y	Y	Y	Y	Y	Y
9 McNerney	Y	Y	Y	N	N	Y
10 Denham	Y	Y	Y	Y	Y	Y
11 DeSaulnier	Y	Y	Y	N	N	Y
12 Pelosi	Y	Y	Y	N	N	Y
13 Lee	Y	Y	Y	N	N	Y
14 Speier	Y	Y	Y	N	N	Y
15 Swalwell	Y	Y	Y	N	N	Y
16 Costa	Y	Y	Y	N	N	Y
17 Khanna	Y	Y	Y	N	N	Y
18 Eshoo	Y	Y	Y	N	N	Y
19 Lofgren	Y	Y	Y	N	N	Y
20 Panetta	Y	Y	Y	N	N	Y
21 Valadao	Y	Y	Y	Y	Y	Y
22 Nunes	Y	Y	Y	Y	Y	?
23 McCarthy	Y	Y	Y	Y	Y	Y
24 Carbajal	+	+	Y	N	Y	Y
25 Knight	Y	Y	Y	Y	Y	Y
26 Brownley	Y	Y	Y	N	N	Y
27 Chu	Y	Y	Y	N	N	Y
28 Schiff	Y	Y	Y	N	N	Y
29 Cardenas	Y	Y	Y	N	N	Y
30 Sherman	Y	Y	Y	N	N	Y
31 Aguilar	Y	Y	Y	N	N	Y
32 Napolitano	Y	Y	Y	N	N	Y
33 Lieu	Y	Y	Y	N	N	Y
34 Gomez	Y	Y	Y	N	N	Y
35 Torres	Y	Y	Y	N	N	Y
36 Ruiz	Y	Y	Y	N	N	Y
37 Bass	?	?	Y	N	N	Y
38 Sánchez, Linda	Y	Y	Y	N	N	Y
39 Royce	Y	Y	Y	Y	Y	Y
40 Roybal-Allard	Y	Y	Y	N	N	Y
41 Takano	Y	Y	Y	N	N	Y
42 Calvert	Y	Y	Y	Y	Y	Y
43 Waters	Y	Y	Y	N	N	Y
44 Barragan	Y	Y	Y	N	N	Y
45 Walters	Y	Y	Y	Y	Y	Y
46 Correa	Y	Y	Y	N	N	Y
47 Lowenthal	Y	Y	Y	N	N	Y
48 Rohrabacher	?	?	Y	Y	Y	Y
49 Issa	Y	Y	Y	Y	Y	Y
50 Hunter	Y	Y	Y	Y	Y	Y
51 Vargas	Y	Y	Y	N	N	Y
52 Peters	Y	Y	Y	N	Y	Y
53 Davis	Y	Y	Y	N	N	Y

	140	141	142	143	144	145
COLORADO						
1 DeGette	Y	Y	Y	N	N	Y
2 Polis	Y	Y	Y	N	N	Y
3 Tipton	Y	Y	Y	Y	Y	Y
4 Buck	Y	Y	Y	Y	Y	Y
5 Lamborn	?	?	Y	Y	Y	Y
6 Coffman	Y	Y	Y	Y	Y	Y
7 Perlmutter	Y	Y	Y	N	N	Y
CONNECTICUT						
1 Larson	Y	Y	Y	N	N	Y
2 Courtney	Y	Y	Y	N	N	Y
3 DeLauro	Y	Y	+	?	?	?
4 Himes	Y	Y	Y	N	N	Y
5 Esty	Y	Y	Y	N	N	Y
DELAWARE						
AL Blunt Rochester	Y	Y	Y	N	N	Y
FLORIDA						
1 Gaetz	Y	Y	Y	Y	Y	Y
2 Dunn	Y	Y	Y	Y	Y	Y
3 Yoho	Y	Y	Y	Y	Y	Y
4 Rutherford	Y	Y	Y	Y	Y	Y
5 Lawson	Y	Y	Y	N	N	Y
6 DeSantis	?	?	Y	Y	Y	Y
7 Murphy	Y	Y	Y	N	N	Y
8 Posey	Y	Y	Y	Y	Y	Y
9 Soto	Y	Y	Y	N	N	Y
10 Demings	Y	Y	Y	N	N	Y
11 Webster	Y	Y	Y	Y	Y	Y
12 Bilirakis	Y	Y	Y	Y	Y	Y
13 Crist	Y	Y	Y	N	N	Y
14 Castor	Y	?	Y	N	N	Y
15 Ross	Y	Y	Y	Y	Y	Y
16 Buchanan	Y	Y	Y	Y	Y	Y
17 Rooney, T.	Y	Y	Y	Y	Y	?
18 Mast	Y	Y	Y	Y	Y	Y
19 Rooney, F.	?	?	Y	Y	Y	Y
20 Hastings	Y	Y	Y	N	N	Y
21 Frankel	?	?	Y	N	N	Y
22 Deutch	Y	Y	Y	N	N	Y
23 Wasserman Schultz	Y	Y	Y	N	N	Y
24 Wilson	?	?	Y	N	N	Y
25 Diaz-Balart	?	?	Y	Y	Y	Y
26 Curbelo	+	+	Y	Y	Y	Y
27 Ros-Lehtinen	Y	Y	Y	Y	Y	Y
GEORGIA						
1 Carter	Y	Y	Y	Y	Y	Y
2 Bishop	Y	Y	Y	N	N	Y
3 Ferguson	Y	Y	Y	Y	Y	Y
4 Johnson	Y	Y	Y	N	N	Y
5 Lewis	Y	Y	Y	N	N	Y
6 Handel	Y	Y	Y	Y	Y	Y
7 Woodall	Y	Y	Y	Y	Y	Y
8 Scott, A.	Y	Y	Y	Y	Y	Y
9 Collins	Y	Y	Y	Y	Y	Y
10 Hice	Y	Y	Y	Y	Y	Y
11 Loudermilk	Y	Y	Y	Y	Y	Y
12 Allen	Y	Y	Y	Y	Y	Y
13 Scott, D.	Y	Y	Y	N	?	Y
14 Graves	Y	Y	Y	Y	Y	Y
HAWAII						
1 Hanabusa	Y	Y	Y	N	N	Y
2 Gabbard	Y	Y	Y	N	N	Y
IDAHO						
1 Labrador	Y	Y	Y	Y	Y	Y
2 Simpson	Y	Y	Y	?	?	?
ILLINOIS						
1 Rush	?	?	Y	N	N	Y
2 Kelly	?	?	Y	N	N	Y
3 Lipinski	Y	Y	Y	N	N	Y
4 Gutierrez	+	+	Y	N	N	Y
5 Quigley	Y	Y	Y	N	N	Y
6 Roskam	Y	Y	Y	Y	Y	Y
7 Davis, D.	Y	Y	Y	N	N	Y
8 Krishnamoorthi	Y	Y	Y	N	N	Y
9 Schakowsky	Y	Y	Y	N	N	Y
10 Schneider	Y	Y	Y	N	Y	Y
11 Foster	Y	Y	Y	N	N	Y
12 Bost	Y	Y	Y	Y	Y	Y
13 Davis, R.	Y	Y	Y	Y	Y	Y

	140	141	142	143	144	145
14 **Hultgren**	Y	Y	Y	Y	Y	Y
15 **Shimkus**	Y	Y	Y	Y	Y	Y
16 **Kinzinger**	Y	Y	Y	Y	Y	Y
17 Bustos	Y	Y	Y	N	N	Y
18 **LaHood**	Y	Y	Y	Y	Y	Y
INDIANA						
1 Visclosky	Y	Y	Y	N	N	Y
2 **Walorski**	Y	Y	Y	Y	Y	Y
3 **Banks**	Y	Y	Y	Y	Y	Y
4 **Rokita**	Y	Y	Y	Y	Y	Y
5 **Brooks**	Y	Y	Y	Y	Y	Y
6 **Messer**	Y	Y	Y	Y	Y	Y
7 Carson	Y	Y	Y	N	N	Y
8 **Bucshon**	Y	Y	Y	Y	Y	Y
9 **Hollingsworth**	Y	Y	Y	Y	Y	Y
IOWA						
1 **Blum**	Y	Y	Y	Y	Y	Y
2 Loebsack	Y	Y	Y	N	N	Y
3 **Young**	Y	Y	Y	Y	Y	Y
4 **King**	Y	Y	Y	Y	Y	Y
KANSAS						
1 **Marshall**	Y	Y	Y	Y	Y	Y
2 **Jenkins**	Y	Y	Y	Y	Y	Y
3 **Yoder**	Y	Y	Y	Y	Y	Y
4 **Estes**	Y	Y	Y	Y	Y	Y
KENTUCKY						
1 **Comer**	Y	Y	Y	Y	Y	Y
2 **Guthrie**	Y	Y	Y	Y	Y	Y
3 Yarmuth	Y	Y	Y	N	N	Y
4 **Massie**	Y	Y	N	Y	N	N
5 **Rogers**	Y	Y	Y	Y	Y	Y
6 **Barr**	Y	Y	Y	Y	Y	Y
LOUISIANA						
1 **Scalise**	+	+	?	+	+	+
2 Richmond	?	Y	Y	N	N	Y
3 **Higgins**	Y	Y	Y	Y	Y	Y
4 **Johnson**	Y	Y	Y	Y	Y	Y
5 **Abraham**	Y	Y	Y	Y	Y	Y
6 **Graves**	Y	Y	Y	Y	Y	Y
MAINE						
1 Pingree	Y	Y	Y	N	N	Y
2 **Poliquin**	Y	Y	Y	Y	Y	Y
MARYLAND						
1 **Harris**	Y	Y	Y	Y	Y	Y
2 Ruppersberger	Y	Y	Y	N	N	Y
3 Sarbanes	Y	Y	Y	N	N	Y
4 Brown	Y	Y	Y	N	N	Y
5 Hoyer	Y	Y	Y	N	N	Y
6 Delaney	Y	Y	Y	?	?	Y
7 Cummings	Y	Y	Y	N	N	Y
8 Raskin	Y	Y	Y	N	N	Y
MASSACHUSETTS						
1 Neal	?	?	Y	N	N	Y
2 McGovern	Y	Y	Y	N	N	Y
3 Tsongas	?	?	Y	N	N	Y
4 Kennedy	?	?	Y	N	N	Y
5 Clark	Y	Y	Y	N	N	Y
6 Moulton	Y	Y	Y	N	N	Y
7 Capuano	Y	Y	Y	N	N	Y
8 Lynch	Y	Y	Y	N	N	Y
9 Keating	Y	Y	Y	?	?	?
MICHIGAN						
1 **Bergman**	Y	Y	Y	Y	Y	Y
2 **Huizenga**	Y	Y	Y	Y	Y	Y
3 *Amash*	N	N	Y	Y	N	N
4 **Moolenaar**	Y	Y	Y	Y	Y	Y
5 Kildee	Y	Y	Y	N	N	Y
6 **Upton**	Y	Y	Y	Y	Y	Y
7 **Walberg**	Y	Y	Y	Y	Y	Y
8 **Bishop**	Y	Y	Y	Y	Y	Y
9 Levin	Y	Y	Y	N	N	Y
10 **Mitchell**	Y	Y	Y	Y	Y	Y
11 **Trott**	Y	Y	Y	Y	Y	Y
12 Dingell	Y	Y	Y	N	N	Y
14 Lawrence	Y	Y	Y	N	N	Y
MINNESOTA						
1 Walz	Y	Y	Y	N	N	Y
2 **Lewis**	Y	Y	Y	Y	Y	Y
3 **Paulsen**	Y	Y	Y	Y	Y	Y
4 McCollum	Y	Y	Y	N	N	Y

	140	141	142	143	144	145
5 Ellison	Y	Y	Y	N	N	Y
6 **Emmer**	Y	Y	Y	Y	Y	Y
7 Peterson	Y	Y	Y	N	N	Y
8 Nolan	Y	Y	Y	N	?	Y
MISSISSIPPI						
1 **Kelly**	Y	Y	Y	Y	Y	Y
2 Thompson	?	?	?	N	N	Y
3 **Harper**	Y	Y	Y	Y	Y	Y
4 **Palazzo**	Y	Y	Y	Y	Y	Y
MISSOURI						
1 Clay	Y	Y	Y	N	N	Y
2 **Wagner**	Y	Y	Y	Y	Y	Y
3 **Luetkemeyer**	Y	Y	Y	Y	Y	Y
4 **Hartzler**	Y	Y	Y	Y	Y	Y
5 Cleaver	Y	Y	Y	N	N	Y
6 **Graves**	Y	Y	Y	Y	Y	Y
7 **Long**	Y	Y	Y	Y	Y	Y
8 **Smith**	Y	Y	Y	Y	Y	Y
MONTANA						
AL **Gianforte**	Y	Y	Y	Y	Y	Y
NEBRASKA						
1 **Fortenberry**	Y	Y	Y	Y	Y	Y
2 **Bacon**	Y	Y	Y	Y	Y	Y
3 **Smith**	Y	Y	Y	Y	Y	Y
NEVADA						
1 Titus	+	+	Y	N	N	Y
2 **Amodei**	Y	Y	Y	Y	Y	?
3 Rosen	Y	Y	Y	N	Y	Y
4 Kihuen	Y	Y	Y	N	N	Y
NEW HAMPSHIRE						
1 Shea-Porter	?	?	Y	N	N	Y
2 Kuster	Y	Y	Y	N	N	Y
NEW JERSEY						
1 Norcross	Y	Y	Y	N	N	Y
2 **LoBiondo**	Y	Y	Y	Y	Y	Y
3 **MacArthur**	Y	Y	Y	Y	Y	Y
4 **Smith**	Y	Y	Y	?	Y	Y
5 Gottheimer	?	?	Y	N	Y	Y
6 Pallone	Y	Y	Y	N	N	Y
7 **Lance**	Y	Y	Y	Y	Y	Y
8 Sires	Y	Y	Y	N	N	Y
9 Pascrell	+	+	Y	N	N	Y
10 Payne	Y	Y	Y	N	N	Y
11 **Frelinghuysen**	Y	Y	Y	Y	Y	Y
12 Watson Coleman	Y	Y	Y	N	N	Y
NEW MEXICO						
1 Lujan Grisham	+	+	Y	N	N	Y
2 **Pearce**	Y	Y	Y	Y	Y	Y
3 Luján	Y	Y	Y	N	N	Y
NEW YORK						
1 **Zeldin**	Y	Y	Y	Y	Y	Y
2 **King**	Y	Y	Y	Y	Y	Y
3 Suozzi	Y	Y	Y	N	Y	Y
4 Rice	?	?	Y	N	N	Y
5 Meeks	Y	Y	Y	N	N	Y
6 Meng	?	?	Y	N	N	Y
7 Velázquez	Y	Y	Y	N	N	Y
8 Jeffries	Y	Y	Y	N	N	Y
9 Clarke	Y	Y	Y	N	N	Y
10 Nadler	Y	Y	Y	N	N	Y
11 **Donovan**	?	?	Y	Y	Y	Y
12 Maloney, C.	Y	Y	Y	N	N	Y
13 Espaillat	Y	Y	Y	N	N	Y
14 Crowley	Y	Y	Y	N	N	Y
15 Serrano	Y	Y	Y	N	N	Y
16 Engel	Y	Y	Y	N	N	Y
17 Lowey	Y	Y	Y	N	N	Y
18 Maloney, S.P.	?	?	Y	N	N	Y
19 **Faso**	Y	Y	Y	Y	Y	Y
20 Tonko	Y	Y	Y	N	N	Y
21 **Stefanik**	Y	Y	Y	Y	Y	Y
22 **Tenney**	Y	Y	Y	Y	Y	Y
23 **Reed**	Y	Y	Y	Y	Y	Y
24 **Katko**	Y	Y	Y	Y	Y	Y
25 **Vacant**						
26 Higgins	Y	Y	Y	N	N	Y
27 **Collins**	Y	Y	Y	Y	Y	Y
NORTH CAROLINA						
1 Butterfield	?	?	Y	N	N	Y
2 **Holding**	Y	Y	Y	Y	Y	Y
3 **Jones**	Y	Y	Y	N	Y	Y
4 Price	Y	Y	Y	N	N	Y

	140	141	142	143	144	145
5 **Foxx**	Y	Y	Y	Y	Y	Y
6 **Walker**	Y	Y	Y	Y	Y	Y
7 **Rouzer**	Y	Y	Y	Y	Y	Y
8 **Hudson**	Y	Y	Y	Y	Y	Y
9 **Pittenger**	N	Y	Y	Y	Y	Y
9 **Vacant**						
10 **McHenry**	Y	Y	Y	Y	Y	Y
11 **Meadows**	Y	Y	Y	Y	Y	Y
12 Adams	Y	Y	Y	N	N	Y
13 **Budd**	Y	Y	Y	Y	Y	Y
NORTH DAKOTA						
AL **Cramer**	?	?	Y	Y	Y	Y
OHIO						
1 **Chabot**	Y	Y	Y	Y	Y	Y
2 **Wenstrup**	Y	Y	Y	Y	Y	Y
3 Beatty	Y	Y	Y	N	N	Y
4 **Jordan**	Y	Y	Y	Y	Y	Y
5 **Latta**	Y	Y	Y	Y	Y	Y
6 **Johnson**	?	?	Y	Y	Y	Y
7 **Gibbs**	Y	Y	Y	Y	Y	Y
8 **Davidson**	Y	Y	Y	Y	Y	Y
9 Kaptur	Y	Y	Y	N	N	Y
10 **Turner**	Y	Y	Y	Y	Y	Y
11 Fudge	Y	Y	Y	N	N	Y
12 **Vacant**						
13 Ryan	Y	Y	Y	N	N	Y
14 **Joyce**	Y	Y	Y	Y	Y	Y
15 **Stivers**	Y	Y	Y	Y	Y	Y
16 **Renacci**	Y	Y	Y	Y	Y	Y
OKLAHOMA						
1 **Bridenstine**	?	?	?	?	?	?
2 **Mullin**	Y	Y	Y	Y	Y	Y
3 **Lucas**	Y	Y	Y	Y	Y	Y
4 **Cole**	Y	Y	Y	Y	Y	Y
5 **Russell**	Y	Y	Y	Y	Y	Y
OREGON						
1 Bonamici	Y	Y	Y	N	N	Y
2 **Walden**	Y	Y	Y	Y	Y	Y
3 Blumenauer	Y	Y	Y	?	?	Y
4 DeFazio	Y	Y	Y	N	N	Y
5 Schrader	Y	Y	Y	N	N	Y
PENNSYLVANIA						
1 Brady	?	?	Y	N	N	Y
2 Evans	Y	Y	Y	N	N	Y
3 **Kelly**	Y	Y	Y	Y	Y	Y
4 **Perry**	Y	Y	Y	Y	Y	Y
5 **Thompson**	Y	Y	Y	Y	Y	Y
6 **Costello**	+	+	Y	Y	Y	Y
7 **Meehan**	Y	Y	Y	Y	Y	Y
8 **Fitzpatrick**	Y	Y	Y	Y	Y	Y
9 **Shuster**	Y	Y	Y	Y	Y	Y
10 **Marino**	Y	Y	Y	Y	Y	Y
11 **Barletta**	Y	Y	Y	?	?	Y
12 **Rothfus**	Y	Y	Y	Y	Y	Y
13 Boyle	Y	Y	Y	N	N	Y
14 Doyle	Y	Y	Y	N	N	Y
15 **Dent**	Y	Y	Y	Y	Y	Y
16 **Smucker**	Y	Y	Y	Y	Y	Y
17 Cartwright	Y	Y	Y	N	N	?
18 Lamb	Y	Y	Y	N	Y	Y
RHODE ISLAND						
1 Cicilline	Y	Y	Y	N	N	Y
2 Langevin	Y	Y	Y	N	N	Y
SOUTH CAROLINA						
1 **Sanford**	Y	Y	Y	Y	Y	N
2 **Wilson**	Y	Y	Y	Y	Y	Y
3 **Duncan**	Y	Y	Y	Y	Y	Y
4 **Gowdy**	?	?	Y	Y	Y	Y
5 **Norman**	Y	Y	Y	Y	Y	Y
6 Clyburn	Y	Y	Y	N	N	Y
7 **Rice**	Y	Y	Y	Y	Y	Y
SOUTH DAKOTA						
AL **Noem**	?	?	Y	Y	Y	Y
TENNESSEE						
1 **Roe**	Y	Y	Y	Y	Y	Y
2 **Duncan**	Y	Y	Y	Y	Y	Y
3 **Fleischmann**	Y	Y	Y	Y	Y	Y
4 **DesJarlais**	Y	Y	Y	Y	Y	Y
5 Cooper	Y	Y	Y	N	N	Y
6 **Black**	?	?	?	?	?	?
7 **Blackburn**	Y	Y	Y	Y	Y	Y
8 **Kustoff**	Y	Y	Y	Y	Y	Y
9 Cohen	Y	Y	Y	N	N	Y

	140	141	142	143	144	145
TEXAS						
1 **Gohmert**	Y	Y	Y	Y	Y	Y
2 **Poe**	Y	Y	Y	Y	Y	Y
3 **Johnson, S.**	Y	Y	Y	Y	Y	Y
4 **Ratcliffe**	Y	Y	Y	Y	Y	Y
5 **Hensarling**	Y	Y	Y	Y	Y	Y
6 **Barton**	Y	Y	Y	Y	Y	Y
7 **Culberson**	Y	Y	Y	Y	Y	Y
8 **Brady**	Y	Y	Y	Y	Y	Y
9 Green, A.	Y	Y	Y	N	N	Y
10 **McCaul**	Y	Y	Y	?	Y	Y
11 **Conaway**	Y	Y	Y	Y	Y	Y
12 **Granger**	Y	Y	Y	Y	Y	Y
13 **Thornberry**	Y	Y	Y	Y	Y	Y
14 **Weber**	Y	Y	?	Y	Y	Y
15 Gonzalez	Y	Y	Y	N	N	Y
16 O'Rourke	Y	Y	Y	N	N	Y
17 **Flores**	Y	Y	Y	Y	Y	Y
18 Jackson Lee	Y	Y	Y	N	N	Y
19 **Arrington**	Y	Y	Y	Y	Y	Y
20 Castro	Y	Y	Y	N	N	Y
21 **Smith**	Y	Y	Y	Y	Y	Y
22 **Olson**	+	+	Y	Y	Y	Y
23 **Hurd**	Y	Y	Y	Y	Y	Y
24 **Marchant**	Y	Y	Y	Y	Y	Y
25 **Williams**	Y	Y	Y	Y	Y	Y
26 **Burgess**	Y	Y	Y	Y	Y	Y
28 Cuellar	Y	Y	Y	N	N	Y
29 Green, G.	Y	Y	Y	N	N	Y
30 Johnson, E.B.	Y	Y	Y	N	N	Y
31 **Carter**	Y	Y	Y	Y	Y	Y
32 **Sessions**	Y	Y	Y	Y	Y	Y
33 Veasey	Y	Y	Y	N	N	Y
34 Vela	Y	Y	Y	N	N	Y
35 Doggett	Y	Y	Y	N	N	Y
36 **Babin**	Y	Y	Y	Y	Y	Y
UTAH						
1 **Bishop**	Y	Y	Y	Y	Y	Y
2 **Stewart**	Y	Y	Y	Y	Y	Y
3 **Curtis**	Y	Y	Y	Y	Y	Y
4 **Love**	Y	Y	Y	Y	Y	Y
VERMONT						
AL Welch	Y	Y	Y	N	N	Y
VIRGINIA						
1 **Wittman**	Y	Y	Y	Y	Y	Y
2 **Taylor**	Y	Y	Y	Y	Y	Y
3 Scott	Y	Y	Y	N	N	Y
4 McEachin	Y	Y	Y	N	N	Y
5 **Garrett**	Y	Y	Y	Y	Y	Y
6 **Goodlatte**	Y	Y	Y	Y	Y	Y
7 **Brat**	Y	Y	Y	Y	Y	Y
8 Beyer	Y	Y	Y	N	N	Y
9 **Griffith**	Y	Y	Y	Y	Y	Y
10 **Comstock**	Y	Y	Y	+	+	+
11 Connolly	Y	Y	Y	N	N	Y
WASHINGTON						
1 DelBene	Y	Y	Y	N	N	Y
2 Larsen	Y	Y	Y	N	N	Y
3 **Herrera Beutler**	Y	Y	Y	Y	Y	Y
4 **Newhouse**	Y	Y	Y	Y	Y	Y
5 **McMorris Rodgers**	Y	Y	Y	Y	Y	Y
6 Kilmer	Y	Y	Y	N	N	Y
7 Jayapal	+	+	Y	N	N	Y
8 **Reichert**	Y	Y	Y	Y	Y	Y
9 Smith	+	+	+	N	N	Y
10 Heck	Y	Y	Y	N	N	Y
WEST VIRGINIA						
1 **McKinley**	Y	Y	Y	Y	Y	Y
2 **Mooney**	Y	Y	Y	Y	Y	Y
3 **Jenkins**	+	+	+	Y	Y	Y
WISCONSIN						
1 **Ryan**						
2 Pocan	+	+	Y	N	N	Y
3 Kind	Y	Y	Y	N	N	Y
4 Moore	Y	Y	Y	?	N	Y
5 **Sensenbrenner**	Y	Y	Y	Y	Y	Y
6 **Grothman**	Y	Y	Y	Y	Y	Y
7 **Duffy**	+	+	Y	Y	Y	Y
8 **Gallagher**	Y	Y	Y	Y	Y	Y
WYOMING						
AL **Cheney**	Y	Y	Y	Y	Y	Y

VOTE NUMBER

146. HR5444. IRS PROCEDURE AND STRUCTURE CHANGES/PASSAGE.
Passage of the bill that would require the Internal Revenue Service to develop a comprehensive customer service strategy that would include expanded offerings for free tax preparation services for low-income taxpayers, waivers for certain fees associated with offers-in-compromise from taxpayers, and a revamped process for appeals. The bill would change the title of the IRS's senior-most official from "Commissioner" to "Administrator" of Internal Revenue, and would require that the administrator submit to Congress by Sept. 30, 2020, a plan to restructure the organization including priorities related to taxpayer contact with the agency and requirements for quick remediation of taxpayer complaints. The bill would eliminate the IRS Oversight Board, and would require the establishment of new rules related to asset seizure and forfeiture by the IRS. Passed 414-0: R 227-0; D 187-0. April 18, 2018.

147. HR2905. IRS IMPERSONATION PENALTIES/PASSAGE. Poe, R-Texas, motion to suspend the rules and pass the bill that would require the Attorney General to establish procedures to expedite the review and indictment of cases in which the defendant misrepresented himself to be an employee of the Internal Revenue Service, or acting on the service's behalf. Motion agreed to 403-3: R 219-2; D 184-1. April 18, 2018.

148. HCONRES111. NORTH AMERICAN WORLD CUP BID/PASSAGE. Royce, R-Calif., motion to suspend the rules and agree to the resolution that would support the efforts of the United Bid committee to bring the 2026 FIFA World Cup to North America and would state that Congress would consider a request by the president to provide the authorizations and appropriations necessary to host the event in North America. Motion agreed to 392-3: R 211-3; D 181-0. April 24, 2018.

149. HR5086. INNOVATION CORPS PROGRAM EXPANSION/PASSAGE.
Webster, R-Fla., motion to suspend the rules and pass the bill that would authorize $5 million for fiscal 2019 and 2020 for the development of a new National Science Foundation Innovation Corps Program course that would support the commercialization of products and services developed through federally funded research. It would also allow grant recipients under the Small Business Innovation Research Program to participate in the I-Corps program. Motion agreed to 379-16: R 199-16; D 180-0. April 24, 2018.

150. HR3144. FAA REAUTHORIZATION AND RIVER POWER SYSTEM MANAGEMENT/PREVIOUS QUESTION. Woodall, R-Ga., motion to order the previous question (thus ending debate and possibility of amendment) on the rule (H Res 839) that would provide for House floor consideration of the bill (HR 4) that would reauthorize the Federal Aviation Administration through fiscal 2023, and would provide for consideration of the bill (HR 3144) related to the operations of the Federal Columbia River Power System. Motion agreed to 225-190: R 225-1; D 0-189. April 25, 2018.

151. HR4. FAA REAUTHORIZATION AND RIVER POWER SYSTEM MANAGEMENT/RULE. Adoption of the rule (H Res 839) that would provide for House floor consideration of the bill (HR 4) that would reauthorize the Federal Aviation Administration through fiscal 2023, and would also provide for consideration of the bill (HR 3144) related to the operations of the Federal Columbia River Power System. Adopted 228-184: R 225-0; D 3-184. April 25, 2018.

	146	147	148	149	150	151
ALABAMA						
1 **Byrne**	Y	Y	Y	Y	Y	Y
2 **Roby**	Y	Y	Y	Y	Y	Y
3 **Rogers**	Y	Y	Y	Y	Y	Y
4 **Aderholt**	Y	Y	Y	Y	Y	Y
5 **Brooks**	Y	Y	Y	N	Y	Y
6 **Palmer**	Y	Y	Y	Y	Y	Y
7 Sewell	Y	Y	Y	Y	N	?
ALASKA						
AL **Young**	Y	Y	Y	Y	Y	Y
ARIZONA						
1 O'Halleran	Y	Y	Y	Y	N	N
2 **McSally**	Y	Y	Y	Y	Y	Y
3 Grijalva	Y	Y	Y	Y	N	N
4 **Gosar**	Y	?	Y	N	Y	Y
5 **Biggs**	Y	Y	Y	N	Y	Y
6 **Schweikert**	Y	Y	Y	Y	Y	Y
7 Gallego	Y	Y	Y	Y	N	N
9 Sinema	Y	Y	Y	Y	N	Y
ARKANSAS						
1 **Crawford**	Y	Y	?	?	?	?
2 **Hill**	Y	Y	Y	Y	Y	Y
3 **Womack**	Y	Y	Y	Y	Y	Y
4 **Westerman**	Y	Y	Y	Y	Y	Y
CALIFORNIA						
1 **LaMalfa**	Y	Y	Y	Y	Y	Y
2 Huffman	Y	Y	Y	Y	N	N
3 Garamendi	?	?	Y	Y	N	N
4 **McClintock**	Y	Y	Y	N	Y	Y
5 Thompson	Y	Y	Y	Y	N	N
6 Matsui	Y	Y	?	?	N	N
7 Bera	Y	Y	Y	Y	N	N
8 **Cook**	Y	Y	Y	Y	Y	Y
9 McNerney	Y	Y	Y	Y	N	N
10 **Denham**	Y	Y	Y	Y	Y	Y
11 DeSaulnier	Y	Y	Y	Y	N	N
12 Pelosi	?	Y	Y	Y	N	N
13 Lee	Y	Y	Y	Y	N	N
14 Speier	?	?	?	Y	N	?
15 Swalwell	Y	Y	+	+	N	N
16 Costa	Y	Y	Y	Y	N	Y
17 Khanna	Y	Y	Y	Y	N	N
18 Eshoo	Y	Y	Y	Y	N	N
19 Lofgren	Y	Y	Y	Y	N	N
20 Panetta	Y	Y	Y	Y	N	N
21 **Valadao**	Y	Y	Y	Y	Y	Y
22 **Nunes**	?	?	Y	Y	Y	Y
23 **McCarthy**	Y	Y	+	+	Y	Y
24 Carbajal	Y	Y	Y	Y	N	N
25 **Knight**	Y	Y	Y	Y	Y	Y
26 Brownley	Y	Y	Y	Y	N	N
27 Chu	Y	Y	Y	Y	N	N
28 Schiff	Y	Y	+	+	N	N
29 Cardenas	Y	Y	Y	Y	N	N
30 Sherman	Y	Y	Y	Y	N	N
31 Aguilar	Y	Y	Y	Y	N	N
32 Napolitano	Y	Y	Y	Y	N	N
33 Lieu	Y	Y	Y	Y	N	N
34 Gomez	Y	Y	Y	Y	N	N
35 Torres	Y	Y	Y	Y	N	N
36 Ruiz	Y	Y	Y	Y	N	N
37 Bass	Y	Y	Y	Y	N	N
38 Sánchez, Linda	Y	Y	Y	Y	N	N
39 **Royce**	Y	Y	?	?	Y	Y
40 Roybal-Allard	Y	+	Y	Y	N	N
41 Takano	Y	Y	Y	Y	N	N
42 **Calvert**	Y	Y	Y	Y	Y	Y
43 Waters	Y	Y	?	?	N	N
44 Barragan	Y	Y	Y	Y	N	N
45 **Walters**	Y	Y	Y	Y	Y	Y
46 Correa	Y	Y	Y	Y	N	N
47 Lowenthal	Y	Y	Y	Y	N	N
48 **Rohrabacher**	Y	Y	Y	N	Y	Y
49 **Issa**	Y	Y	Y	Y	Y	?
50 **Hunter**	Y	Y	Y	Y	Y	Y
51 Vargas	Y	Y	Y	Y	N	N
52 Peters	Y	Y	Y	Y	N	N
53 Davis	Y	Y	Y	Y	N	N
COLORADO						
1 DeGette	Y	Y	Y	Y	N	N
2 Polis	Y	Y	Y	Y	N	N
3 **Tipton**	Y	Y	Y	Y	Y	Y
4 **Buck**	Y	Y	N	Y	N	Y
5 **Lamborn**	Y	Y	?	?	Y	Y
6 **Coffman**	Y	Y	Y	Y	Y	Y
7 Perlmutter	Y	Y	Y	Y	N	N
CONNECTICUT						
1 Larson	Y	Y	Y	Y	N	N
2 Courtney	Y	Y	Y	Y	N	N
3 DeLauro	?	?	Y	Y	N	N
4 Himes	Y	Y	Y	Y	N	N
5 Esty	Y	Y	Y	Y	N	N
DELAWARE						
AL Blunt Rochester	Y	Y	Y	Y	N	N
FLORIDA						
1 **Gaetz**	Y	Y	Y	Y	Y	Y
2 **Dunn**	?	?	?	?	Y	Y
3 **Yoho**	Y	Y	?	?	Y	Y
4 **Rutherford**	Y	Y	Y	Y	Y	Y
5 Lawson	Y	Y	Y	Y	N	N
6 **DeSantis**	Y	Y	Y	Y	Y	Y
7 Murphy	Y	Y	Y	Y	N	N
8 **Posey**	Y	Y	+	+	Y	Y
9 Soto	Y	Y	Y	Y	N	N
10 Demings	Y	Y	Y	Y	N	N
11 **Webster**	Y	Y	Y	Y	Y	Y
12 **Bilirakis**	Y	Y	Y	Y	Y	Y
13 Crist	Y	Y	Y	Y	N	N
14 Castor	Y	?	Y	Y	N	N
15 **Ross**	Y	Y	Y	Y	Y	Y
16 **Buchanan**	Y	Y	Y	Y	Y	Y
17 **Rooney, T.**	?	?	?	?	?	?
18 **Mast**	Y	Y	Y	Y	Y	Y
19 **Rooney, F.**	Y	Y	Y	Y	Y	Y
20 Hastings	Y	Y	Y	Y	N	N
21 Frankel	Y	Y	Y	Y	N	N
22 Deutch	Y	Y	Y	Y	N	N
23 Wasserman Schultz	Y	Y	Y	Y	N	N
24 Wilson	Y	Y	Y	Y	N	N
25 **Diaz-Balart**	Y	Y	Y	Y	Y	Y
26 **Curbelo**	Y	Y	Y	Y	Y	Y
27 **Ros-Lehtinen**	Y	Y	Y	Y	Y	Y
GEORGIA						
1 **Carter**	Y	Y	Y	Y	Y	Y
2 Bishop	Y	Y	Y	Y	N	N
3 **Ferguson**	Y	Y	Y	Y	Y	Y
4 Johnson	Y	Y	Y	Y	N	N
5 Lewis	Y	Y	Y	Y	?	?
6 **Handel**	Y	Y	Y	Y	Y	Y
7 **Woodall**	Y	Y	Y	Y	Y	Y
8 **Scott, A.**	Y	Y	Y	Y	Y	Y
9 **Collins**	Y	Y	Y	Y	Y	Y
10 **Hice**	Y	Y	Y	Y	Y	Y
11 **Loudermilk**	Y	Y	Y	Y	Y	Y
12 **Allen**	Y	Y	Y	Y	Y	Y
13 Scott, D.	Y	Y	Y	Y	N	N
14 **Graves**	Y	Y	Y	Y	Y	Y
HAWAII						
1 Hanabusa	Y	Y	Y	Y	N	N
2 Gabbard	Y	Y	Y	Y	N	N
IDAHO						
1 **Labrador**	Y	Y	?	?	?	?
2 **Simpson**	?	?	Y	Y	Y	Y
ILLINOIS						
1 Rush	Y	Y	Y	Y	N	N
2 Kelly	Y	Y	Y	Y	N	N
3 Lipinski	Y	Y	Y	Y	N	N
4 Gutierrez	Y	Y	+	+	N	N
5 Quigley	Y	Y	Y	Y	N	N
6 **Roskam**	Y	Y	Y	Y	Y	Y
7 Davis, D.	Y	Y	Y	Y	N	N
8 Krishnamoorthi	Y	Y	Y	Y	N	N
9 Schakowsky	Y	Y	Y	Y	N	N
10 Schneider	Y	Y	Y	Y	N	N
11 Foster	Y	Y	Y	Y	N	N
12 **Bost**	Y	Y	Y	Y	Y	Y
13 **Davis, R.**	Y	Y	Y	Y	Y	Y

KEY   **Republicans**   Democrats   *Independents*

Y	Voted for (yea)	X	Paired against
#	Paired for	–	Announced against
+	Announced for	P	Voted "present"
N	Voted against (nay)		
C	Voted "present" to avoid possible conflict of interest		
?	Did not vote or otherwise make a position known		

	146	147	148	149	150	151
14 **Hultgren**	Y	Y	Y	Y	Y	Y
15 **Shimkus**	Y	Y	Y	Y	Y	Y
16 **Kinzinger**	Y	Y	Y	Y	Y	Y
17 Bustos	Y	Y	Y	Y	N	N
18 **LaHood**	Y	Y	Y	Y	Y	Y
INDIANA						
1 Visclosky	Y	Y	Y	Y	N	N
2 **Walorski**	Y	Y	Y	Y	Y	Y
3 **Banks**	Y	Y	Y	Y	Y	Y
4 **Rokita**	Y	Y	Y	Y	Y	Y
5 **Brooks**	Y	Y	Y	Y	Y	Y
6 **Messer**	Y	Y	?	?	Y	Y
7 Carson	Y	Y	Y	Y	N	N
8 **Bucshon**	Y	Y	Y	Y	Y	Y
9 **Hollingsworth**	Y	Y	Y	Y	Y	Y
IOWA						
1 **Blum**	Y	Y	Y	Y	Y	Y
2 Loebsack	Y	Y	Y	Y	N	N
3 **Young**	Y	Y	Y	Y	Y	Y
4 **King**	Y	Y	Y	Y	Y	Y
KANSAS						
1 **Marshall**	Y	Y	Y	Y	Y	Y
2 **Jenkins**	Y	Y	Y	Y	Y	Y
3 **Yoder**	Y	Y	Y	Y	Y	Y
4 **Estes**	Y	Y	Y	Y	Y	Y
KENTUCKY						
1 **Comer**	Y	Y	Y	Y	Y	Y
2 **Guthrie**	Y	Y	Y	Y	Y	Y
3 Yarmuth	Y	Y	Y	Y	N	N
4 **Massie**	Y	N	Y	N	Y	Y
5 **Rogers**	Y	Y	Y	Y	Y	Y
6 **Barr**	Y	Y	Y	Y	Y	Y
LOUISIANA						
1 **Scalise**	+	+	+	+	+	+
2 Richmond	Y	Y	Y	Y	N	N
3 **Higgins**	Y	Y	Y	Y	Y	Y
4 **Johnson**	Y	Y	?	?	Y	Y
5 **Abraham**	Y	Y	Y	Y	Y	Y
6 **Graves**	Y	Y	Y	Y	Y	Y
MAINE						
1 Pingree	Y	Y	Y	Y	N	N
2 **Poliquin**	Y	Y	Y	Y	Y	Y
MARYLAND						
1 **Harris**	Y	Y	Y	Y	Y	Y
2 Ruppersberger	Y	Y	Y	Y	N	N
3 Sarbanes	Y	Y	Y	Y	N	N
4 Brown	Y	Y	Y	Y	N	N
5 Hoyer	Y	Y	Y	Y	N	N
6 Delaney	Y	Y	Y	Y	N	N
7 Cummings	Y	Y	?	?	N	N
8 Raskin	Y	Y	Y	Y	N	N
MASSACHUSETTS						
1 Neal	Y	Y	Y	Y	N	N
2 McGovern	Y	Y	Y	Y	N	N
3 Tsongas	Y	Y	Y	Y	N	N
4 Kennedy	Y	Y	Y	Y	N	N
5 Clark	Y	Y	Y	Y	N	N
6 Moulton	Y	Y	Y	Y	N	N
7 Capuano	Y	Y	Y	Y	?	?
8 Lynch	Y	Y	Y	?	N	N
9 Keating	?	?	Y	Y	N	N
MICHIGAN						
1 **Bergman**	Y	Y	Y	Y	Y	Y
2 **Huizenga**	Y	Y	Y	Y	Y	Y
3 *Amash*	Y	N	N	N	Y	Y
4 **Moolenaar**	Y	Y	Y	Y	Y	Y
5 Kildee	Y	Y	Y	Y	N	N
6 **Upton**	Y	Y	Y	Y	Y	Y
7 **Walberg**	Y	Y	Y	Y	Y	Y
8 **Bishop**	Y	Y	Y	Y	Y	Y
9 Levin	Y	Y	Y	Y	N	N
10 **Mitchell**	Y	Y	Y	Y	Y	Y
11 **Trott**	Y	Y	Y	Y	Y	Y
12 Dingell	Y	Y	Y	Y	N	N
14 Lawrence	Y	Y	Y	Y	N	N
MINNESOTA						
1 Walz	Y	?	Y	Y	?	?
2 **Lewis**	Y	Y	Y	Y	Y	Y
3 **Paulsen**	Y	Y	Y	Y	Y	Y
4 McCollum	Y	Y	Y	Y	N	N

	146	147	148	149	150	151
5 Ellison	Y	Y	Y	Y	N	N
6 **Emmer**	Y	Y	Y	Y	Y	Y
7 Peterson	Y	Y	Y	Y	N	N
8 Nolan	Y	Y	Y	Y	N	N
MISSISSIPPI						
1 **Kelly**	Y	Y	Y	Y	Y	Y
2 Thompson	Y	N	Y	Y	N	N
3 **Harper**	Y	Y	Y	Y	Y	Y
4 **Palazzo**	Y	Y	Y	Y	Y	Y
MISSOURI						
1 Clay	Y	Y	Y	Y	N	N
2 **Wagner**	Y	Y	Y	Y	Y	Y
3 **Luetkemeyer**	Y	Y	Y	Y	Y	Y
4 **Hartzler**	Y	Y	?	Y	Y	Y
5 Cleaver	Y	Y	Y	Y	N	N
6 **Graves**	Y	Y	Y	Y	Y	Y
7 **Long**	Y	Y	Y	Y	Y	Y
8 **Smith**	Y	Y	Y	Y	Y	Y
MONTANA						
AL **Gianforte**	Y	Y	Y	Y	Y	Y
NEBRASKA						
1 **Fortenberry**	Y	Y	Y	Y	Y	Y
2 **Bacon**	Y	Y	Y	Y	Y	Y
3 **Smith**	Y	Y	Y	Y	Y	Y
NEVADA						
1 Titus	Y	Y	Y	Y	N	N
2 **Amodei**	?	?	Y	Y	Y	Y
3 Rosen	Y	Y	Y	Y	N	N
4 Kihuen	Y	Y	Y	Y	N	N
NEW HAMPSHIRE						
1 Shea-Porter	Y	Y	Y	Y	N	N
2 Kuster	Y	Y	+	+	–	–
NEW JERSEY						
1 Norcross	Y	Y	Y	Y	N	N
2 **LoBiondo**	Y	Y	Y	Y	Y	Y
3 **MacArthur**	Y	Y	Y	Y	Y	Y
4 **Smith**	Y	Y	Y	Y	Y	Y
5 Gottheimer	Y	Y	Y	Y	N	N
6 Pallone	Y	Y	Y	Y	N	N
7 **Lance**	Y	Y	Y	Y	Y	Y
8 Sires	Y	Y	Y	Y	N	N
9 Pascrell	Y	Y	Y	Y	N	N
10 Payne	Y	Y	Y	Y	N	N
11 **Frelinghuysen**	Y	Y	Y	Y	Y	Y
12 Watson Coleman	Y	Y	Y	Y	N	N
NEW MEXICO						
1 Lujan Grisham	Y	Y	Y	Y	N	N
2 **Pearce**	Y	Y	Y	Y	Y	Y
3 Luján	Y	Y	Y	Y	N	N
NEW YORK						
1 **Zeldin**	Y	Y	Y	Y	Y	Y
2 **King**	Y	Y	Y	Y	Y	Y
3 Suozzi	Y	Y	Y	Y	N	N
4 Rice	Y	Y	Y	Y	N	N
5 Meeks	Y	Y	Y	Y	N	N
6 Meng	Y	Y	?	?	N	N
7 Velázquez	Y	Y	Y	Y	N	N
8 Jeffries	Y	Y	Y	Y	N	N
9 Clarke	Y	Y	Y	Y	N	N
10 Nadler	Y	Y	Y	Y	N	N
11 **Donovan**	Y	Y	Y	Y	Y	Y
12 Maloney, C.	Y	Y	Y	Y	N	N
13 Espaillat	Y	Y	Y	Y	N	N
14 Crowley	Y	Y	Y	Y	N	N
15 Serrano	Y	Y	Y	Y	N	N
16 Engel	Y	Y	?	?	N	N
17 Lowey	Y	Y	Y	Y	N	N
18 Maloney, S.P.	Y	Y	Y	Y	N	N
19 **Faso**	Y	Y	Y	Y	Y	Y
20 Tonko	Y	Y	Y	Y	N	N
21 **Stefanik**	Y	Y	Y	Y	Y	Y
22 **Tenney**	Y	Y	Y	Y	Y	Y
23 **Reed**	Y	Y	Y	Y	Y	Y
24 **Katko**	Y	Y	Y	Y	Y	Y
25 **Vacant**						
26 Higgins	Y	Y	Y	Y	N	N
27 **Collins**	Y	Y	Y	Y	Y	Y
NORTH CAROLINA						
1 Butterfield	Y	Y	?	?	N	N
2 **Holding**	Y	Y	Y	Y	Y	Y
3 **Jones**	Y	Y	Y	N	N	Y
4 Price	Y	Y	Y	Y	N	N

	146	147	148	149	150	151
5 **Foxx**	Y	Y	Y	N	Y	Y
6 **Walker**	Y	?	Y	Y	Y	Y
7 **Rouzer**	Y	Y	Y	Y	Y	Y
8 **Hudson**	Y	Y	Y	Y	Y	Y
9 **Pittenger**	Y	Y	Y	Y	Y	Y
9 **Vacant**						
10 **McHenry**	Y	Y	Y	Y	Y	Y
11 **Meadows**	Y	Y	Y	Y	Y	Y
12 Adams	Y	Y	Y	Y	N	N
13 **Budd**	Y	Y	Y	Y	Y	Y
NORTH DAKOTA						
AL **Cramer**	Y	Y	Y	Y	Y	Y
OHIO						
1 **Chabot**	Y	Y	?	?	Y	Y
2 **Wenstrup**	Y	Y	Y	Y	Y	Y
3 Beatty	Y	Y	Y	Y	N	N
4 **Jordan**	Y	Y	Y	Y	Y	Y
5 **Latta**	Y	Y	Y	Y	Y	Y
6 **Johnson**	Y	Y	Y	Y	Y	Y
7 **Gibbs**	Y	Y	Y	Y	Y	Y
8 **Davidson**	Y	Y	Y	Y	Y	Y
9 Kaptur	Y	Y	Y	Y	N	N
10 **Turner**	Y	Y	Y	Y	Y	Y
11 Fudge	Y	Y	Y	Y	N	N
12 **Vacant**						
13 Ryan	Y	Y	Y	Y	N	N
14 **Joyce**	Y	Y	Y	Y	Y	Y
15 **Stivers**	Y	Y	Y	Y	Y	Y
16 **Renacci**	Y	Y	Y	Y	Y	Y
OKLAHOMA						
2 **Mullin**	Y	Y	Y	Y	Y	Y
3 **Lucas**	Y	Y	Y	Y	Y	Y
4 **Cole**	Y	Y	Y	Y	Y	Y
5 **Russell**	Y	Y	Y	Y	Y	Y
OREGON						
1 Bonamici	Y	Y	Y	Y	N	N
2 **Walden**	Y	Y	Y	Y	Y	Y
3 Blumenauer	Y	Y	Y	Y	N	N
4 DeFazio	Y	Y	Y	Y	N	N
5 Schrader	Y	Y	Y	Y	N	N
PENNSYLVANIA						
1 Brady	Y	Y	?	?	N	N
2 Evans	Y	Y	Y	Y	N	N
3 **Kelly**	Y	Y	Y	Y	Y	Y
4 **Perry**	Y	Y	Y	Y	Y	Y
5 **Thompson**	Y	Y	Y	Y	Y	Y
6 **Costello**	Y	Y	Y	Y	Y	Y
7 **Meehan**	Y	Y	Y	Y	Y	Y
8 **Fitzpatrick**	Y	Y	Y	Y	Y	Y
9 **Shuster**	Y	Y	Y	Y	Y	Y
10 **Marino**	Y	Y	Y	Y	Y	Y
11 **Barletta**	Y	Y	Y	Y	Y	Y
12 **Rothfus**	Y	Y	Y	Y	Y	Y
13 Boyle	Y	Y	Y	Y	N	N
14 Doyle	Y	Y	Y	Y	N	N
15 **Dent**	Y	Y	Y	Y	Y	Y
16 **Smucker**	Y	Y	Y	Y	Y	Y
17 Cartwright	?	?	Y	Y	N	N
18 Lamb	Y	Y	Y	Y	N	Y
RHODE ISLAND						
1 Cicilline	Y	Y	Y	Y	N	N
2 Langevin	Y	Y	Y	Y	N	N
SOUTH CAROLINA						
1 **Sanford**	Y	Y	Y	N	Y	Y
2 **Wilson**	Y	Y	Y	Y	Y	Y
3 **Duncan**	Y	Y	Y	Y	Y	Y
4 **Gowdy**	Y	?	?	?	?	?
5 **Norman**	Y	Y	Y	N	Y	Y
6 Clyburn	Y	Y	Y	Y	N	N
7 **Rice**	Y	Y	Y	N	Y	Y
SOUTH DAKOTA						
AL **Noem**	Y	Y	?	?	?	?
TENNESSEE						
1 **Roe**	Y	Y	Y	Y	Y	Y
2 **Duncan**	Y	Y	Y	Y	Y	Y
3 **Fleischmann**	Y	Y	Y	Y	Y	Y
4 **DesJarlais**	Y	?	Y	Y	Y	Y
5 Cooper	Y	Y	Y	Y	N	N
6 **Black**	?	?	?	?	?	?
7 **Blackburn**	Y	Y	?	?	Y	Y
8 **Kustoff**	Y	Y	Y	Y	Y	Y
9 Cohen	Y	Y	Y	Y	N	N

	146	147	148	149	150	151
TEXAS						
1 **Gohmert**	Y	Y	N	N	Y	Y
2 **Poe**	Y	?	Y	Y	Y	Y
3 **Johnson, S.**	Y	Y	Y	Y	Y	Y
4 **Ratcliffe**	Y	Y	?	?	Y	Y
5 **Hensarling**	Y	Y	Y	Y	Y	Y
6 **Barton**	Y	Y	Y	Y	Y	Y
7 **Culberson**	Y	Y	Y	Y	Y	Y
8 **Brady**	Y	Y	Y	Y	Y	Y
9 Green, A.	Y	Y	Y	Y	N	N
10 **McCaul**	Y	Y	Y	Y	Y	Y
11 **Conaway**	Y	Y	Y	Y	Y	Y
12 **Granger**	Y	Y	Y	Y	Y	Y
13 **Thornberry**	Y	Y	Y	Y	Y	Y
14 **Weber**	Y	Y	Y	Y	Y	Y
15 Gonzalez	Y	Y	Y	Y	N	N
16 O'Rourke	Y	Y	Y	Y	N	N
17 **Flores**	Y	Y	Y	Y	Y	Y
18 Jackson Lee	Y	Y	Y	Y	N	N
19 **Arrington**	Y	Y	Y	Y	Y	Y
20 Castro	Y	Y	Y	Y	N	N
21 **Smith**	Y	Y	Y	Y	Y	Y
22 **Olson**	Y	Y	Y	Y	Y	Y
23 **Hurd**	Y	Y	Y	Y	Y	Y
24 **Marchant**	Y	?	Y	Y	Y	Y
25 **Williams**	Y	Y	Y	Y	Y	Y
26 **Burgess**	Y	Y	Y	Y	Y	Y
28 Cuellar	Y	Y	Y	Y	N	N
29 Green, G.	Y	Y	Y	Y	N	N
30 Johnson, E.B.	Y	Y	Y	Y	N	N
31 **Carter**	Y	Y	Y	Y	Y	Y
32 **Sessions**	Y	Y	Y	Y	Y	Y
33 Veasey	Y	Y	Y	Y	N	N
34 Vela	Y	Y	Y	Y	N	N
35 Doggett	Y	Y	Y	Y	N	N
36 **Babin**	Y	Y	Y	Y	Y	Y
UTAH						
1 **Bishop**	Y	Y	Y	Y	Y	Y
2 **Stewart**	Y	Y	Y	Y	Y	Y
3 **Curtis**	Y	Y	Y	Y	Y	Y
4 **Love**	Y	Y	Y	Y	Y	Y
VERMONT						
AL Welch	Y	Y	Y	Y	N	N
VIRGINIA						
1 **Wittman**	Y	Y	Y	Y	Y	Y
2 **Taylor**	Y	Y	Y	Y	Y	Y
3 Scott	Y	Y	Y	Y	N	N
4 McEachin	Y	Y	Y	Y	N	N
5 **Garrett**	Y	Y	N	N	Y	Y
6 **Goodlatte**	Y	Y	Y	Y	Y	Y
7 **Brat**	Y	Y	Y	Y	Y	Y
8 Beyer	Y	Y	Y	Y	N	N
9 **Griffith**	Y	Y	Y	N	Y	Y
10 **Comstock**	+	+	+	+	Y	Y
11 Connolly	Y	Y	Y	Y	N	N
WASHINGTON						
1 DelBene	Y	Y	Y	Y	N	N
2 Larsen	Y	Y	Y	Y	N	N
3 **Herrera Beutler**	Y	Y	Y	Y	Y	Y
4 **Newhouse**	Y	Y	Y	Y	Y	Y
5 **McMorris Rodgers**	Y	Y	Y	Y	Y	Y
6 Kilmer	Y	Y	Y	Y	N	N
7 Jayapal	Y	Y	Y	Y	N	N
8 **Reichert**	Y	Y	Y	Y	Y	Y
9 Smith	Y	Y	Y	Y	N	N
10 Heck	Y	Y	Y	Y	N	N
WEST VIRGINIA						
1 **McKinley**	Y	Y	Y	Y	Y	Y
2 **Mooney**	Y	Y	Y	Y	Y	Y
3 **Jenkins**	Y	Y	+	+	?	?
WISCONSIN						
1 **Ryan**						
2 Pocan	Y	Y	Y	Y	N	N
3 Kind	Y	Y	Y	Y	N	N
4 Moore	Y	Y	Y	Y	N	N
5 **Sensenbrenner**	Y	Y	Y	Y	Y	Y
6 **Grothman**	Y	Y	Y	Y	?	?
7 **Duffy**	Y	Y	Y	Y	Y	Y
8 **Gallagher**	Y	Y	Y	Y	Y	Y
WYOMING						
AL **Cheney**	Y	Y	Y	Y	Y	Y

VOTE NUMBER

152. HR3144. RIVER POWER SYSTEM MANAGEMENT/RECOMMIT. Jayapal, D-Wash., motion to recommit the bill to the House Natural Resources Committee with instructions to report it back immediately with an amendment that would prohibit any of the bill's provisions from preventing the sale of power generated by the Federal Columbia River Power System at the lowest possible rate. Motion rejected 190-226: R 2-225; D 188-1. April 25, 2018.

153. HR3144. RIVER POWER SYSTEM MANAGEMENT/PASSAGE. Passage of the bill that would require the Federal Columbia River Power System to be operated under specifications that allow for lower water flow until Sept. 30, 2022, or until the power system is issued a final environmental impact statement. The power system would be allowed to operate under different specifications if it would be necessary for public safety or grid reliability. Passed 225-189: R 217-8; D 8-181. April 25, 2018.

154. HR5447. MUSIC LICENSING/PASSAGE. Goodlatte, R-Va., motion to suspend the rules and pass the bill that would create a licensing collective for music streaming and downloads, which would grant music works copyright owners blanket licenses for streaming and download services. It would allow pre-1972 sound recordings to be licensed under the same system as other recordings. It would also allow streaming companies to receive retroactive protection from statutory damages for potential copyright infringement prior to Jan. 1, 2018. Motion agreed to 415-0: R 227-0; D 188-0. April 25, 2018.

155. HR4. FAA REAUTHORIZATION/LITHIUM BATTERIES. DeFazio, D-Ore., amendment that would remove a prohibition on the Department of Transportation instituting regulations more stringent than the international standard on the transportation of lithium metal and lithium ion batteries in non-passenger-carrying aircraft. Rejected in Committee of the Whole 192-223: R 10-219; D 182-4. April 26, 2018.

156. HR4. FAA REAUTHORIZATION/OCEAN-TO-LAND ALTITUDES. Rohrabacher, R-Calif., amendment that would require the Federal Aviation Administration to ensure that all aircraft transitioning from flight over ocean to flight over land fly at a safe altitude. Rejected in Committee of the Whole 37-375: R 27-201; D 10-174. April 26, 2018.

157. HR4. FAA REAUTHORIZATION/PREVAILING WAGE RATE REQUIREMENTS. King, R-Iowa, amendment that would prohibit any funds authorized by the bill to be used to implement or enforce the prevailing wage rate requirements established by the Davis-Bacon Act. Rejected in Committee of the Whole 172-243: R 172-57; D 0-186. April 26, 2018.

	152	153	154	155	156	157
ALABAMA						
1 Byrne	N	Y	Y	N	N	Y
2 Roby	N	Y	Y	N	N	Y
3 Rogers	N	Y	Y	N	N	Y
4 Aderholt	N	Y	Y	N	Y	Y
5 Brooks	N	Y	Y	N	N	Y
6 Palmer	N	Y	Y	N	N	Y
7 Sewell	+	–	+	+	–	–
ALASKA						
AL Young	N	Y	Y	N	N	N
ARIZONA						
1 O'Halleran	Y	N	Y	Y	N	N
2 McSally	N	Y	Y	N	N	Y
3 Grijalva	Y	N	Y	N	N	N
4 Gosar	N	Y	Y	N	N	Y
5 Biggs	N	Y	Y	N	N	Y
6 Schweikert	N	Y	Y	N	Y	Y
7 Gallego	Y	N	Y	N	N	N
9 Sinema	Y	N	Y	N	N	N
ARKANSAS						
1 Crawford	N	Y	Y	N	N	Y
2 Hill	N	Y	Y	N	N	Y
3 Womack	N	Y	Y	N	N	Y
4 Westerman	N	Y	Y	N	N	Y
CALIFORNIA						
1 LaMalfa	N	Y	Y	N	Y	Y
2 Huffman	Y	N	Y	Y	N	N
3 Garamendi	Y	N	Y	Y	N	N
4 McClintock	N	Y	Y	N	Y	Y
5 Thompson	Y	N	Y	Y	N	N
6 Matsui	Y	N	Y	Y	N	N
7 Bera	Y	N	Y	Y	N	N
8 Cook	N	Y	Y	N	N	N
9 McNerney	Y	N	Y	Y	N	N
10 Denham	N	Y	Y	N	N	N
11 DeSaulnier	Y	N	Y	Y	N	N
12 Pelosi	Y	N	Y	Y	N	N
13 Lee	Y	N	Y	Y	N	N
14 Speier	Y	N	Y	Y	N	N
15 Swalwell	Y	N	Y	Y	N	N
16 Costa	Y	Y	Y	Y	N	N
17 Khanna	Y	N	Y	Y	N	N
18 Eshoo	Y	N	Y	Y	N	N
19 Lofgren	Y	N	Y	+	–	–
20 Panetta	Y	N	Y	Y	N	N
21 Valadao	N	Y	Y	N	N	N
22 Nunes	N	Y	Y	N	N	Y
23 McCarthy	N	Y	Y	N	N	Y
24 Carbajal	Y	N	Y	Y	N	N
25 Knight	N	Y	Y	N	N	Y
26 Brownley	Y	N	Y	Y	N	N
27 Chu	Y	N	Y	Y	N	N
28 Schiff	Y	N	Y	Y	Y	N
29 Cardenas	?	?	?	Y	N	N
30 Sherman	Y	N	Y	Y	Y	N
31 Aguilar	Y	N	Y	Y	N	N
32 Napolitano	Y	N	Y	Y	N	N
33 Lieu	Y	N	Y	Y	N	N
34 Gomez	Y	N	Y	Y	N	N
35 Torres	Y	N	Y	Y	N	N
36 Ruiz	Y	N	Y	N	N	N
37 Bass	Y	N	Y	Y	Y	N
38 Sánchez, Linda	Y	N	Y	Y	N	N
39 Royce	N	Y	Y	N	Y	Y
40 Roybal-Allard	Y	N	Y	Y	N	N
41 Takano	Y	N	Y	Y	N	N
42 Calvert	N	Y	Y	N	Y	Y
43 Waters	Y	N	Y	Y	N	N
44 Barragan	Y	N	Y	Y	N	N
45 Walters	N	Y	Y	N	Y	Y
46 Correa	Y	Y	Y	Y	N	N
47 Lowenthal	Y	N	Y	Y	N	N
48 Rohrabacher	N	Y	Y	N	Y	Y
49 Issa	?	?	Y	N	N	Y
50 Hunter	N	Y	Y	N	Y	Y
51 Vargas	Y	N	Y	Y	N	N
52 Peters	Y	N	Y	N	N	N
53 Davis	Y	N	Y	Y	N	N

	152	153	154	155	156	157
COLORADO						
1 DeGette	Y	Y	Y	Y	N	N
2 Polis	Y	N	Y	N	N	N
3 Tipton	N	Y	Y	N	N	Y
4 Buck	N	Y	Y	N	N	Y
5 Lamborn	N	Y	Y	N	Y	Y
6 Coffman	N	Y	Y	N	N	Y
7 Perlmutter	Y	N	Y	Y	N	N
CONNECTICUT						
1 Larson	Y	N	Y	Y	N	N
2 Courtney	Y	N	Y	Y	N	N
3 DeLauro	Y	N	Y	Y	N	N
4 Himes	Y	N	Y	Y	N	N
5 Esty	Y	N	Y	Y	N	N
DELAWARE						
AL Blunt Rochester	Y	N	Y	Y	N	N
FLORIDA						
1 Gaetz	N	Y	Y	N	N	Y
2 Dunn	N	Y	Y	N	N	Y
3 Yoho	N	Y	Y	N	N	Y
4 Rutherford	N	Y	Y	N	N	Y
5 Lawson	Y	N	Y	N	N	N
6 DeSantis	N	Y	Y	N	N	Y
7 Murphy	Y	N	Y	Y	N	N
8 Posey	N	Y	Y	N	N	Y
9 Soto	Y	N	Y	N	N	N
10 Demings	Y	N	Y	Y	N	N
11 Webster	N	Y	Y	N	Y	Y
12 Bilirakis	N	Y	Y	N	N	Y
13 Crist	Y	N	Y	N	N	N
14 Castor	Y	N	Y	Y	N	N
15 Ross	N	Y	Y	N	N	Y
16 Buchanan	N	Y	Y	N	N	Y
17 Rooney, T.	N	Y	Y	N	Y	Y
18 Mast	N	Y	Y	N	N	Y
19 Rooney, F.	N	Y	Y	N	Y	Y
20 Hastings	Y	N	Y	Y	N	N
21 Frankel	Y	N	Y	Y	N	N
22 Deutch	Y	N	Y	Y	N	N
23 Wasserman Schultz	Y	N	Y	Y	N	N
24 Wilson	Y	N	Y	+	–	–
25 Diaz-Balart	N	Y	Y	N	N	N
26 Curbelo	N	N	Y	N	N	N
27 Ros-Lehtinen	N	N	Y	N	N	N
GEORGIA						
1 Carter	N	Y	Y	N	N	Y
2 Bishop	Y	Y	Y	Y	N	N
3 Ferguson	N	Y	Y	N	N	Y
4 Johnson	Y	N	Y	Y	N	N
5 Lewis	Y	N	Y	?	?	?
6 Handel	N	Y	Y	N	N	Y
7 Woodall	N	Y	Y	N	N	Y
8 Scott, A.	N	Y	Y	N	N	N
9 Collins	N	Y	Y	N	N	Y
10 Hice	N	Y	Y	N	N	Y
11 Loudermilk	N	?	Y	N	N	Y
12 Allen	N	Y	Y	N	N	Y
13 Scott, D.	Y	N	Y	N	N	N
14 Graves	N	Y	Y	N	N	Y
HAWAII						
1 Hanabusa	Y	N	Y	Y	N	N
2 Gabbard	Y	N	Y	Y	N	N
IDAHO						
1 Labrador	?	?	?	?	?	?
2 Simpson	N	Y	Y	N	N	Y
ILLINOIS						
1 Rush	Y	N	Y	Y	N	N
2 Kelly	Y	N	Y	Y	N	N
3 Lipinski	Y	N	Y	Y	N	N
4 Gutierrez	Y	N	?	Y	–	N
5 Quigley	Y	N	Y	Y	N	N
6 Roskam	N	Y	Y	N	N	N
7 Davis, D.	Y	N	Y	Y	N	N
8 Krishnamoorthi	Y	N	Y	Y	N	N
9 Schakowsky	Y	N	Y	Y	N	N
10 Schneider	Y	N	Y	Y	N	N
11 Foster	Y	N	Y	Y	N	N
12 Bost	N	Y	Y	N	N	N
13 Davis, R.	N	Y	Y	N	N	N

	152	153	154	155	156	157
14 **Hultgren**	N	Y	Y	N	Y	N
15 **Shimkus**	N	Y	Y	N	N	N
16 **Kinzinger**	N	Y	Y	N	N	N
17 Bustos	Y	N	Y	Y	N	N
18 **LaHood**	N	Y	Y	N	N	N
INDIANA						
1 Visclosky	Y	N	Y	Y	N	N
2 **Walorski**	N	Y	Y	N	N	Y
3 **Banks**	N	Y	Y	N	N	Y
4 **Rokita**	N	Y	Y	N	N	Y
5 **Brooks**	N	Y	Y	N	N	Y
6 **Messer**	N	Y	Y	N	N	Y
7 Carson	Y	N	Y	+	–	–
8 **Bucshon**	N	Y	Y	N	N	N
9 **Hollingsworth**	N	Y	Y	N	N	Y
IOWA						
1 **Blum**	N	Y	Y	N	N	Y
2 Loebsack	Y	N	Y	Y	N	N
3 **Young**	N	Y	Y	N	N	Y
4 **King**	N	Y	Y	N	N	Y
KANSAS						
1 **Marshall**	N	Y	Y	N	N	Y
2 **Jenkins**	N	Y	Y	N	N	Y
3 **Yoder**	N	Y	Y	N	N	Y
4 **Estes**	N	Y	+	N	N	Y
KENTUCKY						
1 **Comer**	N	Y	Y	N	N	Y
2 **Guthrie**	N	Y	Y	N	N	Y
3 Yarmuth	Y	N	Y	Y	N	N
4 **Massie**	N	Y	Y	Y	N	Y
5 **Rogers**	N	Y	Y	N	N	Y
6 **Barr**	N	Y	Y	N	N	Y
LOUISIANA						
1 **Scalise**	N	Y	Y	N	N	Y
2 Richmond	Y	N	Y	Y	N	N
3 **Higgins**	N	Y	Y	N	N	Y
4 **Johnson**	N	Y	Y	N	N	Y
5 **Abraham**	N	Y	Y	N	N	Y
6 **Graves**	N	Y	Y	N	N	Y
MAINE						
1 Pingree	Y	N	Y	Y	N	N
2 **Poliquin**	N	Y	Y	N	N	Y
MARYLAND						
1 **Harris**	N	Y	Y	N	Y	Y
2 Ruppersberger	Y	N	Y	Y	N	N
3 Sarbanes	Y	N	Y	Y	N	N
4 Brown	Y	N	Y	Y	N	N
5 Hoyer	Y	N	Y	Y	N	N
6 Delaney	Y	N	Y	Y	N	N
7 Cummings	Y	N	Y	Y	N	N
8 Raskin	Y	N	Y	Y	Y	N
MASSACHUSETTS						
1 Neal	Y	N	Y	Y	N	N
2 McGovern	Y	N	Y	Y	N	N
3 Tsongas	Y	N	Y	Y	N	N
4 Kennedy	Y	N	Y	Y	N	N
5 Clark	Y	N	Y	Y	N	N
6 Moulton	Y	N	Y	Y	N	N
7 Capuano	Y	N	Y	Y	N	N
8 Lynch	Y	N	Y	Y	Y	N
9 Keating	Y	N	Y	Y	N	N
MICHIGAN						
1 **Bergman**	N	Y	Y	N	N	Y
2 **Huizenga**	N	Y	Y	N	N	Y
3 *Amash*	N	N	Y	N	N	Y
4 **Moolenaar**	N	Y	Y	N	Y	Y
5 Kildee	Y	N	Y	Y	N	N
6 **Upton**	N	Y	Y	Y	N	N
7 **Walberg**	N	Y	Y	N	N	Y
8 **Bishop**	N	Y	Y	N	N	N
9 Levin	Y	N	Y	Y	N	N
10 **Mitchell**	N	Y	Y	N	N	Y
11 **Trott**	N	Y	Y	N	N	Y
12 Dingell	Y	N	Y	Y	N	N
14 Lawrence	Y	N	Y	Y	N	N
MINNESOTA						
1 Walz	Y	N	Y	Y	N	N
2 **Lewis**	N	Y	Y	N	N	N
3 **Paulsen**	N	Y	Y	N	N	Y
4 McCollum	Y	N	Y	Y	N	N

	152	153	154	155	156	157
5 Ellison	Y	N	Y	Y	N	N
6 **Emmer**	N	Y	Y	N	N	N
7 Peterson	Y	Y	Y	Y	Y	N
8 Nolan	Y	N	Y	Y	N	N
MISSISSIPPI						
1 **Kelly**	N	Y	Y	N	Y	Y
2 Thompson	Y	N	Y	Y	N	N
3 **Harper**	N	Y	Y	N	N	Y
4 **Palazzo**	N	Y	Y	N	N	Y
MISSOURI						
1 Clay	Y	N	Y	Y	N	N
2 **Wagner**	N	Y	Y	N	N	Y
3 **Luetkemeyer**	N	Y	Y	N	N	Y
4 **Hartzler**	N	Y	Y	N	N	Y
5 Cleaver	Y	N	Y	Y	N	N
6 **Graves**	N	Y	Y	N	N	N
7 **Long**	N	Y	Y	N	N	N
8 **Smith**	N	Y	Y	N	N	Y
MONTANA						
AL **Gianforte**	N	Y	Y	N	N	N
NEBRASKA						
1 **Fortenberry**	N	Y	Y	N	N	Y
2 **Bacon**	N	Y	Y	N	N	N
3 **Smith**	N	Y	Y	N	N	Y
NEVADA						
1 Titus	Y	N	Y	Y	N	N
2 **Amodei**	N	Y	Y	N	N	N
3 Rosen	Y	N	Y	Y	N	N
4 Kihuen	Y	N	Y	Y	N	N
NEW HAMPSHIRE						
1 Shea-Porter	Y	N	Y	Y	N	N
2 Kuster	+	–	+	?	–	–
NEW JERSEY						
1 Norcross	Y	N	Y	Y	N	N
2 **LoBiondo**	N	N	Y	Y	N	N
3 **MacArthur**	N	Y	Y	N	N	N
4 **Smith**	N	N	Y	Y	N	N
5 Gottheimer	Y	N	Y	Y	N	N
6 Pallone	Y	N	Y	Y	N	N
7 **Lance**	N	N	Y	N	N	N
8 Sires	?	?	?	?	?	?
9 Pascrell	Y	N	Y	Y	N	N
10 Payne	Y	N	Y	Y	N	N
11 **Frelinghuysen**	N	+	Y	N	N	Y
12 Watson Coleman	Y	N	Y	Y	N	N
NEW MEXICO						
1 Lujan Grisham	Y	N	Y	Y	N	N
2 **Pearce**	N	Y	Y	N	N	Y
3 Luján	Y	N	Y	Y	N	N
NEW YORK						
1 **Zeldin**	N	Y	Y	N	N	N
2 **King**	N	Y	Y	N	N	N
3 Suozzi	Y	N	Y	Y	N	N
4 Rice	Y	N	Y	Y	N	N
5 Meeks	Y	N	Y	Y	N	N
6 Meng	Y	N	Y	Y	N	N
7 Velázquez	Y	N	Y	Y	N	N
8 Jeffries	Y	N	Y	Y	N	N
9 Clarke	Y	N	Y	Y	N	N
10 Nadler	Y	N	Y	Y	N	N
11 **Donovan**	N	Y	Y	N	N	N
12 Maloney, C.	Y	N	Y	Y	N	N
13 Espaillat	Y	N	Y	Y	N	N
14 Crowley	Y	N	Y	Y	N	N
15 Serrano	Y	N	Y	Y	N	N
16 Engel	Y	N	Y	Y	N	N
17 Lowey	Y	N	Y	Y	N	N
18 Maloney, S.P.	Y	N	Y	Y	N	N
19 **Faso**	N	Y	Y	N	N	N
20 Tonko	Y	N	Y	Y	N	N
21 **Stefanik**	N	Y	Y	N	N	N
22 **Tenney**	N	Y	Y	N	N	N
23 **Reed**	N	Y	Y	N	N	N
24 **Katko**	N	Y	Y	N	N	N
25 **Vacant**						
26 Higgins	Y	N	Y	Y	Y	N
27 **Collins**	N	Y	Y	N	N	Y
NORTH CAROLINA						
1 Butterfield	Y	N	Y	Y	N	N
2 **Holding**	N	Y	Y	N	N	Y
3 **Jones**	Y	Y	Y	N	N	Y
4 Price	Y	N	Y	Y	N	N

	152	153	154	155	156	157
5 **Foxx**	N	Y	Y	N	N	Y
6 **Walker**	N	Y	Y	N	N	Y
7 **Rouzer**	N	Y	Y	N	N	Y
8 **Hudson**	N	Y	Y	N	N	Y
9 **Pittenger**	N	Y	Y	N	N	Y
9 **Vacant**						
10 **McHenry**	N	Y	Y	N	N	Y
11 **Meadows**	N	Y	Y	N	N	Y
12 Adams	Y	N	Y	Y	N	N
13 **Budd**	N	Y	Y	N	N	Y
NORTH DAKOTA						
AL **Cramer**	N	Y	Y	N	N	Y
OHIO						
1 **Chabot**	N	Y	Y	N	N	Y
2 **Wenstrup**	N	Y	Y	N	N	Y
3 Beatty	Y	N	Y	Y	N	N
4 **Jordan**	N	Y	Y	N	N	Y
5 **Latta**	N	Y	Y	N	N	Y
6 **Johnson**	N	Y	Y	N	N	N
7 **Gibbs**	N	Y	Y	N	N	Y
8 **Davidson**	N	Y	Y	N	Y	Y
9 Kaptur	Y	N	Y	Y	N	N
10 **Turner**	N	Y	Y	N	N	N
11 Fudge	Y	N	Y	Y	N	N
12 **Vacant**						
13 Ryan	Y	N	Y	Y	N	N
14 **Joyce**	N	Y	Y	Y	N	N
15 **Stivers**	N	Y	Y	N	Y	N
16 **Renacci**	?	?	?	N	N	N
OKLAHOMA						
1 **Vacant**						
2 **Mullin**	N	Y	Y	N	N	Y
3 **Lucas**	N	Y	Y	N	N	Y
4 **Cole**	N	Y	Y	N	N	Y
5 **Russell**	N	Y	Y	N	N	Y
OREGON						
1 Bonamici	Y	N	Y	Y	N	N
2 **Walden**	N	Y	Y	Y	N	N
3 Blumenauer	Y	N	Y	Y	N	N
4 DeFazio	Y	N	Y	Y	N	N
5 Schrader	N	Y	Y	Y	N	N
PENNSYLVANIA						
1 Brady	Y	N	Y	Y	N	N
2 Evans	Y	N	Y	Y	N	N
3 **Kelly**	N	Y	Y	N	N	N
4 **Perry**	N	Y	Y	N	N	Y
5 **Thompson**	N	Y	Y	N	N	Y
6 **Costello**	N	Y	Y	N	?	N
7 **Meehan**	N	Y	Y	N	N	N
8 **Fitzpatrick**	N	N	Y	Y	N	N
9 **Shuster**	N	Y	Y	N	N	N
10 **Marino**	N	Y	Y	N	N	N
11 **Barletta**	N	Y	Y	N	N	N
12 **Rothfus**	N	Y	Y	N	N	Y
13 Boyle	Y	N	Y	Y	N	N
14 Doyle	Y	N	Y	Y	N	N
15 **Dent**	N	Y	Y	N	N	Y
16 **Smucker**	N	Y	Y	N	N	Y
17 Cartwright	Y	N	Y	Y	N	N
18 Lamb	Y	N	Y	Y	N	N
RHODE ISLAND						
1 Cicilline	Y	N	Y	Y	?	N
2 Langevin	Y	N	Y	Y	N	N
SOUTH CAROLINA						
1 **Sanford**	N	N	Y	N	N	Y
2 **Wilson**	N	Y	Y	N	Y	Y
3 **Duncan**	N	Y	Y	N	Y	Y
4 **Gowdy**	?	?	?	?	?	?
5 **Norman**	N	Y	Y	N	N	Y
6 Clyburn	Y	N	Y	Y	N	N
7 **Rice**	N	Y	Y	N	N	Y
SOUTH DAKOTA						
AL **Noem**	?	?	?	?	?	?
TENNESSEE						
1 **Roe**	N	Y	Y	N	N	Y
2 **Duncan**	N	Y	Y	N	N	Y
3 **Fleischmann**	N	Y	Y	N	N	Y
4 **DesJarlais**	N	Y	Y	N	N	Y
5 Cooper	Y	N	Y	Y	N	N
6 **Black**	?	?	+	?	?	?
7 **Blackburn**	N	Y	Y	?	?	?
8 **Kustoff**	N	Y	Y	?	?	?
9 Cohen	Y	N	Y	N	N	N

	152	153	154	155	156	157
TEXAS						
1 **Gohmert**	Y	Y	Y	N	Y	Y
2 **Poe**	N	Y	Y	N	Y	Y
3 **Johnson, S.**	N	Y	Y	N	N	Y
4 **Ratcliffe**	N	Y	Y	N	N	Y
5 **Hensarling**	N	Y	Y	N	N	Y
6 **Barton**	N	Y	Y	N	N	Y
7 **Culberson**	N	Y	Y	N	N	Y
8 **Brady**	N	Y	Y	N	Y	Y
9 Green, A.	Y	N	Y	Y	N	N
10 **McCaul**	N	Y	Y	N	N	Y
11 **Conaway**	N	Y	Y	N	N	Y
12 **Granger**	N	Y	Y	N	N	Y
13 **Thornberry**	N	Y	Y	N	N	Y
14 **Weber**	N	Y	Y	N	N	Y
15 Gonzalez	Y	N	Y	Y	N	N
16 O'Rourke	Y	N	Y	Y	N	N
17 **Flores**	N	Y	Y	N	N	Y
18 Jackson Lee	Y	N	Y	Y	N	N
19 **Arrington**	N	Y	Y	N	N	Y
20 Castro	Y	N	Y	Y	N	N
21 **Smith**	N	Y	Y	N	N	Y
22 **Olson**	N	Y	Y	N	N	Y
23 **Hurd**	N	Y	Y	N	N	Y
24 **Marchant**	N	Y	Y	N	N	Y
25 **Williams**	N	Y	Y	N	N	Y
26 **Burgess**	N	Y	Y	Y	N	Y
28 Cuellar	Y	Y	Y	Y	N	N
29 Green, G.	Y	Y	Y	Y	N	N
30 Johnson, E.B.	Y	N	Y	Y	N	N
31 **Carter**	N	Y	Y	N	N	Y
32 **Sessions**	N	Y	Y	N	N	Y
33 Veasey	Y	N	Y	Y	N	N
34 Vela	Y	N	Y	Y	N	N
35 Doggett	Y	N	Y	Y	N	N
36 **Babin**	N	Y	Y	N	N	Y
UTAH						
1 **Bishop**	N	Y	Y	N	N	Y
2 **Stewart**	N	Y	Y	N	Y	N
3 **Curtis**	N	Y	Y	N	N	Y
4 **Love**	N	Y	Y	N	N	Y
VERMONT						
AL Welch	Y	N	Y	Y	N	N
VIRGINIA						
1 **Wittman**	N	Y	Y	N	N	Y
2 **Taylor**	N	Y	Y	N	Y	Y
3 Scott	Y	N	Y	Y	N	N
4 McEachin	Y	N	Y	Y	N	N
5 **Garrett**	N	Y	Y	N	Y	Y
6 **Goodlatte**	N	Y	Y	N	N	Y
7 **Brat**	N	Y	Y	N	N	Y
8 Beyer	Y	N	Y	Y	Y	N
9 **Griffith**	N	Y	Y	N	N	Y
10 **Comstock**	N	Y	Y	N	N	Y
11 Connolly	Y	N	Y	Y	N	N
WASHINGTON						
1 DelBene	Y	N	Y	Y	N	N
2 Larsen	Y	N	Y	Y	N	N
3 **Herrera Beutler**	N	Y	Y	N	N	Y
4 **Newhouse**	N	Y	Y	N	N	N
5 **McMorris Rodgers**	N	Y	Y	N	N	Y
6 Kilmer	Y	N	Y	Y	N	N
7 Jayapal	Y	N	Y	Y	N	N
8 **Reichert**	N	Y	Y	N	N	N
9 Smith	Y	N	Y	Y	N	N
10 Heck	Y	N	Y	Y	N	N
WEST VIRGINIA						
1 **McKinley**	N	Y	Y	Y	N	N
2 **Mooney**	N	Y	Y	N	N	Y
3 **Jenkins**	?	?	?	N	N	Y
WISCONSIN						
1 **Ryan**						
2 Pocan	Y	N	Y	Y	N	N
3 Kind	Y	N	Y	Y	N	N
4 Moore	Y	N	Y	Y	N	N
5 **Sensenbrenner**	N	Y	Y	N	N	Y
6 **Grothman**	?	?	?	N	N	Y
7 **Duffy**	N	Y	Y	N	N	Y
8 **Gallagher**	N	Y	Y	N	N	Y
WYOMING						
AL **Cheney**	N	Y	Y	N	N	Y

VOTE NUMBER

158. HR4. FAA REAUTHORIZATION/FLIGHT CANCELLATION REQUIREMENTS. Lipinski, D-Ill., amendment that would require the Transportation Department to issue a rule that would require an air carrier, in the event of a flight cancellation, misconnection or delay exceeding three hours, to seek alternative transportation for displaced passengers, including aboard another air carrier, and would require an air carrier to accept passengers of another air carrier that have been displaced following an event within an air carriers control. It would require the department to also issue a rule that would require air carriers adopt contingency plans for lengthy terminal delays at each airport where it operates, including essential needs, meal vouchers and lodging and transportation options for displaced passengers. Rejected in Committee of the Whole 92-323: R 13-216; D 79-107. April 26, 2018.

159. HR4. FAA REAUTHORIZATION/MOTOR CARRIER EMPLOYERS. Denham, R-Calif., amendment that would state that a local or state government may not enact a law that would prohibit motor carrier employees from working to the full extent they are allowed to work, and would prohibit the enactment of additional obligations on motor carriers. Adopted in Committee of the Whole 222-193: R 217-12; D 5-181. April 26, 2018.

160. HR4. FAA REAUTHORIZATION/AIRCRAFT NOISE MITIGATION. Lynch, D-Mass., amendment that would require the Federal Aviation Administration to work with air carriers to identify and facilitate opportunities for air carriers to retrofit aircraft with devices that mitigate noise, including vortex generators. Rejected in Committee of the Whole 187-227: R 7-222; D 180-5. April 26, 2018.

161. HR4744. IRAN SANCTIONS/PASSAGE. Royce, R-Calif., motion to suspend the rules and pass the bill that would impose sanctions on any Iranian individual that engages in politically-motivated harassment, abuse or extortion of a U.S. citizen or another Iranian individual. It would require the president to determine whether any senior officials within the Iranian government would qualify for such sanctions. Motion agreed to 410-2: R 224-2; D 186-0. April 26, 2018.

162. HR4. FAA REAUTHORIZATION/ESSENTIAL AIR SERVICE. McClintock, R-Calif., amendment that would eliminate the bill's authorization of funding for the essential air service program. Rejected in Committee of the Whole 113-293: R 109-115; D 4-178. April 27, 2018.

163. HR4. FAA REAUTHORIZATION/MOTOR CARRIER HIRING STANDARDS. Duncan, R-Tenn., amendment that would require an entity hiring a motor carrier verify that certain standards are met, including that the motor carrier has a certain amount of insurance and has not been issued an unsatisfactory safety fitness determination. Adopted in Committee of the Whole 212-191: R 210-13; D 2-178. April 27, 2018.

	158	159	160	161	162	163
ALABAMA						
1 Byrne	N	Y	N	Y	Y	Y
2 Roby	N	Y	N	Y	N	Y
3 Rogers	N	Y	N	Y	N	Y
4 Aderholt	N	Y	N	Y	N	Y
5 Brooks	N	Y	N	Y	Y	Y
6 Palmer	N	Y	N	Y	Y	Y
7 Sewell	–	–	+	+	–	–
ALASKA						
AL Young	N	Y	N	Y	?	?
ARIZONA						
1 O'Halleran	N	Y	Y	Y	N	N
2 McSally	N	Y	N	Y	Y	Y
3 Grijalva	Y	N	Y	N	N	N
4 Gosar	N	Y	N	Y	N	Y
5 Biggs	N	Y	N	Y	Y	Y
6 Schweikert	N	Y	N	Y	Y	Y
7 Gallego	N	N	Y	N	N	N
9 Sinema	N	N	N	Y	N	N
ARKANSAS						
1 Crawford	N	Y	N	Y	Y	Y
2 Hill	N	Y	N	Y	N	Y
3 Womack	N	Y	N	Y	N	Y
4 Westerman	N	Y	N	Y	N	Y
CALIFORNIA						
1 LaMalfa	N	Y	N	Y	N	Y
2 Huffman	Y	N	Y	N	Y	–
3 Garamendi	N	N	Y	Y	N	Y
4 McClintock	N	Y	Y	Y	Y	Y
5 Thompson	Y	N	Y	Y	N	N
6 Matsui	Y	N	Y	N	N	N
7 Bera	N	N	Y	Y	N	N
8 Cook	N	Y	N	Y	N	Y
9 McNerney	N	N	Y	Y	N	N
10 Denham	N	Y	N	Y	–	+
11 DeSaulnier	Y	N	Y	Y	N	N
12 Pelosi	N	N	Y	Y	N	N
13 Lee	N	N	Y	Y	N	N
14 Speier	Y	N	Y	Y	N	N
15 Swalwell	N	N	Y	Y	N	N
16 Costa	N	Y	Y	Y	N	N
17 Khanna	Y	N	Y	Y	N	N
18 Eshoo	Y	N	Y	Y	N	N
19 Lofgren	+	–	+	+	–	–
20 Panetta	N	N	Y	Y	N	N
21 Valadao	N	Y	N	Y	N	Y
22 Nunes	N	Y	N	Y	N	Y
23 McCarthy	N	Y	N	Y	N	Y
24 Carbajal	Y	N	Y	Y	N	N
25 Knight	N	Y	N	Y	N	Y
26 Brownley	N	N	Y	Y	N	N
27 Chu	Y	N	Y	Y	N	N
28 Schiff	Y	N	Y	Y	N	N
29 Cardenas	N	N	Y	Y	N	N
30 Sherman	Y	N	Y	Y	N	N
31 Aguilar	Y	N	Y	Y	N	N
32 Napolitano	Y	N	Y	Y	N	N
33 Lieu	Y	N	Y	Y	N	N
34 Gomez	N	N	Y	Y	N	N
35 Torres	N	N	Y	Y	N	N
36 Ruiz	Y	N	Y	Y	N	N
37 Bass	Y	N	Y	Y	N	N
38 Sánchez, Linda	N	N	Y	Y	–	–
39 Royce	N	Y	N	Y	Y	Y
40 Roybal-Allard	N	N	Y	Y	N	N
41 Takano	Y	N	Y	Y	N	N
42 Calvert	N	Y	N	Y	Y	Y
43 Waters	Y	N	Y	Y	N	N
44 Barragan	Y	N	Y	Y	N	N
45 Walters	N	Y	N	Y	Y	Y
46 Correa	N	N	N	Y	N	N
47 Lowenthal	Y	N	Y	Y	N	N
48 Rohrabacher	Y	Y	Y	Y	Y	Y
49 Issa	N	Y	N	Y	Y	Y
50 Hunter	Y	Y	N	Y	Y	Y
51 Vargas	N	N	Y	Y	N	N
52 Peters	Y	N	Y	Y	Y	N
53 Davis	Y	N	Y	Y	N	N

	158	159	160	161	162	163
COLORADO						
1 DeGette	N	N	Y	Y	N	N
2 Polis	Y	N	Y	Y	N	N
3 Tipton	N	Y	N	Y	N	N
4 Buck	N	Y	N	Y	Y	Y
5 Lamborn	N	Y	N	Y	Y	Y
6 Coffman	N	Y	N	Y	N	Y
7 Perlmutter	Y	N	Y	Y	N	N
CONNECTICUT						
1 Larson	N	N	Y	Y	N	N
2 Courtney	N	N	Y	Y	N	N
3 DeLauro	Y	N	Y	Y	N	N
4 Himes	N	N	Y	Y	N	N
5 Esty	N	N	Y	Y	N	N
DELAWARE						
AL Blunt Rochester	N	N	Y	Y	N	N
FLORIDA						
1 Gaetz	N	Y	N	Y	Y	Y
2 Dunn	N	Y	N	Y	Y	Y
3 Yoho	N	Y	N	Y	Y	Y
4 Rutherford	N	Y	N	Y	N	Y
5 Lawson	N	N	Y	Y	N	N
6 DeSantis	N	Y	N	Y	Y	Y
7 Murphy	N	N	Y	Y	N	N
8 Posey	Y	Y	N	Y	Y	Y
9 Soto	Y	N	Y	N	N	N
10 Demings	N	N	Y	Y	N	N
11 Webster	N	Y	N	Y	Y	Y
12 Bilirakis	N	Y	N	Y	N	Y
13 Crist	Y	N	Y	N	N	N
14 Castor	N	N	Y	Y	N	N
15 Ross	N	Y	N	Y	N	Y
16 Buchanan	N	Y	N	Y	N	Y
17 Rooney, T.	N	Y	N	Y	N	Y
18 Mast	N	Y	N	Y	N	Y
19 Rooney, F.	N	Y	N	Y	Y	Y
20 Hastings	N	N	Y	Y	N	N
21 Frankel	N	N	Y	Y	N	N
22 Deutch	Y	N	Y	Y	N	N
23 Wasserman Schultz	N	N	Y	Y	N	N
24 Wilson	–	–	+	?	–	+
25 Diaz-Balart	N	Y	N	Y	N	Y
26 Curbelo	N	Y	N	Y	N	Y
27 Ros-Lehtinen	N	Y	N	Y	N	Y
GEORGIA						
1 Carter	N	Y	N	Y	Y	Y
2 Bishop	N	N	Y	Y	N	N
3 Ferguson	N	Y	N	Y	N	Y
4 Johnson	N	N	Y	Y	N	N
5 Lewis	?	?	?	?	?	?
6 Handel	N	Y	N	Y	Y	Y
7 Woodall	N	Y	N	Y	Y	Y
8 Scott, A.	Y	Y	N	Y	N	Y
9 Collins	N	Y	N	Y	Y	Y
10 Hice	N	Y	N	Y	Y	Y
11 Loudermilk	N	Y	N	Y	Y	Y
12 Allen	N	Y	N	Y	Y	Y
13 Scott, D.	N	N	?	Y	N	N
14 Graves	N	Y	N	Y	Y	Y
HAWAII						
1 Hanabusa	N	N	Y	Y	N	N
2 Gabbard	Y	N	Y	?	N	N
IDAHO						
1 Labrador	?	?	?	?	?	?
2 Simpson	N	Y	N	Y	N	Y
ILLINOIS						
1 Rush	Y	N	Y	Y	N	N
2 Kelly	N	N	Y	Y	N	N
3 Lipinski	Y	N	N	Y	N	N
4 Gutierrez	Y	N	Y	Y	N	N
5 Quigley	N	N	Y	Y	N	N
6 Roskam	N	Y	N	Y	Y	Y
7 Davis, D.	Y	N	Y	Y	N	N
8 Krishnamoorthi	N	N	Y	Y	N	N
9 Schakowsky	Y	N	Y	Y	N	N
10 Schneider	Y	N	Y	Y	N	N
11 Foster	N	N	Y	Y	N	N
12 Bost	N	Y	N	Y	N	Y
13 Davis, R.	N	Y	N	Y	N	Y

KEY	**Republicans**	*Democrats*	*Independents*
Y Voted for (yea)	X Paired against		C Voted "present" to avoid possible conflict of interest
# Paired for	– Announced against		? Did not vote or otherwise make a position known
+ Announced for	P Voted "present"		
N Voted against (nay)			

	158	159	160	161	162	163
14 **Hultgren**	Y	Y	N	Y	Y	Y
15 **Shimkus**	N	Y	N	Y	N	Y
16 **Kinzinger**	Y	Y	N	Y	N	Y
17 Bustos	Y	N	Y	Y	N	N
18 **LaHood**	N	Y	N	Y	N	Y
INDIANA						
1 Visclosky	N	N	Y	Y	N	N
2 **Walorski**	N	Y	N	Y	Y	Y
3 **Banks**	N	Y	N	Y	Y	Y
4 **Rokita**	N	Y	N	Y	Y	Y
5 **Brooks**	N	Y	N	Y	N	Y
6 **Messer**	N	Y	N	Y	Y	Y
7 Carson	+	–	+	Y	N	N
8 **Bucshon**	N	Y	N	Y	N	Y
9 **Hollingsworth**	N	Y	N	Y	Y	Y
IOWA						
1 **Blum**	N	Y	N	Y	N	Y
2 Loebsack	Y	N	Y	Y	N	N
3 **Young**	N	Y	N	Y	N	Y
4 **King**	N	Y	N	Y	N	Y
KANSAS						
1 **Marshall**	N	Y	N	Y	N	Y
2 **Jenkins**	N	Y	N	Y	N	Y
3 **Yoder**	N	Y	N	Y	N	Y
4 **Estes**	N	Y	N	Y	N	Y
KENTUCKY						
1 **Comer**	N	Y	N	Y	N	Y
2 **Guthrie**	N	Y	N	Y	N	Y
3 Yarmuth	Y	N	Y	Y	N	N
4 **Massie**	N	Y	N	N	Y	N
5 **Rogers**	N	Y	N	Y	N	Y
6 **Barr**	N	Y	N	Y	N	Y
LOUISIANA						
1 **Scalise**	N	Y	N	Y	Y	Y
2 Richmond	N	N	Y	Y	N	N
3 **Higgins**	N	Y	N	Y	N	N
4 **Johnson**	N	Y	N	Y	N	Y
5 **Abraham**	N	Y	N	Y	Y	Y
6 **Graves**	N	Y	N	Y	Y	Y
MAINE						
1 Pingree	Y	N	Y	Y	N	N
2 **Poliquin**	N	Y	N	Y	N	Y
MARYLAND						
1 **Harris**	Y	Y	Y	Y	Y	Y
2 Ruppersberger	N	N	Y	Y	–	–
3 Sarbanes	N	N	Y	Y	N	N
4 Brown	N	N	Y	Y	N	N
5 Hoyer	N	N	Y	Y	N	N
6 Delaney	N	N	Y	Y	N	N
7 Cummings	N	N	Y	Y	N	N
8 Raskin	Y	N	Y	Y	N	N
MASSACHUSETTS						
1 Neal	Y	N	Y	Y	N	N
2 McGovern	Y	N	Y	Y	N	N
3 Tsongas	Y	N	Y	Y	N	N
4 Kennedy	Y	N	Y	Y	N	N
5 Clark	Y	N	Y	Y	N	N
6 Moulton	N	N	Y	Y	N	N
7 Capuano	Y	N	Y	Y	N	N
8 Lynch	Y	N	Y	Y	N	N
9 Keating	N	N	Y	Y	N	N
MICHIGAN						
1 **Bergman**	N	Y	N	Y	N	Y
2 **Huizenga**	N	Y	N	Y	Y	Y
3 *Amash*	N	Y	N	N	Y	N
4 **Moolenaar**	N	Y	N	Y	N	Y
5 Kildee	N	N	Y	Y	N	N
6 **Upton**	N	Y	N	Y	Y	Y
7 **Walberg**	N	Y	N	Y	Y	Y
8 **Bishop**	N	Y	N	Y	Y	Y
9 Levin	N	N	Y	Y	N	N
10 **Mitchell**	N	Y	N	Y	N	Y
11 **Trott**	N	Y	N	Y	Y	Y
12 Dingell	N	N	Y	Y	N	N
14 Lawrence	N	N	Y	Y	N	N
MINNESOTA						
1 Walz	Y	N	Y	Y	?	?
2 **Lewis**	N	Y	N	Y	Y	Y
3 **Paulsen**	N	Y	Y	Y	Y	Y
4 McCollum	Y	N	Y	Y	N	N

	158	159	160	161	162	163
5 Ellison	Y	N	Y	Y	N	N
6 **Emmer**	N	Y	N	Y	Y	Y
7 Peterson	Y	N	Y	Y	N	N
8 Nolan	Y	N	Y	Y	N	N
MISSISSIPPI						
1 **Kelly**	N	Y	N	Y	N	Y
2 Thompson	N	N	Y	Y	N	N
3 **Harper**	N	Y	N	Y	?	?
4 **Palazzo**	N	Y	N	Y	N	Y
MISSOURI						
1 Clay	N	N	Y	Y	N	N
2 **Wagner**	N	Y	N	Y	Y	Y
3 **Luetkemeyer**	N	Y	N	Y	N	Y
4 **Hartzler**	N	Y	N	Y	N	Y
5 Cleaver	Y	N	Y	Y	N	?
6 **Graves**	N	Y	N	Y	N	Y
7 **Long**	N	Y	N	Y	N	Y
8 **Smith**	N	Y	N	Y	Y	Y
MONTANA						
AL **Gianforte**	N	Y	N	Y	N	Y
NEBRASKA						
1 **Fortenberry**	Y	Y	N	?	N	Y
2 **Bacon**	N	Y	N	Y	N	Y
3 **Smith**	N	Y	N	Y	N	Y
NEVADA						
1 Titus	N	N	Y	Y	N	N
2 **Amodei**	N	Y	N	Y	N	Y
3 Rosen	N	N	Y	Y	N	N
4 Kihuen	Y	N	Y	Y	N	N
NEW HAMPSHIRE						
1 Shea-Porter	Y	N	Y	Y	N	N
2 Kuster	–	–	+	+	–	–
NEW JERSEY						
1 Norcross	N	N	Y	Y	N	N
2 **LoBiondo**	N	Y	N	Y	N	Y
3 **MacArthur**	N	N	N	Y	N	N
4 **Smith**	Y	N	N	Y	N	N
5 Gottheimer	N	N	Y	Y	N	N
6 Pallone	N	N	Y	Y	N	N
7 **Lance**	N	Y	Y	Y	N	Y
8 Sires	?	?	?	?	?	?
9 Pascrell	N	N	Y	Y	N	N
10 Payne	N	N	Y	Y	N	N
11 **Frelinghuysen**	N	Y	N	Y	N	Y
12 Watson Coleman	N	N	Y	Y	N	N
NEW MEXICO						
1 Lujan Grisham	N	N	Y	Y	N	N
2 **Pearce**	N	Y	N	Y	N	Y
3 Luján	Y	N	Y	Y	N	N
NEW YORK						
1 **Zeldin**	N	N	N	Y	Y	Y
2 **King**	N	N	N	Y	N	N
3 Suozzi	N	N	Y	Y	N	N
4 Rice	N	N	Y	Y	N	N
5 Meeks	N	N	Y	Y	N	N
6 Meng	N	N	Y	Y	N	N
7 Velázquez	N	N	Y	Y	N	N
8 Jeffries	N	N	Y	Y	N	N
9 Clarke	N	N	Y	Y	N	N
10 Nadler	Y	N	Y	Y	N	N
11 **Donovan**	N	N	N	Y	N	N
12 Maloney, C.	N	N	Y	Y	N	N
13 Espaillat	N	N	Y	Y	N	N
14 Crowley	N	N	Y	Y	N	N
15 Serrano	N	N	Y	Y	N	N
16 Engel	N	N	Y	Y	N	N
17 Lowey	N	N	Y	Y	N	N
18 Maloney, S.P.	N	N	N	Y	N	N
19 **Faso**	N	Y	N	Y	N	Y
20 Tonko	Y	N	Y	Y	N	N
21 **Stefanik**	N	Y	N	Y	N	Y
22 **Tenney**	N	Y	N	Y	N	Y
23 **Reed**	N	Y	N	Y	N	Y
24 **Katko**	N	N	N	Y	N	Y
25 **Vacant**						
26 Higgins	N	N	Y	Y	N	N
27 **Collins**	N	Y	N	Y	Y	Y
NORTH CAROLINA						
1 Butterfield	N	N	Y	Y	?	?
2 **Holding**	N	Y	N	Y	Y	Y
3 **Jones**	Y	N	N	Y	?	?
4 Price	N	N	Y	Y	N	N

	158	159	160	161	162	163
5 **Foxx**	N	Y	N	Y	Y	Y
6 **Walker**	N	Y	N	Y	Y	Y
7 **Rouzer**	N	Y	N	Y	N	Y
8 **Hudson**	N	Y	N	Y	Y	Y
9 **Pittenger**	N	Y	N	Y	Y	Y
9 **Vacant**						
10 **McHenry**	N	Y	N	Y	Y	Y
11 **Meadows**	N	Y	N	Y	N	Y
12 Adams	N	N	Y	Y	N	N
13 **Budd**	N	Y	N	Y	Y	Y
NORTH DAKOTA						
AL **Cramer**	N	Y	N	Y	N	Y
OHIO						
1 **Chabot**	N	Y	N	Y	Y	Y
2 **Wenstrup**	N	Y	Y	Y	Y	Y
3 Beatty	Y	N	Y	Y	N	N
4 **Jordan**	N	Y	N	Y	Y	Y
5 **Latta**	N	Y	N	Y	Y	Y
6 **Johnson**	N	Y	N	Y	N	Y
7 **Gibbs**	N	Y	N	Y	N	Y
8 **Davidson**	N	Y	N	Y	Y	Y
9 Kaptur	Y	N	Y	Y	N	N
10 **Turner**	N	Y	N	Y	N	Y
11 Fudge	N	N	Y	Y	N	N
12 **Vacant**						
13 Ryan	N	N	Y	Y	N	N
14 **Joyce**	N	Y	N	Y	N	N
15 **Stivers**	N	Y	N	Y	N	Y
16 **Renacci**	N	Y	N	Y	Y	N
OKLAHOMA						
1 **Vacant**						
2 **Mullin**	N	Y	N	Y	N	Y
3 **Lucas**	N	Y	N	Y	N	Y
4 **Cole**	N	Y	N	Y	N	Y
5 **Russell**	N	N	N	Y	Y	N
OREGON						
1 Bonamici	Y	N	Y	Y	N	N
2 **Walden**	N	Y	N	Y	N	Y
3 Blumenauer	N	N	Y	Y	N	N
4 DeFazio	N	N	Y	Y	N	N
5 Schrader	N	N	Y	Y	N	N
PENNSYLVANIA						
1 Brady	N	N	Y	Y	N	N
2 Evans	N	N	Y	Y	N	N
3 **Kelly**	N	Y	N	Y	N	Y
4 **Perry**	N	Y	N	Y	Y	Y
5 **Thompson**	N	Y	N	Y	N	Y
6 **Costello**	N	Y	N	Y	N	Y
7 **Meehan**	N	Y	N	Y	N	Y
8 **Fitzpatrick**	N	N	N	Y	N	N
9 **Shuster**	N	Y	N	Y	N	Y
10 **Marino**	N	Y	N	Y	N	Y
11 **Barletta**	N	Y	N	Y	N	Y
12 **Rothfus**	N	Y	N	Y	N	Y
13 Boyle	N	N	Y	Y	?	?
14 Doyle	N	N	Y	Y	N	N
15 **Dent**	N	Y	N	Y	N	Y
16 **Smucker**	N	Y	N	Y	N	Y
17 Cartwright	N	N	Y	Y	N	N
18 Lamb	N	N	Y	Y	N	N
RHODE ISLAND						
1 Cicilline	N	N	Y	Y	N	N
2 Langevin	N	N	Y	Y	N	N
SOUTH CAROLINA						
1 **Sanford**	N	Y	N	Y	Y	Y
2 **Wilson**	Y	Y	N	Y	Y	Y
3 **Duncan**	N	Y	N	Y	Y	Y
4 **Gowdy**	?	?	?	?	?	?
5 **Norman**	N	Y	N	Y	Y	Y
6 Clyburn	N	N	Y	Y	N	N
7 **Rice**	N	Y	N	Y	Y	N
SOUTH DAKOTA						
AL **Noem**	?	?	?	?	?	?
TENNESSEE						
1 **Roe**	N	Y	N	Y	Y	Y
2 **Duncan**	N	Y	N	Y	Y	Y
3 **Fleischmann**	N	Y	N	Y	N	Y
4 **DesJarlais**	N	N	N	Y	Y	Y
5 Cooper	Y	Y	N	Y	Y	N
6 **Black**	?	?	?	?	?	?
7 **Blackburn**	?	?	?	?	?	?
8 **Kustoff**	?	?	?	?	?	?
9 Cohen	N	N	Y	Y	N	N

	158	159	160	161	162	163
TEXAS						
1 **Gohmert**	Y	Y	N	Y	Y	Y
2 **Poe**	N	Y	N	Y	Y	Y
3 **Johnson, S.**	N	Y	N	Y	Y	Y
4 **Ratcliffe**	N	Y	N	Y	Y	Y
5 **Hensarling**	N	Y	N	Y	Y	Y
6 **Barton**	N	Y	N	Y	N	Y
7 **Culberson**	N	Y	N	Y	Y	Y
8 **Brady**	N	Y	N	Y	N	Y
9 Green, A.	Y	N	Y	Y	N	N
10 **McCaul**	N	Y	N	Y	N	Y
11 **Conaway**	N	Y	N	Y	Y	Y
12 **Granger**	N	Y	N	Y	N	Y
13 **Thornberry**	N	Y	N	Y	N	Y
14 **Weber**	N	Y	N	Y	Y	Y
15 Gonzalez	Y	N	Y	Y	N	N
16 O'Rourke	Y	N	Y	Y	N	N
17 **Flores**	N	Y	N	Y	Y	Y
18 Jackson Lee	Y	N	Y	Y	N	N
19 **Arrington**	N	Y	N	Y	Y	Y
20 Castro	Y	N	Y	Y	N	N
21 **Smith**	N	Y	N	Y	Y	Y
22 **Olson**	N	Y	N	Y	Y	Y
23 **Hurd**	N	Y	N	Y	N	Y
24 **Marchant**	N	Y	N	Y	N	?
25 **Williams**	N	Y	N	Y	Y	Y
26 **Burgess**	N	Y	N	Y	Y	Y
28 Cuellar	N	Y	Y	Y	N	Y
29 Green, G.	Y	N	Y	Y	N	N
30 Johnson, E.B.	N	N	Y	Y	N	N
31 **Carter**	N	Y	N	Y	N	Y
32 **Sessions**	N	Y	N	Y	Y	Y
33 Veasey	N	N	Y	Y	N	N
34 Vela	Y	N	Y	Y	N	N
35 Doggett	Y	N	Y	Y	N	N
36 **Babin**	N	Y	N	?	Y	Y
UTAH						
1 **Bishop**	N	Y	N	Y	N	Y
2 **Stewart**	N	Y	N	Y	Y	Y
3 **Curtis**	N	Y	N	Y	N	Y
4 **Love**	N	Y	N	Y	N	Y
VERMONT						
AL Welch	N	N	Y	Y	N	N
VIRGINIA						
1 **Wittman**	N	Y	N	Y	Y	Y
2 **Taylor**	N	Y	N	Y	N	Y
3 Scott	Y	N	Y	Y	N	N
4 McEachin	N	N	Y	Y	N	N
5 **Garrett**	N	Y	N	Y	Y	Y
6 **Goodlatte**	N	Y	Y	Y	Y	Y
7 **Brat**	N	Y	N	Y	Y	Y
8 Beyer	Y	N	Y	Y	N	N
9 **Griffith**	N	N	N	Y	Y	N
10 **Comstock**	N	Y	N	?	N	Y
11 Connolly	Y	N	Y	Y	N	N
WASHINGTON						
1 DelBene	N	N	Y	Y	N	N
2 Larsen	N	N	Y	Y	N	N
3 **Herrera Beutler**	Y	Y	N	Y	Y	Y
4 **Newhouse**	N	Y	N	Y	N	Y
5 **McMorris Rodgers**	N	Y	N	Y	Y	Y
6 Kilmer	N	N	Y	Y	N	N
7 Jayapal	Y	N	Y	Y	N	N
8 **Reichert**	N	Y	N	Y	N	Y
9 Smith	Y	N	Y	Y	N	N
10 Heck	N	N	Y	Y	N	N
WEST VIRGINIA						
1 **McKinley**	N	N	N	Y	N	Y
2 **Mooney**	N	Y	N	Y	N	Y
3 **Jenkins**	N	Y	N	Y	–	+
WISCONSIN						
1 **Ryan**						
2 Pocan	Y	N	Y	Y	N	N
3 Kind	Y	Y	Y	Y	N	N
4 Moore	Y	N	Y	Y	N	N
5 **Sensenbrenner**	N	Y	N	Y	Y	Y
6 **Grothman**	N	Y	N	Y	N	Y
7 **Duffy**	N	Y	N	Y	N	Y
8 **Gallagher**	N	Y	N	Y	Y	Y
WYOMING						
AL **Cheney**	N	Y	N	Y	N	Y

VOTE NUMBER

164. HR4. FAA REAUTHORIZATION/RECOMMIT. Velazquez, D-N.Y., motion to recommit the bill to the House Transportation and Infrastructure Committee with instructions to report it back immediately with an amendment that would require that direct federal assistance cover 100 percent of eligible costs in any state or U.S. territory impacted by Hurricanes Harvey, Irma and Maria, or the wildfires in California. Motion rejected 182-223: R 0-223; D 182-0. April 27, 2018.

165. HR4. FAA REAUTHORIZATION/PASSAGE. Passage of the bill that would reauthorize federal aviation programs through fiscal 2023. The measure would authorize $10.2 billion in fiscal 2018, which would gradually increase to $11.3 billion in fiscal 2023, for Federal Aviation Administration operations; $3.4 billion annually for the Aviation Trust Fund for the Airport Improvement Program; $2.9 billion in fiscal 2018, which would gradually increase to $3.3 billion in fiscal 2023, for facilities and equipment; and $181 million in fiscal 2018, which would gradually increase to $204 million in fiscal 2023, for research and development. It would extend for six years the authorization for unmanned aircraft test ranges. It would also ban e-cigarettes and talking on a cell phone during a passenger flight. It would prohibit airlines from involuntarily removing passengers from a plane after they have checked in and taken their seats. The bill would modify the Federal Emergency Management Agency's operations and procedures, including allowing a portion of funds appropriated for major disaster assistance to be used for hazard mitigation. It would require FEMA to give greater weight and consideration to areas suffering a severe impact from a disaster when making recommendations to the president regarding the declaration of a major disaster. Passed 393-13: R 217-7; D 176-6. April 27, 2018"

166. HRES856. HOUSE CHAPLAIN/MOTION TO TABLE. McCarthy, R-Calif., motion to table (kill) a resolution that would establish a House select committee to investigate the resignation of the Chaplain of the House of Representatives, Patrick J. Conroy. Motion agreed to 215-171: R 215-2; D 0-169. April 27, 2018.

167. HR4910. BURIAL RECEPTACLE PROVISION/PASSAGE. Roe, R-Tenn., motion to suspend the rules and pass the bill that would require the Interior Department to provide an outer burial receptacle for new graves in open cemeteries that are controlled by the National Park Service, and would require the Department to reimburse veterans' survivors who had purchased one on their own. Motion agreed to 388-0: R 218-0; D 170-0. May 7, 2018.

168. HR4335. MILITARY DEPENDENT BURIAL RIGHTS/PASSAGE. Roe, R-Tenn., motion to suspend the rules and pass the bill that would authorize the Veterans Affairs Department to provide spouses and children of member of the armed forces serving on active duty with headstones or markers when buried in a national cemetery. Motion agreed to 389-0: R 217-0; D 172-0. May 7, 2018.

169. HRES872. MERGER REGULATION ENFORCEMENT, GRANT REPORTING, AND DISAPPROVAL OF LOAN RULES/PREVIOUS QUESTION. Buck, R-Colo., motion to order the previous question (thus ending debate and possibility of amendment) on the rule (H Res 872) that would provide for consideration of the bill (HR 5645) that would synchronize antitrust standards between the Federal Trade Commission and the Justice Department; would provide for consideration of the bill (HR 2152) that would require certain Justice Department grantees to report on the use of funds they received, and would provide for consideration of a joint resolution (S J Res 57) that would disapprove of certain Consumer Financial Regulatory Commission rules related to indirect automotive loans. Motion agreed to 226-177: R 226-0; D 0-177. May 8, 2018.

	164	165	166	167	168	169
ALABAMA						
1 **Byrne**	N	Y	Y	Y	Y	Y
2 **Roby**	N	Y	Y	Y	Y	Y
3 **Rogers**	N	Y	Y	Y	Y	Y
4 **Aderholt**	N	Y	Y	Y	Y	Y
5 **Brooks**	N	Y	Y	Y	Y	Y
6 **Palmer**	N	Y	Y	Y	Y	Y
7 Sewell	+	+	–	Y	Y	N
ALASKA						
AL **Young**	?	?	?	Y	Y	Y
ARIZONA						
1 O'Halleran	Y	Y	N	Y	Y	N
2 **McSally**	N	Y	Y	Y	Y	Y
3 Grijalva	Y	Y	N	Y	Y	N
4 **Gosar**	N	Y	Y	Y	Y	Y
5 **Biggs**	N	Y	Y	Y	Y	Y
6 **Schweikert**	N	Y	Y	Y	Y	Y
7 Gallego	Y	Y	N	Y	Y	N
9 Sinema	Y	Y	N	Y	Y	N
ARKANSAS						
1 **Crawford**	N	Y	Y	Y	Y	Y
2 **Hill**	N	Y	Y	Y	Y	Y
3 **Womack**	N	Y	Y	Y	Y	Y
4 **Westerman**	N	Y	Y	Y	Y	Y
CALIFORNIA						
1 **LaMalfa**	N	Y	Y	Y	Y	Y
2 Huffman	+	+	–	Y	Y	N
3 Garamendi	Y	Y	?	Y	Y	N
4 **McClintock**	N	N	Y	Y	Y	Y
5 Thompson	Y	Y	N	Y	Y	N
6 Matsui	Y	Y	N	Y	Y	N
7 Bera	Y	Y	N	Y	Y	N
8 **Cook**	N	Y	Y	Y	Y	Y
9 McNerney	Y	Y	N	?	Y	N
10 **Denham**	–	+	+	Y	Y	Y
11 DeSaulnier	Y	Y	N	Y	Y	N
12 Pelosi	Y	Y	N	Y	Y	N
13 Lee	Y	Y	N	Y	Y	N
14 Speier	Y	N	N	Y	Y	N
15 Swalwell	Y	N	N	Y	Y	N
16 Costa	Y	Y	N	Y	Y	N
17 Khanna	Y	Y	N	Y	Y	N
18 Eshoo	Y	N	N	Y	Y	N
19 Lofgren	+	+	–	Y	Y	N
20 Panetta	Y	N	N	Y	Y	N
21 **Valadao**	N	Y	Y	Y	Y	Y
22 **Nunes**	N	Y	Y	Y	Y	Y
23 **McCarthy**	N	Y	Y	Y	Y	Y
24 Carbajal	Y	Y	N	Y	Y	N
25 **Knight**	N	Y	Y	Y	Y	Y
26 Brownley	Y	Y	?	Y	Y	N
27 Chu	Y	Y	N	Y	Y	N
28 Schiff	Y	Y	N	Y	Y	–
29 Cardenas	Y	Y	N	Y	Y	N
30 Sherman	Y	Y	N	Y	Y	N
31 Aguilar	Y	Y	N	Y	Y	N
32 Napolitano	Y	Y	?	Y	Y	N
33 Lieu	Y	Y	N	Y	Y	N
34 Gomez	Y	Y	N	Y	Y	N
35 Torres	Y	Y	N	Y	Y	N
36 Ruiz	Y	Y	N	Y	Y	N
37 Bass	Y	Y	N	Y	Y	N
38 Sánchez, Linda	+	+	–	Y	Y	N
39 **Royce**	N	Y	Y	Y	Y	Y
40 Roybal-Allard	Y	Y	–	Y	Y	N
41 Takano	Y	Y	N	Y	Y	N
42 **Calvert**	N	Y	Y	Y	Y	Y
43 Waters	Y	Y	N	?	?	?
44 Barragan	Y	Y	N	Y	Y	N
45 **Walters**	N	Y	Y	Y	Y	Y
46 Correa	Y	Y	N	Y	Y	N
47 Lowenthal	Y	N	N	Y	Y	N
48 **Rohrabacher**	N	N	Y	?	?	Y
49 **Issa**	N	Y	Y	Y	?	Y
50 **Hunter**	N	Y	Y	Y	Y	Y
51 Vargas	Y	Y	N	Y	Y	N
52 Peters	Y	Y	N	Y	Y	N
53 Davis	Y	Y	N	Y	Y	N

	164	165	166	167	168	169
COLORADO						
1 DeGette	Y	Y	N	Y	Y	N
2 Polis	Y	Y	N	Y	Y	N
3 **Tipton**	N	Y	Y	Y	Y	Y
4 **Buck**	N	N	Y	Y	Y	Y
5 **Lamborn**	N	Y	Y	Y	Y	Y
6 **Coffman**	N	Y	Y	Y	Y	Y
7 Perlmutter	Y	Y	N	Y	Y	N
CONNECTICUT						
1 Larson	Y	Y	–	Y	Y	N
2 Courtney	Y	Y	?	Y	Y	N
3 DeLauro	Y	Y	N	Y	Y	N
4 Himes	Y	Y	N	Y	Y	N
5 Esty	Y	Y	N	?	?	N
DELAWARE						
AL Blunt Rochester	Y	Y	N	Y	Y	N
FLORIDA						
1 **Gaetz**	N	Y	Y	Y	Y	Y
2 **Dunn**	N	Y	Y	Y	Y	Y
3 **Yoho**	N	Y	Y	Y	Y	Y
4 **Rutherford**	N	Y	Y	Y	Y	Y
5 Lawson	Y	Y	N	Y	Y	N
6 **DeSantis**	N	Y	Y	Y	Y	Y
7 Murphy	Y	Y	N	Y	Y	N
8 **Posey**	N	Y	Y	Y	Y	Y
9 Soto	Y	Y	N	Y	Y	N
10 Demings	Y	Y	N	Y	Y	N
11 **Webster**	N	Y	Y	Y	Y	Y
12 **Bilirakis**	N	Y	Y	Y	Y	Y
13 Crist	Y	Y	N	Y	Y	N
14 Castor	Y	Y	N	Y	Y	N
15 **Ross**	N	Y	Y	Y	Y	Y
16 **Buchanan**	N	Y	?	Y	Y	Y
17 **Rooney, T.**	N	Y	P	?	?	Y
18 **Mast**	N	Y	Y	Y	Y	Y
19 **Rooney, F.**	N	Y	Y	?	?	Y
20 Hastings	Y	Y	N	Y	Y	N
21 Frankel	Y	Y	N	Y	+	–
22 Deutch	Y	Y	N	Y	Y	N
23 Wasserman Schultz	Y	Y	N	Y	Y	N
24 Wilson	+	+	–	Y	Y	N
25 **Diaz-Balart**	N	Y	Y	Y	Y	Y
26 **Curbelo**	N	Y	Y	Y	Y	Y
27 **Ros-Lehtinen**	N	Y	Y	Y	Y	Y
GEORGIA						
1 **Carter**	N	Y	Y	Y	Y	Y
2 Bishop	Y	Y	N	Y	Y	N
3 **Ferguson**	N	Y	Y	Y	Y	Y
4 Johnson	Y	Y	?	Y	Y	?
5 Lewis	?	?	?	Y	Y	N
6 **Handel**	N	Y	Y	Y	Y	Y
7 **Woodall**	N	Y	Y	Y	Y	Y
8 **Scott, A.**	N	Y	Y	Y	Y	Y
9 **Collins**	N	Y	Y	Y	Y	Y
10 **Hice**	N	Y	Y	Y	Y	Y
11 **Loudermilk**	N	Y	Y	Y	Y	Y
12 **Allen**	N	Y	Y	Y	Y	Y
13 Scott, D.	Y	Y	?	Y	Y	N
14 **Graves**	N	Y	Y	Y	Y	Y
HAWAII						
1 Hanabusa	Y	Y	N	Y	Y	N
2 Gabbard	Y	Y	N	Y	Y	N
IDAHO						
1 **Labrador**	?	?	?	?	?	?
2 **Simpson**	N	Y	Y	Y	Y	Y
ILLINOIS						
1 Rush	Y	Y	N	Y	Y	N
2 Kelly	Y	Y	N	Y	Y	N
3 Lipinski	Y	Y	N	Y	Y	?
4 Gutierrez	Y	Y	N	+	+	–
5 Quigley	Y	Y	N	Y	Y	N
6 **Roskam**	N	Y	Y	Y	Y	Y
7 Davis, D.	Y	Y	?	Y	Y	N
8 Krishnamoorthi	Y	Y	N	Y	Y	N
9 Schakowsky	Y	Y	N	Y	Y	N
10 Schneider	Y	Y	N	Y	Y	N
11 Foster	Y	Y	N	Y	Y	N
12 **Bost**	N	Y	Y	Y	Y	Y
13 **Davis, R.**	N	Y	Y	Y	+	Y

	164	165	166	167	168	169
14 **Hultgren**	N	Y	Y	Y	Y	Y
15 **Shimkus**	N	Y	Y	Y	Y	Y
16 **Kinzinger**	N	Y	Y	Y	Y	Y
17 Bustos	Y	Y	N	Y	Y	N
18 **LaHood**	N	Y	Y	Y	Y	Y
INDIANA						
1 Visclosky	Y	Y	N	Y	Y	N
2 **Walorski**	N	Y	Y	Y	Y	Y
3 **Banks**	N	Y	Y	Y	Y	Y
4 **Rokita**	N	Y	Y	?	?	?
5 **Brooks**	N	Y	Y	+	+	Y
6 **Messer**	N	Y	Y	?	?	?
7 Carson	Y	Y	N	+	+	–
8 **Bucshon**	N	Y	Y	Y	Y	Y
9 **Hollingsworth**	N	Y	Y	Y	Y	Y
IOWA						
1 **Blum**	N	Y	Y	Y	Y	Y
2 Loebsack	Y	Y	N	Y	Y	N
3 **Young**	N	Y	Y	Y	Y	Y
4 **King**	N	Y	Y	Y	Y	Y
KANSAS						
1 **Marshall**	N	Y	Y	Y	Y	Y
2 **Jenkins**	N	Y	Y	Y	Y	Y
3 **Yoder**	N	Y	Y	Y	Y	Y
4 **Estes**	N	Y	Y	Y	Y	Y
KENTUCKY						
1 **Comer**	N	Y	Y	Y	Y	Y
2 **Guthrie**	N	Y	Y	Y	Y	Y
3 Yarmuth	Y	Y	N	Y	Y	N
4 **Massie**	N	Y	Y	Y	Y	Y
5 **Rogers**	N	Y	Y	+	+	+
6 **Barr**	N	Y	Y	Y	Y	Y
LOUISIANA						
1 **Scalise**	N	Y	Y	Y	Y	Y
2 Richmond	Y	Y	?	?	Y	?
3 **Higgins**	N	Y	Y	Y	Y	Y
4 **Johnson**	N	Y	Y	Y	Y	Y
5 **Abraham**	N	Y	Y	Y	Y	Y
6 **Graves**	N	Y	Y	Y	Y	Y
MAINE						
1 Pingree	Y	Y	N	Y	Y	N
2 **Poliquin**	N	Y	Y	?	?	Y
MARYLAND						
1 **Harris**	N	Y	Y	Y	Y	Y
2 Ruppersberger	+	+	–	Y	Y	N
3 Sarbanes	Y	Y	N	Y	Y	N
4 Brown	Y	Y	N	Y	Y	N
5 Hoyer	Y	Y	N	Y	Y	N
6 Delaney	Y	Y	N	Y	+	N
7 Cummings	Y	Y	N	?	?	?
8 Raskin	Y	Y	N	Y	Y	N
MASSACHUSETTS						
1 Neal	Y	Y	N	Y	Y	?
2 McGovern	Y	Y	N	Y	Y	N
3 Tsongas	Y	Y	N	Y	Y	N
4 Kennedy	Y	Y	N	Y	Y	N
5 Clark	Y	Y	N	+	+	N
6 Moulton	Y	Y	N	Y	Y	N
7 Capuano	Y	Y	N	+	+	N
8 Lynch	Y	Y	N	?	?	N
9 Keating	Y	Y	N	Y	Y	N
MICHIGAN						
1 **Bergman**	N	Y	Y	Y	Y	Y
2 **Huizenga**	N	Y	Y	Y	Y	Y
3 *Amash*	N	N	Y	Y	Y	Y
4 **Moolenaar**	N	Y	Y	Y	Y	Y
5 Kildee	Y	Y	N	Y	Y	N
6 **Upton**	N	Y	Y	Y	Y	Y
7 **Walberg**	N	Y	Y	Y	Y	Y
8 **Bishop**	N	Y	Y	?	?	Y
9 Levin	Y	Y	N	Y	Y	N
10 **Mitchell**	N	Y	Y	Y	Y	Y
11 **Trott**	N	Y	Y	Y	Y	Y
12 Dingell	Y	Y	N	Y	Y	N
14 Lawrence	Y	Y	N	Y	Y	N
MINNESOTA						
1 Walz	?	+	?	Y	Y	N
2 **Lewis**	N	Y	Y	Y	Y	Y
3 **Paulsen**	N	Y	Y	Y	Y	Y
4 McCollum	Y	Y	N	Y	Y	?

	164	165	166	167	168	169
5 Ellison	Y	N	N	Y	Y	N
6 **Emmer**	N	Y	Y	Y	Y	Y
7 Peterson	Y	Y	N	Y	Y	N
8 Nolan	Y	Y	N	Y	Y	N
MISSISSIPPI						
1 **Kelly**	N	Y	Y	Y	Y	Y
2 Thompson	Y	Y	N	Y	Y	N
3 **Harper**	?	?	?	Y	Y	Y
4 **Palazzo**	?	Y	Y	Y	Y	Y
MISSOURI						
1 Clay	Y	Y	N	Y	Y	N
2 **Wagner**	N	Y	Y	Y	Y	Y
3 **Luetkemeyer**	N	Y	Y	Y	Y	Y
4 **Hartzler**	N	Y	Y	Y	Y	Y
5 Cleaver	Y	Y	N	Y	Y	N
6 **Graves**	N	Y	Y	Y	Y	Y
7 **Long**	N	Y	Y	Y	Y	Y
8 **Smith**	N	Y	Y	Y	Y	Y
MONTANA						
AL **Gianforte**	N	Y	Y	Y	Y	Y
NEBRASKA						
1 **Fortenberry**	N	Y	Y	Y	Y	Y
2 **Bacon**	N	Y	Y	Y	Y	Y
3 **Smith**	N	Y	Y	Y	Y	Y
NEVADA						
1 Titus	Y	Y	N	Y	Y	N
2 **Amodei**	N	Y	Y	Y	Y	Y
3 Rosen	Y	Y	N	Y	Y	N
4 Kihuen	Y	Y	N	Y	Y	N
NEW HAMPSHIRE						
1 Shea-Porter	Y	Y	N	Y	Y	N
2 Kuster	+	+	–	+	+	–
NEW JERSEY						
1 Norcross	Y	Y	N	Y	Y	N
2 **LoBiondo**	N	Y	Y	Y	Y	Y
3 **MacArthur**	N	Y	Y	Y	Y	Y
4 **Smith**	N	Y	Y	Y	Y	Y
5 Gottheimer	Y	Y	N	Y	Y	N
6 Pallone	Y	Y	N	Y	Y	N
7 **Lance**	N	Y	Y	Y	Y	Y
8 Sires	?	?	?	Y	Y	N
9 Pascrell	Y	Y	N	Y	Y	N
10 Payne	Y	Y	N	Y	Y	N
11 **Frelinghuysen**	N	Y	Y	Y	Y	Y
12 Watson Coleman	Y	Y	N	Y	Y	N
NEW MEXICO						
1 Lujan Grisham	Y	Y	N	+	+	–
2 **Pearce**	N	Y	Y	Y	Y	Y
3 Luján	Y	Y	N	Y	Y	N
NEW YORK						
1 **Zeldin**	N	Y	Y	Y	Y	Y
2 **King**	N	Y	Y	Y	Y	Y
3 Suozzi	Y	Y	N	Y	Y	N
4 Rice	Y	Y	N	Y	Y	N
5 Meeks	Y	Y	N	Y	Y	N
6 Meng	Y	Y	N	Y	Y	N
7 Velázquez	Y	Y	N	Y	Y	N
8 Jeffries	Y	Y	N	?	Y	N
9 Clarke	Y	Y	N	Y	Y	N
10 Nadler	Y	Y	N	?	Y	N
11 **Donovan**	N	Y	Y	Y	Y	Y
12 Maloney, C.	Y	Y	N	?	?	N
13 Espaillat	Y	Y	N	Y	Y	N
14 Crowley	Y	Y	N	Y	Y	N
15 Serrano	Y	Y	N	Y	Y	N
16 Engel	Y	Y	N	Y	Y	N
17 Lowey	Y	Y	N	Y	Y	N
18 Maloney, S.P.	Y	Y	N	Y	Y	N
19 **Faso**	N	Y	Y	Y	Y	Y
20 Tonko	Y	Y	N	+	+	N
21 **Stefanik**	N	Y	Y	Y	Y	Y
22 **Tenney**	N	Y	Y	Y	Y	Y
23 **Reed**	N	Y	N	Y	Y	Y
24 **Katko**	N	Y	Y	Y	Y	Y
25 **Vacant**						
26 Higgins	Y	Y	?	Y	Y	N
27 **Collins**	N	Y	Y	Y	Y	Y
NORTH CAROLINA						
1 Butterfield	?	?	?	?	?	N
2 **Holding**	N	Y	Y	Y	Y	Y
3 **Jones**	?	?	?	?	?	?
4 Price	Y	Y	N	+	+	N

	164	165	166	167	168	169
5 **Foxx**	N	Y	Y	Y	Y	Y
6 **Walker**	N	Y	Y	Y	Y	Y
7 **Rouzer**	N	Y	Y	Y	Y	Y
8 **Hudson**	N	Y	Y	Y	Y	Y
9 **Pittenger**	N	Y	Y	?	?	?
9 **Vacant**						
10 **McHenry**	N	Y	Y	Y	Y	Y
11 **Meadows**	N	Y	Y	Y	Y	Y
12 Adams	Y	Y	N	?	?	?
13 **Budd**	N	Y	Y	Y	Y	Y
NORTH DAKOTA						
AL **Cramer**	N	Y	Y	Y	Y	Y
OHIO						
1 **Chabot**	N	Y	Y	Y	Y	Y
2 **Wenstrup**	N	Y	Y	Y	Y	Y
3 Beatty	Y	Y	N	Y	Y	N
4 **Jordan**	N	Y	Y	Y	Y	Y
5 **Latta**	N	Y	Y	Y	Y	Y
6 **Johnson**	N	Y	Y	Y	Y	Y
7 **Gibbs**	N	Y	?	Y	Y	Y
8 **Davidson**	N	Y	Y	Y	Y	Y
9 Kaptur	Y	Y	N	Y	Y	N
10 **Turner**	N	Y	Y	Y	Y	Y
11 Fudge	Y	Y	N	Y	Y	N
12 **Vacant**						
13 Ryan	Y	Y	N	Y	Y	N
14 **Joyce**	N	Y	P	Y	Y	Y
15 **Stivers**	N	Y	Y	Y	Y	Y
16 **Renacci**	N	Y	Y	Y	Y	+
OKLAHOMA						
1 **Vacant**						
2 **Mullin**	N	Y	Y	Y	Y	Y
3 **Lucas**	N	Y	Y	Y	Y	Y
4 **Cole**	N	Y	Y	Y	Y	Y
5 **Russell**	N	Y	Y	Y	Y	Y
OREGON						
1 Bonamici	Y	Y	N	Y	Y	N
2 **Walden**	N	Y	Y	Y	Y	Y
3 Blumenauer	Y	Y	N	Y	Y	N
4 DeFazio	Y	Y	N	Y	Y	N
5 Schrader	Y	Y	N	Y	Y	N
PENNSYLVANIA						
1 Brady	Y	Y	N	?	?	N
2 Evans	Y	Y	N	Y	Y	N
3 **Kelly**	N	Y	Y	Y	Y	Y
4 **Perry**	N	Y	Y	Y	Y	Y
5 **Thompson**	N	Y	Y	Y	Y	Y
6 **Costello**	N	Y	Y	Y	Y	Y
8 **Fitzpatrick**	N	Y	Y	Y	Y	Y
9 **Shuster**	N	Y	?	Y	Y	Y
10 **Marino**	N	Y	Y	Y	Y	Y
11 **Barletta**	N	Y	Y	Y	Y	Y
12 **Rothfus**	N	Y	Y	Y	Y	Y
13 Boyle	Y	Y	N	Y	Y	N
14 Doyle	Y	Y	N	Y	Y	N
15 **Dent**	N	Y	Y	Y	Y	Y
16 **Smucker**	N	Y	Y	Y	Y	Y
17 Cartwright	Y	Y	N	Y	Y	N
18 Lamb	Y	Y	N	Y	Y	N
RHODE ISLAND						
1 Cicilline	Y	Y	N	Y	Y	N
2 Langevin	Y	Y	N	Y	Y	N
SOUTH CAROLINA						
1 **Sanford**	N	Y	Y	Y	Y	Y
2 **Wilson**	N	Y	Y	Y	Y	Y
3 **Duncan**	N	Y	Y	Y	Y	Y
4 **Gowdy**	?	?	?	?	?	Y
5 **Norman**	N	N	Y	Y	Y	Y
6 Clyburn	Y	Y	N	Y	Y	?
7 **Rice**	N	Y	Y	Y	Y	Y
SOUTH DAKOTA						
AL **Noem**	?	?	?	Y	Y	Y
TENNESSEE						
1 **Roe**	N	Y	Y	Y	Y	Y
2 **Duncan**	N	Y	Y	Y	Y	Y
3 **Fleischmann**	N	Y	Y	Y	Y	Y
4 **DesJarlais**	N	Y	Y	Y	Y	Y
5 Cooper	Y	Y	N	Y	Y	N
6 **Black**	?	?	?	Y	Y	Y
7 **Blackburn**	?	?	?	?	?	Y
8 **Kustoff**	?	?	?	Y	Y	Y
9 Cohen	Y	Y	N	Y	Y	N

	164	165	166	167	168	169
TEXAS						
1 **Gohmert**	N	N	Y	Y	Y	Y
2 **Poe**	N	Y	Y	?	?	?
3 **Johnson, S.**	N	Y	Y	Y	Y	Y
4 **Ratcliffe**	N	Y	Y	Y	Y	Y
5 **Hensarling**	N	Y	Y	Y	Y	Y
6 **Barton**	N	Y	Y	Y	Y	Y
7 **Culberson**	N	Y	Y	Y	Y	Y
8 **Brady**	N	Y	Y	Y	Y	Y
9 Green, A.	Y	Y	N	Y	Y	N
10 **McCaul**	N	Y	Y	Y	Y	Y
11 **Conaway**	N	Y	Y	Y	Y	Y
12 **Granger**	N	Y	Y	Y	Y	Y
13 **Thornberry**	N	Y	Y	Y	Y	Y
14 **Weber**	N	Y	Y	Y	Y	Y
15 Gonzalez	Y	Y	N	+	+	N
16 O'Rourke	Y	Y	N	Y	Y	N
17 **Flores**	N	Y	Y	Y	Y	Y
18 Jackson Lee	Y	Y	N	+	Y	N
19 **Arrington**	N	Y	Y	Y	Y	Y
20 Castro	Y	Y	N	Y	Y	N
21 **Smith**	N	Y	Y	Y	Y	Y
22 **Olson**	N	Y	Y	Y	Y	Y
23 **Hurd**	N	Y	Y	Y	Y	Y
24 **Marchant**	N	Y	Y	Y	Y	Y
25 **Williams**	N	Y	Y	Y	Y	Y
26 **Burgess**	N	Y	Y	Y	Y	Y
28 Cuellar	Y	Y	N	Y	Y	N
29 Green, G.	Y	Y	N	Y	Y	N
30 Johnson, E.B.	Y	Y	N	?	?	?
31 **Carter**	N	Y	Y	Y	Y	Y
32 **Sessions**	N	Y	Y	Y	Y	Y
33 Veasey	Y	Y	N	Y	Y	N
34 Vela	Y	Y	?	Y	Y	N
35 Doggett	Y	Y	?	Y	Y	N
36 **Babin**	N	Y	Y	Y	Y	Y
UTAH						
1 **Bishop**	N	Y	Y	Y	Y	Y
2 **Stewart**	N	Y	Y	Y	Y	Y
3 **Curtis**	N	Y	Y	Y	Y	Y
4 **Love**	N	Y	Y	Y	Y	Y
VERMONT						
AL Welch	Y	Y	N	Y	Y	N
VIRGINIA						
1 **Wittman**	N	Y	Y	Y	Y	Y
2 **Taylor**	N	Y	P	Y	Y	Y
3 Scott	Y	Y	N	Y	Y	N
4 McEachin	Y	Y	N	Y	Y	N
5 **Garrett**	N	Y	Y	Y	Y	Y
6 **Goodlatte**	N	Y	Y	Y	Y	Y
7 **Brat**	N	Y	Y	Y	Y	Y
8 Beyer	Y	Y	N	Y	Y	N
9 **Griffith**	N	Y	Y	Y	Y	Y
10 **Comstock**	N	Y	Y	Y	Y	Y
11 Connolly	Y	Y	N	Y	Y	N
WASHINGTON						
1 DelBene	Y	Y	N	Y	Y	N
2 Larsen	Y	Y	N	Y	Y	N
3 **Herrera Beutler**	N	Y	Y	Y	Y	Y
4 **Newhouse**	N	Y	Y	Y	Y	Y
5 **McMorris Rodgers**	N	Y	Y	Y	Y	Y
6 Kilmer	Y	Y	N	Y	Y	N
7 Jayapal	Y	Y	N	Y	Y	N
8 **Reichert**	N	Y	?	Y	Y	Y
9 Smith	Y	Y	N	Y	Y	N
10 Heck	Y	Y	N	Y	Y	N
WEST VIRGINIA						
1 **McKinley**	N	Y	Y	Y	Y	Y
2 **Mooney**	N	Y	Y	Y	Y	Y
3 **Jenkins**	–	+	?	+	+	+
WISCONSIN						
1 **Ryan**						
2 Pocan	Y	Y	N	Y	Y	N
3 Kind	Y	Y	N	Y	Y	N
4 Moore	Y	Y	N	+	Y	N
5 **Sensenbrenner**	N	N	Y	Y	Y	Y
6 **Grothman**	N	Y	Y	Y	Y	Y
7 **Duffy**	N	Y	Y	Y	Y	Y
8 **Gallagher**	N	Y	Y	Y	Y	Y
WYOMING						
AL **Cheney**	N	Y	Y	Y	Y	Y

III HOUSE VOTES

VOTE NUMBER

170. SJRES57. MERGER REGULATION ENFORCEMENT, GRANT REPORTING, AND DISAPPROVAL OF LOAN RULES/RULE. Adoption of the rule (H Res 872) that would provide for consideration of the bill (HR 5645) that would synchronize antitrust standards between the Federal Trade Commission and the Justice Department; would provide for consideration of the bill (HR 2152) that would require certain Justice Department grantees to report on the use of funds they received, and would provide for consideration of a joint resolution (S J Res 57) that would disapprove of certain Consumer Financial Regulatory Commission rules related to indirect automotive loans. Adopted 227-181: R 226-0; D 1-181. May 8, 2018.

171. SJRES57. INDIRECT AUTOMOBILE LOAN RULE DISAPPROVAL/ PASSAGE. Passage of the joint resolution that would nullify and disapprove of a Consumer Financial Protection Bureau rule that provides guidance to third parties that offer indirect financing for automobile loans. The rule states that such third party lenders are treated as creditors under the Equal Credit Opportunity Act and the lenders may not mark up the rate of an indirect loan in relation to a borrower's race, color, religion, national origin, sex, marital status, age or receipt of income from any public assistance program. Passed 234-175: R 223-1; D 11-174. May 8, 2018.

172. HRES878. HOUSE CHAPLAIN/MOTION TO TABLE. McCarthy, R-Calif., motion to table (kill) the Crowley, D-N.Y., resolution that would establish a select committee to investigate the resignation of Chaplain of the House of Representatives, Patrick J. Conroy. Motion agreed to 223-182: R 223-1; D 0-181. May 8, 2018.

173. HR3053. YUCCA MOUNTAIN AND NUCLEAR WASTE POLICY/ PREVIOUS QUESTION. Newhouse, R-Wash., motion to order the previous question (thus ending debate and possibility of amendment) on the rule (H Res 879) that would provide for consideration of the bill (HR 3053) that would provide for the ongoing licensing process and authorize the continued construction of the nuclear waste repository at Yucca Mountain, and would also modify other nuclear waste policies. Motion agreed to 223-189: R 223-0; D 0-189. May 9, 2018.

174. HRES879. YUCCA MOUNTAIN AND NUCLEAR WASTE POLICY/RULE. Adoption of the rule (H Res 879) that would provide for consideration of the bill (HR 3053) that would provide for the ongoing licensing process and authorize the continued construction of the nuclear waste repository at Yucca Mountain, and would also modify other nuclear waste policies. Adopted 224-184: R 221-0; D 3-184. May 9, 2018.

175. HR2152. PRETRIAL SERVICE GRANT REPORTING/PASSAGE. Passage of the bill would require state and local governments that receive Justice Department grants for pretrial services to submit annually a report to the attorney general that would include the names of defendants who received services, their prior convictions where applicable, and the amount of money that had been allocated for pretrial services. The bill also states that if a state or local government were to fail to submit such a report, it could lose grant funding for the following year. Passed 221-197: R 219-8; D 2-189. May 9, 2018.

	170	171	172	173	174	175
ALABAMA						
1 Byrne	Y	Y	Y	Y	Y	Y
2 Roby	Y	Y	Y	Y	Y	Y
3 Rogers	Y	Y	Y	Y	Y	Y
4 Aderholt	Y	Y	Y	Y	Y	Y
5 Brooks	Y	Y	Y	Y	Y	Y
6 Palmer	Y	Y	Y	Y	Y	Y
7 Sewell	N	N	N	N	N	N
ALASKA						
AL Young	Y	Y	Y	Y	Y	Y
ARIZONA						
1 O'Halleran	N	N	N	N	N	N
2 McSally	Y	Y	Y	Y	Y	Y
3 Grijalva	N	N	N	N	N	N
4 Gosar	Y	Y	Y	Y	Y	Y
5 Biggs	Y	Y	Y	Y	Y	N
6 Schweikert	Y	Y	Y	Y	Y	Y
7 Gallego	N	N	N	N	N	N
8 Lesko	Y	Y	Y	Y	Y	Y
9 Sinema	N	N	N	N	Y	Y
ARKANSAS						
1 Crawford	Y	Y	Y	Y	Y	Y
2 Hill	Y	Y	Y	Y	Y	Y
3 Womack	Y	Y	Y	Y	Y	Y
4 Westerman	Y	Y	Y	Y	Y	Y
CALIFORNIA						
1 LaMalfa	Y	Y	Y	?	Y	Y
2 Huffman	N	N	N	N	N	N
3 Garamendi	N	N	N	N	N	N
4 McClintock	Y	Y	Y	Y	Y	Y
5 Thompson	N	N	N	N	N	N
6 Matsui	N	N	N	N	N	N
7 Bera	N	N	N	N	N	N
8 Cook	Y	Y	Y	Y	Y	Y
9 McNerney	N	N	N	N	N	N
10 Denham	Y	Y	Y	Y	Y	Y
11 DeSaulnier	N	N	N	N	N	N
12 Pelosi	N	N	N	N	N	N
13 Lee	N	N	N	N	N	N
14 Speier	N	N	N	N	N	N
15 Swalwell	N	N	N	N	N	N
16 Costa	N	Y	N	N	N	N
17 Khanna	N	N	N	N	N	N
18 Eshoo	N	N	N	N	N	N
19 Lofgren	N	N	N	N	N	N
20 Panetta	N	N	N	N	N	N
21 Valadao	Y	Y	Y	Y	Y	Y
22 Nunes	Y	Y	Y	Y	Y	Y
23 McCarthy	Y	Y	Y	Y	Y	Y
24 Carbajal	N	N	N	N	N	N
25 Knight	Y	Y	Y	Y	Y	Y
26 Brownley	N	N	N	N	N	N
27 Chu	N	N	N	N	N	N
28 Schiff	N	N	N	N	N	N
29 Cardenas	N	N	N	N	N	N
30 Sherman	N	N	N	N	N	N
31 Aguilar	N	N	N	N	N	N
32 Napolitano	N	N	?	N	N	N
33 Lieu	N	N	N	N	N	N
34 Gomez	N	N	N	N	N	N
35 Torres	N	N	N	N	N	N
36 Ruiz	N	N	N	N	N	N
37 Bass	N	N	N	N	N	N
38 Sánchez, Linda	N	N	N	N	N	N
39 Royce	Y	Y	Y	?	?	Y
40 Roybal-Allard	N	N	N	N	N	N
41 Takano	N	N	N	N	N	N
42 Calvert	Y	Y	Y	Y	Y	Y
43 Waters	N	N	N	N	N	N
44 Barragan	N	N	N	N	N	N
45 Walters	Y	Y	Y	Y	Y	Y
46 Correa	N	Y	N	N	N	N
47 Lowenthal	N	N	N	N	N	N
48 Rohrabacher	Y	Y	Y	Y	Y	Y
49 Issa	Y	Y	Y	Y	Y	Y
50 Hunter	Y	Y	Y	Y	Y	Y
51 Vargas	N	N	N	N	N	N
52 Peters	N	N	N	N	N	N
53 Davis	N	N	N	N	N	N
COLORADO						
1 DeGette	N	N	N	N	N	N
2 Polis	N	N	N	N	N	N
3 Tipton	Y	Y	Y	Y	Y	Y
4 Buck	Y	Y	Y	Y	Y	Y
5 Lamborn	Y	Y	Y	Y	Y	Y
6 Coffman	Y	Y	Y	Y	Y	Y
7 Perlmutter	N	N	N	N	N	N
CONNECTICUT						
1 Larson	N	N	N	N	N	N
2 Courtney	N	N	N	N	N	N
3 DeLauro	N	N	N	N	N	N
4 Himes	N	N	N	N	N	N
5 Esty	N	N	N	N	N	N
DELAWARE						
AL Blunt Rochester	N	N	?	N	N	N
FLORIDA						
1 Gaetz	Y	Y	Y	Y	Y	Y
2 Dunn	Y	Y	Y	Y	Y	Y
3 Yoho	Y	Y	Y	Y	Y	Y
4 Rutherford	Y	Y	Y	Y	Y	Y
5 Lawson	N	N	N	N	N	N
6 DeSantis	Y	Y	Y	Y	Y	Y
7 Murphy	N	Y	N	N	N	N
8 Posey	Y	Y	Y	Y	Y	Y
9 Soto	N	N	N	N	N	N
10 Demings	N	N	N	N	N	N
11 Webster	Y	Y	Y	Y	Y	Y
12 Bilirakis	Y	Y	Y	Y	Y	Y
13 Crist	N	N	N	N	N	N
14 Castor	N	N	N	?	?	N
15 Ross	Y	Y	Y	Y	Y	Y
16 Buchanan	Y	P	Y	Y	Y	Y
17 Rooney, T.	Y	Y	Y	Y	Y	Y
18 Mast	Y	Y	Y	Y	Y	Y
19 Rooney, F.	Y	Y	Y	Y	Y	Y
20 Hastings	N	N	N	N	N	N
21 Frankel	N	N	N	N	N	N
22 Deutch	N	N	N	N	N	?
23 Wasserman Schultz	N	N	N	N	N	N
24 Wilson	N	N	N	N	N	N
25 Diaz-Balart	Y	Y	Y	Y	Y	Y
26 Curbelo	Y	Y	Y	Y	Y	Y
27 Ros-Lehtinen	Y	N	Y	Y	Y	N
GEORGIA						
1 Carter	Y	Y	Y	Y	Y	Y
2 Bishop	N	N	N	N	N	N
3 Ferguson	Y	Y	Y	Y	Y	Y
4 Johnson	N	N	N	N	N	N
5 Lewis	N	N	N	N	N	N
6 Handel	Y	Y	Y	Y	Y	Y
7 Woodall	Y	Y	Y	Y	?	Y
8 Scott, A.	Y	Y	Y	Y	Y	Y
9 Collins	Y	Y	Y	Y	Y	Y
10 Hice	Y	Y	Y	Y	Y	Y
11 Loudermilk	Y	Y	Y	Y	Y	Y
12 Allen	Y	Y	Y	Y	Y	Y
13 Scott, D.	N	Y	?	N	N	N
14 Graves	Y	Y	Y	Y	Y	Y
HAWAII						
1 Hanabusa	N	N	N	N	N	N
2 Gabbard	N	N	N	N	N	N
IDAHO						
1 Labrador	?	?	?	?	?	?
2 Simpson	Y	Y	Y	Y	Y	Y
ILLINOIS						
1 Rush	N	N	N	N	N	N
2 Kelly	N	N	N	N	N	N
3 Lipinski	?	?	?	N	N	N
4 Gutierrez	-	-	-	-	-	N
5 Quigley	N	N	N	N	N	N
6 Roskam	Y	Y	Y	Y	Y	Y
7 Davis, D.	N	N	N	N	N	N
8 Krishnamoorthi	N	N	N	N	N	N
9 Schakowsky	N	N	N	N	N	N
10 Schneider	N	N	N	N	Y	N
11 Foster	N	N	N	N	N	N
12 Bost	Y	Y	Y	Y	Y	Y
13 Davis, R.	Y	Y	Y	Y	Y	Y

	170	171	172	173	174	175
14 **Hultgren**	Y	Y	Y	Y	Y	Y
15 **Shimkus**	Y	Y	Y	Y	Y	Y
16 **Kinzinger**	Y	Y	Y	Y	Y	Y
17 Bustos	N	N	N	N	N	N
18 **LaHood**	Y	Y	Y	Y	Y	Y
INDIANA						
1 Visclosky	N	N	N	N	N	N
2 **Walorski**	Y	Y	Y	Y	Y	Y
3 **Banks**	Y	Y	Y	Y	Y	Y
4 **Rokita**	?	?	?	?	?	?
5 **Brooks**	Y	Y	Y	Y	Y	Y
6 **Messer**	?	?	?	?	?	?
7 Carson	–	–	–	N	N	N
8 **Bucshon**	Y	Y	Y	Y	Y	Y
9 **Hollingsworth**	Y	Y	Y	Y	Y	Y
IOWA						
1 **Blum**	Y	Y	Y	Y	Y	Y
2 Loebsack	N	N	N	N	N	N
3 **Young**	Y	Y	Y	Y	Y	Y
4 **King**	Y	Y	Y	Y	Y	Y
KANSAS						
1 **Marshall**	Y	Y	Y	Y	Y	Y
2 **Jenkins**	Y	Y	Y	Y	Y	Y
3 **Yoder**	Y	Y	Y	Y	Y	Y
4 **Estes**	Y	Y	Y	Y	Y	Y
KENTUCKY						
1 **Comer**	Y	Y	Y	Y	Y	Y
2 **Guthrie**	Y	Y	Y	Y	Y	Y
3 Yarmuth	N	N	N	N	N	N
4 **Massie**	Y	Y	Y	Y	Y	N
5 **Rogers**	+	+	+	+	+	+
6 **Barr**	Y	Y	Y	Y	Y	Y
LOUISIANA						
1 **Scalise**	Y	+	+	Y	Y	Y
2 Richmond	N	N	N	N	N	N
3 **Higgins**	Y	Y	Y	Y	Y	Y
4 **Johnson**	Y	Y	Y	Y	Y	Y
5 **Abraham**	Y	Y	Y	Y	Y	Y
6 **Graves**	Y	Y	Y	Y	Y	Y
MAINE						
1 Pingree	N	N	N	N	N	N
2 **Poliquin**	Y	Y	Y	Y	Y	Y
MARYLAND						
1 **Harris**	Y	Y	Y	?	Y	Y
2 Ruppersberger	N	N	N	N	N	N
3 Sarbanes	N	N	N	N	N	N
4 Brown	N	N	N	N	N	N
5 Hoyer	N	N	N	?	?	N
6 Delaney	N	N	N	N	N	N
7 Cummings	?	?	?	N	N	N
8 Raskin	N	N	N	N	N	N
MASSACHUSETTS						
1 Neal	N	N	N	N	N	N
2 McGovern	N	N	N	N	N	N
3 Tsongas	N	N	N	N	N	N
4 Kennedy	N	N	N	N	N	N
5 Clark	N	N	N	N	N	N
6 Moulton	N	N	N	N	N	N
7 Capuano	N	N	N	N	N	N
8 Lynch	N	N	N	N	N	N
9 Keating	N	N	N	N	N	N
MICHIGAN						
1 **Bergman**	Y	Y	Y	Y	Y	Y
2 **Huizenga**	Y	Y	Y	Y	+	Y
3 *Amash*	Y	Y	N	Y	Y	N
4 **Moolenaar**	Y	Y	Y	Y	Y	Y
5 Kildee	N	N	N	N	N	N
6 **Upton**	Y	Y	Y	Y	Y	Y
7 **Walberg**	Y	Y	Y	Y	Y	Y
8 **Bishop**	Y	Y	Y	Y	Y	Y
9 Levin	N	N	N	N	N	N
10 **Mitchell**	Y	Y	Y	Y	Y	Y
11 **Trott**	Y	Y	Y	Y	Y	Y
12 Dingell	N	N	N	N	N	N
14 Lawrence	N	N	N	N	N	N
MINNESOTA						
1 Walz	N	N	N	N	N	N
2 **Lewis**	Y	Y	Y	Y	Y	N
3 **Paulsen**	Y	Y	Y	Y	Y	N
4 McCollum	?	–	?	N	N	N

	170	171	172	173	174	175
5 Ellison	N	N	N	N	N	N
6 **Emmer**	Y	Y	Y	Y	Y	Y
7 Peterson	Y	Y	N	N	N	N
8 Nolan	N	N	N	N	N	N
MISSISSIPPI						
1 **Kelly**	Y	Y	Y	Y	Y	Y
2 Thompson	N	N	N	N	N	N
3 **Harper**	Y	Y	Y	Y	Y	Y
4 **Palazzo**	Y	Y	Y	Y	Y	Y
MISSOURI						
1 Clay	N	N	N	N	N	N
2 **Wagner**	Y	Y	Y	Y	Y	Y
3 **Luetkemeyer**	Y	Y	Y	Y	Y	Y
4 **Hartzler**	Y	Y	Y	Y	Y	Y
5 Cleaver	N	N	N	N	N	N
6 **Graves**	Y	Y	Y	Y	Y	Y
7 **Long**	Y	Y	Y	Y	Y	Y
8 **Smith**	Y	Y	Y	Y	Y	Y
MONTANA						
AL **Gianforte**	Y	Y	Y	Y	Y	Y
NEBRASKA						
1 **Fortenberry**	Y	Y	Y	Y	Y	Y
2 **Bacon**	Y	Y	Y	Y	Y	Y
3 **Smith**	Y	Y	Y	Y	+	Y
NEVADA						
1 Titus	N	N	N	N	N	N
2 **Amodei**	Y	Y	Y	Y	P	Y
3 Rosen	N	N	?	N	N	N
4 Kihuen	N	N	N	N	N	N
NEW HAMPSHIRE						
1 Shea-Porter	N	N	N	N	N	N
2 Kuster	–	–	–	–	–	–
NEW JERSEY						
1 Norcross	N	N	N	N	N	N
2 **LoBiondo**	Y	Y	Y	Y	Y	Y
3 **MacArthur**	Y	Y	Y	Y	Y	Y
4 **Smith**	Y	Y	Y	Y	Y	Y
5 Gottheimer	N	N	N	N	N	N
6 Pallone	N	N	N	N	N	N
7 **Lance**	Y	Y	Y	Y	Y	Y
8 Sires	N	N	N	N	N	N
9 Pascrell	N	N	N	N	N	N
10 Payne	N	N	N	N	N	N
11 **Frelinghuysen**	Y	Y	Y	Y	Y	Y
12 Watson Coleman	N	N	N	N	N	N
NEW MEXICO						
1 Lujan Grisham	–	N	N	N	N	N
2 **Pearce**	Y	Y	Y	Y	Y	Y
3 Luján	N	N	N	N	N	N
NEW YORK						
1 **Zeldin**	Y	Y	Y	+	Y	Y
2 **King**	Y	Y	Y	Y	Y	Y
3 Suozzi	N	N	N	N	N	N
4 Rice	N	N	N	N	N	N
5 Meeks	N	N	N	N	N	N
6 Meng	N	N	N	N	N	N
7 Velázquez	N	N	N	N	N	N
8 Jeffries	N	N	N	N	N	N
9 Clarke	N	N	N	N	N	N
10 Nadler	N	N	N	N	N	N
11 **Donovan**	Y	Y	Y	Y	Y	Y
12 Maloney, C.	N	N	N	N	N	N
13 Espaillat	N	N	N	N	N	N
14 Crowley	N	N	N	N	N	N
15 Serrano	N	N	N	N	N	N
16 Engel	N	N	N	N	N	N
17 Lowey	N	N	N	N	N	N
18 Maloney, S.P.	N	N	N	N	N	N
19 **Faso**	Y	Y	Y	Y	Y	Y
20 Tonko	N	N	N	N	N	N
21 **Stefanik**	Y	Y	Y	Y	Y	Y
22 **Tenney**	Y	Y	Y	Y	Y	Y
23 **Reed**	Y	Y	Y	Y	Y	Y
24 **Katko**	Y	Y	Y	Y	Y	Y
25 **Vacant**						
26 Higgins	N	N	N	N	N	N
27 **Collins**	Y	Y	Y	Y	Y	Y
NORTH CAROLINA						
1 Butterfield	N	N	N	N	N	N
2 **Holding**	Y	Y	Y	Y	Y	Y
3 **Jones**	?	?	?	?	?	?
4 Price	N	N	N	N	N	N

	170	171	172	173	174	175
5 **Foxx**	Y	Y	Y	Y	Y	Y
6 **Walker**	Y	Y	Y	Y	Y	Y
7 **Rouzer**	Y	Y	Y	Y	Y	Y
8 **Hudson**	Y	Y	Y	Y	Y	Y
9 **Pittenger**	?	?	?	?	?	?
9 **Vacant**						
10 **McHenry**	Y	Y	Y	Y	Y	Y
11 **Meadows**	Y	Y	Y	Y	Y	Y
12 Adams	?	?	?	N	N	N
13 **Budd**	Y	Y	Y	Y	Y	Y
NORTH DAKOTA						
AL **Cramer**	Y	Y	Y	Y	Y	Y
OHIO						
1 **Chabot**	Y	Y	Y	Y	Y	Y
2 **Wenstrup**	Y	Y	Y	Y	Y	Y
3 Beatty	N	N	N	N	N	N
4 **Jordan**	Y	Y	Y	Y	Y	Y
5 **Latta**	Y	Y	Y	Y	Y	Y
6 **Johnson**	Y	Y	Y	Y	Y	Y
7 **Gibbs**	Y	Y	Y	Y	Y	Y
8 **Davidson**	Y	Y	Y	Y	?	Y
9 Kaptur	N	N	N	N	N	N
10 **Turner**	Y	Y	Y	Y	Y	Y
11 Fudge	N	N	N	N	N	N
12 **Vacant**						
13 Ryan	N	N	N	N	N	N
14 **Joyce**	Y	Y	Y	Y	Y	Y
15 **Stivers**	Y	Y	Y	Y	Y	Y
16 **Renacci**	+	+	+	Y	Y	Y
OKLAHOMA						
1 **Vacant**						
2 **Mullin**	Y	Y	Y	Y	Y	Y
3 **Lucas**	Y	Y	Y	Y	Y	Y
4 **Cole**	Y	Y	Y	Y	Y	Y
5 **Russell**	Y	Y	Y	Y	Y	Y
OREGON						
1 Bonamici	N	N	N	N	N	N
2 **Walden**	Y	Y	Y	Y	Y	Y
3 Blumenauer	N	N	N	N	N	N
4 DeFazio	N	N	N	N	N	N
5 Schrader	?	Y	N	N	N	N
PENNSYLVANIA						
1 Brady	N	N	N	N	N	N
2 Evans	N	N	N	N	N	N
3 **Kelly**	Y	Y	Y	Y	Y	Y
4 **Perry**	Y	Y	Y	Y	Y	Y
5 **Thompson**	Y	Y	Y	Y	Y	Y
6 **Costello**	Y	Y	Y	Y	Y	Y
7 **Vacant**						
8 **Fitzpatrick**	Y	Y	Y	Y	Y	Y
9 **Shuster**	Y	Y	Y	Y	Y	Y
10 **Marino**	Y	Y	Y	Y	Y	Y
11 **Barletta**	Y	Y	Y	Y	Y	Y
12 **Rothfus**	Y	Y	Y	Y	Y	Y
13 Boyle	N	N	N	N	N	N
14 Doyle	N	N	N	N	N	N
15 **Dent**	Y	Y	Y	Y	Y	Y
16 **Smucker**	Y	Y	Y	Y	Y	Y
17 Cartwright	N	N	N	N	N	N
18 Lamb	N	N	N	N	Y	N
RHODE ISLAND						
1 Cicilline	N	N	N	N	N	N
2 Langevin	N	N	N	N	N	N
SOUTH CAROLINA						
1 **Sanford**	Y	Y	Y	Y	Y	N
2 **Wilson**	Y	Y	Y	Y	Y	+
3 **Duncan**	Y	Y	Y	Y	Y	Y
4 **Gowdy**	Y	Y	Y	Y	Y	Y
5 **Norman**	Y	Y	Y	Y	Y	Y
6 Clyburn	?	N	N	N	N	N
7 **Rice**	Y	Y	Y	Y	Y	Y
SOUTH DAKOTA						
AL **Noem**	Y	Y	Y	Y	Y	Y
TENNESSEE						
1 **Roe**	Y	Y	Y	Y	Y	Y
2 **Duncan**	Y	Y	Y	Y	Y	Y
3 **Fleischmann**	Y	Y	Y	Y	Y	Y
4 **DesJarlais**	Y	Y	Y	Y	Y	Y
5 Cooper	N	Y	N	N	N	N
6 **Black**	Y	Y	Y	Y	Y	Y
7 **Blackburn**	Y	Y	Y	Y	Y	Y
8 **Kustoff**	Y	Y	Y	Y	Y	Y
9 Cohen	N	N	N	N	?	N

	170	171	172	173	174	175
TEXAS						
1 **Gohmert**	Y	Y	Y	Y	Y	Y
2 **Poe**	?	?	?	Y	Y	Y
3 **Johnson, S.**	Y	Y	Y	Y	Y	Y
4 **Ratcliffe**	Y	Y	Y	Y	Y	Y
5 **Hensarling**	Y	Y	Y	Y	Y	Y
6 **Barton**	Y	Y	Y	Y	Y	Y
7 **Culberson**	Y	Y	Y	Y	Y	Y
8 **Brady**	Y	Y	Y	Y	Y	Y
9 Green, A.	N	N	N	N	N	N
10 **McCaul**	Y	Y	Y	Y	Y	Y
11 **Conaway**	Y	Y	Y	Y	Y	Y
12 **Granger**	Y	Y	Y	Y	Y	Y
13 **Thornberry**	Y	Y	Y	Y	Y	Y
14 **Weber**	Y	Y	Y	Y	Y	Y
15 Gonzalez	N	Y	N	N	N	N
16 O'Rourke	N	N	N	N	N	N
17 **Flores**	Y	Y	Y	Y	Y	Y
18 Jackson Lee	N	N	N	N	N	N
19 **Arrington**	Y	Y	Y	Y	Y	Y
20 Castro	N	N	N	N	N	N
21 **Smith**	Y	Y	Y	?	Y	Y
22 **Olson**	Y	Y	Y	Y	Y	Y
23 **Hurd**	Y	Y	Y	Y	Y	Y
24 **Marchant**	Y	Y	Y	Y	Y	Y
25 **Williams**	Y	Y	Y	Y	Y	Y
26 **Burgess**	Y	Y	Y	Y	Y	Y
28 Cuellar	N	Y	N	N	N	Y
29 Green, G.	N	Y	N	N	N	N
30 Johnson, E.B.	?	?	?	N	N	N
31 **Carter**	Y	Y	Y	Y	Y	Y
32 **Sessions**	Y	Y	Y	Y	Y	Y
33 Veasey	N	N	N	N	N	N
34 Vela	N	Y	N	N	N	N
35 Doggett	N	N	N	N	?	N
36 **Babin**	Y	Y	Y	Y	Y	Y
UTAH						
1 **Bishop**	Y	Y	Y	Y	Y	Y
2 **Stewart**	Y	Y	Y	Y	Y	Y
3 **Curtis**	Y	Y	Y	Y	Y	N
4 **Love**	Y	Y	Y	Y	Y	Y
VERMONT						
AL Welch	N	N	N	N	N	N
VIRGINIA						
1 **Wittman**	Y	Y	Y	Y	Y	Y
2 **Taylor**	Y	Y	Y	Y	Y	Y
3 Scott	N	N	N	N	N	N
4 McEachin	N	N	N	N	N	N
5 **Garrett**	Y	Y	Y	Y	Y	Y
6 **Goodlatte**	Y	Y	Y	Y	Y	Y
7 **Brat**	Y	Y	?	Y	Y	Y
8 Beyer	N	N	N	N	N	N
9 **Griffith**	Y	Y	Y	Y	Y	Y
10 **Comstock**	Y	Y	Y	Y	Y	Y
11 Connolly	N	N	N	N	N	N
WASHINGTON						
1 DelBene	N	N	N	N	N	N
2 Larsen	N	N	N	N	N	N
3 **Herrera Beutler**	Y	Y	Y	Y	Y	Y
4 **Newhouse**	Y	Y	Y	Y	Y	Y
5 **McMorris Rodgers**	Y	Y	Y	Y	Y	Y
6 Kilmer	N	N	N	N	N	N
7 Jayapal	N	N	N	N	N	N
8 **Reichert**	Y	Y	Y	Y	Y	Y
9 Smith	N	N	N	N	N	N
10 Heck	N	N	N	N	N	N
WEST VIRGINIA						
1 **McKinley**	Y	Y	Y	Y	Y	Y
2 **Mooney**	Y	Y	Y	Y	Y	Y
3 **Jenkins**	+	+	+	+	+	+
WISCONSIN						
1 **Ryan**						
2 Pocan	N	N	N	N	N	N
3 Kind	N	N	N	N	N	N
4 Moore	N	N	N	N	N	N
5 **Sensenbrenner**	Y	Y	Y	Y	Y	Y
6 **Grothman**	Y	Y	Y	Y	Y	Y
7 **Duffy**	Y	Y	Y	Y	?	Y
8 **Gallagher**	Y	Y	Y	Y	Y	Y
WYOMING						
AL **Cheney**	Y	Y	Y	Y	Y	Y

⫿ HOUSE VOTES

VOTE NUMBER

176. HR5645. FTC MERGER REGULATION PROCEDURES/RECOMMIT. Doggett, D-Texas, motion to recommit the bill to the House Judiciary Committee with instructions to report back immediately with an amendment that would prohibit provisions in the bill from applying to mergers that would unreasonably increase the costs of pharmaceutical drugs. Motion rejected 193-220: R 2-220; D 191-0. May 9, 2018.

177. HR5645. FTC MERGER REGULATION PROCEDURES/PASSAGE. Passage of the bill that would reconcile differences in anti-trust injunction standards between the Federal Trade Commission and the Justice Department. It would also require FTC cases related to unfair methods of competition to be processed through federal courts as opposed to the commission's administrative process. The bill would allow the FTC to issue judicial actions when resolving a case and would require the commission to notify state attorneys general in instances in which the state would be entitled to bring an action. Passed 230-185: R 226-1; D 4-184. May 9, 2018.

178. HR3053. YUCCA MOUNTAIN AND NUCLEAR WASTE POLICY/LOCAL GOVERNMENT CONSENT. Titus, D-Nev., amendment that would strike all provisions in the bill and would require consent form state, local, and tribal governments before spent nuclear fuel or high-level radioactive waste could be transported through the entity's jurisdiction. Rejected in Committee of the Whole 80-332: R 1-225; D 79-107. May 10, 2018.

179. HR3053. YUCCA MOUNTAIN AND NUCLEAR WASTE POLICY/ PASSAGE. Passage of the bill that would require a decision within 30 months of enactment by the Nuclear Regulatory Commission on the licensing process and construction relating to the nuclear repository at Yucca Mountain. It would also authorize the establishment of interim storage facilities to be operated by the Energy Department until the repository is finished, and would additionally authorize a rail line to connect Yucca Mountain with the national rail system. The bill would also increase from 70,000 metric tons to 110,000, the allowable storage for the repository and provide additional financing mechanisms for the Yucca Mountain project as well as the compensation to Nevada for hosting the national nuclear waste repository. Passed 340-72: R 221-5; D 119-67. May 10, 2018.

180. PROCEDURAL MOTION/JOURNAL. Approval of the House Journal of May 9, 2018. Approved 207-179: R 127-85; D 80-94. May 10, 2018.

181. HR613. CORRECTIONAL OFFICER FIREARM STORAGE/PASSAGE. Goodlatte, R-Va., motion to suspend the rules and pass the bill that would require the director of the Bureau of Prisons to ensure that each federal penal and correctional institution has a secure storage area outside of the secure perimeter for employees to use in storing personal firearms, or allow employees to store firearms in a Bureau of Prisons-approved vehicle lockbox. The bill would allow authorized employees to carry personal firearms on prison grounds outside the secure perimeter of the institution. Motion agreed to 378-0: R 214-0; D 164-0. May 15, 2018.

		176	177	178	179	180	181
ALABAMA							
1	Byrne	N	Y	N	Y	Y	Y
2	Roby	-	Y	N	Y	Y	Y
3	Rogers	N	Y	N	Y	N	Y
4	Aderholt	N	Y	N	Y	N	Y
5	Brooks	N	Y	N	Y	N	Y
6	Palmer	N	Y	N	Y	N	Y
7	Sewell	Y	N	N	Y	N	Y
ALASKA							
AL	Young	N	Y	N	Y	N	Y
ARIZONA							
1	O'Halleran	Y	N	Y	Y	N	Y
2	McSally	N	Y	N	Y	N	?
3	Grijalva	Y	N	Y	?	N	Y
4	Gosar	N	Y	N	Y	Y	Y
5	Biggs	N	Y	N	Y	N	Y
6	Schweikert	N	Y	N	Y	N	Y
7	Gallego	Y	N	Y	N	Y	Y
8	Lesko	N	Y	N	Y	Y	Y
9	Sinema	Y	Y	N	Y	N	+
ARKANSAS							
1	Crawford	N	Y	N	Y	Y	Y
2	Hill	N	Y	N	Y	N	Y
3	Womack	N	Y	N	Y	Y	Y
4	Westerman	N	Y	N	Y	Y	Y
CALIFORNIA							
1	LaMalfa	N	Y	N	Y	?	Y
2	Huffman	Y	N	Y	N	Y	Y
3	Garamendi	Y	N	Y	N	Y	Y
4	McClintock	N	Y	N	Y	Y	Y
5	Thompson	Y	N	Y	N	N	Y
6	Matsui	Y	N	N	Y	Y	Y
7	Bera	Y	N	N	Y	N	Y
8	Cook	N	Y	N	Y	Y	Y
9	McNerney	Y	N	N	Y	Y	?
10	Denham	N	Y	N	Y	N	Y
11	DeSaulnier	Y	N	Y	N	Y	Y
12	Pelosi	Y	N	Y	N	Y	Y
13	Lee	Y	N	Y	N	N	Y
14	Speier	Y	N	?	?	?	Y
15	Swalwell	Y	N	N	Y	N	Y
16	Costa	Y	N	N	Y	N	Y
17	Khanna	Y	N	N	Y	N	Y
18	Eshoo	Y	N	Y	N	Y	Y
19	Lofgren	Y	N	Y	N	N	Y
20	Panetta	Y	N	N	Y	N	Y
21	Valadao	N	Y	N	Y	N	Y
22	Nunes	N	Y	N	Y	Y	Y
23	McCarthy	N	Y	N	Y	Y	Y
24	Carbajal	Y	N	N	Y	N	Y
25	Knight	N	Y	N	Y	N	Y
26	Brownley	Y	N	N	Y	N	Y
27	Chu	Y	N	Y	Y	Y	Y
28	Schiff	Y	N	Y	Y	Y	Y
29	Cardenas	Y	N	N	Y	N	Y
30	Sherman	Y	N	Y	Y	Y	Y
31	Aguilar	Y	N	N	Y	N	Y
32	Napolitano	Y	N	Y	N	N	+
33	Lieu	Y	N	Y	Y	N	Y
34	Gomez	Y	N	Y	Y	N	Y
35	Torres	Y	N	N	Y	N	Y
36	Ruiz	Y	N	N	Y	N	Y
37	Bass	Y	N	Y	Y	Y	Y
38	Sánchez, Linda	Y	?	Y	Y	N	Y
39	Royce	N	Y	N	Y	Y	Y
40	Roybal-Allard	Y	N	Y	N	N	+
41	Takano	Y	N	N	N	Y	Y
42	Calvert	N	Y	N	Y	Y	Y
43	Waters	Y	N	Y	N	Y	Y
44	Barragan	Y	N	N	Y	N	Y
45	Walters	N	Y	N	Y	Y	Y
46	Correa	Y	N	Y	N	N	Y
47	Lowenthal	Y	N	Y	Y	Y	Y
48	Rohrabacher	N	Y	N	Y	Y	?
49	Issa	N	Y	N	Y	Y	Y
50	Hunter	N	Y	N	Y	Y	Y
51	Vargas	Y	N	Y	N	N	Y
52	Peters	Y	Y	N	Y	Y	Y
53	Davis	Y	N	N	Y	Y	Y
COLORADO							
1	DeGette	Y	N	N	Y	Y	?
2	Polis	Y	N	Y	N	Y	Y
3	Tipton	N	Y	N	Y	N	Y
4	Buck	N	Y	N	Y	N	Y
5	Lamborn	N	Y	N	Y	Y	Y
6	Coffman	N	Y	N	Y	N	Y
7	Perlmutter	Y	N	Y	N	Y	Y
CONNECTICUT							
1	Larson	Y	N	N	Y	?	Y
2	Courtney	Y	N	N	Y	?	Y
3	DeLauro	Y	N	+	-	?	Y
4	Himes	Y	N	N	Y	Y	Y
5	Esty	Y	N	N	Y	N	Y
DELAWARE							
AL	Blunt Rochester	Y	N	N	Y	Y	?
FLORIDA							
1	Gaetz	N	Y	N	Y	N	Y
2	Dunn	N	Y	N	Y	?	Y
3	Yoho	N	Y	N	Y	N	Y
4	Rutherford	N	Y	N	Y	N	Y
5	Lawson	Y	N	N	Y	N	Y
6	DeSantis	N	Y	N	Y	N	Y
7	Murphy	Y	N	N	Y	N	Y
8	Posey	N	Y	N	Y	N	Y
9	Soto	Y	N	Y	N	N	Y
10	Demings	Y	N	N	Y	N	Y
11	Webster	?	Y	N	Y	Y	+
12	Bilirakis	N	Y	N	Y	N	Y
13	Crist	Y	N	N	N	N	Y
14	Castor	Y	N	N	Y	N	Y
15	Ross	N	Y	N	Y	Y	Y
16	Buchanan	N	Y	N	Y	Y	Y
17	Rooney, T.	N	Y	N	Y	Y	Y
18	Mast	N	Y	N	Y	N	Y
19	Rooney, F.	N	Y	N	Y	Y	Y
20	Hastings	Y	N	Y	N	N	Y
21	Frankel	Y	N	N	Y	N	Y
22	Deutch	?	?	?	?	?	Y
23	Wasserman Schultz	Y	N	Y	N	Y	Y
24	Wilson	Y	?	Y	Y	Y	?
25	Diaz-Balart	N	Y	N	Y	N	Y
26	Curbelo	N	Y	N	Y	N	Y
27	Ros-Lehtinen	N	Y	N	Y	N	Y
GEORGIA							
1	Carter	N	Y	N	Y	N	Y
2	Bishop	Y	N	N	Y	N	Y
3	Ferguson	N	Y	N	Y	Y	Y
4	Johnson	Y	N	N	Y	N	Y
5	Lewis	Y	N	N	Y	N	Y
6	Handel	N	Y	N	Y	Y	Y
7	Woodall	N	Y	N	Y	N	?
8	Scott, A.	N	Y	N	Y	Y	Y
9	Collins	N	Y	N	Y	Y	Y
10	Hice	N	Y	N	Y	?	Y
11	Loudermilk	N	Y	N	Y	Y	Y
12	Allen	N	Y	N	Y	Y	Y
13	Scott, D.	Y	N	N	Y	Y	Y
14	Graves	N	Y	N	Y	N	Y
HAWAII							
1	Hanabusa	Y	N	N	Y	N	Y
2	Gabbard	Y	N	Y	N	Y	Y
IDAHO							
1	Labrador	?	?	?	?	?	?
2	Simpson	N	Y	N	Y	Y	Y
ILLINOIS							
1	Rush	Y	N	-	N	Y	Y
2	Kelly	Y	N	Y	Y	Y	Y
3	Lipinski	Y	N	N	Y	Y	Y
4	Gutierrez	Y	N	N	N	N	+
5	Quigley	Y	N	N	Y	?	Y
6	Roskam	N	Y	N	Y	N	Y
7	Davis, D.	Y	N	Y	N	Y	?
8	Krishnamoorthi	Y	N	N	Y	N	Y
9	Schakowsky	Y	N	N	N	N	Y
10	Schneider	Y	N	N	Y	Y	Y
11	Foster	Y	N	N	Y	Y	Y
12	Bost	N	Y	N	Y	N	Y
13	Davis, R.	N	Y	N	Y	Y	Y

	176	177	178	179	180	181
14 **Hultgren**	N	Y	N	Y	Y	Y
15 **Shimkus**	N	Y	N	Y	Y	Y
16 **Kinzinger**	N	Y	N	Y	N	Y
17 Bustos	Y	N	N	Y	Y	?
18 **LaHood**	N	Y	N	Y	N	Y
INDIANA						
1 Visclosky	Y	N	N	Y	N	+
2 **Walorski**	N	Y	N	Y	Y	Y
3 **Banks**	N	Y	N	Y	Y	Y
4 **Rokita**	?	?	N	Y	Y	Y
5 **Brooks**	N	Y	N	Y	Y	+
6 **Messer**	?	?	N	Y	Y	?
7 Carson	Y	N	Y	Y	N	Y
8 **Bucshon**	N	Y	N	Y	Y	Y
9 **Hollingsworth**	N	Y	N	Y	Y	Y
IOWA						
1 **Blum**	Y	Y	N	Y	N	Y
2 Loebsack	Y	N	Y	N	N	Y
3 **Young**	N	Y	N	Y	Y	Y
4 **King**	N	Y	N	Y	+	Y
KANSAS						
1 **Marshall**	N	Y	N	Y	N	Y
2 **Jenkins**	N	Y	N	Y	N	Y
3 **Yoder**	N	Y	N	Y	N	Y
4 **Estes**	N	Y	N	Y	Y	Y
KENTUCKY						
1 **Comer**	N	Y	N	Y	Y	Y
2 **Guthrie**	N	Y	N	Y	Y	Y
3 Yarmuth	Y	N	N	N	Y	Y
4 **Massie**	N	Y	N	N	?	Y
5 **Rogers**	–	+	–	+	+	+
6 **Barr**	N	Y	N	Y	Y	Y
LOUISIANA						
1 **Scalise**	N	Y	N	Y	Y	Y
2 Richmond	Y	N	N	Y	N	?
3 **Higgins**	N	Y	N	Y	Y	Y
4 **Johnson**	N	Y	N	Y	Y	Y
5 **Abraham**	N	Y	N	Y	Y	Y
6 **Graves**	N	Y	N	Y	N	Y
MAINE						
1 Pingree	Y	N	N	N	Y	Y
2 **Poliquin**	N	Y	N	Y	N	Y
MARYLAND						
1 **Harris**	N	Y	N	Y	?	Y
2 Ruppersberger	Y	N	N	Y	Y	Y
3 Sarbanes	Y	N	N	Y	N	Y
4 Brown	Y	N	Y	Y	Y	+
5 Hoyer	Y	N	N	Y	N	Y
6 Delaney	Y	N	N	Y	N	Y
7 Cummings	Y	N	N	Y	Y	?
8 Raskin	Y	N	Y	Y	N	Y
MASSACHUSETTS						
1 Neal	Y	N	N	Y	N	Y
2 McGovern	Y	N	Y	N	?	Y
3 Tsongas	Y	N	N	Y	Y	?
4 Kennedy	Y	N	N	Y	Y	Y
5 Clark	Y	N	N	Y	N	Y
6 Moulton	Y	N	N	Y	Y	Y
7 Capuano	Y	N	Y	Y	N	+
8 Lynch	Y	N	N	Y	N	Y
9 Keating	Y	N	N	Y	?	Y
MICHIGAN						
1 **Bergman**	N	Y	N	Y	N	Y
2 **Huizenga**	N	Y	N	Y	Y	Y
3 *Amash*	N	Y	N	N	N	Y
4 **Moolenaar**	N	Y	N	Y	Y	Y
5 Kildee	Y	N	N	Y	Y	Y
6 **Upton**	N	Y	N	Y	N	Y
7 **Walberg**	N	Y	N	Y	N	Y
8 **Bishop**	N	Y	N	Y	N	Y
9 Levin	Y	N	N	Y	N	Y
10 **Mitchell**	N	Y	N	Y	Y	Y
11 **Trott**	N	Y	N	Y	Y	Y
12 Dingell	Y	N	N	Y	Y	Y
14 Lawrence	Y	N	N	Y	Y	Y
MINNESOTA						
1 Walz	Y	N	N	Y	Y	?
2 **Lewis**	N	Y	N	Y	Y	Y
3 **Paulsen**	N	Y	N	Y	N	Y
4 McCollum	Y	N	Y	Y	Y	Y
5 Ellison	Y	N	Y	N	Y	Y
6 **Emmer**	N	Y	N	Y	N	+
7 Peterson	Y	Y	N	Y	N	Y
8 Nolan	Y	N	N	Y	N	Y
MISSISSIPPI						
1 **Kelly**	N	Y	N	Y	N	Y
2 Thompson	Y	N	N	Y	N	Y
3 **Harper**	N	Y	N	Y	Y	Y
4 **Palazzo**	N	Y	N	Y	Y	Y
MISSOURI						
1 Clay	Y	N	N	Y	Y	Y
2 **Wagner**	N	Y	N	Y	Y	Y
3 **Luetkemeyer**	N	Y	N	Y	Y	Y
4 **Hartzler**	N	Y	N	Y	Y	Y
5 Cleaver	Y	N	Y	Y	N	Y
6 **Graves**	N	Y	N	Y	N	+
7 **Long**	N	Y	N	Y	Y	Y
8 **Smith**	N	Y	N	Y	?	Y
MONTANA						
AL **Gianforte**	N	Y	N	Y	Y	Y
NEBRASKA						
1 **Fortenberry**	N	Y	N	Y	Y	Y
2 **Bacon**	N	Y	N	Y	Y	Y
3 **Smith**	N	Y	N	Y	Y	Y
NEVADA						
1 Titus	Y	N	Y	N	Y	Y
2 **Amodei**	N	Y	Y	N	N	Y
3 Rosen	Y	N	Y	N	N	Y
4 Kihuen	Y	N	Y	N	N	Y
NEW HAMPSHIRE						
1 Shea-Porter	Y	N	Y	N	Y	Y
2 Kuster	+	–	–	+	?	Y
NEW JERSEY						
1 Norcross	Y	N	N	Y	N	Y
2 **LoBiondo**	N	Y	N	Y	N	Y
3 **MacArthur**	N	Y	N	Y	N	Y
4 **Smith**	N	Y	N	Y	Y	Y
5 Gottheimer	Y	N	?	?	?	Y
6 Pallone	Y	N	N	Y	N	Y
7 **Lance**	N	Y	N	Y	N	Y
8 Sires	Y	N	N	Y	N	Y
9 Pascrell	Y	N	N	Y	?	Y
10 Payne	Y	N	Y	Y	N	Y
11 **Frelinghuysen**	N	Y	N	Y	Y	Y
12 Watson Coleman	Y	N	N	Y	N	Y
NEW MEXICO						
1 Lujan Grisham	Y	N	Y	N	Y	+
2 **Pearce**	N	Y	N	Y	N	Y
3 Luján	Y	N	Y	N	N	Y
NEW YORK						
1 **Zeldin**	N	Y	N	Y	N	Y
2 **King**	N	Y	N	Y	Y	Y
3 Suozzi	Y	N	Y	N	?	Y
4 Rice	Y	N	N	Y	?	Y
5 Meeks	Y	N	Y	N	Y	Y
6 Meng	Y	N	Y	N	Y	Y
7 Velázquez	Y	N	Y	N	Y	Y
8 Jeffries	Y	N	N	N	N	Y
9 Clarke	Y	N	Y	N	N	Y
10 Nadler	Y	N	Y	N	Y	Y
11 **Donovan**	N	Y	N	Y	Y	Y
12 Maloney, C.	Y	N	Y	N	N	Y
13 Espaillat	Y	N	Y	N	N	Y
14 Crowley	Y	N	+	–	–	Y
15 Serrano	Y	N	Y	N	N	?
16 Engel	Y	N	Y	N	N	Y
17 Lowey	Y	N	N	Y	Y	Y
18 Maloney, S.P.	Y	N	N	Y	N	Y
19 **Faso**	N	Y	N	Y	N	Y
20 Tonko	Y	N	N	Y	P	Y
21 **Stefanik**	N	Y	N	Y	Y	Y
22 **Tenney**	N	Y	N	Y	N	Y
23 **Reed**	N	Y	N	Y	N	Y
24 **Katko**	N	Y	N	Y	N	Y
25 **Vacant**						
26 Higgins	Y	N	N	Y	?	Y
27 **Collins**	N	Y	N	Y	Y	Y
NORTH CAROLINA						
1 Butterfield	Y	N	N	Y	Y	?
2 **Holding**	N	Y	N	Y	N	Y
3 **Jones**	?	?	?	?	?	Y
4 Price	Y	N	N	Y	N	Y
5 **Foxx**	N	Y	N	Y	N	Y
6 **Walker**	N	Y	N	Y	Y	Y
7 **Rouzer**	N	Y	N	Y	N	Y
8 **Hudson**	N	Y	N	Y	N	Y
9 **Pittenger**	?	?	?	?	?	Y
9 **Vacant**						
10 **McHenry**	N	Y	N	Y	Y	Y
11 **Meadows**	N	Y	N	Y	Y	Y
12 Adams	Y	N	N	Y	N	Y
13 **Budd**	N	Y	?	?	?	Y
NORTH DAKOTA						
AL **Cramer**	N	Y	N	Y	Y	Y
OHIO						
1 **Chabot**	N	Y	N	Y	Y	Y
2 **Wenstrup**	N	Y	N	Y	N	Y
3 Beatty	Y	N	N	Y	Y	Y
4 **Jordan**	N	Y	N	Y	N	Y
5 **Latta**	N	Y	N	Y	N	Y
6 **Johnson**	N	Y	N	Y	N	Y
7 **Gibbs**	N	Y	N	Y	?	Y
8 **Davidson**	N	Y	N	Y	Y	Y
9 Kaptur	Y	N	Y	Y	Y	Y
10 **Turner**	N	Y	N	Y	N	Y
11 Fudge	Y	N	N	Y	N	Y
12 **Vacant**						
13 Ryan	Y	N	Y	N	N	Y
14 **Joyce**	N	Y	N	Y	N	Y
15 **Stivers**	N	Y	N	Y	N	Y
16 **Renacci**	N	Y	N	Y	N	Y
OKLAHOMA						
1 **Vacant**						
2 **Mullin**	N	Y	N	Y	Y	+
3 **Lucas**	N	Y	N	Y	Y	Y
4 **Cole**	N	Y	N	Y	Y	+
5 **Russell**	N	Y	N	Y	Y	Y
OREGON						
1 Bonamici	Y	N	Y	Y	Y	Y
2 **Walden**	N	Y	N	Y	Y	Y
3 Blumenauer	Y	N	N	N	N	Y
4 DeFazio	Y	N	Y	N	N	Y
5 Schrader	Y	N	N	Y	N	Y
PENNSYLVANIA						
1 Brady	Y	N	N	Y	N	?
2 Evans	Y	N	N	Y	Y	+
3 **Kelly**	N	Y	N	Y	Y	Y
4 **Perry**	N	Y	N	Y	N	Y
5 **Thompson**	N	Y	N	Y	N	+
6 **Costello**	N	Y	N	Y	N	Y
7 **Vacant**						
8 **Fitzpatrick**	N	Y	N	Y	N	Y
9 **Shuster**	N	Y	N	Y	Y	?
10 **Marino**	N	Y	N	Y	Y	+
11 **Barletta**	N	Y	N	Y	Y	?
12 **Rothfus**	N	Y	N	Y	Y	Y
13 Boyle	Y	N	Y	N	N	+
14 Doyle	Y	N	N	Y	N	?
16 **Smucker**	N	Y	N	Y	Y	+
17 Cartwright	Y	N	N	Y	Y	Y
18 Lamb	Y	N	N	Y	Y	Y
RHODE ISLAND						
1 Cicilline	Y	N	Y	N	Y	Y
2 Langevin	Y	N	N	Y	N	Y
SOUTH CAROLINA						
1 **Sanford**	N	Y	N	Y	N	Y
2 **Wilson**	N	Y	N	Y	Y	Y
3 **Duncan**	N	Y	N	Y	N	Y
4 **Gowdy**	N	Y	N	Y	Y	?
5 **Norman**	N	Y	N	Y	Y	Y
6 Clyburn	Y	N	N	Y	Y	?
7 **Rice**	N	Y	N	Y	P	Y
SOUTH DAKOTA						
AL **Noem**	N	Y	N	Y	Y	Y
TENNESSEE						
1 **Roe**	N	Y	N	Y	N	Y
2 **Duncan**	Y	N	N	Y	?	Y
3 **Fleischmann**	N	Y	N	Y	Y	Y
4 **DesJarlais**	N	Y	N	Y	Y	?
5 Cooper	Y	N	N	Y	Y	Y
6 **Black**	?	Y	?	?	?	Y
7 **Blackburn**	**N**	**Y**	**N**	**Y**	**Y**	**Y**
8 **Kustoff**	N	Y	N	Y	Y	Y
9 Cohen	Y	N	N	Y	?	Y
TEXAS						
1 **Gohmert**	N	Y	N	Y	N	Y
2 **Poe**	N	Y	N	Y	N	Y
3 **Johnson, S.**	N	Y	N	Y	Y	Y
4 **Ratcliffe**	N	Y	N	Y	N	Y
5 **Hensarling**	N	Y	N	Y	Y	Y
6 **Barton**	?	Y	N	Y	Y	Y
7 **Culberson**	N	Y	N	Y	Y	Y
8 **Brady**	N	Y	N	Y	Y	Y
9 Green, A.	Y	N	Y	N	N	Y
10 **McCaul**	N	Y	N	Y	Y	Y
11 **Conaway**	N	Y	N	Y	N	Y
12 **Granger**	N	Y	–	+	+	Y
13 **Thornberry**	N	Y	N	Y	Y	Y
14 **Weber**	N	Y	N	Y	N	Y
15 Gonzalez	Y	N	N	Y	N	Y
16 O'Rourke	Y	N	Y	N	?	+
17 **Flores**	N	Y	N	Y	N	Y
18 Jackson Lee	Y	N	Y	N	N	Y
19 **Arrington**	?	?	N	Y	Y	Y
20 Castro	Y	N	Y	N	Y	Y
21 **Smith**	N	Y	N	Y	Y	Y
22 **Olson**	N	Y	N	Y	Y	Y
23 **Hurd**	N	Y	N	Y	N	Y
24 **Marchant**	N	Y	?	?	?	Y
25 **Williams**	N	Y	N	Y	Y	Y
26 **Burgess**	N	Y	N	Y	N	Y
28 Cuellar	Y	Y	N	Y	N	?
29 Green, G.	Y	N	N	Y	N	Y
30 Johnson, E.B.	Y	N	N	Y	N	?
31 **Carter**	N	Y	N	Y	Y	?
32 **Sessions**	N	Y	N	Y	Y	Y
33 Veasey	Y	N	Y	N	Y	Y
34 Vela	Y	N	N	Y	N	Y
35 Doggett	Y	N	Y	N	Y	Y
36 **Babin**	N	Y	N	Y	N	Y
UTAH						
1 **Bishop**	N	Y	N	N	Y	Y
2 **Stewart**	N	Y	N	Y	Y	Y
3 **Curtis**	N	Y	N	Y	Y	Y
4 **Love**	N	Y	N	N	N	Y
VERMONT						
AL Welch	Y	N	N	Y	Y	Y
VIRGINIA						
1 **Wittman**	N	Y	N	Y	N	Y
2 **Taylor**	?	Y	N	Y	?	Y
3 Scott	Y	N	N	Y	Y	Y
4 McEachin	Y	N	N	Y	Y	Y
5 **Garrett**	N	Y	N	Y	Y	Y
6 **Goodlatte**	N	Y	N	Y	Y	Y
7 **Brat**	N	Y	N	Y	Y	Y
8 Beyer	Y	?	N	Y	N	?
9 **Griffith**	N	Y	N	Y	?	Y
10 **Comstock**	N	Y	N	Y	Y	Y
11 Connolly	Y	N	N	Y	?	Y
WASHINGTON						
1 DelBene	Y	N	N	Y	Y	Y
2 Larsen	Y	N	N	Y	Y	Y
3 **Herrera Beutler**	N	Y	N	Y	Y	Y
4 **Newhouse**	N	Y	N	Y	Y	Y
5 **McMorris Rodgers**	N	Y	N	Y	N	Y
6 Kilmer	Y	N	N	Y	N	Y
7 Jayapal	Y	N	N	N	N	Y
8 **Reichert**	N	Y	N	Y	?	Y
9 Smith	Y	N	Y	N	Y	Y
10 Heck	Y	N	N	Y	Y	Y
WEST VIRGINIA						
1 **McKinley**	N	Y	N	Y	N	Y
2 **Mooney**	N	Y	N	Y	Y	Y
3 **Jenkins**	–	+	–	+	+	Y
WISCONSIN						
1 **Ryan**						
2 Pocan	Y	N	Y	N	Y	Y
3 Kind	Y	N	N	Y	N	Y
4 Moore	Y	N	Y	Y	Y	Y
5 **Sensenbrenner**	N	Y	N	Y	Y	Y
6 **Grothman**	N	Y	N	Y	Y	Y
7 **Duffy**	N	Y	N	Y	Y	Y
8 **Gallagher**	N	Y	N	Y	N	Y
WYOMING						
AL **Cheney**	N	Y	N	Y	?	Y

||| HOUSE VOTES

VOTE NUMBER

182. HR4854. DNA BACKLOG GRANTS/PASSAGE. Goodlatte, R-Va., motion to suspend the rules and pass the bill that would require the Justice Department, in fiscal 2019 through fiscal 2022, to award five to seven percent of grants given to prosecutors to be awarded for the purpose of increasing the capacity of state and local prosecutors to address cold cases involving violent crime, in which suspects have been identified through DNA evidence. Motion agreed to 377-1: R 213-1; D 164-0. May 15, 2018.

183. HRES285. POLICE AND COMMUNITY ALLIANCES/PASSAGE. Goodlatte, R-Va., motion to suspend the rules and agree to the resolution that would express the sense of the U.S. House of Representatives that Congress and the president should empower the creation of police and community alliances designed to enhance and improve communication and collaboration between members of the law enforcement community and the public they serve. Motion agreed to 377-2: R 213-2; D 164-0. May 15, 2018.

184. HR5698. ASSAULT OF LAW ENFORCEMENT PENALTIES, VETERANS' HEALTH CARE, AND AGRICULTURAL PROGRAMS/QUESTION OF CONSIDERATION. Question of wether the House should consider the rule (H Res 891) that would provide for consideration of the bill (HR 5698) that would permit federal prosecution of, and set certain penalties for, crimes in which a person knowingly causes harm to a law enforcement officer; would provide for consideration of the bill (S 2372) that would establish a single program for veterans seeking healthcare outside of the VA system; and would provide consideration for the bill (HR 2) that would reauthorize many federal farm, nutrition assistance, rural development and other Agriculture Department programs. Agreed to consider 223-181: R 223-2; D 0-179. May 16, 2018.

185. HR5698. ASSAULT OF LAW ENFORCEMENT PENALTIES, VETERANS' HEALTH CARE, AND AGRICULTURAL PROGRAMS/PREVIOUS QUESTION. Woodall, R-Ga., motion to order the previous question (thus ending debate and possibility of amendment) on the rule (H Res 891) that would provide for consideration of the bill (HR 5698) that would permit federal prosecution of, and set certain penalties for, crimes in which a person knowingly causes harm to a law enforcement officer; would provide for consideration of the bill (S 2372) that would establish a single program for veterans seeking healthcare outside of the VA system; and would provide consideration for the bill (HR 2) that would reauthorize many federal farm, nutrition assistance, rural development and other Agriculture Department programs. Motion agreed to 230-184: R 230-1; D 0-183. May 16, 2018.

186. HR2. ASSAULT OF LAW ENFORCEMENT PENALTIES, VETERANS' HEALTH CARE, AND AGRICULTURAL PROGRAMS/RULE. Adoption of the rule (H Res 891) that would provide for consideration of the bill (HR 5698) that would permit federal prosecution of, and set certain penalties for, crimes in which a person knowingly causes harm to a law enforcement officer; would provide for consideration of the bill (S 2372) that would establish a single program for veterans seeking healthcare outside of the VA system; and would provide consideration for the bill (HR 2) that would reauthorize many federal farm, nutrition assistance, rural development and other Agriculture Department programs. Adopted 229-185: R 228-1; D 1-184. May 16, 2018.

187. S35. LAND TRANSFER FOR CEMETARY EXPANSION/PASSAGE. Bishop, R-Utah, motion to suspend the rules and pass the bill that would transfer approximately 200 acres in Sturgis, S.D. from the Bureau of Land Management to the Veterans Affairs Department to expand the Black Hills National Cemetery. Motion agreed to 407-0: R 223-0; D 184-0. May 16, 2018.

	182	183	184	185	186	187
ALABAMA						
1 Byrne	Y	Y	Y	Y	Y	Y
2 Roby	Y	Y	Y	Y	Y	Y
3 Rogers	Y	Y	Y	Y	Y	Y
4 Aderholt	Y	Y	Y	Y	Y	Y
5 Brooks	Y	Y	Y	Y	Y	Y
6 Palmer	Y	Y	Y	Y	Y	Y
7 Sewell	Y	Y	N	N	N	Y
ALASKA						
AL Young	Y	Y	Y	Y	Y	Y
ARIZONA						
1 O'Halleran	Y	Y	N	N	N	Y
2 McSally	?	?	Y	Y	Y	Y
3 Grijalva	Y	Y	N	N	N	Y
4 Gosar	Y	Y	Y	Y	Y	Y
5 Biggs	Y	Y	Y	Y	Y	Y
6 Schweikert	Y	Y	Y	Y	Y	Y
7 Gallego	Y	Y	N	N	N	Y
8 Lesko	Y	Y	Y	Y	Y	Y
9 Sinema	+	+	N	N	N	Y
ARKANSAS						
1 Crawford	Y	Y	Y	Y	Y	Y
2 Hill	Y	Y	Y	Y	Y	Y
3 Womack	Y	Y	Y	Y	Y	Y
4 Westerman	Y	Y	Y	Y	Y	Y
CALIFORNIA						
1 LaMalfa	Y	Y	Y	Y	Y	Y
2 Huffman	Y	Y	N	N	N	?
3 Garamendi	Y	Y	N	N	N	Y
4 McClintock	Y	Y	Y	Y	Y	Y
5 Thompson	Y	Y	N	N	N	Y
6 Matsui	Y	Y	N	N	N	Y
7 Bera	Y	Y	N	N	N	Y
8 Cook	Y	Y	Y	Y	Y	Y
9 McNerney	?	?	?	?	?	?
10 Denham	Y	Y	Y	Y	Y	Y
11 DeSaulnier	Y	Y	N	N	N	Y
12 Pelosi	Y	Y	N	N	N	Y
13 Lee	Y	Y	N	N	N	Y
14 Speier	Y	Y	N	N	N	Y
15 Swalwell	Y	Y	N	N	N	Y
16 Costa	Y	Y	N	N	N	Y
17 Khanna	Y	Y	N	N	N	Y
18 Eshoo	Y	Y	N	N	N	Y
19 Lofgren	Y	Y	N	N	N	Y
20 Panetta	Y	Y	N	N	N	Y
21 Valadao	Y	Y	Y	Y	Y	Y
22 Nunes	Y	Y	Y	Y	Y	Y
23 McCarthy	Y	Y	Y	Y	Y	?
24 Carbajal	Y	Y	N	N	N	Y
25 Knight	Y	Y	Y	Y	Y	Y
26 Brownley	Y	Y	N	N	N	Y
27 Chu	Y	Y	?	N	N	Y
28 Schiff	Y	Y	N	N	N	Y
29 Cardenas	Y	Y	?	N	N	Y
30 Sherman	Y	Y	N	N	N	Y
31 Aguilar	Y	Y	N	N	N	Y
32 Napolitano	+	Y	N	N	N	Y
33 Lieu	Y	Y	N	N	N	Y
34 Gomez	Y	Y	N	N	N	Y
35 Torres	Y	Y	N	N	N	Y
36 Ruiz	Y	Y	N	N	N	Y
37 Bass	Y	Y	N	N	N	Y
38 Sánchez, Linda	Y	Y	N	N	N	Y
39 Royce	Y	Y	Y	Y	Y	Y
40 Roybal-Allard	+	+	N	N	N	Y
41 Takano	Y	Y	N	N	N	Y
42 Calvert	Y	Y	Y	Y	Y	Y
43 Waters	Y	Y	N	N	N	Y
44 Barragan	Y	Y	N	N	N	Y
45 Walters	Y	Y	Y	Y	Y	Y
46 Correa	Y	Y	N	N	N	Y
47 Lowenthal	Y	Y	N	N	N	Y
48 Rohrabacher	?	?	Y	Y	Y	Y
49 Issa	?	?	Y	Y	?	?
50 Hunter	Y	Y	Y	Y	Y	Y
51 Vargas	Y	Y	N	N	N	Y
52 Peters	Y	Y	N	N	N	Y
53 Davis	Y	Y	N	N	N	Y

	182	183	184	185	186	187
COLORADO						
1 DeGette	?	?	?	?	?	?
2 Polis	Y	Y	N	N	N	Y
3 Tipton	Y	Y	Y	Y	Y	Y
4 Buck	Y	Y	Y	Y	Y	Y
5 Lamborn	Y	Y	Y	Y	Y	Y
6 Coffman	Y	Y	Y	Y	Y	Y
7 Perlmutter	Y	Y	N	N	N	Y
CONNECTICUT						
1 Larson	Y	Y	N	N	N	Y
2 Courtney	Y	Y	N	N	N	Y
3 DeLauro	Y	Y	N	N	N	Y
4 Himes	Y	Y	N	N	N	?
5 Esty	Y	Y	N	N	N	Y
DELAWARE						
AL Blunt Rochester	?	?	N	N	N	Y
FLORIDA						
1 Gaetz	Y	Y	Y	Y	Y	Y
2 Dunn	Y	Y	Y	Y	Y	Y
3 Yoho	Y	Y	Y	Y	Y	Y
4 Rutherford	Y	Y	Y	Y	Y	Y
5 Lawson	Y	Y	N	N	N	Y
6 DeSantis	Y	Y	Y	Y	Y	Y
7 Murphy	Y	Y	N	N	N	Y
8 Posey	Y	Y	Y	Y	Y	Y
9 Soto	Y	Y	N	N	N	Y
10 Demings	Y	Y	N	N	N	Y
11 Webster	+	+	+	+	+	+
12 Bilirakis	Y	Y	Y	Y	Y	Y
13 Crist	Y	Y	N	N	N	Y
14 Castor	Y	Y	N	N	N	Y
15 Ross	Y	Y	Y	Y	Y	Y
16 Buchanan	Y	Y	Y	Y	Y	Y
17 Rooney, T.	Y	Y	Y	Y	Y	Y
18 Mast	Y	Y	Y	Y	Y	Y
19 Rooney, F.	Y	Y	Y	Y	Y	Y
20 Hastings	Y	Y	N	N	N	Y
21 Frankel	Y	Y	N	N	N	Y
22 Deutch	Y	Y	N	N	N	Y
23 Wasserman Schultz	Y	Y	N	N	N	Y
24 Wilson	?	?	?	N	N	Y
25 Diaz-Balart	Y	Y	Y	Y	Y	Y
26 Curbelo	Y	Y	Y	Y	Y	Y
27 Ros-Lehtinen	Y	Y	Y	Y	Y	Y
GEORGIA						
1 Carter	Y	Y	Y	Y	Y	Y
2 Bishop	Y	Y	N	N	N	Y
3 Ferguson	Y	Y	Y	Y	Y	Y
4 Johnson	Y	Y	N	?	N	Y
5 Lewis	Y	Y	N	N	N	Y
6 Handel	Y	Y	Y	Y	Y	Y
7 Woodall	?	?	Y	Y	Y	Y
8 Scott, A.	Y	Y	Y	Y	Y	Y
9 Collins	Y	Y	Y	Y	Y	Y
10 Hice	Y	Y	Y	Y	Y	Y
11 Loudermilk	Y	Y	Y	Y	Y	Y
12 Allen	Y	Y	Y	Y	Y	Y
13 Scott, D.	Y	Y	N	N	N	Y
14 Graves	Y	Y	Y	Y	Y	Y
HAWAII						
1 Hanabusa	Y	Y	N	N	N	Y
2 Gabbard	Y	Y	?	?	?	?
IDAHO						
1 Labrador	?	?	?	?	?	?
2 Simpson	Y	Y	Y	Y	Y	Y
ILLINOIS						
1 Rush	Y	Y	N	?	Y	Y
2 Kelly	Y	Y	N	N	N	Y
3 Lipinski	Y	Y	?	N	N	Y
4 Gutierrez	+	+	?	N	N	Y
5 Quigley	Y	Y	N	N	N	Y
6 Roskam	Y	Y	?	Y	Y	Y
7 Davis, D.	?	?	N	N	N	Y
8 Krishnamoorthi	Y	Y	N	N	N	Y
9 Schakowsky	Y	Y	N	N	N	Y
10 Schneider	Y	Y	N	N	N	Y
11 Foster	Y	Y	N	N	N	Y
12 Bost	Y	Y	Y	Y	Y	Y
13 Davis, R.	Y	Y	Y	Y	Y	Y

	182	183	184	185	186	187
14 **Hultgren**	Y	Y	Y	Y	Y	Y
15 **Shimkus**	Y	Y	Y	Y	Y	Y
16 **Kinzinger**	Y	Y	Y	Y	Y	Y
17 Bustos	?	?	N	N	N	Y
18 **LaHood**	Y	Y	Y	Y	Y	Y
INDIANA						
1 Visclosky	+	+	N	N	N	Y
2 **Walorski**	Y	Y	Y	Y	Y	Y
3 **Banks**	Y	Y	Y	Y	Y	Y
4 **Rokita**	Y	Y	Y	Y	Y	Y
5 **Brooks**	+	Y	Y	Y	Y	?
6 **Messer**	?	?	Y	Y	Y	Y
7 Carson	Y	Y	N	N	N	Y
8 **Bucshon**	Y	Y	Y	Y	Y	Y
9 **Hollingsworth**	Y	Y	Y	Y	Y	Y
IOWA						
1 **Blum**	Y	Y	Y	Y	Y	Y
2 Loebsack	Y	Y	N	N	N	Y
3 **Young**	Y	Y	Y	Y	Y	Y
4 **King**	Y	Y	Y	Y	Y	Y
KANSAS						
1 **Marshall**	?	Y	Y	Y	Y	Y
2 **Jenkins**	Y	Y	Y	Y	Y	Y
3 **Yoder**	Y	Y	Y	Y	Y	Y
4 **Estes**	Y	Y	Y	Y	Y	Y
KENTUCKY						
1 **Comer**	Y	Y	Y	Y	Y	Y
2 **Guthrie**	Y	Y	Y	Y	Y	Y
3 Yarmuth	Y	Y	N	N	N	Y
4 **Massie**	Y	N	Y	Y	Y	Y
5 **Rogers**	+	+	+	+	+	+
6 **Barr**	Y	Y	Y	Y	Y	Y
LOUISIANA						
1 **Scalise**	Y	Y	Y	Y	Y	Y
2 Richmond	?	?	?	?	?	?
3 **Higgins**	Y	Y	Y	Y	Y	Y
4 **Johnson**	Y	Y	Y	Y	Y	Y
5 **Abraham**	Y	Y	Y	Y	Y	Y
6 **Graves**	Y	Y	Y	Y	Y	Y
MAINE						
1 Pingree	Y	Y	N	N	N	Y
2 **Poliquin**	Y	Y	Y	Y	Y	Y
MARYLAND						
1 **Harris**	Y	Y	Y	Y	Y	Y
2 Ruppersberger	Y	Y	N	N	N	Y
3 Sarbanes	Y	Y	N	N	N	Y
4 Brown	+	+	–	–	–	+
5 Hoyer	Y	Y	N	N	N	Y
6 Delaney	Y	+	N	N	N	Y
7 Cummings	?	?	N	N	N	Y
8 Raskin	Y	Y	N	N	N	Y
MASSACHUSETTS						
1 Neal	Y	Y	N	N	N	Y
2 McGovern	Y	Y	N	N	N	Y
3 Tsongas	?	?	N	N	N	Y
4 Kennedy	Y	Y	N	N	N	Y
5 Clark	Y	Y	N	N	N	Y
6 Moulton	Y	Y	N	N	N	Y
7 Capuano	+	+	N	N	N	Y
8 Lynch	Y	Y	N	N	N	Y
9 Keating	Y	Y	N	N	N	Y
MICHIGAN						
1 **Bergman**	Y	Y	Y	Y	Y	Y
2 **Huizenga**	Y	Y	Y	Y	Y	Y
3 *Amash*	N	N	N	Y	N	Y
4 **Moolenaar**	Y	Y	Y	Y	Y	Y
5 Kildee	Y	Y	N	N	N	Y
6 **Upton**	Y	Y	Y	Y	Y	Y
7 **Walberg**	Y	Y	Y	Y	Y	Y
8 **Bishop**	Y	Y	Y	Y	Y	Y
9 Levin	Y	Y	N	N	N	Y
10 **Mitchell**	Y	Y	Y	Y	Y	Y
11 **Trott**	Y	Y	Y	Y	Y	Y
12 Dingell	Y	Y	N	N	N	Y
14 Lawrence	Y	Y	N	N	N	Y
MINNESOTA						
1 Walz	?	?	N	N	N	Y
2 **Lewis**	Y	Y	Y	Y	Y	Y
3 **Paulsen**	Y	Y	Y	Y	Y	Y
4 McCollum	Y	Y	N	N	N	Y

	182	183	184	185	186	187
5 Ellison	Y	Y	N	N	N	Y
6 **Emmer**	+	+	Y	Y	Y	Y
7 Peterson	Y	Y	N	N	N	Y
8 Nolan	Y	Y	N	N	N	Y
MISSISSIPPI						
1 **Kelly**	Y	Y	Y	Y	Y	Y
2 Thompson	Y	Y	N	N	N	Y
3 **Harper**	Y	Y	Y	Y	Y	Y
4 **Palazzo**	Y	Y	Y	Y	Y	Y
MISSOURI						
1 Clay	Y	Y	N	N	N	Y
2 **Wagner**	Y	Y	Y	Y	Y	Y
3 **Luetkemeyer**	Y	Y	?	Y	Y	Y
4 **Hartzler**	Y	Y	Y	Y	Y	Y
5 Cleaver	Y	Y	N	N	N	Y
6 **Graves**	Y	Y	Y	Y	Y	Y
7 **Long**	Y	Y	Y	Y	Y	Y
8 **Smith**	Y	Y	Y	Y	Y	Y
MONTANA						
AL **Gianforte**	Y	Y	Y	Y	Y	Y
NEBRASKA						
1 **Fortenberry**	Y	Y	Y	Y	Y	Y
2 **Bacon**	Y	Y	Y	Y	Y	Y
3 **Smith**	Y	Y	Y	Y	Y	Y
NEVADA						
1 Titus	Y	Y	N	N	N	Y
2 **Amodei**	Y	Y	Y	Y	Y	Y
3 Rosen	Y	Y	N	N	N	Y
4 Kihuen	Y	Y	N	N	N	Y
NEW HAMPSHIRE						
1 Shea-Porter	Y	Y	?	N	N	Y
2 Kuster	Y	Y	N	N	N	Y
NEW JERSEY						
1 Norcross	Y	Y	N	N	N	Y
2 **LoBiondo**	Y	Y	Y	Y	Y	Y
3 **MacArthur**	Y	Y	Y	Y	Y	Y
4 **Smith**	Y	Y	Y	Y	Y	Y
5 Gottheimer	Y	Y	N	N	N	Y
6 Pallone	Y	Y	N	N	N	Y
7 **Lance**	Y	Y	Y	Y	Y	Y
8 Sires	Y	Y	N	N	N	Y
9 Pascrell	Y	Y	N	N	N	Y
10 Payne	Y	Y	N	N	N	Y
11 **Frelinghuysen**	Y	Y	Y	Y	Y	Y
12 Watson Coleman	Y	Y	N	N	N	Y
NEW MEXICO						
1 Lujan Grisham	+	+	–	N	N	Y
2 **Pearce**	Y	Y	Y	Y	Y	Y
3 Luján	Y	Y	N	N	N	Y
NEW YORK						
1 **Zeldin**	Y	Y	Y	Y	Y	Y
2 **King**	Y	Y	Y	Y	Y	Y
3 Suozzi	Y	Y	N	N	N	Y
4 Rice	Y	Y	N	N	N	Y
5 Meeks	Y	Y	N	N	N	Y
6 Meng	Y	Y	N	N	N	Y
7 Velázquez	Y	Y	N	N	N	Y
8 Jeffries	Y	Y	N	N	N	Y
9 Clarke	Y	Y	N	N	N	Y
10 Nadler	Y	Y	N	N	N	Y
11 **Donovan**	Y	Y	Y	Y	Y	Y
12 Maloney, C.	Y	Y	N	N	N	Y
13 Espaillat	Y	Y	N	N	N	Y
14 Crowley	Y	Y	N	N	N	Y
15 Serrano	Y	Y	N	N	N	Y
16 Engel	Y	Y	?	N	N	Y
17 Lowey	Y	Y	N	N	N	Y
18 Maloney, S.P.	Y	Y	N	N	N	Y
19 **Faso**	Y	Y	Y	Y	Y	?
20 Tonko	Y	Y	N	N	N	Y
21 **Stefanik**	Y	Y	Y	Y	Y	Y
22 **Tenney**	Y	Y	Y	Y	Y	Y
23 **Reed**	Y	Y	?	Y	Y	Y
24 **Katko**	Y	Y	Y	Y	Y	Y
25 **Vacant**						
26 Higgins	Y	Y	N	N	N	Y
27 **Collins**	Y	Y	Y	Y	Y	Y
NORTH CAROLINA						
1 Butterfield	?	?	N	N	?	?
2 **Holding**	Y	Y	Y	Y	Y	Y
3 **Jones**	Y	Y	N	N	Y	Y
4 Price	Y	Y	N	N	N	Y

	182	183	184	185	186	187
5 **Foxx**	Y	Y	Y	Y	Y	Y
6 **Walker**	Y	Y	Y	Y	Y	Y
7 **Rouzer**	Y	Y	Y	Y	Y	Y
8 **Hudson**	Y	Y	Y	Y	Y	Y
9 Pittenger	Y	Y	Y	Y	Y	Y
9 **Vacant**						
10 **McHenry**	Y	Y	Y	Y	Y	Y
11 **Meadows**	Y	Y	Y	Y	Y	Y
12 Adams	Y	Y	N	N	N	Y
13 **Budd**	Y	Y	Y	Y	Y	Y
NORTH DAKOTA						
AL **Cramer**	Y	Y	Y	Y	Y	Y
OHIO						
1 **Chabot**	Y	Y	Y	Y	Y	Y
2 **Wenstrup**	Y	Y	Y	Y	Y	Y
3 Beatty	Y	Y	N	N	N	Y
4 **Jordan**	Y	Y	Y	Y	Y	Y
5 **Latta**	Y	Y	Y	Y	Y	Y
6 **Johnson**	Y	Y	Y	Y	Y	?
7 **Gibbs**	Y	Y	Y	Y	Y	Y
8 **Davidson**	Y	Y	Y	Y	Y	Y
9 Kaptur	Y	Y	N	N	N	Y
10 **Turner**	Y	Y	Y	Y	Y	Y
11 Fudge	Y	Y	N	N	N	Y
12 **Vacant**						
13 Ryan	Y	Y	N	N	N	Y
14 **Joyce**	Y	Y	Y	Y	Y	Y
15 **Stivers**	Y	Y	Y	Y	Y	Y
16 **Renacci**	Y	Y	Y	Y	Y	Y
OKLAHOMA						
1 **Vacant**						
2 **Mullin**	+	+	Y	Y	Y	Y
3 **Lucas**	Y	Y	Y	Y	Y	Y
4 **Cole**	+	+	Y	Y	Y	Y
5 **Russell**	Y	Y	Y	Y	Y	Y
OREGON						
1 Bonamici	Y	Y	N	N	N	Y
2 **Walden**	Y	Y	Y	Y	Y	Y
3 Blumenauer	Y	Y	N	N	N	Y
4 DeFazio	Y	Y	N	N	N	Y
5 Schrader	Y	Y	N	N	N	Y
PENNSYLVANIA						
1 Brady	?	?	N	N	N	Y
2 Evans	+	+	N	N	N	Y
3 **Kelly**	Y	Y	Y	Y	Y	Y
4 **Perry**	Y	Y	Y	Y	Y	?
5 **Thompson**	+	+	Y	Y	Y	Y
6 **Costello**	Y	Y	Y	Y	Y	Y
7 **Vacant**						
8 **Fitzpatrick**	Y	Y	Y	Y	Y	Y
9 **Shuster**	?	?	?	Y	Y	Y
10 **Marino**	+	+	Y	Y	Y	Y
11 **Barletta**	?	?	Y	Y	Y	Y
12 **Rothfus**	Y	Y	Y	Y	Y	Y
13 Boyle	+	+	N	N	N	Y
14 Doyle	?	?	N	N	N	Y
15 **Vacant**						
16 **Smucker**	+	+	Y	Y	Y	Y
17 Cartwright	Y	Y	N	N	N	Y
18 Lamb	Y	Y	N	N	N	Y
RHODE ISLAND						
1 Cicilline	Y	Y	N	–	N	Y
2 Langevin	Y	Y	N	N	N	Y
SOUTH CAROLINA						
1 **Sanford**	Y	Y	Y	Y	Y	Y
2 **Wilson**	Y	?	Y	Y	Y	Y
3 **Duncan**	Y	Y	Y	Y	Y	Y
4 **Gowdy**	?	?	Y	Y	Y	Y
5 **Norman**	Y	Y	Y	Y	Y	Y
6 Clyburn	?	?	N	N	N	Y
7 **Rice**	Y	Y	Y	Y	Y	Y
SOUTH DAKOTA						
AL **Noem**	Y	Y	Y	Y	Y	Y
TENNESSEE						
1 **Roe**	Y	Y	Y	Y	Y	Y
2 **Duncan**	Y	Y	Y	Y	Y	Y
3 **Fleischmann**	Y	Y	Y	Y	Y	Y
4 **DesJarlais**	Y	Y	Y	Y	Y	Y
5 Cooper	Y	Y	N	N	?	Y
6 **Black**	Y	Y	Y	Y	Y	Y
7 **Blackburn**	Y	Y	Y	Y	Y	Y
8 **Kustoff**	Y	Y	Y	Y	Y	Y
9 Cohen	Y	Y	N	N	N	Y

	182	183	184	185	186	187
TEXAS						
1 **Gohmert**	Y	Y	Y	Y	Y	Y
2 **Poe**	Y	Y	Y	Y	?	?
3 **Johnson, S.**	Y	Y	Y	Y	Y	Y
4 **Ratcliffe**	Y	Y	Y	Y	Y	?
5 **Hensarling**	Y	Y	Y	Y	Y	Y
6 **Barton**	Y	Y	Y	Y	Y	Y
7 **Culberson**	Y	Y	Y	Y	Y	Y
8 **Brady**	?	Y	Y	Y	Y	Y
9 Green, A.	Y	Y	N	N	N	Y
10 **McCaul**	Y	Y	Y	Y	Y	Y
11 **Conaway**	Y	Y	Y	Y	Y	Y
12 **Granger**	Y	Y	Y	Y	Y	Y
13 **Thornberry**	Y	Y	?	Y	Y	Y
14 **Weber**	Y	Y	Y	Y	Y	Y
15 Gonzalez	Y	Y	N	?	N	Y
16 O'Rourke	+	+	N	N	N	Y
17 **Flores**	Y	Y	Y	Y	Y	Y
18 Jackson Lee	Y	Y	N	N	N	Y
19 **Arrington**	Y	Y	Y	Y	Y	Y
20 Castro	Y	Y	N	N	N	Y
21 **Smith**	Y	Y	Y	Y	Y	Y
22 **Olson**	Y	Y	Y	Y	Y	Y
23 **Hurd**	Y	Y	Y	Y	Y	Y
24 **Marchant**	Y	Y	Y	Y	Y	Y
25 **Williams**	Y	Y	Y	Y	Y	Y
26 **Burgess**	Y	Y	Y	Y	Y	Y
28 Cuellar	?	?	N	N	N	Y
29 Green, G.	Y	Y	N	N	N	Y
30 Johnson, E.B.	?	?	N	N	N	Y
31 **Carter**	Y	Y	Y	Y	Y	Y
32 **Sessions**	Y	Y	Y	Y	Y	Y
33 Veasey	Y	Y	N	N	N	Y
34 Vela	Y	Y	N	N	N	Y
35 Doggett	Y	Y	N	N	N	Y
36 **Babin**	Y	Y	Y	Y	Y	Y
UTAH						
1 **Bishop**	Y	Y	Y	Y	Y	Y
2 **Stewart**	Y	Y	Y	Y	Y	Y
3 **Curtis**	Y	Y	Y	Y	Y	Y
4 **Love**	Y	Y	Y	Y	Y	Y
VERMONT						
AL Welch	Y	Y	N	N	N	Y
VIRGINIA						
1 **Wittman**	Y	Y	Y	Y	Y	Y
2 **Taylor**	Y	Y	Y	Y	Y	Y
3 Scott	Y	Y	N	N	N	Y
4 McEachin	Y	Y	N	N	N	Y
5 **Garrett**	Y	Y	Y	Y	Y	Y
6 **Goodlatte**	Y	Y	Y	Y	Y	Y
7 **Brat**	Y	Y	Y	Y	Y	Y
8 Beyer	?	?	?	?	?	?
9 **Griffith**	Y	Y	Y	Y	Y	Y
10 **Comstock**	Y	Y	Y	Y	Y	Y
11 Connolly	Y	Y	N	N	N	Y
WASHINGTON						
1 DelBene	Y	Y	N	N	N	Y
2 Larsen	?	?	N	N	N	Y
3 **Herrera Beutler**	Y	Y	Y	Y	Y	Y
4 **Newhouse**	Y	Y	Y	Y	Y	Y
5 **McMorris Rodgers**	Y	Y	Y	Y	Y	Y
6 Kilmer	Y	Y	N	N	N	Y
7 Jayapal	Y	Y	N	N	N	Y
8 **Reichert**	Y	Y	?	Y	Y	Y
9 Smith	Y	Y	N	N	N	Y
10 Heck	Y	Y	N	N	N	Y
WEST VIRGINIA						
1 **McKinley**	Y	Y	Y	Y	Y	Y
2 **Mooney**	Y	Y	Y	Y	Y	Y
3 **Jenkins**	Y	Y	Y	Y	Y	Y
WISCONSIN						
1 **Ryan**						
2 Pocan	Y	Y	N	N	N	Y
3 Kind	Y	Y	N	N	N	Y
4 Moore	Y	Y	N	N	N	Y
5 **Sensenbrenner**	Y	Y	Y	Y	Y	Y
6 **Grothman**	Y	Y	Y	Y	Y	Y
7 **Duffy**	Y	Y	Y	Y	Y	Y
8 **Gallagher**	Y	Y	Y	Y	Y	Y
WYOMING						
AL **Cheney**	Y	Y	Y	Y	Y	Y

VOTE NUMBER

188. HR5698. PENALTIES FOR ASSAULTING LAW ENFORCEMENT/ PASSAGE. Passage of the bill that would limit the punishment of knowingly causing harm to a law enforcement officer to 10 years in imprisonment and a fine, which would increase to life imprisonment if the offence includes death, kidnapping, attempted kidnapping, or an attempt to kill. The bill would also allow for federal prosecution of the stated crime in certain situations including if the offence crosses state lines, the state verdict demonstrably does not serve the federal interest in protecting the public, or prosecution by the federal government is in the public interest. Passed 382-35: R 220-11; D 162-24. May 16, 2018.

189. S2372. VETERANS' HEALTH CARE/PASSAGE. Passage of the bill that would consolidate programs that allow veterans to seek medical care outside of the VA into a new singular entity, the Veterans Community Care Program. The bill would continue the current VA Choice Program for one year, and would authorize an additional $5.2 billion for the costs of providing non-VA medical care through the old program and for transitioning to the new program. It would also authorize the VA to enter into Veterans Care Agreements that would include care standards for providers and private facilities, and would allow veterans to access care at federally-qualified health centers walk-in clinics. The bill would also create a commission to review VA modernization proposals and includes other provisions related to the recruitment of health care professionals. The bill would also require the Interior Department to provide an outer burial receptacle for new graves in open cemeteries that are controlled by the National Park Service, and would require the Department to reimburse veterans' survivors who had purchased one on their own. Passed 347-70: R 231-0; D 116-70. May 16, 2018.

190. HR2. FARM PROGRAMS/PREVIOUS QUESTION. Woodall, R-Ga., motion to order the previous question (thus ending debate and possibility of amendment) on the rule (H Res 900) that would provide for consideration of the bill (HR 2) that would reauthorize many federal farm, nutrition assistance, rural development and other Agriculture Department programs. Motion agreed to 228-189: R 228-1; D 0-188. May 17, 2018.

191. HRES900. FARM PROGRAMS/RULE. Adoption of the rule (H Res 900) that would provide for consideration of the bill (HR 2) that would reauthorize many federal farm, nutrition assistance, rural development and other Agriculture Department programs. Adopted 228-188: R 228-0; D 0-188. May 17, 2018.

192. PROCEDURAL MOTION/JOURNAL. Approval of the House journal of May 16, 2018. Approved 217-188: R 141-80; D 76-108. May 17, 2018.

193. HR2. FARM PROGRAMS/SUGAR PROGRAMS. Foxx, R-N.C., amendment that would adjust loan rates for the sugar program, would terminate the feedstock flexibility program, and would establish tariff rate quotas for raw cane sugar and refined sugar. Rejected in Committee of the Whole 137-278: R 96-132; D 41-146. May 17, 2018.

	188	189	190	191	192	193
ALABAMA						
1 **Byrne**	Y	Y	Y	Y	Y	N
2 **Roby**	Y	Y	Y	Y	Y	N
3 **Rogers**	Y	Y	Y	Y	?	N
4 **Aderholt**	Y	Y	Y	Y	Y	N
5 **Brooks**	Y	Y	Y	N	N	N
6 **Palmer**	Y	Y	Y	Y	Y	N
7 Sewell	Y	Y	N	N	N	N
ALASKA						
AL **Young**	Y	Y	Y	Y	N	N
ARIZONA						
1 O'Halleran	Y	Y	N	N	N	N
2 **McSally**	Y	Y	Y	N	N	N
3 Grijalva	Y	N	N	N	N	N
4 **Gosar**	N	Y	Y	Y	N	Y
5 **Biggs**	N	Y	Y	Y	?	Y
6 **Schweikert**	N	Y	Y	Y	Y	Y
7 Gallego	Y	N	N	N	Y	N
8 **Lesko**	Y	Y	Y	Y	Y	Y
9 Sinema	Y	Y	N	N	N	N
ARKANSAS						
1 **Crawford**	Y	Y	Y	Y	Y	N
2 **Hill**	Y	Y	Y	Y	N	N
3 **Womack**	Y	Y	Y	Y	Y	Y
4 **Westerman**	Y	Y	Y	Y	Y	N
CALIFORNIA						
1 **LaMalfa**	Y	Y	Y	Y	Y	N
2 Huffman	Y	Y	N	N	Y	N
3 Garamendi	Y	Y	N	N	Y	Y
4 **McClintock**	Y	Y	Y	Y	Y	Y
5 Thompson	Y	Y	N	N	N	N
6 Matsui	Y	Y	N	N	N	N
7 Bera	Y	Y	N	N	N	N
8 **Cook**	Y	Y	Y	Y	Y	N
9 McNerney	Y	Y	N	N	Y	N
10 **Denham**	Y	Y	Y	Y	N	N
11 DeSaulnier	N	N	N	N	N	N
12 Pelosi	Y	Y	N	N	Y	N
13 Lee	N	N	N	N	N	Y
14 Speier	Y	Y	N	N	Y	Y
15 Swalwell	Y	Y	N	N	N	Y
16 Costa	Y	Y	N	N	N	N
17 Khanna	Y	N	N	N	N	N
18 Eshoo	Y	N	N	N	N	N
19 Lofgren	Y	N	N	N	N	N
20 Panetta	Y	Y	N	N	N	N
21 **Valadao**	Y	Y	Y	Y	Y	N
22 Nunes	Y	Y	Y	Y	Y	N
23 McCarthy	Y	Y	Y	Y	Y	N
24 Carbajal	Y	Y	N	N	N	N
25 Knight	Y	Y	Y	N	N	N
26 Brownley	Y	N	N	N	N	N
27 Chu	Y	N	N	N	Y	N
28 Schiff	Y	Y	N	N	N	Y
29 Cardenas	Y	Y	N	N	N	N
30 Sherman	Y	N	N	Y	N	N
31 Aguilar	Y	Y	N	N	N	N
32 Napolitano	Y	Y	N	N	N	N
33 Lieu	Y	N	N	N	N	N
34 Gomez	?	?	N	N	N	N
35 Torres	Y	Y	N	N	N	N
36 Ruiz	Y	Y	N	N	N	N
37 Bass	N	N	N	N	N	N
38 Sánchez, Linda	Y	N	N	N	N	N
39 Royce	Y	Y	Y	Y	Y	Y
40 Roybal-Allard	Y	N	N	N	N	N
41 Takano	Y	N	N	N	Y	N
42 Calvert	Y	Y	Y	Y	?	N
43 Waters	N	Y	N	N	Y	N
44 Barragan	N	Y	N	N	N	N
45 Walters	Y	Y	Y	Y	Y	N
46 Correa	Y	Y	N	N	N	N
47 Lowenthal	Y	Y	N	N	N	N
48 Rohrabacher	Y	Y	Y	Y	Y	N
49 Issa	Y	Y	Y	Y	?	Y
50 Hunter	Y	Y	Y	Y	Y	N
51 Vargas	Y	Y	N	N	N	N
52 Peters	Y	Y	N	N	Y	Y
53 Davis	Y	Y	N	N	Y	N

	188	189	190	191	192	193
COLORADO						
1 DeGette	?	?	?	?	?	N
2 Polis	N	Y	?	?	?	?
3 **Tipton**	Y	Y	Y	Y	Y	N
4 **Buck**	Y	Y	Y	Y	N	?
5 **Lamborn**	Y	Y	Y	Y	Y	N
6 **Coffman**	Y	Y	Y	Y	N	Y
7 Perlmutter	Y	Y	N	N	Y	N
CONNECTICUT						
1 Larson	Y	N	N	N	N	N
2 Courtney	Y	Y	N	N	N	N
3 DeLauro	Y	N	N	N	Y	N
4 Himes	Y	Y	N	N	Y	Y
5 Esty	Y	Y	N	N	N	N
DELAWARE						
AL Blunt Rochester	Y	Y	N	N	Y	N
FLORIDA						
1 **Gaetz**	Y	Y	Y	Y	N	N
2 **Dunn**	Y	Y	Y	Y	Y	N
3 **Yoho**	Y	Y	Y	Y	Y	N
4 **Rutherford**	Y	Y	Y	Y	Y	N
5 Lawson	Y	N	N	N	N	N
6 **DeSantis**	Y	Y	Y	Y	N	Y
7 Murphy	Y	N	N	N	N	N
8 **Posey**	Y	Y	Y	Y	Y	N
9 Soto	Y	N	N	N	N	N
10 Demings	Y	N	N	N	Y	N
11 **Webster**	+	+	?	?	?	N
12 **Bilirakis**	Y	Y	Y	Y	Y	N
13 Crist	Y	N	N	N	N	N
14 Castor	Y	N	N	N	N	N
15 **Ross**	Y	Y	Y	Y	Y	N
16 **Buchanan**	Y	Y	Y	Y	Y	N
17 **Rooney, T.**	Y	Y	Y	Y	Y	N
18 **Mast**	Y	Y	Y	Y	N	Y
19 **Rooney, F.**	Y	Y	Y	Y	Y	Y
20 Hastings	N	N	N	N	N	N
21 Frankel	N	N	N	Y	N	N
22 Deutch	Y	N	N	N	Y	N
23 Wasserman Schultz	Y	N	N	N	Y	N
24 Wilson	–	N	N	N	Y	N
25 **Diaz-Balart**	Y	Y	Y	Y	N	N
26 **Curbelo**	Y	Y	Y	Y	N	N
27 **Ros-Lehtinen**	Y	Y	Y	Y	N	N
GEORGIA						
1 **Carter**	Y	Y	Y	Y	N	N
2 Bishop	Y	N	N	N	N	N
3 **Ferguson**	Y	Y	Y	Y	Y	N
4 Johnson	Y	Y	N	N	N	N
5 Lewis	Y	N	N	N	N	N
6 **Handel**	Y	Y	Y	Y	Y	N
7 **Woodall**	Y	Y	Y	Y	N	Y
8 **Scott, A.**	Y	Y	Y	Y	Y	N
9 **Collins**	Y	Y	Y	Y	Y	N
10 **Hice**	Y	Y	Y	Y	N	Y
11 **Loudermilk**	Y	Y	Y	Y	Y	Y
12 **Allen**	Y	Y	Y	Y	Y	N
13 **Scott, D.**	Y	Y	N	N	Y	N
14 **Graves**	Y	Y	Y	N	Y	Y
HAWAII						
1 Hanabusa	Y	Y	N	N	N	N
2 Gabbard	?	?	N	N	Y	N
IDAHO						
1 **Labrador**	?	?	?	?	?	?
2 **Simpson**	Y	Y	Y	Y	Y	N
ILLINOIS						
1 Rush	Y	N	N	N	N	Y
2 Kelly	N	N	N	N	N	N
3 Lipinski	Y	Y	N	N	Y	Y
4 Gutierrez	Y	N	N	N	N	Y
5 Quigley	Y	N	N	N	N	Y
6 **Roskam**	Y	Y	Y	Y	?	Y
7 Davis, D.	Y	?	N	N	Y	N
8 Krishnamoorthi	Y	N	N	N	Y	N
9 Schakowsky	Y	N	N	N	N	N
10 Schneider	Y	N	N	N	Y	Y
11 Foster	N	Y	N	N	Y	Y
12 **Bost**	Y	Y	Y	Y	N	N
13 **Davis, R.**	Y	Y	Y	Y	Y	N

	188	189	190	191	192	193
16 Kinzinger	Y	Y	Y	N	Y	N
17 Bustos	Y	Y	N	N	Y	N
18 LaHood	Y	Y	Y	Y	N	N
INDIANA						
1 Visclosky	N	Y	N	N	N	Y
2 Walorski	Y	Y	Y	Y	Y	Y
3 Banks	Y	Y	Y	Y	Y	Y
4 Rokita	Y	Y	Y	Y	N	Y
5 Brooks	Y	Y	Y	Y	Y	Y
6 Messer	Y	Y	Y	Y	Y	Y
7 Carson	Y	Y	N	N	Y	N
8 Bucshon	Y	Y	Y	Y	Y	Y
9 Hollingsworth	Y	Y	Y	Y	Y	Y
IOWA						
1 Blum	Y	Y	Y	Y	Y	Y
2 Loebsack	Y	Y	N	N	N	N
3 Young	Y	Y	Y	Y	Y	N
4 King	Y	Y	Y	Y	Y	N
KANSAS						
1 Marshall	Y	Y	Y	Y	N	N
2 Jenkins	Y	Y	Y	Y	N	Y
3 Yoder	Y	Y	Y	Y	Y	N
4 Estes	Y	Y	Y	Y	Y	N
KENTUCKY						
1 Comer	Y	Y	Y	Y	N	N
2 Guthrie	Y	Y	Y	Y	Y	N
3 Yarmuth	Y	N	N	N	?	Y
4 Massie	N	Y	Y	Y	Y	Y
5 Rogers	+	+	+	+	+	-
6 Barr	Y	Y	Y	Y	Y	Y
LOUISIANA						
1 Scalise	Y	Y	Y	Y	N	N
2 Richmond	?	?	N	N	N	N
3 Higgins	Y	Y	Y	Y	N	N
4 Johnson	Y	Y	Y	Y	N	N
5 Abraham	Y	Y	Y	Y	Y	N
6 Graves	Y	Y	Y	Y	N	N
MAINE						
1 Pingree	Y	Y	N	N	Y	N
2 Poliquin	Y	Y	Y	Y	N	N
MARYLAND						
1 Harris	Y	Y	Y	Y	Y	Y
2 Ruppersberger	Y	Y	N	N	Y	N
3 Sarbanes	Y	Y	N	N	N	N
4 Brown	+	-	-	-	-	-
5 Hoyer	Y	N	N	N	N	N
6 Delaney	Y	Y	N	N	N	Y
7 Cummings	Y	N	N	N	Y	N
8 Raskin	Y	Y	N	?	Y	Y
MASSACHUSETTS						
1 Neal	Y	Y	N	N	N	N
2 McGovern	Y	N	N	N	N	Y
3 Tsongas	Y	Y	N	N	Y	N
4 Kennedy	Y	N	N	N	N	N
5 Clark	Y	N	N	N	N	Y
6 Moulton	Y	N	N	N	N	N
7 Capuano	Y	N	N	N	N	N
8 Lynch	Y	Y	N	N	N	N
9 Keating	Y	Y	N	N	N	N
MICHIGAN						
1 Bergman	Y	Y	Y	Y	N	N
2 Huizenga	Y	Y	Y	Y	Y	N
3 Amash	N	Y	N	N	N	Y
4 Moolenaar	Y	Y	Y	Y	Y	N
5 Kildee	Y	Y	N	N	Y	N
6 Upton	Y	Y	Y	Y	Y	N
7 Walberg	Y	Y	Y	Y	N	Y
8 Bishop	Y	Y	Y	Y	Y	N
9 Levin	Y	Y	N	N	N	N
10 Mitchell	Y	Y	Y	Y	Y	N
11 Trott	Y	Y	Y	Y	Y	N
12 Dingell	Y	Y	N	N	Y	N
14 Lawrence	Y	Y	N	N	Y	N
MINNESOTA						
1 Walz	Y	N	?	?	?	?
2 Lewis	Y	Y	Y	Y	Y	N
3 Paulsen	Y	Y	Y	Y	Y	N
4 McCollum	Y	N	N	N	N	N
5 Ellison	Y	N	N	N	Y	N
6 Emmer	Y	Y	Y	Y	Y	N
7 Peterson	Y	N	N	N	N	N
8 Nolan	Y	N	N	N	Y	N
MISSISSIPPI						
1 Kelly	Y	Y	Y	Y	N	N
2 Thompson	Y	N	N	N	N	N
3 Harper	Y	Y	Y	Y	Y	N
4 Palazzo	Y	Y	Y	Y	Y	N
MISSOURI						
1 Clay	N	N	N	Y	N	?
2 Wagner	Y	Y	Y	Y	Y	Y
3 Luetkemeyer	Y	Y	Y	Y	Y	N
4 Hartzler	Y	Y	Y	Y	Y	N
5 Cleaver	Y	N	N	N	N	N
6 Graves	Y	Y	Y	Y	Y	N
7 Long	Y	Y	Y	Y	Y	N
8 Smith	Y	Y	Y	Y	Y	N
MONTANA						
AL Gianforte	Y	Y	Y	Y	Y	N
NEBRASKA						
1 Fortenberry	Y	Y	Y	Y	Y	N
2 Bacon	Y	Y	Y	Y	Y	N
3 Smith	Y	Y	Y	Y	Y	N
NEVADA						
1 Titus	Y	N	N	N	Y	Y
2 Amodei	Y	Y	Y	Y	Y	N
3 Rosen	Y	N	N	N	Y	N
4 Kihuen	Y	N	N	N	N	N
NEW HAMPSHIRE						
1 Shea-Porter	Y	Y	N	N	Y	Y
2 Kuster	Y	Y	N	N	Y	Y
NEW JERSEY						
1 Norcross	Y	N	N	N	N	N
2 LoBiondo	Y	Y	Y	Y	N	Y
3 MacArthur	Y	Y	Y	Y	N	N
4 Smith	Y	Y	Y	Y	Y	Y
5 Gottheimer	Y	Y	N	N	N	Y
6 Pallone	N	N	N	N	N	Y
7 Lance	Y	Y	Y	Y	N	Y
8 Sires	Y	N	N	N	N	N
9 Pascrell	Y	N	N	N	Y	Y
10 Payne	N	N	N	N	N	N
11 Frelinghuysen	Y	Y	Y	Y	Y	Y
12 Watson Coleman	N	N	N	N	N	N
NEW MEXICO						
1 Lujan Grisham	Y	Y	N	N	Y	N
2 Pearce	Y	Y	Y	Y	N	N
3 Luján	Y	N	N	N	Y	N
NEW YORK						
1 Zeldin	Y	Y	Y	Y	N	N
2 King	Y	Y	Y	Y	Y	Y
3 Suozzi	Y	N	N	N	N	N
4 Rice	Y	Y	N	N	N	N
5 Meeks	Y	N	N	N	Y	N
6 Meng	Y	N	N	N	N	N
7 Velázquez	N	N	N	N	N	N
8 Jeffries	Y	N	N	N	N	N
9 Clarke	N	N	N	N	N	N
10 Nadler	Y	N	N	N	N	N
11 Donovan	Y	Y	Y	Y	N	N
12 Maloney, C.	Y	N	N	N	N	N
13 Espaillat	N	N	N	N	N	N
14 Crowley	Y	N	N	N	N	N
15 Serrano	N	N	N	N	N	N
16 Engel	Y	N	N	N	N	N
17 Lowey	Y	N	N	N	N	N
18 Maloney, S.P.	Y	N	N	N	N	N
19 Faso	Y	Y	Y	Y	?	N
20 Tonko	N	N	N	P	N	N
21 Stefanik	Y	Y	Y	Y	N	N
22 Tenney	Y	Y	Y	Y	N	N
23 Reed	Y	Y	Y	Y	N	N
24 Katko	Y	Y	Y	Y	N	N
25 Vacant						
26 Higgins	Y	N	N	N	N	N
27 Collins	Y	Y	Y	Y	Y	Y
NORTH CAROLINA						
1 Butterfield	Y	Y	N	N	Y	N
2 Holding	Y	Y	Y	Y	N	Y
3 Jones	Y	Y	N	Y	Y	N
4 Price	Y	N	N	N	N	N
5 Foxx	Y	Y	Y	Y	N	Y
6 Walker	Y	Y	Y	Y	N	N
7 Rouzer	Y	Y	Y	Y	N	N
8 Hudson	Y	Y	Y	Y	N	N
9 Pittenger	Y	Y	Y	Y	N	N
10 McHenry	Y	Y	Y	Y	Y	N
11 Meadows	Y	Y	Y	Y	Y	?
12 Adams	Y	N	N	N	N	N
13 Budd	Y	Y	Y	Y	Y	Y
NORTH DAKOTA						
AL Cramer	Y	Y	Y	Y	Y	N
OHIO						
1 Chabot	Y	Y	Y	Y	Y	Y
2 Wenstrup	Y	Y	Y	Y	Y	Y
3 Beatty	Y	Y	N	N	Y	N
4 Jordan	N	Y	Y	Y	N	Y
5 Latta	Y	Y	Y	Y	Y	Y
6 Johnson	Y	Y	Y	Y	Y	Y
7 Gibbs	Y	Y	Y	Y	N	N
8 Davidson	N	Y	Y	Y	N	Y
9 Kaptur	Y	Y	N	N	Y	N
10 Turner	Y	Y	N	N	Y	N
11 Fudge	Y	N	N	N	N	N
12 Vacant						
13 Ryan	Y	Y	N	N	N	N
14 Joyce	Y	Y	Y	Y	N	Y
15 Stivers	Y	Y	Y	Y	N	Y
16 Renacci	Y	Y	Y	Y	N	Y
OKLAHOMA						
1 Vacant						
2 Mullin	Y	Y	Y	Y	Y	N
3 Lucas	Y	Y	Y	Y	Y	N
4 Cole	Y	Y	Y	Y	Y	N
5 Russell	Y	Y	Y	Y	Y	Y
OREGON						
1 Bonamici	Y	N	N	N	Y	N
2 Walden	Y	Y	Y	Y	Y	N
3 Blumenauer	N	N	N	N	Y	N
4 DeFazio	Y	Y	N	N	?	N
5 Schrader	Y	Y	N	N	N	N
PENNSYLVANIA						
1 Brady	Y	N	N	N	N	N
2 Evans	Y	N	N	N	N	N
3 Kelly	Y	Y	Y	Y	Y	Y
4 Perry	N	Y	Y	Y	N	Y
5 Thompson	Y	Y	Y	Y	N	N
6 Costello	Y	Y	Y	Y	N	N
7 Vacant						
8 Fitzpatrick	Y	Y	Y	Y	N	N
9 Shuster	Y	Y	Y	Y	N	N
10 Marino	Y	Y	Y	Y	N	N
11 Barletta	Y	Y	Y	Y	N	N
12 Rothfus	Y	Y	Y	Y	N	N
13 Boyle	Y	N	N	N	N	?
14 Doyle	Y	N	N	N	N	N
15 Vacant						
16 Smucker	Y	Y	Y	Y	N	N
17 Cartwright	Y	N	N	N	Y	N
18 Lamb	Y	N	N	N	N	N
RHODE ISLAND						
1 Cicilline	Y	Y	N	N	Y	?
2 Langevin	Y	Y	N	N	N	Y
SOUTH CAROLINA						
1 Sanford	N	Y	Y	Y	N	Y
2 Wilson	Y	Y	Y	Y	Y	N
3 Duncan	Y	Y	Y	Y	Y	N
4 Gowdy	Y	Y	Y	Y	Y	N
5 Norman	Y	Y	Y	Y	Y	N
6 Clyburn	Y	Y	N	N	N	N
7 Rice	Y	Y	Y	Y	P	N
SOUTH DAKOTA						
AL Noem	Y	Y	Y	Y	Y	N
TENNESSEE						
1 Roe	Y	Y	Y	Y	Y	N
2 Duncan	Y	Y	Y	Y	Y	N
3 Fleischmann	Y	Y	Y	Y	Y	N
4 DesJarlais	Y	Y	Y	Y	Y	Y
5 Cooper	Y	Y	N	N	Y	Y
6 Black	Y	Y	Y	?	?	Y
7 Blackburn	Y	Y	?	?	?	?
8 Kustoff	Y	Y	Y	Y	Y	N
9 Cohen	Y	N	N	N	N	N
TEXAS						
1 Gohmert	Y	Y	?	?	?	?
2 Poe	Y	Y	Y	Y	N	Y
3 Johnson, S.	Y	Y	Y	Y	Y	Y
4 Ratcliffe	Y	Y	Y	Y	Y	Y
5 Hensarling	Y	Y	Y	Y	Y	Y
6 Barton	Y	Y	Y	Y	Y	N
7 Culberson	Y	Y	Y	Y	Y	N
8 Brady	Y	Y	Y	Y	Y	N
9 Green, A.	Y	Y	N	N	N	N
10 McCaul	Y	Y	Y	Y	Y	N
11 Conaway	Y	Y	Y	Y	Y	N
12 Granger	Y	Y	Y	Y	Y	N
13 Thornberry	Y	Y	Y	Y	Y	Y
14 Weber	Y	Y	Y	Y	Y	N
15 Gonzalez	Y	N	N	N	N	N
16 O'Rourke	Y	N	N	N	N	N
17 Flores	Y	Y	Y	Y	N	N
18 Jackson Lee	Y	N	N	N	N	N
19 Arrington	Y	Y	Y	Y	N	N
20 Castro	Y	N	N	N	N	N
21 Smith	Y	Y	Y	Y	Y	N
22 Olson	Y	Y	Y	Y	Y	N
23 Hurd	Y	Y	Y	Y	N	N
24 Marchant	Y	Y	Y	Y	Y	N
25 Williams	Y	Y	Y	Y	Y	Y
26 Burgess	Y	Y	Y	Y	Y	N
28 Cuellar	Y	N	N	N	N	N
29 Green, G.	Y	N	N	N	N	N
30 Johnson, E.B.	N	N	N	N	N	N
31 Carter	Y	Y	Y	Y	Y	N
32 Sessions	Y	Y	Y	Y	Y	N
33 Veasey	Y	N	N	N	N	N
34 Vela	Y	N	N	N	N	N
35 Doggett	Y	N	N	N	Y	N
36 Babin	Y	Y	Y	Y	N	N
UTAH						
1 Bishop	Y	Y	Y	Y	Y	N
2 Stewart	Y	Y	Y	Y	Y	Y
3 Curtis	Y	Y	Y	Y	Y	N
4 Love	Y	Y	Y	Y	Y	Y
VERMONT						
AL Welch	Y	N	N	N	Y	Y
VIRGINIA						
1 Wittman	Y	Y	Y	Y	Y	N
2 Taylor	Y	Y	Y	Y	Y	N
3 Scott	N	N	N	N	Y	N
4 McEachin	Y	N	N	N	Y	N
5 Garrett	N	Y	Y	Y	N	Y
6 Goodlatte	Y	Y	Y	Y	Y	N
7 Brat	Y	Y	Y	Y	Y	Y
8 Beyer	?	?	?	?	?	?
9 Griffith	Y	Y	Y	Y	Y	Y
10 Comstock	Y	Y	Y	Y	Y	Y
11 Connolly	Y	Y	N	N	N	N
WASHINGTON						
1 DelBene	Y	Y	N	N	Y	N
2 Larsen	Y	Y	N	N	Y	N
3 Herrera Beutler	Y	Y	Y	Y	N	N
4 Newhouse	Y	Y	Y	Y	Y	N
5 McMorris Rodgers	Y	Y	Y	Y	Y	N
6 Kilmer	Y	Y	N	N	Y	N
7 Jayapal	N	N	N	N	N	Y
8 Reichert	Y	Y	Y	Y	Y	N
9 Smith	N	N	N	N	N	Y
10 Heck	Y	Y	N	N	Y	N
WEST VIRGINIA						
1 McKinley	Y	Y	Y	Y	N	N
2 Mooney	Y	Y	Y	Y	N	Y
3 Jenkins	Y	Y	Y	Y	N	N
WISCONSIN						
1 Ryan						
2 Pocan	N	N	N	N	Y	N
3 Kind	Y	Y	N	N	Y	N
4 Moore	N	N	N	N	N	Y
5 Sensenbrenner	Y	Y	Y	Y	Y	N
6 Grothman	Y	Y	Y	Y	Y	N
7 Duffy	Y	Y	Y	Y	Y	N
8 Gallagher	Y	Y	Y	Y	Y	N
WYOMING						
AL Cheney	Y	Y	Y	Y	N	N

VOTE NUMBER

194. HR2. FARM PROGRAMS/ENDING AGRICULTURE SUBSIDIES. McClintock, R-Calif., amendment that would phase out agricultural crop subsidies by 2030. Rejected in Committee of the Whole 34-380: R 34-194; D 0-186. May 17, 2018.

195. HR2. FARM PROGRAMS/SNAP BENEFITS WORK REQUIREMENTS. McClintock, R-Calif., amendment that would reduce work-requirement exemptions from 15 percent to five percent of SNAP benefit recipients; would reduce the qualifying age of children from three-years-old to six-years-old with respect to work requirement-exempted parents; would set the same hour-per-week work requirement for married parents as for single parents; and would require employment and training program participants to have their work eligibility electronically verified through the E-verify system. Rejected in Committee of the Whole 83-330: R 83-145; D 0-185. May 17, 2018.

196. HR2. FARM PROGRAMS/STATES' ABILITY TO RUN SNAP. Faso, R-N.Y., amendment that would allow states to carry out program eligibility and other administrative functions of the Supplemental Nutrition Assistance Program in a number of different ways, including the use of non-governmental contractors, as long as such personnel have no direct or indirect financial interest in an approved retail food store. Adopted in Committee of the Whole 222-192: R 222-6; D 0-186. May 17, 2018.

197. HR2. FARM PROGRAMS/BIOMASS AND BIOENERGY PROGRAMS. Biggs, R-Ariz., amendment that would repeal the Department of Agriculture biomass and bioenergy subsidy programs. Rejected in Committee of the Whole 75-340: R 74-154; D 1-186. May 17, 2018.

198. HR2. FARM PROGRAMS/FOREST MANAGEMENT STUDIES. Westerman, R-Ark., amendment that would require environmental impact statements for certain forest management activities to only study and describe the forest management activity in question and the alternative of not taking any action. Adopted in Committee of the Whole 224-191: R 220-8; D 4-183. May 17, 2018.

199. HR2. FARM PROGRAMS/FOREST SERVICE RULE EXEMPTION. Young R-Alaska, amendment that would exempt Alaska from a 2001 Forest Service rule that prohibits road construction and timber harvesting on approximately 58.5 million acres of roadless Forest Service lands. Adopted in Committee of the Whole 208-207: R 206-23; D 2-184. May 17, 2018.

	194	195	196	197	198	199
ALABAMA						
1 **Byrne**	N	Y	Y	N	Y	Y
2 **Roby**	N	Y	Y	N	Y	Y
3 **Rogers**	N	N	Y	N	Y	N
4 **Aderholt**	N	Y	Y	N	Y	Y
5 **Brooks**	N	N	Y	N	Y	N
6 **Palmer**	N	Y	Y	Y	Y	Y
7 Sewell	N	N	N	N	N	N
ALASKA						
AL **Young**	N	N	Y	N	Y	Y
ARIZONA						
1 O'Halleran	N	N	N	N	N	N
2 **McSally**	N	N	Y	Y	Y	Y
3 Grijalva	N	N	N	N	N	N
4 **Gosar**	Y	Y	Y	Y	Y	Y
5 **Biggs**	Y	Y	Y	Y	Y	Y
6 **Schweikert**	Y	Y	Y	Y	Y	Y
7 Gallego	?	N	N	N	N	N
8 **Lesko**	Y	Y	Y	Y	Y	Y
9 Sinema	N	N	N	N	N	N
ARKANSAS						
1 **Crawford**	N	N	Y	N	Y	N
2 **Hill**	N	N	Y	N	Y	N
3 **Womack**	N	N	Y	N	Y	Y
4 **Westerman**	N	Y	Y	N	Y	Y
CALIFORNIA						
1 **LaMalfa**	N	N	Y	N	Y	Y
2 Huffman	N	N	N	N	N	N
3 Garamendi	N	N	N	N	N	N
4 **McClintock**	Y	Y	Y	Y	Y	Y
5 Thompson	N	N	N	N	N	N
6 Matsui	N	N	N	N	N	N
7 Bera	N	N	N	N	N	N
8 **Cook**	Y	Y	Y	N	Y	Y
9 McNerney	N	N	N	N	N	N
10 **Denham**	N	N	Y	N	Y	Y
11 DeSaulnier	N	N	N	N	N	N
12 Pelosi	N	N	N	N	N	N
13 Lee	N	N	N	N	N	N
14 Speier	N	?	N	N	N	N
15 Swalwell	N	N	N	N	N	N
16 Costa	N	N	N	N	N	N
17 Khanna	N	N	N	N	N	N
18 Eshoo	N	?	N	N	N	N
19 Lofgren	N	N	N	N	N	N
20 Panetta	N	N	N	N	N	N
21 **Valadao**	N	N	Y	N	Y	Y
22 **Nunes**	N	N	Y	N	Y	Y
23 **McCarthy**	N	N	Y	N	Y	Y
24 Carbajal	N	N	N	N	N	N
25 **Knight**	N	N	Y	N	Y	Y
26 Brownley	N	N	N	N	N	N
27 Chu	N	N	N	N	N	N
28 Schiff	N	N	N	N	N	N
29 Cardenas	N	N	N	N	N	N
30 Sherman	N	N	N	N	N	N
31 Aguilar	N	N	N	N	N	N
32 Napolitano	N	N	N	N	N	?
33 Lieu	N	N	N	N	N	N
34 Gomez	N	N	N	N	N	N
35 Torres	N	N	N	N	N	N
36 Ruiz	N	N	N	N	N	N
37 Bass	N	N	N	N	N	N
38 Sánchez, Linda	N	N	N	N	N	N
39 **Royce**	Y	N	Y	Y	Y	Y
40 Roybal-Allard	N	N	N	N	N	N
41 Takano	N	N	N	N	N	N
42 **Calvert**	N	Y	Y	N	Y	Y
43 Waters	N	N	N	N	N	N
44 Barragan	N	N	N	N	N	N
45 **Walters**	N	N	Y	Y	Y	Y
46 Correa	N	N	N	N	N	N
47 Lowenthal	N	N	N	N	N	N
48 **Rohrabacher**	Y	Y	Y	Y	Y	Y
49 **Issa**	Y	Y	Y	Y	Y	Y
50 **Hunter**	N	Y	Y	Y	Y	Y
51 Vargas	N	N	N	N	N	N
52 Peters	N	N	N	N	N	N
53 Davis	N	N	N	N	N	N

	194	195	196	197	198	199
COLORADO						
1 DeGette	N	N	N	N	N	N
2 Polis	?	?	?	?	?	?
3 Tipton	N	N	Y	N	Y	Y
4 **Buck**	?	?	?	?	?	?
5 **Lamborn**	N	Y	Y	N	Y	Y
6 **Coffman**	Y	N	Y	Y	Y	Y
7 Perlmutter	N	N	N	N	N	N
CONNECTICUT						
1 Larson	N	N	N	N	N	N
2 Courtney	N	N	N	N	N	N
3 DeLauro	N	N	N	N	N	N
4 Himes	N	N	N	N	N	N
5 Esty	N	N	N	N	N	N
DELAWARE						
AL Blunt Rochester	N	N	N	N	N	N
FLORIDA						
1 **Gaetz**	Y	Y	Y	N	Y	N
2 **Dunn**	N	N	Y	N	Y	Y
3 **Yoho**	N	N	Y	N	Y	Y
4 **Rutherford**	N	N	Y	N	Y	Y
5 Lawson	N	N	N	N	N	N
6 **DeSantis**	Y	Y	Y	Y	Y	Y
7 Murphy	N	N	N	N	N	N
8 **Posey**	Y	N	Y	Y	Y	Y
9 Soto	N	N	N	N	N	N
10 Demings	N	N	N	N	N	N
11 **Webster**	N	N	Y	Y	Y	Y
12 **Bilirakis**	N	N	Y	Y	Y	Y
13 Crist	N	N	N	N	N	N
14 Castor	N	N	N	N	N	N
15 **Ross**	N	N	Y	N	Y	Y
16 **Buchanan**	N	N	Y	N	Y	Y
17 **Rooney, T.**	N	N	Y	N	Y	Y
18 **Mast**	N	Y	Y	N	Y	Y
19 **Rooney, F.**	Y	Y	Y	Y	Y	N
20 Hastings	N	N	N	N	N	N
21 Frankel	N	N	N	N	N	N
22 Deutch	N	N	N	N	N	N
23 Wasserman Schultz	N	N	N	N	N	N
24 Wilson	N	N	N	N	N	N
25 **Diaz-Balart**	N	N	Y	N	Y	Y
26 **Curbelo**	N	N	Y	N	N	Y
27 **Ros-Lehtinen**	N	N	Y	N	N	N
GEORGIA						
1 **Carter**	N	Y	Y	Y	Y	Y
2 Bishop	N	N	N	N	N	N
3 **Ferguson**	N	Y	Y	N	Y	Y
4 Johnson	N	N	N	N	N	N
5 Lewis	N	N	N	N	N	N
6 **Handel**	N	N	Y	N	Y	Y
7 **Woodall**	N	Y	Y	Y	Y	Y
8 **Scott, A.**	N	N	Y	N	Y	Y
9 **Collins**	N	Y	Y	Y	Y	Y
10 **Hice**	Y	Y	Y	Y	Y	Y
11 **Loudermilk**	Y	Y	Y	Y	Y	Y
12 **Allen**	N	N	Y	N	Y	Y
13 Scott, D.	N	N	N	N	N	N
14 **Graves**	N	Y	Y	Y	Y	Y
HAWAII						
1 Hanabusa	N	N	N	N	N	N
2 Gabbard	N	N	N	N	N	N
IDAHO						
1 **Labrador**	?	?	?	?	?	?
2 **Simpson**	N	N	Y	N	Y	Y
ILLINOIS						
1 Rush	N	N	N	N	N	N
2 Kelly	N	N	N	N	N	N
3 Lipinski	N	N	N	N	N	N
4 Gutierrez	N	N	N	N	N	N
5 Quigley	N	N	N	N	N	N
6 **Roskam**	N	N	Y	N	Y	Y
7 Davis, D.	N	N	N	N	N	N
8 Krishnamoorthi	N	N	N	N	N	N
9 Schakowsky	N	N	N	N	N	N
10 Schneider	N	N	N	N	N	N
11 Foster	N	N	N	N	N	N
12 **Bost**	N	N	Y	N	Y	Y
13 **Davis, R.**	N	N	Y	N	Y	Y

	194	195	196	197	198	199
14 **Hultgren**	N	N	Y	N	Y	Y
15 **Shimkus**	N	N	Y	N	Y	Y
16 **Kinzinger**	N	N	Y	N	Y	Y
17 Bustos	N	N	N	N	N	N
18 **LaHood**	N	Y	Y	N	Y	Y
INDIANA						
1 Visclosky	N	N	N	N	N	N
2 **Walorski**	N	N	Y	N	Y	Y
3 **Banks**	Y	Y	Y	Y	Y	Y
4 **Rokita**	N	Y	Y	Y	Y	Y
5 **Brooks**	N	N	Y	N	Y	Y
6 **Messer**	Y	Y	Y	N	Y	Y
7 Carson	N	N	N	N	N	N
8 **Bucshon**	N	N	Y	N	Y	Y
9 **Hollingsworth**	N	N	Y	N	Y	Y
IOWA						
1 **Blum**	N	Y	Y	N	Y	Y
2 Loebsack	N	N	N	N	N	N
3 **Young**	N	N	Y	N	Y	Y
4 **King**	N	Y	Y	N	Y	N
KANSAS						
1 **Marshall**	N	N	Y	N	Y	Y
2 **Jenkins**	N	N	Y	N	Y	Y
3 **Yoder**	N	N	Y	N	Y	Y
4 **Estes**	N	Y	Y	Y	Y	Y
KENTUCKY						
1 **Comer**	N	Y	Y	Y	Y	Y
2 **Guthrie**	N	Y	Y	N	Y	Y
3 Yarmuth	N	N	N	N	N	N
4 **Massie**	N	N	Y	Y	Y	Y
5 **Rogers**	–	–	?	–	?	?
6 **Barr**	N	Y	Y	N	Y	Y
LOUISIANA						
1 **Scalise**	N	Y	Y	Y	Y	Y
2 Richmond	N	N	N	N	N	N
3 **Higgins**	N	N	Y	N	Y	Y
4 **Johnson**	N	Y	Y	N	Y	N
5 **Abraham**	N	N	Y	N	Y	Y
6 **Graves**	N	Y	Y	N	Y	Y
MAINE						
1 Pingree	N	N	N	N	N	N
2 **Poliquin**	N	N	Y	N	Y	Y
MARYLAND						
1 **Harris**	N	Y	Y	Y	Y	Y
2 Ruppersberger	N	N	N	N	N	N
3 Sarbanes	N	N	N	N	N	N
4 Brown	–	–	–	–	–	–
5 Hoyer	N	N	N	N	N	N
6 Delaney	N	N	N	N	N	N
7 Cummings	N	N	N	N	N	N
8 Raskin	N	N	N	N	N	N
MASSACHUSETTS						
1 Neal	N	N	N	N	N	N
2 McGovern	N	N	N	N	N	N
3 Tsongas	N	N	N	N	N	N
4 Kennedy	N	N	N	N	N	N
5 Clark	N	N	N	N	N	N
6 Moulton	N	N	N	N	N	N
7 Capuano	N	N	N	N	N	N
8 Lynch	N	N	N	N	N	N
9 Keating	N	N	N	N	N	N
MICHIGAN						
1 **Bergman**	N	N	Y	N	Y	Y
2 **Huizenga**	N	Y	Y	Y	Y	Y
3 *Amash*	Y	N	Y	Y	Y	N
4 **Moolenaar**	N	N	Y	N	Y	Y
5 Kildee	N	N	N	N	N	N
6 **Upton**	N	N	Y	N	Y	N
7 **Walberg**	N	N	Y	N	Y	Y
8 **Bishop**	N	N	Y	N	Y	Y
9 Levin	N	N	N	N	N	N
10 **Mitchell**	N	N	Y	N	Y	Y
11 **Trott**	N	N	Y	N	Y	Y
12 Dingell	N	N	N	N	N	N
14 Lawrence	N	N	N	N	N	N
MINNESOTA						
1 Walz	?	?	?	?	?	?
2 **Lewis**	N	N	Y	N	Y	Y
3 **Paulsen**	N	N	Y	N	Y	N
4 McCollum	N	N	N	N	N	N

	194	195	196	197	198	199
5 Ellison	N	N	N	N	N	N
6 **Emmer**	N	N	Y	N	Y	Y
7 Peterson	N	N	N	N	Y	Y
8 Nolan	N	N	N	N	N	N
MISSISSIPPI						
1 **Kelly**	N	N	Y	N	Y	Y
2 Thompson	N	N	N	N	N	N
3 **Harper**	N	N	Y	N	Y	Y
4 **Palazzo**	N	Y	Y	N	Y	Y
MISSOURI						
1 Clay	?	?	?	?	?	?
2 **Wagner**	N	N	Y	Y	Y	Y
3 **Luetkemeyer**	N	N	Y	N	Y	Y
4 **Hartzler**	N	N	Y	Y	Y	Y
5 Cleaver	N	N	N	N	N	N
6 **Graves**	N	N	Y	N	Y	Y
7 **Long**	N	N	Y	N	Y	Y
8 **Smith**	N	N	Y	N	Y	Y
MONTANA						
AL **Gianforte**	N	N	Y	Y	Y	Y
NEBRASKA						
1 **Fortenberry**	N	N	Y	N	Y	Y
2 **Bacon**	N	Y	Y	N	Y	Y
3 **Smith**	N	N	Y	N	Y	Y
NEVADA						
1 Titus	N	N	N	N	Y	N
2 **Amodei**	N	N	Y	N	Y	Y
3 Rosen	N	N	N	N	N	N
4 Kihuen	N	N	N	N	N	N
NEW HAMPSHIRE						
1 Shea-Porter	N	N	N	N	N	N
2 Kuster	N	N	N	N	N	N
NEW JERSEY						
1 Norcross	N	N	N	N	N	N
2 **LoBiondo**	Y	N	N	N	N	N
3 **MacArthur**	N	N	Y	N	N	Y
4 **Smith**	N	N	N	N	N	N
5 Gottheimer	N	N	N	N	N	N
6 Pallone	N	N	N	N	N	N
7 **Lance**	Y	N	N	N	N	N
8 Sires	N	N	N	N	N	N
9 Pascrell	N	N	N	N	N	N
10 Payne	N	N	N	N	N	N
11 **Frelinghuysen**	Y	N	Y	Y	Y	Y
12 Watson Coleman	N	N	N	N	N	N
NEW MEXICO						
1 Lujan Grisham	N	N	N	N	N	N
2 **Pearce**	N	N	Y	N	Y	Y
3 Luján	N	N	N	N	N	N
NEW YORK						
1 **Zeldin**	N	Y	Y	Y	Y	Y
2 **King**	N	N	Y	N	Y	Y
3 Suozzi	N	N	N	N	N	N
4 Rice	N	N	N	N	N	N
5 Meeks	N	N	N	N	N	N
6 Meng	N	N	N	N	N	N
7 Velázquez	N	N	N	N	N	N
8 Jeffries	N	N	N	N	N	N
9 Clarke	N	N	N	N	N	N
10 Nadler	N	N	N	N	N	N
11 **Donovan**	N	N	Y	N	Y	Y
12 Maloney, C.	N	N	N	N	N	N
13 Espaillat	N	N	N	N	N	N
14 Crowley	N	N	N	N	N	N
15 Serrano	N	N	N	N	N	N
16 Engel	N	N	N	N	N	N
17 Lowey	N	N	N	N	N	N
18 Maloney, S.P.	N	N	N	N	N	N
19 **Faso**	N	N	Y	N	Y	N
20 Tonko	N	N	N	N	N	N
21 **Stefanik**	N	N	Y	N	N	N
22 **Tenney**	N	N	Y	N	Y	Y
23 **Reed**	N	N	Y	N	Y	Y
24 **Katko**	N	N	Y	N	Y	Y
25 **Vacant**						
26 Higgins	N	N	N	N	N	N
27 **Collins**	N	N	Y	N	Y	Y
NORTH CAROLINA						
1 Butterfield	N	N	N	N	N	N
2 **Holding**	N	Y	Y	Y	Y	Y
3 **Jones**	N	N	Y	N	Y	Y
4 Price	N	N	N	N	N	N

	194	195	196	197	198	199
5 **Foxx**	Y	Y	Y	Y	Y	Y
6 **Walker**	N	Y	Y	Y	Y	Y
7 **Rouzer**	N	Y	Y	N	Y	Y
8 **Hudson**	N	N	Y	N	Y	Y
9 **Pittenger**	N	Y	Y	N	Y	Y
9 **Vacant**						
10 **McHenry**	N	N	Y	Y	Y	Y
11 **Meadows**	?	?	?	?	?	Y
12 Adams	N	N	N	N	N	N
13 **Budd**	Y	Y	Y	Y	Y	N
NORTH DAKOTA						
AL **Cramer**	N	N	Y	N	Y	Y
OHIO						
1 **Chabot**	Y	Y	Y	Y	Y	N
2 **Wenstrup**	N	N	Y	N	Y	Y
3 Beatty	N	N	N	N	N	N
4 **Jordan**	N	Y	Y	Y	Y	Y
5 **Latta**	N	N	Y	N	Y	Y
6 **Johnson**	N	N	Y	N	Y	Y
7 **Gibbs**	N	N	Y	N	Y	Y
8 **Davidson**	N	Y	Y	Y	Y	Y
9 Kaptur	N	N	N	N	N	Y
10 **Turner**	N	N	N	N	Y	Y
11 Fudge	N	N	N	N	N	N
12 **Vacant**						
13 Ryan	N	N	N	N	N	N
14 **Joyce**	N	N	Y	N	Y	Y
15 **Stivers**	N	N	Y	N	Y	Y
16 **Renacci**	N	N	Y	N	Y	Y
OKLAHOMA						
1 **Vacant**						
2 **Mullin**	N	N	Y	Y	Y	Y
3 **Lucas**	N	N	Y	N	Y	Y
4 **Cole**	N	N	Y	N	Y	Y
5 **Russell**	N	Y	Y	Y	Y	Y
OREGON						
1 Bonamici	N	N	N	N	N	N
2 **Walden**	N	N	N	Y	Y	N
3 Blumenauer	N	N	N	N	N	N
4 DeFazio	N	N	N	N	N	N
5 Schrader	N	N	N	N	Y	N
PENNSYLVANIA						
1 Brady	N	N	N	N	N	N
2 Evans	N	N	N	N	N	N
3 **Kelly**	N	N	Y	N	Y	Y
4 **Perry**	Y	Y	Y	N	Y	Y
5 **Thompson**	N	N	Y	N	Y	Y
6 **Costello**	N	N	N	N	N	Y
7 **Vacant**						
8 **Fitzpatrick**	N	N	Y	N	N	N
9 **Shuster**	N	N	Y	N	Y	Y
10 **Marino**	N	N	Y	N	Y	Y
11 **Barletta**	N	N	Y	N	Y	Y
12 **Rothfus**	Y	N	Y	Y	Y	Y
13 Boyle	?	?	?	?	?	?
14 Doyle	N	N	N	N	N	N
15 **Vacant**						
16 **Smucker**	N	Y	Y	N	Y	Y
17 Cartwright	N	N	N	N	N	N
18 Lamb	N	N	N	N	N	N
RHODE ISLAND						
1 Cicilline	N	N	N	N	N	N
2 Langevin	N	N	N	N	N	N
SOUTH CAROLINA						
1 **Sanford**	Y	Y	Y	Y	Y	N
2 **Wilson**	N	N	Y	N	Y	Y
3 **Duncan**	N	Y	Y	Y	Y	Y
4 **Gowdy**	N	N	Y	N	Y	Y
5 **Norman**	N	Y	Y	Y	Y	Y
6 Clyburn	N	N	N	N	N	N
7 **Rice**	N	Y	Y	N	Y	Y
SOUTH DAKOTA						
AL **Noem**	N	N	Y	N	Y	Y
TENNESSEE						
1 **Roe**	N	N	Y	Y	Y	Y
2 **Duncan**	Y	Y	Y	Y	Y	Y
3 **Fleischmann**	N	Y	Y	Y	Y	Y
4 **DesJarlais**	N	Y	Y	Y	Y	Y
5 Cooper	N	N	N	Y	N	N
6 **Black**	N	Y	Y	N	Y	Y
7 **Blackburn**	?	?	?	?	?	?
8 **Kustoff**	N	Y	Y	N	Y	Y
9 Cohen	N	N	N	N	N	N

	194	195	196	197	198	199
TEXAS						
1 **Gohmert**	?	?	?	?	?	?
2 **Poe**	N	Y	Y	Y	Y	Y
3 **Johnson, S.**	Y	Y	Y	Y	Y	Y
4 **Ratcliffe**	N	Y	Y	Y	Y	Y
5 **Hensarling**	Y	Y	Y	Y	Y	Y
6 **Barton**	N	N	Y	N	Y	N
7 **Culberson**	N	N	Y	Y	Y	Y
8 **Brady**	N	N	Y	N	Y	Y
9 Green, A.	N	N	N	N	N	N
10 **McCaul**	N	N	Y	N	Y	Y
11 **Conaway**	N	N	Y	N	Y	Y
12 **Granger**	N	N	Y	N	Y	Y
13 **Thornberry**	N	N	Y	N	Y	Y
14 **Weber**	N	N	Y	N	Y	Y
15 Gonzalez	N	N	N	N	N	N
16 O'Rourke	N	N	N	N	N	N
17 **Flores**	N	N	Y	N	Y	Y
18 Jackson Lee	N	N	N	N	N	N
19 **Arrington**	N	Y	Y	N	Y	Y
20 Castro	N	N	N	N	N	N
21 **Smith**	N	N	Y	N	Y	Y
22 **Olson**	N	N	Y	N	Y	Y
23 **Hurd**	N	N	Y	N	Y	Y
24 **Marchant**	N	N	Y	N	Y	Y
25 **Williams**	N	Y	Y	Y	Y	Y
26 **Burgess**	N	N	Y	Y	Y	Y
28 Cuellar	N	N	N	N	N	N
29 Green, G.	N	N	?	N	N	N
30 Johnson, E.B.	N	N	N	N	N	N
31 **Carter**	N	N	Y	N	Y	Y
32 **Sessions**	N	N	Y	Y	Y	Y
33 Veasey	N	N	N	N	N	N
34 Vela	N	N	N	N	Y	N
35 Doggett	N	N	N	N	N	N
36 **Babin**	N	N	Y	N	Y	Y
UTAH						
1 **Bishop**	N	Y	Y	Y	Y	Y
2 **Stewart**	N	N	Y	N	Y	Y
3 **Curtis**	N	Y	Y	Y	Y	Y
4 **Love**	N	N	Y	N	Y	Y
VERMONT						
AL Welch	N	N	N	N	N	N
VIRGINIA						
1 **Wittman**	N	Y	Y	Y	Y	Y
2 **Taylor**	N	N	Y	N	Y	Y
3 Scott	N	N	N	N	N	N
4 McEachin	N	N	N	N	N	N
5 **Garrett**	Y	Y	Y	Y	Y	Y
6 **Goodlatte**	N	N	Y	N	Y	Y
7 **Brat**	N	Y	Y	Y	Y	Y
8 Beyer	?	?	?	?	?	?
9 **Griffith**	N	N	Y	N	Y	Y
10 **Comstock**	N	N	Y	N	Y	Y
11 Connolly	N	N	N	N	N	N
WASHINGTON						
1 DelBene	N	N	N	N	N	N
2 Larsen	N	N	N	N	N	N
3 **Herrera Beutler**	Y	N	Y	N	Y	Y
4 **Newhouse**	N	N	N	N	Y	Y
5 **McMorris Rodgers**	N	N	Y	N	Y	Y
6 Kilmer	N	N	N	N	N	N
7 Jayapal	N	N	N	N	N	N
8 **Reichert**	N	N	Y	N	Y	N
9 Smith	N	N	N	N	N	N
10 Heck	N	N	N	N	N	N
WEST VIRGINIA						
1 **McKinley**	N	N	Y	N	Y	Y
2 **Mooney**	Y	Y	Y	Y	Y	Y
3 **Jenkins**	N	N	Y	N	Y	Y
WISCONSIN						
1 **Ryan**						
2 Pocan	N	N	N	N	N	N
3 Kind	N	N	N	N	N	N
4 Moore	N	N	N	N	N	N
5 **Sensenbrenner**	Y	Y	Y	Y	Y	Y
6 **Grothman**	N	Y	Y	Y	Y	Y
7 **Duffy**	N	Y	Y	N	Y	Y
8 **Gallagher**	N	Y	Y	Y	Y	Y
WYOMING						
AL **Cheney**	N	Y	Y	N	Y	Y

VOTE NUMBER

200. HR2. FARM PROGRAMS/VALUE-ADDED AGRICULTURAL PRODUCTS.
Russell, R-Okla., amendment that would exclude beer, wine, distilled spirits, hard cider, and other alcoholic products from counting as value-added agricultural products, thus making such products ineligible for agricultural product market development grants, and would rescind $8 million in unobligated funds from value-added agricultural product market development grant program. Rejected in Committee of the Whole 54-356: R 53-175; D 1-181. May 18, 2018.

201. HR2. FARM PROGRAMS/UNPASTEURIZED MILK PRODUCT TRANSPORTATION. Massie, R-Ky., amendment that would prohibit federal interference in the interstate transportation of unpasteurized milk and milk products between states that allow for the distribution of such products for direct human consumption. Rejected in Committee of the Whole 79-331: R 72-156; D 7-175. May 18, 2018.

202. HR2. FARM PROGRAMS/ANIMAL FIGHTING PROHIBITIONS. Roskam, R-Ill., amendment that would extend the prohibition on animal fighting ventures to all states and U.S. territories. Adopted in Committee of the Whole 359-51: R 204-23; D 155-28. May 18, 2018.

203. HR2. FARM PROGRAMS/EPA WATER RULE. Banks, R-Ind., amendment that would repeal the EPA's rule regarding the definition of the "Waters of the United States" under the Clean Water Act. Adopted in Committee of the Whole 238-173: R 225-3; D 13-170. May 18, 2018.

204. HR2. FARM PROGRAMS/RECOMMIT. Maloney, D-N.Y., motion to recommit the bill to the House Agriculture Committee with instructions to report back immediately with an amendment. Motion rejected 183-226: R 0-226; D 183-0. May 18, 2018.

205. HR2. FARM PROGRAMS/PASSAGE. Passage of the bill that would reauthorize and extend federal farm and nutrition programs through fiscal 2023, including crop subsidies, conservation, rural development and agricultural trade programs and the Supplemental Nutritional Assistance Program. It would require individuals receiving SNAP benefits, who are 18-59 years old, to work or participate in work training programs for a minimum of 20 hours per week, and would require the Department of Agriculture to establish a database to track individuals receiving SNAP benefits. The bill would reauthorize and extend supplemental agricultural disaster assistance programs, the current sugar policies and loan rates, several international food aid programs, nonrecourse marketing assistance loans for loan commodities, several dairy programs, including the dairy risk management program (previously the margin protection program) and would modify certain utility standards in the Home Energy Assistance Program to require SNAP benefits recipients to provide documentation of such expenses in order to receive increased benefits using the Standard Utility Allowance. The bill would authorize, with modifications, the farm risk-management program, which gives agriculture producers a choice of receiving price loss coverage or agriculture risk coverage, on a covered-commodity-by-covered-commodity basis, for the 2019 through 2023 crop years. The bill would reauthorize several conservation programs, and would increase the conservation reserve program from 24 to 29 million acres and reduce from 750,000 to 500,000 acres the cap for Farmable Wetland Program enrollment. It would also increase the amount authorized annually for the Environmental Quality Incentives Program for the 2019 through 2023 crop years, with a maximum authorization of $3 billion in 2023. It would eliminate the conservation stewardship program and would also allow the Environmental Protection Agency to determine whether a pesticide is likely to jeopardize the survival of a federally designated threatened or endangered species, or the habitat of such a species, without having to consult with federal agencies. Rejected 198-213: R 198-30; D 0-183. May 18, 2018.

		200	201	202	203	204	205
ALABAMA							
1	**Byrne**	N	N	Y	Y	N	Y
2	**Roby**	N	N	Y	Y	N	Y
3	**Rogers**	N	N	N	Y	N	Y
4	**Aderholt**	N	N	Y	Y	N	Y
5	**Brooks**	Y	Y	Y	Y	N	Y
6	**Palmer**	Y	Y	Y	Y	N	Y
7	Sewell	–	N	Y	N	Y	N
ALASKA							
AL	**Young**	Y	N	N	Y	N	Y
ARIZONA							
1	O'Halleran	N	N	Y	Y	Y	N
2	**McSally**	N	Y	Y	Y	N	Y
3	Grijalva	N	N	Y	N	Y	N
4	**Gosar**	Y	Y	Y	Y	N	N
5	**Biggs**	Y	Y	Y	Y	N	N
6	**Schweikert**	Y	Y	Y	Y	N	Y
7	Gallego	N	N	Y	N	Y	N
8	**Lesko**	N	Y	Y	Y	N	Y
9	Sinema	N	N	Y	N	Y	N
ARKANSAS							
1	**Crawford**	N	N	Y	Y	N	Y
2	**Hill**	N	N	Y	Y	N	Y
3	**Womack**	N	N	Y	Y	N	Y
4	**Westerman**	N	N	Y	Y	N	Y
CALIFORNIA							
1	**LaMalfa**	N	N	N	Y	N	Y
2	Huffman	N	Y	Y	N	Y	N
3	Garamendi	N	N	Y	N	Y	N
4	**McClintock**	Y	Y	N	Y	N	N
5	Thompson	N	N	Y	N	Y	N
6	Matsui	N	N	N	N	Y	N
7	Bera	N	N	Y	N	Y	N
8	**Cook**	N	N	Y	Y	N	Y
9	McNerney	N	Y	Y	N	Y	N
10	**Denham**	N	N	Y	Y	N	Y
11	DeSaulnier	N	N	Y	N	Y	N
12	Pelosi	N	N	Y	N	Y	N
13	Lee	N	N	N	N	Y	N
14	Speier	–	–	+	–	+	–
15	Swalwell	N	N	Y	N	Y	N
16	Costa	N	N	Y	N	Y	N
17	Khanna	N	N	Y	N	Y	N
18	Eshoo	N	N	Y	N	Y	N
19	Lofgren	N	Y	Y	N	Y	N
20	Panetta	N	N	Y	N	Y	N
21	**Valadao**	N	N	Y	Y	N	?
22	**Nunes**	N	N	Y	Y	N	Y
23	**McCarthy**	N	N	Y	Y	N	Y
24	Carbajal	N	N	Y	N	Y	N
25	**Knight**	N	N	Y	Y	N	Y
26	Brownley	N	N	Y	N	Y	N
27	Chu	N	N	Y	N	Y	N
28	Schiff	N	N	Y	N	Y	N
29	Cardenas	N	N	Y	N	Y	N
30	Sherman	N	N	Y	N	Y	N
31	Aguilar	N	N	Y	N	Y	N
32	Napolitano	N	N	Y	N	Y	N
33	Lieu	?	?	?	?	?	?
34	Gomez	N	N	Y	N	Y	N
35	Torres	N	N	Y	N	Y	N
36	Ruiz	N	N	Y	N	Y	N
37	Bass	N	N	N	N	Y	N
38	Sánchez, Linda	N	N	Y	N	Y	N
39	**Royce**	N	N	Y	Y	N	Y
40	Roybal-Allard	N	N	Y	N	Y	N
41	Takano	N	N	Y	N	Y	N
42	**Calvert**	N	N	Y	Y	N	Y
43	Waters	N	N	N	N	Y	N
44	Barragan	N	N	Y	N	Y	N
45	**Walters**	N	N	Y	Y	N	Y
46	Correa	N	N	Y	N	Y	N
47	Lowenthal	N	N	Y	N	Y	N
48	**Rohrabacher**	Y	Y	N	Y	N	N
49	**Issa**	Y	Y	Y	Y	N	N
50	**Hunter**	N	N	Y	N	Y	N
51	Vargas	N	N	Y	N	Y	N
52	Peters	N	N	Y	N	Y	N
53	Davis	N	N	Y	N	Y	N

		200	201	202	203	204	205
COLORADO							
1	DeGette	N	N	Y	N	Y	N
2	Polis	?	?	?	?	?	–
3	**Tipton**	N	Y	Y	Y	N	Y
4	**Buck**	?	?	?	?	?	?
5	**Lamborn**	N	Y	Y	Y	N	Y
6	**Coffman**	N	N	Y	Y	N	Y
7	Perlmutter	N	N	Y	N	Y	N
CONNECTICUT							
1	Larson	N	N	Y	N	Y	N
2	Courtney	N	N	Y	N	Y	N
3	DeLauro	N	N	Y	N	Y	N
4	Himes	N	N	Y	N	Y	N
5	Esty	N	N	Y	N	Y	N
DELAWARE							
AL	Blunt Rochester	N	N	Y	N	Y	N
FLORIDA							
1	**Gaetz**	Y	Y	Y	Y	N	N
2	**Dunn**	N	N	Y	Y	N	Y
3	**Yoho**	N	N	Y	Y	N	Y
4	**Rutherford**	N	N	Y	Y	N	Y
5	Lawson	N	N	Y	N	Y	N
6	**DeSantis**	Y	Y	Y	Y	N	Y
7	Murphy	N	N	Y	N	Y	N
8	**Posey**	Y	Y	Y	Y	N	Y
9	Soto	N	N	Y	N	Y	N
10	Demings	N	N	Y	N	Y	N
11	**Webster**	Y	Y	Y	Y	N	Y
12	**Bilirakis**	Y	N	Y	Y	N	Y
13	Crist	N	N	Y	N	Y	N
14	Castor	N	N	Y	N	Y	N
15	**Ross**	N	N	Y	Y	N	Y
16	**Buchanan**	N	N	Y	Y	N	Y
17	**Rooney, T.**	N	N	?	Y	N	Y
18	**Mast**	N	N	Y	Y	N	Y
19	**Rooney, F.**	Y	Y	Y	Y	N	Y
20	Hastings	N	N	Y	N	Y	N
21	Frankel	N	N	Y	N	Y	N
22	Deutch	N	N	Y	N	Y	N
23	Wasserman Schultz	N	N	Y	N	Y	N
24	Wilson	N	N	Y	N	Y	N
25	**Diaz-Balart**	N	N	Y	Y	N	Y
26	**Curbelo**	?	?	?	?	?	?
27	**Ros-Lehtinen**	N	N	Y	Y	?	N
GEORGIA							
1	**Carter**	N	N	Y	Y	N	Y
2	Bishop	N	N	Y	Y	Y	N
3	**Ferguson**	N	N	Y	Y	N	Y
4	Johnson	N	N	N	N	Y	N
5	Lewis	N	N	Y	N	Y	N
6	**Handel**	N	N	Y	Y	N	Y
7	**Woodall**	Y	Y	Y	Y	N	Y
8	**Scott, A.**	N	N	N	Y	N	Y
9	**Collins**	N	N	Y	Y	N	Y
10	**Hice**	Y	Y	Y	Y	N	Y
11	**Loudermilk**	N	Y	Y	Y	N	Y
12	**Allen**	Y	N	Y	Y	N	Y
13	Scott, D.	N	N	Y	Y	Y	N
14	**Graves**	N	Y	Y	Y	N	Y
HAWAII							
1	Hanabusa	N	N	N	Y	N	N
2	Gabbard	Y	Y	Y	N	Y	N
IDAHO							
1	**Labrador**	?	?	?	?	?	?
2	**Simpson**	N	N	Y	Y	N	Y
ILLINOIS							
1	Rush	N	N	N	N	Y	N
2	Kelly	N	N	N	N	Y	N
3	Lipinski	N	N	Y	N	Y	N
4	Gutierrez	N	N	N	N	Y	N
5	Quigley	N	N	Y	N	Y	N
6	**Roskam**	N	N	Y	Y	N	Y
7	Davis, D.	N	N	Y	N	Y	N
8	Krishnamoorthi	N	N	Y	N	Y	N
9	Schakowsky	N	N	Y	N	Y	N
10	Schneider	?	?	?	?	?	?
11	Foster	N	N	Y	N	Y	N
12	**Bost**	N	N	Y	Y	N	Y
13	**Davis, R.**	N	N	Y	Y	N	Y

	200	201	202	203	204	205
14 **Hultgren**	N	N	Y	Y	N	Y
15 **Shimkus**	N	N	Y	Y	N	Y
16 **Kinzinger**	N	N	Y	Y	N	Y
17 Bustos	N	N	Y	Y	Y	N
18 **LaHood**	N	N	Y	Y	N	Y
INDIANA						
1 Visclosky	N	N	Y	N	Y	N
2 **Walorski**	N	N	Y	Y	N	Y
3 **Banks**	Y	Y	N	Y	N	Y
4 **Rokita**	N	N	Y	Y	N	Y
5 **Brooks**	N	N	Y	Y	N	Y
6 **Messer**	N	N	Y	Y	?	Y
7 Carson	N	N	N	N	Y	N
8 **Bucshon**	N	N	Y	Y	N	Y
9 **Hollingsworth**	N	N	Y	Y	N	Y
IOWA						
1 **Blum**	N	N	Y	Y	N	Y
2 Loebsack	N	N	Y	N	Y	N
3 **Young**	N	N	Y	Y	N	Y
4 **King**	N	N	N	Y	N	Y
KANSAS						
1 **Marshall**	N	N	Y	Y	N	Y
2 **Jenkins**	N	N	Y	Y	N	Y
3 **Yoder**	?	?	?	?	?	?
4 **Estes**	N	N	Y	Y	N	Y
KENTUCKY						
1 **Comer**	N	Y	Y	Y	N	Y
2 **Guthrie**	N	Y	Y	Y	N	Y
3 Yarmuth	N	N	Y	N	Y	N
4 **Massie**	Y	Y	N	Y	N	N
5 **Rogers**	–	–	?	?	–	?
6 **Barr**	N	N	Y	Y	N	Y
LOUISIANA						
1 **Scalise**	Y	Y	Y	Y	N	Y
2 Richmond	N	N	N	N	Y	N
3 **Higgins**	N	Y	Y	Y	N	Y
4 **Johnson**	Y	Y	Y	Y	N	Y
5 **Abraham**	Y	N	Y	Y	N	Y
6 **Graves**	Y	Y	Y	Y	N	Y
MAINE						
1 Pingree	N	Y	Y	N	Y	N
2 **Poliquin**	N	N	Y	Y	N	Y
MARYLAND						
1 **Harris**	N	Y	Y	Y	N	N
2 Ruppersberger	N	N	Y	N	Y	N
3 Sarbanes	N	N	Y	N	Y	N
4 Brown	–	–	+	–	+	–
5 Hoyer	N	N	Y	N	Y	N
6 Delaney	N	N	Y	N	Y	N
7 Cummings	N	N	Y	N	Y	N
8 Raskin	N	N	Y	N	Y	N
MASSACHUSETTS						
1 Neal	N	N	Y	N	Y	N
2 McGovern	N	N	Y	N	Y	N
3 Tsongas	?	?	?	?	?	?
4 Kennedy	N	N	Y	N	Y	N
5 Clark	N	N	Y	N	Y	N
6 Moulton	N	N	Y	N	Y	N
7 Capuano	N	N	Y	N	Y	N
8 Lynch	N	N	Y	N	Y	N
9 Keating	N	N	Y	N	Y	N
MICHIGAN						
1 **Bergman**	N	N	Y	Y	N	Y
2 **Huizenga**	N	Y	Y	Y	N	Y
3 *Amash*	N	Y	N	Y	N	N
4 **Moolenaar**	N	N	Y	Y	N	Y
5 Kildee	N	N	Y	N	Y	N
6 **Upton**	N	N	Y	Y	N	N
7 **Walberg**	N	N	Y	Y	N	Y
8 **Bishop**	N	N	Y	Y	N	Y
9 Levin	N	N	Y	N	Y	N
10 **Mitchell**	N	N	Y	Y	N	Y
11 **Trott**	N	N	Y	Y	N	Y
12 Dingell	N	N	Y	N	Y	N
14 Lawrence	N	N	Y	N	Y	N
MINNESOTA						
1 Walz	?	?	?	?	?	–
2 **Lewis**	N	N	Y	Y	N	Y
3 **Paulsen**	N	N	Y	Y	N	Y
4 McCollum	N	N	Y	N	Y	N

	200	201	202	203	204	205
5 Ellison	N	N	Y	N	Y	N
6 **Emmer**	N	N	Y	Y	N	Y
7 Peterson	N	N	N	Y	Y	N
8 Nolan	N	N	Y	N	Y	N
MISSISSIPPI						
1 **Kelly**	N	N	Y	Y	N	Y
2 Thompson	N	N	N	N	Y	N
3 **Harper**	N	N	Y	Y	N	Y
4 **Palazzo**	N	N	Y	Y	N	Y
MISSOURI						
1 Clay	?	?	?	?	?	?
2 **Wagner**	N	N	Y	Y	N	Y
3 **Luetkemeyer**	N	N	Y	Y	N	Y
4 **Hartzler**	Y	N	N	Y	N	Y
5 Cleaver	N	?	N	N	Y	N
6 **Graves**	N	N	Y	Y	N	Y
7 **Long**	N	N	Y	Y	N	Y
8 **Smith**	N	Y	N	Y	N	Y
MONTANA						
AL **Gianforte**	Y	N	Y	Y	N	Y
NEBRASKA						
1 **Fortenberry**	N	N	Y	Y	N	Y
2 **Bacon**	N	N	Y	Y	N	Y
3 **Smith**	N	Y	Y	Y	N	Y
NEVADA						
1 Titus	N	N	Y	N	Y	N
2 **Amodei**	N	N	Y	Y	N	Y
3 Rosen	N	N	Y	N	Y	N
4 Kihuen	N	N	N	N	Y	N
NEW HAMPSHIRE						
1 Shea-Porter	N	N	Y	N	Y	N
2 Kuster	N	N	Y	N	Y	N
NEW JERSEY						
1 Norcross	?	?	?	?	?	?
2 **LoBiondo**	Y	N	Y	Y	N	N
3 **MacArthur**	N	N	Y	Y	N	Y
4 **Smith**	N	N	Y	N	N	N
5 Gottheimer	N	N	Y	N	Y	N
6 Pallone	N	N	Y	N	Y	N
7 **Lance**	N	N	Y	Y	N	N
8 Sires	N	N	Y	N	Y	N
9 Pascrell	N	N	Y	N	Y	N
10 Payne	N	N	Y	N	Y	N
11 **Frelinghuysen**	N	N	Y	Y	N	N
12 Watson Coleman	N	N	N	N	Y	N
NEW MEXICO						
1 Lujan Grisham	N	N	Y	N	Y	N
2 **Pearce**	N	N	Y	Y	N	Y
3 Luján	N	N	Y	N	Y	N
NEW YORK						
1 **Zeldin**	Y	Y	Y	Y	N	Y
2 **King**	N	N	Y	Y	N	N
3 Suozzi	N	N	Y	N	Y	N
4 Rice	N	N	Y	N	Y	N
5 Meeks	N	N	Y	N	Y	N
6 Meng	N	N	Y	N	Y	N
7 Velázquez	N	N	N	N	Y	N
8 Jeffries	N	N	N	N	Y	N
9 Clarke	N	N	N	N	Y	N
10 Nadler	N	N	Y	N	Y	N
11 **Donovan**	N	N	Y	Y	N	Y
12 Maloney, C.	N	N	Y	N	Y	N
13 Espaillat	N	N	Y	N	Y	N
14 Crowley	N	N	Y	N	Y	N
15 Serrano	N	N	Y	N	Y	N
16 Engel	N	N	Y	N	Y	N
17 Lowey	N	N	Y	N	Y	N
18 Maloney, S.P.	N	N	Y	N	Y	N
19 **Faso**	N	N	Y	Y	N	Y
20 Tonko	N	N	Y	N	Y	N
21 **Stefanik**	N	N	Y	Y	N	Y
22 **Tenney**	N	N	Y	Y	N	Y
23 **Reed**	N	N	Y	Y	N	Y
24 **Katko**	N	N	Y	Y	N	N
25 **Vacant**						
26 Higgins	N	N	Y	N	Y	N
27 **Collins**	N	N	Y	Y	N	Y
NORTH CAROLINA						
1 Butterfield	N	N	N	N	Y	N
2 **Holding**	N	N	Y	Y	N	Y
3 **Jones**	Y	Y	Y	Y	N	N
4 Price	N	N	Y	N	Y	N

	200	201	202	203	204	205
5 **Foxx**	Y	N	N	Y	N	Y
6 **Walker**	Y	N	Y	Y	N	Y
7 **Rouzer**	N	N	Y	Y	N	Y
8 **Hudson**	N	N	Y	Y	N	Y
9 **Pittenger**	Y	N	Y	Y	N	Y
9 **Vacant**						
10 **McHenry**	N	Y	Y	Y	N	Y
11 **Meadows**	N	Y	Y	Y	N	N
12 Adams	N	N	Y	N	Y	N
13 **Budd**	Y	Y	Y	Y	N	N
NORTH DAKOTA						
AL **Cramer**	N	Y	Y	Y	N	Y
OHIO						
1 **Chabot**	Y	N	Y	Y	N	Y
2 **Wenstrup**	N	N	Y	Y	N	Y
3 Beatty	N	N	N	N	Y	N
4 **Jordan**	Y	Y	Y	Y	N	N
5 **Latta**	N	N	Y	Y	N	Y
6 **Johnson**	N	N	Y	Y	N	Y
7 **Gibbs**	N	N	Y	Y	N	Y
8 **Davidson**	N	Y	Y	Y	N	N
9 Kaptur	N	N	Y	N	Y	N
10 **Turner**	N	N	Y	Y	N	Y
11 Fudge	N	N	N	N	Y	N
12 **Vacant**						
13 Ryan	N	N	Y	N	Y	N
14 **Joyce**	N	N	Y	Y	N	Y
15 **Stivers**	N	N	Y	Y	N	Y
16 **Renacci**	N	N	Y	Y	N	Y
OKLAHOMA						
1 **Vacant**						
2 **Mullin**	N	Y	N	Y	N	Y
3 **Lucas**	N	N	Y	Y	N	Y
4 **Cole**	N	N	Y	Y	N	Y
5 **Russell**	Y	N	Y	Y	N	Y
OREGON						
1 Bonamici	N	N	Y	N	Y	N
2 **Walden**	N	N	Y	Y	N	Y
3 Blumenauer	N	Y	Y	N	Y	N
4 DeFazio	N	N	Y	N	Y	N
5 Schrader	N	N	Y	Y	Y	N
PENNSYLVANIA						
1 Brady	N	N	Y	N	Y	N
2 Evans	N	N	N	N	Y	N
3 **Kelly**	N	N	Y	Y	N	Y
4 **Perry**	Y	Y	Y	Y	N	N
5 **Thompson**	N	N	Y	Y	N	Y
6 **Costello**	N	N	Y	N	N	Y
7 **Vacant**						
8 **Fitzpatrick**	N	N	Y	N	N	N
9 **Shuster**	N	N	Y	Y	N	Y
10 **Marino**	N	Y	Y	Y	N	Y
11 **Barletta**	N	Y	Y	Y	N	Y
12 **Rothfus**	Y	Y	Y	Y	N	N
13 Boyle	?	?	?	?	?	?
14 Doyle	N	N	Y	N	Y	N
15 **Vacant**						
16 **Smucker**	N	Y	Y	Y	N	Y
17 Cartwright	N	N	Y	N	Y	N
18 Lamb	N	N	Y	Y	Y	N
RHODE ISLAND						
1 Cicilline	N	N	Y	N	Y	N
2 Langevin	N	N	N	N	Y	N
SOUTH CAROLINA						
1 **Sanford**	Y	Y	N	Y	N	N
2 **Wilson**	N	N	Y	Y	N	Y
3 **Duncan**	Y	Y	Y	Y	N	Y
4 **Gowdy**	N	N	Y	Y	N	Y
5 **Norman**	Y	Y	Y	Y	N	Y
6 Clyburn	N	N	N	N	Y	N
7 **Rice**	N	Y	Y	Y	N	Y
SOUTH DAKOTA						
AL **Noem**	N	Y	N	Y	N	Y
TENNESSEE						
1 **Roe**	N	N	Y	Y	N	Y
2 **Duncan**	Y	Y	Y	Y	N	N
3 **Fleischmann**	N	N	Y	Y	N	Y
4 **DesJarlais**	N	N	Y	Y	N	Y
5 Cooper	N	N	Y	Y	Y	N
6 **Black**	N	Y	Y	Y	N	Y
7 **Blackburn**	N	Y	Y	Y	N	Y
8 **Kustoff**	N	N	Y	Y	N	Y
9 Cohen	N	N	Y	N	Y	N

	200	201	202	203	204	205
TEXAS						
1 **Gohmert**	?	?	?	?	?	?
2 **Poe**	Y	Y	N	Y	N	Y
3 **Johnson, S.**	N	N	Y	Y	N	Y
4 **Ratcliffe**	N	N	Y	Y	N	Y
5 **Hensarling**	Y	N	Y	Y	N	Y
6 **Barton**	N	Y	Y	Y	N	Y
7 **Culberson**	N	Y	Y	Y	N	Y
8 **Brady**	N	N	Y	Y	N	Y
9 Green, A.	N	N	Y	N	Y	N
10 **McCaul**	N	N	Y	Y	N	Y
11 **Conaway**	N	N	Y	Y	N	Y
12 **Granger**	N	N	Y	Y	N	Y
13 **Thornberry**	N	N	Y	Y	N	Y
14 **Weber**	N	N	Y	Y	N	Y
15 Gonzalez	N	N	Y	Y	Y	N
16 O'Rourke	N	N	Y	N	Y	N
17 **Flores**	N	N	Y	Y	N	Y
18 Jackson Lee	N	N	Y	N	Y	N
19 **Arrington**	N	N	Y	Y	N	Y
20 Castro	N	N	Y	N	Y	N
21 **Smith**	N	N	Y	Y	N	Y
22 **Olson**	N	N	Y	Y	N	Y
23 **Hurd**	N	N	Y	Y	N	Y
24 **Marchant**	N	N	Y	Y	N	Y
25 **Williams**	N	N	Y	Y	N	Y
26 **Burgess**	Y	N	Y	Y	N	Y
28 Cuellar	N	N	Y	Y	Y	N
29 Green, G.	N	N	Y	N	Y	N
30 Johnson, E.B.	N	N	N	N	Y	N
31 **Carter**	N	N	Y	Y	N	Y
32 **Sessions**	N	N	N	Y	N	Y
33 Veasey	N	N	Y	Y	Y	N
34 Vela	N	N	Y	Y	Y	N
35 Doggett	N	N	Y	N	Y	N
36 **Babin**	N	N	N	Y	N	Y
UTAH						
1 **Bishop**	Y	Y	Y	Y	N	Y
2 **Stewart**	N	N	Y	Y	N	Y
3 **Curtis**	Y	Y	Y	Y	N	Y
4 **Love**	Y	N	N	Y	N	Y
VERMONT						
AL Welch	N	Y	Y	N	Y	N
VIRGINIA						
1 **Wittman**	N	Y	Y	Y	N	Y
2 **Taylor**	N	Y	Y	Y	N	Y
3 Scott	N	N	Y	N	Y	N
4 McEachin	N	N	Y	N	Y	N
5 **Garrett**	N	Y	Y	Y	N	Y
6 **Goodlatte**	N	N	N	Y	N	Y
7 **Brat**	Y	Y	Y	Y	N	N
8 Beyer	N	N	Y	N	Y	N
9 **Griffith**	Y	Y	Y	Y	N	Y
10 **Comstock**	N	N	Y	Y	N	Y
11 Connolly	N	N	Y	N	Y	N
WASHINGTON						
1 DelBene	N	N	Y	N	Y	N
2 Larsen	N	N	Y	N	Y	N
3 **Herrera Beutler**	N	Y	Y	Y	N	Y
4 **Newhouse**	N	N	N	Y	N	Y
5 **McMorris Rodgers**	N	N	Y	Y	N	Y
6 Kilmer	N	N	Y	N	Y	N
7 Jayapal	N	N	Y	N	Y	N
8 **Reichert**	N	N	Y	Y	N	Y
9 Smith	N	N	Y	N	Y	N
10 Heck	N	N	Y	N	Y	N
WEST VIRGINIA						
1 **McKinley**	N	N	Y	Y	N	Y
2 **Mooney**	Y	Y	Y	Y	N	Y
3 **Jenkins**	N	Y	Y	Y	N	Y
WISCONSIN						
1 **Ryan**						N
2 Pocan	N	N	Y	N	Y	N
3 Kind	N	N	Y	N	Y	N
4 Moore	N	N	Y	N	Y	N
5 **Sensenbrenner**	Y	Y	Y	Y	N	Y
6 **Grothman**	Y	Y	Y	Y	N	Y
7 **Duffy**	N	N	Y	Y	N	Y
8 **Gallagher**	N	N	Y	Y	N	Y
WYOMING						
AL **Cheney**	N	Y	Y	Y	N	Y

VOTE NUMBER

206. PROCEDURAL MOTION/JOURNAL. Approval of the House Journal of May 17, 2018. Approved 183-163: R 142-60; D 41-103. May 18, 2018.

207. HR4830. LATE GI BILL PAYMENTS/PASSAGE. Dunn, R-Fla., motion to suspend the rules and pass the bill that would prohibit an institution of higher learning from penalizing any student whose GI Bill payments have not been received by the institution. It would make institutions with such penalties in place ineligible for GI Bill benefits. Motion agreed to 382-0: R 212-0; D 170-0. May 21, 2018.

208. HR4451. SERVICES FOR HOMELESS VETERANS/PASSAGE. Roe, R-Tenn., motion to suspend the rules and pass the bill that would allow veterans who are homeless and participating in the HUD-Veterans Affairs Supportive Housing voucher program, those who are transitioning from being incarcerated, and other eligible homeless or recently homeless veterans to be eligible for training services under the Homeless Veteran Reintegration Program. Motion agreed to 377-1: R 210-0; D 167-1. May 21, 2018.

209. HR3832. PRESCRIPTION DRUG DATA SHARING/PASSAGE. Dunn, R-Fla., motion to suspend the rules and pass the bill that would require VA health care providers to share prescription drug data across a national network of interstate prescription drug monitoring programs, and would require VA providers to seek information from prescription drug monitoring programs before prescribing controlled substances. Motion agreed to 377-2: R 208-2; D 169-0. May 21, 2018.

210. HRES905. BANK REGULATION THRESHOLDS, EXPERIMENTAL DRUGS FOR TERMINAL ILLNESSES AND FISCAL 2019 DEFENSE AUTHORIZATION/ PREVIOUS QUESTION. Burgess, R-Texas, motion to order the previous question (thus ending debate and possibility of amendment) on the rule (H Res 905) that would provide for House floor consideration of the bill (S 2155) related to banking regulations, would provide for consideration of the bill (S 204) that would allow individuals with terminal illnesses access to experimental and investigational drugs, and would provide for consideration of the bill (HR 5515) that would authorize $708.1 billion in discretionary funding for defense programs in fiscal 2019. Motion agreed to 222-184: R 222-1; D 0-183. May 22, 2018.

211. S2155. BANK REGULATION THRESHOLDS, EXPERIMENTAL DRUGS FOR TERMINAL ILLNESSES AND FISCAL 2019 DEFENSE AUTHORIZATION/ RULE. Adoption of the rule (H Res 905) that would provide for House floor consideration of the bill (S 2155) that would apply the more stringent bank regulation provisions of the 2010 financial overhaul to banks with $250 billion in assets, instead of those with at least $50 billion in assets, would provide for consideration of the bill (S 204) that would allow individuals with terminal illnesses access to experimental and investigational drugs, and would provide for consideration of the bill (HR 5515) that would authorize $708.1 billion in discretionary funding for defense programs in fiscal 2019. Adopted 227-180: R 222-2; D 5-178. May 22, 2018.

	206	207	208	209	210	211
ALABAMA						
1 Byrne	Y	Y	Y	Y	Y	Y
2 Roby	Y	Y	Y	Y	Y	Y
3 Rogers	N	Y	Y	Y	Y	Y
4 Aderholt	?	Y	Y	Y	Y	Y
5 Brooks	?	Y	Y	Y	Y	Y
6 Palmer	Y	Y	Y	Y	Y	Y
7 Sewell	N	Y	Y	Y	N	N
ALASKA						
AL Young	N	Y	Y	Y	Y	Y
ARIZONA						
1 O'Halleran	N	Y	Y	Y	N	Y
2 McSally	N	?	Y	Y	Y	Y
3 Grijalva	?	Y	Y	Y	N	N
4 Gosar	Y	Y	Y	Y	Y	Y
5 Biggs	N	Y	Y	Y	Y	Y
6 Schweikert	Y	Y	Y	?	Y	Y
7 Gallego	?	Y	Y	Y	N	N
8 Lesko	Y	Y	Y	Y	Y	Y
9 Sinema	N	Y	Y	Y	N	Y
ARKANSAS						
1 Crawford	N	Y	Y	Y	Y	Y
2 Hill	Y	Y	Y	Y	Y	Y
3 Womack	Y	Y	Y	Y	Y	Y
4 Westerman	Y	+	+	+	Y	Y
CALIFORNIA						
1 LaMalfa	Y	Y	Y	Y	Y	Y
2 Huffman	Y	Y	Y	N	N	N
3 Garamendi	?	Y	Y	Y	?	?
4 McClintock	Y	Y	Y	Y	Y	Y
5 Thompson	N	Y	Y	N	N	N
6 Matsui	N	Y	Y	N	N	N
7 Bera	N	Y	Y	N	N	N
8 Cook	Y	Y	Y	Y	Y	Y
9 McNerney	N	Y	Y	N	N	N
10 Denham	N	Y	Y	Y	Y	Y
11 DeSaulnier	Y	Y	Y	N	N	N
12 Pelosi	?	Y	Y	N	N	N
13 Lee	N	Y	Y	?	N	N
14 Speier	?	?	?	?	?	?
15 Swalwell	?	Y	Y	N	N	N
16 Costa	N	Y	Y	N	N	N
17 Khanna	?	Y	Y	N	N	N
18 Eshoo	N	Y	Y	N	N	N
19 Lofgren	N	Y	Y	N	N	N
20 Panetta	Y	Y	Y	N	N	N
21 Valadao	N	Y	Y	Y	Y	Y
22 Nunes	Y	Y	Y	Y	Y	Y
23 McCarthy	Y	Y	Y	Y	Y	Y
24 Carbajal	N	Y	Y	N	N	N
25 Knight	N	Y	Y	Y	Y	Y
26 Brownley	N	Y	Y	N	N	N
27 Chu	Y	Y	Y	N	N	N
28 Schiff	N	Y	Y	N	N	N
29 Cardenas	N	Y	Y	N	N	N
30 Sherman	Y	Y	Y	N	N	N
31 Aguilar	N	Y	Y	N	N	N
32 Napolitano	N	Y	Y	N	N	N
33 Lieu	?	Y	Y	N	N	N
34 Gomez	N	Y	Y	N	N	N
35 Torres	N	Y	Y	N	N	N
36 Ruiz	N	Y	Y	N	N	N
37 Bass	?	Y	Y	N	?	?
38 Sánchez, Linda	N	Y	Y	N	N	N
39 Royce	Y	Y	Y	Y	Y	Y
40 Roybal-Allard	N	Y	Y	N	N	N
41 Takano	N	Y	Y	N	N	N
42 Calvert	Y	Y	Y	Y	Y	Y
43 Waters	Y	Y	Y	N	N	N
44 Barragan	N	Y	Y	N	N	N
45 Walters	Y	Y	Y	Y	Y	Y
46 Correa	N	Y	Y	N	N	N
47 Lowenthal	N	Y	Y	N	N	N
48 Rohrabacher	Y	?	?	?	Y	Y
49 Issa	?	Y	?	?	Y	Y
50 Hunter	N	Y	Y	Y	Y	Y
51 Vargas	N	?	?	?	N	N
52 Peters	?	Y	Y	N	N	N
53 Davis	Y	Y	Y	N	N	N

	206	207	208	209	210	211
COLORADO						
1 DeGette	N	Y	Y	Y	N	N
2 Polis	?	Y	Y	Y	N	N
3 Tipton	Y	Y	Y	Y	Y	Y
4 Buck	?	Y	Y	Y	Y	Y
5 Lamborn	Y	Y	Y	Y	Y	Y
6 Coffman	N	Y	Y	Y	Y	Y
7 Perlmutter	Y	Y	Y	N	N	N
CONNECTICUT						
1 Larson	N	Y	Y	N	N	N
2 Courtney	Y	Y	Y	N	N	N
3 DeLauro	Y	+	+	+	N	N
4 Himes	Y	Y	Y	N	N	N
5 Esty	N	Y	Y	N	N	N
DELAWARE						
AL Blunt Rochester	N	Y	Y	Y	N	N
FLORIDA						
1 Gaetz	N	Y	Y	Y	?	?
2 Dunn	Y	Y	Y	Y	Y	Y
3 Yoho	N	Y	Y	Y	Y	Y
4 Rutherford	Y	Y	Y	Y	Y	Y
5 Lawson	?	Y	Y	Y	N	N
6 DeSantis	N	?	?	Y	Y	Y
7 Murphy	Y	Y	Y	Y	N	Y
8 Posey	Y	Y	Y	Y	Y	Y
9 Soto	N	Y	Y	N	N	N
10 Demings	Y	Y	Y	N	N	N
11 Webster	Y	Y	Y	Y	Y	Y
12 Bilirakis	Y	Y	Y	Y	Y	Y
13 Crist	N	Y	Y	N	N	N
14 Castor	N	?	?	?	N	N
15 Ross	Y	+	+	+	Y	Y
16 Buchanan	Y	?	?	Y	Y	Y
17 Rooney, T.	Y	Y	Y	Y	Y	Y
18 Mast	N	Y	Y	Y	Y	Y
19 Rooney, F.	Y	Y	Y	Y	Y	Y
20 Hastings	N	Y	Y	N	N	N
21 Frankel	Y	Y	Y	N	N	N
22 Deutch	Y	?	?	?	?	?
23 Wasserman Schultz	Y	Y	Y	N	N	N
24 Wilson	?	Y	Y	?	N	N
25 Diaz-Balart	Y	Y	Y	Y	Y	Y
26 Curbelo	?	Y	Y	Y	Y	Y
27 Ros-Lehtinen	N	Y	Y	Y	Y	Y
GEORGIA						
1 Carter	N	Y	Y	Y	Y	Y
2 Bishop	N	Y	Y	N	N	N
3 Ferguson	Y	Y	Y	?	Y	Y
4 Johnson	?	Y	Y	N	N	N
5 Lewis	N	?	?	?	N	N
6 Handel	Y	Y	Y	Y	Y	Y
7 Woodall	N	Y	Y	Y	Y	Y
8 Scott, A.	Y	Y	Y	Y	Y	Y
9 Collins	Y	Y	Y	Y	Y	Y
10 Hice	N	Y	Y	Y	Y	Y
11 Loudermilk	?	Y	Y	Y	Y	Y
12 Allen	Y	Y	Y	Y	?	?
13 Scott, D.	?	Y	Y	N	N	N
14 Graves	Y	?	Y	Y	Y	Y
HAWAII						
1 Hanabusa	N	Y	Y	Y	N	N
2 Gabbard	?	?	?	?	?	?
IDAHO						
1 Labrador	?	Y	Y	Y	Y	Y
2 Simpson	Y	Y	Y	Y	Y	Y
ILLINOIS						
1 Rush	N	?	?	N	N	N
2 Kelly	N	?	?	N	N	N
3 Lipinski	Y	Y	Y	N	N	N
4 Gutierrez	N	+	+	+	N	N
5 Quigley	?	Y	Y	N	N	N
6 Roskam	N	Y	Y	Y	?	Y
7 Davis, D.	N	Y	Y	N	N	N
8 Krishnamoorthi	N	Y	Y	N	N	N
9 Schakowsky	N	Y	Y	N	N	N
10 Schneider	?	Y	Y	N	N	Y
11 Foster	Y	Y	Y	N	N	N
12 Bost	N	Y	Y	Y	Y	Y
13 Davis, R.	Y	Y	Y	Y	Y	Y

	206	207	208	209	210	211
14 **Hultgren**	Y	Y	Y	Y	Y	Y
15 **Shimkus**	Y	Y	Y	Y	Y	Y
16 **Kinzinger**	N	+	+	+	Y	Y
17 Bustos	Y	Y	Y	Y	N	N
18 **LaHood**	N	Y	Y	Y	Y	Y
INDIANA						
1 Visclosky	N	Y	Y	Y	N	N
2 **Walorski**	Y	Y	Y	Y	Y	Y
3 **Banks**	Y	Y	Y	Y	Y	Y
4 **Rokita**	N	Y	Y	Y	Y	Y
5 **Brooks**	Y	Y	Y	Y	Y	Y
6 **Messer**	Y	Y	?	?	Y	Y
7 Carson	N	Y	Y	Y	N	N
8 **Bucshon**	Y	Y	Y	Y	Y	Y
9 **Hollingsworth**	Y	Y	Y	Y	Y	Y
IOWA						
1 **Blum**	N	+	+	+	Y	Y
2 Loebsack	N	+	+	+	N	N
3 **Young**	Y	Y	Y	Y	Y	Y
4 **King**	+	Y	Y	Y	Y	Y
KANSAS						
1 **Marshall**	Y	Y	Y	Y	Y	Y
2 **Jenkins**	N	Y	Y	Y	Y	Y
3 **Yoder**	?	Y	Y	Y	Y	Y
4 **Estes**	?	Y	Y	Y	Y	Y
KENTUCKY						
1 **Comer**	N	Y	Y	Y	Y	Y
2 **Guthrie**	Y	Y	Y	Y	Y	Y
3 Yarmuth	?	Y	Y	Y	N	N
4 **Massie**	Y	Y	Y	N	Y	N
5 **Rogers**	?	?	?	?	?	?
6 **Barr**	N	Y	Y	Y	Y	Y
LOUISIANA						
1 **Scalise**	Y	Y	Y	Y	Y	Y
2 Richmond	N	Y	Y	Y	?	N
3 **Higgins**	Y	+	+	+	+	+
4 **Johnson**	Y	Y	Y	Y	Y	Y
5 **Abraham**	Y	Y	Y	Y	Y	Y
6 **Graves**	Y	Y	Y	Y	Y	Y
MAINE						
1 Pingree	N	Y	Y	Y	N	N
2 **Poliquin**	N	Y	Y	Y	Y	Y
MARYLAND						
1 **Harris**	Y	Y	Y	Y	Y	Y
2 Ruppersberger	Y	Y	Y	Y	N	N
3 Sarbanes	?	Y	Y	Y	N	N
4 Brown	?	+	+	+	-	-
5 Hoyer	N	Y	Y	Y	?	?
6 Delaney	?	Y	Y	Y	N	N
7 Cummings	N	?	?	?	N	N
8 Raskin	N	Y	Y	Y	N	N
MASSACHUSETTS						
1 Neal	?	Y	Y	Y	N	N
2 McGovern	N	Y	Y	Y	N	N
3 Tsongas	?	?	?	?	N	N
4 Kennedy	Y	Y	Y	Y	N	N
5 Clark	N	Y	Y	Y	N	N
6 Moulton	N	Y	Y	Y	N	N
7 Capuano	N	Y	Y	Y	N	N
8 Lynch	N	Y	?	Y	N	N
9 Keating	?	Y	Y	Y	N	N
MICHIGAN						
1 **Bergman**	N	Y	Y	Y	Y	Y
2 **Huizenga**	Y	Y	Y	Y	Y	Y
3 *Amash*	N	Y	Y	N	Y	N
4 **Moolenaar**	?	Y	Y	Y	Y	Y
5 Kildee	Y	Y	Y	Y	N	N
6 **Upton**	N	Y	Y	Y	Y	Y
7 **Walberg**	N	Y	Y	Y	Y	Y
8 **Bishop**	N	Y	Y	Y	Y	Y
9 Levin	N	Y	Y	Y	N	N
10 **Mitchell**	Y	Y	Y	Y	Y	Y
11 **Trott**	Y	Y	Y	Y	Y	Y
12 Dingell	N	Y	Y	Y	N	N
14 Lawrence	?	Y	Y	Y	N	N
MINNESOTA						
1 Walz	?	Y	Y	Y	?	?
2 **Lewis**	Y	Y	Y	Y	Y	Y
3 **Paulsen**	N	Y	Y	Y	Y	Y
4 McCollum	Y	Y	Y	Y	N	N

	206	207	208	209	210	211
5 Ellison	Y	Y	Y	Y	N	N
6 **Emmer**	N	Y	Y	Y	Y	Y
7 Peterson	N	Y	Y	Y	N	N
8 Nolan	N	Y	Y	Y	N	N
MISSISSIPPI						
1 **Kelly**	Y	Y	Y	Y	Y	Y
2 Thompson	N	?	?	?	N	N
3 **Harper**	Y	Y	Y	Y	Y	Y
4 **Palazzo**	Y	Y	Y	Y	Y	Y
MISSOURI						
1 Clay	?	Y	Y	Y	N	N
2 **Wagner**	Y	Y	Y	Y	Y	Y
3 **Luetkemeyer**	Y	Y	Y	Y	Y	Y
4 **Hartzler**	Y	+	+	+	Y	Y
5 Cleaver	N	Y	Y	Y	N	N
6 **Graves**	N	Y	Y	Y	Y	Y
7 **Long**	Y	Y	Y	Y	Y	Y
8 **Smith**	Y	Y	Y	Y	Y	Y
MONTANA						
AL **Gianforte**	Y	Y	Y	Y	Y	Y
NEBRASKA						
1 **Fortenberry**	Y	Y	Y	Y	Y	Y
2 **Bacon**	Y	Y	Y	Y	Y	Y
3 **Smith**	Y	Y	+	Y	Y	Y
NEVADA						
1 Titus	Y	Y	Y	Y	N	N
2 **Amodei**	Y	Y	Y	Y	Y	Y
3 Rosen	N	Y	Y	Y	N	N
4 Kihuen	N	Y	Y	Y	N	N
NEW HAMPSHIRE						
1 Shea-Porter	Y	Y	Y	Y	N	N
2 Kuster	N	Y	Y	Y	N	N
NEW JERSEY						
1 Norcross	?	Y	Y	Y	?	?
2 **LoBiondo**	N	Y	Y	Y	Y	Y
3 **MacArthur**	N	Y	Y	Y	Y	Y
4 **Smith**	Y	Y	Y	Y	Y	Y
5 Gottheimer	N	Y	Y	Y	N	Y
6 Pallone	N	Y	Y	Y	N	N
7 **Lance**	N	Y	Y	Y	Y	Y
8 Sires	?	?	?	?	N	N
9 Pascrell	?	Y	Y	Y	N	N
10 Payne	N	Y	Y	Y	N	N
11 **Frelinghuysen**	Y	+	Y	Y	+	+
12 Watson Coleman	N	Y	Y	Y	N	N
NEW MEXICO						
1 Lujan Grisham	Y	+	+	+	N	N
2 **Pearce**	N	?	?	?	?	?
3 Luján	N	Y	Y	Y	N	N
NEW YORK						
1 **Zeldin**	Y	Y	Y	Y	Y	Y
2 **King**	?	Y	Y	Y	Y	Y
3 Suozzi	Y	Y	Y	Y	N	N
4 Rice	?	Y	Y	Y	N	N
5 Meeks	?	Y	Y	Y	N	N
6 Meng	Y	Y	Y	Y	N	N
7 Velázquez	?	Y	Y	Y	N	N
8 Jeffries	Y	Y	Y	Y	N	N
9 Clarke	N	Y	Y	Y	N	N
10 Nadler	Y	Y	?	Y	N	N
11 **Donovan**	Y	Y	Y	Y	Y	Y
12 Maloney, C.	N	Y	N	Y	N	N
13 Espaillat	?	Y	Y	Y	N	N
14 Crowley	N	Y	Y	Y	N	N
15 Serrano	N	Y	Y	Y	N	N
16 Engel	N	Y	Y	Y	N	N
17 Lowey	N	Y	Y	Y	N	N
18 Maloney, S.P.	?	Y	Y	Y	N	N
19 **Faso**	Y	Y	Y	Y	Y	Y
20 Tonko	P	Y	Y	Y	N	N
21 **Stefanik**	Y	Y	Y	Y	Y	Y
22 **Tenney**	Y	Y	Y	Y	Y	Y
23 **Reed**	?	Y	Y	Y	Y	Y
24 **Katko**	Y	Y	Y	Y	Y	Y
25 **Vacant**						
26 Higgins	?	Y	Y	Y	N	N
27 **Collins**	Y	Y	Y	Y	Y	Y
NORTH CAROLINA						
1 Butterfield	Y	Y	Y	Y	N	N
2 **Holding**	N	Y	Y	Y	Y	Y
3 **Jones**	N	Y	Y	Y	N	Y
4 Price	N	Y	Y	Y	N	N

	206	207	208	209	210	211
5 **Foxx**	N	Y	Y	Y	Y	Y
6 **Walker**	?	Y	Y	Y	Y	Y
7 **Rouzer**	Y	Y	Y	Y	Y	Y
8 **Hudson**	N	Y	Y	Y	Y	Y
9 **Pittenger**	?	Y	Y	Y	Y	Y
9 **Vacant**						
10 **McHenry**	Y	Y	Y	Y	Y	Y
11 **Meadows**	Y	Y	Y	Y	Y	Y
12 Adams	N	Y	Y	Y	N	N
13 **Budd**	Y	Y	Y	Y	Y	Y
NORTH DAKOTA						
AL **Cramer**	Y	Y	Y	Y	Y	Y
OHIO						
1 **Chabot**	Y	Y	Y	Y	Y	Y
2 **Wenstrup**	N	Y	Y	Y	Y	Y
3 Beatty	?	Y	Y	Y	N	N
4 **Jordan**	N	Y	Y	Y	Y	Y
5 **Latta**	Y	Y	Y	Y	Y	Y
6 **Johnson**	N	Y	Y	Y	Y	Y
7 **Gibbs**	Y	Y	Y	Y	Y	Y
8 **Davidson**	Y	Y	Y	Y	Y	Y
9 Kaptur	?	Y	?	Y	N	N
10 **Turner**	Y	+	+	+	Y	Y
11 Fudge	N	Y	Y	Y	N	N
12 **Vacant**						
13 Ryan	N	Y	Y	Y	N	N
14 **Joyce**	N	Y	Y	Y	Y	Y
15 **Stivers**	Y	Y	Y	Y	?	?
16 **Renacci**	N	Y	Y	Y	Y	Y
OKLAHOMA						
1 **Vacant**						
2 **Mullin**	Y	Y	Y	Y	Y	Y
3 **Lucas**	Y	Y	Y	Y	Y	Y
4 **Cole**	Y	Y	Y	Y	Y	Y
5 **Russell**	Y	Y	Y	Y	Y	Y
OREGON						
1 Bonamici	Y	Y	Y	Y	N	N
2 **Walden**	Y	Y	Y	Y	Y	Y
3 Blumenauer	N	Y	Y	Y	N	N
4 DeFazio	N	Y	Y	Y	N	N
5 Schrader	N	Y	Y	Y	N	N
PENNSYLVANIA						
1 Brady	N	?	?	?	N	N
2 Evans	N	Y	Y	Y	N	N
3 **Kelly**	Y	Y	Y	Y	Y	Y
4 **Perry**	N	Y	Y	Y	Y	Y
5 **Thompson**	Y	Y	Y	Y	Y	Y
6 **Costello**	?	Y	Y	Y	Y	Y
7 **Vacant**						
8 **Fitzpatrick**	N	Y	Y	Y	Y	Y
9 **Shuster**	Y	Y	Y	Y	Y	Y
10 **Marino**	?	Y	Y	Y	Y	Y
11 **Barletta**	Y	Y	Y	Y	Y	Y
12 **Rothfus**	Y	Y	Y	Y	Y	Y
13 Boyle	?	Y	Y	Y	N	N
14 Doyle	?	?	?	?	N	N
15 **Vacant**						
16 **Smucker**	Y	Y	Y	Y	Y	Y
17 Cartwright	Y	Y	Y	Y	N	N
18 Lamb	N	Y	Y	Y	N	N
RHODE ISLAND						
1 Cicilline	N	+	+	+	N	N
2 Langevin	N	Y	Y	Y	N	N
SOUTH CAROLINA						
1 **Sanford**	Y	Y	Y	Y	Y	Y
2 **Wilson**	Y	Y	Y	Y	Y	Y
3 **Duncan**	N	Y	Y	Y	Y	Y
4 **Gowdy**	?	?	?	?	Y	Y
5 **Norman**	Y	Y	Y	Y	Y	Y
6 Clyburn	?	Y	Y	Y	N	N
7 **Rice**	Y	Y	Y	Y	Y	Y
SOUTH DAKOTA						
AL **Noem**	Y	Y	Y	Y	Y	Y
TENNESSEE						
1 **Roe**	N	Y	Y	Y	Y	Y
2 **Duncan**	?	Y	Y	Y	Y	Y
3 **Fleischmann**	Y	Y	Y	Y	Y	Y
4 **DesJarlais**	Y	+	+	+	+	+
5 Cooper	Y	Y	Y	Y	N	N
6 **Black**	Y	?	?	?	?	?
7 **Blackburn**	?	Y	Y	Y	Y	Y
8 **Kustoff**	Y	Y	Y	Y	Y	Y
9 Cohen	N	Y	Y	Y	N	N

	206	207	208	209	210	211
TEXAS						
1 **Gohmert**	?	Y	Y	Y	Y	?
2 **Poe**	N	?	?	?	Y	Y
3 **Johnson, S.**	?	Y	Y	Y	Y	Y
4 **Ratcliffe**	?	Y	?	?	Y	Y
5 **Hensarling**	Y	Y	Y	Y	Y	Y
6 **Barton**	?	Y	Y	Y	Y	Y
7 **Culberson**	Y	Y	Y	Y	Y	Y
8 **Brady**	Y	Y	Y	Y	Y	Y
9 Green, A.	N	Y	Y	Y	N	N
10 **McCaul**	Y	Y	Y	Y	Y	Y
11 **Conaway**	Y	Y	Y	Y	Y	Y
12 **Granger**	?	Y	+	Y	Y	Y
13 **Thornberry**	Y	+	+	+	Y	Y
14 **Weber**	Y	Y	Y	Y	Y	Y
15 Gonzalez	?	Y	Y	Y	N	N
16 O'Rourke	?	+	+	+	?	?
17 **Flores**	Y	Y	Y	Y	Y	Y
18 Jackson Lee	N	Y	Y	Y	N	N
19 **Arrington**	?	Y	Y	Y	Y	Y
20 Castro	?	Y	Y	Y	N	N
21 **Smith**	?	Y	Y	Y	Y	Y
22 **Olson**	Y	+	+	+	Y	Y
23 **Hurd**	Y	Y	Y	Y	Y	Y
24 **Marchant**	?	Y	Y	Y	Y	Y
25 **Williams**	Y	Y	Y	Y	Y	Y
26 **Burgess**	Y	Y	Y	Y	+	Y
28 Cuellar	N	Y	Y	Y	N	N
29 Green, G.	N	?	Y	Y	N	N
30 Johnson, E.B.	N	Y	Y	Y	N	N
31 **Carter**	Y	Y	Y	Y	Y	Y
32 **Sessions**	Y	?	?	?	Y	Y
33 Veasey	N	Y	Y	Y	N	N
34 Vela	Y	Y	Y	Y	N	N
35 Doggett	?	Y	Y	Y	N	N
36 **Babin**	Y	Y	Y	Y	Y	Y
UTAH						
1 **Bishop**	Y	Y	Y	Y	Y	Y
2 **Stewart**	Y	Y	Y	Y	Y	Y
3 **Curtis**	Y	Y	Y	Y	Y	Y
4 **Love**	Y	Y	Y	Y	Y	Y
VERMONT						
AL Welch	Y	Y	Y	Y	N	N
VIRGINIA						
1 **Wittman**	N	Y	Y	Y	Y	Y
2 **Taylor**	Y	Y	Y	Y	Y	Y
3 Scott	N	Y	Y	Y	N	N
4 McEachin	N	Y	Y	Y	N	N
5 **Garrett**	N	Y	Y	Y	Y	Y
6 **Goodlatte**	?	Y	Y	Y	Y	Y
7 **Brat**	Y	Y	Y	Y	Y	Y
8 Beyer	N	Y	Y	Y	N	N
9 **Griffith**	Y	Y	Y	Y	Y	Y
10 **Comstock**	Y	Y	Y	Y	Y	Y
11 Connolly	N	Y	Y	Y	N	N
WASHINGTON						
1 DelBene	N	Y	Y	Y	N	N
2 Larsen	N	?	?	?	N	N
3 **Herrera Beutler**	N	Y	Y	Y	Y	Y
4 **Newhouse**	?	Y	Y	Y	Y	Y
5 **McMorris Rodgers**	Y	Y	Y	Y	Y	Y
6 Kilmer	N	Y	Y	Y	N	N
7 Jayapal	N	Y	Y	Y	N	N
8 **Reichert**	Y	Y	Y	Y	Y	Y
9 Smith	Y	Y	Y	Y	N	N
10 Heck	Y	Y	Y	Y	N	N
WEST VIRGINIA						
1 **McKinley**	N	Y	Y	Y	Y	Y
2 **Mooney**	Y	Y	Y	Y	Y	Y
3 **Jenkins**	N	Y	Y	Y	Y	Y
WISCONSIN						
1 **Ryan**						
2 Pocan	Y	Y	Y	Y	N	N
3 Kind	?	Y	Y	Y	N	N
4 Moore	?	Y	Y	Y	N	N
5 **Sensenbrenner**	Y	Y	Y	Y	Y	Y
6 **Grothman**	Y	Y	Y	Y	Y	Y
7 **Duffy**	Y	Y	Y	Y	Y	Y
8 **Gallagher**	N	Y	Y	Y	Y	Y
WYOMING						
AL **Cheney**	Y	Y	Y	Y	Y	Y

VOTE NUMBER

212. PROCEDURAL MOTION/JOURNAL. Approval of the House Journal of May 21, 2018. Approved 219-179: R 142-78; D 77-101. May 22, 2018.

213. S204. EXPERIMENTAL DRUGS FOR TERMINAL ILLNESSES/RECOMMIT. Schakowsky, D-Ill., motion to recommit the bill to the House Energy and Commerce Committee with instructions to report it back immediately with an amendment that would require both the Food and Drug Administration and the manufacturers of drugs eligible under the bill to produce annual summaries on the usage of such drugs. Motion rejected 187-231: R 0-227; D 187-4. May 22, 2018.

214. S204. EXPERIMENTAL DRUGS FOR TERMINAL ILLNESS/PASSAGE. Passage of the bill that would allow patients with life-threatening diseases or conditions who are not participating in clinical trials to seek access to experimental and investigational drugs directly from a drug manufacturer, without approval by the Food and Drug Administration. It would require that in order for the patient to be eligible, the patient must first try all approved treatment options and be unable to participate in a clinical trial. Only drugs that have completed phase 1 clinical trials, that have not been approved or licensed for any use, and that are currently under an active FDA application or are undergoing clinical trials would be eligible for use under the bill's provisions. Passed (thus cleared for the president) 250-169: R 228-0; D 22-169. May 22, 2018.

215. HR5682. PRISONER RECIDIVISM RISK/PASSAGE. Goodlatte, R-Va., motion to suspend the rules and pass the bill that would require the Justice Department to develop a system to determine the risk of recidivism for each prisoner. It would authorize $50 million annually in fiscal 2019 through fiscal 2023 to carry out the system. It would require the Justice Department to provide incentives for inmates to participate in certain recidivism reduction programs. It would also generally prohibit the use of restrains on pregnant prisoners. Motion agreed to 360-59: R 226-2; D 134-57. May 22, 2018.

216. S2155. BANK REGULATION THRESHOLDS/PASSAGE. Passage of the bill that would apply the more stringent bank regulation provisions of the 2010 financial overhaul to banks with $250 billion in assets, instead of those with at least $50 billion in assets. It would also allow banks with less than $10 billion in assets to trade with depositors' money. The bill would lift the threshold for disclosure requirements to $10 million for employee-owned securities and would allow venture capital funds to have up to 250 investors and be exempt from certain registering requirements. It would provide consumers with the right to request a "security freeze" on their credit reports, which would prohibit a consumer reporting agency from releasing information from the consumer's credit report without express authorization. It would define a "qualified mortgage" as any residential mortgage loan held by a bank, removing the requirement that for a "qualified mortgage," a bank must determine that a mortgage recipient has the ability to repay. Passed (thus cleared for the president) 258-159: R 225-1; D 33-158. May 22, 2018.

217. HRES908. FISCAL 2019 DEFENSE AUTHORIZATION/PREVIOUS QUESTION. Byrne, R-Ala., motion to order the previous question (thus ending debate and possibility of amendment) on the rule (H Res 908) that would provide for further House floor consideration of the bill (HR 5515) that would authorize $708.1 billion in discretionary funding for defense programs in fiscal 2019. Motion agreed to 222-189: R 222-0; D 0-189. May 23, 2018.

	212	213	214	215	216	217
ALABAMA						
1 **Byrne**	Y	N	Y	Y	Y	Y
2 **Roby**	Y	N	Y	Y	Y	Y
3 **Rogers**	N	N	Y	Y	Y	Y
4 **Aderholt**	Y	N	Y	Y	Y	Y
5 **Brooks**	N	N	Y	Y	Y	Y
6 **Palmer**	Y	N	Y	Y	Y	Y
7 Sewell	Y	Y	N	Y	Y	N
ALASKA						
AL **Young**	N	N	Y	Y	Y	Y
ARIZONA						
1 O'Halleran	N	Y	Y	Y	Y	N
2 **McSally**	N	N	Y	Y	Y	Y
3 Grijalva	?	Y	N	N	N	N
4 **Gosar**	N	N	Y	Y	Y	?
5 **Biggs**	N	N	Y	Y	Y	Y
6 **Schweikert**	Y	N	Y	Y	Y	Y
7 Gallego	Y	Y	N	Y	N	N
8 **Lesko**	Y	N	Y	Y	Y	Y
9 Sinema	N	N	Y	Y	Y	N
ARKANSAS						
1 **Crawford**	Y	N	Y	Y	Y	Y
2 **Hill**	N	N	Y	Y	Y	Y
3 **Womack**	Y	N	Y	Y	Y	Y
4 **Westerman**	Y	N	Y	Y	Y	Y
CALIFORNIA						
1 **LaMalfa**	Y	N	Y	Y	Y	Y
2 Huffman	Y	Y	N	Y	N	N
3 Garamendi	?	Y	N	Y	N	N
4 **McClintock**	N	Y	Y	Y	Y	Y
5 Thompson	N	Y	N	Y	N	N
6 Matsui	N	Y	N	Y	N	N
7 Bera	N	Y	N	Y	N	N
8 **Cook**	Y	N	Y	Y	Y	Y
9 McNerney	Y	Y	N	Y	N	N
10 **Denham**	N	N	Y	Y	Y	Y
11 DeSaulnier	Y	Y	N	N	N	N
12 Pelosi	Y	Y	N	N	N	N
13 Lee	N	Y	N	N	N	N
14 Speier	?	?	?	?	?	?
15 Swalwell	N	Y	N	Y	N	N
16 Costa	N	Y	Y	Y	Y	N
17 Khanna	N	Y	N	N	N	N
18 Eshoo	N	Y	N	Y	N	N
19 Lofgren	N	Y	N	N	N	N
20 Panetta	Y	Y	N	Y	N	N
21 **Valadao**	N	N	Y	Y	Y	Y
22 **Nunes**	Y	N	Y	Y	Y	Y
23 **McCarthy**	Y	N	Y	Y	Y	Y
24 Carbajal	N	Y	N	Y	N	N
25 **Knight**	Y	N	Y	Y	Y	Y
26 Brownley	N	Y	N	Y	N	N
27 Chu	Y	Y	N	N	N	N
28 Schiff	N	Y	N	Y	N	N
29 Cardenas	N	Y	N	Y	N	N
30 Sherman	N	Y	N	Y	N	N
31 Aguilar	N	Y	N	Y	N	N
32 Napolitano	N	Y	N	N	N	N
33 Lieu	N	Y	Y	Y	N	N
34 Gomez	N	Y	N	N	N	N
35 Torres	N	Y	N	N	N	N
36 Ruiz	N	Y	N	Y	N	N
37 Bass	?	Y	N	Y	N	?
38 Sánchez, Linda	N	Y	N	Y	N	N
39 **Royce**	Y	N	Y	Y	Y	Y
40 Roybal-Allard	N	Y	N	N	N	N
41 Takano	N	Y	N	N	N	N
42 **Calvert**	Y	N	Y	Y	Y	Y
43 Waters	Y	Y	N	N	N	N
44 Barragan	N	Y	N	Y	N	N
45 **Walters**	Y	N	Y	Y	Y	Y
46 Correa	N	Y	N	Y	N	N
47 Lowenthal	N	Y	N	N	N	N
48 **Rohrabacher**	Y	N	Y	Y	Y	Y
49 **Issa**	Y	N	Y	Y	Y	Y
50 **Hunter**	N	N	Y	Y	Y	Y
51 Vargas	N	Y	N	N	N	N
52 Peters	Y	Y	N	Y	Y	N
53 Davis	Y	Y	N	Y	N	N

	212	213	214	215	216	217
COLORADO						
1 DeGette	Y	Y	N	N	N	N
2 Polis	Y	Y	N	N	N	N
3 **Tipton**	N	N	Y	Y	Y	Y
4 **Buck**	N	N	Y	Y	Y	Y
5 **Lamborn**	Y	N	Y	Y	Y	Y
6 **Coffman**	N	N	Y	Y	Y	Y
7 Perlmutter	Y	Y	Y	N	N	N
CONNECTICUT						
1 Larson	N	Y	Y	Y	N	N
2 Courtney	Y	Y	N	Y	N	N
3 DeLauro	Y	Y	N	N	N	N
4 Himes	Y	Y	Y	Y	Y	N
5 Esty	N	Y	N	Y	N	N
DELAWARE						
AL Blunt Rochester	Y	Y	N	Y	Y	N
FLORIDA						
1 **Gaetz**	?	N	Y	Y	Y	Y
2 **Dunn**	Y	N	Y	Y	Y	Y
3 **Yoho**	?	N	Y	Y	Y	Y
4 **Rutherford**	N	N	Y	Y	Y	Y
5 Lawson	N	Y	N	Y	N	N
6 **DeSantis**	N	N	Y	Y	Y	Y
7 Murphy	Y	Y	N	Y	Y	N
8 **Posey**	Y	N	Y	Y	Y	Y
9 Soto	N	Y	N	N	N	N
10 Demings	Y	Y	N	Y	N	N
11 **Webster**	Y	N	Y	Y	Y	Y
12 **Bilirakis**	Y	N	Y	Y	Y	Y
13 Crist	N	Y	N	N	N	N
14 Castor	N	Y	N	N	N	N
15 **Ross**	Y	N	Y	Y	Y	Y
16 **Buchanan**	Y	N	Y	Y	Y	Y
17 **Rooney, T.**	Y	N	Y	Y	Y	Y
18 **Mast**	N	N	Y	Y	Y	Y
19 **Rooney, F.**	Y	N	Y	Y	Y	?
20 Hastings	N	Y	N	Y	N	N
21 Frankel	Y	Y	N	Y	N	N
22 Deutch	?	Y	N	N	N	N
23 Wasserman Schultz	Y	Y	N	N	N	N
24 Wilson	Y	Y	N	Y	N	N
25 **Diaz-Balart**	Y	N	Y	Y	Y	Y
26 **Curbelo**	Y	N	Y	Y	Y	Y
27 Ros-Lehtinen	N	N	Y	Y	Y	Y
GEORGIA						
1 **Carter**	N	N	Y	Y	+	Y
2 Bishop	N	Y	Y	Y	Y	N
3 **Ferguson**	Y	N	Y	Y	Y	Y
4 Johnson	Y	Y	N	N	N	N
5 Lewis	N	Y	N	N	N	?
6 **Handel**	Y	N	Y	Y	Y	Y
7 **Woodall**	N	N	Y	Y	Y	Y
8 **Scott, A.**	Y	N	Y	Y	Y	Y
9 **Collins**	Y	N	Y	Y	Y	Y
10 **Hice**	N	N	Y	Y	Y	Y
11 **Loudermilk**	Y	N	Y	Y	Y	Y
12 **Allen**	?	N	Y	Y	Y	Y
13 Scott, D.	Y	Y	N	Y	N	N
14 **Graves**	N	N	Y	Y	Y	Y
HAWAII						
1 Hanabusa	Y	Y	N	Y	N	N
2 Gabbard	?	Y	Y	Y	N	N
IDAHO						
1 **Labrador**	Y	N	Y	Y	Y	?
2 **Simpson**	Y	N	Y	Y	Y	Y
ILLINOIS						
1 Rush	N	Y	N	N	N	N
2 Kelly	Y	Y	N	Y	N	N
3 Lipinski	Y	Y	N	Y	N	N
4 Gutierrez	N	Y	N	N	N	N
5 Quigley	N	Y	N	N	N	N
6 **Roskam**	N	N	Y	Y	Y	Y
7 Davis, D.	Y	Y	N	N	N	N
8 Krishnamoorthi	Y	Y	N	N	N	N
9 Schakowsky	N	Y	N	N	N	N
10 Schneider	Y	Y	N	Y	N	N
11 Foster	Y	Y	N	Y	N	N
12 **Bost**	N	N	Y	Y	Y	Y
13 **Davis, R.**	Y	N	Y	Y	Y	Y

	212	213	214	215	216	217
14 **Hultgren**	Y	N	Y	Y	Y	Y
15 **Shimkus**	Y	N	Y	Y	Y	Y
16 **Kinzinger**	N	N	Y	Y	Y	Y
17 Bustos	Y	Y	N	N	N	N
18 **LaHood**	N	N	Y	Y	Y	Y
INDIANA						
1 Visclosky	N	Y	N	Y	N	N
2 **Walorski**	Y	N	Y	Y	Y	Y
3 **Banks**	Y	N	Y	Y	Y	Y
4 **Rokita**	N	N	Y	Y	Y	Y
5 **Brooks**	Y	N	Y	Y	Y	Y
6 **Messer**	Y	N	Y	Y	Y	Y
7 Carson	Y	Y	Y	Y	Y	N
8 **Bucshon**	Y	N	Y	Y	Y	Y
9 **Hollingsworth**	Y	N	Y	Y	Y	Y
IOWA						
1 **Blum**	N	N	Y	Y	Y	Y
2 Loebsack	?	Y	N	Y	N	N
3 **Young**	Y	N	Y	Y	Y	Y
4 **King**	Y	N	Y	N	Y	Y
KANSAS						
1 **Marshall**	Y	N	Y	Y	Y	Y
2 **Jenkins**	N	N	Y	Y	Y	Y
3 **Yoder**	N	N	Y	Y	Y	Y
4 **Estes**	Y	N	Y	Y	Y	Y
KENTUCKY						
1 **Comer**	Y	N	Y	Y	Y	Y
2 **Guthrie**	Y	N	Y	Y	Y	Y
3 Yarmuth	Y	Y	N	N	N	N
4 **Massie**	Y	N	Y	Y	Y	Y
5 **Rogers**	?	?	?	?	?	?
6 **Barr**	Y	N	Y	Y	Y	Y
LOUISIANA						
1 **Scalise**	Y	N	Y	Y	Y	Y
2 Richmond	N	Y	N	Y	N	N
3 **Higgins**	+	–	+	+	+	+
4 **Johnson**	Y	N	Y	Y	Y	Y
5 **Abraham**	Y	N	Y	Y	Y	Y
6 **Graves**	N	N	Y	Y	Y	Y
MAINE						
1 Pingree	?	Y	N	Y	N	N
2 **Poliquin**	N	N	Y	Y	Y	Y
MARYLAND						
1 **Harris**	Y	N	Y	Y	Y	Y
2 Ruppersberger	Y	Y	N	Y	N	N
3 Sarbanes	N	Y	N	N	N	N
4 Brown	?	Y	N	N	N	N
5 Hoyer	?	Y	N	Y	N	N
6 Delaney	N	Y	N	Y	Y	N
7 Cummings	Y	Y	N	N	N	N
8 Raskin	Y	Y	N	N	N	N
MASSACHUSETTS						
1 Neal	N	Y	N	N	N	N
2 McGovern	N	Y	N	N	N	N
3 Tsongas	Y	Y	N	Y	N	N
4 Kennedy	Y	Y	N	N	N	N
5 Clark	N	Y	N	Y	N	N
6 Moulton	Y	Y	N	Y	N	N
7 Capuano	N	Y	N	N	N	N
8 Lynch	N	Y	Y	Y	N	N
9 Keating	Y	Y	N	Y	N	N
MICHIGAN						
1 **Bergman**	N	N	Y	Y	Y	Y
2 **Huizenga**	N	N	Y	N	Y	Y
3 *Amash*	N	N	Y	Y	Y	Y
4 **Moolenaar**	Y	N	Y	Y	Y	Y
5 Kildee	N	Y	N	Y	N	N
6 **Upton**	N	N	Y	Y	Y	Y
7 **Walberg**	N	N	Y	Y	Y	Y
8 **Bishop**	Y	N	Y	Y	Y	Y
9 Levin	N	Y	N	N	N	N
10 **Mitchell**	N	N	Y	Y	Y	Y
11 **Trott**	Y	N	Y	Y	Y	?
12 Dingell	N	Y	N	Y	N	N
14 Lawrence	N	Y	N	Y	N	N
MINNESOTA						
1 Walz	?	?	?	?	?	?
2 **Lewis**	Y	N	Y	Y	Y	Y
3 **Paulsen**	N	N	Y	Y	Y	Y
4 McCollum	Y	Y	N	Y	N	N
5 Ellison	Y	Y	N	Y	N	N
6 **Emmer**	N	N	Y	Y	Y	Y
7 Peterson	N	Y	Y	Y	Y	N
8 Nolan	N	Y	N	Y	Y	N
MISSISSIPPI						
1 **Kelly**	N	N	Y	Y	Y	Y
2 Thompson	N	Y	N	Y	N	N
3 **Harper**	Y	N	Y	Y	Y	Y
4 **Palazzo**	Y	N	Y	Y	Y	Y
MISSOURI						
1 Clay	Y	Y	N	Y	N	N
2 **Wagner**	Y	N	Y	Y	Y	Y
3 **Luetkemeyer**	Y	N	Y	Y	Y	Y
4 **Hartzler**	Y	N	Y	Y	Y	Y
5 Cleaver	?	Y	N	Y	N	N
6 **Graves**	N	N	Y	Y	Y	Y
7 **Long**	Y	N	Y	Y	Y	Y
8 **Smith**	N	N	Y	Y	+	Y
MONTANA						
AL **Gianforte**	Y	N	Y	Y	Y	Y
NEBRASKA						
1 **Fortenberry**	Y	N	Y	Y	Y	Y
2 **Bacon**	Y	N	Y	Y	Y	Y
3 **Smith**	Y	N	Y	Y	Y	Y
NEVADA						
1 Titus	Y	Y	N	N	N	N
2 **Amodei**	Y	N	Y	Y	Y	Y
3 Rosen	N	Y	N	Y	N	N
4 Kihuen	N	Y	N	N	N	N
NEW HAMPSHIRE						
1 Shea-Porter	Y	Y	N	Y	N	N
2 Kuster	N	Y	Y	Y	Y	N
NEW JERSEY						
1 Norcross	?	Y	N	N	N	N
2 **LoBiondo**	N	N	Y	Y	Y	Y
3 **MacArthur**	N	N	Y	Y	Y	Y
4 **Smith**	Y	N	Y	Y	Y	Y
5 Gottheimer	N	Y	Y	Y	Y	N
6 Pallone	N	Y	N	N	N	N
7 **Lance**	N	N	Y	Y	Y	Y
8 Sires	N	Y	N	N	N	N
9 Pascrell	Y	Y	N	Y	N	N
10 Payne	N	Y	N	N	N	N
11 **Frelinghuysen**	+	–	+	+	+	Y
12 Watson Coleman	N	Y	N	N	N	N
NEW MEXICO						
1 Lujan Grisham	Y	Y	N	Y	N	N
2 **Pearce**	?	?	?	?	?	?
3 Luján	Y	Y	N	Y	N	N
NEW YORK						
1 **Zeldin**	N	N	Y	Y	Y	+
2 **King**	Y	N	Y	Y	Y	?
3 Suozzi	N	Y	N	Y	Y	N
4 Rice	N	Y	N	Y	Y	N
5 Meeks	N	Y	N	Y	N	N
6 Meng	Y	Y	N	Y	N	N
7 Velázquez	N	Y	N	Y	N	N
8 Jeffries	N	Y	N	Y	N	N
9 Clarke	N	Y	N	Y	N	N
10 Nadler	Y	Y	N	N	N	N
11 **Donovan**	Y	N	Y	Y	Y	?
12 Maloney, C.	N	Y	N	N	N	N
13 Espaillat	N	Y	N	Y	N	N
14 Crowley	N	Y	N	Y	N	N
15 Serrano	N	Y	N	Y	N	N
16 Engel	Y	Y	N	Y	N	N
17 Lowey	N	Y	N	Y	N	N
18 Maloney, S.P.	N	Y	Y	Y	Y	N
19 **Faso**	Y	N	Y	Y	Y	Y
20 Tonko	P	Y	N	Y	N	N
21 **Stefanik**	Y	N	Y	Y	Y	Y
22 **Tenney**	N	N	Y	Y	Y	Y
23 **Reed**	N	N	Y	Y	Y	Y
24 **Katko**	Y	N	Y	Y	Y	Y
25 **Vacant**						
26 Higgins	N	Y	N	Y	N	N
27 **Collins**	Y	N	Y	Y	Y	Y
NORTH CAROLINA						
1 Butterfield	Y	Y	N	Y	N	N
2 **Holding**	N	N	Y	Y	Y	Y
3 **Jones**	N	N	Y	Y	N	Y
4 Price	N	Y	N	Y	N	N
5 **Foxx**	N	N	Y	Y	Y	Y
6 **Walker**	Y	N	Y	Y	Y	Y
7 **Rouzer**	N	N	Y	Y	Y	Y
8 **Hudson**	N	N	Y	Y	Y	Y
9 **Pittenger**	?	N	Y	Y	Y	Y
9 **Vacant**						
10 **McHenry**	Y	N	Y	Y	Y	Y
11 **Meadows**	Y	N	Y	Y	Y	Y
12 Adams	Y	Y	N	Y	N	N
13 **Budd**	Y	N	Y	Y	Y	Y
NORTH DAKOTA						
AL **Cramer**	N	N	Y	Y	Y	Y
OHIO						
1 **Chabot**	Y	N	Y	Y	Y	Y
2 **Wenstrup**	Y	N	Y	Y	Y	Y
3 Beatty	N	Y	N	Y	N	N
4 **Jordan**	N	N	Y	Y	Y	Y
5 **Latta**	Y	N	Y	Y	Y	Y
6 **Johnson**	N	N	Y	Y	Y	Y
7 **Gibbs**	N	N	Y	Y	Y	Y
8 **Davidson**	Y	N	Y	Y	Y	Y
9 Kaptur	Y	N	N	Y	N	N
10 **Turner**	N	N	Y	Y	Y	Y
11 Fudge	N	Y	N	Y	N	N
12 **Vacant**						
13 Ryan	N	Y	N	Y	N	N
14 **Joyce**	Y	N	Y	Y	Y	Y
15 **Stivers**	?	?	?	?	?	?
16 **Renacci**	N	N	Y	Y	Y	Y
OKLAHOMA						
1 **Vacant**						
2 **Mullin**	Y	N	Y	Y	Y	Y
3 **Lucas**	Y	N	Y	Y	Y	Y
4 **Cole**	Y	N	Y	Y	Y	Y
5 **Russell**	Y	N	Y	Y	Y	Y
OREGON						
1 Bonamici	Y	Y	N	N	N	N
2 **Walden**	Y	N	Y	Y	Y	Y
3 Blumenauer	Y	Y	N	N	N	N
4 DeFazio	N	Y	N	Y	N	N
5 Schrader	N	Y	N	Y	Y	N
PENNSYLVANIA						
1 Brady	N	Y	N	N	N	N
2 Evans	Y	Y	N	N	N	N
3 **Kelly**	Y	N	Y	Y	Y	Y
4 **Perry**	N	N	Y	Y	Y	Y
5 **Thompson**	N	N	Y	Y	Y	Y
6 **Costello**	N	N	Y	Y	Y	Y
7 **Vacant**						
8 **Fitzpatrick**	N	N	Y	Y	Y	Y
9 **Shuster**	Y	N	Y	Y	Y	Y
10 **Marino**	Y	N	Y	Y	Y	Y
11 **Barletta**	Y	N	Y	Y	Y	Y
12 **Rothfus**	Y	N	Y	Y	Y	Y
13 Boyle	N	Y	N	N	N	N
14 Doyle	N	Y	N	Y	N	N
15 **Vacant**						
16 **Smucker**	Y	N	Y	Y	Y	Y
17 Cartwright	Y	Y	N	Y	N	N
18 Lamb	Y	Y	N	Y	N	N
RHODE ISLAND						
1 Cicilline	Y	Y	N	Y	N	N
2 Langevin	N	Y	N	Y	N	N
SOUTH CAROLINA						
1 **Sanford**	Y	N	Y	Y	Y	Y
2 **Wilson**	Y	N	Y	Y	Y	Y
3 **Duncan**	N	N	Y	Y	Y	Y
4 **Gowdy**	Y	N	Y	Y	Y	Y
5 **Norman**	Y	N	Y	Y	Y	Y
6 Clyburn	N	Y	N	Y	N	N
7 **Rice**	Y	N	Y	Y	Y	Y
SOUTH DAKOTA						
AL **Noem**	N	N	Y	Y	Y	Y
TENNESSEE						
1 **Roe**	Y	N	Y	Y	Y	Y
2 **Duncan**	Y	N	Y	Y	Y	Y
3 **Fleischmann**	Y	N	Y	Y	Y	Y
4 **DesJarlais**	+	N	Y	Y	Y	Y
5 Cooper	Y	Y	Y	Y	N	N
6 **Black**	?	?	?	?	+	?
7 **Blackburn**	N	N	Y	Y	Y	Y
8 **Kustoff**	Y	N	Y	Y	Y	Y
9 Cohen	N	Y	N	Y	N	N
TEXAS						
1 **Gohmert**	N	N	Y	Y	Y	Y
2 **Poe**	N	N	Y	Y	Y	Y
3 **Johnson, S.**	Y	N	Y	Y	Y	Y
4 **Ratcliffe**	?	N	Y	Y	Y	Y
5 **Hensarling**	Y	N	Y	Y	Y	Y
6 **Barton**	Y	N	Y	Y	Y	Y
7 **Culberson**	Y	N	Y	Y	Y	Y
8 **Brady**	Y	N	Y	Y	Y	Y
9 Green, A.	N	Y	N	N	N	N
10 **McCaul**	Y	N	Y	Y	Y	Y
11 **Conaway**	N	N	Y	Y	Y	Y
12 **Granger**	Y	N	Y	Y	Y	Y
13 **Thornberry**	Y	N	Y	Y	Y	Y
14 **Weber**	N	N	Y	Y	Y	Y
15 Gonzalez	Y	N	N	Y	Y	N
16 O'Rourke	?	Y	Y	Y	N	N
17 **Flores**	N	N	Y	Y	Y	Y
18 Jackson Lee	N	Y	N	N	N	N
19 **Arrington**	Y	N	Y	Y	Y	Y
20 Castro	Y	Y	N	Y	N	N
21 **Smith**	Y	N	Y	Y	Y	Y
22 **Olson**	Y	N	Y	Y	Y	Y
23 **Hurd**	N	N	Y	Y	Y	Y
24 **Marchant**	Y	N	Y	Y	Y	Y
25 **Williams**	?	N	Y	Y	Y	Y
26 **Burgess**	Y	N	Y	Y	Y	Y
28 Cuellar	N	Y	Y	Y	Y	N
29 Green, G.	N	Y	N	N	N	N
30 Johnson, E.B.	Y	Y	N	Y	N	N
31 **Carter**	Y	N	Y	Y	Y	Y
32 **Sessions**	Y	N	Y	Y	Y	Y
33 Veasey	N	Y	Y	Y	Y	N
34 Vela	Y	Y	N	Y	Y	N
35 Doggett	Y	Y	N	N	N	N
36 **Babin**	Y	N	Y	Y	Y	Y
UTAH						
1 **Bishop**	Y	N	Y	Y	Y	Y
2 **Stewart**	Y	N	Y	Y	Y	Y
3 **Curtis**	Y	N	Y	Y	Y	Y
4 **Love**	Y	N	Y	Y	Y	Y
VERMONT						
AL Welch	Y	Y	N	Y	N	N
VIRGINIA						
1 **Wittman**	N	N	Y	Y	Y	Y
2 **Taylor**	N	N	Y	Y	Y	Y
3 Scott	N	Y	N	Y	N	N
4 McEachin	Y	Y	N	Y	N	N
5 **Garrett**	Y	N	Y	Y	Y	Y
6 **Goodlatte**	Y	N	Y	Y	Y	Y
7 **Brat**	Y	N	Y	Y	Y	Y
8 Beyer	N	Y	N	Y	N	N
9 **Griffith**	Y	N	Y	Y	Y	Y
10 **Comstock**	Y	N	Y	Y	Y	Y
11 Connolly	N	Y	N	Y	N	N
WASHINGTON						
1 DelBene	Y	Y	N	Y	N	N
2 Larsen	N	Y	N	N	Y	N
3 **Herrera Beutler**	N	N	Y	Y	Y	Y
4 **Newhouse**	Y	N	Y	Y	Y	Y
5 **McMorris Rodgers**	Y	N	Y	Y	Y	Y
6 Kilmer	N	Y	N	Y	N	N
7 Jayapal	N	Y	N	N	N	N
8 **Reichert**	Y	N	Y	Y	Y	Y
9 Smith	Y	Y	N	N	N	N
10 Heck	N	Y	N	Y	N	N
WEST VIRGINIA						
1 **McKinley**	N	N	Y	Y	Y	Y
2 **Mooney**	Y	?	Y	Y	Y	Y
3 **Jenkins**	N	N	Y	Y	Y	Y
WISCONSIN						
1 **Ryan**						
2 Pocan	Y	Y	N	Y	N	N
3 Kind	N	Y	Y	Y	Y	N
4 Moore	Y	Y	N	Y	N	N
5 **Sensenbrenner**	Y	N	Y	Y	Y	Y
6 **Grothman**	?	N	Y	Y	Y	Y
7 **Duffy**	Y	N	Y	Y	Y	Y
8 **Gallagher**	N	N	Y	Y	Y	Y
WYOMING						
AL **Cheney**	Y	N	Y	Y	Y	Y

VOTE NUMBER

218. HRES908. FISCAL 2019 DEFENSE AUTHORIZATION/RULE.
Adoption of the rule (H Res 908) that would provide for further House floor consideration of the bill (HR 5515) that would authorize $708.1 billion in discretionary funding for defense programs in fiscal 2019. Adopted 229-183: R 223-1; D 6-182. May 23, 2018.

219. HR5515. FISCAL 2019 DEFENSE AUTHORIZATION/OVERSEAS CONTINGENCY OPERATIONS FUNDING ELIMINATION. Nolan, D-Minn., amendment that would eliminate the authorization of appropriations for overseas contingency operations. Rejected in Committee of the Whole 62-351: R 7-217; D 55-134. May 23, 2018.

220. HR5515. FISCAL 2019 DEFENSE AUTHORIZATION/FOREIGN PARTNERSHIPS COUNTERING IRAN. Gabbard, D-Hawaii, amendment that would eliminate the authorization for the Defense Department to develop and implement a strategy with foreign partners to counter destabilizing activities undertaken by Iran. Rejected in Committee of the Whole 60-355: R 8-217; D 52-138. May 23, 2018.

221. HR5515. FISCAL 2019 DEFENSE AUTHORIZATION/NUCLEAR WEAPON LIFECYCLE COST. Aguilar, D-Calif., amendment that would require the annual report on the plan for U.S. nuclear weapons to include an estimate of the projected future total lifecycle cost of each type of nuclear weapon and delivery platform. Rejected in Committee of the Whole 198-217: R 9-216; D 189-1. May 23, 2018.

222. HR5515. FISCAL 2019 DEFENSE AUTHORIZATION/LOW-YIELD NUCLEAR WEAPONS. Garamendi, D-Calif., for Blumenauer, D-Ore., amendment that would eliminate the bill's repeal of the requirement that the secretary of Energy may not commence the development of a low-yield nuclear weapon unless specifically authorized by Congress. It would also limit funding to the W76-2 warhead modification until the Defense Department reports to Congress on the potential effects of certain low-yield nuclear warheads. Rejected in Committee of the Whole 188-226: R 5-219; D 183-7. May 23, 2018.

223. HR5515. FISCAL 2019 DEFENSE AUTHORIZATION/EXPEDITED REVIEWS FOR MINING PROJECTS. Amodei, R-Nev., amendment that would expedite the environmental review process for certain domestic mine projects if the minerals in the mine are deemed necessary for strategic or national security purposes. Adopted in Committee of the Whole 229-183: R 224-1; D 5-182. May 23, 2018.

	218	219	220	221	222	223
ALABAMA						
1 **Byrne**	Y	N	N	N	N	Y
2 **Roby**	Y	N	N	N	N	Y
3 **Rogers**	Y	N	N	N	N	Y
4 **Aderholt**	Y	N	N	N	N	Y
5 **Brooks**	Y	N	N	N	N	Y
6 **Palmer**	Y	N	N	N	N	Y
7 Sewell	N	N	N	Y	Y	N
ALASKA						
AL **Young**	Y	N	N	N	N	Y
ARIZONA						
1 O'Halleran	Y	N	N	Y	Y	N
2 **McSally**	Y	N	N	N	N	Y
3 Grijalva	N	Y	Y	Y	Y	N
4 **Gosar**	Y	Y	N	N	N	Y
5 **Biggs**	Y	N	N	N	N	Y
6 **Schweikert**	Y	N	N	N	N	Y
7 Gallego	N	N	N	Y	Y	N
8 **Lesko**	Y	N	N	N	N	Y
9 Sinema	Y	N	N	Y	Y	N
ARKANSAS						
1 **Crawford**	Y	N	N	N	N	Y
2 **Hill**	Y	N	N	N	N	Y
3 **Womack**	Y	N	N	N	N	Y
4 **Westerman**	Y	N	N	N	N	Y
CALIFORNIA						
1 **LaMalfa**	Y	N	N	N	N	Y
2 Huffman	N	Y	Y	Y	Y	N
3 Garamendi	N	N	N	Y	Y	N
4 **McClintock**	Y	N	N	N	N	Y
5 Thompson	N	Y	Y	Y	Y	N
6 Matsui	N	Y	Y	Y	Y	N
7 Bera	N	N	N	Y	Y	N
8 **Cook**	Y	N	N	N	N	Y
9 McNerney	N	N	Y	Y	Y	N
10 **Denham**	Y	N	N	N	N	Y
11 DeSaulnier	N	Y	Y	Y	Y	N
12 Pelosi	N	N	N	Y	Y	N
13 Lee	N	Y	Y	Y	Y	N
14 Speier	?	?	?	?	?	N
15 Swalwell	N	N	Y	Y	Y	N
16 Costa	?	?	N	Y	Y	Y
17 Khanna	N	Y	Y	Y	Y	N
18 Eshoo	N	Y	Y	Y	Y	N
19 Lofgren	N	Y	Y	Y	Y	N
20 Panetta	N	N	N	Y	Y	N
21 **Valadao**	Y	N	N	N	N	Y
22 **Nunes**	Y	N	N	N	N	Y
23 **McCarthy**	Y	N	N	N	N	Y
24 Carbajal	N	N	N	Y	Y	N
25 **Knight**	Y	N	N	N	N	Y
26 Brownley	N	N	N	Y	Y	N
27 Chu	N	Y	Y	Y	Y	N
28 Schiff	N	N	N	Y	Y	N
29 Cardenas	N	N	Y	Y	Y	N
30 Sherman	N	N	N	Y	Y	N
31 Aguilar	N	N	N	Y	Y	N
32 Napolitano	N	Y	Y	Y	Y	N
33 Lieu	N	N	N	Y	Y	N
34 Gomez	N	Y	N	Y	Y	N
35 Torres	N	N	N	Y	Y	N
36 Ruiz	N	N	N	Y	Y	N
37 Bass	N	N	N	Y	Y	N
38 Sánchez, Linda	N	N	Y	Y	Y	N
39 **Royce**	Y	N	N	N	N	Y
40 Roybal-Allard	N	N	N	Y	Y	N
41 Takano	N	Y	Y	Y	Y	N
42 **Calvert**	Y	N	N	N	N	Y
43 Waters	N	Y	Y	Y	Y	N
44 Barragan	N	Y	N	Y	Y	N
45 **Walters**	Y	N	N	N	N	Y
46 Correa	N	N	N	Y	Y	N
47 Lowenthal	N	Y	N	Y	Y	N
48 **Rohrabacher**	Y	N	N	N	N	Y
49 **Issa**	Y	N	N	N	N	Y
50 **Hunter**	Y	N	N	N	N	Y
51 Vargas	N	Y	N	Y	Y	N
52 Peters	N	N	N	Y	Y	N
53 Davis	N	N	N	Y	Y	N

	218	219	220	221	222	223
COLORADO						
1 DeGette	N	Y	Y	Y	Y	N
2 Polis	N	Y	Y	Y	Y	N
3 **Tipton**	Y	N	N	N	N	Y
4 **Buck**	Y	Y	N	N	N	Y
5 **Lamborn**	Y	N	N	N	N	Y
6 **Coffman**	Y	N	N	Y	N	Y
7 Perlmutter	N	N	N	Y	Y	N
CONNECTICUT						
1 Larson	N	N	N	Y	Y	N
2 Courtney	N	N	N	Y	Y	N
3 DeLauro	N	N	N	Y	Y	N
4 Himes	N	N	N	Y	Y	N
5 Esty	N	N	N	Y	Y	N
DELAWARE						
AL Blunt Rochester	N	N	N	Y	Y	N
FLORIDA						
1 **Gaetz**	Y	N	N	N	N	Y
2 **Dunn**	Y	N	N	N	N	Y
3 Yoho	Y	N	Y	N	N	Y
4 **Rutherford**	Y	N	N	N	N	Y
5 Lawson	N	N	N	Y	Y	N
6 **DeSantis**	Y	N	N	N	N	Y
7 Murphy	N	N	Y	Y	Y	N
8 **Posey**	Y	N	N	N	N	Y
9 Soto	N	N	N	Y	Y	N
10 Demings	N	N	N	Y	Y	N
11 **Webster**	Y	Y	N	N	N	Y
12 **Bilirakis**	Y	N	N	N	N	Y
13 Crist	N	N	N	Y	Y	N
14 Castor	N	Y	Y	Y	Y	?
15 **Ross**	Y	N	N	N	N	Y
16 **Buchanan**	Y	N	N	N	N	Y
17 **Rooney, T.**	Y	N	N	N	N	Y
18 **Mast**	Y	N	N	N	N	Y
19 **Rooney, F.**	?	?	N	N	N	Y
20 Hastings	N	N	N	Y	Y	N
21 Frankel	N	N	N	Y	Y	N
22 Deutch	N	N	N	Y	Y	N
23 Wasserman Schultz	N	N	N	Y	Y	N
24 Wilson	N	Y	Y	Y	N	N
25 **Diaz-Balart**	Y	N	N	N	N	Y
26 **Curbelo**	Y	N	N	N	N	Y
27 **Ros-Lehtinen**	Y	N	N	N	N	Y
GEORGIA						
1 **Carter**	Y	N	N	N	N	Y
2 Bishop	N	N	N	Y	Y	N
3 **Ferguson**	Y	N	N	N	N	Y
4 Johnson	N	Y	Y	Y	Y	N
5 Lewis	?	?	?	?	?	?
6 **Handel**	Y	N	N	N	N	Y
7 **Woodall**	Y	N	N	N	N	Y
8 **Scott, A.**	Y	N	N	N	N	Y
9 **Collins**	Y	N	N	N	N	Y
10 **Hice**	Y	N	N	N	N	Y
11 **Loudermilk**	Y	N	N	N	N	Y
12 **Allen**	Y	N	N	N	N	Y
13 Scott, D.	N	N	N	Y	Y	N
14 **Graves**	Y	N	N	N	N	Y
HAWAII						
1 Hanabusa	N	N	N	Y	Y	N
2 Gabbard	N	Y	Y	Y	Y	N
IDAHO						
1 **Labrador**	Y	N	Y	N	N	Y
2 **Simpson**	Y	N	N	N	N	Y
ILLINOIS						
1 Rush	N	N	N	Y	Y	N
2 Kelly	N	N	N	Y	Y	N
3 Lipinski	N	N	N	Y	Y	N
4 Gutierrez	?	N	Y	Y	Y	N
5 Quigley	N	N	N	Y	Y	N
6 **Roskam**	Y	N	N	N	N	Y
7 Davis, D.	N	N	Y	Y	Y	N
8 Krishnamoorthi	N	N	N	Y	Y	N
9 Schakowsky	N	Y	Y	Y	Y	N
10 Schneider	N	N	N	Y	Y	N
11 Foster	N	N	N	Y	Y	N
12 **Bost**	Y	N	N	N	N	Y
13 **Davis, R.**	Y	N	Y	N	Y	Y

KEY	Republicans	Democrats	Independents

Y	Voted for (yea)	X Paired against	C Voted "present" to avoid possible conflict of interest
#	Paired for	– Announced against	
+	Announced for	P Voted "present"	? Did not vote or otherwise make a position known
N	Voted against (nay)		

	218	219	220	221	222	223
14 **Hultgren**	Y	N	N	N	N	Y
15 **Shimkus**	Y	N	N	N	N	Y
16 **Kinzinger**	Y	N	N	N	N	Y
17 Bustos	N	N	N	Y	Y	N
18 **LaHood**	Y	N	N	N	N	Y
INDIANA						
1 Visclosky	N	N	N	Y	Y	N
2 **Walorski**	Y	N	N	N	N	Y
3 **Banks**	Y	N	N	N	N	Y
4 **Rokita**	Y	N	N	N	N	Y
5 **Brooks**	Y	N	N	N	N	Y
6 **Messer**	Y	N	N	N	N	Y
7 Carson	N	N	N	Y	Y	N
8 **Bucshon**	Y	N	N	N	N	Y
9 **Hollingsworth**	Y	N	N	N	N	Y
IOWA						
1 **Blum**	Y	N	N	N	N	Y
2 Loebsack	N	N	N	Y	Y	N
3 **Young**	Y	N	N	N	N	Y
4 **King**	Y	N	N	N	N	Y
KANSAS						
1 **Marshall**	Y	N	N	N	N	Y
2 **Jenkins**	Y	N	N	N	N	Y
3 **Yoder**	Y	N	N	N	N	Y
4 **Estes**	Y	N	N	N	N	Y
KENTUCKY						
1 **Comer**	Y	N	N	N	N	Y
2 **Guthrie**	Y	N	N	N	N	Y
3 Yarmuth	N	N	N	Y	Y	N
4 **Massie**	N	Y	Y	Y	Y	Y
5 **Rogers**	?	?	?	?	?	?
6 **Barr**	Y	N	N	N	N	Y
LOUISIANA						
1 **Scalise**	Y	N	N	N	N	Y
2 Richmond	N	Y	Y	Y	Y	N
3 **Higgins**	+	–	–	–	–	+
4 **Johnson**	Y	N	N	N	N	Y
5 **Abraham**	Y	N	N	N	N	Y
6 **Graves**	Y	N	N	N	N	Y
MAINE						
1 Pingree	N	Y	Y	Y	Y	N
2 **Poliquin**	Y	N	N	N	N	Y
MARYLAND						
1 **Harris**	Y	N	N	N	N	Y
2 Ruppersberger	N	N	N	Y	Y	N
3 Sarbanes	N	N	Y	Y	Y	N
4 Brown	N	N	N	Y	Y	+
5 Hoyer	N	N	N	Y	Y	N
6 Delaney	N	N	N	Y	Y	?
7 Cummings	N	N	N	Y	Y	N
8 Raskin	N	Y	Y	Y	Y	N
MASSACHUSETTS						
1 Neal	N	N	N	Y	Y	N
2 McGovern	N	Y	Y	Y	Y	N
3 Tsongas	N	N	N	Y	Y	N
4 Kennedy	N	N	N	Y	Y	N
5 Clark	N	Y	Y	Y	Y	N
6 Moulton	N	N	N	Y	Y	N
7 Capuano	N	Y	Y	Y	Y	N
8 Lynch	N	N	N	Y	Y	N
9 Keating	N	N	N	Y	Y	N
MICHIGAN						
1 **Bergman**	Y	N	N	N	N	Y
2 **Huizenga**	Y	N	N	N	N	Y
3 *Amash*	Y	Y	Y	Y	Y	Y
4 **Moolenaar**	Y	N	N	N	N	Y
5 Kildee	N	N	N	Y	Y	N
6 **Upton**	Y	N	N	N	N	Y
7 **Walberg**	Y	N	N	N	N	Y
8 **Bishop**	Y	N	N	N	N	Y
9 Levin	N	N	N	Y	Y	N
10 **Mitchell**	Y	N	N	N	N	Y
11 **Trott**	?	?	?	?	?	?
12 Dingell	N	N	Y	Y	Y	N
14 Lawrence	N	N	N	Y	Y	N
MINNESOTA						
1 Walz	?	?	?	?	?	?
2 **Lewis**	Y	N	N	N	N	Y
3 **Paulsen**	Y	N	N	N	N	Y
4 McCollum	N	N	N	Y	Y	N
5 Ellison	N	Y	Y	Y	Y	N
6 **Emmer**	Y	N	N	N	N	Y
7 Peterson	N	N	N	Y	Y	N
8 Nolan	N	Y	Y	Y	Y	N
MISSISSIPPI						
1 **Kelly**	Y	N	N	N	N	Y
2 Thompson	N	N	N	Y	Y	N
3 **Harper**	Y	N	N	N	?	Y
4 **Palazzo**	Y	N	N	N	N	Y
MISSOURI						
1 Clay	N	Y	Y	Y	Y	N
2 **Wagner**	Y	N	N	N	N	Y
3 **Luetkemeyer**	Y	N	N	N	N	Y
4 **Hartzler**	Y	N	N	N	N	Y
5 Cleaver	N	N	Y	Y	Y	N
6 **Graves**	Y	N	N	N	N	Y
7 **Long**	Y	N	N	N	N	Y
8 **Smith**	Y	N	N	N	N	Y
MONTANA						
AL **Gianforte**	Y	N	N	N	N	Y
NEBRASKA						
1 **Fortenberry**	Y	N	N	Y	N	Y
2 **Bacon**	Y	N	N	N	N	Y
3 **Smith**	Y	N	N	N	N	Y
NEVADA						
1 Titus	N	N	N	Y	Y	Y
2 **Amodei**	Y	N	N	N	N	Y
3 Rosen	N	N	N	Y	Y	Y
4 Kihuen	N	N	N	Y	Y	Y
NEW HAMPSHIRE						
1 Shea-Porter	N	N	N	Y	Y	N
2 Kuster	N	N	N	Y	Y	N
NEW JERSEY						
1 Norcross	N	N	N	Y	Y	N
2 **LoBiondo**	Y	N	N	N	N	Y
3 **MacArthur**	Y	N	N	N	N	Y
4 **Smith**	Y	N	N	N	N	Y
5 Gottheimer	Y	N	N	Y	N	N
6 Pallone	N	Y	N	Y	Y	N
7 **Lance**	Y	N	N	N	N	Y
8 Sires	N	N	N	Y	Y	N
9 Pascrell	N	Y	N	Y	Y	N
10 Payne	N	N	N	Y	Y	N
11 **Frelinghuysen**	Y	N	N	N	N	Y
12 Watson Coleman	N	Y	N	Y	Y	N
NEW MEXICO						
1 Lujan Grisham	N	N	N	Y	Y	N
2 **Pearce**	?	?	?	?	?	?
3 Luján	N	N	N	Y	Y	N
NEW YORK						
1 **Zeldin**	+	–	–	–	–	+
2 **King**	?	?	?	?	?	?
3 Suozzi	N	N	N	Y	Y	N
4 Rice	N	N	N	Y	Y	N
5 Meeks	N	N	N	Y	Y	N
6 Meng	N	N	N	Y	Y	N
7 Velázquez	N	N	N	Y	Y	N
8 Jeffries	N	Y	Y	Y	Y	N
9 Clarke	N	Y	N	Y	Y	N
10 Nadler	N	Y	N	Y	Y	N
11 **Donovan**	?	?	?	?	?	?
12 Maloney, C.	N	N	N	Y	Y	N
13 Espaillat	N	Y	Y	Y	Y	N
14 Crowley	N	Y	Y	Y	Y	N
15 Serrano	N	Y	Y	Y	Y	N
16 Engel	N	Y	N	Y	Y	N
17 Lowey	N	N	N	Y	Y	N
18 Maloney, S.P.	N	N	N	Y	Y	N
19 **Faso**	Y	N	N	N	N	Y
20 Tonko	N	N	Y	Y	Y	N
21 **Stefanik**	Y	N	N	N	N	Y
22 **Tenney**	Y	N	N	N	N	Y
23 **Reed**	Y	N	N	N	N	Y
24 **Katko**	Y	N	N	N	N	Y
25 **Vacant**						
26 Higgins	N	N	N	Y	Y	N
27 **Collins**	Y	N	N	N	N	Y
NORTH CAROLINA						
1 Butterfield	N	N	N	Y	Y	N
2 **Holding**	Y	N	N	N	N	Y
3 **Jones**	Y	Y	Y	Y	Y	Y
4 Price	N	N	N	Y	Y	N
5 **Foxx**	Y	N	N	N	N	Y
6 **Walker**	Y	N	N	N	N	Y
7 **Rouzer**	Y	N	N	N	N	Y
8 **Hudson**	Y	N	N	N	N	Y
9 **Pittenger**	Y	N	N	N	N	Y
9 **Vacant**						
10 **McHenry**	Y	N	N	N	N	Y
11 **Meadows**	Y	N	N	N	N	Y
12 Adams	N	N	N	Y	Y	N
13 **Budd**	Y	N	N	N	N	Y
NORTH DAKOTA						
AL **Cramer**	Y	N	N	N	N	Y
OHIO						
1 **Chabot**	Y	N	N	N	N	Y
2 **Wenstrup**	Y	N	N	N	N	Y
3 Beatty	N	N	N	Y	Y	N
4 **Jordan**	Y	N	N	N	N	Y
5 **Latta**	Y	N	N	N	N	Y
6 **Johnson**	Y	N	N	N	N	Y
7 **Gibbs**	Y	N	N	N	N	Y
8 **Davidson**	Y	N	N	N	N	Y
9 Kaptur	N	N	N	Y	Y	N
10 **Turner**	Y	N	N	N	N	Y
11 Fudge	N	N	Y	Y	Y	N
12 **Vacant**						
13 Ryan	N	N	N	Y	Y	N
14 **Joyce**	Y	N	N	N	N	Y
15 **Stivers**	?	?	?	?	?	?
16 **Renacci**	Y	N	N	N	N	Y
OKLAHOMA						
1 **Vacant**						
2 **Mullin**	Y	N	N	N	N	Y
3 **Lucas**	Y	N	N	N	N	Y
4 **Cole**	Y	N	N	N	N	Y
5 **Russell**	Y	N	N	N	N	Y
OREGON						
1 Bonamici	N	Y	N	Y	Y	N
2 **Walden**	Y	N	N	N	N	Y
3 Blumenauer	N	N	N	Y	Y	N
4 DeFazio	N	Y	N	Y	Y	N
5 Schrader	N	Y	N	Y	Y	N
PENNSYLVANIA						
1 Brady	N	N	N	Y	Y	N
2 Evans	N	Y	Y	Y	Y	N
3 **Kelly**	Y	N	N	N	N	Y
4 **Perry**	Y	N	N	N	N	Y
5 **Thompson**	Y	N	N	N	N	Y
6 **Costello**	Y	N	N	N	N	Y
7 **Vacant**						
8 **Fitzpatrick**	Y	N	N	N	N	N
9 **Shuster**	Y	N	N	N	N	Y
10 **Marino**	Y	N	N	N	N	Y
11 **Barletta**	Y	N	N	N	N	Y
12 **Rothfus**	Y	N	N	N	N	Y
13 Boyle	N	N	N	Y	Y	N
14 Doyle	N	Y	N	Y	Y	N
15 **Vacant**						
16 **Smucker**	Y	N	N	N	N	Y
17 Cartwright	N	N	N	Y	Y	N
18 Lamb	Y	N	N	Y	Y	N
RHODE ISLAND						
1 Cicilline	N	Y	N	Y	Y	N
2 Langevin	N	N	N	Y	Y	N
SOUTH CAROLINA						
1 **Sanford**	Y	N	Y	Y	Y	Y
2 **Wilson**	Y	N	N	N	N	Y
3 **Duncan**	Y	N	N	N	N	Y
4 **Gowdy**	Y	N	N	N	N	Y
5 **Norman**	Y	N	N	N	N	Y
6 Clyburn	N	N	N	Y	Y	N
7 **Rice**	Y	N	N	N	N	Y
SOUTH DAKOTA						
AL **Noem**	Y	N	N	N	N	Y
TENNESSEE						
1 **Roe**	Y	N	N	N	N	Y
2 **Duncan**	Y	Y	Y	N	N	Y
3 **Fleischmann**	Y	N	N	N	N	Y
4 **DesJarlais**	Y	N	N	N	N	Y
5 Cooper	N	N	N	Y	Y	N
6 **Black**	?	–	–	–	–	+
7 **Blackburn**	Y	N	N	N	N	Y
8 **Kustoff**	Y	N	N	N	N	Y
9 Cohen	N	N	N	Y	Y	N
TEXAS						
1 **Gohmert**	Y	N	N	N	N	Y
2 **Poe**	Y	N	N	N	N	Y
3 **Johnson, S.**	Y	N	N	N	N	Y
4 **Ratcliffe**	Y	N	N	N	N	Y
5 **Hensarling**	Y	N	N	N	N	Y
6 **Barton**	Y	N	N	N	N	Y
7 **Culberson**	Y	N	N	N	N	Y
8 **Brady**	Y	N	N	N	N	Y
9 Green, A.	N	N	N	Y	N	N
10 **McCaul**	Y	N	N	N	N	Y
11 **Conaway**	Y	N	N	N	N	Y
12 **Granger**	Y	N	N	N	N	Y
13 **Thornberry**	Y	N	N	N	N	Y
14 **Weber**	Y	N	N	N	N	Y
15 Gonzalez	N	N	N	Y	Y	N
16 O'Rourke	N	N	Y	Y	Y	N
17 **Flores**	Y	N	N	N	N	Y
18 Jackson Lee	N	N	N	Y	N	N
19 **Arrington**	Y	N	N	N	N	Y
20 Castro	N	N	N	Y	Y	N
21 **Smith**	Y	N	N	N	N	Y
22 **Olson**	Y	N	N	N	N	Y
23 **Hurd**	Y	N	N	N	N	Y
24 **Marchant**	Y	N	N	N	N	Y
25 **Williams**	Y	N	N	N	N	Y
26 **Burgess**	Y	N	Y	N	N	Y
28 Cuellar	N	N	N	Y	Y	N
29 Green, G.	N	Y	N	Y	Y	N
30 Johnson, E.B.	N	N	N	Y	Y	N
31 **Carter**	Y	N	N	N	N	Y
32 **Sessions**	Y	N	N	N	N	Y
33 Veasey	N	N	N	Y	Y	N
34 Vela	N	N	N	Y	Y	N
35 Doggett	N	N	Y	Y	Y	N
36 **Babin**	Y	N	N	N	N	Y
UTAH						
1 **Bishop**	Y	N	N	N	N	Y
2 **Stewart**	Y	N	N	N	N	Y
3 **Curtis**	Y	N	N	N	N	Y
4 **Love**	Y	N	N	N	N	Y
VERMONT						
AL Welch	N	Y	Y	Y	Y	N
VIRGINIA						
1 **Wittman**	Y	N	N	N	N	Y
2 **Taylor**	Y	N	N	N	N	Y
3 Scott	N	N	N	Y	Y	N
4 McEachin	N	N	N	Y	Y	N
5 **Garrett**	Y	N	N	N	N	Y
6 **Goodlatte**	Y	N	N	N	N	Y
7 **Brat**	Y	N	N	N	N	Y
8 Beyer	N	N	N	Y	Y	?
9 **Griffith**	Y	N	N	N	N	Y
10 **Comstock**	Y	N	N	N	N	Y
11 Connolly	N	N	N	Y	N	N
WASHINGTON						
1 DelBene	N	N	N	Y	Y	N
2 Larsen	N	N	Y	Y	Y	N
3 **Herrera Beutler**	Y	N	N	N	N	Y
4 **Newhouse**	Y	N	N	N	N	Y
5 **McMorris Rodgers**	Y	N	N	N	N	Y
6 Kilmer	N	N	N	Y	Y	N
7 Jayapal	N	Y	Y	Y	Y	N
8 **Reichert**	Y	N	N	N	N	Y
9 Smith	N	N	N	Y	Y	N
10 Heck	N	N	N	Y	Y	N
WEST VIRGINIA						
1 **McKinley**	Y	N	N	N	N	Y
2 **Mooney**	Y	N	N	Y	N	Y
3 **Jenkins**	Y	N	N	N	N	Y
WISCONSIN						
1 **Ryan**						
2 Pocan	N	Y	Y	Y	Y	N
3 Kind	N	Y	N	Y	Y	N
4 Moore	N	Y	Y	Y	Y	N
5 **Sensenbrenner**	Y	N	N	N	N	Y
6 **Grothman**	Y	N	N	N	N	Y
7 **Duffy**	Y	N	N	N	N	Y
8 **Gallagher**	Y	N	N	N	N	Y
WYOMING						
AL **Cheney**	Y	N	N	N	N	Y

VOTE NUMBER

224. HR5515. FISCAL 2019 DEFENSE AUTHORIZATION/RADIATION-EXPOSED VETERANS MEDAL. McGovern, D-Mass., amendment that would require the Defense Department to produce a service medal to honor retired and former members of the armed forces who participated in radiation-risk activities. Adopted in Committee of the Whole 408-1: R 221-1; D 187-0. May 23, 2018.

225. HR5515. FISCAL 2019 DEFENSE AUTHORIZATION/DOMESTICALLY-SOURCED DINNER WARE. McKinley, R-W.Va., amendment that would establish a domestic sourcing requirement at the Department of Defense for dinner ware and would provide for a one-year phase-in period. Rejected in Committee of the Whole 160-252: R 36-188; D 124-64. May 23, 2018.

226. HR5515. FISCAL 2019 DEFENSE AUTHORIZATION/DOMESTICALLY-SOURCED STAINLESS STEEL FLATWARE. Tenney, R-N.Y., amendment that would establish a domestic sourcing requirement at the Department of Defense for stainless steel flatware and would provide for a one-year phase-in period. Rejected in Committee of the Whole 174-239: R 47-177; D 127-62. May 23, 2018.

227. HR5515. FISCAL 2019 DEFENSE AUTHORIZATION/BURMESE MILITARY SANCTIONS. Engel, D-N.Y., amendment that would prohibit the United States from providing security assistance to the Burmese military until the secretary of State affirms that Burma has demonstrated progress in abiding by international human rights standards and would impose sanctions against current and former senior officials of the Burmese military who perpetrated humans rights offenses. Adopted in Committee of the Whole 382-30: R 194-30; D 188-0. May 23, 2018.

228. HR5515. FISCAL 2019 DEFENSE AUTHORIZATION/NATIONAL NUCLEAR SECURITY ADMINISTRATION. Polis, D-Colo., amendment that would reduce the amount authorized for the National Nuclear Security Administration by $198 million. Rejected in Committee of the Whole 174-239: R 8-216; D 166-23. May 23, 2018.

229. HR5515. FISCAL 2019 DEFENSE AUTHORIZATION/MOTION TO TABLE. Thornberry, R-Texas, motion to table (kill) the Thompson, D-Calif., motion to appeal the ruling of the Chair that the Thompson motion to recommit the bill would violate clause 10 of Rule XXI. Motion agreed to 224-191: R 223-3; D 1-188. May 24, 2018.

	224	225	226	227	228	229
ALABAMA						
1 **Byrne**	Y	N	N	N	N	Y
2 **Roby**	Y	N	N	N	N	Y
3 **Rogers**	Y	N	N	Y	N	Y
4 **Aderholt**	Y	N	N	Y	N	Y
5 **Brooks**	Y	N	N	Y	N	Y
6 **Palmer**	Y	N	N	Y	N	Y
7 Sewell	Y	N	Y	Y	Y	N
ALASKA						
AL **Young**	Y	Y	Y	Y	N	Y
ARIZONA						
1 O'Halleran	Y	Y	Y	Y	N	N
2 **McSally**	Y	Y	Y	Y	N	Y
3 Grijalva	Y	Y	Y	Y	Y	N
4 **Gosar**	Y	N	N	Y	N	Y
5 **Biggs**	Y	N	N	N	N	Y
6 **Schweikert**	Y	N	N	Y	N	Y
7 Gallego	Y	N	N	Y	Y	N
8 **Lesko**	Y	N	N	N	N	Y
9 Sinema	Y	Y	Y	Y	N	N
ARKANSAS						
1 **Crawford**	Y	N	N	Y	N	Y
2 **Hill**	Y	N	N	Y	N	Y
3 **Womack**	Y	N	N	Y	N	Y
4 **Westerman**	Y	N	N	Y	N	Y
CALIFORNIA						
1 **LaMalfa**	Y	N	Y	Y	N	Y
2 Huffman	Y	Y	Y	Y	Y	N
3 Garamendi	Y	Y	Y	Y	Y	N
4 **McClintock**	Y	N	N	N	N	Y
5 Thompson	Y	Y	Y	Y	Y	N
6 Matsui	Y	Y	Y	Y	Y	N
7 Bera	Y	Y	Y	Y	Y	N
8 **Cook**	Y	N	N	Y	N	Y
9 McNerney	Y	Y	Y	Y	Y	N
10 **Denham**	Y	N	N	Y	N	Y
11 DeSaulnier	Y	N	N	Y	Y	N
12 Pelosi	Y	Y	Y	Y	Y	N
13 Lee	Y	N	N	Y	Y	N
14 Speier	Y	N	N	Y	Y	N
15 Swalwell	Y	Y	Y	Y	N	N
16 Costa	Y	N	N	Y	N	N
17 Khanna	Y	Y	Y	Y	Y	N
18 Eshoo	Y	Y	Y	Y	Y	N
19 Lofgren	Y	N	N	Y	N	N
20 Panetta	Y	N	N	Y	Y	N
21 **Valadao**	Y	N	N	Y	N	Y
22 **Nunes**	Y	N	N	Y	N	Y
23 **McCarthy**	Y	N	N	Y	N	Y
24 Carbajal	Y	Y	Y	Y	Y	N
25 **Knight**	Y	N	N	Y	N	Y
26 Brownley	Y	Y	Y	Y	Y	N
27 Chu	Y	Y	Y	Y	Y	N
28 Schiff	Y	Y	Y	Y	Y	N
29 Cardenas	Y	N	N	Y	Y	N
30 Sherman	Y	Y	Y	Y	Y	N
31 Aguilar	Y	N	N	Y	N	N
32 Napolitano	Y	Y	Y	Y	Y	N
33 Lieu	Y	N	N	Y	Y	N
34 Gomez	Y	N	N	Y	Y	N
35 Torres	Y	Y	Y	Y	Y	N
36 Ruiz	Y	Y	Y	Y	Y	N
37 Bass	Y	N	N	Y	Y	N
38 Sánchez, Linda	Y	Y	Y	Y	Y	N
39 **Royce**	Y	N	N	Y	N	Y
40 Roybal-Allard	Y	Y	Y	Y	Y	N
41 Takano	Y	Y	Y	Y	Y	N
42 **Calvert**	Y	N	N	Y	N	Y
43 Waters	Y	Y	Y	Y	Y	N
44 Barragan	Y	N	N	Y	Y	N
45 **Walters**	Y	N	N	Y	N	Y
46 Correa	Y	Y	Y	Y	Y	N
47 Lowenthal	Y	Y	Y	Y	Y	N
48 **Rohrabacher**	Y	N	N	Y	N	Y
49 **Issa**	Y	N	N	Y	N	Y
50 **Hunter**	Y	Y	Y	Y	N	Y
51 Vargas	Y	N	Y	Y	Y	N
52 Peters	Y	N	N	Y	N	N
53 Davis	Y	N	N	Y	Y	N

	224	225	226	227	228	229
COLORADO						
1 DeGette	Y	N	N	Y	Y	N
2 Polis	Y	N	N	Y	Y	N
3 **Tipton**	Y	Y	Y	Y	N	Y
4 **Buck**	Y	N	N	Y	N	Y
5 **Lamborn**	Y	N	N	Y	N	Y
6 **Coffman**	+	N	N	Y	N	Y
7 Perlmutter	Y	Y	Y	Y	Y	N
CONNECTICUT						
1 Larson	Y	Y	Y	Y	Y	N
2 Courtney	Y	Y	Y	Y	Y	N
3 DeLauro	Y	Y	Y	Y	Y	N
4 Himes	Y	N	N	Y	N	N
5 Esty	Y	Y	Y	Y	Y	N
DELAWARE						
AL Blunt Rochester	Y	N	N	Y	Y	N
FLORIDA						
1 **Gaetz**	Y	N	N	N	N	Y
2 **Dunn**	N	N	N	N	N	Y
3 Yoho	Y	N	N	Y	N	Y
4 **Rutherford**	Y	N	N	Y	N	Y
5 Lawson	Y	N	Y	Y	Y	N
6 **DeSantis**	Y	N	N	Y	N	Y
7 Murphy	Y	N	N	Y	N	N
8 **Posey**	Y	N	Y	Y	N	Y
9 Soto	Y	Y	Y	Y	Y	N
10 Demings	Y	N	N	Y	Y	N
11 **Webster**	Y	N	N	Y	N	Y
12 **Bilirakis**	Y	Y	Y	Y	N	Y
13 Crist	Y	Y	Y	Y	Y	N
14 Castor	?	?	?	?	?	N
15 **Ross**	Y	N	N	Y	N	Y
16 **Buchanan**	Y	Y	Y	Y	N	Y
17 **Rooney, T.**	Y	Y	Y	Y	N	Y
18 **Mast**	Y	Y	Y	Y	N	Y
19 **Rooney, F.**	Y	N	N	Y	N	Y
20 Hastings	Y	Y	Y	Y	Y	N
21 Frankel	Y	Y	Y	Y	Y	N
22 Deutch	Y	Y	Y	Y	Y	N
23 Wasserman Schultz	Y	Y	Y	Y	Y	N
24 Wilson	Y	Y	Y	?	Y	N
25 **Diaz-Balart**	Y	N	N	Y	N	Y
26 **Curbelo**	Y	N	N	Y	N	Y
27 **Ros-Lehtinen**	Y	N	Y	Y	N	Y
GEORGIA						
1 **Carter**	Y	N	N	Y	N	Y
2 Bishop	Y	Y	Y	Y	Y	N
3 **Ferguson**	Y	N	N	Y	N	Y
4 Johnson	Y	Y	Y	Y	Y	N
5 Lewis	?	?	?	?	?	?
6 **Handel**	Y	N	N	N	N	Y
7 **Woodall**	Y	N	N	Y	N	Y
8 **Scott, A.**	Y	N	N	N	N	Y
9 **Collins**	Y	N	N	Y	N	Y
10 **Hice**	Y	N	N	Y	N	Y
11 **Loudermilk**	Y	N	N	Y	N	Y
12 **Allen**	Y	N	N	Y	N	Y
13 Scott, D.	Y	N	N	Y	Y	N
14 **Graves**	Y	N	N	N	N	Y
HAWAII						
1 Hanabusa	Y	N	N	Y	Y	N
2 Gabbard	Y	Y	Y	Y	Y	N
IDAHO						
1 **Labrador**	Y	N	N	Y	N	Y
2 **Simpson**	Y	N	N	Y	N	Y
ILLINOIS						
1 Rush	Y	Y	Y	Y	Y	N
2 Kelly	Y	Y	Y	Y	Y	N
3 Lipinski	Y	Y	Y	Y	Y	N
4 Gutierrez	Y	N	N	Y	Y	N
5 Quigley	Y	N	N	Y	Y	N
6 **Roskam**	Y	N	N	Y	N	Y
7 Davis, D.	Y	Y	Y	Y	Y	N
8 Krishnamoorthi	Y	Y	Y	Y	Y	N
9 Schakowsky	Y	Y	Y	Y	Y	N
10 Schneider	Y	N	N	Y	N	N
11 Foster	Y	N	N	Y	Y	N
12 **Bost**	Y	N	N	Y	N	Y
13 **Davis, R.**	Y	N	N	Y	N	Y

	224	225	226	227	228	229
14 **Hultgren**	Y	N	N	Y	N	Y
15 **Shimkus**	Y	N	N	Y	N	Y
16 **Kinzinger**	Y	N	N	Y	N	Y
17 Bustos	Y	Y	Y	Y	Y	N
18 **LaHood**	Y	N	N	Y	N	Y
INDIANA						
1 Visclosky	Y	Y	Y	Y	Y	N
2 **Walorski**	Y	N	N	Y	N	Y
3 **Banks**	Y	N	N	Y	N	Y
4 **Rokita**	Y	N	N	?	N	Y
5 **Brooks**	Y	N	N	Y	N	Y
6 **Messer**	Y	N	N	Y	N	Y
7 Carson	Y	Y	Y	Y	Y	N
8 **Bucshon**	Y	N	N	Y	N	Y
9 **Hollingsworth**	Y	N	N	Y	N	Y
IOWA						
1 **Blum**	Y	N	N	Y	N	Y
2 Loebsack	Y	Y	Y	Y	N	N
3 **Young**	Y	N	N	Y	N	Y
4 **King**	Y	N	Y	N	N	Y
KANSAS						
1 **Marshall**	Y	Y	Y	N	N	Y
2 **Jenkins**	Y	N	N	Y	N	Y
3 **Yoder**	Y	N	N	Y	N	Y
4 **Estes**	Y	N	N	Y	N	Y
KENTUCKY						
1 **Comer**	Y	N	N	N	Y	Y
2 **Guthrie**	Y	N	N	Y	N	Y
3 Yarmuth	Y	Y	Y	Y	Y	N
4 **Massie**	Y	Y	Y	N	Y	Y
5 **Rogers**	?	?	?	?	?	?
6 **Barr**	Y	N	N	Y	N	Y
LOUISIANA						
1 **Scalise**	Y	N	N	Y	N	Y
2 Richmond	Y	Y	Y	Y	Y	N
3 **Higgins**	+	+	+	+	–	+
4 **Johnson**	Y	N	N	Y	N	Y
5 **Abraham**	Y	N	N	N	N	Y
6 **Graves**	Y	N	N	Y	N	Y
MAINE						
1 Pingree	Y	Y	Y	Y	Y	N
2 **Poliquin**	Y	Y	Y	Y	N	Y
MARYLAND						
1 **Harris**	Y	N	Y	Y	N	Y
2 Ruppersberger	Y	N	N	Y	N	N
3 Sarbanes	Y	N	N	Y	Y	N
4 Brown	?	–	+	–	–	N
5 Hoyer	Y	N	Y	Y	Y	N
6 Delaney	?	Y	Y	Y	Y	N
7 Cummings	Y	N	N	Y	Y	N
8 Raskin	Y	Y	Y	Y	Y	N
MASSACHUSETTS						
1 Neal	Y	Y	Y	Y	Y	N
2 McGovern	Y	Y	Y	Y	Y	N
3 Tsongas	Y	Y	Y	Y	Y	N
4 Kennedy	Y	Y	Y	Y	Y	N
5 Clark	Y	Y	Y	Y	Y	N
6 Moulton	Y	N	N	Y	Y	N
7 Capuano	Y	Y	Y	Y	Y	N
8 Lynch	Y	Y	Y	Y	N	N
9 Keating	Y	Y	Y	Y	Y	N
MICHIGAN						
1 **Bergman**	Y	Y	Y	Y	N	Y
2 **Huizenga**	Y	N	N	Y	N	Y
3 *Amash*	Y	N	N	Y	Y	Y
4 **Moolenaar**	Y	N	N	Y	N	Y
5 Kildee	Y	Y	Y	Y	Y	N
6 **Upton**	Y	Y	N	Y	N	Y
7 **Walberg**	Y	N	N	Y	N	Y
8 **Bishop**	Y	N	N	Y	N	Y
9 Levin	Y	Y	Y	Y	Y	N
10 **Mitchell**	+	N	N	Y	N	Y
11 **Trott**	?	?	?	?	?	Y
12 Dingell	Y	Y	Y	Y	Y	N
14 Lawrence	Y	Y	N	Y	Y	N
MINNESOTA						
1 Walz	?	?	?	?	?	?
2 **Lewis**	Y	N	N	Y	Y	Y
3 **Paulsen**	Y	N	N	Y	N	Y
4 McCollum	Y	Y	Y	Y	Y	N

	224	225	226	227	228	229
5 Ellison	Y	Y	Y	Y	Y	N
6 **Emmer**	Y	N	N	Y	N	N
7 Peterson	Y	Y	Y	Y	Y	Y
8 Nolan	Y	Y	Y	Y	Y	N
MISSISSIPPI						
1 **Kelly**	Y	N	N	N	N	Y
2 Thompson	Y	N	Y	Y	Y	N
3 **Harper**	Y	N	N	Y	N	Y
4 **Palazzo**	Y	N	N	Y	N	Y
MISSOURI						
1 Clay	Y	Y	Y	Y	Y	N
2 **Wagner**	Y	N	N	Y	N	Y
3 **Luetkemeyer**	Y	N	N	Y	N	Y
4 **Hartzler**	Y	N	N	Y	N	Y
5 Cleaver	Y	N	N	Y	Y	N
6 **Graves**	Y	N	N	Y	N	Y
7 **Long**	Y	N	N	Y	N	Y
8 **Smith**	Y	N	N	N	N	Y
MONTANA						
AL **Gianforte**	Y	N	N	Y	N	Y
NEBRASKA						
1 **Fortenberry**	Y	Y	Y	Y	N	Y
2 **Bacon**	Y	N	N	N	N	Y
3 **Smith**	Y	N	N	N	N	Y
NEVADA						
1 Titus	Y	Y	Y	Y	N	N
2 **Amodei**	Y	N	N	Y	N	Y
3 Rosen	Y	N	N	Y	N	N
4 Kihuen	Y	N	N	Y	Y	N
NEW HAMPSHIRE						
1 Shea-Porter	Y	Y	Y	Y	Y	N
2 Kuster	Y	Y	Y	Y	Y	N
NEW JERSEY						
1 Norcross	Y	Y	Y	Y	N	N
2 **LoBiondo**	Y	Y	Y	Y	N	Y
3 **MacArthur**	Y	N	N	Y	N	Y
4 **Smith**	Y	Y	Y	Y	N	Y
5 Gottheimer	Y	Y	Y	Y	N	N
6 Pallone	Y	N	N	Y	Y	N
7 **Lance**	Y	N	N	Y	N	Y
8 Sires	Y	Y	Y	Y	Y	N
9 Pascrell	Y	Y	Y	Y	Y	N
10 Payne	Y	N	N	Y	Y	N
11 **Frelinghuysen**	Y	N	N	Y	N	Y
12 Watson Coleman	Y	Y	Y	Y	Y	N
NEW MEXICO						
1 Lujan Grisham	Y	N	N	Y	N	N
2 **Pearce**	?	?	?	?	?	Y
3 Luján	Y	N	N	Y	N	?
NEW YORK						
1 **Zeldin**	+	–	–	+	–	Y
2 **King**	?	?	?	?	?	Y
3 Suozzi	Y	N	Y	Y	Y	N
4 Rice	Y	N	N	Y	Y	N
5 Meeks	Y	N	N	Y	Y	N
6 Meng	Y	Y	Y	Y	Y	N
7 Velázquez	Y	Y	Y	Y	Y	N
8 Jeffries	Y	N	N	Y	N	N
9 Clarke	Y	Y	Y	Y	Y	N
10 Nadler	Y	Y	Y	Y	Y	N
11 **Donovan**	?	?	?	?	?	Y
12 Maloney, C.	Y	Y	Y	Y	Y	N
13 Espaillat	Y	Y	N	Y	Y	N
14 Crowley	Y	Y	Y	Y	Y	N
15 Serrano	Y	Y	Y	Y	Y	N
16 Engel	Y	Y	Y	Y	Y	N
17 Lowey	Y	Y	Y	Y	Y	N
18 Maloney, S.P.	Y	Y	Y	Y	Y	N
19 **Faso**	Y	Y	Y	Y	N	Y
20 Tonko	Y	Y	Y	Y	Y	N
21 **Stefanik**	Y	Y	Y	Y	N	Y
22 **Tenney**	Y	Y	Y	Y	N	Y
23 **Reed**	Y	Y	Y	Y	N	Y
24 **Katko**	Y	Y	Y	Y	N	Y
25 **Vacant**						
26 Higgins	Y	N	Y	Y	Y	N
27 **Collins**	Y	Y	Y	Y	N	Y
NORTH CAROLINA						
1 Butterfield	Y	Y	Y	Y	Y	N
2 **Holding**	Y	N	N	Y	N	Y
3 **Jones**	Y	Y	Y	Y	Y	N
4 Price	Y	Y	Y	Y	Y	N

	224	225	226	227	228	229
5 **Foxx**	Y	N	N	Y	N	Y
6 **Walker**	Y	N	N	Y	N	Y
7 **Rouzer**	Y	N	N	Y	N	Y
8 **Hudson**	Y	N	N	Y	N	?
9 **Pittenger**	Y	N	N	Y	N	Y
9 **Vacant**						
10 **McHenry**	Y	Y	Y	Y	N	Y
11 **Meadows**	Y	N	N	Y	N	Y
12 Adams	Y	Y	Y	Y	Y	N
13 **Budd**	Y	N	N	Y	N	Y
NORTH DAKOTA						
AL **Cramer**	Y	Y	Y	Y	N	Y
OHIO						
1 **Chabot**	Y	N	N	Y	N	Y
2 **Wenstrup**	Y	N	N	N	N	Y
3 Beatty	Y	Y	Y	Y	Y	N
4 **Jordan**	Y	N	N	Y	N	Y
5 **Latta**	Y	N	N	Y	N	Y
6 **Johnson**	Y	N	N	Y	N	Y
7 **Gibbs**	Y	N	N	Y	N	Y
8 **Davidson**	Y	N	N	Y	N	Y
9 Kaptur	Y	Y	Y	Y	Y	N
10 **Turner**	Y	N	N	Y	N	Y
11 Fudge	Y	Y	Y	Y	Y	N
12 **Vacant**						
13 Ryan	Y	Y	Y	Y	N	N
14 **Joyce**	Y	N	N	Y	?	N
15 **Stivers**	?	?	?	?	?	?
16 **Renacci**	Y	N	N	Y	N	Y
OKLAHOMA						
1 **Vacant**						
2 **Mullin**	Y	N	N	Y	N	Y
3 **Lucas**	Y	N	N	Y	N	Y
4 **Cole**	Y	Y	Y	Y	N	Y
5 **Russell**	Y	N	N	N	N	Y
OREGON						
1 Bonamici	Y	Y	Y	Y	Y	N
2 **Walden**	Y	N	N	Y	N	Y
3 Blumenauer	Y	N	N	Y	N	N
4 DeFazio	Y	Y	Y	Y	Y	N
5 Schrader	Y	N	N	Y	Y	N
PENNSYLVANIA						
1 Brady	Y	Y	Y	Y	Y	N
2 Evans	Y	Y	Y	Y	Y	N
3 **Kelly**	Y	Y	Y	N	N	Y
4 **Perry**	Y	N	N	Y	N	Y
5 **Thompson**	Y	N	N	N	N	Y
6 **Costello**	Y	N	N	Y	N	Y
7 **Vacant**						
8 **Fitzpatrick**	Y	Y	Y	Y	N	Y
9 **Shuster**	Y	N	Y	Y	N	Y
10 **Marino**	Y	N	N	N	N	Y
11 **Barletta**	Y	N	N	N	N	Y
12 **Rothfus**	Y	N	N	Y	N	Y
13 Boyle	Y	Y	Y	Y	Y	N
14 Doyle	Y	Y	Y	Y	Y	N
15 **Vacant**						
16 **Smucker**	Y	N	N	Y	N	Y
17 Cartwright	Y	Y	Y	Y	Y	N
18 Lamb	Y	Y	Y	Y	Y	N
RHODE ISLAND						
1 Cicilline	Y	Y	Y	Y	Y	N
2 Langevin	Y	Y	Y	Y	Y	N
SOUTH CAROLINA						
1 **Sanford**	Y	N	N	N	Y	Y
2 **Wilson**	Y	N	N	Y	N	Y
3 **Duncan**	Y	N	Y	Y	N	Y
4 **Gowdy**	Y	N	N	Y	N	Y
5 **Norman**	Y	N	N	Y	N	Y
6 Clyburn	Y	Y	Y	Y	Y	N
7 **Rice**	Y	N	N	Y	N	Y
SOUTH DAKOTA						
AL **Noem**	Y	N	N	N	N	?
TENNESSEE						
1 **Roe**	Y	N	N	Y	N	Y
2 **Duncan**	Y	Y	Y	Y	Y	Y
3 **Fleischmann**	Y	N	N	Y	N	Y
4 **DesJarlais**	Y	N	N	Y	N	Y
5 Cooper	Y	N	N	Y	N	N
6 **Black**	+	–	–	+	–	?
7 **Blackburn**	Y	N	N	Y	N	Y
8 **Kustoff**	Y	N	N	Y	N	Y
9 Cohen	Y	Y	Y	Y	Y	N

	224	225	226	227	228	229
TEXAS						
1 **Gohmert**	Y	N	N	Y	N	Y
2 **Poe**	Y	Y	Y	Y	N	Y
3 **Johnson, S.**	Y	N	N	Y	N	Y
4 **Ratcliffe**	Y	N	N	Y	N	Y
5 **Hensarling**	Y	N	N	Y	N	Y
6 **Barton**	Y	N	N	Y	N	Y
7 **Culberson**	Y	N	N	Y	N	Y
8 **Brady**	Y	N	?	N	N	Y
9 Green, A.	Y	Y	Y	Y	Y	N
10 **McCaul**	Y	N	N	Y	N	Y
11 **Conaway**	Y	N	N	Y	N	Y
12 **Granger**	Y	N	N	Y	N	Y
13 **Thornberry**	Y	N	N	Y	N	Y
14 **Weber**	Y	N	N	Y	N	?
15 Gonzalez	Y	N	N	Y	Y	N
16 O'Rourke	Y	Y	Y	Y	Y	N
17 **Flores**	Y	N	N	Y	N	Y
18 Jackson Lee	Y	Y	Y	Y	Y	N
19 **Arrington**	Y	N	N	Y	N	Y
20 Castro	Y	Y	Y	Y	Y	N
21 **Smith**	Y	N	Y	Y	N	Y
22 **Olson**	Y	N	N	Y	N	Y
23 **Hurd**	Y	N	N	Y	N	Y
24 **Marchant**	Y	N	N	Y	N	Y
25 **Williams**	Y	N	N	Y	N	Y
26 **Burgess**	Y	N	Y	Y	N	Y
28 Cuellar	Y	N	N	Y	N	N
29 Green, G.	Y	Y	Y	Y	Y	N
30 Johnson, E.B.	Y	N	N	Y	Y	N
31 **Carter**	Y	N	N	Y	N	Y
32 **Sessions**	Y	N	N	Y	N	Y
33 Veasey	Y	Y	Y	Y	Y	N
34 Vela	Y	N	N	Y	Y	N
35 Doggett	Y	N	N	Y	Y	N
36 **Babin**	Y	N	N	Y	N	Y
UTAH						
1 **Bishop**	Y	Y	Y	Y	N	Y
2 **Stewart**	Y	N	N	Y	N	Y
3 **Curtis**	Y	N	N	Y	N	Y
4 **Love**	Y	N	N	Y	N	Y
VERMONT						
AL Welch	Y	Y	Y	Y	Y	N
VIRGINIA						
1 **Wittman**	Y	N	N	Y	N	Y
2 **Taylor**	Y	N	Y	Y	N	Y
3 Scott	Y	N	N	Y	Y	N
4 McEachin	Y	N	N	Y	Y	N
5 **Garrett**	Y	N	N	Y	N	Y
6 **Goodlatte**	+	–	N	Y	N	Y
7 **Brat**	Y	N	N	Y	N	Y
8 Beyer	?	?	N	Y	Y	N
9 **Griffith**	Y	Y	Y	Y	N	Y
10 **Comstock**	Y	N	N	Y	N	Y
11 Connolly	Y	N	N	Y	Y	N
WASHINGTON						
1 DelBene	Y	Y	Y	Y	Y	N
2 Larsen	Y	N	N	Y	Y	N
3 **Herrera Beutler**	Y	N	N	Y	N	Y
4 **Newhouse**	Y	N	N	Y	N	Y
5 **McMorris Rodgers**	Y	N	Y	Y	N	Y
6 Kilmer	Y	Y	Y	Y	Y	N
7 Jayapal	Y	Y	Y	Y	Y	N
8 **Reichert**	Y	N	N	Y	N	Y
9 Smith	Y	N	N	Y	Y	N
10 Heck	Y	N	N	Y	Y	N
WEST VIRGINIA						
1 **McKinley**	Y	Y	Y	Y	N	Y
2 **Mooney**	Y	Y	N	Y	N	Y
3 **Jenkins**	Y	Y	Y	Y	N	+
WISCONSIN						
1 **Ryan**						
2 Pocan	Y	Y	Y	Y	Y	N
3 Kind	Y	N	N	Y	Y	N
4 Moore	Y	N	N	Y	Y	–
5 **Sensenbrenner**	Y	N	Y	Y	N	Y
6 **Grothman**	Y	N	N	Y	N	Y
7 **Duffy**	Y	Y	Y	N	N	Y
8 **Gallagher**	Y	N	N	N	N	Y
WYOMING						
AL **Cheney**	Y	N	N	Y	N	Y

VOTE NUMBER

230. HR5515. FISCAL 2019 DEFENSE AUTHORIZATION/PASSAGE. Passage of the bill that would authorize $708.1 billion in discretionary funding for defense programs in fiscal 2019. The total would include $69 billion for overseas contingency operations; $241.2 billion for operations and maintenance; $11.3 billion for military construction; $185.8 billion for military personnel; and $33.6 billion for defense health care programs. It would authorize $65 million for the development of a low-yield nuclear warhead for submarine-launched ballistic missiles. It would prohibit the Defense Department from reducing the number of intercontinental ballistic missiles, and would withhold funding for certain White House functions until the implementation of certain congressionally-mandated sanctions on Russia for violations of the Intermediate Nuclear Forces Treaty. It would require the Defense Department to establish a comprehensive oversight plan for implementation of the department's new harassment prevention and response policy. Passed 351-66: R 220-7; D 131-59. May 24, 2018.

231. HR5005. JAMES WELDON JOHNSON BIRTHPLACE/PASSAGE. Bishop, R-Utah, motion to suspend the rules and pass the bill that would require the Interior Department to conduct a special resource study on the suitability and feasibility of including the birthplace of James Weldon Johnson in Jacksonville, Fla., in the National Park System. Motion agreed to 374-5: R 212-5; D 162-0. June 5, 2018.

232. HR2991. SUSQUEHANNA NATIONAL HERITAGE AREA/PASSAGE. Bishop, R-Utah, motion to suspend the rules and pass the bill that would establish the Susquehanna National Heritage Area in Lancaster and York Counties, Pa. Motion agreed to 373-9: R 211-9; D 162-0. June 5, 2018.

233. HR5655. CAMP NELSON HERITAGE NATIONAL MONUMENT/PASSAGE. Bishop, R-Utah, motion to suspend the rules and pass the bill that would establish the Camp Nelson Heritage National Monument in Nicholasville, Ky. The site would become a unit of the National Park System. Motion agreed to 376-4: R 214-4; D 162-0. June 5, 2018.

234. HRES918. LAW ENFORCEMENT PARTNERSHIP GRANTS, WATER INFRASTRUCTURE PROJECTS AUTHORIZATION, AND FISCAL 2019 APPROPRIATIONS PACKAGE/PREVIOUS QUESTION. Woodall, R-Ga., motion to order the previous question (thus ending debate and possibility of amendment) on the rule (H Res 918) that would provide for House floor consideration of the Senate amendment to the bill (HR 3249) that would create partnerships between local, state and federal law enforcement agencies to fight criminal street gangs; would provide for consideration of the bill (HR 8) that would authorize certain water resource projects; and would provide for consideration of the legislative vehicle for a fiscal 2019 minibus appropriations bill (HR 5895) that would make certain appropriations for the fiscal year ending Sept. 30, 2019, and would provide for consideration of amendments to the Energy-Water division of the bill. Motion agreed to 224-176: R 224-0; D 0-176. June 6, 2018.

235. HRES918. LAW ENFORCEMENT PARTNERSHIP GRANTS, WATER INFRASTRUCTURE PROJECTS AUTHORIZATION, AND FISCAL 2019 APPROPRIATIONS PACKAGE/RULE. Adoption of the rule (H Res 918) that would provide for House floor consideration of the Senate amendment to the bill (HR 3249) that would create partnerships between local, state and federal law enforcement agencies to fight criminal street gangs; would provide for consideration of the bill (HR 8) that would authorize certain water resource projects; and would provide for consideration of the legislative vehicle for a fiscal 2019 minibus appropriations bill (HR 5895) that would make certain appropriations for the fiscal year ending Sept. 30, 2019, and would provide for consideration of amendments to the Energy-Water division of the bill. Adopted 223-175: R 220-3; D 3-172. June 6, 2018.

	230	231	232	233	234	235
ALABAMA						
1 Byrne	Y	Y	Y	Y	Y	Y
2 Roby	Y	?	?	?	?	?
3 Rogers	Y	Y	Y	Y	Y	Y
4 Aderholt	Y	Y	Y	Y	Y	Y
5 Brooks	Y	?	?	?	?	?
6 Palmer	Y	Y	Y	Y	Y	Y
7 Sewell	Y	Y	Y	Y	N	N
ALASKA						
AL Young	Y	Y	Y	Y	Y	Y
ARIZONA						
1 O'Halleran	Y	Y	Y	Y	N	N
2 McSally	Y	Y	Y	Y	Y	Y
3 Grijalva	N	Y	Y	Y	N	?
4 Gosar	Y	Y	N	Y	Y	Y
5 Biggs	Y	N	N	Y	Y	Y
6 Schweikert	Y	Y	Y	Y	Y	Y
7 Gallego	Y	Y	Y	Y	N	N
8 Lesko	Y	Y	Y	Y	Y	Y
9 Sinema	Y	Y	Y	Y	N	N
ARKANSAS						
1 Crawford	Y	Y	Y	Y	Y	Y
2 Hill	Y	Y	Y	Y	Y	Y
3 Womack	Y	Y	Y	Y	Y	Y
4 Westerman	Y	Y	Y	Y	Y	Y
CALIFORNIA						
1 LaMalfa	Y	Y	Y	Y	Y	Y
2 Huffman	N	Y	Y	Y	N	N
3 Garamendi	Y	Y	Y	Y	N	N
4 McClintock	Y	Y	Y	Y	Y	Y
5 Thompson	N	Y	Y	Y	N	N
6 Matsui	N	Y	Y	Y	N	N
7 Bera	Y	Y	Y	Y	N	N
8 Cook	Y	Y	Y	Y	Y	Y
9 McNerney	Y	?	?	?	?	?
10 Denham	Y	?	?	?	Y	Y
11 DeSaulnier	N	Y	Y	Y	N	N
12 Pelosi	Y	Y	Y	Y	?	?
13 Lee	N	Y	Y	Y	–	–
14 Speier	Y	Y	Y	Y	N	N
15 Swalwell	N	?	?	Y	N	N
16 Costa	Y	Y	Y	Y	N	Y
17 Khanna	N	Y	Y	Y	N	N
18 Eshoo	N	Y	Y	Y	N	N
19 Lofgren	N	Y	Y	Y	N	N
20 Panetta	Y	Y	Y	Y	N	N
21 Valadao	Y	Y	Y	Y	Y	Y
22 Nunes	Y	Y	Y	Y	Y	Y
23 McCarthy	Y	Y	Y	Y	Y	Y
24 Carbajal	Y	Y	Y	Y	N	N
25 Knight	Y	Y	Y	Y	Y	Y
26 Brownley	Y	?	?	?	N	N
27 Chu	N	Y	Y	Y	N	N
28 Schiff	Y	Y	Y	Y	N	N
29 Cardenas	Y	?	?	?	?	?
30 Sherman	Y	+	+	+	–	–
31 Aguilar	Y	Y	Y	Y	N	N
32 Napolitano	N	Y	Y	Y	N	N
33 Lieu	Y	?	?	?	N	N
34 Gomez	N	?	?	?	?	?
35 Torres	Y	?	?	?	N	N
36 Ruiz	Y	Y	Y	Y	N	N
37 Bass	N	?	?	?	N	N
38 Sánchez, Linda	N	?	?	?	?	?
39 Royce	Y	Y	Y	Y	Y	Y
40 Roybal-Allard	Y	Y	Y	Y	N	N
41 Takano	N	Y	Y	Y	N	N
42 Calvert	Y	Y	Y	Y	Y	Y
43 Waters	N	?	?	?	?	?
44 Barragan	N	?	?	?	N	N
45 Walters	Y	?	?	?	Y	Y
46 Correa	Y	Y	Y	Y	N	N
47 Lowenthal	N	Y	Y	Y	N	N
48 Rohrabacher	Y	?	?	?	?	?
49 Issa	Y	?	?	?	?	?
50 Hunter	Y	?	?	?	?	?
51 Vargas	Y	Y	Y	Y	N	N
52 Peters	Y	Y	Y	Y	N	N
53 Davis	Y	Y	Y	Y	N	N

	230	231	232	233	234	235
COLORADO						
1 DeGette	N	Y	Y	Y	N	N
2 Polis	N	?	?	?	?	?
3 Tipton	Y	Y	Y	Y	Y	Y
4 Buck	N	Y	N	Y	Y	Y
5 Lamborn	Y	Y	Y	Y	Y	Y
6 Coffman	Y	Y	Y	Y	Y	Y
7 Perlmutter	Y	?	?	?	?	?
CONNECTICUT						
1 Larson	Y	Y	Y	Y	N	N
2 Courtney	Y	Y	Y	Y	N	N
3 DeLauro	Y	Y	Y	Y	N	N
4 Himes	Y	Y	Y	Y	N	N
5 Esty	Y	Y	Y	Y	N	N
DELAWARE						
AL Blunt Rochester	Y	Y	Y	Y	N	N
FLORIDA						
1 Gaetz	Y	?	Y	Y	Y	Y
2 Dunn	Y	Y	Y	Y	Y	Y
3 Yoho	Y	Y	Y	Y	Y	Y
4 Rutherford	Y	Y	Y	Y	Y	Y
5 Lawson	Y	Y	Y	Y	N	N
6 DeSantis	Y	Y	Y	Y	Y	Y
7 Murphy	Y	Y	Y	Y	N	Y
8 Posey	Y	Y	Y	Y	Y	Y
9 Soto	Y	Y	Y	Y	N	N
10 Demings	Y	Y	Y	Y	N	N
11 Webster	Y	Y	Y	Y	Y	Y
12 Bilirakis	Y	+	+	+	+	+
13 Crist	Y	Y	Y	Y	N	N
14 Castor	Y	Y	Y	Y	N	N
15 Ross	Y	Y	Y	Y	Y	Y
16 Buchanan	Y	Y	Y	Y	Y	Y
17 Rooney, T.	Y	Y	Y	Y	Y	Y
18 Mast	Y	Y	Y	Y	Y	Y
19 Rooney, F.	Y	Y	Y	Y	Y	Y
20 Hastings	Y	Y	Y	Y	N	N
21 Frankel	Y	Y	Y	Y	N	N
22 Deutch	Y	Y	Y	Y	N	N
23 Wasserman Schultz	Y	Y	Y	Y	N	N
24 Wilson	N	+	+	+	–	–
25 Diaz-Balart	Y	Y	Y	Y	Y	Y
26 Curbelo	Y	Y	Y	Y	Y	Y
27 Ros-Lehtinen	Y	Y	Y	Y	Y	Y
GEORGIA						
1 Carter	Y	Y	Y	Y	Y	Y
2 Bishop	Y	Y	Y	Y	N	N
3 Ferguson	Y	Y	Y	Y	Y	Y
4 Johnson	N	Y	Y	Y	N	N
5 Lewis	?	Y	Y	Y	N	N
6 Handel	Y	Y	Y	Y	Y	Y
7 Woodall	Y	Y	Y	Y	Y	Y
8 Scott, A.	Y	Y	Y	Y	Y	Y
9 Collins	Y	Y	Y	?	Y	Y
10 Hice	Y	Y	Y	Y	Y	Y
11 Loudermilk	Y	Y	Y	Y	Y	Y
12 Allen	Y	Y	Y	Y	Y	Y
13 Scott, D.	Y	Y	Y	Y	N	N
14 Graves	Y	Y	Y	Y	Y	Y
HAWAII						
1 Hanabusa	Y	Y	Y	Y	N	N
2 Gabbard	N	Y	Y	Y	N	N
IDAHO						
1 Labrador	N	Y	Y	Y	Y	Y
2 Simpson	Y	Y	Y	Y	Y	Y
ILLINOIS						
1 Rush	Y	Y	Y	Y	N	N
2 Kelly	Y	Y	Y	Y	N	N
3 Lipinski	Y	Y	Y	Y	N	N
4 Gutierrez	N	+	+	+	?	?
5 Quigley	Y	Y	Y	Y	N	N
6 Roskam	Y	Y	Y	Y	Y	Y
7 Davis, D.	Y	Y	Y	Y	N	N
8 Krishnamoorthi	Y	Y	Y	Y	N	N
9 Schakowsky	N	Y	Y	Y	N	N
10 Schneider	Y	Y	Y	Y	N	N
11 Foster	Y	Y	Y	Y	N	N
12 Bost	Y	Y	Y	Y	Y	Y
13 Davis, R.	Y	Y	Y	Y	+	Y

	230	231	232	233	234	235
14 **Hultgren**	Y	Y	Y	Y	Y	Y
15 **Shimkus**	Y	Y	Y	Y	Y	Y
16 **Kinzinger**	Y	Y	Y	Y	Y	Y
17 Bustos	Y	Y	Y	Y	N	N
18 **LaHood**	Y	Y	Y	Y	Y	Y
INDIANA						
1 Visclosky	Y	Y	Y	Y	N	N
2 **Walorski**	Y	Y	Y	Y	Y	Y
3 **Banks**	Y	Y	Y	Y	Y	Y
4 **Rokita**	Y	?	?	?	Y	Y
5 **Brooks**	Y	Y	Y	Y	Y	Y
6 **Messer**	Y	Y	Y	Y	Y	Y
7 Carson	Y	Y	Y	Y	N	N
8 **Bucshon**	Y	Y	Y	Y	Y	Y
9 **Hollingsworth**	Y	Y	Y	Y	Y	Y
IOWA						
1 **Blum**	Y	Y	Y	Y	Y	Y
2 Loebsack	Y	Y	Y	Y	N	N
3 **Young**	Y	Y	Y	Y	Y	Y
4 **King**	Y	Y	Y	Y	Y	Y
KANSAS						
1 **Marshall**	Y	Y	Y	Y	Y	Y
2 **Jenkins**	Y	Y	Y	Y	Y	Y
3 **Yoder**	Y	Y	Y	Y	Y	Y
4 **Estes**	Y	Y	Y	Y	Y	Y
KENTUCKY						
1 **Comer**	Y	Y	Y	Y	Y	Y
2 **Guthrie**	Y	Y	Y	Y	Y	Y
3 Yarmuth	N	Y	Y	Y	N	N
4 **Massie**	N	N	N	Y	Y	N
5 **Rogers**	?	Y	Y	Y	Y	Y
6 **Barr**	Y	Y	Y	Y	Y	Y
LOUISIANA						
1 **Scalise**	Y	Y	Y	Y	Y	Y
2 Richmond	Y	?	?	?	N	N
3 **Higgins**	+	Y	Y	Y	Y	Y
4 **Johnson**	Y	Y	Y	Y	Y	Y
5 **Abraham**	Y	Y	Y	Y	Y	Y
6 **Graves**	Y	Y	Y	Y	Y	Y
MAINE						
1 Pingree	Y	Y	Y	Y	N	N
2 **Poliquin**	Y	Y	Y	Y	Y	Y
MARYLAND						
1 **Harris**	Y	N	Y	N	Y	Y
2 Ruppersberger	Y	Y	Y	Y	N	N
3 Sarbanes	Y	Y	Y	Y	N	N
4 Brown	Y	Y	Y	Y	N	N
5 Hoyer	Y	Y	Y	Y	N	N
6 Delaney	Y	Y	Y	Y	N	N
7 Cummings	Y	?	?	?	N	N
8 Raskin	N	Y	Y	Y	N	N
MASSACHUSETTS						
1 Neal	Y	Y	Y	Y	N	N
2 McGovern	N	Y	Y	Y	N	N
3 Tsongas	Y	?	?	?	N	N
4 Kennedy	N	Y	Y	Y	N	N
5 Clark	N	Y	Y	Y	N	N
6 Moulton	Y	Y	Y	Y	N	N
7 Capuano	N	Y	Y	Y	N	N
8 Lynch	Y	Y	Y	Y	N	N
9 Keating	Y	Y	Y	Y	N	N
MICHIGAN						
1 **Bergman**	Y	Y	Y	Y	Y	Y
2 **Huizenga**	Y	Y	Y	Y	Y	Y
3 *Amash*	N	N	N	N	Y	N
4 **Moolenaar**	Y	Y	Y	Y	Y	Y
5 Kildee	N	Y	Y	Y	N	N
6 **Upton**	Y	Y	Y	Y	Y	Y
7 **Walberg**	Y	Y	Y	Y	Y	Y
8 **Bishop**	Y	Y	Y	Y	?	?
9 Levin	Y	Y	Y	Y	N	N
10 **Mitchell**	Y	Y	Y	Y	Y	Y
11 **Trott**	Y	Y	Y	Y	Y	Y
12 Dingell	Y	Y	Y	Y	N	N
14 Lawrence	Y	Y	Y	Y	N	N
MINNESOTA						
1 Walz	?	?	?	?	?	?
2 **Lewis**	Y	Y	Y	Y	Y	Y
3 **Paulsen**	Y	Y	Y	Y	Y	Y
4 McCollum	N	Y	Y	Y	N	?

	230	231	232	233	234	235
5 Ellison	N	?	?	?	?	?
6 **Emmer**	Y	Y	Y	Y	Y	Y
7 Peterson	Y	Y	Y	Y	N	N
8 Nolan	N	Y	Y	Y	N	N
MISSISSIPPI						
1 **Kelly**	Y	Y	Y	Y	Y	Y
2 Thompson	Y	Y	Y	Y	N	N
3 **Harper**	Y	Y	Y	Y	Y	Y
4 **Palazzo**	Y	?	?	?	?	?
MISSOURI						
1 Clay	Y	Y	Y	Y	N	N
2 **Wagner**	Y	Y	Y	Y	Y	Y
3 **Luetkemeyer**	Y	Y	Y	Y	Y	Y
4 **Hartzler**	Y	Y	Y	Y	Y	Y
5 Cleaver	N	Y	Y	Y	N	N
6 **Graves**	Y	Y	Y	Y	Y	Y
7 **Long**	Y	Y	Y	Y	Y	Y
8 **Smith**	Y	?	?	?	Y	Y
MONTANA						
AL **Gianforte**	Y	Y	Y	Y	Y	Y
NEBRASKA						
1 **Fortenberry**	Y	Y	Y	Y	?	?
2 **Bacon**	Y	Y	Y	Y	Y	Y
3 **Smith**	Y	Y	Y	Y	Y	Y
NEVADA						
1 Titus	Y	?	?	?	N	N
2 **Amodei**	Y	Y	Y	Y	Y	Y
3 Rosen	Y	?	?	?	N	N
4 Kihuen	Y	Y	Y	Y	N	N
NEW HAMPSHIRE						
1 Shea-Porter	Y	Y	Y	Y	N	N
2 Kuster	Y	Y	Y	Y	N	N
NEW JERSEY						
1 Norcross	Y	Y	Y	Y	N	N
2 **LoBiondo**	Y	Y	Y	Y	Y	Y
3 **MacArthur**	Y	Y	Y	Y	Y	Y
4 **Smith**	Y	Y	Y	Y	Y	Y
5 Gottheimer	Y	Y	Y	Y	N	N
6 Pallone	N	Y	Y	Y	N	N
7 **Lance**	Y	Y	Y	Y	Y	Y
8 Sires	Y	?	?	?	N	N
9 Pascrell	Y	Y	Y	Y	N	N
10 Payne	N	Y	Y	Y	N	N
11 **Frelinghuysen**	Y	Y	Y	Y	Y	Y
12 Watson Coleman	N	Y	Y	Y	N	N
NEW MEXICO						
1 Lujan Grisham	Y	+	+	+	?	?
2 **Pearce**	Y	Y	Y	Y	Y	Y
3 Luján	Y	Y	Y	Y	N	N
NEW YORK						
1 **Zeldin**	Y	Y	Y	Y	Y	Y
2 **King**	Y	Y	Y	Y	Y	Y
3 Suozzi	Y	Y	Y	Y	N	N
4 Rice	Y	Y	Y	Y	N	N
5 Meeks	Y	Y	Y	Y	N	N
6 Meng	Y	Y	Y	Y	N	N
7 Velázquez	N	Y	Y	Y	N	N
8 Jeffries	N	Y	Y	Y	N	N
9 Clarke	N	Y	Y	Y	N	N
10 Nadler	N	Y	Y	Y	N	N
11 **Donovan**	Y	Y	Y	Y	Y	Y
12 Maloney, C.	N	Y	Y	Y	N	N
13 Espaillat	N	Y	Y	Y	N	N
14 Crowley	N	Y	Y	Y	N	N
15 Serrano	N	Y	Y	Y	N	N
16 Engel	Y	Y	Y	Y	N	N
17 Lowey	Y	Y	Y	Y	N	N
18 Maloney, S.P.	Y	Y	Y	Y	N	N
19 **Faso**	Y	Y	Y	Y	Y	Y
20 Tonko	Y	Y	Y	Y	N	N
21 **Stefanik**	Y	Y	Y	Y	Y	Y
22 **Tenney**	Y	Y	Y	Y	Y	Y
23 **Reed**	Y	Y	Y	Y	Y	Y
24 **Katko**	Y	Y	Y	Y	Y	Y
25 **Vacant**						
26 Higgins	Y	Y	Y	Y	N	N
27 **Collins**	Y	Y	Y	Y	Y	Y
NORTH CAROLINA						
1 Butterfield	Y	?	?	?	N	N
2 **Holding**	Y	Y	Y	Y	Y	Y
3 **Jones**	N	N	N	N	Y	N
4 Price	Y	Y	Y	Y	N	N

	230	231	232	233	234	235
5 **Foxx**	Y	Y	Y	Y	Y	Y
6 **Walker**	Y	Y	Y	Y	Y	Y
7 **Rouzer**	Y	Y	Y	Y	Y	Y
8 **Hudson**	Y	Y	Y	Y	Y	Y
9 **Pittenger**	Y	Y	Y	Y	Y	?
9 **Vacant**						
10 **McHenry**	Y	Y	Y	Y	Y	Y
11 **Meadows**	Y	Y	Y	Y	Y	Y
12 Adams	Y	Y	Y	Y	N	N
13 **Budd**	Y	Y	Y	Y	Y	Y
NORTH DAKOTA						
AL **Cramer**	Y	Y	Y	Y	Y	Y
OHIO						
1 **Chabot**	Y	Y	Y	Y	Y	Y
2 **Wenstrup**	Y	Y	Y	Y	Y	Y
3 Beatty	N	+	+	+	–	–
4 **Jordan**	Y	Y	Y	Y	Y	Y
5 **Latta**	Y	Y	Y	Y	Y	Y
6 **Johnson**	Y	Y	Y	Y	Y	Y
7 **Gibbs**	Y	Y	Y	Y	Y	Y
8 **Davidson**	Y	Y	Y	Y	Y	Y
9 Kaptur	Y	Y	Y	Y	N	N
10 **Turner**	Y	Y	Y	Y	Y	Y
11 Fudge	Y	Y	Y	Y	N	N
12 **Vacant**						
13 Ryan	Y	Y	Y	Y	N	N
14 **Joyce**	Y	Y	Y	Y	Y	Y
15 **Stivers**	?	Y	Y	Y	Y	Y
16 **Renacci**	Y	Y	Y	Y	Y	Y
OKLAHOMA						
1 **Vacant**						
2 **Mullin**	Y	Y	Y	Y	Y	Y
3 **Lucas**	Y	Y	Y	Y	Y	Y
4 **Cole**	Y	Y	Y	Y	Y	Y
5 **Russell**	Y	Y	Y	Y	Y	Y
OREGON						
1 Bonamici	N	Y	Y	Y	N	N
2 **Walden**	Y	Y	Y	Y	Y	Y
3 Blumenauer	N	Y	Y	Y	N	N
4 DeFazio	N	Y	Y	Y	N	N
5 Schrader	Y	Y	Y	Y	N	N
PENNSYLVANIA						
1 Brady	Y	?	?	?	N	N
2 Evans	Y	Y	Y	Y	N	N
3 **Kelly**	Y	Y	Y	Y	Y	Y
4 **Perry**	Y	Y	Y	Y	Y	Y
5 **Thompson**	Y	Y	Y	Y	Y	Y
6 **Costello**	Y	Y	Y	Y	Y	Y
7 **Vacant**						
8 **Fitzpatrick**	Y	Y	Y	Y	Y	Y
9 **Shuster**	Y	Y	Y	Y	Y	Y
10 **Marino**	Y	Y	Y	Y	Y	Y
11 **Barletta**	Y	Y	Y	Y	Y	Y
12 **Rothfus**	Y	Y	Y	Y	Y	Y
13 Boyle	Y	Y	Y	Y	N	N
14 Doyle	N	Y	Y	Y	N	N
15 **Vacant**						
16 **Smucker**	Y	Y	Y	Y	Y	Y
17 Cartwright	Y	Y	Y	Y	N	N
18 Lamb	Y	Y	Y	Y	N	Y
RHODE ISLAND						
1 Cicilline	N	Y	Y	Y	N	N
2 Langevin	Y	Y	Y	Y	N	N
SOUTH CAROLINA						
1 **Sanford**	Y	Y	N	Y	Y	Y
2 **Wilson**	Y	Y	Y	Y	Y	Y
3 **Duncan**	Y	Y	Y	Y	Y	Y
4 **Gowdy**	Y	?	?	?	Y	Y
5 **Norman**	Y	Y	Y	Y	Y	Y
6 Clyburn	Y	Y	Y	Y	N	N
7 **Rice**	Y	Y	Y	Y	Y	Y
SOUTH DAKOTA						
AL **Noem**	?	?	?	?	?	?
TENNESSEE						
1 **Roe**	Y	Y	Y	Y	Y	Y
2 **Duncan**	N	?	?	?	Y	Y
3 **Fleischmann**	Y	Y	Y	Y	Y	Y
4 **DesJarlais**	Y	Y	Y	Y	Y	Y
5 Cooper	Y	Y	Y	Y	N	N
6 **Black**	+	Y	Y	?	Y	Y
7 **Blackburn**	Y	Y	Y	Y	Y	Y
8 **Kustoff**	Y	Y	Y	Y	Y	Y
9 Cohen	N	Y	Y	Y	?	N

	230	231	232	233	234	235
TEXAS						
1 **Gohmert**	Y	Y	Y	Y	Y	Y
2 **Poe**	Y	Y	Y	Y	Y	Y
3 **Johnson, S.**	Y	Y	Y	Y	Y	Y
4 **Ratcliffe**	Y	Y	Y	Y	Y	Y
5 **Hensarling**	Y	Y	Y	Y	Y	Y
6 **Barton**	Y	Y	Y	Y	Y	Y
7 **Culberson**	Y	Y	Y	Y	Y	Y
8 **Brady**	Y	Y	Y	Y	Y	?
9 Green, A.	Y	Y	Y	Y	N	N
10 **McCaul**	Y	Y	Y	Y	Y	Y
11 **Conaway**	Y	Y	Y	Y	Y	Y
12 **Granger**	Y	Y	Y	Y	Y	Y
13 **Thornberry**	Y	Y	Y	Y	Y	Y
14 **Weber**	?	Y	Y	Y	Y	Y
15 Gonzalez	Y	+	+	+	N	N
16 O'Rourke	Y	+	+	+	N	N
17 **Flores**	Y	Y	Y	Y	Y	Y
18 Jackson Lee	Y	Y	Y	Y	N	N
19 **Arrington**	Y	Y	Y	Y	Y	Y
20 Castro	Y	Y	Y	Y	N	N
21 **Smith**	Y	Y	Y	Y	Y	Y
22 **Olson**	Y	Y	Y	Y	Y	Y
23 **Hurd**	Y	+	Y	Y	Y	Y
24 **Marchant**	Y	Y	Y	Y	Y	Y
25 **Williams**	Y	Y	Y	Y	Y	Y
26 **Burgess**	Y	Y	Y	Y	Y	Y
28 Cuellar	Y	Y	Y	Y	N	N
29 Green, G.	Y	Y	Y	Y	N	N
30 Johnson, E.B.	Y	Y	Y	Y	N	N
31 **Carter**	Y	Y	Y	Y	Y	Y
32 **Sessions**	Y	Y	Y	Y	Y	Y
33 Veasey	Y	Y	Y	Y	N	N
34 Vela	Y	?	?	?	N	N
35 Doggett	+	Y	Y	Y	N	N
36 **Babin**	Y	Y	Y	Y	Y	Y
UTAH						
1 **Bishop**	Y	Y	Y	Y	Y	Y
2 **Stewart**	Y	Y	Y	Y	Y	Y
3 **Curtis**	Y	Y	Y	Y	Y	Y
4 **Love**	Y	Y	Y	Y	Y	Y
VERMONT						
AL Welch	N	Y	Y	Y	N	N
VIRGINIA						
1 **Wittman**	Y	Y	Y	Y	Y	Y
2 **Taylor**	Y	Y	Y	Y	Y	Y
3 Scott	Y	Y	Y	Y	N	N
4 McEachin	Y	Y	Y	Y	N	N
5 **Garrett**	Y	Y	N	Y	Y	Y
6 **Goodlatte**	Y	Y	Y	Y	Y	Y
7 **Brat**	Y	Y	Y	Y	Y	Y
8 Beyer	Y	Y	Y	Y	N	N
9 **Griffith**	N	Y	N	N	Y	Y
10 **Comstock**	Y	Y	Y	Y	Y	Y
11 Connolly	Y	Y	Y	Y	N	N
WASHINGTON						
1 DelBene	Y	Y	Y	Y	N	N
2 Larsen	Y	Y	Y	Y	N	N
3 **Herrera Beutler**	Y	Y	Y	Y	Y	Y
4 **Newhouse**	Y	Y	Y	Y	Y	Y
5 **McMorris Rodgers**	Y	Y	Y	Y	Y	Y
6 Kilmer	Y	Y	Y	Y	N	N
7 Jayapal	N	Y	Y	Y	N	N
8 **Reichert**	Y	Y	Y	Y	Y	Y
9 Smith	Y	Y	Y	Y	N	N
10 Heck	Y	Y	Y	Y	N	N
WEST VIRGINIA						
1 **McKinley**	Y	?	Y	Y	Y	Y
2 **Mooney**	Y	Y	Y	Y	Y	Y
3 **Jenkins**	+	Y	Y	Y	Y	Y
WISCONSIN						
1 **Ryan**						
2 Pocan	N	Y	Y	Y	N	N
3 Kind	Y	Y	Y	Y	N	N
4 Moore	N	Y	Y	Y	N	N
5 **Sensenbrenner**	Y	Y	Y	Y	Y	Y
6 **Grothman**	Y	Y	Y	Y	Y	Y
7 **Duffy**	Y	Y	Y	Y	Y	Y
8 **Gallagher**	Y	Y	Y	Y	Y	Y
WYOMING						
AL **Cheney**	Y	Y	Y	Y	Y	Y

VOTE NUMBER

236. PROCEDURAL MOTION/JOURNAL. Approval of the House Journal of June 5, 2018. Approved 219-177: R 141-79; D 78-98. June 6, 2018.

237. HR8. WATER INFRASTRUCTURE PROJECTS AUTHORIZATION/ RECOMMIT. Velazquez, D-N.Y., motion to recommit the bill to the House Transportation and Infrastructure Committee with instructions to report it back immediately with an amendment that would require the secretary of the Army to restore and improve the public infrastructure in the continental United States, Puerto Rico, and the U.S. Virgin Islands that was damaged as a result of Hurricane Harvey, Hurricane Irma or Hurricane Maria. Motion rejected 180-227: R 1-227; D 179-0. June 6, 2018.

238. HR8. WATER INFRASTRUCTURE PROJECTS AUTHORIZATION/ PASSAGE. Passage of the bill that would authorize nine new Army Corps of Engineers water resources projects, including navigation, flood control, harbor expansion and natural disaster damage projects. It would also deauthorize four projects, would authorize the corps to conduct feasibility studies for 12 possible projects, and would require the corps to expedite feasibility studies for more than 20 projects. It would require that most watershed assessments that take place after a major disaster be conducted at federal expense. It would require the corps to conduct a study on the ability of the corps to carry out its missions and the potential effects of transferring the corps from the Defense Department to another federal agency. Passed 408-2: R 227-2; D 181-0. June 6, 2018.

239. HR3249. LAW ENFORCEMENT PARTNERSHIP GRANTS/MOTION TO CONCUR. Goodlatte, R-Va., motion to concur in the Senate amendment to the bill that would establish a Project Safe Neighborhoods Block Grant Program within the Justice Department to create partnerships between local, state and federal law enforcement agencies to fight criminal street gangs. It would authorize $50 million a year from fiscal 2019 through fiscal 2021 for the program to assist law enforcement agencies in combating gang crimes, and to develop intervention and prevention initiatives. The bill would not contain a provision barring the authorization of funds for certain other Justice Department programs related to gun crime and gang violence. Motion agreed to 394-13: R 216-13; D 178-0. June 6, 2018.

240. HR5895. ANTICIPATED LEGISLATIVE VEHICLE FOR FISCAL 2019 ENERGY-WATER, LEGISLATIVE BRANCH, MIL CON-VA APPROPRIATIONS AND RESCISSIONS/PREVIOUS QUESTION. Burgess, R-Texas, motion to order the previous question (thus ending debate and possibility of amendment) on the the rule (H Res 923) that would provide for further House floor consideration of the bill (HR 5895) that would make certain appropriations for the fiscal year ending Sept. 30, 2019, and would provide for consideration the bill (HR 3) that would cancel approximately $14.8 billion in previously approved appropriations. Motion agreed to 227-185: R 227-1; D 0-184. June 7, 2018.

241. HR5895. LEGISLATIVE VEHICLE FOR FISCAL 2019 ENERGY-WATER, LEGISLATIVE BRANCH, MIL CON-VA APPROPRIATIONS AND RESCISSION OF APPROPRIATIONS/RULE. Adoption of the rule (H Res 923) that would provide for further House floor consideration of the bill (HR 5895) that would make certain appropriations for the fiscal year ending Sept. 30, 2019, and would provide for consideration of amendments to the Energy-Water, Legislative Branch and Military Construction-VA divisions of the bill, and would provide for consideration the bill (HR 3) that would cancel approximately $14.8 billion in previously approved appropriations. Adopted 225-187: R 225-3; D 0-184. June 7, 2018.

	236	237	238	239	240	241
ALABAMA						
1 **Byrne**	Y	N	Y	Y	Y	Y
2 **Roby**	?	N	Y	Y	Y	Y
3 **Rogers**	N	N	Y	Y	Y	Y
4 **Aderholt**	Y	N	Y	Y	Y	Y
5 **Brooks**	?	N	Y	Y	Y	Y
6 **Palmer**	N	N	Y	Y	Y	Y
7 Sewell	N	Y	Y	Y	N	N
ALASKA						
AL **Young**	N	N	Y	Y	Y	Y
ARIZONA						
1 O'Halleran	N	Y	Y	Y	N	N
2 **McSally**	N	N	Y	Y	Y	Y
3 Grijalva	N	Y	Y	Y	N	N
4 **Gosar**	N	N	Y	N	Y	Y
5 **Biggs**	N	N	Y	N	Y	Y
6 **Schweikert**	Y	N	Y	Y	Y	Y
7 Gallego	Y	+	Y	Y	N	N
8 **Lesko**	Y	N	Y	Y	Y	Y
9 Sinema	N	Y	Y	Y	N	N
ARKANSAS						
1 **Crawford**	Y	N	Y	Y	Y	Y
2 **Hill**	N	N	Y	Y	Y	Y
3 **Womack**	Y	N	Y	Y	Y	Y
4 **Westerman**	Y	N	Y	Y	Y	Y
CALIFORNIA						
1 **LaMalfa**	Y	N	Y	Y	Y	Y
2 Huffman	Y	Y	Y	Y	N	N
3 Garamendi	Y	Y	Y	Y	N	N
4 **McClintock**	Y	N	Y	N	Y	Y
5 Thompson	N	Y	Y	Y	N	N
6 Matsui	N	Y	Y	Y	N	N
7 Bera	N	Y	Y	Y	N	N
8 **Cook**	Y	N	Y	Y	Y	Y
9 McNerney	?	?	?	?	N	N
10 **Denham**	N	N	Y	Y	Y	Y
11 DeSaulnier	Y	Y	Y	Y	N	N
12 Pelosi	Y	Y	Y	Y	N	N
13 Lee	–	+	+	+	N	N
14 Speier	Y	Y	Y	Y	N	N
15 Swalwell	N	Y	Y	Y	N	N
16 Costa	N	Y	Y	Y	N	N
17 Khanna	N	Y	Y	Y	N	N
18 Eshoo	Y	Y	Y	Y	N	N
19 Lofgren	N	Y	Y	Y	N	N
20 Panetta	N	Y	Y	Y	N	N
21 **Valadao**	N	N	Y	Y	Y	Y
22 **Nunes**	Y	N	Y	Y	Y	Y
23 **McCarthy**	Y	N	Y	Y	Y	Y
24 Carbajal	N	Y	Y	Y	–	–
25 **Knight**	Y	N	Y	Y	Y	Y
26 Brownley	N	Y	Y	Y	N	N
27 Chu	Y	Y	Y	Y	N	N
28 Schiff	N	Y	Y	Y	N	N
29 Cardenas	?	Y	Y	Y	N	N
30 Sherman	+	+	+	+	N	N
31 Aguilar	Y	Y	Y	?	N	N
32 Napolitano	Y	Y	Y	Y	N	N
33 Lieu	N	Y	Y	Y	N	N
34 Gomez	?	Y	Y	Y	N	N
35 Torres	N	Y	Y	Y	N	N
36 Ruiz	N	Y	Y	Y	N	N
37 Bass	N	Y	Y	Y	N	N
38 Sánchez, Linda	?	Y	Y	Y	N	N
39 **Royce**	Y	N	Y	Y	Y	Y
40 Roybal-Allard	N	Y	Y	Y	N	N
41 Takano	Y	Y	Y	Y	N	N
42 **Calvert**	Y	N	Y	Y	Y	Y
43 Waters	?	?	?	?	N	N
44 Barragan	N	Y	Y	Y	N	N
45 **Walters**	Y	N	Y	Y	Y	Y
46 Correa	N	Y	Y	Y	N	N
47 Lowenthal	N	Y	Y	Y	N	N
48 **Rohrabacher**	?	N	Y	Y	Y	Y
49 **Issa**	Y	N	Y	Y	Y	Y
50 **Hunter**	?	N	Y	Y	Y	Y
51 Vargas	N	Y	Y	Y	?	?
52 Peters	Y	Y	Y	Y	N	N
53 Davis	Y	Y	Y	Y	N	N

	236	237	238	239	240	241
COLORADO						
1 DeGette	Y	Y	Y	Y	N	N
2 Polis	?	?	+	?	?	?
3 **Tipton**	N	N	Y	Y	Y	Y
4 **Buck**	N	N	Y	N	Y	Y
5 **Lamborn**	Y	N	Y	Y	Y	Y
6 **Coffman**	N	N	Y	Y	Y	Y
7 Perlmutter	?	?	+	+	N	N
CONNECTICUT						
1 Larson	Y	Y	Y	Y	N	N
2 Courtney	Y	Y	Y	Y	N	N
3 DeLauro	Y	Y	Y	Y	N	N
4 Himes	Y	Y	Y	Y	N	N
5 Esty	N	Y	Y	Y	N	N
DELAWARE						
AL Blunt Rochester	Y	Y	Y	Y	N	N
FLORIDA						
1 **Gaetz**	N	N	Y	N	Y	Y
2 **Dunn**	?	N	Y	Y	Y	Y
3 **Yoho**	N	N	Y	Y	Y	Y
4 **Rutherford**	N	N	Y	Y	Y	Y
5 Lawson	N	Y	Y	Y	N	N
6 **DeSantis**	N	N	Y	Y	Y	Y
7 Murphy	Y	Y	Y	Y	N	N
8 **Posey**	Y	Y	Y	Y	Y	Y
9 Soto	N	Y	Y	Y	N	N
10 Demings	Y	Y	Y	Y	N	N
11 **Webster**	Y	N	Y	Y	Y	Y
12 **Bilirakis**	+	+	+	+	+	+
13 Crist	N	Y	Y	Y	N	N
14 Castor	N	Y	Y	Y	N	N
15 **Ross**	Y	N	Y	Y	Y	Y
16 **Buchanan**	Y	N	Y	Y	Y	Y
17 **Rooney, T.**	Y	N	Y	Y	Y	Y
18 **Mast**	N	N	Y	Y	Y	Y
19 **Rooney, F.**	Y	N	Y	Y	Y	Y
20 Hastings	N	Y	Y	Y	N	N
21 Frankel	Y	Y	Y	Y	N	N
22 Deutch	Y	Y	Y	Y	N	N
23 Wasserman Schultz	Y	Y	Y	Y	N	N
24 Wilson	–	+	+	+	N	?
25 **Diaz-Balart**	N	N	Y	Y	Y	Y
26 **Curbelo**	N	N	Y	Y	Y	Y
27 **Ros-Lehtinen**	N	N	Y	Y	Y	Y
GEORGIA						
1 **Carter**	N	N	Y	Y	Y	Y
2 Bishop	N	Y	Y	N	N	N
3 **Ferguson**	N	N	Y	Y	Y	Y
4 Johnson	Y	Y	Y	Y	N	N
5 Lewis	N	Y	Y	Y	N	N
6 **Handel**	Y	N	Y	Y	Y	Y
7 **Woodall**	N	N	Y	Y	Y	Y
8 **Scott, A.**	Y	N	Y	Y	Y	Y
9 **Collins**	?	N	Y	Y	Y	Y
10 **Hice**	N	N	Y	Y	Y	Y
11 **Loudermilk**	Y	N	Y	Y	Y	Y
12 **Allen**	Y	N	Y	Y	Y	Y
13 Scott, D.	Y	Y	Y	N	N	N
14 **Graves**	N	N	Y	Y	Y	Y
HAWAII						
1 Hanabusa	Y	Y	Y	Y	N	N
2 Gabbard	Y	Y	Y	Y	N	N
IDAHO						
1 **Labrador**	Y	N	Y	N	Y	Y
2 **Simpson**	Y	N	Y	Y	Y	Y
ILLINOIS						
1 Rush	N	Y	Y	Y	N	N
2 Kelly	N	Y	Y	Y	N	N
3 Lipinski	Y	Y	Y	Y	N	N
4 Gutierrez	?	Y	Y	Y	N	N
5 Quigley	N	Y	Y	Y	N	N
6 **Roskam**	N	N	Y	Y	Y	Y
7 Davis, D.	Y	?	Y	Y	–	–
8 Krishnamoorthi	Y	Y	Y	Y	N	N
9 Schakowsky	N	Y	Y	Y	N	N
10 Schneider	Y	Y	Y	Y	N	N
11 Foster	Y	Y	Y	Y	N	N
12 **Bost**	N	N	Y	Y	Y	Y
13 **Davis, R.**	Y	N	Y	Y	Y	Y

	236	237	238	239	240	241
14 **Hultgren**	Y	N	Y	Y	Y	Y
15 **Shimkus**	Y	N	Y	Y	Y	Y
16 **Kinzinger**	N	N	Y	Y	Y	Y
17 Bustos	Y	Y	Y	Y	N	N
18 **LaHood**	N	N	Y	Y	Y	Y
INDIANA						
1 Visclosky	N	Y	Y	Y	N	N
2 **Walorski**	Y	N	Y	Y	Y	Y
3 **Banks**	Y	N	Y	Y	Y	Y
4 **Rokita**	N	N	Y	Y	Y	?
5 **Brooks**	Y	N	Y	Y	Y	Y
6 **Messer**	Y	N	Y	Y	Y	Y
7 Carson	N	Y	Y	Y	N	N
8 **Bucshon**	Y	N	Y	Y	Y	Y
9 **Hollingsworth**	Y	N	Y	Y	Y	Y
IOWA						
1 **Blum**	Y	N	Y	Y	Y	Y
2 Loebsack	N	Y	Y	Y	N	N
3 **Young**	Y	N	Y	Y	Y	Y
4 **King**	Y	N	Y	Y	Y	Y
KANSAS						
1 **Marshall**	Y	N	Y	Y	Y	Y
2 **Jenkins**	N	N	Y	Y	Y	Y
3 **Yoder**	N	N	Y	Y	Y	Y
4 **Estes**	Y	N	Y	Y	Y	Y
KENTUCKY						
1 **Comer**	N	N	Y	Y	Y	Y
2 **Guthrie**	Y	N	Y	Y	Y	Y
3 Yarmuth	Y	Y	Y	Y	N	N
4 **Massie**	Y	N	Y	N	Y	N
5 **Rogers**	Y	N	Y	Y	Y	Y
6 **Barr**	Y	N	Y	Y	Y	Y
LOUISIANA						
1 **Scalise**	Y	N	Y	Y	Y	Y
2 Richmond	N	Y	Y	P	N	N
3 **Higgins**	Y	N	Y	Y	Y	Y
4 **Johnson**	Y	N	Y	Y	Y	Y
5 **Abraham**	Y	N	Y	Y	Y	Y
6 **Graves**	N	N	Y	Y	Y	Y
MAINE						
1 Pingree	Y	Y	Y	Y	N	N
2 **Poliquin**	N	N	Y	Y	+	Y
MARYLAND						
1 **Harris**	Y	N	Y	Y	Y	Y
2 Ruppersberger	Y	Y	Y	Y	N	N
3 Sarbanes	N	Y	Y	Y	N	N
4 Brown	Y	Y	Y	Y	N	N
5 Hoyer	N	Y	Y	Y	N	N
6 Delaney	N	Y	Y	Y	N	N
7 Cummings	Y	Y	Y	Y	N	N
8 Raskin	N	Y	Y	Y	N	N
MASSACHUSETTS						
1 Neal	N	Y	Y	Y	N	N
2 McGovern	N	Y	Y	Y	N	N
3 Tsongas	Y	Y	Y	Y	N	N
4 Kennedy	Y	Y	Y	Y	N	N
5 Clark	N	Y	Y	Y	N	N
6 Moulton	Y	Y	Y	Y	N	N
7 Capuano	N	Y	Y	Y	N	N
8 Lynch	?	?	?	?	?	?
9 Keating	N	Y	Y	Y	N	N
MICHIGAN						
1 **Bergman**	N	N	Y	Y	Y	Y
2 **Huizenga**	N	N	Y	Y	Y	Y
3 *Amash*	N	N	N	N	Y	N
4 **Moolenaar**	N	N	Y	Y	Y	Y
5 Kildee	Y	Y	Y	Y	N	N
6 **Upton**	N	N	Y	Y	Y	Y
7 **Walberg**	N	N	Y	Y	Y	Y
8 **Bishop**	?	?	?	?	Y	Y
9 Levin	N	Y	Y	Y	N	N
10 **Mitchell**	N	N	Y	Y	Y	Y
11 **Trott**	Y	N	Y	Y	Y	Y
12 Dingell	Y	Y	Y	Y	N	N
14 Lawrence	N	Y	Y	Y	N	N
MINNESOTA						
1 Walz	?	?	?	?	?	?
2 **Lewis**	Y	N	Y	Y	Y	Y
3 **Paulsen**	N	N	Y	Y	Y	Y
4 McCollum	Y	Y	Y	Y	N	N
5 Ellison	?	?	?	?	N	N
6 **Emmer**	Y	N	Y	Y	Y	Y
7 Peterson	N	Y	Y	Y	N	N
8 Nolan	N	Y	Y	Y	N	N
MISSISSIPPI						
1 **Kelly**	Y	N	Y	Y	Y	Y
2 Thompson	N	Y	Y	Y	?	N
3 **Harper**	Y	N	Y	Y	Y	Y
4 **Palazzo**	?	?	?	?	?	?
MISSOURI						
1 Clay	Y	Y	Y	Y	N	N
2 **Wagner**	Y	N	Y	Y	Y	Y
3 **Luetkemeyer**	Y	N	Y	Y	Y	Y
4 **Hartzler**	Y	N	Y	Y	Y	Y
5 Cleaver	N	Y	Y	Y	N	N
6 **Graves**	N	N	Y	Y	Y	Y
7 **Long**	Y	N	Y	Y	Y	Y
8 **Smith**	Y	N	Y	Y	Y	Y
MONTANA						
AL **Gianforte**	Y	N	Y	Y	Y	Y
NEBRASKA						
1 **Fortenberry**	?	?	?	?	?	?
2 **Bacon**	Y	N	Y	Y	Y	Y
3 **Smith**	Y	N	Y	Y	Y	Y
NEVADA						
1 Titus	Y	Y	Y	Y	N	N
2 **Amodei**	Y	N	Y	Y	Y	Y
3 Rosen	N	Y	Y	Y	N	N
4 Kihuen	N	Y	Y	Y	N	N
NEW HAMPSHIRE						
1 Shea-Porter	Y	Y	Y	Y	N	N
2 Kuster	Y	Y	Y	Y	N	N
NEW JERSEY						
1 Norcross	N	Y	Y	Y	N	N
2 **LoBiondo**	N	N	Y	Y	Y	Y
3 **MacArthur**	N	N	Y	Y	Y	Y
4 **Smith**	Y	N	Y	Y	Y	Y
5 Gottheimer	N	Y	Y	Y	N	N
6 Pallone	N	Y	Y	Y	N	N
7 **Lance**	N	N	Y	Y	Y	Y
8 Sires	N	Y	Y	Y	N	N
9 Pascrell	Y	Y	Y	Y	N	N
10 Payne	N	Y	Y	Y	N	N
11 **Frelinghuysen**	Y	N	Y	Y	Y	Y
12 Watson Coleman	N	Y	Y	Y	N	N
NEW MEXICO						
1 Lujan Grisham	?	Y	Y	Y	N	N
2 **Pearce**	N	N	Y	Y	Y	Y
3 Luján	N	Y	Y	Y	N	N
NEW YORK						
1 **Zeldin**	Y	N	Y	Y	Y	Y
2 **King**	Y	N	Y	Y	Y	Y
3 Suozzi	N	Y	Y	Y	N	N
4 Rice	N	Y	Y	Y	N	N
5 Meeks	Y	Y	Y	Y	N	N
6 Meng	Y	Y	Y	Y	N	N
7 Velázquez	N	Y	Y	Y	N	N
8 Jeffries	Y	Y	Y	Y	N	N
9 Clarke	N	Y	Y	Y	N	N
10 Nadler	Y	Y	Y	Y	N	N
11 **Donovan**	Y	N	Y	Y	Y	Y
12 Maloney, C.	N	Y	Y	Y	N	N
13 Espaillat	N	Y	Y	Y	N	N
14 Crowley	N	Y	Y	Y	N	N
15 Serrano	N	Y	Y	Y	N	N
16 Engel	Y	Y	Y	Y	N	N
17 Lowey	N	Y	Y	P	N	N
18 Maloney, S.P.	N	Y	Y	Y	N	N
19 **Faso**	N	N	Y	Y	Y	Y
20 Tonko	P	Y	Y	Y	N	N
21 **Stefanik**	Y	N	Y	Y	Y	Y
22 **Tenney**	N	N	Y	Y	Y	Y
23 **Reed**	N	N	Y	Y	Y	Y
24 **Katko**	Y	N	Y	Y	Y	Y
25 **Vacant**						
26 Higgins	Y	Y	Y	Y	N	N
27 **Collins**	Y	N	Y	Y	Y	Y
NORTH CAROLINA						
1 Butterfield	Y	Y	Y	Y	N	N
2 **Holding**	N	N	Y	Y	Y	Y
3 **Jones**	N	N	N	N	N	N
4 Price	N	Y	Y	Y	N	N
5 **Foxx**	N	N	Y	Y	Y	Y
6 **Walker**	Y	N	Y	Y	Y	Y
7 **Rouzer**	N	N	Y	Y	Y	Y
8 **Hudson**	N	N	Y	Y	Y	Y
9 **Pittenger**	?	N	Y	Y	Y	Y
9 **Vacant**						
10 **McHenry**	Y	N	Y	Y	Y	Y
11 **Meadows**	Y	N	Y	Y	Y	Y
12 Adams	N	Y	Y	Y	N	N
13 **Budd**	Y	N	Y	Y	Y	Y
NORTH DAKOTA						
AL **Cramer**	Y	N	Y	Y	Y	Y
OHIO						
1 **Chabot**	Y	N	Y	Y	Y	Y
2 **Wenstrup**	N	N	Y	Y	Y	Y
3 Beatty	–	–	+	+	–	–
4 **Jordan**	N	N	Y	N	Y	Y
5 **Latta**	N	N	Y	Y	Y	Y
6 **Johnson**	N	N	Y	Y	Y	Y
7 **Gibbs**	N	N	Y	Y	Y	Y
8 **Davidson**	Y	N	Y	Y	Y	Y
9 Kaptur	Y	Y	Y	Y	N	N
10 **Turner**	Y	N	Y	Y	Y	Y
11 Fudge	N	Y	Y	Y	N	N
12 **Vacant**						
13 Ryan	N	Y	Y	Y	N	N
14 **Joyce**	Y	N	Y	Y	Y	Y
15 **Stivers**	Y	N	Y	Y	Y	Y
16 **Renacci**	N	N	Y	Y	Y	Y
OKLAHOMA						
1 **Vacant**						
2 **Mullin**	Y	N	Y	Y	Y	Y
3 **Lucas**	Y	N	Y	Y	Y	Y
4 **Cole**	Y	N	Y	Y	Y	Y
5 **Russell**	Y	N	Y	Y	Y	Y
OREGON						
1 Bonamici	Y	Y	Y	Y	N	N
2 **Walden**	Y	N	Y	Y	Y	Y
3 Blumenauer	Y	Y	Y	Y	N	N
4 DeFazio	N	+	+	+	N	N
5 Schrader	N	Y	Y	Y	N	N
PENNSYLVANIA						
1 Brady	N	Y	Y	Y	N	N
2 Evans	N	Y	Y	Y	N	N
3 **Kelly**	Y	N	Y	Y	Y	Y
4 **Perry**	N	N	Y	N	Y	Y
5 **Thompson**	N	N	Y	Y	Y	Y
6 **Costello**	Y	N	Y	Y	Y	Y
7 **Vacant**						
8 **Fitzpatrick**	N	N	Y	Y	Y	Y
9 **Shuster**	Y	N	Y	Y	Y	Y
10 **Marino**	Y	N	Y	Y	Y	Y
11 **Barletta**	Y	N	Y	Y	Y	Y
12 **Rothfus**	Y	N	Y	Y	Y	Y
13 Boyle	N	Y	Y	Y	+	+
14 Doyle	N	Y	Y	Y	N	N
15 **Vacant**						
16 **Smucker**	Y	N	Y	Y	Y	Y
17 Cartwright	Y	Y	Y	Y	N	N
18 Lamb	Y	Y	Y	Y	N	N
RHODE ISLAND						
1 Cicilline	Y	Y	Y	Y	N	N
2 Langevin	N	Y	Y	Y	N	N
SOUTH CAROLINA						
1 **Sanford**	Y	N	Y	N	Y	Y
2 **Wilson**	Y	N	Y	Y	Y	Y
3 **Duncan**	N	N	Y	Y	Y	Y
4 **Gowdy**	Y	N	Y	Y	Y	Y
5 **Norman**	Y	N	Y	Y	Y	Y
6 Clyburn	Y	Y	Y	Y	N	N
7 **Rice**	Y	N	Y	Y	Y	Y
SOUTH DAKOTA						
AL **Noem**	?	?	?	?	?	?
TENNESSEE						
1 **Roe**	N	N	Y	Y	Y	Y
2 **Duncan**	Y	N	Y	Y	Y	Y
3 **Fleischmann**	Y	N	Y	Y	Y	Y
4 **DesJarlais**	N	N	Y	Y	Y	Y
5 Cooper	Y	Y	Y	Y	N	N
6 **Black**	Y	N	Y	Y	Y	Y
7 **Blackburn**	N	N	Y	Y	Y	Y
8 **Kustoff**	Y	N	Y	Y	Y	Y
9 Cohen	N	Y	Y	Y	N	N
TEXAS						
1 **Gohmert**	N	N	Y	N	Y	Y
2 **Poe**	N	N	Y	Y	Y	Y
3 **Johnson, S.**	Y	N	Y	Y	Y	Y
4 **Ratcliffe**	?	N	Y	Y	Y	Y
5 **Hensarling**	Y	N	Y	Y	Y	Y
6 **Barton**	Y	N	Y	Y	Y	Y
7 **Culberson**	Y	N	Y	Y	Y	Y
8 **Brady**	?	N	Y	Y	Y	Y
9 Green, A.	N	Y	Y	Y	N	N
10 **McCaul**	Y	N	Y	Y	Y	Y
11 **Conaway**	N	N	Y	Y	Y	Y
12 **Granger**	Y	?	Y	Y	Y	Y
13 **Thornberry**	Y	N	Y	Y	Y	Y
14 **Weber**	Y	N	Y	Y	Y	Y
15 Gonzalez	Y	Y	Y	Y	N	N
16 O'Rourke	Y	Y	Y	Y	N	N
17 **Flores**	Y	N	Y	Y	?	?
18 Jackson Lee	N	Y	Y	Y	N	N
19 **Arrington**	Y	N	Y	Y	Y	Y
20 Castro	Y	Y	Y	Y	N	N
21 **Smith**	Y	N	Y	Y	Y	Y
22 **Olson**	Y	N	Y	Y	Y	Y
23 **Hurd**	N	N	Y	Y	Y	Y
24 **Marchant**	Y	N	Y	Y	Y	Y
25 **Williams**	Y	N	Y	Y	Y	Y
26 **Burgess**	N	N	Y	Y	Y	Y
28 Cuellar	N	Y	Y	Y	N	N
29 Green, G.	N	Y	Y	Y	N	N
30 Johnson, E.B.	Y	Y	Y	Y	N	N
31 **Carter**	Y	N	Y	Y	Y	Y
32 **Sessions**	Y	N	Y	Y	Y	Y
33 Veasey	N	Y	Y	Y	N	N
34 Vela	Y	Y	Y	Y	N	N
35 Doggett	Y	Y	Y	Y	N	N
36 **Babin**	Y	N	Y	Y	Y	Y
UTAH						
1 **Bishop**	Y	N	Y	Y	Y	Y
2 **Stewart**	Y	N	Y	Y	Y	Y
3 **Curtis**	Y	N	Y	Y	Y	Y
4 **Love**	Y	N	Y	Y	Y	Y
VERMONT						
AL Welch	Y	Y	Y	Y	N	N
VIRGINIA						
1 **Wittman**	Y	N	Y	Y	Y	Y
2 **Taylor**	N	N	Y	Y	Y	Y
3 Scott	N	Y	Y	Y	N	N
4 McEachin	Y	Y	Y	Y	N	N
5 **Garrett**	Y	N	Y	Y	Y	Y
6 **Goodlatte**	Y	N	Y	Y	Y	Y
7 **Brat**	Y	N	Y	Y	Y	Y
8 Beyer	N	Y	Y	Y	N	N
9 **Griffith**	Y	N	Y	Y	Y	Y
10 **Comstock**	Y	N	Y	Y	Y	Y
11 Connolly	N	Y	Y	Y	N	N
WASHINGTON						
1 DelBene	Y	Y	Y	Y	N	N
2 Larsen	Y	Y	Y	Y	N	N
3 **Herrera Beutler**	N	N	Y	Y	Y	Y
4 **Newhouse**	Y	N	Y	Y	Y	Y
5 **McMorris Rodgers**	Y	N	Y	Y	Y	Y
6 Kilmer	N	Y	Y	Y	N	N
7 Jayapal	N	Y	Y	Y	N	N
8 **Reichert**	Y	N	Y	Y	Y	Y
9 Smith	Y	Y	Y	Y	N	N
10 Heck	Y	Y	Y	Y	N	N
WEST VIRGINIA						
1 **McKinley**	N	N	Y	Y	Y	Y
2 **Mooney**	Y	N	Y	Y	Y	Y
3 **Jenkins**	N	N	Y	Y	Y	Y
WISCONSIN						
1 **Ryan**						
2 Pocan	Y	Y	Y	Y	N	N
3 Kind	N	Y	Y	Y	N	N
4 Moore	N	Y	Y	Y	N	N
5 **Sensenbrenner**	Y	N	Y	Y	Y	Y
6 **Grothman**	N	N	Y	Y	Y	Y
7 **Duffy**	Y	N	Y	Y	Y	Y
8 **Gallagher**	N	N	Y	Y	Y	Y
WYOMING						
AL **Cheney**	Y	N	Y	Y	Y	Y

VOTE NUMBER

242. PROCEDURAL MOTION/JOURNAL. Approval of the House Journal of June 6, 2018. Approved 213-197: R 133-93; D 80-104. June 7, 2018.

243. HR3. RESCISSION OF APPROPRIATIONS/PASSAGE. Passage of the bill that would cancel approximately $14.8 billion in previously approved spending, including reductions in budget authority for mandatory programs. It would rescind allocated funding across various departments and programs, including $7 billion from the Children's Health Insurance Program, $4.3 billion from the Energy Department?s Advanced Technology Vehicles Manufacturing Loan Program, $683 million from Innovative Technology Loan Guarantees, and $800 million in mandatory funding from the Center for Medicare and Medicaid Innovation. It would not rescind any of the funding provided by the fiscal 2018 omnibus appropriations measure. Passed 210-206: R 210-19; D 0-187. June 7, 2018.

244. HR5895. LEGISLATIVE VEHICLE FOR FISCAL 2019 ENERGY-WATER, LEGISLATIVE BRANCH, MIL CON-VA APPROPRIATIONS/RENEWABLE ENERGY ACTIVITIES. Tsongas, D-Mass., amendment that would increase funding for energy efficiency and renewable energy activities at the Energy Department by $5 million and would decrease funding for the salaries and expenses at the Energy Department by the same amount. Rejected in Committee of the Whole 201-217: R 23-208; D 178-9. June 7, 2018.

245. HR5895. LEGISLATIVE VEHICLE FOR FISCAL 2019 ENERGY-WATER, LEGISLATIVE BRANCH, MILITARY CONSTRUCTION-VA APPROPRIATIONS/ADVANCED RESEARCH PROJECTS FUNDING INCREASE. Beyer, D-Va., amendment that would decrease funding for fossil energy research and development at the Energy Department by $28.3 million, and would increase funding for advanced research projects at the department by the same amount. Rejected in Committee of the Whole 204-214: R 24-207; D 180-7. June 7, 2018.

246. HR5895. LEGISLATIVE VEHICLE FOR FISCAL 2019 ENERGY-WATER, LEGISLATIVE BRANCH, MILITARY CONSTRUCTION-VA APPROPRIATIONS/ADVANCED RESEARCH PROJECTS FUNDING ELIMINATION. Gosar, R-Ariz., amendment that would eliminate all funding for the Energy Department's Advanced Research Project Agency, and would allocate $325 million to the spending reduction account. Rejected in Committee of the Whole 123-295: R 123-108; D 0-187. June 7, 2018.

247. HR5895. LEGISLATIVE VEHICLE FOR FISCAL 2019 ENERGY-WATER, LEGISLATIVE BRANCH, MILITARY CONSTRUCTION-VA APPROPRIATIONS/NUCLEAR NONPROLIFERATION ACTIVITIES. Lee, D-Calif., amendment that would decrease funding for atomic energy defense weapons activities at the National Nuclear Security Administration by $65 million, and would increase funding for NNSA defense nuclear nonproliferation activities by that same amount. Rejected in Committee of the Whole 177-241: R 5-226; D 172-15. June 7, 2018.

	242	243	244	245	246	247
ALABAMA						
1 **Byrne**	Y	Y	N	N	Y	N
2 **Roby**	Y	Y	N	N	N	N
3 **Rogers**	N	Y	N	N	Y	N
4 **Aderholt**	Y	Y	N	N	Y	N
5 **Brooks**	N	Y	N	N	Y	N
6 **Palmer**	N	Y	N	N	Y	N
7 Sewell	Y	–	+	+	–	+
ALASKA						
AL **Young**	N	Y	N	N	N	N
ARIZONA						
1 O'Halleran	N	N	Y	Y	N	N
2 **McSally**	N	Y	N	N	N	N
3 Grijalva	N	N	Y	Y	N	Y
4 **Gosar**	N	Y	N	N	Y	N
5 **Biggs**	N	Y	N	N	Y	N
6 **Schweikert**	Y	Y	N	N	Y	N
7 Gallego	N	N	Y	Y	N	Y
8 **Lesko**	Y	Y	N	N	Y	N
9 Sinema	N	N	Y	N	N	N
ARKANSAS						
1 **Crawford**	Y	Y	N	N	N	N
2 **Hill**	N	Y	N	N	N	N
3 **Womack**	Y	Y	N	N	N	N
4 **Westerman**	Y	Y	N	Y	N	N
CALIFORNIA						
1 **LaMalfa**	Y	Y	N	N	N	N
2 Huffman	Y	N	Y	Y	N	Y
3 Garamendi	Y	N	Y	Y	N	Y
4 **McClintock**	Y	Y	N	N	Y	N
5 Thompson	N	N	Y	Y	N	Y
6 Matsui	N	N	Y	Y	N	Y
7 Bera	N	N	Y	Y	N	Y
8 **Cook**	Y	Y	N	N	Y	N
9 McNerney	Y	N	Y	Y	N	Y
10 **Denham**	N	Y	N	N	N	N
11 DeSaulnier	Y	N	Y	Y	N	Y
12 Pelosi	Y	N	Y	Y	N	Y
13 Lee	N	N	Y	Y	N	Y
14 Speier	Y	N	Y	Y	N	Y
15 Swalwell	N	N	Y	Y	N	Y
16 Costa	N	N	Y	N	N	Y
17 Khanna	N	N	Y	Y	N	Y
18 Eshoo	N	N	Y	Y	N	Y
19 Lofgren	N	N	Y	Y	N	Y
20 Panetta	Y	N	Y	Y	N	Y
21 **Valadao**	N	Y	N	N	N	N
22 **Nunes**	Y	Y	N	N	Y	N
23 **McCarthy**	Y	Y	N	N	N	N
24 Carbajal	–	–	+	+	–	+
25 **Knight**	N	Y	N	N	Y	N
26 Brownley	N	N	Y	Y	N	Y
27 Chu	Y	N	Y	Y	N	Y
28 Schiff	N	N	Y	Y	N	Y
29 Cardenas	N	N	Y	Y	N	Y
30 Sherman	Y	N	Y	Y	N	Y
31 Aguilar	N	N	Y	Y	N	Y
32 Napolitano	N	N	Y	Y	N	Y
33 Lieu	N	N	Y	Y	N	Y
34 Gomez	N	N	Y	Y	N	Y
35 Torres	N	N	Y	Y	N	Y
36 Ruiz	N	N	Y	Y	N	Y
37 Bass	N	N	Y	Y	N	Y
38 Sánchez, Linda	N	N	Y	Y	N	Y
39 **Royce**	Y	Y	N	N	N	N
40 Roybal-Allard	N	N	Y	Y	N	Y
41 Takano	N	N	Y	Y	N	Y
42 **Calvert**	Y	Y	N	N	N	N
43 Waters	Y	N	Y	Y	N	Y
44 Barragan	N	N	Y	Y	N	Y
45 **Walters**	Y	?	?	?	?	?
46 Correa	N	N	Y	N	N	Y
47 Lowenthal	Y	N	Y	Y	N	Y
48 **Rohrabacher**	Y	Y	N	Y	N	Y
49 **Issa**	Y	Y	N	N	Y	N
50 **Hunter**	N	Y	N	N	Y	N
51 Vargas	?	?	?	?	?	?
52 Peters	Y	N	Y	Y	N	Y
53 Davis	Y	N	Y	N	N	Y

	242	243	244	245	246	247
COLORADO						
1 DeGette	Y	N	Y	Y	N	Y
2 Polis	?	–	?	?	?	?
3 **Tipton**	N	Y	N	N	N	N
4 **Buck**	N	Y	N	N	N	N
5 **Lamborn**	Y	Y	N	N	Y	N
6 **Coffman**	N	Y	N	Y	N	N
7 Perlmutter	Y	N	Y	Y	N	Y
CONNECTICUT						
1 Larson	Y	N	Y	Y	N	Y
2 Courtney	Y	N	Y	Y	N	Y
3 DeLauro	Y	N	Y	Y	N	Y
4 Himes	Y	N	Y	Y	N	Y
5 Esty	N	N	Y	Y	N	Y
DELAWARE						
AL Blunt Rochester	Y	N	Y	Y	N	Y
FLORIDA						
1 **Gaetz**	N	Y	N	N	N	N
2 **Dunn**	Y	Y	N	N	Y	N
3 Yoho	N	Y	N	N	Y	N
4 **Rutherford**	Y	Y	N	N	Y	N
5 Lawson	N	N	Y	Y	N	Y
6 **DeSantis**	N	Y	N	Y	N	N
7 Murphy	Y	N	Y	Y	N	Y
8 **Posey**	Y	Y	N	N	Y	N
9 Soto	N	N	Y	Y	N	Y
10 Demings	Y	N	Y	Y	N	Y
11 **Webster**	Y	Y	N	N	Y	N
12 **Bilirakis**	+	Y	N	N	Y	N
13 Crist	N	N	Y	Y	N	Y
14 Castor	N	N	Y	Y	N	Y
15 **Ross**	Y	Y	N	N	N	N
16 **Buchanan**	Y	N	N	N	N	N
17 **Rooney, T.**	Y	Y	N	N	N	N
18 **Mast**	N	N	Y	N	N	N
19 **Rooney, F.**	Y	Y	N	N	N	N
20 Hastings	N	N	Y	Y	N	Y
21 Frankel	Y	N	Y	Y	N	Y
22 Deutch	Y	N	Y	Y	N	Y
23 Wasserman Schultz	Y	N	Y	Y	N	Y
24 Wilson	N	N	Y	Y	N	Y
25 **Diaz-Balart**	N	N	N	N	N	N
26 **Curbelo**	N	N	Y	Y	N	N
27 **Ros-Lehtinen**	N	N	Y	Y	N	N
GEORGIA						
1 **Carter**	N	Y	N	N	Y	N
2 Bishop	N	N	Y	N	N	N
3 **Ferguson**	N	Y	N	N	N	N
4 Johnson	N	N	Y	Y	N	Y
5 Lewis	N	N	Y	Y	N	Y
6 **Handel**	Y	Y	N	N	Y	N
7 **Woodall**	N	Y	N	N	N	N
8 **Scott, A.**	?	Y	N	N	N	N
9 **Collins**	Y	Y	N	N	Y	N
10 **Hice**	N	Y	N	N	Y	N
11 **Loudermilk**	Y	Y	N	N	Y	N
12 **Allen**	Y	Y	N	?	N	?
13 Scott, D.	Y	N	Y	Y	N	Y
14 **Graves**	N	Y	N	N	Y	N
HAWAII						
1 Hanabusa	N	N	Y	Y	N	Y
2 Gabbard	Y	N	Y	Y	N	Y
IDAHO						
1 **Labrador**	?	Y	N	N	Y	N
2 **Simpson**	Y	Y	N	N	N	N
ILLINOIS						
1 Rush	N	N	Y	Y	N	Y
2 Kelly	N	N	Y	Y	N	Y
3 Lipinski	Y	N	Y	Y	N	Y
4 Gutierrez	N	N	Y	Y	N	Y
5 Quigley	N	N	Y	Y	N	Y
6 **Roskam**	N	N	N	N	N	N
7 Davis, D.	+	N	Y	Y	N	Y
8 Krishnamoorthi	Y	N	Y	Y	N	Y
9 Schakowsky	N	N	Y	Y	N	Y
10 Schneider	N	N	Y	Y	N	Y
11 Foster	Y	N	Y	Y	N	Y
12 **Bost**	N	Y	N	N	N	N
13 **Davis, R.**	Y	Y	N	N	Y	N

Y Voted for (yea)	X Paired against	C Voted "present" to avoid possible conflict of interest
# Paired for	– Announced against	
+ Announced for	P Voted "present"	? Did not vote or otherwise make a position known
N Voted against (nay)		

	242	243	244	245	246	247
14 **Hultgren**	Y	Y	N	N	N	N
15 **Shimkus**	Y	?	N	N	N	N
16 **Kinzinger**	N	Y	N	Y	N	N
17 Bustos	Y	N	Y	Y	N	Y
18 **LaHood**	N	Y	N	N	Y	N
INDIANA						
1 Visclosky	N	N	Y	Y	N	Y
2 **Walorski**	Y	N	N	N	Y	N
3 **Banks**	Y	Y	N	N	Y	N
4 **Rokita**	Y	Y	N	N	Y	N
5 **Brooks**	Y	Y	N	N	N	N
6 **Messer**	Y	Y	N	N	Y	N
7 Carson	Y	N	Y	Y	N	Y
8 **Bucshon**	Y	Y	N	N	Y	N
9 **Hollingsworth**	Y	Y	Y	N	Y	N
IOWA						
1 **Blum**	N	Y	N	N	Y	N
2 Loebsack	N	N	Y	Y	N	Y
3 **Young**	Y	Y	N	Y	N	N
4 **King**	Y	Y	Y	N	N	N
KANSAS						
1 **Marshall**	N	Y	N	N	N	N
2 **Jenkins**	N	Y	N	N	Y	N
3 **Yoder**	N	N	N	N	Y	N
4 **Estes**	Y	Y	N	N	Y	N
KENTUCKY						
1 **Comer**	Y	Y	N	N	Y	N
2 **Guthrie**	Y	Y	N	N	Y	N
3 Yarmuth	Y	N	Y	Y	N	Y
4 **Massie**	Y	Y	N	N	Y	N
5 **Rogers**	Y	Y	N	N	N	N
6 **Barr**	N	Y	N	N	Y	N
LOUISIANA						
1 **Scalise**	Y	Y	N	N	Y	N
2 Richmond	N	N	Y	Y	N	Y
3 **Higgins**	Y	Y	N	N	Y	N
4 **Johnson**	Y	Y	N	N	Y	N
5 **Abraham**	Y	Y	N	N	Y	N
6 **Graves**	N	Y	Y	N	Y	N
MAINE						
1 Pingree	Y	N	Y	Y	N	Y
2 **Poliquin**	N	Y	Y	N	N	N
MARYLAND						
1 **Harris**	Y	Y	N	N	Y	N
2 Ruppersberger	Y	N	Y	Y	N	N
3 Sarbanes	N	N	Y	Y	N	Y
4 Brown	Y	N	Y	Y	N	Y
5 Hoyer	N	N	Y	Y	N	Y
6 Delaney	N	N	Y	Y	N	Y
7 Cummings	N	N	Y	Y	N	Y
8 Raskin	N	N	Y	Y	N	Y
MASSACHUSETTS						
1 Neal	N	N	Y	Y	N	Y
2 McGovern	N	N	Y	Y	N	Y
3 Tsongas	Y	N	Y	Y	N	Y
4 Kennedy	Y	N	Y	Y	N	N
5 Clark	N	N	Y	Y	N	Y
6 Moulton	Y	N	Y	Y	N	Y
7 Capuano	N	N	Y	Y	N	Y
8 Lynch	?	N	Y	Y	N	Y
9 Keating	N	N	Y	Y	N	Y
MICHIGAN						
1 **Bergman**	N	Y	N	N	N	N
2 **Huizenga**	N	Y	N	N	Y	N
3 *Amash*	N	Y	N	N	Y	Y
4 **Moolenaar**	Y	Y	N	N	N	N
5 Kildee	Y	N	Y	Y	N	Y
6 **Upton**	N	N	Y	N	N	N
7 **Walberg**	N	Y	N	N	Y	N
8 **Bishop**	N	Y	N	N	Y	N
9 Levin	N	N	Y	Y	N	Y
10 **Mitchell**	Y	Y	N	N	N	N
11 **Trott**	Y	Y	N	N	N	N
12 Dingell	Y	N	Y	Y	N	Y
14 Lawrence	Y	N	Y	Y	N	Y
MINNESOTA						
1 Walz	?	?	?	?	?	?
2 **Lewis**	Y	Y	N	N	Y	N
3 **Paulsen**	N	Y	N	Y	N	N
4 McCollum	Y	N	Y	Y	N	Y

	242	243	244	245	246	247
5 Ellison	Y	N	Y	Y	N	Y
6 **Emmer**	N	Y	N	N	Y	N
7 Peterson	N	N	Y	N	N	N
8 Nolan	N	N	Y	Y	N	Y
MISSISSIPPI						
1 **Kelly**	Y	Y	N	N	Y	N
2 Thompson	N	N	Y	Y	N	Y
3 **Harper**	Y	Y	N	N	N	N
4 **Palazzo**	?	?	?	?	?	?
MISSOURI						
1 Clay	Y	N	Y	Y	N	Y
2 **Wagner**	Y	Y	N	N	Y	N
3 **Luetkemeyer**	Y	Y	N	N	Y	N
4 **Hartzler**	N	Y	N	N	Y	N
5 Cleaver	N	N	Y	Y	N	Y
6 **Graves**	N	Y	N	N	Y	N
7 **Long**	Y	Y	N	N	Y	N
8 **Smith**	N	Y	N	N	N	N
MONTANA						
AL **Gianforte**	Y	Y	N	N	Y	N
NEBRASKA						
1 **Fortenberry**	?	Y	N	Y	N	N
2 **Bacon**	Y	Y	Y	N	N	N
3 **Smith**	Y	Y	N	N	N	N
NEVADA						
1 Titus	Y	N	Y	Y	N	Y
2 **Amodei**	Y	Y	N	N	N	N
3 Rosen	N	N	Y	Y	N	Y
4 Kihuen	N	N	Y	Y	N	Y
NEW HAMPSHIRE						
1 Shea-Porter	Y	N	Y	Y	N	Y
2 Kuster	Y	N	Y	Y	N	Y
NEW JERSEY						
1 Norcross	N	N	N	Y	N	N
2 **LoBiondo**	N	Y	Y	Y	N	N
3 **MacArthur**	N	N	Y	N	N	N
4 **Smith**	Y	Y	Y	N	N	N
5 Gottheimer	N	N	N	Y	N	N
6 Pallone	N	N	N	Y	N	Y
7 **Lance**	N	N	Y	Y	N	N
8 Sires	N	N	N	Y	N	N
9 Pascrell	Y	N	Y	Y	N	Y
10 Payne	N	N	Y	Y	N	Y
11 **Frelinghuysen**	Y	Y	N	N	N	N
12 Watson Coleman	N	N	Y	Y	N	Y
NEW MEXICO						
1 Lujan Grisham	Y	N	Y	Y	N	Y
2 **Pearce**	N	Y	N	N	Y	N
3 Luján	Y	N	Y	Y	N	Y
NEW YORK						
1 **Zeldin**	N	Y	N	Y	N	N
2 **King**	Y	Y	N	Y	N	N
3 Suozzi	N	N	Y	Y	N	Y
4 Rice	N	N	Y	Y	N	Y
5 Meeks	Y	N	Y	Y	N	Y
6 Meng	Y	N	Y	Y	N	Y
7 Velázquez	N	N	Y	Y	N	Y
8 Jeffries	N	N	Y	Y	N	Y
9 Clarke	N	N	Y	Y	N	Y
10 Nadler	Y	N	Y	Y	N	Y
11 **Donovan**	Y	Y	Y	Y	N	N
12 Maloney, C.	N	N	Y	Y	N	Y
13 Espaillat	N	N	Y	Y	N	Y
14 Crowley	N	N	Y	Y	N	Y
15 Serrano	N	N	Y	Y	N	Y
16 Engel	Y	N	Y	Y	N	Y
17 Lowey	Y	N	Y	Y	N	Y
18 Maloney, S.P.	N	N	Y	Y	N	N
19 **Faso**	N	Y	Y	Y	N	N
20 Tonko	P	N	Y	Y	N	Y
21 **Stefanik**	Y	N	Y	Y	N	N
22 **Tenney**	N	Y	N	N	Y	N
23 **Reed**	Y	Y	Y	Y	N	N
24 **Katko**	N	N	Y	Y	N	N
25 **Vacant**						
26 Higgins	Y	N	Y	Y	N	Y
27 **Collins**	Y	Y	N	N	N	N
NORTH CAROLINA						
1 Butterfield	Y	N	Y	Y	N	Y
2 **Holding**	N	Y	N	N	Y	N
3 **Jones**	N	Y	Y	Y	Y	Y
4 Price	N	N	Y	Y	N	Y

	242	243	244	245	246	247
5 **Foxx**	N	Y	N	N	Y	N
6 **Walker**	Y	Y	N	N	Y	N
7 **Rouzer**	N	Y	N	N	Y	N
8 **Hudson**	N	Y	N	N	Y	N
9 **Pittenger**	N	Y	N	N	Y	N
9 **Vacant**						
10 **McHenry**	Y	Y	N	N	Y	N
11 **Meadows**	Y	Y	N	N	Y	N
12 Adams	N	N	Y	Y	N	Y
13 **Budd**	Y	Y	N	N	Y	N
NORTH DAKOTA						
AL **Cramer**	Y	Y	N	N	N	N
OHIO						
1 **Chabot**	Y	Y	N	N	Y	N
2 **Wenstrup**	Y	Y	N	N	Y	N
3 Beatty	–	–	+	+	–	+
4 **Jordan**	N	Y	N	N	Y	N
5 **Latta**	Y	Y	N	N	Y	N
6 **Johnson**	N	Y	N	N	Y	N
7 **Gibbs**	Y	Y	N	N	Y	N
8 **Davidson**	Y	Y	N	N	Y	N
9 Kaptur	Y	N	Y	Y	N	Y
10 **Turner**	N	N	N	N	N	N
11 Fudge	N	N	N	Y	N	Y
12 **Vacant**						
13 Ryan	N	N	N	Y	N	N
14 **Joyce**	Y	Y	N	N	N	N
15 **Stivers**	Y	Y	N	N	N	N
16 **Renacci**	N	Y	N	N	N	N
OKLAHOMA						
1 **Vacant**						
2 **Mullin**	Y	Y	N	N	N	N
3 **Lucas**	Y	Y	N	N	N	N
4 **Cole**	Y	Y	N	N	N	N
5 **Russell**	Y	Y	N	N	Y	N
OREGON						
1 Bonamici	Y	N	Y	Y	N	Y
2 **Walden**	N	Y	N	N	N	N
3 Blumenauer	Y	N	Y	Y	N	Y
4 DeFazio	N	N	Y	Y	N	Y
5 Schrader	N	N	Y	Y	N	Y
PENNSYLVANIA						
1 Brady	N	N	N	Y	N	Y
2 Evans	N	N	Y	Y	N	Y
3 **Kelly**	Y	N	N	N	N	N
4 **Perry**	N	Y	N	N	Y	N
5 **Thompson**	N	Y	N	N	N	N
6 **Costello**	N	Y	Y	N	N	N
7 **Vacant**						
8 **Fitzpatrick**	N	N	Y	Y	N	N
9 **Shuster**	N	?	N	N	Y	N
10 **Marino**	Y	Y	N	N	N	N
11 **Barletta**	Y	Y	N	N	N	N
12 **Rothfus**	Y	N	N	N	Y	N
13 Boyle	?	N	N	Y	N	Y
14 Doyle	N	N	Y	Y	N	Y
15 **Vacant**						
16 **Smucker**	Y	Y	N	N	N	N
17 Cartwright	Y	N	Y	Y	N	Y
18 Lamb	Y	N	Y	N	N	Y
RHODE ISLAND						
1 Cicilline	Y	N	Y	Y	N	Y
2 Langevin	N	N	Y	Y	N	Y
SOUTH CAROLINA						
1 **Sanford**	N	Y	N	N	Y	Y
2 **Wilson**	Y	Y	N	N	N	N
3 **Duncan**	N	Y	N	N	Y	N
4 **Gowdy**	N	Y	N	N	N	N
5 **Norman**	Y	Y	N	N	Y	N
6 Clyburn	N	N	Y	Y	N	Y
7 **Rice**	N	Y	N	N	Y	N
SOUTH DAKOTA						
AL **Noem**	?	?	?	?	?	?
TENNESSEE						
1 **Roe**	Y	Y	N	N	N	N
2 **Duncan**	Y	Y	N	N	Y	Y
3 **Fleischmann**	Y	Y	N	N	N	N
4 **DesJarlais**	Y	Y	N	N	N	N
5 Cooper	Y	N	Y	Y	N	N
6 **Black**	Y	Y	N	N	N	N
7 **Blackburn**	N	Y	N	N	N	N
8 **Kustoff**	Y	Y	N	N	Y	N
9 Cohen	N	N	Y	Y	N	Y

	242	243	244	245	246	247
TEXAS						
1 **Gohmert**	N	Y	N	N	Y	N
2 **Poe**	N	Y	N	N	Y	N
3 **Johnson, S.**	Y	Y	N	N	Y	N
4 **Ratcliffe**	N	Y	N	N	Y	N
5 **Hensarling**	Y	Y	N	N	Y	N
6 **Barton**	Y	Y	N	N	N	N
7 **Culberson**	Y	Y	N	N	N	N
8 **Brady**	Y	Y	N	N	N	N
9 Green, A.	N	N	Y	Y	N	N
10 **McCaul**	Y	Y	N	N	N	N
11 **Conaway**	N	Y	N	N	N	N
12 **Granger**	N	Y	N	N	N	N
13 **Thornberry**	Y	Y	N	N	N	N
14 **Weber**	N	Y	N	N	N	N
15 Gonzalez	N	N	Y	Y	N	Y
16 O'Rourke	Y	N	Y	Y	N	Y
17 **Flores**	?	Y	N	N	N	N
18 Jackson Lee	N	N	Y	Y	N	Y
19 **Arrington**	Y	Y	N	N	Y	N
20 Castro	Y	N	Y	Y	N	Y
21 **Smith**	?	Y	N	N	N	N
22 **Olson**	Y	Y	N	N	Y	N
23 **Hurd**	N	N	N	N	N	N
24 **Marchant**	Y	Y	N	N	N	N
25 **Williams**	Y	Y	N	N	Y	N
26 **Burgess**	N	Y	N	N	Y	N
28 Cuellar	Y	N	Y	N	N	N
29 Green, G.	N	N	Y	Y	N	N
30 Johnson, E.B.	N	N	Y	Y	N	Y
31 **Carter**	Y	Y	N	N	N	N
32 **Sessions**	Y	Y	N	N	Y	N
33 Veasey	N	N	Y	Y	N	Y
34 Vela	N	N	Y	Y	N	Y
35 Doggett	Y	N	Y	Y	N	Y
36 **Babin**	N	Y	N	N	N	N
UTAH						
1 **Bishop**	Y	Y	N	N	Y	N
2 **Stewart**	Y	Y	N	N	Y	N
3 **Curtis**	Y	Y	N	N	Y	N
4 **Love**	Y	Y	N	Y	N	N
VERMONT						
AL Welch	N	N	Y	Y	N	Y
VIRGINIA						
1 **Wittman**	N	Y	N	N	Y	N
2 **Taylor**	N	Y	N	N	Y	N
3 Scott	Y	N	Y	Y	N	Y
4 McEachin	Y	N	Y	Y	N	Y
5 **Garrett**	Y	Y	N	N	Y	N
6 **Goodlatte**	Y	Y	N	N	Y	N
7 **Brat**	Y	Y	N	N	Y	N
8 Beyer	N	N	Y	Y	N	Y
9 **Griffith**	Y	Y	Y	N	Y	N
10 **Comstock**	Y	Y	N	N	N	N
11 Connolly	N	N	Y	Y	N	Y
WASHINGTON						
1 DelBene	Y	N	Y	Y	N	Y
2 Larsen	Y	N	Y	Y	N	Y
3 **Herrera Beutler**	N	Y	N	Y	N	N
4 **Newhouse**	Y	Y	N	N	Y	N
5 **McMorris Rodgers**	Y	Y	N	N	N	N
6 Kilmer	N	N	Y	Y	N	Y
7 Jayapal	N	N	Y	Y	N	Y
8 **Reichert**	Y	Y	Y	Y	N	N
9 Smith	Y	N	Y	Y	N	Y
10 Heck	Y	N	Y	Y	N	Y
WEST VIRGINIA						
1 **McKinley**	N	N	N	N	N	N
2 **Mooney**	Y	Y	N	N	Y	N
3 **Jenkins**	N	Y	N	N	N	N
WISCONSIN						
1 **Ryan**						
2 Pocan	Y	N	Y	Y	N	Y
3 Kind	N	N	Y	Y	N	Y
4 Moore	N	N	Y	Y	N	Y
5 **Sensenbrenner**	N	Y	N	N	Y	N
6 **Grothman**	Y	Y	N	N	Y	N
7 **Duffy**	Y	Y	N	N	Y	N
8 **Gallagher**	N	Y	N	N	Y	N
WYOMING						
AL **Cheney**	Y	Y	N	N	Y	N

VOTE NUMBER

248. HR5895. LEGISLATIVE VEHICLE FOR FISCAL 2019 ENERGY-WATER, LEGISLATIVE BRANCH, MILITARY CONSTRUCTION-VA APPROPRIATIONS/ NUCLEAR NONPROLIFERATION ACTIVITIES. Connolly, D-Va., amendment that would decrease funding for atomic energy defense weapons activities at the National Nuclear Security Administration by $97.2 million, and would increase funding for NNSA defense nuclear nonproliferation activities by that same amount. Rejected in Committee of the Whole 179-239: R 5-226; D 174-13. June 7, 2018.

249. HR5895. LEGISLATIVE VEHICLE FOR FISCAL 2019 ENERGY-WATER, LEGISLATIVE BRANCH, MILITARY CONSTRUCTION-VA APPROPRIATIONS/ MARK GABRIEL SALARY REDUCTION. Gosar, R-Ariz., amendment that would reduce the salary of the administrator of the Western Area Power Administration, Mark Gabriel, to $1. Rejected in Committee of the Whole 139-276: R 138-90; D 1-186. June 7, 2018.

250. HR5895. LEGISLATIVE VEHICLE FOR FISCAL 2019 ENERGY-WATER, LEGISLATIVE BRANCH, MILITARY CONSTRUCTION-VA APPROPRIATIONS/ MARINE PLANNING PROJECTS. Lowenthal, D-Calif., for Beyer, D-Va., amendment that would remove a ban on the use of funds appropriated by the bill to further implement certain coastal and marine spatial planning and ecosystem-based management projects. Rejected in Committee of the Whole 195-223: R 9-222; D 186-1. June 7, 2018.

251. HR5895. LEGISLATIVE VEHICLE FOR FISCAL 2019 ENERGY-WATER, LEGISLATIVE BRANCH, MILITARY CONSTRUCTION-VA APPROPRIATIONS/ ONE PERCENT REDUCTION. Blackburn, R-Tenn., amendment that would reduce all funds appropriated in Energy-Water division of the bill by one percent. Rejected in Committee of the Whole 155-262: R 154-77; D 1-185. June 7, 2018.

252. HR5895. LEGISLATIVE VEHICLE FOR FISCAL 2019 ENERGY-WATER, LEGISLATIVE BRANCH, MILITARY CONSTRUCTION-VA APPROPRIATIONS/ ENERGY-WATER REDUCTION. Norman, R-S.C., amendment that would reduce the total amount of appropriations for the Energy-Water division of the bill by $1.5 billion. Rejected in Committee of the Whole 128-289: R 127-103; D 1-186. June 7, 2018.

253. HR5895. LEGISLATIVE VEHICLE FOR FISCAL 2019 ENERGY-WATER, LEGISLATIVE BRANCH, MILITARY CONSTRUCTION-VA APPROPRIATIONS/ SOCIAL COST OF CARBON. Gohmert, R-Texas, amendment that would prohibit appropriated funds from being used to prepare, propose or promulgate any regulation or guidance which would rely on the analyses found in various documents published by the Interagency Working Group on the Social Cost of Carbon. Adopted in Committee of the Whole 212-201: R 210-16; D 2-185. June 8, 2018.

	248	249	250	251	252	253
ALABAMA						
1 Byrne	N	Y	N	Y	Y	Y
2 Roby	N	N	N	N	N	Y
3 Rogers	N	N	N	N	N	Y
4 Aderholt	N	Y	N	N	N	Y
5 Brooks	N	Y	N	Y	Y	Y
6 Palmer	N	Y	N	Y	Y	Y
7 Sewell	+	–	+	–	–	–
ALASKA						
AL Young	N	Y	N	N	N	Y
ARIZONA						
1 O'Halleran	Y	N	Y	N	N	N
2 McSally	N	Y	N	Y	N	Y
3 Grijalva	Y	N	Y	N	N	N
4 Gosar	N	Y	N	Y	Y	Y
5 Biggs	N	Y	N	Y	Y	Y
6 Schweikert	N	Y	N	Y	Y	Y
7 Gallego	Y	N	Y	N	N	N
8 Lesko	N	Y	N	Y	Y	Y
9 Sinema	N	N	Y	?	N	N
ARKANSAS						
1 Crawford	N	N	N	Y	N	Y
2 Hill	N	N	N	Y	Y	Y
3 Womack	N	N	N	Y	N	Y
4 Westerman	N	Y	N	Y	Y	Y
CALIFORNIA						
1 LaMalfa	N	Y	N	N	N	Y
2 Huffman	Y	N	Y	N	N	N
3 Garamendi	Y	N	Y	N	N	N
4 McClintock	N	Y	N	Y	Y	Y
5 Thompson	Y	N	Y	N	N	N
6 Matsui	Y	N	Y	N	N	N
7 Bera	Y	N	Y	N	N	N
8 Cook	N	Y	N	Y	Y	Y
9 McNerney	Y	N	Y	N	N	N
10 Denham	N	N	N	N	N	Y
11 DeSaulnier	Y	N	Y	N	N	N
12 Pelosi	Y	N	Y	N	N	N
13 Lee	Y	N	Y	N	N	N
14 Speier	Y	N	Y	N	N	N
15 Swalwell	Y	N	Y	N	N	N
16 Costa	Y	N	Y	N	N	N
17 Khanna	Y	N	Y	N	N	N
18 Eshoo	Y	N	Y	N	N	N
19 Lofgren	Y	N	Y	N	N	N
20 Panetta	Y	N	Y	N	N	N
21 Valadao	N	N	N	N	N	Y
22 Nunes	N	N	N	N	N	Y
23 McCarthy	N	Y	N	Y	Y	Y
24 Carbajal	+	–	+	–	–	N
25 Knight	N	Y	N	Y	N	Y
26 Brownley	Y	N	Y	N	N	N
27 Chu	Y	N	Y	N	N	N
28 Schiff	Y	N	Y	N	N	N
29 Cardenas	Y	N	Y	N	N	N
30 Sherman	Y	N	Y	N	N	N
31 Aguilar	Y	N	Y	N	N	N
32 Napolitano	Y	N	Y	N	N	N
33 Lieu	Y	N	Y	N	N	N
34 Gomez	Y	N	Y	N	N	N
35 Torres	Y	N	Y	N	N	N
36 Ruiz	Y	N	Y	N	N	N
37 Bass	Y	N	Y	N	N	N
38 Sánchez, Linda	Y	N	Y	N	N	N
39 Royce	N	N	N	Y	N	N
40 Roybal-Allard	Y	N	Y	N	N	N
41 Takano	Y	N	Y	N	N	N
42 Calvert	N	N	N	N	N	Y
43 Waters	Y	N	Y	N	N	N
44 Barragan	Y	N	Y	N	N	N
45 Walters	?	?	?	?	?	?
46 Correa	N	N	Y	N	N	N
47 Lowenthal	Y	N	Y	N	N	N
48 Rohrabacher	Y	Y	Y	Y	Y	Y
49 Issa	N	N	N	Y	?	Y
50 Hunter	N	Y	N	Y	N	Y
51 Vargas	?	?	?	?	?	N
52 Peters	Y	N	Y	N	N	N
53 Davis	Y	N	Y	N	N	N

	248	249	250	251	252	253
COLORADO						
1 DeGette	Y	N	Y	N	N	N
2 Polis	?	?	?	?	?	?
3 Tipton	N	Y	N	Y	Y	Y
4 Buck	N	Y	N	Y	Y	Y
5 Lamborn	N	Y	N	Y	Y	Y
6 Coffman	N	Y	N	Y	N	N
7 Perlmutter	Y	N	Y	N	N	N
CONNECTICUT						
1 Larson	Y	Y	Y	N	N	N
2 Courtney	Y	N	Y	N	N	N
3 DeLauro	Y	N	Y	N	N	N
4 Himes	Y	N	Y	N	N	N
5 Esty	Y	N	Y	N	N	N
DELAWARE						
AL Blunt Rochester	Y	N	Y	N	N	N
FLORIDA						
1 Gaetz	N	Y	N	Y	Y	Y
2 Dunn	N	Y	N	N	Y	Y
3 Yoho	N	Y	N	Y	Y	Y
4 Rutherford	N	N	N	N	N	Y
5 Lawson	Y	N	Y	N	N	N
6 DeSantis	N	Y	N	Y	Y	Y
7 Murphy	Y	N	Y	N	N	N
8 Posey	N	Y	N	Y	Y	Y
9 Soto	Y	N	Y	N	N	N
10 Demings	Y	N	Y	N	N	N
11 Webster	N	Y	N	Y	Y	Y
12 Bilirakis	N	Y	N	Y	Y	Y
13 Crist	Y	N	Y	N	N	N
14 Castor	Y	N	Y	N	N	N
15 Ross	N	N	N	N	N	Y
16 Buchanan	N	N	Y	N	Y	N
17 Rooney, T.	N	P	N	N	N	N
18 Mast	N	N	Y	N	N	N
19 Rooney, F.	Y	Y	Y	Y	Y	N
20 Hastings	Y	N	Y	N	N	N
21 Frankel	Y	N	Y	N	N	N
22 Deutch	Y	N	Y	N	N	N
23 Wasserman Schultz	Y	N	Y	N	N	N
24 Wilson	Y	N	Y	N	N	N
25 Diaz-Balart	N	N	N	N	N	?
26 Curbelo	N	N	N	N	N	N
27 Ros-Lehtinen	N	N	N	N	N	N
GEORGIA						
1 Carter	N	Y	N	Y	Y	Y
2 Bishop	N	N	Y	N	N	N
3 Ferguson	N	Y	N	Y	Y	Y
4 Johnson	Y	N	Y	N	N	N
5 Lewis	Y	N	Y	N	N	N
6 Handel	N	Y	N	Y	Y	Y
7 Woodall	N	N	N	Y	Y	Y
8 Scott, A.	N	Y	N	Y	Y	Y
9 Collins	N	Y	N	Y	N	Y
10 Hice	N	Y	N	Y	Y	Y
11 Loudermilk	N	Y	N	Y	Y	Y
12 Allen	N	Y	N	Y	Y	Y
13 Scott, D.	Y	N	N	N	N	N
14 Graves	N	N	N	Y	Y	Y
HAWAII						
1 Hanabusa	Y	N	Y	N	N	N
2 Gabbard	Y	N	Y	N	N	N
IDAHO						
1 Labrador	N	Y	N	Y	Y	Y
2 Simpson	N	N	N	N	N	Y
ILLINOIS						
1 Rush	Y	N	Y	N	N	N
2 Kelly	Y	N	Y	N	N	N
3 Lipinski	N	N	Y	N	N	N
4 Gutierrez	Y	N	Y	N	N	N
5 Quigley	Y	N	Y	N	N	N
6 Roskam	N	N	N	N	N	N
7 Davis, D.	Y	N	Y	N	N	N
8 Krishnamoorthi	Y	N	Y	N	N	N
9 Schakowsky	Y	N	Y	N	N	N
10 Schneider	Y	N	Y	N	N	N
11 Foster	Y	N	Y	N	N	N
12 Bost	N	N	N	N	N	Y
13 Davis, R.	N	Y	N	N	N	Y

	248	249	250	251	252	253
14 **Hultgren**	N	Y	N	Y	Y	Y
15 **Shimkus**	N	N	N	N	N	Y
16 **Kinzinger**	N	N	N	N	N	Y
17 Bustos	Y	N	Y	N	N	N
18 **LaHood**	N	Y	N	Y	Y	Y
INDIANA						
1 Visclosky	Y	N	Y	N	N	N
2 **Walorski**	N	Y	N	Y	N	Y
3 **Banks**	N	Y	N	Y	Y	Y
4 Rokita	N	Y	N	Y	Y	Y
5 **Brooks**	N	N	N	Y	N	Y
6 **Messer**	N	Y	N	Y	Y	Y
7 Carson	Y	N	Y	N	N	N
8 **Bucshon**	N	Y	N	Y	N	Y
9 **Hollingsworth**	N	Y	N	N	Y	Y
IOWA						
1 **Blum**	N	Y	N	Y	Y	Y
2 Loebsack	Y	N	Y	N	N	N
3 **Young**	N	Y	N	Y	N	Y
4 **King**	N	N	N	Y	Y	Y
KANSAS						
1 **Marshall**	N	Y	N	N	Y	Y
2 **Jenkins**	N	Y	N	Y	Y	Y
3 **Yoder**	N	Y	N	Y	Y	Y
4 **Estes**	N	Y	N	Y	Y	Y
KENTUCKY						
1 **Comer**	N	Y	N	Y	Y	Y
2 **Guthrie**	N	Y	N	Y	Y	Y
3 Yarmuth	Y	N	Y	N	N	N
4 **Massie**	N	Y	N	Y	Y	Y
5 **Rogers**	N	N	N	N	N	Y
6 **Barr**	N	N	N	N	Y	Y
LOUISIANA						
1 **Scalise**	N	Y	N	Y	Y	Y
2 Richmond	Y	N	N	N	N	N
3 **Higgins**	N	Y	N	Y	Y	Y
4 **Johnson**	N	Y	N	Y	Y	Y
5 **Abraham**	N	Y	N	Y	Y	Y
6 **Graves**	N	N	N	Y	Y	Y
MAINE						
1 Pingree	Y	N	Y	N	Y	N
2 **Poliquin**	N	N	Y	Y	N	Y
MARYLAND						
1 **Harris**	N	Y	N	Y	Y	Y
2 Ruppersberger	N	N	Y	N	N	N
3 Sarbanes	Y	N	Y	N	N	N
4 Brown	Y	N	Y	N	N	N
5 Hoyer	Y	N	Y	N	N	N
6 Delaney	Y	N	Y	N	N	N
7 Cummings	Y	N	Y	N	N	N
8 Raskin	Y	N	Y	N	N	N
MASSACHUSETTS						
1 Neal	Y	N	Y	N	N	N
2 McGovern	Y	N	Y	N	N	N
3 Tsongas	Y	N	Y	N	N	?
4 Kennedy	Y	N	Y	N	N	?
5 Clark	Y	N	Y	N	N	N
6 Moulton	Y	N	Y	N	N	N
7 Capuano	Y	N	Y	N	N	N
8 Lynch	Y	N	Y	N	N	N
9 Keating	Y	N	Y	N	N	N
MICHIGAN						
1 **Bergman**	N	N	N	Y	Y	N
2 **Huizenga**	N	Y	N	Y	N	Y
3 *Amash*	Y	P	N	Y	Y	Y
4 **Moolenaar**	N	Y	N	N	N	Y
5 Kildee	Y	N	Y	N	N	N
6 **Upton**	N	N	N	Y	N	Y
7 **Walberg**	N	Y	N	Y	Y	Y
8 **Bishop**	N	N	N	Y	Y	Y
9 Levin	Y	N	Y	N	N	N
10 **Mitchell**	N	N	N	Y	N	Y
11 **Trott**	N	N	N	N	N	N
12 Dingell	Y	N	Y	N	N	N
14 Lawrence	Y	N	Y	N	N	N
MINNESOTA						
1 Walz	?	?	?	?	?	?
2 **Lewis**	N	Y	N	Y	Y	Y
3 **Paulsen**	N	N	N	Y	N	N
4 McCollum	Y	N	Y	N	N	N
5 Ellison	Y	N	Y	N	N	N
6 **Emmer**	N	Y	N	N	N	Y
7 Peterson	Y	N	Y	N	N	N
8 Nolan	Y	N	Y	N	N	N
MISSISSIPPI						
1 **Kelly**	N	Y	N	Y	Y	Y
2 Thompson	Y	N	Y	N	N	N
3 **Harper**	N	N	N	N	N	Y
4 **Palazzo**	?	?	?	?	?	?
MISSOURI						
1 Clay	Y	N	Y	N	N	N
2 **Wagner**	N	Y	N	Y	Y	Y
3 **Luetkemeyer**	N	N	N	N	N	Y
4 **Hartzler**	N	N	N	N	N	Y
5 Cleaver	Y	N	Y	N	N	N
6 **Graves**	N	N	N	N	N	Y
7 **Long**	N	N	N	Y	Y	Y
8 **Smith**	N	Y	N	Y	Y	Y
MONTANA						
AL **Gianforte**	N	Y	N	Y	Y	Y
NEBRASKA						
1 **Fortenberry**	N	N	Y	N	N	Y
2 **Bacon**	N	Y	N	Y	Y	Y
3 **Smith**	N	Y	N	Y	N	Y
NEVADA						
1 Titus	Y	N	Y	N	N	N
2 **Amodei**	N	Y	N	N	N	N
3 Rosen	N	N	Y	N	N	N
4 Kihuen	Y	N	Y	N	N	N
NEW HAMPSHIRE						
1 Shea-Porter	Y	N	Y	N	N	N
2 Kuster	Y	N	Y	N	N	N
NEW JERSEY						
1 Norcross	N	N	Y	N	N	N
2 **LoBiondo**	N	N	N	N	N	Y
3 **MacArthur**	N	N	N	N	N	Y
4 **Smith**	N	N	N	N	N	Y
5 Gottheimer	N	N	Y	N	N	N
6 Pallone	Y	N	Y	N	N	N
7 **Lance**	N	N	N	Y	N	N
8 Sires	Y	N	Y	N	N	N
9 Pascrell	Y	N	Y	N	N	N
10 Payne	Y	N	Y	N	N	N
11 **Frelinghuysen**	N	N	N	N	N	Y
12 Watson Coleman	Y	N	Y	N	N	N
NEW MEXICO						
1 Lujan Grisham	Y	N	Y	N	N	N
2 **Pearce**	N	Y	N	Y	N	Y
3 Luján	Y	N	Y	N	N	N
NEW YORK						
1 **Zeldin**	N	Y	N	Y	Y	Y
2 **King**	N	N	N	N	N	Y
3 Suozzi	Y	N	Y	N	N	N
4 Rice	Y	N	Y	N	N	N
5 Meeks	Y	N	Y	N	N	N
6 Meng	Y	N	Y	N	N	N
7 Velázquez	Y	N	Y	N	N	N
8 Jeffries	Y	N	Y	N	N	N
9 Clarke	Y	N	Y	N	N	N
10 Nadler	Y	N	Y	N	N	N
11 **Donovan**	N	N	N	N	N	Y
12 Maloney, C.	Y	N	Y	N	N	N
13 Espaillat	Y	N	Y	N	N	N
14 Crowley	Y	N	Y	N	N	N
15 Serrano	Y	N	Y	N	N	N
16 Engel	Y	N	Y	N	N	N
17 Lowey	Y	N	Y	N	N	N
18 Maloney, S.P.	N	N	Y	N	N	N
19 **Faso**	N	N	N	N	N	N
20 Tonko	Y	N	Y	N	N	N
21 **Stefanik**	N	N	Y	N	N	N
22 **Tenney**	N	N	N	N	N	Y
23 **Reed**	N	N	N	N	N	Y
24 **Katko**	N	N	Y	N	N	Y
25 **Vacant**						
26 Higgins	Y	N	Y	N	N	N
27 **Collins**	N	N	N	N	N	Y
NORTH CAROLINA						
1 Butterfield	Y	N	Y	N	N	N
2 **Holding**	N	Y	N	Y	Y	Y
3 **Jones**	Y	Y	N	Y	Y	Y
4 Price	Y	N	Y	N	N	N
5 **Foxx**	N	N	N	Y	Y	Y
6 **Walker**	N	Y	N	Y	Y	Y
7 **Rouzer**	N	Y	N	Y	Y	Y
8 **Hudson**	N	Y	N	Y	Y	Y
9 **Pittenger**	N	N	N	N	Y	Y
9 **Vacant**						
10 **McHenry**	N	N	N	Y	N	Y
11 **Meadows**	N	Y	N	Y	Y	Y
12 Adams	Y	N	Y	N	N	N
13 **Budd**	N	Y	N	Y	Y	Y
NORTH DAKOTA						
AL **Cramer**	N	Y	N	Y	Y	Y
OHIO						
1 **Chabot**	N	Y	N	Y	Y	Y
2 **Wenstrup**	N	N	N	Y	N	Y
3 Beatty	+	–	+	–	–	–
4 **Jordan**	N	Y	N	Y	Y	Y
5 **Latta**	N	Y	N	Y	Y	Y
6 **Johnson**	N	Y	N	Y	Y	Y
7 **Gibbs**	N	Y	N	Y	N	Y
8 **Davidson**	N	Y	N	Y	Y	Y
9 Kaptur	Y	N	Y	N	N	N
10 **Turner**	N	N	N	N	N	Y
11 Fudge	Y	N	Y	N	N	N
12 **Vacant**						
13 Ryan	N	N	Y	N	N	N
14 **Joyce**	N	N	N	N	N	Y
15 **Stivers**	N	N	N	N	N	Y
16 **Renacci**	N	N	N	N	Y	Y
OKLAHOMA						
1 **Vacant**						
2 **Mullin**	N	Y	N	Y	Y	Y
3 **Lucas**	N	N	N	Y	N	Y
4 **Cole**	N	N	N	N	N	Y
5 **Russell**	N	N	N	Y	Y	Y
OREGON						
1 Bonamici	Y	N	Y	N	N	N
2 **Walden**	N	Y	N	N	N	Y
3 Blumenauer	Y	N	Y	N	N	N
4 DeFazio	N	N	Y	N	N	N
5 Schrader	Y	N	Y	N	N	N
PENNSYLVANIA						
1 Brady	Y	N	Y	N	N	N
2 Evans	Y	N	Y	N	N	N
3 **Kelly**	N	N	N	N	N	Y
4 **Perry**	N	Y	N	Y	Y	Y
5 **Thompson**	N	N	N	N	N	Y
6 **Costello**	Y	N	N	N	N	?
7 **Vacant**						
8 **Fitzpatrick**	N	N	Y	N	N	N
9 **Shuster**	N	N	N	N	N	?
10 **Marino**	N	N	N	N	N	Y
11 **Barletta**	N	N	N	N	N	Y
12 **Rothfus**	N	Y	N	Y	Y	Y
13 Boyle	Y	N	Y	N	N	N
14 Doyle	Y	N	Y	N	N	N
15 **Vacant**						
16 **Smucker**	N	Y	N	Y	Y	Y
17 Cartwright	Y	N	Y	N	N	N
18 Lamb	Y	N	Y	N	N	N
RHODE ISLAND						
1 Cicilline	Y	N	Y	N	N	N
2 Langevin	Y	N	Y	N	N	N
SOUTH CAROLINA						
1 **Sanford**	N	Y	N	Y	Y	Y
2 **Wilson**	N	Y	N	N	N	Y
3 **Duncan**	N	Y	N	Y	Y	Y
4 **Gowdy**	N	Y	N	Y	Y	Y
5 **Norman**	N	Y	N	Y	Y	Y
6 Clyburn	Y	N	Y	N	N	N
7 **Rice**	N	Y	N	Y	Y	N
SOUTH DAKOTA						
AL **Noem**	?	?	?	?	?	?
TENNESSEE						
1 **Roe**	N	N	N	Y	N	Y
2 **Duncan**	Y	Y	N	Y	Y	Y
3 **Fleischmann**	N	N	N	N	N	Y
4 **DesJarlais**	N	Y	N	Y	N	Y
5 Cooper	N	N	Y	Y	N	N
6 **Black**	N	N	N	Y	Y	Y
7 **Blackburn**	N	N	N	Y	Y	Y
8 **Kustoff**	N	Y	N	Y	Y	Y
9 Cohen	Y	N	Y	N	N	N
TEXAS						
1 **Gohmert**	N	Y	N	Y	Y	Y
2 **Poe**	N	Y	N	Y	Y	Y
3 **Johnson, S.**	N	Y	N	Y	Y	Y
4 **Ratcliffe**	N	Y	N	Y	Y	Y
5 **Hensarling**	N	Y	N	Y	Y	Y
6 **Barton**	N	Y	N	Y	Y	Y
7 **Culberson**	N	Y	N	Y	N	Y
8 **Brady**	N	N	N	Y	Y	+
9 Green, A.	Y	N	Y	N	N	N
10 **McCaul**	N	Y	N	Y	Y	Y
11 **Conaway**	N	N	N	Y	N	Y
12 **Granger**	N	N	N	N	N	Y
13 **Thornberry**	N	N	N	N	N	Y
14 **Weber**	N	Y	N	Y	Y	Y
15 Gonzalez	Y	N	Y	N	N	Y
16 O'Rourke	Y	N	Y	N	N	N
17 **Flores**	N	Y	N	Y	Y	Y
18 Jackson Lee	Y	N	Y	N	N	N
19 **Arrington**	N	Y	N	Y	Y	Y
20 Castro	Y	N	Y	N	N	N
21 **Smith**	N	Y	N	Y	Y	Y
22 **Olson**	N	Y	N	Y	Y	Y
23 **Hurd**	N	N	N	N	N	Y
24 Marchant	N	Y	N	Y	Y	Y
25 **Williams**	N	N	N	Y	Y	Y
26 **Burgess**	N	Y	N	Y	N	Y
28 Cuellar	N	N	Y	N	N	Y
29 Green, G.	Y	N	Y	N	N	N
30 Johnson, E.B.	Y	N	Y	N	N	N
31 **Carter**	N	N	N	N	N	Y
32 **Sessions**	N	Y	N	Y	Y	Y
33 Veasey	Y	N	Y	N	N	N
34 Vela	Y	N	Y	N	N	N
35 Doggett	Y	N	Y	N	N	N
36 **Babin**	N	Y	N	Y	Y	Y
UTAH						
1 **Bishop**	N	N	N	Y	Y	Y
2 **Stewart**	N	Y	N	Y	Y	Y
3 **Curtis**	N	Y	N	Y	Y	Y
4 **Love**	N	Y	N	N	N	Y
VERMONT						
AL Welch	Y	N	Y	N	N	N
VIRGINIA						
1 **Wittman**	N	Y	N	Y	Y	Y
2 **Taylor**	N	Y	N	Y	Y	Y
3 Scott	Y	N	Y	N	N	N
4 McEachin	Y	N	Y	N	N	N
5 **Garrett**	N	Y	N	Y	Y	Y
6 **Goodlatte**	N	N	N	Y	Y	Y
7 **Brat**	N	Y	N	Y	Y	Y
8 Beyer	Y	N	Y	N	N	N
9 **Griffith**	N	?	N	Y	Y	Y
10 **Comstock**	N	N	N	N	N	Y
11 Connolly	Y	N	Y	N	N	N
WASHINGTON						
1 DelBene	Y	N	Y	N	N	N
2 Larsen	Y	N	Y	N	N	N
3 **Herrera Beutler**	N	Y	N	N	N	Y
4 **Newhouse**	N	Y	N	N	N	Y
5 **McMorris Rodgers**	N	Y	N	Y	N	Y
6 Kilmer	Y	N	Y	N	N	N
7 Jayapal	Y	N	Y	N	N	N
8 **Reichert**	N	N	N	N	N	Y
9 Smith	Y	N	Y	N	N	N
10 Heck	Y	N	Y	N	N	N
WEST VIRGINIA						
1 **McKinley**	N	Y	N	N	N	Y
2 **Mooney**	N	Y	N	Y	Y	Y
3 **Jenkins**	N	N	N	N	N	Y
WISCONSIN						
1 **Ryan**						
2 Pocan	Y	N	Y	N	N	N
3 Kind	Y	N	Y	N	N	N
4 Moore	Y	N	Y	N	N	N
5 **Sensenbrenner**	N	Y	N	Y	Y	Y
6 **Grothman**	N	Y	N	Y	Y	Y
7 **Duffy**	N	Y	N	Y	Y	Y
8 **Gallagher**	N	Y	N	N	Y	Y
WYOMING						
AL **Cheney**	N	Y	N	N	N	?

VOTE NUMBER

254. HR5895. LEGISLATIVE VEHICLE FOR FISCAL 2019 ENERGY-WATER, LEGISLATIVE BRANCH, MILITARY CONSTRUCTION-VA APPROPRIATIONS/ INDEPENDENT COUNSEL AUDITS. Meadows, R-N.C., amendment that would prohibit appropriated funds from being used to enforce the repeal of the Government Accountability Office's ability to perform semiannual financial reviews of expenditures from the Independent Counsel permanent indefinite appropriation. Adopted in Committee of the Whole 207-201: R 202-22; D 5-179. June 8, 2018.

255. HR5895. LEGISLATIVE VEHICLE FOR FISCAL 2019 ENERGY-WATER, LEGISLATIVE BRANCH, MILITARY CONSTRUCTION-VA APPROPRIATIONS/ OFFICE OF TECHNOLOGY ASSESSMENT. Takano, D-Calif., amendment that would appropriate $2.5 million for the Office of Technology Assessment and would decrease funding for the Architect of the Capitol's capital construction and operations projects by $3.5 million. Rejected in Committee of the Whole 195-217: R 15-211; D 180-6. June 8, 2018.

256. HR5895. LEGISLATIVE VEHICLE FOR FISCAL 2019 ENERGY-WATER, LEGISLATIVE BRANCH, MILITARY CONSTRUCTION-VA APPROPRIATIONS/ RECOMMIT. Kuster, D-N.H., motion to recommit the bill to the House Appropriations Committee with instructions to report back it back immediately with an amendment that would decrease funding for VA administration by $10.2 million and would increase funding for medical funding at the Veterans Health Administration by $10 million, to be available on Oct 1, 2018. Motion rejected 187-225: R 2-225; D 185-0. June 8, 2018.

257. HR5895. FISCAL 2019 ENERGY-WATER, LEGISLATIVE BRANCH, MILITARY CONSTRUCTION-VA APPROPRIATIONS/PASSAGE. Passage of the bill, as amended, that would provide $146.5 billion in discretionary funding for fiscal 2019 to various departments, agencies and legislative operations, including $44.7 billion for the Energy Department, the Army Corps of Engineers, the Interior Department's Bureau of Reclamation; $98 billion for military construction activities and for VA programs and activities; and $3.8 billion for operations of the House of Representatives, joint House-Senate items and legislative branch entities such as the Library of Congress, the Capitol Police, and the Government Accountability Office. It would provide $11.2 billion for programs that maintain and refurbish nuclear weapons in the United States' stockpile. As amended, it would provide $1.1 billion in funding for the Veterans Community Care Program. Passed 235-179: R 212-16; D 23-163. June 8, 2018.

258. HR5327. OPIOID-USE DISORDERS TREATMENT GRANTS/PASSAGE. Carter, R-Ga., motion to suspend the rules and pass the bill that would authorize $10 million annually, for fiscal 2019 through fiscal 2023, for Health and Human Services Department grants for to providers that offer treatment services for people with opioid use disorders. It would require that there be at least 10 grants awarded to qualified providers. Motion agreed to 383-13: R 204-13; D 179-0. June 12, 2018.

259. HR5041. CONTROLLED SUBSTANCES DISPOSAL/PASSAGE. Walden, R-Ore., motion to suspend the rules and pass the bill that would authorize hospice program employees to dispose of a deceased hospice patient's controlled substances if the hospice program has written policies and procedures related to the disposal of controlled substances. Motion agreed to 398-0: R 219-0; D 179-0. June 12, 2018.

	254	255	256	257	258	259
ALABAMA						
1 Byrne	Y	N	N	Y	Y	Y
2 Roby	Y	N	N	Y	Y	Y
3 Rogers	Y	N	N	Y	Y	Y
4 Aderholt	Y	N	N	Y	Y	Y
5 Brooks	Y	N	N	N	N	Y
6 Palmer	Y	N	N	Y	Y	Y
7 Sewell	–	+	+	–	Y	Y
ALASKA						
AL Young	Y	N	N	Y	Y	Y
ARIZONA						
1 O'Halleran	?	Y	Y	Y	Y	Y
2 McSally	Y	N	?	Y	Y	Y
3 Grijalva	N	Y	N	N	Y	Y
4 Gosar	Y	N	N	N	N	Y
5 Biggs	Y	N	N	N	N	Y
6 Schweikert	N	N	N	N	Y	Y
7 Gallego	N	Y	N	N	Y	Y
8 Lesko	Y	N	N	Y	Y	Y
9 Sinema	Y	Y	Y	Y	Y	Y
ARKANSAS						
1 Crawford	Y	N	N	Y	?	?
2 Hill	Y	N	N	Y	Y	Y
3 Womack	Y	N	N	Y	Y	Y
4 Westerman	Y	N	N	Y	Y	Y
CALIFORNIA						
1 LaMalfa	Y	N	N	Y	Y	Y
2 Huffman	–	+	+	–	Y	Y
3 Garamendi	N	Y	Y	Y	Y	Y
4 McClintock	N	N	N	N	N	Y
5 Thompson	N	Y	Y	N	Y	Y
6 Matsui	N	Y	Y	N	Y	Y
7 Bera	N	Y	Y	Y	Y	Y
8 Cook	Y	N	N	Y	Y	Y
9 McNerney	Y	Y	Y	N	Y	Y
10 Denham	Y	N	N	Y	Y	Y
11 DeSaulnier	N	Y	Y	N	Y	Y
12 Pelosi	N	Y	Y	N	Y	Y
13 Lee	N	Y	Y	N	Y	Y
14 Speier	N	Y	Y	N	Y	Y
15 Swalwell	N	Y	Y	N	?	?
16 Costa	Y	Y	?	Y	Y	Y
17 Khanna	N	Y	Y	N	Y	Y
18 Eshoo	N	Y	Y	N	Y	Y
19 Lofgren	N	Y	Y	N	Y	Y
20 Panetta	N	Y	Y	N	Y	Y
21 Valadao	Y	N	N	Y	Y	Y
22 Nunes	Y	N	N	Y	Y	Y
23 McCarthy	Y	N	N	Y	Y	Y
24 Carbajal	N	Y	Y	Y	Y	Y
25 Knight	Y	N	N	Y	Y	Y
26 Brownley	N	Y	Y	Y	Y	Y
27 Chu	N	Y	Y	N	Y	Y
28 Schiff	N	Y	Y	N	Y	Y
29 Cardenas	N	Y	Y	N	Y	Y
30 Sherman	N	Y	Y	N	Y	Y
31 Aguilar	N	Y	Y	N	Y	Y
32 Napolitano	N	Y	Y	N	Y	Y
33 Lieu	Y	Y	Y	N	Y	Y
34 Gomez	N	Y	Y	N	Y	Y
35 Torres	N	Y	Y	N	Y	Y
36 Ruiz	N	Y	Y	Y	Y	Y
37 Bass	N	Y	Y	N	Y	Y
38 Sánchez, Linda	N	Y	Y	N	Y	Y
39 Royce	Y	N	N	Y	Y	Y
40 Roybal-Allard	N	Y	Y	N	Y	Y
41 Takano	N	Y	Y	N	Y	Y
42 Calvert	Y	N	N	Y	Y	Y
43 Waters	N	Y	Y	N	Y	Y
44 Barragan	N	Y	Y	N	Y	Y
45 Walters	?	?	?	?	Y	Y
46 Correa	N	N	N	Y	Y	Y
47 Lowenthal	N	Y	Y	N	Y	Y
48 Rohrabacher	Y	N	N	Y	N	Y
49 Issa	Y	N	N	Y	Y	Y
50 Hunter	Y	N	N	Y	Y	Y
51 Vargas	N	Y	Y	N	Y	Y
52 Peters	N	Y	Y	Y	Y	Y
53 Davis	N	Y	Y	N	Y	Y

	254	255	256	257	258	259
COLORADO						
1 DeGette	N	Y	Y	N	Y	Y
2 Polis	?	?	?	–	Y	Y
3 Tipton	Y	N	N	Y	N	Y
4 Buck	Y	N	N	Y	N	Y
5 Lamborn	Y	N	N	Y	Y	Y
6 Coffman	Y	Y	N	Y	Y	Y
7 Perlmutter	N	Y	Y	N	Y	Y
CONNECTICUT						
1 Larson	N	N	Y	N	Y	Y
2 Courtney	N	Y	Y	N	Y	Y
3 DeLauro	N	Y	Y	N	?	?
4 Himes	N	Y	Y	N	Y	Y
5 Esty	N	Y	Y	N	Y	Y
DELAWARE						
AL Blunt Rochester	N	Y	Y	N	Y	Y
FLORIDA						
1 Gaetz	Y	N	N	Y	N	Y
2 Dunn	Y	N	N	Y	Y	Y
3 Yoho	Y	N	N	Y	Y	Y
4 Rutherford	Y	N	N	Y	Y	Y
5 Lawson	N	Y	Y	N	Y	Y
6 DeSantis	Y	N	N	Y	Y	Y
7 Murphy	N	Y	Y	Y	?	?
8 Posey	Y	N	N	Y	Y	Y
9 Soto	N	Y	Y	N	Y	Y
10 Demings	N	Y	Y	N	Y	Y
11 Webster	Y	N	N	Y	Y	Y
12 Bilirakis	Y	N	N	Y	+	+
13 Crist	N	Y	Y	Y	Y	Y
14 Castor	N	Y	Y	N	Y	Y
15 Ross	Y	N	N	Y	Y	Y
16 Buchanan	Y	N	N	Y	Y	Y
17 Rooney, T.	Y	N	N	Y	?	?
18 Mast	Y	N	N	Y	Y	Y
19 Rooney, F.	Y	N	N	Y	?	?
20 Hastings	N	Y	Y	N	Y	Y
21 Frankel	N	Y	Y	N	Y	Y
22 Deutch	N	Y	Y	N	Y	Y
23 Wasserman Schultz	N	Y	Y	N	Y	Y
24 Wilson	N	Y	Y	N	?	?
25 Diaz-Balart	Y	N	N	Y	Y	Y
26 Curbelo	N	Y	Y	N	Y	Y
27 Ros-Lehtinen	N	Y	Y	N	Y	Y
GEORGIA						
1 Carter	Y	N	N	Y	Y	Y
2 Bishop	N	Y	Y	N	Y	Y
3 Ferguson	Y	N	N	Y	Y	Y
4 Johnson	N	Y	Y	N	Y	Y
5 Lewis	N	Y	Y	N	Y	Y
6 Handel	N	N	N	Y	Y	Y
7 Woodall	?	N	N	Y	Y	Y
8 Scott, A.	Y	N	N	Y	Y	Y
9 Collins	Y	?	N	Y	Y	Y
10 Hice	Y	N	N	Y	N	Y
11 Loudermilk	Y	N	N	Y	Y	Y
12 Allen	Y	N	N	Y	Y	Y
13 Scott, D.	N	Y	N	Y	Y	Y
14 Graves	Y	N	N	Y	Y	Y
HAWAII						
1 Hanabusa	N	Y	Y	N	Y	Y
2 Gabbard	N	Y	Y	N	Y	Y
IDAHO						
1 Labrador	Y	N	N	N	Y	Y
2 Simpson	Y	N	N	Y	Y	Y
ILLINOIS						
1 Rush	N	Y	Y	N	Y	Y
2 Kelly	N	Y	Y	N	Y	Y
3 Lipinski	N	Y	Y	N	Y	Y
4 Gutierrez	?	Y	Y	N	Y	Y
5 Quigley	N	Y	Y	N	Y	Y
6 Roskam	N	N	N	Y	+	+
7 Davis, D.	N	Y	Y	N	?	?
8 Krishnamoorthi	N	Y	Y	N	Y	Y
9 Schakowsky	N	Y	Y	N	Y	Y
10 Schneider	N	Y	Y	N	Y	Y
11 Foster	N	Y	Y	N	Y	Y
12 Bost	Y	N	N	Y	Y	Y
13 Davis, R.	Y	N	N	Y	Y	Y

	254	255	256	257	258	259
14 **Hultgren**	Y	Y	N	Y	Y	Y
15 **Shimkus**	Y	N	N	Y	Y	Y
16 **Kinzinger**	N	N	N	Y	Y	Y
17 Bustos	N	Y	Y	N	Y	Y
18 **LaHood**	Y	N	N	Y	Y	Y
INDIANA						
1 Visclosky	N	Y	Y	N	+	+
2 **Walorski**	N	N	N	Y	Y	Y
3 **Banks**	N	N	N	Y	Y	Y
4 Rokita	Y	N	N	Y	Y	Y
5 **Brooks**	N	N	N	Y	Y	Y
6 **Messer**	Y	N	N	Y	Y	Y
7 Carson	N	Y	Y	N	Y	Y
8 **Bucshon**	Y	N	N	Y	Y	Y
9 **Hollingsworth**	N	N	N	N	Y	Y
IOWA						
1 **Blum**	Y	N	Y	Y	Y	Y
2 Loebsack	N	Y	Y	Y	Y	Y
3 **Young**	Y	N	N	Y	Y	Y
4 **King**	Y	N	N	Y	Y	Y
KANSAS						
1 **Marshall**	Y	N	N	Y	Y	Y
2 **Jenkins**	Y	N	N	Y	Y	Y
3 **Yoder**	Y	N	N	Y	Y	Y
4 **Estes**	Y	N	N	Y	+	+
KENTUCKY						
1 **Comer**	Y	N	N	Y	Y	Y
2 **Guthrie**	Y	N	N	Y	Y	Y
3 Yarmuth	N	Y	Y	N	Y	Y
4 **Massie**	Y	N	N	N	N	Y
5 **Rogers**	Y	N	N	Y	Y	Y
6 **Barr**	Y	N	N	Y	Y	Y
LOUISIANA						
1 **Scalise**	Y	N	N	Y	Y	Y
2 Richmond	N	Y	Y	N	Y	Y
3 **Higgins**	Y	N	N	Y	Y	Y
4 **Johnson**	Y	N	N	Y	Y	Y
5 **Abraham**	Y	N	N	Y	Y	Y
6 **Graves**	Y	N	N	Y	Y	Y
MAINE						
1 Pingree	N	Y	Y	N	Y	Y
2 **Poliquin**	N	N	N	Y	Y	Y
MARYLAND						
1 **Harris**	Y	N	N	Y	Y	Y
2 Ruppersberger	N	Y	Y	N	Y	Y
3 Sarbanes	N	Y	Y	N	Y	Y
4 Brown	N	Y	Y	N	Y	Y
5 Hoyer	N	Y	Y	N	?	?
6 Delaney	N	Y	Y	N	Y	Y
7 Cummings	N	Y	Y	N	Y	Y
8 Raskin	N	Y	Y	N	Y	Y
MASSACHUSETTS						
1 Neal	N	N	Y	N	Y	Y
2 McGovern	N	Y	Y	N	Y	Y
3 Tsongas	?	?	?	?	Y	Y
4 Kennedy	?	?	?	?	Y	Y
5 Clark	N	Y	Y	N	Y	Y
6 Moulton	N	Y	Y	N	Y	Y
7 Capuano	N	Y	Y	N	Y	Y
8 Lynch	N	N	Y	Y	Y	Y
9 Keating	N	Y	Y	Y	Y	Y
MICHIGAN						
1 **Bergman**	Y	N	N	Y	Y	Y
2 **Huizenga**	Y	N	N	Y	Y	Y
3 *Amash*	Y	Y	N	N	N	Y
4 **Moolenaar**	Y	N	N	Y	Y	Y
5 Kildee	N	Y	Y	N	Y	Y
6 **Upton**	N	N	N	Y	Y	Y
7 **Walberg**	Y	N	N	Y	Y	Y
8 **Bishop**	Y	N	N	Y	Y	Y
9 Levin	N	Y	Y	N	Y	Y
10 **Mitchell**	Y	N	N	Y	Y	Y
11 **Trott**	Y	N	N	Y	Y	Y
12 Dingell	N	Y	Y	N	Y	Y
14 Lawrence	N	Y	Y	N	Y	Y
MINNESOTA						
1 Walz	?	?	?	?	?	?
2 **Lewis**	Y	N	N	Y	Y	Y
3 **Paulsen**	N	N	N	Y	Y	Y
4 McCollum	N	Y	Y	N	Y	Y
5 Ellison	N	Y	Y	N	?	?
6 **Emmer**	Y	N	N	Y	Y	Y
7 Peterson	N	Y	Y	Y	Y	Y
8 Nolan	N	Y	Y	N	Y	Y
MISSISSIPPI						
1 **Kelly**	Y	N	N	Y	Y	Y
2 Thompson	N	Y	Y	N	Y	Y
3 **Harper**	Y	N	N	Y	?	?
4 **Palazzo**	?	?	?	?	Y	Y
MISSOURI						
1 Clay	N	Y	Y	N	Y	Y
2 **Wagner**	Y	N	N	Y	Y	Y
3 **Luetkemeyer**	Y	N	N	Y	Y	Y
4 **Hartzler**	Y	N	N	Y	Y	Y
5 Cleaver	N	Y	Y	N	Y	Y
6 **Graves**	Y	N	N	Y	Y	Y
7 **Long**	Y	N	N	Y	Y	Y
8 **Smith**	Y	N	N	Y	Y	Y
MONTANA						
AL **Gianforte**	Y	N	N	Y	Y	Y
NEBRASKA						
1 **Fortenberry**	Y	N	N	Y	Y	Y
2 **Bacon**	Y	N	N	Y	Y	Y
3 **Smith**	Y	N	N	Y	Y	Y
NEVADA						
1 Titus	N	Y	Y	N	+	+
2 **Amodei**	Y	N	N	Y	Y	Y
3 Rosen	N	Y	Y	N	Y	Y
4 Kihuen	N	Y	Y	N	Y	Y
NEW HAMPSHIRE						
1 Shea-Porter	N	Y	Y	N	Y	Y
2 Kuster	N	Y	Y	Y	Y	Y
NEW JERSEY						
1 Norcross	N	Y	Y	N	Y	Y
2 **LoBiondo**	Y	Y	N	Y	Y	Y
3 **MacArthur**	N	N	N	Y	Y	Y
4 **Smith**	Y	N	N	Y	Y	Y
5 Gottheimer	N	N	Y	Y	Y	Y
6 Pallone	N	Y	Y	N	Y	Y
7 **Lance**	N	Y	N	Y	Y	Y
8 Sires	N	Y	Y	N	?	?
9 Pascrell	N	Y	Y	N	Y	Y
10 Payne	N	Y	Y	N	Y	Y
11 **Frelinghuysen**	Y	N	N	Y	Y	Y
12 Watson Coleman	N	Y	Y	N	Y	Y
NEW MEXICO						
1 Lujan Grisham	N	Y	Y	N	Y	Y
2 **Pearce**	Y	N	N	Y	Y	Y
3 Luján	N	Y	Y	N	Y	Y
NEW YORK						
1 **Zeldin**	Y	N	N	Y	Y	Y
2 **King**	Y	N	N	Y	?	?
3 Suozzi	N	Y	Y	N	Y	Y
4 Rice	N	Y	Y	N	Y	Y
5 Meeks	N	Y	Y	N	Y	Y
6 Meng	N	Y	Y	N	Y	Y
7 Velázquez	N	Y	Y	N	Y	Y
8 Jeffries	N	Y	Y	N	Y	Y
9 Clarke	N	Y	Y	N	Y	Y
10 Nadler	N	Y	Y	N	Y	Y
11 **Donovan**	Y	N	N	Y	Y	Y
12 Maloney, C.	N	Y	Y	N	Y	Y
13 Espaillat	N	Y	Y	N	Y	Y
14 Crowley	N	Y	Y	N	Y	Y
15 Serrano	N	Y	Y	N	Y	Y
16 Engel	N	N	Y	N	Y	Y
17 Lowey	N	Y	Y	N	Y	Y
18 Maloney, S.P.	N	Y	Y	N	Y	Y
19 **Faso**	Y	N	N	Y	Y	Y
20 Tonko	N	Y	Y	N	Y	Y
21 **Stefanik**	N	Y	N	Y	Y	Y
22 **Tenney**	Y	Y	N	Y	Y	Y
23 **Reed**	+	N	N	Y	Y	Y
24 **Katko**	N	N	N	Y	Y	Y
25 **Vacant**						
26 Higgins	N	Y	Y	N	Y	Y
27 **Collins**	Y	Y	N	Y	Y	Y
NORTH CAROLINA						
1 Butterfield	N	Y	Y	N	Y	Y
2 **Holding**	Y	N	N	Y	Y	Y
3 **Jones**	Y	N	Y	N	N	Y
4 Price	N	Y	Y	N	Y	Y
5 **Foxx**	Y	N	N	Y	Y	Y
6 **Walker**	Y	N	N	Y	Y	Y
7 **Rouzer**	Y	N	N	Y	Y	Y
8 **Hudson**	Y	N	N	Y	Y	Y
9 **Pittenger**	Y	N	N	Y	Y	Y
9 **Vacant**						
10 **McHenry**	Y	N	N	Y	Y	Y
11 **Meadows**	Y	N	N	Y	Y	Y
12 Adams	N	Y	Y	N	Y	Y
13 **Budd**	Y	N	N	Y	Y	Y
NORTH DAKOTA						
AL **Cramer**	Y	N	N	Y	Y	Y
OHIO						
1 **Chabot**	Y	N	N	Y	Y	Y
2 **Wenstrup**	Y	N	N	Y	Y	Y
3 Beatty	–	+	+	–	+	+
4 **Jordan**	Y	N	N	N	Y	Y
5 **Latta**	Y	N	N	Y	Y	Y
6 **Johnson**	Y	N	N	Y	Y	Y
7 **Gibbs**	Y	N	N	Y	Y	Y
8 **Davidson**	Y	N	N	N	Y	Y
9 Kaptur	N	Y	Y	N	Y	Y
10 **Turner**	Y	N	N	Y	Y	Y
11 Fudge	N	Y	Y	N	Y	Y
12 **Vacant**						
13 Ryan	N	Y	Y	N	Y	Y
14 **Joyce**	Y	N	N	Y	Y	Y
15 **Stivers**	Y	N	N	Y	Y	Y
16 **Renacci**	Y	N	N	Y	Y	Y
OKLAHOMA						
1 **Vacant**						
2 **Mullin**	Y	N	N	Y	Y	Y
3 **Lucas**	Y	N	N	Y	Y	Y
4 **Cole**	Y	N	N	Y	Y	Y
5 **Russell**	Y	Y	N	Y	Y	Y
OREGON						
1 Bonamici	N	Y	Y	N	Y	Y
2 **Walden**	Y	Y	N	Y	Y	Y
3 Blumenauer	N	Y	Y	N	Y	Y
4 DeFazio	N	Y	Y	N	Y	Y
5 Schrader	N	Y	Y	Y	Y	Y
PENNSYLVANIA						
1 Brady	N	Y	Y	N	?	?
2 Evans	N	Y	Y	N	Y	Y
3 **Kelly**	Y	N	N	Y	Y	Y
4 **Perry**	Y	N	N	N	Y	Y
5 **Thompson**	N	N	N	Y	Y	Y
6 **Costello**	?	?	?	?	?	?
7 **Vacant**						
8 **Fitzpatrick**	N	Y	N	Y	Y	Y
9 **Shuster**	?	?	N	Y	Y	Y
10 **Marino**	N	N	N	Y	Y	Y
11 **Barletta**	Y	N	N	Y	Y	Y
12 **Rothfus**	Y	N	N	Y	Y	Y
13 Boyle	N	Y	Y	N	Y	Y
14 Doyle	N	Y	Y	N	Y	Y
15 **Vacant**						
16 **Smucker**	Y	N	N	Y	Y	Y
17 Cartwright	N	Y	Y	N	Y	Y
18 Lamb	N	Y	Y	Y	Y	Y
RHODE ISLAND						
1 Cicilline	N	Y	Y	N	Y	Y
2 Langevin	N	Y	Y	N	Y	Y
SOUTH CAROLINA						
1 **Sanford**	Y	N	N	N	–	–
2 **Wilson**	Y	N	N	Y	+	+
3 **Duncan**	Y	N	N	Y	Y	Y
4 **Gowdy**	Y	N	N	Y	?	?
5 **Norman**	Y	N	N	Y	Y	Y
6 Clyburn	N	Y	Y	N	Y	Y
7 **Rice**	Y	N	N	Y	Y	Y
SOUTH DAKOTA						
AL **Noem**	?	?	?	?	Y	Y
TENNESSEE						
1 **Roe**	Y	N	N	Y	Y	Y
2 **Duncan**	Y	N	N	N	N	Y
3 **Fleischmann**	Y	N	N	Y	Y	Y
4 **DesJarlais**	Y	N	N	Y	Y	Y
5 Cooper	N	Y	Y	N	Y	Y
6 **Black**	Y	N	N	Y	Y	Y
7 **Blackburn**	Y	N	N	Y	?	?
8 **Kustoff**	Y	N	N	Y	Y	Y
9 Cohen	N	Y	Y	N	Y	Y
TEXAS						
1 **Gohmert**	Y	N	N	Y	?	Y
2 **Poe**	Y	N	N	Y	Y	Y
3 **Johnson, S.**	Y	N	N	Y	Y	Y
4 **Ratcliffe**	Y	N	N	Y	Y	Y
5 **Hensarling**	Y	N	N	Y	Y	Y
6 **Barton**	?	N	N	Y	Y	Y
7 **Culberson**	Y	N	N	Y	Y	Y
8 **Brady**	+	–	–	+	Y	Y
9 Green, A.	N	Y	Y	N	+	+
10 **McCaul**	Y	N	N	Y	Y	Y
11 **Conaway**	Y	N	N	Y	Y	Y
12 **Granger**	Y	N	N	Y	Y	Y
13 **Thornberry**	Y	N	N	Y	Y	Y
14 **Weber**	Y	N	N	Y	Y	Y
15 Gonzalez	N	Y	Y	N	Y	Y
16 O'Rourke	N	Y	Y	Y	Y	Y
17 **Flores**	Y	N	N	Y	Y	Y
18 Jackson Lee	N	Y	Y	N	Y	Y
19 **Arrington**	Y	N	N	Y	Y	Y
20 Castro	N	Y	Y	N	Y	Y
21 **Smith**	Y	N	N	Y	Y	Y
22 **Olson**	Y	N	N	Y	Y	Y
23 **Hurd**	N	N	N	Y	Y	Y
24 Marchant	Y	N	N	Y	?	?
25 **Williams**	Y	N	N	Y	Y	Y
26 **Burgess**	Y	N	N	Y	Y	Y
28 Cuellar	N	Y	Y	N	Y	Y
29 Green, G.	Y	Y	Y	N	Y	Y
30 Johnson, E.B.	N	Y	Y	N	Y	Y
31 **Carter**	Y	N	N	Y	Y	Y
32 **Sessions**	Y	N	N	Y	Y	Y
33 Veasey	N	Y	Y	N	Y	Y
34 Vela	N	Y	Y	Y	Y	Y
35 Doggett	N	Y	Y	N	Y	Y
36 **Babin**	Y	N	N	Y	Y	Y
UTAH						
1 **Bishop**	Y	N	N	Y	Y	Y
2 **Stewart**	Y	N	N	Y	Y	Y
3 **Curtis**	Y	N	N	Y	Y	Y
4 **Love**	Y	N	N	Y	Y	Y
VERMONT						
AL Welch	N	Y	Y	N	Y	Y
VIRGINIA						
1 **Wittman**	Y	N	N	Y	Y	Y
2 **Taylor**	Y	N	N	Y	+	+
3 Scott	N	Y	Y	N	Y	Y
4 McEachin	N	Y	Y	N	Y	Y
5 **Garrett**	Y	N	N	Y	N	Y
6 **Goodlatte**	Y	N	N	Y	Y	Y
7 **Brat**	Y	N	N	Y	Y	Y
8 Beyer	N	Y	Y	N	Y	Y
9 **Griffith**	Y	N	N	Y	Y	Y
10 **Comstock**	Y	N	N	Y	Y	Y
11 Connolly	N	Y	Y	N	Y	Y
WASHINGTON						
1 DelBene	N	Y	Y	N	Y	Y
2 Larsen	N	Y	Y	Y	Y	Y
3 **Herrera Beutler**	Y	N	N	Y	Y	Y
4 **Newhouse**	Y	N	N	Y	Y	Y
5 **McMorris Rodgers**	Y	N	N	Y	Y	Y
6 Kilmer	N	Y	Y	N	Y	Y
7 Jayapal	N	Y	Y	N	Y	Y
8 **Reichert**	N	N	N	Y	Y	Y
9 Smith	N	Y	Y	N	Y	Y
10 Heck	N	Y	Y	N	Y	Y
WEST VIRGINIA						
1 **McKinley**	Y	N	N	Y	Y	Y
2 **Mooney**	Y	N	N	Y	Y	Y
3 **Jenkins**	Y	N	N	Y	+	+
WISCONSIN						
1 **Ryan**						
2 Pocan	N	Y	Y	N	Y	Y
3 Kind	N	Y	Y	N	Y	Y
4 Moore	N	Y	Y	N	Y	Y
5 **Sensenbrenner**	Y	N	N	N	Y	Y
6 **Grothman**	Y	Y	N	Y	Y	Y
7 **Duffy**	Y	N	N	Y	Y	Y
8 **Gallagher**	Y	Y	N	Y	Y	Y
WYOMING						
AL **Cheney**	?	?	?	?	Y	Y

VOTE NUMBER

260. PROCEDURAL MOTION/JOURNAL. Approval of the House Journal of June 8, 2018. Approved 224-159: R 130-79; D 94-80. June 12, 2018.

261. HR5788. CONTROLLED SUBSTANCES EXPANSION, TRANSITIONAL HOUSING PILOT PROGRAM AND SHIPMENT DATA/PREVIOUS QUESTION. Buck, R-Colo., motion to order the previous question (thus ending debate and possibility of amendment) on the rule (H Res 934) that would provide for House floor consideration of the bill (HR 2851) that would create a new category of controlled substances, provide for consideration of the bill (HR 5735) that would create a transitional substance abuse recovery housing pilot program, and would provide for consideration of the bill (HR 5788) that would require packages entering the United States to have advance electronic tracking data about the shipment's contents. Motion agreed to 230-183: R 230-0; D 0-183. June 13, 2018.

262. HR5788. CONTROLLED SUBSTANCES EXPANSION, TRANSITIONAL HOUSING PILOT PROGRAM AND SHIPMENT DATA/RULE. Adoption of the rule (H Res 934) that would provide for House floor consideration for the bill (HR 2851) that would create a new category of controlled substances, provide for consideration of the bill (HR 5735) that would create a transitional substance abuse recovery housing pilot program, and would provide for consideration of the bill (HR 5788) that would require packages entering the United States to have advance electronic tracking data about the shipment's contents. Adopted 233-175: R 229-0; D 4-175. June 13, 2018.

263. HR5890. INFANT CARE PLANS/PASSAGE. Garrett, R-Va., motion to suspend the rules and pass the bill that would require the Health and Human Services Department to provide written and technical assistance to assist states in complying with and implementing a plan of safe care for infants born and identified as being affected by substance abuse or withdrawal symptoms, or a fetal alcohol spectrum disorder. Motion agreed to 406-3: R 222-3; D 184-0. June 13, 2018.

264. HR5891. SUBSTANCE ABUSE TASK FORCE/PASSAGE. Grothman, R-Wis., motion to suspend the rules and pass the bill that would establish an interagency task force to develop a federal strategy on how agencies can implement a coordinated approach to responding to substance abuse disorders and opioid abuse, with a focus on coordinating existing programs that support infants, children and families. Motion agreed to 409-8: R 223-8; D 186-0. June 13, 2018.

265. HR5788. SHIPMENT DATA/PASSAGE. Passage of the bill that would require the U.S. Postal Service to obtain advance electronic tracking data, including the shipment's contents and intended recipients, for packages entering the United States. The bill would require the U.S. Postal Service to pass information about such packages to U.S. Customs and Border Protection and would authorize a customs fee of $1 per piece of inbound express mail to cover the cost of screening international mail. The bill would require the U.S Customs and Border Protection to develop technology for the detection of controlled substances in mail. Passed 353-52: R 222-3; D 131-49. June 14, 2018.

	260	261	262	263	264	265
ALABAMA						
1 Byrne	Y	Y	Y	Y	Y	Y
2 Roby	Y	Y	Y	Y	Y	Y
3 Rogers	N	Y	Y	Y	Y	Y
4 Aderholt	Y	Y	Y	Y	Y	Y
5 Brooks	N	Y	Y	Y	Y	Y
6 Palmer	N	Y	Y	Y	Y	Y
7 Sewell	N	N	N	Y	Y	Y
ALASKA						
AL Young	N	Y	Y	?	Y	N
ARIZONA						
1 O'Halleran	N	N	N	Y	Y	Y
2 McSally	N	Y	Y	Y	Y	Y
3 Grijalva	?	?	?	?	?	N
4 Gosar	N	Y	?	Y	N	Y
5 Biggs	N	Y	Y	N	N	Y
6 Schweikert	?	Y	Y	Y	Y	Y
7 Gallego	Y	N	N	Y	Y	Y
8 Lesko	Y	Y	Y	Y	Y	Y
9 Sinema	N	N	Y	Y	Y	Y
ARKANSAS						
1 Crawford	?	Y	Y	Y	Y	Y
2 Hill	N	Y	Y	Y	Y	Y
3 Womack	Y	Y	Y	Y	Y	Y
4 Westerman	?	Y	Y	Y	Y	Y
CALIFORNIA						
1 LaMalfa	Y	Y	Y	Y	Y	Y
2 Huffman	Y	N	?	Y	Y	?
3 Garamendi	N	N	N	Y	Y	Y
4 McClintock	Y	Y	Y	Y	Y	Y
5 Thompson	N	N	N	Y	Y	Y
6 Matsui	Y	N	N	Y	Y	Y
7 Bera	N	N	N	Y	Y	Y
8 Cook	Y	Y	Y	Y	Y	Y
9 McNerney	Y	N	N	Y	Y	Y
10 Denham	N	Y	Y	Y	Y	Y
11 DeSaulnier	Y	N	N	Y	Y	N
12 Pelosi	Y	N	N	Y	Y	Y
13 Lee	N	N	N	Y	Y	–
14 Speier	Y	N	N	Y	Y	Y
15 Swalwell	?	N	N	Y	Y	Y
16 Costa	N	N	N	Y	Y	Y
17 Khanna	N	N	N	?	Y	N
18 Eshoo	N	N	N	Y	Y	Y
19 Lofgren	N	N	N	Y	Y	Y
20 Panetta	N	N	N	Y	Y	Y
21 Valadao	N	Y	Y	Y	Y	Y
22 Nunes	Y	Y	Y	Y	Y	Y
23 McCarthy	Y	Y	Y	Y	Y	Y
24 Carbajal	N	N	N	Y	Y	Y
25 Knight	N	Y	Y	Y	Y	Y
26 Brownley	N	N	N	Y	Y	Y
27 Chu	Y	?	?	Y	N	N
28 Schiff	Y	N	N	Y	Y	Y
29 Cardenas	N	N	N	Y	Y	Y
30 Sherman	Y	N	N	Y	Y	Y
31 Aguilar	N	N	N	Y	Y	Y
32 Napolitano	Y	N	N	Y	Y	N
33 Lieu	N	N	N	Y	Y	Y
34 Gomez	N	?	?	Y	Y	Y
35 Torres	Y	N	N	Y	Y	Y
36 Ruiz	N	N	N	Y	Y	Y
37 Bass	N	N	N	Y	Y	N
38 Sánchez, Linda	N	N	N	Y	Y	Y
39 Royce	Y	Y	Y	Y	Y	Y
40 Roybal-Allard	Y	N	N	Y	Y	N
41 Takano	N	N	N	Y	Y	Y
42 Calvert	Y	Y	Y	Y	Y	Y
43 Waters	Y	N	N	Y	Y	N
44 Barragan	N	N	N	Y	Y	Y
45 Walters	Y	Y	Y	Y	Y	Y
46 Correa	N	N	N	Y	Y	Y
47 Lowenthal	Y	N	N	Y	Y	N
48 Rohrabacher	Y	Y	?	Y	Y	Y
49 Issa	?	Y	Y	Y	Y	Y
50 Hunter	N	Y	Y	Y	Y	Y
51 Vargas	N	N	N	Y	Y	Y
52 Peters	Y	N	N	Y	Y	Y
53 Davis	Y	N	N	Y	Y	Y

	260	261	262	263	264	265
COLORADO						
1 DeGette	Y	N	N	Y	Y	Y
2 Polis	Y	N	N	Y	Y	N
3 Tipton	N	Y	Y	Y	Y	Y
4 Buck	N	Y	Y	Y	Y	Y
5 Lamborn	Y	Y	Y	Y	Y	Y
6 Coffman	N	Y	Y	Y	Y	Y
7 Perlmutter	Y	N	N	Y	?	Y
CONNECTICUT						
1 Larson	Y	N	N	Y	Y	Y
2 Courtney	Y	N	N	Y	Y	Y
3 DeLauro	?	N	N	Y	Y	Y
4 Himes	Y	N	N	Y	Y	+
5 Esty	N	N	N	Y	Y	Y
DELAWARE						
AL Blunt Rochester	Y	N	N	Y	Y	Y
FLORIDA						
1 Gaetz	N	Y	Y	Y	N	Y
2 Dunn	Y	Y	Y	Y	Y	Y
3 Yoho	Y	Y	Y	Y	Y	Y
4 Rutherford	Y	Y	Y	Y	Y	Y
5 Lawson	N	N	N	Y	Y	Y
6 DeSantis	Y	Y	Y	Y	Y	Y
7 Murphy	?	N	N	Y	Y	Y
8 Posey	N	Y	Y	Y	Y	Y
9 Soto	N	N	N	Y	Y	N
10 Demings	Y	N	N	Y	Y	N
11 Webster	Y	Y	Y	Y	Y	Y
12 Bilirakis	+	#	#	#	+	Y
13 Crist	N	N	N	Y	Y	Y
14 Castor	N	N	N	Y	Y	Y
15 Ross	Y	Y	Y	Y	Y	Y
16 Buchanan	Y	Y	Y	Y	Y	Y
17 Rooney, T.	Y	Y	Y	Y	Y	?
18 Mast	N	Y	Y	Y	Y	Y
19 Rooney, F.	?	Y	Y	Y	Y	Y
20 Hastings	N	N	N	Y	Y	N
21 Frankel	Y	N	N	Y	Y	Y
22 Deutch	Y	N	N	Y	Y	Y
23 Wasserman Schultz	Y	N	N	Y	Y	Y
24 Wilson	?	N	N	+	Y	Y
25 Diaz-Balart	N	Y	Y	Y	Y	Y
26 Curbelo	N	Y	Y	Y	Y	Y
27 Ros-Lehtinen	N	Y	Y	Y	Y	Y
GEORGIA						
1 Carter	N	Y	Y	Y	Y	Y
2 Bishop	N	N	N	Y	Y	Y
3 Ferguson	Y	Y	Y	Y	Y	Y
4 Johnson	Y	N	N	Y	Y	N
5 Lewis	N	N	?	Y	Y	N
6 Handel	Y	Y	Y	Y	Y	Y
7 Woodall	N	Y	Y	Y	Y	Y
8 Scott, A.	Y	Y	Y	Y	Y	Y
9 Collins	Y	Y	Y	Y	Y	Y
10 Hice	N	Y	Y	Y	Y	Y
11 Loudermilk	Y	Y	Y	Y	Y	Y
12 Allen	Y	Y	Y	Y	Y	Y
13 Scott, D.	Y	N	N	Y	Y	Y
14 Graves	N	Y	Y	Y	Y	Y
HAWAII						
1 Hanabusa	Y	N	N	Y	Y	?
2 Gabbard	Y	N	N	Y	Y	Y
IDAHO						
1 Labrador	Y	Y	Y	Y	Y	?
2 Simpson	Y	Y	Y	Y	Y	Y
Illinois						
1 Rush	Y	N	N	Y	Y	N
2 Kelly	N	N	N	Y	Y	N
3 Lipinski	Y	N	N	Y	Y	Y
4 Gutierrez	?	–	–	Y	Y	Y
5 Quigley	N	N	N	Y	Y	?
6 Roskam	+	Y	Y	Y	Y	Y
7 Davis, D.	?	N	N	Y	Y	N
8 Krishnamoorthi	Y	N	N	Y	Y	Y
9 Schakowsky	N	N	+	Y	Y	N
10 Schneider	Y	N	N	Y	Y	Y
11 Foster	Y	N	N	Y	Y	Y
12 Bost	?	Y	Y	Y	Y	Y
13 Davis, R.	Y	Y	Y	Y	Y	Y

KEY	Republicans	Democrats	Independents

Y Voted for (yea)	X Paired against	C Voted "present" to avoid possible conflict of interest
# Paired for	– Announced against	
+ Announced for	P Voted "present"	? Did not vote or otherwise make a position known
N Voted against (nay)		

	260	261	262	263	264	265
14 **Hultgren**	Y	Y	Y	Y	Y	Y
15 **Shimkus**	Y	Y	Y	Y	Y	Y
16 **Kinzinger**	N	Y	Y	Y	Y	Y
17 Bustos	Y	N	N	Y	Y	Y
18 **LaHood**	Y	Y	Y	Y	Y	Y
INDIANA						
1 Visclosky	–	N	N	Y	Y	Y
2 **Walorski**	Y	Y	Y	Y	Y	Y
3 **Banks**	Y	Y	Y	Y	Y	Y
4 Rokita	N	Y	Y	Y	Y	Y
5 **Brooks**	Y	Y	Y	Y	Y	Y
6 **Messer**	?	Y	Y	Y	Y	Y
7 Carson	Y	N	N	Y	Y	N
8 **Bucshon**	Y	Y	Y	Y	Y	Y
9 **Hollingsworth**	Y	Y	Y	Y	Y	Y
IOWA						
1 **Blum**	N	Y	Y	Y	Y	Y
2 Loebsack	N	N	N	Y	Y	Y
3 **Young**	Y	Y	Y	Y	Y	Y
4 **King**	Y	Y	Y	Y	Y	Y
KANSAS						
1 **Marshall**	Y	Y	Y	Y	Y	Y
2 **Jenkins**	N	Y	Y	Y	Y	Y
3 **Yoder**	N	Y	Y	Y	Y	Y
4 **Estes**	?	Y	Y	Y	Y	Y
KENTUCKY						
1 **Comer**	N	Y	Y	Y	Y	Y
2 **Guthrie**	Y	Y	Y	Y	Y	Y
3 Yarmuth	Y	N	N	?	Y	Y
4 **Massie**	Y	Y	Y	N	N	Y
5 **Rogers**	Y	Y	Y	Y	Y	Y
6 **Barr**	Y	Y	Y	Y	Y	Y
LOUISIANA						
1 **Scalise**	Y	Y	Y	Y	+	Y
2 Richmond	N	N	N	Y	Y	N
3 **Higgins**	Y	Y	Y	Y	Y	Y
4 **Johnson**	Y	Y	Y	Y	Y	Y
5 **Abraham**	Y	Y	Y	Y	Y	Y
6 **Graves**	Y	Y	Y	+	+	Y
MAINE						
1 Pingree	Y	N	N	Y	Y	Y
2 **Poliquin**	N	Y	+	Y	Y	Y
MARYLAND						
1 **Harris**	Y	Y	Y	Y	Y	Y
2 Ruppersberger	Y	N	N	Y	Y	Y
3 Sarbanes	N	N	N	Y	Y	Y
4 Brown	Y	N	N	Y	Y	N
5 Hoyer	?	N	N	Y	Y	Y
6 Delaney	N	N	N	Y	Y	Y
7 Cummings	N	N	N	Y	Y	Y
8 Raskin	Y	N	N	Y	Y	N
MASSACHUSETTS						
1 Neal	N	N	N	Y	Y	Y
2 McGovern	N	N	N	Y	Y	Y
3 Tsongas	Y	N	N	Y	Y	?
4 Kennedy	Y	N	N	Y	Y	Y
5 Clark	N	N	N	Y	Y	Y
6 Moulton	Y	N	N	Y	Y	Y
7 Capuano	N	N	N	Y	Y	Y
8 Lynch	N	N	N	?	?	Y
9 Keating	N	N	N	Y	Y	Y
MICHIGAN						
1 **Bergman**	N	Y	Y	Y	Y	Y
2 **Huizenga**	N	Y	Y	Y	Y	Y
3 *Amash*	N	Y	Y	N	N	N
4 **Moolenaar**	N	Y	Y	Y	Y	Y
5 Kildee	Y	N	N	Y	Y	Y
6 **Upton**	N	Y	Y	Y	Y	Y
7 **Walberg**	N	Y	Y	Y	Y	Y
8 **Bishop**	N	Y	Y	Y	Y	Y
9 Levin	N	N	N	Y	Y	Y
10 **Mitchell**	Y	Y	Y	Y	Y	Y
11 **Trott**	Y	Y	Y	Y	Y	?
12 Dingell	Y	N	N	Y	Y	Y
14 Lawrence	Y	N	N	Y	Y	N
MINNESOTA						
1 Walz	?	?	?	?	?	?
2 **Lewis**	Y	Y	Y	Y	Y	Y
3 **Paulsen**	N	Y	Y	Y	Y	Y
4 McCollum	Y	N	N	Y	Y	N

	260	261	262	263	264	265
5 Ellison	?	?	?	?	?	?
6 **Emmer**	N	Y	Y	Y	Y	Y
7 Peterson	N	N	N	Y	Y	Y
8 Nolan	N	N	N	Y	Y	N
MISSISSIPPI						
1 **Kelly**	Y	Y	Y	Y	Y	Y
2 Thompson	N	N	N	Y	Y	N
3 **Harper**	?	Y	Y	Y	Y	Y
4 **Palazzo**	N	Y	Y	Y	Y	Y
MISSOURI						
1 Clay	Y	N	N	Y	Y	N
2 **Wagner**	Y	Y	Y	Y	Y	Y
3 **Luetkemeyer**	Y	Y	Y	Y	Y	Y
4 **Hartzler**	Y	Y	Y	Y	Y	Y
5 Cleaver	N	N	N	Y	Y	N
6 **Graves**	N	Y	Y	Y	Y	Y
7 **Long**	Y	Y	Y	?	Y	Y
8 **Smith**	Y	Y	Y	Y	Y	Y
MONTANA						
AL **Gianforte**	Y	Y	Y	Y	Y	Y
NEBRASKA						
1 **Fortenberry**	Y	Y	Y	Y	Y	Y
2 **Bacon**	Y	Y	Y	Y	Y	Y
3 **Smith**	Y	Y	Y	Y	Y	Y
NEVADA						
1 Titus	+	N	N	Y	Y	N
2 **Amodei**	Y	Y	Y	Y	Y	Y
3 Rosen	N	N	N	Y	Y	Y
4 Kihuen	N	N	N	Y	Y	Y
NEW HAMPSHIRE						
1 Shea-Porter	Y	N	N	Y	Y	Y
2 Kuster	Y	N	N	Y	Y	Y
NEW JERSEY						
1 Norcross	N	N	N	Y	Y	N
2 **LoBiondo**	N	Y	Y	Y	Y	Y
3 **MacArthur**	N	Y	Y	Y	Y	Y
4 **Smith**	Y	Y	Y	Y	Y	Y
5 Gottheimer	N	N	Y	Y	Y	Y
6 Pallone	N	N	N	Y	Y	Y
7 **Lance**	N	Y	Y	Y	Y	Y
8 Sires	?	N	N	Y	Y	Y
9 Pascrell	Y	N	N	Y	Y	Y
10 Payne	N	N	N	Y	Y	N
11 **Frelinghuysen**	Y	Y	Y	Y	Y	Y
12 Watson Coleman	N	N	N	Y	Y	N
NEW MEXICO						
1 Lujan Grisham	Y	N	N	Y	Y	Y
2 **Pearce**	?	Y	Y	Y	Y	Y
3 Luján	Y	N	N	Y	Y	Y
NEW YORK						
1 **Zeldin**	N	Y	Y	Y	Y	Y
2 **King**	?	Y	Y	Y	Y	Y
3 Suozzi	Y	N	N	Y	Y	Y
4 Rice	Y	N	N	Y	Y	Y
5 Meeks	Y	N	N	Y	Y	Y
6 Meng	Y	N	N	Y	Y	Y
7 Velázquez	Y	N	N	Y	Y	N
8 Jeffries	N	N	N	Y	Y	N
9 Clarke	N	N	N	Y	Y	N
10 Nadler	Y	N	N	Y	Y	Y
11 **Donovan**	Y	Y	Y	Y	Y	?
12 Maloney, C.	Y	N	N	Y	Y	Y
13 Espaillat	N	?	?	Y	Y	Y
14 Crowley	N	–	–	+	+	Y
15 Serrano	N	N	N	Y	Y	Y
16 Engel	Y	N	N	Y	Y	Y
17 Lowey	Y	N	N	Y	Y	?
18 Maloney, S.P.	N	N	N	Y	Y	Y
19 **Faso**	N	Y	Y	Y	Y	Y
20 Tonko	P	N	N	Y	Y	Y
21 **Stefanik**	Y	Y	Y	Y	Y	Y
22 **Tenney**	N	Y	Y	Y	Y	Y
23 **Reed**	N	Y	Y	Y	Y	Y
24 **Katko**	Y	Y	Y	?	Y	Y
25 **Vacant**						
26 Higgins	Y	N	N	Y	Y	N
27 **Collins**	Y	Y	Y	Y	Y	Y
NORTH CAROLINA						
1 Butterfield	Y	N	N	Y	Y	Y
2 **Holding**	N	Y	Y	Y	Y	Y
3 **Jones**	N	Y	Y	Y	N	?
4 Price	N	N	N	Y	Y	Y

	260	261	262	263	264	265
5 **Foxx**	N	Y	Y	Y	Y	Y
6 **Walker**	Y	Y	Y	Y	Y	Y
7 **Rouzer**	N	Y	Y	Y	Y	Y
8 **Hudson**	N	Y	Y	Y	Y	Y
9 **Pittenger**	N	Y	Y	Y	Y	Y
9 **Vacant**						
10 **McHenry**	Y	Y	Y	Y	Y	Y
11 **Meadows**	Y	Y	Y	Y	Y	Y
12 Adams	Y	N	N	Y	Y	Y
13 **Budd**	Y	Y	Y	Y	Y	Y
NORTH DAKOTA						
AL **Cramer**	Y	Y	Y	Y	Y	Y
OHIO						
1 **Chabot**	Y	Y	Y	Y	Y	Y
2 **Wenstrup**	?	Y	Y	Y	Y	Y
3 Beatty	–	–	–	+	+	+
4 **Jordan**	N	Y	Y	Y	Y	Y
5 **Latta**	Y	Y	Y	Y	Y	Y
6 **Johnson**	N	Y	Y	Y	Y	Y
7 **Gibbs**	Y	Y	Y	Y	Y	Y
8 **Davidson**	Y	Y	Y	Y	Y	Y
9 Kaptur	Y	N	N	Y	Y	Y
10 **Turner**	?	Y	Y	Y	Y	Y
11 Fudge	N	N	N	Y	Y	N
12 **Vacant**						
13 Ryan	Y	N	N	Y	Y	Y
14 **Joyce**	N	Y	Y	Y	Y	Y
15 **Stivers**	N	Y	Y	Y	Y	Y
16 **Renacci**	Y	Y	Y	Y	Y	Y
OKLAHOMA						
1 **Vacant**						
2 **Mullin**	Y	Y	Y	Y	Y	Y
3 **Lucas**	Y	Y	Y	Y	Y	Y
4 **Cole**	Y	Y	Y	Y	Y	Y
5 **Russell**	Y	Y	Y	Y	Y	Y
OREGON						
1 Bonamici	Y	N	N	Y	Y	Y
2 **Walden**	Y	Y	Y	Y	Y	Y
3 Blumenauer	Y	N	N	Y	Y	Y
4 DeFazio	N	N	N	Y	Y	+
5 Schrader	N	N	N	Y	Y	Y
PENNSYLVANIA						
1 Brady	?	N	N	Y	Y	Y
2 Evans	Y	N	N	Y	Y	Y
3 **Kelly**	Y	Y	Y	Y	Y	Y
4 **Perry**	N	Y	Y	Y	Y	Y
5 **Thompson**	N	Y	Y	Y	Y	Y
6 **Costello**	?	Y	Y	Y	Y	Y
7 **Vacant**						
8 **Fitzpatrick**	N	Y	Y	Y	Y	Y
9 **Shuster**	?	?	?	Y	Y	Y
10 **Marino**	Y	Y	Y	Y	Y	Y
11 **Barletta**	Y	Y	Y	+	Y	Y
12 **Rothfus**	Y	Y	Y	Y	Y	Y
13 Boyle	N	N	N	Y	Y	Y
14 Doyle	N	N	N	Y	Y	Y
15 **Vacant**						
16 **Smucker**	Y	Y	Y	Y	Y	Y
17 Cartwright	Y	N	N	Y	Y	Y
18 Lamb	Y	N	Y	Y	Y	Y
RHODE ISLAND						
1 Cicilline	N	N	N	Y	Y	Y
2 Langevin	N	N	N	Y	Y	Y
SOUTH CAROLINA						
1 **Sanford**	+	Y	Y	Y	N	Y
2 **Wilson**	?	Y	Y	Y	Y	Y
3 **Duncan**	N	Y	Y	+	Y	Y
4 **Gowdy**	?	Y	Y	Y	Y	Y
5 **Norman**	Y	Y	Y	Y	Y	Y
6 Clyburn	Y	N	N	Y	Y	Y
7 **Rice**	Y	Y	Y	Y	Y	Y
SOUTH DAKOTA						
AL **Noem**	Y	Y	Y	Y	Y	Y
TENNESSEE						
1 **Roe**	Y	Y	Y	Y	Y	Y
2 **Duncan**	Y	Y	Y	Y	Y	Y
3 **Fleischmann**	Y	Y	Y	Y	Y	Y
4 **DesJarlais**	Y	Y	Y	Y	Y	Y
5 Cooper	Y	N	N	Y	Y	Y
6 **Black**	Y	Y	Y	Y	Y	?
7 **Blackburn**	?	Y	Y	Y	Y	Y
8 **Kustoff**	Y	Y	Y	Y	Y	Y
9 Cohen	N	N	N	Y	Y	N

	260	261	262	263	264	265
TEXAS						
1 **Gohmert**	N	Y	Y	Y	N	Y
2 **Poe**	N	Y	Y	Y	Y	Y
3 **Johnson, S.**	Y	Y	Y	Y	Y	Y
4 **Ratcliffe**	N	Y	Y	Y	Y	Y
5 **Hensarling**	Y	Y	Y	Y	Y	Y
6 **Barton**	Y	Y	Y	Y	Y	Y
7 **Culberson**	Y	Y	Y	Y	Y	Y
8 **Brady**	Y	Y	Y	Y	Y	Y
9 Green, A.	+	–	–	Y	Y	N
10 **McCaul**	Y	Y	Y	Y	Y	Y
11 **Conaway**	N	Y	Y	Y	Y	Y
12 **Granger**	Y	Y	Y	Y	Y	Y
13 **Thornberry**	Y	Y	Y	Y	Y	Y
14 **Weber**	N	Y	Y	Y	Y	Y
15 Gonzalez	Y	N	N	Y	Y	N
16 O'Rourke	Y	N	N	Y	Y	+
17 **Flores**	N	Y	Y	Y	Y	Y
18 Jackson Lee	N	N	N	Y	Y	N
19 **Arrington**	Y	Y	Y	Y	Y	Y
20 Castro	Y	N	N	Y	Y	Y
21 **Smith**	Y	Y	Y	Y	Y	Y
22 **Olson**	Y	Y	Y	Y	Y	Y
23 **Hurd**	N	Y	Y	+	Y	Y
24 Marchant	?	Y	Y	Y	Y	Y
25 **Williams**	Y	Y	Y	Y	Y	Y
26 **Burgess**	N	Y	Y	Y	Y	Y
28 Cuellar	?	N	N	Y	Y	Y
29 Green, G.	N	N	N	Y	Y	N
30 Johnson, E.B.	N	N	N	Y	Y	Y
31 **Carter**	Y	Y	Y	Y	Y	?
32 **Sessions**	Y	Y	Y	Y	Y	Y
33 Veasey	N	N	N	Y	Y	N
34 Vela	Y	N	N	Y	Y	Y
35 Doggett	?	N	N	Y	Y	N
36 **Babin**	N	+	Y	Y	Y	Y
UTAH						
1 **Bishop**	Y	Y	Y	Y	Y	Y
2 **Stewart**	Y	Y	Y	Y	Y	Y
3 **Curtis**	Y	Y	Y	Y	Y	Y
4 **Love**	N	Y	Y	Y	Y	Y
VERMONT						
AL Welch	Y	N	N	Y	Y	Y
VIRGINIA						
1 **Wittman**	?	Y	Y	Y	Y	Y
2 **Taylor**	+	Y	Y	Y	Y	Y
3 Scott	Y	N	N	Y	Y	N
4 McEachin	Y	N	N	Y	Y	N
5 **Garrett**	N	Y	Y	Y	Y	Y
6 **Goodlatte**	Y	Y	Y	Y	Y	Y
7 **Brat**	Y	Y	Y	Y	Y	Y
8 Beyer	N	N	N	Y	Y	Y
9 **Griffith**	Y	Y	Y	Y	Y	?
10 **Comstock**	Y	Y	Y	Y	Y	?
11 Connolly	N	N	N	Y	Y	Y
WASHINGTON						
1 DelBene	Y	N	N	Y	Y	Y
2 Larsen	Y	N	N	Y	Y	Y
3 **Herrera Beutler**	N	Y	Y	Y	Y	Y
4 **Newhouse**	Y	Y	Y	Y	Y	Y
5 **McMorris Rodgers**	Y	Y	Y	Y	Y	Y
6 Kilmer	N	N	N	Y	Y	Y
7 Jayapal	Y	N	?	Y	Y	N
8 **Reichert**	N	Y	Y	Y	Y	Y
9 Smith	Y	N	N	Y	Y	+
10 **Heck**	Y	N	N	Y	Y	Y
WEST VIRGINIA						
1 **McKinley**	N	Y	Y	Y	Y	Y
2 **Mooney**	Y	Y	Y	Y	Y	N
3 **Jenkins**	?	Y	Y	Y	Y	Y
WISCONSIN						
1 **Ryan**						
2 Pocan	Y	N	N	Y	Y	N
3 Kind	N	N	N	Y	Y	Y
4 Moore	Y	N	N	Y	Y	N
5 **Sensenbrenner**	Y	Y	Y	Y	Y	Y
6 **Grothman**	Y	+	Y	Y	Y	Y
7 **Duffy**	Y	Y	Y	Y	Y	Y
8 **Gallagher**	N	Y	Y	Y	Y	Y
WYOMING						
AL **Cheney**	Y	Y	Y	?	Y	Y

VOTE NUMBER

266. HR5735. TRANSITIONAL HOUSING PILOT PROGRAM/PASSAGE.
Passage of the bill that would establish a pilot program that would provide 10,000 Section 8 Housing Choice vouchers, or 0.5 percent of such available vouchers, whichever is less, to nonprofit entities to pay for individuals to live in supportive and transitional housing programs that provide treatment for opioid use disorders or other substance use disorders. Non-profit entities would be required to provide an evidence-based treatment program and a jobs skills training program, and meet various other standards to qualify for vouchers under the pilot program. Passed 230-173: R 218-7; D 12-166. June 14, 2018.

267. HR2851. CONTROLLED SUBSTANCES EXPANSION/HUMAN CONSUMPTION GUIDELINES. Thornberry, R-Texas, amendment that would set guidelines for how law enforcement should determine if a controlled substance analogue is intended for human consumption. Adopted in Committee of the Whole 223-158: R 203-6; D 20-152. June 15, 2018.

268. HR2851. CONTROLLED SUBSTANCES EXPANSION/PASSAGE.
Passage of the bill that would create a new category of controlled substances, "schedule A," for drugs or substances that have similar chemical structures or effects as controlled substances in schedules I through V. It would immediately classify certain fentanyl analogues as schedule A drugs. The bill would establish maximum penalties for the manufacture, distribution or dispensing of schedule A drugs, though possession of such substances alone would not constitute a basis for criminal or civil penalties. Passed 239-142: R 197-12; D 42-130. June 15, 2018.

269. HR5687. PRESCRIPTION DRUG PACKAGING/PASSAGE. Walden, R-Ore., motion to suspend the rules and pass the bill that would allow the Food and Drug Administration to require that the packaging for prescription drugs contain mechanisms that would mitigate the risk of abuse of such drugs. Motion agreed to 342-13: R 190-13; D 152-0. June 19, 2018.

270. HR5676. PHARMACIES SUSPECTED OF FRAUD/PASSAGE. Roskam, R-Ill., motion to suspend the rules and pass the bill that would allow the Health and Human Services Department to suspend Medicare prescription drug and Medicare Advantage reimbursement payments to pharmacies who are under investigation for possible fraud. Motion agreed to 356-3: R 203-3; D 153-0. June 19, 2018.

271. PROCEDURAL MOTION/JOURNAL. Approval of the House Journal of June 15, 2018. Approved 195-152: R 125-75; D 70-77. June 19, 2018.

	266	267	268	269	270	271
ALABAMA						
1 **Byrne**	Y	Y	Y	Y	Y	Y
2 **Roby**	Y	+	Y	Y	Y	Y
3 **Rogers**	Y	Y	Y	Y	Y	N
4 **Aderholt**	Y	Y	Y	Y	Y	Y
5 **Brooks**	N	Y	N	N	N	N
6 **Palmer**	Y	Y	Y	Y	Y	N
7 Sewell	N	N	N	+	+	?
ALASKA						
AL **Young**	Y	Y	Y	Y	Y	N
Arizona						
1 O'Halleran	Y	Y	Y	Y	Y	N
2 **McSally**	Y	Y	Y	?	?	?
3 Grijalva	N	N	N	Y	Y	?
4 **Gosar**	Y	?	?	Y	Y	N
5 **Biggs**	Y	N	N	N	Y	Y
6 **Schweikert**	Y	Y	Y	Y	Y	Y
7 Gallego	N	N	N	Y	Y	N
8 **Lesko**	Y	Y	Y	Y	Y	Y
9 Sinema	Y	Y	Y	Y	Y	N
ARKANSAS						
1 **Crawford**	Y	Y	Y	?	?	?
2 **Hill**	Y	Y	Y	Y	Y	Y
3 **Womack**	Y	Y	Y	Y	Y	Y
4 **Westerman**	Y	Y	Y	Y	Y	Y
CALIFORNIA						
1 **LaMalfa**	Y	Y	Y	Y	Y	Y
2 Huffman	?	?	?	Y	Y	Y
3 Garamendi	N	Y	Y	Y	Y	Y
4 **McClintock**	Y	N	N	N	Y	Y
5 Thompson	N	N	N	Y	Y	Y
6 Matsui	N	N	N	Y	Y	N
7 Bera	Y	N	Y	Y	Y	N
8 **Cook**	Y	Y	Y	Y	Y	Y
9 McNerney	N	N	N	Y	Y	Y
10 **Denham**	Y	Y	Y	Y	Y	N
11 DeSaulnier	N	N	N	Y	Y	Y
12 Pelosi	N	N	N	Y	Y	Y
13 Lee	–	N	N	Y	Y	N
14 Speier	N	?	?	Y	Y	Y
15 Swalwell	N	N	N	Y	Y	N
16 Costa	N	Y	Y	Y	Y	N
17 Khanna	N	N	N	Y	Y	Y
18 Eshoo	N	N	N	Y	Y	Y
19 Lofgren	N	N	N	Y	Y	N
20 Panetta	Y	Y	Y	Y	Y	Y
21 **Valadao**	Y	Y	Y	Y	Y	N
22 **Nunes**	Y	Y	Y	Y	Y	Y
23 **McCarthy**	Y	Y	Y	+	+	+
24 Carbajal	N	N	Y	Y	Y	N
25 **Knight**	Y	Y	Y	Y	Y	Y
26 Brownley	N	N	Y	Y	Y	Y
27 Chu	N	N	N	Y	Y	Y
28 Schiff	N	N	N	Y	Y	Y
29 Cardenas	N	N	N	Y	Y	N
30 Sherman	N	N	N	Y	Y	Y
31 Aguilar	N	Y	N	Y	Y	N
32 Napolitano	N	N	Y	?	?	Y
33 Lieu	N	Y	N	Y	?	N
34 Gomez	N	N	N	Y	Y	N
35 Torres	N	N	Y	Y	Y	N
36 Ruiz	N	N	N	Y	Y	N
37 Bass	N	?	?	Y	Y	N
38 Sánchez, Linda	N	?	?	Y	?	N
39 **Royce**	Y	Y	Y	Y	Y	Y
40 Roybal-Allard	N	N	N	Y	Y	N
41 Takano	N	N	N	Y	Y	Y
42 **Calvert**	Y	Y	Y	Y	Y	Y
43 Waters	N	N	N	Y	Y	Y
44 Barragan	N	N	N	Y	Y	N
45 **Walters**	Y	Y	Y	Y	Y	Y
46 Correa	N	N	Y	Y	Y	N
47 Lowenthal	N	N	N	Y	Y	Y
48 **Rohrabacher**	Y	N	N	Y	Y	N
49 **Issa**	Y	Y	Y	?	?	?
50 **Hunter**	Y	Y	Y	Y	Y	Y
51 Vargas	N	N	N	Y	Y	N
52 Peters	Y	N	Y	Y	Y	Y
53 Davis	N	N	N	Y	Y	?

	266	267	268	269	270	271
COLORADO						
1 DeGette	N	N	N	Y	Y	Y
2 Polis	N	N	N	?	?	?
3 **Tipton**	Y	?	?	Y	Y	N
4 **Buck**	Y	Y	Y	Y	Y	Y
5 **Lamborn**	Y	Y	Y	Y	Y	Y
6 **Coffman**	Y	Y	Y	Y	Y	N
7 Perlmutter	N	N	N	Y	Y	Y
CONNECTICUT						
1 Larson	N	–	–	Y	Y	Y
2 Courtney	N	N	N	Y	Y	Y
3 DeLauro	N	N	N	Y	Y	?
4 Himes	–	N	Y	Y	Y	Y
5 Esty	N	N	N	Y	Y	N
DELAWARE						
AL Blunt Rochester	N	–	–	Y	Y	Y
FLORIDA						
1 **Gaetz**	N	Y	N	N	Y	N
2 **Dunn**	Y	Y	Y	Y	Y	?
3 **Yoho**	Y	?	N	Y	N	N
4 **Rutherford**	Y	Y	Y	Y	Y	Y
5 Lawson	N	N	N	Y	Y	N
6 **DeSantis**	Y	Y	Y	Y	Y	Y
7 Murphy	N	Y	?	?	?	?
8 **Posey**	Y	Y	Y	+	+	+
9 Soto	N	N	N	Y	Y	N
10 Demings	N	N	N	Y	Y	Y
11 **Webster**	Y	?	?	?	?	?
12 **Bilirakis**	Y	Y	Y	Y	Y	Y
13 Crist	N	Y	Y	Y	Y	N
14 Castor	N	N	N	Y	Y	N
15 **Ross**	Y	Y	Y	?	?	?
16 **Buchanan**	Y	Y	Y	?	?	?
17 **Rooney, T.**	?	?	?	Y	Y	Y
18 **Mast**	Y	Y	Y	Y	Y	N
19 **Rooney, F.**	Y	Y	Y	Y	Y	Y
20 Hastings	N	N	N	Y	Y	N
21 Frankel	N	N	N	?	?	?
22 Deutch	N	N	N	Y	Y	Y
23 Wasserman Schultz	N	N	N	?	?	?
24 Wilson	N	N	N	?	?	?
25 **Diaz-Balart**	Y	Y	Y	Y	Y	N
26 **Curbelo**	Y	?	?	Y	Y	Y
27 **Ros-Lehtinen**	Y	Y	Y	Y	Y	N
GEORGIA						
1 **Carter**	Y	Y	Y	+	Y	N
2 Bishop	N	N	N	Y	Y	N
3 **Ferguson**	Y	Y	Y	Y	Y	Y
4 Johnson	N	N	N	Y	Y	Y
5 Lewis	?	?	?	Y	Y	N
6 **Handel**	Y	Y	Y	Y	Y	Y
7 **Woodall**	Y	Y	Y	Y	Y	Y
8 **Scott, A.**	Y	Y	Y	Y	Y	Y
9 **Collins**	Y	Y	Y	+	+	?
10 **Hice**	Y	Y	N	Y	Y	N
11 **Loudermilk**	Y	Y	Y	?	Y	Y
12 **Allen**	Y	Y	Y	Y	Y	Y
13 Scott, D.	N	N	N	Y	Y	N
14 **Graves**	Y	Y	Y	Y	Y	N
HAWAII						
1 Hanabusa	?	?	?	Y	Y	N
2 Gabbard	N	N	N	Y	Y	?
IDAHO						
1 **Labrador**	?	?	?	N	Y	Y
2 **Simpson**	Y	Y	Y	?	?	?
ILLINOIS						
1 Rush	N	N	N	Y	Y	N
2 Kelly	N	N	N	?	?	?
3 Lipinski	N	Y	Y	?	?	?
4 Gutierrez	N	?	?	+	+	?
5 Quigley	?	?	?	?	?	?
6 **Roskam**	Y	Y	Y	Y	Y	N
7 Davis, D.	N	?	?	?	?	?
8 Krishnamoorthi	N	N	N	Y	Y	Y
9 Schakowsky	N	N	N	Y	Y	N
10 Schneider	Y	Y	Y	Y	Y	Y
11 Foster	N	N	N	?	?	?
12 **Bost**	Y	Y	Y	Y	Y	N
13 **Davis, R.**	Y	Y	Y	Y	Y	N

	266	267	268	269	270	271
14 **Hultgren**	Y	Y	Y	Y	Y	Y
15 **Shimkus**	Y	?	?	Y	Y	Y
16 **Kinzinger**	Y	Y	Y	Y	Y	N
17 Bustos	N	N	Y	Y	Y	Y
18 **LaHood**	Y	Y	Y	+	+	?
INDIANA						
1 Visclosky	N	Y	Y	Y	Y	N
2 **Walorski**	Y	Y	Y	Y	Y	Y
3 **Banks**	Y	Y	Y	+	+	+
4 Rokita	Y	Y	Y	Y	Y	N
5 **Brooks**	Y	Y	Y	Y	Y	Y
6 **Messer**	Y	Y	Y	Y	Y	?
7 Carson	N	N	N	Y	Y	N
8 **Bucshon**	Y	Y	Y	Y	Y	Y
9 **Hollingsworth**	Y	Y	Y	Y	Y	Y
IOWA						
1 **Blum**	Y	Y	Y	+	+	+
2 Loebsack	N	N	Y	?	?	?
3 **Young**	Y	Y	Y	Y	Y	Y
4 **King**	Y	Y	Y	Y	Y	Y
KANSAS						
1 **Marshall**	Y	Y	Y	Y	Y	Y
2 **Jenkins**	Y	Y	Y	Y	Y	N
3 **Yoder**	Y	Y	Y	Y	Y	N
4 **Estes**	Y	+	+	Y	Y	Y
KENTUCKY						
1 **Comer**	Y	Y	Y	Y	Y	N
2 **Guthrie**	Y	Y	Y	Y	Y	Y
3 Yarmuth	N	N	N	Y	Y	Y
4 **Massie**	N	Y	N	N	N	Y
5 **Rogers**	Y	Y	Y	Y	Y	Y
6 **Barr**	Y	Y	Y	Y	Y	Y
LOUISIANA						
1 **Scalise**	Y	?	?	Y	Y	Y
2 Richmond	N	N	N	Y	Y	Y
3 **Higgins**	Y	Y	Y	Y	Y	Y
4 **Johnson**	Y	?	?	Y	Y	Y
5 **Abraham**	Y	Y	Y	Y	Y	Y
6 **Graves**	Y	Y	Y	Y	Y	?
MAINE						
1 Pingree	N	N	N	Y	Y	Y
2 **Poliquin**	Y	Y	Y	Y	Y	N
MARYLAND						
1 **Harris**	Y	Y	Y	Y	Y	Y
2 Ruppersberger	N	N	Y	Y	Y	Y
3 Sarbanes	N	N	N	Y	Y	N
4 Brown	N	N	N	Y	Y	Y
5 Hoyer	N	N	N	Y	Y	N
6 Delaney	N	N	Y	Y	Y	N
7 Cummings	N	N	N	?	?	?
8 Raskin	N	N	N	Y	Y	N
MASSACHUSETTS						
1 Neal	N	?	?	?	?	?
2 McGovern	N	N	N	Y	Y	N
3 Tsongas	?	?	?	?	?	?
4 Kennedy	N	N	N	Y	Y	Y
5 Clark	N	N	N	+	Y	N
6 Moulton	Y	N	N	?	Y	Y
7 Capuano	N	N	N	+	+	?
8 Lynch	N	N	Y	?	Y	N
9 Keating	N	N	Y	?	?	?
MICHIGAN						
1 **Bergman**	Y	Y	Y	+	+	–
2 **Huizenga**	Y	Y	Y	Y	Y	N
3 *Amash*	N	N	N	N	N	N
4 **Moolenaar**	Y	Y	Y	Y	+	Y
5 Kildee	N	N	N	Y	Y	Y
6 **Upton**	Y	Y	Y	Y	Y	N
7 **Walberg**	Y	Y	Y	Y	Y	N
8 **Bishop**	Y	Y	Y	Y	Y	N
9 Levin	N	N	N	Y	Y	N
10 **Mitchell**	Y	Y	Y	Y	Y	Y
11 Trott	?	?	?	Y	Y	Y
12 Dingell	N	N	N	Y	Y	Y
14 Lawrence	N	N	N	Y	Y	N
MINNESOTA						
1 Walz	?	?	?	?	?	?
2 **Lewis**	Y	N	N	Y	Y	Y
3 **Paulsen**	Y	Y	Y	Y	Y	N
4 McCollum	N	N	N	Y	Y	Y
5 Ellison	?	?	?	?	?	?
6 **Emmer**	Y	Y	Y	Y	Y	N
7 Peterson	Y	Y	Y	Y	Y	N
8 Nolan	N	N	N	Y	Y	N
MISSISSIPPI						
1 **Kelly**	Y	?	?	Y	Y	Y
2 Thompson	N	N	N	?	?	?
3 **Harper**	Y	Y	Y	Y	Y	Y
4 **Palazzo**	Y	Y	Y	Y	Y	N
MISSOURI						
1 Clay	N	N	N	Y	Y	Y
2 **Wagner**	Y	Y	Y	Y	Y	Y
3 **Luetkemeyer**	Y	Y	Y	Y	Y	Y
4 **Hartzler**	Y	Y	Y	Y	Y	Y
5 Cleaver	N	N	N	Y	Y	N
6 **Graves**	Y	Y	Y	+	+	?
7 **Long**	Y	Y	Y	Y	Y	Y
8 **Smith**	Y	Y	Y	Y	Y	Y
MONTANA						
AL **Gianforte**	Y	Y	Y	Y	Y	Y
NEBRASKA						
1 **Fortenberry**	Y	Y	Y	Y	Y	Y
2 **Bacon**	Y	Y	Y	Y	Y	Y
3 **Smith**	Y	Y	Y	Y	Y	Y
NEVADA						
1 Titus	N	N	N	Y	Y	Y
2 **Amodei**	Y	Y	Y	Y	Y	Y
3 Rosen	Y	Y	Y	Y	Y	N
4 Kihuen	N	N	N	Y	Y	N
NEW HAMPSHIRE						
1 Shea-Porter	N	N	N	Y	Y	Y
2 Kuster	N	N	Y	Y	Y	Y
NEW JERSEY						
1 Norcross	N	N	N	Y	Y	N
2 **LoBiondo**	Y	Y	Y	Y	Y	N
3 **MacArthur**	Y	Y	Y	Y	Y	N
4 **Smith**	Y	Y	Y	Y	Y	Y
5 Gottheimer	Y	Y	Y	Y	Y	N
6 Pallone	N	N	N	Y	Y	N
7 **Lance**	Y	Y	Y	Y	Y	N
8 Sires	N	N	N	Y	Y	N
9 Pascrell	N	N	N	Y	Y	Y
10 Payne	N	N	N	Y	Y	N
11 **Frelinghuysen**	Y	Y	Y	Y	Y	Y
12 Watson Coleman	N	N	N	Y	Y	N
NEW MEXICO						
1 Lujan Grisham	N	N	N	Y	Y	Y
2 **Pearce**	Y	?	?	Y	Y	N
3 Luján	N	N	N	Y	Y	Y
NEW YORK						
1 **Zeldin**	Y	Y	Y	Y	Y	N
2 **King**	Y	Y	Y	Y	Y	Y
3 Suozzi	N	Y	Y	Y	Y	N
4 Rice	N	Y	Y	?	?	?
5 Meeks	N	N	N	?	?	?
6 Meng	N	N	N	Y	Y	Y
7 Velázquez	N	N	N	Y	Y	N
8 Jeffries	N	N	N	Y	Y	Y
9 Clarke	N	N	N	Y	Y	N
10 Nadler	?	N	N	Y	Y	Y
11 **Donovan**	?	Y	Y	Y	Y	Y
12 Maloney, C.	N	N	N	Y	Y	N
13 Espaillat	N	N	N	Y	Y	N
14 Crowley	N	N	N	Y	Y	N
15 Serrano	N	N	N	Y	Y	N
16 Engel	N	N	N	Y	Y	Y
17 Lowey	?	N	N	Y	Y	Y
18 Maloney, S.P.	N	N	Y	Y	Y	N
19 **Faso**	Y	Y	Y	Y	Y	N
20 Tonko	N	–	–	Y	Y	P
21 **Stefanik**	Y	Y	Y	Y	Y	Y
22 **Tenney**	Y	Y	Y	Y	Y	N
23 **Reed**	Y	Y	Y	Y	Y	N
24 **Katko**	Y	Y	Y	?	?	?
25 **Vacant**						
26 Higgins	N	N	N	Y	Y	Y
27 **Collins**	Y	Y	Y	Y	Y	Y
NORTH CAROLINA						
1 Butterfield	N	N	N	?	?	?
2 **Holding**	Y	Y	Y	Y	Y	?
3 **Jones**	?	?	?	Y	Y	Y
4 Price	N	N	N	+	+	?
5 **Foxx**	Y	Y	Y	Y	Y	N
6 **Walker**	Y	Y	Y	Y	Y	Y
7 **Rouzer**	Y	Y	Y	Y	Y	N
8 **Hudson**	Y	Y	Y	Y	Y	N
9 **Pittenger**	Y	Y	Y	?	?	?
9 **Vacant**						
10 **McHenry**	Y	Y	Y	Y	Y	Y
11 **Meadows**	Y	Y	Y	Y	Y	Y
12 Adams	N	N	N	Y	Y	N
13 **Budd**	Y	Y	Y	Y	Y	Y
NORTH DAKOTA						
AL **Cramer**	Y	Y	Y	Y	Y	Y
OHIO						
1 **Chabot**	Y	Y	Y	Y	Y	Y
2 **Wenstrup**	Y	Y	Y	Y	Y	Y
3 Beatty	–	–	–	+	+	–
4 **Jordan**	Y	Y	Y	Y	Y	N
5 **Latta**	Y	Y	Y	Y	Y	N
6 **Johnson**	Y	Y	Y	Y	Y	N
7 **Gibbs**	Y	Y	Y	+	+	+
8 **Davidson**	Y	Y	Y	N	Y	Y
9 Kaptur	N	N	Y	Y	Y	Y
10 **Turner**	Y	Y	Y	Y	Y	N
11 Fudge	N	N	N	?	?	?
12 **Vacant**						
13 Ryan	N	N	N	Y	Y	N
14 **Joyce**	Y	Y	Y	?	?	?
15 **Stivers**	Y	Y	Y	?	?	?
16 **Renacci**	Y	Y	Y	+	+	?
OKLAHOMA						
1 **Vacant**						
2 **Mullin**	Y	?	?	Y	Y	Y
3 **Lucas**	Y	Y	Y	Y	Y	Y
4 **Cole**	Y	Y	Y	Y	Y	Y
5 **Russell**	Y	Y	Y	Y	Y	Y
OREGON						
1 Bonamici	N	N	N	+	+	?
2 **Walden**	Y	Y	Y	Y	Y	N
3 Blumenauer	N	N	N	+	+	Y
4 DeFazio	?	–	–	Y	Y	Y
5 Schrader	N	N	Y	?	?	?
PENNSYLVANIA						
1 Brady	N	N	N	?	?	?
2 Evans	N	N	N	Y	Y	Y
3 **Kelly**	Y	Y	Y	Y	Y	Y
4 **Perry**	Y	Y	Y	N	Y	N
5 **Thompson**	Y	Y	Y	Y	Y	N
6 **Costello**	Y	Y	Y	Y	Y	Y
7 **Vacant**						
8 **Fitzpatrick**	Y	Y	Y	Y	Y	N
9 **Shuster**	Y	Y	Y	Y	Y	?
10 **Marino**	Y	Y	Y	Y	Y	Y
11 **Barletta**	Y	Y	Y	?	?	?
12 **Rothfus**	Y	Y	Y	Y	Y	Y
13 Boyle	N	N	N	?	?	?
14 Doyle	N	N	N	Y	Y	N
15 **Vacant**						
16 **Smucker**	Y	Y	Y	Y	Y	Y
17 Cartwright	N	N	N	Y	Y	Y
18 Lamb	Y	Y	Y	Y	Y	Y
RHODE ISLAND						
1 Cicilline	N	N	Y	Y	Y	Y
2 Langevin	N	N	Y	Y	Y	?
SOUTH CAROLINA						
1 **Sanford**	N	N	N	–	–	–
2 **Wilson**	Y	Y	Y	Y	Y	Y
3 **Duncan**	Y	Y	Y	Y	Y	N
4 **Gowdy**	Y	Y	Y	Y	Y	Y
5 **Norman**	Y	Y	Y	+	+	+
6 Clyburn	N	N	N	?	?	?
7 **Rice**	Y	Y	Y	Y	Y	Y
SOUTH DAKOTA						
AL **Noem**	Y	Y	Y	Y	Y	Y
TENNESSEE						
1 **Roe**	Y	Y	Y	Y	Y	Y
2 **Duncan**	N	Y	Y	Y	Y	Y
3 **Fleischmann**	Y	Y	Y	Y	Y	Y
4 **DesJarlais**	Y	Y	Y	Y	Y	N
5 Cooper	N	Y	Y	Y	Y	Y
6 **Black**	+	?	+	?	?	?
7 **Blackburn**	Y	Y	Y	?	?	?
8 **Kustoff**	Y	Y	Y	Y	Y	Y
9 Cohen	N	N	N	Y	Y	Y
TEXAS						
1 **Gohmert**	Y	?	?	N	Y	N
2 **Poe**	Y	Y	Y	N	Y	N
3 **Johnson, S.**	Y	Y	Y	Y	Y	Y
4 **Ratcliffe**	Y	Y	Y	Y	Y	N
5 **Hensarling**	Y	Y	Y	?	?	?
6 **Barton**	Y	Y	Y	Y	Y	Y
7 **Culberson**	Y	+	+	?	Y	Y
8 **Brady**	Y	Y	Y	Y	Y	Y
9 Green, A.	N	N	N	+	+	?
10 **McCaul**	Y	Y	Y	Y	Y	Y
11 **Conaway**	Y	Y	Y	Y	Y	N
12 **Granger**	Y	Y	Y	Y	Y	Y
13 **Thornberry**	Y	Y	Y	Y	Y	Y
14 **Weber**	Y	Y	Y	Y	Y	N
15 Gonzalez	N	N	Y	+	+	+
16 O'Rourke	–	–	–	Y	Y	Y
17 **Flores**	Y	Y	Y	Y	Y	N
18 Jackson Lee	N	N	N	Y	Y	N
19 **Arrington**	Y	Y	Y	Y	Y	Y
20 Castro	N	N	N	Y	Y	N
21 **Smith**	Y	Y	Y	Y	Y	?
22 **Olson**	Y	Y	Y	Y	Y	Y
23 **Hurd**	Y	Y	Y	Y	Y	N
24 Marchant	Y	+	+	Y	Y	N
25 **Williams**	Y	Y	N	Y	Y	Y
26 **Burgess**	Y	Y	Y	Y	Y	N
28 Cuellar	N	Y	Y	Y	Y	Y
29 Green, G.	N	?	?	+	+	?
30 Johnson, E.B.	N	N	N	Y	Y	N
31 **Carter**	?	?	?	Y	Y	Y
32 **Sessions**	Y	+	+	Y	Y	Y
33 Veasey	N	N	N	Y	Y	N
34 Vela	N	N	N	?	?	?
35 Doggett	N	N	N	Y	Y	Y
36 **Babin**	Y	Y	Y	Y	Y	N
UTAH						
1 **Bishop**	Y	Y	?	Y	Y	Y
2 **Stewart**	Y	Y	Y	Y	Y	Y
3 **Curtis**	Y	Y	Y	Y	Y	Y
4 **Love**	Y	Y	Y	Y	Y	Y
VERMONT						
AL Welch	N	N	N	Y	Y	Y
VIRGINIA						
1 **Wittman**	Y	+	+	Y	Y	N
2 **Taylor**	Y	Y	Y	Y	Y	N
3 Scott	N	N	N	Y	Y	Y
4 McEachin	N	N	N	Y	Y	Y
5 **Garrett**	N	Y	N	N	Y	N
6 **Goodlatte**	Y	Y	Y	Y	Y	Y
7 **Brat**	Y	Y	Y	Y	Y	Y
8 Beyer	N	N	N	Y	Y	?
9 **Griffith**	?	Y	Y	Y	Y	Y
10 **Comstock**	?	Y	Y	Y	Y	Y
11 Connolly	N	N	N	Y	Y	N
WASHINGTON						
1 DelBene	N	N	N	Y	Y	Y
2 Larsen	N	N	N	Y	Y	N
3 **Herrera Beutler**	Y	Y	Y	?	Y	N
4 **Newhouse**	Y	Y	Y	Y	Y	Y
5 **McMorris Rodgers**	Y	Y	Y	Y	Y	Y
6 Kilmer	N	N	Y	Y	Y	N
7 Jayapal	N	N	N	Y	Y	?
8 **Reichert**	Y	+	+	Y	Y	Y
9 Smith	–	–	–	Y	Y	Y
10 Heck	N	N	N	Y	Y	Y
WEST VIRGINIA						
1 **McKinley**	Y	Y	Y	Y	Y	N
2 **Mooney**	Y	Y	Y	Y	Y	Y
3 **Jenkins**	Y	Y	Y	Y	Y	N
WISCONSIN						
1 **Ryan**						
2 Pocan	N	N	N	Y	Y	Y
3 Kind	Y	N	Y	Y	Y	N
4 Moore	N	N	N	Y	Y	N
5 **Sensenbrenner**	Y	Y	Y	Y	Y	Y
6 **Grothman**	Y	Y	Y	Y	Y	N
7 **Duffy**	Y	Y	Y	Y	Y	Y
8 **Gallagher**	Y	Y	Y	Y	Y	N
WYOMING						
AL **Cheney**	Y	Y	Y	Y	Y	Y

⦀ HOUSE VOTES

VOTE NUMBER

272. PROCEDURAL MOTION/CHANGE CONVENING TIME. Burgess, R-Texas, motion to change the time that the House would convene for legislative business on Thursday, June 21, 2018, to 10 a.m. Motion agreed to 222-184: R 221-1; D 1-183. June 20, 2018.

273. HR6082. MEDICAL FILE ACCESS, MEDICAID COVERAGE OF SUBSTANCE ABUSE TREATMENT, AND OPIOID ABUSE PREVENTION AND HEALTH PROGRAMS/PREVIOUS QUESTION. Burgess, R-Texas, motion to order the previous question (thus ending debate and possibility of amendment) on the rule (H Res 949) that would provide for House floor consideration of the bill (HR 6082) that would allow certain medical professionals to access patients' medical files related to substance abuse without their explicit consent, provide for consideration of the bill (HR 5797) that would temporarily allow the use of Medicaid funds to pay for substance use disorder treatment at certain inpatient mental health treatment facilities, and provide for consideration of the bill (HR 6) that would modify Medicare and Medicaid and a variety of other health programs in relation to opioid abuse. Motion agreed to 221-185: R 221-0; D 0-185. June 20, 2018.

274. HR6. MEDICAL FILE ACCESS, MEDICAID COVERAGE OF SUBSTANCE ABUSE TREATMENT, AND OPIOID ABUSE PREVENTION AND HEALTH PROGRAMS/RULE. Adoption of the rule (H Res 949) that would provide for House floor consideration of the bill (HR 6082) that would allow certain medical professionals to access patients' medical files related to substance abuse without their explicit consent, provide for consideration of the bill (HR 5797) that would temporarily allow the use of Medicaid funds to pay for substance use disorder treatment at certain inpatient mental health treatment facilities, and provide for consideration of the bill (HR 6) that would modify Medicare and Medicaid and a variety of other health programs in relation to opioid abuse. The rule would provide for the texts of HR 2851, HR 5735 and HR 5797, as passed the House, to be incorporated into the text of HR 6 during the engrossment of HR 6. Adopted 225-180: R 220-3; D 5-177. June 20, 2018.

275. HR5797. MEDICAID COVERAGE OF SUBSTANCE ABUSE TREATMENT/ RECOMMIT. Castor, D-Fla., motion to recommit the bill to the House Energy and Commerce Committee with instructions to report it back immediately with an amendment that would replace the bill's provisions with a program that would provide federal matching funds for the treatment for eligible individuals suffering from substance abuse disorders. It would require that states extend Medicaid eligibility to receive such federal funds. Motion rejected 190-226: R 0-226; D 190-0. June 20, 2018.

276. HR5797. MEDICAID COVERAGE OF SUBSTANCE ABUSE TREATMENT/ PASSAGE. Passge of the bill that would temporarily allow, until 2023, the use of Medicaid funds to pay for substance use disorder treatment at certain inpatient mental health treatment facilities. It would require states, to be eligible for such funds, to include in their state Medicaid plan information on how the state will improve access to outpatient care, the process to be used for transitioning individuals to appropriate outpatient care, and how individuals will be screened and assessed. The bill would limit an individual to a maximum of 30 days of inpatient treatment in a 12-month period that could be covered by Medicaid. Passed 261-155: R 211-15; D 50-140. June 20, 2018.

277. HR6082. MEDICAL FILE ACCESS/RECOMMIT. Pallone, D-N.J., motion to recommit the bill to the House Energy and Commerce Committee with instructions to report it back immediately with an amendment that would remove the bill's provisions that would allow certain medical professionals to access patients' medical files related to substance abuse without their explicit consent and would instead require the secretary of Health and Human Services to identify model programs for training health care providers in the appropriate use and disclosure of patient health records. Motion rejected 175-240: R 0-225; D 175-15. June 20, 2018.

	272	273	274	275	276	277
ALABAMA						
1 Byrne	Y	Y	Y	N	Y	N
2 Roby	Y	Y	Y	N	Y	N
3 Rogers	Y	Y	Y	N	Y	N
4 Aderholt	Y	Y	Y	N	Y	N
5 Brooks	Y	Y	Y	N	N	N
6 Palmer	Y	Y	Y	N	Y	N
7 Sewell	N	N	N	Y	Y	Y
ALASKA						
AL Young	Y	Y	Y	N	Y	N
ARIZONA						
1 O'Halleran	N	N	N	Y	Y	N
2 McSally	Y	Y	Y	N	Y	N
3 Grijalva	N	N	N	Y	N	Y
4 Gosar	Y	Y	Y	N	N	N
5 Biggs	Y	Y	Y	N	N	N
6 Schweikert	Y	Y	Y	N	Y	N
7 Gallego	N	N	N	Y	N	Y
8 Lesko	Y	Y	Y	N	Y	N
9 Sinema	N	N	+	Y	Y	N
ARKANSAS						
1 Crawford	Y	Y	Y	N	Y	N
2 Hill	Y	Y	Y	N	Y	N
3 Womack	Y	Y	Y	N	Y	N
4 Westerman	Y	Y	Y	N	Y	N
CALIFORNIA						
1 LaMalfa	Y	Y	Y	N	Y	N
2 Huffman	N	N	N	Y	N	N
3 Garamendi	N	N	N	Y	Y	Y
4 McClintock	Y	Y	Y	N	N	N
5 Thompson	N	N	N	Y	N	Y
6 Matsui	N	N	N	Y	N	Y
7 Bera	N	N	N	Y	Y	Y
8 Cook	Y	Y	Y	N	Y	N
9 McNerney	N	N	N	Y	N	Y
10 Denham	Y	Y	Y	N	Y	–
11 DeSaulnier	N	N	N	Y	N	Y
12 Pelosi	?	?	?	Y	N	Y
13 Lee	N	N	N	Y	Y	Y
14 Speier	N	N	N	Y	N	Y
15 Swalwell	N	N	N	Y	N	Y
16 Costa	N	N	N	Y	N	Y
17 Khanna	N	N	N	Y	N	Y
18 Eshoo	N	N	N	Y	N	Y
19 Lofgren	N	N	N	Y	N	Y
20 Panetta	N	N	N	Y	Y	Y
21 Valadao	Y	Y	Y	N	Y	N
22 Nunes	Y	Y	Y	N	N	N
23 McCarthy	Y	Y	Y	?	?	?
24 Carbajal	N	N	N	Y	N	N
25 Knight	Y	Y	Y	N	Y	N
26 Brownley	N	N	N	Y	N	Y
27 Chu	N	N	N	Y	N	Y
28 Schiff	N	N	N	Y	N	Y
29 Cardenas	N	N	N	Y	N	Y
30 Sherman	N	N	N	Y	N	Y
31 Aguilar	N	N	N	Y	Y	Y
32 Napolitano	N	N	N	Y	N	Y
33 Lieu	N	N	N	Y	Y	Y
34 Gomez	N	N	N	Y	N	Y
35 Torres	N	N	N	Y	Y	Y
36 Ruiz	N	N	N	Y	N	Y
37 Bass	N	N	N	Y	Y	Y
38 Sánchez, Linda	N	N	N	Y	N	Y
39 Royce	Y	Y	Y	N	Y	N
40 Roybal-Allard	N	N	N	Y	N	Y
41 Takano	N	N	N	Y	N	Y
42 Calvert	Y	Y	Y	N	Y	N
43 Waters	N	N	N	Y	N	Y
44 Barragan	N	N	N	Y	N	Y
45 Walters	Y	Y	Y	N	Y	N
46 Correa	N	N	N	Y	Y	Y
47 Lowenthal	N	N	N	Y	N	Y
48 Rohrabacher	Y	Y	Y	N	Y	N
49 Issa	Y	Y	Y	N	Y	N
50 Hunter	Y	Y	Y	N	Y	N
51 Vargas	N	N	N	Y	N	Y
52 Peters	N	N	N	Y	N	Y
53 Davis	N	N	N	Y	N	Y

	272	273	274	275	276	277
COLORADO						
1 DeGette	N	N	N	Y	N	Y
2 Polis	?	?	?	?	–	?
3 Tipton	Y	Y	Y	N	Y	N
4 Buck	Y	Y	Y	N	Y	N
5 Lamborn	Y	Y	Y	N	Y	N
6 Coffman	Y	Y	Y	N	Y	N
7 Perlmutter	N	N	N	Y	N	Y
CONNECTICUT						
1 Larson	N	N	N	Y	Y	Y
2 Courtney	N	N	N	Y	Y	Y
3 DeLauro	N	N	N	Y	Y	Y
4 Himes	N	N	N	Y	Y	Y
5 Esty	N	N	N	Y	Y	Y
DELAWARE						
AL Blunt Rochester	N	N	N	Y	Y	Y
FLORIDA						
1 Gaetz	Y	Y	Y	N	N	N
2 Dunn	Y	Y	Y	N	Y	N
3 Yoho	Y	Y	Y	N	Y	N
4 Rutherford	Y	Y	Y	N	Y	N
5 Lawson	N	N	N	Y	Y	Y
6 DeSantis	Y	Y	Y	N	Y	N
7 Murphy	N	N	Y	Y	N	Y
8 Posey	Y	Y	Y	N	Y	N
9 Soto	N	N	N	Y	N	Y
10 Demings	N	N	N	Y	N	Y
11 Webster	Y	Y	Y	N	Y	N
12 Bilirakis	Y	Y	Y	N	Y	N
13 Crist	N	N	N	Y	Y	Y
14 Castor	N	N	N	Y	N	Y
15 Ross	Y	Y	Y	N	Y	N
16 Buchanan	Y	Y	Y	N	Y	N
17 Rooney, T.	Y	Y	Y	N	Y	N
18 Mast	Y	Y	Y	N	Y	N
19 Rooney, F.	Y	Y	Y	N	Y	N
20 Hastings	N	N	N	Y	N	Y
21 Frankel	?	?	?	Y	N	N
22 Deutch	N	N	N	Y	N	N
23 Wasserman Schultz	N	N	N	Y	N	Y
24 Wilson	P	N	N	Y	N	Y
25 Diaz-Balart	Y	Y	Y	N	Y	N
26 Curbelo	Y	Y	Y	N	Y	N
27 Ros-Lehtinen	Y	Y	Y	N	Y	N
GEORGIA						
1 Carter	Y	Y	Y	N	Y	N
2 Bishop	N	N	N	Y	N	Y
3 Ferguson	Y	Y	Y	N	Y	N
4 Johnson	N	N	N	Y	N	Y
5 Lewis	N	N	N	Y	N	Y
6 Handel	Y	Y	Y	N	Y	N
7 Woodall	Y	Y	Y	N	Y	N
8 Scott, A.	Y	Y	Y	N	Y	N
9 Collins	+	+	+	–	+	–
10 Hice	Y	Y	Y	N	Y	N
11 Loudermilk	Y	Y	Y	N	N	N
12 Allen	Y	Y	Y	N	Y	N
13 Scott, D.	N	N	N	Y	N	Y
14 Graves	Y	Y	Y	N	Y	N
HAWAII						
1 Hanabusa	N	N	N	Y	N	Y
2 Gabbard	N	N	N	Y	N	Y
IDAHO						
1 Labrador	Y	Y	Y	N	N	N
2 Simpson	Y	Y	Y	N	Y	N
ILLINOIS						
1 Rush	N	N	?	Y	Y	Y
2 Kelly	N	N	N	Y	Y	Y
3 Lipinski	N	N	N	Y	Y	Y
4 Gutierrez	N	N	N	Y	N	Y
5 Quigley	N	N	N	Y	N	Y
6 Roskam	Y	Y	Y	N	Y	N
7 Davis, D.	N	N	N	Y	N	Y
8 Krishnamoorthi	N	N	N	Y	N	Y
9 Schakowsky	N	N	N	Y	N	Y
10 Schneider	N	N	Y	Y	Y	Y
11 Foster	N	N	N	Y	N	Y
12 Bost	Y	Y	Y	N	Y	N
13 Davis, R.	Y	Y	Y	N	Y	N

KEY	Republicans	Democrats	Independents
Y Voted for (yea)		**X** Paired against	**C** Voted "present" to avoid possible conflict of interest
# Paired for		**–** Announced against	
+ Announced for		**P** Voted "present"	**?** Did not vote or otherwise make a position known
N Voted against (nay)			

	272	273	274	275	276	277
14 **Hultgren**	Y	Y	Y	N	Y	N
15 **Shimkus**	Y	Y	Y	N	Y	N
16 **Kinzinger**	+	+	+	N	Y	N
17 Bustos	N	N	N	Y	N	N
18 **LaHood**	Y	Y	Y	N	Y	N
INDIANA						
1 Visclosky	N	N	N	Y	N	Y
2 **Walorski**	Y	Y	Y	N	Y	N
3 **Banks**	Y	Y	Y	N	Y	N
4 Rokita	Y	Y	Y	N	Y	N
5 **Brooks**	Y	Y	Y	N	Y	N
6 **Messer**	Y	Y	Y	N	Y	N
7 Carson	N	N	N	Y	N	Y
8 **Bucshon**	Y	Y	Y	N	Y	N
9 **Hollingsworth**	Y	Y	Y	N	Y	N
IOWA						
1 **Blum**	?	?	?	-	+	-
2 Loebsack	N	N	N	Y	N	Y
3 **Young**	Y	Y	Y	N	Y	N
4 **King**	Y	Y	Y	N	N	N
KANSAS						
1 **Marshall**	Y	Y	Y	N	Y	N
2 **Jenkins**	Y	Y	Y	N	Y	N
3 **Yoder**	Y	Y	Y	N	Y	N
4 **Estes**	Y	Y	Y	N	Y	N
KENTUCKY						
1 **Comer**	Y	Y	Y	N	Y	N
2 **Guthrie**	Y	Y	Y	N	Y	N
3 Yarmuth	N	N	N	Y	N	N
4 **Massie**	Y	Y	N	N	N	N
5 **Rogers**	Y	Y	Y	N	Y	N
6 **Barr**	Y	Y	Y	N	Y	N
LOUISIANA						
1 **Scalise**	Y	Y	Y	N	Y	N
2 Richmond	N	N	N	Y	N	Y
3 **Higgins**	Y	Y	Y	N	Y	N
4 **Johnson**	Y	Y	Y	N	Y	N
5 **Abraham**	Y	Y	Y	N	Y	N
6 **Graves**	Y	Y	Y	N	N	N
MAINE						
1 Pingree	N	N	N	Y	N	Y
2 **Poliquin**	Y	Y	Y	N	Y	N
MARYLAND						
1 **Harris**	Y	Y	Y	N	Y	N
2 Ruppersberger	N	N	N	Y	N	Y
3 Sarbanes	N	N	N	Y	N	Y
4 Brown	N	N	N	Y	N	Y
5 Hoyer	N	N	N	Y	N	Y
6 Delaney	N	N	N	Y	Y	Y
7 Cummings	N	N	N	Y	N	Y
8 Raskin	N	N	N	Y	N	Y
MASSACHUSETTS						
1 Neal	N	N	N	Y	N	Y
2 McGovern	N	N	N	Y	N	Y
3 Tsongas	N	N	N	Y	N	Y
4 Kennedy	N	N	N	Y	N	Y
5 Clark	N	N	N	Y	N	Y
6 Moulton	N	N	N	Y	N	Y
7 Capuano	N	N	N	Y	N	Y
8 Lynch	N	N	N	Y	N	Y
9 Keating	N	N	N	Y	N	Y
MICHIGAN						
1 **Bergman**	Y	Y	?	N	Y	N
2 **Huizenga**	Y	Y	Y	N	Y	N
3 *Amash*	N	Y	N	N	N	N
4 **Moolenaar**	Y	Y	Y	N	Y	N
5 Kildee	N	N	N	Y	N	Y
6 **Upton**	Y	Y	Y	N	Y	N
7 **Walberg**	Y	Y	Y	N	Y	N
8 **Bishop**	Y	Y	Y	N	Y	N
9 Levin	N	N	N	Y	N	Y
10 **Mitchell**	Y	Y	Y	N	Y	N
11 **Trott**	Y	Y	Y	N	Y	N
12 Dingell	N	N	N	Y	N	Y
14 Lawrence	N	N	N	Y	N	Y
MINNESOTA						
1 Walz	?	?	?	Y	Y	Y
2 **Lewis**	Y	Y	Y	?	+	?
3 **Paulsen**	Y	Y	Y	N	Y	N
4 McCollum	N	N	N	Y	N	Y

	272	273	274	275	276	277
5 Ellison	?	?	?	?	?	?
6 **Emmer**	Y	Y	Y	?	?	?
7 Peterson	N	N	N	Y	Y	Y
8 Nolan	N	N	N	Y	Y	Y
MISSISSIPPI						
1 **Kelly**	Y	Y	Y	N	Y	N
2 Thompson	?	?	?	Y	N	Y
3 **Harper**	Y	Y	Y	N	Y	N
4 **Palazzo**	Y	Y	Y	N	Y	N
MISSOURI						
1 Clay	N	N	N	Y	N	Y
2 **Wagner**	Y	Y	Y	N	Y	N
3 **Luetkemeyer**	Y	Y	Y	N	Y	N
4 **Hartzler**	Y	Y	Y	N	Y	N
5 Cleaver	N	N	N	Y	N	Y
6 **Graves**	?	?	?	?	?	?
7 **Long**	Y	Y	Y	N	Y	N
8 **Smith**	Y	Y	Y	N	Y	N
MONTANA						
AL **Gianforte**	Y	Y	Y	N	Y	N
NEBRASKA						
1 **Fortenberry**	Y	Y	Y	N	Y	N
2 **Bacon**	Y	Y	Y	N	Y	N
3 **Smith**	Y	Y	Y	N	Y	N
NEVADA						
1 Titus	N	N	N	Y	N	Y
2 **Amodei**	Y	Y	Y	N	Y	N
3 Rosen	N	N	N	Y	Y	N
4 Kihuen	N	N	N	Y	N	Y
NEW HAMPSHIRE						
1 Shea-Porter	N	N	N	Y	Y	Y
2 Kuster	N	N	N	Y	Y	Y
NEW JERSEY						
1 Norcross	N	N	N	Y	N	Y
2 **LoBiondo**	Y	Y	Y	N	Y	N
3 **MacArthur**	Y	Y	Y	N	Y	N
4 **Smith**	Y	Y	Y	N	Y	N
5 Gottheimer	N	N	Y	Y	Y	Y
6 Pallone	N	N	N	Y	N	Y
7 **Lance**	Y	Y	Y	N	Y	N
8 Sires	N	N	N	Y	N	Y
9 Pascrell	N	N	?	Y	N	Y
10 Payne	N	N	N	Y	N	Y
11 **Frelinghuysen**	Y	Y	Y	N	Y	N
12 Watson Coleman	N	N	N	Y	N	Y
NEW MEXICO						
1 Lujan Grisham	N	N	N	Y	Y	Y
2 **Pearce**	Y	Y	Y	N	Y	N
3 Luján	N	N	N	Y	N	Y
NEW YORK						
1 **Zeldin**	Y	Y	Y	N	Y	N
2 **King**	Y	Y	Y	N	Y	N
3 Suozzi	N	N	Y	Y	Y	N
4 Rice	N	N	N	Y	Y	Y
5 Meeks	N	N	N	Y	N	Y
6 Meng	N	N	N	Y	N	Y
7 Velázquez	N	N	N	Y	N	Y
8 Jeffries	N	N	N	Y	N	Y
9 Clarke	N	N	N	Y	N	Y
10 Nadler	N	N	N	Y	N	Y
11 **Donovan**	Y	Y	Y	N	Y	N
12 Maloney, C.	N	N	N	Y	N	Y
13 Espaillat	N	N	N	Y	N	Y
14 Crowley	N	N	N	Y	N	Y
15 Serrano	N	N	N	Y	N	Y
16 Engel	N	N	N	Y	N	Y
17 Lowey	N	N	N	Y	N	Y
18 Maloney, S.P.	N	N	N	Y	Y	Y
19 **Faso**	Y	Y	Y	N	Y	N
20 Tonko	N	N	N	Y	Y	Y
21 **Stefanik**	Y	Y	Y	N	Y	N
22 **Tenney**	Y	Y	Y	N	Y	N
23 **Reed**	Y	Y	Y	N	Y	N
24 **Katko**	Y	Y	Y	N	Y	N
25 **Vacant**						
26 Higgins	N	N	N	Y	N	Y
27 **Collins**	?	Y	Y	N	Y	N
NORTH CAROLINA						
1 Butterfield	N	N	N	Y	N	Y
2 **Holding**	Y	Y	Y	N	Y	N
3 **Jones**	Y	Y	N	N	N	N
4 Price	N	N	N	Y	N	Y

	272	273	274	275	276	277
5 **Foxx**	Y	Y	Y	N	Y	N
6 **Walker**	Y	Y	Y	N	Y	N
7 **Rouzer**	Y	Y	Y	N	Y	N
8 **Hudson**	Y	Y	Y	N	Y	N
9 **Pittenger**	Y	Y	Y	N	Y	N
9 **Vacant**						
10 **McHenry**	Y	Y	Y	N	Y	N
11 **Meadows**	Y	Y	Y	N	Y	N
12 Adams	N	N	N	Y	N	Y
13 **Budd**	Y	Y	Y	N	Y	N
NORTH DAKOTA						
AL **Cramer**	Y	Y	Y	N	Y	N
OHIO						
1 **Chabot**	Y	Y	Y	N	Y	N
2 **Wenstrup**	Y	Y	Y	N	Y	N
3 Beatty	N	N	N	Y	N	Y
4 **Jordan**	?	?	?	N	Y	N
5 **Latta**	Y	Y	Y	N	Y	N
6 **Johnson**	Y	Y	Y	N	Y	N
7 **Gibbs**	Y	Y	Y	N	Y	N
8 **Davidson**	?	?	Y	N	Y	N
9 Kaptur	N	N	N	Y	N	Y
10 **Turner**	+	+	+	N	Y	N
11 Fudge	N	N	N	Y	Y	Y
12 **Vacant**						
13 Ryan	N	N	N	Y	N	Y
14 **Joyce**	Y	Y	Y	N	Y	N
15 **Stivers**	Y	Y	Y	N	Y	N
16 **Renacci**	Y	Y	Y	N	Y	N
OKLAHOMA						
1 **Vacant**						
2 **Mullin**	Y	Y	Y	N	Y	N
3 **Lucas**	Y	Y	Y	N	Y	N
4 **Cole**	Y	Y	Y	N	Y	N
5 **Russell**	Y	Y	Y	N	Y	N
OREGON						
1 Bonamici	N	N	N	Y	N	N
2 **Walden**	Y	Y	Y	N	Y	N
3 Blumenauer	N	N	N	Y	N	N
4 DeFazio	N	N	N	Y	N	Y
5 Schrader	N	N	N	Y	N	Y
PENNSYLVANIA						
1 Brady	N	N	N	Y	N	Y
2 Evans	N	N	N	Y	N	Y
3 **Kelly**	Y	Y	Y	N	Y	N
4 **Perry**	Y	Y	Y	N	Y	N
5 **Thompson**	Y	Y	Y	N	Y	N
6 **Costello**	Y	Y	Y	N	Y	N
7 **Vacant**						
8 **Fitzpatrick**	Y	Y	Y	N	Y	N
9 **Shuster**	Y	Y	Y	N	Y	N
10 **Marino**	Y	Y	Y	N	Y	N
11 **Barletta**	Y	Y	Y	N	Y	N
12 **Rothfus**	Y	Y	Y	N	Y	N
13 Boyle	N	N	N	Y	N	Y
14 Doyle	N	N	N	Y	N	Y
15 **Vacant**						
16 **Smucker**	Y	Y	Y	N	Y	N
17 Cartwright	N	N	N	Y	N	Y
18 Lamb	Y	N	Y	Y	Y	Y
RHODE ISLAND						
1 Cicilline	N	N	N	Y	N	Y
2 Langevin	N	N	N	Y	N	Y
SOUTH CAROLINA						
1 **Sanford**	Y	Y	Y	N	N	N
2 **Wilson**	Y	Y	Y	N	Y	N
3 **Duncan**	Y	?	Y	N	Y	N
4 **Gowdy**	Y	Y	Y	N	Y	N
5 **Norman**	Y	Y	Y	N	Y	N
6 Clyburn	N	N	N	Y	N	Y
7 **Rice**	Y	Y	Y	N	Y	N
SOUTH DAKOTA						
AL **Noem**	Y	Y	Y	N	Y	N
TENNESSEE						
1 **Roe**	Y	Y	Y	N	Y	N
2 **Duncan**	Y	Y	Y	N	Y	N
3 **Fleischmann**	Y	Y	Y	N	Y	N
4 **DesJarlais**	Y	Y	Y	N	Y	N
5 Cooper	N	N	N	Y	Y	Y
6 **Black**	?	?	?	?	?	?
7 **Blackburn**	Y	Y	Y	N	Y	N
8 **Kustoff**	Y	Y	Y	N	Y	N
9 Cohen	N	N	N	Y	N	N

	272	273	274	275	276	277
TEXAS						
1 **Gohmert**	Y	Y	Y	N	N	N
2 **Poe**	Y	Y	Y	N	Y	N
3 **Johnson, S.**	Y	Y	Y	N	Y	N
4 **Ratcliffe**	Y	Y	Y	N	Y	N
5 **Hensarling**	Y	Y	Y	N	Y	N
6 **Barton**	Y	Y	Y	N	Y	N
7 **Culberson**	Y	Y	Y	N	Y	N
8 **Brady**	Y	Y	Y	N	Y	N
9 Green, A.	N	N	N	Y	N	Y
10 **McCaul**	Y	Y	Y	N	Y	N
11 **Conaway**	Y	Y	Y	N	Y	N
12 **Granger**	Y	Y	Y	N	Y	N
13 **Thornberry**	?	?	?	N	Y	N
14 **Weber**	Y	Y	Y	N	Y	N
15 Gonzalez	N	N	N	Y	Y	Y
16 O'Rourke	N	N	N	Y	Y	Y
17 **Flores**	Y	Y	Y	N	Y	N
18 Jackson Lee	N	N	N	Y	Y	Y
19 **Arrington**	Y	Y	Y	N	Y	N
20 Castro	N	N	N	Y	N	Y
21 **Smith**	Y	Y	Y	N	Y	N
22 **Olson**	Y	Y	Y	N	Y	N
23 **Hurd**	Y	Y	Y	N	Y	N
24 Marchant	Y	Y	Y	N	Y	N
25 **Williams**	Y	Y	Y	N	Y	N
26 **Burgess**	Y	Y	Y	N	Y	N
28 Cuellar	N	N	N	Y	Y	Y
29 Green, G.	N	N	N	Y	N	Y
30 Johnson, E.B.	?	?	?	Y	N	Y
31 **Carter**	Y	Y	Y	N	Y	N
32 **Sessions**	Y	Y	Y	N	Y	N
33 Veasey	N	N	N	Y	N	Y
34 Vela	?	?	?	?	?	?
35 Doggett	N	N	N	Y	N	Y
36 **Babin**	Y	Y	Y	N	Y	N
UTAH						
1 **Bishop**	Y	?	Y	N	Y	N
2 **Stewart**	Y	Y	Y	N	Y	N
3 **Curtis**	Y	Y	Y	N	Y	N
4 **Love**	Y	Y	Y	N	Y	N
VERMONT						
AL Welch	N	N	N	Y	N	Y
VIRGINIA						
1 **Wittman**	Y	Y	Y	N	Y	N
2 **Taylor**	Y	Y	Y	N	Y	N
3 Scott	N	N	N	Y	Y	Y
4 McEachin	N	N	N	Y	N	Y
5 **Garrett**	Y	Y	Y	N	N	N
6 **Goodlatte**	Y	Y	Y	N	Y	N
7 **Brat**	Y	Y	Y	N	Y	N
8 Beyer	N	N	N	Y	Y	Y
9 **Griffith**	Y	Y	Y	N	Y	N
10 **Comstock**	Y	Y	Y	N	Y	N
11 Connolly	N	N	N	Y	Y	Y
WASHINGTON						
1 DelBene	N	N	N	Y	N	Y
2 Larsen	N	N	N	Y	N	Y
3 **Herrera Beutler**	Y	Y	Y	N	Y	N
4 **Newhouse**	Y	Y	Y	N	Y	N
5 **McMorris Rodgers**	Y	Y	Y	N	Y	N
6 Kilmer	N	N	N	Y	Y	Y
7 Jayapal	N	N	N	Y	N	Y
8 **Reichert**	Y	Y	Y	N	Y	N
9 Smith	N	N	N	Y	N	Y
10 Heck	N	N	N	Y	N	Y
WEST VIRGINIA						
1 **McKinley**	Y	Y	Y	N	Y	N
2 **Mooney**	Y	Y	Y	N	Y	N
3 **Jenkins**	Y	Y	Y	N	Y	N
WISCONSIN						
1 **Ryan**						
2 Pocan	N	N	N	Y	N	Y
3 Kind	N	N	N	Y	Y	Y
4 Moore	N	N	N	Y	N	Y
5 **Sensenbrenner**	Y	Y	Y	N	Y	N
6 **Grothman**	Y	Y	Y	N	Y	N
7 **Duffy**	Y	Y	Y	-	+	-
8 **Gallagher**	?	?	?	N	Y	N
WYOMING						
AL **Cheney**	?	?	?	N	Y	N

III HOUSE VOTES

VOTE NUMBER

278. HR6082. MEDICAL FILE ACCESS/PASSAGE. Passage of the bill that would allow certain medical professionals to access patients' medical files related to substance abuse without their explicit consent if they are treating a patient for a substance abuse disorder. The bill would allow disclosure of such medical records to public health authorities if an individual's identifying information is not included. The bill would prohibit disclosure of such records as part of law enforcement activities. Passed 357-57: R 217-7; D 140-50. June 20, 2018.

279. HRES954. IMMIGRATION PROGRAMS AND AUTHORIZATIONS/ PREVIOUS QUESTION. Burgess, R-Texas, motion to order the previous question (thus ending debate and possibility of amendment) on the rule (H Res 954) that would provide for House floor consideration of the bill (HR 4760) that would authorize $24.8 billion for fiscal 2018 through fiscal 2022 for various border security activities and would provide individuals registered under the Deferred Action for Childhood Arrivals program with a three-year, renewable contingent non-immigrant legal status but with no special path to citizenship. Adoption of the rule would provide for the automatic adoption of an amendment that would modify funds authorized for border activities under the bill; authorizing $24.8 billion for fiscal 2018 through fiscal 2022, instead of authorizing $24.8 billion annually for fiscal 2018 through fiscal 2022. Motion agreed to 232-190: R 231-0; D 1-190. June 21, 2018.

280. HRES954. IMMIGRATION PROGRAMS AND AUTHORIZATIONS/ RULE. Adoption of the rule (H Res 954) that would provide for House floor consideration of the bill (HR 4760) that would authorize $24.8 billion for fiscal 2018 through fiscal 2022 for various border security activities and would provide individuals registered under the Deferred Action for Childhood Arrivals program with a three-year, renewable contingent non-immigrant legal status but with no special path to citizenship. Adoption of the rule would provide for the automatic adoption of an amendment that would modify funds authorized for border activities under the bill; authorizing $24.8 billion for fiscal 2018 through fiscal 2022, instead of authorizing $24.8 billion annually for fiscal 2018 through fiscal 2022. Adopted 226-195: R 226-5; D 0-190. June 21, 2018.

281. HR4760. IMMIGRATION PROGRAMS AND AUTHORIZATIONS/ RECOMMIT. Lujan Grisham, D-N.M., motion to recommit the bill to the House Judiciary Committee with instructions to report it back immediately with an amendment that would replace the bill's provisions with a system that would provide a pathway to citizenship for recipients of the Deferred Action for Childhood Arrivals program. Motion rejected 191-234: R 0-234; D 191-0. June 21, 2018.

282. HR4760. IMMIGRATION PROGRAMS AND AUTHORIZATIONS/ PASSAGE. Passage of the bill that would authorize $24.8 billion for fiscal 2018 through fiscal 2022 for various border security activities, including $9.3 billion for a border wall and other physical barriers and would provide individuals registered under the Deferred Action for Childhood Arrivals program with a three-year, renewable contingent non-immigrant legal status but with no special path to citizenship. It would modify legal immigration by ending the diversity visa program and restricting most family-based immigration to allow only spouses and minor children of legal permanent residents to receive green cards. It would increase enforcement of immigration laws within the United States, including by requiring all employers to verify the immigration status and eligibility of individuals seeking jobs in the United States. Rejected 193-231: R 193-41; D 0-190. June 21, 2018.

283. HR2. FARM PROGRAMS/MOTION TO RECONSIDER. Ryan, R-Wis., motion to reconsider the vote on passage of the bill. Motion agreed to 233-191: R 233-0; D 0-191. June 21, 2018.

	278	279	280	281	282	283
ALABAMA						
1 **Byrne**	Y	Y	Y	N	Y	Y
2 **Roby**	Y	Y	Y	N	Y	Y
3 **Rogers**	Y	Y	Y	N	Y	Y
4 **Aderholt**	Y	Y	Y	N	Y	Y
5 **Brooks**	Y	Y	Y	N	Y	Y
6 **Palmer**	Y	Y	Y	N	Y	Y
7 Sewell	Y	N	N	Y	N	N
ALASKA						
AL **Young**	Y	Y	Y	N	Y	Y
ARIZONA						
1 O'Halleran	Y	N	N	Y	N	N
2 **McSally**	Y	Y	Y	N	Y	Y
3 Grijalva	N	N	N	Y	N	N
4 **Gosar**	Y	Y	Y	N	N	Y
5 **Biggs**	Y	Y	Y	N	N	Y
6 **Schweikert**	Y	Y	Y	N	Y	Y
7 Gallego	Y	N	N	Y	N	N
8 **Lesko**	Y	Y	Y	N	Y	Y
9 Sinema	Y	N	N	Y	N	N
ARKANSAS						
1 **Crawford**	Y	Y	Y	N	Y	Y
2 **Hill**	Y	Y	Y	N	Y	Y
3 **Womack**	Y	Y	Y	N	Y	Y
4 **Westerman**	Y	Y	Y	N	Y	Y
CALIFORNIA						
1 **LaMalfa**	Y	Y	Y	N	Y	Y
2 Huffman	Y	N	N	Y	N	N
3 Garamendi	Y	N	N	Y	N	N
4 **McClintock**	N	Y	Y	N	Y	Y
5 Thompson	Y	N	N	Y	N	N
6 Matsui	N	N	N	Y	N	N
7 Bera	Y	N	N	Y	N	N
8 **Cook**	Y	Y	Y	N	Y	Y
9 McNerney	N	N	N	Y	N	N
10 **Denham**	+	Y	Y	N	N	Y
11 DeSaulnier	N	N	N	Y	N	N
12 Pelosi	Y	N	N	Y	N	N
13 Lee	N	N	N	Y	N	N
14 Speier	N	N	N	Y	N	N
15 Swalwell	Y	N	N	Y	N	N
16 Costa	Y	N	N	Y	N	N
17 Khanna	N	N	N	Y	N	N
18 Eshoo	Y	N	N	Y	N	N
19 Lofgren	Y	N	N	Y	N	N
20 Panetta	Y	N	N	Y	N	N
21 **Valadao**	Y	Y	Y	N	N	Y
22 **Nunes**	Y	Y	Y	N	Y	Y
23 **McCarthy**	?	Y	Y	N	Y	Y
24 Carbajal	Y	N	N	Y	N	N
25 **Knight**	Y	Y	Y	N	N	Y
26 Brownley	Y	N	N	Y	N	N
27 Chu	N	N	N	Y	N	N
28 Schiff	Y	N	N	Y	N	N
29 Cardenas	Y	N	N	Y	N	N
30 Sherman	Y	N	N	Y	N	N
31 Aguilar	Y	N	N	Y	N	N
32 Napolitano	N	N	N	Y	N	N
33 Lieu	Y	N	N	Y	N	N
34 Gomez	Y	N	N	Y	N	N
35 Torres	Y	N	N	Y	N	N
36 Ruiz	Y	N	N	Y	N	N
37 Bass	Y	N	N	Y	N	N
38 Sánchez, Linda	N	N	N	Y	N	N
39 **Royce**	Y	Y	Y	N	Y	Y
40 Roybal-Allard	N	N	N	Y	N	N
41 Takano	Y	N	N	Y	N	N
42 **Calvert**	Y	Y	Y	N	Y	Y
43 Waters	N	N	N	Y	N	N
44 Barragan	Y	N	N	Y	N	N
45 **Walters**	Y	Y	Y	N	Y	Y
46 Correa	Y	N	N	Y	N	N
47 Lowenthal	Y	N	N	Y	N	N
48 **Rohrabacher**	Y	Y	Y	N	N	Y
49 **Issa**	Y	Y	Y	N	Y	Y
50 **Hunter**	Y	Y	Y	N	Y	Y
51 Vargas	N	N	N	Y	N	N
52 Peters	Y	N	N	Y	N	N
53 Davis	N	N	N	Y	N	N
COLORADO						
1 DeGette	N	N	Y	N	N	N
2 Polis	-	N	N	Y	N	N
3 **Tipton**	Y	Y	Y	N	Y	Y
4 **Buck**	Y	Y	Y	N	Y	Y
5 **Lamborn**	Y	Y	Y	N	Y	Y
6 **Coffman**	Y	Y	Y	N	N	Y
7 Perlmutter	Y	N	N	Y	N	N
CONNECTICUT						
1 Larson	Y	N	N	Y	N	N
2 Courtney	Y	N	N	Y	N	N
3 DeLauro	Y	N	N	Y	N	N
4 Himes	Y	N	N	Y	N	N
5 Esty	Y	N	N	Y	N	N
DELAWARE						
AL Blunt Rochester	Y	N	N	Y	N	N
FLORIDA						
1 **Gaetz**	Y	Y	Y	N	Y	Y
2 **Dunn**	Y	Y	Y	N	Y	Y
3 **Yoho**	Y	Y	Y	N	Y	Y
4 **Rutherford**	Y	Y	Y	N	Y	Y
5 Lawson	Y	N	N	Y	N	N
6 **DeSantis**	Y	Y	Y	N	Y	Y
7 Murphy	Y	N	N	Y	N	N
8 **Posey**	Y	Y	Y	N	Y	Y
9 Soto	Y	N	N	Y	N	N
10 Demings	Y	N	N	Y	N	N
11 **Webster**	Y	Y	Y	N	Y	Y
12 **Bilirakis**	Y	Y	Y	N	Y	Y
13 Crist	Y	N	N	Y	N	N
14 Castor	N	N	N	Y	N	N
15 **Ross**	Y	Y	Y	N	Y	Y
16 **Buchanan**	Y	Y	Y	N	Y	Y
17 **Rooney, T.**	Y	Y	Y	N	Y	Y
18 **Mast**	Y	Y	Y	N	Y	Y
19 **Rooney, F.**	Y	Y	Y	N	Y	Y
20 Hastings	Y	N	N	Y	N	N
21 Frankel	Y	N	N	Y	N	N
22 Deutch	Y	N	N	Y	N	N
23 Wasserman Schultz	N	N	N	Y	N	N
24 Wilson	Y	N	N	Y	N	N
25 **Diaz-Balart**	Y	Y	Y	N	N	Y
26 **Curbelo**	Y	Y	Y	N	N	Y
27 **Ros-Lehtinen**	Y	Y	Y	N	N	Y
GEORGIA						
1 **Carter**	Y	Y	Y	N	Y	Y
2 Bishop	Y	N	N	Y	N	N
3 **Ferguson**	Y	Y	Y	N	N	Y
4 Johnson	N	N	N	Y	N	N
5 Lewis	N	N	N	Y	N	N
6 **Handel**	Y	Y	Y	N	Y	Y
7 **Woodall**	Y	Y	Y	N	Y	Y
8 **Scott, A.**	Y	Y	Y	N	Y	Y
9 **Collins**	+	?	?	N	Y	Y
10 **Hice**	Y	Y	Y	N	Y	Y
11 **Loudermilk**	Y	Y	Y	N	Y	Y
12 **Allen**	Y	Y	Y	N	Y	Y
13 Scott, D.	N	N	N	Y	N	N
14 **Graves**	Y	Y	Y	N	Y	Y
HAWAII						
1 Hanabusa	Y	N	N	Y	N	N
2 Gabbard	Y	N	N	Y	N	N
IDAHO						
1 **Labrador**	N	Y	Y	N	Y	?
2 **Simpson**	Y	Y	Y	N	N	Y
ILLINOIS						
1 Rush	N	N	N	Y	N	N
2 Kelly	N	N	N	Y	N	N
3 Lipinski	N	N	N	Y	N	N
4 Gutierrez	N	N	N	Y	N	N
5 Quigley	Y	N	N	Y	N	N
6 **Roskam**	Y	Y	Y	N	N	Y
7 Davis, D.	Y	N	N	Y	N	N
8 Krishnamoorthi	Y	N	N	Y	N	N
9 Schakowsky	N	N	N	Y	N	N
10 Schneider	Y	N	N	Y	N	N
11 Foster	Y	N	N	Y	N	N
12 **Bost**	Y	Y	Y	N	Y	Y
13 **Davis, R.**	Y	Y	Y	N	Y	Y

	278	279	280	281	282	283
14 **Hultgren**	Y	Y	Y	N	Y	Y
15 **Shimkus**	Y	Y	Y	N	Y	Y
16 **Kinzinger**	Y	Y	Y	N	Y	Y
17 Bustos	Y	N	N	Y	N	N
18 **LaHood**	Y	Y	Y	N	Y	Y
INDIANA						
1 Visclosky	Y	N	N	Y	N	N
2 **Walorski**	Y	Y	Y	N	Y	Y
3 **Banks**	Y	Y	Y	N	Y	Y
4 Rokita	Y	Y	Y	N	Y	Y
5 **Brooks**	Y	Y	Y	N	Y	Y
6 **Messer**	Y	Y	Y	N	Y	Y
7 Carson	N	N	N	Y	N	N
8 **Bucshon**	Y	Y	Y	N	Y	Y
9 **Hollingsworth**	Y	Y	Y	N	Y	Y
IOWA						
1 **Blum**	+	Y	Y	N	Y	Y
2 Loebsack	Y	N	N	Y	N	N
3 **Young**	Y	Y	Y	N	Y	Y
4 **King**	Y	Y	N	N	N	Y
KANSAS						
1 **Marshall**	Y	Y	Y	N	Y	Y
2 **Jenkins**	Y	Y	Y	N	Y	Y
3 **Yoder**	Y	Y	Y	N	Y	Y
4 **Estes**	Y	Y	Y	N	Y	Y
KENTUCKY						
1 **Comer**	Y	Y	Y	N	Y	Y
2 **Guthrie**	Y	Y	Y	N	Y	Y
3 Yarmuth	Y	N	N	Y	?	N
4 **Massie**	N	Y	N	N	N	Y
5 **Rogers**	Y	Y	Y	N	Y	Y
6 **Barr**	Y	Y	Y	N	Y	Y
LOUISIANA						
1 **Scalise**	Y	Y	Y	N	Y	Y
2 Richmond	Y	N	N	Y	N	N
3 **Higgins**	Y	Y	Y	N	Y	Y
4 **Johnson**	Y	Y	Y	N	Y	Y
5 **Abraham**	Y	Y	Y	N	Y	Y
6 **Graves**	Y	Y	Y	N	Y	Y
MAINE						
1 Pingree	Y	N	N	Y	N	N
2 **Poliquin**	Y	Y	Y	N	Y	Y
MARYLAND						
1 **Harris**	Y	Y	Y	N	Y	Y
2 Ruppersberger	Y	N	N	Y	N	N
3 Sarbanes	N	N	N	Y	N	N
4 Brown	Y	N	N	Y	N	N
5 Hoyer	Y	N	N	Y	N	N
6 Delaney	Y	N	N	Y	N	N
7 Cummings	N	N	N	Y	N	N
8 Raskin	Y	N	N	Y	N	N
MASSACHUSETTS						
1 Neal	Y	N	N	Y	N	N
2 McGovern	N	N	N	Y	N	N
3 Tsongas	Y	N	N	Y	N	N
4 Kennedy	N	N	N	Y	N	N
5 Clark	Y	N	N	Y	N	N
6 Moulton	Y	N	N	Y	N	N
7 Capuano	Y	N	N	Y	N	N
8 Lynch	Y	N	N	Y	N	N
9 Keating	Y	N	N	Y	N	N
MICHIGAN						
1 **Bergman**	Y	Y	Y	N	Y	Y
2 **Huizenga**	Y	Y	Y	N	Y	Y
3 *Amash*	N	Y	N	N	N	Y
4 **Moolenaar**	Y	Y	Y	N	Y	Y
5 Kildee	Y	N	N	Y	N	N
6 **Upton**	Y	Y	Y	N	N	Y
7 **Walberg**	Y	Y	Y	N	Y	Y
8 **Bishop**	Y	Y	Y	N	Y	Y
9 Levin	N	N	N	Y	N	N
10 **Mitchell**	Y	Y	Y	N	Y	Y
11 **Trott**	Y	Y	Y	N	Y	Y
12 Dingell	N	N	N	Y	N	N
14 Lawrence	Y	N	N	Y	N	N
MINNESOTA						
1 Walz	Y	N	N	Y	N	N
2 **Lewis**	+	Y	Y	N	Y	Y
3 **Paulsen**	Y	Y	Y	N	N	Y
4 McCollum	Y	N	N	Y	N	N

	278	279	280	281	282	283
5 Ellison	?	N	N	Y	N	N
6 **Emmer**	?	Y	Y	N	Y	Y
7 Peterson	Y	N	N	Y	N	N
8 Nolan	Y	N	N	Y	N	N
MISSISSIPPI						
1 **Kelly**	Y	Y	Y	N	Y	Y
2 Thompson	Y	N	N	Y	N	N
3 **Harper**	Y	Y	Y	N	Y	Y
4 **Palazzo**	Y	Y	Y	N	Y	Y
MISSOURI						
1 Clay	Y	N	N	Y	N	N
2 **Wagner**	Y	Y	Y	N	Y	Y
3 **Luetkemeyer**	Y	Y	Y	N	Y	Y
4 **Hartzler**	Y	Y	Y	N	Y	Y
5 Cleaver	Y	N	N	Y	N	N
6 **Graves**	?	Y	Y	N	Y	Y
7 **Long**	Y	Y	Y	N	Y	Y
8 **Smith**	Y	Y	Y	N	Y	Y
MONTANA						
AL **Gianforte**	Y	Y	Y	N	Y	Y
NEBRASKA						
1 **Fortenberry**	Y	Y	Y	N	Y	Y
2 **Bacon**	Y	Y	Y	N	Y	Y
3 **Smith**	Y	Y	Y	N	Y	Y
NEVADA						
1 Titus	Y	N	N	Y	N	N
2 **Amodei**	Y	Y	Y	N	Y	Y
3 Rosen	Y	N	N	Y	N	N
4 Kihuen	N	N	N	Y	N	N
NEW HAMPSHIRE						
1 Shea-Porter	N	N	N	Y	N	N
2 Kuster	N	N	N	Y	N	N
NEW JERSEY						
1 Norcross	Y	N	N	Y	N	N
2 **LoBiondo**	Y	Y	Y	N	N	Y
3 **MacArthur**	Y	Y	Y	N	N	Y
4 **Smith**	Y	Y	Y	N	N	Y
5 Gottheimer	Y	N	N	Y	N	N
6 Pallone	N	N	N	Y	N	N
7 **Lance**	Y	Y	Y	N	N	Y
8 Sires	N	N	N	Y	N	N
9 Pascrell	N	N	N	Y	N	N
10 Payne	Y	–	–	+	–	–
11 **Frelinghuysen**	Y	Y	Y	N	N	Y
12 Watson Coleman	N	N	N	Y	N	N
NEW MEXICO						
1 Lujan Grisham	Y	N	N	Y	N	N
2 **Pearce**	Y	Y	Y	N	Y	Y
3 Luján	N	N	N	Y	N	N
NEW YORK						
1 **Zeldin**	Y	Y	Y	N	Y	Y
2 **King**	Y	Y	Y	N	N	Y
3 Suozzi	Y	N	N	Y	N	N
4 Rice	Y	N	N	Y	N	N
5 Meeks	Y	N	N	Y	N	N
6 Meng	N	N	N	Y	N	N
7 Velázquez	N	N	N	Y	N	N
8 Jeffries	Y	–	–	+	–	–
9 Clarke	N	N	N	Y	N	N
10 Nadler	N	N	N	Y	N	N
11 **Donovan**	Y	Y	Y	N	Y	Y
12 Maloney, C.	Y	N	N	Y	N	N
13 Espaillat	N	N	N	Y	N	N
14 Crowley	Y	N	N	Y	N	N
15 Serrano	N	N	N	Y	N	N
16 Engel	N	N	N	Y	N	N
17 Lowey	N	N	N	Y	N	N
18 Maloney, S.P.	Y	N	N	Y	N	N
19 **Faso**	Y	Y	Y	N	N	Y
20 Tonko	Y	N	N	Y	N	N
21 **Stefanik**	Y	Y	Y	N	N	Y
22 **Tenney**	Y	Y	Y	N	Y	Y
23 **Reed**	Y	Y	Y	N	N	Y
24 **Katko**	Y	Y	Y	N	N	Y
25 **Vacant**						
26 Higgins	Y	N	N	Y	N	N
27 **Collins**	Y	Y	Y	N	Y	Y
NORTH CAROLINA						
1 Butterfield	Y	N	N	Y	N	N
2 **Holding**	Y	Y	Y	N	Y	Y
3 **Jones**	N	Y	Y	N	Y	Y
4 Price	Y	N	N	Y	N	N

	278	279	280	281	282	283
5 **Foxx**	Y	Y	Y	N	Y	Y
6 **Walker**	Y	Y	Y	N	Y	Y
7 **Rouzer**	Y	Y	Y	N	Y	Y
8 **Hudson**	Y	Y	Y	N	Y	Y
9 **Pittenger**	Y	Y	Y	N	Y	Y
9 **Vacant**						
10 **McHenry**	Y	Y	Y	N	Y	Y
11 **Meadows**	Y	Y	Y	N	Y	Y
12 Adams	Y	N	N	Y	N	N
13 **Budd**	Y	Y	Y	N	Y	Y
NORTH DAKOTA						
AL **Cramer**	Y	Y	Y	N	Y	Y
OHIO						
1 **Chabot**	Y	Y	Y	N	Y	Y
2 **Wenstrup**	Y	Y	Y	N	Y	Y
3 Beatty	Y	N	N	Y	N	N
4 **Jordan**	Y	Y	Y	N	Y	Y
5 **Latta**	Y	Y	Y	N	Y	Y
6 **Johnson**	Y	Y	Y	N	Y	Y
7 **Gibbs**	Y	Y	Y	N	Y	Y
8 **Davidson**	Y	Y	Y	N	Y	Y
9 Kaptur	N	N	N	Y	N	N
10 **Turner**	Y	Y	Y	N	N	Y
11 Fudge	Y	N	N	Y	N	N
12 **Vacant**						
13 Ryan	Y	N	N	Y	N	N
14 **Joyce**	Y	Y	Y	N	Y	Y
15 **Stivers**	Y	Y	Y	N	Y	Y
16 **Renacci**	Y	Y	Y	N	Y	Y
OKLAHOMA						
1 **Vacant**						
2 **Mullin**	Y	Y	Y	N	Y	Y
3 **Lucas**	Y	Y	Y	N	Y	Y
4 **Cole**	Y	Y	Y	N	Y	Y
5 **Russell**	Y	Y	Y	N	N	Y
OREGON						
1 Bonamici	Y	N	N	Y	N	N
2 **Walden**	Y	Y	Y	N	Y	Y
3 Blumenauer	Y	N	N	Y	N	N
4 DeFazio	Y	N	N	Y	N	N
5 Schrader	Y	N	N	Y	N	N
PENNSYLVANIA						
1 Brady	Y	N	N	Y	N	N
2 Evans	Y	N	N	Y	N	N
3 **Kelly**	Y	Y	Y	N	Y	Y
4 **Perry**	Y	Y	Y	N	Y	Y
5 **Thompson**	Y	Y	Y	N	Y	Y
6 **Costello**	Y	Y	Y	N	N	Y
7 **Vacant**						
8 **Fitzpatrick**	Y	Y	Y	N	N	Y
9 **Shuster**	Y	Y	Y	N	N	Y
10 **Marino**	Y	Y	Y	N	Y	Y
11 **Barletta**	?	Y	Y	N	Y	Y
12 **Rothfus**	Y	Y	Y	N	Y	Y
13 Boyle	Y	N	N	Y	N	N
14 Doyle	Y	N	N	Y	N	N
15 **Vacant**						
16 **Smucker**	Y	Y	Y	N	Y	Y
17 Cartwright	Y	N	N	Y	N	N
18 Lamb	Y	N	N	Y	N	N
RHODE ISLAND						
1 Cicilline	Y	N	N	Y	N	N
2 Langevin	Y	N	N	Y	N	N
SOUTH CAROLINA						
1 **Sanford**	Y	Y	Y	N	Y	Y
2 **Wilson**	Y	Y	Y	N	Y	Y
3 **Duncan**	Y	Y	Y	N	Y	Y
4 **Gowdy**	Y	Y	Y	N	Y	Y
5 **Norman**	Y	Y	Y	N	Y	Y
6 Clyburn	Y	N	N	Y	N	N
7 **Rice**	Y	Y	Y	N	Y	Y
SOUTH DAKOTA						
AL **Noem**	Y	Y	Y	N	N	Y
TENNESSEE						
1 **Roe**	Y	Y	Y	N	Y	Y
2 **Duncan**	Y	Y	Y	N	Y	Y
3 **Fleischmann**	Y	Y	Y	N	Y	Y
4 **DesJarlais**	Y	Y	Y	N	Y	Y
5 Cooper	Y	N	N	Y	N	N
6 **Black**	?	?	?	N	Y	Y
7 **Blackburn**	Y	Y	Y	N	Y	Y
8 **Kustoff**	Y	?	?	N	Y	Y
9 Cohen	Y	N	N	Y	N	N

	278	279	280	281	282	283
TEXAS						
1 **Gohmert**	N	Y	N	N	N	Y
2 **Poe**	Y	Y	Y	N	Y	Y
3 **Johnson, S.**	Y	Y	Y	N	Y	Y
4 **Ratcliffe**	Y	Y	Y	N	Y	Y
5 **Hensarling**	Y	Y	Y	N	Y	Y
6 **Barton**	Y	Y	Y	N	Y	Y
7 **Culberson**	Y	Y	Y	N	Y	Y
8 **Brady**	Y	Y	Y	N	Y	Y
9 Green, A.	Y	N	N	Y	N	N
10 **McCaul**	Y	Y	Y	N	Y	Y
11 **Conaway**	Y	Y	Y	N	Y	Y
12 **Granger**	Y	Y	Y	N	Y	Y
13 **Thornberry**	Y	Y	Y	N	Y	Y
14 **Weber**	Y	Y	Y	N	Y	Y
15 Gonzalez	Y	N	N	Y	N	N
16 O'Rourke	Y	N	?	Y	N	N
17 **Flores**	Y	Y	Y	N	Y	Y
18 Jackson Lee	N	N	N	Y	N	N
19 **Arrington**	Y	Y	Y	N	Y	Y
20 Castro	Y	N	N	Y	N	N
21 **Smith**	Y	Y	Y	N	Y	Y
22 **Olson**	Y	Y	Y	N	Y	Y
23 **Hurd**	Y	Y	Y	N	N	Y
24 Marchant	Y	Y	Y	N	Y	Y
25 **Williams**	Y	Y	Y	N	Y	Y
26 **Burgess**	Y	Y	Y	N	Y	Y
28 Cuellar	Y	N	N	Y	N	N
29 Green, G.	Y	N	N	Y	N	N
30 Johnson, E.B.	Y	N	N	Y	N	N
31 **Carter**	Y	Y	Y	N	Y	Y
32 **Sessions**	Y	Y	Y	N	Y	Y
33 Veasey	Y	N	N	Y	N	N
34 Vela	?	N	N	Y	N	N
35 Doggett	Y	N	N	Y	N	N
36 **Babin**	Y	Y	Y	N	Y	Y
UTAH						
1 **Bishop**	Y	Y	Y	N	Y	Y
2 **Stewart**	Y	Y	Y	N	Y	Y
3 **Curtis**	Y	Y	Y	N	Y	Y
4 **Love**	Y	Y	Y	N	N	Y
VERMONT						
AL Welch	Y	N	N	Y	N	N
VIRGINIA						
1 **Wittman**	Y	Y	Y	N	Y	Y
2 **Taylor**	Y	Y	Y	N	Y	Y
3 Scott	Y	N	N	Y	N	N
4 McEachin	Y	N	N	Y	N	N
5 **Garrett**	N	Y	Y	N	Y	Y
6 **Goodlatte**	Y	Y	Y	N	Y	Y
7 **Brat**	Y	Y	Y	N	Y	Y
8 Beyer	Y	N	N	Y	N	N
9 **Griffith**	Y	Y	Y	N	Y	Y
10 **Comstock**	Y	Y	Y	N	N	Y
11 Connolly	Y	N	N	Y	N	N
WASHINGTON						
1 DelBene	Y	N	N	Y	N	N
2 Larsen	Y	N	N	Y	N	N
3 **Herrera Beutler**	Y	Y	Y	N	Y	Y
4 **Newhouse**	Y	Y	Y	N	N	Y
5 **McMorris Rodgers**	Y	Y	Y	N	N	Y
6 Kilmer	Y	N	N	Y	N	N
7 Jayapal	Y	N	N	Y	N	N
8 **Reichert**	Y	Y	Y	N	N	Y
9 Smith	Y	N	N	Y	N	N
10 Heck	Y	N	N	Y	N	N
WEST VIRGINIA						
1 **McKinley**	Y	Y	Y	N	Y	Y
2 **Mooney**	Y	Y	Y	N	Y	Y
3 **Jenkins**	Y	Y	Y	N	Y	Y
WISCONSIN						
1 **Ryan**						
2 Pocan	Y	N	N	Y	N	N
3 Kind	Y	N	N	Y	N	N
4 Moore	N	N	N	Y	N	N
5 **Sensenbrenner**	Y	Y	Y	N	Y	Y
6 **Grothman**	Y	Y	Y	N	Y	Y
7 **Duffy**	+	Y	Y	N	Y	Y
8 **Gallagher**	Y	Y	Y	N	Y	Y
WYOMING						
AL **Cheney**	Y	Y	Y	N	Y	Y

VOTE NUMBER

284. HR2. FARM PROGRAMS/PASSAGE. Passage of the bill that would reauthorize and extend federal farm and nutrition programs through fiscal 2023, including crop subsidies, conservation, rural development and agricultural trade programs and the Supplemental Nutritional Assistance Program. (Truncated, visit cq.com for more.) Passed 213-211: R 213-20; D 0-191. June 21, 2018.

285. HRES953. IMMIGRATION PROGRAMS AND APPROPRIATIONS/ PREVIOUS QUESTION. Newhouse, R-Wash., motion to order the previous question (thus ending debate and possibility of amendment) on the rule (H Res 953) that would provide for House floor consideration of the bill (HR 6136) that would appropriate $23.4 billion for various border security activities. Included would be $16.6 billion for a "border wall system," which would be available from fiscal 2019 through fiscal 2027, and $6.8 billion for border security investments, which would be available from fiscal 2019 through fiscal 2023. It would provide those with Deferred Action for Childhood Arrivals status a six-year renewable contingent non-immigrant legal status and would allow them to apply for a green card after five years thereby providing a path to citizenship. Motion agreed to 233-191: R 233-0; D 0-191. June 21, 2018.

286. HR6136. IMMIGRATION PROGRAMS AND APPROPRIATIONS/ RULE. Adoption of the rule (H Res 953) that would provide for House floor consideration of the bill (HR 6136) that would appropriate $23.4 billion for various border security activities. Included would be $16.6 billion for a "border wall system," which would be available from fiscal 2019 through fiscal 2027, and $6.8 billion for border security investments, which would be available from fiscal 2019 through fiscal 2023. It would provide those with Deferred Action for Childhood Arrivals status a six-year renewable contingent non-immigrant legal status and would allow them to apply for a green card after five years thereby providing a path to citizenship. Adopted 227-195: R 227-5; D 0-190. June 21, 2018.

287. HR6. OPIOID ABUSE PREVENTION AND HEALTH PROGRAMS/ RECOMMIT. Tonko, D-N.Y., motion to recommit the bill to the House Energy and Commerce Committee and the House Ways and Means Committee with instructions to report it back immediately with an amendment that would appropriate $995 million annually, for fiscal 2019 through 2021, for state opioid grant programs and would allow the Health and Human Services Department to increase the number of residency positions at hospitals that have established programs related to addiction. Motion rejected 185-226: R 1-226; D 184-0. June 22, 2018.

288. HR6. OPIOID ABUSE PREVENTION AND HEALTH PROGRAMS/ PASSAGE. Passage of the bill that would modify Medicare and Medicaid and a variety of other health programs in relation to opioid abuse. It would expand both Medicare and Medicaid to cover medication-assisted treatment for substance use disorder, would require all state Medicaid programs, beginning Jan 1, 2020, to operate pharmacy programs that identify people at high risk of abusing controlled substance, and would place new requirements on states regarding Medicaid drug review and utilization requirements. It would appropriate $15 million annually, from fiscal 2019 through 2023, to support the establishment or operation of public health laboratories to detect synthetic opioids. Passed 396-14: R 214-13; D 182-1. June 22, 2018.

289. HR299. PRESUMED AGENT ORANGE EXPOSURE AND VA HOME LOANS/PASSAGE. Roe, R-Tenn., motion to suspend the rules and pass the bill that would allow veterans who served off the shore of Vietnam between Jan. 9, 1962, and May 7, 1975, to be eligible for a presumption of exposure to certain herbicides, including Agent Orange, for the purpose of VA disability compensation and would authorize retroactive payments to veterans who have previously been denied a claim for a eligible condition caused by presumed exposure to Agent Orange. The bill would eliminate the use of the Freddie Mac conforming loan limit with regard to the VA home loan program, would eliminate the additional fee that members of the National Guard and Reserve pay on home loans, and would impose a fee on certain veteran borrowers who have service-connected disabilities. Motion agreed to 382-0: R 221-0; D 161-0. June 25, 2018.

	284	285	286	287	288	289
ALABAMA						
1 Byrne	Y	Y	Y	N	Y	Y
2 Roby	Y	Y	Y	N	Y	Y
3 Rogers	Y	Y	Y	N	Y	Y
4 Aderholt	?	Y	Y	N	Y	Y
5 Brooks	Y	Y	Y	N	N	Y
6 Palmer	Y	Y	Y	N	Y	Y
7 Sewell	N	N	N	Y	Y	+
ALASKA						
AL Young	Y	Y	Y	N	Y	Y
ARIZONA						
1 O'Halleran	N	N	N	Y	Y	Y
2 McSally	Y	Y	Y	N	Y	Y
3 Grijalva	N	N	N	Y	Y	Y
4 Gosar	Y	Y	Y	N	N	Y
5 Biggs	N	Y	Y	N	N	Y
6 Schweikert	Y	Y	Y	N	Y	Y
7 Gallego	N	N	N	Y	Y	Y
8 Lesko	Y	Y	Y	N	Y	Y
9 Sinema	N	N	N	Y	Y	Y
ARKANSAS						
1 Crawford	Y	Y	Y	N	Y	Y
2 Hill	Y	Y	Y	N	Y	Y
3 Womack	Y	Y	Y	N	Y	Y
4 Westerman	Y	Y	Y	N	Y	Y
CALIFORNIA						
1 LaMalfa	Y	Y	?	N	Y	Y
2 Huffman	N	N	N	Y	Y	Y
3 Garamendi	N	N	N	Y	Y	Y
4 McClintock	N	Y	Y	N	N	Y
5 Thompson	N	N	N	Y	Y	Y
6 Matsui	N	N	N	Y	Y	Y
7 Bera	N	N	N	Y	Y	Y
8 Cook	Y	Y	Y	N	Y	Y
9 McNerney	N	N	N	Y	Y	Y
10 Denham	Y	Y	Y	N	Y	Y
11 DeSaulnier	N	N	N	Y	Y	Y
12 Pelosi	N	N	N	Y	Y	Y
13 Lee	N	N	N	Y	Y	Y
14 Speier	N	N	N	Y	Y	Y
15 Swalwell	N	N	N	Y	Y	Y
16 Costa	N	N	N	Y	Y	Y
17 Khanna	N	N	N	Y	Y	Y
18 Eshoo	N	N	N	Y	Y	Y
19 Lofgren	N	N	N	Y	Y	Y
20 Panetta	N	N	N	Y	Y	Y
21 Valadao	Y	Y	Y	N	Y	Y
22 Nunes	Y	Y	Y	N	Y	Y
23 McCarthy	Y	Y	Y	N	Y	Y
24 Carbajal	N	N	N	Y	Y	+
25 Knight	Y	Y	Y	N	Y	Y
26 Brownley	N	N	N	Y	Y	Y
27 Chu	N	N	N	Y	Y	?
28 Schiff	N	N	N	Y	Y	Y
29 Cardenas	N	N	N	Y	Y	Y
30 Sherman	N	N	N	Y	Y	Y
31 Aguilar	N	N	N	Y	Y	Y
32 Napolitano	N	N	N	Y	Y	Y
33 Lieu	N	N	N	Y	Y	Y
34 Gomez	N	N	N	Y	Y	?
35 Torres	N	N	N	Y	Y	Y
36 Ruiz	N	N	N	Y	Y	Y
37 Bass	N	N	N	Y	Y	Y
38 Sánchez, Linda	N	N	N	Y	Y	Y
39 Royce	Y	Y	Y	N	Y	Y
40 Roybal-Allard	N	N	N	Y	Y	Y
41 Takano	N	N	N	Y	Y	Y
42 Calvert	Y	Y	Y	N	Y	Y
43 Waters	N	N	N	Y	Y	Y
44 Barragan	N	N	N	Y	Y	Y
45 Walters	Y	Y	Y	N	Y	Y
46 Correa	N	N	N	Y	Y	Y
47 Lowenthal	N	N	N	Y	Y	Y
48 Rohrabacher	N	Y	Y	N	Y	Y
49 Issa	Y	Y	Y	N	Y	Y
50 Hunter	Y	Y	Y	N	Y	Y
51 Vargas	N	N	N	Y	Y	Y
52 Peters	N	N	N	Y	Y	Y
53 Davis	N	N	N	Y	Y	Y

	284	285	286	287	288	289
COLORADO						
1 DeGette	N	N	N	Y	Y	?
2 Polis	N	N	N	Y	Y	?
3 Tipton	Y	Y	?	N	Y	Y
4 Buck	Y	Y	Y	N	Y	Y
5 Lamborn	Y	Y	Y	N	Y	Y
6 Coffman	Y	Y	Y	N	Y	Y
7 Perlmutter	N	N	N	Y	Y	Y
CONNECTICUT						
1 Larson	N	N	N	Y	Y	Y
2 Courtney	N	N	N	Y	Y	Y
3 DeLauro	N	N	N	Y	Y	Y
4 Himes	N	N	N	Y	Y	Y
5 Esty	N	N	N	Y	Y	Y
DELAWARE						
AL Blunt Rochester	N	N	N	Y	Y	Y
FLORIDA						
1 Gaetz	N	Y	Y	N	N	Y
2 Dunn	Y	Y	Y	N	Y	Y
3 Yoho	Y	Y	Y	N	Y	Y
4 Rutherford	Y	+	Y	N	Y	Y
5 Lawson	N	N	N	Y	Y	Y
6 DeSantis	Y	Y	Y	N	Y	?
7 Murphy	N	N	N	Y	Y	Y
8 Posey	Y	Y	Y	N	Y	Y
9 Soto	N	N	N	Y	Y	Y
10 Demings	N	N	N	Y	Y	Y
11 Webster	Y	Y	Y	N	Y	Y
12 Bilirakis	Y	Y	Y	N	Y	Y
13 Crist	N	N	N	Y	Y	Y
14 Castor	N	N	N	Y	Y	Y
15 Ross	Y	Y	Y	N	Y	?
16 Buchanan	Y	Y	Y	N	Y	Y
17 Rooney, T.	Y	Y	Y	?	?	+
18 Mast	Y	Y	Y	N	Y	Y
19 Rooney, F.	Y	Y	Y	N	Y	Y
20 Hastings	N	N	N	Y	Y	Y
21 Frankel	N	N	N	Y	Y	Y
22 Deutch	N	N	N	Y	Y	Y
23 Wasserman Schultz	N	N	N	Y	Y	Y
24 Wilson	N	N	N	Y	Y	Y
25 Diaz-Balart	Y	Y	Y	N	Y	Y
26 Curbelo	Y	Y	Y	N	Y	Y
27 Ros-Lehtinen	N	Y	Y	N	Y	Y
GEORGIA						
1 Carter	Y	Y	Y	N	Y	Y
2 Bishop	N	N	N	Y	Y	Y
3 Ferguson	Y	Y	Y	N	Y	Y
4 Johnson	N	N	N	Y	Y	Y
5 Lewis	N	N	N	Y	Y	Y
6 Handel	Y	Y	Y	N	Y	Y
7 Woodall	Y	Y	Y	N	Y	Y
8 Scott, A.	Y	Y	Y	N	Y	Y
9 Collins	Y	Y	Y	–	+	Y
10 Hice	Y	Y	Y	N	Y	Y
11 Loudermilk	Y	Y	Y	N	N	Y
12 Allen	Y	Y	Y	N	Y	Y
13 Scott, D.	N	N	N	Y	Y	?
14 Graves	Y	Y	Y	N	Y	Y
HAWAII						
1 Hanabusa	N	N	N	?	?	Y
2 Gabbard	N	N	N	Y	Y	Y
IDAHO						
1 Labrador	Y	Y	Y	N	N	Y
2 Simpson	Y	Y	Y	N	Y	Y
Illinois						
1 Rush	N	N	N	Y	Y	?
2 Kelly	N	N	N	Y	Y	Y
3 Lipinski	N	N	N	Y	Y	Y
4 Gutierrez	N	N	N	Y	Y	+
5 Quigley	N	N	N	Y	Y	Y
6 Roskam	Y	Y	Y	N	Y	Y
7 Davis, D.	N	N	N	Y	Y	Y
8 Krishnamoorthi	N	N	N	Y	Y	Y
9 Schakowsky	N	N	N	Y	Y	Y
10 Schneider	N	N	N	Y	Y	Y
11 Foster	N	N	N	Y	Y	Y
12 Bost	Y	Y	Y	N	Y	Y
13 Davis, R.	Y	Y	Y	N	Y	Y

	284	285	286	287	288	289
14 **Hultgren**	Y	Y	Y	N	Y	Y
15 **Shimkus**	Y	Y	Y	N	Y	Y
16 **Kinzinger**	Y	Y	Y	N	Y	Y
17 Bustos	N	N	N	Y	Y	Y
18 **LaHood**	Y	Y	Y	N	Y	Y
INDIANA						
1 Visclosky	N	N	N	Y	Y	Y
2 **Walorski**	Y	Y	Y	N	Y	Y
3 **Banks**	Y	Y	Y	N	Y	Y
4 Rokita	Y	Y	Y	–	+	Y
5 **Brooks**	Y	Y	Y	N	Y	Y
6 **Messer**	Y	Y	Y	N	Y	Y
7 Carson	N	N	N	Y	Y	Y
8 **Bucshon**	Y	Y	Y	N	Y	Y
9 **Hollingsworth**	Y	Y	Y	N	Y	Y
IOWA						
1 **Blum**	Y	Y	Y	Y	Y	Y
2 Loebsack	N	N	N	Y	Y	Y
3 **Young**	Y	Y	Y	N	Y	Y
4 **King**	Y	Y	N	N	Y	Y
KANSAS						
1 **Marshall**	Y	Y	Y	N	Y	Y
2 **Jenkins**	Y	Y	Y	N	Y	Y
3 **Yoder**	Y	Y	Y	N	Y	Y
4 **Estes**	Y	Y	Y	N	Y	Y
KENTUCKY						
1 **Comer**	Y	Y	Y	N	Y	Y
2 **Guthrie**	Y	Y	Y	N	Y	Y
3 Yarmuth	N	N	N	Y	Y	Y
4 **Massie**	N	Y	N	N	N	Y
5 **Rogers**	Y	Y	Y	N	Y	Y
6 **Barr**	Y	Y	Y	N	Y	Y
LOUISIANA						
1 **Scalise**	Y	Y	Y	N	Y	Y
2 Richmond	N	N	N	Y	Y	Y
3 **Higgins**	Y	Y	Y	N	Y	Y
4 **Johnson**	Y	Y	Y	N	Y	Y
5 **Abraham**	Y	Y	Y	N	Y	Y
6 **Graves**	Y	Y	Y	N	Y	Y
MAINE						
1 Pingree	N	N	N	Y	Y	Y
2 **Poliquin**	Y	Y	Y	N	Y	Y
MARYLAND						
1 **Harris**	Y	Y	Y	N	Y	Y
2 Ruppersberger	N	N	N	Y	Y	?
3 Sarbanes	N	N	N	Y	Y	Y
4 Brown	N	N	?	Y	Y	Y
5 Hoyer	N	N	N	Y	Y	Y
6 Delaney	N	N	N	+	+	+
7 Cummings	N	N	N	Y	Y	?
8 Raskin	N	N	N	Y	Y	Y
MASSACHUSETTS						
1 Neal	N	N	N	Y	Y	Y
2 McGovern	N	N	N	Y	Y	Y
3 Tsongas	N	N	N	Y	Y	?
4 Kennedy	N	N	N	Y	Y	Y
5 Clark	N	N	N	Y	Y	Y
6 Moulton	N	N	N	Y	Y	Y
7 Capuano	N	N	N	Y	Y	Y
8 Lynch	N	N	N	Y	Y	Y
9 Keating	N	N	N	Y	Y	Y
MICHIGAN						
1 **Bergman**	Y	Y	Y	N	Y	Y
2 **Huizenga**	Y	Y	Y	N	Y	Y
3 *Amash*	N	Y	N	N	N	Y
4 **Moolenaar**	Y	Y	Y	N	Y	Y
5 Kildee	N	N	N	Y	Y	Y
6 **Upton**	N	Y	Y	N	Y	Y
7 **Walberg**	Y	Y	Y	N	Y	Y
8 **Bishop**	Y	Y	Y	N	Y	Y
9 Levin	N	N	N	Y	Y	Y
10 **Mitchell**	Y	Y	Y	N	Y	Y
11 **Trott**	Y	Y	Y	N	Y	Y
12 Dingell	N	N	N	Y	Y	Y
14 Lawrence	N	N	N	Y	Y	Y
MINNESOTA						
1 Walz	N	N	N	?	?	?
2 **Lewis**	Y	Y	Y	N	Y	Y
3 **Paulsen**	Y	Y	Y	N	Y	Y
4 McCollum	N	N	N	Y	Y	Y

	284	285	286	287	288	289
5 Ellison	N	N	N	?	?	?
6 **Emmer**	Y	Y	Y	N	Y	Y
7 Peterson	N	N	N	Y	Y	Y
8 Nolan	N	N	N	Y	Y	Y
MISSISSIPPI						
1 **Kelly**	Y	Y	Y	N	Y	Y
2 Thompson	N	N	N	Y	Y	?
3 **Harper**	Y	Y	Y	N	Y	Y
4 **Palazzo**	Y	Y	Y	N	Y	Y
MISSOURI						
1 Clay	N	N	N	Y	Y	Y
2 **Wagner**	Y	Y	Y	N	Y	Y
3 **Luetkemeyer**	Y	Y	Y	N	Y	Y
4 **Hartzler**	Y	Y	Y	N	Y	Y
5 Cleaver	N	N	N	Y	Y	Y
6 **Graves**	Y	Y	Y	N	Y	Y
7 **Long**	Y	Y	Y	N	Y	Y
8 **Smith**	Y	Y	Y	N	Y	Y
MONTANA						
AL **Gianforte**	Y	Y	Y	N	Y	Y
NEBRASKA						
1 **Fortenberry**	Y	Y	Y	N	Y	Y
2 **Bacon**	Y	Y	Y	N	Y	Y
3 **Smith**	Y	Y	Y	N	Y	Y
NEVADA						
1 Titus	N	N	N	?	?	Y
2 **Amodei**	Y	Y	Y	N	Y	Y
3 Rosen	N	N	N	Y	Y	+
4 Kihuen	N	N	N	Y	Y	Y
NEW HAMPSHIRE						
1 Shea-Porter	N	N	N	Y	Y	?
2 Kuster	N	N	N	Y	Y	Y
NEW JERSEY						
1 Norcross	N	N	N	Y	Y	Y
2 **LoBiondo**	N	Y	Y	N	Y	Y
3 **MacArthur**	Y	Y	Y	N	Y	Y
4 **Smith**	N	Y	Y	N	Y	Y
5 Gottheimer	N	N	N	Y	Y	Y
6 Pallone	N	N	N	Y	Y	Y
7 **Lance**	N	Y	Y	N	Y	Y
8 Sires	N	N	N	Y	Y	?
9 Pascrell	N	N	N	Y	Y	Y
10 Payne	–	–	–	?	?	?
11 **Frelinghuysen**	N	Y	Y	N	Y	Y
12 Watson Coleman	N	N	N	Y	Y	Y
NEW MEXICO						
1 Lujan Grisham	N	N	N	Y	Y	?
2 **Pearce**	Y	Y	Y	N	Y	?
3 Luján	N	N	N	Y	Y	Y
NEW YORK						
1 **Zeldin**	Y	Y	Y	N	Y	Y
2 **King**	N	Y	Y	N	Y	Y
3 Suozzi	N	N	N	Y	Y	Y
4 Rice	N	N	N	Y	Y	Y
5 Meeks	N	N	N	Y	Y	?
6 Meng	N	N	N	?	?	Y
7 Velázquez	N	N	N	Y	Y	Y
8 Jeffries	–	–	–	Y	Y	Y
9 Clarke	N	N	N	Y	Y	+
10 Nadler	N	N	N	Y	Y	Y
11 **Donovan**	Y	Y	Y	N	Y	?
12 Maloney, C.	N	N	N	Y	Y	?
13 Espaillat	N	N	N	Y	Y	Y
14 Crowley	N	N	N	+	+	Y
15 Serrano	N	N	N	Y	Y	Y
16 Engel	N	N	N	Y	Y	?
17 Lowey	N	N	N	Y	Y	Y
18 Maloney, S.P.	N	N	N	Y	Y	Y
19 **Faso**	Y	Y	Y	N	Y	Y
20 Tonko	N	N	N	Y	Y	Y
21 **Stefanik**	Y	Y	Y	N	Y	Y
22 **Tenney**	Y	Y	Y	N	Y	Y
23 **Reed**	Y	Y	Y	–	+	Y
24 **Katko**	N	Y	Y	N	Y	Y
25 **Vacant**						
26 Higgins	N	N	N	Y	Y	Y
27 **Collins**	Y	Y	Y	N	Y	Y
NORTH CAROLINA						
1 Butterfield	N	N	N	Y	Y	Y
2 **Holding**	Y	Y	Y	N	Y	Y
3 **Jones**	N	Y	N	N	N	Y
4 Price	N	N	N	Y	Y	Y

	284	285	286	287	288	289
5 **Foxx**	Y	Y	Y	N	Y	Y
6 **Walker**	Y	Y	Y	N	Y	Y
7 **Rouzer**	Y	Y	Y	N	Y	Y
8 **Hudson**	Y	Y	Y	N	Y	Y
9 **Pittenger**	Y	Y	Y	N	Y	Y
9 **Vacant**						
10 **McHenry**	Y	Y	Y	N	Y	Y
11 **Meadows**	Y	Y	Y	N	Y	Y
12 Adams	N	N	N	Y	Y	Y
13 **Budd**	Y	Y	Y	N	Y	Y
NORTH DAKOTA						
AL **Cramer**	Y	Y	Y	N	Y	Y
OHIO						
1 **Chabot**	Y	Y	Y	N	Y	Y
2 **Wenstrup**	Y	Y	Y	N	Y	Y
3 Beatty	N	N	N	Y	Y	Y
4 **Jordan**	Y	Y	Y	N	Y	Y
5 **Latta**	Y	Y	Y	N	Y	Y
6 **Johnson**	Y	Y	Y	N	Y	Y
7 **Gibbs**	Y	Y	Y	N	Y	Y
8 **Davidson**	Y	Y	Y	N	Y	Y
9 Kaptur	N	N	N	Y	Y	Y
10 **Turner**	Y	Y	Y	N	Y	Y
11 Fudge	N	N	N	Y	Y	Y
12 **Vacant**						
13 Ryan	N	N	N	Y	Y	Y
14 **Joyce**	Y	Y	Y	N	Y	Y
15 **Stivers**	Y	Y	Y	N	Y	Y
16 **Renacci**	Y	Y	Y	N	Y	Y
OKLAHOMA						
1 **Vacant**						
2 **Mullin**	Y	Y	Y	N	Y	Y
3 **Lucas**	Y	Y	Y	N	Y	Y
4 **Cole**	Y	Y	Y	N	Y	Y
5 **Russell**	Y	Y	Y	N	Y	Y
OREGON						
1 Bonamici	N	N	N	Y	Y	Y
2 **Walden**	Y	Y	Y	N	Y	Y
3 Blumenauer	N	N	N	Y	Y	Y
4 DeFazio	N	N	N	Y	Y	Y
5 Schrader	N	N	N	Y	Y	Y
PENNSYLVANIA						
1 Brady	N	N	N	Y	Y	?
2 Evans	N	N	N	Y	Y	Y
3 **Kelly**	Y	Y	Y	N	Y	Y
4 **Perry**	–	Y	Y	N	Y	Y
5 **Thompson**	Y	Y	Y	N	Y	Y
6 **Costello**	Y	Y	Y	N	Y	Y
7 **Vacant**						
8 **Fitzpatrick**	N	Y	Y	N	Y	Y
9 **Shuster**	Y	Y	Y	N	Y	Y
10 **Marino**	Y	Y	Y	N	Y	Y
11 **Barletta**	Y	Y	Y	N	Y	Y
12 **Rothfus**	N	Y	Y	N	Y	Y
13 Boyle	N	N	N	Y	Y	Y
14 Doyle	N	N	N	Y	Y	Y
15 **Vacant**						
16 **Smucker**	Y	Y	Y	N	Y	Y
17 Cartwright	N	N	N	Y	Y	Y
18 Lamb	N	N	N	Y	Y	Y
RHODE ISLAND						
1 Cicilline	N	N	N	Y	Y	Y
2 Langevin	N	N	N	Y	Y	Y
SOUTH CAROLINA						
1 **Sanford**	N	Y	Y	N	N	Y
2 **Wilson**	Y	Y	Y	N	Y	?
3 **Duncan**	Y	Y	Y	N	Y	Y
4 **Gowdy**	Y	Y	Y	N	Y	?
5 **Norman**	Y	Y	Y	N	Y	Y
6 Clyburn	N	N	N	Y	Y	Y
7 **Rice**	Y	Y	Y	N	Y	?
SOUTH DAKOTA						
AL **Noem**	Y	Y	Y	?	?	Y
TENNESSEE						
1 **Roe**	Y	Y	Y	N	Y	Y
2 **Duncan**	N	Y	Y	N	Y	Y
3 **Fleischmann**	Y	Y	Y	N	Y	Y
4 **DesJarlais**	Y	Y	Y	N	Y	Y
5 Cooper	N	N	N	Y	Y	Y
6 **Black**	Y	Y	Y	?	?	?
7 **Blackburn**	Y	Y	Y	N	Y	?
8 **Kustoff**	Y	Y	Y	N	Y	Y
9 Cohen	N	N	N	Y	Y	Y

	284	285	286	287	288	289
TEXAS						
1 **Gohmert**	Y	Y	N	N	N	Y
2 **Poe**	Y	Y	Y	N	Y	Y
3 **Johnson, S.**	Y	Y	Y	N	Y	?
4 **Ratcliffe**	Y	Y	Y	N	Y	Y
5 **Hensarling**	Y	Y	Y	N	Y	Y
6 **Barton**	Y	Y	Y	N	Y	Y
7 **Culberson**	Y	Y	Y	N	Y	Y
8 **Brady**	Y	Y	Y	N	Y	Y
9 Green, A.	N	N	N	Y	Y	Y
10 **McCaul**	Y	Y	Y	N	Y	Y
11 **Conaway**	Y	Y	Y	N	Y	Y
12 **Granger**	Y	Y	Y	N	Y	Y
13 **Thornberry**	Y	Y	Y	N	Y	Y
14 **Weber**	Y	Y	Y	N	Y	Y
15 Gonzalez	N	N	N	Y	N	Y
16 O'Rourke	N	N	N	Y	?	?
17 **Flores**	Y	Y	Y	N	Y	Y
18 Jackson Lee	N	N	N	Y	Y	Y
19 **Arrington**	Y	Y	Y	N	Y	Y
20 Castro	N	N	N	Y	Y	Y
21 **Smith**	Y	Y	Y	N	Y	Y
22 **Olson**	Y	Y	Y	N	Y	Y
23 **Hurd**	Y	Y	Y	N	Y	Y
24 Marchant	Y	Y	Y	–	+	+
25 **Williams**	Y	Y	Y	N	Y	Y
26 **Burgess**	Y	Y	Y	N	Y	Y
28 Cuellar	N	N	N	Y	Y	+
29 Green, G.	N	N	N	Y	Y	Y
30 Johnson, E.B.	N	N	N	Y	Y	Y
31 **Carter**	Y	Y	Y	N	Y	Y
32 **Sessions**	Y	Y	Y	N	Y	Y
33 Veasey	N	N	N	?	+	Y
34 Vela	N	N	N	Y	Y	Y
35 Doggett	N	N	N	Y	Y	+
36 **Babin**	Y	Y	Y	N	Y	Y
UTAH						
1 **Bishop**	Y	Y	Y	N	Y	Y
2 **Stewart**	Y	Y	Y	N	Y	Y
3 **Curtis**	Y	Y	Y	N	Y	?
4 **Love**	Y	Y	Y	N	Y	Y
VERMONT						
AL Welch	N	N	N	Y	Y	Y
VIRGINIA						
1 **Wittman**	Y	Y	Y	N	Y	Y
2 **Taylor**	Y	Y	Y	N	Y	Y
3 Scott	N	N	N	Y	Y	?
4 McEachin	N	N	N	Y	Y	Y
5 **Garrett**	N	Y	Y	N	N	Y
6 **Goodlatte**	Y	Y	Y	N	Y	Y
7 **Brat**	Y	Y	Y	N	Y	Y
8 Beyer	N	N	N	Y	Y	Y
9 **Griffith**	Y	Y	Y	N	Y	Y
10 **Comstock**	Y	Y	Y	N	Y	Y
11 Connolly	N	N	N	Y	Y	Y
WASHINGTON						
1 DelBene	N	N	N	Y	Y	Y
2 Larsen	N	N	N	Y	Y	Y
3 **Herrera Beutler**	Y	Y	Y	N	Y	Y
4 **Newhouse**	Y	Y	Y	N	Y	Y
5 **McMorris Rodgers**	Y	Y	Y	N	Y	Y
6 Kilmer	N	N	N	Y	Y	Y
7 Jayapal	N	N	N	Y	Y	Y
8 **Reichert**	Y	Y	Y	N	Y	Y
9 Smith	N	N	N	Y	Y	Y
10 Heck	N	N	N	Y	Y	Y
WEST VIRGINIA						
1 **McKinley**	Y	Y	Y	N	Y	Y
2 **Mooney**	Y	Y	Y	N	Y	Y
3 **Jenkins**	Y	Y	Y	N	Y	Y
WISCONSIN						
1 **Ryan**	Y					
2 Pocan	N	N	N	Y	Y	+
3 Kind	N	N	N	Y	Y	Y
4 Moore	N	N	N	Y	Y	+
5 **Sensenbrenner**	Y	Y	Y	N	Y	Y
6 **Grothman**	Y	Y	Y	N	Y	Y
7 **Duffy**	Y	Y	Y	N	Y	Y
8 **Gallagher**	Y	Y	Y	N	Y	Y
WYOMING						
AL **Cheney**	Y	Y	Y	N	Y	Y

VOTE NUMBER

290. HR5783. FINANCIAL INSTITUTION LIABILITY PROTECTION/PASSAGE. Hill, R-Ark., motion to suspend the rules and pass the bill that would provide legal protection for a bank or financial institution that keeps open a customer account at the written request of a local, state or federal law enforcement agency. Motion agreed to 379-4: R 217-4; D 162-0. June 25, 2018.

291. HR2083. FISCAL 2019 DEFENSE APPROPRIATIONS AND PREDATORY MARINE MAMMALS HUNTING PERMITS/PREVIOUS QUESTION. Cheney, R-Wyo., motion to order the previous question (thus ending debate and possibility of amendment) on the rule (H Res 961) that would provide for House floor consideration of the fiscal 2019 defense appropriations (HR 6157) and would provide for consideration of the bill (HR 2083) that would authorize the National Oceanic and Atmospheric Administration to issue permits for certain state governments to hunt certain predatory marine mammals. Motion agreed to 219-172: R 217-0; D 2-172. June 26, 2018.

292. HRES961. FISCAL 2019 DEFENSE APPROPRIATIONS AND PREDATORY MARINE MAMMALS HUNTING PERMITS/RULE. Adopted of the rule (H Res 961) that would provide for House floor consideration of the fiscal 2019 defense appropriations (HR 6157) and would provide for consideration of the bill (HR 2083) that would authorize the National Oceanic and Atmospheric Administration to issue permits for certain state governments to hunt certain predatory marine mammals. Adopted 222-172: R 215-3; D 7-169. June 26, 2018.

293. HR4294. FINANCIAL INSTITUTION PROPRIETARY INFORMATION DISCLOSURE/PASSAGE. Hill, R-Ark., motion to suspend the rules and pass the bill that would establish criminal penalties for the unauthorized disclosure of proprietary information related to a financial institution by an employee of a federal banking regulator. Motion agreed to 392-2: R 216-0; D 176-0. June 26, 2018.

294. HR2083. PREDATORY SEA LIONS AND SALMON FISH STOCK/PASSAGE. Passage of the bill that would authorize the National Oceanic and Atmospheric Administration to issue permits for certain state governments to hunt for sea lions. The states that would be eligible for the permits would be Washington, Oregon, Idaho, and American Indian Tribes with lands surrounding the Columbia River and its tributaries, and each permit would authorize the taking of up to 100 sea lions. Passed 288-116: R 220-5; D 68-111. June 26, 2018.

295. HR5841. EXPORT LICENSES AND CRITICAL INFRATRUCTURE/PASSAGE. Royce, R-Calif., motion to suspend the rules and pass the bill that would expand the types of transactions covered by the Committee on Foreign Investment in the U.S. to include critical infrastructure projects and land deals near sensitive government properties and facilities. The bill would authorize the Commerce Department to request disclosures of data about foreign persons or companies with a stake in companies that partner with U.S. firms in overseas joint ventures that apply for export licenses to allow for the transfer of sensitive technology. The bill would also authorize $20 million annually for fiscal 2019 through fiscal 2023 for operations of the committee. Motion agreed to 400-2: R 222-2; D 178-0. June 26, 2018.

	290	291	292	293	294	295
ALABAMA						
1 **Byrne**	Y	Y	Y	Y	Y	Y
2 **Roby**	Y	+	+	+	Y	Y
3 **Rogers**	Y	Y	Y	Y	Y	Y
4 **Aderholt**	Y	?	?	?	Y	Y
5 **Brooks**	Y	Y	Y	Y	Y	Y
6 **Palmer**	Y	Y	Y	Y	Y	Y
7 Sewell	+	–	–	+	+	+
ALASKA						
AL **Young**	Y	Y	Y	Y	Y	?
ARIZONA						
1 O'Halleran	Y	N	Y	Y	Y	Y
2 **McSally**	Y	Y	Y	Y	?	?
3 Grijalva	Y	N	N	Y	N	Y
4 **Gosar**	Y	Y	Y	Y	Y	Y
5 **Biggs**	Y	Y	Y	Y	Y	Y
6 **Schweikert**	Y	Y	Y	Y	Y	Y
7 Gallego	Y	N	N	Y	N	Y
8 **Lesko**	Y	Y	Y	Y	Y	Y
9 Sinema	Y	N	Y	Y	Y	Y
ARKANSAS						
1 **Crawford**	Y	Y	Y	Y	Y	Y
2 **Hill**	Y	Y	Y	Y	Y	Y
3 **Womack**	Y	Y	Y	Y	Y	Y
4 **Westerman**	Y	Y	Y	Y	Y	Y
CALIFORNIA						
1 **LaMalfa**	Y	Y	Y	Y	Y	Y
2 Huffman	Y	N	N	Y	Y	Y
3 Garamendi	Y	N	N	Y	Y	Y
4 **McClintock**	Y	Y	Y	Y	Y	Y
5 Thompson	Y	N	N	Y	Y	Y
6 Matsui	Y	N	N	Y	Y	Y
7 Bera	Y	N	N	Y	Y	Y
8 **Cook**	Y	Y	Y	Y	Y	Y
9 McNerney	Y	N	N	Y	N	Y
10 **Denham**	Y	Y	Y	Y	Y	Y
11 DeSaulnier	Y	N	N	Y	N	Y
12 Pelosi	Y	N	N	Y	N	Y
13 Lee	Y	N	N	Y	N	Y
14 Speier	Y	N	N	Y	N	Y
15 Swalwell	Y	N	N	Y	N	Y
16 Costa	Y	N	Y	Y	Y	Y
17 Khanna	Y	N	N	Y	N	Y
18 Eshoo	Y	N	N	Y	Y	Y
19 Lofgren	Y	N	N	Y	N	Y
20 Panetta	Y	N	N	Y	N	Y
21 **Valadao**	Y	Y	Y	Y	Y	Y
22 **Nunes**	Y	Y	Y	Y	Y	Y
23 **McCarthy**	Y	Y	Y	Y	Y	Y
24 Carbajal	+	N	N	Y	N	Y
25 **Knight**	?	Y	Y	Y	Y	Y
26 Brownley	Y	N	N	Y	N	Y
27 Chu	?	N	N	Y	N	Y
28 Schiff	Y	N	N	Y	N	Y
29 Cardenas	Y	N	N	Y	N	Y
30 Sherman	Y	N	N	Y	Y	Y
31 Aguilar	Y	N	N	Y	N	Y
32 Napolitano	Y	N	N	Y	N	Y
33 Lieu	Y	N	N	Y	N	Y
34 Gomez	?	N	N	Y	N	Y
35 Torres	Y	N	N	Y	N	Y
36 Ruiz	Y	N	N	Y	Y	Y
37 Bass	Y	N	N	Y	N	?
38 Sánchez, Linda	Y	N	N	Y	Y	Y
39 **Royce**	Y	Y	Y	Y	Y	Y
40 Roybal-Allard	Y	N	N	Y	N	Y
41 Takano	Y	N	N	Y	N	Y
42 **Calvert**	Y	Y	Y	Y	Y	Y
43 Waters	Y	N	N	Y	N	Y
44 Barragan	Y	N	N	Y	N	Y
45 **Walters**	Y	Y	Y	Y	Y	Y
46 Correa	Y	N	N	Y	N	Y
47 Lowenthal	Y	N	N	Y	N	Y
48 **Rohrabacher**	Y	Y	Y	Y	Y	Y
49 **Issa**	Y	Y	Y	Y	Y	Y
50 **Hunter**	Y	Y	Y	Y	Y	Y
51 Vargas	Y	N	N	Y	N	Y
52 Peters	Y	N	N	Y	Y	Y
53 Davis	Y	N	N	Y	Y	Y

	290	291	292	293	294	295
COLORADO						
1 DeGette	?	?	?	?	?	?
2 Polis	?	?	?	?	?	?
3 **Tipton**	Y	Y	Y	Y	Y	Y
4 **Buck**	Y	Y	Y	Y	Y	Y
5 **Lamborn**	Y	Y	Y	Y	Y	Y
6 **Coffman**	Y	Y	Y	Y	Y	Y
7 Perlmutter	Y	N	N	Y	Y	Y
CONNECTICUT						
1 Larson	Y	N	N	Y	Y	Y
2 Courtney	Y	N	N	Y	Y	Y
3 DeLauro	Y	N	N	Y	N	Y
4 Himes	Y	N	N	Y	Y	Y
5 Esty	Y	N	N	Y	Y	Y
DELAWARE						
AL Blunt Rochester	Y	N	N	Y	N	Y
FLORIDA						
1 **Gaetz**	Y	Y	Y	Y	Y	Y
2 **Dunn**	Y	Y	Y	Y	Y	Y
3 **Yoho**	Y	Y	Y	Y	Y	Y
4 **Rutherford**	Y	Y	Y	Y	Y	Y
5 Lawson	Y	N	N	Y	N	Y
6 **DeSantis**	?	Y	Y	Y	Y	Y
7 Murphy	Y	N	N	Y	Y	Y
8 **Posey**	Y	Y	Y	Y	Y	Y
9 Soto	Y	N	N	Y	N	Y
10 Demings	Y	N	N	Y	N	Y
11 **Webster**	Y	Y	Y	Y	Y	Y
12 **Bilirakis**	Y	Y	Y	Y	Y	Y
13 Crist	Y	N	N	Y	Y	Y
14 Castor	Y	N	N	Y	N	Y
15 Ross	?	Y	Y	Y	Y	Y
16 **Buchanan**	Y	Y	Y	Y	N	Y
17 **Rooney, T.**	Y	Y	Y	Y	Y	Y
18 **Mast**	Y	Y	Y	Y	Y	Y
19 **Rooney, F.**	Y	Y	Y	Y	Y	Y
20 Hastings	Y	N	N	Y	N	Y
21 Frankel	Y	N	N	Y	N	Y
22 Deutch	Y	N	N	Y	N	Y
23 Wasserman Schultz	Y	N	N	Y	N	Y
24 Wilson	Y	N	N	Y	Y	Y
25 **Diaz-Balart**	Y	?	?	?	Y	Y
26 **Curbelo**	Y	Y	Y	Y	Y	Y
27 **Ros-Lehtinen**	Y	Y	Y	Y	Y	Y
GEORGIA						
1 **Carter**	Y	Y	Y	Y	+	+
2 Bishop	Y	N	N	Y	Y	Y
3 **Ferguson**	Y	Y	Y	Y	Y	Y
4 Johnson	Y	N	N	Y	N	Y
5 Lewis	Y	N	N	Y	N	Y
6 **Handel**	Y	Y	Y	Y	Y	Y
7 **Woodall**	Y	Y	Y	Y	Y	Y
8 **Scott, A.**	Y	Y	Y	Y	Y	Y
9 **Collins**	Y	Y	Y	Y	Y	Y
10 **Hice**	Y	Y	Y	Y	Y	Y
11 **Loudermilk**	Y	Y	Y	Y	Y	Y
12 **Allen**	Y	Y	Y	Y	Y	Y
13 Scott, D.	?	N	N	Y	N	Y
14 **Graves**	Y	+	+	+	Y	Y
HAWAII						
1 Hanabusa	Y	N	N	Y	Y	Y
2 Gabbard	Y	N	N	Y	N	Y
IDAHO						
1 **Labrador**	Y	Y	Y	Y	Y	Y
2 **Simpson**	Y	Y	Y	Y	Y	Y
ILLINOIS						
1 Rush	?	?	?	?	?	?
2 Kelly	Y	N	N	Y	N	Y
3 Lipinski	Y	N	N	Y	Y	Y
4 Gutierrez	+	+	+	+	+	+
5 Quigley	Y	N	N	Y	N	Y
6 **Roskam**	Y	Y	Y	Y	Y	Y
7 Davis, D.	Y	N	N	Y	N	Y
8 Krishnamoorthi	Y	N	N	Y	N	Y
9 Schakowsky	Y	N	N	Y	N	Y
10 Schneider	Y	N	N	Y	N	Y
11 Foster	Y	N	N	Y	N	Y
12 **Bost**	Y	Y	Y	Y	Y	Y
13 **Davis, R.**	Y	Y	Y	Y	Y	Y

KEY   **Republicans**   Democrats   *Independents*

Y Voted for (yea)	X Paired against	C Voted "present" to avoid possible conflict of interest
# Paired for	– Announced against	
+ Announced for	P Voted "present"	? Did not vote or otherwise make a position known
N Voted against (nay)		

	290	291	292	293	294	295
14 **Hultgren**	Y	Y	Y	Y	Y	Y
15 **Shimkus**	Y	Y	Y	?	Y	Y
16 **Kinzinger**	Y	Y	Y	Y	Y	Y
17 Bustos	Y	N	N	Y	Y	Y
18 **LaHood**	Y	Y	Y	Y	Y	Y
INDIANA						
1 Visclosky	Y	N	N	Y	N	Y
2 **Walorski**	Y	Y	Y	Y	Y	Y
3 **Banks**	Y	Y	Y	Y	Y	Y
4 Rokita	Y	Y	Y	Y	Y	Y
5 **Brooks**	Y	Y	Y	Y	Y	Y
6 **Messer**	Y	Y	Y	Y	Y	Y
7 Carson	Y	N	N	Y	N	Y
8 **Bucshon**	Y	Y	Y	Y	Y	Y
9 **Hollingsworth**	Y	Y	Y	Y	Y	Y
IOWA						
1 **Blum**	Y	Y	Y	Y	Y	Y
2 Loebsack	Y	N	N	Y	Y	Y
3 **Young**	Y	Y	Y	Y	Y	Y
4 **King**	Y	Y	Y	Y	Y	Y
KANSAS						
1 **Marshall**	Y	Y	Y	Y	Y	Y
2 **Jenkins**	Y	Y	Y	Y	Y	Y
3 **Yoder**	Y	+	+	+	Y	Y
4 **Estes**	Y	Y	Y	Y	Y	Y
KENTUCKY						
1 **Comer**	Y	Y	Y	Y	?	?
2 **Guthrie**	Y	Y	Y	Y	Y	Y
3 Yarmuth	Y	N	N	Y	N	Y
4 **Massie**	N	Y	N	N	Y	N
5 **Rogers**	Y	?	?	?	Y	Y
6 **Barr**	Y	Y	Y	Y	Y	Y
LOUISIANA						
1 **Scalise**	Y	Y	Y	Y	Y	Y
2 Richmond	Y	?	N	Y	N	Y
3 **Higgins**	Y	Y	Y	Y	Y	Y
4 **Johnson**	Y	Y	Y	Y	Y	Y
5 **Abraham**	Y	Y	Y	Y	Y	Y
6 **Graves**	Y	Y	Y	Y	Y	Y
MAINE						
1 Pingree	Y	N	N	Y	N	Y
2 **Poliquin**	Y	Y	Y	Y	Y	Y
MARYLAND						
1 **Harris**	Y	Y	Y	Y	Y	Y
2 Ruppersberger	?	N	N	Y	Y	Y
3 Sarbanes	Y	N	N	Y	N	Y
4 Brown	Y	N	N	Y	Y	Y
5 Hoyer	Y	?	?	?	N	Y
6 Delaney	+	–	–	+	N	Y
7 Cummings	?	N	N	Y	N	Y
8 Raskin	Y	N	N	Y	N	Y
MASSACHUSETTS						
1 Neal	Y	N	N	Y	N	Y
2 McGovern	Y	N	N	Y	N	Y
3 Tsongas	?	N	N	Y	N	Y
4 Kennedy	Y	N	N	Y	N	Y
5 Clark	Y	N	N	Y	N	Y
6 Moulton	Y	N	N	Y	Y	Y
7 Capuano	Y	N	N	Y	N	Y
8 Lynch	Y	N	N	Y	N	Y
9 Keating	Y	N	N	Y	N	Y
MICHIGAN						
1 **Bergman**	Y	Y	Y	Y	Y	Y
2 **Huizenga**	Y	Y	Y	Y	Y	Y
3 *Amash*	N	Y	N	N	N	N
4 **Moolenaar**	Y	Y	Y	Y	Y	Y
5 Kildee	Y	N	N	Y	Y	Y
6 **Upton**	Y	Y	Y	Y	Y	Y
7 **Walberg**	Y	Y	Y	Y	Y	Y
8 **Bishop**	Y	Y	Y	Y	Y	Y
9 Levin	Y	N	N	Y	Y	Y
10 **Mitchell**	Y	Y	Y	Y	Y	Y
11 **Trott**	Y	Y	Y	Y	Y	Y
12 Dingell	Y	N	N	Y	Y	Y
14 Lawrence	Y	N	N	Y	N	Y
MINNESOTA						
1 Walz	?	N	N	Y	N	Y
2 **Lewis**	Y	Y	Y	Y	Y	Y
3 **Paulsen**	Y	Y	Y	Y	Y	Y
4 McCollum	Y	N	N	Y	Y	Y

	290	291	292	293	294	295
5 Ellison	?	?	?	?	?	?
6 **Emmer**	Y	Y	Y	Y	Y	Y
7 Peterson	Y	Y	Y	Y	Y	Y
8 Nolan	Y	N	N	Y	Y	Y
MISSISSIPPI						
1 **Kelly**	Y	Y	Y	Y	Y	Y
2 Thompson	?	?	?	?	?	?
3 **Harper**	Y	Y	Y	Y	Y	Y
4 **Palazzo**	Y	Y	Y	Y	Y	Y
MISSOURI						
1 Clay	Y	N	N	Y	N	Y
2 **Wagner**	Y	Y	Y	Y	Y	Y
3 **Luetkemeyer**	Y	Y	Y	Y	Y	Y
4 **Hartzler**	Y	Y	Y	Y	Y	Y
5 Cleaver	Y	N	N	Y	N	Y
6 **Graves**	Y	Y	Y	Y	Y	Y
7 **Long**	Y	Y	Y	Y	Y	Y
8 **Smith**	Y	Y	Y	Y	Y	Y
MONTANA						
AL **Gianforte**	Y	Y	Y	Y	Y	Y
NEBRASKA						
1 **Fortenberry**	Y	Y	Y	Y	Y	Y
2 **Bacon**	Y	Y	Y	Y	Y	Y
3 **Smith**	Y	Y	Y	Y	Y	Y
NEVADA						
1 Titus	Y	N	N	Y	N	Y
2 **Amodei**	Y	Y	Y	Y	Y	Y
3 Rosen	+	N	N	Y	N	Y
4 Kihuen	Y	N	N	Y	N	Y
NEW HAMPSHIRE						
1 Shea-Porter	?	?	?	?	?	?
2 Kuster	Y	N	N	Y	Y	Y
NEW JERSEY						
1 Norcross	Y	N	N	Y	N	Y
2 **LoBiondo**	Y	Y	Y	Y	Y	Y
3 **MacArthur**	Y	Y	Y	Y	Y	Y
4 **Smith**	Y	Y	Y	Y	Y	Y
5 Gottheimer	Y	N	Y	Y	Y	Y
6 Pallone	Y	N	N	Y	N	Y
7 **Lance**	Y	Y	Y	Y	Y	Y
8 Sires	?	N	N	Y	N	Y
9 Pascrell	Y	N	N	Y	N	Y
10 Payne	?	?	?	?	N	Y
11 **Frelinghuysen**	Y	?	?	?	Y	Y
12 Watson Coleman	Y	N	N	Y	N	Y
NEW MEXICO						
1 Lujan Grisham	?	?	?	?	Y	Y
2 **Pearce**	?	Y	Y	Y	Y	Y
3 Luján	Y	N	N	Y	Y	Y
NEW YORK						
1 **Zeldin**	Y	Y	Y	Y	Y	Y
2 **King**	Y	Y	Y	Y	Y	Y
3 Suozzi	Y	N	N	Y	Y	Y
4 Rice	Y	N	N	Y	Y	Y
5 Meeks	?	?	?	?	?	?
6 Meng	Y	N	N	Y	Y	Y
7 Velázquez	Y	N	N	Y	N	Y
8 Jeffries	Y	N	N	Y	N	Y
9 Clarke	+	–	–	+	–	+
10 Nadler	Y	N	N	Y	N	Y
11 **Donovan**	?	?	?	?	?	?
12 Maloney, C.	?	?	?	?	?	?
13 Espaillat	Y	N	N	Y	N	Y
14 Crowley	Y	?	?	?	?	?
15 Serrano	Y	N	N	Y	N	Y
16 Engel	?	?	?	?	?	?
17 Lowey	Y	N	N	Y	N	Y
18 Maloney, S.P.	Y	N	N	Y	N	Y
19 **Faso**	Y	Y	Y	Y	Y	Y
20 Tonko	Y	N	N	Y	N	Y
21 **Stefanik**	Y	Y	Y	Y	Y	Y
22 **Tenney**	Y	Y	Y	Y	Y	Y
23 **Reed**	Y	Y	Y	Y	Y	Y
24 **Katko**	Y	Y	Y	Y	Y	Y
25 **Vacant**						
26 Higgins	Y	N	N	Y	N	Y
27 **Collins**	Y	Y	Y	Y	Y	Y
NORTH CAROLINA						
1 Butterfield	Y	?	N	Y	N	Y
2 **Holding**	Y	+	Y	Y	Y	Y
3 **Jones**	Y	Y	N	Y	Y	Y
4 Price	Y	N	N	Y	N	Y

	290	291	292	293	294	295
5 **Foxx**	Y	Y	Y	Y	Y	Y
6 **Walker**	Y	Y	Y	Y	Y	Y
7 **Rouzer**	Y	Y	Y	Y	Y	Y
8 **Hudson**	Y	Y	Y	Y	Y	Y
9 **Pittenger**	Y	Y	Y	Y	Y	Y
9 **Vacant**						
10 **McHenry**	Y	Y	Y	Y	Y	Y
11 **Meadows**	Y	Y	Y	Y	Y	Y
12 Adams	Y	N	N	Y	N	Y
13 **Budd**	Y	Y	Y	Y	Y	Y
NORTH DAKOTA						
AL **Cramer**	Y	Y	Y	Y	Y	Y
OHIO						
1 **Chabot**	Y	Y	Y	Y	Y	Y
2 **Wenstrup**	Y	Y	Y	Y	Y	Y
3 Beatty	Y	N	N	Y	Y	Y
4 **Jordan**	Y	Y	Y	Y	Y	Y
5 **Latta**	Y	Y	Y	Y	Y	Y
6 **Johnson**	Y	Y	Y	Y	Y	Y
7 **Gibbs**	Y	Y	Y	Y	Y	Y
8 **Davidson**	Y	Y	Y	Y	N	Y
9 Kaptur	Y	N	N	Y	N	Y
10 **Turner**	Y	Y	Y	Y	Y	Y
11 Fudge	Y	N	N	Y	N	Y
12 **Vacant**						
13 Ryan	Y	N	N	Y	N	Y
14 **Joyce**	Y	Y	Y	Y	Y	Y
15 **Stivers**	Y	Y	Y	Y	Y	Y
16 **Renacci**	Y	Y	Y	Y	Y	Y
OKLAHOMA						
1 **Vacant**						
2 **Mullin**	Y	Y	Y	Y	Y	Y
3 **Lucas**	Y	Y	Y	Y	Y	Y
4 **Cole**	Y	+	+	+	Y	Y
5 **Russell**	Y	Y	Y	Y	Y	Y
OREGON						
1 Bonamici	Y	N	N	Y	Y	Y
2 **Walden**	Y	Y	Y	Y	Y	Y
3 Blumenauer	Y	N	N	Y	Y	Y
4 DeFazio	Y	N	N	Y	Y	Y
5 Schrader	Y	N	N	Y	Y	Y
PENNSYLVANIA						
1 Brady	?	N	N	Y	N	Y
2 Evans	Y	N	N	Y	N	Y
3 **Kelly**	Y	Y	Y	Y	Y	Y
4 **Perry**	Y	Y	Y	Y	Y	Y
5 **Thompson**	Y	Y	Y	Y	Y	Y
6 **Costello**	Y	Y	Y	Y	Y	Y
7 **Vacant**						
8 **Fitzpatrick**	Y	Y	Y	Y	N	Y
9 **Shuster**	Y	Y	Y	Y	Y	Y
10 **Marino**	Y	Y	Y	Y	Y	Y
11 **Barletta**	Y	?	Y	Y	Y	Y
12 **Rothfus**	Y	Y	Y	Y	Y	Y
13 Boyle	Y	N	N	Y	N	Y
14 Doyle	Y	N	N	Y	N	Y
15 **Vacant**						
16 **Smucker**	Y	Y	Y	Y	Y	Y
17 Cartwright	Y	N	N	Y	N	Y
18 Lamb	Y	N	Y	Y	Y	Y
RHODE ISLAND						
1 Cicilline	Y	N	N	Y	N	Y
2 Langevin	Y	N	N	Y	N	Y
SOUTH CAROLINA						
1 **Sanford**	Y	Y	Y	Y	N	Y
2 **Wilson**	?	?	?	?	?	?
3 **Duncan**	Y	Y	Y	Y	Y	Y
4 **Gowdy**	?	?	?	?	?	?
5 **Norman**	Y	Y	Y	Y	Y	Y
6 Clyburn	Y	N	N	Y	N	Y
7 **Rice**	?	Y	Y	Y	Y	Y
SOUTH DAKOTA						
AL **Noem**	Y	Y	Y	Y	Y	Y
TENNESSEE						
1 **Roe**	Y	Y	Y	Y	Y	Y
2 **Duncan**	Y	Y	Y	Y	Y	Y
3 **Fleischmann**	Y	Y	Y	Y	Y	Y
4 **DesJarlais**	Y	Y	Y	Y	Y	Y
5 Cooper	Y	N	N	Y	Y	Y
6 **Black**	?	?	?	?	?	?
7 **Blackburn**	?	Y	Y	Y	Y	Y
8 **Kustoff**	Y	Y	Y	Y	Y	Y
9 Cohen	Y	N	N	Y	N	Y

	290	291	292	293	294	295
TEXAS						
1 **Gohmert**	Y	Y	Y	Y	Y	Y
2 **Poe**	Y	Y	Y	Y	Y	Y
3 **Johnson, S.**	?	?	?	?	?	+
4 **Ratcliffe**	Y	Y	Y	Y	Y	Y
5 **Hensarling**	Y	Y	Y	Y	Y	Y
6 **Barton**	Y	Y	Y	Y	Y	Y
7 **Culberson**	Y	Y	Y	Y	Y	Y
8 **Brady**	Y	Y	Y	Y	Y	Y
9 Green, A.	Y	N	N	Y	N	Y
10 **McCaul**	Y	Y	Y	Y	Y	Y
11 **Conaway**	Y	Y	Y	Y	Y	Y
12 **Granger**	Y	Y	Y	Y	Y	Y
13 **Thornberry**	Y	Y	Y	Y	Y	Y
14 **Weber**	Y	Y	Y	Y	Y	Y
15 Gonzalez	Y	N	N	Y	Y	Y
16 O'Rourke	?	N	N	Y	Y	Y
17 **Flores**	Y	Y	Y	Y	Y	Y
18 Jackson Lee	Y	N	N	Y	N	Y
19 **Arrington**	Y	Y	Y	Y	Y	Y
20 Castro	Y	N	N	Y	Y	Y
21 **Smith**	Y	Y	Y	Y	Y	Y
22 **Olson**	Y	Y	Y	Y	Y	Y
23 **Hurd**	Y	Y	Y	Y	Y	Y
24 Marchant	+	Y	Y	Y	Y	Y
25 **Williams**	Y	Y	Y	Y	Y	Y
26 **Burgess**	Y	Y	Y	Y	Y	Y
28 Cuellar	Y	N	N	Y	Y	Y
29 Green, G.	Y	N	N	Y	Y	Y
30 Johnson, E.B.	Y	N	N	Y	Y	Y
31 **Carter**	Y	Y	?	Y	Y	Y
32 **Sessions**	Y	Y	Y	Y	Y	Y
33 Veasey	Y	N	N	Y	Y	Y
34 Vela	Y	Y	N	Y	Y	Y
35 Doggett	?	N	N	Y	N	Y
36 **Babin**	Y	Y	Y	Y	Y	Y
UTAH						
1 **Bishop**	Y	Y	Y	Y	Y	Y
2 **Stewart**	Y	Y	Y	Y	Y	Y
3 **Curtis**	?	?	?	?	?	?
4 **Love**	Y	Y	Y	Y	Y	Y
VERMONT						
AL Welch	Y	N	N	Y	N	Y
VIRGINIA						
1 **Wittman**	Y	Y	Y	Y	Y	Y
2 **Taylor**	Y	+	+	+	Y	Y
3 Scott	?	N	N	Y	N	Y
4 McEachin	Y	N	N	Y	N	Y
5 **Garrett**	N	Y	Y	Y	Y	Y
6 **Goodlatte**	Y	Y	Y	Y	Y	Y
7 **Brat**	Y	Y	Y	Y	Y	Y
8 Beyer	Y	N	N	Y	Y	Y
9 **Griffith**	N	Y	Y	Y	Y	Y
10 **Comstock**	Y	Y	Y	Y	Y	Y
11 Connolly	Y	N	N	Y	N	Y
WASHINGTON						
1 DelBene	Y	N	N	Y	Y	Y
2 Larsen	Y	N	N	Y	Y	Y
3 **Herrera Beutler**	Y	Y	Y	Y	Y	Y
4 **Newhouse**	Y	Y	Y	Y	Y	Y
5 **McMorris Rodgers**	Y	Y	Y	Y	Y	Y
6 Kilmer	Y	N	N	Y	Y	Y
7 Jayapal	Y	N	N	Y	Y	Y
8 **Reichert**	Y	Y	Y	Y	Y	Y
9 Smith	Y	N	N	Y	Y	Y
10 Heck	Y	N	N	Y	Y	Y
WEST VIRGINIA						
1 **McKinley**	Y	Y	Y	Y	Y	Y
2 **Mooney**	Y	Y	Y	Y	Y	Y
3 **Jenkins**	Y	Y	Y	Y	Y	Y
WISCONSIN						
1 **Ryan**						
2 Pocan	+	N	N	Y	N	Y
3 Kind	Y	N	N	Y	Y	Y
4 Moore	+	N	N	Y	?	+
5 **Sensenbrenner**	Y	Y	Y	Y	Y	Y
6 **Grothman**	Y	Y	Y	Y	Y	Y
7 **Duffy**	Y	Y	Y	Y	Y	Y
8 **Gallagher**	Y	Y	Y	Y	Y	Y
WYOMING						
AL **Cheney**	Y	Y	Y	Y	Y	Y

VOTE NUMBER

296. HR6136. DACA AND BORDER SECURITY/RECOMMIT. Espaillat, D-N.Y., motion to recommit the bill to the House Judiciary Committee with instructions to report it back immediately with an amendment that would prohibit law enforcement from detaining, separately from their child, any individual accused of illegally entering the United States with a child, in cases in which the child is under the age of 18. Motion rejected 190-230: R 1-230; D 189-0. June 27, 2018.

297. HR6136. DACA AND BORDER SECURITY/PASSAGE. Passage of the bill that would appropriate $23.4 billion for various border security activities. Included would be $16.6 billion for a "border wall system," which would be available from fiscal 2019 through fiscal 2027, and $6.8 billion for border security investments, which would be available from fiscal 2019 through fiscal 2023. It would provide those with Deferred Action for Childhood Arrivals status a six-year renewable contingent non-immigrant legal status and would allow them to apply for a green card after five years, providing a path to citizenship. It would modify legal immigration by ending the diversity visa program and reallocating those visas to other classifications.The bill would require that undocumented immigrants who are charged with a misdemeanor offense for improper entry into the United States be detained with their minor children. Rejected 121-301: R 121-112; D 0-189. June 27, 2018.

298. HRES964. FISCAL 2019 DEFENSE APPROPRIATIONS/PREVIOUS QUESTION. Cheney, R-Wyo., motion to order the previous question (thus ending debate and possibility of amendment) on the rule (H Res 964) that would provide for further consideration of the fiscal 2019 defense appropriations bill (HR 6157). Motion agreed to 231-188: R 231-0; D 0-188. June 27, 2018.

299. HRES964. FISCAL 2019 DEFENSE APPROPRIATIONS/RULE. Adoption of the rule (H Res 964) that would provide for further consideration of the fiscal 2019 defense appropriations bill (HR 6157). Adopted 230-185: R 225-3; D 5-182. June 27, 2018.

300. HR5515. FISCAL 2019 DEFENSE AUTHORIZATION/MOTION TO INSTRUCT. Carbajal, D-Calif., motion to instruct conferees on the part of the House to agree to section 703 of the Senate bill, which is the provision related to contraception coverage parity under the TRICARE Program. Motion rejected 188-231: R 0-231; D 188-0. June 27, 2018.

301. HR5515. FISCAL 2019 DEFENSE AUTHORIZATION/MOTION TO CLOSE. Thornberry, R-Texas, motion that the meetings of the conference between the House and the Senate on the bill may be closed to the public at such times as classified national security information may be discussed, provided that any sitting member of Congress shall be entitled to attend any meeting of the conference. Motion agreed to 403-15: R 227-3; D 176-12. June 27, 2018.

	296	297	298	299	300	301
ALABAMA						
1 Byrne	N	N	Y	Y	N	Y
2 Roby	N	N	Y	Y	N	Y
3 Rogers	N	N	Y	Y	N	Y
4 Aderholt	N	N	Y	Y	N	Y
5 Brooks	N	N	Y	Y	N	Y
6 Palmer	N	N	Y	Y	N	Y
7 Sewell	Y	N	N	N	Y	Y
ALASKA						
AL Young	N	Y	Y	Y	N	Y
ARIZONA						
1 O'Halleran	Y	N	N	Y	Y	Y
2 McSally	N	Y	Y	Y	N	Y
3 Grijalva	Y	N	N	N	Y	Y
4 Gosar	N	N	Y	Y	?	?
5 Biggs	N	N	Y	Y	N	Y
6 Schweikert	N	N	Y	Y	N	Y
7 Gallego	Y	N	N	N	Y	Y
8 Lesko	N	N	Y	Y	N	Y
9 Sinema	Y	N	N	Y	Y	Y
ARKANSAS						
1 Crawford	N	N	Y	Y	N	Y
2 Hill	N	Y	Y	Y	N	Y
3 Womack	N	Y	Y	Y	N	Y
4 Westerman	N	N	Y	Y	N	Y
CALIFORNIA						
1 LaMalfa	N	N	Y	Y	N	Y
2 Huffman	Y	N	N	N	Y	Y
3 Garamendi	Y	N	N	N	Y	Y
4 McClintock	N	N	Y	Y	N	Y
5 Thompson	Y	N	N	N	Y	Y
6 Matsui	Y	N	N	N	Y	Y
7 Bera	Y	N	N	N	Y	Y
8 Cook	N	N	Y	Y	N	Y
9 McNerney	Y	N	N	N	Y	Y
10 Denham	N	Y	Y	Y	N	Y
11 DeSaulnier	Y	N	N	N	Y	Y
12 Pelosi	Y	N	N	N	Y	Y
13 Lee	Y	N	N	N	Y	N
14 Speier	Y	N	N	N	Y	Y
15 Swalwell	Y	N	N	N	Y	Y
16 Costa	Y	N	N	N	Y	Y
17 Khanna	Y	N	N	N	Y	Y
18 Eshoo	Y	N	N	N	Y	Y
19 Lofgren	Y	N	N	N	Y	Y
20 Panetta	Y	N	N	N	Y	Y
21 Valadao	N	Y	Y	Y	N	Y
22 Nunes	N	Y	Y	Y	N	Y
23 McCarthy	N	Y	Y	Y	N	Y
24 Carbajal	Y	N	N	N	Y	Y
25 Knight	N	Y	Y	Y	N	Y
26 Brownley	Y	N	N	N	Y	Y
27 Chu	Y	N	N	N	Y	Y
28 Schiff	Y	N	N	N	Y	Y
29 Cardenas	Y	N	N	N	Y	Y
30 Sherman	Y	N	N	N	Y	Y
31 Aguilar	Y	N	N	N	Y	Y
32 Napolitano	Y	N	N	N	Y	Y
33 Lieu	Y	N	N	N	Y	Y
34 Gomez	Y	N	N	N	Y	Y
35 Torres	Y	N	N	N	Y	Y
36 Ruiz	Y	N	N	N	Y	Y
37 Bass	Y	N	N	N	Y	Y
38 Sánchez, Linda	Y	N	N	N	Y	Y
39 Royce	N	Y	Y	Y	N	Y
40 Roybal-Allard	Y	N	N	N	Y	Y
41 Takano	Y	N	N	N	Y	Y
42 Calvert	N	Y	Y	Y	N	Y
43 Waters	Y	N	N	N	Y	Y
44 Barragan	Y	N	N	N	Y	Y
45 Walters	N	Y	Y	Y	N	Y
46 Correa	Y	N	N	N	Y	Y
47 Lowenthal	Y	N	N	N	Y	N
48 Rohrabacher	N	N	Y	Y	N	Y
49 Issa	N	Y	Y	Y	N	Y
50 Hunter	N	N	Y	Y	N	Y
51 Vargas	Y	N	N	N	Y	Y
52 Peters	Y	N	N	N	Y	Y
53 Davis	Y	N	N	N	Y	Y

	296	297	298	299	300	301
COLORADO						
1 DeGette	?	?	?	?	Y	Y
2 Polis	Y	N	N	N	Y	N
3 Tipton	N	N	Y	Y	N	Y
4 Buck	N	N	Y	Y	N	Y
5 Lamborn	N	N	Y	Y	N	Y
6 Coffman	N	Y	Y	Y	N	Y
7 Perlmutter	Y	N	N	N	Y	Y
CONNECTICUT						
1 Larson	Y	N	N	N	Y	Y
2 Courtney	Y	N	N	N	Y	Y
3 DeLauro	Y	N	N	N	Y	Y
4 Himes	Y	N	N	N	Y	Y
5 Esty	Y	N	N	N	Y	Y
DELAWARE						
AL Blunt Rochester	Y	N	N	N	Y	Y
FLORIDA						
1 Gaetz	N	N	Y	Y	N	Y
2 Dunn	N	Y	Y	Y	N	Y
3 Yoho	N	N	Y	Y	N	Y
4 Rutherford	N	Y	Y	Y	N	Y
5 Lawson	Y	N	N	N	Y	Y
6 DeSantis	N	N	Y	Y	N	Y
7 Murphy	Y	N	N	N	Y	Y
8 Posey	N	N	Y	Y	N	Y
9 Soto	Y	N	N	N	Y	Y
10 Demings	Y	N	N	N	Y	Y
11 Webster	N	N	Y	Y	N	Y
12 Bilirakis	N	Y	Y	Y	N	Y
13 Crist	Y	N	N	N	Y	Y
14 Castor	Y	N	N	N	Y	Y
15 Ross	N	Y	Y	Y	N	Y
16 Buchanan	N	N	Y	Y	N	Y
17 Rooney, T.	N	Y	Y	Y	N	Y
18 Mast	N	Y	Y	Y	N	Y
19 Rooney, F.	N	Y	Y	Y	N	Y
20 Hastings	Y	N	N	N	Y	Y
21 Frankel	Y	N	N	N	Y	Y
22 Deutch	Y	N	N	N	Y	Y
23 Wasserman Schultz	Y	N	N	N	Y	Y
24 Wilson	Y	N	N	N	Y	Y
25 Diaz-Balart	N	Y	Y	Y	N	Y
26 Curbelo	N	Y	Y	Y	N	Y
27 Ros-Lehtinen	N	Y	Y	Y	N	Y
GEORGIA						
1 Carter	N	N	Y	Y	N	Y
2 Bishop	Y	N	N	N	Y	Y
3 Ferguson	N	N	Y	Y	N	Y
4 Johnson	Y	N	N	N	Y	Y
5 Lewis	Y	N	N	N	Y	Y
6 Handel	N	Y	Y	Y	N	Y
7 Woodall	N	Y	Y	Y	N	Y
8 Scott, A.	N	Y	Y	Y	N	Y
9 Collins	N	Y	Y	Y	N	Y
10 Hice	N	N	Y	Y	N	Y
11 Loudermilk	N	N	Y	Y	N	Y
12 Allen	N	N	Y	Y	N	Y
13 Scott, D.	Y	N	N	N	Y	Y
14 Graves	N	N	Y	Y	N	Y
HAWAII						
1 Hanabusa	Y	N	N	N	Y	Y
2 Gabbard	Y	N	N	N	Y	Y
IDAHO						
1 Labrador	N	N	Y	Y	N	Y
2 Simpson	N	Y	Y	Y	N	Y
ILLINOIS						
1 Rush	?	?	?	?	?	?
2 Kelly	Y	N	N	N	Y	Y
3 Lipinski	Y	N	N	N	Y	Y
4 Gutierrez	Y	N	N	N	Y	Y
5 Quigley	Y	N	N	N	Y	Y
6 Roskam	N	Y	Y	Y	N	Y
7 Davis, D.	Y	N	N	N	Y	Y
8 Krishnamoorthi	Y	N	N	N	Y	Y
9 Schakowsky	Y	N	N	N	Y	Y
10 Schneider	Y	N	N	N	Y	Y
11 Foster	Y	N	N	N	Y	Y
12 Bost	N	Y	Y	Y	N	Y
13 Davis, R.	N	Y	Y	Y	N	Y

KEY   Republicans   Democrats   *Independents*

Y	Voted for (yea)	X	Paired against
#	Paired for	–	Announced against
+	Announced for	P	Voted "present"
N	Voted against (nay)		

C	Voted "present" to avoid possible conflict of interest
?	Did not vote or otherwise make a position known

	296	297	298	299	300	301
14 **Hultgren**	N	Y	Y	Y	N	Y
15 **Shimkus**	N	Y	Y	Y	N	Y
16 **Kinzinger**	N	Y	Y	Y	N	Y
17 Bustos	Y	N	N	N	Y	Y
18 **LaHood**	N	N	Y	Y	N	Y
INDIANA						
1 Visclosky	Y	N	N	N	Y	Y
2 **Walorski**	N	Y	Y	Y	N	Y
3 **Banks**	N	N	Y	Y	N	Y
4 Rokita	N	N	Y	Y	N	Y
5 **Brooks**	N	Y	Y	Y	N	Y
6 **Messer**	?	?	?	?	N	Y
7 Carson	Y	N	N	N	Y	Y
8 **Bucshon**	N	Y	Y	Y	N	Y
9 **Hollingsworth**	N	N	Y	Y	N	Y
IOWA						
1 **Blum**	Y	N	Y	Y	N	Y
2 Loebsack	Y	N	N	N	Y	Y
3 **Young**	N	Y	Y	Y	N	Y
4 **King**	N	N	Y	Y	N	Y
KANSAS						
1 **Marshall**	N	Y	Y	Y	N	Y
2 **Jenkins**	N	Y	Y	Y	N	Y
3 **Yoder**	N	Y	Y	Y	N	Y
4 **Estes**	N	N	Y	Y	N	Y
KENTUCKY						
1 **Comer**	N	N	Y	Y	N	Y
2 **Guthrie**	N	Y	Y	Y	N	Y
3 Yarmuth	Y	N	N	N	Y	Y
4 **Massie**	N	N	Y	N	N	N
5 **Rogers**	N	Y	Y	Y	N	Y
6 **Barr**	N	Y	Y	Y	N	Y
LOUISIANA						
1 **Scalise**	N	Y	Y	Y	N	Y
2 Richmond	Y	N	N	?	Y	Y
3 **Higgins**	N	Y	Y	Y	N	Y
4 **Johnson**	N	N	Y	Y	N	Y
5 **Abraham**	N	N	Y	Y	N	Y
6 **Graves**	N	N	Y	Y	N	Y
MAINE						
1 Pingree	Y	N	N	N	Y	Y
2 **Poliquin**	N	Y	Y	Y	N	Y
MARYLAND						
1 **Harris**	N	N	Y	Y	N	Y
2 Ruppersberger	Y	N	N	N	Y	Y
3 Sarbanes	Y	N	N	N	Y	Y
4 Brown	Y	N	N	N	Y	Y
5 Hoyer	Y	N	N	N	Y	Y
6 Delaney	Y	N	N	N	Y	Y
7 Cummings	Y	N	N	N	Y	Y
8 Raskin	Y	N	N	N	Y	Y
MASSACHUSETTS						
1 Neal	Y	N	N	N	Y	Y
2 McGovern	Y	N	N	N	Y	N
3 Tsongas	Y	N	N	N	?	?
4 Kennedy	Y	N	N	N	Y	Y
5 Clark	Y	N	N	N	Y	Y
6 Moulton	Y	N	N	N	Y	Y
7 Capuano	Y	N	N	N	Y	Y
8 Lynch	Y	N	N	?	Y	Y
9 Keating	Y	N	N	N	Y	Y
MICHIGAN						
1 **Bergman**	N	Y	Y	Y	N	Y
2 **Huizenga**	N	Y	Y	Y	N	Y
3 *Amash*	N	N	Y	N	N	N
4 **Moolenaar**	N	Y	Y	Y	N	Y
5 Kildee	Y	N	N	N	Y	Y
6 **Upton**	N	Y	Y	Y	N	Y
7 **Walberg**	N	Y	Y	Y	N	Y
8 **Bishop**	N	Y	Y	?	N	Y
9 Levin	Y	N	N	N	Y	Y
10 **Mitchell**	N	Y	Y	Y	N	Y
11 **Trott**	N	Y	Y	Y	N	Y
12 Dingell	Y	N	N	N	Y	Y
14 Lawrence	Y	N	N	N	Y	Y
MINNESOTA						
1 Walz	Y	N	N	N	?	?
2 **Lewis**	N	Y	Y	Y	N	Y
3 **Paulsen**	N	Y	Y	Y	N	Y
4 McCollum	Y	N	N	N	Y	Y

	296	297	298	299	300	301
5 Ellison	Y	N	N	N	Y	N
6 **Emmer**	N	N	Y	Y	N	Y
7 Peterson	Y	N	N	N	Y	Y
8 Nolan	Y	N	N	N	Y	Y
MISSISSIPPI						
1 **Kelly**	N	N	Y	Y	N	Y
2 Thompson	?	?	?	?	?	?
3 **Harper**	N	Y	Y	Y	N	Y
4 **Palazzo**	N	N	Y	Y	N	Y
MISSOURI						
1 Clay	Y	N	N	N	Y	Y
2 **Wagner**	N	Y	Y	Y	N	Y
3 **Luetkemeyer**	N	Y	Y	Y	N	Y
4 **Hartzler**	N	Y	Y	Y	N	Y
5 Cleaver	Y	N	N	N	Y	Y
6 **Graves**	N	N	Y	Y	N	Y
7 **Long**	N	N	Y	Y	N	Y
8 **Smith**	N	N	Y	Y	N	Y
MONTANA						
AL **Gianforte**	N	Y	Y	Y	N	Y
NEBRASKA						
1 **Fortenberry**	N	Y	Y	Y	N	Y
2 **Bacon**	N	Y	Y	Y	N	Y
3 **Smith**	N	N	Y	Y	N	Y
NEVADA						
1 Titus	Y	N	N	N	Y	Y
2 **Amodei**	N	Y	Y	Y	N	Y
3 Rosen	Y	N	N	N	Y	Y
4 Kihuen	Y	N	N	N	Y	Y
NEW HAMPSHIRE						
1 Shea-Porter	Y	N	N	N	Y	Y
2 Kuster	Y	N	N	N	Y	Y
NEW JERSEY						
1 Norcross	Y	N	?	N	Y	Y
2 **LoBiondo**	N	Y	Y	Y	N	Y
3 **MacArthur**	N	Y	Y	Y	N	Y
4 **Smith**	N	Y	Y	Y	N	Y
5 Gottheimer	Y	N	N	Y	Y	Y
6 Pallone	Y	N	N	N	Y	Y
7 **Lance**	N	Y	Y	Y	N	Y
8 Sires	Y	N	N	N	Y	Y
9 Pascrell	Y	N	N	N	Y	Y
10 Payne	Y	N	N	N	Y	Y
11 **Frelinghuysen**	N	Y	Y	Y	N	Y
12 Watson Coleman	Y	N	N	N	Y	N
NEW MEXICO						
1 Lujan Grisham	Y	N	N	N	Y	Y
2 **Pearce**	N	Y	Y	Y	N	Y
3 Luján	Y	N	N	N	Y	Y
NEW YORK						
1 **Zeldin**	N	N	Y	Y	N	Y
2 **King**	N	Y	Y	Y	N	Y
3 Suozzi	Y	N	N	N	Y	Y
4 Rice	Y	N	N	N	Y	Y
5 Meeks	Y	N	N	N	Y	Y
6 Meng	Y	N	N	N	Y	Y
7 Velázquez	Y	N	N	N	Y	Y
8 Jeffries	Y	N	N	N	Y	Y
9 Clarke	Y	N	N	N	Y	Y
10 Nadler	Y	N	N	N	Y	Y
11 **Donovan**	N	Y	Y	Y	N	Y
12 Maloney, C.	Y	N	N	N	Y	Y
13 Espaillat	Y	N	N	N	Y	Y
14 Crowley	?	?	?	?	?	?
15 Serrano	Y	N	N	N	Y	Y
16 Engel	Y	N	N	N	Y	Y
17 Lowey	Y	N	N	N	Y	Y
18 Maloney, S.P.	Y	N	N	N	Y	Y
19 **Faso**	N	Y	Y	Y	N	Y
20 Tonko	Y	N	N	N	Y	N
21 **Stefanik**	N	Y	Y	Y	N	Y
22 **Tenney**	N	N	Y	Y	N	Y
23 **Reed**	N	Y	Y	Y	N	Y
24 **Katko**	N	Y	Y	Y	N	Y
25 **Vacant**						
26 Higgins	Y	N	N	N	Y	Y
27 **Collins**	N	Y	Y	Y	N	Y
NORTH CAROLINA						
1 Butterfield	Y	N	N	N	Y	Y
2 **Holding**	N	N	Y	Y	N	Y
3 **Jones**	N	N	Y	N	N	N
4 Price	Y	N	N	N	Y	Y

	296	297	298	299	300	301
5 **Foxx**	N	N	Y	Y	N	Y
6 **Walker**	N	N	Y	Y	N	Y
7 **Rouzer**	N	N	Y	Y	N	Y
8 **Hudson**	N	N	Y	Y	N	Y
9 **Pittenger**	N	Y	Y	Y	N	Y
9 **Vacant**						
10 **McHenry**	N	Y	Y	Y	N	Y
11 **Meadows**	N	N	Y	?	N	Y
12 Adams	Y	N	N	N	Y	Y
13 **Budd**	N	N	Y	Y	N	Y
NORTH DAKOTA						
AL **Cramer**	N	Y	Y	Y	?	?
OHIO						
1 **Chabot**	N	Y	Y	Y	N	Y
2 **Wenstrup**	N	Y	Y	Y	N	Y
3 Beatty	Y	N	N	N	Y	Y
4 **Jordan**	N	N	Y	Y	N	Y
5 **Latta**	N	N	Y	Y	N	Y
6 **Johnson**	N	Y	Y	Y	N	Y
7 **Gibbs**	N	Y	Y	Y	N	Y
8 **Davidson**	N	N	Y	Y	N	Y
9 Kaptur	Y	N	N	N	Y	Y
10 **Turner**	N	Y	Y	Y	N	Y
11 Fudge	Y	N	N	N	Y	Y
12 **Vacant**						
13 Ryan	Y	N	N	N	Y	Y
14 **Joyce**	N	Y	Y	Y	N	Y
15 **Stivers**	N	Y	Y	Y	N	Y
16 **Renacci**	N	Y	Y	Y	N	Y
OKLAHOMA						
1 **Vacant**						
2 **Mullin**	N	N	Y	Y	N	Y
3 **Lucas**	N	Y	Y	Y	N	Y
4 **Cole**	N	Y	Y	Y	N	Y
5 **Russell**	N	N	Y	Y	N	Y
OREGON						
1 Bonamici	Y	N	N	N	Y	Y
2 **Walden**	N	Y	Y	Y	N	Y
3 Blumenauer	Y	N	N	N	Y	N
4 DeFazio	Y	N	N	N	Y	N
5 Schrader	Y	N	N	N	Y	Y
PENNSYLVANIA						
1 Brady	Y	N	N	N	Y	Y
2 Evans	Y	N	N	N	Y	Y
3 **Kelly**	N	Y	Y	Y	N	Y
4 **Perry**	N	N	Y	Y	N	Y
5 **Thompson**	N	Y	Y	Y	N	Y
6 **Costello**	N	Y	Y	Y	N	Y
7 **Vacant**						
8 **Fitzpatrick**	N	Y	Y	Y	N	Y
9 **Shuster**	N	Y	Y	Y	N	Y
10 **Marino**	N	Y	Y	Y	N	Y
11 **Barletta**	N	N	Y	Y	N	Y
12 **Rothfus**	N	N	Y	Y	N	Y
13 Boyle	Y	N	N	N	Y	Y
14 Doyle	Y	N	N	N	Y	Y
15 **Vacant**						
16 **Smucker**	N	N	Y	Y	N	Y
17 Cartwright	Y	N	N	N	Y	Y
18 Lamb	Y	N	N	N	Y	Y
RHODE ISLAND						
1 Cicilline	Y	N	N	N	Y	Y
2 Langevin	Y	N	N	N	Y	Y
SOUTH CAROLINA						
1 **Sanford**	N	N	Y	Y	N	Y
2 **Wilson**	N	Y	Y	Y	N	Y
3 **Duncan**	N	N	Y	Y	N	Y
4 **Gowdy**	N	N	Y	Y	N	Y
5 **Norman**	N	N	Y	Y	N	Y
6 Clyburn	Y	N	N	N	Y	Y
7 **Rice**	N	N	Y	Y	N	Y
SOUTH DAKOTA						
AL **Noem**	N	N	Y	Y	N	Y
TENNESSEE						
1 **Roe**	N	N	Y	Y	N	Y
2 **Duncan**	N	N	Y	Y	N	Y
3 **Fleischmann**	N	N	Y	Y	N	Y
4 **DesJarlais**	N	N	Y	Y	N	Y
5 Cooper	Y	N	N	N	Y	Y
6 **Black**	?	?	?	?	?	?
7 **Blackburn**	N	N	Y	Y	N	Y
8 **Kustoff**	N	N	Y	Y	N	Y
9 Cohen	Y	N	N	N	Y	Y

	296	297	298	299	300	301
TEXAS						
1 **Gohmert**	N	N	Y	Y	N	Y
2 **Poe**	N	N	Y	Y	N	Y
3 **Johnson, S.**	N	N	Y	Y	N	Y
4 **Ratcliffe**	N	N	Y	Y	N	Y
5 **Hensarling**	N	Y	Y	Y	N	Y
6 **Barton**	N	Y	Y	Y	N	Y
7 **Culberson**	N	N	Y	Y	N	Y
8 **Brady**	N	Y	Y	Y	N	Y
9 Green, A.	Y	N	N	N	Y	Y
10 **McCaul**	N	Y	Y	Y	N	Y
11 **Conaway**	N	Y	Y	Y	N	Y
12 **Granger**	N	N	Y	Y	N	Y
13 **Thornberry**	N	Y	Y	Y	N	Y
14 **Weber**	N	N	Y	Y	N	Y
15 Gonzalez	Y	N	N	N	Y	Y
16 O'Rourke	Y	N	N	N	Y	Y
17 **Flores**	N	Y	Y	Y	N	Y
18 Jackson Lee	Y	N	N	N	Y	Y
19 **Arrington**	N	N	Y	Y	N	Y
20 Castro	Y	N	N	N	Y	Y
21 **Smith**	N	N	Y	Y	N	?
22 **Olson**	N	N	Y	?	N	Y
23 **Hurd**	N	N	Y	Y	N	Y
24 Marchant	N	N	?	Y	N	Y
25 **Williams**	N	N	Y	Y	N	Y
26 **Burgess**	N	N	Y	Y	N	Y
28 Cuellar	Y	N	N	N	Y	Y
29 Green, G.	Y	N	N	N	Y	Y
30 Johnson, E.B.	Y	N	N	N	Y	Y
31 **Carter**	?	N	Y	Y	N	Y
32 **Sessions**	N	N	Y	Y	N	Y
33 Veasey	Y	N	N	N	Y	Y
34 Vela	Y	N	N	N	Y	Y
35 Doggett	Y	N	N	N	Y	Y
36 **Babin**	N	N	Y	Y	N	Y
UTAH						
1 **Bishop**	N	Y	Y	Y	N	Y
2 **Stewart**	N	Y	Y	Y	N	Y
3 **Curtis**	N	Y	Y	Y	N	Y
4 **Love**	N	Y	Y	Y	N	Y
VERMONT						
AL Welch	Y	N	N	N	Y	Y
VIRGINIA						
1 **Wittman**	N	N	Y	Y	N	Y
2 **Taylor**	N	N	Y	Y	N	Y
3 Scott	Y	N	N	N	Y	Y
4 McEachin	Y	N	N	N	Y	Y
5 **Garrett**	N	N	Y	?	N	Y
6 **Goodlatte**	N	Y	Y	Y	N	Y
7 **Brat**	N	N	Y	Y	N	Y
8 Beyer	Y	N	N	N	Y	Y
9 **Griffith**	N	Y	Y	Y	N	Y
10 **Comstock**	N	Y	Y	Y	N	Y
11 Connolly	Y	N	N	N	Y	Y
WASHINGTON						
1 DelBene	Y	N	N	N	Y	Y
2 Larsen	Y	N	N	N	Y	Y
3 **Herrera Beutler**	N	Y	Y	Y	N	Y
4 **Newhouse**	N	Y	Y	Y	N	Y
5 **McMorris Rodgers**	N	Y	Y	Y	N	Y
6 Kilmer	Y	N	N	N	Y	Y
7 Jayapal	Y	N	N	N	Y	N
8 **Reichert**	N	Y	Y	Y	N	Y
9 Smith	Y	N	N	N	Y	Y
10 Heck	Y	N	N	N	Y	Y
WEST VIRGINIA						
1 **McKinley**	N	Y	Y	Y	N	Y
2 **Mooney**	N	N	Y	Y	N	Y
3 **Jenkins**	N	N	Y	Y	N	Y
WISCONSIN						
1 **Ryan**		Y				
2 Pocan	Y	N	N	N	Y	N
3 Kind	Y	N	N	N	Y	Y
4 Moore	Y	N	N	N	Y	N
5 **Sensenbrenner**	N	N	Y	Y	N	Y
6 **Grothman**	N	N	Y	Y	N	Y
7 **Duffy**	N	Y	Y	Y	N	Y
8 **Gallagher**	N	N	Y	Y	N	Y
WYOMING						
AL **Cheney**	N	N	Y	Y	N	Y

VOTE NUMBER

302. HR6157. FISCAL 2019 DEFENSE APPROPRIATIONS/ARMY AND NAVY SCIENTIFIC RESEARCH. Langevin, D-R.I., amendment that would decrease funding for operations and maintenance, defense-wide, and research and development, defense-wide, by $40 million, increase funding for Army scientific research and development by $10 million and increase Naval scientific research and development by $30 million. Rejected in Committee of the Whole 188-228: R 87-141; D 101-87. June 27, 2018.

303. HR6157. FISCAL 2019 DEFENSE APPROPRIATIONS/COOPERATING NATIONS MILITARY SUPPORT. Poe, R-Texas, amendment that would reduce funding for payments to key cooperating nations for logistical and military support by $200 million and would allocate the same amount to the spending reduction account. Rejected in Committee of the Whole 175-241: R 156-73; D 19-168. June 27, 2018.

304. HRES971. SUBPOENAS REQUESTED FROM JUSTICE DEPARTMENT/ PREVIOUS QUESTION. Collins, R-Ga., motion to order the previous question (thus ending debate and possibility of amendment) on the rule (H Res 971) that would provide for consideration of the resolution (H Res 970) that would insist that the Justice Department fully comply with the document requests and subpoenas issued by the Intelligence and Judiciary committees with regard to potential violations of the Foreign Intelligence Surveillance Act (FISA) by Justice Department personnel and related matters, by Friday, July 6, 2018. Motion agreed to 224-186: R 224-0; D 0-186. June 28, 2018.

305. HRES971. SUBPOENAS REQUESTED FROM JUSTICE DEPARTMENT/ RULE. Adoption of the rule (H Res 971) that would provide for consideration of the resolution (H Res 970) that would insist that the Justice Department fully comply with the document requests and subpoenas issued by the Intelligence and Judiciary committees with regard to potential violations of the Foreign Intelligence Surveillance Act (FISA) by Justice Department personnel and related matters, by Friday, July 6, 2018. Adopted 224-184: R 224-0; D 0-184. June 28, 2018.

306. HRES970. SUBPOENAS REQUESTED FROM JUSTICE DEPARTMENT/ PASSAGE. Adoption of the resolution that would insist that the Justice Department fully comply with the document requests and subpoenas issued by the Intelligence and Judiciary committees with regard to potential violations of the Foreign Intelligence Surveillance Act (FISA) by Justice Department personnel and related matters, by Friday, July 6, 2018. Adopted 226-183: R 226-0; D 0-183. June 28, 2018.

307. HR6157. FISCAL 2019 DEFENSE APPROPRIATIONS/NAVAL WEAPON PROCUREMENT. Gallagher, R-Wis., amendment that would decrease funding for non-military Defense Department activities by $23.8 million and increase funding for naval weapons procurement by the same amount. Rejected in Committee of the Whole 116-296: R 90-138; D 26-158. June 28, 2018.

	302	303	304	305	306	307
ALABAMA						
1 **Byrne**	N	N	Y	Y	Y	Y
2 **Roby**	N	N	Y	Y	Y	N
3 **Rogers**	Y	N	Y	Y	Y	Y
4 **Aderholt**	N	N	Y	Y	?	?
5 **Brooks**	Y	Y	Y	Y	Y	Y
6 **Palmer**	N	Y	Y	Y	Y	Y
7 Sewell	Y	N	N	N	N	N
ALASKA						
AL **Young**	N	Y	Y	Y	Y	Y
ARIZONA						
1 O'Halleran	Y	N	N	N	N	Y
2 **McSally**	Y	Y	Y	Y	Y	Y
3 Grijalva	N	N	N	N	?	N
4 **Gosar**	N	Y	Y	Y	Y	Y
5 **Biggs**	N	Y	Y	Y	Y	Y
6 **Schweikert**	Y	Y	?	Y	Y	N
7 Gallego	Y	N	N	N	N	Y
8 **Lesko**	N	Y	Y	Y	Y	Y
9 Sinema	Y	N	N	N	N	Y
ARKANSAS						
1 **Crawford**	N	Y	Y	Y	Y	N
2 **Hill**	N	Y	Y	Y	Y	N
3 **Womack**	N	N	Y	Y	Y	N
4 **Westerman**	N	Y	Y	Y	Y	N
CALIFORNIA						
1 **LaMalfa**	N	Y	Y	Y	Y	Y
2 Huffman	N	N	N	N	N	N
3 Garamendi	Y	N	N	N	N	Y
4 **McClintock**	N	Y	Y	Y	Y	Y
5 Thompson	N	N	N	N	N	N
6 Matsui	N	N	N	N	N	N
7 Bera	Y	N	N	N	N	Y
8 **Cook**	Y	Y	Y	Y	Y	Y
9 McNerney	Y	N	N	N	N	N
10 **Denham**	N	N	Y	Y	Y	N
11 DeSaulnier	N	N	N	N	N	N
12 Pelosi	Y	N	N	?	?	?
13 Lee	N	N	N	N	N	N
14 Speier	Y	N	N	–	–	
15 Swalwell	N	N	N	N	N	N
16 Costa	Y	N	N	N	N	N
17 Khanna	Y	N	N	N	N	N
18 Eshoo	N	N	N	–	–	
19 Lofgren	N	Y	N	N	N	N
20 Panetta	Y	N	N	N	N	Y
21 **Valadao**	N	N	Y	Y	Y	N
22 **Nunes**	N	N	Y	Y	Y	N
23 **McCarthy**	N	N	Y	Y	Y	Y
24 Carbajal	Y	N	N	N	N	N
25 **Knight**	Y	Y	Y	Y	Y	Y
26 Brownley	N	N	N	N	N	N
27 Chu	N	N	N	N	N	N
28 Schiff	N	N	N	N	N	N
29 Cardenas	N	N	N	N	N	N
30 Sherman	Y	Y	N	N	N	N
31 Aguilar	N	N	N	N	N	N
32 Napolitano	Y	Y	N	N	N	N
33 Lieu	Y	N	N	N	N	Y
34 Gomez	N	N	N	N	N	N
35 Torres	Y	N	N	N	N	N
36 Ruiz	Y	N	N	N	N	N
37 Bass	Y	N	N	N	N	N
38 Sánchez, Linda	Y	N	N	N	N	N
39 **Royce**	N	Y	Y	Y	Y	N
40 Roybal-Allard	N	N	N	N	N	N
41 Takano	N	N	N	N	N	N
42 **Calvert**	N	N	Y	Y	Y	N
43 Waters	N	N	N	N	N	N
44 Barragan	N	N	N	N	N	N
45 **Walters**	N	Y	Y	Y	Y	Y
46 Correa	Y	N	N	N	N	N
47 Lowenthal	N	N	N	N	N	N
48 **Rohrabacher**	Y	Y	Y	Y	Y	N
49 **Issa**	?	?	Y	Y	Y	N
50 **Hunter**	Y	Y	Y	Y	Y	Y
51 Vargas	N	Y	N	N	N	N
52 Peters	Y	N	N	N	N	N
53 Davis	Y	N	N	N	N	N

	302	303	304	305	306	307
COLORADO						
1 DeGette	Y	N	N	N	N	N
2 Polis	N	N	N	N	N	N
3 **Tipton**	N	Y	Y	Y	Y	Y
4 **Buck**	N	Y	?	?	Y	N
5 **Lamborn**	Y	N	Y	Y	Y	Y
6 **Coffman**	Y	Y	Y	Y	Y	Y
7 Perlmutter	Y	N	N	N	N	N
CONNECTICUT						
1 Larson	Y	N	N	N	N	N
2 Courtney	Y	N	N	N	N	Y
3 DeLauro	Y	N	N	N	N	N
4 Himes	Y	N	N	N	N	N
5 Esty	Y	N	N	N	N	N
DELAWARE						
AL Blunt Rochester	Y	N	N	N	N	N
FLORIDA						
1 **Gaetz**	Y	Y	Y	Y	Y	N
2 **Dunn**	N	N	Y	Y	Y	N
3 **Yoho**	Y	Y	Y	Y	Y	N
4 **Rutherford**	N	N	Y	Y	Y	N
5 Lawson	N	N	N	N	N	N
6 **DeSantis**	Y	Y	Y	Y	Y	N
7 Murphy	Y	N	N	N	N	Y
8 **Posey**	Y	Y	Y	Y	Y	Y
9 Soto	Y	N	N	N	N	N
10 Demings	Y	N	N	N	N	N
11 **Webster**	Y	Y	Y	Y	Y	Y
12 **Bilirakis**	Y	Y	Y	Y	Y	Y
13 Crist	N	N	N	N	N	N
14 Castor	N	Y	N	N	N	N
15 **Ross**	N	Y	Y	Y	Y	N
16 **Buchanan**	Y	N	Y	Y	Y	N
17 **Rooney, T.**	N	N	Y	Y	Y	N
18 **Mast**	N	Y	Y	Y	Y	Y
19 **Rooney, F.**	Y	Y	Y	Y	Y	Y
20 Hastings	Y	N	N	N	N	N
21 Frankel	N	N	N	N	N	N
22 Deutch	N	N	N	N	N	N
23 Wasserman Schultz	Y	N	N	N	N	N
24 Wilson	N	N	N	?	N	N
25 **Diaz-Balart**	N	Y	Y	Y	Y	N
26 **Curbelo**	N	Y	Y	Y	Y	Y
27 Ros-Lehtinen	Y	Y	Y	Y	Y	Y
GEORGIA						
1 **Carter**	N	Y	Y	Y	Y	N
2 Bishop	Y	N	N	N	N	N
3 **Ferguson**	N	Y	Y	Y	Y	N
4 Johnson	Y	N	N	N	N	N
5 Lewis	N	N	N	N	N	N
6 **Handel**	N	N	Y	Y	Y	N
7 **Woodall**	Y	Y	Y	Y	Y	Y
8 **Scott, A.**	N	Y	Y	Y	Y	Y
9 **Collins**	N	Y	Y	Y	Y	Y
10 **Hice**	Y	Y	Y	Y	Y	Y
11 **Loudermilk**	N	Y	Y	Y	Y	N
12 **Allen**	Y	Y	Y	Y	Y	Y
13 Scott, D.	N	N	N	N	N	N
14 **Graves**	Y	Y	Y	Y	Y	N
HAWAII						
1 Hanabusa	Y	N	N	N	N	N
2 Gabbard	Y	Y	N	N	N	N
IDAHO						
1 **Labrador**	?	?	?	?	?	?
2 **Simpson**	N	N	Y	Y	Y	N
ILLINOIS						
1 Rush	?	?	?	?	N	N
2 Kelly	N	N	N	N	N	N
3 Lipinski	Y	N	N	N	N	Y
4 Gutierrez	Y	N	N	N	N	N
5 Quigley	Y	N	N	N	N	N
6 **Roskam**	N	N	Y	Y	Y	N
7 Davis, D.	N	N	N	N	N	N
8 Krishnamoorthi	N	N	N	N	N	N
9 Schakowsky	N	N	N	N	N	N
10 Schneider	N	N	N	N	N	N
11 Foster	Y	N	N	N	N	N
12 **Bost**	N	N	Y	Y	Y	N
13 **Davis, R.**	N	Y	Y	Y	Y	N

	302	303	304	305	306	307
14 **Hultgren**	N	Y	Y	Y	Y	N
15 **Shimkus**	N	N	Y	Y	Y	N
16 **Kinzinger**	N	N	Y	Y	Y	N
17 Bustos	N	N	N	N	N	N
18 **LaHood**	N	Y	Y	Y	Y	N
INDIANA						
1 Visclosky	N	N	N	N	N	N
2 **Walorski**	Y	N	Y	Y	Y	N
3 **Banks**	Y	Y	Y	Y	Y	Y
4 Rokita	N	Y	Y	Y	Y	N
5 **Brooks**	Y	N	Y	Y	Y	N
6 **Messer**	Y	Y	Y	Y	Y	N
7 Carson	Y	N	N	N	N	N
8 **Bucshon**	N	Y	Y	Y	Y	N
9 **Hollingsworth**	N	N	Y	Y	Y	N
IOWA						
1 **Blum**	N	Y	Y	Y	Y	N
2 Loebsack	N	N	N	N	N	N
3 **Young**	N	N	Y	Y	Y	Y
4 **King**	N	Y	Y	Y	Y	Y
KANSAS						
1 **Marshall**	N	N	Y	Y	Y	N
2 **Jenkins**	N	Y	Y	Y	Y	N
3 **Yoder**	N	Y	Y	Y	Y	Y
4 **Estes**	Y	Y	Y	Y	Y	N
KENTUCKY						
1 **Comer**	N	Y	Y	Y	Y	Y
2 **Guthrie**	N	Y	Y	Y	Y	N
3 Yarmuth	N	N	N	N	N	N
4 **Massie**	N	Y	Y	Y	Y	N
5 **Rogers**	N	N	Y	Y	Y	N
6 **Barr**	N	N	Y	Y	Y	N
LOUISIANA						
1 **Scalise**	N	Y	Y	Y	Y	N
2 Richmond	Y	N	?	N	N	N
3 **Higgins**	Y	Y	Y	Y	Y	Y
4 **Johnson**	N	Y	Y	Y	Y	N
5 **Abraham**	Y	Y	Y	Y	Y	Y
6 **Graves**	N	Y	Y	Y	Y	N
MAINE						
1 Pingree	Y	N	N	N	N	N
2 **Poliquin**	Y	Y	Y	Y	Y	N
MARYLAND						
1 **Harris**	N	N	Y	Y	Y	N
2 Ruppersberger	Y	N	N	N	N	N
3 Sarbanes	N	N	N	N	N	N
4 Brown	Y	N	N	N	N	N
5 Hoyer	Y	N	N	N	N	N
6 Delaney	Y	N	N	N	N	N
7 Cummings	Y	Y	N	N	N	N
8 Raskin	N	N	N	N	N	N
MASSACHUSETTS						
1 Neal	Y	N	N	N	N	N
2 McGovern	Y	N	N	N	N	Y
3 Tsongas	?	?	?	?	?	?
4 Kennedy	Y	N	N	N	N	N
5 Clark	N	N	N	N	N	N
6 Moulton	Y	Y	N	N	N	Y
7 Capuano	Y	N	N	N	N	N
8 Lynch	Y	N	N	N	N	N
9 Keating	Y	Y	N	N	N	Y
MICHIGAN						
1 **Bergman**	Y	N	Y	Y	Y	Y
2 **Huizenga**	N	Y	Y	Y	Y	N
3 *Amash*	N	Y	Y	Y	P	N
4 **Moolenaar**	N	N	Y	Y	Y	N
5 Kildee	N	N	N	N	N	N
6 **Upton**	N	Y	Y	Y	Y	N
7 **Walberg**	N	Y	Y	Y	Y	N
8 **Bishop**	N	Y	Y	Y	Y	N
9 Levin	N	N	N	N	N	N
10 **Mitchell**	Y	N	Y	Y	Y	Y
11 **Trott**	N	Y	Y	Y	Y	N
12 Dingell	Y	N	N	N	N	N
14 Lawrence	Y	N	N	N	N	N
MINNESOTA						
1 Walz	?	?	?	?	?	?
2 **Lewis**	Y	Y	Y	Y	Y	Y
3 **Paulsen**	Y	Y	Y	Y	Y	N
4 McCollum	N	N	N	N	N	N

	302	303	304	305	306	307
5 Ellison	N	N	?	?	?	?
6 **Emmer**	Y	Y	Y	Y	Y	Y
7 Peterson	Y	N	N	N	N	Y
8 Nolan	Y	Y	N	N	N	N
MISSISSIPPI						
1 **Kelly**	Y	Y	Y	Y	Y	Y
2 Thompson	?	?	?	?	?	?
3 **Harper**	Y	Y	Y	Y	Y	N
4 **Palazzo**	Y	Y	Y	Y	Y	N
MISSOURI						
1 Clay	Y	N	N	N	N	N
2 **Wagner**	Y	Y	Y	Y	Y	Y
3 **Luetkemeyer**	N	Y	Y	Y	+	N
4 **Hartzler**	Y	Y	Y	Y	Y	Y
5 Cleaver	Y	N	N	N	N	N
6 **Graves**	Y	Y	Y	Y	Y	Y
7 **Long**	N	Y	Y	Y	Y	N
8 **Smith**	Y	Y	Y	Y	Y	N
MONTANA						
AL **Gianforte**	Y	Y	Y	Y	Y	Y
NEBRASKA						
1 **Fortenberry**	N	N	Y	Y	Y	N
2 **Bacon**	Y	Y	Y	Y	Y	Y
3 **Smith**	Y	Y	Y	Y	Y	N
NEVADA						
1 Titus	N	N	N	N	N	N
2 **Amodei**	N	N	Y	Y	Y	N
3 Rosen	Y	N	N	N	N	Y
4 Kihuen	Y	N	N	N	N	N
NEW HAMPSHIRE						
1 Shea-Porter	N	N	N	N	N	Y
2 Kuster	N	N	N	N	N	Y
NEW JERSEY						
1 Norcross	Y	N	N	N	N	Y
2 **LoBiondo**	Y	N	Y	Y	Y	Y
3 **MacArthur**	N	N	Y	Y	Y	N
4 **Smith**	Y	Y	Y	Y	Y	N
5 Gottheimer	Y	Y	N	N	N	Y
6 Pallone	N	N	N	N	N	N
7 **Lance**	Y	N	Y	Y	Y	N
8 Sires	N	N	N	N	N	N
9 Pascrell	Y	N	N	N	N	N
10 Payne	N	N	N	N	N	N
11 **Frelinghuysen**	N	N	Y	Y	Y	N
12 Watson Coleman	N	N	N	N	N	N
NEW MEXICO						
1 Lujan Grisham	N	N	N	N	N	Y
2 **Pearce**	N	Y	Y	Y	Y	N
3 Luján	N	N	N	N	N	Y
NEW YORK						
1 **Zeldin**	Y	Y	Y	Y	Y	N
2 **King**	Y	Y	Y	Y	Y	Y
3 Suozzi	Y	N	N	N	N	?
4 Rice	N	N	N	N	N	N
5 Meeks	Y	N	N	N	N	N
6 Meng	N	N	N	N	N	N
7 Velázquez	N	N	N	N	N	N
8 Jeffries	Y	N	N	N	N	N
9 Clarke	N	N	N	N	N	N
10 Nadler	N	Y	N	N	N	N
11 **Donovan**	Y	Y	Y	Y	Y	Y
12 Maloney, C.	Y	N	N	N	N	N
13 Espaillat	N	N	N	N	N	N
14 Crowley	?	?	N	N	?	?
15 Serrano	N	N	N	N	N	N
16 Engel	N	N	N	N	N	N
17 Lowey	Y	N	N	N	N	N
18 Maloney, S.P.	Y	N	N	N	N	N
19 **Faso**	N	N	Y	Y	Y	N
20 Tonko	N	Y	N	N	N	N
21 **Stefanik**	Y	Y	Y	Y	Y	Y
22 **Tenney**	Y	Y	Y	Y	Y	Y
23 **Reed**	N	Y	Y	Y	Y	N
24 **Katko**	Y	Y	Y	Y	Y	Y
25 **Vacant**						
26 Higgins	Y	Y	N	N	N	N
27 **Collins**	N	Y	Y	Y	Y	N
NORTH CAROLINA						
1 Butterfield	Y	N	N	N	N	N
2 **Holding**	N	Y	Y	Y	Y	N
3 **Jones**	N	Y	?	?	?	?
4 Price	N	N	N	N	N	N

	302	303	304	305	306	307
5 **Foxx**	N	Y	Y	Y	Y	N
6 **Walker**	N	Y	Y	Y	Y	Y
7 **Rouzer**	N	Y	Y	Y	Y	N
8 **Hudson**	N	Y	Y	Y	Y	N
9 **Pittenger**	N	N	Y	Y	Y	N
9 **Vacant**						
10 **McHenry**	N	N	Y	Y	Y	N
11 **Meadows**	N	Y	Y	Y	Y	Y
12 Adams	N	N	N	N	N	N
13 **Budd**	Y	Y	Y	Y	Y	Y
NORTH DAKOTA						
AL **Cramer**	?	?	Y	Y	Y	N
OHIO						
1 **Chabot**	N	Y	Y	Y	Y	Y
2 **Wenstrup**	Y	Y	Y	Y	Y	Y
3 Beatty	Y	N	N	N	N	N
4 **Jordan**	N	Y	Y	Y	Y	Y
5 **Latta**	N	N	Y	Y	Y	N
6 **Johnson**	N	Y	+	+	Y	N
7 **Gibbs**	N	Y	Y	Y	Y	N
8 **Davidson**	N	Y	Y	Y	Y	Y
9 Kaptur	N	N	N	N	N	N
10 **Turner**	Y	N	Y	Y	Y	Y
11 Fudge	Y	N	N	N	N	N
12 **Vacant**						
13 Ryan	Y	N	N	N	N	Y
14 **Joyce**	N	N	Y	Y	Y	N
15 **Stivers**	N	Y	Y	Y	Y	Y
16 **Renacci**	N	Y	Y	Y	Y	N
OKLAHOMA						
1 **Vacant**						
2 **Mullin**	N	Y	Y	Y	Y	N
3 **Lucas**	N	N	Y	Y	Y	N
4 **Cole**	N	N	Y	Y	Y	N
5 **Russell**	Y	Y	Y	Y	Y	Y
OREGON						
1 Bonamici	N	N	N	N	N	N
2 **Walden**	Y	Y	Y	Y	Y	N
3 Blumenauer	N	N	–	N	N	N
4 DeFazio	Y	N	N	N	N	N
5 Schrader	N	N	N	N	N	N
PENNSYLVANIA						
1 Brady	Y	N	N	N	N	N
2 Evans	N	N	N	N	N	N
3 **Kelly**	N	N	Y	Y	Y	N
4 **Perry**	N	Y	Y	Y	Y	N
5 **Thompson**	N	Y	Y	Y	Y	N
6 **Costello**	Y	N	?	?	?	?
7 **Vacant**						
8 **Fitzpatrick**	Y	N	Y	Y	Y	Y
9 **Shuster**	N	N	Y	Y	Y	Y
10 **Marino**	N	Y	Y	Y	Y	Y
11 **Barletta**	N	N	?	?	Y	N
12 **Rothfus**	N	Y	Y	Y	Y	N
13 Boyle	N	N	N	N	N	N
14 Doyle	N	N	N	N	N	N
15 **Vacant**						
16 **Smucker**	N	N	Y	Y	Y	N
17 Cartwright	Y	N	N	?	N	N
18 Lamb	Y	N	N	N	N	Y
RHODE ISLAND						
1 Cicilline	Y	N	N	?	N	N
2 Langevin	Y	N	N	N	N	N
SOUTH CAROLINA						
1 **Sanford**	Y	Y	Y	Y	Y	N
2 **Wilson**	Y	N	Y	Y	Y	Y
3 **Duncan**	N	Y	Y	Y	Y	N
4 **Gowdy**	N	Y	Y	Y	Y	N
5 **Norman**	N	Y	Y	Y	Y	Y
6 Clyburn	Y	N	N	N	N	N
7 **Rice**	N	Y	Y	Y	Y	N
SOUTH DAKOTA						
AL **Noem**	N	N	Y	Y	Y	N
TENNESSEE						
1 **Roe**	N	Y	Y	Y	Y	N
2 **Duncan**	N	Y	Y	Y	Y	N
3 **Fleischmann**	N	N	Y	Y	Y	N
4 **DesJarlais**	N	Y	Y	Y	Y	Y
5 Cooper	N	?	N	N	N	N
6 **Black**	?	?	?	?	+	?
7 **Blackburn**	N	Y	Y	Y	Y	N
8 **Kustoff**	N	Y	Y	Y	Y	N
9 Cohen	Y	Y	N	N	N	N

	302	303	304	305	306	307
TEXAS						
1 **Gohmert**	Y	Y	Y	Y	Y	Y
2 **Poe**	Y	Y	Y	Y	Y	N
3 **Johnson, S.**	N	Y	Y	Y	Y	N
4 **Ratcliffe**	N	Y	Y	Y	Y	N
5 **Hensarling**	N	N	Y	Y	Y	N
6 **Barton**	N	Y	Y	?	Y	N
7 **Culberson**	Y	Y	Y	Y	Y	N
8 **Brady**	N	Y	+	+	Y	Y
9 Green, A.	N	N	N	N	N	N
10 **McCaul**	Y	N	Y	Y	Y	Y
11 **Conaway**	Y	N	Y	Y	Y	Y
12 **Granger**	N	N	Y	Y	Y	N
13 **Thornberry**	Y	N	Y	Y	Y	Y
14 **Weber**	Y	Y	Y	Y	Y	N
15 Gonzalez	Y	N	N	N	N	N
16 O'Rourke	N	Y	N	N	N	N
17 **Flores**	Y	N	Y	Y	Y	Y
18 Jackson Lee	N	N	N	N	N	N
19 **Arrington**	N	Y	Y	Y	Y	N
20 Castro	Y	N	N	N	N	N
21 **Smith**	?	?	Y	Y	Y	N
22 **Olson**	Y	Y	Y	Y	Y	N
23 **Hurd**	N	N	Y	Y	Y	N
24 Marchant	Y	Y	Y	Y	Y	N
25 **Williams**	N	Y	Y	Y	Y	N
26 **Burgess**	N	Y	Y	Y	Y	N
28 Cuellar	Y	N	N	N	N	N
29 Green, G.	Y	Y	N	N	N	N
30 Johnson, E.B.	Y	N	N	N	N	N
31 **Carter**	Y	N	Y	Y	Y	N
32 **Sessions**	N	N	Y	Y	Y	N
33 Veasey	Y	N	N	N	N	N
34 Vela	Y	N	N	N	N	N
35 Doggett	N	Y	N	N	N	N
36 **Babin**	Y	Y	Y	Y	Y	N
UTAH						
1 **Bishop**	Y	N	Y	Y	Y	Y
2 **Stewart**	Y	N	Y	Y	Y	N
3 **Curtis**	?	N	Y	Y	Y	N
4 **Love**	Y	N	Y	Y	Y	N
VERMONT						
AL Welch	N	N	N	N	N	N
VIRGINIA						
1 **Wittman**	N	Y	Y	Y	Y	Y
2 **Taylor**	N	N	Y	Y	Y	N
3 Scott	N	N	N	?	N	N
4 McEachin	Y	N	N	N	N	N
5 **Garrett**	Y	Y	Y	Y	Y	Y
6 **Goodlatte**	N	Y	Y	Y	Y	N
7 **Brat**	N	Y	Y	Y	Y	N
8 Beyer	N	N	N	N	N	N
9 **Griffith**	N	Y	Y	Y	Y	Y
10 **Comstock**	Y	Y	Y	Y	Y	Y
11 Connolly	N	N	N	N	N	N
WASHINGTON						
1 DelBene	N	N	N	N	N	N
2 Larsen	Y	N	N	N	N	Y
3 **Herrera Beutler**	N	Y	Y	Y	Y	Y
4 **Newhouse**	Y	Y	Y	Y	Y	N
5 **McMorris Rodgers**	N	Y	Y	Y	Y	Y
6 Kilmer	N	N	N	N	N	N
7 Jayapal	N	N	N	N	N	N
8 **Reichert**	N	N	Y	Y	Y	N
9 Smith	Y	N	N	N	N	N
10 Heck	N	N	N	N	N	N
WEST VIRGINIA						
1 **McKinley**	N	Y	Y	Y	Y	Y
2 **Mooney**	Y	Y	Y	Y	Y	Y
3 **Jenkins**	N	Y	Y	Y	Y	Y
WISCONSIN						
1 **Ryan**						
2 Pocan	N	N	N	N	N	N
3 Kind	N	Y	N	N	N	N
4 Moore	N	N	N	N	N	N
5 **Sensenbrenner**	Y	Y	Y	Y	Y	Y
6 **Grothman**	N	Y	+	+	+	–
7 **Duffy**	Y	Y	Y	Y	Y	Y
8 **Gallagher**	Y	Y	Y	Y	Y	Y
WYOMING						
AL **Cheney**	Y	N	Y	Y	Y	Y

☰ HOUSE VOTES

VOTE NUMBER

308. HR6157. FISCAL 2019 DEFENSE APPROPRIATIONS/AIR FORCE MISSILE PROCUREMENT. Gallagher, R-Wis., amendment that would decrease funding for non-military Defense Department activities by $33 million and increase funding for Air Force missile procurement by the same amount. Rejected in Committee of the Whole 115-296: R 90-137; D 25-159. June 28, 2018.

309. HR6157. FISCAL 2019 DEFENSE APPROPRIATIONS/DEFENSE-WIDE RESEARCH AND DEVELOPMENT. Clark, D-Mass., amendment that would reduce, and then increase, by $14 million funds made available in the bill for defense-wide research, development, test and evaluation. Adopted in Committee of the Whole 252-157: R 96-132; D 156-25. June 28, 2018.

310. HR6157. FISCAL 2019 DEFENSE APPROPRIATIONS/PROHIBITION OF SPACED-BASED BALLISTIC MISSILE INTERCEPT LAYER. Foster, D-Ill., amendment that would prohibit any funds appropriated by the bill to be used to procure, develop, research or test a space-based ballistic missile intercept layer. Rejected in Committee of the Whole 160-251: R 0-227; D 160-24. June 28, 2018.

311. HR6157. FISCAL 2019 DEFENSE APPROPRIATIONS/VIRGINIA-CLASS SUBMARINES. Courtney, D-Conn., amendment that would decrease funding for several programs and would provide funding for long lead time materials needed to construct additional Virginia-class submarines. Rejected in Committee of the Whole 144-267: R 50-177; D 94-90. June 28, 2018.

312. HR6157. FISCAL 2019 DEFENSE APPROPRIATIONS/RECOMMIT. Lieu, D-Calif., motion to recommit the bill to the House Appropriations Committee with instruction to report it back immediately with an amendment that would decrease funding for defense-wide operations and maintenance by $25 million and would increase funding for Defense Health Programs by the same amount. Motion rejected 186-224: R 2-224; D 184-0. June 28, 2018.

313. HR6157. FISCAL 2019 DEFENSE APPROPRIATIONS/PASSAGE. Passage of the bill that would make a total of $674.6 billion in discretionary defense spending for fiscal 2019, which would include $605.5 billion in discretionary spending subject to spending caps for fiscal 2019 and $68.1 billion in uncapped Overseas Contingency Operations funding. Passed 359-49: R 222-3; D 137-46. June 28, 2018.

	308	309	310	311	312	313
ALABAMA						
1 Byrne	Y	N	N	Y	N	Y
2 Roby	N	N	N	N	N	Y
3 Rogers	Y	Y	N	Y	N	Y
4 Aderholt	?	?	?	?	?	?
5 Brooks	Y	N	N	Y	N	Y
6 Palmer	Y	N	N	N	N	Y
7 Sewell	N	?	Y	N	Y	Y
ALASKA						
AL Young	Y	Y	N	N	N	Y
ARIZONA						
1 O'Halleran	Y	Y	N	Y	Y	Y
2 McSally	Y	Y	N	N	N	Y
3 Grijalva	N	N	Y	Y	Y	N
4 Gosar	Y	N	N	N	N	Y
5 Biggs	Y	N	N	Y	N	Y
6 Schweikert	Y	N	N	N	N	Y
7 Gallego	Y	Y	Y	Y	Y	Y
8 Lesko	Y	N	N	N	N	Y
9 Sinema	Y	Y	N	Y	Y	Y
ARKANSAS						
1 Crawford	N	N	N	N	N	Y
2 Hill	N	N	N	N	N	Y
3 Womack	N	N	N	N	N	Y
4 Westerman	N	N	N	N	N	Y
CALIFORNIA						
1 LaMalfa	Y	Y	N	N	N	Y
2 Huffman	N	Y	Y	N	Y	N
3 Garamendi	Y	Y	Y	Y	Y	Y
4 McClintock	Y	N	N	N	N	Y
5 Thompson	N	N	Y	N	Y	Y
6 Matsui	N	N	Y	N	Y	Y
7 Bera	Y	Y	Y	N	Y	Y
8 Cook	Y	Y	N	N	N	Y
9 McNerney	N	Y	Y	N	Y	Y
10 Denham	N	N	N	N	N	Y
11 DeSaulnier	N	Y	Y	N	Y	N
12 Pelosi	?	?	?	?	?	?
13 Lee	N	Y	Y	N	Y	N
14 Speier	–	+	+	–	+	–
15 Swalwell	N	Y	Y	N	Y	N
16 Costa	N	N	N	N	N	Y
17 Khanna	N	Y	N	N	Y	Y
18 Eshoo	–	+	+	–	+	–
19 Lofgren	N	Y	Y	N	Y	Y
20 Panetta	Y	Y	Y	Y	Y	Y
21 Valadao	N	N	N	N	N	Y
22 Nunes	N	N	N	N	N	Y
23 McCarthy	Y	Y	N	N	N	Y
24 Carbajal	N	Y	Y	Y	Y	Y
25 Knight	Y	Y	N	N	N	Y
26 Brownley	N	Y	Y	N	Y	Y
27 Chu	N	N	Y	N	Y	Y
28 Schiff	N	Y	Y	Y	Y	Y
29 Cardenas	N	Y	Y	Y	Y	Y
30 Sherman	N	Y	Y	N	Y	Y
31 Aguilar	N	Y	N	N	N	Y
32 Napolitano	N	Y	Y	N	Y	N
33 Lieu	Y	Y	N	Y	Y	Y
34 Gomez	N	Y	Y	Y	Y	N
35 Torres	N	Y	Y	Y	Y	Y
36 Ruiz	N	Y	N	N	Y	Y
37 Bass	N	N	Y	Y	Y	N
38 Sánchez, Linda	N	Y	Y	Y	Y	Y
39 Royce	N	N	N	N	N	Y
40 Roybal-Allard	N	Y	Y	N	Y	Y
41 Takano	N	N	Y	N	Y	N
42 Calvert	N	Y	N	N	N	Y
43 Waters	N	Y	Y	N	Y	Y
44 Barragan	N	Y	Y	Y	Y	Y
45 Walters	Y	Y	N	N	N	Y
46 Correa	Y	N	N	Y	Y	Y
47 Lowenthal	N	Y	Y	N	Y	N
48 Rohrabacher	N	N	N	N	N	Y
49 Issa	N	Y	N	N	N	Y
50 Hunter	Y	Y	N	N	N	Y
51 Vargas	N	Y	Y	Y	Y	Y
52 Peters	N	Y	N	Y	Y	Y
53 Davis	N	Y	Y	Y	Y	Y

	308	309	310	311	312	313
COLORADO						
1 DeGette	N	N	Y	N	Y	N
2 Polis	N	Y	Y	Y	Y	N
3 Tipton	Y	N	N	N	N	Y
4 Buck	N	N	N	N	N	Y
5 Lamborn	Y	Y	N	Y	N	Y
6 Coffman	Y	Y	N	N	N	Y
7 Perlmutter	N	Y	Y	Y	Y	Y
CONNECTICUT						
1 Larson	N	Y	Y	Y	Y	Y
2 Courtney	Y	Y	Y	Y	Y	Y
3 DeLauro	N	Y	Y	Y	Y	Y
4 Himes	N	Y	Y	Y	Y	Y
5 Esty	N	Y	Y	Y	Y	Y
DELAWARE						
AL Blunt Rochester	N	Y	Y	N	Y	Y
FLORIDA						
1 Gaetz	N	Y	N	Y	N	Y
2 Dunn	N	N	N	N	N	Y
3 Yoho	N	Y	N	N	N	Y
4 Rutherford	N	Y	N	N	N	Y
5 Lawson	N	N	Y	N	Y	Y
6 DeSantis	N	Y	N	N	N	Y
7 Murphy	Y	Y	Y	Y	Y	Y
8 Posey	Y	N	N	Y	N	Y
9 Soto	N	Y	Y	Y	Y	Y
10 Demings	Y	Y	Y	Y	Y	Y
11 Webster	Y	Y	N	N	N	?
12 Bilirakis	Y	N	N	N	N	Y
13 Crist	Y	Y	N	N	Y	Y
14 Castor	N	N	Y	N	Y	Y
15 Ross	N	N	N	N	N	Y
16 Buchanan	N	N	N	N	N	Y
17 Rooney, T.	N	N	N	N	N	Y
18 Mast	Y	N	N	N	N	Y
19 Rooney, F.	Y	Y	N	N	N	Y
20 Hastings	N	Y	Y	Y	Y	Y
21 Frankel	N	Y	Y	N	Y	Y
22 Deutch	N	Y	Y	Y	Y	Y
23 Wasserman Schultz	N	Y	Y	N	Y	Y
24 Wilson	N	Y	Y	N	Y	Y
25 Diaz-Balart	N	N	N	N	N	Y
26 Curbelo	Y	Y	N	N	N	Y
27 Ros-Lehtinen	Y	Y	N	N	N	Y
GEORGIA						
1 Carter	N	Y	N	Y	N	Y
2 Bishop	N	Y	Y	N	Y	Y
3 Ferguson	N	N	N	N	N	Y
4 Johnson	N	N	N	N	Y	N
5 Lewis	N	Y	Y	N	Y	N
6 Handel	Y	Y	N	N	N	Y
7 Woodall	Y	N	?	N	Y	Y
8 Scott, A.	Y	Y	N	N	N	Y
9 Collins	Y	N	N	N	N	Y
10 Hice	Y	Y	N	Y	N	Y
11 Loudermilk	Y	Y	N	N	N	Y
12 Allen	N	Y	N	N	N	Y
13 Scott, D.	N	Y	Y	N	Y	Y
14 Graves	N	Y	N	N	N	Y
HAWAII						
1 Hanabusa	N	Y	Y	Y	Y	Y
2 Gabbard	N	Y	Y	Y	Y	Y
IDAHO						
1 Labrador	?	?	?	?	?	?
2 Simpson	N	N	N	N	N	Y
ILLINOIS						
1 Rush	N	Y	Y	N	Y	Y
2 Kelly	N	Y	Y	N	Y	Y
3 Lipinski	Y	Y	N	Y	Y	Y
4 Gutierrez	N	Y	Y	N	Y	N
5 Quigley	N	Y	Y	Y	Y	Y
6 Roskam	N	N	N	N	N	Y
7 Davis, D.	N	Y	Y	Y	Y	N
8 Krishnamoorthi	N	Y	Y	Y	Y	Y
9 Schakowsky	N	Y	Y	Y	Y	N
10 Schneider	N	Y	Y	N	Y	Y
11 Foster	N	Y	Y	Y	Y	Y
12 Bost	N	N	N	N	N	Y
13 Davis, R.	N	N	N	N	N	Y

KEY	Republicans	Democrats	Independents

- **Y** Voted for (yea)
- **#** Paired for
- **+** Announced for
- **N** Voted against (nay)
- **X** Paired against
- **–** Announced against
- **P** Voted "present"
- **C** Voted "present" to avoid possible conflict of interest
- **?** Did not vote or otherwise make a position known

	308	309	310	311	312	313
14 **Hultgren**	N	N	N	Y	N	Y
15 **Shimkus**	N	N	N	Y	N	?
16 **Kinzinger**	N	N	N	?	N	Y
17 Bustos	N	Y	N	N	Y	Y
18 **LaHood**	N	N	N	N	N	Y
INDIANA						
1 Visclosky	N	N	Y	N	Y	Y
2 **Walorski**	N	Y	N	Y	N	Y
3 **Banks**	Y	Y	N	N	N	Y
4 Rokita	N	N	N	N	N	Y
5 **Brooks**	N	N	N	N	N	Y
6 **Messer**	N	N	N	N	N	Y
7 Carson	N	Y	Y	Y	Y	N
8 **Bucshon**	N	N	N	N	N	Y
9 **Hollingsworth**	N	N	N	N	N	Y
IOWA						
1 **Blum**	N	Y	N	N	Y	Y
2 Loebsack	N	Y	Y	N	Y	Y
3 **Young**	Y	Y	N	N	N	Y
4 **King**	+	Y	N	N	N	Y
KANSAS						
1 **Marshall**	N	N	N	N	N	Y
2 **Jenkins**	N	N	N	N	N	Y
3 **Yoder**	Y	Y	N	N	N	Y
4 **Estes**	N	N	N	N	N	Y
KENTUCKY						
1 **Comer**	Y	N	N	N	N	Y
2 **Guthrie**	N	N	N	N	N	Y
3 Yarmuth	N	N	Y	N	Y	N
4 **Massie**	N	Y	N	N	N	N
5 **Rogers**	N	N	N	N	N	Y
6 **Barr**	N	N	N	N	N	Y
LOUISIANA						
1 **Scalise**	N	N	N	N	N	Y
2 Richmond	N	Y	Y	N	Y	Y
3 **Higgins**	Y	Y	N	N	N	Y
4 **Johnson**	N	N	N	N	N	Y
5 **Abraham**	Y	Y	N	N	N	Y
6 **Graves**	N	Y	N	N	N	Y
MAINE						
1 Pingree	N	Y	Y	N	Y	Y
2 **Poliquin**	N	Y	N	N	N	Y
MARYLAND						
1 **Harris**	N	N	N	N	N	Y
2 Ruppersberger	N	N	N	N	Y	Y
3 Sarbanes	N	N	Y	N	Y	Y
4 Brown	N	Y	Y	Y	Y	Y
5 Hoyer	N	Y	Y	Y	Y	Y
6 Delaney	N	Y	N	N	Y	Y
7 Cummings	N	Y	Y	Y	Y	Y
8 Raskin	N	N	Y	N	Y	N
MASSACHUSETTS						
1 Neal	N	Y	Y	Y	Y	Y
2 McGovern	N	Y	Y	Y	Y	N
3 Tsongas	?	?	?	?	?	?
4 Kennedy	N	Y	Y	Y	Y	N
5 Clark	N	Y	Y	Y	Y	N
6 Moulton	Y	Y	Y	Y	Y	Y
7 Capuano	N	Y	Y	Y	Y	N
8 Lynch	N	Y	Y	Y	Y	Y
9 Keating	Y	Y	Y	Y	Y	Y
MICHIGAN						
1 **Bergman**	Y	Y	N	Y	N	Y
2 **Huizenga**	N	N	N	N	N	Y
3 *Amash*	N	Y	N	N	N	N
4 **Moolenaar**	N	N	N	N	N	Y
5 Kildee	N	Y	Y	N	Y	Y
6 **Upton**	N	N	N	N	N	Y
7 **Walberg**	N	N	N	N	N	Y
8 **Bishop**	Y	N	N	Y	N	Y
9 Levin	N	Y	Y	Y	Y	Y
10 **Mitchell**	Y	Y	N	N	N	Y
11 **Trott**	N	N	N	N	N	Y
12 Dingell	N	Y	Y	Y	Y	Y
14 Lawrence	N	Y	Y	Y	Y	Y
MINNESOTA						
1 Walz	?	?	?	?	?	?
2 **Lewis**	Y	N	N	N	N	Y
3 **Paulsen**	N	Y	N	N	N	Y
4 McCollum	N	N	Y	N	Y	Y

	308	309	310	311	312	313
5 Ellison	?	?	?	?	?	?
6 **Emmer**	Y	N	N	N	N	Y
7 Peterson	Y	Y	N	Y	Y	Y
8 Nolan	N	Y	Y	N	Y	Y
MISSISSIPPI						
1 **Kelly**	Y	Y	N	N	N	Y
2 Thompson	?	?	?	?	?	?
3 **Harper**	N	N	N	N	N	Y
4 **Palazzo**	N	N	N	N	N	Y
MISSOURI						
1 Clay	N	Y	Y	N	Y	Y
2 **Wagner**	Y	N	N	N	N	Y
3 **Luetkemeyer**	N	N	N	N	N	Y
4 **Hartzler**	Y	Y	N	Y	N	Y
5 Cleaver	N	Y	Y	N	Y	Y
6 **Graves**	Y	Y	N	Y	N	Y
7 **Long**	N	N	N	N	N	Y
8 **Smith**	N	N	N	N	N	Y
MONTANA						
AL **Gianforte**	Y	N	N	N	N	Y
NEBRASKA						
1 **Fortenberry**	N	Y	N	N	N	Y
2 **Bacon**	Y	Y	N	N	N	Y
3 **Smith**	N	N	N	N	N	Y
NEVADA						
1 Titus	N	N	Y	Y	Y	Y
2 **Amodei**	N	Y	N	N	N	Y
3 Rosen	Y	Y	N	Y	Y	Y
4 Kihuen	N	Y	Y	N	Y	Y
NEW HAMPSHIRE						
1 Shea-Porter	Y	Y	Y	Y	Y	Y
2 Kuster	Y	Y	Y	Y	Y	Y
NEW JERSEY						
1 Norcross	Y	Y	Y	Y	Y	Y
2 **LoBiondo**	Y	Y	N	N	N	Y
3 **MacArthur**	N	N	N	N	N	Y
4 **Smith**	N	N	N	Y	N	Y
5 Gottheimer	Y	Y	Y	Y	Y	Y
6 Pallone	N	Y	Y	Y	Y	N
7 **Lance**	N	N	N	N	N	Y
8 Sires	N	Y	Y	Y	Y	Y
9 Pascrell	N	Y	Y	Y	Y	Y
10 Payne	N	Y	Y	N	Y	N
11 **Frelinghuysen**	N	N	N	N	N	Y
12 Watson Coleman	N	Y	Y	Y	Y	N
NEW MEXICO						
1 Lujan Grisham	Y	Y	Y	N	Y	Y
2 **Pearce**	N	Y	N	N	N	Y
3 Luján	Y	Y	Y	N	Y	Y
NEW YORK						
1 **Zeldin**	N	N	N	N	N	Y
2 **King**	Y	Y	N	Y	N	Y
3 Suozzi	?	?	?	?	?	?
4 Rice	N	N	Y	N	Y	Y
5 Meeks	N	Y	Y	Y	Y	N
6 Meng	N	Y	Y	N	Y	Y
7 Velázquez	N	N	Y	Y	Y	N
8 Jeffries	N	Y	Y	Y	Y	Y
9 Clarke	N	Y	Y	N	Y	N
10 Nadler	N	Y	Y	N	Y	N
11 **Donovan**	Y	Y	N	N	N	Y
12 Maloney, C.	N	?	Y	Y	Y	N
13 Espaillat	N	Y	Y	Y	Y	N
14 Crowley	?	?	?	?	?	?
15 Serrano	N	N	Y	Y	Y	N
16 Engel	N	Y	Y	N	Y	Y
17 Lowey	N	Y	Y	N	Y	Y
18 Maloney, S.P.	N	Y	N	Y	Y	?
19 **Faso**	N	Y	N	N	N	Y
20 Tonko	N	Y	Y	Y	Y	Y
21 **Stefanik**	Y	Y	N	Y	N	Y
22 **Tenney**	Y	N	N	N	N	Y
23 **Reed**	N	N	N	N	N	Y
24 **Katko**	Y	N	N	N	N	Y
25 **Vacant**						
26 Higgins	N	Y	Y	Y	Y	Y
27 **Collins**	N	N	N	N	N	Y
NORTH CAROLINA						
1 Butterfield	N	Y	Y	Y	Y	Y
2 **Holding**	N	N	N	N	N	Y
3 **Jones**	?	?	?	?	?	?
4 Price	N	Y	Y	N	Y	Y

	308	309	310	311	312	313
5 **Foxx**	N	N	N	N	N	Y
6 **Walker**	Y	N	N	N	N	Y
7 **Rouzer**	N	N	N	N	N	Y
8 **Hudson**	N	Y	N	N	N	Y
9 **Pittenger**	N	Y	N	Y	N	Y
9 **Vacant**						
10 **McHenry**	N	Y	N	N	N	Y
11 **Meadows**	Y	N	N	N	N	Y
12 Adams	N	Y	Y	Y	Y	Y
13 **Budd**	Y	N	N	N	N	Y
NORTH DAKOTA						
AL **Cramer**	N	N	N	Y	N	Y
OHIO						
1 **Chabot**	Y	Y	N	N	N	Y
2 **Wenstrup**	Y	Y	N	N	N	Y
3 Beatty	N	Y	Y	N	Y	Y
4 **Jordan**	Y	N	N	N	N	Y
5 **Latta**	N	N	N	N	N	Y
6 **Johnson**	N	N	N	N	N	Y
7 **Gibbs**	N	N	N	N	N	Y
8 **Davidson**	Y	Y	N	N	N	Y
9 Kaptur	N	Y	Y	N	Y	Y
10 **Turner**	Y	Y	N	N	N	Y
11 Fudge	N	Y	Y	Y	Y	Y
12 **Vacant**						
13 Ryan	Y	Y	N	N	Y	Y
14 **Joyce**	N	N	N	N	N	Y
15 **Stivers**	Y	Y	N	N	N	Y
16 **Renacci**	N	N	N	N	N	Y
OKLAHOMA						
1 **Vacant**						
2 **Mullin**	N	N	N	N	N	Y
3 **Lucas**	N	N	N	N	N	Y
4 **Cole**	N	N	N	N	N	Y
5 **Russell**	Y	Y	N	N	N	Y
OREGON						
1 Bonamici	N	Y	Y	Y	Y	N
2 **Walden**	N	Y	N	N	N	Y
3 Blumenauer	N	Y	Y	N	Y	N
4 DeFazio	N	Y	Y	Y	Y	N
5 Schrader	N	Y	Y	N	Y	Y
PENNSYLVANIA						
1 Brady	N	Y	Y	Y	Y	Y
2 Evans	N	Y	Y	Y	Y	Y
3 **Kelly**	N	Y	N	Y	N	Y
4 **Perry**	N	Y	N	Y	N	Y
5 **Thompson**	N	N	N	N	N	Y
6 **Costello**	?	?	?	?	?	?
7 **Vacant**						
8 **Fitzpatrick**	Y	Y	N	N	N	Y
9 **Shuster**	Y	N	N	Y	N	Y
10 **Marino**	Y	Y	N	Y	N	Y
11 **Barletta**	N	N	N	Y	N	Y
12 **Rothfus**	N	N	N	N	N	Y
13 Boyle	N	Y	N	Y	Y	Y
14 Doyle	N	Y	Y	Y	Y	Y
15 **Vacant**						
16 **Smucker**	N	N	N	Y	N	Y
17 Cartwright	N	Y	Y	Y	Y	Y
18 Lamb	Y	Y	Y	Y	Y	Y
RHODE ISLAND						
1 Cicilline	N	Y	Y	Y	Y	N
2 Langevin	N	Y	Y	Y	Y	Y
SOUTH CAROLINA						
1 **Sanford**	N	N	N	Y	N	Y
2 **Wilson**	Y	Y	N	N	N	Y
3 **Duncan**	N	N	N	N	N	Y
4 **Gowdy**	N	N	N	N	N	Y
5 **Norman**	Y	N	N	N	N	Y
6 Clyburn	N	Y	Y	N	Y	Y
7 **Rice**	N	N	N	N	N	Y
SOUTH DAKOTA						
AL **Noem**	N	N	N	N	N	Y
TENNESSEE						
1 **Roe**	N	N	N	N	N	Y
2 **Duncan**	N	Y	N	N	?	?
3 **Fleischmann**	N	Y	N	N	N	Y
4 **DesJarlais**	Y	Y	N	N	N	Y
5 Cooper	N	N	Y	N	Y	Y
6 **Black**	?	?	?	?	?	?
7 **Blackburn**	N	N	N	N	N	Y
8 **Kustoff**	N	N	N	N	N	Y
9 Cohen	N	Y	Y	N	Y	N

	308	309	310	311	312	313
TEXAS						
1 **Gohmert**	Y	N	N	N	N	Y
2 **Poe**	N	N	N	N	N	Y
3 **Johnson, S.**	N	N	N	N	N	Y
4 **Ratcliffe**	N	Y	N	N	N	Y
5 **Hensarling**	N	N	N	N	N	Y
6 **Barton**	N	N	N	N	N	Y
7 **Culberson**	N	Y	N	N	N	Y
8 **Brady**	Y	Y	N	Y	?	Y
9 Green, A.	N	Y	Y	Y	Y	Y
10 **McCaul**	Y	Y	N	N	N	Y
11 **Conaway**	Y	Y	N	N	N	Y
12 **Granger**	N	N	N	N	N	Y
13 **Thornberry**	Y	Y	N	Y	N	Y
14 **Weber**	N	Y	N	N	N	Y
15 Gonzalez	N	Y	N	N	Y	Y
16 O'Rourke	N	Y	Y	N	Y	Y
17 **Flores**	Y	N	N	Y	N	Y
18 Jackson Lee	N	Y	Y	N	Y	Y
19 **Arrington**	N	N	N	N	N	Y
20 Castro	N	Y	Y	N	Y	Y
21 **Smith**	N	N	N	N	N	Y
22 **Olson**	N	N	N	N	N	Y
23 **Hurd**	N	Y	N	N	N	Y
24 Marchant	N	N	N	N	N	Y
25 **Williams**	N	Y	N	N	N	Y
26 **Burgess**	N	N	N	N	N	Y
28 Cuellar	N	Y	Y	N	Y	Y
29 Green, G.	N	Y	N	N	Y	Y
30 Johnson, E.B.	N	Y	Y	Y	Y	Y
31 **Carter**	N	Y	N	N	N	Y
32 **Sessions**	N	N	N	N	N	Y
33 Veasey	N	Y	Y	Y	Y	Y
34 Vela	N	Y	Y	N	Y	Y
35 Doggett	N	?	Y	N	Y	Y
36 **Babin**	N	Y	N	N	N	Y
UTAH						
1 **Bishop**	Y	Y	N	N	N	Y
2 **Stewart**	N	N	N	N	N	Y
3 **Curtis**	N	N	N	N	N	Y
4 **Love**	N	Y	N	N	N	Y
VERMONT						
AL Welch	N	N	Y	N	Y	N
VIRGINIA						
1 **Wittman**	Y	Y	N	Y	N	Y
2 **Taylor**	N	N	N	Y	N	Y
3 Scott	N	Y	N	Y	Y	Y
4 McEachin	N	Y	Y	Y	Y	Y
5 **Garrett**	Y	N	N	Y	N	Y
6 **Goodlatte**	N	Y	N	Y	N	Y
7 **Brat**	N	N	N	Y	N	Y
8 Beyer	N	N	Y	N	Y	Y
9 **Griffith**	N	N	N	Y	N	Y
10 **Comstock**	Y	N	N	Y	N	Y
11 Connolly	N	Y	Y	N	Y	Y
WASHINGTON						
1 DelBene	N	Y	Y	N	Y	Y
2 Larsen	N	Y	Y	Y	Y	Y
3 **Herrera Beutler**	N	N	N	N	N	Y
4 **Newhouse**	N	Y	N	N	N	Y
5 **McMorris Rodgers**	Y	Y	N	N	N	Y
6 Kilmer	N	Y	N	N	Y	Y
7 Jayapal	N	Y	Y	N	Y	N
8 **Reichert**	N	N	N	N	N	Y
9 Smith	N	Y	Y	Y	Y	Y
10 Heck	N	Y	Y	N	Y	Y
WEST VIRGINIA						
1 **McKinley**	Y	N	N	N	N	Y
2 **Mooney**	Y	N	N	Y	N	Y
3 **Jenkins**	Y	Y	N	N	N	Y
WISCONSIN						
1 **Ryan**						
2 Pocan	N	Y	Y	N	Y	N
3 Kind	N	Y	Y	N	Y	Y
4 Moore	N	Y	Y	N	Y	N
5 **Sensenbrenner**	Y	Y	N	Y	N	Y
6 **Grothman**	–	–	–	–	–	+
7 **Duffy**	Y	Y	N	Y	N	Y
8 **Gallagher**	Y	Y	N	Y	N	Y
WYOMING						
AL **Cheney**	Y	Y	N	Y	N	Y

⫿ HOUSE VOTES

VOTE NUMBER

314. HR5793. PUBLIC HOUSING VOUCHERS/PASSAGE. Huizenga, R-Mich., motion to suspend the rules and pass the bill that would permit the Housing and Urban Development Department to allow public housing authorities to use administrative fees, fee reserves and funding from certain private entities to provide public housing vouchers and certain housing assistance services for the purpose of incentivizing families that receive vouchers to move to lower-poverty areas. Motion agreed to 368-19: R 195-19; D 173-0. July 10, 2018.

315. HR5749. RISK-ADJUSTED DERIVATIVES CAPITAL/PASSAGE. Huizenga, R-Mich., motion to suspend the rules and pass the bill that would require the Federal Reserve System to develop a rule by which the amount of capital required to be held to insure certain derivatives and options would be calculated on a risk-adjusted basis. Motion agreed to 385-0: R 213-0; D 172-0. July 10, 2018.

316. HRES965. REGIONAL FISHERY MANAGEMENT/PREVIOUS QUESTION. Byrne, R-Ala., motion to order the previous question (thus ending debate and possibility of amendment) on the rule (H Res 965) that would provide for House floor consideration of the bill (HR 200) that would reauthorize the Magnuson-Stevens Fishery Conservation and Management Act through fiscal 2022 and would provide greater authority to regional fishery management councils in setting the conditions under which overfished or depleted fisheries are to be restored. Motion agreed to 225-186: R 225-1; D 0-185. July 11, 2018.

317. HR200. REGIONAL FISHERY MANAGEMENT/RULE. Adoption of the rule (H Res 965) that would provide for House floor consideration of the bill (HR 200) that would reauthorize the Magnuson-Stevens Fishery Conservation and Management Act through fiscal 2022 and would provide greater authority to regional fishery management councils in setting the conditions under which overfished or depleted fisheries are to be restored. Adopted 227-184: R 227-0; D 0-184. July 11, 2018.

318. HRES985. UNFUNDED MANDATES AND WATER INFRASTRUCTURE PROJECTS/PREVIOUS QUESTION. Collins, R-Ga., motion to order the previous question (thus ending debate and possibility of amendment) on the rule (H Res 961) that would provide for House floor consideration of the bill (HR 50) that would require that independent agencies conduct analyses of their proposed rules on the private sector and state and local governments, and would require all federal agencies to consult with the private sector when developing rules, and would provide for consideration of the bill (HR 3281) that would permit the Bureau of Reclamation to transfer ownership of certain federal water infrastructure facilities to certain nonfederal entities without the need for Congress to enact project-specific legislation. Motion agreed to 228-184: R 228-0; D 0-184. July 11, 2018.

319. HR3281. UNFUNDED MANDATES AND WATER INFRASTRUCTURE PROJECTS/RULE. Adoption of the rule (H Res 961) that would provide for House floor consideration of the bill (HR 50) that would require that independent agencies conduct analyses of their proposed rules on the private sector and state and local governments, and would require all federal agencies to consult with the private sector when developing rules, and would provide for consideration of the bill (HR 3281) that would permit the Bureau of Reclamation to transfer ownership of certain federal water infrastructure facilities to certain nonfederal entities without the need for Congress to enact project-specific legislation. Adopted 229-183: R 229-0; D 0-183. July 11, 2018.

	314	315	316	317	318	319
ALABAMA						
1 Byrne	Y	Y	Y	Y	Y	Y
2 Roby	Y	Y	Y	Y	Y	Y
3 Rogers	Y	Y	Y	Y	Y	Y
4 Aderholt	Y	Y	Y	Y	Y	Y
5 Brooks	N	Y	Y	Y	Y	Y
6 Palmer	Y	Y	Y	Y	Y	Y
7 Sewell	Y	Y	N	N	N	N
ALASKA						
AL Young	Y	Y	Y	Y	Y	Y
ARIZONA						
1 O'Halleran	Y	Y	N	N	N	N
2 McSally	Y	Y	Y	Y	Y	Y
3 Grijalva	?	?	N	N	N	N
4 Gosar	N	Y	Y	Y	Y	Y
5 Biggs	N	Y	Y	Y	Y	Y
6 Schweikert	Y	Y	Y	Y	Y	Y
7 Gallego	Y	Y	N	N	N	N
8 Lesko	Y	Y	Y	Y	Y	Y
9 Sinema	Y	Y	N	N	N	N
ARKANSAS						
1 Crawford	Y	Y	Y	Y	Y	Y
2 Hill	Y	Y	Y	Y	Y	Y
3 Womack	Y	Y	Y	Y	Y	Y
4 Westerman	Y	Y	Y	Y	Y	Y
CALIFORNIA						
1 LaMalfa	Y	Y	Y	Y	Y	Y
2 Huffman	Y	Y	N	N	N	N
3 Garamendi	Y	Y	N	N	N	N
4 McClintock	Y	Y	Y	Y	Y	Y
5 Thompson	Y	Y	N	N	N	N
6 Matsui	Y	Y	N	N	N	N
7 Bera	Y	Y	N	N	N	N
8 Cook	Y	Y	Y	Y	Y	Y
9 McNerney	Y	Y	N	N	N	N
10 Denham	Y	Y	Y	Y	Y	Y
11 DeSaulnier	Y	Y	N	N	N	N
12 Pelosi	Y	Y	N	N	N	N
13 Lee	Y	Y	N	N	N	N
14 Speier	Y	Y	?	?	?	?
15 Swalwell	Y	Y	N	N	N	N
16 Costa	?	?	?	?	?	?
17 Khanna	Y	Y	N	N	N	N
18 Eshoo	Y	Y	N	N	N	N
19 Lofgren	Y	Y	N	N	N	N
20 Panetta	Y	Y	N	N	N	N
21 Valadao	Y	Y	Y	Y	Y	Y
22 Nunes	Y	Y	Y	Y	Y	Y
23 McCarthy	Y	Y	Y	Y	Y	Y
24 Carbajal	Y	Y	N	N	N	N
25 Knight	Y	Y	Y	Y	Y	Y
26 Brownley	Y	Y	N	N	N	N
27 Chu	Y	Y	N	N	N	N
28 Schiff	Y	Y	N	N	N	N
29 Cardenas	Y	Y	N	N	N	N
30 Sherman	Y	Y	N	N	N	N
31 Aguilar	?	Y	N	N	N	N
32 Napolitano	+	+	-	-	-	-
33 Lieu	Y	Y	N	N	N	N
34 Gomez	Y	Y	N	N	N	N
35 Torres	Y	Y	N	N	N	N
36 Ruiz	Y	Y	N	N	N	N
37 Bass	Y	Y	N	N	N	N
38 Sánchez, Linda	Y	Y	N	N	N	N
39 Royce	Y	?	Y	Y	Y	Y
40 Roybal-Allard	Y	Y	N	N	N	N
41 Takano	Y	Y	N	N	N	N
42 Calvert	Y	Y	Y	Y	Y	Y
43 Waters	Y	Y	N	N	N	N
44 Barragan	Y	Y	N	N	N	N
45 Walters	Y	Y	Y	Y	Y	Y
46 Correa	Y	Y	N	N	N	N
47 Lowenthal	Y	?	N	N	N	N
48 Rohrabacher	?	?	Y	Y	Y	Y
49 Issa	?	?	Y	Y	Y	Y
50 Hunter	?	?	Y	Y	Y	Y
51 Vargas	Y	Y	N	N	N	N
52 Peters	Y	Y	N	N	N	N
53 Davis	Y	Y	N	N	N	N

	314	315	316	317	318	319
COLORADO						
1 DeGette	Y	Y	N	N	N	N
2 Polis	Y	Y	N	N	N	N
3 Tipton	Y	Y	Y	Y	Y	Y
4 Buck	N	Y	Y	Y	Y	Y
5 Lamborn	Y	Y	Y	Y	Y	Y
6 Coffman	Y	Y	Y	Y	Y	Y
7 Perlmutter	?	?	?	?	?	?
CONNECTICUT						
1 Larson	Y	Y	N	N	N	N
2 Courtney	Y	Y	N	N	N	N
3 DeLauro	Y	Y	N	N	N	N
4 Himes	Y	Y	N	N	N	N
5 Esty	Y	Y	N	N	N	N
DELAWARE						
AL Blunt Rochester	Y	Y	N	N	N	N
FLORIDA						
1 Gaetz	N	Y	Y	Y	Y	Y
2 Dunn	Y	Y	Y	Y	Y	Y
3 Yoho	Y	Y	Y	Y	Y	Y
4 Rutherford	Y	Y	Y	Y	Y	Y
5 Lawson	Y	Y	N	N	N	N
6 DeSantis	Y	Y	Y	Y	Y	Y
7 Murphy	Y	Y	N	N	N	N
8 Posey	Y	Y	Y	Y	Y	Y
9 Soto	Y	Y	N	N	N	N
10 Demings	Y	Y	N	N	N	N
11 Webster	Y	Y	Y	Y	Y	Y
12 Bilirakis	+	+	Y	Y	Y	Y
13 Crist	Y	Y	N	N	N	N
14 Castor	Y	Y	N	N	N	N
15 Ross	Y	Y	Y	Y	Y	Y
16 Buchanan	Y	Y	Y	Y	Y	Y
17 Rooney, T.	?	?	Y	Y	Y	Y
18 Mast	?	?	Y	Y	Y	Y
19 Rooney, F.	Y	Y	Y	Y	Y	Y
20 Hastings	?	?	N	N	N	N
21 Frankel	?	?	N	N	N	N
22 Deutch	Y	Y	N	N	N	N
23 Wasserman Schultz	Y	Y	N	N	N	N
24 Wilson	?	?	N	N	N	N
25 Diaz-Balart	Y	Y	Y	Y	Y	Y
26 Curbelo	Y	Y	Y	Y	Y	Y
27 Ros-Lehtinen	Y	Y	Y	Y	Y	Y
GEORGIA						
1 Carter	Y	Y	Y	Y	Y	Y
2 Bishop	Y	Y	N	N	N	N
3 Ferguson	Y	Y	Y	Y	Y	Y
4 Johnson	Y	Y	N	N	N	N
5 Lewis	Y	Y	N	N	N	?
6 Handel	Y	Y	Y	Y	Y	Y
7 Woodall	Y	Y	Y	Y	Y	Y
8 Scott, A.	Y	Y	Y	Y	Y	Y
9 Collins	Y	Y	Y	Y	Y	Y
10 Hice	N	Y	Y	Y	Y	Y
11 Loudermilk	Y	Y	Y	Y	Y	Y
12 Allen	?	?	Y	Y	Y	Y
13 Scott, D.	Y	Y	N	?	N	N
14 Graves	Y	Y	Y	Y	Y	Y
HAWAII						
1 Hanabusa	?	?	?	?	?	?
2 Gabbard	Y	Y	N	N	N	N
IDAHO						
1 Labrador	N	Y	Y	Y	Y	Y
2 Simpson	Y	Y	Y	Y	Y	Y
ILLINOIS						
1 Rush	?	?	?	?	?	?
2 Kelly	Y	Y	N	N	N	N
3 Lipinski	Y	Y	N	N	N	N
4 Gutierrez	+	+	N	N	N	N
5 Quigley	Y	Y	N	N	N	N
6 Roskam	Y	Y	Y	Y	Y	Y
7 Davis, D.	Y	Y	N	N	N	N
8 Krishnamoorthi	Y	Y	N	N	N	N
9 Schakowsky	Y	Y	N	N	N	N
10 Schneider	Y	Y	N	N	N	N
11 Foster	Y	Y	N	N	N	N
12 Bost	Y	Y	Y	Y	Y	Y
13 Davis, R.	Y	Y	Y	Y	Y	Y

KEY	**Republicans**	Democrats	*Independents*
Y Voted for (yea)	X Paired against	C Voted "present" to avoid possible conflict of interest
# Paired for	– Announced against	
+ Announced for	P Voted "present"	? Did not vote or otherwise make a position known
N Voted against (nay)		

	314	315	316	317	318	319
14 **Hultgren**	Y	Y	Y	Y	Y	Y
15 **Shimkus**	Y	Y	Y	Y	Y	Y
16 **Kinzinger**	Y	Y	Y	Y	Y	Y
17 Bustos	Y	Y	N	N	N	N
18 **LaHood**	Y	Y	Y	Y	Y	Y
INDIANA						
1 Visclosky	Y	Y	N	N	N	N
2 **Walorski**	Y	Y	Y	Y	Y	Y
3 **Banks**	Y	Y	Y	Y	Y	Y
4 Rokita	Y	Y	Y	Y	Y	Y
5 **Brooks**	Y	Y	Y	Y	Y	Y
6 **Messer**	Y	Y	?	?	Y	Y
7 Carson	Y	Y	N	N	N	N
8 **Bucshon**	Y	Y	Y	Y	Y	Y
9 **Hollingsworth**	Y	Y	Y	Y	Y	Y
IOWA						
1 **Blum**	N	Y	?	?	?	?
2 Loebsack	Y	Y	N	N	N	N
3 **Young**	Y	Y	Y	Y	Y	Y
4 **King**	Y	Y	Y	Y	Y	Y
KANSAS						
1 **Marshall**	Y	Y	Y	Y	Y	Y
2 **Jenkins**	+	+	+	+	+	+
3 **Yoder**	Y	Y	Y	Y	Y	Y
4 **Estes**	Y	Y	Y	Y	Y	Y
KENTUCKY						
1 **Comer**	Y	Y	Y	Y	Y	Y
2 **Guthrie**	Y	Y	Y	Y	Y	Y
3 Yarmuth	Y	Y	N	N	N	N
4 **Massie**	N	Y	Y	Y	Y	Y
5 **Rogers**	Y	Y	Y	Y	Y	Y
6 **Barr**	Y	Y	Y	Y	Y	Y
LOUISIANA						
1 **Scalise**	Y	Y	Y	Y	Y	Y
2 Richmond	Y	Y	N	N	N	N
3 **Higgins**	Y	Y	Y	Y	Y	Y
4 **Johnson**	Y	Y	Y	Y	Y	Y
5 **Abraham**	Y	Y	Y	Y	Y	Y
6 **Graves**	+	+	Y	Y	Y	Y
MAINE						
1 Pingree	Y	Y	N	N	N	N
2 **Poliquin**	Y	Y	Y	Y	Y	Y
MARYLAND						
1 **Harris**	N	Y	Y	Y	Y	Y
2 Ruppersberger	Y	Y	N	N	N	?
3 Sarbanes	Y	Y	N	N	N	N
4 Brown	Y	Y	N	N	N	N
5 Hoyer	?	?	N	N	N	N
6 Delaney	Y	Y	N	N	N	N
7 Cummings	?	?	N	N	N	N
8 Raskin	Y	Y	N	N	N	N
MASSACHUSETTS						
1 Neal	?	?	N	N	N	N
2 McGovern	Y	Y	N	N	N	N
3 Tsongas	Y	Y	N	N	N	N
4 Kennedy	Y	Y	N	N	N	N
5 Clark	Y	Y	N	N	N	N
6 Moulton	Y	Y	N	N	N	N
7 Capuano	Y	Y	N	N	N	N
8 Lynch	Y	Y	N	N	N	N
9 Keating	Y	Y	N	N	N	N
MICHIGAN						
1 **Bergman**	Y	Y	Y	Y	Y	Y
2 **Huizenga**	Y	Y	Y	Y	Y	Y
3 *Amash*	N	Y	Y	Y	Y	Y
4 **Moolenaar**	Y	Y	Y	Y	Y	Y
5 Kildee	Y	Y	N	N	N	N
6 **Upton**	?	?	Y	Y	Y	Y
7 **Walberg**	Y	Y	Y	Y	Y	Y
8 **Bishop**	Y	Y	Y	Y	Y	Y
9 Levin	Y	Y	N	N	N	N
10 **Mitchell**	Y	Y	Y	Y	Y	Y
11 **Trott**	Y	Y	Y	Y	Y	Y
12 Dingell	Y	Y	N	N	N	N
14 Lawrence	Y	Y	N	N	N	N
MINNESOTA						
1 Walz	?	?	?	?	?	?
2 **Lewis**	Y	Y	Y	Y	Y	Y
3 **Paulsen**	Y	Y	Y	Y	Y	Y
4 McCollum	Y	Y	N	N	N	N
5 Ellison	?	?	?	?	?	?
6 **Emmer**	Y	Y	Y	Y	Y	Y
7 Peterson	Y	Y	N	N	N	N
8 Nolan	Y	Y	N	N	N	N
MISSISSIPPI						
1 **Kelly**	Y	Y	Y	Y	Y	Y
2 Thompson	Y	Y	N	N	N	N
3 **Harper**	?	?	?	?	?	?
4 **Palazzo**	Y	Y	Y	Y	Y	Y
MISSOURI						
1 Clay	Y	Y	N	N	N	N
2 **Wagner**	Y	Y	Y	Y	Y	Y
3 **Luetkemeyer**	Y	Y	Y	Y	Y	Y
4 **Hartzler**	Y	Y	Y	Y	Y	Y
5 Cleaver	Y	Y	N	N	N	N
6 **Graves**	Y	Y	Y	Y	Y	Y
7 **Long**	Y	Y	Y	Y	Y	Y
8 **Smith**	Y	Y	Y	Y	Y	Y
MONTANA						
AL **Gianforte**	Y	Y	Y	Y	Y	Y
NEBRASKA						
1 **Fortenberry**	Y	Y	Y	Y	Y	Y
2 **Bacon**	Y	Y	Y	Y	Y	Y
3 **Smith**	Y	Y	Y	Y	Y	Y
NEVADA						
1 Titus	Y	Y	N	N	N	N
2 **Amodei**	Y	Y	?	Y	Y	Y
3 Rosen	Y	Y	N	N	N	N
4 Kihuen	Y	Y	N	N	N	N
NEW HAMPSHIRE						
1 Shea-Porter	?	?	N	N	N	N
2 Kuster	Y	Y	N	N	N	N
NEW JERSEY						
1 Norcross	Y	Y	N	N	N	N
2 **LoBiondo**	Y	Y	Y	Y	Y	Y
3 **MacArthur**	Y	Y	Y	Y	Y	Y
4 **Smith**	Y	Y	Y	Y	Y	Y
5 Gottheimer	Y	Y	N	N	N	N
6 Pallone	Y	Y	N	N	N	N
7 **Lance**	Y	Y	Y	Y	Y	Y
8 Sires	Y	Y	N	N	N	N
9 Pascrell	Y	Y	N	N	N	N
10 Payne	Y	Y	N	N	N	N
11 **Frelinghuysen**	Y	Y	Y	Y	Y	Y
12 Watson Coleman	Y	Y	N	N	N	N
NEW MEXICO						
1 Lujan Grisham	Y	Y	N	N	N	N
2 **Pearce**	Y	Y	Y	Y	Y	Y
3 Luján	Y	Y	N	N	N	N
NEW YORK						
1 **Zeldin**	Y	Y	Y	Y	Y	Y
2 **King**	Y	Y	Y	Y	Y	Y
3 Suozzi	Y	?	N	N	N	N
4 Rice	Y	Y	N	N	N	N
5 Meeks	?	?	N	N	N	N
6 Meng	Y	Y	N	N	N	N
7 Velázquez	Y	Y	N	N	N	N
8 Jeffries	Y	Y	N	N	N	N
9 Clarke	Y	Y	N	N	N	N
10 Nadler	Y	Y	N	N	N	N
11 **Donovan**	Y	Y	Y	Y	Y	Y
12 Maloney, C.	Y	Y	N	N	N	N
13 Espaillat	Y	Y	N	N	N	N
14 Crowley	Y	Y	N	N	N	N
15 Serrano	Y	Y	N	N	?	N
16 Engel	Y	Y	N	N	N	N
17 Lowey	?	?	N	N	N	N
18 Maloney, S.P.	Y	Y	N	N	N	N
19 **Faso**	Y	Y	Y	Y	Y	Y
20 Tonko	Y	Y	N	N	N	N
21 **Stefanik**	Y	Y	Y	Y	Y	Y
22 **Tenney**	Y	Y	Y	Y	Y	Y
23 **Reed**	Y	Y	Y	Y	Y	Y
24 **Katko**	Y	Y	Y	Y	Y	Y
25 **Vacant**						
26 Higgins	Y	Y	N	N	N	N
27 **Collins**	Y	Y	Y	Y	Y	Y
NORTH CAROLINA						
1 Butterfield	Y	Y	N	N	N	N
2 **Holding**	Y	Y	Y	Y	Y	Y
3 **Jones**	N	?	N	Y	Y	Y
4 Price	Y	Y	N	N	N	N
5 **Foxx**	Y	Y	Y	Y	Y	Y
6 **Walker**	Y	Y	Y	Y	Y	Y
7 **Rouzer**	Y	Y	Y	Y	Y	Y
8 **Hudson**	Y	Y	Y	Y	Y	Y
9 **Pittenger**	Y	Y	Y	Y	Y	Y
9 **Vacant**						
10 **McHenry**	Y	Y	Y	Y	Y	Y
11 **Meadows**	Y	Y	Y	Y	Y	Y
12 Adams	Y	Y	N	N	N	N
13 **Budd**	Y	Y	Y	Y	Y	Y
NORTH DAKOTA						
AL **Cramer**	Y	Y	Y	Y	Y	Y
OHIO						
1 **Chabot**	Y	Y	Y	Y	Y	Y
2 **Wenstrup**	Y	Y	Y	Y	Y	Y
3 Beatty	Y	Y	N	N	N	N
4 **Jordan**	Y	Y	Y	Y	Y	Y
5 **Latta**	Y	Y	Y	Y	Y	Y
6 **Johnson**	Y	Y	Y	Y	Y	Y
7 **Gibbs**	Y	Y	Y	Y	Y	Y
8 **Davidson**	Y	Y	Y	Y	Y	Y
9 Kaptur	Y	Y	N	N	N	N
10 **Turner**	Y	Y	Y	Y	Y	Y
11 Fudge	Y	Y	N	N	N	N
12 **Vacant**						
13 Ryan	Y	Y	N	N	N	N
14 **Joyce**	Y	Y	Y	Y	Y	Y
15 **Stivers**	Y	Y	Y	Y	Y	Y
16 **Renacci**	Y	Y	Y	Y	Y	Y
OKLAHOMA						
1 **Vacant**						
2 **Mullin**	Y	Y	Y	Y	Y	Y
3 **Lucas**	Y	Y	Y	Y	Y	Y
4 **Cole**	Y	Y	Y	Y	Y	Y
5 **Russell**	+	+	Y	Y	Y	Y
OREGON						
1 Bonamici	Y	Y	N	N	N	N
2 **Walden**	Y	Y	Y	Y	Y	Y
3 Blumenauer	Y	Y	N	N	N	N
4 DeFazio	Y	Y	N	N	N	N
5 Schrader	Y	Y	N	N	N	N
PENNSYLVANIA						
1 Brady	?	?	N	N	N	N
2 Evans	Y	Y	N	N	N	N
3 **Kelly**	Y	Y	Y	Y	Y	Y
4 **Perry**	N	Y	Y	Y	Y	Y
5 **Thompson**	Y	Y	Y	Y	Y	Y
6 **Costello**	?	?	Y	Y	Y	Y
7 **Vacant**						
8 **Fitzpatrick**	Y	Y	Y	Y	Y	Y
9 **Shuster**	Y	Y	?	?	?	?
10 **Marino**	Y	Y	Y	Y	Y	Y
11 **Barletta**	Y	Y	Y	Y	Y	Y
12 **Rothfus**	Y	Y	Y	Y	Y	Y
13 Boyle	Y	Y	N	N	N	N
14 Doyle	Y	Y	N	N	N	N
15 **Vacant**						
16 **Smucker**	Y	Y	Y	Y	Y	Y
17 Cartwright	Y	Y	N	N	N	N
18 Lamb	Y	Y	N	N	N	N
RHODE ISLAND						
1 Cicilline	Y	Y	N	N	N	N
2 Langevin	Y	Y	N	N	N	N
SOUTH CAROLINA						
1 **Sanford**	N	Y	Y	Y	Y	Y
2 **Wilson**	Y	Y	Y	Y	Y	Y
3 **Duncan**	Y	Y	Y	Y	Y	Y
4 **Gowdy**	?	?	Y	Y	Y	Y
5 **Norman**	Y	?	Y	Y	Y	Y
6 Clyburn	Y	Y	N	N	N	N
7 **Rice**	Y	Y	Y	Y	Y	Y
SOUTH DAKOTA						
AL **Noem**	?	Y	Y	Y	Y	Y
TENNESSEE						
1 **Roe**	Y	Y	Y	Y	Y	Y
2 **Duncan**	N	Y	Y	Y	Y	Y
3 **Fleischmann**	Y	Y	Y	Y	Y	Y
4 **DesJarlais**	Y	Y	Y	Y	Y	Y
5 Cooper	Y	Y	N	N	N	N
6 **Black**	Y	Y	Y	Y	Y	Y
7 **Blackburn**	?	?	Y	Y	Y	Y
8 **Kustoff**	Y	Y	Y	Y	Y	Y
9 Cohen	Y	Y	N	N	N	N
TEXAS						
1 **Gohmert**	N	Y	Y	Y	Y	Y
2 **Poe**	Y	Y	Y	Y	Y	Y
3 **Johnson, S.**	Y	Y	Y	Y	Y	Y
4 **Ratcliffe**	Y	Y	Y	Y	Y	Y
5 **Hensarling**	Y	Y	Y	Y	Y	Y
6 **Barton**	Y	Y	Y	Y	Y	Y
7 **Culberson**	Y	Y	Y	Y	Y	Y
8 **Brady**	Y	Y	Y	Y	Y	Y
9 Green, A.	Y	Y	N	N	N	N
10 **McCaul**	Y	Y	Y	Y	Y	Y
11 **Conaway**	Y	Y	Y	Y	Y	Y
12 **Granger**	Y	Y	Y	Y	Y	Y
13 **Thornberry**	Y	Y	Y	Y	Y	Y
14 **Weber**	?	?	?	?	?	Y
15 Gonzalez	Y	Y	N	N	N	N
16 O'Rourke	Y	Y	N	N	N	N
17 **Flores**	Y	Y	Y	Y	Y	Y
18 Jackson Lee	Y	Y	N	N	N	N
19 **Arrington**	Y	Y	Y	Y	Y	Y
20 Castro	Y	Y	N	N	N	N
21 **Smith**	Y	Y	Y	Y	Y	Y
22 **Olson**	Y	Y	Y	Y	Y	Y
23 **Hurd**	Y	Y	Y	Y	Y	Y
24 Marchant	Y	Y	Y	Y	Y	Y
25 **Williams**	Y	Y	Y	Y	Y	Y
26 **Burgess**	Y	Y	Y	Y	Y	Y
27 Cloud		Y	Y	Y	Y	Y
28 Cuellar	Y	Y	N	N	N	N
29 Green, G.	Y	Y	N	N	N	N
30 Johnson, E.B.	Y	Y	N	N	N	N
31 **Carter**	Y	Y	Y	Y	Y	Y
32 **Sessions**	Y	Y	Y	Y	Y	Y
33 Veasey	Y	Y	N	N	N	N
34 Vela	Y	Y	N	N	N	N
35 Doggett	Y	Y	N	N	N	N
36 **Babin**	Y	Y	Y	Y	Y	Y
UTAH						
1 **Bishop**	Y	Y	Y	Y	Y	Y
2 **Stewart**	Y	Y	Y	Y	Y	Y
3 **Curtis**	Y	Y	Y	Y	Y	Y
4 **Love**	Y	Y	Y	Y	Y	Y
VERMONT						
AL Welch	Y	Y	N	N	N	N
VIRGINIA						
1 **Wittman**	Y	Y	Y	Y	Y	Y
2 **Taylor**	Y	Y	Y	Y	Y	Y
3 Scott	Y	Y	N	N	N	N
4 McEachin	Y	Y	N	N	N	N
5 **Garrett**	N	Y	Y	Y	Y	Y
6 **Goodlatte**	Y	Y	Y	Y	Y	Y
7 **Brat**	Y	Y	Y	Y	Y	Y
8 Beyer	Y	Y	N	N	N	N
9 **Griffith**	Y	Y	Y	Y	Y	Y
10 **Comstock**	Y	Y	Y	Y	Y	Y
11 Connolly	Y	Y	N	N	N	N
WASHINGTON						
1 DelBene	Y	Y	N	N	N	N
2 Larsen	Y	Y	N	N	N	N
3 **Herrera Beutler**	Y	Y	Y	Y	Y	Y
4 **Newhouse**	Y	Y	Y	Y	Y	Y
5 **McMorris Rodgers**	Y	Y	Y	Y	Y	Y
6 Kilmer	Y	Y	N	N	N	N
7 Jayapal	Y	Y	N	N	N	N
8 **Reichert**	Y	Y	Y	Y	Y	Y
9 Smith	Y	Y	N	N	N	N
10 Heck	Y	Y	N	N	N	N
WEST VIRGINIA						
1 **McKinley**	Y	Y	Y	Y	Y	Y
2 **Mooney**	+	+	Y	Y	Y	Y
3 **Jenkins**	Y	Y	Y	Y	Y	Y
WISCONSIN						
1 **Ryan**						
2 Pocan	Y	Y	N	N	N	N
3 Kind	Y	Y	N	N	N	N
4 Moore	Y	Y	N	N	N	N
5 **Sensenbrenner**	N	Y	Y	Y	Y	Y
6 **Grothman**	N	Y	Y	Y	Y	Y
7 **Duffy**	Y	Y	Y	Y	Y	Y
8 **Gallagher**	?	?	?	?	?	?
WYOMING						
AL **Cheney**	?	?	?	?	?	?

VOTE NUMBER

320. HR200. REGIONAL FISHERY MANAGEMENT/RECOMMIT. Gomez, D-Calif., motion to recommit the bill to the House Natural Resources Committee with instructions to report it back immediately with an amendment that would require the Commerce Department, or a relevant state government, to declare a fishery disaster if any unilateral tariffs imposed by any countries on U.S. seafood exports affect the economic viability of the U.S. fishing industry. Motion rejected 187-228: R 1-227; D 186-1. July 11, 2018.

321. HR200. REGIONAL FISHERY MANAGEMENT/PASSAGE. Passage of the bill that would reauthorize and modify the Magnuson-Stevens Fishery Conservation and Management Act through fiscal 2022 and would provide greater authority to regional fishery management councils in setting the conditions under which overfished or depleted fisheries are to be restored. The bill would eliminate the current 10-year requirement for rebuilding overfished or depleted fisheries and would allow fishery councils to set rebuilding periods that reflect the individual fish species' ability to recover. The bill would also modify catch limits for specific species and would prohibit fisheries councils in four regions from implementing any new "catch share" programs unless such plans had been approved by an industry referendum vote. The bill would authorize $397 million annually for fiscal 2018 through fiscal 2022 to carry out the bill's provisions. Passed 222-193: R 213-15; D 9-178. July 11, 2018.

322. HR6237. FISCAL 2018 AND 2019 INTELLIGENCE AUTHORIZATION/ PREVIOUS QUESTION. Collins, R-Ga., motion to order the previous question (thus ending debate and possibility of amendment) on the rule (H Res 989) that would provide for House floor consideration of the bill (HR 6237) that would authorize classified amounts in fiscal 2018 and fiscal 2019 for 16 U.S. intelligence agencies and intelligence-related activities of the U.S. government, which would cover general intelligence operations, clandestine human intelligence programs and analysis, and covert action programs. Motion agreed to 229-182: R 229-0; D 0-182. July 12, 2018.

323. HR6237. FISCAL 2018 AND 2019 INTELLIGENCE AUTHORIZATION/ RULE. Adoption of the rule (H Res 989) that would provide for House floor consideration of the bill (HR 6237) that would authorize classified amounts in fiscal 2018 and fiscal 2019 for 16 U.S. intelligence agencies and intelligence-related activities of the U.S. government, which would cover general intelligence operations, clandestine human intelligence programs and analysis, and covert action programs. Adopted 235-178: R 228-1; D 7-177. July 12, 2018.

324. HR3281. WATER INFRASTRUCTURE PROJECTS/RECOMMIT. Huffman, D-Calif., motion to recommit the bill to the House Natural Resources Committee with instructions to report it back immediately with an amendment that would prohibit a conveyance under the bill's provisions if the qualifying entity to which the facility would be conveyed had employed the secretary or deputy secretary of the Interior Department as federally registered lobbyist in the last three years. Motion rejected 187-230: R 1-229; D 186-1. July 12, 2018.

325. HR3281. WATER INFRASTRUCTURE PROJECTS/PASSAGE. Passage of the bill that would permit the Bureau of Reclamation to transfer ownership of certain federal water infrastructure facilities to certain nonfederal entities without the need for Congress to enact project-specific legislation, provided that the entity to which ownership would be transferred has a water service contract with BOR. The bill would require that, for a transfer to take place, the agency must notify Congress in writing of the proposed conveyance and the reason for the conveyance at least 90 days before it would occur, and Congress must not pass a joint resolution disapproving the conveyance before that date. The bill would require BOR to establish criteria for determining which facilities are eligible for such title transfers, including that a proposed transfer would not have an "unmitigated significant effect on the environment," and that the receiving entity would need to intend to use the property for substantially the same purposes as it had been used for prior to the transfer. The bill would also prohibit any conveyance that would adversely impact power rates or repayment obligations. Passed 233-184: R 224-6; D 9-178. July 12, 2018.

	320	321	322	323	324	325
ALABAMA						
1 **Byrne**	N	Y	Y	Y	N	Y
2 **Roby**	N	Y	Y	Y	N	Y
3 **Rogers**	N	Y	Y	Y	N	Y
4 **Aderholt**	N	Y	Y	Y	N	Y
5 **Brooks**	N	Y	Y	Y	N	Y
6 **Palmer**	N	Y	Y	Y	N	Y
7 Sewell	Y	N	N	N	Y	N
ALASKA						
AL **Young**	N	Y	Y	Y	N	Y
ARIZONA						
1 O'Halleran	Y	N	N	Y	Y	N
2 **McSally**	N	Y	Y	Y	N	Y
3 Grijalva	Y	N	N	N	Y	N
4 **Gosar**	N	Y	Y	Y	N	Y
5 **Biggs**	N	Y	Y	Y	N	Y
6 **Schweikert**	N	Y	Y	Y	N	Y
7 Gallego	Y	N	N	N	Y	N
8 **Lesko**	N	Y	Y	Y	N	Y
9 Sinema	Y	N	N	Y	Y	N
ARKANSAS						
1 **Crawford**	N	Y	Y	Y	N	Y
2 **Hill**	N	Y	Y	Y	N	Y
3 **Womack**	N	Y	Y	Y	N	Y
4 **Westerman**	N	Y	Y	Y	N	Y
CALIFORNIA						
1 **LaMalfa**	N	Y	Y	Y	N	Y
2 Huffman	Y	N	N	N	Y	N
3 Garamendi	Y	N	N	N	Y	Y
4 **McClintock**	N	Y	Y	Y	N	Y
5 Thompson	Y	N	N	N	Y	N
6 Matsui	Y	N	N	N	Y	N
7 Bera	Y	N	N	N	Y	N
8 **Cook**	N	Y	Y	Y	N	Y
9 McNerney	Y	N	N	?	Y	N
10 **Denham**	N	Y	Y	Y	N	Y
11 DeSaulnier	Y	N	N	N	Y	N
12 Pelosi	Y	N	?	?	Y	N
13 Lee	Y	N	N	N	Y	N
14 Speier	?	?	?	?	?	?
15 Swalwell	Y	N	N	N	Y	N
16 Costa	N	N	N	Y	N	Y
17 Khanna	Y	N	N	N	Y	N
18 Eshoo	Y	N	N	N	Y	N
19 Lofgren	Y	N	N	N	Y	N
20 Panetta	Y	N	N	N	Y	N
21 **Valadao**	N	Y	Y	Y	N	Y
22 **Nunes**	N	Y	Y	Y	N	Y
23 **McCarthy**	N	Y	Y	Y	N	Y
24 Carbajal	Y	N	N	N	Y	N
25 **Knight**	N	Y	Y	Y	N	Y
26 Brownley	Y	N	N	N	Y	N
27 Chu	Y	N	N	N	Y	N
28 Schiff	Y	N	N	N	Y	N
29 Cardenas	Y	N	N	N	Y	N
30 Sherman	Y	N	N	N	Y	N
31 Aguilar	Y	N	N	N	Y	N
32 Napolitano	+	–	N	N	Y	N
33 Lieu	Y	N	N	N	Y	N
34 Gomez	Y	N	?	N	Y	N
35 Torres	Y	N	N	N	Y	N
36 Ruiz	Y	N	N	N	Y	N
37 Bass	Y	N	N	N	Y	N
38 Sánchez, Linda	Y	N	N	N	Y	N
39 **Royce**	N	Y	Y	Y	N	Y
40 Roybal-Allard	Y	N	N	N	Y	N
41 Takano	Y	N	N	N	Y	N
42 **Calvert**	N	Y	Y	Y	N	Y
43 Waters	Y	N	N	N	Y	N
44 Barragan	Y	N	N	N	Y	N
45 **Walters**	N	Y	Y	Y	N	Y
46 Correa	Y	N	N	N	Y	N
47 Lowenthal	Y	N	N	N	Y	N
48 **Rohrabacher**	N	Y	Y	Y	N	Y
49 **Issa**	N	Y	Y	?	Y	?
50 **Hunter**	N	Y	Y	Y	N	Y
51 Vargas	Y	N	N	N	Y	N
52 Peters	Y	N	N	N	Y	N
53 Davis	Y	N	N	N	Y	N
COLORADO						
1 DeGette	Y	N	N	N	Y	N
2 Polis	Y	N	N	N	Y	N
3 **Tipton**	N	Y	Y	Y	N	Y
4 **Buck**	N	Y	Y	Y	N	Y
5 **Lamborn**	N	Y	Y	Y	N	Y
6 **Coffman**	N	Y	Y	Y	N	Y
7 Perlmutter	?	–	?	?	?	–
CONNECTICUT						
1 Larson	Y	N	N	N	Y	N
2 Courtney	Y	Y	N	N	Y	N
3 DeLauro	Y	N	N	N	Y	N
4 Himes	Y	N	N	N	Y	N
5 Esty	Y	N	N	N	Y	N
DELAWARE						
AL Blunt Rochester	Y	N	N	N	Y	N
FLORIDA						
1 **Gaetz**	N	Y	Y	Y	N	Y
2 **Dunn**	N	Y	Y	Y	N	Y
3 **Yoho**	N	Y	Y	Y	N	Y
4 **Rutherford**	N	Y	Y	Y	N	Y
5 Lawson	Y	N	N	N	Y	N
6 **DeSantis**	N	Y	Y	Y	N	Y
7 Murphy	Y	N	N	N	Y	N
8 **Posey**	N	Y	Y	Y	N	Y
9 Soto	Y	N	N	N	Y	N
10 Demings	Y	N	N	N	Y	N
11 **Webster**	N	Y	Y	Y	N	Y
12 **Bilirakis**	N	Y	Y	Y	N	Y
13 Crist	Y	N	N	N	Y	N
14 Castor	Y	N	N	N	Y	N
15 **Ross**	N	Y	Y	Y	N	Y
16 **Buchanan**	N	N	Y	Y	N	Y
17 **Rooney, T.**	N	Y	Y	Y	N	Y
18 **Mast**	N	Y	Y	Y	N	Y
19 **Rooney, F.**	N	Y	Y	Y	N	Y
20 Hastings	Y	N	N	N	Y	N
21 Frankel	Y	N	?	?	Y	N
22 Deutch	Y	N	N	N	Y	N
23 Wasserman Schultz	Y	N	N	N	Y	N
24 Wilson	Y	N	N	N	Y	N
25 **Diaz-Balart**	N	Y	Y	Y	N	Y
26 **Curbelo**	N	Y	Y	Y	N	Y
27 **Ros-Lehtinen**	N	Y	Y	Y	N	Y
GEORGIA						
1 **Carter**	N	Y	Y	Y	N	Y
2 Bishop	Y	N	?	?	Y	Y
3 **Ferguson**	N	Y	Y	Y	N	Y
4 Johnson	Y	N	N	N	Y	N
5 Lewis	Y	N	N	N	Y	N
6 **Handel**	N	Y	Y	Y	N	Y
7 **Woodall**	N	Y	Y	Y	N	Y
8 **Scott, A.**	N	Y	Y	Y	N	Y
9 **Collins**	N	Y	Y	Y	N	Y
10 **Hice**	N	Y	Y	Y	N	Y
11 **Loudermilk**	N	Y	Y	Y	N	Y
12 **Allen**	N	Y	Y	Y	N	Y
13 Scott, D.	Y	N	N	N	Y	N
14 **Graves**	N	Y	Y	Y	N	Y
HAWAII						
1 Hanabusa	?	?	?	?	?	?
2 Gabbard	Y	N	N	N	Y	N
IDAHO						
1 **Labrador**	N	Y	Y	Y	N	Y
2 **Simpson**	N	Y	Y	Y	N	Y
ILLINOIS						
1 Rush	?	?	N	N	Y	N
2 Kelly	Y	N	N	N	Y	N
3 Lipinski	Y	N	N	N	Y	N
4 Gutierrez	Y	N	N	N	Y	N
5 Quigley	Y	N	N	N	Y	N
6 **Roskam**	N	Y	Y	Y	N	Y
7 Davis, D.	Y	N	N	N	Y	N
8 Krishnamoorthi	Y	N	N	N	Y	N
9 Schakowsky	Y	N	N	N	Y	N
10 Schneider	Y	N	N	N	Y	N
11 Foster	Y	N	N	N	Y	N
12 **Bost**	N	Y	Y	Y	N	Y
13 **Davis, R.**	N	Y	Y	Y	N	Y

KEY	Republicans	Democrats	Independents
Y Voted for (yea)		X Paired against	C Voted "present" to avoid possible conflict of interest
# Paired for		– Announced against	
+ Announced for		P Voted "present"	? Did not vote or otherwise make a position known
N Voted against (nay)			

	320	321	322	323	324	325
14 **Hultgren**	N	Y	Y	Y	N	Y
15 **Shimkus**	N	Y	Y	Y	N	Y
16 **Kinzinger**	N	Y	Y	Y	N	Y
17 Bustos	Y	N	N	N	Y	N
18 **LaHood**	N	Y	Y	Y	N	Y
INDIANA						
1 Visclosky	Y	N	N	N	Y	N
2 **Walorski**	N	Y	Y	Y	N	Y
3 **Banks**	N	Y	Y	Y	N	Y
4 Rokita	N	Y	Y	Y	N	Y
5 **Brooks**	N	Y	Y	Y	N	Y
6 **Messer**	N	Y	Y	Y	N	Y
7 Carson	Y	N	N	N	Y	N
8 **Bucshon**	N	Y	Y	Y	N	Y
9 **Hollingsworth**	N	Y	Y	Y	N	Y
IOWA						
1 **Blum**	–	+	Y	Y	N	Y
2 Loebsack	Y	N	N	N	Y	N
3 **Young**	N	Y	Y	Y	N	Y
4 **King**	N	Y	Y	Y	N	Y
KANSAS						
1 **Marshall**	N	Y	Y	Y	N	Y
2 **Jenkins**	–	+	Y	Y	N	Y
3 **Yoder**	N	Y	Y	Y	N	Y
4 **Estes**	N	Y	Y	Y	N	Y
KENTUCKY						
1 **Comer**	N	Y	Y	Y	N	Y
2 **Guthrie**	N	Y	Y	Y	N	Y
3 Yarmuth	Y	N	N	N	Y	N
4 **Massie**	N	Y	Y	Y	N	N
5 **Rogers**	N	Y	Y	Y	N	Y
6 **Barr**	N	Y	Y	Y	N	Y
LOUISIANA						
1 **Scalise**	–	+	Y	Y	N	Y
2 Richmond	Y	N	?	N	Y	N
3 **Higgins**	N	Y	Y	Y	N	Y
4 **Johnson**	N	Y	Y	Y	N	Y
5 **Abraham**	N	Y	Y	Y	N	Y
6 **Graves**	N	Y	Y	Y	N	Y
MAINE						
1 Pingree	Y	N	N	N	Y	N
2 **Poliquin**	N	Y	Y	Y	N	Y
MARYLAND						
1 **Harris**	N	Y	Y	Y	N	Y
2 Ruppersberger	Y	N	N	N	Y	N
3 Sarbanes	Y	N	N	N	Y	N
4 Brown	Y	N	N	N	Y	N
5 Hoyer	Y	N	N	N	Y	N
6 Delaney	Y	N	N	N	Y	N
7 Cummings	Y	N	N	N	Y	N
8 Raskin	Y	N	N	N	Y	N
MASSACHUSETTS						
1 Neal	Y	N	N	N	Y	N
2 McGovern	Y	N	N	N	Y	N
3 Tsongas	Y	N	N	N	Y	N
4 Kennedy	Y	N	N	N	Y	N
5 Clark	Y	N	N	N	Y	N
6 Moulton	Y	N	–	–	+	–
7 Capuano	Y	N	N	N	Y	N
8 Lynch	Y	Y	N	N	Y	N
9 Keating	Y	N	N	N	Y	N
MICHIGAN						
1 **Bergman**	N	Y	Y	Y	N	Y
2 **Huizenga**	N	Y	Y	Y	N	Y
3 *Amash*	N	Y	Y	Y	N	N
4 **Moolenaar**	N	Y	Y	Y	N	Y
5 Kildee	Y	N	N	N	Y	N
6 **Upton**	N	Y	Y	Y	N	Y
7 **Walberg**	N	Y	Y	Y	N	Y
8 **Bishop**	N	Y	Y	Y	N	Y
9 Levin	Y	N	N	N	Y	N
10 **Mitchell**	N	Y	Y	Y	N	Y
11 **Trott**	N	Y	Y	Y	N	Y
12 Dingell	Y	N	N	N	Y	N
14 Lawrence	Y	N	N	N	Y	N
MINNESOTA						
1 Walz	Y	N	N	N	?	?
2 **Lewis**	N	Y	Y	Y	N	Y
3 **Paulsen**	N	N	Y	Y	N	Y
4 McCollum	Y	N	N	N	Y	N

	320	321	322	323	324	325
5 Ellison	?	?	?	?	?	?
6 **Emmer**	N	Y	Y	Y	N	Y
7 Peterson	Y	Y	N	N	Y	Y
8 Nolan	Y	N	N	N	Y	N
MISSISSIPPI						
1 **Kelly**	N	Y	Y	Y	N	Y
2 Thompson	Y	N	N	N	Y	N
3 **Harper**	?	?	?	?	?	?
4 **Palazzo**	N	Y	Y	Y	N	Y
MISSOURI						
1 Clay	Y	N	N	N	Y	N
2 **Wagner**	N	Y	Y	Y	N	Y
3 **Luetkemeyer**	N	Y	Y	Y	N	Y
4 **Hartzler**	N	Y	Y	Y	N	Y
5 Cleaver	Y	N	N	N	Y	N
6 **Graves**	N	Y	Y	Y	N	Y
7 **Long**	N	Y	Y	Y	N	Y
8 **Smith**	N	Y	Y	Y	N	Y
MONTANA						
AL **Gianforte**	N	Y	Y	Y	N	Y
NEBRASKA						
1 **Fortenberry**	N	Y	Y	Y	N	Y
2 **Bacon**	N	Y	Y	Y	N	Y
3 **Smith**	N	Y	Y	Y	N	Y
NEVADA						
1 Titus	Y	N	N	N	Y	N
2 **Amodei**	N	Y	Y	Y	N	Y
3 Rosen	Y	N	N	N	Y	N
4 Kihuen	Y	N	N	N	Y	N
NEW HAMPSHIRE						
1 Shea-Porter	Y	N	N	N	Y	N
2 Kuster	Y	N	N	N	Y	N
NEW JERSEY						
1 Norcross	Y	N	N	N	Y	Y
2 **LoBiondo**	N	Y	?	?	N	Y
3 **MacArthur**	N	Y	Y	Y	N	Y
4 **Smith**	N	Y	Y	Y	N	Y
5 Gottheimer	Y	N	N	Y	Y	Y
6 Pallone	Y	N	N	N	Y	N
7 **Lance**	N	N	Y	Y	N	Y
8 Sires	Y	N	N	N	Y	N
9 Pascrell	Y	N	N	N	Y	N
10 Payne	Y	N	N	N	Y	N
11 **Frelinghuysen**	N	Y	Y	Y	N	Y
12 Watson Coleman	Y	N	N	N	Y	N
NEW MEXICO						
1 Lujan Grisham	Y	N	N	N	Y	N
2 **Pearce**	N	Y	Y	Y	N	Y
3 Luján	Y	N	N	N	Y	N
NEW YORK						
1 **Zeldin**	N	Y	Y	Y	N	Y
2 **King**	N	Y	Y	Y	N	Y
3 Suozzi	Y	N	N	Y	Y	N
4 Rice	Y	N	N	N	Y	N
5 Meeks	Y	N	N	N	Y	N
6 Meng	Y	N	N	N	Y	N
7 Velázquez	Y	N	N	N	Y	N
8 Jeffries	Y	N	N	N	Y	N
9 Clarke	Y	N	N	N	Y	N
10 Nadler	Y	N	N	N	Y	N
11 **Donovan**	N	Y	Y	Y	N	Y
12 Maloney, C.	Y	N	N	N	Y	N
13 Espaillat	Y	N	N	N	Y	N
14 Crowley	Y	N	N	N	Y	N
15 Serrano	Y	N	N	N	Y	N
16 Engel	Y	N	N	N	Y	N
17 Lowey	Y	N	N	N	Y	N
18 Maloney, S.P.	Y	N	N	N	Y	N
19 **Faso**	N	Y	Y	Y	N	Y
20 Tonko	Y	N	N	N	Y	N
21 **Stefanik**	N	Y	Y	Y	N	Y
22 **Tenney**	N	Y	Y	Y	N	Y
23 **Reed**	N	Y	Y	Y	N	Y
24 **Katko**	N	Y	Y	Y	N	Y
25 **Vacant**						
26 Higgins	Y	Y	N	N	Y	N
27 **Collins**	N	Y	Y	Y	N	Y
NORTH CAROLINA						
1 Butterfield	Y	N	N	N	Y	N
2 **Holding**	N	Y	Y	Y	N	Y
3 **Jones**	Y	Y	Y	N	Y	N
4 Price	Y	N	N	N	Y	N

	320	321	322	323	324	325
5 **Foxx**	N	Y	Y	Y	N	Y
6 **Walker**	N	Y	Y	Y	N	Y
7 **Rouzer**	N	Y	Y	Y	N	Y
8 **Hudson**	N	Y	Y	Y	N	Y
9 **Pittenger**	N	Y	Y	Y	N	Y
9 **Vacant**						
10 **McHenry**	N	Y	Y	Y	N	Y
11 **Meadows**	N	Y	Y	Y	N	Y
12 Adams	Y	N	N	N	Y	N
13 **Budd**	N	Y	Y	Y	N	Y
NORTH DAKOTA						
AL **Cramer**	N	Y	Y	Y	N	Y
OHIO						
1 **Chabot**	N	Y	Y	Y	N	Y
2 **Wenstrup**	N	Y	Y	Y	N	Y
3 Beatty	Y	N	N	N	Y	N
4 **Jordan**	N	Y	Y	Y	N	Y
5 **Latta**	N	Y	Y	Y	N	Y
6 **Johnson**	N	Y	Y	Y	N	Y
7 **Gibbs**	N	Y	Y	Y	N	Y
8 **Davidson**	N	Y	Y	Y	N	Y
9 Kaptur	Y	N	N	N	Y	N
10 **Turner**	N	Y	Y	Y	N	Y
11 Fudge	Y	N	N	N	Y	N
12 **Vacant**						
13 Ryan	Y	N	N	N	Y	N
14 **Joyce**	N	Y	Y	Y	N	Y
15 **Stivers**	N	Y	Y	Y	N	Y
16 **Renacci**	N	Y	Y	Y	N	Y
OKLAHOMA						
1 **Vacant**						
2 **Mullin**	N	Y	Y	Y	N	Y
3 **Lucas**	N	Y	Y	Y	N	Y
4 **Cole**	N	Y	Y	Y	N	Y
5 **Russell**	N	Y	Y	Y	N	N
OREGON						
1 Bonamici	Y	N	N	N	Y	N
2 **Walden**	N	Y	Y	Y	N	Y
3 Blumenauer	Y	N	N	N	Y	N
4 DeFazio	Y	N	N	N	Y	N
5 Schrader	Y	N	N	N	Y	Y
PENNSYLVANIA						
1 Brady	Y	N	N	N	Y	N
2 Evans	Y	N	N	N	Y	N
3 **Kelly**	N	Y	Y	Y	N	Y
4 **Perry**	N	Y	Y	Y	N	Y
5 **Thompson**	N	Y	Y	Y	N	Y
6 **Costello**	N	N	Y	Y	N	Y
7 **Vacant**						
8 **Fitzpatrick**	N	N	Y	Y	N	N
9 **Shuster**	N	Y	Y	Y	N	Y
10 **Marino**	N	Y	Y	Y	N	Y
11 **Barletta**	N	Y	Y	Y	N	Y
12 **Rothfus**	N	Y	Y	Y	N	Y
13 Boyle	Y	N	N	N	Y	N
14 Doyle	Y	N	N	N	Y	N
15 **Vacant**						
16 **Smucker**	N	Y	Y	Y	N	Y
17 Cartwright	Y	N	N	N	Y	N
18 Lamb	Y	N	N	Y	Y	N
RHODE ISLAND						
1 Cicilline	Y	N	N	N	Y	N
2 Langevin	Y	N	N	N	Y	N
SOUTH CAROLINA						
1 **Sanford**	N	N	?	?	N	N
2 **Wilson**	N	Y	Y	Y	N	Y
3 **Duncan**	N	Y	Y	Y	N	Y
4 **Gowdy**	N	Y	Y	Y	N	Y
5 **Norman**	N	Y	Y	Y	N	Y
6 Clyburn	Y	N	N	N	Y	N
7 **Rice**	N	Y	Y	Y	N	Y
SOUTH DAKOTA						
AL **Noem**	N	Y	Y	Y	N	Y
TENNESSEE						
1 **Roe**	N	Y	Y	Y	N	Y
2 **Duncan**	N	Y	Y	Y	N	Y
3 **Fleischmann**	N	Y	Y	Y	N	Y
4 **DesJarlais**	N	Y	Y	Y	N	Y
5 Cooper	Y	N	N	N	Y	N
6 **Black**	N	Y	?	?	?	?
7 **Blackburn**	?	?	Y	Y	N	Y
8 **Kustoff**	N	Y	?	?	?	?
9 Cohen	Y	N	N	N	Y	N

	320	321	322	323	324	325
TEXAS						
1 **Gohmert**	N	Y	Y	Y	N	Y
2 **Poe**	N	Y	Y	Y	N	Y
3 **Johnson, S.**	N	Y	Y	Y	N	Y
4 **Ratcliffe**	N	Y	Y	Y	N	Y
5 **Hensarling**	N	Y	Y	Y	N	Y
6 **Barton**	N	Y	Y	Y	N	Y
7 **Culberson**	N	N	Y	Y	N	Y
8 **Brady**	N	Y	Y	Y	N	Y
9 Green, A.	Y	N	N	N	Y	N
10 **McCaul**	N	Y	Y	Y	N	Y
11 **Conaway**	N	Y	Y	Y	N	Y
12 **Granger**	N	N	Y	Y	N	Y
13 **Thornberry**	N	Y	Y	Y	N	Y
14 **Weber**	N	N	Y	Y	N	Y
15 Gonzalez	Y	Y	N	N	Y	N
16 O'Rourke	Y	N	N	N	Y	N
17 **Flores**	N	Y	Y	Y	N	Y
18 Jackson Lee	Y	N	N	N	Y	N
19 **Arrington**	N	Y	Y	Y	N	Y
20 Castro	Y	N	N	N	Y	N
21 **Smith**	N	Y	Y	Y	N	Y
22 **Olson**	N	Y	Y	Y	N	Y
23 **Hurd**	N	Y	Y	Y	N	Y
24 Marchant	N	Y	Y	Y	N	Y
25 **Williams**	N	Y	Y	Y	N	Y
26 **Burgess**	N	Y	Y	Y	N	Y
27 Cloud	N	Y	Y	Y	N	Y
28 Cuellar	Y	Y	N	N	Y	Y
29 Green, G.	Y	Y	N	N	Y	N
30 Johnson, E.B.	Y	N	N	N	Y	N
31 **Carter**	N	N	Y	Y	N	Y
32 **Sessions**	N	Y	Y	Y	N	Y
33 Veasey	Y	Y	?	N	Y	N
34 Vela	Y	N	N	N	Y	Y
35 Doggett	Y	N	N	N	Y	N
36 **Babin**	N	Y	Y	Y	N	Y
UTAH						
1 **Bishop**	N	Y	Y	Y	N	Y
2 **Stewart**	N	Y	Y	Y	N	Y
3 **Curtis**	N	Y	Y	Y	N	Y
4 **Love**	N	Y	Y	Y	N	Y
VERMONT						
AL Welch	Y	N	N	N	Y	N
VIRGINIA						
1 **Wittman**	N	Y	Y	Y	N	Y
2 **Taylor**	N	Y	Y	Y	N	Y
3 Scott	Y	N	N	N	Y	N
4 McEachin	Y	N	N	N	Y	N
5 **Garrett**	N	Y	Y	Y	N	Y
6 **Goodlatte**	N	Y	Y	Y	N	Y
7 **Brat**	N	Y	Y	Y	N	Y
8 Beyer	Y	N	N	N	Y	N
9 **Griffith**	N	Y	Y	Y	N	Y
10 **Comstock**	N	Y	Y	Y	N	Y
11 Connolly	Y	N	N	N	Y	N
WASHINGTON						
1 DelBene	Y	N	N	N	Y	N
2 Larsen	Y	N	N	N	Y	N
3 **Herrera Beutler**	N	Y	Y	Y	N	Y
4 **Newhouse**	N	Y	Y	Y	N	Y
5 **McMorris Rodgers**	N	Y	Y	Y	N	Y
6 Kilmer	Y	N	N	N	Y	N
7 Jayapal	Y	N	N	N	Y	N
8 **Reichert**	N	Y	Y	Y	N	Y
9 Smith	Y	N	N	N	Y	N
10 Heck	Y	N	N	N	Y	N
WEST VIRGINIA						
1 **McKinley**	N	Y	Y	Y	N	Y
2 **Mooney**	N	Y	Y	Y	N	Y
3 **Jenkins**	N	Y	Y	Y	N	Y
WISCONSIN						
1 **Ryan**						
2 Pocan	Y	N	N	N	Y	N
3 Kind	Y	N	N	N	Y	N
4 Moore	Y	N	N	N	Y	N
5 **Sensenbrenner**	N	Y	Y	Y	N	Y
6 **Grothman**	N	Y	Y	Y	N	Y
7 **Duffy**	N	Y	Y	Y	N	Y
8 **Gallagher**	?	?	Y	Y	N	Y
WYOMING						
AL **Cheney**	?	?	?	?	?	?

VOTE NUMBER

326. HR6237. FISCAL 2018 AND 2019 INTELLIGENCE AUTHORIZATION/ PASSAGE. Passage of the bill that would authorize classified amounts in fiscal 2018 and fiscal 2019 for 16 U.S. intelligence agencies and intelligence-related activities of the U.S. government, which would cover general intelligence operations, clandestine human intelligence programs and analysis, and covert action programs. The bill would authorize $547 million in fiscal 2018 and $515 million in fiscal 2019 for the Intelligence Community Management account. The bill would require several reports on foreign malign influencers, including Russia, North Korea and Iran, and activities related to funding or carrying out a cyber or terrorist attack. The bill would also require the Director of National Intelligence to electronically publish an unclassified report on foreign counterintelligence and cybersecurity threats to U.S. election campaigns for federal offices. Passed 363-54: R 222-8; D 141-46. July 12, 2018.

327. HR50. UNFUNDED MANDATES/RECOMMIT. Beatty, D-Ohio, motion to recommit the bill to the House Oversight and Governmental Reform Committee with instructions to report it back immediately with an amendment that would exempt from the bill's provisions the actions and mandates of agencies tasked with protection of children against sex offenders, protection of domestic violence victims, protection against rape and sexual assault, and those that assist in background checks for school employees. Motion rejected 180-219: R 1-219; D 179-0. July 13, 2018.

328. HR50. UNFUNDED MANDATES/PASSAGE. Passage of the bill that would require independent agencies to conduct analyses of their proposed rules and the effect thereof on the private sector and on state and local governments. The bill would require that independent federal regulatory agencies, except for the Federal Reserve, conduct unfunded mandate analyses of their proposed rules and would require all agencies that conduct unfunded mandate reviews, including both independent and non-independent federal agencies, to consult with private-sector stakeholders on the potential impact of regulations being developed. The bill would also require federal agencies, if requested by a committee chairman or ranking member, to conduct retrospective unfunded mandate analyses of existing regulations. The bill would transfer authority for oversight of UMRA activities to the Office of Information and Regulatory Affairs within the Office of Management and Budget. Passed 230-168: R 220-0; D 10-168. July 13, 2018.

329. HR4946. SPECIALIST TREVOR A. WIN'E POST OFFICE/PASSAGE. Walker, R-N.C., motion to suspend the rules and pass the bill that would designate the postal facility located at 1075 North Tustin Street in Orange, Calif., as the "Specialist Trevor A. Win'E Post Office." Motion agreed to 368-0: R 211-0; D 157-0. July 16, 2018.

330. HR4960. SPC. STERLING WILLIAM WYATT POST OFFICE BUILDING/ PASSAGE. Walker, R-N.C., motion to suspend the rules and pass the bill that would designate the postal facility located at 511 East Walnut Street in Columbia, Mo., as the "Spc. Sterling William Wyatt Post Office Building." Motion agreed to 368-0: R 212-0; D 156-0. July 16, 2018.

331. HRES996. FISCAL 2019 INTERIOR-ENVIRONMENT AND FINANCIAL SERVICES APPROPRIATIONS PACKAGE/PREVIOUS QUESTION. Cole, R-Okla., motion to order the previous question (thus ending debate and possibility of amendment) on the rule (Res 966) that would provide for House floor consideration of the bill (HR 6147) that would make available $58.7 billion through fiscal 2019, with $35.3 billion for the Department of Interior, environment portion, and $23.4 billion for the Financial Services and related agencies portion. Motion agreed to 230-183: R 230-0; D 0-183. July 17, 2018.

	326	327	328	329	330	331
ALABAMA						
1 **Byrne**	Y	N	Y	Y	Y	Y
2 **Roby**	Y	N	Y	?	?	?
3 **Rogers**	Y	N	Y	Y	Y	Y
4 **Aderholt**	Y	N	Y	?	?	Y
5 **Brooks**	Y	N	Y	Y	Y	Y
6 **Palmer**	Y	N	Y	?	Y	Y
7 Sewell	Y	+	–	Y	Y	N
ALASKA						
AL **Young**	Y	N	Y	Y	Y	Y
ARIZONA						
1 O'Halleran	Y	Y	Y	Y	Y	N
2 **McSally**	Y	N	Y	Y	Y	Y
3 Grijalva	N	Y	N	?	?	N
4 **Gosar**	Y	N	Y	Y	Y	Y
5 **Biggs**	N	N	Y	Y	Y	Y
6 **Schweikert**	Y	N	Y	Y	Y	Y
7 Gallego	Y	Y	N	Y	Y	N
8 **Lesko**	Y	N	Y	Y	Y	Y
9 Sinema	Y	Y	Y	Y	Y	N
ARKANSAS						
1 **Crawford**	Y	N	Y	Y	Y	Y
2 **Hill**	Y	N	Y	Y	Y	+
3 **Womack**	Y	N	Y	Y	Y	Y
4 **Westerman**	Y	N	Y	Y	Y	Y
CALIFORNIA						
1 **LaMalfa**	Y	N	Y	Y	Y	Y
2 Huffman	N	Y	N	Y	Y	N
3 Garamendi	Y	Y	N	Y	Y	N
4 **McClintock**	Y	N	Y	Y	Y	Y
5 Thompson	Y	Y	N	Y	Y	N
6 Matsui	Y	Y	N	Y	Y	N
7 Bera	Y	Y	N	Y	Y	N
8 **Cook**	Y	N	Y	Y	Y	Y
9 McNerney	Y	Y	N	Y	Y	N
10 **Denham**	Y	N	Y	Y	Y	Y
11 DeSaulnier	N	Y	N	Y	Y	N
12 Pelosi	Y	Y	N	Y	Y	N
13 Lee	N	Y	N	Y	Y	N
14 Speier	?	?	?	?	?	?
15 Swalwell	Y	Y	N	Y	Y	N
16 Costa	Y	Y	Y	Y	Y	N
17 Khanna	N	Y	N	Y	Y	N
18 Eshoo	Y	Y	N	Y	Y	N
19 Lofgren	N	?	?	Y	Y	N
20 Panetta	Y	Y	N	Y	Y	N
21 **Valadao**	Y	N	Y	Y	Y	Y
22 **Nunes**	Y	N	Y	Y	Y	Y
23 **McCarthy**	Y	N	Y	Y	Y	Y
24 Carbajal	Y	Y	N	Y	Y	N
25 **Knight**	Y	N	Y	Y	Y	Y
26 Brownley	Y	Y	N	Y	Y	N
27 Chu	N	Y	N	Y	Y	N
28 Schiff	Y	Y	N	Y	Y	N
29 Cardenas	Y	Y	N	?	?	?
30 Sherman	Y	Y	N	Y	Y	N
31 Aguilar	Y	Y	N	Y	Y	N
32 Napolitano	N	Y	N	Y	Y	N
33 Lieu	N	Y	N	Y	Y	N
34 Gomez	N	Y	N	Y	Y	N
35 Torres	Y	Y	N	Y	Y	N
36 Ruiz	Y	Y	N	Y	Y	N
37 Bass	N	Y	N	Y	Y	N
38 Sánchez, Linda	Y	Y	N	Y	Y	N
39 **Royce**	Y	N	Y	Y	Y	Y
40 Roybal-Allard	Y	Y	N	Y	Y	N
41 Takano	N	Y	N	Y	Y	N
42 **Calvert**	Y	N	Y	Y	Y	Y
43 Waters	Y	?	?	Y	Y	N
44 Barragan	Y	Y	N	Y	Y	N
45 **Walters**	Y	N	Y	Y	Y	Y
46 Correa	Y	Y	Y	Y	Y	N
47 Lowenthal	N	Y	N	Y	Y	N
48 **Rohrabacher**	Y	N	Y	?	?	Y
49 **Issa**	?	?	?	Y	Y	Y
50 **Hunter**	Y	N	Y	Y	Y	Y
51 Vargas	Y	Y	N	Y	Y	N
52 Peters	Y	Y	N	Y	Y	N
53 Davis	Y	Y	N	Y	Y	N

	326	327	328	329	330	331
COLORADO						
1 DeGette	Y	Y	N	Y	Y	N
2 Polis	N	Y	N	Y	Y	N
3 Tipton	Y	N	Y	Y	Y	Y
4 **Buck**	N	N	Y	Y	Y	Y
5 **Lamborn**	Y	N	Y	Y	Y	Y
6 **Coffman**	Y	N	Y	Y	Y	Y
7 Perlmutter	+	?	–	Y	Y	N
CONNECTICUT						
1 Larson	Y	Y	N	Y	Y	N
2 Courtney	Y	Y	N	Y	Y	N
3 DeLauro	Y	Y	N	Y	Y	N
4 Himes	Y	Y	N	Y	Y	N
5 Esty	Y	Y	N	Y	Y	N
DELAWARE						
AL Blunt Rochester	Y	Y	N	Y	Y	N
FLORIDA						
1 **Gaetz**	Y	N	Y	Y	Y	Y
2 **Dunn**	Y	N	Y	Y	Y	Y
3 **Yoho**	Y	N	Y	Y	Y	Y
4 **Rutherford**	Y	N	Y	Y	Y	Y
5 Lawson	Y	Y	N	Y	Y	N
6 **DeSantis**	Y	N	Y	?	?	Y
7 Murphy	Y	Y	Y	Y	Y	N
8 **Posey**	Y	N	Y	Y	Y	Y
9 Soto	Y	Y	N	Y	Y	N
10 Demings	Y	Y	N	Y	Y	N
11 **Webster**	Y	N	Y	Y	Y	Y
12 **Bilirakis**	Y	N	Y	Y	Y	Y
13 Crist	Y	Y	N	Y	Y	N
14 Castor	Y	Y	N	Y	Y	N
15 **Ross**	Y	N	Y	Y	Y	Y
16 **Buchanan**	Y	N	Y	Y	Y	Y
17 **Rooney, T.**	Y	?	?	?	?	Y
18 **Mast**	Y	N	Y	Y	Y	Y
19 **Rooney, F.**	Y	N	Y	Y	Y	Y
20 Hastings	Y	Y	N	Y	Y	N
21 Frankel	Y	Y	N	Y	Y	N
22 Deutch	Y	Y	N	Y	Y	N
23 Wasserman Schultz	Y	Y	N	?	?	N
24 Wilson	Y	Y	N	Y	Y	N
25 **Diaz-Balart**	Y	N	Y	Y	Y	Y
26 **Curbelo**	Y	N	Y	Y	Y	Y
27 **Ros-Lehtinen**	Y	N	Y	Y	Y	Y
GEORGIA						
1 **Carter**	Y	N	Y	Y	Y	Y
2 Bishop	Y	Y	N	?	?	N
3 **Ferguson**	Y	N	Y	Y	Y	Y
4 Johnson	Y	Y	N	Y	Y	N
5 Lewis	N	Y	N	Y	Y	N
6 **Handel**	Y	N	Y	Y	Y	Y
7 **Woodall**	Y	N	Y	Y	Y	Y
8 **Scott, A.**	Y	N	Y	Y	Y	Y
9 **Collins**	Y	N	Y	Y	Y	Y
10 **Hice**	Y	N	Y	Y	Y	Y
11 **Loudermilk**	Y	N	Y	Y	Y	Y
12 **Allen**	Y	N	Y	Y	Y	Y
13 Scott, D.	Y	Y	N	Y	Y	N
14 **Graves**	Y	N	Y	Y	Y	Y
HAWAII						
1 Hanabusa	?	?	?	?	?	?
2 Gabbard	N	Y	N	Y	Y	N
IDAHO						
1 **Labrador**	N	N	Y	Y	Y	Y
2 **Simpson**	Y	–	+	?	?	+
ILLINOIS						
1 Rush	N	Y	N	?	?	N
2 Kelly	Y	Y	N	?	?	N
3 Lipinski	Y	Y	N	?	?	N
4 Gutierrez	N	Y	N	+	+	–
5 Quigley	Y	Y	N	Y	Y	N
6 **Roskam**	Y	N	Y	Y	Y	Y
7 Davis, D.	N	Y	N	?	?	N
8 Krishnamoorthi	Y	Y	N	Y	Y	N
9 Schakowsky	N	Y	N	Y	Y	N
10 Schneider	Y	Y	N	Y	Y	N
11 Foster	Y	Y	N	Y	Y	N
12 **Bost**	Y	N	Y	Y	Y	Y
13 **Davis, R.**	Y	N	Y	Y	Y	Y

	326	327	328	329	330	331
14 **Hultgren**	Y	N	Y	Y	Y	Y
15 **Shimkus**	Y	N	Y	Y	Y	Y
16 **Kinzinger**	Y	–	+	+	+	Y
17 Bustos	Y	Y	N	Y	Y	N
18 **LaHood**	Y	N	Y	Y	Y	Y
INDIANA						
1 Visclosky	Y	Y	N	+	+	N
2 **Walorski**	Y	N	Y	Y	Y	Y
3 **Banks**	Y	N	Y	Y	Y	Y
4 Rokita	Y	N	Y	Y	Y	Y
5 **Brooks**	Y	N	Y	Y	Y	Y
6 **Messer**	Y	N	Y	Y	Y	Y
7 Carson	N	Y	N	Y	Y	N
8 **Bucshon**	Y	N	Y	Y	Y	Y
9 **Hollingsworth**	Y	N	Y	Y	Y	Y
IOWA						
1 **Blum**	Y	Y	Y	Y	Y	Y
2 Loebsack	N	Y	N	?	?	N
3 **Young**	Y	N	Y	Y	Y	Y
4 **King**	Y	N	Y	Y	Y	Y
KANSAS						
1 **Marshall**	Y	N	Y	Y	Y	Y
2 **Jenkins**	Y	N	Y	Y	?	Y
3 **Yoder**	Y	N	Y	Y	Y	Y
4 **Estes**	Y	N	Y	Y	Y	Y
KENTUCKY						
1 **Comer**	Y	N	Y	Y	Y	Y
2 **Guthrie**	Y	N	Y	Y	Y	Y
3 Yarmuth	Y	Y	N	?	?	N
4 **Massie**	N	N	Y	?	?	Y
5 **Rogers**	Y	N	Y	Y	Y	Y
6 **Barr**	Y	N	Y	Y	Y	Y
LOUISIANA						
1 **Scalise**	Y	N	Y	Y	Y	Y
2 Richmond	Y	Y	N	?	?	N
3 **Higgins**	Y	N	Y	Y	Y	Y
4 **Johnson**	Y	N	Y	Y	Y	Y
5 **Abraham**	Y	N	Y	Y	Y	Y
6 **Graves**	Y	N	Y	Y	Y	Y
MAINE						
1 Pingree	Y	Y	N	?	?	N
2 **Poliquin**	Y	N	Y	Y	Y	Y
MARYLAND						
1 **Harris**	Y	N	Y	Y	Y	Y
2 Ruppersberger	Y	Y	N	Y	Y	N
3 Sarbanes	Y	Y	N	Y	Y	N
4 Brown	Y	Y	N	Y	Y	N
5 Hoyer	Y	?	?	Y	Y	N
6 Delaney	Y	Y	N	Y	Y	N
7 Cummings	Y	Y	N	Y	Y	N
8 Raskin	N	Y	N	Y	Y	N
MASSACHUSETTS						
1 Neal	Y	Y	N	?	?	N
2 McGovern	N	Y	N	Y	Y	N
3 Tsongas	Y	Y	N	?	?	N
4 Kennedy	Y	Y	N	Y	Y	N
5 Clark	N	Y	N	Y	Y	N
6 Moulton	+	?	?	Y	Y	N
7 Capuano	N	Y	N	Y	Y	N
8 Lynch	Y	Y	N	Y	Y	N
9 Keating	Y	Y	N	Y	Y	N
MICHIGAN						
1 **Bergman**	Y	N	Y	Y	Y	Y
2 **Huizenga**	Y	N	+	+	+	Y
3 *Amash*	N	N	Y	Y	Y	Y
4 **Moolenaar**	Y	N	Y	Y	Y	Y
5 Kildee	Y	Y	N	Y	Y	N
6 **Upton**	Y	N	Y	Y	Y	Y
7 **Walberg**	Y	N	Y	Y	Y	Y
8 **Bishop**	Y	N	Y	Y	Y	Y
9 Levin	Y	Y	N	Y	Y	N
10 **Mitchell**	Y	N	Y	Y	Y	Y
11 **Trott**	Y	N	Y	?	?	Y
12 Dingell	Y	Y	N	Y	Y	N
14 Lawrence	Y	Y	N	?	?	N
MINNESOTA						
1 Walz	?	?	?	?	?	?
2 **Lewis**	Y	N	Y	Y	Y	Y
3 **Paulsen**	Y	N	Y	Y	Y	Y
4 McCollum	N	Y	N	Y	Y	N

	326	327	328	329	330	331
5 Ellison	?	?	?	?	?	?
6 **Emmer**	Y	N	Y	Y	Y	Y
7 Peterson	Y	Y	Y	Y	Y	N
8 Nolan	Y	Y	?	Y	Y	N
MISSISSIPPI						
1 **Kelly**	Y	N	Y	Y	Y	Y
2 Thompson	Y	?	?	Y	Y	N
3 **Harper**	?	?	?	Y	Y	Y
4 **Palazzo**	Y	N	Y	Y	Y	Y
MISSOURI						
1 Clay	Y	Y	N	Y	Y	N
2 **Wagner**	Y	N	Y	Y	Y	Y
3 **Luetkemeyer**	Y	N	Y	?	?	?
4 **Hartzler**	Y	N	Y	Y	Y	Y
5 Cleaver	Y	Y	N	+	+	N
6 **Graves**	Y	N	Y	Y	Y	Y
7 **Long**	Y	N	Y	Y	Y	Y
8 **Smith**	Y	N	Y	Y	Y	Y
MONTANA						
AL **Gianforte**	Y	N	Y	Y	Y	Y
NEBRASKA						
1 **Fortenberry**	Y	N	Y	Y	Y	Y
2 **Bacon**	Y	N	Y	Y	Y	Y
3 **Smith**	Y	N	Y	Y	Y	Y
NEVADA						
1 Titus	Y	Y	N	Y	Y	N
2 **Amodei**	Y	N	Y	Y	Y	Y
3 Rosen	Y	Y	N	Y	Y	N
4 Kihuen	Y	Y	N	Y	Y	N
NEW HAMPSHIRE						
1 Shea-Porter	Y	Y	N	?	?	?
2 Kuster	Y	Y	N	Y	Y	N
NEW JERSEY						
1 Norcross	Y	Y	N	Y	Y	N
2 **LoBiondo**	Y	N	Y	Y	Y	Y
3 **MacArthur**	Y	N	Y	Y	Y	Y
4 **Smith**	Y	N	Y	Y	Y	Y
5 Gottheimer	Y	Y	Y	Y	Y	N
6 Pallone	Y	Y	N	Y	Y	N
7 **Lance**	Y	N	Y	Y	Y	Y
8 Sires	Y	Y	N	Y	Y	N
9 Pascrell	Y	Y	N	Y	Y	N
10 Payne	Y	Y	N	Y	Y	N
11 **Frelinghuysen**	Y	N	Y	Y	Y	Y
12 Watson Coleman	N	Y	N	Y	Y	N
NEW MEXICO						
1 Lujan Grisham	Y	Y	N	+	+	?
2 **Pearce**	Y	N	Y	Y	Y	Y
3 Luján	Y	Y	N	Y	Y	N
NEW YORK						
1 **Zeldin**	Y	N	Y	Y	Y	Y
2 **King**	Y	N	Y	Y	Y	Y
3 Suozzi	Y	Y	Y	Y	Y	N
4 Rice	Y	Y	N	?	?	N
5 Meeks	Y	Y	N	?	?	N
6 Meng	Y	Y	N	Y	Y	N
7 Velázquez	N	Y	N	Y	Y	N
8 Jeffries	N	Y	N	Y	Y	N
9 Clarke	N	Y	N	Y	Y	N
10 Nadler	Y	Y	N	Y	Y	N
11 **Donovan**	Y	N	Y	Y	Y	Y
12 Maloney, C.	Y	Y	N	Y	Y	N
13 Espaillat	N	Y	N	Y	Y	N
14 Crowley	Y	Y	N	Y	Y	?
15 Serrano	Y	Y	N	Y	Y	N
16 Engel	Y	Y	N	Y	Y	N
17 Lowey	Y	?	?	?	?	N
18 Maloney, S.P.	Y	Y	N	Y	Y	N
19 **Faso**	Y	N	Y	Y	Y	Y
20 Tonko	Y	Y	N	Y	Y	N
21 **Stefanik**	Y	N	Y	Y	Y	Y
22 **Tenney**	Y	N	Y	Y	Y	Y
23 **Reed**	Y	N	Y	?	?	Y
24 **Katko**	Y	N	Y	Y	Y	Y
25 **Vacant**						
26 Higgins	Y	Y	N	Y	Y	N
27 **Collins**	Y	N	Y	Y	Y	Y
NORTH CAROLINA						
1 Butterfield	Y	Y	N	Y	?	N
2 **Holding**	Y	N	Y	+	+	Y
3 **Jones**	N	?	?	Y	Y	Y
4 Price	Y	Y	N	Y	Y	N

	326	327	328	329	330	331
5 **Foxx**	Y	N	Y	Y	Y	Y
6 **Walker**	Y	N	Y	Y	Y	Y
7 **Rouzer**	Y	N	Y	Y	Y	Y
8 **Hudson**	Y	N	Y	Y	Y	Y
9 **Pittenger**	Y	N	Y	Y	Y	Y
9 **Vacant**						
10 **McHenry**	Y	N	Y	Y	Y	Y
11 **Meadows**	Y	N	Y	Y	Y	Y
12 Adams	Y	Y	N	Y	Y	N
13 **Budd**	Y	N	Y	Y	Y	Y
NORTH DAKOTA						
AL **Cramer**	Y	N	Y	Y	Y	Y
OHIO						
1 **Chabot**	Y	N	Y	Y	Y	Y
2 **Wenstrup**	Y	N	Y	Y	Y	Y
3 Beatty	Y	Y	N	Y	Y	N
4 **Jordan**	Y	N	Y	Y	Y	Y
5 **Latta**	Y	N	Y	Y	Y	Y
6 **Johnson**	Y	N	Y	Y	Y	Y
7 **Gibbs**	Y	N	Y	Y	Y	Y
8 **Davidson**	Y	N	Y	Y	Y	Y
9 Kaptur	Y	Y	N	?	?	N
10 **Turner**	Y	N	Y	Y	Y	Y
11 Fudge	Y	Y	N	Y	Y	N
12 **Vacant**						
13 Ryan	N	Y	N	?	?	N
14 **Joyce**	Y	N	Y	Y	Y	Y
15 **Stivers**	Y	?	?	Y	Y	Y
16 **Renacci**	Y	N	Y	+	+	Y
OKLAHOMA						
1 **Vacant**						
2 **Mullin**	Y	?	Y	Y	Y	Y
3 **Lucas**	Y	N	Y	Y	Y	Y
4 **Cole**	Y	N	Y	Y	Y	Y
5 **Russell**	Y	N	Y	Y	Y	Y
OREGON						
1 Bonamici	Y	Y	N	Y	Y	N
2 **Walden**	Y	N	Y	Y	Y	Y
3 Blumenauer	N	Y	N	Y	Y	N
4 DeFazio	N	Y	N	Y	Y	N
5 Schrader	Y	Y	Y	Y	Y	N
PENNSYLVANIA						
1 Brady	Y	Y	N	?	?	N
2 Evans	Y	Y	N	Y	Y	N
3 **Kelly**	Y	N	Y	?	?	Y
4 **Perry**	Y	N	Y	Y	Y	Y
5 **Thompson**	Y	N	Y	Y	Y	Y
6 **Costello**	Y	N	Y	Y	Y	Y
7 **Vacant**						
8 **Fitzpatrick**	Y	N	Y	Y	Y	Y
9 **Shuster**	Y	N	Y	Y	Y	Y
10 **Marino**	Y	N	Y	Y	Y	Y
11 **Barletta**	Y	?	?	Y	Y	Y
12 **Rothfus**	Y	N	Y	Y	Y	Y
13 Boyle	Y	Y	N	Y	Y	N
14 Doyle	N	Y	N	?	?	N
15 **Vacant**						
16 **Smucker**	Y	N	Y	Y	Y	Y
17 Cartwright	Y	Y	N	Y	Y	N
18 Lamb	Y	Y	N	?	?	N
RHODE ISLAND						
1 Cicilline	Y	Y	N	Y	?	N
2 Langevin	Y	Y	N	Y	Y	N
SOUTH CAROLINA						
1 **Sanford**	N	N	Y	Y	Y	Y
2 **Wilson**	Y	N	Y	Y	Y	Y
3 **Duncan**	Y	N	Y	Y	Y	Y
4 **Gowdy**	Y	N	Y	?	?	Y
5 **Norman**	Y	N	Y	Y	Y	Y
6 Clyburn	Y	Y	N	Y	Y	N
7 **Rice**	Y	N	Y	Y	Y	Y
SOUTH DAKOTA						
AL **Noem**	Y	N	Y	Y	Y	Y
TENNESSEE						
1 **Roe**	Y	N	Y	?	?	Y
2 **Duncan**	N	N	Y	Y	Y	Y
3 **Fleischmann**	Y	N	Y	Y	Y	Y
4 **DesJarlais**	Y	N	Y	Y	Y	Y
5 Cooper	Y	Y	N	Y	Y	N
6 **Black**	+	?	+	?	?	?
7 **Blackburn**	Y	N	Y	Y	Y	Y
8 **Kustoff**	?	?	?	Y	Y	Y
9 Cohen	Y	Y	N	Y	Y	N

	326	327	328	329	330	331
TEXAS						
1 **Gohmert**	Y	N	Y	Y	Y	Y
2 **Poe**	Y	N	Y	?	?	Y
3 **Johnson, S.**	Y	N	Y	?	?	Y
4 **Ratcliffe**	Y	N	Y	Y	Y	Y
5 **Hensarling**	Y	N	Y	Y	Y	Y
6 **Barton**	Y	N	Y	?	?	Y
7 **Culberson**	Y	N	Y	Y	Y	Y
8 **Brady**	Y	N	Y	Y	Y	Y
9 Green, A.	N	Y	N	Y	Y	N
10 **McCaul**	Y	N	Y	Y	Y	Y
11 **Conaway**	Y	N	Y	Y	Y	Y
12 **Granger**	Y	N	Y	Y	Y	Y
13 **Thornberry**	Y	N	Y	Y	Y	Y
14 **Weber**	Y	N	Y	Y	Y	Y
15 Gonzalez	Y	Y	N	Y	Y	N
16 O'Rourke	N	Y	N	+	+	N
17 **Flores**	Y	N	Y	Y	Y	Y
18 Jackson Lee	N	Y	N	+	+	?
19 **Arrington**	Y	N	Y	Y	Y	Y
20 Castro	N	Y	N	Y	Y	N
21 **Smith**	Y	N	Y	Y	Y	Y
22 **Olson**	Y	N	Y	Y	Y	Y
23 **Hurd**	Y	N	Y	Y	Y	Y
24 Marchant	Y	–	+	+	+	Y
25 **Williams**	Y	N	Y	Y	Y	Y
26 **Burgess**	Y	N	Y	Y	Y	Y
27 Cloud	Y	N	Y	Y	Y	Y
28 Cuellar	Y	Y	Y	Y	Y	N
29 Green, G.	Y	Y	N	Y	Y	N
30 Johnson, E.B.	Y	Y	N	Y	Y	N
31 **Carter**	Y	N	Y	Y	Y	Y
32 **Sessions**	Y	N	Y	Y	Y	Y
33 Veasey	Y	Y	N	Y	Y	N
34 Vela	Y	Y	N	Y	Y	N
35 Doggett	N	Y	N	Y	Y	N
36 **Babin**	Y	N	Y	Y	Y	Y
UTAH						
1 **Bishop**	Y	N	Y	Y	Y	Y
2 **Stewart**	Y	?	?	Y	Y	Y
3 **Curtis**	Y	N	Y	Y	Y	Y
4 **Love**	Y	N	Y	Y	Y	Y
VERMONT						
AL Welch	N	Y	N	Y	Y	N
VIRGINIA						
1 **Wittman**	Y	N	Y	Y	Y	Y
2 **Taylor**	Y	N	Y	Y	Y	Y
3 Scott	Y	Y	N	?	?	N
4 McEachin	Y	?	?	Y	Y	N
5 **Garrett**	Y	?	?	Y	Y	Y
6 **Goodlatte**	Y	N	Y	Y	Y	Y
7 **Brat**	Y	N	Y	Y	Y	Y
8 Beyer	Y	Y	N	Y	Y	N
9 **Griffith**	Y	N	Y	Y	Y	Y
10 **Comstock**	Y	N	Y	Y	Y	Y
11 Connolly	Y	Y	N	Y	Y	N
WASHINGTON						
1 DelBene	N	Y	N	Y	Y	N
2 Larsen	Y	Y	N	Y	Y	N
3 **Herrera Beutler**	Y	N	Y	Y	Y	Y
4 **Newhouse**	Y	N	Y	Y	Y	Y
5 **McMorris Rodgers**	Y	N	Y	Y	Y	Y
6 Kilmer	Y	Y	N	Y	Y	N
7 Jayapal	N	Y	N	Y	Y	N
8 **Reichert**	Y	N	Y	Y	Y	Y
9 Smith	N	Y	N	Y	Y	N
10 Heck	Y	Y	N	Y	Y	N
WEST VIRGINIA						
1 **McKinley**	Y	N	Y	Y	Y	Y
2 **Mooney**	Y	N	Y	Y	Y	Y
3 **Jenkins**	Y	N	Y	Y	Y	Y
WISCONSIN						
1 **Ryan**						
2 Pocan	N	Y	N	Y	Y	N
3 Kind	Y	Y	N	Y	Y	N
4 Moore	N	+	–	+	+	N
5 **Sensenbrenner**	Y	N	Y	Y	Y	Y
6 **Grothman**	Y	N	Y	Y	Y	Y
7 **Duffy**	Y	N	Y	+	Y	Y
8 **Gallagher**	Y	N	Y	Y	Y	Y
WYOMING						
AL **Cheney**	?	?	?	Y	Y	Y

VOTE NUMBER

332. HRES996. FISCAL 2019 INTERIOR-ENVIRONMENT AND FINANCIAL SERVICES APPROPRIATIONS PACKAGE/RULE. Adoption of the rule (H Res 996) that would provide for House floor consideration of the bill (HR 6147) that would make available $58.7 billion through fiscal 2019, with $35.3 billion for the Department of Interior, environment portion, and $23.4 billion for the Financial Services and related agencies portion. Adopted 229-184: R 229-3; D 0-181. July 17, 2018.

333. S488. FINANCIAL SERVICE MEASURE PACKAGE/PASSAGE. Hensarling, R-Texas, motion to suspend the rules and pass the bill that is comprised of 32 financial services-related measures that would, in various cases, codify and modify rules related to SEC oversight of financial institutions, impose requirements on the Consumer Financial Protection Bureau, and require actions by the Federal Reserve, the FDIC and the Office of the Comptroller of Currency. Among other provisions, the bill would establish criminal penalties for the unauthorized disclosure of proprietary information by federal banking regulators, and would require a number of reports on the use of cryptocurrencies and online marketplaces by human traffickers. Motion agreed to 406-4: R 227-2; D 179-2. July 17, 2018.

334. HR3030. GENOCIDE PREVENTION/PASSAGE. Royce, R-Calif., motion to suspend the rules and pass the bill that would state as policy of the U.S. the purpose of preventing genocide and other mass atrocities. The bill would also require additional training for Foreign Service Officers to recognize atrocities. Motion agreed to 406-5: R 224-5; D 182-0. July 17, 2018.

335. HR4989. LOCATION TRACKING AT DIPLOMATIC FACILITIES/ PASSAGE. Royce, R-Calif., motion to suspend the rules and pass the bill that would require the secretary of State to establish a policy on the use of location-tracking consumer devices, including GPS-enabled devices, at U.S. diplomatic and consular facilities by government employees, contractors, locally employed staff and members of other agencies deployed to or stationed at such facilities. Motion agreed to 412-0: R 227-0; D 185-0. July 17, 2018.

336. HR2. FARM PROGRAMS/MOTION TO INSTRUCT. Peterson, D-Minn., motion to instruct House conferees to insist on provisions related to mandatory funding for animal disease preparedness and response programs. Motion agreed to 392-20: R 207-20; D 185-0. July 18, 2018.

337. HRES990. LAW ENFORCEMENT AT THE BORDER/PASSAGE. Goodlatte, R-Va., motion to suspend the rules and agree to the resolution that would express the House of Representative's continued support for U.S. Immigration and Customs Enforcement and all government entities tasked with law enforcement duties on or near the nation's borders. It would also denounce calls to abolish ICE. Motion agreed to 244-35: R 226-1; D 18-34. July 18, 2018.

	332	333	334	335	336	337
ALABAMA						
1 **Byrne**	Y	Y	Y	Y	Y	Y
2 **Roby**	?	?	?	?	?	?
3 **Rogers**	Y	Y	Y	Y	Y	Y
4 **Aderholt**	Y	Y	Y	Y	Y	Y
5 **Brooks**	Y	Y	Y	Y	N	Y
6 **Palmer**	Y	Y	Y	Y	Y	Y
7 Sewell	N	Y	Y	Y	Y	P
ALASKA						
AL **Young**	Y	Y	Y	Y	Y	Y
ARIZONA						
1 O'Halleran	N	Y	Y	Y	Y	Y
2 **McSally**	Y	Y	Y	Y	Y	Y
3 Grijalva	N	Y	Y	Y	Y	N
4 **Gosar**	Y	Y	Y	Y	N	Y
5 **Biggs**	Y	Y	N	Y	N	Y
6 **Schweikert**	Y	Y	Y	Y	Y	Y
7 Gallego	N	?	Y	Y	Y	P
8 **Lesko**	Y	Y	Y	Y	Y	Y
9 Sinema	N	Y	Y	Y	Y	Y
ARKANSAS						
1 **Crawford**	Y	Y	Y	Y	Y	Y
2 **Hill**	Y	Y	Y	Y	Y	Y
3 **Womack**	Y	Y	Y	Y	Y	Y
4 **Westerman**	Y	Y	Y	Y	Y	Y
CALIFORNIA						
1 **LaMalfa**	Y	Y	Y	Y	Y	Y
2 Huffman	N	Y	Y	Y	N	N
3 Garamendi	?	?	Y	Y	Y	P
4 **McClintock**	Y	Y	Y	N	Y	N
5 Thompson	N	Y	Y	Y	Y	P
6 Matsui	N	Y	Y	Y	Y	P
7 Bera	N	Y	Y	Y	Y	Y
8 **Cook**	Y	Y	Y	Y	Y	Y
9 McNerney	N	Y	?	Y	Y	P
10 **Denham**	Y	Y	Y	Y	Y	Y
11 DeSaulnier	N	Y	Y	Y	N	N
12 Pelosi	N	Y	Y	Y	Y	P
13 Lee	N	Y	Y	Y	Y	P
14 Speier	?	?	?	?	?	?
15 Swalwell	N	Y	Y	Y	N	N
16 Costa	N	Y	Y	Y	Y	Y
17 Khanna	N	Y	Y	Y	Y	P
18 Eshoo	N	Y	Y	Y	Y	P
19 Lofgren	N	Y	Y	Y	Y	P
20 Panetta	N	Y	Y	Y	Y	Y
21 **Valadao**	Y	Y	Y	Y	Y	Y
22 **Nunes**	Y	Y	Y	Y	Y	Y
23 **McCarthy**	Y	Y	Y	Y	Y	Y
24 Carbajal	N	Y	Y	Y	Y	P
25 **Knight**	Y	Y	Y	Y	Y	Y
26 Brownley	N	Y	Y	Y	Y	P
27 Chu	N	Y	Y	Y	Y	P
28 Schiff	N	Y	Y	Y	Y	N
29 Cardenas	?	?	?	?	?	?
30 Sherman	N	Y	Y	Y	Y	P
31 Aguilar	N	Y	Y	Y	Y	P
32 Napolitano	N	Y	Y	Y	Y	P
33 Lieu	N	Y	Y	Y	Y	P
34 Gomez	N	Y	Y	Y	N	N
35 Torres	N	Y	Y	Y	Y	P
36 Ruiz	N	Y	Y	Y	Y	P
37 Bass	N	Y	Y	Y	?	?
38 Sánchez, Linda	N	Y	Y	Y	Y	P
39 **Royce**	Y	Y	Y	Y	Y	Y
40 Roybal-Allard	N	Y	Y	Y	Y	P
41 Takano	N	Y	Y	Y	Y	P
42 **Calvert**	Y	Y	Y	Y	Y	Y
43 Waters	N	Y	Y	Y	Y	P
44 Barragan	N	Y	Y	Y	Y	P
45 **Walters**	Y	Y	Y	Y	Y	Y
46 Correa	N	Y	Y	Y	Y	N
47 Lowenthal	N	Y	Y	Y	Y	P
48 **Rohrabacher**	Y	Y	Y	Y	Y	Y
49 **Issa**	Y	Y	Y	Y	Y	Y
50 **Hunter**	Y	Y	Y	Y	Y	Y
51 Vargas	N	Y	Y	Y	Y	N
52 Peters	N	Y	Y	Y	Y	P
53 Davis	N	Y	Y	Y	Y	P

	332	333	334	335	336	337
COLORADO						
1 DeGette	N	Y	Y	Y	Y	P
2 Polis	N	Y	Y	Y	Y	P
3 Tipton	Y	Y	Y	Y	Y	Y
4 **Buck**	Y	Y	Y	Y	Y	Y
5 **Lamborn**	Y	Y	Y	Y	Y	Y
6 **Coffman**	Y	Y	Y	?	Y	Y
7 Perlmutter	N	Y	Y	Y	Y	P
CONNECTICUT						
1 Larson	N	Y	Y	Y	Y	P
2 Courtney	N	Y	Y	Y	Y	P
3 DeLauro	N	Y	Y	Y	Y	P
4 Himes	N	Y	Y	Y	Y	P
5 Esty	N	Y	Y	Y	Y	P
DELAWARE						
AL Rochester	N	Y	Y	Y	Y	P
FLORIDA						
1 **Gaetz**	Y	Y	Y	Y	?	?
2 **Dunn**	Y	Y	Y	Y	Y	Y
3 **Yoho**	Y	Y	Y	Y	Y	Y
4 **Rutherford**	Y	Y	Y	Y	Y	Y
5 Lawson	N	Y	Y	Y	Y	Y
6 **DeSantis**	Y	Y	Y	Y	?	?
7 Murphy	N	Y	Y	Y	Y	Y
8 **Posey**	Y	Y	Y	N	Y	N
9 Soto	N	Y	Y	Y	Y	N
10 Demings	N	Y	Y	Y	N	N
11 **Webster**	Y	Y	Y	Y	Y	Y
12 **Bilirakis**	Y	Y	Y	Y	Y	Y
13 Crist	N	Y	Y	Y	Y	Y
14 Castor	N	Y	Y	Y	?	?
15 **Ross**	Y	Y	Y	Y	Y	Y
16 **Buchanan**	Y	Y	Y	Y	Y	Y
17 **Rooney, T.**	Y	Y	Y	Y	Y	Y
18 **Mast**	Y	Y	Y	Y	Y	Y
19 **Rooney, F.**	Y	?	?	?	Y	Y
20 Hastings	N	Y	Y	Y	Y	P
21 Frankel	N	Y	Y	Y	Y	P
22 Deutch	N	Y	Y	Y	Y	P
23 Wasserman Schultz	N	Y	Y	Y	Y	P
24 Wilson	N	Y	Y	Y	Y	P
25 **Diaz-Balart**	Y	Y	Y	Y	Y	Y
26 **Curbelo**	Y	Y	Y	Y	Y	Y
27 **Ros-Lehtinen**	Y	Y	Y	Y	Y	Y
GEORGIA						
1 **Carter**	Y	Y	Y	Y	Y	Y
2 Bishop	N	?	?	Y	Y	P
3 **Ferguson**	Y	Y	Y	Y	Y	Y
4 Johnson	N	Y	Y	Y	Y	P
5 Lewis	N	Y	Y	Y	Y	P
6 **Handel**	Y	Y	Y	Y	Y	Y
7 **Woodall**	Y	Y	Y	Y	Y	Y
8 **Scott, A.**	Y	Y	Y	Y	Y	Y
9 **Collins**	Y	Y	Y	Y	Y	Y
10 **Hice**	Y	Y	Y	Y	N	Y
11 **Loudermilk**	Y	Y	Y	Y	Y	Y
12 **Allen**	Y	Y	Y	Y	Y	+
13 **Scott, D.**	N	Y	Y	Y	Y	Y
14 **Graves**	Y	Y	Y	Y	Y	Y
HAWAII						
1 Hanabusa	?	?	?	?	?	?
2 Gabbard	N	Y	Y	Y	Y	P
IDAHO						
1 Labrador	Y	Y	Y	N	N	Y
2 **Simpson**	+	+	+	+	Y	Y
ILLINOIS						
1 Rush	N	Y	Y	Y	Y	N
2 Kelly	N	Y	Y	Y	Y	P
3 Lipinski	N	Y	Y	Y	Y	P
4 Gutierrez	–	+	+	+	Y	N
5 Quigley	N	Y	Y	Y	Y	P
6 **Roskam**	Y	Y	Y	Y	Y	Y
7 Davis, D.	N	Y	Y	Y	Y	N
8 Krishnamoorthi	N	Y	Y	Y	Y	P
9 Schakowsky	N	N	Y	Y	Y	N
10 Schneider	N	Y	Y	Y	Y	P
11 Foster	N	Y	Y	Y	Y	P
12 **Bost**	Y	Y	Y	Y	Y	Y
13 **Davis, R.**	Y	Y	Y	Y	Y	Y

	332	333	334	335	336	337
14 **Hultgren**	Y	Y	Y	Y	Y	Y
15 **Shimkus**	Y	Y	Y	Y	Y	Y
16 **Kinzinger**	Y	Y	Y	Y	Y	Y
17 Bustos	N	Y	Y	Y	Y	P
18 **LaHood**	Y	Y	Y	Y	Y	Y
INDIANA						
1 Visclosky	N	Y	Y	Y	Y	Y
2 **Walorski**	Y	Y	Y	Y	Y	Y
3 **Banks**	Y	Y	Y	Y	Y	Y
4 Rokita	Y	Y	Y	Y	N	Y
5 **Brooks**	Y	Y	Y	Y	Y	Y
6 **Messer**	Y	Y	Y	Y	Y	Y
7 Carson	N	Y	Y	Y	Y	P
8 **Bucshon**	Y	Y	Y	Y	Y	Y
9 **Hollingsworth**	Y	Y	Y	Y	Y	Y
IOWA						
1 **Blum**	Y	Y	Y	Y	Y	Y
2 Loebsack	N	Y	Y	Y	Y	P
3 **Young**	Y	Y	Y	Y	Y	Y
4 **King**	Y	Y	Y	Y	Y	Y
KANSAS						
1 **Marshall**	Y	Y	Y	Y	Y	Y
2 **Jenkins**	Y	Y	Y	Y	Y	Y
3 **Yoder**	Y	Y	Y	Y	Y	Y
4 **Estes**	Y	Y	Y	Y	Y	Y
KENTUCKY						
1 **Comer**	Y	Y	Y	Y	Y	Y
2 **Guthrie**	Y	Y	Y	Y	Y	Y
3 Yarmuth	N	Y	Y	Y	Y	P
4 **Massie**	N	N	N	Y	N	Y
5 **Rogers**	Y	Y	Y	Y	Y	Y
6 **Barr**	Y	Y	Y	Y	Y	Y
LOUISIANA						
1 **Scalise**	Y	Y	Y	Y	Y	Y
2 Richmond	N	Y	Y	Y	?	?
3 **Higgins**	Y	Y	Y	Y	Y	Y
4 **Johnson**	Y	Y	Y	Y	Y	Y
5 **Abraham**	Y	Y	Y	Y	Y	Y
6 **Graves**	Y	Y	Y	Y	Y	Y
MAINE						
1 Pingree	N	Y	Y	Y	Y	P
2 **Poliquin**	Y	Y	Y	Y	Y	Y
MARYLAND						
1 **Harris**	Y	Y	Y	Y	N	Y
2 Ruppersberger	N	Y	Y	Y	Y	P
3 Sarbanes	N	Y	Y	Y	Y	P
4 Brown	N	Y	Y	Y	Y	N
5 Hoyer	N	Y	Y	Y	Y	P
6 Delaney	N	Y	Y	Y	Y	P
7 Cummings	N	Y	Y	Y	Y	P
8 Raskin	N	Y	Y	Y	Y	P
MASSACHUSETTS						
1 Neal	N	Y	Y	Y	Y	P
2 McGovern	N	Y	Y	Y	Y	P
3 Tsongas	N	Y	Y	Y	Y	P
4 Kennedy	N	Y	Y	Y	Y	P
5 Clark	–	Y	Y	Y	Y	P
6 Moulton	N	Y	Y	Y	Y	P
7 Capuano	N	Y	Y	Y	Y	P
8 Lynch	N	Y	Y	Y	Y	Y
9 Keating	N	Y	Y	Y	Y	P
MICHIGAN						
1 **Bergman**	Y	Y	Y	Y	Y	Y
2 **Huizenga**	Y	Y	Y	Y	Y	Y
3 *Amash*	N	N	N	Y	N	N
4 **Moolenaar**	Y	Y	Y	Y	Y	Y
5 Kildee	N	Y	Y	Y	Y	P
6 **Upton**	Y	Y	Y	Y	Y	Y
7 **Walberg**	Y	Y	Y	Y	Y	Y
8 **Bishop**	Y	Y	Y	Y	Y	Y
9 Levin	N	Y	Y	Y	Y	P
10 **Mitchell**	Y	Y	Y	Y	Y	Y
11 **Trott**	Y	Y	Y	Y	Y	Y
12 Dingell	N	Y	Y	Y	Y	P
14 Lawrence	N	Y	Y	Y	Y	P
MINNESOTA						
1 Walz	?	?	?	?	?	?
2 **Lewis**	Y	Y	Y	Y	Y	Y
3 **Paulsen**	Y	Y	Y	Y	Y	Y
4 McCollum	N	?	Y	Y	Y	P

	332	333	334	335	336	337
5 Ellison	?	?	?	?	Y	P
6 **Emmer**	Y	Y	Y	Y	Y	Y
7 Peterson	N	Y	Y	Y	Y	?
8 Nolan	N	Y	Y	Y	Y	P
MISSISSIPPI						
1 **Kelly**	Y	Y	Y	Y	N	Y
2 Thompson	N	Y	Y	Y	Y	N
3 **Harper**	Y	Y	Y	Y	Y	Y
4 **Palazzo**	Y	Y	Y	Y	Y	Y
MISSOURI						
1 Clay	N	Y	Y	Y	Y	N
2 **Wagner**	Y	Y	Y	Y	Y	Y
3 **Luetkemeyer**	Y	Y	Y	Y	Y	Y
4 **Hartzler**	Y	Y	Y	Y	Y	Y
5 Cleaver	N	Y	Y	Y	Y	N
6 **Graves**	Y	Y	Y	Y	Y	Y
7 **Long**	Y	Y	Y	Y	Y	Y
8 **Smith**	Y	Y	Y	Y	Y	Y
MONTANA						
AL **Gianforte**	Y	Y	Y	Y	Y	Y
NEBRASKA						
1 **Fortenberry**	Y	Y	Y	Y	Y	Y
2 **Bacon**	Y	Y	Y	Y	Y	Y
3 **Smith**	Y	Y	Y	Y	Y	Y
NEVADA						
1 Titus	N	Y	?	Y	Y	P
2 **Amodei**	Y	Y	Y	Y	Y	Y
3 Rosen	N	Y	Y	Y	Y	Y
4 Kihuen	N	Y	Y	Y	Y	P
NEW HAMPSHIRE						
1 Shea-Porter	?	Y	Y	Y	Y	P
2 Kuster	N	Y	Y	Y	Y	P
NEW JERSEY						
1 Norcross	N	Y	Y	Y	Y	P
2 **LoBiondo**	Y	Y	Y	Y	Y	Y
3 **MacArthur**	Y	Y	Y	?	Y	Y
4 **Smith**	Y	Y	Y	Y	Y	Y
5 Gottheimer	N	Y	Y	Y	Y	Y
6 Pallone	N	Y	Y	Y	Y	P
7 **Lance**	Y	Y	Y	Y	Y	Y
8 Sires	N	Y	Y	Y	Y	P
9 Pascrell	N	Y	Y	Y	Y	P
10 Payne	N	Y	Y	Y	Y	P
11 **Frelinghuysen**	Y	Y	Y	Y	Y	Y
12 Watson Coleman	N	Y	Y	Y	Y	P
NEW MEXICO						
1 Lujan Grisham	?	Y	Y	Y	Y	P
2 **Pearce**	Y	Y	Y	Y	Y	Y
3 Luján	N	Y	Y	Y	Y	P
NEW YORK						
1 **Zeldin**	Y	Y	Y	Y	Y	Y
2 **King**	Y	Y	Y	Y	Y	Y
3 Suozzi	N	Y	Y	Y	Y	Y
4 Rice	N	Y	Y	Y	Y	P
5 Meeks	N	Y	Y	Y	Y	N
6 Meng	N	Y	Y	Y	Y	P
7 Velázquez	N	Y	Y	Y	Y	N
8 Jeffries	N	Y	Y	Y	Y	P
9 Clarke	N	Y	Y	Y	Y	N
10 Nadler	N	N	Y	Y	Y	P
11 **Donovan**	Y	Y	Y	Y	Y	Y
12 Maloney, C.	N	Y	Y	Y	Y	P
13 Espaillat	N	Y	Y	Y	Y	N
14 Crowley	?	Y	Y	Y	Y	N
15 Serrano	N	Y	Y	Y	Y	N
16 Engel	N	Y	Y	Y	Y	P
17 Lowey	N	Y	Y	Y	Y	P
18 Maloney, S.P.	N	Y	Y	Y	Y	P
19 **Faso**	Y	Y	Y	Y	Y	Y
20 Tonko	N	Y	Y	Y	Y	N
21 **Stefanik**	Y	Y	Y	Y	Y	Y
22 **Tenney**	Y	Y	Y	Y	Y	Y
23 **Reed**	Y	Y	Y	Y	Y	Y
24 **Katko**	Y	Y	Y	Y	Y	Y
25 **Vacant**						
26 Higgins	N	Y	Y	Y	Y	P
27 **Collins**	Y	Y	Y	Y	Y	Y
NORTH CAROLINA						
1 Butterfield	N	?	?	?	Y	P
2 **Holding**	Y	Y	Y	Y	Y	Y
3 **Jones**	N	Y	N	Y	N	Y
4 Price	N	Y	Y	Y	Y	P

	332	333	334	335	336	337
5 **Foxx**	Y	Y	Y	Y	Y	Y
6 **Walker**	Y	Y	Y	Y	Y	Y
7 **Rouzer**	Y	Y	Y	Y	Y	Y
8 **Hudson**	Y	Y	Y	Y	Y	Y
9 **Pittenger**	Y	Y	Y	Y	Y	Y
9 **Vacant**						
10 **McHenry**	Y	Y	Y	Y	Y	Y
11 **Meadows**	Y	Y	Y	Y	Y	Y
12 Adams	N	Y	Y	Y	Y	P
13 **Budd**	Y	Y	Y	Y	Y	Y
NORTH DAKOTA						
AL **Cramer**	Y	Y	Y	Y	Y	Y
OHIO						
1 **Chabot**	Y	Y	Y	Y	Y	Y
2 **Wenstrup**	Y	Y	Y	Y	Y	Y
3 Beatty	N	Y	Y	Y	Y	P
4 **Jordan**	Y	Y	Y	Y	N	Y
5 **Latta**	Y	Y	Y	Y	Y	Y
6 **Johnson**	Y	Y	Y	Y	Y	Y
7 **Gibbs**	Y	Y	Y	Y	Y	Y
8 **Davidson**	Y	Y	Y	Y	Y	Y
9 Kaptur	N	Y	Y	Y	Y	P
10 **Turner**	Y	Y	Y	Y	Y	Y
11 Fudge	N	Y	Y	Y	Y	P
12 **Vacant**						
13 Ryan	N	Y	Y	Y	Y	P
14 **Joyce**	Y	Y	?	?	Y	Y
15 **Stivers**	Y	Y	Y	Y	Y	Y
16 **Renacci**	Y	Y	Y	Y	Y	Y
OKLAHOMA						
1 **Vacant**						
2 **Mullin**	Y	Y	Y	Y	Y	Y
3 **Lucas**	Y	Y	Y	Y	Y	Y
4 **Cole**	Y	Y	Y	Y	Y	Y
5 **Russell**	Y	Y	Y	Y	Y	Y
OREGON						
1 Bonamici	N	Y	Y	Y	Y	P
2 **Walden**	Y	Y	Y	Y	Y	Y
3 Blumenauer	N	+	+	+	Y	P
4 DeFazio	N	Y	Y	Y	Y	P
5 Schrader	N	Y	Y	Y	Y	Y
PENNSYLVANIA						
1 Brady	N	Y	Y	Y	Y	P
2 Evans	N	Y	Y	Y	Y	P
3 **Kelly**	Y	Y	Y	Y	Y	Y
4 **Perry**	Y	Y	Y	Y	N	Y
5 **Thompson**	Y	Y	Y	Y	Y	Y
6 **Costello**	Y	?	Y	Y	Y	Y
7 **Vacant**						
8 **Fitzpatrick**	Y	Y	Y	Y	Y	Y
9 **Shuster**	Y	?	?	?	?	?
10 **Marino**	Y	Y	Y	Y	Y	Y
11 **Barletta**	Y	Y	Y	Y	Y	Y
12 **Rothfus**	Y	Y	Y	Y	Y	Y
13 Boyle	N	Y	Y	Y	Y	P
14 Doyle	N	Y	Y	Y	Y	P
15 **Vacant**						
16 **Smucker**	Y	Y	Y	Y	Y	Y
17 Cartwright	N	Y	Y	Y	Y	Y
18 Lamb	N	Y	Y	Y	Y	Y
RHODE ISLAND						
1 Cicilline	N	Y	Y	Y	Y	P
2 Langevin	N	Y	Y	Y	Y	P
SOUTH CAROLINA						
1 **Sanford**	Y	Y	N	Y	N	Y
2 **Wilson**	Y	Y	Y	Y	Y	Y
3 **Duncan**	Y	Y	Y	Y	?	?
4 **Gowdy**	Y	Y	Y	Y	Y	Y
5 **Norman**	Y	Y	Y	Y	Y	Y
6 Clyburn	N	Y	Y	Y	Y	P
7 **Rice**	Y	Y	Y	Y	Y	Y
SOUTH DAKOTA						
AL **Noem**	Y	Y	Y	Y	Y	Y
TENNESSEE						
1 **Roe**	Y	Y	Y	Y	Y	Y
2 **Duncan**	Y	Y	Y	Y	Y	Y
3 **Fleischmann**	Y	Y	Y	Y	Y	Y
4 **DesJarlais**	Y	Y	Y	Y	Y	Y
5 Cooper	N	Y	Y	Y	Y	P
6 **Black**	?	Y	Y	Y	?	+
7 **Blackburn**	Y	Y	Y	Y	?	?
8 **Kustoff**	Y	Y	Y	Y	Y	Y
9 Cohen	N	Y	Y	Y	Y	P

	332	333	334	335	336	337
TEXAS						
1 **Gohmert**	Y	Y	Y	Y	N	Y
2 **Poe**	Y	Y	Y	Y	Y	Y
3 **Johnson, S.**	Y	Y	Y	Y	Y	Y
4 **Ratcliffe**	Y	Y	Y	Y	Y	Y
5 **Hensarling**	Y	Y	Y	Y	Y	Y
6 **Barton**	Y	Y	Y	Y	Y	Y
7 **Culberson**	Y	Y	Y	Y	Y	Y
8 **Brady**	Y	Y	Y	Y	Y	Y
9 Green, A.	N	Y	Y	Y	Y	N
10 **McCaul**	Y	Y	Y	Y	Y	Y
11 **Conaway**	Y	Y	Y	Y	Y	Y
12 **Granger**	Y	Y	Y	Y	Y	Y
13 **Thornberry**	Y	Y	Y	Y	Y	Y
14 **Weber**	Y	Y	Y	Y	Y	Y
15 Gonzalez	N	Y	Y	Y	Y	P
16 O'Rourke	N	Y	Y	Y	Y	N
17 **Flores**	Y	?	?	?	Y	Y
18 Jackson Lee	?	Y	Y	Y	Y	N
19 **Arrington**	Y	Y	Y	Y	Y	Y
20 Castro	N	Y	Y	Y	Y	N
21 **Smith**	Y	Y	Y	Y	Y	Y
22 **Olson**	Y	Y	Y	Y	Y	Y
23 **Hurd**	Y	Y	Y	Y	Y	Y
24 **Marchant**	Y	Y	Y	Y	Y	Y
25 **Williams**	Y	Y	Y	Y	Y	Y
26 **Burgess**	Y	Y	Y	Y	Y	Y
27 **Cloud**	Y	Y	Y	Y	Y	Y
28 Cuellar	N	Y	Y	Y	Y	Y
29 Green, G.	N	Y	Y	Y	Y	P
30 Johnson, E.B.	N	Y	Y	Y	Y	N
31 **Carter**	Y	Y	Y	Y	Y	Y
32 **Sessions**	Y	Y	Y	Y	Y	Y
33 Veasey	N	Y	Y	Y	Y	N
34 Vela	N	Y	Y	Y	Y	N
35 Doggett	N	Y	Y	Y	Y	N
36 **Babin**	Y	Y	Y	Y	Y	Y
UTAH						
1 **Bishop**	Y	Y	Y	Y	Y	Y
2 **Stewart**	Y	Y	Y	Y	Y	Y
3 **Curtis**	Y	Y	Y	Y	Y	Y
4 **Love**	Y	Y	Y	Y	Y	Y
VERMONT						
AL Welch	N	Y	Y	Y	Y	P
VIRGINIA						
1 **Wittman**	Y	Y	Y	Y	Y	Y
2 **Taylor**	Y	Y	Y	Y	Y	Y
3 Scott	N	Y	Y	Y	Y	P
4 McEachin	N	Y	Y	Y	Y	P
5 **Garrett**	Y	Y	Y	Y	N	Y
6 **Goodlatte**	Y	Y	Y	Y	+	Y
7 **Brat**	Y	Y	Y	Y	N	Y
8 Beyer	N	Y	Y	Y	Y	P
9 **Griffith**	Y	Y	Y	Y	N	Y
10 **Comstock**	Y	Y	Y	Y	Y	Y
11 Connolly	N	Y	Y	Y	Y	P
WASHINGTON						
1 DelBene	N	Y	Y	Y	Y	P
2 Larsen	N	Y	Y	Y	Y	P
3 **Herrera Beutler**	Y	Y	Y	Y	Y	Y
4 **Newhouse**	Y	Y	Y	Y	Y	Y
5 **McMorris Rodgers**	Y	Y	Y	Y	Y	Y
6 Kilmer	N	Y	Y	Y	Y	P
7 Jayapal	N	Y	Y	Y	Y	P
8 **Reichert**	Y	Y	Y	Y	Y	Y
9 Smith	N	Y	Y	Y	Y	P
10 Heck	N	Y	Y	Y	Y	P
WEST VIRGINIA						
1 **McKinley**	Y	Y	Y	Y	Y	Y
2 **Mooney**	Y	Y	Y	Y	Y	Y
3 **Jenkins**	Y	Y	Y	Y	Y	Y
WISCONSIN						
1 **Ryan**						
2 Pocan	N	Y	Y	Y	Y	P
3 Kind	N	Y	Y	Y	Y	Y
4 Moore	N	Y	Y	Y	?	P
5 **Sensenbrenner**	Y	Y	Y	Y	Y	Y
6 **Grothman**	Y	Y	Y	Y	Y	Y
7 **Duffy**	Y	Y	Y	Y	Y	Y
8 **Gallagher**	Y	Y	Y	Y	Y	Y
WYOMING						
AL **Cheney**	Y	Y	Y	Y	Y	Y

VOTE NUMBER

338. HR1037. NATIONAL EMERGENCY MEDICAL SERVICES MEMORIAL/ PASSAGE. McClintock, R-Calif., motion to suspend the rules and pass the bill that would permit the National Emergency Medical Services Memorial Foundation to establish a memorial on federal land in or near the District of Columbia to commemorate the commitment and service of emergency medical service providers. Motion agreed to 414-0: R 228-0; D 186-0. July 18, 2018.

339. HCONRES119. CARBON TAX RESOLUTION/PREVIOUS QUESTION. Newhouse, R-Wash., motion to order the previous question (thus limiting debate and the possibility of amendment) on the rule that would provide for House floor consideration of the concurrent resolution (H Con Res 119) expressing the sense of Congress that a carbon tax would be detrimental to the United States economy. Motion agreed to 226-186: R 226-0; D 0-186. July 18, 2018.

340. HCONRES119. CARBON TAX RESOLUTION/RULE. Adoption of rule (H Res 1001) that would provide for House floor consideration of the concurrent resolution (H Con Res 119) expressing the sense of Congress that a carbon tax would be detrimental to the United States economy. Adopted 229-183: R 226-0; D 3-183. July 18, 2018.

341. HR6147. FISCAL 2019 INTERIOR-ENVIRONMENT AND FINANCIAL SERVICES APPROPRIATIONS PACKAGE/LAND ACQUISITION FUNDING. Biggs, R-Ariz., amendment that would increase funding for the operations and maintenance of the National Park Service by $2.4 million and would decrease funding for land acquisition activities by an equal amount. Rejected in Committee of the Whole 172-237: R 172-52; D 0-185. July 18, 2018.

342. HR6147. FISCAL 2019 INTERIOR-ENVIRONMENT AND FINANCIAL SERVICES APPROPRIATIONS PACKAGE/INTERIOR DEPARTMENT FUNDING. Grijalva, D-Ariz., amendment that would increase funding for the Interior Department Inspector General's Office by $2.5 million, and would decrease funding for the Office of the Interior Secretary by an equal amount. Rejected in Committee of the Whole 190-223: R 5-222; D 185-1. July 18, 2018.

343. HR6147. FISCAL 2019 INTERIOR-ENVIRONMENT AND FINANCIAL SERVICES APPROPRIATIONS PACKAGE/NATIVE AMERICAN OFFICE FUNDING. O'Halleran, D-Ariz., amendment that would increase funding for the Office of Navajo and Hopi Indian Relocation by $3 million, and would decrease funding for Office of the Special Trustee for American Indians by an equal amount. Adopted in Committee of the Whole 217-196: R 31-196; D 186-0. July 18, 2018.

	338	339	340	341	342	343
ALABAMA						
1 **Byrne**	Y	Y	Y	Y	N	N
2 **Roby**	?	?	?	?	?	?
3 **Rogers**	Y	Y	Y	Y	N	N
4 **Aderholt**	Y	Y	Y	Y	N	N
5 **Brooks**	Y	Y	Y	Y	N	N
6 **Palmer**	Y	Y	Y	Y	N	N
7 Sewell	Y	N	N	N	Y	N
ALASKA						
AL **Young**	Y	Y	Y	N	N	Y
ARIZONA						
1 O'Halleran	Y	N	N	N	Y	Y
2 **McSally**	Y	Y	Y	Y	N	Y
3 Grijalva	Y	N	N	N	Y	Y
4 **Gosar**	Y	Y	Y	Y	N	N
5 **Biggs**	Y	Y	Y	Y	N	Y
6 **Schweikert**	Y	Y	Y	Y	N	Y
7 Gallego	Y	N	N	N	Y	Y
8 **Lesko**	Y	Y	Y	Y	N	N
9 Sinema	Y	N	N	N	Y	Y
ARKANSAS						
1 **Crawford**	Y	Y	Y	Y	N	N
2 **Hill**	Y	Y	Y	Y	N	N
3 **Womack**	Y	Y	Y	Y	N	N
4 **Westerman**	Y	Y	Y	Y	N	N
CALIFORNIA						
1 **LaMalfa**	Y	Y	Y	?	N	N
2 Huffman	Y	N	N	N	Y	Y
3 Garamendi	Y	N	N	N	Y	Y
4 **McClintock**	Y	Y	Y	Y	N	N
5 Thompson	Y	N	N	N	Y	Y
6 Matsui	Y	N	N	N	Y	Y
7 Bera	Y	N	N	N	Y	Y
8 **Cook**	Y	Y	Y	Y	N	N
9 McNerney	Y	N	N	N	Y	Y
10 **Denham**	Y	Y	Y	Y	N	Y
11 DeSaulnier	Y	N	N	N	Y	Y
12 Pelosi	Y	N	N	N	Y	Y
13 Lee	Y	N	N	N	Y	Y
14 Speier	?	?	?	?	?	?
15 Swalwell	Y	N	N	N	Y	Y
16 Costa	Y	N	N	N	Y	Y
17 Khanna	Y	N	N	N	Y	Y
18 Eshoo	Y	N	N	N	Y	Y
19 Lofgren	Y	N	N	N	Y	Y
20 Panetta	Y	N	N	N	Y	Y
21 **Valadao**	Y	Y	Y	Y	N	N
22 **Nunes**	Y	Y	Y	Y	N	N
23 **McCarthy**	Y	Y	Y	Y	N	N
24 Carbajal	Y	N	N	N	Y	Y
25 **Knight**	Y	Y	Y	N	N	N
26 Brownley	Y	N	N	N	Y	Y
27 Chu	Y	N	N	N	Y	Y
28 Schiff	Y	N	N	N	Y	Y
29 Cardenas	?	?	?	?	?	?
30 Sherman	Y	N	N	N	Y	Y
31 Aguilar	Y	N	N	N	Y	Y
32 Napolitano	Y	N	N	N	Y	Y
33 Lieu	Y	N	N	N	Y	Y
34 Gomez	Y	N	N	N	Y	Y
35 Torres	Y	N	N	N	Y	Y
36 Ruiz	Y	N	N	N	Y	Y
37 Bass	?	?	?	?	?	?
38 Sánchez, Linda	Y	N	N	N	Y	Y
39 **Royce**	Y	Y	Y	Y	N	N
40 Roybal-Allard	Y	N	N	N	Y	Y
41 Takano	Y	N	N	N	Y	Y
42 **Calvert**	Y	Y	Y	Y	N	N
43 Waters	Y	N	N	N	Y	Y
44 Barragan	Y	N	N	N	Y	Y
45 **Walters**	Y	Y	Y	Y	N	N
46 Correa	Y	N	N	N	Y	Y
47 Lowenthal	Y	N	N	N	Y	Y
48 **Rohrabacher**	Y	Y	Y	Y	N	N
49 **Issa**	Y	Y	Y	Y	N	N
50 **Hunter**	Y	Y	Y	Y	N	N
51 Vargas	Y	N	N	N	Y	Y
52 Peters	Y	N	N	N	Y	Y
53 Davis	Y	N	N	N	Y	Y

	338	339	340	341	342	343
COLORADO						
1 DeGette	Y	N	N	N	Y	Y
2 Polis	Y	N	N	N	Y	Y
3 **Tipton**	Y	Y	Y	N	N	N
4 **Buck**	Y	Y	Y	Y	N	N
5 **Lamborn**	Y	Y	?	Y	N	N
6 **Coffman**	Y	Y	Y	Y	Y	N
7 Perlmutter	Y	N	N	N	Y	Y
CONNECTICUT						
1 Larson	Y	N	N	N	Y	Y
2 Courtney	Y	N	N	N	Y	Y
3 DeLauro	Y	N	N	N	Y	Y
4 Himes	Y	N	N	N	Y	Y
5 Esty	Y	N	N	N	Y	Y
DELAWARE						
AL Blunt Rochester	Y	N	N	N	Y	Y
FLORIDA						
1 **Gaetz**	?	?	?	?	?	?
2 **Dunn**	Y	Y	Y	Y	N	Y
3 Yoho	Y	Y	Y	Y	N	N
4 **Rutherford**	Y	Y	Y	Y	N	Y
5 Lawson	Y	N	N	N	Y	Y
6 **DeSantis**	?	?	?	?	?	?
7 Murphy	Y	N	N	N	Y	Y
8 **Posey**	Y	Y	Y	Y	N	N
9 Soto	Y	N	N	N	Y	Y
10 Demings	Y	N	N	N	Y	Y
11 **Webster**	Y	Y	Y	Y	N	N
12 **Bilirakis**	Y	Y	Y	Y	N	Y
13 Crist	Y	N	N	N	Y	Y
14 Castor	Y	N	N	N	Y	Y
15 **Ross**	Y	Y	Y	Y	N	N
16 **Buchanan**	Y	Y	Y	N	N	N
17 **Rooney, T.**	Y	Y	Y	N	N	N
18 **Mast**	Y	Y	Y	N	N	N
19 **Rooney, F.**	Y	Y	Y	N	N	N
20 Hastings	Y	N	N	N	Y	Y
21 Frankel	Y	N	N	N	Y	Y
22 Deutch	Y	N	N	N	Y	Y
23 Wasserman Schultz	Y	N	N	N	Y	Y
24 Wilson	Y	N	N	N	Y	Y
25 **Diaz-Balart**	Y	Y	Y	N	N	N
26 **Curbelo**	Y	Y	Y	N	N	N
27 **Ros-Lehtinen**	Y	Y	Y	N	N	N
GEORGIA						
1 **Carter**	Y	Y	Y	N	N	N
2 Bishop	Y	N	N	N	Y	Y
3 **Ferguson**	Y	Y	Y	N	N	N
4 Johnson	Y	N	N	N	Y	Y
5 Lewis	Y	N	N	N	Y	Y
6 **Handel**	Y	Y	Y	N	N	N
7 **Woodall**	Y	Y	Y	N	N	N
8 **Scott, A.**	Y	Y	Y	N	N	N
9 **Collins**	Y	Y	Y	N	N	N
10 **Hice**	Y	Y	Y	N	N	N
11 **Loudermilk**	Y	Y	Y	N	N	N
12 **Allen**	Y	Y	Y	N	N	N
13 Scott, D.	Y	N	N	N	Y	Y
14 **Graves**	Y	Y	Y	N	N	N
HAWAII						
1 Hanabusa	?	?	?	?	?	?
2 Gabbard	Y	N	N	N	Y	Y
IDAHO						
1 **Labrador**	Y	Y	Y	Y	N	N
2 **Simpson**	Y	Y	Y	N	N	Y
ILLINOIS						
1 Rush	Y	N	N	N	Y	Y
2 Kelly	Y	N	N	N	Y	Y
3 Lipinski	Y	N	N	N	Y	Y
4 Gutierrez	Y	N	N	N	Y	Y
5 Quigley	Y	N	N	N	Y	Y
6 **Roskam**	Y	Y	Y	Y	N	N
7 Davis, D.	Y	N	N	N	Y	Y
8 Krishnamoorthi	Y	N	N	N	Y	Y
9 Schakowsky	Y	N	N	N	Y	Y
10 Schneider	Y	N	N	N	Y	Y
11 Foster	Y	N	N	N	Y	Y
12 **Bost**	Y	Y	Y	Y	N	N
13 **Davis, R.**	Y	Y	Y	N	N	N

	338	339	340	341	342	343
14 **Hultgren**	Y	Y	Y	Y	N	N
15 **Shimkus**	Y	Y	Y	Y	N	N
16 **Kinzinger**	Y	Y	Y	Y	N	N
17 Bustos	Y	N	N	N	Y	Y
18 **LaHood**	Y	Y	Y	Y	N	N
INDIANA						
1 Visclosky	Y	N	N	N	Y	Y
2 **Walorski**	Y	Y	Y	Y	N	N
3 **Banks**	Y	Y	Y	Y	N	N
4 Rokita	Y	Y	Y	Y	N	N
5 **Brooks**	Y	Y	Y	N	N	N
6 **Messer**	Y	Y	Y	Y	N	N
7 Carson	Y	N	N	N	Y	Y
8 **Bucshon**	Y	Y	Y	Y	N	N
9 **Hollingsworth**	Y	Y	Y	Y	N	Y
IOWA						
1 **Blum**	Y	Y	Y	P	N	N
2 Loebsack	Y	N	N	N	Y	Y
3 **Young**	Y	Y	Y	Y	N	Y
4 **King**	Y	Y	Y	Y	N	N
KANSAS						
1 **Marshall**	Y	Y	Y	N	N	N
2 **Jenkins**	Y	Y	Y	Y	N	N
3 **Yoder**	Y	Y	Y	Y	N	N
4 **Estes**	Y	Y	Y	Y	N	N
KENTUCKY						
1 **Comer**	Y	Y	Y	Y	N	N
2 **Guthrie**	Y	Y	Y	Y	N	N
3 Yarmuth	Y	N	N	N	Y	Y
4 **Massie**	Y	Y	Y	Y	Y	Y
5 **Rogers**	Y	Y	Y	Y	N	N
6 **Barr**	Y	Y	Y	Y	N	N
LOUISIANA						
1 **Scalise**	Y	Y	+	+	–	–
2 Richmond	?	?	?	?	?	?
3 **Higgins**	Y	Y	Y	Y	N	N
4 **Johnson**	Y	Y	Y	N	N	N
5 **Abraham**	Y	Y	Y	Y	N	N
6 **Graves**	Y	Y	Y	Y	N	N
MAINE						
1 Pingree	Y	N	N	N	Y	Y
2 **Poliquin**	Y	Y	Y	N	N	N
MARYLAND						
1 **Harris**	Y	Y	Y	Y	N	N
2 Ruppersberger	Y	N	N	N	Y	Y
3 Sarbanes	Y	N	N	N	Y	Y
4 Brown	Y	N	N	N	Y	Y
5 Hoyer	Y	N	N	N	Y	Y
6 Delaney	Y	N	N	N	Y	Y
7 Cummings	Y	N	N	N	Y	Y
8 Raskin	Y	N	N	N	Y	Y
MASSACHUSETTS						
1 Neal	Y	N	N	N	Y	Y
2 McGovern	Y	N	N	N	Y	Y
3 Tsongas	Y	N	N	N	Y	Y
4 Kennedy	Y	N	N	N	Y	Y
5 Clark	Y	N	N	N	Y	Y
6 Moulton	Y	N	N	N	Y	Y
7 Capuano	Y	N	N	N	Y	Y
8 Lynch	Y	N	N	N	Y	Y
9 Keating	Y	N	N	N	Y	Y
MICHIGAN						
1 **Bergman**	Y	Y	Y	N	N	Y
2 **Huizenga**	Y	Y	Y	Y	N	N
3 *Amash*	Y	Y	Y	Y	N	Y
4 **Moolenaar**	Y	Y	Y	Y	N	N
5 Kildee	Y	N	N	N	Y	Y
6 **Upton**	Y	Y	Y	Y	N	N
7 **Walberg**	Y	Y	Y	Y	N	N
8 **Bishop**	Y	Y	Y	Y	N	N
9 Levin	Y	N	N	N	Y	Y
10 **Mitchell**	Y	Y	Y	Y	N	N
11 **Trott**	Y	Y	Y	Y	N	N
12 Dingell	Y	N	N	N	Y	Y
14 Lawrence	Y	N	N	N	Y	Y
MINNESOTA						
1 Walz	?	?	?	?	?	?
2 **Lewis**	Y	Y	Y	Y	N	N
3 **Paulsen**	Y	Y	Y	N	N	N
4 McCollum	Y	N	N	N	Y	Y

	338	339	340	341	342	343
5 Ellison	Y	N	N	N	Y	Y
6 **Emmer**	Y	Y	Y	Y	N	N
7 Peterson	?	?	?	?	?	?
8 Nolan	Y	N	N	N	Y	Y
MISSISSIPPI						
1 **Kelly**	Y	Y	Y	Y	N	N
2 Thompson	Y	N	N	N	Y	Y
3 **Harper**	Y	Y	Y	Y	N	N
4 **Palazzo**	Y	Y	Y	Y	N	N
MISSOURI						
1 Clay	Y	N	N	N	Y	Y
2 **Wagner**	Y	Y	Y	Y	N	N
3 **Luetkemeyer**	Y	Y	Y	Y	N	N
4 **Hartzler**	Y	Y	Y	Y	N	N
5 Cleaver	Y	N	N	N	Y	Y
6 **Graves**	Y	Y	Y	Y	N	N
7 **Long**	Y	Y	Y	N	N	N
8 **Smith**	Y	Y	Y	Y	N	N
MONTANA						
AL **Gianforte**	Y	Y	Y	N	N	N
NEBRASKA						
1 **Fortenberry**	Y	Y	Y	N	N	Y
2 **Bacon**	Y	Y	Y	Y	N	N
3 **Smith**	Y	Y	Y	Y	N	N
NEVADA						
1 Titus	Y	N	N	N	Y	Y
2 **Amodei**	Y	Y	Y	Y	N	N
3 Rosen	Y	N	N	N	Y	Y
4 Kihuen	Y	N	N	N	Y	Y
NEW HAMPSHIRE						
1 Shea-Porter	Y	N	N	N	Y	Y
2 Kuster	Y	N	N	N	Y	Y
NEW JERSEY						
1 Norcross	Y	N	N	N	Y	Y
2 **LoBiondo**	Y	Y	Y	N	N	Y
3 **MacArthur**	Y	Y	Y	N	N	N
4 **Smith**	Y	Y	Y	N	N	Y
5 Gottheimer	Y	N	N	N	Y	Y
6 Pallone	Y	N	N	N	Y	Y
7 **Lance**	Y	Y	Y	N	Y	N
8 Sires	Y	N	N	N	Y	Y
9 Pascrell	Y	N	N	N	Y	Y
10 Payne	Y	N	N	N	Y	Y
11 **Frelinghuysen**	Y	Y	Y	Y	N	N
12 Watson Coleman	Y	N	N	N	Y	Y
NEW MEXICO						
1 Lujan Grisham	Y	N	N	N	Y	Y
2 **Pearce**	Y	Y	Y	Y	N	Y
3 Luján	Y	N	N	N	Y	Y
NEW YORK						
1 **Zeldin**	Y	Y	Y	N	N	N
2 **King**	Y	Y	Y	N	N	Y
3 Suozzi	Y	N	N	N	Y	Y
4 Rice	Y	N	N	N	Y	Y
5 Meeks	Y	N	N	N	Y	Y
6 Meng	Y	N	N	N	Y	Y
7 Velázquez	Y	N	N	N	Y	Y
8 Jeffries	Y	N	N	N	Y	Y
9 Clarke	Y	N	N	N	Y	Y
10 Nadler	Y	N	N	N	Y	Y
11 **Donovan**	Y	Y	Y	N	N	N
12 Maloney, C.	Y	N	N	N	Y	Y
13 Espaillat	Y	N	N	N	Y	Y
14 Crowley	Y	N	N	N	Y	Y
15 Serrano	Y	N	N	N	Y	Y
16 Engel	Y	N	N	N	Y	Y
17 Lowey	Y	N	N	N	Y	Y
18 Maloney, S.P.	Y	N	N	N	Y	Y
19 **Faso**	Y	Y	Y	N	N	Y
20 Tonko	Y	N	N	N	Y	Y
21 **Stefanik**	Y	Y	Y	N	N	Y
22 **Tenney**	Y	Y	Y	N	N	N
23 **Reed**	Y	Y	Y	Y	N	N
24 **Katko**	Y	Y	Y	N	N	Y
25 **Vacant**						
26 Higgins	Y	N	N	N	Y	Y
27 **Collins**	Y	Y	Y	N	N	N
NORTH CAROLINA						
1 Butterfield	Y	N	N	N	Y	Y
2 **Holding**	Y	Y	Y	N	N	N
3 **Jones**	Y	Y	Y	Y	Y	Y
4 Price	Y	N	N	N	Y	Y

	338	339	340	341	342	343
5 **Foxx**	Y	Y	Y	Y	N	N
6 **Walker**	Y	Y	Y	Y	N	N
7 **Rouzer**	Y	Y	Y	N	N	N
8 **Hudson**	Y	Y	Y	Y	N	N
9 **Pittenger**	Y	Y	Y	Y	N	N
9 **Vacant**						
10 **McHenry**	Y	Y	Y	N	N	N
11 **Meadows**	Y	?	Y	Y	N	N
12 Adams	Y	N	N	N	Y	Y
13 **Budd**	Y	Y	Y	Y	N	N
NORTH DAKOTA						
AL **Cramer**	Y	Y	Y	Y	N	N
OHIO						
1 **Chabot**	Y	Y	Y	Y	N	N
2 **Wenstrup**	Y	Y	Y	Y	N	N
3 Beatty	Y	N	N	N	Y	Y
4 **Jordan**	Y	Y	Y	Y	N	N
5 **Latta**	Y	Y	Y	Y	N	N
6 **Johnson**	Y	Y	Y	Y	N	N
7 **Gibbs**	Y	Y	Y	Y	N	N
8 **Davidson**	Y	Y	Y	Y	N	N
9 Kaptur	Y	N	N	N	Y	Y
10 **Turner**	Y	Y	Y	Y	N	N
11 Fudge	Y	N	N	N	Y	Y
12 **Vacant**						
13 Ryan	Y	N	N	N	Y	Y
14 **Joyce**	Y	Y	Y	N	N	N
15 **Stivers**	Y	Y	Y	N	N	N
16 **Renacci**	Y	Y	Y	Y	N	N
OKLAHOMA						
1 **Vacant**						
2 **Mullin**	Y	Y	Y	Y	N	Y
3 **Lucas**	Y	Y	Y	Y	N	N
4 **Cole**	Y	Y	Y	Y	N	Y
5 **Russell**	Y	Y	Y	Y	N	Y
OREGON						
1 Bonamici	Y	N	N	N	Y	Y
2 **Walden**	Y	Y	Y	Y	N	N
3 Blumenauer	Y	N	N	N	Y	Y
4 DeFazio	Y	N	N	N	Y	Y
5 Schrader	Y	N	N	?	Y	Y
PENNSYLVANIA						
1 Brady	Y	N	N	N	Y	Y
2 Evans	Y	N	N	N	Y	Y
3 **Kelly**	Y	Y	Y	Y	N	N
4 **Perry**	Y	Y	Y	Y	N	N
5 **Thompson**	Y	Y	Y	Y	N	Y
6 **Costello**	Y	Y	Y	N	N	N
7 **Vacant**						
8 **Fitzpatrick**	Y	Y	Y	N	Y	Y
9 **Shuster**	?	?	?	?	?	?
10 **Marino**	Y	Y	Y	N	N	N
11 **Barletta**	Y	Y	Y	N	N	N
12 **Rothfus**	Y	Y	Y	Y	N	N
13 Boyle	Y	N	N	N	Y	Y
14 Doyle	Y	N	N	N	Y	Y
15 **Vacant**						
16 **Smucker**	Y	Y	Y	Y	N	N
17 Cartwright	Y	N	N	N	Y	Y
18 Lamb	Y	N	Y	N	Y	Y
RHODE ISLAND						
1 Cicilline	Y	N	N	N	Y	Y
2 Langevin	Y	N	N	N	Y	Y
SOUTH CAROLINA						
1 **Sanford**	Y	Y	Y	N	N	N
2 **Wilson**	Y	Y	Y	Y	N	N
3 **Duncan**	?	?	?	?	?	?
4 **Gowdy**	Y	Y	Y	Y	N	N
5 **Norman**	Y	Y	Y	Y	N	N
6 Clyburn	Y	N	N	N	Y	Y
7 **Rice**	Y	Y	Y	Y	N	N
SOUTH DAKOTA						
AL **Noem**	Y	Y	Y	Y	N	N
TENNESSEE						
1 **Roe**	Y	Y	Y	Y	N	N
2 **Duncan**	Y	Y	Y	Y	N	N
3 **Fleischmann**	Y	Y	Y	Y	N	N
4 **DesJarlais**	Y	Y	Y	Y	N	N
5 Cooper	Y	N	N	N	Y	Y
6 **Black**	?	?	?	?	?	?
7 **Blackburn**	?	?	?	?	?	?
8 **Kustoff**	Y	Y	Y	Y	N	N
9 Cohen	Y	N	N	N	Y	Y

	338	339	340	341	342	343
TEXAS						
1 **Gohmert**	Y	Y	Y	Y	N	N
2 **Poe**	Y	Y	Y	Y	N	N
3 **Johnson, S.**	Y	Y	Y	Y	N	N
4 **Ratcliffe**	Y	Y	Y	Y	N	N
5 **Hensarling**	Y	Y	Y	Y	N	N
6 **Barton**	Y	Y	Y	Y	N	N
7 **Culberson**	Y	Y	Y	Y	N	N
8 **Brady**	Y	Y	Y	Y	N	N
9 Green, A.	Y	N	N	N	Y	Y
10 **McCaul**	Y	Y	Y	Y	N	N
11 **Conaway**	Y	Y	Y	Y	N	N
12 **Granger**	Y	Y	Y	Y	N	N
13 **Thornberry**	Y	Y	Y	Y	N	N
14 **Weber**	Y	Y	Y	Y	N	N
15 Gonzalez	Y	N	Y	N	Y	Y
16 O'Rourke	Y	N	N	N	Y	Y
17 **Flores**	Y	Y	Y	Y	N	N
18 Jackson Lee	Y	N	N	N	Y	Y
19 **Arrington**	Y	Y	Y	Y	N	N
20 Castro	Y	N	N	N	Y	Y
21 **Smith**	Y	Y	Y	Y	N	Y
22 **Olson**	Y	Y	Y	Y	N	N
23 **Hurd**	Y	Y	Y	N	N	N
24 Marchant	Y	Y	Y	Y	N	N
25 **Williams**	Y	Y	Y	Y	N	N
26 **Burgess**	Y	Y	Y	Y	N	N
27 Cloud	Y	Y	Y	Y	N	N
28 Cuellar	Y	N	N	N	Y	Y
29 Green, G.	Y	N	Y	N	Y	Y
30 Johnson, E.B.	Y	N	N	N	Y	Y
31 **Carter**	Y	Y	Y	Y	N	N
32 **Sessions**	Y	Y	Y	N	N	N
33 Veasey	Y	N	N	N	Y	Y
34 Vela	Y	N	N	N	Y	Y
35 Doggett	Y	N	N	N	Y	Y
36 **Babin**	Y	Y	Y	Y	N	N
UTAH						
1 **Bishop**	Y	Y	Y	Y	N	N
2 **Stewart**	Y	Y	Y	N	N	N
3 **Curtis**	Y	Y	Y	Y	N	N
4 **Love**	Y	Y	Y	N	N	N
VERMONT						
AL Welch	Y	N	N	N	Y	Y
VIRGINIA						
1 **Wittman**	Y	?	Y	N	N	N
2 **Taylor**	Y	Y	Y	Y	N	N
3 Scott	Y	N	N	N	Y	Y
4 McEachin	Y	N	N	N	Y	Y
5 **Garrett**	Y	Y	Y	Y	N	N
6 **Goodlatte**	Y	Y	Y	Y	N	N
7 **Brat**	Y	Y	Y	Y	N	N
8 Beyer	Y	N	N	N	Y	Y
9 **Griffith**	Y	Y	Y	Y	N	N
10 **Comstock**	Y	Y	Y	N	N	N
11 Connolly	Y	N	N	N	Y	Y
WASHINGTON						
1 DelBene	Y	N	N	N	Y	Y
2 Larsen	Y	N	N	N	Y	Y
3 **Herrera Beutler**	Y	Y	Y	Y	N	Y
4 **Newhouse**	Y	Y	Y	N	N	N
5 **McMorris Rodgers**	Y	Y	Y	Y	N	N
6 Kilmer	Y	N	N	N	Y	Y
7 Jayapal	Y	N	N	N	Y	Y
8 **Reichert**	Y	Y	Y	?	N	N
9 Smith	Y	N	N	N	Y	Y
10 Heck	Y	N	N	N	Y	Y
WEST VIRGINIA						
1 **McKinley**	Y	Y	Y	N	N	N
2 **Mooney**	Y	Y	Y	Y	N	N
3 **Jenkins**	Y	Y	Y	N	N	N
WISCONSIN						
1 **Ryan**						
2 Pocan	Y	N	N	N	Y	Y
3 Kind	Y	N	N	N	Y	Y
4 Moore	Y	N	N	N	Y	Y
5 **Sensenbrenner**	Y	Y	Y	Y	N	N
6 **Grothman**	Y	Y	Y	Y	N	N
7 **Duffy**	Y	Y	Y	Y	N	N
8 **Gallagher**	Y	Y	Y	Y	N	N
WYOMING						
AL **Cheney**	Y	Y	Y	Y	N	N

III HOUSE VOTES

VOTE NUMBER

344. HR6147. FISCAL 2019 INTERIOR-ENVIRONMENT AND FINANCIAL SERVICES APPROPRIATIONS PACKAGE/EPA PROGRAMS FUNDING. Adams, D-N.C., amendment that would decrease, then increase, funding for Environmental Protection Agency environmental programs and management by $742,000. Rejected in Committee of the Whole 194-218: R 8-218; D 186-0. July 18, 2018.

345. HR6147. FISCAL 2019 INTERIOR-ENVIRONMENT AND FINANCIAL SERVICES APPROPRIATIONS PACKAGE/ARTS AND HUMANITIES FUNDING. Grothman, R-Wis., amendment that would increase funding for the spending reduction account by $46.5 million, and would decrease funding for funding for the National Endowment on the Arts and the Humanities by the same amount. Rejected in Committee of the Whole 114-297: R 113-112; D 1-185. July 18, 2018.

346. HR6147. FISCAL 2019 INTERIOR-ENVIRONMENT AND FINANCIAL SERVICES APPROPRIATIONS PACKAGE/EMISSIONS STANDARDS ENFORCEMENT. Mullin, R-Okla., amendment that would prohibit appropriated funds from being used to enforce the EPA's "Oil and Natural Gas Sector: Emission Standards for New, Reconstructed, and Modified Sources" rule. Adopted in Committee of the Whole 215-194: R 213-16; D 2-178. July 18, 2018.

347. HR6147. FISCAL 2019 INTERIOR-ENVIRONMENT AND FINANCIAL SERVICES APPROPRIATIONS PACKAGE/SOCIAL COST OF CARBON REGULATIONS. Mullin, R-Okla., amendment that would prohibit appropriated funds from being used to prepare, propose or promulgate any regulation or guidance which would rely on the analyses found in various documents published by the Interagency Working Group on the Social Cost of Carbon. Adopted in Committee of the Whole 215-199: R 213-16; D 2-183. July 18, 2018.

348. HR6147. FISCAL 2019 INTERIOR-ENVIRONMENT AND FINANCIAL SERVICES APPROPRIATIONS PACKAGE/WASHINGTON STATE WATER QUALITY STANDARDS. McMorris Rodgers, R-Wash., amendment that would prohibit appropriated funds from being used to implement Washington state's revised water quality standard. Adopted in Committee of the Whole 227-185: R 223-7; D 4-178. July 18, 2018.

349. HR6147. FISCAL 2019 INTERIOR-ENVIRONMENT AND FINANCIAL SERVICES APPROPRIATIONS PACKAGE/PREBLE'S MEADOW JUMPING MOUSE. Lamborn, R-Colo., amendment that would prohibit appropriated funds from being used to implement or enforce the threatened species listing of the Preble's meadow jumping mouse under the Endangered Species Act. Adopted in Committee of the Whole 213-202: R 213-17; D 0-185. July 18, 2018.

	344	345	346	347	348	349
Alabama						
1 **Byrne**	N	Y	Y	Y	Y	Y
2 **Roby**	?	?	Y	Y	Y	Y
3 **Rogers**	N	Y	Y	Y	Y	Y
4 **Aderholt**	N	N	Y	Y	Y	Y
5 **Brooks**	N	Y	Y	Y	Y	N
6 **Palmer**	N	Y	Y	Y	Y	Y
7 Sewell	Y	N	N	N	N	N
ALASKA						
AL **Young**	N	N	Y	Y	Y	Y
ARIZONA						
1 O'Halleran	Y	N	N	N	N	N
2 **McSally**	N	Y	Y	Y	Y	Y
3 Grijalva	Y	N	N	N	?	N
4 **Gosar**	N	Y	Y	Y	Y	Y
5 **Biggs**	N	Y	Y	Y	Y	Y
6 **Schweikert**	N	Y	Y	Y	Y	Y
7 Gallego	Y	N	N	N	N	N
8 **Lesko**	N	Y	Y	Y	Y	Y
9 Sinema	Y	N	–	N	N	N
ARKANSAS						
1 **Crawford**	N	N	Y	Y	Y	Y
2 **Hill**	N	N	Y	Y	Y	Y
3 **Womack**	N	N	Y	Y	Y	Y
4 **Westerman**	N	Y	Y	Y	Y	Y
CALIFORNIA						
1 **LaMalfa**	N	Y	Y	Y	Y	Y
2 Huffman	Y	N	N	N	N	N
3 Garamendi	Y	N	N	N	N	N
4 **McClintock**	N	Y	Y	Y	Y	Y
5 Thompson	Y	N	N	N	N	N
6 Matsui	Y	N	N	N	N	N
7 Bera	Y	N	N	N	N	N
8 **Cook**	N	N	Y	Y	Y	Y
9 McNerney	Y	N	N	N	N	N
10 **Denham**	N	N	Y	Y	Y	Y
11 DeSaulnier	Y	N	N	N	N	N
12 Pelosi	Y	N	N	N	N	N
13 Lee	Y	N	N	N	N	N
14 Speier	?	?	?	?	?	?
15 Swalwell	Y	N	N	N	N	N
16 Costa	Y	N	N	N	N	N
17 Khanna	Y	N	N	N	N	N
18 Eshoo	Y	N	N	N	N	N
19 Lofgren	Y	N	N	N	N	N
20 Panetta	Y	N	N	N	N	N
21 **Valadao**	N	N	Y	Y	Y	Y
22 **Nunes**	N	Y	Y	Y	Y	Y
23 **McCarthy**	N	Y	Y	Y	Y	Y
24 Carbajal	Y	N	N	N	N	N
25 **Knight**	N	N	Y	Y	Y	Y
26 Brownley	Y	N	N	N	N	N
27 Chu	Y	N	N	N	N	N
28 Schiff	Y	N	N	N	N	N
29 Cardenas	?	?	?	?	?	?
30 Sherman	Y	N	N	N	N	N
31 Aguilar	Y	N	–	N	N	N
32 Napolitano	Y	N	N	N	N	N
33 Lieu	Y	N	N	N	N	N
34 Gomez	Y	N	N	N	N	N
35 Torres	Y	N	N	N	N	N
36 Ruiz	Y	N	N	N	N	N
37 Bass	?	?	?	?	?	?
38 Sánchez, Linda	Y	N	N	N	N	N
39 **Royce**	N	Y	Y	N	Y	Y
40 Roybal-Allard	Y	N	N	N	N	N
41 Takano	Y	N	N	N	N	N
42 **Calvert**	N	N	Y	Y	N	Y
43 Waters	Y	N	N	N	Y	N
44 Barragan	Y	N	N	N	N	N
45 **Walters**	N	Y	Y	Y	Y	Y
46 Correa	Y	N	N	N	N	N
47 Lowenthal	Y	N	N	N	N	N
48 **Rohrabacher**	N	Y	Y	Y	Y	Y
49 **Issa**	N	Y	Y	Y	Y	Y
50 **Hunter**	N	Y	Y	Y	Y	Y
51 Vargas	Y	N	N	N	N	N
52 Peters	Y	N	–	N	N	N
53 Davis	Y	N	N	N	N	N

	344	345	346	347	348	349
COLORADO						
1 DeGette	Y	N	N	N	N	N
2 Polis	Y	N	N	N	N	N
3 **Tipton**	N	N	Y	Y	Y	Y
4 **Buck**	N	Y	Y	Y	Y	Y
5 **Lamborn**	N	Y	Y	Y	Y	Y
6 **Coffman**	N	N	N	Y	Y	Y
7 Perlmutter	Y	N	N	N	N	N
CONNECTICUT						
1 Larson	Y	N	N	N	N	N
2 Courtney	Y	N	N	N	N	N
3 DeLauro	Y	N	N	N	N	N
4 Himes	Y	N	N	N	N	N
5 Esty	Y	N	N	N	N	N
DELAWARE						
AL Blunt Rochester	Y	N	N	N	N	N
FLORIDA						
1 **Gaetz**	?	?	?	?	?	?
2 **Dunn**	N	Y	Y	Y	Y	Y
3 **Yoho**	N	Y	Y	Y	Y	Y
4 **Rutherford**	N	N	Y	Y	Y	Y
5 Lawson	Y	N	N	N	N	N
6 **DeSantis**	?	?	?	?	?	?
7 Murphy	Y	N	N	N	N	N
8 **Posey**	N	Y	Y	Y	Y	Y
9 Soto	Y	N	N	N	N	N
10 Demings	Y	N	N	N	N	N
11 **Webster**	N	Y	Y	Y	Y	Y
12 **Bilirakis**	N	Y	Y	Y	Y	Y
13 Crist	Y	N	N	N	N	N
14 Castor	Y	N	N	N	N	N
15 **Ross**	N	N	Y	Y	Y	Y
16 **Buchanan**	N	N	Y	Y	Y	N
17 **Rooney, T.**	N	Y	Y	Y	Y	Y
18 **Mast**	N	N	Y	Y	Y	Y
19 **Rooney, F.**	N	Y	N	Y	Y	Y
20 Hastings	Y	N	N	N	N	N
21 Frankel	Y	N	N	N	N	N
22 Deutch	Y	N	N	N	N	N
23 Wasserman Schultz	Y	N	N	N	N	N
24 Wilson	Y	N	N	N	N	N
25 **Diaz-Balart**	N	N	Y	Y	Y	Y
26 **Curbelo**	Y	N	N	N	N	N
27 **Ros-Lehtinen**	Y	N	N	N	Y	N
GEORGIA						
1 **Carter**	N	Y	Y	Y	Y	Y
2 Bishop	Y	N	Y	Y	N	N
3 **Ferguson**	N	Y	Y	Y	Y	Y
4 Johnson	Y	N	N	N	N	N
5 Lewis	Y	N	N	N	N	N
6 **Handel**	N	Y	Y	Y	Y	Y
7 **Woodall**	N	Y	Y	Y	Y	Y
8 **Scott, A.**	N	Y	Y	Y	Y	Y
9 **Collins**	N	Y	Y	Y	Y	Y
10 **Hice**	N	Y	Y	Y	Y	Y
11 **Loudermilk**	N	Y	Y	Y	Y	Y
12 **Allen**	N	Y	Y	Y	Y	Y
13 Scott, D.	Y	N	N	N	?	N
14 **Graves**	N	Y	Y	Y	Y	Y
HAWAII						
1 Hanabusa	?	?	?	?	?	?
2 Gabbard	Y	N	N	N	N	N
IDAHO						
1 **Labrador**	N	?	Y	Y	Y	Y
2 **Simpson**	N	N	Y	Y	Y	Y
ILLINOIS						
1 Rush	Y	N	N	N	N	N
2 Kelly	Y	N	N	N	N	N
3 Lipinski	Y	N	N	N	N	N
4 Gutierrez	Y	N	N	N	?	N
5 Quigley	Y	N	N	N	N	N
6 **Roskam**	Y	N	N	N	Y	Y
7 Davis, D.	Y	N	N	N	N	N
8 Krishnamoorthi	Y	N	N	N	N	N
9 Schakowsky	Y	N	N	N	N	N
10 Schneider	Y	N	N	N	N	N
11 Foster	Y	N	N	N	N	N
12 **Bost**	N	N	Y	Y	Y	Y
13 **Davis, R.**	N	N	Y	Y	Y	Y

KEY	**Republicans**	Democrats	*Independents*	
Y	Voted for (yea)	X Paired against	C Voted "present" to avoid possible conflict of interest	
#	Paired for	– Announced against		
+	Announced for	P Voted "present"	? Did not vote or otherwise make a position known	
N	Voted against (nay)			

	344	345	346	347	348	349
14 **Hultgren**	N	N	Y	Y	Y	Y
15 **Shimkus**	N	N	Y	Y	Y	Y
16 **Kinzinger**	N	N	Y	Y	Y	Y
17 Bustos	Y	N	N	N	N	N
18 **LaHood**	N	N	Y	Y	Y	Y
INDIANA						
1 Visclosky	Y	N	N	N	N	N
2 **Walorski**	N	N	Y	Y	Y	Y
3 **Banks**	N	Y	Y	Y	Y	Y
4 Rokita	N	Y	Y	Y	Y	Y
5 **Brooks**	N	N	Y	Y	Y	Y
6 **Messer**	N	Y	Y	Y	Y	Y
7 Carson	Y	N	N	N	N	N
8 **Bucshon**	N	N	Y	Y	Y	Y
9 **Hollingsworth**	N	N	Y	Y	Y	Y
IOWA						
1 **Blum**	N	N	Y	Y	Y	Y
2 Loebsack	Y	N	N	N	N	N
3 **Young**	N	N	Y	Y	Y	Y
4 **King**	N	Y	Y	Y	Y	Y
KANSAS						
1 **Marshall**	N	N	Y	Y	Y	Y
2 **Jenkins**	N	Y	Y	Y	Y	Y
3 **Yoder**	N	N	Y	Y	Y	Y
4 **Estes**	N	Y	Y	Y	Y	Y
KENTUCKY						
1 **Comer**	N	Y	Y	Y	Y	Y
2 **Guthrie**	N	Y	Y	Y	Y	Y
3 Yarmuth	Y	N	N	N	N	N
4 **Massie**	N	Y	Y	Y	Y	Y
5 **Rogers**	N	N	Y	Y	Y	Y
6 **Barr**	N	Y	Y	Y	Y	Y
LOUISIANA						
1 **Scalise**	–	+	Y	Y	Y	Y
2 Richmond	?	?	?	?	?	?
3 **Higgins**	N	Y	Y	Y	Y	Y
4 **Johnson**	N	Y	Y	Y	Y	Y
5 **Abraham**	N	Y	Y	Y	Y	Y
6 **Graves**	N	Y	Y	Y	Y	Y
MAINE						
1 Pingree	Y	N	N	N	N	N
2 **Poliquin**	N	N	Y	Y	Y	Y
MARYLAND						
1 **Harris**	N	Y	Y	Y	Y	Y
2 Ruppersberger	Y	N	N	N	N	N
3 Sarbanes	Y	N	N	N	N	N
4 Brown	Y	N	N	N	N	N
5 Hoyer	Y	N	?	?	?	?
6 Delaney	Y	N	N	N	N	N
7 Cummings	Y	N	N	N	N	N
8 Raskin	Y	N	N	N	N	N
MASSACHUSETTS						
1 Neal	Y	N	N	N	N	N
2 McGovern	Y	N	N	N	N	N
3 Tsongas	Y	N	N	N	N	N
4 Kennedy	Y	N	N	N	N	N
5 Clark	Y	N	N	N	N	N
6 Moulton	Y	N	N	N	N	N
7 Capuano	Y	N	N	N	N	N
8 Lynch	Y	N	N	N	N	N
9 Keating	Y	N	N	N	N	N
MICHIGAN						
1 **Bergman**	N	N	Y	N	Y	Y
2 **Huizenga**	N	Y	Y	Y	Y	Y
3 *Amash*	N	Y	Y	Y	N	N
4 **Moolenaar**	N	N	Y	Y	Y	Y
5 Kildee	Y	N	N	N	N	N
6 **Upton**	Y	N	N	Y	Y	N
7 **Walberg**	N	Y	Y	Y	Y	Y
8 **Bishop**	N	Y	Y	Y	Y	Y
9 Levin	Y	N	N	N	N	N
10 **Mitchell**	N	N	Y	Y	Y	Y
11 **Trott**	N	N	Y	Y	Y	Y
12 Dingell	Y	N	N	N	N	N
14 Lawrence	Y	N	N	N	N	N
MINNESOTA						
1 Walz	?	?	?	?	?	?
2 **Lewis**	N	Y	Y	Y	Y	Y
3 **Paulsen**	N	N	+	N	Y	N
4 McCollum	Y	N	N	N	N	N

	344	345	346	347	348	349
5 Ellison	Y	N	N	N	N	N
6 **Emmer**	N	Y	Y	Y	Y	Y
7 Peterson	?	?	?	?	?	?
8 Nolan	Y	N	N	N	N	N
MISSISSIPPI						
1 **Kelly**	N	Y	Y	Y	Y	Y
2 Thompson	Y	N	N	N	N	N
3 **Harper**	N	N	Y	Y	Y	Y
4 **Palazzo**	N	N	Y	Y	Y	Y
MISSOURI						
1 Clay	Y	N	N	N	N	N
2 **Wagner**	?	?	Y	Y	Y	Y
3 **Luetkemeyer**	N	Y	Y	Y	Y	Y
4 **Hartzler**	N	Y	Y	Y	Y	Y
5 Cleaver	Y	N	N	N	N	N
6 **Graves**	N	Y	Y	Y	Y	Y
7 **Long**	N	N	Y	Y	Y	Y
8 **Smith**	N	Y	Y	Y	Y	Y
MONTANA						
AL **Gianforte**	N	N	Y	Y	Y	Y
NEBRASKA						
1 **Fortenberry**	N	N	Y	Y	Y	N
2 **Bacon**	N	N	Y	Y	Y	Y
3 **Smith**	N	Y	Y	Y	Y	Y
NEVADA						
1 Titus	Y	N	N	N	N	N
2 **Amodei**	N	N	Y	N	Y	Y
3 Rosen	Y	N	N	N	N	N
4 Kihuen	Y	N	N	N	N	N
NEW HAMPSHIRE						
1 Shea-Porter	Y	N	?	N	N	N
2 Kuster	Y	N	N	N	N	N
NEW JERSEY						
1 Norcross	Y	N	N	N	N	N
2 **LoBiondo**	N	N	Y	Y	N	N
3 **MacArthur**	N	N	Y	Y	Y	Y
4 **Smith**	N	N	N	Y	N	N
5 Gottheimer	Y	N	N	N	N	N
6 Pallone	Y	N	N	N	N	N
7 **Lance**	Y	N	N	N	N	N
8 Sires	Y	N	N	N	N	N
9 Pascrell	Y	N	N	N	N	N
10 Payne	Y	N	N	N	N	N
11 **Frelinghuysen**	N	N	Y	Y	Y	Y
12 Watson Coleman	Y	N	N	N	N	N
NEW MEXICO						
1 Lujan Grisham	Y	N	N	N	N	N
2 **Pearce**	N	N	Y	Y	Y	Y
3 Luján	Y	N	N	N	N	N
NEW YORK						
1 **Zeldin**	N	N	Y	Y	Y	Y
2 **King**	N	N	Y	Y	Y	N
3 Suozzi	Y	N	N	N	N	N
4 Rice	Y	N	–	N	N	N
5 Meeks	Y	N	N	N	N	N
6 Meng	Y	N	N	N	N	N
7 Velázquez	Y	N	N	N	N	N
8 Jeffries	Y	N	N	N	N	N
9 Clarke	Y	N	N	N	N	N
10 Nadler	Y	N	N	N	N	N
11 **Donovan**	N	N	Y	Y	Y	N
12 Maloney, C.	Y	N	N	N	Y	N
13 Espaillat	Y	N	N	N	N	N
14 Crowley	Y	N	N	N	N	N
15 Serrano	Y	N	N	N	N	N
16 Engel	Y	N	N	N	N	N
17 Lowey	Y	N	N	N	N	N
18 Maloney, S.P.	Y	N	N	N	N	N
19 **Faso**	N	N	N	N	Y	Y
20 Tonko	Y	N	N	N	N	N
21 **Stefanik**	N	N	N	N	Y	Y
22 **Tenney**	N	N	Y	Y	Y	Y
23 **Reed**	N	N	Y	N	Y	Y
24 **Katko**	N	N	N	N	Y	Y
25 **Vacant**						
26 Higgins	Y	N	N	N	N	N
27 **Collins**	N	N	Y	Y	Y	Y
NORTH CAROLINA						
1 Butterfield	Y	N	N	N	N	N
2 **Holding**	N	Y	Y	Y	Y	Y
3 **Jones**	Y	Y	Y	Y	Y	Y
4 Price	Y	N	N	N	N	N

	344	345	346	347	348	349
5 **Foxx**	N	Y	Y	Y	Y	Y
6 **Walker**	N	Y	Y	Y	Y	Y
7 **Rouzer**	N	Y	Y	Y	Y	Y
8 **Hudson**	N	Y	Y	Y	Y	Y
9 **Pittenger**	N	Y	Y	Y	Y	Y
9 **Vacant**						
10 **McHenry**	N	Y	Y	N	Y	Y
11 **Meadows**	N	Y	Y	Y	Y	Y
12 Adams	Y	N	N	N	N	N
13 **Budd**	N	Y	Y	Y	Y	Y
NORTH DAKOTA						
AL **Cramer**	N	N	Y	Y	Y	Y
OHIO						
1 **Chabot**	N	Y	Y	Y	Y	Y
2 **Wenstrup**	N	Y	Y	Y	Y	Y
3 Beatty	Y	N	N	N	N	N
4 **Jordan**	N	Y	Y	Y	Y	Y
5 **Latta**	N	Y	Y	Y	Y	Y
6 **Johnson**	N	N	Y	Y	Y	Y
7 **Gibbs**	N	Y	Y	Y	Y	Y
8 **Davidson**	N	Y	Y	Y	Y	Y
9 Kaptur	Y	N	N	N	N	N
10 **Turner**	N	N	Y	Y	Y	Y
11 Fudge	Y	N	N	N	N	N
12 **Vacant**						
13 Ryan	Y	N	N	N	N	N
14 **Joyce**	N	N	Y	?	Y	Y
15 **Stivers**	N	N	Y	Y	Y	Y
16 **Renacci**	N	N	Y	Y	Y	Y
OKLAHOMA						
1 **Vacant**						
2 **Mullin**	N	Y	Y	Y	Y	Y
3 **Lucas**	N	N	Y	Y	Y	Y
4 **Cole**	N	N	Y	Y	N	Y
5 **Russell**	N	Y	Y	Y	Y	Y
OREGON						
1 Bonamici	Y	N	N	N	N	N
2 **Walden**	N	N	Y	Y	Y	Y
3 Blumenauer	Y	N	N	N	N	N
4 DeFazio	Y	N	N	N	N	N
5 Schrader	Y	N	N	N	Y	N
PENNSYLVANIA						
1 Brady	Y	N	N	N	N	N
2 Evans	Y	N	N	N	N	N
3 **Kelly**	N	N	Y	Y	Y	Y
4 **Perry**	N	Y	Y	Y	Y	Y
5 **Thompson**	N	N	Y	Y	Y	Y
6 **Costello**	Y	N	N	N	Y	N
7 **Vacant**						
8 **Fitzpatrick**	Y	N	N	N	N	N
9 **Shuster**	?	?	?	?	?	?
10 **Marino**	N	N	Y	Y	Y	Y
11 **Barletta**	N	N	Y	Y	Y	Y
12 **Rothfus**	N	Y	Y	Y	Y	Y
13 Boyle	Y	N	N	N	N	N
14 Doyle	Y	N	N	N	N	N
15 **Vacant**						
16 **Smucker**	N	Y	Y	Y	Y	Y
17 Cartwright	Y	N	N	N	N	N
18 Lamb	Y	N	N	N	N	N
RHODE ISLAND						
1 Cicilline	Y	N	N	N	N	N
2 Langevin	Y	N	N	N	N	N
SOUTH CAROLINA						
1 **Sanford**	N	Y	N	Y	N	N
2 **Wilson**	N	Y	Y	Y	Y	Y
3 **Duncan**	?	?	Y	Y	Y	Y
4 **Gowdy**	N	N	Y	Y	Y	Y
5 **Norman**	N	Y	Y	Y	Y	Y
6 Clyburn	Y	N	N	N	N	N
7 **Rice**	N	Y	Y	Y	Y	Y
SOUTH DAKOTA						
AL **Noem**	N	Y	Y	Y	Y	Y
TENNESSEE						
1 **Roe**	N	Y	Y	Y	Y	Y
2 **Duncan**	N	Y	Y	Y	Y	Y
3 **Fleischmann**	N	N	Y	Y	Y	Y
4 **DesJarlais**	N	Y	Y	Y	Y	Y
5 Cooper	Y	N	N	N	N	N
6 **Black**	?	?	?	?	?	?
7 **Blackburn**	?	?	?	?	?	?
8 **Kustoff**	N	Y	Y	Y	Y	Y
9 Cohen	Y	N	N	N	N	N

	344	345	346	347	348	349
TEXAS						
1 **Gohmert**	N	N	Y	Y	Y	Y
2 **Poe**	N	N	Y	Y	Y	Y
3 **Johnson, S.**	N	Y	Y	Y	Y	Y
4 **Ratcliffe**	N	N	Y	Y	Y	Y
5 **Hensarling**	N	Y	Y	Y	Y	Y
6 **Barton**	N	N	Y	Y	Y	Y
7 **Culberson**	N	N	Y	Y	Y	Y
8 **Brady**	N	Y	Y	Y	Y	Y
9 Green, A.	Y	N	N	N	N	N
10 **McCaul**	N	N	Y	Y	Y	Y
11 **Conaway**	N	N	Y	Y	Y	Y
12 **Granger**	N	N	Y	Y	Y	Y
13 **Thornberry**	N	N	Y	Y	Y	Y
14 **Weber**	N	N	Y	Y	Y	Y
15 Gonzalez	Y	Y	N	N	N	N
16 O'Rourke	Y	N	N	N	N	N
17 **Flores**	N	Y	Y	Y	Y	Y
18 Jackson Lee	Y	N	N	N	N	N
19 **Arrington**	N	Y	Y	Y	Y	Y
20 Castro	Y	N	N	N	N	N
21 **Smith**	N	N	Y	Y	Y	Y
22 **Olson**	N	N	Y	Y	Y	Y
23 **Hurd**	N	N	Y	Y	Y	Y
24 Marchant	N	Y	Y	Y	Y	Y
25 **Williams**	N	N	Y	Y	Y	Y
26 **Burgess**	N	Y	Y	Y	Y	Y
27 Cloud	N	Y	Y	Y	Y	Y
28 Cuellar	Y	N	Y	Y	Y	N
29 Green, G.	Y	N	N	N	N	N
30 Johnson, E.B.	Y	N	N	N	N	N
31 **Carter**	N	N	Y	Y	Y	Y
32 **Sessions**	N	N	Y	Y	Y	Y
33 Veasey	Y	N	N	N	N	N
34 Vela	Y	N	N	N	N	N
35 Doggett	Y	N	N	N	N	N
36 **Babin**	N	Y	Y	Y	Y	Y
UTAH						
1 **Bishop**	N	Y	Y	Y	Y	Y
2 **Stewart**	N	N	Y	Y	Y	Y
3 **Curtis**	N	Y	Y	Y	Y	Y
4 **Love**	N	N	Y	Y	Y	Y
VERMONT						
AL Welch	Y	N	N	N	N	N
VIRGINIA						
1 **Wittman**	N	Y	Y	Y	Y	Y
2 **Taylor**	N	N	Y	Y	Y	Y
3 Scott	Y	N	N	N	N	N
4 McEachin	Y	N	N	N	N	N
5 **Garrett**	N	Y	Y	Y	Y	Y
6 **Goodlatte**	N	Y	Y	Y	Y	Y
7 **Brat**	N	Y	Y	Y	Y	Y
8 Beyer	Y	N	N	N	N	N
9 **Griffith**	N	Y	Y	Y	Y	Y
10 **Comstock**	N	N	Y	Y	Y	Y
11 Connolly	Y	N	N	N	N	N
WASHINGTON						
1 DelBene	Y	N	N	N	N	N
2 Larsen	Y	N	N	N	N	N
3 **Herrera Beutler**	N	N	Y	Y	Y	Y
4 **Newhouse**	N	N	Y	Y	Y	Y
5 **McMorris Rodgers**	N	Y	Y	Y	Y	Y
6 Kilmer	Y	N	N	N	N	N
7 Jayapal	Y	N	N	N	N	N
8 **Reichert**	N	N	N	Y	Y	N
9 Smith	Y	N	N	N	N	N
10 Heck	Y	N	N	N	N	N
WEST VIRGINIA						
1 **McKinley**	N	N	Y	Y	Y	Y
2 **Mooney**	N	Y	Y	Y	Y	Y
3 **Jenkins**	N	N	Y	Y	Y	Y
WISCONSIN						
1 **Ryan**						
2 Pocan	Y	N	N	N	N	N
3 Kind	Y	N	N	N	N	N
4 Moore	Y	N	N	N	N	N
5 **Sensenbrenner**	N	Y	Y	Y	Y	Y
6 **Grothman**	N	Y	Y	Y	Y	Y
7 **Duffy**	N	N	Y	Y	Y	Y
8 **Gallagher**	N	Y	Y	Y	Y	Y
WYOMING						
AL **Cheney**	N	N	Y	Y	Y	Y

ⅠⅠⅠ HOUSE VOTES

VOTE NUMBER

350. HR6147. FISCAL 2019 INTERIOR-ENVIRONMENT AND FINANCIAL SERVICES APPROPRIATIONS PACKAGE/ENDANGERED AND THREATENED SPECIES. Lamborn, R-Colo., amendment that would prohibit appropriated funds from being used to implement or enforce the threatened species or endangered species listing of any plant or wildlife that has not undergone a review as required by the Endangered Species Act. Adopted in Committee of the Whole 213-201: R 210-19; D 3-182. July 18, 2018.

351. HR6147. FISCAL 2019 INTERIOR-ENVIRONMENT AND FINANCIAL SERVICES APPROPRIATIONS PACKAGE/WATERSHED REGULATION. Goodlatte, R-Va., amendment that would prohibit appropriated funds from being used by the EPA to take any actions described as a "backstop" in a Dec. 2009 letter from the EPA's regional administrator to the states in the watershed and the District of Columbia. Adopted in Committee of the Whole 213-202: R 211-19; D 2-183. July 18, 2018.

352. HR6147. FISCAL 2019 INTERIOR-ENVIRONMENT AND FINANCIAL SERVICES APPROPRIATIONS PACKAGE/GRAZING PERMIT QUALIFICATIONS. Gallego, D-Ariz., amendment that would prohibit appropriated funds from being used to issue a grazing permit or lease that violates the mandatory qualifications for such permits. Rejected in Committee of the Whole 203-212: R 19-211; D 184-1. July 18, 2018.

353. HR6147. FISCAL 2019 INTERIOR-ENVIRONMENT AND FINANCIAL SERVICES APPROPRIATIONS PACKAGE/MEADOW JUMPING MOUSE. Pearce, R-N.M., amendment that would prohibit appropriated funds from being used to treat the New Mexico meadow jumping mouse as an endangered species. Rejected in Committee of the Whole 206-209: R 206-24; D 0-185. July 18, 2018.

354. HR6147. FISCAL 2019 INTERIOR-ENVIRONMENT AND FINANCIAL SERVICES APPROPRIATIONS PACKAGE/LESSER PRAIRIE CHICKEN. Pearce, R-N.M., amendment that would prohibit appropriated funds from being used to propose, implement or enforce any rulemaking on the lesser prairie chicken. Adopted in Committee of the Whole 216-199: R 215-15; D 1-184. July 18, 2018.

355. HR6147. FISCAL 2019 INTERIOR-ENVIRONMENT AND FINANCIAL SERVICES APPROPRIATIONS PACKAGE/IRONWOOD FOREST NATIONAL MONUMENT. Gosar, R-Ariz., amendment that would prohibit appropriated funds from being used to carry out the establishment of the Ironwood Forest National Monument. Rejected in Committee of the Whole 193-220: R 193-35; D 0-185. July 18, 2018.

	350	351	352	353	354	355
ALABAMA						
1 Byrne	Y	Y	N	Y	Y	Y
2 Roby	Y	Y	N	Y	Y	Y
3 Rogers	Y	Y	N	Y	Y	Y
4 Aderholt	Y	Y	N	Y	Y	Y
5 Brooks	N	N	Y	N	N	Y
6 Palmer	Y	Y	N	Y	Y	Y
7 Sewell	N	N	Y	N	N	N
ALASKA						
AL Young	Y	Y	N	Y	Y	Y
ARIZONA						
1 O'Halleran	N	N	Y	N	N	N
2 McSally	Y	Y	N	Y	Y	N
3 Grijalva	N	N	Y	N	N	N
4 Gosar	Y	Y	N	Y	Y	Y
5 Biggs	Y	Y	N	Y	Y	Y
6 Schweikert	Y	Y	N	Y	Y	Y
7 Gallego	N	N	Y	N	N	N
8 Lesko	Y	Y	N	Y	Y	Y
9 Sinema	N	N	Y	N	N	N
ARKANSAS						
1 Crawford	Y	Y	N	Y	Y	?
2 Hill	Y	Y	N	Y	Y	Y
3 Womack	Y	Y	N	Y	Y	Y
4 Westerman	Y	Y	N	Y	Y	Y
CALIFORNIA						
1 LaMalfa	Y	Y	N	Y	Y	Y
2 Huffman	N	N	Y	N	N	N
3 Garamendi	N	N	Y	N	N	N
4 McClintock	Y	Y	N	Y	Y	Y
5 Thompson	N	N	Y	N	N	N
6 Matsui	N	N	Y	N	N	N
7 Bera	N	N	Y	N	N	N
8 Cook	Y	Y	N	Y	Y	Y
9 McNerney	N	N	Y	N	N	N
10 Denham	Y	Y	N	Y	Y	Y
11 DeSaulnier	N	N	Y	N	N	N
12 Pelosi	N	N	Y	N	N	N
13 Lee	N	N	Y	N	N	N
14 Speier	?	?	?	?	?	?
15 Swalwell	N	N	Y	N	N	N
16 Costa	Y	N	Y	N	N	N
17 Khanna	N	N	Y	N	N	N
18 Eshoo	N	N	Y	N	N	N
19 Lofgren	N	N	Y	N	N	N
20 Panetta	N	N	Y	N	N	N
21 Valadao	Y	Y	N	Y	Y	Y
22 Nunes	Y	Y	N	Y	Y	Y
23 McCarthy	Y	Y	N	Y	Y	Y
24 Carbajal	N	N	Y	N	N	N
25 Knight	Y	Y	N	Y	Y	N
26 Brownley	N	N	Y	N	N	N
27 Chu	N	N	Y	N	N	N
28 Schiff	N	N	Y	N	N	N
29 Cardenas	?	?	?	?	?	?
30 Sherman	N	N	Y	N	N	N
31 Aguilar	N	N	Y	N	N	N
32 Napolitano	N	N	Y	N	N	N
33 Lieu	N	N	Y	N	N	N
34 Gomez	N	N	Y	N	N	N
35 Torres	N	N	Y	N	N	N
36 Ruiz	N	N	Y	N	N	N
37 Bass	?	?	?	?	?	?
38 Sánchez, Linda	N	N	Y	N	N	N
39 Royce	Y	Y	N	Y	Y	Y
40 Roybal-Allard	N	N	Y	N	N	N
41 Takano	N	N	Y	N	N	N
42 Calvert	Y	Y	N	Y	Y	Y
43 Waters	N	N	Y	N	N	N
44 Barragan	N	N	N	N	N	N
45 Walters	Y	Y	N	Y	Y	Y
46 Correa	N	N	Y	N	N	N
47 Lowenthal	N	N	Y	N	N	N
48 Rohrabacher	Y	Y	N	Y	Y	Y
49 Issa	Y	Y	N	Y	Y	Y
50 Hunter	Y	Y	N	Y	Y	Y
51 Vargas	N	N	Y	N	N	N
52 Peters	N	N	Y	N	N	N
53 Davis	N	N	Y	N	N	N

	350	351	352	353	354	355
COLORADO						
1 DeGette	N	N	Y	N	N	N
2 Polis	N	N	Y	N	N	N
3 Tipton	Y	Y	N	Y	Y	?
4 Buck	Y	Y	N	Y	Y	Y
5 Lamborn	Y	Y	N	Y	Y	Y
6 Coffman	Y	N	Y	Y	Y	N
7 Perlmutter	N	N	Y	N	N	N
CONNECTICUT						
1 Larson	N	N	Y	N	N	N
2 Courtney	N	N	Y	N	N	N
3 DeLauro	N	N	Y	N	N	N
4 Himes	N	N	Y	N	N	N
5 Esty	N	N	Y	N	N	N
DELAWARE						
AL Blunt Rochester	N	N	Y	N	N	N
FLORIDA						
1 Gaetz	?	?	?	?	?	?
2 Dunn	Y	Y	N	Y	Y	Y
3 Yoho	Y	Y	N	Y	Y	Y
4 Rutherford	Y	Y	N	Y	Y	Y
5 Lawson	N	N	Y	N	N	N
6 DeSantis	?	?	?	?	?	?
7 Murphy	N	N	Y	N	N	N
8 Posey	Y	Y	N	Y	Y	Y
9 Soto	N	N	Y	N	N	N
10 Demings	N	N	Y	N	N	N
11 Webster	Y	Y	N	Y	Y	Y
12 Bilirakis	Y	Y	N	Y	Y	N
13 Crist	N	N	Y	N	N	N
14 Castor	N	N	Y	N	N	N
15 Ross	Y	Y	N	Y	Y	Y
16 Buchanan	N	Y	N	N	N	N
17 Rooney, T.	Y	Y	N	Y	Y	Y
18 Mast	N	Y	N	N	N	Y
19 Rooney, F.	Y	Y	N	Y	Y	Y
20 Hastings	N	N	Y	N	N	N
21 Frankel	N	N	Y	N	N	N
22 Deutch	N	N	Y	N	N	N
23 Wasserman Schultz	N	N	Y	N	N	N
24 Wilson	N	N	Y	N	N	N
25 Diaz-Balart	Y	Y	N	Y	Y	Y
26 Curbelo	N	N	Y	N	Y	N
27 Ros-Lehtinen	N	N	Y	N	Y	N
GEORGIA						
1 Carter	Y	Y	N	Y	Y	Y
2 Bishop	N	N	Y	N	N	N
3 Ferguson	Y	Y	N	Y	Y	Y
4 Johnson	N	N	Y	N	N	N
5 Lewis	N	N	Y	N	N	N
6 Handel	Y	Y	N	Y	Y	Y
7 Woodall	Y	Y	N	Y	Y	Y
8 Scott, A.	Y	Y	N	Y	Y	Y
9 Collins	Y	Y	N	Y	Y	Y
10 Hice	Y	Y	N	Y	Y	Y
11 Loudermilk	Y	Y	N	Y	Y	Y
12 Allen	Y	Y	N	Y	Y	?
13 Scott, D.	N	N	Y	N	N	N
14 Graves	Y	Y	N	Y	Y	Y
HAWAII						
1 Hanabusa	?	?	?	?	?	?
2 Gabbard	N	N	Y	N	N	N
IDAHO						
1 Labrador	Y	Y	N	Y	Y	Y
2 Simpson	Y	Y	N	Y	Y	N
ILLINOIS						
1 Rush	N	N	Y	N	N	N
2 Kelly	N	N	Y	N	N	N
3 Lipinski	N	N	Y	N	N	N
4 Gutierrez	N	N	Y	N	N	N
5 Quigley	N	N	Y	N	N	N
6 Roskam	Y	Y	Y	Y	Y	N
7 Davis, D.	N	N	Y	N	N	N
8 Krishnamoorthi	N	N	Y	N	N	N
9 Schakowsky	N	N	Y	N	N	N
10 Schneider	N	N	Y	N	N	N
11 Foster	N	N	Y	N	N	N
12 Bost	Y	Y	N	Y	Y	Y
13 Davis, R.	Y	Y	N	Y	Y	Y

	350	351	352	353	354	355
14 **Hultgren**	Y	Y	N	Y	Y	Y
15 **Shimkus**	Y	Y	N	Y	Y	Y
16 **Kinzinger**	Y	Y	N	Y	Y	Y
17 Bustos	N	N	Y	N	N	N
18 **LaHood**	Y	Y	N	Y	Y	Y
INDIANA						
1 Visclosky	N	N	Y	N	N	N
2 **Walorski**	Y	Y	N	Y	Y	Y
3 **Banks**	Y	Y	N	Y	Y	Y
4 Rokita	Y	Y	N	Y	Y	Y
5 **Brooks**	Y	Y	N	Y	Y	Y
6 **Messer**	Y	Y	N	Y	Y	Y
7 Carson	N	N	Y	N	N	N
8 **Bucshon**	Y	Y	N	Y	Y	Y
9 **Hollingsworth**	Y	Y	N	Y	Y	Y
IOWA						
1 **Blum**	Y	Y	N	Y	Y	Y
2 Loebsack	N	N	Y	N	N	N
3 **Young**	Y	Y	N	Y	Y	Y
4 **King**	Y	Y	N	Y	Y	Y
KANSAS						
1 **Marshall**	Y	Y	N	Y	Y	Y
2 **Jenkins**	Y	Y	N	Y	Y	Y
3 **Yoder**	Y	Y	N	Y	Y	Y
4 Estes	Y	Y	N	Y	Y	Y
KENTUCKY						
1 **Comer**	Y	Y	N	Y	Y	Y
2 **Guthrie**	Y	Y	N	Y	Y	Y
3 Yarmuth	N	N	Y	N	N	N
4 **Massie**	Y	Y	N	Y	Y	Y
5 **Rogers**	Y	Y	N	Y	Y	Y
6 **Barr**	Y	Y	N	Y	Y	Y
LOUISIANA						
1 **Scalise**	Y	Y	N	Y	Y	Y
2 Richmond	?	?	?	?	?	?
3 **Higgins**	Y	Y	N	Y	Y	Y
4 **Johnson**	Y	Y	N	Y	Y	Y
5 **Abraham**	Y	Y	N	Y	Y	Y
6 **Graves**	Y	Y	N	Y	Y	Y
MAINE						
1 Pingree	N	N	Y	N	N	N
2 **Poliquin**	Y	Y	N	Y	Y	N
MARYLAND						
1 **Harris**	Y	N	N	Y	Y	Y
2 Ruppersberger	N	N	Y	N	N	N
3 Sarbanes	N	N	Y	N	N	N
4 Brown	N	N	Y	N	N	N
5 Hoyer	?	?	?	?	?	?
6 Delaney	N	N	Y	N	N	N
7 Cummings	N	N	Y	N	N	N
8 Raskin	N	N	Y	N	N	N
MASSACHUSETTS						
1 Neal	N	N	Y	N	N	N
2 McGovern	N	N	Y	N	N	N
3 Tsongas	N	N	Y	N	N	N
4 Kennedy	N	N	Y	N	N	N
5 Clark	N	N	Y	N	N	N
6 Moulton	N	N	Y	N	N	N
7 Capuano	N	N	Y	N	N	N
8 Lynch	N	N	Y	N	N	N
9 Keating	N	N	Y	N	N	N
MICHIGAN						
1 **Bergman**	Y	Y	N	Y	Y	Y
2 **Huizenga**	Y	Y	N	Y	Y	Y
3 *Amash*	Y	Y	Y	N	Y	Y
4 **Moolenaar**	Y	Y	N	Y	Y	Y
5 Kildee	N	N	Y	N	N	N
6 **Upton**	N	N	N	N	N	N
7 **Walberg**	Y	Y	N	Y	Y	Y
8 **Bishop**	Y	Y	N	Y	Y	Y
9 Levin	N	N	Y	N	N	N
10 **Mitchell**	Y	Y	N	Y	Y	Y
11 **Trott**	Y	Y	N	Y	Y	N
12 Dingell	N	N	Y	N	N	N
14 Lawrence	N	N	Y	N	N	N
MINNESOTA						
1 Walz	?	?	?	?	?	?
2 **Lewis**	Y	Y	N	Y	Y	Y
3 **Paulsen**	N	N	Y	N	Y	N
4 McCollum	N	N	Y	N	N	N

	350	351	352	353	354	355
5 Ellison	N	N	Y	N	N	N
6 **Emmer**	Y	Y	N	Y	Y	Y
7 Peterson	?	?	?	?	?	?
8 Nolan	N	N	Y	N	N	N
MISSISSIPPI						
1 **Kelly**	Y	Y	N	Y	Y	Y
2 Thompson	N	N	Y	N	N	N
3 **Harper**	Y	Y	N	Y	Y	Y
4 **Palazzo**	?	Y	N	Y	Y	Y
MISSOURI						
1 Clay	N	N	Y	N	N	N
2 **Wagner**	Y	Y	N	Y	Y	Y
3 **Luetkemeyer**	Y	Y	N	Y	Y	Y
4 **Hartzler**	Y	Y	N	Y	Y	Y
5 Cleaver	N	N	Y	N	N	N
6 **Graves**	Y	Y	N	Y	Y	Y
7 **Long**	Y	Y	N	Y	Y	Y
8 **Smith**	Y	Y	N	Y	Y	Y
MONTANA						
AL **Gianforte**	Y	Y	N	Y	Y	Y
NEBRASKA						
1 **Fortenberry**	N	Y	Y	N	N	N
2 **Bacon**	Y	Y	N	Y	Y	Y
3 **Smith**	Y	Y	N	Y	Y	Y
NEVADA						
1 Titus	N	N	Y	N	N	N
2 **Amodei**	Y	Y	N	Y	Y	Y
3 Rosen	N	N	Y	N	N	N
4 Kihuen	N	N	Y	N	N	N
NEW HAMPSHIRE						
1 Shea-Porter	N	N	Y	N	N	N
2 Kuster	N	N	Y	N	N	N
NEW JERSEY						
1 Norcross	N	N	Y	N	N	N
2 **LoBiondo**	N	N	Y	N	Y	N
3 **MacArthur**	Y	N	N	Y	Y	Y
4 **Smith**	N	N	Y	N	N	N
5 Gottheimer	N	N	Y	N	N	N
6 Pallone	N	N	Y	N	N	N
7 **Lance**	N	N	Y	N	N	N
8 Sires	N	N	Y	N	N	N
9 Pascrell	N	N	Y	N	N	N
10 Payne	N	N	Y	N	N	N
11 **Frelinghuysen**	Y	Y	N	N	Y	N
12 Watson Coleman	N	N	Y	N	N	N
NEW MEXICO						
1 Lujan Grisham	N	N	Y	N	N	N
2 **Pearce**	Y	Y	N	Y	Y	Y
3 Luján	N	N	Y	N	N	N
NEW YORK						
1 **Zeldin**	Y	Y	N	Y	Y	Y
2 **King**	N	Y	N	N	N	N
3 Suozzi	N	N	Y	N	N	N
4 Rice	N	N	Y	N	N	N
5 Meeks	N	N	Y	N	N	N
6 Meng	N	N	Y	N	N	N
7 Velázquez	N	N	Y	N	N	N
8 Jeffries	N	N	Y	N	N	N
9 Clarke	N	N	Y	N	N	N
10 Nadler	N	N	Y	N	N	N
11 **Donovan**	N	Y	N	N	N	N
12 Maloney, C.	N	N	Y	N	N	N
13 Espaillat	N	N	Y	N	N	N
14 Crowley	N	N	Y	N	N	N
15 Serrano	N	N	Y	N	N	N
16 Engel	N	N	Y	N	N	N
17 Lowey	N	N	Y	N	N	N
18 Maloney, S.P.	N	N	Y	N	N	N
19 **Faso**	N	N	Y	N	N	N
20 Tonko	N	N	Y	N	N	N
21 **Stefanik**	N	N	Y	N	N	N
22 **Tenney**	Y	Y	N	Y	Y	Y
23 **Reed**	Y	N	N	Y	Y	Y
24 **Katko**	N	Y	Y	Y	Y	N
25 **Vacant**						
26 Higgins	N	N	Y	N	N	N
27 **Collins**	Y	Y	N	Y	Y	Y
NORTH CAROLINA						
1 Butterfield	N	N	Y	N	N	N
2 **Holding**	Y	Y	N	Y	Y	Y
3 **Jones**	Y	Y	Y	Y	Y	N
4 Price	N	N	Y	N	N	N

	350	351	352	353	354	355
5 **Foxx**	Y	Y	N	Y	Y	Y
6 **Walker**	Y	Y	N	Y	Y	Y
7 **Rouzer**	Y	Y	N	Y	Y	Y
8 **Hudson**	Y	Y	N	Y	Y	Y
9 **Pittenger**	Y	Y	N	Y	Y	Y
9 **Vacant**						
10 **McHenry**	Y	Y	N	Y	Y	N
11 **Meadows**	Y	Y	N	Y	Y	Y
12 Adams	N	N	Y	N	N	N
13 **Budd**	Y	Y	N	Y	Y	Y
NORTH DAKOTA						
AL **Cramer**	Y	Y	N	Y	Y	Y
OHIO						
1 **Chabot**	Y	Y	N	Y	Y	Y
2 **Wenstrup**	Y	Y	N	Y	Y	Y
3 Beatty	N	N	Y	N	N	N
4 **Jordan**	Y	Y	N	Y	Y	Y
5 **Latta**	Y	Y	N	Y	Y	Y
6 **Johnson**	Y	Y	N	Y	Y	Y
7 **Gibbs**	Y	Y	N	Y	Y	Y
8 **Davidson**	Y	Y	N	Y	Y	Y
9 Kaptur	N	N	Y	N	N	N
10 **Turner**	Y	Y	N	Y	Y	N
11 Fudge	N	N	Y	N	N	N
12 **Vacant**						
13 Ryan	N	N	Y	N	N	N
14 **Joyce**	Y	N	N	Y	Y	N
15 **Stivers**	Y	Y	N	Y	Y	N
16 **Renacci**	Y	Y	N	Y	Y	Y
OKLAHOMA						
1 **Vacant**						
2 **Mullin**	Y	Y	N	Y	Y	Y
3 **Lucas**	Y	Y	N	Y	Y	Y
4 **Cole**	Y	Y	N	Y	Y	Y
5 **Russell**	Y	Y	N	Y	Y	Y
OREGON						
1 Bonamici	N	N	Y	N	N	N
2 **Walden**	Y	Y	N	Y	Y	Y
3 Blumenauer	N	N	Y	N	N	N
4 DeFazio	N	N	Y	N	N	N
5 Schrader	Y	Y	Y	N	N	N
PENNSYLVANIA						
1 Brady	N	N	Y	N	N	N
2 Evans	N	N	Y	N	N	N
3 **Kelly**	Y	Y	N	Y	Y	Y
4 **Perry**	Y	Y	N	Y	Y	Y
5 **Thompson**	Y	Y	N	Y	Y	Y
6 **Costello**	N	Y	Y	N	Y	N
7 **Vacant**						
8 **Fitzpatrick**	N	N	Y	N	N	N
9 **Shuster**	?	?	?	?	?	?
10 **Marino**	Y	Y	N	Y	Y	Y
11 **Barletta**	Y	Y	N	Y	Y	Y
12 **Rothfus**	Y	Y	N	Y	Y	Y
13 Boyle	N	N	Y	N	N	N
14 Doyle	N	N	Y	N	N	N
15 **Vacant**						
16 **Smucker**	Y	Y	N	Y	Y	Y
17 Cartwright	N	N	Y	N	N	N
18 Lamb	N	N	Y	N	N	N
RHODE ISLAND						
1 Cicilline	N	N	Y	N	N	N
2 Langevin	N	N	Y	N	N	N
SOUTH CAROLINA						
1 **Sanford**	Y	Y	Y	N	N	Y
2 **Wilson**	Y	Y	N	Y	Y	Y
3 **Duncan**	Y	Y	N	Y	Y	Y
4 **Gowdy**	Y	Y	N	Y	Y	Y
5 **Norman**	Y	Y	N	Y	Y	Y
6 Clyburn	N	N	Y	N	N	N
7 **Rice**	Y	Y	N	Y	Y	Y
SOUTH DAKOTA						
AL **Noem**	Y	Y	N	Y	Y	Y
TENNESSEE						
1 **Roe**	Y	Y	N	Y	Y	Y
2 **Duncan**	Y	Y	N	Y	Y	Y
3 **Fleischmann**	Y	Y	N	Y	Y	Y
4 **DesJarlais**	Y	Y	N	Y	Y	Y
5 Cooper	N	N	Y	N	N	N
6 **Black**	?	?	?	?	?	?
7 **Blackburn**	?	?	?	?	?	?
8 **Kustoff**	Y	Y	N	Y	Y	Y
9 Cohen	N	N	Y	N	N	N

	350	351	352	353	354	355
TEXAS						
1 **Gohmert**	Y	Y	N	Y	Y	Y
2 **Poe**	Y	Y	N	Y	Y	Y
3 **Johnson, S.**	Y	Y	N	Y	Y	Y
4 **Ratcliffe**	Y	Y	N	Y	Y	Y
5 **Hensarling**	Y	Y	N	Y	Y	Y
6 **Barton**	Y	Y	N	Y	Y	Y
7 **Culberson**	Y	Y	N	Y	Y	Y
8 **Brady**	Y	Y	N	Y	Y	Y
9 Green, A.	N	N	Y	N	N	N
10 **McCaul**	Y	Y	N	Y	Y	Y
11 **Conaway**	Y	Y	N	Y	Y	Y
12 **Granger**	Y	Y	N	Y	Y	Y
13 **Thornberry**	Y	Y	N	Y	Y	Y
14 **Weber**	Y	Y	N	Y	Y	Y
15 Gonzalez	N	N	Y	N	N	N
16 O'Rourke	N	N	Y	N	N	N
17 **Flores**	Y	Y	N	Y	Y	Y
18 Jackson Lee	N	N	Y	N	N	N
19 **Arrington**	Y	Y	N	Y	Y	Y
20 Castro	N	N	Y	N	N	N
21 **Smith**	Y	Y	N	Y	Y	Y
22 **Olson**	Y	Y	N	Y	Y	Y
23 **Hurd**	Y	Y	N	Y	Y	N
24 Marchant	Y	Y	N	Y	Y	Y
25 **Williams**	Y	Y	N	Y	Y	Y
26 **Burgess**	Y	Y	N	Y	Y	Y
27 Cloud	Y	Y	N	Y	Y	Y
28 Cuellar	Y	Y	Y	N	Y	N
29 Green, G.	N	N	Y	N	N	N
30 Johnson, E.B.	N	N	Y	N	N	N
31 **Carter**	Y	Y	N	Y	Y	Y
32 **Sessions**	Y	Y	N	Y	Y	Y
33 Veasey	N	N	Y	N	N	N
34 Vela	N	N	Y	N	N	N
35 Doggett	N	N	Y	N	N	N
36 **Babin**	Y	Y	N	Y	Y	Y
UTAH						
1 **Bishop**	Y	Y	N	Y	Y	Y
2 **Stewart**	Y	Y	N	Y	Y	Y
3 **Curtis**	Y	Y	N	Y	Y	Y
4 **Love**	Y	Y	N	Y	Y	Y
VERMONT						
AL Welch	N	N	Y	N	N	N
VIRGINIA						
1 **Wittman**	Y	N	N	Y	Y	Y
2 **Taylor**	Y	N	N	Y	Y	N
3 Scott	N	N	Y	N	N	N
4 McEachin	N	N	Y	N	N	N
5 **Garrett**	Y	Y	N	N	Y	Y
6 **Goodlatte**	Y	Y	N	Y	Y	Y
7 **Brat**	Y	Y	N	Y	Y	Y
8 Beyer	N	N	Y	N	N	N
9 **Griffith**	Y	Y	N	N	Y	Y
10 **Comstock**	Y	N	N	Y	Y	N
11 Connolly	N	N	Y	N	N	N
WASHINGTON						
1 DelBene	N	N	Y	N	N	N
2 Larsen	N	N	Y	N	N	N
3 **Herrera Beutler**	Y	Y	N	Y	N	N
4 **Newhouse**	Y	Y	N	Y	Y	Y
5 **McMorris Rodgers**	Y	Y	N	Y	Y	Y
6 Kilmer	N	N	Y	N	N	N
7 Jayapal	N	N	Y	N	N	N
8 **Reichert**	N	Y	N	N	Y	N
9 Smith	N	N	Y	N	N	N
10 Heck	N	N	Y	N	N	N
WEST VIRGINIA						
1 **McKinley**	Y	Y	N	Y	Y	Y
2 **Mooney**	Y	Y	N	Y	Y	Y
3 **Jenkins**	Y	Y	N	Y	Y	Y
WISCONSIN						
1 **Ryan**						
2 Pocan	N	N	Y	N	N	N
3 Kind	N	N	Y	N	N	N
4 Moore	N	N	Y	N	N	N
5 **Sensenbrenner**	Y	Y	N	Y	Y	Y
6 **Grothman**	Y	Y	N	Y	N	Y
7 **Duffy**	Y	Y	N	Y	Y	Y
8 **Gallagher**	Y	Y	N	Y	Y	Y
WYOMING						
AL **Cheney**	Y	Y	N	Y	Y	Y

VOTE NUMBER

356. HR6147. FISCAL 2019 INTERIOR-ENVIRONMENT AND FINANCIAL SERVICES APPROPRIATIONS PACKAGE/ENVIRONMENTAL JUSTICE SMALL GRANTS PROGRAM. Hice, R-Ga., amendment that would prohibit appropriated funds from being used for Environmental Justice Small Grants Program. Rejected in Committee of the Whole 174-240: R 173-57; D 1-183. July 18, 2018.

357. HR6147. FISCAL 2019 INTERIOR-ENVIRONMENT AND FINANCIAL SERVICES APPROPRIATIONS PACKAGE/ENVIRONMENTAL REGULATION SETTLEMENTS. Smith, R-Mo., amendment that would prohibit appropriated funds from being used to pay attorney's fees in a settlement related to the Clean Air Act, the Federal Water Pollution Control Act or the Endangered Species Act. Adopted in Committee of the Whole 215-199: R 215-14; D 0-185. July 18, 2018.

358. HR6147. FISCAL 2019 INTERIOR-ENVIRONMENT AND FINANCIAL SERVICES APPROPRIATIONS PACKAGE/POLICIAL CONTRIBUTION DISCLOSURE. Carbajal, D-Calif., for Capuano, D-Mass, amendment that would remove the bill's ban on the use of funds by the Securities and Exchange Commission to issue rules on the disclosure of political contributions. Rejected in Committee of the Whole 190-224: R 6-223; D 184-1. July 18, 2018.

359. HR6147. FISCAL 2019 INTERIOR-ENVIRONMENT AND FINANCIAL SERVICES APPROPRIATIONS PACKAGE/DISTRICT OF COLUMBIA HEALTH INSURANCE. Palmer, R-Ala., amendment that would prohibit the District of Columbia from using funds appropriated by the bill to enforce certain health insurance requirements. Adopted in Committee of the Whole 226-189: R 226-4; D 0-185. July 18, 2018.

360. HR6147. FISCAL 2019 INTERIOR-ENVIRONMENT AND FINANCIAL SERVICES APPROPRIATIONS PACKAGE/HEALTH CARE FUNDS. Meadows, R-N.C., amendment that would prohibit any funds appropriated by the bill from being used for the multi-state plan program created by the 2010 health care overhaul. Adopted in Committee of the Whole 223-192: R 222-8; D 1-184. July 18, 2018.

361. HR6147. FISCAL 2019 INTERIOR-ENVIRONMENT AND FINANCIAL SERVICES APPROPRIATIONS PACKAGE/DISTRICT OF COLUMBIA INDIVIDUAL MANDATE. Rothfus, R-Pa., amendment that would prohibit funds appropriated by the bill from being used to seize property as a means of enforcing the liability provisions of the District of Columbia's individual mandate. Adopted in Committee of the Whole 231-184: R 230-0; D 1-184. July 18, 2018.

	356	357	358	359	360	361
ALABAMA						
1 **Byrne**	Y	Y	N	Y	Y	Y
2 **Roby**	N	Y	N	Y	Y	Y
3 **Rogers**	Y	Y	N	Y	Y	Y
4 **Aderholt**	Y	Y	N	Y	Y	Y
5 **Brooks**	Y	Y	N	Y	Y	Y
6 **Palmer**	Y	Y	N	Y	Y	Y
7 Sewell	N	N	Y	N	N	N
ALASKA						
AL **Young**	Y	Y	N	Y	Y	Y
ARIZONA						
1 O'Halleran	N	N	Y	N	N	N
2 **McSally**	N	Y	N	Y	Y	Y
3 Grijalva	N	N	Y	N	N	N
4 **Gosar**	Y	Y	N	Y	Y	Y
5 **Biggs**	Y	Y	N	Y	Y	Y
6 **Schweikert**	Y	Y	N	Y	Y	Y
7 Gallego	N	N	Y	N	N	N
8 **Lesko**	Y	Y	N	Y	Y	Y
9 Sinema	N	N	Y	N	Y	N
ARKANSAS						
1 **Crawford**	Y	Y	N	Y	Y	Y
2 **Hill**	Y	Y	N	Y	N	Y
3 **Womack**	N	Y	N	Y	Y	Y
4 **Westerman**	Y	Y	N	Y	Y	Y
CALIFORNIA						
1 **LaMalfa**	Y	Y	N	Y	Y	Y
2 Huffman	N	N	Y	N	N	N
3 Garamendi	N	N	Y	N	N	N
4 **McClintock**	Y	Y	N	Y	Y	Y
5 Thompson	N	N	Y	N	N	N
6 Matsui	N	N	Y	N	N	N
7 Bera	N	N	Y	N	N	N
8 **Cook**	Y	Y	N	Y	Y	Y
9 McNerney	N	N	N	N	N	N
10 **Denham**	N	Y	N	Y	Y	Y
11 DeSaulnier	N	N	Y	N	N	N
12 Pelosi	N	N	Y	N	N	N
13 Lee	N	N	Y	N	N	N
14 Speier	?	?	?	?	?	?
15 Swalwell	N	N	Y	N	N	N
16 Costa	N	N	Y	N	N	N
17 Khanna	N	N	Y	N	N	N
18 Eshoo	N	N	Y	N	N	N
19 Lofgren	N	N	Y	N	N	N
20 Panetta	N	N	Y	N	N	N
21 **Valadao**	N	Y	N	Y	Y	Y
22 **Nunes**	N	Y	N	Y	Y	Y
23 **McCarthy**	Y	Y	N	Y	Y	Y
24 Carbajal	N	N	Y	N	N	N
25 **Knight**	N	Y	N	Y	Y	Y
26 Brownley	N	N	Y	N	N	N
27 Chu	N	N	Y	N	N	N
28 Schiff	N	N	Y	N	N	N
29 Cardenas	?	?	?	?	?	?
30 Sherman	N	N	Y	N	N	N
31 Aguilar	N	N	Y	N	N	N
32 Napolitano	N	N	Y	N	N	N
33 Lieu	N	N	Y	N	N	N
34 Gomez	N	N	Y	N	N	N
35 Torres	N	N	Y	N	N	N
36 Ruiz	N	N	Y	N	N	N
37 Bass	?	?	?	?	?	?
38 Sánchez, Linda	N	N	Y	N	N	N
39 **Royce**	N	Y	N	Y	Y	Y
40 Roybal-Allard	N	N	Y	N	N	N
41 Takano	N	N	Y	N	N	N
42 **Calvert**	N	Y	N	Y	Y	Y
43 Waters	N	N	Y	N	N	N
44 Barragan	N	N	Y	N	N	N
45 **Walters**	Y	Y	N	Y	Y	Y
46 Correa	N	N	Y	N	N	N
47 Lowenthal	N	N	Y	N	N	N
48 **Rohrabacher**	Y	Y	N	Y	N	Y
49 **Issa**	Y	Y	N	Y	Y	Y
50 **Hunter**	Y	Y	N	Y	Y	Y
51 Vargas	N	N	Y	N	N	N
52 Peters	N	N	Y	N	N	N
53 Davis	N	N	Y	N	N	N
COLORADO						
1 DeGette	N	N	Y	N	N	N
2 Polis	N	N	Y	N	N	N
3 **Tipton**	N	Y	N	Y	Y	Y
4 **Buck**	Y	Y	N	Y	Y	Y
5 **Lamborn**	Y	Y	N	Y	Y	Y
6 **Coffman**	N	Y	N	Y	Y	Y
7 Perlmutter	N	N	Y	N	N	N
CONNECTICUT						
1 Larson	N	N	Y	N	N	N
2 Courtney	N	N	Y	N	N	N
3 DeLauro	N	N	Y	N	N	N
4 Himes	N	N	Y	N	N	N
5 Esty	N	N	Y	N	N	N
DELAWARE						
AL Blunt Rochester	N	N	Y	N	N	N
FLORIDA						
1 **Gaetz**	?	?	?	?	?	?
2 **Dunn**	Y	Y	N	Y	Y	Y
3 **Yoho**	Y	Y	N	Y	Y	Y
4 **Rutherford**	N	Y	N	Y	Y	Y
5 Lawson	N	N	Y	N	N	N
6 **DeSantis**	?	?	?	?	?	?
7 Murphy	N	N	Y	N	N	N
8 **Posey**	Y	Y	N	Y	Y	Y
9 Soto	N	N	Y	N	N	N
10 Demings	N	N	Y	N	N	N
11 **Webster**	Y	Y	N	Y	Y	Y
12 **Bilirakis**	Y	Y	N	Y	Y	Y
13 Crist	N	N	Y	N	N	N
14 Castor	N	N	Y	N	N	N
15 **Ross**	Y	Y	N	Y	Y	Y
16 **Buchanan**	N	N	Y	Y	Y	Y
17 **Rooney, T.**	Y	Y	N	Y	Y	Y
18 **Mast**	Y	Y	N	Y	Y	Y
19 **Rooney, F.**	Y	Y	N	Y	Y	Y
20 Hastings	N	N	Y	N	N	N
21 Frankel	N	N	Y	N	N	N
22 Deutch	N	N	Y	N	N	N
23 Wasserman Schultz	N	N	Y	N	N	N
24 Wilson	N	N	Y	N	N	N
25 **Diaz-Balart**	N	Y	N	Y	Y	Y
26 **Curbelo**	N	N	Y	N	Y	Y
27 **Ros-Lehtinen**	N	N	N	N	Y	Y
GEORGIA						
1 **Carter**	Y	Y	N	Y	Y	Y
2 Bishop	N	N	Y	N	N	N
3 **Ferguson**	Y	Y	N	Y	Y	Y
4 Johnson	N	N	Y	N	N	N
5 Lewis	N	N	Y	N	N	N
6 **Handel**	Y	Y	N	Y	Y	Y
7 **Woodall**	Y	Y	N	Y	Y	Y
8 **Scott, A.**	Y	Y	Y	Y	Y	Y
9 **Collins**	Y	Y	N	Y	Y	Y
10 **Hice**	Y	Y	N	Y	Y	Y
11 **Loudermilk**	Y	Y	N	Y	Y	Y
12 **Allen**	Y	Y	N	Y	Y	Y
13 Scott, D.	N	N	Y	N	N	N
14 **Graves**	Y	Y	N	Y	Y	Y
HAWAII						
1 Hanabusa	?	?	?	?	?	?
2 Gabbard	N	N	Y	N	N	N
IDAHO						
1 **Labrador**	Y	Y	N	Y	Y	Y
2 **Simpson**	N	Y	N	Y	Y	Y
ILLINOIS						
1 Rush	N	N	Y	N	N	N
2 Kelly	N	N	Y	N	N	N
3 Lipinski	N	N	Y	N	N	N
4 Gutierrez	N	N	Y	N	N	N
5 Quigley	N	N	Y	N	N	N
6 **Roskam**	N	Y	N	Y	Y	Y
7 Davis, D.	N	N	Y	N	N	N
8 Krishnamoorthi	N	N	Y	N	N	N
9 Schakowsky	N	N	Y	N	N	N
10 Schneider	N	N	Y	N	N	N
11 Foster	N	N	Y	N	N	N
12 **Bost**	Y	Y	N	Y	Y	Y
13 **Davis, R.**	N	Y	N	Y	Y	Y

KEY	Republicans		Democrats		Independents	
Y Voted for (yea)		X Paired against		C Voted "present" to avoid possible conflict of interest		
# Paired for		– Announced against				
+ Announced for		P Voted "present"		? Did not vote or otherwise make a position known		
N Voted against (nay)						

	356	357	358	359	360	361
14 **Hultgren**	Y	Y	N	Y	Y	Y
15 **Shimkus**	N	Y	N	Y	Y	Y
16 **Kinzinger**	Y	Y	N	Y	Y	Y
17 Bustos	N	N	Y	N	N	N
18 **LaHood**	Y	Y	N	Y	Y	Y
INDIANA						
1 Visclosky	N	N	Y	N	N	N
2 **Walorski**	Y	Y	N	Y	Y	Y
3 **Banks**	Y	Y	N	Y	Y	Y
4 Rokita	Y	Y	N	Y	Y	Y
5 Brooks	Y	Y	N	Y	Y	Y
6 **Messer**	Y	Y	N	Y	Y	Y
7 Carson	N	N	Y	N	N	N
8 **Bucshon**	N	Y	N	Y	Y	Y
9 **Hollingsworth**	N	Y	N	Y	Y	Y
IOWA						
1 **Blum**	Y	Y	N	Y	Y	Y
2 Loebsack	N	N	Y	N	N	N
3 **Young**	Y	Y	N	Y	Y	Y
4 **King**	Y	Y	N	Y	Y	Y
KANSAS						
1 **Marshall**	Y	Y	N	Y	Y	Y
2 **Jenkins**	Y	Y	N	Y	Y	Y
3 **Yoder**	Y	Y	N	Y	Y	Y
4 **Estes**	Y	Y	N	Y	Y	Y
KENTUCKY						
1 **Comer**	Y	Y	Y	Y	Y	Y
2 **Guthrie**	Y	Y	N	Y	Y	Y
3 Yarmuth	N	N	Y	N	N	N
4 **Massie**	Y	Y	N	Y	Y	Y
5 **Rogers**	N	Y	N	Y	Y	Y
6 **Barr**	Y	Y	N	Y	Y	Y
LOUISIANA						
1 **Scalise**	Y	Y	N	Y	Y	Y
2 Richmond	?	?	?	?	?	?
3 **Higgins**	Y	Y	N	Y	Y	Y
4 **Johnson**	Y	Y	N	Y	Y	Y
5 **Abraham**	Y	Y	N	Y	Y	Y
6 **Graves**	Y	Y	N	Y	Y	Y
MAINE						
1 Pingree	N	N	Y	N	N	N
2 **Poliquin**	Y	Y	Y	Y	Y	Y
MARYLAND						
1 **Harris**	Y	Y	Y	Y	Y	Y
2 Ruppersberger	N	N	Y	N	N	N
3 Sarbanes	N	N	Y	N	N	N
4 Brown	N	N	Y	N	N	N
5 Hoyer	?	?	?	?	?	?
6 Delaney	N	N	Y	N	N	N
7 Cummings	N	N	Y	N	N	N
8 Raskin	N	N	Y	N	N	N
MASSACHUSETTS						
1 Neal	N	N	Y	N	N	N
2 McGovern	N	N	Y	N	N	N
3 Tsongas	N	N	Y	N	N	N
4 Kennedy	N	N	Y	N	N	N
5 Clark	N	N	Y	N	N	N
6 Moulton	N	N	Y	N	N	N
7 Capuano	N	N	Y	N	N	N
8 Lynch	N	N	Y	N	N	N
9 Keating	N	N	Y	N	N	N
MICHIGAN						
1 **Bergman**	Y	Y	N	Y	Y	Y
2 **Huizenga**	Y	Y	N	Y	Y	Y
3 *Amash*	Y	Y	N	Y	Y	Y
4 **Moolenaar**	N	Y	N	Y	Y	Y
5 Kildee	N	N	Y	N	N	N
6 **Upton**	N	Y	N	Y	Y	Y
7 **Walberg**	Y	Y	N	Y	Y	Y
8 **Bishop**	Y	Y	N	Y	Y	Y
9 Levin	N	N	Y	N	N	N
10 **Mitchell**	Y	Y	N	Y	Y	Y
11 **Trott**	N	Y	N	Y	Y	Y
12 Dingell	N	N	Y	N	N	N
14 Lawrence	N	N	Y	N	N	N
MINNESOTA						
1 Walz	?	?	?	?	?	?
2 **Lewis**	Y	Y	N	Y	Y	Y
3 **Paulsen**	N	Y	N	Y	Y	Y
4 McCollum	N	N	Y	N	N	N

	356	357	358	359	360	361
5 Ellison	N	N	Y	N	N	N
6 **Emmer**	Y	Y	N	Y	Y	Y
7 Peterson	?	?	?	?	?	?
8 Nolan	?	N	Y	N	N	N
MISSISSIPPI						
1 **Kelly**	Y	Y	N	Y	Y	Y
2 Thompson	N	N	Y	N	N	N
3 **Harper**	Y	Y	N	Y	Y	Y
4 **Palazzo**	Y	Y	N	Y	Y	Y
MISSOURI						
1 Clay	N	N	Y	N	N	N
2 **Wagner**	Y	Y	N	Y	Y	Y
3 **Luetkemeyer**	Y	Y	N	Y	Y	Y
4 **Hartzler**	Y	Y	N	Y	Y	Y
5 Cleaver	N	N	Y	N	N	N
6 **Graves**	Y	Y	N	Y	Y	Y
7 **Long**	Y	Y	N	Y	Y	Y
8 **Smith**	Y	Y	N	Y	Y	Y
MONTANA						
AL **Gianforte**	Y	Y	N	Y	Y	Y
NEBRASKA						
1 **Fortenberry**	Y	Y	N	Y	Y	Y
2 **Bacon**	N	Y	Y	Y	Y	Y
3 **Smith**	Y	Y	N	Y	Y	Y
NEVADA						
1 Titus	N	N	Y	N	N	N
2 **Amodei**	N	Y	N	Y	Y	Y
3 Rosen	N	N	Y	N	N	N
4 Kihuen	N	N	Y	N	N	N
NEW HAMPSHIRE						
1 Shea-Porter	N	N	Y	N	N	N
2 Kuster	N	N	Y	N	N	N
NEW JERSEY						
1 Norcross	N	N	Y	N	N	N
2 **LoBiondo**	N	N	N	Y	Y	Y
3 **MacArthur**	N	N	N	Y	N	Y
4 **Smith**	N	N	N	Y	Y	Y
5 Gottheimer	N	N	Y	N	N	N
6 Pallone	N	N	Y	N	N	N
7 **Lance**	N	N	N	Y	N	Y
8 Sires	N	N	Y	N	N	N
9 Pascrell	N	N	Y	N	N	N
10 Payne	N	N	Y	N	N	N
11 **Frelinghuysen**	N	Y	N	Y	Y	Y
12 Watson Coleman	N	N	Y	N	N	N
NEW MEXICO						
1 Lujan Grisham	N	N	Y	N	N	N
2 **Pearce**	Y	Y	N	Y	Y	Y
3 Luján	N	N	Y	N	N	N
NEW YORK						
1 **Zeldin**	Y	N	N	Y	Y	Y
2 **King**	N	N	N	Y	Y	Y
3 Suozzi	N	N	Y	N	N	N
4 Rice	N	N	Y	N	N	N
5 Meeks	N	N	Y	N	N	N
6 Meng	N	N	Y	N	N	N
7 Velázquez	N	N	Y	N	N	N
8 Jeffries	N	N	Y	N	N	N
9 Clarke	N	N	Y	N	N	N
10 Nadler	N	N	Y	N	N	N
11 **Donovan**	N	N	N	Y	Y	Y
12 Maloney, C.	N	N	Y	N	N	N
13 Espaillat	N	N	Y	N	N	N
14 Crowley	N	N	Y	N	N	N
15 Serrano	N	N	Y	N	N	N
16 Engel	N	N	Y	N	N	N
17 Lowey	N	N	Y	N	N	N
18 Maloney, S.P.	N	N	Y	N	N	N
19 **Faso**	N	Y	N	N	N	Y
20 Tonko	N	N	Y	N	N	N
21 **Stefanik**	N	N	N	Y	N	Y
22 **Tenney**	N	Y	N	Y	Y	Y
23 **Reed**	N	Y	N	Y	N	Y
24 **Katko**	N	N	N	Y	N	Y
25 **Vacant**						
26 Higgins	N	N	Y	N	N	N
27 **Collins**	N	Y	N	Y	Y	Y
NORTH CAROLINA						
1 Butterfield	N	N	Y	N	N	N
2 **Holding**	Y	Y	N	Y	Y	Y
3 **Jones**	Y	Y	Y	Y	Y	Y
4 Price	N	N	Y	N	N	N

	356	357	358	359	360	361
5 **Foxx**	N	Y	N	Y	Y	Y
6 **Walker**	Y	Y	N	Y	Y	Y
7 **Rouzer**	Y	Y	N	Y	Y	Y
8 **Hudson**	Y	Y	N	Y	Y	Y
9 **Pittenger**	Y	Y	N	Y	Y	Y
9 **Vacant**						
10 **McHenry**	Y	Y	N	Y	Y	Y
11 **Meadows**	Y	Y	N	Y	Y	Y
12 Adams	N	N	Y	N	N	N
13 **Budd**	Y	Y	N	Y	Y	Y
NORTH DAKOTA						
AL **Cramer**	Y	Y	N	Y	Y	Y
OHIO						
1 **Chabot**	Y	Y	N	Y	Y	Y
2 **Wenstrup**	Y	Y	N	Y	Y	Y
3 Beatty	N	N	Y	N	N	N
4 **Jordan**	Y	Y	N	Y	Y	Y
5 **Latta**	Y	Y	N	Y	Y	Y
6 **Johnson**	Y	Y	N	Y	Y	Y
7 **Gibbs**	Y	Y	N	Y	Y	Y
8 **Davidson**	Y	Y	N	Y	Y	Y
9 Kaptur	N	N	Y	N	N	N
10 **Turner**	N	Y	N	Y	Y	Y
11 Fudge	N	N	Y	N	N	N
12 **Vacant**						
13 Ryan	N	N	Y	N	N	N
14 **Joyce**	N	Y	N	Y	Y	Y
15 **Stivers**	N	Y	N	Y	Y	Y
16 **Renacci**	Y	Y	N	Y	Y	Y
OKLAHOMA						
1 **Vacant**						
2 **Mullin**	Y	Y	N	Y	Y	Y
3 **Lucas**	N	Y	N	Y	Y	Y
4 **Cole**	N	Y	N	Y	Y	Y
5 **Russell**	Y	Y	N	Y	Y	Y
OREGON						
1 Bonamici	N	N	Y	N	N	N
2 **Walden**	N	Y	N	Y	Y	Y
3 Blumenauer	N	N	Y	N	N	N
4 DeFazio	N	N	Y	N	N	N
5 Schrader	N	N	Y	N	N	Y
PENNSYLVANIA						
1 Brady	N	N	Y	N	N	N
2 Evans	N	N	Y	N	N	N
3 **Kelly**	Y	Y	N	Y	Y	Y
4 **Perry**	Y	Y	N	Y	Y	Y
5 **Thompson**	Y	Y	N	Y	Y	Y
6 **Costello**	N	N	N	Y	Y	Y
7 **Vacant**						
8 **Fitzpatrick**	N	N	N	N	N	Y
9 **Shuster**	?	?	?	?	?	?
10 **Marino**	Y	Y	N	Y	Y	Y
11 **Barletta**	Y	Y	N	Y	Y	Y
12 **Rothfus**	Y	Y	N	Y	Y	Y
13 Boyle	N	N	Y	N	N	N
14 Doyle	N	N	Y	N	N	N
15 **Vacant**						
16 **Smucker**	Y	Y	N	Y	Y	Y
17 Cartwright	N	N	Y	N	N	N
18 Lamb	N	N	Y	N	N	N
RHODE ISLAND						
1 Cicilline	N	N	Y	N	N	N
2 Langevin	N	N	Y	N	N	N
SOUTH CAROLINA						
1 **Sanford**	Y	Y	N	Y	Y	Y
2 **Wilson**	Y	Y	N	Y	Y	Y
3 **Duncan**	Y	Y	N	Y	Y	Y
4 **Gowdy**	Y	Y	N	Y	Y	Y
5 **Norman**	Y	Y	N	Y	Y	Y
6 Clyburn	N	N	Y	N	N	N
7 **Rice**	Y	Y	N	Y	Y	Y
SOUTH DAKOTA						
AL **Noem**	Y	Y	N	Y	Y	Y
TENNESSEE						
1 **Roe**	Y	Y	N	Y	Y	Y
2 **Duncan**	Y	Y	N	Y	Y	Y
3 **Fleischmann**	Y	Y	N	Y	Y	Y
4 **DesJarlais**	Y	Y	N	Y	Y	Y
5 Cooper	N	N	Y	N	N	N
6 **Black**	?	?	?	?	?	?
7 **Blackburn**	?	?	?	?	?	?
8 **Kustoff**	Y	Y	N	Y	Y	Y
9 Cohen	N	N	Y	N	N	N

	356	357	358	359	360	361
TEXAS						
1 **Gohmert**	Y	Y	N	Y	Y	Y
2 **Poe**	Y	Y	N	Y	Y	Y
3 **Johnson, S.**	Y	Y	N	Y	Y	Y
4 **Ratcliffe**	Y	Y	N	Y	Y	Y
5 **Hensarling**	Y	Y	N	Y	Y	Y
6 **Barton**	Y	Y	N	Y	Y	Y
7 **Culberson**	Y	Y	N	Y	Y	Y
8 **Brady**	Y	?	?	Y	Y	Y
9 Green, A.	N	N	Y	N	N	N
10 **McCaul**	Y	Y	N	Y	Y	Y
11 **Conaway**	Y	Y	N	Y	Y	Y
12 **Granger**	Y	Y	N	Y	Y	Y
13 **Thornberry**	Y	Y	N	Y	Y	Y
14 **Weber**	Y	Y	N	Y	Y	Y
15 Gonzalez	Y	N	Y	N	N	N
16 O'Rourke	N	N	Y	N	N	N
17 **Flores**	Y	Y	N	Y	Y	Y
18 Jackson Lee	N	N	Y	N	N	N
19 **Arrington**	Y	Y	N	Y	Y	Y
20 Castro	N	N	Y	N	N	N
21 **Smith**	Y	Y	N	Y	Y	Y
22 **Olson**	Y	Y	N	Y	Y	Y
23 **Hurd**	N	Y	N	Y	Y	Y
24 Marchant	Y	Y	N	Y	Y	Y
25 **Williams**	Y	Y	N	Y	Y	Y
26 **Burgess**	Y	Y	N	Y	Y	Y
27 Cloud	Y	Y	N	Y	Y	Y
28 Cuellar	N	N	Y	N	N	N
29 Green, G.	N	N	Y	N	N	N
30 Johnson, E.B.	N	N	Y	N	N	N
31 **Carter**	Y	Y	N	Y	Y	Y
32 **Sessions**	Y	Y	N	Y	Y	Y
33 Veasey	N	N	Y	N	N	N
34 Vela	N	N	Y	N	N	N
35 Doggett	N	N	Y	N	N	N
36 **Babin**	Y	Y	N	Y	Y	Y
UTAH						
1 **Bishop**	Y	Y	N	Y	Y	Y
2 **Stewart**	Y	Y	N	Y	Y	Y
3 **Curtis**	Y	Y	N	Y	Y	Y
4 **Love**	Y	Y	N	Y	Y	Y
VERMONT						
AL Welch	N	N	Y	N	N	N
VIRGINIA						
1 **Wittman**	Y	Y	N	Y	Y	Y
2 **Taylor**	N	Y	N	Y	Y	Y
3 Scott	N	N	Y	N	N	N
4 McEachin	N	N	Y	N	N	N
5 **Garrett**	Y	Y	N	Y	Y	Y
6 **Goodlatte**	Y	Y	N	Y	Y	Y
7 **Brat**	Y	Y	N	Y	Y	Y
8 Beyer	N	N	Y	N	N	N
9 **Griffith**	Y	Y	N	Y	Y	Y
10 **Comstock**	Y	Y	N	Y	Y	Y
11 Connolly	N	N	Y	N	N	N
WASHINGTON						
1 DelBene	N	N	Y	N	N	N
2 Larsen	N	N	Y	N	N	N
3 **Herrera Beutler**	N	Y	N	Y	Y	Y
4 **Newhouse**	Y	Y	N	Y	Y	Y
5 **McMorris Rodgers**	Y	Y	N	Y	Y	Y
6 Kilmer	N	N	Y	N	N	N
7 Jayapal	N	N	Y	N	N	N
8 **Reichert**	N	Y	N	Y	Y	Y
9 Smith	N	N	Y	N	N	N
10 Heck	N	N	Y	N	N	N
WEST VIRGINIA						
1 **McKinley**	N	Y	N	Y	Y	Y
2 **Mooney**	Y	Y	N	Y	Y	Y
3 **Jenkins**	N	Y	N	Y	Y	Y
WISCONSIN						
1 **Ryan**						
2 Pocan	N	N	Y	N	N	N
3 Kind	N	N	Y	N	N	N
4 Moore	N	N	Y	N	N	N
5 **Sensenbrenner**	Y	Y	N	Y	Y	Y
6 **Grothman**	Y	Y	N	Y	Y	Y
7 **Duffy**	Y	Y	N	Y	Y	Y
8 **Gallagher**	Y	Y	N	Y	Y	Y
WYOMING						
AL **Cheney**	Y	Y	N	Y	Y	Y

VOTE NUMBER

362. HR6147. FISCAL 2019 INTERIOR-ENVIRONMENT AND FINANCIAL SERVICES APPROPRIATIONS PACKAGE/POSTAL SERVICE FINANCE PRODUCTS. McHenry, R-N.C, amendment that would prohibit funds appropriated by the bill from being used by the Postal Service to provide additional financial products or services. Rejected in Committee of the Whole 201-212: R 201-28; D 0-184. July 18, 2018.

363. HCONRES119. CARBON TAX RESOLUTION/ADOPTION. Adoption of the concurrent resolution that would express the sense of Congress that a carbon tax would be detrimental to American families and businesses, and is not in the best interest of the United States. Adopted 229-180: R 222-6; D 7-174. July 19, 2018.

364. HR6147. FISCAL 2019 INTERIOR-ENVIRONMENT AND FINANCIAL SERVICES APPROPRIATIONS PACKAGE/RECOMMIT. Quigley, D-Ill., motion to recommit the bill to the House Appropriations Committee with instructions to report it back immediately with an amendment that would increase funding for the Election Assistance Commission by $380 million, and would decrease funding for the "Fund for America's Kids and Grandkids" by the same amount. Motion rejected 182-232: R 0-232; D 182-0. July 19, 2018.

365. HR6147. FISCAL 2019 INTERIOR-ENVIRONMENT AND FINANCIAL SERVICES APPROPRIATIONS PACKAGE/PASSAGE. Passage of the bill that would make available $58.7 billion through fiscal 2019, with $35.3 billion for the Department of Interior and environmental programs, and $23.4 billion for financial services matters and related agencies. Specifically, it would provide $8 billion for the Environmental Protection Agency, $3.1 billion for the U.S. Forest Service, non-wildfire, core functions, $13 billion for the Interior Department, and $11.6 billion for the Internal Revenue Service. It would also place $585 million into a "savings account" that could not be used until the federal budget is balanced. As amended, it would also restrict greenhouse gas emissions regulations and would limit funding for enforcement of endangered species-protections for certain animals. Other amendments would also prohibit the District of Columbia from enforcing certain health care-related provisions. Passed 217-199: R 217-15; D 0-184. July 19, 2018.

366. HR2345. MENTAL HEALTH PHONE NUMBERS/PASSAGE. Lance, R-N.J., motion to suspend the rules and pass the bill that would require the Federal Communications Commission, in coordination with the Veterans Affairs Department and the Health and Human Services Department, to study the feasibility of designating an N11 or other simple dialing code for the national suicide prevention and mental health crisis hotline system. It would also require that the study include an assessment of the effectiveness of the National Suicide Prevention Lifeline, including how it addresses the needs of veterans. Motion agreed to 379-1: R 211-1; D 168-0. July 23, 2018.

367. HR4881. AGRICULTURE CONNECTIVITY TASK FORCE/PASSAGE. Lance, R-N.J., motion to suspend the rules and pass the bill that would require the Federal Communications Commission to establish a task force that, with the Agriculture Department, would work with public and private stakeholders to review and develop recommendations regarding the connectivity and technology needs of precision agriculture in the United States. Motion agreed to 378-4: R 210-4; D 168-0. July 23, 2018.

	362	363	364	365	366	367
ALABAMA						
1 **Byrne**	Y	Y	N	Y	Y	Y
2 **Roby**	Y	Y	N	Y	?	?
3 **Rogers**	Y	Y	N	Y	Y	Y
4 **Aderholt**	Y	Y	N	Y	Y	Y
5 **Brooks**	Y	Y	N	N	Y	Y
6 **Palmer**	Y	Y	N	Y	Y	Y
7 Sewell	N	N	Y	N	Y	Y
ALASKA						
AL **Young**	N	Y	N	Y	Y	Y
ARIZONA						
1 O'Halleran	N	Y	Y	N	Y	Y
2 **McSally**	Y	Y	N	Y	Y	Y
3 Grijalva	N	N	Y	N	?	?
4 **Gosar**	Y	Y	N	Y	Y	Y
5 **Biggs**	Y	Y	N	N	Y	N
6 **Schweikert**	Y	Y	N	Y	Y	Y
7 Gallego	N	N	Y	N	Y	Y
8 **Lesko**	Y	Y	N	Y	Y	Y
9 Sinema	?	Y	Y	N	Y	Y
ARKANSAS						
1 **Crawford**	Y	Y	N	Y	Y	Y
2 **Hill**	Y	Y	N	Y	Y	Y
3 **Womack**	Y	Y	N	Y	Y	Y
4 **Westerman**	Y	Y	N	Y	Y	Y
CALIFORNIA						
1 **LaMalfa**	Y	Y	N	Y	Y	Y
2 Huffman	N	N	Y	N	Y	Y
3 Garamendi	N	N	Y	N	Y	Y
4 **McClintock**	Y	Y	N	Y	Y	Y
5 Thompson	N	N	Y	N	Y	Y
6 Matsui	N	N	Y	N	Y	Y
7 Bera	N	N	Y	N	Y	Y
8 **Cook**	N	Y	N	Y	Y	Y
9 McNerney	N	N	Y	N	Y	Y
10 **Denham**	N	Y	N	Y	Y	Y
11 DeSaulnier	N	N	Y	N	Y	Y
12 Pelosi	N	N	Y	N	Y	Y
13 Lee	N	N	Y	N	Y	Y
14 Speier	?	?	?	?	?	?
15 Swalwell	N	N	Y	N	Y	Y
16 Costa	N	N	Y	N	Y	Y
17 Khanna	N	N	Y	N	Y	Y
18 Eshoo	N	N	Y	N	Y	Y
19 Lofgren	N	N	Y	N	Y	Y
20 Panetta	N	N	Y	N	Y	Y
21 **Valadao**	N	Y	N	Y	Y	Y
22 **Nunes**	Y	Y	N	Y	Y	Y
23 **McCarthy**	Y	Y	N	Y	Y	Y
24 Carbajal	N	N	Y	N	Y	Y
25 **Knight**	N	Y	N	Y	Y	Y
26 Brownley	N	N	Y	N	Y	Y
27 Chu	N	N	Y	N	Y	Y
28 Schiff	N	N	Y	N	Y	Y
29 Cardenas	?	?	?	?	Y	Y
30 Sherman	N	N	Y	N	Y	Y
31 Aguilar	N	N	Y	N	Y	Y
32 Napolitano	N	N	Y	N	Y	Y
33 Lieu	N	N	Y	N	Y	Y
34 Gomez	N	N	Y	N	Y	Y
35 Torres	N	N	Y	N	Y	Y
36 Ruiz	N	N	Y	N	Y	Y
37 Bass	?	N	Y	N	Y	Y
38 Sánchez, Linda	N	N	Y	N	Y	Y
39 **Royce**	Y	?	N	Y	Y	Y
40 Roybal-Allard	N	N	Y	N	Y	Y
41 Takano	N	N	Y	N	Y	Y
42 **Calvert**	Y	Y	N	Y	Y	Y
43 Waters	N	N	Y	N	Y	Y
44 Barragan	N	N	Y	N	Y	Y
45 **Walters**	Y	Y	N	Y	Y	Y
46 Correa	N	N	Y	N	Y	Y
47 Lowenthal	N	N	Y	N	Y	Y
48 **Rohrabacher**	Y	Y	N	Y	?	?
49 **Issa**	Y	Y	N	Y	?	?
50 **Hunter**	Y	Y	N	Y	?	?
51 Vargas	N	N	Y	N	Y	Y
52 Peters	N	N	Y	N	Y	Y
53 Davis	N	N	Y	N	Y	Y

	362	363	364	365	366	367
COLORADO						
1 DeGette	N	N	Y	N	Y	Y
2 Polis	N	N	Y	N	Y	Y
3 **Tipton**	Y	Y	N	Y	Y	Y
4 **Buck**	Y	Y	N	Y	Y	Y
5 **Lamborn**	Y	Y	N	Y	Y	Y
6 **Coffman**	Y	Y	N	Y	Y	Y
7 Perlmutter	N	N	Y	N	?	?
CONNECTICUT						
1 Larson	N	N	Y	N	Y	Y
2 Courtney	N	N	Y	N	Y	Y
3 DeLauro	N	N	Y	N	Y	Y
4 Himes	N	N	Y	N	Y	Y
5 Esty	N	N	Y	N	Y	Y
DELAWARE						
AL Blunt Rochester	N	N	Y	N	Y	Y
FLORIDA						
1 **Gaetz**	?	Y	N	Y	Y	Y
2 **Dunn**	Y	Y	N	Y	Y	Y
3 **Yoho**	Y	Y	N	Y	Y	Y
4 **Rutherford**	Y	Y	N	Y	Y	Y
5 Lawson	N	–	Y	N	Y	Y
6 **DeSantis**	?	Y	N	Y	Y	Y
7 Murphy	N	Y	Y	N	Y	Y
8 **Posey**	Y	Y	N	Y	Y	Y
9 Soto	N	N	Y	N	Y	Y
10 Demings	N	N	Y	N	Y	Y
11 **Webster**	Y	Y	N	Y	?	Y
12 **Bilirakis**	Y	Y	N	Y	Y	Y
13 Crist	N	N	Y	N	Y	Y
14 Castor	N	N	Y	N	Y	Y
15 **Ross**	Y	Y	N	Y	Y	Y
16 **Buchanan**	Y	Y	N	N	?	?
17 **Rooney, T.**	Y	Y	N	Y	?	?
18 **Mast**	N	Y	N	Y	Y	Y
19 **Rooney, F.**	Y	Y	N	Y	Y	Y
20 Hastings	N	N	Y	N	Y	Y
21 Frankel	N	N	Y	N	Y	Y
22 Deutch	N	N	Y	N	Y	Y
23 Wasserman Schultz	N	N	Y	N	Y	Y
24 Wilson	N	N	Y	N	?	?
25 **Diaz-Balart**	Y	Y	N	Y	Y	Y
26 **Curbelo**	N	N	Y	N	Y	Y
27 **Ros-Lehtinen**	N	N	N	N	Y	Y
GEORGIA						
1 **Carter**	Y	Y	N	Y	Y	Y
2 Bishop	N	Y	Y	N	Y	Y
3 **Ferguson**	Y	Y	N	Y	Y	Y
4 Johnson	N	N	Y	N	Y	Y
5 Lewis	N	N	Y	N	Y	Y
6 **Handel**	Y	Y	N	Y	Y	Y
7 **Woodall**	Y	Y	N	Y	Y	Y
8 **Scott, A.**	Y	Y	N	Y	Y	Y
9 **Collins**	Y	Y	N	Y	Y	Y
10 **Hice**	Y	Y	N	Y	Y	Y
11 **Loudermilk**	Y	Y	N	Y	Y	Y
12 **Allen**	Y	Y	N	Y	Y	Y
13 Scott, D.	N	N	Y	N	Y	Y
14 **Graves**	Y	Y	N	Y	Y	Y
HAWAII						
1 Hanabusa	?	?	?	?	?	?
2 Gabbard	N	N	Y	N	Y	Y
IDAHO						
1 **Labrador**	Y	Y	N	N	Y	Y
2 **Simpson**	Y	Y	N	Y	Y	Y
ILLINOIS						
1 Rush	N	N	Y	N	Y	Y
2 Kelly	N	N	Y	N	Y	Y
3 Lipinski	N	N	Y	N	?	?
4 Gutierrez	N	N	?	N	+	+
5 Quigley	N	N	Y	N	Y	Y
6 **Roskam**	Y	Y	N	Y	Y	Y
7 Davis, D.	N	N	Y	N	Y	Y
8 Krishnamoorthi	N	N	Y	N	Y	Y
9 Schakowsky	N	N	Y	N	Y	Y
10 Schneider	N	N	Y	N	Y	Y
11 Foster	N	N	Y	N	Y	Y
12 **Bost**	N	Y	N	Y	Y	Y
13 **Davis, R.**	N	Y	N	Y	Y	Y

	362	363	364	365	366	367
14 **Hultgren**	Y	Y	N	Y	Y	Y
15 **Shimkus**	Y	Y	N	Y	Y	Y
16 **Kinzinger**	Y	Y	N	Y	Y	Y
17 Bustos	N	N	Y	N	Y	Y
18 **LaHood**	Y	Y	N	Y	Y	Y
INDIANA						
1 Visclosky	N	N	Y	N	Y	Y
2 **Walorski**	Y	Y	N	Y	Y	Y
3 **Banks**	Y	Y	N	Y	Y	Y
4 Rokita	Y	Y	N	Y	Y	Y
5 **Brooks**	Y	Y	N	Y	Y	Y
6 **Messer**	Y	Y	N	Y	Y	Y
7 Carson	N	N	Y	N	Y	Y
8 **Bucshon**	Y	Y	N	Y	Y	Y
9 **Hollingsworth**	Y	N	N	N	Y	Y
IOWA						
1 **Blum**	Y	Y	N	N	Y	Y
2 Loebsack	N	N	Y	N	Y	Y
3 **Young**	Y	Y	N	Y	Y	Y
4 **King**	Y	Y	N	Y	+	+
KANSAS						
1 **Marshall**	Y	Y	N	Y	Y	Y
2 **Jenkins**	Y	Y	N	Y	Y	Y
3 **Yoder**	Y	Y	N	Y	Y	Y
4 **Estes**	Y	Y	N	Y	Y	Y
KENTUCKY						
1 **Comer**	Y	Y	N	Y	Y	Y
2 **Guthrie**	Y	Y	N	Y	Y	Y
3 Yarmuth	N	N	Y	N	Y	Y
4 **Massie**	Y	Y	N	N	Y	N
5 **Rogers**	Y	Y	N	Y	Y	Y
6 **Barr**	Y	Y	N	Y	Y	Y
LOUISIANA						
1 **Scalise**	Y	Y	N	Y	Y	Y
2 Richmond	?	?	?	?	Y	Y
3 **Higgins**	Y	Y	N	Y	Y	Y
4 **Johnson**	Y	Y	N	Y	Y	Y
5 **Abraham**	Y	Y	N	Y	Y	Y
6 **Graves**	Y	Y	N	Y	+	+
MAINE						
1 Pingree	N	N	Y	N	Y	Y
2 **Poliquin**	Y	Y	N	Y	Y	Y
MARYLAND						
1 **Harris**	Y	Y	N	Y	Y	Y
2 Ruppersberger	N	N	Y	N	Y	Y
3 Sarbanes	N	N	Y	N	Y	Y
4 Brown	N	N	Y	N	Y	Y
5 Hoyer	?	N	Y	N	Y	Y
6 Delaney	N	N	Y	N	Y	Y
7 Cummings	N	N	Y	N	?	?
8 Raskin	N	N	Y	N	Y	Y
MASSACHUSETTS						
1 Neal	N	N	Y	N	Y	Y
2 McGovern	N	N	Y	N	Y	Y
3 Tsongas	N	N	Y	N	?	?
4 Kennedy	N	N	Y	N	Y	Y
5 Clark	N	N	Y	N	Y	Y
6 Moulton	N	N	Y	N	Y	Y
7 Capuano	N	N	Y	N	Y	Y
8 Lynch	N	N	Y	N	Y	Y
9 Keating	N	N	Y	N	Y	Y
MICHIGAN						
1 **Bergman**	Y	?	?	?	Y	Y
2 **Huizenga**	Y	Y	N	Y	Y	Y
3 *Amash*	Y	Y	N	N	N	N
4 **Moolenaar**	Y	Y	N	Y	Y	Y
5 Kildee	N	N	Y	N	Y	Y
6 **Upton**	Y	Y	N	Y	Y	Y
7 **Walberg**	Y	Y	N	Y	Y	Y
8 **Bishop**	Y	Y	N	Y	Y	Y
9 Levin	N	N	Y	N	Y	Y
10 **Mitchell**	Y	Y	N	Y	Y	Y
11 **Trott**	Y	Y	N	Y	Y	Y
12 Dingell	N	N	Y	N	Y	Y
14 Lawrence	N	N	Y	N	Y	Y
MINNESOTA						
1 Walz	?	?	?	?	?	?
2 **Lewis**	Y	Y	N	Y	Y	Y
3 **Paulsen**	Y	Y	N	Y	Y	Y
4 McCollum	N	N	Y	N	Y	Y

	362	363	364	365	366	367
5 Ellison	N	?	?	?	?	?
6 **Emmer**	Y	Y	N	Y	Y	Y
7 Peterson	?	?	?	?	Y	Y
8 Nolan	N	N	Y	N	Y	Y
MISSISSIPPI						
1 **Kelly**	Y	Y	N	Y	Y	Y
2 Thompson	N	N	Y	N	?	?
3 **Harper**	Y	Y	N	Y	Y	Y
4 **Palazzo**	Y	Y	N	Y	Y	Y
MISSOURI						
1 Clay	N	N	Y	N	Y	Y
2 **Wagner**	Y	Y	N	Y	Y	Y
3 **Luetkemeyer**	Y	Y	N	Y	Y	Y
4 **Hartzler**	Y	Y	N	Y	Y	Y
5 Cleaver	N	N	Y	N	Y	Y
6 **Graves**	Y	Y	N	Y	+	+
7 **Long**	Y	Y	N	Y	Y	Y
8 **Smith**	Y	Y	N	Y	Y	Y
MONTANA						
AL **Gianforte**	Y	Y	N	Y	Y	Y
NEBRASKA						
1 **Fortenberry**	N	Y	N	Y	Y	Y
2 **Bacon**	Y	Y	N	Y	Y	Y
3 **Smith**	Y	Y	N	Y	Y	Y
NEVADA						
1 Titus	N	N	Y	N	Y	Y
2 **Amodei**	?	Y	N	Y	Y	Y
3 Rosen	N	N	Y	N	Y	Y
4 Kihuen	N	N	Y	N	Y	Y
NEW HAMPSHIRE						
1 Shea-Porter	N	N	Y	N	Y	Y
2 Kuster	N	N	Y	N	Y	Y
NEW JERSEY						
1 Norcross	N	N	Y	N	Y	Y
2 **LoBiondo**	N	Y	N	N	Y	Y
3 **MacArthur**	Y	Y	N	Y	Y	Y
4 **Smith**	N	Y	N	Y	Y	Y
5 Gottheimer	N	N	Y	N	Y	Y
6 Pallone	N	N	Y	N	Y	Y
7 **Lance**	N	Y	N	Y	Y	Y
8 Sires	N	N	Y	N	Y	Y
9 Pascrell	N	N	Y	N	Y	Y
10 Payne	N	N	Y	N	Y	Y
11 **Frelinghuysen**	Y	Y	N	Y	Y	Y
12 Watson Coleman	N	N	Y	N	Y	Y
NEW MEXICO						
1 Lujan Grisham	N	P	Y	N	Y	Y
2 **Pearce**	Y	Y	N	Y	Y	Y
3 Luján	N	N	Y	N	Y	Y
NEW YORK						
1 **Zeldin**	Y	Y	N	Y	Y	Y
2 **King**	N	Y	N	Y	Y	Y
3 Suozzi	N	N	Y	N	Y	Y
4 Rice	N	N	Y	N	Y	Y
5 Meeks	N	N	Y	N	Y	Y
6 Meng	N	N	Y	N	Y	Y
7 Velázquez	N	N	Y	N	Y	?
8 Jeffries	N	N	Y	N	Y	Y
9 Clarke	N	N	Y	N	+	+
10 Nadler	N	N	Y	N	Y	Y
11 **Donovan**	N	Y	N	Y	Y	Y
12 Maloney, C.	N	N	Y	N	?	?
13 Espaillat	N	N	Y	N	Y	Y
14 Crowley	N	–	+	N	Y	Y
15 Serrano	N	N	Y	N	Y	Y
16 Engel	N	N	Y	N	Y	Y
17 Lowey	N	N	Y	N	Y	Y
18 Maloney, S.P.	N	N	Y	N	?	?
19 **Faso**	N	Y	N	Y	Y	Y
20 Tonko	N	N	Y	N	Y	Y
21 **Stefanik**	N	Y	N	Y	Y	Y
22 **Tenney**	Y	Y	N	Y	Y	Y
23 **Reed**	Y	Y	N	Y	Y	Y
24 **Katko**	N	Y	N	N	Y	Y
25 **Vacant**						
26 Higgins	N	N	Y	N	Y	Y
27 **Collins**	Y	Y	N	Y	Y	Y
NORTH CAROLINA						
1 Butterfield	N	N	Y	N	?	?
2 **Holding**	Y	Y	N	Y	Y	Y
3 **Jones**	N	?	?	?	Y	Y
4 Price	N	N	Y	N	Y	Y

	362	363	364	365	366	367
5 **Foxx**	Y	Y	N	Y	Y	Y
6 **Walker**	Y	Y	N	Y	Y	Y
7 **Rouzer**	Y	Y	N	Y	Y	Y
8 **Hudson**	Y	Y	N	Y	Y	Y
9 **Pittenger**	Y	Y	N	Y	?	?
9 **Vacant**						
10 **McHenry**	Y	Y	N	Y	+	+
11 **Meadows**	N	Y	N	Y	Y	Y
12 Adams	N	N	Y	N	Y	Y
13 **Budd**	Y	Y	N	Y	Y	Y
NORTH DAKOTA						
AL **Cramer**	Y	Y	N	Y	Y	Y
OHIO						
1 **Chabot**	Y	Y	N	Y	Y	Y
2 **Wenstrup**	Y	Y	N	Y	Y	Y
3 Beatty	N	N	Y	N	Y	Y
4 **Jordan**	Y	Y	N	Y	Y	Y
5 **Latta**	Y	Y	N	Y	Y	Y
6 **Johnson**	N	Y	N	Y	Y	Y
7 **Gibbs**	Y	Y	N	Y	Y	Y
8 **Davidson**	Y	Y	N	Y	Y	Y
9 Kaptur	N	N	Y	N	Y	Y
10 **Turner**	N	Y	N	Y	+	+
11 Fudge	N	?	?	?	Y	Y
12 **Vacant**						
13 Ryan	N	N	Y	N	?	?
14 **Joyce**	N	Y	N	Y	Y	Y
15 **Stivers**	Y	Y	N	Y	Y	Y
16 **Renacci**	Y	Y	N	Y	Y	Y
OKLAHOMA						
1 **Vacant**						
2 **Mullin**	Y	Y	N	Y	Y	Y
3 **Lucas**	Y	Y	N	Y	Y	Y
4 **Cole**	Y	Y	N	Y	Y	Y
5 **Russell**	Y	Y	N	Y	?	Y
OREGON						
1 Bonamici	N	N	Y	N	+	Y
2 **Walden**	Y	Y	N	Y	Y	Y
3 Blumenauer	N	N	Y	N	+	+
4 DeFazio	N	N	Y	N	Y	Y
5 Schrader	N	N	Y	N	Y	Y
PENNSYLVANIA						
1 Brady	N	?	?	?	?	?
2 Evans	N	N	Y	N	Y	Y
3 **Kelly**	Y	Y	N	Y	Y	Y
4 **Perry**	N	Y	N	Y	Y	+
5 **Thompson**	Y	Y	N	Y	Y	Y
6 **Costello**	N	P	N	Y	Y	Y
7 **Vacant**						
8 **Fitzpatrick**	N	N	N	N	Y	Y
9 **Shuster**	?	Y	N	Y	Y	Y
10 **Marino**	Y	Y	N	Y	Y	Y
11 **Barletta**	Y	Y	N	Y	?	?
12 **Rothfus**	Y	Y	N	Y	Y	Y
13 Boyle	N	N	Y	N	Y	Y
14 Doyle	N	N	Y	N	Y	Y
15 **Vacant**						
16 **Smucker**	Y	Y	N	Y	Y	Y
17 Cartwright	N	N	Y	N	Y	Y
18 Lamb	N	Y	Y	N	Y	Y
RHODE ISLAND						
1 Cicilline	N	N	Y	N	Y	Y
2 Langevin	N	N	Y	N	+	+
SOUTH CAROLINA						
1 **Sanford**	Y	Y	N	Y	Y	N
2 **Wilson**	Y	Y	N	Y	Y	Y
3 **Duncan**	Y	Y	N	Y	Y	Y
4 **Gowdy**	Y	Y	N	Y	Y	Y
5 **Norman**	Y	Y	N	Y	Y	Y
6 Clyburn	N	N	Y	N	Y	Y
7 **Rice**	Y	Y	N	Y	Y	Y
SOUTH DAKOTA						
AL **Noem**	Y	Y	N	Y	?	?
TENNESSEE						
1 **Roe**	Y	Y	N	Y	Y	Y
2 **Duncan**	Y	Y	N	N	?	?
3 **Fleischmann**	Y	Y	N	Y	Y	Y
4 **DesJarlais**	Y	Y	N	Y	Y	Y
5 Cooper	N	N	Y	N	Y	Y
6 **Black**	?	+	?	?	?	?
7 **Blackburn**	?	Y	N	Y	?	?
8 **Kustoff**	Y	Y	N	Y	?	?
9 Cohen	N	N	Y	N	Y	Y

	362	363	364	365	366	367
TEXAS						
1 **Gohmert**	Y	Y	N	Y	Y	Y
2 **Poe**	Y	Y	N	Y	Y	Y
3 **Johnson, S.**	Y	Y	N	Y	Y	Y
4 **Ratcliffe**	Y	Y	N	Y	Y	Y
5 **Hensarling**	Y	Y	N	Y	Y	Y
6 **Barton**	Y	Y	N	Y	?	?
7 **Culberson**	Y	Y	N	Y	Y	Y
8 **Brady**	Y	Y	N	Y	Y	Y
9 Green, A.	N	N	Y	N	Y	Y
10 **McCaul**	Y	Y	N	Y	Y	Y
11 **Conaway**	Y	Y	N	Y	Y	Y
12 **Granger**	Y	+	N	Y	Y	Y
13 **Thornberry**	Y	Y	N	Y	Y	Y
14 **Weber**	Y	Y	N	Y	Y	Y
15 Gonzalez	N	Y	Y	N	Y	Y
16 O'Rourke	N	N	Y	N	Y	Y
17 **Flores**	Y	Y	N	Y	Y	Y
18 Jackson Lee	N	N	Y	N	Y	Y
19 **Arrington**	Y	Y	N	Y	?	?
20 Castro	N	N	Y	N	Y	Y
21 **Smith**	Y	Y	N	Y	Y	Y
22 **Olson**	Y	Y	N	Y	Y	Y
23 **Hurd**	Y	Y	N	Y	Y	Y
24 Marchant	Y	Y	N	Y	Y	Y
25 **Williams**	Y	Y	N	Y	Y	Y
26 **Burgess**	Y	Y	N	Y	Y	Y
27 Cloud	Y	Y	N	Y	Y	Y
28 Cuellar	N	Y	Y	N	Y	Y
29 Green, G.	N	N	Y	N	Y	Y
30 Johnson, E.B.	N	N	Y	N	Y	Y
31 **Carter**	Y	Y	N	Y	Y	Y
32 **Sessions**	Y	Y	N	Y	Y	Y
33 Veasey	N	N	Y	N	Y	Y
34 Vela	N	N	Y	N	?	?
35 Doggett	N	N	Y	N	Y	Y
36 **Babin**	Y	Y	N	Y	Y	Y
UTAH						
1 **Bishop**	Y	Y	N	Y	Y	Y
2 **Stewart**	Y	Y	N	Y	Y	Y
3 **Curtis**	Y	Y	N	Y	Y	Y
4 **Love**	Y	N	N	Y	Y	Y
VERMONT						
AL Welch	N	N	Y	N	Y	Y
VIRGINIA						
1 **Wittman**	Y	Y	N	Y	Y	Y
2 **Taylor**	Y	Y	N	Y	Y	Y
3 Scott	N	N	Y	N	Y	Y
4 McEachin	N	N	Y	N	Y	Y
5 **Garrett**	Y	?	N	N	Y	Y
6 **Goodlatte**	Y	Y	N	Y	Y	Y
7 **Brat**	Y	Y	N	Y	Y	Y
8 Beyer	N	N	Y	N	Y	Y
9 **Griffith**	Y	Y	N	Y	Y	Y
10 **Comstock**	Y	Y	N	Y	Y	Y
11 Connolly	N	N	Y	N	Y	Y
WASHINGTON						
1 DelBene	N	N	Y	N	Y	Y
2 Larsen	N	N	Y	N	Y	Y
3 **Herrera Beutler**	Y	Y	N	Y	+	Y
4 **Newhouse**	Y	Y	N	Y	Y	Y
5 **McMorris Rodgers**	Y	Y	N	Y	Y	Y
6 Kilmer	N	N	Y	N	Y	Y
7 Jayapal	N	N	Y	N	+	+
8 **Reichert**	Y	Y	N	Y	Y	Y
9 Smith	N	N	Y	N	Y	Y
10 Heck	N	N	Y	N	Y	Y
WEST VIRGINIA						
1 **McKinley**	N	Y	N	Y	Y	Y
2 **Mooney**	Y	Y	N	Y	Y	Y
3 **Jenkins**	Y	Y	N	Y	Y	Y
WISCONSIN						
1 **Ryan**						
2 Pocan	N	N	Y	N	+	+
3 Kind	N	N	Y	N	Y	Y
4 Moore	N	N	Y	N	+	+
5 **Sensenbrenner**	Y	Y	N	N	Y	Y
6 **Grothman**	Y	Y	N	Y	Y	Y
7 **Duffy**	Y	Y	N	Y	Y	Y
8 **Gallagher**	Y	Y	N	Y	Y	Y
WYOMING						
AL **Cheney**	Y	Y	N	Y	Y	Y

III HOUSE VOTES

VOTE NUMBER

368. HR6199. EXPANDING HEALTH SAVINGS ACCOUNTS/PREVIOUS QUESTION. Burgess, R-Texas, motion to order the previous question (thus ending debate and possibility of amendment) on the rule (H Res 1012) that would provide for House floor consideration of the bill (HR 6199) that would make a number of changes to expand the allowable uses of health savings accounts under the 2010 health care overhaul, and would provide for House floor proceedings during the period from July 27 through Sept. 3, 2018. Motion agreed to 224-184: R 224-0; D 0-184. July 24, 2018.

369. HRES1012. EXPANDING HEALTH SAVINGS ACCOUNTS/RULE. Adoption of the rule (H Res 1012) that would provide for consideration of the bill (HR 6199) that would make a number of changes to expand the allowable uses of health savings accounts under the 2010 health care overhaul, and would provide for House floor proceedings during the period from July 27 through Sept. 3, 2018. Adopted 229-179: R 223-0; D 6-179. July 24, 2018.

370. HR6311. MEDICAL DEVICE TAX AND HEALTH CARE LAW CHANGES/ PREVIOUS QUESTION. Burgess, R-Texas, motion to order the previous question (thus ending debate and possibility of amendment) on the rule (H Res 1011) that would provide for consideration of the bill (HR 184) that would fully repeal the medical device tax, and would provide for consideration of the bill (HR 6311) that would modify the 2010 health care law to allow anyone to purchase a catastrophic plan, known as "copper" plans, through the law's insurance exchanges and would extend, through 2021, the suspension of the annual tax on health insurers. Motion agreed to 223-188: R 223-1; D 0-187. July 24, 2018.

371. HR184. MEDICAL DEVICE TAX AND HEALTH CARE LAW CHANGES/ RULE. Adoption of the rule (H Res 1011) that would provide for consideration of the bill (HR 184) that would fully repeal the medical device tax, and would provide for consideration of the bill (HR 6311) that would modify the 2010 health care law to allow anyone to purchase a catastrophic plan, known as "copper" plans, through the law's insurance exchanges and would extend, through 2021, the suspension of the annual tax on health insurers. Adopted 225-184: R 223-0; D 2-184. July 24, 2018.

372. HR184. MEDICAL DEVICE TAX REPEAL/PASSAGE. Passage of the bill that would fully repeal the 2.3 percent excise tax on the sale of a medical device by the manufacturer, producer, or importer after Dec. 31, 2019. Passed 283-132: R 226-1; D 57-131. July 24, 2018.

373. S1182. FLOOD INSURANCE EXTENSION/PASSAGE. Hensarling, R-Texas, motion to suspend the rules and pass the bill that would extend the authorization of the National Flood Insurance Program through November 30, 2018. Motion agreed to 366-52: R 179-51; D 187-1. July 25, 2018.

	368	369	370	371	372	373
ALABAMA						
1 **Byrne**	Y	Y	Y	Y	Y	Y
2 **Roby**	Y	Y	Y	Y	Y	Y
3 **Rogers**	Y	Y	Y	Y	Y	Y
4 **Aderholt**	Y	Y	Y	Y	Y	Y
5 **Brooks**	Y	Y	Y	Y	Y	Y
6 **Palmer**	Y	Y	Y	Y	Y	N
7 Sewell	N	N	N	N	Y	Y
ALASKA						
AL **Young**	Y	Y	Y	Y	Y	Y
ARIZONA						
1 O'Halleran	N	N	N	N	Y	Y
2 **McSally**	Y	Y	Y	Y	Y	Y
3 Grijalva	N	N	N	N	N	Y
4 **Gosar**	Y	Y	Y	Y	Y	N
5 **Biggs**	Y	Y	Y	Y	Y	N
6 **Schweikert**	Y	Y	Y	Y	Y	N
7 Gallego	N	N	N	N	N	Y
8 **Lesko**	Y	Y	Y	Y	Y	N
9 Sinema	N	Y	N	Y	Y	Y
ARKANSAS						
1 **Crawford**	Y	Y	Y	Y	Y	Y
2 **Hill**	Y	Y	Y	Y	Y	Y
3 **Womack**	Y	Y	Y	Y	Y	Y
4 **Westerman**	Y	Y	Y	Y	Y	N
CALIFORNIA						
1 **LaMalfa**	Y	Y	Y	Y	Y	Y
2 Huffman	N	N	N	N	N	Y
3 Garamendi	N	N	N	N	N	Y
4 **McClintock**	Y	Y	Y	Y	Y	N
5 Thompson	N	N	N	N	N	Y
6 Matsui	N	N	N	N	N	Y
7 Bera	N	N	N	N	Y	Y
8 **Cook**	Y	Y	Y	Y	Y	Y
9 McNerney	N	N	N	N	N	Y
10 **Denham**	Y	Y	Y	Y	Y	Y
11 DeSaulnier	N	N	N	N	N	Y
12 Pelosi	N	N	N	N	N	Y
13 Lee	N	N	N	N	N	Y
14 Speier	?	?	?	?	+	?
15 Swalwell	N	N	N	N	Y	Y
16 Costa	N	N	N	N	N	Y
17 Khanna	N	N	N	N	Y	Y
18 Eshoo	–	N	N	N	N	Y
19 Lofgren	N	N	N	N	N	Y
20 Panetta	N	N	N	N	Y	Y
21 **Valadao**	Y	Y	Y	Y	Y	Y
22 **Nunes**	Y	Y	Y	Y	Y	Y
23 **McCarthy**	Y	Y	Y	Y	Y	Y
24 Carbajal	N	N	N	N	Y	Y
25 **Knight**	Y	Y	Y	Y	Y	Y
26 Brownley	N	N	N	N	Y	Y
27 Chu	N	N	N	N	N	Y
28 Schiff	N	N	N	N	N	Y
29 Cardenas	N	N	N	N	Y	Y
30 Sherman	N	N	N	N	N	Y
31 Aguilar	N	N	N	N	N	Y
32 Napolitano	N	N	N	N	N	Y
33 Lieu	N	N	N	N	Y	Y
34 Gomez	N	N	N	N	Y	Y
35 Torres	N	N	N	N	Y	Y
36 Ruiz	N	N	N	N	Y	Y
37 Bass	N	N	N	N	N	Y
38 Sánchez, Linda	N	N	N	N	N	Y
39 **Royce**	Y	Y	Y	Y	Y	N
40 Roybal-Allard	N	N	N	N	N	Y
41 Takano	N	N	N	N	N	Y
42 **Calvert**	Y	Y	Y	Y	Y	Y
43 Waters	N	N	N	N	N	Y
44 Barragan	N	N	N	N	Y	Y
45 **Walters**	Y	Y	Y	Y	Y	Y
46 Correa	N	N	N	N	Y	Y
47 Lowenthal	N	N	N	N	N	Y
48 **Rohrabacher**	Y	Y	Y	Y	Y	N
49 **Issa**	Y	Y	Y	Y	Y	Y
50 **Hunter**	Y	Y	Y	Y	Y	Y
51 Vargas	N	N	N	N	Y	Y
52 Peters	N	N	N	N	Y	Y
53 Davis	N	N	N	N	Y	Y

	368	369	370	371	372	373
COLORADO						
1 DeGette	N	N	N	N	N	Y
2 Polis	N	N	N	N	Y	Y
3 **Tipton**	Y	Y	Y	Y	Y	Y
4 **Buck**	Y	Y	Y	Y	Y	Y
5 **Lamborn**	Y	Y	Y	Y	Y	N
6 **Coffman**	Y	Y	Y	Y	Y	Y
7 Perlmutter	N	N	N	N	N	Y
CONNECTICUT						
1 Larson	N	N	N	N	N	Y
2 Courtney	N	N	N	N	N	Y
3 DeLauro	N	N	N	N	N	Y
4 Himes	N	N	N	N	N	Y
5 Esty	N	N	N	N	N	Y
DELAWARE						
AL Blunt Rochester	N	N	N	N	N	Y
FLORIDA						
1 **Gaetz**	Y	Y	Y	Y	Y	Y
2 **Dunn**	Y	Y	Y	Y	Y	Y
3 **Yoho**	Y	Y	Y	Y	Y	Y
4 **Rutherford**	Y	Y	Y	Y	Y	Y
5 Lawson	N	N	N	N	Y	Y
6 **DeSantis**	Y	Y	Y	Y	Y	Y
7 Murphy	N	Y	N	Y	Y	Y
8 **Posey**	Y	Y	Y	Y	Y	Y
9 Soto	N	N	N	N	N	Y
10 Demings	N	N	N	N	N	Y
11 **Webster**	Y	Y	Y	Y	Y	Y
12 **Bilirakis**	Y	Y	Y	Y	Y	Y
13 Crist	N	N	N	N	Y	Y
14 Castor	N	N	N	N	N	Y
15 **Ross**	Y	Y	Y	Y	Y	N
16 **Buchanan**	Y	Y	Y	Y	Y	Y
17 **Rooney, T.**	Y	Y	Y	Y	Y	Y
18 **Mast**	Y	Y	Y	Y	Y	Y
19 **Rooney, F.**	Y	Y	Y	Y	Y	Y
20 Hastings	N	N	N	N	N	Y
21 Frankel	N	N	N	N	N	Y
22 Deutch	N	N	N	N	N	Y
23 Wasserman Schultz	N	N	N	N	N	Y
24 Wilson	N	N	N	N	N	Y
25 **Diaz-Balart**	Y	?	Y	Y	Y	Y
26 **Curbelo**	Y	Y	Y	Y	Y	Y
27 **Ros-Lehtinen**	Y	Y	Y	Y	Y	Y
GEORGIA						
1 **Carter**	Y	Y	Y	Y	Y	Y
2 Bishop	N	N	N	N	N	Y
3 **Ferguson**	Y	Y	Y	Y	Y	Y
4 Johnson	N	N	N	N	N	Y
5 Lewis	N	N	N	N	N	Y
6 **Handel**	Y	Y	Y	Y	Y	Y
7 **Woodall**	Y	Y	Y	Y	Y	Y
8 **Scott, A.**	Y	Y	Y	Y	Y	Y
9 **Collins**	Y	Y	Y	Y	Y	Y
10 **Hice**	Y	Y	Y	Y	Y	N
11 **Loudermilk**	Y	Y	Y	Y	Y	N
12 **Allen**	Y	Y	Y	Y	Y	Y
13 Scott, D.	N	N	N	N	N	Y
14 **Graves**	Y	Y	Y	Y	Y	Y
HAWAII						
1 Hanabusa	?	?	?	?	?	?
2 Gabbard	N	N	N	N	Y	Y
IDAHO						
1 **Labrador**	Y	Y	Y	Y	Y	N
2 **Simpson**	Y	Y	Y	Y	Y	?
ILLINOIS						
1 Rush	N	N	N	N	N	Y
2 Kelly	N	N	N	N	N	Y
3 Lipinski	?	?	N	N	Y	Y
4 Gutierrez	N	N	N	N	N	Y
5 Quigley	N	N	N	N	N	Y
6 **Roskam**	Y	Y	Y	Y	Y	Y
7 Davis, D.	N	N	N	N	N	Y
8 Krishnamoorthi	N	N	N	N	N	Y
9 Schakowsky	N	N	N	N	N	Y
10 Schneider	N	Y	N	N	Y	Y
11 Foster	N	N	N	N	N	Y
12 **Bost**	Y	Y	Y	Y	Y	Y
13 **Davis, R.**	Y	Y	Y	Y	Y	Y

KEY	Republicans	Democrats	Independents

Y Voted for (yea)	X Paired against	C Voted "present" to avoid possible conflict of interest
# Paired for	– Announced against	
+ Announced for	P Voted "present"	? Did not vote or otherwise make a position known
N Voted against (nay)		

	368	369	370	371	372	373
14 **Hultgren**	Y	Y	Y	Y	Y	Y
15 **Shimkus**	Y	Y	Y	Y	Y	Y
16 **Kinzinger**	Y	Y	Y	Y	Y	Y
17 Bustos	N	N	N	N	Y	Y
18 **LaHood**	Y	Y	Y	Y	Y	Y
INDIANA						
1 Visclosky	N	N	N	N	N	Y
2 **Walorski**	Y	Y	Y	Y	Y	Y
3 **Banks**	Y	Y	Y	Y	Y	N
4 Rokita	?	?	?	?	Y	N
5 **Brooks**	Y	Y	Y	Y	Y	Y
6 **Messer**	?	?	?	?	Y	N
7 Carson	N	N	N	N	N	Y
8 **Bucshon**	Y	Y	Y	Y	Y	Y
9 **Hollingsworth**	Y	Y	Y	Y	Y	N
IOWA						
1 **Blum**	Y	Y	Y	Y	Y	Y
2 Loebsack	N	N	N	N	Y	Y
3 **Young**	Y	Y	Y	Y	Y	Y
4 **King**	+	+	+	+	Y	Y
KANSAS						
1 **Marshall**	Y	Y	Y	Y	Y	Y
2 **Jenkins**	Y	Y	Y	Y	Y	Y
3 **Yoder**	?	?	?	?	?	Y
4 **Estes**	Y	Y	Y	Y	Y	Y
KENTUCKY						
1 **Comer**	Y	Y	Y	Y	Y	Y
2 **Guthrie**	Y	Y	Y	Y	Y	Y
3 Yarmuth	N	N	N	N	N	Y
4 **Massie**	Y	Y	Y	Y	Y	N
5 **Rogers**	Y	Y	Y	Y	Y	Y
6 **Barr**	Y	Y	Y	Y	Y	Y
LOUISIANA						
1 **Scalise**	Y	Y	Y	Y	Y	Y
2 Richmond	N	N	N	N	N	Y
3 **Higgins**	Y	Y	Y	Y	Y	Y
4 **Johnson**	Y	Y	Y	Y	Y	Y
5 **Abraham**	Y	Y	Y	Y	Y	Y
6 **Graves**	Y	Y	Y	Y	Y	Y
MAINE						
1 Pingree	N	N	N	N	N	Y
2 **Poliquin**	Y	Y	Y	Y	Y	Y
MARYLAND						
1 **Harris**	Y	Y	Y	Y	Y	Y
2 Ruppersberger	N	?	N	N	N	Y
3 Sarbanes	N	N	N	N	N	Y
4 Brown	N	N	N	N	N	Y
5 Hoyer	N	N	N	N	N	Y
6 Delaney	N	N	N	N	Y	Y
7 Cummings	N	N	N	N	N	Y
8 Raskin	N	N	N	N	N	Y
MASSACHUSETTS						
1 Neal	N	N	N	N	N	Y
2 McGovern	N	N	N	N	N	Y
3 Tsongas	N	N	N	N	N	Y
4 Kennedy	N	N	N	N	N	Y
5 Clark	N	N	N	N	Y	Y
6 Moulton	N	N	N	N	Y	Y
7 Capuano	N	N	N	N	N	Y
8 Lynch	N	N	N	N	Y	Y
9 Keating	N	N	N	N	Y	Y
MICHIGAN						
1 **Bergman**	Y	Y	Y	Y	Y	Y
2 **Huizenga**	Y	Y	Y	Y	Y	Y
3 *Amash*	Y	Y	Y	Y	Y	N
4 **Moolenaar**	Y	Y	Y	Y	Y	Y
5 Kildee	N	N	N	N	N	Y
6 **Upton**	Y	Y	Y	Y	Y	Y
7 **Walberg**	Y	Y	Y	Y	Y	Y
8 **Bishop**	Y	Y	Y	Y	Y	Y
9 Levin	N	N	N	?	N	Y
10 **Mitchell**	Y	Y	Y	Y	Y	Y
11 **Trott**	Y	Y	Y	Y	Y	Y
12 Dingell	N	N	N	N	Y	Y
14 Lawrence	N	N	N	N	N	Y
MINNESOTA						
1 Walz	?	?	?	?	?	?
2 **Lewis**	Y	Y	Y	Y	Y	Y
3 **Paulsen**	Y	Y	Y	Y	Y	Y
4 McCollum	N	N	N	N	N	Y

	368	369	370	371	372	373
5 Ellison	?	?	?	?	?	?
6 **Emmer**	Y	Y	Y	Y	Y	Y
7 Peterson	N	N	N	N	Y	Y
8 Nolan	N	N	N	N	Y	Y
MISSISSIPPI						
1 **Kelly**	Y	Y	Y	Y	Y	N
2 Thompson	N	N	N	N	N	Y
3 **Harper**	Y	Y	Y	Y	Y	Y
4 **Palazzo**	Y	Y	Y	Y	Y	Y
MISSOURI						
1 Clay	N	N	N	N	N	Y
2 **Wagner**	Y	Y	Y	Y	Y	Y
3 **Luetkemeyer**	Y	Y	Y	Y	Y	N
4 **Hartzler**	+	+	+	+	+	Y
5 Cleaver	N	N	N	N	N	Y
6 **Graves**	+	+	+	+	+	Y
7 **Long**	+	+	+	+	+	Y
8 **Smith**	?	?	?	?	?	N
MONTANA						
AL **Gianforte**	Y	Y	Y	Y	Y	Y
NEBRASKA						
1 **Fortenberry**	Y	Y	Y	Y	Y	Y
2 **Bacon**	Y	Y	Y	Y	Y	Y
3 **Smith**	Y	Y	Y	Y	Y	N
NEVADA						
1 Titus	N	N	N	N	N	Y
2 **Amodei**	Y	Y	Y	Y	Y	Y
3 Rosen	N	N	N	N	Y	Y
4 Kihuen	N	N	N	N	N	Y
NEW HAMPSHIRE						
1 Shea-Porter	N	N	N	N	N	Y
2 Kuster	N	N	N	N	Y	Y
NEW JERSEY						
1 Norcross	N	N	N	N	Y	Y
2 **LoBiondo**	Y	Y	Y	Y	Y	Y
3 **MacArthur**	Y	Y	Y	Y	Y	Y
4 **Smith**	Y	Y	Y	Y	Y	Y
5 Gottheimer	N	Y	N	N	Y	Y
6 Pallone	N	N	N	N	N	Y
7 **Lance**	Y	Y	Y	Y	Y	Y
8 Sires	N	N	N	N	Y	Y
9 Pascrell	N	N	N	N	N	Y
10 Payne	N	N	N	N	N	Y
11 **Frelinghuysen**	Y	Y	Y	Y	Y	Y
12 Watson Coleman	N	N	N	N	N	Y
NEW MEXICO						
1 Lujan Grisham	N	N	N	N	N	Y
2 **Pearce**	Y	Y	Y	Y	Y	Y
3 Luján	N	N	N	N	N	Y
NEW YORK						
1 **Zeldin**	Y	Y	Y	Y	Y	Y
2 **King**	Y	Y	Y	Y	Y	Y
3 Suozzi	N	Y	N	N	Y	Y
4 Rice	N	N	N	N	Y	Y
5 Meeks	N	N	N	N	N	Y
6 Meng	N	N	N	N	N	Y
7 Velázquez	N	N	N	N	N	Y
8 Jeffries	?	N	N	N	N	Y
9 Clarke	N	N	N	N	N	Y
10 Nadler	N	N	N	N	N	Y
11 **Donovan**	Y	Y	Y	Y	Y	Y
12 Maloney, C.	N	N	N	N	N	Y
13 Espaillat	N	N	N	N	N	Y
14 Crowley	N	N	N	N	N	Y
15 Serrano	N	N	N	N	N	Y
16 Engel	N	N	N	N	N	Y
17 Lowey	N	N	N	N	N	Y
18 Maloney, S.P.	N	N	N	N	Y	Y
19 **Faso**	Y	Y	Y	Y	Y	Y
20 Tonko	N	N	N	N	Y	Y
21 **Stefanik**	Y	Y	Y	Y	Y	Y
22 **Tenney**	Y	Y	Y	Y	Y	Y
23 **Reed**	Y	Y	Y	Y	Y	Y
24 **Katko**	Y	Y	Y	Y	Y	Y
25 **Vacant**						
26 Higgins	N	N	N	N	N	Y
27 **Collins**	Y	Y	Y	Y	Y	Y
NORTH CAROLINA						
1 Butterfield	N	N	N	N	N	Y
2 **Holding**	Y	Y	Y	Y	Y	N
3 **Jones**	Y	Y	N	Y	N	Y
4 Price	?	?	?	?	N	Y

	368	369	370	371	372	373
5 **Foxx**	Y	Y	Y	Y	Y	N
6 **Walker**	Y	Y	Y	Y	Y	N
7 **Rouzer**	Y	Y	Y	Y	Y	Y
8 **Hudson**	Y	Y	Y	Y	Y	N
9 **Pittenger**	Y	Y	Y	Y	Y	Y
9 **Vacant**						
10 **McHenry**	Y	Y	Y	Y	Y	Y
11 **Meadows**	Y	Y	Y	Y	Y	Y
12 Adams	N	N	N	N	N	Y
13 **Budd**	Y	Y	Y	Y	Y	N
NORTH DAKOTA						
AL **Cramer**	Y	Y	Y	Y	Y	?
OHIO						
1 **Chabot**	Y	Y	Y	Y	Y	N
2 **Wenstrup**	Y	Y	Y	Y	Y	N
3 Beatty	N	N	N	N	N	Y
4 **Jordan**	Y	Y	Y	Y	Y	N
5 **Latta**	Y	Y	Y	Y	Y	Y
6 **Johnson**	Y	Y	Y	Y	Y	Y
7 **Gibbs**	Y	Y	Y	Y	Y	Y
8 **Davidson**	Y	Y	Y	Y	Y	N
9 Kaptur	N	N	N	N	N	Y
10 **Turner**	Y	Y	Y	Y	Y	Y
11 Fudge	N	N	N	N	N	Y
12 **Vacant**						
13 Ryan	N	N	N	N	N	Y
14 **Joyce**	Y	Y	Y	Y	Y	Y
15 **Stivers**	Y	Y	Y	Y	Y	Y
16 **Renacci**	Y	Y	Y	Y	Y	Y
OKLAHOMA						
1 **Vacant**						
2 **Mullin**	Y	Y	Y	Y	Y	Y
3 **Lucas**	Y	Y	Y	Y	Y	Y
4 **Cole**	Y	Y	Y	Y	Y	Y
5 **Russell**	Y	Y	Y	Y	Y	Y
OREGON						
1 Bonamici	N	N	N	N	N	Y
2 **Walden**	Y	Y	Y	Y	Y	Y
3 Blumenauer	N	N	N	N	N	N
4 DeFazio	N	N	N	N	N	Y
5 Schrader	N	N	N	N	N	Y
PENNSYLVANIA						
1 Brady	N	N	N	N	N	Y
2 Evans	N	N	N	N	N	Y
3 **Kelly**	Y	Y	Y	Y	Y	Y
4 **Perry**	Y	Y	Y	Y	Y	Y
5 **Thompson**	Y	Y	Y	Y	Y	Y
6 **Costello**	Y	Y	Y	Y	Y	Y
7 **Vacant**						
8 **Fitzpatrick**	Y	Y	Y	Y	Y	Y
9 **Shuster**	Y	Y	Y	Y	Y	Y
10 **Marino**	Y	Y	Y	Y	Y	Y
11 **Barletta**	Y	Y	Y	Y	Y	Y
12 **Rothfus**	Y	Y	Y	Y	Y	Y
13 Boyle	N	N	N	N	Y	Y
14 Doyle	N	N	N	N	N	Y
15 **Vacant**						
16 **Smucker**	Y	Y	Y	Y	Y	Y
17 Cartwright	N	N	N	N	N	Y
18 Lamb	N	Y	N	Y	Y	Y
RHODE ISLAND						
1 Cicilline	N	N	N	N	N	Y
2 Langevin	N	N	N	N	N	Y
SOUTH CAROLINA						
1 **Sanford**	Y	Y	Y	Y	Y	Y
2 **Wilson**	Y	Y	Y	Y	Y	Y
3 **Duncan**	Y	Y	Y	Y	Y	N
4 **Gowdy**	Y	Y	Y	Y	Y	Y
5 **Norman**	Y	Y	Y	Y	Y	Y
6 Clyburn	N	N	N	N	N	Y
7 **Rice**	Y	Y	Y	Y	Y	Y
SOUTH DAKOTA						
AL **Noem**	?	?	?	?	?	?
TENNESSEE						
1 **Roe**	Y	Y	Y	Y	Y	Y
2 **Duncan**	Y	Y	Y	Y	Y	N
3 **Fleischmann**	Y	Y	Y	Y	Y	Y
4 **DesJarlais**	Y	Y	Y	Y	Y	Y
5 Cooper	N	N	N	N	N	Y
6 **Black**	?	?	?	?	?	?
7 **Blackburn**	?	?	?	?	?	Y
8 **Kustoff**	Y	Y	Y	Y	Y	Y
9 Cohen	N	N	N	N	N	Y

	368	369	370	371	372	373
TEXAS						
1 **Gohmert**	Y	Y	Y	Y	Y	N
2 **Poe**	Y	Y	Y	Y	Y	Y
3 **Johnson, S.**	Y	Y	Y	Y	Y	N
4 **Ratcliffe**	Y	Y	Y	?	Y	N
5 **Hensarling**	Y	Y	Y	Y	Y	N
6 **Barton**	Y	Y	Y	Y	Y	N
7 **Culberson**	Y	Y	Y	Y	Y	Y
8 **Brady**	Y	Y	Y	Y	Y	Y
9 Green, A.	N	N	N	N	N	Y
10 **McCaul**	Y	Y	Y	Y	Y	Y
11 **Conaway**	Y	Y	Y	Y	Y	N
12 **Granger**	Y	Y	Y	Y	Y	Y
13 **Thornberry**	Y	Y	Y	Y	Y	Y
14 **Weber**	Y	Y	Y	Y	Y	Y
15 Gonzalez	N	N	N	N	Y	Y
16 O'Rourke	N	N	N	N	N	Y
17 **Flores**	Y	Y	Y	Y	Y	Y
18 Jackson Lee	N	N	N	N	N	Y
19 **Arrington**	Y	Y	Y	Y	Y	Y
20 Castro	N	N	N	N	N	Y
21 **Smith**	Y	Y	Y	Y	Y	?
22 **Olson**	Y	Y	Y	Y	Y	Y
23 **Hurd**	Y	Y	Y	Y	Y	Y
24 Marchant	Y	Y	Y	Y	Y	Y
25 **Williams**	Y	Y	Y	Y	Y	N
26 **Burgess**	Y	Y	Y	Y	Y	Y
27 Cloud	Y	Y	Y	Y	Y	Y
28 Cuellar	N	N	N	N	Y	Y
29 Green, G.	N	N	N	N	Y	Y
30 Johnson, E.B.	N	N	N	N	N	Y
31 **Carter**	Y	Y	Y	Y	Y	Y
32 **Sessions**	Y	Y	Y	Y	Y	Y
33 Veasey	N	N	N	N	Y	Y
34 Vela	N	N	N	N	Y	Y
35 Doggett	N	N	N	N	N	Y
36 **Babin**	Y	Y	Y	Y	Y	Y
UTAH						
1 **Bishop**	Y	Y	Y	Y	Y	Y
2 **Stewart**	Y	Y	Y	Y	Y	Y
3 **Curtis**	Y	Y	Y	Y	Y	Y
4 **Love**	Y	Y	Y	Y	Y	Y
VERMONT						
AL Welch	N	N	N	N	N	Y
VIRGINIA						
1 **Wittman**	Y	Y	Y	Y	Y	Y
2 **Taylor**	Y	Y	Y	Y	Y	Y
3 Scott	N	N	N	N	N	Y
4 McEachin	N	N	N	N	N	Y
5 **Garrett**	Y	Y	Y	Y	Y	N
6 **Goodlatte**	Y	Y	Y	Y	Y	Y
7 **Brat**	Y	Y	Y	Y	Y	N
8 Beyer	N	N	N	N	N	Y
9 **Griffith**	Y	Y	Y	Y	Y	Y
10 **Comstock**	Y	Y	Y	Y	Y	Y
11 Connolly	N	N	N	N	N	Y
WASHINGTON						
1 DelBene	N	N	N	N	Y	Y
2 Larsen	N	N	N	N	N	Y
3 **Herrera Beutler**	Y	Y	Y	Y	Y	Y
4 **Newhouse**	Y	Y	Y	Y	Y	Y
5 McMorris Rodgers	Y	Y	Y	Y	Y	Y
6 Kilmer	N	N	N	N	Y	Y
7 Jayapal	N	N	N	N	N	Y
8 **Reichert**	Y	Y	Y	Y	Y	Y
9 Smith	N	N	N	N	N	Y
10 Heck	N	N	N	N	N	Y
WEST VIRGINIA						
1 **McKinley**	Y	Y	Y	Y	Y	Y
2 **Mooney**	Y	Y	Y	Y	Y	N
3 **Jenkins**	Y	Y	Y	Y	Y	Y
WISCONSIN						
1 **Ryan**						
2 Pocan	N	N	N	N	N	Y
3 Kind	N	N	N	N	N	Y
4 Moore	–	–	–	–	–	+
5 **Sensenbrenner**	Y	Y	Y	Y	Y	N
6 **Grothman**	Y	Y	Y	Y	Y	N
7 **Duffy**	Y	Y	Y	Y	Y	N
8 **Gallagher**	Y	Y	Y	Y	Y	N
WYOMING						
AL **Cheney**	Y	Y	Y	Y	Y	N

||| HOUSE VOTES

VOTE NUMBER

374. HR5864. VA HUMAN RESOURCES STANDARDS/PASSAGE. Roe, R-Tenn., motion to suspend the rules and pass the bill that would require the Veterans Affairs Department to establish qualifications and standardized performance metrics for human resources positions within the Veterans Health Administration. Motion agreed to 417-0: R 229-0; D 188-0. July 25, 2018.

375. HR6311. HEALTH CARE LAW CHANGES/RECOMMIT. Frankel, D-Fla., motion to recommit the bill to the House Ways and Means Committee with instructions to report it back immediately with an amendment that would prohibit enactment of the bill's provisions until the annual reports from the Board of the Trustees of the Federal Hospital Insurance Trust Fund and the Federal Supplementary Medical Insurance Trust Fund indicate that such funds are solvent. Motion rejected 187-229: R 2-227; D 185-2. July 25, 2018.

376. HR6311. HEALTH CARE LAW CHANGES/PASSAGE. Passage of the bill that would modify the 2010 health care overhaul law to allow anyone to purchase a "copper" (catastrophic) plan through the law's insurance exchanges, and would extend the suspension of the annual tax on health insurers through 2021. It would also allow individuals on certain plans to use health savings accounts associated with their plans and would also increase the contribution limit for certain HSAs. Passed 242-176: R 230-1; D 12-175. July 25, 2018.

377. HR6199. EXPANDING HEALTH SAVINGS ACCOUNTS/PASSAGE. Passage of the bill that would make a number of changes to health savings accounts. It would permit certain plans to pay for initial medical services before the plan's deductible kicks in, and would allow an individual to have an HSA in addition even if they also have certain other types of health care coverage in addition to a high deductible plan. It would also permit an individual to contribute to an HSA even if their spouse has a flexible spending account, and would allow the use of HSAs to pay for over-the-counter medical products, as well as some sport and fitness expenses. Passed 277-142: R 231-1; D 46-141. July 25, 2018.

378. HRES1027. FISCAL 2019 DEFENSE AUTHORIZATION/PREVIOUS QUESTION. Byrne, R-Ala., motion to order the previous question (thus ending debate and the possibility of amendment) on the rule (H Res 1027) that would provide for house floor consideration of the conference report to accompany the fiscal 2019 NDAA (HR 5515) that would authorize $708.1 billion for the Defense Department and related programs. The rule would also provide, through 3 p.m. on August 2, 2018, that the Committee on Appropriations may file privileged reports to accompany measures making appropriations for the fiscal 2019. Motion agreed to 226-183: R 224-0; D 2-183. July 26, 2018.

379. HR5515. FISCAL 2019 DEFENSE AUTHORIZATION/CONFERENCE REPORT. Adoption of the conference report on the bill that would authorize $708.1 billion for defense-related programs, with $639.1 billion for the Defense Department's base budget, and $69 billion for overseas contingency operations. Specifically, it would authorize $65 million for the development of low-yield nuclear weapons. It would also authorize $18.8 billion for Navy aircraft procurement, $16.5 billion for Air Force aircraft, and 24.1 billion for Navy shipbuilding. It would prohibit any U.S. government agency from using technology produced by the Chinese companies ZTE or Huawei, but would not reimpose a ban on U.S. exports to ZTE. Adopted (thus sent to the Senate) 359-54: R 220-5; D 139-49. July 26, 2018.

	374	375	376	377	378	379
ALABAMA						
1 **Byrne**	Y	N	Y	Y	Y	Y
2 **Roby**	Y	N	Y	Y	Y	Y
3 **Rogers**	Y	N	Y	Y	Y	Y
4 **Aderholt**	Y	N	Y	Y	Y	Y
5 **Brooks**	Y	N	Y	Y	Y	Y
6 **Palmer**	Y	N	Y	Y	Y	Y
7 Sewell	Y	Y	N	N	N	Y
ALASKA						
AL **Young**	Y	N	Y	Y	Y	Y
ARIZONA						
1 O'Halleran	Y	Y	Y	Y	N	Y
2 **McSally**	Y	N	Y	Y	Y	Y
3 Grijalva	Y	Y	N	N	N	N
4 **Gosar**	Y	N	Y	Y	Y	Y
5 **Biggs**	Y	N	Y	Y	Y	Y
6 **Schweikert**	Y	N	Y	Y	Y	Y
7 Gallego	Y	Y	N	N	N	Y
8 **Lesko**	Y	N	Y	Y	Y	Y
9 Sinema	Y	N	Y	Y	N	Y
ARKANSAS						
1 **Crawford**	Y	N	Y	Y	Y	Y
2 **Hill**	Y	N	Y	Y	Y	Y
3 **Womack**	Y	N	Y	Y	Y	Y
4 **Westerman**	Y	N	Y	Y	Y	Y
CALIFORNIA						
1 **LaMalfa**	Y	N	Y	Y	Y	Y
2 Huffman	Y	Y	N	N	N	N
3 Garamendi	Y	Y	N	N	N	Y
4 **McClintock**	Y	N	Y	Y	Y	Y
5 Thompson	Y	Y	N	N	N	Y
6 Matsui	Y	Y	N	N	N	N
7 Bera	Y	Y	Y	Y	N	Y
8 **Cook**	Y	N	Y	Y	Y	Y
9 McNerney	Y	Y	N	N	N	Y
10 **Denham**	Y	N	Y	Y	Y	Y
11 DeSaulnier	Y	Y	N	N	N	N
12 Pelosi	Y	Y	N	?	N	Y
13 Lee	Y	Y	N	N	N	N
14 Speier	?	?	?	?	?	?
15 Swalwell	Y	Y	N	Y	N	N
16 Costa	Y	Y	N	N	N	Y
17 Khanna	Y	Y	N	N	N	N
18 Eshoo	Y	Y	N	N	N	N
19 Lofgren	Y	Y	N	N	N	N
20 Panetta	Y	Y	N	Y	N	Y
21 **Valadao**	Y	N	Y	Y	Y	Y
22 **Nunes**	Y	N	Y	Y	Y	Y
23 **McCarthy**	Y	N	Y	Y	Y	Y
24 Carbajal	Y	Y	N	Y	N	Y
25 **Knight**	Y	N	Y	Y	Y	Y
26 Brownley	Y	Y	N	Y	N	Y
27 Chu	Y	Y	N	N	N	N
28 Schiff	Y	Y	N	N	N	Y
29 Cardenas	Y	Y	N	N	N	Y
30 Sherman	Y	Y	N	N	N	Y
31 Aguilar	Y	Y	N	Y	N	Y
32 Napolitano	Y	Y	N	N	N	N
33 Lieu	Y	Y	N	N	N	Y
34 Gomez	Y	Y	N	N	N	N
35 Torres	Y	Y	N	Y	N	Y
36 Ruiz	Y	Y	N	Y	N	Y
37 Bass	Y	?	?	?	N	N
38 Sánchez, Linda	Y	Y	N	N	N	Y
39 **Royce**	Y	N	Y	Y	Y	Y
40 Roybal-Allard	Y	Y	N	N	N	Y
41 Takano	Y	Y	N	N	N	N
42 **Calvert**	Y	N	Y	Y	Y	Y
43 Waters	Y	Y	N	N	N	Y
44 Barragan	Y	Y	N	N	N	Y
45 **Walters**	Y	N	Y	Y	Y	Y
46 Correa	Y	Y	N	N	N	Y
47 Lowenthal	Y	Y	N	N	N	N
48 **Rohrabacher**	Y	N	Y	Y	Y	Y
49 **Issa**	Y	N	Y	Y	Y	Y
50 **Hunter**	Y	N	Y	Y	Y	Y
51 Vargas	Y	Y	N	N	N	Y
52 Peters	Y	Y	N	N	N	Y
53 Davis	Y	Y	N	N	N	Y

	374	375	376	377	378	379
COLORADO						
1 DeGette	Y	Y	N	N	N	N
2 Polis	Y	Y	N	N	N	Y
3 **Tipton**	Y	N	Y	Y	Y	Y
4 **Buck**	Y	N	Y	Y	Y	Y
5 **Lamborn**	Y	N	Y	Y	Y	Y
6 **Coffman**	Y	N	Y	Y	Y	Y
7 Perlmutter	Y	Y	N	Y	N	Y
CONNECTICUT						
1 Larson	Y	Y	N	N	N	Y
2 Courtney	Y	Y	N	N	N	Y
3 DeLauro	Y	Y	N	N	N	Y
4 Himes	Y	Y	N	N	N	Y
5 Esty	Y	Y	N	N	N	Y
DELAWARE						
AL Blunt Rochester	Y	Y	N	N	N	Y
FLORIDA						
1 **Gaetz**	Y	N	Y	Y	Y	Y
2 **Dunn**	Y	–	Y	Y	Y	Y
3 **Yoho**	Y	N	Y	Y	Y	Y
4 **Rutherford**	Y	N	Y	Y	Y	Y
5 Lawson	Y	Y	N	N	N	Y
6 **DeSantis**	Y	N	Y	Y	Y	Y
7 Murphy	Y	Y	Y	Y	N	Y
8 **Posey**	Y	N	Y	Y	Y	Y
9 Soto	Y	Y	N	N	N	Y
10 Demings	Y	Y	N	N	N	Y
11 **Webster**	Y	N	Y	Y	Y	Y
12 **Bilirakis**	Y	N	Y	Y	Y	Y
13 Crist	Y	Y	N	Y	N	Y
14 Castor	Y	Y	N	N	N	Y
15 **Ross**	Y	N	Y	Y	Y	Y
16 **Buchanan**	Y	N	Y	Y	Y	Y
17 **Rooney, T.**	Y	N	Y	Y	Y	Y
18 **Mast**	Y	N	Y	Y	Y	Y
19 **Rooney, F.**	Y	N	Y	Y	Y	Y
20 Hastings	Y	Y	N	N	N	Y
21 Frankel	Y	Y	N	N	N	Y
22 Deutch	Y	Y	N	N	N	Y
23 Wasserman Schultz	Y	Y	N	N	N	Y
24 Wilson	Y	Y	N	N	N	Y
25 **Diaz-Balart**	Y	N	Y	Y	Y	Y
26 **Curbelo**	Y	N	Y	Y	Y	Y
27 **Ros-Lehtinen**	Y	N	Y	Y	Y	Y
GEORGIA						
1 **Carter**	Y	N	Y	Y	Y	Y
2 Bishop	Y	Y	N	N	N	Y
3 **Ferguson**	Y	N	Y	Y	Y	Y
4 Johnson	Y	Y	N	N	N	N
5 Lewis	Y	Y	N	N	N	N
6 **Handel**	Y	N	Y	Y	Y	Y
7 **Woodall**	Y	N	Y	Y	Y	Y
8 **Scott, A.**	Y	N	Y	Y	Y	Y
9 **Collins**	Y	N	Y	Y	Y	Y
10 **Hice**	Y	N	Y	Y	Y	Y
11 **Loudermilk**	Y	N	Y	Y	Y	Y
12 **Allen**	Y	N	Y	Y	Y	Y
13 Scott, D.	Y	Y	N	N	N	Y
14 **Graves**	Y	N	Y	Y	Y	Y
HAWAII						
1 Hanabusa	?	?	?	?	?	?
2 Gabbard	Y	Y	N	N	N	N
IDAHO						
1 **Labrador**	Y	N	Y	Y	?	?
2 **Simpson**	Y	N	Y	Y	Y	Y
ILLINOIS						
1 Rush	Y	Y	N	N	N	N
2 Kelly	Y	Y	N	N	N	Y
3 Lipinski	Y	Y	N	N	N	Y
4 Gutierrez	Y	Y	N	N	N	N
5 Quigley	Y	Y	N	N	N	Y
6 **Roskam**	Y	N	Y	Y	Y	Y
7 Davis, D.	Y	Y	N	N	?	?
8 Krishnamoorthi	Y	Y	N	Y	N	Y
9 Schakowsky	Y	Y	N	N	N	N
10 Schneider	Y	Y	N	N	N	Y
11 Foster	Y	Y	N	N	N	Y
12 **Bost**	Y	N	Y	Y	+	+
13 **Davis, R.**	Y	N	Y	Y	?	?

KEY	Republicans	Democrats	Independents
Y Voted for (yea)	**X** Paired against		**C** Voted "present" to avoid possible conflict of interest
# Paired for	**~** Announced against		
+ Announced for	**P** Voted "present"		**?** Did not vote or otherwise make a position known
N Voted against (nay)			

	374	375	376	377	378	379
14 **Hultgren**	Y	N	Y	Y	Y	Y
15 **Shimkus**	Y	N	Y	Y	Y	Y
16 **Kinzinger**	Y	N	Y	Y	Y	Y
17 Bustos	Y	Y	Y	Y	N	Y
18 **LaHood**	?	N	Y	Y	Y	Y
INDIANA						
1 Visclosky	Y	Y	N	N	N	Y
2 **Walorski**	Y	N	Y	Y	Y	Y
3 **Banks**	Y	N	Y	Y	Y	Y
4 Rokita	Y	N	Y	Y	?	?
5 **Brooks**	Y	N	Y	Y	Y	Y
6 **Messer**	Y	N	Y	Y	Y	Y
7 Carson	Y	Y	N	N	N	Y
8 **Bucshon**	Y	N	Y	Y	Y	Y
9 **Hollingsworth**	Y	N	Y	Y	Y	Y
IOWA						
1 **Blum**	Y	Y	Y	Y	?	?
2 Loebsack	Y	Y	N	Y	N	Y
3 **Young**	Y	N	Y	Y	Y	Y
4 **King**	Y	N	Y	Y	Y	Y
KANSAS						
1 **Marshall**	Y	N	Y	Y	Y	Y
2 **Jenkins**	Y	N	Y	Y	Y	Y
3 **Yoder**	Y	N	Y	Y	Y	Y
4 **Estes**	Y	N	Y	Y	Y	Y
KENTUCKY						
1 **Comer**	Y	N	Y	Y	Y	Y
2 **Guthrie**	Y	N	Y	Y	Y	Y
3 Yarmuth	Y	Y	N	N	N	N
4 **Massie**	Y	N	Y	Y	Y	N
5 **Rogers**	Y	N	Y	Y	Y	Y
6 **Barr**	Y	N	Y	Y	Y	Y
LOUISIANA						
1 **Scalise**	Y	N	Y	Y	Y	Y
2 Richmond	Y	Y	N	N	N	Y
3 **Higgins**	Y	N	Y	Y	Y	Y
4 **Johnson**	Y	N	Y	Y	Y	Y
5 **Abraham**	Y	N	Y	Y	Y	Y
6 **Graves**	Y	N	Y	Y	Y	Y
MAINE						
1 Pingree	Y	Y	N	Y	N	Y
2 **Poliquin**	Y	N	Y	Y	Y	Y
MARYLAND						
1 **Harris**	Y	N	Y	Y	Y	Y
2 Ruppersberger	Y	Y	N	N	N	Y
3 Sarbanes	Y	Y	N	N	N	Y
4 Brown	Y	Y	N	N	N	Y
5 Hoyer	Y	Y	N	N	N	Y
6 Delaney	Y	Y	N	Y	N	Y
7 Cummings	Y	Y	N	N	N	Y
8 Raskin	Y	Y	N	N	N	N
MASSACHUSETTS						
1 Neal	Y	Y	N	N	N	Y
2 McGovern	Y	Y	N	N	N	N
3 Tsongas	Y	Y	N	N	N	Y
4 Kennedy	Y	Y	N	N	N	N
5 Clark	Y	Y	N	N	N	N
6 Moulton	Y	Y	N	N	N	Y
7 Capuano	Y	Y	N	N	N	N
8 Lynch	Y	Y	N	Y	N	Y
9 Keating	Y	Y	N	N	N	Y
MICHIGAN						
1 **Bergman**	Y	N	Y	Y	Y	Y
2 **Huizenga**	Y	N	Y	Y	Y	Y
3 *Amash*	Y	N	Y	Y	Y	N
4 **Moolenaar**	Y	N	Y	Y	Y	Y
5 Kildee	Y	Y	N	N	N	N
6 **Upton**	Y	N	Y	Y	Y	Y
7 **Walberg**	Y	N	Y	Y	Y	Y
8 **Bishop**	Y	N	Y	Y	Y	Y
9 Levin	Y	Y	N	N	N	Y
10 **Mitchell**	Y	N	Y	Y	Y	Y
11 **Trott**	Y	N	Y	Y	Y	Y
12 Dingell	Y	Y	N	N	N	Y
14 Lawrence	Y	Y	N	N	N	Y
MINNESOTA						
1 Walz	?	?	?	?	?	?
2 **Lewis**	Y	N	Y	Y	Y	Y
3 **Paulsen**	Y	N	Y	Y	Y	Y
4 McCollum	Y	Y	N	N	N	N
5 Ellison	?	?	?	?	?	?
6 **Emmer**	Y	N	Y	Y	Y	Y
7 Peterson	Y	Y	Y	Y	N	Y
8 Nolan	Y	Y	N	Y	N	N
MISSISSIPPI						
1 **Kelly**	Y	N	Y	Y	Y	Y
2 Thompson	Y	Y	N	N	N	Y
3 **Harper**	Y	N	Y	Y	Y	Y
4 **Palazzo**	Y	–	+	Y	Y	Y
MISSOURI						
1 Clay	Y	Y	N	N	N	Y
2 **Wagner**	Y	N	Y	Y	Y	Y
3 **Luetkemeyer**	Y	N	Y	Y	Y	Y
4 **Hartzler**	Y	N	Y	Y	Y	Y
5 Cleaver	Y	Y	N	Y	N	Y
6 **Graves**	Y	N	Y	Y	Y	Y
7 **Long**	Y	N	Y	Y	Y	Y
8 **Smith**	Y	N	Y	Y	Y	Y
MONTANA						
AL **Gianforte**	Y	N	Y	Y	Y	Y
NEBRASKA						
1 **Fortenberry**	Y	N	Y	Y	Y	Y
2 **Bacon**	Y	N	Y	Y	Y	Y
3 **Smith**	Y	N	Y	Y	Y	Y
NEVADA						
1 Titus	Y	Y	N	N	N	Y
2 **Amodei**	Y	N	Y	Y	Y	Y
3 Rosen	Y	Y	Y	Y	N	Y
4 Kihuen	Y	Y	N	N	N	Y
NEW HAMPSHIRE						
1 Shea-Porter	Y	Y	N	Y	N	Y
2 Kuster	Y	Y	Y	Y	N	Y
NEW JERSEY						
1 Norcross	Y	Y	N	N	N	Y
2 **LoBiondo**	Y	N	Y	Y	Y	Y
3 **MacArthur**	Y	N	Y	Y	Y	Y
4 **Smith**	Y	N	Y	Y	Y	Y
5 Gottheimer	Y	Y	Y	Y	N	Y
6 Pallone	Y	Y	N	N	N	N
7 **Lance**	Y	N	Y	Y	Y	Y
8 Sires	Y	Y	N	N	N	Y
9 Pascrell	Y	Y	N	N	N	Y
10 Payne	Y	Y	N	N	N	Y
11 **Frelinghuysen**	+	–	Y	Y	Y	Y
12 Watson Coleman	Y	Y	N	N	N	N
NEW MEXICO						
1 Lujan Grisham	Y	Y	N	Y	N	Y
2 **Pearce**	Y	N	Y	Y	Y	Y
3 Luján	Y	Y	N	N	N	Y
NEW YORK						
1 **Zeldin**	Y	N	Y	Y	Y	Y
2 **King**	Y	N	Y	Y	Y	Y
3 Suozzi	Y	Y	N	Y	N	Y
4 Rice	Y	Y	N	Y	?	Y
5 Meeks	Y	Y	N	Y	N	Y
6 Meng	Y	Y	N	Y	N	Y
7 Velázquez	Y	Y	N	N	N	N
8 Jeffries	Y	Y	N	N	N	N
9 Clarke	Y	Y	N	N	N	N
10 Nadler	Y	Y	N	N	N	N
11 **Donovan**	Y	N	Y	Y	Y	Y
12 Maloney, C.	Y	Y	N	N	N	N
13 Espaillat	Y	Y	N	N	N	N
14 Crowley	Y	Y	N	N	N	Y
15 Serrano	Y	Y	N	N	N	N
16 Engel	Y	Y	N	N	N	Y
17 Lowey	Y	Y	N	N	N	Y
18 Maloney, S.P.	Y	?	?	?	N	Y
19 **Faso**	Y	N	Y	Y	Y	Y
20 Tonko	Y	Y	N	N	N	Y
21 **Stefanik**	Y	N	Y	Y	Y	Y
22 **Tenney**	Y	N	Y	Y	Y	Y
23 **Reed**	Y	N	Y	Y	Y	Y
24 **Katko**	Y	N	Y	Y	Y	Y
25 **Vacant**						
26 Higgins	Y	Y	N	N	N	Y
27 **Collins**	Y	N	Y	Y	Y	Y
NORTH CAROLINA						
1 Butterfield	Y	Y	N	N	N	Y
2 **Holding**	Y	N	Y	Y	Y	Y
3 **Jones**	Y	Y	N	N	?	?
4 Price	Y	Y	N	N	N	Y
5 **Foxx**	Y	N	Y	Y	Y	Y
6 **Walker**	Y	N	Y	Y	Y	Y
7 **Rouzer**	Y	N	Y	Y	Y	Y
8 **Hudson**	Y	N	Y	Y	?	Y
9 **Pittenger**	Y	N	Y	Y	Y	Y
9 **Vacant**						
10 **McHenry**	Y	N	Y	Y	Y	Y
11 **Meadows**	Y	N	Y	Y	Y	Y
12 Adams	Y	Y	N	N	N	Y
13 **Budd**	Y	N	Y	Y	Y	Y
NORTH DAKOTA						
AL **Cramer**	?	?	?	?	Y	Y
OHIO						
1 **Chabot**	Y	N	Y	Y	Y	Y
2 **Wenstrup**	Y	N	Y	Y	Y	Y
3 Beatty	Y	Y	N	N	N	Y
4 **Jordan**	Y	N	Y	Y	Y	Y
5 **Latta**	Y	N	Y	Y	Y	Y
6 **Johnson**	Y	N	Y	Y	Y	Y
7 **Gibbs**	Y	N	Y	Y	Y	Y
8 **Davidson**	Y	N	Y	Y	Y	Y
9 Kaptur	Y	Y	N	N	N	Y
10 **Turner**	Y	N	Y	Y	Y	Y
11 Fudge	Y	Y	N	N	N	Y
12 **Vacant**						
13 Ryan	Y	Y	N	N	N	Y
14 **Joyce**	Y	N	Y	Y	Y	Y
15 **Stivers**	Y	N	Y	Y	Y	Y
16 **Renacci**	Y	N	Y	Y	Y	Y
OKLAHOMA						
1 **Vacant**						
2 **Mullin**	Y	N	Y	Y	Y	Y
3 **Lucas**	Y	N	Y	Y	Y	Y
4 **Cole**	Y	N	Y	Y	Y	Y
5 **Russell**	Y	N	Y	Y	Y	Y
OREGON						
1 Bonamici	Y	Y	N	Y	N	N
2 **Walden**	Y	N	Y	Y	Y	Y
3 Blumenauer	Y	Y	N	Y	N	N
4 DeFazio	Y	Y	N	Y	N	N
5 Schrader	Y	Y	N	Y	N	Y
PENNSYLVANIA						
1 Brady	Y	Y	N	N	N	Y
2 Evans	Y	Y	N	N	N	Y
3 **Kelly**	Y	N	Y	Y	Y	Y
4 **Perry**	Y	N	Y	Y	Y	Y
5 **Thompson**	Y	N	Y	Y	Y	Y
6 **Costello**	Y	N	Y	Y	Y	Y
7 **Vacant**						
8 **Fitzpatrick**	Y	N	Y	Y	Y	Y
9 **Shuster**	Y	N	Y	Y	Y	Y
10 **Marino**	Y	N	Y	Y	+	+
11 **Barletta**	Y	N	Y	Y	Y	Y
12 **Rothfus**	Y	N	Y	Y	Y	Y
13 Boyle	Y	Y	N	N	N	Y
14 Doyle	Y	Y	N	N	N	Y
15 **Vacant**						
16 **Smucker**	Y	N	Y	Y	Y	Y
17 Cartwright	Y	Y	N	N	N	Y
18 Lamb	Y	N	Y	Y	N	Y
RHODE ISLAND						
1 Cicilline	Y	Y	N	N	N	Y
2 Langevin	Y	Y	N	N	N	Y
SOUTH CAROLINA						
1 **Sanford**	Y	N	Y	Y	Y	Y
2 **Wilson**	Y	N	Y	Y	Y	Y
3 **Duncan**	Y	N	Y	Y	Y	Y
4 **Gowdy**	Y	N	Y	Y	Y	Y
5 **Norman**	Y	N	Y	Y	Y	Y
6 Clyburn	Y	Y	N	N	N	Y
7 **Rice**	Y	N	Y	Y	Y	Y
SOUTH DAKOTA						
AL **Noem**	?	N	Y	Y	Y	Y
TENNESSEE						
1 **Roe**	Y	N	Y	Y	Y	Y
2 **Duncan**	Y	N	Y	Y	Y	N
3 **Fleischmann**	Y	N	Y	Y	Y	Y
4 **DesJarlais**	Y	N	Y	Y	Y	Y
5 Cooper	Y	Y	N	N	N	Y
6 **Black**	?	?	?	+	+	?
7 **Blackburn**	Y	?	?	?	?	?
8 **Kustoff**	Y	N	Y	Y	Y	Y
9 Cohen	Y	Y	N	N	N	N
TEXAS						
1 **Gohmert**	Y	N	Y	Y	?	?
2 **Poe**	Y	N	Y	Y	Y	Y
3 **Johnson, S.**	Y	N	Y	Y	Y	Y
4 **Ratcliffe**	Y	N	Y	Y	Y	Y
5 **Hensarling**	Y	N	Y	Y	Y	Y
6 **Barton**	Y	N	Y	Y	Y	Y
7 **Culberson**	Y	N	Y	Y	Y	Y
8 **Brady**	Y	N	Y	Y	Y	Y
9 Green, A.	Y	Y	N	N	N	Y
10 **McCaul**	Y	N	Y	Y	Y	Y
11 **Conaway**	Y	N	Y	Y	Y	Y
12 **Granger**	Y	N	Y	Y	Y	Y
13 **Thornberry**	Y	N	Y	Y	Y	Y
14 **Weber**	Y	N	Y	Y	Y	Y
15 Gonzalez	Y	Y	Y	Y	N	Y
16 O'Rourke	Y	Y	N	Y	N	Y
17 **Flores**	Y	N	Y	Y	Y	Y
18 Jackson Lee	Y	Y	N	N	N	Y
19 **Arrington**	Y	N	Y	Y	Y	Y
20 Castro	Y	Y	N	N	N	Y
21 **Smith**	?	N	Y	Y	Y	Y
22 **Olson**	Y	N	Y	Y	Y	Y
23 **Hurd**	Y	N	Y	Y	Y	Y
24 Marchant	Y	N	Y	Y	Y	Y
25 **Williams**	Y	N	Y	Y	Y	Y
26 **Burgess**	Y	N	Y	Y	Y	Y
27 Cloud	Y	N	Y	Y	Y	Y
28 Cuellar	Y	Y	Y	Y	N	Y
29 Green, G.	Y	Y	N	Y	Y	Y
30 Johnson, E.B.	Y	Y	N	N	N	Y
31 **Carter**	Y	N	Y	Y	Y	Y
32 **Sessions**	Y	N	Y	Y	Y	Y
33 Veasey	Y	Y	N	N	N	Y
34 Vela	Y	Y	N	Y	Y	Y
35 Doggett	Y	Y	N	N	N	Y
36 **Babin**	Y	N	Y	Y	Y	Y
UTAH						
1 **Bishop**	Y	N	Y	Y	Y	Y
2 **Stewart**	Y	N	Y	Y	Y	Y
3 **Curtis**	Y	N	Y	Y	Y	Y
4 **Love**	Y	N	Y	Y	Y	Y
VERMONT						
AL Welch	Y	Y	N	N	N	N
VIRGINIA						
1 **Wittman**	Y	N	Y	Y	Y	Y
2 **Taylor**	Y	N	Y	Y	Y	Y
3 Scott	Y	Y	N	N	N	Y
4 McEachin	Y	Y	N	N	N	Y
5 **Garrett**	Y	N	Y	Y	Y	Y
6 **Goodlatte**	Y	N	Y	Y	Y	Y
7 **Brat**	Y	N	Y	Y	Y	Y
8 Beyer	Y	Y	N	N	N	Y
9 **Griffith**	Y	N	Y	Y	Y	N
10 **Comstock**	Y	N	Y	Y	Y	Y
11 Connolly	Y	Y	N	N	N	Y
WASHINGTON						
1 DelBene	Y	Y	N	N	N	Y
2 Larsen	Y	Y	N	N	N	Y
3 **Herrera Beutler**	Y	N	Y	Y	Y	Y
4 **Newhouse**	Y	N	Y	Y	Y	Y
5 **McMorris Rodgers**	Y	N	Y	Y	Y	Y
6 Kilmer	Y	Y	N	N	N	Y
7 Jayapal	Y	Y	N	N	N	N
8 **Reichert**	Y	N	Y	Y	Y	Y
9 Smith	Y	Y	N	N	N	Y
10 Heck	Y	Y	N	N	N	Y
WEST VIRGINIA						
1 **McKinley**	Y	N	Y	Y	Y	Y
2 **Mooney**	Y	N	Y	Y	Y	Y
3 **Jenkins**	Y	N	Y	Y	Y	Y
WISCONSIN						
1 **Ryan**						
2 Pocan	Y	Y	N	N	N	N
3 Kind	Y	Y	N	N	N	Y
4 Moore	+	Y	N	N	?	Y
5 **Sensenbrenner**	Y	N	Y	Y	Y	Y
6 **Grothman**	Y	N	Y	Y	Y	Y
7 **Duffy**	Y	N	Y	Y	Y	Y
8 **Gallagher**	Y	N	Y	Y	Y	Y
WYOMING						
AL **Cheney**	Y	N	Y	Y	Y	Y

VOTE NUMBER

380. HR6157. FISCAL 2019 DEFENSE, LABOR-HHS-EDUCATION APPROPRIATIONS/MOTION TO INSTRUCT. DeLauro, D-Conn., motion to instruct House conferees to agree with the Labor-HHS-Education division of the Senate amendment to the bill. Motion rejected 171-221: R 0-221; D 171-0. Oct. 4, 2018.

381. HR6439. BIOMETRIC IDENTIFICATION PROGRAM/PASSAGE. McCaul, R-Texas, motion to suspend the rules and pass the bill that would formally authorize the Biometric Identification Transnational Migration Alert Program within the Department of Homeland Security. The program would direct DHS to coordinate with other federal agencies as well as foreign governments to collect and share biometric and biographical data on foreign nationals who may pose a terrorist threat or a threat to national or border security. Motion agreed to 272-119: R 213-8; D 59-111. Oct. 4, 2018.

382. HR1635. STUDENT LOAN COUNSELING AND NATURAL GAS EXPORTS/ PREVIOUS QUESTION. Cheney, R-Wyo., motion to order the previous question (thus ending debate and possibility of amendment) on the rule (H Res 1049) that would provide for House floor consideration of the bill (HR 1635) that would modify counseling requirements for federal student loan recipients, and would provide for House floor consideration of the bill (HR 4606) that would allow certain small-scale imports and exports of natural gas to be automatically approved. Motion agreed to 221-186: R 221-0; D 0-186. Oct. 5, 2018.

383. HR1635. STUDENT LOAN COUNSELING AND NATURAL GAS EXPORTS/RULE. Adoption of the rule (H Res 1049) that would provide for House floor consideration of the bill (HR 1635) that would modify counseling requirements for federal student loan recipients, and would provide for House floor consideration of the bill (HR 4606) that would allow certain small-scale imports and exports of natural gas to be automatically approved. Adopted 224-180: R 222-0; D 2-180. Oct. 5, 2018.

384. HR1635. STUDENT LOAN COUNSELING/RECOMMIT. Lamb, D-Pa., motion to recommit the bill to the House Education and the Workforce Committee with instructions to report it back immediately with an amendment that would require that the bill's study on the effectiveness of student loan counseling include information on the veteran status of borrowers. Motion rejected 187-224: R 2-224; D 185-0. Oct. 5, 2018.

385. HR1635. STUDENT LOAN COUNSELING/PASSAGE. Passage of the bill that would require institutions of higher education to ensure that students and parents who receive federal student loans or Pell grants receive annual financial counseling. It would require that exit counseling be tailored to a borrower's loans and potential income. It would authorize $2 million for the Department of Education to develop an online student loan counseling tool for institutions of higher education to use to meet the bill's annual requirements. Passed 406-4: R 222-4; D 184-0. Oct. 5, 2018.

	380	381	382	383	384	385
ALABAMA						
1 **Byrne**	N	Y	Y	Y	N	Y
2 **Roby**	N	Y	Y	Y	N	Y
3 **Rogers**	N	Y	Y	Y	N	Y
4 **Aderholt**	N	Y	Y	Y	N	Y
5 **Brooks**	N	Y	Y	Y	N	Y
6 **Palmer**	N	Y	Y	Y	N	Y
7 **Sewell**	Y	Y	N	N	Y	Y
ALASKA						
AL **Young**	N	Y	Y	Y	N	Y
ARIZONA						
1 O'Halleran	Y	Y	N	N	Y	Y
2 **McSally**	N	Y	Y	Y	N	Y
3 Grijalva	?	?	N	N	Y	Y
4 **Gosar**	?	?	Y	Y	N	Y
5 **Biggs**	N	N	Y	Y	N	N
6 **Schweikert**	N	Y	Y	Y	N	Y
7 Gallego	?	?	N	N	Y	Y
8 **Lesko**	N	Y	Y	Y	N	Y
9 Sinema	Y	Y	N	N	Y	Y
ARKANSAS						
1 **Crawford**	N	Y	Y	Y	N	Y
2 **Hill**	N	Y	Y	Y	N	Y
3 **Womack**	N	Y	Y	Y	N	Y
4 **Westerman**	N	Y	Y	Y	N	Y
CALIFORNIA						
1 **LaMalfa**	N	Y	Y	Y	N	Y
2 Huffman	Y	N	N	N	Y	Y
3 Garamendi	Y	Y	N	N	Y	Y
4 **McClintock**	N	Y	Y	Y	N	Y
5 Thompson	Y	N	N	N	Y	Y
6 Matsui	Y	N	N	N	Y	Y
7 Bera	Y	Y	N	N	Y	Y
8 **Cook**	N	Y	Y	Y	N	Y
9 McNerney	?	?	N	N	Y	Y
10 **Denham**	N	Y	Y	Y	N	Y
11 DeSaulnier	Y	N	N	N	Y	Y
12 Pelosi	Y	N	N	?	Y	Y
13 Lee	Y	N	N	N	Y	Y
14 Speier	?	?	?	?	?	?
15 Swalwell	+	+	N	N	Y	Y
16 Costa	Y	Y	N	Y	Y	Y
17 Khanna	Y	N	N	N	Y	Y
18 Eshoo	+	-	-	-	+	+
19 Lofgren	Y	N	N	N	Y	Y
20 Panetta	Y	Y	N	N	Y	Y
21 **Valadao**	N	Y	Y	Y	N	Y
22 **Nunes**	N	Y	Y	Y	N	Y
23 **McCarthy**	N	Y	Y	Y	N	Y
24 Carbajal	Y	Y	N	N	Y	Y
25 **Knight**	N	Y	Y	Y	N	Y
26 Brownley	Y	Y	N	N	Y	Y
27 Chu	Y	N	N	N	Y	Y
28 Schiff	Y	N	N	N	Y	Y
29 Cardenas	Y	N	N	N	Y	Y
30 Sherman	Y	N	N	N	Y	Y
31 Aguilar	?	?	N	N	Y	Y
32 Napolitano	Y	N	N	N	Y	Y
33 Lieu	Y	N	N	N	Y	Y
34 Gomez	Y	N	N	N	Y	Y
35 Torres	Y	Y	N	N	Y	Y
36 Ruiz	Y	N	N	N	Y	Y
37 Bass	Y	N	N	N	Y	Y
38 Sánchez, Linda	Y	N	N	N	Y	Y
39 **Royce**	N	Y	Y	Y	N	Y
40 Roybal-Allard	Y	N	N	N	Y	Y
41 Takano	Y	N	N	N	Y	Y
42 **Calvert**	N	Y	Y	Y	N	Y
43 Waters	Y	N	N	N	Y	Y
44 Barragan	Y	N	N	N	Y	Y
45 **Walters**	N	Y	Y	Y	N	Y
46 Correa	Y	Y	N	N	Y	Y
47 Lowenthal	Y	N	N	N	Y	Y
48 **Rohrabacher**	?	?	Y	Y	N	Y
49 **Issa**	N	Y	Y	Y	N	Y
50 **Hunter**	?	?	Y	Y	N	Y
51 Vargas	Y	N	N	N	Y	Y
52 Peters	Y	Y	N	N	Y	Y
53 Davis	Y	N	N	N	Y	Y

	380	381	382	383	384	385
COLORADO						
1 DeGette	Y	N	N	N	Y	Y
2 Polis	Y	N	N	N	Y	Y
3 **Tipton**	?	?	Y	Y	N	Y
4 **Buck**	N	Y	Y	Y	N	Y
5 **Lamborn**	N	Y	Y	Y	N	Y
6 **Coffman**	N	Y	Y	Y	N	Y
7 Perlmutter	Y	N	N	N	Y	Y
CONNECTICUT						
1 Larson	Y	N	N	N	Y	Y
2 Courtney	Y	N	N	N	Y	Y
3 DeLauro	Y	N	N	N	Y	Y
4 Himes	Y	Y	N	N	Y	Y
5 Esty	Y	N	N	N	Y	Y
DELAWARE						
AL Blunt Rochester	Y	Y	N	N	Y	Y
FLORIDA						
1 **Gaetz**	N	Y	Y	Y	N	Y
2 **Dunn**	N	Y	Y	Y	N	Y
3 **Yoho**	N	Y	Y	Y	N	Y
4 **Rutherford**	N	Y	Y	Y	N	Y
5 Lawson	Y	Y	N	N	Y	Y
6 **DeSantis**	?	?	?	?	?	?
7 Murphy	Y	Y	N	N	Y	Y
8 **Posey**	N	Y	Y	Y	N	Y
9 Soto	Y	N	N	N	Y	Y
10 Demings	Y	N	N	N	Y	Y
11 **Webster**	N	Y	Y	Y	N	Y
12 **Bilirakis**	N	Y	Y	Y	N	Y
13 Crist	Y	N	N	N	Y	Y
14 Castor	?	?	N	N	Y	Y
15 **Ross**	N	Y	Y	Y	N	Y
16 **Buchanan**	N	Y	Y	Y	N	Y
17 **Rooney, T.**	?	?	?	?	?	?
18 **Mast**	N	Y	Y	Y	N	Y
19 **Rooney, F.**	N	Y	Y	Y	N	Y
20 Hastings	Y	N	N	N	Y	Y
21 Frankel	Y	N	N	N	Y	Y
22 Deutch	Y	N	N	N	Y	Y
23 Wasserman Schultz	Y	N	N	N	Y	Y
24 Wilson	?	?	N	N	Y	Y
25 **Diaz-Balart**	N	Y	Y	Y	N	Y
26 **Curbelo**	N	Y	Y	Y	N	Y
27 **Ros-Lehtinen**	N	Y	?	?	?	?
GEORGIA						
1 **Carter**	N	Y	Y	Y	N	Y
2 Bishop	Y	N	N	N	Y	Y
3 **Ferguson**	N	Y	Y	Y	N	Y
4 Johnson	Y	Y	N	?	Y	Y
5 Lewis	Y	N	N	N	Y	Y
6 **Handel**	N	Y	Y	Y	N	Y
7 **Woodall**	N	Y	Y	Y	N	Y
8 **Scott, A.**	N	Y	Y	Y	N	Y
9 **Collins**	N	Y	Y	Y	N	Y
10 **Hice**	N	Y	Y	Y	N	Y
11 **Loudermilk**	N	Y	Y	Y	N	Y
12 **Allen**	N	Y	Y	Y	N	Y
13 Scott, D.	Y	Y	N	N	Y	Y
14 **Graves**	N	Y	Y	Y	N	Y
HAWAII						
1 Hanabusa	Y	N	N	N	Y	Y
2 Gabbard	Y	N	N	N	Y	Y
IDAHO						
1 **Labrador**	N	N	Y	Y	N	Y
2 **Simpson**	N	Y	Y	Y	N	Y
ILLINOIS						
1 Rush	?	?	N	N	Y	Y
2 Kelly	Y	N	N	N	Y	Y
3 Lipinski	Y	Y	N	N	Y	Y
4 Gutierrez	-	-	N	N	Y	Y
5 Quigley	Y	Y	N	N	Y	Y
6 **Roskam**	N	Y	Y	Y	N	Y
7 Davis, D.	Y	N	N	N	Y	Y
8 Krishnamoorthi	Y	N	N	N	Y	Y
9 Schakowsky	Y	N	N	N	Y	Y
10 Schneider	Y	Y	N	N	Y	Y
11 Foster	Y	Y	N	N	Y	Y
12 **Bost**	N	Y	Y	Y	N	Y
13 **Davis, R.**	N	Y	Y	Y	N	Y

KEY	**Republicans**	Democrats	*Independents*
Y Voted for (yea)		X Paired against	C Voted "present" to avoid possible conflict of interest
# Paired for		– Announced against	
+ Announced for		P Voted "present"	? Did not vote or otherwise make a position known
N Voted against (nay)			

	380	381	382	383	384	385
14 **Hultgren**	N	Y	Y	Y	N	Y
15 **Shimkus**	N	Y	Y	Y	N	Y
16 **Kinzinger**	N	Y	Y	Y	N	Y
17 Bustos	Y	Y	N	N	Y	Y
18 **LaHood**	N	Y	Y	Y	N	Y
INDIANA						
1 Visclosky	Y	Y	N	N	Y	Y
2 **Walorski**	N	Y	Y	Y	N	Y
3 **Banks**	N	Y	Y	Y	N	Y
4 Rokita	?	?	Y	Y	N	Y
5 **Brooks**	N	Y	Y	Y	N	Y
6 **Messer**	N	Y	?	?	N	Y
7 Carson	Y	N	N	N	Y	Y
8 **Bucshon**	N	Y	Y	Y	N	Y
9 **Hollingsworth**	N	Y	Y	Y	N	Y
IOWA						
1 **Blum**	N	Y	Y	Y	Y	Y
2 Loebsack	Y	Y	N	?	Y	Y
3 **Young**	N	Y	Y	Y	N	Y
4 **King**	N	Y	Y	Y	N	Y
KANSAS						
1 **Marshall**	N	Y	Y	Y	N	Y
2 **Jenkins**	N	Y	Y	Y	N	Y
3 **Yoder**	N	Y	Y	Y	N	Y
4 **Estes**	N	Y	Y	Y	N	Y
KENTUCKY						
1 **Comer**	N	Y	Y	Y	N	Y
2 **Guthrie**	N	Y	Y	Y	N	Y
3 Yarmuth	Y	N	N	?	Y	Y
4 **Massie**	N	N	Y	Y	N	N
5 **Rogers**	N	Y	Y	Y	N	Y
6 **Barr**	N	Y	Y	Y	N	Y
LOUISIANA						
1 **Scalise**	N	Y	Y	Y	N	Y
2 Richmond	Y	N	N	N	Y	Y
3 **Higgins**	N	Y	Y	Y	N	Y
4 **Johnson**	N	Y	Y	Y	N	Y
5 **Abraham**	N	Y	Y	Y	N	Y
6 **Graves**	N	Y	Y	Y	N	Y
MAINE						
1 Pingree	Y	N	N	N	Y	Y
2 **Poliquin**	N	Y	Y	Y	N	Y
MARYLAND						
1 **Harris**	N	Y	Y	Y	N	Y
2 Ruppersberger	Y	Y	N	N	Y	Y
3 Sarbanes	Y	N	N	N	Y	Y
4 Brown	Y	Y	N	N	Y	Y
5 Hoyer	Y	N	N	N	Y	Y
6 Delaney	Y	Y	N	N	Y	Y
7 Cummings	Y	N	N	N	Y	Y
8 Raskin	Y	N	N	N	Y	Y
MASSACHUSETTS						
1 Neal	?	?	N	N	Y	Y
2 McGovern	Y	N	N	N	Y	Y
3 Tsongas	?	?	N	N	Y	Y
4 Kennedy	?	?	N	N	Y	Y
5 Clark	Y	N	N	N	Y	Y
6 Moulton	Y	Y	N	N	Y	Y
7 Capuano	?	?	?	?	?	?
8 Lynch	Y	Y	N	N	Y	Y
9 Keating	?	+	N	N	Y	Y
MICHIGAN						
1 **Bergman**	N	Y	Y	Y	N	Y
2 **Huizenga**	N	Y	Y	Y	N	Y
3 *Amash*	N	N	Y	Y	N	N
4 **Moolenaar**	N	Y	Y	Y	N	Y
5 Kildee	Y	N	N	N	Y	Y
6 **Upton**	N	Y	Y	Y	N	Y
7 **Walberg**	N	Y	Y	Y	N	Y
8 **Bishop**	N	Y	?	Y	N	Y
9 Levin	Y	N	N	N	Y	Y
10 **Mitchell**	N	Y	Y	Y	N	Y
11 **Trott**	N	Y	Y	Y	N	Y
12 Dingell	Y	N	N	N	Y	Y
14 Lawrence	Y	N	N	N	Y	Y
MINNESOTA						
1 Walz	?	?	N	N	?	?
2 **Lewis**	N	Y	Y	Y	N	Y
3 **Paulsen**	N	Y	Y	Y	N	Y
4 McCollum	Y	Y	N	N	Y	Y
5 Ellison	?	?	?	?	?	?
6 **Emmer**	N	Y	Y	Y	N	Y
7 Peterson	Y	Y	N	N	Y	Y
8 Nolan	Y	N	N	N	Y	Y
MISSISSIPPI						
1 **Kelly**	N	Y	Y	Y	N	Y
2 Thompson	Y	N	N	N	Y	Y
3 **Harper**	N	Y	Y	Y	N	Y
4 **Palazzo**	?	?	+	+	–	+
MISSOURI						
1 Clay	Y	N	N	N	Y	Y
2 **Wagner**	N	Y	Y	Y	N	Y
3 **Luetkemeyer**	N	Y	Y	Y	N	Y
4 **Hartzler**	N	Y	Y	Y	N	Y
5 Cleaver	Y	N	N	N	Y	Y
6 **Graves**	N	Y	Y	Y	N	Y
7 **Long**	N	Y	Y	Y	N	Y
8 **Smith**	N	Y	Y	Y	N	Y
MONTANA						
AL **Gianforte**	N	Y	Y	Y	N	Y
NEBRASKA						
1 **Fortenberry**	N	Y	Y	Y	N	Y
2 **Bacon**	N	Y	Y	Y	N	Y
3 **Smith**	N	Y	Y	Y	N	Y
NEVADA						
1 Titus	+	–	–	–	+	+
2 **Amodei**	N	Y	Y	Y	N	Y
3 Rosen	Y	Y	N	N	Y	Y
4 Kihuen	Y	N	N	N	Y	Y
NEW HAMPSHIRE						
1 Shea-Porter	Y	Y	N	N	Y	Y
2 Kuster	Y	Y	N	N	Y	Y
NEW JERSEY						
1 Norcross	Y	Y	N	N	Y	Y
2 **LoBiondo**	N	Y	Y	Y	N	Y
3 **MacArthur**	N	Y	Y	Y	N	Y
4 **Smith**	N	Y	Y	Y	N	Y
5 Gottheimer	Y	Y	N	N	Y	Y
6 Pallone	Y	N	N	N	Y	Y
7 **Lance**	N	Y	Y	Y	N	Y
8 Sires	Y	N	N	N	Y	Y
9 Pascrell	Y	N	N	N	Y	Y
10 Payne	Y	?	N	N	Y	Y
11 **Frelinghuysen**	N	Y	Y	Y	N	Y
12 Watson Coleman	Y	N	N	N	Y	Y
NEW MEXICO						
1 Lujan Grisham	Y	N	N	N	Y	Y
2 **Pearce**	N	Y	Y	Y	N	Y
3 Luján	Y	N	N	N	Y	Y
NEW YORK						
1 **Zeldin**	N	Y	Y	Y	N	Y
2 **King**	N	Y	Y	Y	N	Y
3 Suozzi	Y	Y	N	N	Y	Y
4 Rice	Y	Y	N	N	Y	Y
5 Meeks	Y	N	N	N	Y	Y
6 Meng	Y	N	N	N	Y	Y
7 Velázquez	Y	N	N	N	Y	Y
8 Jeffries	Y	N	N	N	Y	Y
9 Clarke	Y	N	N	N	Y	Y
10 Nadler	Y	N	N	N	Y	Y
11 **Donovan**	N	Y	Y	Y	N	Y
12 Maloney, C.	Y	N	N	N	Y	Y
13 Espaillat	Y	N	N	N	Y	Y
14 Crowley	Y	N	N	N	Y	Y
15 Serrano	Y	N	N	N	Y	Y
16 Engel	Y	N	N	N	Y	Y
17 Lowey	Y	N	N	N	Y	Y
18 Maloney, S.P.	?	?	?	?	?	?
19 **Faso**	N	Y	Y	Y	N	Y
20 Tonko	Y	Y	N	N	Y	Y
21 **Stefanik**	N	Y	Y	Y	N	Y
22 **Tenney**	N	Y	Y	Y	N	Y
23 **Reed**	N	Y	Y	Y	N	Y
24 **Katko**	N	Y	Y	Y	N	Y
25 **Vacant**						
26 Higgins	Y	Y	N	N	Y	Y
27 **Collins**	N	Y	Y	Y	N	Y
NORTH CAROLINA						
1 Butterfield	Y	N	N	N	Y	Y
2 **Holding**	N	Y	Y	Y	N	Y
3 **Jones**	?	?	Y	Y	Y	Y
4 Price	Y	N	N	N	Y	Y
5 **Foxx**	N	Y	Y	Y	N	Y
6 **Walker**	N	Y	Y	Y	N	Y
7 **Rouzer**	N	Y	Y	Y	N	Y
8 **Hudson**	N	Y	Y	Y	N	Y
9 **Pittenger**	N	Y	Y	Y	N	Y
9 **Vacant**						
10 **McHenry**	N	Y	Y	Y	N	Y
11 **Meadows**	N	Y	Y	Y	N	Y
12 Adams	Y	N	N	N	Y	Y
13 **Budd**	N	Y	Y	Y	N	Y
NORTH DAKOTA						
AL **Cramer**	N	Y	Y	Y	N	Y
OHIO						
1 **Chabot**	N	Y	Y	Y	N	Y
2 **Wenstrup**	N	Y	Y	Y	N	Y
3 Beatty	Y	N	N	N	Y	Y
4 **Jordan**	N	Y	Y	Y	N	Y
5 **Latta**	N	Y	Y	Y	N	Y
6 **Johnson**	N	Y	Y	Y	N	Y
7 **Gibbs**	N	Y	Y	Y	N	Y
8 **Davidson**	N	Y	Y	Y	N	Y
9 Kaptur	Y	Y	N	N	Y	Y
10 **Turner**	N	Y	Y	Y	N	Y
11 Fudge	Y	N	N	N	Y	Y
12 **Vacant**						
13 Ryan	Y	Y	N	N	Y	Y
14 **Joyce**	N	Y	Y	Y	N	Y
15 **Stivers**	N	Y	Y	Y	N	Y
16 **Renacci**	N	Y	Y	Y	N	Y
OKLAHOMA						
1 **Vacant**						
2 **Mullin**	N	Y	Y	Y	N	Y
3 **Lucas**	N	Y	Y	Y	N	Y
4 **Cole**	N	Y	Y	Y	N	Y
5 **Russell**	N	Y	Y	Y	N	Y
OREGON						
1 Bonamici	Y	N	N	N	Y	Y
2 ~~**Walden**~~	N	Y	Y	Y	N	Y
3 Blumenauer	Y	N	N	N	Y	Y
4 DeFazio	Y	Y	N	N	Y	Y
5 Schrader	Y	Y	N	N	Y	Y
PENNSYLVANIA						
1 Brady	?	?	N	N	Y	Y
2 Evans	Y	Y	N	N	Y	Y
3 **Kelly**	N	Y	Y	Y	N	Y
4 **Perry**	N	Y	Y	Y	N	Y
5 **Thompson**	N	Y	Y	Y	N	Y
6 **Costello**	N	Y	Y	Y	N	Y
7 **Vacant**						
8 **Fitzpatrick**	N	Y	Y	Y	N	Y
9 **Shuster**	N	Y	Y	Y	N	Y
10 **Marino**	N	Y	Y	Y	N	Y
11 **Barletta**	N	Y	?	?	N	Y
12 **Rothfus**	N	Y	Y	Y	N	Y
13 Boyle	Y	Y	?	?	?	?
14 Doyle	Y	N	N	N	Y	Y
15 **Vacant**						
16 **Smucker**	N	Y	Y	Y	N	Y
17 Cartwright	Y	Y	N	N	Y	Y
18 Lamb	Y	Y	N	Y	Y	Y
RHODE ISLAND						
1 Cicilline	Y	N	N	N	Y	Y
2 Langevin	Y	Y	N	N	Y	Y
SOUTH CAROLINA						
1 **Sanford**	N	N	?	?	N	N
2 **Wilson**	N	Y	Y	Y	N	Y
3 **Duncan**	N	Y	Y	Y	N	Y
4 **Gowdy**	?	?	Y	Y	N	Y
5 **Norman**	N	Y	Y	Y	N	Y
6 Clyburn	Y	N	N	N	Y	Y
7 **Rice**	N	Y	Y	?	N	Y
SOUTH DAKOTA						
AL **Noem**	N	Y	Y	Y	N	Y
TENNESSEE						
1 **Roe**	N	Y	Y	Y	N	Y
2 **Duncan**	N	N	Y	Y	N	Y
3 **Fleischmann**	N	Y	Y	Y	N	Y
4 **DesJarlais**	N	Y	Y	Y	N	Y
5 Cooper	Y	Y	N	N	Y	Y
6 **Black**	N	Y	Y	Y	N	Y
7 **Blackburn**	?	?	?	?	?	?
8 **Kustoff**	N	Y	Y	Y	N	Y
9 Cohen	Y	N	N	N	Y	Y
TEXAS						
1 **Gohmert**	N	Y	?	?	N	Y
2 **Poe**	?	?	?	?	?	?
3 **Johnson, S.**	N	Y	Y	Y	N	Y
4 **Ratcliffe**	N	Y	Y	Y	N	Y
5 **Hensarling**	N	Y	Y	Y	N	Y
6 **Barton**	N	Y	?	Y	N	Y
7 **Culberson**	?	?	Y	Y	N	Y
8 **Brady**	N	Y	Y	Y	N	Y
9 Green, A.	Y	N	N	N	Y	Y
10 **McCaul**	N	Y	Y	Y	N	Y
11 **Conaway**	N	Y	Y	Y	N	Y
12 **Granger**	N	Y	Y	Y	N	Y
13 **Thornberry**	N	Y	Y	Y	?	+
14 **Weber**	N	Y	Y	Y	N	Y
15 Gonzalez	Y	Y	N	N	Y	Y
16 O'Rourke	?	?	N	N	Y	Y
17 **Flores**	N	Y	Y	Y	N	Y
18 Jackson Lee	Y	N	N	N	Y	Y
19 **Arrington**	N	Y	Y	Y	N	Y
20 Castro	Y	N	N	N	Y	Y
21 **Smith**	N	Y	Y	Y	N	Y
22 **Olson**	N	Y	Y	Y	N	Y
23 **Hurd**	N	Y	Y	Y	N	Y
24 Marchant	N	Y	Y	Y	N	Y
25 **Williams**	N	Y	Y	Y	N	Y
26 **Burgess**	N	Y	Y	Y	N	Y
27 Cloud	N	Y	Y	Y	N	Y
28 Cuellar	Y	Y	N	N	Y	Y
29 Green, G.	Y	Y	N	N	Y	Y
30 Johnson, E.B.	Y	N	N	N	Y	Y
31 **Carter**	N	Y	Y	Y	N	Y
32 **Sessions**	N	Y	Y	Y	N	Y
33 Veasey	Y	N	N	N	Y	Y
34 Vela	Y	N	N	N	Y	?
35 Doggett	Y	N	N	N	Y	Y
36 **Babin**	N	Y	Y	Y	N	?
UTAH						
1 **Bishop**	N	Y	Y	Y	N	Y
2 **Stewart**	N	Y	Y	Y	N	Y
3 **Curtis**	N	Y	Y	Y	N	Y
4 **Love**	N	Y	Y	Y	N	Y
VERMONT						
AL Welch	Y	N	N	N	Y	Y
VIRGINIA						
1 **Wittman**	N	Y	Y	Y	N	Y
2 **Taylor**	N	Y	Y	Y	N	Y
3 Scott	Y	N	N	N	Y	Y
4 McEachin	Y	N	N	N	Y	Y
5 **Garrett**	N	N	Y	Y	N	Y
6 **Goodlatte**	N	Y	Y	Y	N	Y
7 **Brat**	N	Y	Y	Y	N	Y
8 Beyer	Y	N	N	N	Y	Y
9 **Griffith**	N	Y	Y	Y	N	Y
10 **Comstock**	N	Y	Y	Y	N	Y
11 Connolly	Y	N	N	N	Y	Y
WASHINGTON						
1 DelBene	Y	N	N	N	Y	Y
2 Larsen	Y	N	N	N	Y	Y
3 **Herrera Beutler**	N	Y	Y	Y	N	Y
4 **Newhouse**	N	Y	Y	Y	N	Y
5 **McMorris Rodgers**	N	Y	Y	Y	N	Y
6 Kilmer	Y	Y	N	N	Y	Y
7 Jayapal	Y	N	N	N	Y	Y
8 **Reichert**	N	Y	Y	Y	N	Y
9 Smith	Y	N	N	N	Y	Y
10 Heck	Y	N	N	N	Y	Y
WEST VIRGINIA						
1 **McKinley**	N	Y	Y	Y	N	Y
2 **Mooney**	N	Y	Y	Y	N	Y
3 **Jenkins**	?	?	?	?	?	?
WISCONSIN						
1 **Ryan**						
2 Pocan	Y	N	N	N	Y	Y
3 Kind	Y	Y	N	N	Y	Y
4 Moore	Y	N	N	N	Y	Y
5 **Sensenbrenner**	N	Y	+	–	?	+
6 **Grothman**	N	N	Y	Y	N	Y
7 **Duffy**	N	Y	Y	Y	N	Y
8 **Gallagher**	N	Y	Y	Y	N	Y
WYOMING						
AL **Cheney**	N	Y	Y	Y	N	Y

VOTE NUMBER

386. HRES1051. "CRIME OF VIOLENCE" DEFINITION/PREVIOUS QUESTION. Buck, R-Colo., motion to order the previous question (thus ending debate and possibility of amendment) on the rule (H Res 1051) that would provide for House floor consideration of the bill (HR 6691) that would modify the definition of the term "crime of violence," and would provide for consideration of motions to suspend the rules. Motion agreed to 224-181: R 224-0; D 0-181. Oct. 6, 2018.

387. HR6691. "CRIME OF VIOLENCE" DEFINITION/RULE. Adoption of the rule (H Res 1051) that would provide for House floor consideration of the bill (HR 6691) that would modify the definition of the term "crime of violence," and would provide for consideration of motions to suspend the rules. Adopted 225-179: R 223-2; D 2-177. Oct. 6, 2018.

388. HR6147. FISCAL 2019 INTERIOR-ENVIRONMENT, FINANCIAL SERVICES, AGRICULTURE, TRANSPORTATION-HUD APPROPRIATIONS/ MOTION TO INSTRUCT. McCollum, D-Minn., motion to instruct the conferees on the part of the House to agree to the Senate amendment to the bill in relation to provisions that would fund the Payments in Lieu of Taxes program that provides federal payments to local governments that have large tracts of federal land that cannot be locally taxed. Motion rejected 187-218: R 5-218; D 182-0. Oct. 6, 2018.

389. HR4606. NATURAL GAS IMPORTS AND EXPORTS/PUBLIC INPUT ON APPLICATIONS. Pallone, D-N.J., amendment that would require an opportunity for hearings and public input before a relevant application could be deemed consistent with the public interest. Rejected in Committee of the Whole 176-227: R 1-222; D 175-5. Oct. 6, 2018.

390. HR4606. NATURAL GAS IMPORTS AND EXPORTS/MINIMIZING METHANE EMISSIONS. DeGette, D-Colo., amendment that would require natural gas export applications covered under the bill to include information to demonstrate that the natural gas was produced using techniques and systems designed to minimize methane emissions from leaks or venting. Rejected in Committee of the Whole 195-210: R 14-209; D 181-1. Oct. 6, 2018.

391. HR4606. NATURAL GAS IMPORTS AND EXPORTS/RECOMMIT. Watson Coleman, D-N.J., motion to recommit the bill to the House Energy and Commerce Committee with instructions to report it back immediately with an amendment that would prohibit any imports or exports from being automatically approved under the bill's provisions if any pipeline involved in the importing or exporting process used land acquired through eminent domain. Motion rejected 178-231: R 1-226; D 177-5. Oct. 6, 2018.

	386	387	388	389	390	391
ALABAMA						
1 Byrne	Y	Y	N	N	N	N
2 Roby	Y	Y	N	N	N	N
3 Rogers	Y	Y	Y	N	N	N
4 Aderholt	Y	Y	N	N	N	N
5 Brooks	Y	Y	N	N	N	N
6 Palmer	Y	Y	N	N	N	N
7 Sewell	N	N	Y	Y	Y	Y
ALASKA						
AL Young	Y	Y	N	N	N	N
ARIZONA						
1 O'Halleran	N	N	Y	Y	Y	Y
2 McSally	Y	Y	N	N	N	N
3 Grijalva	N	N	Y	Y	Y	Y
4 Gosar	Y	Y	N	N	N	N
5 Biggs	Y	Y	N	N	N	N
6 Schweikert	Y	Y	N	N	N	N
7 Gallego	N	N	Y	Y	Y	Y
8 Lesko	Y	Y	N	N	N	N
9 Sinema	N	N	Y	Y	Y	Y
ARKANSAS						
1 Crawford	Y	Y	N	N	N	N
2 Hill	Y	Y	N	N	N	N
3 Womack	Y	Y	N	N	N	N
4 Westerman	Y	Y	N	N	N	N
CALIFORNIA						
1 LaMalfa	Y	Y	N	N	N	N
2 Huffman	?	?	?	?	?	?
3 Garamendi	N	N	Y	Y	Y	Y
4 McClintock	Y	Y	N	N	N	N
5 Thompson	N	N	Y	Y	Y	Y
6 Matsui	N	N	Y	Y	Y	Y
7 Bera	N	N	Y	Y	Y	Y
8 Cook	Y	Y	N	N	N	N
9 McNerney	N	N	Y	Y	Y	Y
10 Denham	Y	Y	N	N	N	N
11 DeSaulnier	N	N	Y	Y	Y	Y
12 Pelosi	N	N	Y	Y	Y	Y
13 Lee	N	N	Y	Y	Y	Y
14 Speier	?	?	?	?	?	?
15 Swalwell	N	N	Y	Y	Y	Y
16 Costa	N	N	Y	Y	Y	Y
17 Khanna	N	N	Y	Y	Y	Y
18 Eshoo	–	–	+	?	+	+
19 Lofgren	N	N	Y	Y	Y	Y
20 Panetta	N	N	Y	Y	Y	Y
21 Valadao	Y	Y	N	N	N	N
22 Nunes	Y	Y	N	N	N	N
23 McCarthy	Y	Y	N	N	N	N
24 Carbajal	N	N	Y	Y	Y	Y
25 Knight	Y	Y	N	N	N	N
26 Brownley	N	N	Y	Y	Y	Y
27 Chu	N	N	Y	Y	Y	Y
28 Schiff	N	N	Y	Y	Y	Y
29 Cardenas	N	N	Y	Y	Y	Y
30 Sherman	N	N	Y	Y	Y	Y
31 Aguilar	N	N	Y	Y	Y	Y
32 Napolitano	N	N	Y	Y	Y	Y
33 Lieu	N	N	Y	Y	Y	Y
34 Gomez	N	N	Y	Y	Y	Y
35 Torres	N	N	Y	Y	Y	Y
36 Ruiz	N	N	Y	Y	Y	Y
37 Bass	N	N	Y	Y	Y	Y
38 Sánchez, Linda	N	N	Y	Y	Y	Y
39 Royce	?	?	?	?	?	?
40 Roybal-Allard	N	N	Y	Y	Y	Y
41 Takano	N	N	Y	Y	Y	Y
42 Calvert	Y	Y	N	N	N	N
43 Waters	N	N	Y	Y	Y	Y
44 Barragan	N	N	Y	Y	Y	Y
45 Walters	Y	Y	N	N	N	N
46 Correa	N	N	Y	Y	Y	Y
47 Lowenthal	N	N	Y	Y	Y	Y
48 Rohrabacher	Y	Y	N	N	N	N
49 Issa	Y	Y	?	?	?	N
50 Hunter	Y	Y	N	N	N	N
51 Vargas	N	N	Y	Y	Y	Y
52 Peters	N	N	Y	Y	Y	Y
53 Davis	N	N	Y	Y	Y	Y

	386	387	388	389	390	391
COLORADO						
1 DeGette	N	N	Y	Y	Y	Y
2 Polis	N	N	Y	Y	Y	Y
3 Tipton	Y	Y	N	N	N	N
4 Buck	Y	Y	N	N	N	N
5 Lamborn	Y	Y	N	N	N	N
6 Coffman	Y	Y	N	N	Y	N
7 Perlmutter	N	N	Y	Y	Y	Y
CONNECTICUT						
1 Larson	N	N	Y	?	Y	Y
2 Courtney	N	N	Y	Y	Y	Y
3 DeLauro	N	N	Y	Y	Y	Y
4 Himes	N	N	Y	Y	Y	Y
5 Esty	N	N	Y	Y	Y	Y
DELAWARE						
AL Blunt Rochester	N	N	Y	Y	Y	Y
FLORIDA						
1 Gaetz	?	Y	N	N	N	N
2 Dunn	Y	Y	N	N	N	N
3 Yoho	Y	Y	N	N	N	N
4 Rutherford	Y	Y	N	N	–	N
5 Lawson	N	N	Y	Y	Y	Y
6 DeSantis	?	?	?	?	?	?
7 Murphy	N	N	Y	Y	Y	Y
8 Posey	Y	Y	N	N	N	N
9 Soto	N	N	Y	Y	Y	Y
10 Demings	N	N	Y	Y	Y	Y
11 Webster	Y	?	N	N	N	N
12 Bilirakis	Y	Y	N	N	N	N
13 Crist	N	Y	Y	Y	Y	Y
14 Castor	N	N	Y	Y	Y	Y
15 Ross	Y	Y	N	N	N	N
16 Buchanan	Y	Y	N	N	N	N
17 Rooney, T.	?	?	?	?	?	?
18 Mast	Y	Y	N	N	N	N
19 Rooney, F.	Y	Y	N	N	Y	N
20 Hastings	N	N	Y	Y	Y	Y
21 Frankel	N	N	Y	Y	Y	Y
22 Deutch	N	N	Y	Y	Y	Y
23 Wasserman Schultz	N	N	Y	Y	Y	Y
24 Wilson	N	N	Y	Y	Y	Y
25 Diaz-Balart	Y	Y	N	N	N	N
26 Curbelo	Y	Y	N	N	N	N
27 Ros-Lehtinen	?	?	?	?	?	?
GEORGIA						
1 Carter	Y	Y	N	N	N	N
2 Bishop	N	N	Y	Y	Y	Y
3 Ferguson	Y	Y	N	N	N	N
4 Johnson	N	?	Y	Y	Y	Y
5 Lewis	N	N	Y	Y	Y	Y
6 Handel	Y	Y	N	N	N	N
7 Woodall	Y	Y	N	N	N	N
8 Scott, A.	Y	Y	N	N	N	N
9 Collins	Y	Y	N	N	N	N
10 Hice	Y	Y	N	N	N	N
11 Loudermilk	Y	Y	N	N	N	N
12 Allen	Y	Y	N	N	N	N
13 Scott, D.	N	N	Y	Y	Y	Y
14 Graves	Y	Y	N	N	N	N
HAWAII						
1 Hanabusa	N	N	Y	Y	Y	Y
2 Gabbard	N	N	Y	Y	Y	Y
IDAHO						
1 Labrador	Y	Y	N	N	N	N
2 Simpson	Y	Y	N	N	N	N
ILLINOIS						
1 Rush	N	N	Y	Y	Y	Y
2 Kelly	N	N	Y	Y	Y	Y
3 Lipinski	N	N	Y	Y	Y	Y
4 Gutierrez	N	N	Y	Y	Y	Y
5 Quigley	N	N	Y	Y	Y	Y
6 Roskam	Y	Y	N	N	N	N
7 Davis, D.	N	N	Y	Y	Y	Y
8 Krishnamoorthi	N	N	Y	Y	Y	Y
9 Schakowsky	N	N	Y	Y	Y	Y
10 Schneider	N	N	Y	Y	Y	Y
11 Foster	N	N	Y	Y	Y	Y
12 Bost	Y	Y	N	N	N	N
13 Davis, R.	Y	Y	N	N	N	N

	386	387	388	389	390	391
14 **Hultgren**	Y	Y	N	N	N	N
15 **Shimkus**	Y	Y	N	N	N	N
16 **Kinzinger**	Y	Y	N	N	N	N
17 Bustos	N	N	Y	Y	Y	Y
18 **LaHood**	Y	Y	N	N	N	N
INDIANA						
1 Visclosky	N	N	Y	Y	Y	Y
2 **Walorski**	Y	Y	N	N	N	N
3 **Banks**	Y	Y	N	N	N	N
4 Rokita	Y	Y	N	N	N	N
5 **Brooks**	Y	Y	N	N	N	N
6 **Messer**	Y	Y	N	N	N	N
7 Carson	N	N	Y	Y	Y	Y
8 **Bucshon**	Y	Y	N	N	N	N
9 **Hollingsworth**	Y	Y	N	N	N	N
IOWA						
1 **Blum**	Y	Y	N	N	N	N
2 Loebsack	N	N	Y	Y	Y	Y
3 **Young**	Y	Y	N	N	N	N
4 **King**	Y	Y	N	N	N	N
KANSAS						
1 **Marshall**	Y	Y	N	N	N	N
2 **Jenkins**	Y	Y	N	N	N	N
3 **Yoder**	Y	Y	N	N	N	N
4 **Estes**	Y	Y	N	N	N	N
KENTUCKY						
1 **Comer**	Y	Y	N	N	N	N
2 **Guthrie**	Y	Y	N	N	N	N
3 Yarmuth	N	N	Y	Y	Y	Y
4 **Massie**	Y	N	N	N	N	N
5 **Rogers**	Y	Y	N	N	N	N
6 **Barr**	Y	Y	N	N	N	N
LOUISIANA						
1 **Scalise**	Y	Y	N	N	N	N
2 Richmond	N	N	Y	Y	Y	Y
3 **Higgins**	Y	Y	N	N	N	N
4 **Johnson**	Y	Y	N	N	N	N
5 **Abraham**	Y	Y	N	N	N	N
6 **Graves**	Y	Y	N	N	N	N
MAINE						
1 Pingree	N	N	Y	Y	Y	Y
2 **Poliquin**	Y	Y	N	N	N	N
MARYLAND						
1 **Harris**	Y	Y	N	N	N	N
2 Ruppersberger	N	N	Y	Y	Y	Y
3 Sarbanes	N	N	Y	Y	Y	Y
4 Brown	N	N	Y	Y	Y	Y
5 Hoyer	N	N	Y	Y	Y	Y
6 Delaney	N	N	Y	Y	Y	Y
7 Cummings	N	N	Y	Y	Y	Y
8 Raskin	N	N	Y	Y	Y	Y
MASSACHUSETTS						
1 Neal	?	?	?	?	?	?
2 McGovern	N	N	Y	Y	Y	Y
3 Tsongas	N	N	Y	Y	Y	Y
4 Kennedy	N	N	Y	Y	Y	Y
5 Clark	N	N	Y	Y	Y	Y
6 Moulton	N	N	Y	Y	Y	Y
7 Capuano	?	?	?	?	?	?
8 Lynch	N	N	Y	Y	Y	Y
9 Keating	N	N	Y	Y	Y	Y
MICHIGAN						
1 **Bergman**	Y	Y	N	N	N	N
2 **Huizenga**	Y	Y	N	N	N	N
3 *Amash*	Y	N	N	N	N	N
4 **Moolenaar**	Y	Y	N	N	N	N
5 Kildee	N	N	Y	Y	Y	Y
6 **Upton**	Y	Y	N	N	Y	N
7 **Walberg**	Y	Y	N	N	N	N
8 **Bishop**	Y	Y	N	N	N	N
9 Levin	N	N	Y	Y	Y	Y
10 **Mitchell**	Y	Y	N	N	N	N
11 **Trott**	Y	Y	N	N	N	N
12 Dingell	N	N	Y	Y	Y	Y
14 Lawrence	N	N	Y	Y	Y	Y
MINNESOTA						
1 Walz	?	?	?	?	?	?
2 **Lewis**	Y	Y	N	N	N	N
3 **Paulsen**	Y	Y	–	N	N	N
4 McCollum	N	N	Y	Y	Y	Y

	386	387	388	389	390	391
5 Ellison	?	?	?	?	?	?
6 **Emmer**	Y	Y	N	N	N	N
7 Peterson	N	N	Y	N	N	N
8 Nolan	N	N	Y	?	Y	Y
MISSISSIPPI						
1 **Kelly**	Y	Y	N	N	N	N
2 Thompson	N	N	Y	Y	Y	Y
3 **Harper**	Y	Y	N	N	N	N
4 **Palazzo**	+	+	–	?	–	?
MISSOURI						
1 Clay	N	N	Y	Y	Y	Y
2 **Wagner**	Y	Y	N	N	N	N
3 **Luetkemeyer**	Y	Y	N	N	N	N
4 **Hartzler**	Y	Y	N	N	N	N
5 Cleaver	N	N	Y	Y	Y	Y
6 **Graves**	Y	Y	N	N	N	N
7 **Long**	Y	Y	N	N	N	N
8 **Smith**	Y	Y	N	N	N	N
MONTANA						
AL **Gianforte**	Y	Y	?	?	?	?
NEBRASKA						
1 **Fortenberry**	Y	Y	N	N	N	N
2 **Bacon**	Y	Y	N	N	N	N
3 **Smith**	Y	Y	N	N	N	N
NEVADA						
1 Titus	–	–	+	+	+	+
2 **Amodei**	?	?	N	N	N	N
3 Rosen	N	N	Y	Y	Y	Y
4 Kihuen	N	N	Y	Y	Y	Y
NEW HAMPSHIRE						
1 Shea-Porter	N	N	Y	Y	Y	Y
2 Kuster	N	N	Y	Y	Y	Y
NEW JERSEY						
1 Norcross	N	N	Y	Y	Y	Y
2 **LoBiondo**	Y	Y	N	N	Y	N
3 **MacArthur**	Y	Y	N	N	Y	N
4 **Smith**	Y	Y	N	N	Y	N
5 Gottheimer	N	N	Y	Y	Y	Y
6 Pallone	N	N	Y	Y	Y	Y
7 **Lance**	Y	Y	N	N	N	N
8 Sires	N	N	Y	Y	Y	Y
9 Pascrell	N	N	Y	Y	Y	Y
10 Payne	N	N	Y	Y	Y	Y
11 **Frelinghuysen**	Y	Y	N	N	N	N
12 Watson Coleman	N	N	Y	Y	Y	Y
NEW MEXICO						
1 Lujan Grisham	N	N	Y	N	Y	Y
2 **Pearce**	Y	Y	N	N	N	N
3 Luján	N	N	Y	N	Y	Y
NEW YORK						
1 **Zeldin**	Y	Y	N	N	N	N
2 **King**	Y	Y	N	N	N	N
3 Suozzi	N	N	Y	Y	Y	Y
4 Rice	N	N	Y	Y	Y	Y
5 Meeks	N	N	Y	Y	Y	Y
6 Meng	N	N	Y	Y	Y	Y
7 Velázquez	N	N	Y	Y	Y	Y
8 Jeffries	N	N	Y	Y	Y	Y
9 Clarke	N	N	Y	Y	Y	Y
10 Nadler	N	N	Y	Y	Y	Y
11 **Donovan**	Y	Y	N	N	N	N
12 Maloney, C.	N	N	Y	Y	Y	Y
13 Espaillat	N	N	Y	Y	Y	Y
14 Crowley	N	N	Y	Y	Y	Y
15 Serrano	N	N	Y	Y	Y	Y
16 Engel	N	N	Y	Y	Y	Y
17 Lowey	N	N	Y	Y	Y	Y
18 Maloney, S.P.	?	?	?	?	?	?
19 **Faso**	Y	Y	N	N	N	N
20 Tonko	N	N	Y	Y	Y	Y
21 **Stefanik**	Y	Y	N	N	Y	N
22 **Tenney**	Y	Y	N	N	N	N
23 **Reed**	Y	Y	N	N	N	N
24 **Katko**	Y	Y	N	N	Y	N
25 **Vacant**						
26 Higgins	N	N	Y	Y	Y	Y
27 **Collins**	Y	Y	N	N	N	N
NORTH CAROLINA						
1 Butterfield	N	N	Y	Y	Y	Y
2 **Holding**	Y	Y	N	N	N	N
3 **Jones**	Y	Y	Y	Y	N	Y
4 Price	N	N	Y	Y	Y	Y

	386	387	388	389	390	391
5 **Foxx**	Y	Y	N	N	N	N
6 **Walker**	Y	Y	N	N	N	N
7 **Rouzer**	Y	Y	N	N	N	N
8 **Hudson**	Y	Y	N	N	N	N
9 **Pittenger**	Y	Y	N	N	N	N
9 **Vacant**						
10 **McHenry**	Y	Y	N	N	N	N
11 **Meadows**	Y	Y	N	N	N	N
12 Adams	N	N	Y	Y	Y	Y
13 **Budd**	Y	Y	N	N	N	N
NORTH DAKOTA						
AL **Cramer**	Y	Y	N	N	N	N
OHIO						
1 **Chabot**	Y	Y	N	N	N	N
2 **Wenstrup**	Y	Y	N	N	N	N
3 Beatty	N	N	Y	Y	Y	Y
4 **Jordan**	Y	Y	N	N	N	N
5 **Latta**	Y	Y	N	N	N	N
6 **Johnson**	Y	Y	N	N	N	N
7 **Gibbs**	Y	Y	N	N	N	N
8 **Davidson**	Y	Y	N	N	N	N
9 Kaptur	N	N	Y	Y	Y	Y
10 **Turner**	Y	Y	N	N	N	N
11 Fudge	N	N	Y	Y	Y	Y
12 Balderson	Y	Y	N	N	N	N
13 Ryan	?	?	?	?	?	?
14 **Joyce**	Y	Y	N	?	N	N
15 **Stivers**	Y	Y	N	N	N	N
16 **Renacci**	Y	Y	N	N	N	N
OKLAHOMA						
1 **Vacant**						
2 **Mullin**	Y	Y	N	N	N	N
3 **Lucas**	Y	Y	N	N	N	N
4 **Cole**	Y	Y	N	N	N	N
5 **Russell**	Y	Y	?	?	?	N
OREGON						
1 Bonamici	N	N	Y	Y	Y	Y
2 **Walden**	Y	Y	N	N	N	N
3 Blumenauer	N	N	Y	Y	Y	Y
4 DeFazio	N	N	Y	Y	Y	Y
5 Schrader	N	N	Y	Y	Y	Y
PENNSYLVANIA						
1 Brady	N	N	Y	Y	Y	Y
2 Evans	N	N	Y	Y	Y	Y
3 **Kelly**	Y	Y	N	N	N	N
4 **Perry**	Y	Y	N	–	N	N
5 **Thompson**	Y	Y	N	N	N	N
6 **Costello**	Y	Y	N	N	Y	N
7 **Vacant**						
8 **Fitzpatrick**	Y	Y	N	N	Y	N
9 **Shuster**	?	Y	?	N	N	N
10 **Marino**	Y	Y	N	N	N	N
11 **Barletta**	?	?	N	N	N	N
12 **Rothfus**	Y	Y	N	N	N	N
13 Boyle	N	N	Y	Y	Y	Y
14 Doyle	N	N	Y	Y	Y	Y
15 **Vacant**						
16 **Smucker**	Y	Y	N	N	N	N
17 Cartwright	N	N	Y	Y	Y	Y
18 Lamb	N	Y	Y	N	Y	N
RHODE ISLAND						
1 Cicilline	N	N	Y	Y	Y	Y
2 Langevin	N	N	Y	Y	Y	Y
SOUTH CAROLINA						
1 **Sanford**	Y	Y	N	N	N	N
2 **Wilson**	Y	Y	N	N	N	N
3 **Duncan**	Y	Y	N	N	N	N
4 **Gowdy**	Y	Y	N	N	N	N
5 **Norman**	Y	Y	N	N	N	N
6 Clyburn	N	N	Y	Y	Y	Y
7 **Rice**	Y	Y	N	N	N	N
SOUTH DAKOTA						
AL **Noem**	Y	Y	?	?	?	?
TENNESSEE						
1 **Roe**	Y	Y	N	N	N	N
2 **Duncan**	Y	Y	Y	N	N	N
3 **Fleischmann**	Y	Y	N	N	N	N
4 **DesJarlais**	Y	Y	N	N	N	N
5 Cooper	N	N	Y	Y	Y	Y
6 **Black**	Y	Y	N	N	N	N
7 **Blackburn**	?	?	?	?	?	?
8 **Kustoff**	Y	Y	N	N	N	N
9 Cohen	N	N	Y	Y	Y	Y

	386	387	388	389	390	391
TEXAS						
1 **Gohmert**	Y	Y	Y	N	N	N
2 **Poe**	?	?	N	N	N	N
3 **Johnson, S.**	Y	Y	N	N	N	N
4 **Ratcliffe**	Y	Y	N	N	N	N
5 **Hensarling**	Y	Y	N	N	N	N
6 **Barton**	Y	Y	N	N	N	N
7 **Culberson**	Y	Y	N	N	N	N
8 **Brady**	Y	Y	N	N	N	N
9 Green, A.	N	N	Y	Y	Y	Y
10 **McCaul**	Y	Y	N	N	N	N
11 **Conaway**	Y	Y	N	N	N	N
12 **Granger**	Y	Y	N	N	N	N
13 **Thornberry**	Y	Y	N	N	N	N
14 **Weber**	Y	Y	N	N	N	N
15 Gonzalez	N	N	Y	Y	Y	N
16 O'Rourke	N	N	Y	Y	Y	Y
17 **Flores**	Y	Y	N	N	?	N
18 Jackson Lee	N	N	Y	Y	Y	Y
19 **Arrington**	Y	Y	N	N	N	N
20 Castro	N	N	Y	Y	Y	Y
21 **Smith**	Y	Y	N	N	N	N
22 **Olson**	Y	Y	N	N	N	N
23 **Hurd**	Y	Y	N	N	N	N
24 Marchant	Y	Y	N	N	N	N
25 **Williams**	Y	Y	N	N	N	N
26 **Burgess**	Y	Y	N	N	N	N
27 Cloud	Y	Y	N	N	N	N
28 Cuellar	N	N	Y	Y	Y	N
29 Green, G.	N	N	Y	N	Y	N
30 Johnson, E.B.	N	N	Y	Y	Y	Y
31 **Carter**	Y	Y	N	N	N	N
32 **Sessions**	Y	Y	N	N	N	N
33 Veasey	N	N	Y	Y	Y	Y
34 Vela	N	N	Y	Y	Y	Y
35 Doggett	N	N	Y	Y	Y	Y
36 **Babin**	Y	Y	N	N	N	N
UTAH						
1 **Bishop**	Y	Y	N	N	N	N
2 **Stewart**	Y	Y	N	N	N	N
3 **Curtis**	Y	Y	N	N	N	N
4 **Love**	Y	Y	N	N	Y	N
VERMONT						
AL Welch	N	?	Y	Y	Y	Y
VIRGINIA						
1 **Wittman**	Y	Y	N	N	N	N
2 **Taylor**	Y	Y	N	N	N	N
3 Scott	N	N	Y	Y	Y	Y
4 McEachin	N	N	?	?	?	?
5 **Garrett**	Y	Y	N	N	N	N
6 **Goodlatte**	Y	Y	N	N	N	N
7 **Brat**	Y	Y	N	N	N	N
8 Beyer	N	N	Y	Y	Y	Y
9 **Griffith**	Y	Y	N	N	N	N
10 **Comstock**	Y	Y	N	N	N	N
11 Connolly	?	?	Y	Y	Y	Y
WASHINGTON						
1 DelBene	N	N	Y	Y	Y	Y
2 Larsen	N	N	Y	Y	Y	Y
3 **Herrera Beutler**	Y	Y	N	N	N	N
4 **Newhouse**	Y	Y	N	N	N	N
5 McMorris Rodgers	Y	Y	N	N	N	N
6 Kilmer	N	N	Y	Y	Y	Y
7 Jayapal	N	N	Y	Y	Y	Y
8 **Reichert**	Y	Y	N	N	Y	N
9 Smith	N	N	Y	Y	Y	Y
10 Heck	N	N	Y	Y	Y	Y
WEST VIRGINIA						
1 **McKinley**	Y	Y	N	N	N	N
2 **Mooney**	Y	Y	N	N	N	N
3 **Jenkins**	?	?	?	?	?	?
WISCONSIN						
1 **Ryan**						
2 Pocan	N	N	Y	Y	Y	Y
3 Kind	N	N	Y	Y	Y	Y
4 Moore	–	–	Y	Y	Y	Y
5 **Sensenbrenner**	Y	Y	N	N	N	N
6 **Grothman**	Y	Y	N	N	N	N
7 **Duffy**	Y	Y	N	N	N	N
8 **Gallagher**	Y	Y	N	N	N	N
WYOMING						
AL **Cheney**	Y	Y	N	N	N	N

VOTE NUMBER

392. HR4606. NATURAL GAS IMPORTS AND EXPORTS/PASSAGE. Passage of the bill that would allow applications for small-scale imports and exports of natural gas to be automatically approved if they would not exceed 0.14 billion cubic feet per day and would not require an environmental impact statement or an environmental assessment. Passed 260-146: R 223-3; D 37-143. Oct. 6, 2018.

393. HR6691. "CRIME OF VIOLENCE" DEFINITION/PASSAGE. Passage of the bill that would specify that any of the following acts would be defined as a "crime of violence" which could be used in determining whether a crime is an aggravated felony, including: murder; voluntary manslaughter; assault; certain types of sexual abuse; abusive sexual contact; child abuse; kidnapping; robbery; carjacking; firearms use; burglary; arson; extortion; communication of threats; coercion; fleeing via a motor vehicle; interference with airline flight crews members; domestic violence; hostage taking; stalking; human trafficking; piracy; certain terrorism offenses; and unlawful possession or use of a weapon of mass destruction. Passed 247-152: R 218-4; D 29-148. Oct. 7, 2018.

394. HR5923. ARKANSAS LAND EXCHANGE/PASSAGE. Gianforte, R-Mont., motion to suspend the rules and pass the bill that would require the U.S. Forest Service to exchange four acres of land within the Ouachita National Forest for six acres of land owned by the Walnut Grove Community Church of Jessieville, Ark. Motion agreed to 379-3: R 208-3; D 171-0. Oct. 12, 2018.

395. HR3186. FEDERAL LAND ACCESS FOR KIDS/PASSAGE. Gianforte, R-Mont., motion to suspend the rules and pass the bill that would direct several federal agencies across four departments to jointly establish the Every Kid Outdoors program to issue all fourth grade students with a pass that would provide free access to publicly accessible federal lands and waters. The passes would be issued as requested by each student. Motion agreed to 383-2: R 211-2; D 172-0. Oct. 12, 2018.

396. HR4689. NORTH PLATTE PROJECT REPAYMENTS/PASSAGE. Gianforte, R-Mont., motion to suspend the rules and pass the bill that would authorize the early repayment of obligations by landowners within the Northport Irrigation District of Nebraska to the Bureau of Reclamation for construction costs of the North Platte Project in Nebraska. Motion agreed to 378-1: R 209-1; D 169-0. Oct. 12, 2018.

397. HRES1059. EMPLOYER-PROVIDED HEALTH CARE AND APPROPRIATIONS PACKAGE/RULE. Adoption of the rule (H Res 1059) that would provide for House floor consideration of the bill (HR 3798) that would modify a number of aspects of the 2010 health care law related to employer provided health care, and would provide for consideration of the conference report to accompany the bill (HR 5895) the Fiscal 2019 Energy-Water, Legislative Branch, Military Construction-VA Appropriations package. Adopted 222-171: R 218-0; D 4-171. Oct. 13, 2018.

	392	393	394	395	396	397
ALABAMA						
1 **Byrne**	Y	Y	Y	Y	Y	Y
2 **Roby**	Y	Y	Y	Y	Y	Y
3 **Rogers**	Y	Y	Y	Y	Y	Y
4 **Aderholt**	Y	Y	Y	Y	?	Y
5 **Brooks**	Y	Y	Y	Y	Y	Y
6 **Palmer**	Y	Y	Y	Y	Y	Y
7 Sewell	Y	N	Y	Y	Y	N
ALASKA						
AL **Young**	Y	Y	?	Y	Y	Y
ARIZONA						
1 O'Halleran	Y	Y	Y	Y	?	Y
2 **McSally**	Y	Y	Y	Y	Y	Y
3 Grijalva	N	N	Y	Y	Y	N
4 **Gosar**	Y	Y	Y	Y	Y	Y
5 **Biggs**	Y	N	N	N	Y	Y
6 **Schweikert**	Y	Y	Y	Y	Y	Y
7 Gallego	N	N	Y	Y	Y	N
8 **Lesko**	Y	Y	Y	Y	Y	+
9 Sinema	Y	Y	Y	Y	Y	Y
ARKANSAS						
1 **Crawford**	Y	Y	Y	Y	Y	Y
2 **Hill**	Y	Y	Y	Y	Y	Y
3 **Womack**	Y	Y	Y	Y	Y	Y
4 **Westerman**	Y	Y	Y	Y	Y	Y
CALIFORNIA						
1 **LaMalfa**	Y	Y	Y	Y	Y	Y
2 Huffman	?	?	Y	Y	Y	N
3 Garamendi	N	Y	Y	Y	Y	N
4 **McClintock**	Y	Y	Y	Y	Y	Y
5 Thompson	N	Y	Y	Y	Y	N
6 Matsui	N	N	Y	Y	Y	N
7 Bera	N	Y	Y	Y	Y	N
8 **Cook**	Y	Y	Y	Y	Y	Y
9 McNerney	Y	N	Y	Y	Y	N
10 **Denham**	Y	Y	Y	Y	Y	Y
11 DeSaulnier	N	N	Y	Y	Y	N
12 Pelosi	N	N	?	?	?	?
13 Lee	N	N	Y	Y	Y	N
14 Speier	?	?	?	?	?	?
15 Swalwell	N	N	Y	Y	Y	N
16 Costa	Y	Y	Y	Y	Y	Y
17 Khanna	N	N	Y	Y	Y	N
18 Eshoo	–	–	+	+	+	–
19 Lofgren	N	P	+	+	+	–
20 Panetta	N	Y	Y	Y	Y	N
21 **Valadao**	Y	Y	Y	Y	Y	Y
22 **Nunes**	Y	Y	Y	Y	Y	Y
23 **McCarthy**	Y	Y	Y	Y	Y	Y
24 Carbajal	N	Y	Y	Y	Y	N
25 **Knight**	Y	Y	Y	Y	Y	Y
26 Brownley	N	N	Y	Y	Y	N
27 Chu	N	N	Y	Y	Y	N
28 Schiff	N	N	Y	Y	Y	N
29 Cardenas	N	N	Y	Y	?	N
30 Sherman	N	N	Y	?	Y	N
31 Aguilar	N	N	Y	Y	Y	N
32 Napolitano	N	N	Y	Y	Y	N
33 Lieu	N	N	Y	Y	Y	N
34 Gomez	N	N	Y	Y	Y	N
35 Torres	N	N	Y	Y	Y	N
36 Ruiz	N	Y	Y	Y	Y	N
37 Bass	N	N	Y	Y	Y	N
38 Sánchez, Linda	N	N	Y	Y	Y	N
39 Royce	?	?	Y	Y	Y	Y
40 Roybal-Allard	N	N	Y	Y	Y	N
41 Takano	N	N	Y	Y	Y	N
42 **Calvert**	Y	Y	Y	Y	Y	Y
43 Waters	N	N	Y	?	Y	N
44 Barragan	N	N	Y	Y	Y	N
45 **Walters**	Y	Y	?	?	?	?
46 Correa	Y	N	Y	Y	Y	N
47 Lowenthal	N	N	Y	Y	Y	N
48 **Rohrabacher**	Y	Y	?	?	?	Y
49 **Issa**	Y	Y	?	?	?	Y
50 **Hunter**	Y	Y	?	?	?	Y
51 Vargas	N	N	Y	Y	Y	N
52 Peters	N	N	Y	Y	Y	N
53 Davis	N	N	Y	Y	Y	N

	392	393	394	395	396	397
COLORADO						
1 DeGette	N	N	Y	Y	Y	N
2 Polis	Y	Y	Y	Y	Y	N
3 **Tipton**	Y	Y	Y	Y	Y	Y
4 **Buck**	Y	Y	Y	Y	Y	Y
5 **Lamborn**	Y	Y	?	Y	Y	Y
6 **Coffman**	?	Y	Y	Y	Y	Y
7 Perlmutter	Y	N	Y	Y	Y	N
CONNECTICUT						
1 Larson	N	N	Y	Y	?	N
2 Courtney	N	N	Y	Y	Y	N
3 DeLauro	N	N	Y	Y	Y	N
4 Himes	Y	N	Y	Y	Y	N
5 Esty	N	N	Y	Y	Y	N
DELAWARE						
AL Blunt Rochester	N	N	Y	Y	Y	N
FLORIDA						
1 **Gaetz**	Y	Y	Y	Y	Y	Y
2 **Dunn**	Y	Y	Y	Y	Y	Y
3 Yoho	Y	Y	Y	Y	Y	Y
4 **Rutherford**	Y	Y	Y	Y	Y	Y
5 Lawson	N	N	Y	Y	Y	N
6 Murphy	Y	Y	Y	Y	Y	Y
7 **Posey**	Y	Y	Y	Y	Y	Y
8 Soto	N	N	Y	Y	Y	N
9 Demings	N	N	Y	Y	Y	N
10 Demings	N	N	Y	Y	Y	N
11 **Webster**	Y	Y	Y	Y	Y	Y
12 **Bilirakis**	Y	Y	Y	Y	Y	Y
13 Crist	N	Y	Y	Y	Y	N
14 Castor	N	N	Y	Y	Y	N
15 **Ross**	Y	Y	?	?	?	Y
16 **Buchanan**	Y	Y	Y	Y	Y	Y
17 **Rooney, T.**	?	?	?	?	?	?
18 **Mast**	Y	Y	Y	Y	Y	Y
19 **Rooney, F.**	Y	Y	Y	Y	Y	Y
20 Hastings	N	Y	Y	Y	Y	N
21 Frankel	N	N	Y	Y	Y	N
22 Deutch	N	N	Y	Y	Y	N
23 Wasserman Schultz	N	N	?	?	?	?
24 Wilson	N	N	?	Y	Y	N
25 **Diaz-Balart**	Y	Y	Y	Y	Y	Y
26 **Curbelo**	Y	Y	Y	Y	Y	Y
27 **Ros-Lehtinen**	?	?	Y	Y	Y	Y
GEORGIA						
1 **Carter**	Y	Y	Y	Y	Y	Y
2 Bishop	Y	N	Y	Y	Y	N
3 **Ferguson**	Y	Y	Y	Y	Y	Y
4 Johnson	N	N	Y	Y	Y	N
5 Lewis	N	N	Y	Y	Y	N
6 **Handel**	Y	Y	Y	Y	Y	Y
7 **Woodall**	Y	Y	Y	Y	Y	Y
8 **Scott, A.**	Y	Y	Y	Y	Y	Y
9 **Collins**	Y	Y	Y	Y	Y	Y
10 **Hice**	Y	Y	?	?	?	?
11 **Loudermilk**	Y	Y	Y	Y	Y	Y
12 **Allen**	Y	Y	Y	Y	Y	Y
13 Scott, D.	N	N	Y	Y	Y	N
14 **Graves**	Y	Y	Y	Y	Y	Y
HAWAII						
1 Hanabusa	N	N	Y	Y	Y	N
2 Gabbard	N	N	Y	Y	Y	N
IDAHO						
1 **Labrador**	Y	N	Y	Y	Y	Y
2 **Simpson**	Y	Y	Y	Y	Y	Y
ILLINOIS						
1 Rush	N	N	Y	Y	Y	N
2 Kelly	N	N	Y	Y	Y	N
3 Lipinski	Y	Y	Y	Y	Y	N
4 Gutierrez	N	N	+	+	+	N
5 Quigley	N	N	Y	Y	Y	N
6 **Roskam**	Y	Y	Y	Y	Y	Y
7 Davis, D.	N	N	Y	Y	Y	N
8 Krishnamoorthi	N	N	Y	Y	Y	N
9 Schakowsky	N	N	Y	Y	Y	N
10 Schneider	N	N	Y	Y	Y	N
11 Foster	N	N	Y	Y	Y	N
12 **Bost**	Y	Y	Y	Y	Y	Y
13 **Davis, R.**	Y	?	Y	Y	Y	Y
14 **Hultgren**	Y	Y	Y	Y	Y	Y

KEY	Republicans		Democrats		Independents	
Y	Voted for (yea)	X	Paired against	C	Voted "present" to avoid possible conflict of interest	
#	Paired for	–	Announced against			
+	Announced for	P	Voted "present"	?	Did not vote or otherwise make a position known	
N	Voted against (nay)					

	392	393	394	395	396	397
15 **Shimkus**	Y	Y	Y	Y	Y	Y
16 **Kinzinger**	Y	Y	Y	Y	Y	Y
17 Bustos	N	Y	Y	Y	Y	N
18 **LaHood**	Y	Y	Y	Y	Y	Y
INDIANA						
1 Visclosky	N	N	Y	Y	Y	N
2 **Walorski**	Y	Y	Y	Y	Y	Y
3 **Banks**	Y	Y	Y	Y	Y	Y
4 Rokita	Y	Y	Y	Y	Y	Y
5 **Brooks**	Y	Y	Y	Y	Y	Y
6 **Messer**	Y	Y	Y	Y	Y	Y
7 Carson	N	N	Y	Y	Y	N
8 **Bucshon**	Y	Y	Y	Y	Y	Y
9 **Hollingsworth**	Y	Y	Y	Y	Y	Y
IOWA						
1 **Blum**	Y	Y	Y	Y	Y	Y
2 Loebsack	?	Y	Y	Y	Y	N
3 **Young**	Y	Y	Y	Y	Y	Y
4 **King**	Y	Y	Y	Y	Y	Y
KANSAS						
1 **Marshall**	Y	Y	Y	Y	Y	Y
2 **Jenkins**	Y	Y	Y	Y	Y	Y
3 **Yoder**	Y	Y	Y	Y	Y	Y
4 **Estes**	Y	Y	Y	Y	Y	Y
KENTUCKY						
1 **Comer**	Y	Y	Y	Y	Y	Y
2 **Guthrie**	Y	Y	Y	Y	Y	Y
3 Yarmuth	N	N	Y	Y	Y	N
4 **Massie**	Y	N	N	Y	Y	Y
5 **Rogers**	Y	Y	Y	Y	Y	Y
6 **Barr**	Y	Y	Y	Y	Y	Y
LOUISIANA						
1 **Scalise**	Y	Y	Y	Y	Y	Y
2 Richmond	Y	?	Y	Y	Y	?
3 **Higgins**	Y	Y	Y	Y	Y	Y
4 **Johnson**	Y	Y	Y	Y	Y	Y
5 **Abraham**	Y	Y	Y	Y	Y	Y
6 **Graves**	Y	Y	Y	Y	Y	Y
MAINE						
1 Pingree	N	N	Y	Y	Y	N
2 **Poliquin**	Y	Y	Y	Y	Y	Y
MARYLAND						
1 **Harris**	Y	Y	Y	Y	Y	Y
2 Ruppersberger	N	N	Y	Y	Y	N
3 Sarbanes	N	N	Y	Y	Y	N
4 Brown	Y	N	Y	Y	Y	N
5 Hoyer	N	N	?	Y	Y	?
6 Delaney	N	N	Y	Y	Y	N
7 Cummings	N	N	Y	Y	Y	?
8 Raskin	N	N	Y	Y	Y	N
MASSACHUSETTS						
1 Neal	?	?	Y	Y	Y	N
2 McGovern	N	N	Y	Y	Y	N
3 Tsongas	N	?	Y	Y	Y	N
4 Kennedy	N	?	Y	Y	Y	N
5 Clark	N	N	Y	Y	Y	N
6 Moulton	N	N	Y	Y	Y	N
7 Capuano	?	?	Y	Y	Y	N
8 Lynch	N	Y	?	?	?	N
9 Keating	N	Y	Y	Y	Y	N
MICHIGAN						
1 **Bergman**	Y	Y	Y	Y	Y	Y
2 **Huizenga**	Y	Y	Y	Y	Y	Y
3 *Amash*	Y	N	N	N	N	Y
4 **Moolenaar**	Y	Y	Y	Y	Y	?
5 Kildee	N	N	Y	Y	Y	N
6 **Upton**	Y	Y	Y	Y	Y	Y
7 **Walberg**	Y	Y	Y	Y	Y	Y
8 **Bishop**	Y	Y	Y	Y	Y	Y
9 Levin	N	N	Y	Y	Y	N
10 **Mitchell**	Y	Y	Y	Y	Y	Y
11 **Trott**	Y	Y	Y	Y	Y	Y
12 Dingell	N	N	Y	Y	Y	N
14 Lawrence	N	N	Y	Y	Y	N
MINNESOTA						
1 Walz	?	?	?	?	?	?
2 **Lewis**	Y	Y	Y	Y	Y	Y
3 **Paulsen**	Y	Y	Y	Y	Y	Y
4 McCollum	N	N	Y	Y	Y	N
5 Ellison	?	?	?	?	?	?
6 **Emmer**	Y	Y	Y	Y	Y	Y
7 Peterson	Y	Y	Y	Y	Y	N
8 Nolan	Y	N	?	?	?	?
MISSISSIPPI						
1 **Kelly**	Y	Y	Y	Y	Y	Y
2 Thompson	Y	N	Y	Y	Y	N
3 **Harper**	Y	Y	Y	Y	Y	Y
4 **Palazzo**	–	Y	Y	Y	Y	Y
MISSOURI						
1 Clay	N	N	Y	Y	Y	N
2 **Wagner**	Y	Y	Y	Y	Y	Y
3 **Luetkemeyer**	Y	Y	Y	Y	Y	Y
4 **Hartzler**	Y	Y	Y	Y	Y	Y
5 Cleaver	N	N	Y	Y	Y	?
6 **Graves**	Y	Y	Y	Y	Y	Y
7 **Long**	Y	Y	Y	Y	Y	Y
8 **Smith**	Y	Y	Y	Y	Y	Y
MONTANA						
AL **Gianforte**	?	?	Y	Y	Y	Y
NEBRASKA						
1 **Fortenberry**	Y	Y	Y	Y	Y	Y
2 **Bacon**	Y	Y	Y	Y	Y	Y
3 **Smith**	Y	Y	Y	Y	Y	Y
NEVADA						
1 Titus	–	–	Y	Y	Y	N
2 **Amodei**	Y	Y	Y	Y	Y	Y
3 Rosen	N	Y	Y	Y	Y	N
4 Kihuen	N	N	Y	Y	Y	N
NEW HAMPSHIRE						
1 Shea-Porter	N	?	?	?	?	N
2 Kuster	N	Y	Y	Y	Y	N
NEW JERSEY						
1 Norcross	Y	N	Y	Y	Y	N
2 **LoBiondo**	Y	Y	Y	Y	Y	Y
3 **MacArthur**	Y	Y	Y	Y	Y	Y
4 **Smith**	N	Y	Y	Y	Y	Y
5 Gottheimer	Y	Y	+	+	+	+
6 Pallone	N	N	Y	Y	Y	N
7 **Lance**	Y	Y	Y	Y	Y	Y
8 Sires	Y	N	Y	Y	Y	N
9 Pascrell	N	N	Y	Y	Y	N
10 Payne	N	N	Y	Y	Y	N
11 **Frelinghuysen**	Y	Y	Y	Y	Y	Y
12 Watson Coleman	N	N	Y	Y	Y	N
NEW MEXICO						
1 Lujan Grisham	Y	Y	Y	Y	Y	N
2 **Pearce**	Y	Y	?	?	?	?
3 Luján	Y	N	Y	Y	Y	N
NEW YORK						
1 **Zeldin**	Y	Y	Y	Y	Y	Y
2 **King**	Y	Y	Y	Y	Y	Y
3 Suozzi	N	Y	Y	Y	Y	N
4 Rice	N	N	Y	Y	Y	N
5 Meeks	N	N	Y	Y	Y	N
6 Meng	N	N	?	?	?	N
7 Velázquez	N	N	Y	Y	?	N
8 Jeffries	N	N	Y	Y	Y	N
9 Clarke	N	N	Y	Y	Y	N
10 Nadler	N	N	Y	Y	Y	N
11 **Donovan**	Y	Y	Y	Y	Y	Y
12 Maloney, C.	N	N	Y	Y	Y	N
13 Espaillat	N	N	Y	Y	Y	N
14 Crowley	N	N	Y	Y	Y	N
15 Serrano	N	N	Y	Y	Y	N
16 Engel	N	N	Y	Y	Y	N
17 Lowey	N	N	Y	Y	Y	N
18 Maloney, S.P.	?	?	?	?	?	?
19 **Faso**	Y	Y	Y	Y	Y	Y
20 Tonko	N	N	Y	Y	Y	N
21 **Stefanik**	Y	Y	Y	Y	Y	Y
22 **Tenney**	Y	Y	Y	Y	Y	Y
23 **Reed**	Y	Y	Y	Y	Y	Y
24 **Katko**	Y	Y	Y	Y	Y	Y
25 **Vacant**						
26 Higgins	N	N	Y	Y	Y	N
27 **Collins**	Y	Y	Y	Y	Y	Y
NORTH CAROLINA						
1 Butterfield	?	N	?	?	?	?
2 **Holding**	Y	Y	+	+	+	?
3 **Jones**	N	?	?	?	?	?
4 Price	N	N	?	?	?	?
5 **Foxx**	Y	Y	Y	Y	Y	Y
6 **Walker**	Y	Y	Y	Y	Y	Y
7 **Rouzer**	Y	Y	?	?	?	?
8 **Hudson**	Y	Y	Y	Y	Y	Y
9 **Pittenger**	Y	Y	?	?	?	?
9 **Vacant**						
10 **McHenry**	Y	Y	Y	Y	Y	Y
11 **Meadows**	Y	Y	Y	Y	Y	Y
12 Adams	N	N	?	?	?	?
13 **Budd**	Y	Y	Y	Y	Y	Y
NORTH DAKOTA						
AL **Cramer**	Y	?	Y	Y	Y	Y
OHIO						
1 **Chabot**	Y	Y	Y	Y	Y	Y
2 **Wenstrup**	Y	Y	Y	Y	Y	Y
3 Beatty	N	N	Y	Y	Y	?
4 **Jordan**	Y	Y	Y	Y	Y	Y
5 **Latta**	Y	Y	Y	Y	Y	Y
6 **Johnson**	Y	Y	Y	Y	Y	Y
7 **Gibbs**	Y	Y	Y	Y	Y	Y
8 **Davidson**	Y	Y	Y	Y	Y	Y
9 Kaptur	N	N	Y	Y	Y	N
10 **Turner**	Y	Y	+	+	+	Y
11 Fudge	N	N	Y	Y	Y	N
12 Balderson	Y	Y	Y	Y	Y	Y
13 Ryan	?	?	Y	Y	Y	N
14 **Joyce**	Y	Y	Y	Y	Y	Y
15 **Stivers**	Y	Y	Y	Y	Y	Y
16 **Renacci**	Y	?	+	+	+	+
OKLAHOMA						
1 **Vacant**						
2 **Mullin**	Y	Y	Y	Y	Y	Y
3 **Lucas**	Y	Y	Y	Y	Y	Y
4 **Cole**	Y	Y	Y	Y	Y	Y
5 **Russell**	Y	Y	Y	Y	Y	Y
OREGON						
1 Bonamici	N	N	Y	Y	Y	N
2 **Walden**	Y	Y	Y	Y	Y	Y
3 Blumenauer	N	N	Y	Y	Y	N
4 DeFazio	N	P	Y	Y	Y	N
5 Schrader	Y	Y	Y	Y	Y	N
PENNSYLVANIA						
1 Brady	Y	N	?	?	?	N
2 Evans	N	N	Y	Y	Y	N
3 **Kelly**	Y	Y	Y	Y	Y	Y
4 **Perry**	Y	Y	Y	Y	Y	Y
5 **Thompson**	Y	Y	Y	Y	Y	Y
6 **Costello**	Y	Y	Y	Y	Y	Y
7 **Vacant**						
8 **Fitzpatrick**	Y	Y	Y	Y	Y	Y
9 **Shuster**	Y	Y	Y	Y	Y	Y
10 **Marino**	Y	Y	Y	Y	Y	Y
11 **Barletta**	Y	Y	?	?	?	Y
12 **Rothfus**	Y	Y	Y	Y	Y	Y
13 Boyle	N	N	Y	Y	Y	N
14 Doyle	Y	N	Y	Y	Y	N
15 **Vacant**						
16 **Smucker**	Y	Y	+	+	+	Y
17 Cartwright	Y	Y	Y	Y	Y	N
18 Lamb	Y	Y	Y	Y	Y	Y
RHODE ISLAND						
1 Cicilline	N	N	?	?	?	N
2 Langevin	N	N	Y	Y	Y	N
SOUTH CAROLINA						
1 **Sanford**	N	Y	?	?	?	?
2 **Wilson**	Y	Y	Y	Y	Y	Y
3 **Duncan**	Y	Y	Y	Y	Y	Y
4 **Gowdy**	Y	Y	Y	Y	Y	Y
5 **Norman**	Y	Y	?	?	?	?
6 Clyburn	N	N	Y	Y	Y	N
7 **Rice**	Y	Y	?	?	?	?
SOUTH DAKOTA						
AL **Noem**	?	?	Y	Y	Y	Y
TENNESSEE						
1 **Roe**	Y	Y	Y	Y	Y	Y
2 **Duncan**	Y	Y	Y	Y	Y	Y
3 **Fleischmann**	Y	Y	Y	Y	Y	Y
4 **DesJarlais**	Y	Y	Y	Y	Y	Y
5 Cooper	Y	N	Y	Y	Y	N
6 **Black**	Y	Y	Y	Y	Y	Y
7 **Blackburn**	?	?	?	?	?	?
8 **Kustoff**	Y	Y	Y	Y	Y	Y
9 Cohen	N	N	Y	Y	Y	N
TEXAS						
1 **Gohmert**	Y	Y	Y	Y	Y	Y
2 **Poe**	Y	Y	Y	Y	Y	Y
3 **Johnson, S.**	Y	Y	Y	Y	Y	Y
4 **Ratcliffe**	Y	Y	Y	Y	Y	Y
5 **Hensarling**	Y	Y	Y	Y	Y	Y
6 **Barton**	Y	Y	Y	Y	Y	Y
7 **Culberson**	Y	?	Y	Y	Y	Y
8 **Brady**	Y	Y	Y	Y	Y	Y
9 Green, A.	Y	N	Y	Y	Y	N
10 **McCaul**	Y	Y	+	Y	Y	Y
11 **Conaway**	Y	Y	Y	Y	Y	Y
12 **Granger**	Y	Y	Y	Y	Y	Y
13 **Thornberry**	Y	Y	Y	Y	Y	Y
14 **Weber**	Y	Y	Y	Y	Y	Y
15 Gonzalez	Y	N	Y	Y	Y	N
16 O'Rourke	Y	N	?	?	?	N
17 **Flores**	Y	Y	Y	Y	Y	Y
18 Jackson Lee	Y	N	Y	Y	Y	N
19 **Arrington**	Y	Y	Y	Y	Y	Y
20 Castro	Y	N	Y	Y	Y	N
21 **Smith**	Y	?	Y	Y	Y	Y
22 **Olson**	Y	Y	Y	Y	?	Y
23 **Hurd**	Y	Y	+	+	+	Y
24 Marchant	Y	Y	Y	Y	Y	Y
25 **Williams**	Y	Y	Y	Y	Y	Y
26 **Burgess**	Y	Y	Y	Y	Y	Y
27 Cloud	Y	Y	Y	Y	Y	Y
28 Cuellar	Y	Y	Y	Y	Y	N
29 Green, G.	Y	N	Y	Y	Y	N
30 Johnson, E.B.	N	N	Y	Y	Y	N
31 **Carter**	Y	Y	Y	Y	Y	Y
32 **Sessions**	Y	Y	Y	Y	Y	Y
33 Veasey	Y	N	Y	Y	Y	N
34 Vela	N	N	Y	Y	Y	N
35 Doggett	N	N	Y	Y	Y	N
36 **Babin**	Y	Y	Y	Y	Y	Y
UTAH						
1 **Bishop**	Y	Y	Y	Y	Y	Y
2 **Stewart**	Y	Y	Y	Y	Y	Y
3 **Curtis**	Y	Y	Y	Y	Y	Y
4 **Love**	Y	Y	Y	Y	Y	Y
VERMONT						
AL Welch	N	N	Y	Y	Y	N
VIRGINIA						
1 **Wittman**	Y	Y	Y	Y	Y	Y
2 **Taylor**	Y	Y	+	+	+	+
3 Scott	N	N	Y	Y	Y	N
4 McEachin	?	N	Y	Y	Y	N
5 **Garrett**	Y	Y	Y	Y	Y	Y
6 **Goodlatte**	Y	Y	Y	Y	Y	Y
7 **Brat**	Y	Y	Y	Y	Y	Y
8 Beyer	N	N	Y	Y	Y	N
9 **Griffith**	Y	N	Y	Y	Y	Y
10 **Comstock**	Y	Y	Y	Y	Y	Y
11 Connolly	N	N	Y	Y	Y	N
WASHINGTON						
1 DelBene	N	N	Y	Y	Y	N
2 Larsen	Y	N	Y	Y	Y	N
3 **Herrera Beutler**	Y	Y	Y	Y	Y	Y
4 **Newhouse**	Y	Y	Y	Y	Y	Y
5 **McMorris Rodgers**	Y	Y	Y	Y	Y	Y
6 Kilmer	N	N	Y	Y	Y	N
7 Jayapal	N	N	Y	Y	Y	N
8 **Reichert**	Y	Y	Y	Y	Y	Y
9 Smith	N	N	Y	Y	Y	N
10 Heck	N	N	Y	Y	Y	N
WEST VIRGINIA						
1 **McKinley**	Y	Y	Y	Y	Y	Y
2 **Mooney**	Y	Y	Y	Y	Y	Y
3 **Jenkins**	?	?	Y	Y	?	?
WISCONSIN						
1 **Ryan**						
2 Pocan	N	N	Y	Y	Y	N
3 Kind	N	Y	Y	Y	Y	N
4 Moore	N	N	Y	Y	Y	N
5 **Sensenbrenner**	Y	Y	Y	Y	Y	Y
6 **Grothman**	Y	Y	Y	Y	Y	Y
7 **Duffy**	Y	Y	Y	Y	Y	Y
8 **Gallagher**	Y	Y	Y	Y	Y	Y
WYOMING						
AL **Cheney**	Y	Y	Y	Y	Y	Y

VOTE NUMBER

398. HR1911. ANTI-SEMITISM SPECIAL ENVOY/PASSAGE. Royce, R-Calif., motion to suspend the rules and pass the bill that would direct the president to appoint the head of the Office to Monitor and Combat Anti-Semitism within the Department of State as a special envoy with the rank of ambassador, who would report directly to the secretary of State. Motion agreed to 393-2: R 218-1; D 175-1. Oct. 13, 2018.

399. HR5895. FISCAL 2019 ENERGY-WATER, LEGISLATIVE BRANCH, MILITARY CONSTRUCTION-VA APPROPRIATIONS/CONFERENCE REPORT. Adoption of the conference report to accompany the fiscal 2019 three-bill spending package: Energy-Water, Legislative Branch, Military Construction-VA that would provide $147.5 billion in discretionary funding for fiscal 2019 to various departments, agencies and legislative operations, including $35.7 billion for the Energy Department, $7 billion for the Army Corps of Engineers, and $1.6 billion for the Interior Department's Bureau of Reclamation. It would provide $98.1 billion for military construction activities and for VA programs and activities, and $4.8 billion for operations of the House, Senate, joint House-Senate items and legislative branch entities such as the Library of Congress, the Capitol Police, and the Government Accountability Office Adopted (thus cleared for the president) 377-20: R 202-18; D 175-2. Oct. 13, 2018.

400. HR6368. SMALL BUSINESS RATINGS/PASSAGE. Chabot, R-Ohio, motion to suspend the rules and pass the bill that would require the Small Business Administration to increase past performance ratings of small business contractors that serve as mentors to other small businesses within certain federal research and technology programs for small businesses. Motion agreed to 389-6: R 214-6; D 175-0. Oct. 25, 2018.

401. HR6369. SMALL BUSINESS SOLE SOURCE CONTRACTS/PASSAGE. Chabot, R-Ohio, motion to suspend the rules and pass the bill that would raise the maximum threshold for sole source contracts that may be awarded to small business that are owned by women or service-disabled veterans, or operate in underutilized business zones. Contracts would not be allowed to exceed $7 million for industrial manufacturing or $4 million for any other contract. It would also modify the eligibility determination process for such contracts. Motion agreed to 392-5: R 216-5; D 176-0. Oct. 25, 2018.

402. HRES1071. FISCAL 2019 DEFENSE, LABOR-HHS-EDUCATION, AND CONTINUING APPROPRIATIONS; AND CONGRESSIONAL STANCE ON "ILLEGAL IMMIGRANT VOTING"/PREVIOUS QUESTION. Cole, R-Okla., motion to order the previous question (thus ending debate and possibility of amendment) on the rule (H Res 1077) that would provide for House floor consideration of the conference report to accompany the Defense and Labor-HHS-Education and continuing appropriations package (HR 6157) and providing for consideration of a resolution (H Res 1071) related to voting by "illegal immigrants," and for motions to suspend the rules. Motion agreed to 230-188: R 230-0; D 0-188. Oct. 26, 2018.

403. HRES1071. FISCAL 2019 DEFENSE, LABOR-HHS-EDUCATION, AND CONTINUING APPROPRIATIONS; AND CONGRESSIONAL STANCE ON "ILLEGAL IMMIGRANT VOTING"/RULE. Adoption of the rule (H Res 1077) that would provide for House floor consideration of the conference report to accompany the Defense and Labor-HHS-Education and continuing appropriations package (HR 6157), providing for a resolution (H Res 1071) related to voting by "illegal immigrants," and providing for motions to suspend the rules. Adopted 230-188: R 223-8; D 7-180. Oct. 26, 2018.

	398	399	400	401	402	403
ALABAMA						
1 **Byrne**	Y	Y	Y	Y	Y	Y
2 **Roby**	Y	Y	Y	Y	Y	Y
3 **Rogers**	Y	Y	Y	Y	Y	Y
4 **Aderholt**	Y	Y	Y	Y	Y	Y
5 **Brooks**	Y	N	Y	Y	Y	Y
6 **Palmer**	Y	Y	Y	Y	Y	Y
7 Sewell	Y	Y	Y	N	N	N
ALASKA						
AL **Young**	Y	Y	Y	Y	Y	Y
ARIZONA						
1 O'Halleran	Y	Y	Y	Y	N	Y
2 **McSally**	Y	Y	Y	Y	Y	Y
3 Grijalva	Y	Y	Y	N	N	N
4 **Gosar**	Y	Y	Y	Y	Y	Y
5 **Biggs**	Y	N	N	N	Y	Y
6 **Schweikert**	Y	Y	Y	Y	Y	Y
7 Gallego	Y	Y	Y	N	N	N
8 **Lesko**	+	Y	Y	Y	Y	Y
9 Sinema	Y	Y	Y	N	N	Y
ARKANSAS						
1 **Crawford**	Y	Y	Y	Y	Y	Y
2 **Hill**	Y	Y	Y	Y	Y	Y
3 **Womack**	Y	Y	Y	Y	Y	Y
4 **Westerman**	Y	Y	Y	Y	Y	Y
CALIFORNIA						
1 **LaMalfa**	Y	Y	Y	Y	Y	Y
2 Huffman	Y	Y	Y	N	N	N
3 Garamendi	Y	Y	Y	N	N	N
4 **McClintock**	Y	N	Y	Y	Y	Y
5 Thompson	Y	Y	Y	N	N	N
6 Matsui	Y	Y	Y	N	N	N
7 Bera	Y	Y	Y	N	N	N
8 **Cook**	Y	Y	Y	Y	Y	Y
9 McNerney	N	Y	Y	N	N	N
10 **Denham**	Y	Y	Y	Y	Y	Y
11 DeSaulnier	Y	Y	Y	N	N	N
12 Pelosi	?	?	Y	Y	N	N
13 Lee	Y	Y	Y	N	N	N
14 Speier	?	?	Y	Y	N	N
15 Swalwell	Y	Y	Y	Y	N	N
16 Costa	Y	Y	Y	N	N	N
17 Khanna	Y	Y	Y	N	N	N
18 Eshoo	+	+	+	+	–	–
19 Lofgren	+	+	Y	N	N	N
20 Panetta	Y	Y	Y	N	N	N
21 **Valadao**	Y	Y	Y	Y	Y	Y
22 **Nunes**	Y	Y	Y	Y	Y	Y
23 **McCarthy**	Y	Y	Y	Y	Y	Y
24 Carbajal	Y	Y	Y	N	N	N
25 **Knight**	Y	Y	Y	Y	Y	Y
26 Brownley	Y	Y	Y	N	N	N
27 Chu	Y	Y	Y	N	N	N
28 Schiff	Y	Y	Y	N	N	N
29 Cardenas	?	Y	Y	N	N	N
30 Sherman	Y	Y	Y	N	N	N
31 Aguilar	Y	Y	Y	N	N	N
32 Napolitano	Y	Y	Y	N	N	N
33 Lieu	Y	N	Y	N	N	N
34 Gomez	Y	Y	Y	N	N	N
35 Torres	Y	Y	Y	N	N	N
36 Ruiz	Y	Y	Y	N	N	N
37 Bass	Y	Y	Y	N	N	N
38 Sánchez, Linda	Y	Y	Y	N	N	N
39 **Royce**	Y	Y	Y	Y	Y	Y
40 Roybal-Allard	Y	Y	Y	N	N	N
41 Takano	Y	Y	Y	N	N	N
42 **Calvert**	Y	Y	Y	Y	Y	Y
43 Waters	Y	Y	Y	N	N	N
44 Barragan	Y	Y	Y	N	N	N
45 **Walters**	?	Y	Y	Y	Y	Y
46 Correa	Y	Y	Y	N	N	N
47 Lowenthal	Y	Y	Y	N	N	N
48 **Rohrabacher**	Y	Y	?	?	Y	Y
49 **Issa**	Y	Y	Y	?	?	Y
50 **Hunter**	Y	Y	Y	Y	Y	Y
51 Vargas	Y	Y	Y	N	N	N
52 Peters	Y	Y	Y	N	N	N
53 Davis	Y	Y	Y	N	N	N

	398	399	400	401	402	403
COLORADO						
1 DeGette	Y	Y	Y	Y	N	?
2 Polis	Y	Y	Y	N	N	N
3 **Tipton**	Y	Y	Y	Y	Y	Y
4 **Buck**	Y	N	Y	Y	Y	Y
5 **Lamborn**	Y	Y	Y	Y	Y	Y
6 **Coffman**	Y	Y	Y	Y	Y	Y
7 Perlmutter	Y	Y	Y	N	N	N
CONNECTICUT						
1 Larson	Y	Y	Y	N	N	N
2 Courtney	Y	Y	Y	N	N	N
3 DeLauro	Y	Y	Y	N	N	N
4 Himes	Y	Y	Y	N	N	N
5 Esty	Y	Y	Y	N	N	N
DELAWARE						
AL Blunt Rochester	Y	Y	Y	N	N	N
FLORIDA						
1 **Gaetz**	Y	Y	?	?	Y	Y
2 **Dunn**	Y	Y	Y	Y	Y	Y
3 **Yoho**	Y	Y	Y	Y	Y	Y
4 **Rutherford**	Y	Y	Y	Y	Y	Y
5 Lawson	Y	Y	Y	N	N	N
6 Vacant						
7 Murphy	Y	Y	Y	N	N	Y
8 **Posey**	Y	Y	Y	Y	Y	Y
9 Soto	Y	Y	Y	N	N	N
10 Demings	Y	Y	Y	N	N	N
11 **Webster**	Y	Y	Y	Y	Y	Y
12 **Bilirakis**	Y	Y	Y	Y	Y	Y
13 Crist	Y	Y	Y	N	N	N
14 Castor	Y	Y	Y	Y	?	?
15 **Ross**	Y	Y	Y	Y	Y	Y
16 **Buchanan**	Y	Y	Y	Y	Y	Y
17 **Rooney, T.**	?	?	?	?	Y	Y
18 **Mast**	Y	Y	Y	Y	Y	Y
19 **Rooney, F.**	Y	Y	Y	Y	Y	Y
20 Hastings	Y	Y	Y	N	N	N
21 Frankel	Y	Y	Y	N	N	N
22 Deutch	Y	Y	?	?	N	N
23 Wasserman Schultz	?	?	Y	Y	N	N
24 Wilson	Y	Y	?	?	N	N
25 **Diaz-Balart**	Y	Y	Y	Y	Y	Y
26 **Curbelo**	Y	Y	Y	Y	Y	Y
27 **Ros-Lehtinen**	Y	Y	Y	Y	?	?
GEORGIA						
1 **Carter**	Y	Y	Y	Y	Y	Y
2 Bishop	Y	Y	Y	N	N	N
3 **Ferguson**	Y	Y	Y	Y	Y	Y
4 Johnson	Y	Y	Y	N	N	N
5 Lewis	Y	Y	Y	N	N	N
6 **Handel**	Y	Y	Y	Y	Y	Y
7 **Woodall**	Y	Y	Y	Y	Y	Y
8 **Scott, A.**	Y	Y	Y	Y	Y	Y
9 **Collins**	Y	Y	Y	Y	Y	Y
10 **Hice**	?	?	Y	Y	Y	Y
11 **Loudermilk**	Y	Y	Y	Y	Y	Y
12 **Allen**	Y	Y	+	Y	Y	Y
13 Scott, D.	Y	Y	Y	N	N	N
14 **Graves**	Y	Y	Y	Y	Y	Y
HAWAII						
1 Hanabusa	Y	Y	Y	N	N	N
2 Gabbard	Y	Y	Y	N	N	N
IDAHO						
1 **Labrador**	Y	N	?	?	Y	Y
2 **Simpson**	Y	Y	Y	Y	Y	Y
ILLINOIS						
1 Rush	Y	Y	Y	N	N	N
2 Kelly	Y	Y	Y	N	N	N
3 Lipinski	Y	Y	Y	N	N	N
4 Gutierrez	Y	Y	+	+	N	N
5 Quigley	Y	Y	Y	N	N	N
6 **Roskam**	Y	Y	Y	Y	Y	Y
7 Davis, D.	Y	Y	?	?	N	N
8 Krishnamoorthi	Y	Y	Y	N	N	N
9 Schakowsky	Y	N	Y	N	N	N
10 Schneider	Y	Y	Y	N	N	N
11 Foster	Y	Y	Y	N	N	N
12 **Bost**	Y	Y	Y	Y	Y	Y
13 **Davis, R.**	Y	Y	Y	Y	Y	Y

KEY	**Republicans**	Democrats	*Independents*
Y Voted for (yea)		**X** Paired against	**C** Voted "present" to avoid possible conflict of interest
# Paired for		**–** Announced against	
+ Announced for		**P** Voted "present"	**?** Did not vote or otherwise make a position known
N Voted against (nay)			

	398	399	400	401	402	403
14 **Hultgren**	Y	Y	Y	Y	Y	Y
15 **Shimkus**	Y	N	Y	Y	Y	Y
16 **Kinzinger**	Y	Y	Y	Y	Y	Y
17 Bustos	Y	Y	Y	Y	N	N
18 **LaHood**	Y	Y	Y	Y	Y	Y
INDIANA						
1 Visclosky	Y	Y	Y	Y	N	N
2 **Walorski**	Y	Y	Y	Y	Y	Y
3 **Banks**	Y	Y	Y	Y	Y	Y
4 Rokita	Y	Y	Y	Y	Y	Y
5 **Brooks**	Y	Y	Y	Y	Y	Y
6 **Messer**	Y	Y	Y	Y	Y	Y
7 Carson	Y	Y	Y	Y	N	N
8 **Bucshon**	Y	Y	Y	Y	Y	Y
9 **Hollingsworth**	Y	N	Y	Y	Y	Y
IOWA						
1 **Blum**	Y	Y	Y	Y	Y	Y
2 Loebsack	Y	Y	Y	Y	N	N
3 **Young**	Y	Y	Y	Y	Y	Y
4 **King**	Y	Y	Y	N	Y	Y
KANSAS						
1 **Marshall**	Y	Y	Y	Y	Y	Y
2 **Jenkins**	Y	Y	Y	Y	Y	Y
3 **Yoder**	Y	Y	Y	Y	Y	Y
4 **Estes**	Y	Y	Y	Y	Y	Y
KENTUCKY						
1 **Comer**	Y	Y	Y	Y	Y	Y
2 **Guthrie**	Y	Y	Y	Y	Y	Y
3 Yarmuth	Y	Y	Y	Y	N	N
4 **Massie**	Y	N	N	N	Y	N
5 **Rogers**	Y	Y	Y	Y	Y	Y
6 **Barr**	Y	Y	Y	Y	Y	Y
LOUISIANA						
1 **Scalise**	Y	Y	Y	Y	Y	Y
2 Richmond	?	?	Y	Y	N	N
3 **Higgins**	Y	Y	Y	Y	Y	Y
4 **Johnson**	Y	Y	Y	Y	Y	Y
5 **Abraham**	Y	Y	Y	Y	Y	Y
6 **Graves**	Y	Y	Y	Y	Y	Y
MAINE						
1 Pingree	Y	Y	Y	Y	N	N
2 **Poliquin**	Y	Y	Y	Y	Y	Y
MARYLAND						
1 **Harris**	Y	N	Y	Y	Y	Y
2 Ruppersberger	Y	Y	Y	Y	N	N
3 Sarbanes	Y	Y	Y	Y	N	N
4 Brown	Y	Y	Y	Y	N	N
5 Hoyer	?	Y	Y	Y	N	N
6 Delaney	Y	Y	Y	Y	N	N
7 Cummings	Y	Y	?	?	N	N
8 Raskin	Y	Y	Y	Y	N	N
MASSACHUSETTS						
1 Neal	Y	Y	Y	Y	N	N
2 McGovern	Y	Y	Y	Y	N	N
3 Tsongas	Y	Y	Y	Y	N	N
4 Kennedy	Y	Y	Y	Y	N	N
5 Clark	Y	Y	Y	Y	N	N
6 Moulton	Y	Y	Y	Y	N	N
7 Capuano	Y	Y	?	Y	N	N
8 Lynch	Y	Y	Y	Y	N	N
9 Keating	Y	Y	Y	Y	N	N
MICHIGAN						
1 **Bergman**	Y	Y	Y	Y	Y	Y
2 **Huizenga**	Y	Y	Y	Y	Y	Y
3 *Amash*	N	N	N	N	Y	N
4 **Moolenaar**	Y	Y	Y	Y	Y	Y
5 Kildee	Y	Y	Y	Y	N	N
6 **Upton**	Y	Y	Y	Y	Y	Y
7 **Walberg**	Y	Y	Y	Y	Y	Y
8 **Bishop**	Y	Y	Y	Y	Y	Y
9 Levin	Y	Y	Y	Y	N	N
10 **Mitchell**	Y	Y	Y	Y	Y	Y
11 **Trott**	Y	Y	Y	Y	Y	Y
12 Dingell	Y	Y	?	?	N	N
14 Lawrence	Y	Y	Y	Y	N	N
MINNESOTA						
1 Walz	?	?	?	?	N	N
2 **Lewis**	Y	Y	Y	Y	Y	Y
3 **Paulsen**	Y	Y	Y	Y	Y	Y
4 McCollum	Y	Y	Y	Y	N	N

	398	399	400	401	402	403
5 Ellison	?	?	?	?	?	?
6 **Emmer**	Y	Y	Y	Y	Y	Y
7 Peterson	Y	Y	Y	Y	N	N
8 Nolan	?	?	?	?	?	?
MISSISSIPPI						
1 **Kelly**	Y	Y	Y	Y	Y	Y
2 Thompson	Y	Y	Y	Y	N	N
3 **Harper**	Y	Y	Y	Y	Y	Y
4 **Palazzo**	Y	Y	Y	Y	Y	Y
MISSOURI						
1 Clay	Y	Y	?	?	N	N
2 **Wagner**	Y	Y	Y	Y	Y	Y
3 **Luetkemeyer**	Y	Y	Y	Y	Y	Y
4 **Hartzler**	Y	Y	Y	Y	Y	Y
5 Cleaver	?	+	Y	Y	N	N
6 **Graves**	Y	Y	Y	Y	Y	Y
7 **Long**	Y	Y	Y	Y	Y	Y
8 **Smith**	Y	Y	Y	Y	Y	Y
MONTANA						
AL **Gianforte**	Y	Y	Y	Y	Y	Y
NEBRASKA						
1 **Fortenberry**	Y	Y	Y	Y	Y	Y
2 **Bacon**	Y	Y	Y	Y	Y	Y
3 **Smith**	Y	Y	Y	Y	Y	Y
NEVADA						
1 Titus	Y	Y	Y	Y	N	N
2 **Amodei**	Y	Y	Y	Y	Y	Y
3 Rosen	Y	Y	Y	Y	N	N
4 Kihuen	Y	Y	Y	Y	N	N
NEW HAMPSHIRE						
1 Shea-Porter	Y	Y	Y	Y	N	N
2 Kuster	Y	Y	Y	Y	N	N
NEW JERSEY						
1 Norcross	Y	Y	Y	Y	N	N
2 **LoBiondo**	Y	Y	Y	Y	Y	Y
3 **MacArthur**	Y	Y	Y	Y	Y	Y
4 **Smith**	Y	Y	?	Y	Y	Y
5 Gottheimer	+	+	Y	Y	N	Y
6 Pallone	Y	Y	Y	Y	N	N
7 **Lance**	Y	Y	Y	Y	Y	Y
8 Sires	Y	Y	Y	Y	N	N
9 Pascrell	Y	Y	Y	Y	N	N
10 Payne	Y	?	Y	Y	N	N
11 **Frelinghuysen**	Y	Y	Y	Y	Y	Y
12 Watson Coleman	Y	Y	Y	Y	N	N
NEW MEXICO						
1 Lujan Grisham	Y	Y	+	+	–	–
2 **Pearce**	?	?	Y	Y	Y	Y
3 Luján	Y	Y	Y	Y	N	N
NEW YORK						
1 **Zeldin**	Y	Y	Y	Y	Y	Y
2 **King**	Y	Y	Y	Y	Y	Y
3 Suozzi	Y	Y	Y	Y	N	Y
4 Rice	Y	Y	Y	Y	N	N
5 Meeks	Y	Y	?	?	N	N
6 Meng	Y	Y	Y	Y	N	N
7 Velázquez	Y	Y	Y	Y	N	N
8 Jeffries	Y	Y	Y	Y	N	N
9 Clarke	Y	Y	Y	Y	N	N
10 Nadler	Y	Y	Y	Y	N	N
11 **Donovan**	Y	Y	Y	Y	Y	Y
12 Maloney, C.	Y	Y	Y	Y	N	N
13 Espaillat	Y	Y	Y	Y	N	N
14 Crowley	Y	Y	Y	Y	N	N
15 Serrano	Y	Y	Y	Y	N	N
16 Engel	Y	Y	Y	Y	N	N
17 Lowey	Y	Y	Y	Y	N	N
18 Maloney, S.P.	?	?	Y	Y	N	N
19 **Faso**	Y	Y	Y	Y	Y	Y
20 Tonko	Y	Y	Y	Y	N	N
21 **Stefanik**	Y	Y	Y	Y	Y	Y
22 **Tenney**	Y	Y	Y	Y	Y	Y
23 **Reed**	Y	Y	Y	Y	Y	Y
24 **Katko**	Y	Y	Y	Y	Y	Y
25 **Vacant**						
26 Higgins	Y	Y	Y	Y	N	N
27 **Collins**	Y	Y	Y	Y	Y	Y
NORTH CAROLINA						
1 Butterfield	?	?	Y	Y	N	N
2 **Holding**	?	?	Y	Y	Y	Y
3 **Jones**	?	?	Y	Y	N	N
4 Price	?	?	Y	Y	N	N

	398	399	400	401	402	403
5 **Foxx**	Y	Y	Y	Y	Y	Y
6 **Walker**	Y	N	Y	Y	Y	Y
7 **Rouzer**	?	?	Y	Y	Y	Y
8 **Hudson**	Y	Y	Y	Y	Y	Y
9 **Pittenger**	?	?	Y	Y	Y	Y
9 **Vacant**						
10 **McHenry**	Y	Y	Y	Y	Y	Y
11 **Meadows**	Y	Y	Y	Y	Y	N
12 Adams	?	?	Y	Y	N	N
13 **Budd**	Y	Y	Y	Y	Y	Y
NORTH DAKOTA						
AL **Cramer**	Y	Y	Y	Y	Y	Y
OHIO						
1 **Chabot**	Y	Y	Y	Y	Y	Y
2 **Wenstrup**	Y	Y	Y	Y	Y	Y
3 Beatty	Y	Y	Y	Y	N	N
4 **Jordan**	Y	Y	?	Y	Y	Y
5 **Latta**	Y	Y	Y	Y	Y	Y
6 **Johnson**	Y	Y	Y	Y	Y	Y
7 **Gibbs**	Y	Y	Y	Y	Y	Y
8 **Davidson**	Y	N	Y	Y	Y	Y
9 Kaptur	Y	Y	Y	Y	N	N
10 **Turner**	Y	Y	Y	Y	Y	Y
11 Fudge	Y	Y	Y	Y	N	N
12 Balderson	Y	Y	Y	Y	Y	Y
13 Ryan	Y	Y	Y	Y	N	N
14 **Joyce**	Y	Y	Y	Y	Y	Y
15 **Stivers**	Y	Y	Y	Y	Y	Y
16 **Renacci**	+	+	+	+	Y	Y
OKLAHOMA						
1 **Vacant**						
2 **Mullin**	Y	Y	Y	Y	Y	Y
3 **Lucas**	Y	Y	Y	Y	Y	Y
4 **Cole**	Y	Y	Y	Y	Y	Y
5 **Russell**	Y	Y	Y	Y	Y	Y
OREGON						
1 Bonamici	Y	Y	Y	Y	N	N
2 **Walden**	Y	Y	Y	Y	Y	Y
3 Blumenauer	Y	Y	Y	Y	N	N
4 DeFazio	Y	Y	Y	Y	N	N
5 Schrader	Y	Y	Y	Y	N	N
PENNSYLVANIA						
1 Brady	Y	Y	?	?	N	N
2 Evans	Y	Y	Y	Y	N	N
3 **Kelly**	Y	Y	Y	Y	Y	Y
4 **Perry**	Y	N	Y	Y	Y	Y
5 **Thompson**	Y	Y	Y	Y	Y	Y
6 **Costello**	Y	Y	Y	Y	Y	Y
7 **Vacant**						
8 **Fitzpatrick**	Y	Y	Y	Y	Y	Y
9 **Shuster**	Y	Y	Y	Y	Y	Y
10 **Marino**	Y	Y	Y	Y	Y	Y
11 **Barletta**	Y	Y	?	?	?	?
12 **Rothfus**	Y	Y	Y	Y	Y	Y
13 Boyle	Y	Y	Y	Y	N	N
14 Doyle	Y	Y	Y	Y	N	N
15 **Vacant**						
16 **Smucker**	Y	Y	Y	Y	Y	Y
17 Cartwright	Y	Y	?	?	N	N
18 Lamb	Y	Y	Y	Y	N	Y
RHODE ISLAND						
1 Cicilline	Y	Y	Y	Y	N	N
2 Langevin	Y	Y	Y	Y	N	N
SOUTH CAROLINA						
1 **Sanford**	?	?	N	N	Y	Y
2 **Wilson**	Y	Y	Y	Y	Y	Y
3 **Duncan**	Y	N	Y	Y	Y	Y
4 **Gowdy**	Y	Y	?	?	Y	Y
5 **Norman**	?	?	Y	Y	Y	Y
6 Clyburn	Y	Y	Y	Y	N	N
7 **Rice**	?	?	Y	Y	Y	Y
SOUTH DAKOTA						
AL **Noem**	Y	Y	Y	Y	Y	Y
TENNESSEE						
1 **Roe**	Y	Y	Y	Y	Y	Y
2 Duncan	Y	N	Y	Y	Y	Y
3 **Fleischmann**	Y	Y	Y	Y	Y	Y
4 **DesJarlais**	Y	Y	Y	Y	Y	Y
5 Cooper	Y	Y	Y	Y	N	N
6 **Black**	Y	Y	Y	Y	Y	Y
7 **Blackburn**	?	?	?	?	?	?
8 **Kustoff**	Y	Y	Y	Y	Y	Y
9 Cohen	Y	Y	Y	Y	N	N

	398	399	400	401	402	403
TEXAS						
1 **Gohmert**	Y	?	Y	Y	Y	N
2 **Poe**	Y	Y	Y	Y	Y	Y
3 **Johnson, S.**	Y	Y	Y	Y	Y	Y
4 **Ratcliffe**	Y	Y	?	?	Y	Y
5 **Hensarling**	Y	Y	Y	Y	Y	Y
6 **Barton**	Y	N	Y	Y	Y	Y
7 **Culberson**	Y	Y	Y	Y	Y	Y
8 **Brady**	Y	Y	Y	Y	Y	Y
9 Green, A.	Y	Y	Y	Y	N	N
10 **McCaul**	Y	Y	Y	Y	Y	Y
11 **Conaway**	Y	Y	Y	Y	Y	Y
12 **Granger**	Y	Y	Y	Y	Y	Y
13 **Thornberry**	Y	Y	Y	Y	Y	Y
14 **Weber**	Y	Y	Y	Y	Y	Y
15 Gonzalez	Y	Y	Y	Y	N	N
16 O'Rourke	Y	Y	?	?	N	N
17 **Flores**	Y	Y	Y	Y	Y	Y
18 Jackson Lee	Y	Y	Y	Y	N	N
19 **Arrington**	Y	Y	Y	Y	Y	Y
20 Castro	Y	Y	?	?	N	N
21 **Smith**	Y	Y	Y	?	Y	Y
22 **Olson**	Y	Y	Y	Y	Y	Y
23 **Hurd**	Y	Y	Y	Y	Y	Y
24 Marchant	Y	Y	Y	Y	Y	Y
25 **Williams**	Y	Y	Y	Y	Y	Y
26 **Burgess**	Y	Y	N	Y	Y	Y
27 Cloud	Y	Y	Y	Y	Y	Y
28 Cuellar	Y	Y	Y	Y	N	N
29 Green, G.	Y	Y	Y	Y	N	N
30 Johnson, E.B.	Y	Y	Y	Y	N	N
31 **Carter**	Y	Y	Y	Y	Y	Y
32 **Sessions**	Y	Y	Y	Y	Y	Y
33 Veasey	Y	Y	Y	Y	N	N
34 Vela	Y	Y	Y	Y	N	N
35 Doggett	Y	Y	Y	Y	N	N
36 **Babin**	Y	Y	Y	Y	Y	Y
UTAH						
1 **Bishop**	Y	Y	?	?	Y	Y
2 **Stewart**	Y	Y	?	?	Y	Y
3 **Curtis**	Y	Y	Y	Y	Y	Y
4 **Love**	Y	Y	Y	Y	Y	Y
VERMONT						
AL Welch	Y	Y	Y	Y	N	N
VIRGINIA						
1 **Wittman**	Y	Y	Y	Y	Y	Y
2 **Taylor**	+	+	Y	Y	Y	Y
3 Scott	Y	Y	Y	Y	N	N
4 McEachin	Y	Y	Y	Y	N	N
5 **Garrett**	Y	N	Y	Y	Y	Y
6 **Goodlatte**	Y	Y	Y	Y	Y	Y
7 **Brat**	Y	Y	Y	Y	Y	Y
8 Beyer	Y	Y	Y	Y	N	N
9 **Griffith**	Y	Y	Y	Y	Y	N
10 **Comstock**	Y	Y	Y	Y	Y	Y
11 Connolly	Y	Y	Y	Y	N	N
WASHINGTON						
1 DelBene	Y	Y	Y	Y	N	N
2 Larsen	Y	Y	Y	Y	N	N
3 **Herrera Beutler**	Y	Y	Y	Y	Y	Y
4 **Newhouse**	Y	Y	Y	Y	Y	Y
5 **McMorris Rodgers**	Y	Y	Y	Y	Y	Y
6 Kilmer	Y	Y	Y	Y	N	N
7 Jayapal	Y	Y	Y	Y	N	N
8 **Reichert**	Y	Y	Y	Y	Y	Y
9 Smith	Y	Y	Y	Y	N	N
10 Heck	Y	Y	Y	Y	N	N
WEST VIRGINIA						
1 **McKinley**	Y	Y	Y	Y	Y	Y
2 **Mooney**	Y	Y	Y	Y	Y	N
3 **Jenkins**	?	?	?	?	?	?
WISCONSIN						
1 **Ryan**						
2 Pocan	Y	Y	Y	Y	N	N
3 Kind	Y	Y	Y	Y	N	N
4 Moore	Y	Y	Y	Y	N	N
5 **Sensenbrenner**	Y	N	Y	Y	Y	Y
6 **Grothman**	Y	Y	N	Y	Y	Y
7 **Duffy**	Y	Y	Y	Y	Y	Y
8 **Gallagher**	Y	Y	Y	Y	Y	Y
WYOMING						
AL **Cheney**	Y	Y	Y	Y	Y	Y

VOTE NUMBER

404. HR5420. FRANKLIN D. ROOSEVELT NATIONAL HISTORIC SITE LAND EXPANSION/PASSAGE. McClintock, R-Calif., motion to suspend the rules and pass the bill that would authorize the National Park Service to acquire 89 acres of land adjacent to the Franklin D. Roosevelt National Historic Site and incorporate such land into the site. Motion agreed to 394-15: R 216-15; D 178-0. Oct. 26, 2018.

405. HR6157. FISCAL 2019 DEFENSE, LABOR-HHS-EDUCATION, AND CONTINUING APPROPRIATIONS/CONFERENCE REPORT. Adoption of the conference report to accompany the bill that would provide $855.1 billion in discretionary funding for fiscal 2019 to various departments and agencies, including $674.4 billion for the Defense Department and $178.1 billion for the Labor, Health and Human Services and Education departments. The Defense Department total would include $606.5 billion in base Defense Department funding subject to spending caps, and would include $67.9 billion in overseas contingency operations funding. The bill would provide $90.3 billion in discretionary spending for the Health and Human Services Department, $71.4 billion for the Education Department and $12.1 billion for the Labor Department. The measure would also provide funding for federal government operations until Dec. 7, 2018, at an annualized rate of approximately $1.3 trillion. Adopted (thus cleared for the president) 361-61: R 176-56; D 185-5. Oct. 26, 2018.

406. HRES1071. CONGRESSIONAL STANCE ON "ILLEGAL IMMIGRANT VOTING"/PASSAGE. Adoption of the resolution that would state that the House of Representatives "recognizes that allowing illegal immigrants the right to vote devalues the franchise and diminishes the voting power of United States citizens." Adopted 279-72: R 230-1; D 49-71. Oct. 26, 2018.

407. HRES1082. FAA REAUTHORIZATION AND SUPPLEMENTAL DISASTER APPROPRIATIONS/ADOPTION. Shuster, R-Pa., motion to suspend the rules and adopt the resolution that would provide for concurrence by the House in the Senate amendment to HR 302, with an amendment that would reauthorize federal aviation programs through fiscal 2023. The measure would authorize $10.2 billion in fiscal 2018, which would gradually increase to $11.6 billion in fiscal 2023, for Federal Aviation Administration operations; $3.4 billion annually for the Aviation Trust Fund for the Airport Improvement Program; $3.3 billion in fiscal 2018, which would gradually increase to $3.7 billion in fiscal 2023, for facilities and equipment; and $189 million in fiscal 2018, which would gradually increase to $214 million in fiscal 2023, for research and development. It would also ban e-cigarettes and talking on a cell phone during a passenger flight. It would prohibit airlines from involuntarily removing passengers from a plane after they have checked in and taken their seats, and would require the FAA to establish minimum seat dimensions on passenger airlines. The bill would also appropriate $1.7 billion in emergency supplemental funding for activities by HUD's Community Development Fund to aid disaster relief and recovery efforts in areas hit by natural disasters. It would also extend medical professional liability insurance coverage to sports medicine professionals who provide certain medical services to athletes outside their home state. Motion agreed to 398-23: R 211-20; D 187-3. Oct. 26, 2018.

408. HR6729. HUMAN TRAFFICKING INFORMATION SHARING/PASSAGE. Tipton, R-Colo., motion to suspend the rules and pass the bill that would allow the Treasury Department to designate certain nonprofit organizations to provide information on suspected human trafficking or related money laundering activities directly to financial institutions without liability. Motion agreed to 297-124: R 202-29; D 95-95. Oct. 26, 2018.

409. HR6756. TAX DEDUCTIONS FOR NEW BUSINESS, TAX-FAVORED RETIREMENT ACCOUNTS, AND PERMANENT TAX EXTENSIONS/PREVIOUS QUESTION. Sessions, R-Texas, motion to order the previous question (thus ending debate and possibility of amendment) on the rule (H Res 1084) that would provide for House floor consideration of a bill related to new-business tax deductions (HR 6756), a bill related to tax-favored retirement accounts (HR 6757), and a bill that would make many temporary aspects of the individual tax code permanent (HR 6760). Motion agreed to 227-189: R 227-0; D 0-189. Oct. 27, 2018.

	404	405	406	407	408	409
ALABAMA						
1 Byrne	Y	Y	Y	Y	Y	Y
2 Roby	Y	Y	Y	Y	Y	Y
3 Rogers	Y	Y	Y	Y	Y	Y
4 Aderholt	Y	Y	Y	Y	Y	Y
5 Brooks	N	Y	Y	N	N	Y
6 Palmer	Y	N	Y	Y	Y	Y
7 Sewell	Y	Y	P	Y	Y	N
ALASKA						
AL Young	N	Y	Y	Y	Y	Y
ARIZONA						
1 O'Halleran	Y	Y	Y	Y	Y	N
2 McSally	Y	Y	Y	Y	Y	Y
3 Grijalva	Y	Y	P	Y	Y	N
4 Gosar	N	N	Y	N	N	Y
5 Biggs	N	N	Y	N	N	Y
6 Schweikert	Y	Y	Y	Y	Y	Y
7 Gallego	Y	Y	P	Y	Y	N
8 Lesko	Y	Y	Y	Y	Y	Y
9 Sinema	Y	Y	Y	Y	Y	N
ARKANSAS						
1 Crawford	Y	Y	Y	Y	Y	Y
2 Hill	Y	Y	Y	Y	Y	Y
3 Womack	Y	Y	Y	Y	Y	Y
4 Westerman	Y	Y	Y	Y	Y	Y
CALIFORNIA						
1 LaMalfa	Y	Y	Y	Y	Y	Y
2 Huffman	Y	Y	N	N	N	N
3 Garamendi	Y	Y	Y	Y	Y	N
4 McClintock	Y	N	Y	N	Y	Y
5 Thompson	Y	Y	P	Y	N	N
6 Matsui	Y	Y	P	Y	N	N
7 Bera	Y	Y	Y	Y	Y	N
8 Cook	Y	Y	Y	Y	Y	Y
9 McNerney	Y	Y	Y	Y	N	N
10 Denham	Y	Y	Y	Y	Y	Y
11 DeSaulnier	Y	N	N	Y	N	N
12 Pelosi	Y	Y	N	Y	N	N
13 Lee	Y	Y	N	Y	N	N
14 Speier	?	Y	Y	N	Y	N
15 Swalwell	Y	Y	N	Y	N	N
16 Costa	Y	Y	Y	Y	Y	N
17 Khanna	Y	N	P	N	N	N
18 Eshoo	+	+	?	–	–	?
19 Lofgren	?	Y	P	Y	N	N
20 Panetta	Y	Y	N	N	Y	N
21 Valadao	Y	Y	Y	Y	Y	Y
22 Nunes	Y	Y	Y	Y	Y	Y
23 McCarthy	Y	Y	Y	Y	Y	Y
24 Carbajal	Y	Y	Y	Y	Y	N
25 Knight	Y	Y	Y	Y	Y	Y
26 Brownley	Y	Y	P	Y	Y	N
27 Chu	Y	Y	P	Y	N	N
28 Schiff	Y	Y	P	Y	N	N
29 Cardenas	Y	Y	P	Y	Y	N
30 Sherman	Y	Y	P	Y	Y	N
31 Aguilar	Y	Y	P	Y	Y	N
32 Napolitano	+	Y	N	Y	N	N
33 Lieu	?	Y	P	Y	N	N
34 Gomez	Y	Y	P	Y	N	N
35 Torres	Y	Y	N	Y	N	N
36 Ruiz	Y	Y	P	Y	Y	N
37 Bass	Y	Y	N	Y	N	N
38 Sánchez, Linda	Y	Y	P	Y	N	N
39 Royce	Y	Y	Y	Y	Y	Y
40 Roybal-Allard	Y	Y	N	Y	N	N
41 Takano	Y	Y	P	Y	N	N
42 Calvert	Y	Y	Y	Y	Y	Y
43 Waters	Y	Y	P	Y	N	N
44 Barragan	Y	Y	P	Y	N	N
45 Walters	Y	Y	Y	Y	Y	Y
46 Correa	Y	Y	N	Y	N	N
47 Lowenthal	Y	Y	P	Y	N	N
48 Rohrabacher	Y	Y	Y	N	N	Y
49 Issa	Y	Y	Y	Y	Y	Y
50 Hunter	Y	Y	Y	Y	Y	Y
51 Vargas	?	Y	N	Y	Y	N
52 Peters	Y	Y	P	Y	Y	N
53 Davis	Y	Y	N	Y	Y	N

	404	405	406	407	408	409
COLORADO						
1 DeGette	Y	Y	N	Y	N	N
2 Polis	Y	Y	Y	N	N	N
3 Tipton	Y	Y	Y	Y	Y	Y
4 Buck	Y	N	N	N	N	Y
5 Lamborn	Y	N	Y	Y	Y	Y
6 Coffman	Y	Y	Y	Y	Y	Y
7 Perlmutter	Y	Y	P	Y	Y	N
CONNECTICUT						
1 Larson	Y	Y	Y	Y	Y	N
2 Courtney	Y	Y	Y	Y	Y	N
3 DeLauro	+	Y	Y	Y	Y	N
4 Himes	Y	Y	Y	Y	Y	N
5 Esty	Y	Y	Y	Y	Y	N
DELAWARE						
AL Blunt Rochester	Y	Y	P	Y	Y	N
FLORIDA						
1 Gaetz	Y	Y	Y	Y	N	Y
2 Dunn	Y	Y	Y	Y	Y	Y
3 Yoho	N	N	Y	Y	N	Y
4 Rutherford	Y	Y	Y	Y	Y	Y
5 Lawson	Y	Y	Y	Y	Y	N
6 Vacant						
7 Murphy	Y	Y	Y	Y	Y	N
8 Posey	Y	Y	Y	Y	Y	Y
9 Soto	Y	Y	N	Y	Y	N
10 Demings	Y	Y	N	Y	Y	N
11 Webster	Y	N	Y	Y	Y	Y
12 Bilirakis	Y	Y	Y	Y	Y	Y
13 Crist	Y	Y	Y	Y	Y	N
14 Castor	?	Y	Y	Y	Y	N
15 Ross	Y	Y	Y	Y	Y	Y
16 Buchanan	Y	Y	Y	Y	Y	Y
17 Rooney, T.	Y	Y	Y	Y	Y	?
18 Mast	Y	Y	Y	Y	Y	Y
19 Rooney, F.	Y	N	Y	Y	Y	Y
20 Hastings	Y	Y	N	Y	N	N
21 Frankel	?	Y	P	Y	Y	N
22 Deutch	Y	Y	P	Y	N	N
23 Wasserman Schultz	Y	Y	P	Y	Y	N
24 Wilson	Y	Y	P	Y	N	N
25 Diaz-Balart	Y	Y	Y	Y	Y	Y
26 Curbelo	Y	Y	Y	Y	Y	Y
27 Ros-Lehtinen	?	Y	Y	Y	Y	Y
GEORGIA						
1 Carter	Y	Y	Y	Y	Y	Y
2 Bishop	Y	Y	Y	Y	N	N
3 Ferguson	Y	Y	Y	Y	Y	Y
4 Johnson	Y	Y	N	Y	N	N
5 Lewis	Y	Y	P	Y	N	N
6 Handel	Y	Y	Y	Y	Y	Y
7 Woodall	Y	Y	Y	Y	Y	Y
8 Scott, A.	Y	Y	Y	Y	Y	Y
9 Collins	Y	Y	Y	Y	Y	Y
10 Hice	Y	N	Y	Y	Y	Y
11 Loudermilk	Y	Y	Y	Y	Y	Y
12 Allen	Y	Y	Y	Y	Y	Y
13 Scott, D.	Y	Y	Y	Y	Y	N
14 Graves	Y	Y	Y	Y	Y	Y
HAWAII						
1 Hanabusa	Y	Y	P	Y	N	N
2 Gabbard	Y	Y	P	Y	N	N
IDAHO						
1 Labrador	Y	?	?	?	?	Y
2 Simpson	Y	Y	Y	Y	Y	Y
ILLINOIS						
1 Rush	+	Y	N	Y	N	N
2 Kelly	Y	Y	N	Y	N	N
3 Lipinski	Y	Y	Y	Y	Y	N
4 Gutierrez	Y	Y	N	Y	N	N
5 Quigley	Y	Y	N	Y	N	N
6 Roskam	Y	Y	Y	Y	Y	Y
7 Davis, D.	Y	Y	N	Y	N	N
8 Krishnamoorthi	Y	Y	P	Y	Y	N
9 Schakowsky	Y	Y	N	Y	N	N
10 Schneider	Y	Y	N	Y	Y	N
11 Foster	Y	Y	N	Y	Y	N
12 Bost	Y	Y	Y	Y	Y	Y
13 Davis, R.	Y	Y	Y	Y	Y	Y

HOUSE VOTES III

	404	405	406	407	408	409
14 **Hultgren**	Y	Y	Y	Y	Y	Y
15 **Shimkus**	Y	Y	Y	Y	Y	Y
16 **Kinzinger**	Y	Y	Y	Y	Y	Y
17 Bustos	Y	Y	Y	Y	Y	N
18 **LaHood**	Y	Y	Y	Y	Y	Y
INDIANA						
1 Visclosky	Y	Y	Y	Y	Y	N
2 **Walorski**	Y	Y	Y	Y	Y	Y
3 **Banks**	Y	N	Y	Y	Y	Y
4 Rokita	Y	?	?	?	?	Y
5 **Brooks**	Y	Y	Y	Y	Y	Y
6 **Messer**	Y	Y	Y	Y	Y	Y
7 Carson	Y	Y	N	Y	Y	N
8 **Bucshon**	Y	Y	Y	Y	Y	Y
9 **Hollingsworth**	Y	N	Y	Y	Y	Y
IOWA						
1 **Blum**	Y	Y	Y	Y	N	Y
2 Loebsack	Y	Y	P	Y	Y	N
3 **Young**	Y	Y	Y	Y	Y	Y
4 **King**	Y	N	Y	Y	Y	Y
KANSAS						
1 **Marshall**	Y	Y	Y	Y	Y	Y
2 **Jenkins**	Y	Y	Y	Y	Y	Y
3 **Yoder**	Y	Y	Y	Y	Y	Y
4 **Estes**	Y	Y	Y	Y	Y	Y
KENTUCKY						
1 **Comer**	Y	Y	Y	Y	Y	Y
2 **Guthrie**	Y	Y	Y	Y	Y	Y
3 Yarmuth	?	Y	Y	Y	N	N
4 **Massie**	N	N	Y	N	N	Y
5 **Rogers**	Y	Y	Y	Y	Y	Y
6 **Barr**	Y	Y	Y	Y	Y	Y
LOUISIANA						
1 **Scalise**	Y	Y	Y	Y	Y	Y
2 Richmond	Y	Y	P	Y	N	N
3 **Higgins**	Y	N	Y	Y	Y	Y
4 **Johnson**	Y	N	Y	Y	N	Y
5 **Abraham**	Y	N	Y	Y	Y	Y
6 **Graves**	Y	Y	Y	Y	Y	Y
MAINE						
1 Pingree	Y	Y	P	Y	N	N
2 **Poliquin**	Y	Y	Y	Y	Y	Y
MARYLAND						
1 **Harris**	N	N	Y	N	N	Y
2 Ruppersberger	Y	Y	P	Y	Y	N
3 Sarbanes	Y	Y	N	Y	Y	N
4 Brown	Y	Y	N	Y	N	N
5 Hoyer	Y	Y	N	Y	N	N
6 Delaney	Y	Y	P	Y	Y	N
7 Cummings	Y	Y	N	Y	N	N
8 Raskin	Y	Y	N	Y	N	N
MASSACHUSETTS						
1 Neal	Y	Y	P	Y	N	N
2 McGovern	Y	Y	N	Y	N	N
3 Tsongas	Y	Y	N	Y	Y	N
4 Kennedy	Y	Y	P	Y	N	N
5 Clark	Y	Y	P	Y	N	N
6 Moulton	Y	Y	N	Y	Y	N
7 Capuano	Y	Y	?	Y	N	N
8 Lynch	Y	Y	Y	Y	Y	N
9 Keating	Y	Y	P	Y	Y	N
MICHIGAN						
1 **Bergman**	Y	Y	Y	Y	Y	Y
2 **Huizenga**	Y	Y	Y	Y	Y	Y
3 *Amash*	N	N	N	N	N	Y
4 **Moolenaar**	Y	Y	Y	Y	Y	Y
5 Kildee	Y	Y	P	Y	Y	N
6 **Upton**	Y	Y	Y	Y	Y	Y
7 **Walberg**	Y	Y	Y	Y	Y	Y
8 **Bishop**	Y	Y	Y	Y	Y	Y
9 Levin	Y	Y	P	Y	Y	N
10 **Mitchell**	Y	Y	Y	Y	Y	Y
11 **Trott**	Y	Y	Y	Y	Y	Y
12 Dingell	Y	Y	P	Y	Y	N
14 Lawrence	Y	Y	P	Y	N	N
MINNESOTA						
1 Walz	Y	Y	Y	Y	N	N
2 **Lewis**	Y	Y	Y	Y	Y	Y
3 **Paulsen**	Y	Y	Y	Y	Y	Y
4 McCollum	Y	Y	Y	Y	N	N

	404	405	406	407	408	409
5 Ellison	?	Y	Y	Y	Y	?
6 **Emmer**	Y	N	Y	N	Y	Y
7 Peterson	Y	Y	Y	Y	Y	N
8 Nolan	?	?	?	?	?	?
MISSISSIPPI						
1 **Kelly**	Y	N	Y	Y	Y	Y
2 Thompson	Y	Y	N	Y	N	N
3 **Harper**	Y	Y	Y	Y	Y	?
4 **Palazzo**	Y	Y	Y	Y	Y	Y
MISSOURI						
1 Clay	Y	Y	P	Y	N	N
2 **Wagner**	Y	Y	Y	N	Y	Y
3 **Luetkemeyer**	Y	Y	Y	Y	Y	Y
4 **Hartzler**	Y	Y	Y	Y	Y	Y
5 Cleaver	Y	Y	P	Y	N	N
6 **Graves**	Y	Y	Y	Y	Y	Y
7 **Long**	Y	Y	Y	Y	Y	Y
8 **Smith**	Y	N	Y	Y	Y	Y
MONTANA						
AL **Gianforte**	Y	N	Y	Y	Y	Y
NEBRASKA						
1 **Fortenberry**	Y	Y	Y	Y	Y	Y
2 **Bacon**	Y	Y	Y	Y	Y	Y
3 **Smith**	Y	N	Y	Y	Y	Y
NEVADA						
1 Titus	Y	Y	P	Y	N	N
2 **Amodei**	Y	Y	Y	Y	Y	Y
3 Rosen	Y	Y	Y	Y	Y	N
4 Kihuen	Y	Y	N	Y	Y	N
NEW HAMPSHIRE						
1 Shea-Porter	Y	Y	Y	Y	Y	N
2 Kuster	Y	Y	Y	Y	Y	N
NEW JERSEY						
1 Norcross	Y	Y	P	Y	Y	N
2 **LoBiondo**	Y	Y	Y	Y	Y	Y
3 **MacArthur**	Y	Y	Y	Y	Y	Y
4 **Smith**	Y	Y	Y	Y	Y	Y
5 Gottheimer	Y	Y	Y	Y	Y	N
6 Pallone	Y	Y	N	Y	N	N
7 **Lance**	Y	Y	Y	Y	Y	Y
8 Sires	Y	Y	P	Y	Y	N
9 Pascrell	Y	Y	N	Y	Y	N
10 Payne	Y	Y	N	Y	N	N
11 **Frelinghuysen**	Y	Y	Y	Y	Y	Y
12 Watson Coleman	Y	Y	N	Y	N	N
NEW MEXICO						
1 Lujan Grisham	+	?	?	?	?	?
2 **Pearce**	Y	Y	Y	Y	Y	Y
3 Luján	Y	Y	P	Y	Y	N
NEW YORK						
1 **Zeldin**	Y	Y	Y	Y	Y	Y
2 **King**	Y	Y	Y	Y	Y	Y
3 Suozzi	Y	N	Y	Y	Y	N
4 Rice	Y	Y	P	Y	Y	N
5 Meeks	Y	Y	N	Y	N	N
6 Meng	Y	Y	N	Y	N	N
7 Velázquez	Y	Y	N	Y	N	N
8 Jeffries	Y	Y	P	Y	N	N
9 Clarke	Y	Y	N	Y	N	N
10 Nadler	Y	Y	N	Y	N	N
11 **Donovan**	Y	Y	Y	Y	Y	Y
12 Maloney, C.	Y	Y	P	Y	Y	N
13 Espaillat	Y	Y	N	Y	N	N
14 Crowley	Y	Y	N	Y	N	N
15 Serrano	Y	Y	N	Y	N	N
16 Engel	Y	Y	P	Y	N	N
17 Lowey	Y	Y	N	Y	N	N
18 Maloney, S.P.	Y	Y	N	Y	Y	N
19 **Faso**	Y	Y	Y	Y	Y	Y
20 Tonko	Y	Y	N	Y	N	N
21 **Stefanik**	Y	Y	Y	Y	Y	Y
22 **Tenney**	Y	Y	Y	Y	Y	Y
23 **Reed**	Y	Y	Y	Y	Y	Y
24 **Katko**	Y	Y	Y	Y	Y	Y
25 **Vacant**						
26 Higgins	Y	Y	N	Y	Y	N
27 **Collins**	Y	Y	Y	Y	Y	Y
NORTH CAROLINA						
1 Butterfield	Y	Y	P	Y	N	N
2 **Holding**	Y	Y	Y	Y	Y	Y
3 **Jones**	N	N	Y	Y	N	?
4 Price	Y	Y	N	Y	N	N

	404	405	406	407	408	409
5 **Foxx**	Y	Y	Y	N	Y	Y
6 **Walker**	Y	N	Y	Y	Y	Y
7 **Rouzer**	Y	Y	Y	Y	Y	Y
8 **Hudson**	Y	Y	Y	Y	Y	Y
9 **Pittenger**	Y	Y	Y	Y	Y	Y
9 **Vacant**						
10 **McHenry**	Y	Y	Y	Y	Y	Y
11 **Meadows**	Y	N	Y	Y	N	Y
12 Adams	Y	Y	P	Y	N	N
13 **Budd**	Y	N	Y	Y	Y	Y
NORTH DAKOTA						
AL **Cramer**	Y	Y	Y	Y	Y	Y
OHIO						
1 **Chabot**	Y	N	Y	Y	Y	Y
2 **Wenstrup**	Y	Y	Y	Y	N	Y
3 Beatty	Y	Y	P	Y	N	N
4 **Jordan**	N	N	Y	N	N	Y
5 **Latta**	Y	Y	Y	Y	Y	Y
6 **Johnson**	Y	Y	Y	Y	Y	Y
7 **Gibbs**	Y	Y	Y	Y	Y	Y
8 **Davidson**	N	N	Y	N	N	Y
9 Kaptur	Y	Y	Y	Y	Y	N
10 **Turner**	Y	Y	Y	Y	Y	Y
11 Fudge	Y	Y	P	Y	N	N
12 Balderson	Y	Y	Y	Y	Y	Y
13 Ryan	Y	Y	Y	Y	Y	N
14 **Joyce**	Y	Y	Y	Y	Y	Y
15 **Stivers**	Y	Y	Y	Y	Y	Y
16 **Renacci**	Y	N	Y	Y	Y	Y
OKLAHOMA						
1 **Vacant**						
2 **Mullin**	Y	N	Y	Y	Y	Y
3 **Lucas**	Y	Y	Y	Y	Y	Y
4 **Cole**	Y	Y	Y	Y	Y	Y
5 **Russell**	Y	Y	Y	Y	Y	Y
OREGON						
1 Bonamici	Y	Y	P	Y	N	N
2 **Walden**	Y	Y	Y	Y	Y	Y
3 Blumenauer	Y	Y	P	Y	Y	N
4 DeFazio	Y	Y	P	Y	Y	N
5 Schrader	Y	Y	Y	Y	Y	N
PENNSYLVANIA						
1 Brady	Y	Y	N	Y	N	N
2 Evans	Y	Y	N	Y	N	N
3 **Kelly**	Y	N	Y	Y	Y	Y
4 **Perry**	N	N	Y	Y	Y	Y
5 **Thompson**	Y	Y	Y	Y	Y	Y
6 **Costello**	Y	Y	Y	Y	Y	Y
7 **Vacant**						
8 **Fitzpatrick**	Y	Y	Y	Y	Y	Y
9 **Shuster**	Y	Y	Y	Y	Y	Y
10 **Marino**	Y	Y	Y	Y	Y	Y
11 **Barletta**	?	Y	Y	Y	Y	?
12 **Rothfus**	Y	N	Y	Y	Y	Y
13 Boyle	Y	Y	P	Y	Y	N
14 Doyle	Y	Y	N	Y	Y	N
15 **Vacant**						
16 **Smucker**	Y	N	Y	Y	Y	Y
17 Cartwright	Y	Y	Y	Y	Y	N
18 Lamb	Y	Y	Y	Y	Y	N
RHODE ISLAND						
1 Cicilline	Y	Y	Y	Y	N	N
2 Langevin	Y	Y	Y	Y	Y	N
SOUTH CAROLINA						
1 **Sanford**	Y	N	Y	Y	N	Y
2 **Wilson**	Y	Y	Y	Y	Y	Y
3 **Duncan**	N	N	Y	N	N	Y
4 **Gowdy**	Y	Y	Y	Y	Y	Y
5 **Norman**	Y	N	Y	N	N	Y
6 Clyburn	Y	Y	Y	Y	N	N
7 **Rice**	Y	Y	Y	Y	Y	Y
SOUTH DAKOTA						
AL **Noem**	Y	Y	Y	Y	Y	Y
TENNESSEE						
1 **Roe**	Y	Y	Y	Y	Y	Y
2 **Duncan**	N	N	Y	Y	N	Y
3 **Fleischmann**	Y	Y	Y	Y	Y	Y
4 **DesJarlais**	Y	N	Y	Y	Y	?
5 Cooper	Y	Y	Y	Y	Y	N
6 **Black**	Y	Y	Y	Y	Y	Y
7 **Blackburn**	?	N	?	?	?	?
8 **Kustoff**	Y	Y	Y	Y	Y	Y
9 Cohen	Y	Y	Y	Y	N	N

	404	405	406	407	408	409
TEXAS						
1 **Gohmert**	N	N	Y	Y	N	Y
2 **Poe**	Y	Y	Y	Y	Y	Y
3 **Johnson, S.**	Y	Y	Y	Y	Y	Y
4 **Ratcliffe**	Y	N	Y	Y	Y	Y
5 **Hensarling**	Y	N	Y	N	Y	Y
6 **Barton**	Y	N	Y	Y	Y	Y
7 **Culberson**	Y	Y	Y	Y	Y	Y
8 **Brady**	Y	Y	Y	Y	Y	Y
9 Green, A.	Y	Y	P	Y	N	N
10 **McCaul**	Y	Y	Y	Y	Y	Y
11 **Conaway**	Y	Y	Y	Y	Y	Y
12 **Granger**	Y	Y	Y	Y	Y	Y
13 **Thornberry**	Y	Y	Y	Y	Y	Y
14 **Weber**	Y	Y	Y	Y	Y	Y
15 Gonzalez	Y	Y	Y	Y	N	N
16 O'Rourke	Y	Y	N	Y	Y	N
17 **Flores**	Y	Y	Y	Y	Y	Y
18 Jackson Lee	+	Y	P	Y	N	N
19 **Arrington**	Y	Y	Y	Y	Y	Y
20 Castro	Y	Y	N	Y	Y	N
21 **Smith**	Y	Y	Y	Y	Y	Y
22 **Olson**	Y	Y	Y	Y	Y	Y
23 **Hurd**	Y	Y	Y	Y	Y	Y
24 Marchant	Y	N	Y	Y	Y	Y
25 **Williams**	Y	Y	Y	Y	Y	Y
26 **Burgess**	Y	Y	Y	Y	N	Y
27 Cloud	Y	N	Y	Y	N	Y
28 Cuellar	Y	Y	Y	Y	Y	N
29 Green, G.	Y	Y	N	Y	Y	N
30 Johnson, E.B.	Y	Y	N	Y	N	N
31 **Carter**	Y	Y	Y	Y	Y	Y
32 **Sessions**	Y	Y	Y	Y	Y	Y
33 Veasey	Y	Y	N	Y	N	N
34 Vela	Y	Y	Y	Y	N	N
35 Doggett	Y	Y	N	Y	N	N
36 **Babin**	Y	Y	Y	Y	Y	Y
UTAH						
1 **Bishop**	Y	Y	Y	Y	Y	Y
2 **Stewart**	Y	Y	Y	Y	Y	Y
3 **Curtis**	Y	N	Y	Y	Y	Y
4 **Love**	Y	N	Y	Y	Y	Y
VERMONT						
AL Welch	Y	Y	N	Y	N	N
VIRGINIA						
1 **Wittman**	Y	Y	Y	Y	N	Y
2 **Taylor**	Y	Y	Y	Y	Y	Y
3 Scott	Y	Y	N	Y	N	N
4 McEachin	Y	Y	N	Y	N	N
5 **Garrett**	Y	N	Y	N	N	Y
6 **Goodlatte**	Y	Y	Y	Y	N	Y
7 **Brat**	Y	N	Y	Y	Y	Y
8 Beyer	Y	Y	N	Y	N	N
9 **Griffith**	Y	Y	Y	N	N	Y
10 **Comstock**	Y	Y	Y	Y	Y	Y
11 Connolly	Y	Y	P	Y	Y	N
WASHINGTON						
1 DelBene	Y	Y	P	Y	Y	N
2 Larsen	Y	Y	Y	Y	Y	N
3 **Herrera Beutler**	Y	Y	Y	Y	Y	Y
4 **Newhouse**	Y	Y	Y	Y	Y	+
5 **McMorris Rodgers**	Y	Y	Y	Y	Y	Y
6 Kilmer	Y	Y	P	Y	Y	N
7 Jayapal	Y	N	N	Y	N	N
8 **Reichert**	Y	Y	Y	Y	Y	Y
9 Smith	Y	Y	N	Y	N	N
10 Heck	Y	Y	P	Y	Y	N
WEST VIRGINIA						
1 **McKinley**	Y	Y	Y	Y	Y	Y
2 **Mooney**	Y	N	Y	Y	Y	Y
3 **Jenkins**	?	?	?	?	?	?
WISCONSIN						
1 **Ryan**						
2 Pocan	Y	Y	N	Y	N	N
3 Kind	Y	Y	Y	Y	Y	N
4 Moore	Y	N	N	Y	Y	N
5 **Sensenbrenner**	Y	N	Y	N	N	Y
6 **Grothman**	Y	Y	Y	Y	Y	Y
7 **Duffy**	Y	N	Y	Y	Y	Y
8 **Gallagher**	Y	Y	Y	Y	Y	Y
WYOMING						
AL **Cheney**	Y	Y	Y	Y	Y	Y

⦚ HOUSE VOTES

VOTE NUMBER

410. HR6760. TAX DEDUCTIONS FOR NEW BUSINESS, TAX-FAVORED RETIREMENT ACCOUNTS, AND PERMANENT TAX EXTENSIONS/RULE. Adoption of the rule (H Res 1084) that would provide for House floor consideration of a bill related to new-business tax deductions (HR 6756), a bill related to tax-favored retirement accounts (HR 6757), and a bill that would make many temporary aspects of the individual tax code permanent (HR 6760). Adopted 226-189: R 226-1; D 0-188. Oct. 27, 2018.

411. HR6757. TAX-FAVORED RETIREMENT ACCOUNTS/PASSAGE. Passage of the bill that would make various modifications related to tax-favored retirement accounts. It would provide for the establishment of "pooled" retirement plans by unrelated small businesses that are not in the same trade or industry. It would allow individuals to continue making contributions to a regular IRA after reaching the age of 70 years and six months, exempt individuals who have less than $50,000 in their retirement accounts from having to take required minimum distributions from those accounts after reaching age of 70 years and six months. It would also allow individuals to withdraw up to $7,500 from their retirement plans, without penalty, to help pay for the expenses of a new baby or adopted child. It would establish tax-favored Universal Savings Accounts that could be used by individuals and families for any purpose. Passed 240-177: R 230-0; D 10-177. Oct. 27, 2018.

412. HR6756. NEW-BUSINESS TAX DEDUCTIONS/PASSAGE. Passage of the bill that would allow individual taxpayers, beginning in tax year 2019, to deduct up to $20,000 during a year in which they start a new business for expenses related to business start-up. It would allow up to $120,000 of such expenses to be amortized over 15 years. It would allow the thresholds to be adjusted for inflation annually, beginning in 2020. Passed 260-156: R 229-0; D 31-156. Oct. 27, 2018.

413. HR6760. PERMANENT TAX EXTENSIONS/RECOMMIT. Larson, D-Conn., motion to recommit the bill to the House Ways and Means Committee with instructions to report it back immediately with an amendment that would prevent enactment of the bill's provisions until actuaries from the Medicare Hospital Insurance Trust Fund and the Old-Age and Survivor Insurance and Disability Insurance Trust Funds certify that the measure would not cause financial harm to such trust funds. Motion rejected 184-226: R 0-226; D 184-0. Oct. 28, 2018.

414. HR6760. PERMANENT TAX EXTENSIONS/PASSAGE. Passage of the bill that would make permanent a number of tax provisions that would otherwise expire in 2025. The provisions from the 2017 tax overhaul (PL 115-97) that would become permanent include: reduced tax rates and modified tax bracket breakpoints for the seven tax brackets, the standard deduction amount, the elimination of personal exemptions for each taxpayer and dependent, and the increased child tax credit. Passed 220-191: R 217-10; D 3-181. Oct. 28, 2018.

415. HRES1099. OPIOID ABUSE PREVENTION AND HEALTH PROGRAMS/ ADOPTION. Walden, R-Ore., motion to suspend the rules and adopt the resolution that would provide for the concurrence by the House in the Senate amendment to HR 6, with an amendment that would modify Medicare and Medicaid and a variety of other health programs in relation to opioid abuse. It would expand both Medicare and Medicaid to cover medication-assisted treatment for substance use disorder and would place new requirements on states regarding Medicaid drug review and utilization requirements. It would appropriate $15 million annually, from fiscal 2019 through 2023, to support the establishment or operation of public health laboratories to detect synthetic opioids. As amended, the bill would allow Medicaid patients with opioid use or cocaine use disorders to stay up to 30 days per year in certain treatment facilities with more than 16 beds. Motion agreed to 393-8: R 215-8; D 178-0. Oct. 28, 2018.

	410	411	412	413	414	415
ALABAMA						
1 **Byrne**	Y	Y	Y	N	Y	Y
2 **Roby**	Y	Y	Y	N	Y	Y
3 **Rogers**	Y	Y	Y	N	Y	Y
4 **Aderholt**	Y	Y	Y	N	Y	Y
5 **Brooks**	Y	Y	Y	N	Y	Y
6 **Palmer**	Y	Y	Y	N	Y	Y
7 Sewell	N	N	N	Y	N	Y
ALASKA						
AL **Young**	Y	Y	Y	N	Y	Y
ARIZONA						
1 O'Halleran	N	N	Y	Y	N	Y
2 **McSally**	Y	Y	Y	N	Y	Y
3 Grijalva	N	N	N	Y	N	Y
4 **Gosar**	Y	Y	Y	N	Y	N
5 **Biggs**	Y	Y	Y	N	Y	N
6 **Schweikert**	Y	Y	Y	N	Y	Y
7 Gallego	N	N	N	Y	N	Y
8 **Lesko**	Y	Y	Y	N	Y	Y
9 Sinema	N	Y	Y	Y	Y	Y
ARKANSAS						
1 **Crawford**	Y	Y	Y	N	Y	Y
2 **Hill**	Y	Y	Y	–	Y	Y
3 **Womack**	Y	Y	Y	N	Y	Y
4 **Westerman**	Y	Y	Y	N	Y	Y
CALIFORNIA						
1 **LaMalfa**	Y	Y	Y	N	Y	Y
2 Huffman	N	N	N	Y	N	Y
3 Garamendi	N	N	N	Y	N	Y
4 **McClintock**	Y	Y	Y	N	Y	N
5 Thompson	N	N	N	Y	N	Y
6 Matsui	N	N	N	Y	N	Y
7 Bera	N	N	Y	Y	N	Y
8 **Cook**	Y	Y	Y	N	Y	Y
9 McNerney	N	N	N	Y	N	Y
10 **Denham**	Y	Y	Y	N	Y	Y
11 DeSaulnier	N	N	N	Y	N	Y
12 Pelosi	N	N	N	Y	N	?
13 Lee	N	N	N	Y	N	Y
14 Speier	N	N	N	Y	N	Y
15 Swalwell	N	N	N	Y	N	Y
16 Costa	N	N	N	Y	N	Y
17 Khanna	N	N	N	Y	N	Y
18 Eshoo	?	?	?	+	–	+
19 Lofgren	N	N	N	Y	N	Y
20 Panetta	N	N	N	Y	N	Y
21 **Valadao**	Y	Y	Y	N	Y	Y
22 **Nunes**	Y	Y	Y	N	Y	Y
23 **McCarthy**	Y	Y	Y	N	Y	Y
24 Carbajal	N	N	Y	Y	N	Y
25 **Knight**	Y	Y	Y	N	Y	Y
26 Brownley	N	N	Y	Y	N	Y
27 Chu	N	N	N	Y	N	Y
28 Schiff	N	N	N	Y	N	Y
29 Cardenas	N	N	N	Y	N	Y
30 Sherman	N	N	N	Y	N	Y
31 Aguilar	N	N	Y	Y	N	Y
32 Napolitano	N	N	N	Y	N	Y
33 Lieu	N	N	N	Y	N	Y
34 Gomez	N	N	N	Y	N	?
35 Torres	N	N	N	Y	N	Y
36 Ruiz	N	N	N	Y	N	Y
37 Bass	N	N	N	Y	N	Y
38 Sánchez, Linda	N	N	N	Y	N	Y
39 **Royce**	Y	Y	Y	N	Y	Y
40 Roybal-Allard	N	N	N	Y	N	Y
41 Takano	N	N	N	Y	N	Y
42 **Calvert**	Y	Y	Y	N	Y	Y
43 Waters	N	N	N	Y	N	Y
44 Barragan	N	N	N	Y	N	Y
45 **Walters**	Y	Y	Y	N	Y	Y
46 Correa	N	Y	Y	Y	N	Y
47 Lowenthal	N	N	N	Y	N	Y
48 **Rohrabacher**	Y	Y	Y	N	Y	Y
49 **Issa**	Y	Y	Y	N	Y	Y
50 **Hunter**	Y	Y	Y	?	?	?
51 Vargas	N	N	N	Y	N	Y
52 Peters	N	N	N	Y	N	Y
53 Davis	N	N	N	Y	N	Y
COLORADO						
1 DeGette	N	N	N	Y	N	Y
2 Polis	N	Y	N	Y	N	Y
3 **Tipton**	Y	Y	Y	N	Y	Y
4 **Buck**	Y	Y	Y	N	Y	Y
5 **Lamborn**	Y	Y	Y	N	Y	Y
6 **Coffman**	Y	Y	Y	N	Y	Y
7 Perlmutter	N	N	N	Y	N	Y
CONNECTICUT						
1 Larson	N	N	N	Y	N	Y
2 Courtney	N	N	N	Y	N	Y
3 DeLauro	N	N	N	Y	N	Y
4 Himes	N	N	N	Y	N	Y
5 Esty	N	N	N	Y	N	Y
DELAWARE						
AL Blunt Rochester	N	N	N	Y	N	Y
FLORIDA						
1 **Gaetz**	Y	Y	Y	N	Y	N
2 **Dunn**	Y	Y	Y	N	Y	Y
3 **Yoho**	Y	Y	Y	N	Y	Y
4 **Rutherford**	Y	Y	Y	N	Y	Y
5 Lawson	N	N	Y	N	Y	N
6 **Vacant**						
7 Murphy	N	Y	Y	Y	N	Y
8 **Posey**	Y	Y	Y	N	Y	Y
9 Soto	N	N	N	Y	N	Y
10 Demings	N	N	N	Y	N	?
11 **Webster**	Y	Y	Y	N	Y	Y
12 **Bilirakis**	Y	Y	Y	N	Y	Y
13 Crist	N	N	Y	Y	N	Y
14 Castor	N	N	N	Y	N	Y
15 **Ross**	Y	Y	Y	N	Y	Y
16 **Buchanan**	Y	Y	Y	N	Y	Y
17 **Rooney, T.**	?	?	?	N	Y	Y
18 **Mast**	Y	Y	Y	N	Y	Y
19 **Rooney, F.**	Y	Y	Y	N	Y	Y
20 Hastings	N	N	N	Y	N	Y
21 Frankel	N	N	N	Y	N	Y
22 Deutch	N	N	N	Y	N	Y
23 Wasserman Schultz	N	N	N	Y	N	Y
24 Wilson	N	N	N	Y	N	?
25 **Diaz-Balart**	Y	Y	Y	N	Y	Y
26 **Curbelo**	Y	Y	Y	N	Y	Y
27 **Ros-Lehtinen**	Y	Y	Y	N	Y	Y
GEORGIA						
1 **Carter**	Y	Y	Y	N	Y	Y
2 Bishop	N	Y	Y	N	Y	Y
3 **Ferguson**	Y	Y	Y	N	Y	Y
4 Johnson	N	N	N	Y	N	Y
5 Lewis	N	N	N	Y	N	Y
6 **Handel**	Y	Y	Y	N	Y	Y
7 **Woodall**	Y	Y	Y	N	Y	Y
8 **Scott, A.**	Y	Y	Y	N	Y	Y
9 **Collins**	Y	Y	Y	N	Y	Y
10 **Hice**	Y	Y	Y	N	Y	Y
11 **Loudermilk**	Y	Y	Y	N	Y	Y
12 **Allen**	Y	Y	Y	N	Y	Y
13 Scott, D.	N	N	N	Y	N	Y
14 **Graves**	Y	Y	Y	N	Y	Y
HAWAII						
1 Hanabusa	N	N	N	Y	N	Y
2 Gabbard	N	N	N	?	?	?
IDAHO						
1 **Labrador**	Y	Y	Y	?	?	?
2 **Simpson**	Y	Y	Y	N	Y	Y
ILLINOIS						
1 Rush	N	?	?	?	?	?
2 Kelly	N	N	N	Y	N	Y
3 Lipinski	N	Y	Y	Y	N	Y
4 Gutierrez	N	N	N	?	?	?
5 Quigley	N	N	N	Y	N	Y
6 **Roskam**	Y	Y	Y	N	Y	Y
7 Davis, D.	N	N	N	Y	N	Y
8 Krishnamoorthi	N	N	N	Y	N	Y
9 Schakowsky	N	N	N	Y	N	Y
10 Schneider	N	N	N	Y	N	Y
11 Foster	N	N	N	Y	N	Y
12 **Bost**	Y	Y	Y	N	Y	Y
13 **Davis, R.**	Y	Y	Y	N	Y	Y

KEY   Republicans   Democrats   *Independents*

Y Voted for (yea)	X Paired against	C Voted "present" to avoid possible conflict of interest
# Paired for	– Announced against	
+ Announced for	P Voted "present"	? Did not vote or otherwise make a position known
N Voted against (nay)		

	410	411	412	413	414	415
14 **Hultgren**	Y	Y	Y	N	Y	Y
15 **Shimkus**	Y	Y	Y	N	Y	Y
16 **Kinzinger**	Y	Y	Y	N	Y	Y
17 Bustos	N	N	N	Y	N	Y
18 **LaHood**	Y	Y	Y	N	Y	Y
INDIANA						
1 Visclosky	N	N	N	Y	N	Y
2 **Walorski**	Y	Y	Y	N	Y	Y
3 **Banks**	Y	Y	Y	N	Y	Y
4 Rokita	Y	Y	Y	?	?	?
5 **Brooks**	Y	Y	Y	N	Y	Y
6 **Messer**	Y	Y	Y	N	Y	Y
7 Carson	N	N	N	Y	N	Y
8 **Bucshon**	Y	Y	Y	N	Y	Y
9 **Hollingsworth**	Y	Y	Y	N	Y	Y
IOWA						
1 **Blum**	Y	Y	Y	N	Y	Y
2 Loebsack	N	N	Y	Y	N	Y
3 **Young**	Y	Y	Y	N	Y	Y
4 **King**	Y	Y	Y	N	Y	Y
KANSAS						
1 **Marshall**	Y	Y	Y	N	Y	Y
2 **Jenkins**	Y	Y	Y	N	Y	Y
3 **Yoder**	Y	Y	Y	N	Y	Y
4 **Estes**	Y	Y	Y	N	Y	Y
KENTUCKY						
1 **Comer**	Y	Y	Y	N	Y	Y
2 **Guthrie**	Y	Y	Y	N	Y	Y
3 Yarmuth	N	N	N	Y	N	Y
4 **Massie**	Y	Y	Y	N	Y	N
5 **Rogers**	Y	Y	Y	N	Y	Y
6 **Barr**	Y	Y	Y	N	Y	Y
LOUISIANA						
1 **Scalise**	Y	Y	Y	N	Y	Y
2 Richmond	N	N	N	Y	N	Y
3 **Higgins**	Y	Y	Y	N	Y	Y
4 **Johnson**	Y	Y	Y	N	Y	Y
5 **Abraham**	Y	Y	Y	N	Y	Y
6 **Graves**	Y	Y	Y	N	Y	Y
MAINE						
1 Pingree	N	N	N	Y	N	Y
2 **Poliquin**	Y	Y	Y	N	Y	Y
MARYLAND						
1 **Harris**	Y	Y	Y	N	Y	Y
2 Ruppersberger	N	N	N	Y	N	Y
3 Sarbanes	N	N	N	Y	N	Y
4 Brown	N	N	N	Y	N	Y
5 Hoyer	N	N	N	Y	N	Y
6 Delaney	N	N	Y	Y	N	Y
7 Cummings	N	N	N	Y	N	Y
8 Raskin	N	N	N	Y	N	Y
MASSACHUSETTS						
1 Neal	N	N	N	Y	N	Y
2 McGovern	N	N	N	Y	N	Y
3 Tsongas	N	N	N	Y	N	Y
4 Kennedy	N	N	N	Y	N	Y
5 Clark	N	N	N	Y	N	Y
6 Moulton	N	N	N	+	–	+
7 Capuano	N	N	N	Y	N	Y
8 Lynch	N	N	N	Y	N	Y
9 Keating	N	N	N	Y	N	Y
MICHIGAN						
1 **Bergman**	Y	Y	Y	N	Y	Y
2 **Huizenga**	Y	Y	Y	N	Y	Y
3 *Amash*	N	Y	Y	N	Y	N
4 **Moolenaar**	Y	Y	Y	N	Y	Y
5 Kildee	N	N	N	Y	N	Y
6 **Upton**	Y	Y	Y	N	Y	Y
7 **Walberg**	Y	Y	Y	N	Y	Y
8 **Bishop**	Y	Y	Y	N	Y	Y
9 Levin	N	N	N	Y	N	Y
10 **Mitchell**	Y	Y	Y	N	Y	Y
11 **Trott**	Y	Y	Y	N	Y	Y
12 Dingell	N	N	N	Y	N	Y
14 Lawrence	N	N	N	Y	N	Y
MINNESOTA						
1 Walz	?	?	?	?	?	?
2 **Lewis**	Y	Y	Y	N	Y	Y
3 **Paulsen**	Y	Y	Y	N	Y	Y
4 McCollum	N	N	N	Y	N	Y
5 Ellison	?	?	?	?	?	?
6 **Emmer**	Y	Y	Y	N	Y	Y
7 Peterson	N	Y	Y	Y	N	Y
8 Nolan	?	?	?	?	?	?
MISSISSIPPI						
1 **Kelly**	Y	Y	Y	N	Y	Y
2 Thompson	N	N	N	Y	N	Y
3 **Harper**	?	?	?	?	?	?
4 **Palazzo**	Y	Y	Y	N	Y	Y
MISSOURI						
1 Clay	N	N	N	Y	N	Y
2 **Wagner**	Y	Y	Y	N	Y	Y
3 **Luetkemeyer**	Y	Y	Y	N	Y	Y
4 **Hartzler**	Y	Y	Y	N	Y	Y
5 Cleaver	N	N	N	Y	N	Y
6 **Graves**	Y	Y	Y	N	Y	Y
7 **Long**	Y	Y	Y	N	Y	Y
8 **Smith**	Y	Y	Y	N	Y	Y
MONTANA						
AL **Gianforte**	Y	Y	Y	N	Y	Y
NEBRASKA						
1 **Fortenberry**	Y	Y	Y	N	Y	Y
2 **Bacon**	Y	Y	Y	N	Y	Y
3 **Smith**	Y	Y	Y	N	Y	Y
NEVADA						
1 Titus	N	N	Y	Y	N	Y
2 **Amodei**	Y	Y	Y	N	Y	Y
3 Rosen	N	N	Y	Y	Y	Y
4 Kihuen	N	N	N	Y	N	Y
NEW HAMPSHIRE						
1 Shea-Porter	N	N	N	Y	N	Y
2 Kuster	N	N	Y	Y	N	Y
NEW JERSEY						
1 Norcross	N	N	N	Y	N	Y
2 **LoBiondo**	Y	Y	Y	N	N	Y
3 **MacArthur**	Y	Y	Y	N	Y	Y
4 **Smith**	Y	Y	Y	N	N	Y
5 Gottheimer	N	Y	Y	Y	N	Y
6 Pallone	N	N	N	Y	N	Y
7 **Lance**	Y	Y	Y	N	N	Y
8 Sires	N	N	N	Y	N	Y
9 Pascrell	N	N	N	Y	N	Y
10 Payne	N	N	N	Y	N	Y
11 **Frelinghuysen**	Y	Y	Y	N	N	Y
12 Watson Coleman	N	N	N	Y	N	Y
NEW MEXICO						
1 Lujan Grisham	?	?	?	?	?	?
2 **Pearce**	Y	Y	Y	N	Y	Y
3 Luján	N	N	N	Y	N	Y
NEW YORK						
1 **Zeldin**	Y	Y	Y	N	N	Y
2 **King**	Y	Y	Y	N	N	Y
3 Suozzi	N	N	Y	Y	N	Y
4 Rice	N	N	Y	Y	N	Y
5 Meeks	N	N	N	Y	N	Y
6 Meng	N	N	N	Y	N	Y
7 Velázquez	N	N	N	Y	N	Y
8 Jeffries	N	N	N	Y	N	Y
9 Clarke	N	N	N	Y	N	Y
10 Nadler	N	N	N	Y	N	Y
11 **Donovan**	Y	Y	Y	N	N	Y
12 Maloney, C.	N	N	N	Y	N	Y
13 Espaillat	N	N	N	Y	N	Y
14 Crowley	N	N	N	Y	N	Y
15 Serrano	N	N	N	Y	N	Y
16 Engel	N	N	N	Y	N	Y
17 Lowey	N	N	N	Y	N	Y
18 Maloney, S.P.	N	N	Y	Y	N	Y
19 **Faso**	Y	Y	Y	N	N	Y
20 Tonko	N	N	N	Y	N	Y
21 **Stefanik**	Y	Y	Y	N	N	Y
22 **Tenney**	Y	Y	Y	N	Y	Y
23 **Reed**	Y	Y	Y	N	Y	Y
24 **Katko**	Y	Y	Y	N	Y	Y
25 **Vacant**						
26 Higgins	N	N	N	Y	N	Y
27 **Collins**	Y	Y	Y	N	Y	Y
NORTH CAROLINA						
1 Butterfield	N	N	N	Y	N	Y
2 **Holding**	Y	Y	Y	N	Y	Y
3 **Jones**	?	?	?	?	?	?
4 Price	N	N	N	Y	N	Y
5 **Foxx**	Y	Y	Y	N	Y	Y
6 **Walker**	Y	Y	Y	N	Y	Y
7 **Rouzer**	Y	Y	Y	N	Y	Y
8 **Hudson**	Y	Y	Y	N	Y	Y
9 **Pittenger**	Y	Y	Y	N	Y	Y
9 **Vacant**						
10 **McHenry**	Y	Y	Y	N	Y	Y
11 **Meadows**	Y	Y	Y	N	Y	Y
12 Adams	N	N	N	Y	N	Y
13 **Budd**	Y	Y	Y	N	Y	Y
NORTH DAKOTA						
AL **Cramer**	Y	Y	Y	N	Y	Y
OHIO						
1 **Chabot**	Y	Y	Y	N	Y	Y
2 **Wenstrup**	Y	Y	Y	N	Y	Y
3 Beatty	N	N	N	Y	N	Y
4 **Jordan**	Y	Y	Y	N	Y	Y
5 **Latta**	Y	Y	Y	N	Y	Y
6 **Johnson**	Y	Y	Y	N	Y	Y
7 **Gibbs**	Y	Y	Y	N	Y	Y
8 **Davidson**	Y	Y	Y	N	Y	Y
9 Kaptur	N	N	N	Y	N	Y
10 **Turner**	Y	Y	Y	N	Y	Y
11 Fudge	N	N	N	Y	N	Y
12 Balderson	Y	Y	Y	N	Y	Y
13 Ryan	N	N	Y	Y	N	Y
14 **Joyce**	Y	Y	Y	N	Y	Y
15 **Stivers**	Y	Y	Y	N	Y	Y
16 **Renacci**	Y	Y	Y	N	Y	Y
OKLAHOMA						
1 **Vacant**						
2 **Mullin**	Y	Y	Y	N	Y	Y
3 **Lucas**	Y	Y	Y	N	Y	Y
4 **Cole**	Y	Y	Y	N	Y	Y
5 **Russell**	Y	Y	Y	N	Y	Y
OREGON						
1 Bonamici	N	N	N	Y	N	Y
2 **Walden**	Y	Y	Y	N	Y	Y
3 Blumenauer	N	N	N	Y	N	Y
4 DeFazio	N	N	N	Y	N	Y
5 Schrader	N	N	N	Y	N	Y
PENNSYLVANIA						
1 Brady	N	N	N	Y	N	Y
2 Evans	N	N	N	Y	N	Y
3 **Kelly**	Y	Y	Y	N	Y	Y
4 **Perry**	Y	Y	Y	N	Y	Y
5 **Thompson**	Y	Y	Y	N	Y	Y
6 **Costello**	Y	Y	Y	N	Y	Y
7 **Vacant**						
8 **Fitzpatrick**	Y	Y	Y	N	Y	Y
9 **Shuster**	Y	Y	Y	N	Y	Y
10 **Marino**	Y	Y	Y	N	Y	Y
11 **Barletta**	?	Y	Y	N	Y	Y
12 **Rothfus**	Y	Y	Y	N	Y	Y
13 Boyle	N	N	N	Y	N	Y
14 Doyle	N	N	Y	Y	N	Y
15 **Vacant**						
16 **Smucker**	Y	Y	Y	N	Y	Y
17 Cartwright	N	N	Y	Y	N	Y
18 Lamb	N	Y	Y	Y	Y	Y
RHODE ISLAND						
1 Cicilline	N	N	N	Y	N	Y
2 Langevin	N	N	N	Y	N	Y
SOUTH CAROLINA						
1 **Sanford**	Y	Y	Y	N	Y	N
2 **Wilson**	Y	Y	Y	N	Y	Y
3 **Duncan**	Y	Y	Y	N	Y	Y
4 **Gowdy**	Y	Y	Y	N	Y	Y
5 **Norman**	Y	Y	Y	N	Y	Y
6 Clyburn	N	N	N	Y	N	?
7 **Rice**	Y	Y	Y	N	Y	Y
SOUTH DAKOTA						
AL **Noem**	Y	Y	Y	N	Y	Y
TENNESSEE						
1 **Roe**	Y	Y	Y	N	Y	Y
2 **Duncan**	Y	Y	Y	N	Y	Y
3 **Fleischmann**	Y	Y	Y	N	Y	Y
4 **DesJarlais**	?	Y	Y	N	Y	Y
5 Cooper	N	N	N	Y	N	Y
6 **Black**	Y	Y	Y	N	Y	Y
7 **Blackburn**	?	?	?	?	?	?
8 **Kustoff**	Y	Y	Y	N	Y	Y
9 Cohen	N	N	N	Y	N	Y
TEXAS						
1 **Gohmert**	Y	Y	Y	N	Y	?
2 **Poe**	Y	Y	Y	N	Y	Y
3 **Johnson, S.**	Y	Y	Y	N	Y	Y
4 **Ratcliffe**	Y	Y	Y	N	Y	Y
5 **Hensarling**	Y	Y	Y	N	Y	Y
6 **Barton**	Y	Y	Y	N	?	?
7 **Culberson**	Y	Y	Y	N	Y	Y
8 **Brady**	Y	Y	Y	N	Y	Y
9 Green, A.	N	N	N	Y	N	Y
10 **McCaul**	Y	Y	Y	N	Y	Y
11 **Conaway**	Y	Y	Y	N	Y	Y
12 **Granger**	Y	Y	Y	N	Y	+
13 **Thornberry**	Y	Y	Y	N	Y	Y
14 **Weber**	Y	Y	Y	N	Y	Y
15 Gonzalez	N	N	N	Y	N	Y
16 O'Rourke	N	N	Y	Y	N	Y
17 **Flores**	Y	Y	Y	N	Y	Y
18 Jackson Lee	N	N	N	Y	N	Y
19 **Arrington**	Y	Y	Y	N	Y	Y
20 Castro	N	N	N	Y	N	?
21 **Smith**	Y	Y	Y	N	Y	Y
22 **Olson**	Y	Y	Y	–	+	+
23 **Hurd**	Y	Y	Y	N	Y	Y
24 Marchant	Y	Y	Y	N	Y	Y
25 **Williams**	Y	Y	Y	?	?	?
26 **Burgess**	Y	Y	Y	N	Y	Y
27 Cloud	Y	Y	Y	N	Y	Y
28 Cuellar	N	Y	Y	Y	N	Y
29 Green, G.	N	N	N	Y	N	Y
30 Johnson, E.B.	N	N	N	Y	N	Y
31 **Carter**	Y	Y	Y	N	Y	Y
32 **Sessions**	Y	Y	Y	N	Y	Y
33 Veasey	N	N	N	Y	N	Y
34 Vela	N	N	N	Y	N	Y
35 Doggett	N	N	N	Y	N	Y
36 **Babin**	Y	Y	Y	N	Y	Y
UTAH						
1 **Bishop**	Y	Y	Y	N	Y	Y
2 **Stewart**	Y	Y	Y	N	Y	Y
3 **Curtis**	Y	Y	Y	N	Y	Y
4 **Love**	Y	Y	Y	N	Y	Y
VERMONT						
AL Welch	N	N	N	Y	N	Y
VIRGINIA						
1 **Wittman**	Y	Y	Y	N	Y	Y
2 **Taylor**	Y	Y	Y	N	Y	Y
3 Scott	N	N	N	Y	N	Y
4 McEachin	N	N	N	Y	N	Y
5 **Garrett**	Y	Y	Y	N	Y	N
6 **Goodlatte**	Y	Y	Y	N	Y	Y
7 **Brat**	Y	Y	Y	N	Y	Y
8 Beyer	N	N	N	Y	N	Y
9 **Griffith**	Y	Y	Y	N	Y	Y
10 **Comstock**	Y	Y	Y	N	Y	Y
11 Connolly	N	N	N	Y	N	Y
WASHINGTON						
1 DelBene	N	N	N	Y	N	Y
2 Larsen	N	N	N	Y	N	Y
3 **Herrera Beutler**	Y	Y	Y	N	Y	Y
4 **Newhouse**	+	+	+	N	Y	Y
5 **McMorris Rodgers**	Y	Y	Y	N	Y	Y
6 Kilmer	N	N	N	Y	N	Y
7 Jayapal	N	N	N	Y	N	Y
8 **Reichert**	Y	Y	Y	N	Y	Y
9 Smith	N	N	N	Y	N	Y
10 Heck	N	N	N	Y	N	Y
WEST VIRGINIA						
1 **McKinley**	Y	Y	Y	N	Y	Y
2 **Mooney**	Y	Y	Y	N	Y	Y
3 **Jenkins**	?	Y	?	N	Y	Y
WISCONSIN						
1 **Ryan**					Y	
2 Pocan	N	N	N	Y	N	Y
3 Kind	N	N	N	Y	N	Y
4 Moore	N	N	N	Y	N	Y
5 **Sensenbrenner**	Y	Y	Y	N	Y	Y
6 **Grothman**	Y	Y	Y	N	Y	Y
7 **Duffy**	Y	Y	Y	N	Y	Y
8 **Gallagher**	Y	Y	Y	N	Y	Y
WYOMING						
AL **Cheney**	Y	Y	Y	N	Y	?

VOTE NUMBER

416. HR6064. WOLFF NATIONAL WILDLIFE REFUGE/PASSAGE. Lamborn, R-Colo., motion to suspend the rules and pass the bill that would rename the Oyster Bay National Wildlife Refuge in Oyster Bay, N.Y. as the "Congressman Lester Wolff National Wildlife Refuge." Motion agreed to 385-4: R 209-4; D 176-0. Sept. 13, 2018.

417. HR2615. GULF ISLANDS NATIONAL SEASHORE LAND CONVEYANCE/ PASSAGE. Gosar, R-Ariz., motion to suspend the rules and concur in the Senate amendment to the bill that would authorize an exchange of certain lands in the Gulf Islands National Seashore, Miss., between the National Park Service and the Veterans of Foreign Wars. Motion agreed to 375-1: R 206-1; D 169-0. Sept. 13, 2018.

418. HR6784. DELISTING GRAY WOLVES AS ENDANGERED SPECIES/RULE. Adoption of the rule (H Res 1142) providing for House floor consideration of the bill (HR 6784) that would provide for removal of the gray wolf in the contiguous 48 States from the List of Endangered and Threatened Wildlife published under the Endangered Species Act of 1973; and providing for proceedings during the period from November 19, 2018, through November 26, 2018. The rule would also waive section 7 of the War Powers Resolution for a resolution (H Con Res 138) that would direct the president to withdraw U.S. armed forces from hostilities in Yemen. Adopted 201-187: R 195-15; D 6-172. Sept. 14, 2018.

419. HR5787. CHAFEE COASTAL BARRIER SYSTEM BOUNDARY UPDATE/ PASSAGE. Lamborn, R-Colo., motion to suspend the rules and pass the bill (HR 5787), as amended, that would formally update maps of the John H. Chafee Coastal Barrier Resources System in Delaware, North Carolina, South Carolina, Florida and Louisiana, and would require the U.S. Fish and Wildlife Service to make updated maps publicly available online. Motion agreed to 375-1: R 198-1; D 177-0. Sept. 16, 2018.

420. HR6784. DELISTING GRAY WOLVES AS ENDANGERED SPECIES/ PASSAGE. Passage of a bill that would direct the U.S. Fish and Wildlife Service to issue a rule removing the gray wolf from the list of endangered and threatened wildlife, thus removing federal protections for the species, in the 48 contiguous United States. It would also direct the Interior Department to reissue a 2011 rule delisting gray wolves in the Western Great Lakes region of Minnesota, Wisconsin, and Michigan, and would exempt both rules, and another rule delisting the species in Wyoming, from judicial review. Passed 196-180: R 187-12; D 9-168. Sept. 16, 2018.

421. HR5273. GLOBAL CONFLICT STABILIZATION/PASSAGE. Royce, R-Calif., motion to suspend the rules and pass the bill, as amended, that would direct the secretary of State to develop an interagency initiative to prevent violence and stabilize conflict-affected areas worldwide, in coordination with relevant federal departments and agencies, including the U.S. Agency for International Development and Department of Defense. It would require the secretary to submit to Congress 10-year plans for stabilization and prevention in at least six regions within 180 days of enactment. Motion agreed to 376-16: R 193-16; D 183-0. Sept. 27, 2018.

	416	417	418	419	420	421
ALABAMA						
1 Byrne	Y	Y	Y	Y	Y	Y
2 Roby	Y	Y	Y	?	?	Y
3 Rogers	Y	Y	Y	Y	Y	Y
4 Aderholt	Y	Y	Y	Y	Y	Y
5 Brooks	Y	Y	Y	Y	Y	N
6 Palmer	Y	Y	Y	Y	Y	Y
7 Sewell	Y	Y	N	Y	N	Y
ALASKA						
AL Young	Y	Y	?	Y	Y	Y
ARIZONA						
1 O'Halleran	Y	?	N	Y	N	Y
2 McSally	?	?	Y	Y	Y	Y
3 Grijalva	?	?	N	Y	N	Y
4 Gosar	Y	Y	Y	Y	Y	N
5 Biggs	N	Y	N	Y	Y	N
6 Schweikert	Y	Y	Y	Y	Y	Y
7 Gallego	Y	Y	N	Y	N	Y
8 Lesko	Y	Y	Y	Y	Y	Y
9 Sinema	Y	Y	N	Y	N	Y
ARKANSAS						
1 Crawford	Y	Y	Y	Y	Y	Y
2 Hill	Y	Y	Y	Y	Y	Y
3 Womack	Y	Y	Y	Y	Y	Y
4 Westerman	Y	Y	Y	Y	Y	Y
CALIFORNIA						
1 LaMalfa	Y	Y	Y	Y	Y	?
2 Huffman	Y	Y	N	Y	N	Y
3 Garamendi	Y	Y	N	Y	N	Y
4 McClintock	Y	Y	Y	Y	Y	Y
5 Thompson	Y	Y	N	Y	N	Y
6 Matsui	Y	?	N	Y	N	Y
7 Bera	Y	Y	N	Y	N	Y
8 Cook	Y	Y	Y	Y	Y	Y
9 McNerney	Y	Y	N	Y	N	Y
10 Denham	Y	Y	?	?	?	?
11 DeSaulnier	+	+	N	Y	N	Y
12 Pelosi	Y	Y	N	Y	N	Y
13 Lee	Y	Y	N	Y	N	Y
14 Speier	Y	?	N	Y	N	Y
15 Swalwell	Y	Y	N	+	-	Y
16 Costa	Y	Y	Y	Y	Y	Y
17 Khanna	Y	Y	N	Y	N	Y
18 Eshoo	Y	Y	N	Y	N	Y
19 Lofgren	Y	Y	N	Y	N	Y
20 Panetta	Y	Y	-	Y	N	Y
21 Valadao	Y	Y	Y	Y	Y	?
22 Nunes	Y	Y	Y	?	?	Y
23 McCarthy	Y	Y	Y	Y	Y	Y
24 Carbajal	Y	Y	N	Y	N	Y
25 Knight	?	?	Y	Y	Y	?
26 Brownley	?	?	?	?	?	Y
27 Chu	Y	Y	N	Y	N	Y
28 Schiff	Y	Y	N	Y	N	Y
29 Cardenas	Y	Y	N	Y	N	Y
30 Sherman	Y	Y	N	Y	N	Y
31 Aguilar	Y	Y	N	Y	N	Y
32 Napolitano	Y	Y	N	Y	N	Y
33 Lieu	Y	?	N	Y	N	Y
34 Gomez	Y	Y	-	Y	N	Y
35 Torres	?	Y	N	Y	N	Y
36 Ruiz	Y	Y	N	Y	N	Y
37 Bass	Y	Y	N	Y	N	Y
38 Sánchez, Linda	Y	Y	N	Y	N	Y
39 Royce	Y	Y	Y	Y	Y	?
40 Roybal-Allard	Y	Y	N	Y	N	Y
41 Takano	Y	Y	N	Y	N	Y
42 Calvert	Y	Y	Y	Y	Y	Y
43 Waters	Y	Y	N	Y	N	Y
44 Barragan	Y	Y	N	Y	N	Y
45 Walters	Y	Y	?	Y	Y	?
46 Correa	Y	Y	N	Y	N	Y
47 Lowenthal	Y	Y	N	Y	N	Y
48 Rohrabacher	Y	Y	Y	Y	Y	Y
49 Issa	Y	?	Y	Y	Y	Y
50 Hunter	Y	Y	Y	Y	?	Y
51 Vargas	Y	Y	N	Y	N	Y
52 Peters	?	?	?	?	?	Y
53 Davis	Y	Y	N	Y	N	Y
COLORADO						
1 DeGette	Y	Y	N	Y	N	Y
2 Polis	?	?	?	?	?	Y
3 Tipton	Y	Y	Y	Y	Y	?
4 Buck	Y	Y	Y	Y	Y	Y
5 Lamborn	Y	Y	Y	Y	Y	Y
6 Coffman	Y	Y	Y	Y	Y	Y
7 Perlmutter	Y	Y	-	Y	N	Y
CONNECTICUT						
1 Larson	Y	Y	-	Y	N	Y
2 Courtney	Y	Y	N	Y	N	Y
3 DeLauro	Y	Y	N	Y	N	Y
4 Himes	?	Y	N	Y	N	Y
5 Esty	Y	Y	-	Y	N	Y
DELAWARE						
AL Blunt Rochester	Y	Y	N	Y	N	Y
FLORIDA						
1 Gaetz	?	?	Y	Y	Y	N
2 Dunn	Y	Y	Y	Y	Y	Y
3 Yoho	Y	Y	Y	?	?	Y
4 Rutherford	Y	Y	Y	Y	Y	Y
5 Lawson	Y	Y	N	Y	N	Y
6 Vacant						
7 Murphy	?	Y	N	Y	N	Y
8 Posey	Y	Y	N	Y	N	Y
9 Soto	Y	Y	N	Y	N	Y
10 Demings	Y	Y	N	Y	N	Y
11 Webster	Y	Y	Y	Y	Y	Y
12 Bilirakis	Y	Y	Y	Y	Y	Y
13 Crist	Y	Y	N	Y	N	Y
14 Castor	Y	Y	N	Y	N	Y
15 Ross	Y	Y	?	?	?	Y
16 Buchanan	Y	?	Y	Y	N	Y
17 Rooney, T.	?	?	Y	?	?	?
18 Mast	Y	Y	Y	Y	Y	Y
19 Rooney, F.	?	?	Y	+	?	Y
20 Hastings	Y	?	?	?	?	?
21 Frankel	Y	Y	N	Y	N	Y
22 Deutch	Y	Y	N	Y	N	Y
23 Wasserman Schultz	Y	Y	N	Y	N	Y
24 Wilson	?	?	?	Y	N	?
25 Diaz-Balart	Y	Y	Y	Y	Y	Y
26 Curbelo	?	?	Y	Y	N	Y
27 Ros-Lehtinen	Y	Y	Y	?	?	Y
GEORGIA						
1 Carter	Y	Y	Y	Y	Y	Y
2 Bishop	Y	Y	N	Y	Y	Y
3 Ferguson	Y	Y	Y	Y	Y	Y
4 Johnson	Y	Y	?	Y	N	Y
5 Lewis	Y	Y	N	?	N	Y
6 Handel	Y	Y	Y	Y	Y	Y
7 Woodall	Y	Y	?	Y	Y	Y
8 Scott, A.	Y	Y	Y	Y	Y	Y
9 Collins	Y	Y	?	Y	Y	Y
10 Hice	Y	Y	Y	Y	Y	N
11 Loudermilk	Y	Y	Y	Y	Y	N
12 Allen	Y	Y	Y	Y	Y	Y
13 Scott, D.	Y	Y	N	Y	N	Y
14 Graves	Y	Y	Y	Y	Y	Y
HAWAII						
1 Hanabusa	Y	Y	N	Y	N	?
2 Gabbard	Y	Y	N	Y	-	Y
IDAHO						
1 Labrador	Y	Y	N	?	?	?
2 Simpson	Y	Y	Y	Y	Y	Y
ILLINOIS						
1 Rush	Y	Y	N	?	?	?
2 Kelly	Y	Y	N	Y	N	Y
3 Lipinski	Y	Y	N	Y	N	Y
4 Gutierrez	+	+	N	?	?	+
5 Quigley	Y	Y	N	Y	N	Y
6 Roskam	Y	Y	Y	?	?	?
7 Davis, D.	Y	Y	N	Y	N	Y
8 Krishnamoorthi	Y	Y	N	Y	N	Y
9 Schakowsky	Y	Y	N	Y	N	Y
10 Schneider	Y	Y	N	Y	N	Y
11 Foster	Y	Y	N	Y	N	Y
12 Bost	Y	Y	Y	Y	Y	Y
13 Davis, R.	Y	Y	Y	Y	Y	Y

KEY	Republicans	Democrats	Independents
Y Voted for (yea)	**X** Paired against	**C** Voted "present" to avoid possible conflict of interest
# Paired for	**–** Announced against	
+ Announced for	**P** Voted "present"	**?** Did not vote or otherwise make a position known
N Voted against (nay)		

	416	417	418	419	420	421
14 **Hultgren**	Y	Y	?	?	?	Y
15 **Shimkus**	Y	Y	Y	Y	Y	Y
16 **Kinzinger**	+	+	Y	Y	Y	Y
17 Bustos	Y	Y	N	Y	N	Y
18 **LaHood**	Y	Y	Y	Y	Y	Y
INDIANA						
1 Visclosky	Y	Y	–	Y	N	Y
2 **Walorski**	Y	Y	Y	Y	Y	Y
3 **Banks**	Y	Y	Y	Y	Y	Y
4 Rokita	Y	Y	Y	Y	Y	Y
5 **Brooks**	Y	Y	+	Y	Y	Y
6 **Messer**	Y	Y	?	?	Y	?
7 Carson	Y	Y	N	Y	N	Y
8 **Bucshon**	?	?	Y	Y	Y	Y
9 **Hollingsworth**	Y	Y	Y	Y	Y	Y
IOWA						
1 **Blum**	?	?	N	Y	Y	N
2 Loebsack	Y	Y	N	Y	N	Y
3 **Young**	Y	Y	Y	Y	Y	Y
4 **King**	Y	Y	Y	Y	Y	Y
KANSAS						
1 **Marshall**	Y	Y	Y	Y	Y	Y
2 **Jenkins**	?	?	?	?	?	Y
3 **Yoder**	Y	Y	Y	Y	Y	Y
4 **Estes**	Y	Y	Y	Y	Y	Y
KENTUCKY						
1 **Comer**	Y	Y	Y	Y	Y	Y
2 **Guthrie**	Y	Y	Y	Y	Y	Y
3 Yarmuth	Y	Y	N	?	N	Y
4 **Massie**	N	Y	N	N	Y	N
5 **Rogers**	Y	Y	Y	Y	Y	Y
6 **Barr**	Y	Y	Y	Y	Y	Y
LOUISIANA						
1 **Scalise**	Y	Y	Y	Y	Y	Y
2 Richmond	Y	Y	N	Y	N	Y
3 **Higgins**	Y	Y	Y	Y	Y	Y
4 **Johnson**	Y	Y	Y	Y	Y	Y
5 **Abraham**	Y	Y	Y	Y	Y	Y
6 **Graves**	Y	Y	Y	Y	Y	Y
MAINE						
1 Pingree	Y	Y	N	Y	N	Y
2 **Poliquin**	?	?	Y	Y	Y	Y
MARYLAND						
1 **Harris**	Y	Y	?	Y	Y	N
2 Ruppersberger	Y	Y	N	Y	N	Y
3 Sarbanes	Y	Y	N	?	N	Y
4 Brown	Y	Y	N	Y	N	Y
5 Hoyer	Y	Y	N	Y	N	Y
6 Delaney	Y	Y	N	Y	N	Y
7 Cummings	Y	Y	N	Y	N	?
8 Raskin	Y	Y	N	Y	N	Y
MASSACHUSETTS						
1 Neal	Y	Y	N	Y	N	Y
2 McGovern	Y	Y	N	Y	N	Y
3 Tsongas	Y	Y	N	?	?	Y
4 Kennedy	Y	Y	N	Y	N	Y
5 Clark	Y	Y	N	Y	N	Y
6 Moulton	Y	Y	N	Y	N	Y
7 Capuano	?	?	N	?	?	Y
8 Lynch	Y	Y	?	?	?	Y
9 Keating	Y	Y	N	Y	N	Y
MICHIGAN						
1 **Bergman**	Y	Y	Y	Y	Y	Y
2 **Huizenga**	Y	+	Y	Y	Y	Y
3 *Amash*	N	N	N	Y	N	N
4 **Moolenaar**	Y	Y	Y	Y	Y	Y
5 Kildee	Y	Y	N	Y	N	Y
6 **Upton**	Y	Y	Y	?	?	Y
7 **Walberg**	Y	Y	Y	Y	Y	Y
8 **Bishop**	Y	Y	Y	Y	N	?
9 Levin	Y	Y	N	Y	N	Y
10 **Mitchell**	Y	Y	Y	Y	Y	Y
11 **Trott**	Y	Y	Y	Y	Y	Y
12 Dingell	Y	Y	N	Y	N	Y
14 Lawrence	Y	Y	N	Y	N	Y
MINNESOTA						
1 Walz	?	?	N	?	?	?
2 **Lewis**	Y	Y	Y	Y	Y	Y
3 **Paulsen**	Y	Y	Y	Y	Y	Y
4 McCollum	Y	Y	N	Y	N	Y

	416	417	418	419	420	421
5 Ellison	?	?	N	?	?	?
6 **Emmer**	Y	Y	Y	Y	Y	Y
7 Peterson	Y	Y	Y	Y	Y	Y
8 Nolan	?	?	N	?	?	?
MISSISSIPPI						
1 **Kelly**	Y	Y	Y	Y	Y	Y
2 Thompson	Y	Y	N	Y	N	Y
3 **Harper**	?	Y	Y	Y	Y	Y
4 **Palazzo**	Y	Y	Y	Y	Y	Y
MISSOURI						
1 Clay	Y	Y	N	Y	N	Y
2 **Wagner**	Y	Y	Y	Y	Y	Y
3 **Luetkemeyer**	Y	Y	Y	Y	Y	Y
4 **Hartzler**	Y	Y	Y	Y	Y	Y
5 Cleaver	Y	Y	N	Y	N	Y
6 **Graves**	Y	Y	Y	Y	Y	Y
7 **Long**	Y	Y	Y	Y	Y	Y
8 **Smith**	Y	Y	Y	Y	Y	Y
MONTANA						
AL **Gianforte**	Y	Y	Y	Y	Y	Y
NEBRASKA						
1 **Fortenberry**	Y	Y	Y	Y	Y	Y
2 **Bacon**	Y	Y	Y	Y	Y	Y
3 **Smith**	Y	Y	Y	Y	Y	Y
NEVADA						
1 Titus	Y	Y	N	Y	N	Y
2 **Amodei**	Y	Y	Y	Y	Y	?
3 Rosen	Y	Y	N	Y	N	Y
4 Kihuen	Y	Y	N	Y	N	Y
NEW HAMPSHIRE						
1 Shea-Porter	Y	Y	N	Y	N	Y
2 Kuster	Y	Y	N	Y	N	Y
NEW JERSEY						
1 Norcross	Y	Y	?	Y	N	Y
2 **LoBiondo**	Y	Y	Y	Y	N	Y
3 **MacArthur**	Y	Y	Y	Y	Y	Y
4 **Smith**	Y	Y	Y	Y	N	Y
5 Gottheimer	Y	Y	N	?	?	Y
6 Pallone	Y	Y	N	Y	N	Y
7 **Lance**	Y	Y	Y	Y	N	Y
8 Sires	Y	Y	N	Y	N	?
9 Pascrell	Y	Y	N	Y	–	Y
10 Payne	Y	Y	N	Y	N	Y
11 **Frelinghuysen**	Y	Y	Y	Y	Y	+
12 Watson Coleman	?	?	N	Y	N	Y
NEW MEXICO						
1 Lujan Grisham	Y	Y	N	Y	N	Y
2 **Pearce**	Y	Y	Y	Y	Y	Y
3 Luján	Y	Y	N	Y	N	Y
NEW YORK						
1 **Zeldin**	Y	Y	Y	Y	Y	Y
2 **King**	Y	Y	Y	?	?	Y
3 Suozzi	Y	Y	N	Y	N	Y
4 Rice	?	Y	N	Y	N	Y
5 Meeks	Y	Y	N	Y	N	Y
6 Meng	Y	Y	N	Y	N	Y
7 Velázquez	Y	Y	N	Y	N	Y
8 Jeffries	Y	Y	N	Y	N	Y
9 Clarke	Y	Y	N	Y	N	Y
10 Nadler	Y	Y	N	Y	N	Y
11 **Donovan**	Y	Y	Y	Y	N	Y
12 Maloney, C.	Y	Y	N	Y	N	Y
13 Espaillat	Y	Y	N	Y	N	Y
14 Crowley	Y	Y	N	?	?	Y
15 Serrano	Y	Y	N	Y	N	Y
16 Engel	Y	Y	N	Y	N	Y
17 Lowey	Y	Y	N	Y	N	Y
18 Maloney, S.P.	Y	?	N	Y	N	?
19 **Faso**	Y	Y	Y	Y	Y	Y
20 Tonko	Y	Y	N	Y	N	Y
21 **Stefanik**	Y	Y	Y	Y	Y	Y
22 **Tenney**	Y	Y	Y	Y	Y	Y
23 **Reed**	Y	Y	?	Y	Y	Y
24 **Katko**	Y	Y	?	Y	N	Y
25 Morelle		Y	N	Y	N	Y
26 Higgins	Y	?	N	Y	N	Y
27 **Collins**	Y	Y	Y	Y	Y	Y
NORTH CAROLINA						
1 Butterfield	Y	Y	N	Y	N	Y
2 **Holding**	Y	Y	Y	?	?	Y
3 **Jones**	?	?	?	?	?	?
4 Price	Y	Y	N	Y	N	Y

	416	417	418	419	420	421
5 **Foxx**	Y	Y	Y	Y	Y	Y
6 **Walker**	Y	Y	Y	Y	Y	Y
7 **Rouzer**	Y	Y	Y	Y	Y	Y
8 **Hudson**	Y	Y	Y	Y	Y	Y
9 **Pittenger**	Y	?	Y	Y	Y	Y
9 **Vacant**						
10 **McHenry**	Y	Y	Y	Y	Y	Y
11 **Meadows**	Y	Y	N	Y	Y	Y
12 Adams	Y	Y	N	Y	N	Y
13 **Budd**	Y	Y	Y	Y	Y	Y
NORTH DAKOTA						
AL **Cramer**	Y	?	Y	Y	Y	Y
OHIO						
1 **Chabot**	Y	Y	Y	Y	Y	Y
2 **Wenstrup**	Y	Y	Y	Y	Y	Y
3 Beatty	Y	Y	N	Y	N	Y
4 **Jordan**	Y	Y	N	Y	Y	Y
5 **Latta**	Y	Y	Y	Y	Y	Y
6 **Johnson**	Y	Y	Y	Y	Y	Y
7 **Gibbs**	Y	Y	Y	Y	Y	Y
8 **Davidson**	Y	Y	Y	Y	Y	Y
9 Kaptur	Y	Y	?	Y	N	Y
10 **Turner**	Y	Y	Y	Y	Y	Y
11 Fudge	Y	Y	N	Y	N	Y
12 Balderson	Y	Y	Y	Y	Y	Y
13 Ryan	Y	?	N	Y	N	Y
14 **Joyce**	Y	Y	Y	?	?	Y
15 **Stivers**	Y	Y	Y	?	?	Y
16 **Renacci**	Y	Y	Y	?	?	?
OKLAHOMA						
1 Hern		Y	Y	Y	Y	Y
2 **Mullin**	Y	Y	Y	Y	Y	Y
3 **Lucas**	Y	Y	Y	Y	Y	Y
4 **Cole**	Y	Y	Y	Y	Y	Y
5 **Russell**	Y	Y	Y	Y	Y	Y
OREGON						
1 Bonamici	Y	Y	N	Y	N	Y
2 **Walden**	Y	Y	Y	Y	Y	Y
3 Blumenauer	Y	Y	N	Y	N	Y
4 DeFazio	Y	?	N	Y	N	Y
5 Schrader	Y	Y	?	Y	N	Y
PENNSYLVANIA						
1 Brady	?	?	N	Y	N	Y
2 Evans	Y	Y	N	Y	N	Y
3 **Kelly**	Y	Y	Y	Y	Y	Y
4 **Perry**	Y	Y	Y	Y	Y	Y
5 **Thompson**	Y	Y	Y	Y	Y	Y
6 **Costello**	Y	?	Y	Y	N	Y
7 Scanlon		Y	N	Y	N	Y
8 **Fitzpatrick**	Y	Y	?	Y	N	Y
9 **Shuster**	Y	Y	?	?	?	Y
10 **Marino**	Y	Y	Y	Y	Y	Y
11 **Barletta**	?	?	Y	Y	Y	?
12 **Rothfus**	Y	Y	Y	Y	Y	Y
13 Boyle	Y	Y	N	Y	N	Y
14 Doyle	Y	Y	N	Y	N	Y
15 **Vacant**						
16 **Smucker**	Y	Y	Y	Y	Y	Y
17 Cartwright	Y	Y	N	Y	N	Y
18 Lamb	Y	Y	N	Y	N	Y
RHODE ISLAND						
1 Cicilline	Y	?	N	Y	N	Y
2 Langevin	Y	Y	N	Y	N	Y
SOUTH CAROLINA						
1 **Sanford**	P	Y	N	Y	N	N
2 **Wilson**	Y	Y	Y	Y	Y	Y
3 **Duncan**	Y	Y	Y	?	?	Y
4 **Gowdy**	?	?	Y	?	?	?
5 **Norman**	Y	Y	N	Y	Y	Y
6 Clyburn	Y	Y	N	Y	N	Y
7 **Rice**	P	Y	Y	Y	Y	N
SOUTH DAKOTA						
AL **Noem**	?	?	?	?	?	?
TENNESSEE						
1 **Roe**	Y	Y	Y	Y	Y	Y
2 **Duncan**	Y	Y	N	Y	Y	N
3 **Fleischmann**	Y	Y	Y	Y	Y	Y
4 **DesJarlais**	Y	Y	?	Y	Y	?
5 Cooper	Y	Y	N	Y	Y	Y
6 **Black**	Y	Y	?	?	?	Y
7 **Blackburn**	Y	Y	Y	?	?	Y
8 **Kustoff**	Y	Y	Y	Y	Y	Y
9 Cohen	Y	?	N	Y	N	Y

	416	417	418	419	420	421
TEXAS						
1 **Gohmert**	Y	Y	N	Y	Y	N
2 **Poe**	Y	Y	Y	?	?	Y
3 **Johnson, S.**	Y	Y	Y	Y	Y	Y
4 **Ratcliffe**	?	?	Y	?	?	?
5 **Hensarling**	Y	Y	Y	?	?	Y
6 **Barton**	Y	Y	?	?	?	?
7 **Culberson**	Y	Y	Y	?	?	?
8 **Brady**	Y	Y	Y	+	+	Y
9 Green, A.	Y	Y	N	Y	N	Y
10 **McCaul**	Y	Y	Y	Y	Y	Y
11 **Conaway**	Y	Y	Y	Y	Y	Y
12 **Granger**	Y	Y	Y	Y	Y	Y
13 **Thornberry**	Y	Y	Y	Y	Y	Y
14 **Weber**	Y	Y	Y	Y	Y	Y
15 Gonzalez	Y	Y	Y	Y	Y	+
16 O'Rourke	Y	Y	N	Y	N	Y
17 **Flores**	Y	Y	Y	Y	Y	Y
18 Jackson Lee	Y	Y	N	Y	N	Y
19 **Arrington**	Y	Y	Y	Y	Y	Y
20 Castro	Y	Y	N	Y	N	Y
21 **Smith**	Y	?	Y	Y	Y	Y
22 **Olson**	?	?	Y	Y	Y	Y
23 **Hurd**	Y	Y	Y	Y	Y	Y
24 Marchant	Y	Y	Y	Y	Y	Y
25 **Williams**	Y	Y	Y	?	?	Y
26 **Burgess**	Y	Y	Y	Y	Y	?
27 Cloud	Y	Y	Y	Y	Y	Y
28 Cuellar	Y	Y	N	Y	Y	Y
29 Green, G.	Y	Y	Y	Y	Y	Y
30 Johnson, E.B.	Y	Y	N	Y	N	Y
31 **Carter**	Y	Y	Y	Y	Y	Y
32 **Sessions**	Y	Y	Y	Y	Y	Y
33 Veasey	Y	Y	N	Y	N	Y
34 Vela	Y	Y	Y	Y	Y	Y
35 Doggett	Y	Y	N	Y	N	Y
36 **Babin**	Y	Y	+	Y	Y	Y
UTAH						
1 **Bishop**	Y	Y	Y	Y	Y	Y
2 **Stewart**	Y	Y	Y	Y	Y	Y
3 **Curtis**	Y	Y	Y	Y	Y	Y
4 **Love**	?	?	Y	?	?	Y
VERMONT						
AL Welch	Y	Y	N	Y	N	Y
VIRGINIA						
1 **Wittman**	Y	Y	Y	Y	Y	Y
2 **Taylor**	Y	Y	Y	Y	Y	Y
3 Scott	Y	Y	N	Y	N	Y
4 McEachin	Y	Y	N	Y	N	Y
5 **Garrett**	Y	Y	?	Y	Y	?
6 **Goodlatte**	Y	?	+	Y	Y	Y
7 **Brat**	Y	Y	N	Y	Y	Y
8 Beyer	Y	Y	?	Y	N	Y
9 **Griffith**	Y	Y	N	Y	Y	Y
10 **Comstock**	Y	?	?	?	?	Y
11 Connolly	Y	?	N	Y	N	Y
WASHINGTON						
1 DelBene	Y	Y	N	Y	N	Y
2 Larsen	Y	?	N	Y	N	Y
3 **Herrera Beutler**	Y	Y	Y	Y	Y	Y
4 **Newhouse**	Y	Y	Y	Y	Y	Y
5 **McMorris Rodgers**	Y	Y	?	Y	Y	Y
6 Kilmer	Y	Y	N	Y	N	Y
7 Jayapal	Y	Y	N	Y	–	Y
8 **Reichert**	Y	Y	Y	Y	Y	Y
9 Smith	Y	Y	N	Y	N	Y
10 Heck	Y	Y	N	Y	N	Y
WEST VIRGINIA						
1 **McKinley**	Y	Y	Y	Y	Y	Y
2 **Mooney**	Y	Y	Y	Y	Y	Y
3 **Vacant**						
WISCONSIN						
1 **Ryan**						
2 Pocan	Y	Y	N	Y	N	Y
3 Kind	Y	Y	N	Y	Y	Y
4 Moore	Y	Y	N	Y	N	Y
5 **Sensenbrenner**	Y	Y	Y	+	+	Y
6 **Grothman**	N	Y	Y	Y	Y	N
7 **Duffy**	Y	Y	Y	Y	Y	?
8 **Gallagher**	Y	Y	Y	Y	Y	Y
WYOMING						
AL **Cheney**	Y	Y	Y	Y	Y	Y

VOTE NUMBER

422. HR6207. DEMOCRATIC REPUBLIC OF CONGO SANCTIONS/ PASSAGE. Royce, R-Calif., motion to suspend the rules and pass the bill, as amended, that would codify for five years sanctions imposed by 2006 and 2014 executive orders on individuals whose actions contribute to ongoing instability and conflict in the Democratic Republic of the Congo, unless the President determines that the DRC has made significant progress towards holding free and fair elections and respecting civil liberties as described in a 2016 United Nations resolution. It would also require the president to determine whether additional DRC senior government officials should be sanctioned under these provisions, and would order a State Department report on DRC government and military complicity in human rights abuses and corruption. Motion agreed to 374-11: R 194-11; D 180-0. Sept. 27, 2018.

423. HRES1160. TAX EXTENSION PACKAGE/RULE. Adoption of the rule (H Res 1160) providing for House floor consideration of a motion to concur in the Senate amendment to a bill (HR 88) that is the expected legislative vehicle for a package of bills that would extend certain tax cuts that lapsed at the end of 2017. It would extend and gradually phase out through 2024 a biodiesel tax credit, make permanent a railroad track maintenance credit at a reduced rate, and extend a range of other tax cuts through the end of 2018. The bill also contains provisions related to retirement savings plans, temporary tax relief for victims of hurricanes and wildfires, and operations of the Internal Revenue Service. Adopted 219-181: R 219-1; D 0-180. Sept. 29, 2018.

424. HR7187. FLOOD INSURANCE EXTENSION/PASSAGE. Hensarling, R-Texas, motion to suspend the rules and pass the bill that would extend the authorization and authorities under the National Flood Insurance Program for one week, through Dec. 7, 2018. The program is administered by the Federal Emergency Management Agency and offers federally-backed flood insurance to individuals and entities in communities that adopt certain flood plain management standards. Motion agreed to 350-46: R 172-46; D 178-0. Sept. 29, 2018.

425. HR6901. FEDERAL IT OFFICE/PASSAGE. Comer, R-Ky., motion to suspend the rules and pass the bill as amended, that would formally authorize and rename the Office of Electronic Government within the Office of Management and Budget as the Office of the Federal Chief Information Officer. The bill would formally codify the position and duties of the Federal CIO and another presidential appointee reporting to the CIO. It would also direct OMB to develop, for all federal agencies, an information technology expenditure reporting system. Motion agreed to 391-0: R 212-0; D 179-0. Sept. 30, 2018.

426. HRES792. ROBERTO CLEMENTE HISTORIC SITE/ADOPTION. Bishop, R-Utah, motion to suspend the rules and agree to the resolution, as amended, the would request that the Interior secretary add Roberto Clemente's place of death in Loiza, Puerto Rico, to the National Register of Historic Places. Motion agreed to 385-1: R 209-1; D 176-0. Dec. 10, 2018.

427. HR3008. GEORGE W. BUSH CHILDHOOD HOME STUDY/PASSAGE. Bishop, R-Utah, motion to suspend the rules and pass the bill that would direct the Interior secretary to conduct a study of the childhood home of former President George W. Bush in Midland, Texas, to determine its suitability for designation as part of the National Park system. Motion agreed to 382-4: R 206-4; D 176-0. Dec. 10, 2018.

	422	423	424	425	426	427
ALABAMA						
1 Byrne	Y	Y	Y	Y	Y	Y
2 Roby	Y	Y	Y	Y	Y	Y
3 Rogers	Y	Y	Y	Y	Y	Y
4 Aderholt	Y	Y	Y	Y	Y	Y
5 Brooks	N	Y	N	Y	Y	Y
6 Palmer	Y	Y	N	Y	Y	Y
7 Sewell	Y	N	Y	Y	Y	Y
ALASKA						
AL Young	Y	Y	Y	Y	Y	Y
ARIZONA						
1 O'Halleran	Y	N	Y	Y	?	?
2 McSally	Y	Y	Y	Y	?	?
3 Grijalva	Y	?	?	Y	?	?
4 Gosar	N	Y	N	Y	Y	Y
5 Biggs	N	Y	N	Y	Y	N
6 Schweikert	Y	Y	Y	Y	Y	Y
7 Gallego	Y	N	Y	Y	Y	Y
8 Lesko	Y	Y	N	Y	Y	Y
9 Sinema	?	N	Y	Y	Y	Y
ARKANSAS						
1 Crawford	Y	Y	Y	Y	Y	Y
2 Hill	Y	Y	N	Y	Y	Y
3 Womack	Y	Y	Y	Y	Y	Y
4 Westerman	Y	Y	Y	Y	Y	Y
CALIFORNIA						
1 LaMalfa	?	Y	Y	Y	Y	Y
2 Huffman	Y	N	Y	Y	Y	Y
3 Garamendi	Y	N	Y	Y	Y	Y
4 McClintock	N	Y	N	Y	Y	Y
5 Thompson	Y	N	Y	Y	Y	Y
6 Matsui	Y	N	Y	Y	Y	Y
7 Bera	Y	N	Y	Y	Y	Y
8 Cook	Y	Y	Y	Y	Y	Y
9 McNerney	Y	N	Y	Y	Y	Y
10 Denham	?	Y	Y	?	?	?
11 DeSaulnier	Y	N	Y	Y	+	+
12 Pelosi	Y	N	Y	Y	Y	Y
13 Lee	Y	N	Y	Y	Y	Y
14 Speier	Y	N	Y	Y	Y	Y
15 Swalwell	Y	N	Y	Y	Y	Y
16 Costa	Y	N	Y	Y	?	?
17 Khanna	Y	N	Y	Y	Y	Y
18 Eshoo	Y	N	Y	Y	Y	Y
19 Lofgren	Y	N	Y	Y	Y	Y
20 Panetta	Y	N	Y	Y	Y	Y
21 Valadao	?	Y	Y	Y	Y	Y
22 Nunes	Y	Y	Y	Y	Y	Y
23 McCarthy	Y	Y	Y	Y	Y	Y
24 Carbajal	Y	N	Y	Y	Y	Y
25 Knight	?	?	?	?	?	?
26 Brownley	Y	N	Y	Y	Y	Y
27 Chu	Y	N	Y	Y	Y	Y
28 Schiff	Y	N	Y	Y	Y	Y
29 Cardenas	Y	N	Y	Y	Y	Y
30 Sherman	Y	N	Y	Y	Y	Y
31 Aguilar	Y	N	Y	Y	Y	Y
32 Napolitano	Y	N	Y	Y	Y	Y
33 Lieu	Y	N	Y	Y	?	?
34 Gomez	Y	N	Y	Y	Y	Y
35 Torres	Y	N	Y	Y	Y	Y
36 Ruiz	Y	N	Y	Y	Y	Y
37 Bass	Y	N	Y	Y	Y	Y
38 Sánchez, Linda	Y	N	Y	Y	Y	Y
39 Royce	?	Y	N	Y	Y	Y
40 Roybal-Allard	Y	N	Y	Y	Y	Y
41 Takano	Y	N	Y	Y	Y	Y
42 Calvert	Y	Y	Y	Y	Y	Y
43 Waters	?	N	Y	?	Y	Y
44 Barragan	Y	N	Y	Y	Y	Y
45 Walters	?	?	?	?	Y	Y
46 Correa	Y	N	Y	Y	Y	Y
47 Lowenthal	Y	N	Y	Y	Y	Y
48 Rohrabacher	Y	Y	Y	Y	Y	N
49 Issa	?	Y	?	Y	Y	Y
50 Hunter	Y	Y	Y	Y	Y	Y
51 Vargas	Y	N	Y	Y	Y	Y
52 Peters	Y	N	Y	Y	Y	Y
53 Davis	Y	N	Y	?	Y	Y

	422	423	424	425	426	427
COLORADO						
1 DeGette	Y	N	Y	Y	Y	Y
2 Polis	Y	?	?	?	?	?
3 Tipton	?	Y	Y	Y	?	?
4 Buck	Y	Y	N	Y	Y	Y
5 Lamborn	Y	Y	Y	Y	?	?
6 Coffman	Y	Y	Y	Y	Y	Y
7 Perlmutter	Y	N	Y	Y	Y	Y
CONNECTICUT						
1 Larson	Y	N	Y	Y	Y	Y
2 Courtney	Y	N	Y	Y	Y	Y
3 DeLauro	Y	N	Y	Y	Y	Y
4 Himes	Y	N	Y	Y	Y	Y
5 Esty	Y	N	Y	Y	Y	Y
DELAWARE						
AL Blunt Rochester	Y	N	Y	Y	Y	Y
FLORIDA						
1 Gaetz	Y	Y	Y	Y	Y	Y
2 Dunn	Y	Y	Y	Y	Y	Y
3 Yoho	N	Y	N	Y	Y	Y
4 Rutherford	Y	Y	Y	Y	Y	Y
5 Lawson	Y	N	Y	Y	Y	Y
6 Vacant						
7 Murphy	Y	N	Y	Y	Y	Y
8 Posey	Y	Y	Y	Y	Y	Y
9 Soto	Y	N	Y	Y	Y	Y
10 Demings	Y	N	Y	Y	Y	Y
11 Webster	Y	Y	Y	Y	Y	Y
12 Bilirakis	Y	Y	Y	Y	Y	Y
13 Crist	Y	N	Y	Y	Y	Y
14 Castor	Y	N	Y	Y	Y	Y
15 Ross	Y	Y	N	Y	?	?
16 Buchanan	Y	?	?	?	?	?
17 Rooney, T.	?	Y	Y	Y	?	?
18 Mast	Y	Y	Y	Y	?	?
19 Rooney, F.	Y	Y	Y	Y	Y	Y
20 Hastings	?	?	?	?	Y	Y
21 Frankel	Y	N	Y	Y	Y	Y
22 Deutch	Y	N	Y	Y	Y	Y
23 Wasserman Schultz	Y	N	Y	Y	Y	Y
24 Wilson	?	?	?	?	Y	Y
25 Diaz-Balart	Y	Y	Y	Y	Y	Y
26 Curbelo	Y	Y	Y	?	?	Y
27 Ros-Lehtinen	Y	Y	Y	?	Y	Y
GEORGIA						
1 Carter	Y	Y	Y	Y	Y	Y
2 Bishop	Y	N	Y	Y	Y	Y
3 Ferguson	Y	Y	Y	Y	Y	Y
4 Johnson	Y	N	Y	Y	Y	Y
5 Lewis	Y	N	Y	Y	?	?
6 Handel	Y	Y	Y	Y	Y	Y
7 Woodall	Y	Y	Y	Y	Y	Y
8 Scott, A.	Y	Y	Y	Y	Y	Y
9 Collins	Y	Y	Y	Y	Y	Y
10 Hice	Y	Y	N	Y	Y	Y
11 Loudermilk	Y	Y	Y	Y	?	Y
12 Allen	Y	Y	Y	Y	Y	Y
13 Scott, D.	Y	N	Y	Y	Y	Y
14 Graves	Y	Y	Y	Y	Y	Y
HAWAII						
1 Hanabusa	?	?	?	?	Y	Y
2 Gabbard	?	N	Y	Y	?	?
IDAHO						
1 Labrador	?	?	?	?	Y	Y
2 Simpson	Y	?	?	Y	?	?
ILLINOIS						
1 Rush	?	N	Y	Y	?	Y
2 Kelly	Y	N	Y	Y	Y	Y
3 Lipinski	Y	?	?	?	?	?
4 Gutierrez	+	-	+	+	+	+
5 Quigley	Y	N	Y	Y	Y	Y
6 Roskam	?	Y	Y	?	?	?
7 Davis, D.	Y	-	+	+	Y	Y
8 Krishnamoorthi	Y	N	Y	Y	Y	Y
9 Schakowsky	Y	N	Y	Y	Y	Y
10 Schneider	Y	N	Y	Y	Y	Y
11 Foster	Y	N	Y	Y	Y	Y
12 Bost	Y	Y	Y	Y	Y	Y
13 Davis, R.	Y	Y	Y	Y	Y	Y

KEY	**Republicans**	Democrats	*Independents*
Y Voted for (yea)		**X** Paired against	**C** Voted "present" to avoid possible conflict of interest
# Paired for		**–** Announced against	
+ Announced for		**P** Voted "present"	**?** Did not vote or otherwise make a position known
N Voted against (nay)			

	422	423	424	425	426	427
14 **Hultgren**	Y	Y	Y	Y	Y	Y
15 **Shimkus**	Y	Y	Y	Y	Y	Y
16 **Kinzinger**	Y	Y	Y	Y	Y	Y
17 Bustos	Y	N	Y	Y	Y	Y
18 **LaHood**	Y	Y	Y	Y	Y	Y
INDIANA						
1 Visclosky	Y	N	Y	Y	Y	Y
2 **Walorski**	Y	Y	Y	Y	Y	Y
3 **Banks**	Y	Y	N	Y	Y	Y
4 Rokita	Y	Y	N	Y	Y	Y
5 **Brooks**	Y	Y	Y	Y	Y	Y
6 **Messer**	?	?	?	?	Y	Y
7 Carson	Y	N	Y	Y	Y	Y
8 **Bucshon**	Y	Y	Y	Y	Y	Y
9 **Hollingsworth**	Y	Y	Y	Y	Y	Y
IOWA						
1 **Blum**	N	Y	Y	Y	Y	Y
2 Loebsack	Y	N	Y	Y	Y	Y
3 **Young**	Y	Y	Y	Y	Y	Y
4 **King**	Y	Y	Y	Y	Y	Y
KANSAS						
1 **Marshall**	Y	Y	Y	Y	Y	Y
2 **Jenkins**	Y	Y	Y	Y	?	?
3 **Yoder**	Y	Y	Y	Y	Y	Y
4 **Estes**	Y	Y	Y	Y	Y	Y
KENTUCKY						
1 **Comer**	Y	Y	Y	Y	Y	Y
2 **Guthrie**	Y	Y	Y	Y	Y	Y
3 Yarmuth	Y	N	Y	Y	Y	Y
4 **Massie**	N	Y	N	Y	Y	N
5 **Rogers**	Y	Y	Y	Y	Y	Y
6 **Barr**	Y	Y	Y	Y	Y	Y
LOUISIANA						
1 **Scalise**	Y	Y	Y	Y	Y	Y
2 Richmond	Y	N	Y	Y	Y	Y
3 **Higgins**	Y	Y	Y	Y	Y	Y
4 **Johnson**	Y	Y	Y	Y	Y	Y
5 **Abraham**	Y	Y	Y	Y	Y	Y
6 **Graves**	Y	Y	Y	Y	Y	Y
MAINE						
1 Pingree	Y	N	Y	Y	Y	Y
2 **Poliquin**	Y	Y	Y	Y	Y	Y
MARYLAND						
1 **Harris**	Y	Y	Y	Y	Y	Y
2 Ruppersberger	Y	–	+	+	Y	Y
3 Sarbanes	Y	N	Y	Y	Y	Y
4 Brown	Y	N	Y	Y	Y	Y
5 Hoyer	Y	N	Y	Y	Y	Y
6 Delaney	Y	N	Y	Y	Y	Y
7 Cummings	?	N	Y	Y	Y	Y
8 Raskin	Y	N	Y	Y	Y	Y
MASSACHUSETTS						
1 Neal	Y	N	Y	Y	Y	Y
2 McGovern	Y	N	Y	Y	Y	Y
3 Tsongas	Y	?	?	?	?	?
4 Kennedy	Y	N	?	Y	Y	Y
5 Clark	Y	N	Y	Y	Y	Y
6 Moulton	Y	N	Y	Y	Y	Y
7 Capuano	Y	N	Y	Y	Y	Y
8 Lynch	Y	N	Y	Y	Y	Y
9 Keating	Y	?	?	?	?	?
MICHIGAN						
1 **Bergman**	Y	Y	Y	Y	Y	Y
2 **Huizenga**	Y	Y	Y	Y	Y	Y
3 *Amash*	N	N	N	Y	N	N
4 **Moolenaar**	Y	Y	Y	Y	Y	Y
5 Kildee	Y	N	Y	Y	Y	Y
6 **Upton**	Y	Y	Y	Y	Y	Y
7 **Walberg**	Y	Y	Y	Y	Y	Y
8 **Bishop**	?	Y	Y	Y	?	?
9 Levin	Y	N	Y	Y	Y	Y
10 **Mitchell**	Y	Y	Y	Y	Y	Y
11 **Trott**	Y	Y	Y	Y	Y	Y
12 Dingell	Y	N	Y	Y	Y	Y
14 Lawrence	Y	N	Y	Y	Y	Y
MINNESOTA						
1 Walz	?	?	?	?	?	?
2 **Lewis**	Y	Y	Y	Y	Y	Y
3 **Paulsen**	Y	Y	Y	Y	Y	Y
4 McCollum	Y	N	Y	Y	Y	Y

	422	423	424	425	426	427
5 Ellison	?	?	?	?	?	?
6 **Emmer**	Y	Y	Y	?	Y	Y
7 Peterson	Y	N	Y	Y	Y	Y
8 Nolan	?	?	?	?	Y	Y
MISSISSIPPI						
1 **Kelly**	Y	Y	Y	Y	Y	Y
2 Thompson	Y	N	Y	Y	Y	Y
3 **Harper**	Y	Y	Y	Y	Y	Y
4 **Palazzo**	Y	Y	Y	Y	Y	Y
MISSOURI						
1 Clay	Y	N	Y	Y	Y	Y
2 **Wagner**	Y	Y	Y	Y	Y	Y
3 **Luetkemeyer**	Y	Y	Y	Y	Y	Y
4 **Hartzler**	Y	Y	Y	Y	Y	Y
5 Cleaver	Y	N	Y	Y	Y	Y
6 **Graves**	Y	Y	Y	+	Y	Y
7 **Long**	Y	Y	Y	Y	Y	Y
8 **Smith**	Y	Y	N	Y	Y	Y
MONTANA						
AL **Gianforte**	Y	Y	Y	Y	Y	Y
NEBRASKA						
1 **Fortenberry**	Y	Y	Y	Y	Y	Y
2 **Bacon**	Y	Y	Y	Y	Y	Y
3 **Smith**	Y	Y	Y	Y	Y	Y
NEVADA						
1 Titus	Y	N	Y	Y	Y	Y
2 **Amodei**	?	Y	Y	?	Y	Y
3 Rosen	Y	N	Y	Y	Y	Y
4 Kihuen	Y	N	Y	Y	Y	Y
NEW HAMPSHIRE						
1 Shea-Porter	Y	N	Y	Y	Y	Y
2 Kuster	Y	N	Y	Y	Y	Y
NEW JERSEY						
1 Norcross	Y	N	Y	Y	Y	Y
2 **LoBiondo**	Y	Y	Y	Y	Y	Y
3 **MacArthur**	Y	Y	Y	Y	Y	Y
4 **Smith**	Y	Y	Y	Y	Y	Y
5 Gottheimer	Y	N	Y	Y	Y	Y
6 Pallone	Y	N	Y	Y	Y	Y
7 **Lance**	Y	Y	Y	Y	Y	Y
8 Sires	?	N	Y	Y	Y	Y
9 Pascrell	Y	N	Y	Y	Y	Y
10 Payne	Y	N	Y	Y	Y	Y
11 **Frelinghuysen**	+	Y	Y	Y	Y	Y
12 Watson Coleman	Y	N	Y	Y	Y	Y
NEW MEXICO						
1 Lujan Grisham	Y	N	Y	Y	?	?
2 **Pearce**	Y	Y	N	Y	Y	Y
3 Luján	Y	N	Y	Y	Y	Y
NEW YORK						
1 **Zeldin**	Y	Y	Y	Y	Y	Y
2 **King**	Y	Y	Y	Y	Y	Y
3 Suozzi	Y	N	Y	Y	Y	Y
4 Rice	Y	?	?	Y	Y	Y
5 Meeks	Y	N	Y	Y	Y	Y
6 Meng	Y	N	Y	Y	Y	Y
7 Velázquez	Y	N	Y	Y	Y	Y
8 Jeffries	Y	N	Y	Y	Y	Y
9 Clarke	Y	N	Y	Y	Y	Y
10 Nadler	Y	N	Y	Y	Y	Y
11 **Donovan**	Y	Y	Y	Y	Y	Y
12 Maloney, C.	Y	N	Y	Y	Y	Y
13 Espaillat	Y	N	Y	Y	Y	Y
14 Crowley	Y	N	Y	?	Y	Y
15 Serrano	Y	N	Y	Y	Y	Y
16 Engel	Y	N	Y	Y	?	?
17 Lowey	Y	N	Y	Y	Y	Y
18 Maloney, S.P.	?	?	?	?	Y	Y
19 **Faso**	Y	Y	Y	Y	Y	Y
20 Tonko	Y	N	Y	Y	Y	Y
21 **Stefanik**	Y	Y	Y	Y	Y	Y
22 **Tenney**	Y	Y	N	Y	Y	Y
23 **Reed**	Y	Y	Y	Y	Y	Y
24 **Katko**	Y	Y	Y	Y	Y	Y
25 Morelle	Y	N	Y	Y	Y	Y
26 Higgins	Y	N	Y	Y	Y	Y
27 **Collins**	Y	Y	Y	Y	Y	Y
NORTH CAROLINA						
1 Butterfield	Y	N	Y	Y	Y	Y
2 **Holding**	Y	Y	Y	Y	Y	Y
3 **Jones**	?	?	?	?	?	?
4 Price	Y	N	Y	Y	?	?

	422	423	424	425	426	427
5 **Foxx**	Y	Y	N	Y	Y	Y
6 **Walker**	Y	Y	N	Y	Y	Y
7 **Rouzer**	Y	Y	Y	Y	Y	Y
8 **Hudson**	Y	Y	N	Y	+	+
9 **Pittenger**	Y	Y	Y	Y	?	?
9 **Vacant**						
10 **McHenry**	Y	Y	Y	Y	Y	Y
11 **Meadows**	Y	Y	Y	Y	Y	Y
12 Adams	Y	N	Y	Y	Y	Y
13 **Budd**	Y	Y	N	Y	Y	Y
NORTH DAKOTA						
AL **Cramer**	Y	Y	Y	Y	Y	Y
OHIO						
1 **Chabot**	Y	Y	Y	Y	Y	Y
2 **Wenstrup**	Y	Y	N	Y	Y	Y
3 Beatty	Y	N	Y	Y	Y	Y
4 **Jordan**	Y	Y	N	Y	Y	Y
5 **Latta**	Y	Y	Y	Y	Y	Y
6 **Johnson**	Y	Y	Y	Y	Y	Y
7 **Gibbs**	Y	Y	Y	Y	Y	Y
8 **Davidson**	Y	Y	N	Y	Y	Y
9 Kaptur	Y	N	Y	Y	Y	Y
10 **Turner**	?	Y	Y	Y	Y	Y
11 Fudge	Y	N	Y	Y	Y	Y
12 Balderson	Y	Y	Y	Y	Y	Y
13 Ryan	Y	N	Y	Y	Y	Y
14 **Joyce**	Y	Y	Y	Y	Y	Y
15 **Stivers**	Y	Y	Y	Y	Y	Y
16 **Renacci**	?	Y	Y	Y	Y	Y
OKLAHOMA						
1 Hern	Y	Y	Y	Y	Y	Y
2 **Mullin**	Y	Y	Y	Y	Y	Y
3 **Lucas**	Y	Y	Y	Y	Y	Y
4 **Cole**	Y	Y	Y	Y	Y	Y
5 **Russell**	Y	Y	Y	Y	Y	Y
OREGON						
1 Bonamici	Y	N	Y	Y	Y	Y
2 **Walden**	Y	Y	Y	Y	Y	Y
3 Blumenauer	Y	N	?	Y	Y	Y
4 DeFazio	?	N	Y	Y	Y	Y
5 Schrader	Y	N	Y	Y	Y	Y
PENNSYLVANIA						
1 Brady	Y	N	Y	?	?	?
2 Evans	Y	N	Y	Y	Y	Y
3 **Kelly**	Y	Y	Y	Y	Y	Y
4 **Perry**	Y	Y	Y	Y	Y	Y
5 **Thompson**	Y	Y	Y	Y	Y	Y
6 **Costello**	Y	Y	Y	Y	Y	Y
7 Scanlon	Y	N	Y	Y	Y	Y
8 **Fitzpatrick**	Y	Y	Y	Y	Y	Y
9 **Shuster**	Y	Y	Y	Y	?	?
10 **Marino**	Y	Y	Y	Y	Y	Y
11 **Barletta**	?	?	?	?	?	?
12 **Rothfus**	Y	Y	Y	Y	Y	Y
13 Boyle	Y	N	Y	Y	Y	Y
14 Doyle	Y	N	Y	Y	Y	Y
15 Wild	Y	N	Y	Y	Y	Y
16 **Smucker**	Y	Y	Y	Y	Y	Y
17 Cartwright	Y	N	Y	Y	Y	Y
18 Lamb	Y	N	Y	Y	Y	Y
RHODE ISLAND						
1 Cicilline	Y	N	Y	Y	Y	Y
2 Langevin	Y	N	Y	Y	Y	Y
SOUTH CAROLINA						
1 **Sanford**	N	Y	N	Y	P	P
2 **Wilson**	Y	Y	Y	Y	Y	Y
3 **Duncan**	Y	Y	N	Y	Y	Y
4 **Gowdy**	?	Y	?	?	?	?
5 **Norman**	Y	Y	N	Y	Y	Y
6 Clyburn	Y	N	Y	Y	Y	Y
7 **Rice**	N	Y	Y	Y	P	P
SOUTH DAKOTA						
AL **Noem**	?	?	?	?	?	?
TENNESSEE						
1 **Roe**	Y	Y	Y	Y	Y	Y
2 **Duncan**	N	Y	N	Y	Y	Y
3 **Fleischmann**	Y	Y	Y	Y	Y	Y
4 **DesJarlais**	?	?	?	?	Y	Y
5 Cooper	Y	N	Y	Y	Y	Y
6 **Black**	?	?	?	?	Y	?
7 **Blackburn**	Y	?	?	?	Y	?
8 **Kustoff**	Y	Y	Y	Y	Y	Y
9 Cohen	Y	N	Y	Y	Y	Y

	422	423	424	425	426	427
TEXAS						
1 **Gohmert**	Y	Y	N	Y	Y	Y
2 **Poe**	Y	Y	Y	?	Y	Y
3 **Johnson, S.**	Y	Y	N	Y	Y	Y
4 **Ratcliffe**	?	Y	N	Y	Y	Y
5 **Hensarling**	Y	Y	N	Y	Y	Y
6 **Barton**	?	Y	N	Y	Y	Y
7 **Culberson**	?	Y	Y	Y	Y	Y
8 **Brady**	Y	Y	Y	Y	Y	Y
9 Green, A.	Y	N	Y	Y	Y	Y
10 **McCaul**	Y	Y	Y	Y	Y	Y
11 **Conaway**	Y	Y	N	Y	Y	Y
12 **Granger**	Y	Y	Y	Y	Y	Y
13 **Thornberry**	Y	Y	N	Y	Y	Y
14 **Weber**	Y	Y	Y	Y	Y	Y
15 Gonzalez	+	N	Y	Y	+	+
16 O'Rourke	Y	N	Y	Y	Y	Y
17 **Flores**	Y	Y	N	Y	Y	Y
18 Jackson Lee	Y	N	Y	Y	Y	Y
19 **Arrington**	Y	Y	Y	Y	Y	Y
20 Castro	Y	N	Y	Y	Y	Y
21 **Smith**	Y	?	?	Y	Y	Y
22 **Olson**	Y	Y	Y	Y	Y	Y
23 **Hurd**	Y	Y	Y	Y	Y	Y
24 Marchant	Y	Y	Y	Y	?	?
25 **Williams**	Y	Y	N	Y	Y	Y
26 **Burgess**	?	Y	Y	Y	Y	Y
27 Cloud	Y	Y	Y	Y	Y	Y
28 Cuellar	Y	N	Y	Y	Y	Y
29 Green, G.	Y	N	Y	Y	Y	Y
30 Johnson, E.B.	Y	N	Y	Y	Y	Y
31 **Carter**	Y	Y	Y	Y	Y	Y
32 **Sessions**	Y	Y	Y	Y	Y	Y
33 Veasey	Y	N	Y	Y	Y	Y
34 Vela	Y	N	Y	?	Y	Y
35 Doggett	Y	N	Y	Y	Y	Y
36 **Babin**	Y	Y	Y	Y	Y	Y
UTAH						
1 **Bishop**	Y	Y	Y	Y	Y	Y
2 **Stewart**	Y	Y	N	Y	Y	Y
3 **Curtis**	Y	Y	Y	Y	Y	Y
4 **Love**	Y	Y	Y	?	Y	Y
VERMONT						
AL Welch	Y	N	Y	Y	Y	Y
VIRGINIA						
1 **Wittman**	Y	Y	Y	Y	Y	Y
2 **Taylor**	Y	?	?	?	Y	Y
3 Scott	Y	N	Y	Y	Y	Y
4 McEachin	Y	N	Y	Y	Y	Y
5 **Garrett**	?	Y	N	Y	Y	Y
6 **Goodlatte**	Y	Y	Y	Y	Y	Y
7 **Brat**	Y	Y	N	Y	Y	Y
8 Beyer	Y	?	?	Y	?	?
9 **Griffith**	Y	Y	Y	Y	Y	Y
10 **Comstock**	Y	Y	Y	?	Y	Y
11 Connolly	Y	N	Y	Y	Y	Y
WASHINGTON						
1 DelBene	Y	N	Y	Y	Y	Y
2 Larsen	Y	N	Y	Y	Y	Y
3 **Herrera Beutler**	Y	Y	Y	Y	Y	Y
4 **Newhouse**	Y	?	?	Y	Y	Y
5 **McMorris Rodgers**	Y	Y	Y	Y	Y	Y
6 Kilmer	Y	N	Y	Y	Y	Y
7 Jayapal	Y	N	Y	Y	Y	Y
8 **Reichert**	Y	Y	Y	Y	Y	Y
9 Smith	Y	N	Y	Y	Y	Y
10 Heck	Y	N	Y	Y	Y	Y
WEST VIRGINIA						
1 **McKinley**	Y	Y	Y	Y	Y	Y
2 **Mooney**	Y	Y	N	Y	Y	Y
3 **Vacant**						
WISCONSIN						
1 **Ryan**						
2 Pocan	Y	N	Y	Y	Y	Y
3 Kind	Y	N	Y	Y	Y	Y
4 Moore	Y	N	Y	Y	Y	Y
5 **Sensenbrenner**	Y	Y	N	Y	Y	Y
6 **Grothman**	Y	Y	Y	Y	Y	Y
7 **Duffy**	?	Y	N	Y	Y	Y
8 **Gallagher**	Y	Y	N	Y	Y	Y
WYOMING						
AL **Cheney**	Y	Y	Y	Y	Y	Y

VOTE NUMBER

428. HR7217. MEDICAID COVERAGE HEALTH HOME PROTOCOL/ PASSAGE. Barton, R-Texas, motion to suspend the rules and pass the bill that would allow states to cover the cost of care for children with complex medical conditions through health homes under Medicaid, beginning Oct. 1, 2022; direct the Health and Human Services Department to establish standards for qualification as a health home; and establish relevant monitoring and reporting requirements for participating states. The bill also includes provisions related to programs for individuals with chronic conditions transitioning out of health care institutions, protecting financial resources of individuals with spouses in nursing homes, state electronic verification of Medicaid eligibility, penalties for misclassification of drugs by manufacturers, and other provisions related to Medicaid and Medicare. Finally, the measure rescinds $22 million from the Medicaid Improvement Fund. Motion agreed to 400-11: R 212-11; D 188-0. Dec. 11, 2018.

429. S3029. PRETERM BIRTH RESEARCH/PASSAGE. Burgess, R-Texas, motion to suspend the rules and pass the bill that would expand and reauthorize Health and Human Services Department research and education activities related to preterm births and direct the agency to study additional strategies to address the issue, in collaboration with other federal agencies. It would authorize $2 million annually through fiscal 2023 for these activities. Motion agreed to 406-3: R 218-3; D 188-0. Dec. 11, 2018.

430. S825. ALASKA HEALTH LAND EXCHANGE/PASSAGE. Young, R-Alaska, motion to suspend the rules and pass the bill that would direct the Health and Human Services secretary to convey 19.07 acres of federal land in Sitka, Alaska to the Southeast Alaska Regional Health Consortium. Motion agreed to 403-3: R 216-3; D 187-0. Dec. 11, 2018.

431. HRES1176. FARM PROGRAMS/PREVIOUS QUESTION. Newhouse, R-Wash., motion to order the previous question (thus ending debate and the possibility of amendment) on the rule (H Res 1176) that would provide for House floor consideration of the conference report to accompany the Farm Bill (HR 2), that would reauthorize and extend federal farm and nutrition programs through fiscal 2023, and would waive section 7 of the War Powers Resolution for a concurrent resolution related to hostilities in Yemen. Motion agreed to 220-191: R 220-0; D 0-191. Dec. 12, 2018.

432. HRES1176. FARM PROGRAMS/RULE. Adoption of the rule (H Res 1176) that would provide for House floor consideration of the conference report to accompany the Farm Bill (HR 2), that would reauthorize and extend federal farm and nutrition programs through fiscal 2023. The rule would also waive section 7 of the War Powers Resolution for a concurrent resolution related to hostilities in Yemen. Adopted 206-203: R 201-18; D 5-185. Dec. 12, 2018.

433. PROCEDURAL MOTION/JOURNAL. Approval of the House Journal of December 12, 2018. Approved 226-169: R 138-77; D 88-92. Dec. 12, 2018.

	428	429	430	431	432	433
ALABAMA						
1 Byrne	Y	Y	Y	Y	Y	Y
2 Roby	Y	Y	Y	Y	Y	Y
3 Rogers	Y	Y	Y	Y	Y	N
4 Aderholt	Y	Y	Y	?	?	?
5 Brooks	N	Y	N	Y	Y	Y
6 Palmer	Y	Y	Y	Y	Y	Y
7 Sewell	Y	Y	Y	N	N	N
ALASKA						
AL Young	Y	Y	Y	Y	Y	N
ARIZONA						
1 O'Halleran	Y	Y	Y	N	N	N
2 McSally	Y	Y	Y	Y	Y	N
3 Grijalva	Y	Y	Y	N	?	?
4 Gosar	N	Y	Y	Y	N	N
5 Biggs	N	Y	Y	Y	N	N
6 Schweikert	Y	?	Y	Y	N	Y
7 Gallego	Y	Y	Y	N	N	Y
8 Lesko	Y	Y	Y	Y	Y	Y
9 Sinema	Y	Y	Y	N	N	N
ARKANSAS						
1 Crawford	Y	Y	Y	Y	Y	Y
2 Hill	Y	Y	Y	Y	Y	N
3 Womack	Y	Y	Y	Y	Y	Y
4 Westerman	Y	Y	Y	Y	Y	Y
CALIFORNIA						
1 LaMalfa	Y	Y	Y	Y	Y	Y
2 Huffman	Y	Y	Y	N	N	Y
3 Garamendi	Y	Y	Y	N	N	Y
4 McClintock	Y	Y	Y	Y	Y	Y
5 Thompson	Y	Y	Y	N	N	N
6 Matsui	Y	Y	Y	N	N	N
7 Bera	Y	Y	Y	N	N	N
8 Cook	Y	Y	Y	Y	Y	Y
9 McNerney	Y	Y	Y	N	N	Y
10 Denham	Y	Y	Y	Y	Y	N
11 DeSaulnier	Y	Y	Y	N	N	Y
12 Pelosi	Y	Y	Y	N	N	N
13 Lee	Y	Y	Y	N	N	N
14 Speier	Y	Y	Y	N	N	Y
15 Swalwell	Y	Y	Y	N	N	N
16 Costa	?	?	?	N	Y	N
17 Khanna	Y	Y	Y	N	N	Y
18 Eshoo	Y	Y	Y	N	N	Y
19 Lofgren	Y	Y	Y	N	N	N
20 Panetta	Y	Y	Y	N	N	N
21 Valadao	Y	Y	Y	Y	Y	N
22 Nunes	Y	Y	Y	Y	Y	Y
23 McCarthy	Y	Y	Y	Y	Y	Y
24 Carbajal	Y	Y	Y	N	N	N
25 Knight	?	?	?	?	?	?
26 Brownley	Y	Y	Y	N	N	N
27 Chu	Y	Y	Y	N	N	Y
28 Schiff	Y	Y	Y	N	N	N
29 Cardenas	Y	Y	Y	N	N	N
30 Sherman	Y	Y	Y	N	N	Y
31 Aguilar	Y	Y	Y	N	N	N
32 Napolitano	Y	Y	Y	N	N	Y
33 Lieu	Y	Y	Y	N	N	?
34 Gomez	Y	Y	Y	N	N	N
35 Torres	Y	Y	Y	N	N	N
36 Ruiz	Y	Y	Y	N	N	N
37 Bass	Y	Y	Y	N	N	N
38 Sánchez, Linda	Y	Y	Y	N	N	N
39 Royce	Y	Y	Y	Y	Y	Y
40 Roybal-Allard	Y	Y	Y	N	N	N
41 Takano	Y	Y	Y	N	N	N
42 Calvert	Y	Y	Y	Y	Y	Y
43 Waters	Y	Y	Y	N	N	?
44 Barragan	Y	Y	Y	N	N	N
45 Walters	?	?	?	Y	Y	Y
46 Correa	Y	Y	Y	N	N	N
47 Lowenthal	Y	Y	Y	N	N	Y
48 Rohrabacher	Y	Y	Y	Y	Y	Y
49 Issa	Y	Y	?	Y	Y	Y
50 Hunter	Y	Y	Y	?	?	?
51 Vargas	Y	Y	Y	N	N	N
52 Peters	?	Y	Y	N	N	Y
53 Davis	Y	Y	Y	N	N	Y

	428	429	430	431	432	433
COLORADO						
1 DeGette	Y	Y	Y	N	N	Y
2 Polis	?	?	?	?	?	?
3 Tipton	Y	Y	Y	Y	Y	N
4 Buck	Y	Y	Y	Y	Y	N
5 Lamborn	Y	Y	Y	Y	Y	Y
6 Coffman	Y	Y	Y	Y	Y	N
7 Perlmutter	Y	Y	Y	N	N	Y
CONNECTICUT						
1 Larson	Y	Y	Y	N	N	Y
2 Courtney	Y	Y	Y	N	N	N
3 DeLauro	Y	Y	Y	N	N	Y
4 Himes	Y	Y	Y	N	N	Y
5 Esty	Y	Y	Y	N	N	Y
DELAWARE						
AL Blunt Rochester	Y	Y	Y	N	N	Y
FLORIDA						
1 Gaetz	N	Y	?	Y	N	Y
2 Dunn	Y	Y	Y	Y	Y	Y
3 Yoho	Y	?	Y	Y	Y	Y
4 Rutherford	Y	Y	Y	Y	Y	Y
5 Lawson	Y	Y	Y	N	Y	N
6 Vacant						
7 Murphy	Y	Y	Y	N	N	Y
8 Posey	Y	Y	Y	N	Y	Y
9 Soto	Y	Y	Y	N	N	N
10 Demings	Y	Y	Y	N	N	N
11 Webster	Y	Y	Y	Y	Y	N
12 Bilirakis	Y	Y	Y	Y	Y	Y
13 Crist	Y	Y	Y	N	N	N
14 Castor	Y	Y	Y	N	N	N
15 Ross	?	?	?	Y	Y	Y
16 Buchanan	?	?	?	?	?	?
17 Rooney, T.	?	?	?	?	?	?
18 Mast	Y	Y	Y	N	N	Y
19 Rooney, F.	N	Y	Y	Y	Y	Y
20 Hastings	Y	Y	Y	?	?	?
21 Frankel	Y	Y	Y	N	N	Y
22 Deutch	Y	Y	Y	N	N	Y
23 Wasserman Schultz	Y	Y	Y	N	N	Y
24 Wilson	Y	Y	Y	N	N	Y
25 Diaz-Balart	Y	Y	Y	Y	Y	?
26 Curbelo	?	?	?	Y	Y	Y
27 Ros-Lehtinen	Y	Y	Y	Y	Y	N
GEORGIA						
1 Carter	Y	Y	Y	Y	Y	N
2 Bishop	Y	Y	Y	N	N	Y
3 Ferguson	Y	Y	Y	Y	Y	Y
4 Johnson	Y	Y	Y	N	N	N
5 Lewis	Y	Y	Y	N	N	N
6 Handel	Y	Y	Y	Y	Y	Y
7 Woodall	Y	Y	Y	Y	Y	N
8 Scott, A.	Y	Y	Y	Y	Y	Y
9 Collins	Y	Y	Y	Y	Y	Y
10 Hice	N	Y	Y	Y	Y	N
11 Loudermilk	Y	Y	Y	Y	Y	Y
12 Allen	Y	Y	Y	Y	Y	Y
13 Scott, D.	Y	Y	Y	N	Y	Y
14 Graves	Y	Y	Y	Y	Y	N
HAWAII						
1 Hanabusa	Y	Y	Y	N	N	Y
2 Gabbard	Y	Y	Y	N	N	Y
IDAHO						
1 Labrador	N	Y	Y	Y	N	Y
2 Simpson	Y	Y	Y	Y	Y	Y
ILLINOIS						
1 Rush	Y	Y	Y	N	N	Y
2 Kelly	Y	Y	Y	N	N	N
3 Lipinski	Y	Y	Y	N	N	Y
4 Gutierrez	Y	Y	Y	N	N	N
5 Quigley	Y	Y	Y	N	N	Y
6 Roskam	Y	Y	Y	?	?	?
7 Davis, D.	Y	Y	?	N	N	Y
8 Krishnamoorthi	Y	Y	Y	N	N	Y
9 Schakowsky	Y	Y	?	N	N	N
10 Schneider	Y	Y	Y	N	N	Y
11 Foster	Y	Y	Y	N	N	Y
12 Bost	Y	Y	Y	Y	Y	Y
13 Davis, R.	Y	Y	Y	Y	Y	Y

KEY   **Republicans**   Democrats   *Independents*

Y Voted for (yea)	X Paired against	C Voted "present" to avoid possible conflict of interest
# Paired for	– Announced against	
+ Announced for	P Voted "present"	? Did not vote or otherwise make a position known
N Voted against (nay)		

	428	429	430	431	432	433
14 **Hultgren**	Y	Y	Y	Y	Y	Y
15 **Shimkus**	Y	Y	Y	Y	Y	Y
16 **Kinzinger**	Y	Y	Y	Y	Y	N
17 Bustos	Y	Y	Y	N	N	Y
18 **LaHood**	Y	Y	Y	Y	Y	N
INDIANA						
1 Visclosky	Y	Y	Y	N	N	N
2 **Walorski**	Y	Y	Y	Y	Y	Y
3 **Banks**	Y	Y	Y	Y	Y	Y
4 Rokita	Y	Y	Y	Y	Y	N
5 **Brooks**	Y	Y	Y	Y	Y	Y
6 **Messer**	Y	Y	Y	Y	Y	Y
7 Carson	Y	Y	Y	N	N	?
8 **Bucshon**	Y	Y	Y	Y	Y	Y
9 **Hollingsworth**	Y	Y	Y	Y	Y	Y
IOWA						
1 **Blum**	Y	Y	Y	Y	N	N
2 Loebsack	Y	Y	Y	N	N	N
3 **Young**	Y	Y	Y	Y	Y	Y
4 **King**	Y	Y	Y	Y	Y	Y
KANSAS						
1 **Marshall**	Y	Y	Y	Y	Y	Y
2 **Jenkins**	?	?	?	Y	Y	N
3 **Yoder**	Y	Y	Y	Y	Y	N
4 **Estes**	Y	Y	Y	Y	Y	Y
KENTUCKY						
1 **Comer**	Y	Y	Y	Y	Y	N
2 **Guthrie**	Y	Y	Y	Y	Y	Y
3 Yarmuth	Y	Y	Y	N	N	Y
4 **Massie**	N	N	Y	Y	N	Y
5 **Rogers**	Y	Y	Y	Y	Y	Y
6 **Barr**	Y	Y	Y	Y	Y	N
LOUISIANA						
1 **Scalise**	Y	Y	Y	Y	Y	Y
2 Richmond	Y	Y	Y	N	N	N
3 **Higgins**	Y	Y	Y	Y	Y	Y
4 **Johnson**	Y	Y	Y	Y	Y	Y
5 **Abraham**	Y	Y	Y	Y	Y	Y
6 **Graves**	Y	Y	Y	Y	N	N
MAINE						
1 Pingree	Y	Y	Y	N	N	Y
2 **Poliquin**	Y	Y	Y	Y	Y	N
MARYLAND						
1 **Harris**	N	Y	Y	Y	Y	Y
2 Ruppersberger	Y	Y	Y	N	Y	Y
3 Sarbanes	Y	Y	Y	N	N	N
4 Brown	Y	Y	Y	N	N	Y
5 Hoyer	Y	Y	Y	N	N	N
6 Delaney	Y	Y	Y	N	N	N
7 Cummings	Y	Y	Y	N	N	N
8 Raskin	Y	Y	Y	N	N	?
MASSACHUSETTS						
1 Neal	Y	Y	Y	N	N	N
2 McGovern	Y	Y	Y	N	N	N
3 Tsongas	Y	Y	Y	N	N	Y
4 Kennedy	Y	Y	Y	N	N	Y
5 Clark	Y	Y	Y	N	N	Y
6 Moulton	Y	Y	Y	N	N	Y
7 Capuano	Y	Y	Y	N	N	N
8 Lynch	Y	Y	Y	N	N	N
9 Keating	?	?	?	–	–	?
MICHIGAN						
1 **Bergman**	Y	Y	Y	Y	Y	N
2 **Huizenga**	Y	Y	Y	Y	Y	N
3 *Amash*	N	N	N	Y	N	N
4 **Moolenaar**	Y	Y	Y	Y	Y	N
5 Kildee	Y	Y	Y	N	N	Y
6 **Upton**	Y	Y	Y	Y	Y	N
7 **Walberg**	Y	Y	Y	Y	Y	N
8 Bishop	?	?	?	Y	Y	Y
9 Levin	Y	Y	Y	N	N	N
10 **Mitchell**	Y	Y	Y	Y	Y	Y
11 **Trott**	Y	Y	Y	Y	Y	Y
12 Dingell	Y	Y	Y	N	N	P
13 Jones	Y	Y	Y	N	N	N
14 Lawrence	Y	Y	Y	N	N	N
MINNESOTA						
1 Walz	?	?	?	?	?	?
2 **Lewis**	Y	Y	Y	Y	Y	Y
3 **Paulsen**	Y	Y	Y	Y	Y	N
4 McCollum	Y	Y	Y	N	N	Y

	428	429	430	431	432	433
5 Ellison	?	?	?	?	?	?
6 **Emmer**	Y	Y	Y	Y	Y	N
7 Peterson	Y	Y	Y	N	Y	N
8 Nolan	Y	Y	Y	N	N	N
MISSISSIPPI						
1 **Kelly**	Y	Y	Y	Y	Y	Y
2 Thompson	Y	Y	Y	N	N	N
3 **Harper**	Y	Y	Y	Y	Y	Y
4 **Palazzo**	Y	Y	Y	Y	Y	Y
MISSOURI						
1 Clay	Y	Y	Y	N	N	Y
2 **Wagner**	Y	Y	Y	Y	Y	Y
3 **Luetkemeyer**	Y	Y	Y	Y	Y	Y
4 **Hartzler**	?	?	?	?	?	?
5 Cleaver	Y	Y	Y	N	N	Y
6 **Graves**	Y	Y	Y	Y	Y	N
7 **Long**	Y	Y	Y	Y	Y	Y
8 **Smith**	Y	Y	Y	Y	Y	Y
MONTANA						
AL **Gianforte**	Y	Y	Y	Y	Y	Y
NEBRASKA						
1 **Fortenberry**	Y	Y	Y	Y	Y	N
2 **Bacon**	Y	Y	Y	Y	Y	Y
3 **Smith**	Y	Y	Y	Y	Y	Y
NEVADA						
1 Titus	Y	Y	Y	N	N	Y
2 **Amodei**	Y	Y	Y	Y	Y	Y
3 Rosen	Y	Y	Y	N	N	N
4 Kihuen	Y	Y	Y	N	N	N
NEW HAMPSHIRE						
1 Shea-Porter	Y	Y	Y	N	N	Y
2 Kuster	Y	Y	Y	N	N	Y
NEW JERSEY						
1 Norcross	Y	Y	Y	N	N	N
2 **LoBiondo**	Y	Y	Y	Y	Y	N
3 **MacArthur**	Y	Y	Y	Y	Y	N
4 **Smith**	Y	Y	Y	Y	?	Y
5 Gottheimer	Y	Y	Y	N	N	N
6 Pallone	Y	Y	Y	N	N	N
7 **Lance**	Y	Y	Y	Y	Y	N
8 Sires	Y	Y	Y	N	N	N
9 Pascrell	Y	Y	Y	N	N	Y
10 Payne	Y	Y	Y	N	N	P
11 **Frelinghuysen**	Y	Y	+	Y	Y	Y
12 Watson Coleman	Y	Y	Y	N	N	N
NEW MEXICO						
1 Lujan Grisham	Y	Y	Y	?	?	?
2 **Pearce**	Y	Y	Y	Y	Y	Y
3 Luján	Y	Y	Y	N	N	Y
NEW YORK						
1 **Zeldin**	Y	Y	Y	Y	Y	N
2 **King**	Y	Y	Y	Y	Y	Y
3 Suozzi	Y	?	Y	N	N	N
4 Rice	Y	Y	Y	N	N	N
5 Meeks	Y	Y	Y	N	N	N
6 Meng	Y	Y	Y	N	N	Y
7 Velázquez	Y	Y	Y	N	N	N
8 Jeffries	Y	Y	Y	N	N	N
9 Clarke	Y	Y	Y	N	N	N
10 Nadler	Y	Y	Y	N	N	Y
11 **Donovan**	Y	Y	Y	Y	Y	Y
12 Maloney, C.	Y	Y	Y	N	N	N
13 Espaillat	Y	Y	Y	N	N	N
14 Crowley	Y	Y	Y	N	N	N
15 Serrano	Y	Y	Y	N	N	N
16 Engel	Y	Y	Y	N	N	Y
17 Lowey	Y	Y	Y	N	N	Y
18 Maloney, S.P.	Y	Y	Y	N	N	N
19 **Faso**	Y	Y	Y	Y	Y	N
20 Tonko	Y	Y	Y	N	N	P
21 **Stefanik**	Y	Y	Y	Y	Y	?
22 **Tenney**	Y	Y	Y	Y	Y	N
23 **Reed**	Y	Y	Y	Y	Y	N
24 **Katko**	Y	Y	Y	Y	Y	Y
25 Morelle	Y	Y	Y	N	N	N
26 Higgins	Y	Y	Y	N	N	N
27 **Collins**	Y	Y	Y	Y	Y	Y
NORTH CAROLINA						
1 Butterfield	Y	Y	Y	N	N	N
2 **Holding**	Y	Y	Y	Y	Y	N
3 **Jones**	?	?	?	?	?	?
4 Price	Y	Y	Y	N	N	N

	428	429	430	431	432	433
5 **Foxx**	Y	Y	Y	Y	Y	N
6 **Walker**	Y	Y	Y	Y	Y	Y
7 **Rouzer**	Y	Y	Y	Y	Y	N
8 **Hudson**	Y	Y	Y	Y	Y	N
9 **Pittenger**	?	?	?	Y	Y	Y
9 **Vacant**						
10 **McHenry**	Y	Y	Y	Y	Y	Y
11 **Meadows**	Y	Y	Y	Y	N	Y
12 Adams	Y	Y	Y	N	N	Y
13 **Budd**	Y	Y	Y	Y	Y	Y
NORTH DAKOTA						
AL **Cramer**	Y	Y	?	Y	Y	?
OHIO						
1 **Chabot**	Y	Y	Y	Y	Y	Y
2 **Wenstrup**	Y	Y	Y	Y	Y	N
3 Beatty	Y	Y	Y	N	N	?
4 **Jordan**	Y	Y	Y	Y	N	N
5 **Latta**	Y	Y	Y	Y	Y	N
6 **Johnson**	Y	Y	Y	Y	Y	N
7 **Gibbs**	Y	Y	Y	Y	Y	Y
8 **Davidson**	Y	Y	Y	Y	?	N
9 Kaptur	Y	Y	Y	N	N	Y
10 **Turner**	Y	Y	Y	Y	Y	N
11 Fudge	Y	Y	Y	N	N	N
12 Balderson	Y	Y	Y	Y	Y	Y
13 Ryan	Y	Y	Y	N	N	N
14 **Joyce**	Y	Y	Y	Y	Y	N
15 **Stivers**	Y	Y	Y	Y	Y	N
16 **Renacci**	Y	Y	Y	Y	Y	N
OKLAHOMA						
1 Hern	Y	Y	Y	Y	Y	Y
2 **Mullin**	Y	Y	Y	Y	Y	Y
3 **Lucas**	Y	Y	Y	Y	Y	Y
4 **Cole**	Y	Y	Y	Y	Y	Y
5 **Russell**	Y	Y	Y	Y	Y	Y
OREGON						
1 Bonamici	Y	Y	Y	N	N	Y
2 **Walden**	Y	Y	Y	Y	Y	Y
3 Blumenauer	Y	Y	Y	N	N	Y
4 DeFazio	?	?	?	N	N	N
5 Schrader	Y	Y	Y	N	N	N
PENNSYLVANIA						
1 Brady	Y	Y	Y	N	N	Y
2 Evans	Y	Y	Y	N	N	Y
3 **Kelly**	Y	Y	Y	Y	Y	Y
4 **Perry**	Y	Y	Y	Y	N	N
5 **Thompson**	Y	Y	Y	Y	Y	N
6 **Costello**	Y	Y	Y	Y	Y	N
7 Scanlon	Y	Y	Y	N	N	Y
8 **Fitzpatrick**	Y	Y	Y	Y	Y	Y
9 **Shuster**	Y	Y	Y	?	?	?
10 **Marino**	Y	Y	Y	Y	Y	Y
11 **Barletta**	Y	Y	Y	?	?	?
12 **Rothfus**	Y	Y	Y	Y	Y	Y
13 Boyle	Y	Y	Y	N	N	N
14 Doyle	Y	Y	Y	N	N	N
15 Wild	Y	Y	Y	N	N	N
16 **Smucker**	Y	Y	Y	Y	Y	Y
17 Cartwright	Y	Y	Y	N	N	Y
18 Lamb	Y	Y	Y	N	N	Y
RHODE ISLAND						
1 Cicilline	Y	Y	Y	N	N	Y
2 Langevin	Y	Y	Y	N	N	N
SOUTH CAROLINA						
1 **Sanford**	Y	Y	Y	Y	N	N
2 **Wilson**	Y	Y	Y	Y	Y	Y
3 **Duncan**	Y	Y	Y	Y	Y	N
4 **Gowdy**	Y	Y	Y	Y	Y	Y
5 **Norman**	Y	Y	Y	Y	Y	Y
6 Clyburn	Y	Y	Y	N	N	Y
7 **Rice**	Y	Y	Y	Y	Y	Y
SOUTH DAKOTA						
AL **Noem**	?	?	?	?	?	?
TENNESSEE						
1 **Roe**	Y	Y	Y	Y	Y	Y
2 **Duncan**	Y	Y	Y	Y	Y	Y
3 **Fleischmann**	Y	Y	Y	Y	Y	Y
4 **DesJarlais**	Y	Y	Y	Y	Y	Y
5 Cooper	Y	Y	Y	N	N	Y
6 **Black**	Y	Y	Y	?	?	?
7 **Blackburn**	Y	Y	Y	?	?	?
8 **Kustoff**	Y	Y	Y	Y	Y	Y
9 Cohen	Y	Y	Y	N	N	Y

	428	429	430	431	432	433
TEXAS						
1 **Gohmert**	Y	Y	Y	Y	N	P
2 **Poe**	Y	Y	Y	Y	Y	N
3 **Johnson, S.**	Y	Y	Y	Y	Y	Y
4 **Ratcliffe**	Y	Y	Y	Y	Y	N
5 **Hensarling**	Y	Y	Y	Y	Y	Y
6 **Barton**	Y	Y	Y	Y	Y	Y
7 **Culberson**	Y	Y	Y	Y	Y	Y
8 **Brady**	Y	Y	Y	Y	Y	Y
9 Green, A.	Y	Y	Y	N	N	N
10 **McCaul**	Y	Y	Y	Y	Y	Y
11 **Conaway**	Y	Y	Y	Y	Y	Y
12 **Granger**	Y	Y	Y	Y	Y	Y
13 **Thornberry**	Y	Y	Y	Y	Y	Y
14 **Weber**	Y	Y	Y	Y	Y	Y
15 Gonzalez	Y	Y	Y	N	N	N
16 O'Rourke	Y	Y	Y	N	N	Y
17 **Flores**	Y	Y	Y	Y	Y	N
18 Jackson Lee	Y	Y	Y	N	N	Y
19 **Arrington**	Y	Y	Y	Y	Y	?
20 Castro	Y	Y	Y	N	N	Y
21 **Smith**	Y	Y	Y	Y	Y	Y
22 **Olson**	Y	Y	Y	Y	Y	Y
23 **Hurd**	Y	Y	Y	Y	Y	N
24 Marchant	Y	Y	Y	Y	Y	Y
25 **Williams**	Y	Y	Y	Y	Y	Y
26 **Burgess**	Y	Y	Y	Y	Y	N
27 Cloud	Y	Y	Y	Y	N	Y
28 Cuellar	Y	Y	Y	N	N	Y
29 Green, G.	Y	Y	Y	N	N	N
30 Johnson, E.B.	Y	Y	Y	N	N	Y
31 **Carter**	Y	Y	Y	Y	Y	Y
32 **Sessions**	Y	Y	Y	Y	Y	Y
33 Veasey	Y	Y	Y	N	N	N
34 Vela	Y	Y	Y	N	N	Y
35 Doggett	?	Y	Y	N	N	Y
36 **Babin**	Y	Y	Y	Y	Y	Y
UTAH						
1 **Bishop**	Y	Y	Y	Y	Y	Y
2 **Stewart**	Y	Y	Y	?	?	?
3 **Curtis**	Y	Y	Y	Y	Y	Y
4 **Love**	Y	Y	Y	Y	Y	Y
VERMONT						
AL Welch	Y	Y	Y	N	N	Y
VIRGINIA						
1 **Wittman**	Y	Y	Y	Y	Y	N
2 **Taylor**	Y	Y	Y	Y	Y	N
3 Scott	Y	Y	Y	N	N	Y
4 McEachin	Y	?	?	N	N	?
5 **Garrett**	N	N	N	Y	N	N
6 **Goodlatte**	Y	Y	Y	Y	Y	Y
7 **Brat**	Y	Y	Y	Y	N	Y
8 Beyer	?	?	?	N	N	N
9 **Griffith**	Y	Y	Y	Y	Y	Y
10 **Comstock**	Y	Y	Y	?	?	?
11 Connolly	Y	Y	Y	N	N	N
WASHINGTON						
1 DelBene	Y	Y	Y	N	N	N
2 Larsen	Y	Y	Y	N	N	?
3 **Herrera Beutler**	Y	Y	Y	Y	Y	N
4 **Newhouse**	Y	Y	Y	Y	Y	Y
5 **McMorris Rodgers**	Y	Y	Y	Y	Y	N
6 Kilmer	Y	Y	Y	N	N	N
7 Jayapal	Y	Y	Y	N	N	N
8 **Reichert**	Y	Y	Y	Y	Y	Y
9 Smith	Y	Y	Y	N	N	Y
10 Heck	Y	Y	Y	N	N	Y
WEST VIRGINIA						
1 **McKinley**	Y	Y	Y	Y	Y	N
2 **Mooney**	Y	Y	Y	Y	Y	Y
3 **Vacant**						
WISCONSIN						
1 **Ryan**					Y	
2 Pocan	Y	Y	Y	N	N	Y
3 Kind	Y	Y	Y	N	N	N
4 Moore	Y	Y	Y	N	N	Y
5 **Sensenbrenner**	Y	Y	Y	Y	Y	Y
6 **Grothman**	Y	Y	Y	Y	Y	Y
7 **Duffy**	Y	Y	Y	Y	Y	N
8 **Gallagher**	Y	Y	Y	Y	Y	N
WYOMING						
AL **Cheney**	Y	Y	Y	Y	Y	Y

III HOUSE VOTES

VOTE NUMBER

434. HR2. FARM PROGRAMS/CONFERENCE REPORT. Adoption of the conference report on the bill that would reauthorize and extend federal farm and nutrition programs through fiscal 2023, including crop subsidies, conservation, rural development and agricultural trade programs and the Supplemental Nutritional Assistance Program. It would reauthorize and extend supplemental agricultural disaster assistance programs, sugar policies and loan rates, several international food aid programs, nonrecourse marketing assistance loans for loan commodities, and several dairy programs, including the dairy risk management program (previously the margin protection program). It would create new pilot programs that would test strategies for improving the accuracy of the SNAP income verification process. It would allow industrial hemp to be grown in the United States, subject to close regulation at the state level. It would modify the activities permitted on land contracted under the conservation reserve program. Adopted (thus cleared for the president) 369-47: R 182-44; D 187-3. Dec. 12, 2018.

435. HRES1091. HUMAN RIGHTS IN BURMA/ADOPTION. Royce, R-Calif., motion to suspend the rules and agree to the resolution, as amended, that would express that the House of Representatives considers Burmese military actions against the Rohingya population to be genocide and call for the Burmese government to release and end prosecution of journalists and other political prisoners. It would urge the secretary of State to determine whether Burmese military actions constitute crimes under international law and urge the president to impose sanctions on Burmese individuals responsible for human rights abuses. Motion agreed to 394-1: R 211-1; D 183-0. Dec. 13, 2018.

436. HR1222. CONGENITAL HEART DISEASE /PASSAGE. Walden, R-Ore., motion to suspend the rules and concur in the Senate amendment to the bill that would authorize Health and Human Services Department activities related to research, surveillance, and public awareness of congenital heart diseases, including a national epidemiology study. Annually through fiscal 2024, it would authorize $10 million for these activities. Motion agreed to 355-7: R 188-7; D 167-0. Dec. 19, 2018.

437. HR6615. BRAIN TRAUMA/PASSAGE. Walden, R-Ore., motion to suspend the rules and concur in the Senate amendment to the bill that would reauthorize several Health and Human Services Department grant programs for state activities related to traumatic brain injury research, treatment, and prevention. Annually through fiscal 2024, it would authorize $11.8 million for grants related to prevention and data collection, $7.3 million for grants related to access to rehabilitation, and $4 million for grants related to protection and advocacy services. Motion agreed to 352-6: R 185-6; D 167-0. Dec. 19, 2018.

438. S2076. ALZHEIMER'S CENTERS/PASSAGE. Walden, R-Ore., motion to suspend the rules and pass the bill that would authorize Health and Human Services Department grants and contracts with state, local, tribal, and educational entities to establish or support regional centers and other activities addressing Alzheimer's and other dementias. Annually through fiscal 2024, it would authorize $20 million for these activities. Motion agreed to 361-3: R 195-3; D 166-0. Dec. 19, 2018.

439. S2278. RURAL HEALTH OFFICES /PASSAGE. Walden, R-Ore., motion to suspend the rules and pass the bill that would reauthorize and modify the Health and Human Services Department grant program for state offices of rural health. It would allow the HHS secretary to waive or reduce the fund matching requirement for states but would increase the required annual state contribution for operation of the office. Annually through fiscal 2022, it would authorize $12.5 million for the grant program. Motion agreed to 357-4: R 191-4; D 166-0. Dec. 19, 2018.

	434	435	436	437	438	439
ALABAMA						
1 Byrne	Y	Y	Y	Y	Y	Y
2 Roby	Y	Y	Y	Y	Y	Y
3 Rogers	Y	Y	Y	Y	Y	Y
4 Aderholt	Y	Y	Y	Y	Y	Y
5 Brooks	Y	Y	Y	Y	Y	Y
6 Palmer	Y	Y	Y	Y	Y	Y
7 Sewell	Y	Y	Y	Y	Y	Y
ALASKA						
AL Young	Y	Y	Y	Y	Y	Y
ARIZONA						
1 O'Halleran	Y	Y	Y	Y	Y	Y
2 McSally	N	Y	?	?	?	?
3 Grijalva	Y	?	Y	Y	Y	Y
4 Gosar	N	Y	Y	Y	Y	Y
5 Biggs	N	N	N	Y	Y	N
6 Schweikert	N	Y	Y	Y	Y	Y
7 Gallego	Y	Y	Y	Y	Y	Y
8 Lesko	N	Y	Y	N	Y	Y
9 Sinema	Y	Y	?	?	?	?
ARKANSAS						
1 Crawford	Y	Y	Y	Y	Y	Y
2 Hill	Y	Y	Y	Y	Y	Y
3 Womack	Y	Y	Y	Y	Y	Y
4 Westerman	Y	Y	Y	Y	Y	Y
CALIFORNIA						
1 LaMalfa	Y	Y	Y	Y	Y	Y
2 Huffman	Y	Y	Y	Y	Y	Y
3 Garamendi	Y	Y	Y	Y	Y	Y
4 McClintock	N	Y	N	N	N	Y
5 Thompson	Y	Y	Y	Y	Y	Y
6 Matsui	Y	Y	Y	Y	Y	Y
7 Bera	Y	Y	Y	Y	Y	Y
8 Cook	Y	Y	Y	Y	Y	Y
9 McNerney	Y	Y	Y	Y	Y	Y
10 Denham	Y	?	?	?	?	?
11 DeSaulnier	Y	Y	Y	Y	Y	Y
12 Pelosi	Y	Y	Y	Y	Y	Y
13 Lee	Y	Y	Y	Y	Y	Y
14 Speier	Y	Y	?	?	?	?
15 Swalwell	Y	Y	Y	Y	Y	Y
16 Costa	Y	Y	?	?	?	?
17 Khanna	Y	Y	Y	Y	Y	Y
18 Eshoo	Y	Y	Y	Y	Y	Y
19 Lofgren	Y	Y	Y	Y	Y	Y
20 Panetta	Y	Y	Y	Y	Y	Y
21 Valadao	Y	Y	?	?	Y	Y
22 Nunes	Y	Y	?	?	?	?
23 McCarthy	Y	Y	Y	Y	Y	Y
24 Carbajal	Y	Y	Y	Y	Y	Y
25 Knight	?	?	Y	Y	Y	Y
26 Brownley	Y	?	Y	Y	Y	Y
27 Chu	Y	Y	Y	Y	Y	Y
28 Schiff	Y	Y	Y	Y	Y	Y
29 Cardenas	Y	Y	?	?	?	?
30 Sherman	Y	Y	Y	Y	Y	Y
31 Aguilar	Y	Y	Y	Y	Y	Y
32 Napolitano	Y	Y	Y	Y	Y	Y
33 Lieu	Y	Y	Y	Y	Y	Y
34 Gomez	Y	Y	Y	Y	Y	Y
35 Torres	Y	Y	Y	Y	Y	Y
36 Ruiz	Y	Y	Y	Y	Y	Y
37 Bass	Y	Y	Y	Y	Y	Y
38 Sánchez, Linda	Y	Y	Y	Y	Y	Y
39 Royce	Y	Y	Y	Y	Y	Y
40 Roybal-Allard	Y	Y	Y	Y	Y	Y
41 Takano	Y	Y	Y	Y	Y	Y
42 Calvert	Y	Y	Y	Y	Y	Y
43 Waters	Y	Y	Y	Y	Y	Y
44 Barragan	Y	Y	Y	Y	Y	Y
45 Walters	Y	Y	?	?	?	?
46 Correa	Y	Y	Y	Y	Y	Y
47 Lowenthal	Y	Y	?	?	?	?
48 Rohrabacher	Y	Y	Y	Y	Y	Y
49 Issa	Y	Y	Y	Y	Y	Y
50 Hunter	Y	Y	Y	Y	Y	Y
51 Vargas	Y	Y	Y	Y	Y	Y
52 Peters	Y	Y	Y	Y	Y	Y
53 Davis	Y	Y	Y	Y	Y	Y
COLORADO						
1 DeGette	Y	Y	Y	Y	Y	Y
2 Polis	?	?	?	?	?	?
3 Tipton	Y	Y	Y	Y	Y	Y
4 Buck	N	Y	Y	Y	Y	Y
5 Lamborn	N	Y	Y	Y	Y	Y
6 Coffman	N	Y	Y	Y	Y	Y
7 Perlmutter	Y	Y	Y	Y	Y	Y
CONNECTICUT						
1 Larson	Y	Y	Y	Y	Y	Y
2 Courtney	Y	Y	Y	Y	Y	Y
3 DeLauro	Y	Y	Y	Y	Y	Y
4 Himes	Y	Y	Y	Y	Y	Y
5 Esty	Y	Y	Y	Y	Y	Y
DELAWARE						
AL Blunt Rochester	Y	Y	Y	Y	Y	Y
FLORIDA						
1 Gaetz	N	Y	Y	Y	Y	Y
2 Dunn	Y	Y	Y	Y	Y	Y
3 Yoho	Y	Y	?	?	?	?
4 Rutherford	Y	Y	Y	Y	Y	Y
5 Lawson	Y	Y	Y	Y	Y	Y
6 Vacant						
7 Murphy	Y	Y	Y	Y	Y	Y
8 Posey	N	Y	Y	Y	Y	Y
9 Soto	Y	Y	Y	Y	Y	Y
10 Demings	Y	Y	Y	Y	Y	Y
11 Webster	Y	Y	Y	Y	Y	Y
12 Bilirakis	Y	Y	Y	Y	Y	Y
13 Crist	Y	Y	Y	Y	Y	Y
14 Castor	Y	Y	Y	Y	Y	Y
15 Ross	Y	Y	?	?	?	?
16 Buchanan	?	?	?	?	?	?
17 Rooney, T.	Y	Y	Y	Y	Y	Y
18 Mast	N	Y	Y	Y	Y	Y
19 Rooney, F.	N	Y	Y	Y	Y	Y
20 Hastings	Y	Y	Y	Y	Y	Y
21 Frankel	Y	Y	Y	Y	Y	Y
22 Deutch	Y	Y	Y	Y	Y	Y
23 Wasserman Schultz	Y	Y	Y	Y	Y	Y
24 Wilson	Y	Y	?	?	?	?
25 Diaz-Balart	Y	Y	Y	Y	Y	Y
26 Curbelo	Y	?	Y	Y	Y	Y
27 Ros-Lehtinen	Y	Y	?	?	?	?
GEORGIA						
1 Carter	N	Y	Y	Y	Y	Y
2 Bishop	Y	Y	Y	Y	Y	Y
3 Ferguson	Y	Y	Y	Y	Y	Y
4 Johnson	Y	Y	Y	Y	Y	Y
5 Lewis	Y	Y	Y	Y	Y	Y
6 Handel	Y	Y	Y	Y	Y	Y
7 Woodall	Y	Y	Y	Y	Y	Y
8 Scott, A.	Y	Y	Y	Y	Y	Y
9 Collins	Y	Y	Y	Y	Y	?
10 Hice	N	Y	Y	Y	Y	Y
11 Loudermilk	N	Y	Y	Y	Y	Y
12 Allen	Y	Y	Y	Y	Y	Y
13 Scott, D.	Y	Y	?	?	?	?
14 Graves	Y	Y	Y	Y	Y	Y
HAWAII						
1 Hanabusa	Y	?	?	?	?	?
2 Gabbard	Y	Y	?	?	?	?
IDAHO						
1 Labrador	?	?	Y	Y	Y	Y
2 Simpson	Y	Y	Y	Y	Y	Y
ILLINOIS						
1 Rush	Y	Y	Y	Y	Y	Y
2 Kelly	Y	Y	Y	Y	Y	Y
3 Lipinski	Y	Y	?	?	?	?
4 Gutierrez	Y	?	?	?	?	?
5 Quigley	Y	Y	Y	Y	Y	Y
6 Roskam	Y	Y	Y	Y	Y	Y
7 Davis, D.	Y	Y	Y	Y	Y	Y
8 Krishnamoorthi	Y	Y	Y	Y	Y	Y
9 Schakowsky	Y	Y	Y	Y	Y	Y
10 Schneider	Y	Y	Y	Y	Y	Y
11 Foster	Y	Y	?	?	?	?
12 Bost	Y	Y	Y	Y	Y	Y
13 Davis, R.	Y	Y	Y	Y	Y	Y

	434	435	436	437	438	439
14 **Hultgren**	Y	Y	Y	Y	Y	Y
15 **Shimkus**	Y	Y	Y	Y	Y	Y
16 **Kinzinger**	Y	Y	Y	Y	Y	Y
17 Bustos	Y	Y	Y	Y	Y	Y
18 **LaHood**	Y	Y	Y	Y	Y	Y
INDIANA						
1 Visclosky	Y	?	Y	Y	Y	Y
2 **Walorski**	Y	Y	Y	Y	Y	Y
3 **Banks**	Y	Y	Y	Y	Y	Y
4 Rokita	Y	?	Y	Y	Y	Y
5 **Brooks**	Y	Y	Y	Y	Y	?
6 **Messer**	Y	Y	?	?	?	?
7 Carson	Y	Y	Y	Y	Y	Y
8 **Bucshon**	Y	Y	Y	Y	Y	Y
9 **Hollingsworth**	Y	Y	Y	Y	Y	?
IOWA						
1 **Blum**	Y	Y	Y	Y	Y	Y
2 Loebsack	Y	Y	Y	Y	Y	Y
3 **Young**	Y	Y	Y	Y	Y	Y
4 **King**	Y	Y	Y	Y	Y	Y
KANSAS						
1 **Marshall**	Y	Y	Y	Y	Y	Y
2 **Jenkins**	Y	?	?	?	?	?
3 **Yoder**	Y	Y	Y	Y	Y	Y
4 **Estes**	Y	Y	Y	Y	Y	Y
KENTUCKY						
1 **Comer**	Y	Y	Y	Y	Y	Y
2 **Guthrie**	Y	Y	Y	Y	Y	Y
3 Yarmuth	Y	Y	Y	Y	Y	Y
4 **Massie**	N	Y	N	N	Y	Y
5 **Rogers**	Y	Y	Y	Y	Y	Y
6 **Barr**	Y	Y	Y	Y	Y	Y
LOUISIANA						
1 **Scalise**	Y	Y	Y	Y	Y	Y
2 Richmond	Y	?	Y	Y	Y	Y
3 **Higgins**	Y	Y	Y	Y	Y	Y
4 **Johnson**	Y	Y	Y	Y	Y	Y
5 **Abraham**	Y	Y	?	?	?	?
6 **Graves**	Y	Y	Y	Y	Y	Y
MAINE						
1 Pingree	Y	Y	Y	Y	Y	Y
2 **Poliquin**	Y	Y	Y	Y	Y	Y
MARYLAND						
1 **Harris**	N	Y	Y	Y	Y	Y
2 Ruppersberger	Y	Y	Y	Y	Y	Y
3 Sarbanes	Y	Y	Y	Y	Y	Y
4 Brown	Y	Y	Y	Y	Y	Y
5 Hoyer	Y	Y	Y	Y	Y	Y
6 Delaney	Y	Y	Y	Y	Y	Y
7 Cummings	Y	Y	Y	Y	Y	Y
8 Raskin	Y	Y	Y	Y	Y	Y
MASSACHUSETTS						
1 Neal	Y	Y	Y	Y	Y	Y
2 McGovern	Y	Y	Y	Y	Y	Y
3 Tsongas	Y	Y	?	?	?	?
4 Kennedy	Y	Y	?	?	?	?
5 Clark	Y	Y	Y	Y	Y	Y
6 Moulton	Y	Y	?	?	?	?
7 Capuano	Y	Y	Y	Y	Y	Y
8 Lynch	Y	Y	Y	Y	Y	Y
9 Keating	+	?	?	?	?	?
MICHIGAN						
1 **Bergman**	Y	Y	Y	Y	Y	Y
2 **Huizenga**	Y	Y	Y	Y	Y	Y
3 *Amash*	N	Y	N	N	N	N
4 **Moolenaar**	Y	Y	Y	Y	Y	Y
5 Kildee	Y	Y	Y	Y	Y	Y
6 **Upton**	Y	Y	Y	Y	Y	Y
7 **Walberg**	Y	Y	Y	Y	Y	Y
8 **Bishop**	Y	Y	?	?	?	?
9 Levin	Y	Y	Y	Y	Y	Y
10 **Mitchell**	Y	Y	Y	Y	Y	Y
11 **Trott**	Y	?	Y	Y	Y	Y
12 Dingell	Y	Y	Y	Y	Y	Y
13 Jones	Y	Y	Y	Y	Y	Y
14 Lawrence	Y	Y	Y	Y	Y	Y
MINNESOTA						
1 Walz	?	?	?	?	?	?
2 **Lewis**	N	Y	Y	Y	Y	Y
3 **Paulsen**	Y	?	?	?	?	?
4 McCollum	Y	Y	Y	Y	Y	Y

	434	435	436	437	438	439
5 Ellison	?	?	?	?	?	?
6 **Emmer**	Y	Y	Y	Y	Y	Y
7 Peterson	Y	Y	Y	Y	Y	Y
8 Nolan	Y	Y	?	?	?	?
MISSISSIPPI						
1 **Kelly**	Y	Y	Y	Y	Y	Y
2 Thompson	Y	Y	?	?	?	?
3 **Harper**	Y	Y	Y	Y	Y	Y
4 **Palazzo**	Y	Y	Y	Y	Y	Y
MISSOURI						
1 Clay	Y	?	Y	Y	Y	Y
2 **Wagner**	Y	?	Y	Y	Y	Y
3 **Luetkemeyer**	Y	Y	?	?	Y	Y
4 **Hartzler**	?	?	Y	Y	Y	Y
5 Cleaver	Y	Y	Y	Y	Y	?
6 **Graves**	Y	Y	Y	Y	Y	Y
7 **Long**	Y	Y	Y	Y	Y	Y
8 **Smith**	Y	Y	Y	Y	Y	Y
MONTANA						
AL **Gianforte**	Y	Y	Y	Y	Y	Y
NEBRASKA						
1 **Fortenberry**	Y	Y	Y	Y	Y	Y
2 **Bacon**	Y	Y	Y	Y	Y	Y
3 **Smith**	Y	Y	Y	Y	Y	Y
NEVADA						
1 Titus	Y	Y	Y	Y	Y	Y
2 **Amodei**	Y	Y	Y	Y	Y	Y
3 Rosen	Y	Y	?	?	?	?
4 Kihuen	Y	Y	Y	Y	Y	Y
NEW HAMPSHIRE						
1 Shea-Porter	Y	Y	+	+	+	+
2 Kuster	Y	Y	Y	Y	Y	Y
NEW JERSEY						
1 Norcross	Y	Y	Y	Y	Y	Y
2 **LoBiondo**	Y	Y	Y	Y	Y	Y
3 **MacArthur**	Y	Y	Y	Y	Y	Y
4 **Smith**	Y	Y	Y	Y	Y	Y
5 Gottheimer	Y	Y	Y	Y	Y	Y
6 Pallone	Y	Y	Y	Y	Y	Y
7 **Lance**	N	Y	Y	Y	Y	Y
8 Sires	Y	Y	Y	Y	Y	Y
9 Pascrell	Y	Y	Y	Y	Y	Y
10 Payne	?	Y	Y	Y	Y	Y
11 **Frelinghuysen**	N	Y	Y	Y	Y	Y
12 Watson Coleman	Y	Y	Y	Y	Y	Y
NEW MEXICO						
1 Lujan Grisham	?	?	?	?	?	?
2 **Pearce**	Y	Y	Y	Y	Y	Y
3 Luján	Y	Y	Y	Y	Y	Y
NEW YORK						
1 **Zeldin**	Y	Y	Y	Y	Y	Y
2 **King**	Y	Y	?	?	?	?
3 Suozzi	Y	Y	Y	Y	Y	Y
4 Rice	Y	Y	?	?	?	?
5 Meeks	Y	Y	Y	Y	Y	Y
6 Meng	Y	Y	Y	Y	Y	Y
7 Velázquez	Y	Y	Y	Y	Y	Y
8 Jeffries	Y	Y	Y	Y	Y	Y
9 Clarke	Y	Y	Y	Y	Y	Y
10 Nadler	Y	Y	Y	Y	Y	Y
11 **Donovan**	?	?	Y	Y	Y	Y
12 Maloney, C.	Y	Y	Y	Y	Y	Y
13 Espaillat	Y	Y	Y	Y	Y	Y
14 Crowley	Y	Y	Y	Y	Y	Y
15 Serrano	Y	Y	Y	Y	Y	Y
16 Engel	Y	Y	Y	Y	Y	Y
17 Lowey	Y	Y	Y	Y	Y	Y
18 Maloney, S.P.	Y	Y	Y	Y	Y	Y
19 **Faso**	Y	Y	Y	Y	Y	Y
20 Tonko	Y	Y	Y	Y	Y	Y
21 **Stefanik**	Y	Y	Y	Y	Y	Y
22 **Tenney**	Y	Y	Y	Y	Y	Y
23 **Reed**	Y	Y	Y	Y	Y	Y
24 **Katko**	Y	Y	Y	Y	Y	Y
25 Morelle	Y	Y	Y	Y	Y	Y
26 Higgins	Y	Y	Y	Y	Y	Y
27 **Collins**	Y	Y	Y	Y	Y	Y
NORTH CAROLINA						
1 Butterfield	Y	Y	Y	Y	Y	Y
2 **Holding**	N	Y	Y	Y	Y	Y
3 **Jones**	?	?	?	?	?	?
4 Price	Y	Y	Y	Y	Y	Y

	434	435	436	437	438	439
5 **Foxx**	N	Y	Y	Y	Y	Y
6 **Walker**	Y	Y	Y	Y	Y	Y
7 **Rouzer**	Y	Y	Y	Y	Y	Y
8 **Hudson**	Y	Y	?	Y	Y	Y
9 **Pittenger**	Y	Y	?	?	?	Y
9 **Vacant**						
10 **McHenry**	Y	Y	?	?	?	?
11 **Meadows**	N	Y	Y	Y	Y	Y
12 Adams	Y	Y	Y	Y	Y	Y
13 **Budd**	N	Y	?	Y	Y	Y
NORTH DAKOTA						
AL **Cramer**	Y	?	?	?	?	?
OHIO						
1 **Chabot**	N	Y	Y	Y	Y	Y
2 **Wenstrup**	Y	Y	Y	Y	Y	Y
3 Beatty	Y	Y	Y	Y	Y	Y
4 **Jordan**	N	Y	Y	Y	Y	Y
5 **Latta**	Y	Y	Y	Y	Y	Y
6 **Johnson**	Y	Y	Y	Y	Y	Y
7 **Gibbs**	Y	Y	Y	Y	Y	Y
8 **Davidson**	N	Y	N	N	Y	Y
9 Kaptur	Y	Y	Y	Y	Y	Y
10 **Turner**	Y	Y	Y	?	Y	Y
11 Fudge	Y	?	Y	Y	Y	Y
12 Balderson	Y	Y	Y	Y	Y	Y
13 Ryan	Y	Y	Y	Y	Y	Y
14 **Joyce**	Y	Y	Y	Y	Y	Y
15 **Stivers**	Y	Y	Y	Y	Y	Y
16 **Renacci**	Y	?	Y	Y	Y	Y
OKLAHOMA						
1 Hern	Y	Y	Y	Y	Y	Y
2 **Mullin**	Y	Y	Y	Y	Y	Y
3 **Lucas**	Y	Y	Y	Y	Y	Y
4 **Cole**	Y	Y	Y	Y	Y	Y
5 **Russell**	Y	Y	Y	Y	Y	Y
OREGON						
1 Bonamici	Y	Y	Y	Y	Y	Y
2 **Walden**	Y	Y	Y	Y	Y	Y
3 Blumenauer	N	Y	Y	Y	Y	Y
4 DeFazio	Y	Y	Y	Y	Y	Y
5 Schrader	Y	Y	Y	Y	Y	Y
PENNSYLVANIA						
1 Brady	Y	Y	?	?	?	?
2 Evans	Y	Y	Y	Y	Y	Y
3 **Kelly**	Y	Y	Y	Y	Y	Y
4 **Perry**	N	Y	Y	Y	Y	Y
5 **Thompson**	Y	Y	Y	Y	Y	Y
6 **Costello**	Y	Y	Y	Y	Y	Y
7 Scanlon	Y	Y	Y	Y	Y	Y
8 **Fitzpatrick**	Y	Y	Y	Y	Y	Y
9 **Shuster**	Y	Y	?	?	?	?
10 **Marino**	Y	?	Y	Y	Y	Y
11 **Barletta**	?	?	?	?	?	?
12 **Rothfus**	N	Y	Y	Y	Y	Y
13 Boyle	Y	Y	?	?	?	?
14 Doyle	Y	Y	Y	Y	Y	Y
15 Wild	Y	Y	?	?	?	?
16 **Smucker**	Y	Y	Y	Y	Y	Y
17 Cartwright	Y	Y	Y	Y	Y	Y
18 Lamb	Y	Y	Y	Y	Y	Y
RHODE ISLAND						
1 Cicilline	Y	Y	Y	Y	Y	Y
2 Langevin	Y	Y	Y	Y	Y	Y
SOUTH CAROLINA						
1 **Sanford**	N	Y	N	N	N	N
2 **Wilson**	N	Y	Y	Y	Y	Y
3 **Duncan**	N	Y	?	?	?	?
4 **Gowdy**	Y	Y	?	?	?	?
5 **Norman**	N	Y	?	?	?	?
6 Clyburn	Y	Y	Y	Y	Y	Y
7 **Rice**	Y	Y	Y	Y	Y	Y
SOUTH DAKOTA						
AL **Noem**	Y	Y	?	?	?	?
TENNESSEE						
1 **Roe**	Y	Y	Y	Y	Y	Y
2 **Duncan**	N	?	Y	Y	Y	Y
3 **Fleischmann**	Y	Y	Y	Y	Y	Y
4 **DesJarlais**	Y	?	Y	Y	Y	Y
5 Cooper	Y	Y	Y	Y	Y	Y
6 **Black**	Y	Y	?	?	?	?
7 **Blackburn**	Y	Y	Y	?	?	?
8 **Kustoff**	Y	Y	Y	Y	Y	Y
9 Cohen	Y	Y	Y	Y	Y	Y

	434	435	436	437	438	439
TEXAS						
1 **Gohmert**	N	Y	Y	Y	Y	Y
2 **Poe**	Y	Y	Y	Y	Y	Y
3 **Johnson, S.**	N	Y	?	?	?	?
4 **Ratcliffe**	N	Y	?	?	?	?
5 **Hensarling**	N	Y	Y	Y	Y	Y
6 **Barton**	?	Y	?	?	?	?
7 **Culberson**	Y	Y	Y	Y	Y	Y
8 **Brady**	Y	Y	Y	Y	Y	Y
9 Green, A.	Y	Y	Y	Y	Y	Y
10 **McCaul**	Y	Y	Y	Y	Y	Y
11 **Conaway**	Y	Y	Y	Y	Y	Y
12 **Granger**	Y	Y	Y	Y	Y	Y
13 **Thornberry**	Y	Y	?	?	?	?
14 **Weber**	Y	Y	Y	Y	Y	Y
15 Gonzalez	Y	Y	Y	Y	?	Y
16 O'Rourke	Y	Y	Y	Y	Y	Y
17 **Flores**	Y	Y	?	?	?	?
18 Jackson Lee	Y	Y	Y	Y	Y	Y
19 **Arrington**	Y	Y	Y	Y	Y	Y
20 Castro	Y	Y	Y	Y	Y	Y
21 **Smith**	Y	Y	Y	Y	Y	Y
22 **Olson**	Y	Y	?	?	?	?
23 **Hurd**	Y	Y	Y	Y	Y	Y
24 Marchant	Y	Y	?	?	?	?
25 **Williams**	Y	Y	Y	?	Y	Y
26 **Burgess**	Y	Y	Y	Y	Y	Y
27 Cloud	Y	Y	Y	Y	Y	Y
28 Cuellar	Y	Y	Y	Y	Y	Y
29 Green, G.	Y	Y	Y	Y	Y	Y
30 Johnson, E.B.	Y	Y	Y	Y	Y	Y
31 **Carter**	Y	Y	Y	Y	Y	Y
32 **Sessions**	Y	Y	Y	Y	Y	Y
33 Veasey	Y	Y	Y	Y	Y	Y
34 Vela	Y	Y	?	?	?	?
35 Doggett	N	Y	Y	Y	Y	Y
36 **Babin**	Y	Y	Y	Y	Y	Y
UTAH						
1 **Bishop**	Y	?	Y	Y	Y	Y
2 **Stewart**	?	?	Y	Y	Y	Y
3 **Curtis**	Y	Y	Y	?	Y	Y
4 **Love**	Y	?	?	?	?	?
VERMONT						
AL Welch	Y	Y	Y	Y	Y	Y
VIRGINIA						
1 **Wittman**	Y	Y	Y	Y	Y	Y
2 **Taylor**	Y	Y	Y	?	Y	Y
3 Scott	Y	Y	Y	Y	Y	Y
4 McEachin	Y	Y	Y	Y	Y	Y
5 **Garrett**	N	Y	N	Y	?	?
6 **Goodlatte**	Y	Y	Y	Y	Y	Y
7 **Brat**	N	Y	?	?	?	?
8 Beyer	Y	?	Y	Y	Y	Y
9 **Griffith**	Y	Y	Y	Y	Y	Y
10 **Comstock**	Y	?	?	?	?	?
11 Connolly	Y	Y	Y	Y	Y	Y
WASHINGTON						
1 DelBene	Y	Y	Y	Y	Y	Y
2 Larsen	Y	Y	Y	Y	Y	Y
3 **Herrera Beutler**	Y	Y	Y	Y	Y	Y
4 **Newhouse**	Y	Y	Y	Y	Y	Y
5 **McMorris Rodgers**	Y	Y	Y	Y	Y	Y
6 Kilmer	Y	Y	Y	Y	Y	Y
7 Jayapal	Y	Y	Y	Y	Y	Y
8 **Reichert**	Y	Y	Y	Y	Y	Y
9 Smith	Y	Y	Y	Y	Y	Y
10 Heck	Y	Y	Y	Y	Y	Y
WEST VIRGINIA						
1 **McKinley**	Y	Y	Y	Y	Y	Y
2 **Mooney**	N	Y	?	?	Y	Y
3 **Vacant**						
WISCONSIN						
1 **Ryan**						
2 Pocan	Y	Y	Y	Y	Y	Y
3 Kind	N	Y	?	?	?	?
4 Moore	+	Y	Y	Y	Y	Y
5 **Sensenbrenner**	N	Y	Y	Y	Y	N
6 **Grothman**	Y	Y	Y	Y	Y	Y
7 **Duffy**	Y	Y	Y	Y	Y	Y
8 **Gallagher**	N	Y	Y	Y	Y	Y
WYOMING						
AL **Cheney**	Y	Y	Y	Y	Y	?

VOTE NUMBER

440. HR7327. FEDERAL IT SECURITY COUNSEL /PASSAGE. Hurd, R-Texas, motion to suspend the rules and pass the bill that would establish a federal security council to mitigate security risks arising from federal acquisition of information technology, telecommunications services, and other goods and services. The council would include representatives from several executive agencies and would be required to develop supply chain risk management standards and practices across agencies and facilitate information sharing to support risk analysis. The bill would require the Homeland Security secretary to establish a policy for collecting reports on security vulnerabilities in the agency's public websites and remediating issues reported. It would also modify certain pay procedures for border patrol agents, including provisions related to pay rate determination and overtime policy. Motion agreed to 362-1: R 198-1; D 164-0. Dec. 19, 2018.

441. HR7279. WATER MANAGEMENT /PASSAGE. Walden, R-Ore., motion to suspend the rules and pass the bill that would formally codify the Environmental Protection Agency's permit process for integrated plans for wastewater and stormwater management by municipalities under the Clean Water Act. It would also establish the position and office of a municipal ombudsman within the EPA to assist municipalities in complying with the Clean Water Act. Motion agreed to 351-10: R 186-10; D 165-0. Dec. 19, 2018.

442. HR6227. QUANTUM SCIENCE RESEARCH /PASSAGE. Smith, R-Texas, motion to suspend the rules and concur in the Senate amendment to the bill that would direct the president to establish a national program to develop and coordinate research into quantum information sciences and quantum-based technologies, establish a quantum coordination office within the White House Office of Science and Technology Policy to oversee the program, and establish an interagency committee to establish the program's goals and strategic plan, chaired by the Energy secretary and directors of the National Institutes of Science and Technology and National Science Foundation. It would direct these agencies, respectively, to allocate up to $25 million, $80 million, and $10 million, annually through fiscal 2023, for grants and research activities related to quantum information science. Motion agreed to 348-11: R 185-11; D 163-0. Dec. 19, 2018.

443. HR6652. IRRIGATION LAND TRANSFER /PASSAGE. McClintock, R-Calif., motion to suspend the rules and pass the bill, as amended, that would authorize the transfer of the Kennewick Division of the the Kennewick Irrigation District in Benton County, Wash. from federal to local ownership. Motion agreed to 359-1: R 197-1; D 162-0. Dec. 19, 2018.

444. S1520. FISHERY MANAGEMENT /PASSAGE. Graves, R-La., motion to suspend the rules and pass the bill that would require several federal studies by the comptroller general, Commerce secretary, and National Academies on the management and operation of fisheries. It would also direct the Commerce Department collect and report data on recreational fisheries and create grants to assist states in complying with data collection. Motion agreed to 350-11: R 189-10; D 161-1. Dec. 19, 2018.

445. S3530. MUSEUM AND LIBRARY SERVICES /PASSAGE. Banks, R-Ind., motion to suspend the rules and pass the bill that would reauthorize through fiscal 2025 federal assistance for museum and library programs administered by the Institute of Museum and Library Service. It would also make tribal libraries eligible for grants, expand the responsibilities of the Institute director, and make other modifications to Institute programs and activities. Motion agreed to 331-28: R 170-28; D 161-0. Dec. 19, 2018.

	440	441	442	443	444	445
ALABAMA						
1 **Byrne**	Y	Y	Y	Y	Y	Y
2 **Roby**	Y	Y	Y	Y	Y	Y
3 **Rogers**	Y	Y	Y	Y	Y	Y
4 **Aderholt**	Y	Y	Y	Y	Y	Y
5 **Brooks**	Y	Y	Y	Y	Y	Y
6 **Palmer**	Y	Y	Y	Y	Y	N
7 Sewell	Y	Y	Y	Y	Y	Y
ALASKA						
AL **Young**	Y	Y	Y	Y	N	Y
ARIZONA						
1 O'Halleran	Y	Y	Y	Y	Y	Y
2 **McSally**	?	?	?	?	?	?
3 Grijalva	Y	Y	Y	Y	Y	?
4 **Gosar**	Y	Y	Y	Y	Y	N
5 **Biggs**	Y	N	Y	Y	N	N
6 **Schweikert**	Y	Y	Y	Y	Y	N
7 Gallego	Y	Y	Y	Y	Y	Y
8 **Lesko**	Y	Y	Y	Y	Y	N
9 Sinema	?	?	?	?	?	?
ARKANSAS						
1 **Crawford**	Y	Y	Y	Y	Y	Y
2 **Hill**	Y	Y	Y	Y	Y	Y
3 **Womack**	Y	Y	Y	Y	Y	Y
4 **Westerman**	Y	Y	Y	Y	Y	Y
CALIFORNIA						
1 **LaMalfa**	Y	Y	Y	Y	Y	Y
2 Huffman	Y	Y	Y	Y	Y	Y
3 Garamendi	Y	Y	Y	Y	Y	Y
4 **McClintock**	Y	Y	N	Y	Y	N
5 Thompson	Y	Y	Y	Y	Y	Y
6 Matsui	Y	Y	Y	Y	Y	Y
7 Bera	Y	Y	Y	Y	Y	Y
8 **Cook**	Y	Y	Y	Y	Y	Y
9 McNerney	Y	Y	Y	Y	Y	Y
10 **Denham**	?	?	?	?	?	?
11 DeSaulnier	Y	Y	Y	Y	Y	Y
12 Pelosi	Y	Y	Y	Y	Y	Y
13 Lee	Y	Y	Y	Y	Y	Y
14 Speier	?	?	?	?	?	?
15 Swalwell	?	?	?	?	?	?
16 Costa	?	?	?	?	?	?
17 Khanna	Y	Y	Y	Y	Y	Y
18 Eshoo	Y	Y	Y	Y	Y	Y
19 Lofgren	Y	Y	Y	Y	Y	Y
20 Panetta	Y	Y	Y	Y	Y	Y
21 **Valadao**	Y	Y	Y	Y	Y	Y
22 **Nunes**	?	?	?	?	?	?
23 **McCarthy**	Y	Y	Y	Y	Y	Y
24 Carbajal	Y	Y	Y	Y	Y	Y
25 **Knight**	Y	Y	Y	Y	Y	Y
26 Brownley	Y	Y	Y	Y	Y	Y
27 Chu	Y	Y	Y	Y	Y	Y
28 Schiff	Y	Y	Y	Y	Y	Y
29 Cardenas	?	?	?	?	?	?
30 Sherman	Y	Y	Y	Y	Y	Y
31 Aguilar	Y	Y	Y	Y	Y	Y
32 Napolitano	Y	Y	Y	Y	Y	Y
33 Lieu	Y	Y	Y	Y	Y	Y
34 Gomez	Y	Y	Y	Y	Y	Y
35 Torres	Y	Y	Y	Y	Y	Y
36 Ruiz	Y	Y	Y	Y	Y	Y
37 Bass	Y	Y	Y	Y	Y	Y
38 Sánchez, Linda	Y	Y	Y	Y	Y	Y
39 **Royce**	Y	Y	Y	Y	Y	Y
40 Roybal-Allard	Y	Y	Y	Y	Y	Y
41 Takano	Y	Y	Y	Y	Y	Y
42 **Calvert**	Y	Y	Y	Y	Y	Y
43 Waters	Y	Y	Y	Y	Y	Y
44 Barragan	Y	Y	Y	Y	Y	Y
45 **Walters**	?	?	?	?	?	?
46 Correa	Y	Y	Y	Y	Y	Y
47 Lowenthal	?	?	?	?	?	?
48 **Rohrabacher**	Y	Y	Y	Y	Y	N
49 **Issa**	Y	?	?	?	?	?
50 **Hunter**	Y	Y	Y	Y	Y	Y
51 Vargas	Y	Y	Y	Y	Y	Y
52 Peters	Y	Y	Y	Y	Y	Y
53 Davis	Y	Y	Y	Y	Y	Y

	440	441	442	443	444	445
COLORADO						
1 DeGette	Y	Y	Y	Y	Y	Y
2 Polis	?	?	?	?	?	?
3 Tipton	Y	Y	Y	Y	Y	Y
4 **Buck**	Y	Y	N	Y	Y	N
5 **Lamborn**	Y	Y	Y	Y	Y	Y
6 **Coffman**	Y	Y	Y	Y	Y	Y
7 Perlmutter	Y	Y	Y	Y	Y	Y
CONNECTICUT						
1 Larson	Y	Y	Y	Y	Y	Y
2 Courtney	Y	Y	Y	Y	Y	Y
3 DeLauro	?	Y	Y	Y	Y	Y
4 Himes	Y	Y	Y	Y	Y	Y
5 Esty	Y	Y	Y	Y	Y	Y
DELAWARE						
AL Blunt Rochester	Y	Y	Y	Y	Y	Y
FLORIDA						
1 **Gaetz**	Y	N	N	Y	N	N
2 **Dunn**	Y	Y	Y	Y	Y	Y
3 **Yoho**	?	?	?	?	?	?
4 **Rutherford**	Y	Y	Y	Y	Y	Y
5 Lawson	Y	Y	Y	Y	Y	Y
6 Vacant						
7 Murphy	Y	Y	Y	Y	Y	Y
8 **Posey**	Y	Y	Y	Y	Y	Y
9 Soto	Y	Y	Y	Y	Y	Y
10 Demings	Y	Y	Y	Y	Y	Y
11 **Webster**	Y	Y	Y	Y	Y	Y
12 **Bilirakis**	Y	Y	Y	Y	Y	Y
13 Crist	Y	Y	Y	Y	Y	Y
14 Castor	Y	Y	Y	Y	Y	Y
15 **Ross**	?	?	?	?	?	?
16 **Buchanan**	?	?	?	?	?	?
17 **Rooney, T.**	?	?	?	?	?	?
18 **Mast**	Y	Y	Y	Y	Y	Y
19 **Rooney, F.**	Y	Y	Y	Y	Y	Y
20 Hastings	Y	Y	Y	Y	Y	Y
21 Frankel	Y	Y	Y	Y	Y	Y
22 Deutch	Y	Y	Y	Y	Y	Y
23 Wasserman Schultz	Y	Y	Y	Y	Y	Y
24 Wilson	?	?	?	?	?	?
25 **Diaz-Balart**	Y	Y	Y	Y	Y	Y
26 **Curbelo**	Y	Y	Y	Y	Y	Y
27 **Ros-Lehtinen**	?	?	?	?	?	?
GEORGIA						
1 **Carter**	Y	Y	Y	Y	Y	Y
2 Bishop	?	?	?	?	Y	Y
3 **Ferguson**	Y	Y	Y	Y	Y	Y
4 Johnson	Y	Y	Y	Y	Y	Y
5 Lewis	Y	Y	Y	Y	Y	Y
6 **Handel**	Y	Y	Y	Y	Y	Y
7 **Woodall**	Y	Y	Y	Y	Y	Y
8 **Scott, A.**	Y	Y	Y	Y	Y	Y
9 **Collins**	Y	Y	Y	Y	Y	Y
10 **Hice**	Y	Y	Y	Y	Y	N
11 **Loudermilk**	Y	Y	Y	Y	Y	Y
12 **Allen**	Y	Y	Y	Y	Y	Y
13 Scott, D.	?	?	?	?	?	?
14 **Graves**	Y	Y	Y	Y	Y	Y
HAWAII						
1 Hanabusa	?	?	?	?	?	?
2 Gabbard	?	?	?	?	?	?
IDAHO						
1 **Labrador**	Y	Y	Y	Y	N	N
2 **Simpson**	Y	Y	Y	Y	Y	Y
ILLINOIS						
1 Rush	Y	Y	?	Y	Y	Y
2 Kelly	Y	Y	Y	Y	Y	Y
3 Lipinski	?	?	?	?	?	?
4 Gutierrez	?	?	?	?	?	?
5 Quigley	Y	Y	Y	Y	Y	Y
6 **Roskam**	Y	Y	Y	Y	Y	Y
7 Davis, D.	Y	Y	Y	Y	Y	Y
8 Krishnamoorthi	Y	Y	Y	Y	Y	Y
9 Schakowsky	Y	Y	Y	Y	Y	Y
10 Schneider	Y	Y	Y	Y	Y	Y
11 Foster	?	?	?	?	?	?
12 **Bost**	Y	Y	Y	Y	Y	Y
13 **Davis, R.**	Y	Y	Y	Y	Y	Y

	440	441	442	443	444	445
14 **Hultgren**	Y	Y	Y	Y	Y	Y
15 **Shimkus**	Y	Y	Y	Y	Y	Y
16 **Kinzinger**	Y	Y	Y	Y	Y	Y
17 Bustos	Y	Y	Y	Y	Y	Y
18 **LaHood**	Y	Y	Y	Y	Y	Y
INDIANA						
1 Visclosky	Y	Y	Y	Y	Y	Y
2 **Walorski**	Y	Y	Y	Y	Y	Y
3 **Banks**	Y	Y	Y	Y	Y	Y
4 Rokita	Y	Y	Y	Y	Y	Y
5 **Brooks**	Y	Y	Y	Y	Y	Y
6 **Messer**	?	?	?	?	?	?
7 Carson	Y	Y	Y	Y	Y	Y
8 **Bucshon**	Y	Y	Y	Y	Y	Y
9 **Hollingsworth**	Y	Y	?	Y	Y	Y
IOWA						
1 **Blum**	Y	N	N	Y	N	N
2 Loebsack	Y	Y	Y	Y	Y	Y
3 **Young**	Y	Y	Y	Y	Y	Y
4 **King**	Y	Y	Y	Y	Y	Y
KANSAS						
1 **Marshall**	Y	Y	Y	Y	Y	Y
2 **Jenkins**	?	?	?	?	?	?
3 **Yoder**	Y	Y	Y	Y	Y	Y
4 **Estes**	Y	Y	Y	Y	Y	Y
KENTUCKY						
1 **Comer**	Y	Y	Y	Y	Y	Y
2 **Guthrie**	Y	Y	Y	Y	Y	Y
3 Yarmuth	Y	Y	?	?	?	?
4 **Massie**	N	N	N	Y	N	N
5 **Rogers**	Y	Y	Y	Y	Y	Y
6 **Barr**	Y	Y	Y	Y	Y	Y
LOUISIANA						
1 **Scalise**	Y	Y	Y	Y	Y	Y
2 Richmond	Y	Y	Y	Y	Y	Y
3 **Higgins**	Y	Y	Y	Y	Y	Y
4 **Johnson**	Y	Y	Y	Y	Y	N
5 **Abraham**	?	?	?	?	?	?
6 **Graves**	Y	?	Y	Y	Y	Y
MAINE						
1 Pingree	Y	Y	Y	Y	Y	Y
2 **Poliquin**	Y	Y	Y	Y	Y	Y
MARYLAND						
1 **Harris**	Y	Y	Y	Y	Y	N
2 Ruppersberger	Y	Y	Y	Y	Y	Y
3 Sarbanes	Y	Y	Y	Y	Y	Y
4 Brown	Y	Y	Y	Y	Y	Y
5 Hoyer	Y	Y	Y	Y	Y	Y
6 Delaney	Y	Y	Y	?	?	?
7 Cummings	Y	Y	Y	Y	Y	Y
8 Raskin	Y	Y	Y	Y	Y	Y
MASSACHUSETTS						
1 Neal	Y	Y	Y	Y	Y	Y
2 McGovern	Y	Y	Y	Y	Y	Y
3 Tsongas	?	?	?	?	?	?
4 Kennedy	?	?	?	?	?	?
5 Clark	Y	Y	Y	Y	Y	Y
6 Moulton	?	?	?	?	?	?
7 Capuano	Y	Y	?	Y	Y	Y
8 Lynch	Y	Y	Y	Y	Y	Y
9 Keating	?	?	?	?	?	?
MICHIGAN						
1 **Bergman**	Y	Y	Y	Y	Y	Y
2 **Huizenga**	Y	Y	Y	Y	Y	Y
3 *Amash*	Y	N	N	N	N	N
4 **Moolenaar**	Y	Y	Y	Y	Y	Y
5 Kildee	Y	Y	Y	Y	Y	Y
6 **Upton**	Y	Y	Y	Y	Y	Y
7 **Walberg**	Y	Y	Y	Y	Y	Y
8 **Bishop**	?	?	?	?	?	?
9 Levin	Y	Y	Y	Y	Y	Y
10 **Mitchell**	Y	Y	Y	Y	Y	Y
11 **Trott**	Y	Y	Y	Y	Y	Y
12 Dingell	Y	Y	Y	Y	Y	Y
13 Jones	Y	Y	Y	Y	Y	Y
14 Lawrence	Y	Y	Y	Y	Y	Y
MINNESOTA						
1 Walz	?	?	?	?	?	?
2 **Lewis**	Y	Y	Y	Y	Y	Y
3 **Paulsen**	?	?	?	?	?	?
4 McCollum	Y	Y	Y	Y	Y	Y

	440	441	442	443	444	445
5 Ellison	?	?	?	?	?	?
6 **Emmer**	Y	Y	Y	Y	Y	Y
7 Peterson	Y	Y	Y	Y	Y	Y
8 Nolan	?	?	?	?	?	?
MISSISSIPPI						
1 **Kelly**	Y	Y	Y	Y	Y	Y
2 Thompson	?	?	?	?	?	?
3 **Harper**	Y	Y	Y	Y	Y	Y
4 **Palazzo**	Y	Y	Y	Y	Y	Y
MISSOURI						
1 Clay	Y	Y	Y	Y	Y	Y
2 **Wagner**	Y	Y	Y	Y	Y	Y
3 **Luetkemeyer**	Y	Y	Y	Y	Y	Y
4 **Hartzler**	Y	Y	Y	Y	Y	Y
5 Cleaver	Y	Y	Y	Y	Y	Y
6 **Graves**	Y	Y	Y	Y	Y	Y
7 **Long**	Y	Y	Y	Y	Y	Y
8 **Smith**	Y	Y	Y	Y	Y	Y
MONTANA						
AL **Gianforte**	Y	Y	Y	Y	Y	Y
NEBRASKA						
1 **Fortenberry**	Y	Y	Y	Y	Y	Y
2 **Bacon**	Y	Y	Y	Y	Y	Y
3 **Smith**	Y	Y	Y	Y	Y	Y
NEVADA						
1 Titus	Y	Y	Y	Y	Y	Y
2 **Amodei**	Y	Y	Y	Y	Y	Y
3 Rosen	?	?	?	?	?	?
4 Kihuen	Y	Y	Y	Y	Y	Y
NEW HAMPSHIRE						
1 Shea-Porter	+	+	+	+	+	+
2 Kuster	Y	Y	Y	Y	Y	Y
NEW JERSEY						
1 Norcross	Y	Y	Y	Y	Y	Y
2 **LoBiondo**	Y	Y	Y	Y	Y	Y
3 **MacArthur**	Y	Y	Y	Y	Y	Y
4 **Smith**	Y	Y	Y	Y	Y	Y
5 Gottheimer	Y	Y	Y	Y	Y	Y
6 Pallone	Y	Y	Y	Y	Y	Y
7 **Lance**	Y	Y	Y	Y	Y	Y
8 Sires	Y	Y	Y	Y	Y	Y
9 Pascrell	Y	Y	Y	Y	Y	Y
10 Payne	Y	Y	Y	Y	Y	Y
11 **Frelinghuysen**	Y	Y	Y	Y	Y	Y
12 Watson Coleman	Y	Y	Y	Y	Y	Y
NEW MEXICO						
1 Lujan Grisham	?	?	?	?	?	?
2 **Pearce**	Y	Y	Y	Y	Y	Y
3 Luján	Y	Y	Y	Y	Y	Y
NEW YORK						
1 **Zeldin**	Y	Y	Y	Y	Y	Y
2 **King**	?	?	?	?	?	?
3 Suozzi	Y	Y	Y	Y	Y	Y
4 Rice	?	?	?	?	?	?
5 Meeks	Y	Y	Y	Y	Y	Y
6 Meng	Y	Y	Y	Y	Y	Y
7 Velázquez	Y	Y	Y	Y	Y	Y
8 Jeffries	Y	Y	Y	Y	Y	Y
9 Clarke	Y	Y	Y	Y	Y	Y
10 Nadler	Y	Y	Y	Y	Y	Y
11 **Donovan**	Y	Y	Y	Y	Y	Y
12 Maloney, C.	Y	Y	Y	Y	Y	Y
13 Espaillat	Y	Y	Y	Y	Y	Y
14 Crowley	Y	Y	Y	Y	Y	Y
15 Serrano	Y	Y	Y	Y	?	Y
16 Engel	Y	Y	Y	Y	Y	Y
17 Lowey	Y	Y	Y	Y	Y	Y
18 Maloney, S.P.	Y	Y	Y	Y	Y	Y
19 **Faso**	Y	Y	Y	Y	Y	Y
20 Tonko	Y	Y	Y	Y	Y	Y
21 **Stefanik**	Y	Y	Y	Y	Y	Y
22 **Tenney**	Y	Y	Y	Y	Y	Y
23 **Reed**	Y	Y	Y	Y	Y	Y
24 **Katko**	Y	Y	Y	Y	Y	Y
25 Morelle	Y	Y	Y	Y	Y	Y
26 Higgins	Y	Y	Y	Y	Y	Y
27 **Collins**	Y	Y	Y	Y	Y	Y
NORTH CAROLINA						
1 Butterfield	Y	Y	Y	Y	Y	Y
2 **Holding**	Y	Y	Y	Y	Y	Y
3 **Jones**	?	?	?	?	?	?
4 Price	Y	Y	Y	Y	Y	Y

	440	441	442	443	444	445
5 **Foxx**	Y	Y	Y	Y	Y	Y
6 **Walker**	Y	Y	Y	Y	Y	Y
7 **Rouzer**	Y	Y	Y	Y	Y	Y
8 **Hudson**	Y	Y	Y	Y	Y	N
9 **Pittenger**	Y	Y	Y	Y	Y	Y
9 **Vacant**						
10 **McHenry**	?	?	?	?	?	?
11 **Meadows**	Y	Y	Y	Y	Y	Y
12 Adams	Y	Y	Y	Y	Y	Y
13 **Budd**	Y	Y	Y	Y	Y	Y
NORTH DAKOTA						
AL **Cramer**	?	?	?	?	?	?
OHIO						
1 **Chabot**	Y	Y	Y	Y	Y	Y
2 **Wenstrup**	Y	Y	Y	Y	Y	Y
3 Beatty	Y	Y	Y	Y	Y	Y
4 **Jordan**	Y	Y	Y	Y	Y	N
5 **Latta**	Y	Y	Y	Y	Y	Y
6 **Johnson**	Y	Y	Y	Y	Y	Y
7 **Gibbs**	Y	Y	Y	Y	Y	Y
8 **Davidson**	Y	Y	N	Y	N	N
9 Kaptur	Y	Y	Y	Y	Y	Y
10 **Turner**	Y	Y	Y	Y	Y	Y
11 Fudge	Y	Y	Y	Y	Y	Y
12 Balderson	Y	Y	Y	Y	Y	?
13 Ryan	Y	Y	Y	Y	Y	Y
14 **Joyce**	Y	Y	Y	Y	Y	Y
15 **Stivers**	Y	Y	Y	Y	Y	Y
16 **Renacci**	Y	Y	Y	Y	Y	Y
OKLAHOMA						
1 Hern	Y	Y	Y	Y	Y	Y
2 **Mullin**	Y	Y	Y	Y	Y	Y
3 **Lucas**	Y	Y	Y	Y	Y	Y
4 **Cole**	Y	Y	Y	Y	Y	Y
5 **Russell**	Y	Y	Y	Y	Y	Y
OREGON						
1 Bonamici	Y	Y	Y	Y	Y	Y
2 **Walden**	Y	Y	Y	Y	Y	Y
3 Blumenauer	Y	Y	Y	?	?	?
4 DeFazio	Y	Y	Y	Y	Y	Y
5 Schrader	Y	Y	Y	Y	N	Y
PENNSYLVANIA						
1 Brady	?	?	?	?	?	?
2 Evans	Y	Y	Y	Y	Y	Y
3 **Kelly**	Y	Y	Y	Y	Y	Y
4 **Perry**	Y	Y	Y	Y	Y	N
5 **Thompson**	Y	Y	Y	Y	Y	Y
6 **Costello**	Y	Y	Y	Y	Y	Y
7 Scanlon	Y	Y	Y	Y	Y	Y
8 **Fitzpatrick**	Y	Y	Y	Y	Y	Y
9 **Shuster**	?	?	?	?	?	?
10 **Marino**	Y	Y	Y	Y	Y	Y
11 **Barletta**	?	?	?	?	?	?
12 **Rothfus**	Y	Y	Y	Y	Y	Y
13 Boyle	?	?	?	?	?	?
14 Doyle	Y	Y	Y	Y	Y	Y
15 Wild	?	?	?	?	?	?
16 **Smucker**	Y	Y	Y	Y	Y	Y
17 Cartwright	Y	Y	Y	Y	Y	Y
18 Lamb	Y	Y	Y	Y	Y	Y
RHODE ISLAND						
1 Cicilline	Y	Y	Y	Y	Y	Y
2 Langevin	Y	Y	Y	Y	Y	Y
SOUTH CAROLINA						
1 **Sanford**	Y	N	Y	Y	N	N
2 **Wilson**	Y	Y	Y	Y	Y	Y
3 **Duncan**	?	?	?	?	?	?
4 **Gowdy**	?	?	?	?	?	?
5 **Norman**	?	?	?	?	Y	Y
6 Clyburn	Y	Y	Y	Y	Y	Y
7 **Rice**	Y	Y	Y	Y	Y	N
SOUTH DAKOTA						
AL **Noem**	?	?	?	?	?	?
TENNESSEE						
1 **Roe**	Y	Y	Y	Y	Y	Y
2 **Duncan**	Y	Y	N	Y	N	N
3 **Fleischmann**	Y	Y	Y	Y	Y	Y
4 **DesJarlais**	Y	Y	Y	Y	Y	Y
5 Cooper	Y	Y	Y	Y	Y	Y
6 **Black**	?	?	?	?	?	?
7 **Blackburn**	?	?	?	?	?	?
8 **Kustoff**	Y	Y	Y	Y	Y	Y
9 Cohen	Y	Y	Y	Y	Y	Y

	440	441	442	443	444	445
TEXAS						
1 **Gohmert**	Y	Y	N	Y	Y	N
2 **Poe**	Y	Y	Y	Y	Y	Y
3 **Johnson, S.**	?	?	?	?	?	?
4 **Ratcliffe**	?	?	?	?	?	?
5 **Hensarling**	Y	Y	Y	Y	Y	Y
6 **Barton**	?	?	?	?	?	?
7 **Culberson**	Y	Y	Y	Y	Y	Y
8 **Brady**	Y	Y	Y	Y	Y	Y
9 Green, A.	Y	Y	Y	Y	Y	Y
10 **McCaul**	Y	Y	Y	Y	Y	Y
11 **Conaway**	Y	Y	Y	Y	Y	Y
12 **Granger**	Y	Y	Y	Y	Y	Y
13 **Thornberry**	?	?	?	?	?	?
14 **Weber**	Y	Y	Y	Y	Y	N
15 Gonzalez	Y	Y	Y	Y	Y	Y
16 O'Rourke	Y	Y	Y	Y	Y	Y
17 **Flores**	?	?	?	?	?	?
18 Jackson Lee	Y	Y	Y	Y	Y	Y
19 **Arrington**	Y	Y	Y	Y	Y	Y
20 Castro	Y	Y	Y	Y	Y	Y
21 **Smith**	Y	Y	Y	Y	Y	Y
22 **Olson**	?	?	?	?	?	?
23 **Hurd**	Y	Y	Y	Y	Y	Y
24 Marchant	?	?	?	?	?	?
25 **Williams**	Y	Y	Y	Y	Y	Y
26 **Burgess**	Y	Y	Y	Y	Y	Y
27 Cloud	Y	Y	Y	Y	Y	Y
28 Cuellar	Y	Y	Y	Y	Y	Y
29 Green, G.	Y	Y	Y	Y	Y	Y
30 Johnson, E.B.	Y	Y	Y	Y	Y	Y
31 **Carter**	Y	Y	Y	Y	Y	Y
32 **Sessions**	Y	Y	Y	Y	Y	Y
33 Veasey	Y	Y	Y	Y	Y	Y
34 Vela	?	?	?	?	?	?
35 Doggett	Y	Y	Y	Y	Y	Y
36 **Babin**	Y	Y	Y	Y	Y	Y
UTAH						
1 **Bishop**	Y	Y	Y	Y	Y	Y
2 **Stewart**	Y	Y	Y	Y	Y	Y
3 **Curtis**	Y	Y	Y	Y	Y	Y
4 **Love**	?	?	?	?	?	?
VERMONT						
AL Welch	Y	Y	Y	Y	Y	Y
VIRGINIA						
1 **Wittman**	Y	Y	Y	Y	Y	Y
2 **Taylor**	Y	Y	Y	Y	Y	Y
3 Scott	Y	Y	Y	Y	Y	Y
4 McEachin	Y	Y	Y	Y	Y	Y
5 **Garrett**	Y	?	?	Y	N	N
6 **Goodlatte**	Y	N	Y	Y	Y	Y
7 **Brat**	?	?	?	?	?	?
8 Beyer	Y	Y	Y	Y	Y	Y
9 **Griffith**	Y	N	Y	Y	Y	Y
10 **Comstock**	?	?	?	?	?	?
11 Connolly	Y	Y	Y	Y	Y	Y
WASHINGTON						
1 DelBene	Y	Y	Y	Y	Y	Y
2 Larsen	Y	Y	Y	Y	Y	Y
3 **Herrera Beutler**	Y	Y	Y	Y	Y	Y
4 **Newhouse**	Y	Y	Y	Y	Y	Y
5 **McMorris Rodgers**	Y	Y	Y	Y	Y	Y
6 Kilmer	Y	Y	Y	Y	Y	Y
7 Jayapal	Y	Y	Y	Y	Y	Y
8 **Reichert**	Y	Y	Y	Y	Y	Y
9 Smith	Y	Y	Y	Y	Y	Y
10 Heck	Y	Y	Y	Y	Y	Y
WEST VIRGINIA						
1 **McKinley**	Y	Y	Y	Y	Y	Y
2 **Mooney**	Y	Y	Y	Y	Y	Y
3 **Vacant**						
WISCONSIN						
1 **Ryan**						
2 Pocan	Y	Y	Y	Y	Y	?
3 Kind	?	?	?	?	?	?
4 Moore	Y	Y	Y	Y	Y	Y
5 **Sensenbrenner**	Y	N	N	Y	Y	N
6 **Grothman**	Y	N	N	Y	Y	N
7 **Duffy**	Y	Y	Y	Y	Y	Y
8 **Gallagher**	Y	Y	Y	Y	Y	Y
WYOMING						
AL **Cheney**	Y	Y	Y	Y	Y	Y

VOTE NUMBER

446. HR88. TAX PROVISION PACKAGE/RULE. Adoption of the rule (H Res 1180) that would provide consideration of the House amendment to the Senate amendment to a bill (HR 88) that is the expected legislative vehicle for a package of tax-related bills. HR 88 would extend and gradually phase out through 2024 a biodiesel tax credit, make permanent a railroad track maintenance credit at a reduced rate, and provide temporary tax relief for victims of hurricanes and wildfires. The rule would also provide for floor proceedings during the period between Dec. 24, 2018 and Jan. 3, 2019. Adopted 207-170: R 207-0; D 0-170. Dec. 20, 2018.

447. HRES1181. SAME-DAY CONSIDERATION/RULE. Adoption of the rule (H Res 1181) that would waive the requirement of a two-thirds vote to consider a rule on the same day it is reported from the Rules Committee, through Dec. 24, and would provide for House consideration of measures under suspension of the rules through Dec. 23, 2018. Adopted 350-30: R 185-24; D 165-6. Dec. 20, 2018.

448. S756. CRIMINAL RECIDIVISM PROGRAMS, JUDICIAL AND PRISON SYSTEM MODIFICATIONS/PASSAGE. Goodlatte, R-Va., motion to suspend the rules and concur in the Senate amendment to the House amendment to the bill that would seek to reduce numbers of federally incarcerated individuals through changes in sentencing laws. The bill would seek to do so, in part, by allowing judges more flexibility when handing down sentences below the mandatory minimum for nonviolent drug offenders. It would also establish programs to provide support for prisoners returning to society in an attempt to reduce rates of recidivation. Motion agreed to 358-36: R 182-36; D 176-0. Dec. 20, 2018.

449. HR7328. PUBLIC HEALTH PREPAREDNESS PROGRAMS/PASSAGE. Burgess, R-Texas, motion to suspend the rules and pass the bill that would reauthorize a number of public health and preparedness programs and would modify regulations relating to non-prescription drugs. Motion agreed to 367-9: R 201-9; D 166-0. Dec. 20, 2018.

450. HR5075. FINDING MISSING ADULTS/PASSAGE. Collins, R-Ga., motion to suspend the rules and concur in the Senate amendment to the bill that would authorize $3 million annually, for fiscal 2019 through fiscal 2022, for the Department of Justice to establish the Ashanti Alert network, a national communications network that would provide assistance to regional and local search efforts for missing adults. Motion agreed to 386-2: R 211-2; D 175-0. Dec. 20, 2018.

451. HR7093. REPEAL OF OUTDATED LAWS/PASSAGE. Collins, R-Ga., motion to suspend the rules and pass the bill that would repeal nine laws that are considered outdated and for which offenders have not been prosecuted in years. Motion agreed to 386-5: R 215-0; D 171-5. Dec. 20, 2018.

	446	447	448	449	450	451
ALABAMA						
1 Byrne	Y	Y	N	Y	Y	Y
2 Roby	Y	Y	N	Y	Y	Y
3 Rogers	Y	Y	N	Y	Y	Y
4 Aderholt	Y	Y	N	Y	Y	Y
5 Brooks	Y	Y	N	N	Y	Y
6 Palmer	Y	N	N	Y	Y	Y
7 Sewell	N	Y	Y	Y	Y	Y
ALASKA						
AL Young	?	?	N	Y	Y	Y
ARIZONA						
1 O'Halleran	N	Y	Y	Y	Y	Y
2 McSally	Y	Y	Y	Y	Y	Y
3 Grijalva	N	Y	Y	Y	Y	Y
4 Gosar	Y	N	N	Y	Y	Y
5 Biggs	Y	N	N	N	Y	Y
6 Schweikert	Y	Y	Y	Y	Y	Y
7 Gallego	N	Y	Y	Y	Y	Y
8 Lesko	Y	Y	Y	Y	Y	Y
9 Sinema	?	?	?	?	?	?
ARKANSAS						
1 Crawford	Y	Y	Y	Y	Y	Y
2 Hill	Y	Y	Y	Y	Y	Y
3 Womack	Y	Y	Y	Y	Y	Y
4 Westerman	Y	Y	Y	Y	Y	Y
CALIFORNIA						
1 LaMalfa	Y	Y	N	Y	Y	Y
2 Huffman	N	Y	Y	Y	Y	Y
3 Garamendi	N	Y	Y	Y	Y	Y
4 McClintock	Y	Y	Y	Y	Y	Y
5 Thompson	N	Y	Y	Y	Y	Y
6 Matsui	N	Y	Y	Y	Y	Y
7 Bera	N	Y	Y	Y	Y	Y
8 Cook	Y	Y	Y	Y	Y	Y
9 McNerney	N	Y	Y	Y	Y	Y
10 Denham	?	?	Y	?	Y	Y
11 DeSaulnier	N	Y	Y	Y	Y	Y
12 Pelosi	N	Y	Y	?	Y	Y
13 Lee	N	Y	Y	Y	Y	Y
14 Speier	N	Y	Y	Y	Y	Y
15 Swalwell	?	?	?	?	?	?
16 Costa	?	?	?	?	?	?
17 Khanna	N	Y	Y	Y	Y	Y
18 Eshoo	N	Y	Y	Y	Y	Y
19 Lofgren	N	Y	Y	?	Y	Y
20 Panetta	N	Y	Y	Y	Y	Y
21 Valadao	Y	Y	Y	Y	Y	Y
22 Nunes	Y	Y	Y	Y	Y	Y
23 McCarthy	Y	Y	Y	Y	Y	Y
24 Carbajal	N	Y	Y	Y	Y	Y
25 Knight	?	?	Y	Y	Y	Y
26 Brownley	N	Y	Y	Y	Y	Y
27 Chu	N	Y	Y	Y	Y	Y
28 Schiff	N	Y	Y	Y	Y	Y
29 Cardenas	N	Y	Y	Y	Y	Y
30 Sherman	N	N	Y	Y	Y	Y
31 Aguilar	N	Y	Y	Y	Y	Y
32 Napolitano	N	Y	Y	Y	Y	Y
33 Lieu	N	Y	Y	Y	Y	Y
34 Gomez	N	Y	Y	Y	Y	Y
35 Torres	N	Y	Y	Y	Y	Y
36 Ruiz	N	Y	Y	Y	Y	Y
37 Bass	N	Y	Y	Y	Y	Y
38 Sánchez, Linda	N	Y	Y	Y	Y	Y
39 Royce	Y	Y	Y	Y	Y	Y
40 Roybal-Allard	N	Y	Y	Y	?	Y
41 Takano	N	Y	Y	Y	Y	Y
42 Calvert	Y	Y	Y	Y	Y	Y
43 Waters	N	Y	Y	Y	Y	Y
44 Barragan	N	Y	Y	Y	Y	Y
45 Walters	?	Y	?	?	?	?
46 Correa	N	Y	Y	Y	Y	Y
47 Lowenthal	?	?	?	?	?	?
48 Rohrabacher	Y	Y	Y	Y	Y	Y
49 Issa	Y	Y	?	?	?	?
50 Hunter	Y	Y	Y	Y	Y	Y
51 Vargas	N	Y	Y	Y	Y	Y
52 Peters	N	Y	Y	Y	Y	Y
53 Davis	N	Y	Y	Y	Y	Y

	446	447	448	449	450	451
COLORADO						
1 DeGette	N	Y	Y	Y	Y	Y
2 Polis	?	?	?	?	?	?
3 Tipton	Y	Y	Y	Y	Y	Y
4 Buck	Y	Y	N	Y	Y	Y
5 Lamborn	Y	Y	Y	Y	Y	Y
6 Coffman	Y	Y	Y	Y	Y	Y
7 Perlmutter	N	Y	Y	Y	N	N
CONNECTICUT						
1 Larson	N	Y	Y	Y	Y	Y
2 Courtney	N	Y	Y	Y	Y	Y
3 DeLauro	N	Y	Y	Y	Y	Y
4 Himes	N	Y	Y	Y	Y	Y
5 Esty	N	Y	Y	Y	Y	Y
DELAWARE						
AL Blunt Rochester	N	Y	Y	Y	Y	Y
FLORIDA						
1 Gaetz	Y	Y	Y	Y	Y	Y
2 Dunn	Y	Y	Y	Y	Y	Y
3 Yoho	Y	N	Y	N	Y	Y
4 Rutherford	Y	Y	Y	?	Y	Y
5 Lawson	N	Y	Y	Y	Y	Y
6 Vacant						
7 Murphy	N	Y	Y	Y	Y	Y
8 Posey	Y	N	Y	N	Y	Y
9 Soto	N	Y	Y	Y	Y	Y
10 Demings	N	Y	Y	Y	Y	Y
11 Webster	?	Y	Y	Y	Y	Y
12 Bilirakis	Y	Y	Y	Y	Y	Y
13 Crist	N	Y	Y	Y	Y	Y
14 Castor	N	Y	Y	Y	Y	N
15 Ross	?	?	?	?	?	?
16 Buchanan	Y	Y	Y	Y	Y	Y
17 Rooney, T.	Y	Y	Y	Y	Y	Y
18 Mast	Y	Y	Y	Y	Y	Y
19 Rooney, F.	Y	Y	Y	Y	Y	Y
20 Hastings	N	Y	?	?	?	?
21 Frankel	N	Y	Y	Y	Y	Y
22 Deutch	N	Y	Y	Y	Y	Y
23 Wasserman Schultz	N	Y	Y	Y	Y	N
24 Wilson	?	?	Y	Y	Y	Y
25 Diaz-Balart	Y	Y	Y	Y	Y	Y
26 Curbelo	Y	Y	Y	Y	Y	Y
27 Ros-Lehtinen	Y	Y	Y	Y	Y	Y
GEORGIA						
1 Carter	Y	Y	Y	Y	Y	Y
2 Bishop	N	Y	Y	Y	Y	Y
3 Ferguson	Y	Y	Y	Y	Y	Y
4 Johnson	N	Y	Y	Y	Y	Y
5 Lewis	N	Y	Y	?	Y	Y
6 Handel	Y	Y	Y	Y	Y	Y
7 Woodall	Y	Y	Y	Y	Y	Y
8 Scott, A.	Y	Y	Y	Y	Y	Y
9 Collins	Y	Y	Y	Y	Y	Y
10 Hice	Y	N	Y	Y	Y	Y
11 Loudermilk	?	Y	Y	Y	Y	Y
12 Allen	Y	Y	Y	Y	Y	Y
13 Scott, D.	?	?	?	?	?	?
14 Graves	Y	Y	Y	Y	Y	Y
HAWAII						
1 Hanabusa	?	?	?	?	?	?
2 Gabbard	N	Y	Y	Y	Y	Y
IDAHO						
1 Labrador	Y	N	Y	Y	Y	Y
2 Simpson	Y	Y	Y	Y	Y	Y
ILLINOIS						
1 Rush	N	Y	Y	Y	Y	?
2 Kelly	N	Y	Y	Y	Y	Y
3 Lipinski	?	?	Y	Y	Y	Y
4 Gutierrez	N	Y	?	Y	Y	Y
5 Quigley	N	Y	Y	Y	Y	Y
6 Roskam	?	?	Y	Y	Y	Y
7 Davis, D.	N	Y	?	?	?	?
8 Krishnamoorthi	N	Y	Y	Y	Y	Y
9 Schakowsky	N	Y	Y	Y	Y	Y
10 Schneider	N	Y	Y	Y	Y	Y
11 Foster	N	Y	Y	Y	Y	Y
12 Bost	Y	Y	Y	Y	Y	Y
13 Davis, R.	Y	Y	Y	Y	Y	Y

	446	447	448	449	450	451
14 **Hultgren**	?	?	?	?	?	?
15 **Shimkus**	Y	Y	Y	Y	Y	Y
16 **Kinzinger**	Y	Y	Y	Y	Y	Y
17 Bustos	N	Y	Y	Y	Y	Y
18 **LaHood**	Y	Y	Y	Y	Y	Y
INDIANA						
1 Visclosky	N	N	Y	Y	Y	Y
2 **Walorski**	Y	Y	Y	Y	Y	Y
3 **Banks**	Y	Y	Y	Y	Y	Y
4 Rokita	Y	Y	N	Y	Y	Y
5 **Brooks**	Y	Y	Y	Y	Y	Y
6 **Messer**	Y	Y	?	?	?	?
7 Carson	N	Y	Y	Y	Y	Y
8 **Bucshon**	Y	Y	Y	Y	Y	Y
9 **Hollingsworth**	Y	Y	Y	Y	Y	Y
IOWA						
1 **Blum**	Y	N	Y	Y	Y	Y
2 Loebsack	N	Y	Y	Y	Y	Y
3 **Young**	Y	Y	Y	Y	Y	Y
4 **King**	Y	Y	N	N	Y	Y
KANSAS						
1 **Marshall**	Y	Y	Y	Y	Y	Y
2 **Jenkins**	?	?	?	?	?	?
3 **Yoder**	Y	Y	Y	Y	Y	Y
4 **Estes**	Y	Y	Y	Y	Y	Y
KENTUCKY						
1 **Comer**	Y	Y	Y	Y	Y	Y
2 **Guthrie**	Y	Y	Y	Y	Y	Y
3 Yarmuth	N	Y	Y	Y	Y	N
4 **Massie**	Y	N	Y	N	N	Y
5 **Rogers**	Y	Y	Y	Y	Y	Y
6 **Barr**	Y	Y	Y	Y	Y	Y
LOUISIANA						
1 **Scalise**	Y	Y	Y	Y	Y	Y
2 Richmond	N	Y	Y	?	Y	Y
3 **Higgins**	Y	Y	N	Y	Y	Y
4 **Johnson**	Y	Y	Y	Y	Y	Y
5 **Abraham**	Y	Y	N	Y	Y	Y
6 **Graves**	Y	Y	Y	Y	Y	Y
MAINE						
1 Pingree	N	Y	Y	Y	Y	Y
2 **Poliquin**	Y	Y	Y	Y	Y	Y
MARYLAND						
1 **Harris**	?	?	Y	Y	Y	Y
2 Ruppersberger	N	Y	Y	Y	Y	Y
3 Sarbanes	N	Y	Y	?	Y	Y
4 Brown	N	Y	Y	Y	Y	Y
5 Hoyer	N	Y	Y	?	Y	Y
6 Delaney	N	Y	Y	Y	Y	Y
7 Cummings	?	?	Y	Y	Y	Y
8 Raskin	N	Y	Y	Y	Y	Y
MASSACHUSETTS						
1 Neal	N	Y	Y	Y	Y	Y
2 McGovern	N	Y	Y	Y	Y	Y
3 Tsongas	?	?	Y	Y	Y	Y
4 Kennedy	N	Y	Y	Y	Y	Y
5 Clark	N	Y	Y	Y	Y	Y
6 Moulton	?	?	Y	Y	Y	Y
7 Capuano	?	?	?	?	?	?
8 Lynch	N	Y	Y	Y	Y	Y
9 Keating	?	?	?	?	?	?
MICHIGAN						
1 **Bergman**	Y	Y	Y	Y	Y	Y
2 **Huizenga**	Y	Y	Y	Y	Y	Y
3 *Amash*	Y	N	Y	N	N	Y
4 **Moolenaar**	Y	Y	Y	Y	Y	Y
5 Kildee	N	Y	Y	Y	Y	Y
6 **Upton**	Y	Y	Y	Y	Y	Y
7 **Walberg**	Y	Y	Y	Y	Y	Y
8 **Bishop**	?	?	?	?	?	?
9 Levin	N	Y	Y	Y	Y	Y
10 **Mitchell**	Y	Y	Y	Y	Y	Y
11 **Trott**	Y	Y	?	?	?	?
12 Dingell	N	Y	Y	Y	Y	Y
13 Jones	N	Y	Y	Y	Y	Y
14 Lawrence	N	Y	Y	Y	Y	Y
MINNESOTA						
1 Walz	?	?	?	?	?	?
2 **Lewis**	Y	Y	Y	Y	Y	Y
3 **Paulsen**	Y	Y	Y	Y	Y	Y
4 McCollum	N	Y	Y	Y	Y	Y
5 Ellison	?	?	Y	Y	Y	Y
6 **Emmer**	Y	Y	Y	Y	Y	Y
7 Peterson	N	Y	?	?	?	?
8 Nolan	?	?	Y	Y	Y	Y
MISSISSIPPI						
1 **Kelly**	Y	Y	Y	Y	Y	Y
2 Thompson	?	?	?	?	?	?
3 **Harper**	Y	Y	Y	Y	Y	Y
4 **Palazzo**	Y	Y	N	Y	Y	Y
MISSOURI						
1 Clay	N	Y	Y	Y	Y	Y
2 **Wagner**	Y	Y	Y	Y	Y	Y
3 **Luetkemeyer**	Y	Y	Y	Y	Y	Y
4 **Hartzler**	Y	Y	Y	Y	Y	Y
5 Cleaver	N	Y	Y	Y	Y	Y
6 **Graves**	Y	Y	Y	Y	Y	Y
7 **Long**	Y	Y	Y	Y	Y	Y
8 **Smith**	Y	Y	N	Y	Y	Y
MONTANA						
AL **Gianforte**	Y	Y	Y	Y	Y	Y
NEBRASKA						
1 **Fortenberry**	Y	Y	Y	Y	Y	Y
2 **Bacon**	Y	Y	Y	Y	Y	Y
3 **Smith**	Y	Y	N	Y	Y	Y
NEVADA						
1 Titus	N	Y	Y	Y	Y	Y
2 **Amodei**	Y	Y	Y	Y	Y	Y
3 Rosen	?	?	?	?	?	?
4 Kihuen	N	Y	Y	?	Y	Y
NEW HAMPSHIRE						
1 Shea-Porter	–	+	+	+	+	+
2 Kuster	N	Y	Y	Y	Y	Y
NEW JERSEY						
1 Norcross	N	Y	Y	Y	Y	Y
2 **LoBiondo**	Y	Y	Y	Y	Y	Y
3 **MacArthur**	Y	Y	Y	Y	Y	Y
4 **Smith**	Y	Y	Y	Y	Y	Y
5 Gottheimer	N	Y	Y	Y	Y	Y
6 Pallone	N	N	Y	Y	Y	Y
7 **Lance**	Y	Y	Y	Y	Y	Y
8 Sires	N	Y	Y	Y	Y	Y
9 Pascrell	N	Y	Y	Y	Y	Y
10 Payne	N	Y	Y	Y	Y	Y
11 **Frelinghuysen**	Y	Y	Y	Y	Y	Y
12 Watson Coleman	N	Y	Y	Y	Y	Y
NEW MEXICO						
1 Lujan Grisham	?	?	?	?	?	?
2 **Pearce**	Y	N	N	Y	Y	Y
3 Luján	N	Y	Y	Y	Y	Y
NEW YORK						
1 **Zeldin**	Y	Y	Y	Y	Y	Y
2 **King**	Y	Y	Y	Y	Y	Y
3 Suozzi	N	Y	Y	Y	Y	Y
4 Rice	?	?	Y	Y	Y	Y
5 Meeks	N	Y	Y	Y	Y	Y
6 Meng	N	Y	Y	Y	Y	Y
7 Velázquez	N	Y	Y	Y	Y	Y
8 Jeffries	N	Y	Y	Y	Y	Y
9 Clarke	N	Y	Y	Y	Y	Y
10 Nadler	N	Y	Y	?	Y	Y
11 **Donovan**	Y	Y	Y	Y	Y	Y
12 Maloney, C.	N	Y	Y	?	Y	Y
13 Espaillat	N	Y	Y	Y	Y	Y
14 Crowley	?	?	?	?	?	?
15 Serrano	N	Y	Y	Y	Y	Y
16 Engel	N	Y	Y	Y	Y	Y
17 Lowey	N	Y	Y	Y	Y	Y
18 Maloney, S.P.	N	Y	Y	Y	Y	Y
19 **Faso**	Y	Y	Y	Y	Y	Y
20 Tonko	N	Y	Y	Y	Y	Y
21 **Stefanik**	Y	Y	Y	Y	Y	Y
22 **Tenney**	Y	Y	Y	Y	Y	Y
23 **Reed**	Y	Y	Y	Y	Y	Y
24 **Katko**	Y	Y	Y	Y	Y	Y
25 Morelle	N	Y	Y	Y	Y	Y
26 Higgins	N	Y	Y	Y	Y	Y
27 **Collins**	Y	Y	Y	Y	Y	Y
NORTH CAROLINA						
1 Butterfield	N	Y	Y	Y	Y	Y
2 **Holding**	Y	Y	N	Y	Y	Y
3 **Jones**	?	?	?	?	?	?
4 Price	N	Y	Y	Y	Y	Y
5 **Foxx**	Y	Y	Y	Y	Y	Y
6 **Walker**	Y	Y	Y	Y	?	Y
7 **Rouzer**	Y	Y	N	Y	Y	Y
8 **Hudson**	Y	Y	N	Y	Y	Y
9 **Pittenger**	?	?	?	?	?	?
9 **Vacant**						
10 **McHenry**	Y	Y	Y	Y	Y	Y
11 **Meadows**	Y	N	Y	Y	Y	Y
12 Adams	N	Y	Y	Y	Y	Y
13 **Budd**	Y	Y	Y	Y	Y	Y
NORTH DAKOTA						
AL **Cramer**	Y	Y	Y	?	?	?
OHIO						
1 **Chabot**	Y	Y	Y	Y	Y	Y
2 **Wenstrup**	Y	Y	Y	Y	Y	Y
3 Beatty	N	Y	Y	Y	Y	Y
4 **Jordan**	Y	N	Y	Y	Y	Y
5 **Latta**	Y	Y	Y	Y	Y	Y
6 **Johnson**	Y	Y	Y	Y	Y	Y
7 **Gibbs**	Y	Y	Y	Y	Y	Y
8 **Davidson**	Y	?	Y	?	Y	Y
9 Kaptur	N	Y	Y	?	?	Y
10 **Turner**	Y	Y	Y	Y	Y	Y
11 Fudge	N	Y	Y	Y	Y	Y
12 Balderson	Y	Y	Y	Y	Y	Y
13 Ryan	N	Y	Y	Y	Y	Y
14 **Joyce**	Y	Y	Y	Y	Y	Y
15 **Stivers**	Y	Y	Y	Y	Y	Y
16 **Renacci**	Y	Y	Y	Y	Y	Y
OKLAHOMA						
1 Hern	Y	Y	Y	Y	Y	Y
2 **Mullin**	Y	Y	N	Y	Y	Y
3 **Lucas**	Y	Y	Y	Y	Y	Y
4 **Cole**	Y	Y	Y	Y	Y	Y
5 **Russell**	Y	Y	Y	?	?	?
OREGON						
1 Bonamici	N	Y	Y	Y	Y	Y
2 **Walden**	Y	Y	Y	Y	Y	Y
3 Blumenauer	N	Y	Y	Y	Y	Y
4 DeFazio	N	N	Y	Y	Y	Y
5 Schrader	N	N	Y	Y	Y	Y
PENNSYLVANIA						
1 Brady	N	Y	Y	Y	Y	Y
2 Evans	N	Y	Y	Y	Y	Y
3 **Kelly**	Y	Y	Y	Y	Y	Y
4 **Perry**	Y	N	Y	N	Y	Y
5 **Thompson**	Y	Y	Y	Y	Y	Y
6 **Costello**	Y	Y	Y	Y	Y	Y
7 Scanlon	N	Y	Y	Y	Y	Y
8 **Fitzpatrick**	Y	Y	Y	Y	Y	Y
9 **Shuster**	?	?	Y	?	Y	Y
10 **Marino**	?	Y	Y	Y	Y	Y
11 **Barletta**	?	?	Y	Y	Y	Y
12 **Rothfus**	Y	Y	Y	Y	Y	Y
13 Boyle	N	Y	Y	Y	Y	Y
14 Doyle	N	Y	Y	Y	Y	Y
15 Wild	N	Y	Y	Y	Y	Y
16 **Smucker**	Y	Y	Y	Y	Y	Y
17 Cartwright	N	Y	Y	?	Y	Y
18 Lamb	N	Y	Y	Y	Y	Y
RHODE ISLAND						
1 Cicilline	N	Y	Y	Y	Y	Y
2 Langevin	?	Y	Y	Y	Y	Y
SOUTH CAROLINA						
1 **Sanford**	Y	N	N	Y	Y	Y
2 **Wilson**	Y	Y	N	Y	Y	Y
3 **Duncan**	?	?	?	?	?	?
4 **Gowdy**	Y	Y	Y	Y	Y	Y
5 **Norman**	Y	N	N	Y	Y	Y
6 Clyburn	N	Y	Y	Y	Y	Y
7 **Rice**	Y	N	N	Y	Y	Y
SOUTH DAKOTA						
AL **Noem**	?	?	?	?	?	?
TENNESSEE						
1 **Roe**	Y	Y	Y	Y	Y	Y
2 **Duncan**	Y	Y	Y	Y	Y	Y
3 **Fleischmann**	Y	Y	Y	Y	Y	Y
4 **DesJarlais**	Y	Y	Y	Y	Y	Y
5 Cooper	N	N	Y	Y	Y	Y
6 **Black**	?	?	?	?	?	?
7 **Blackburn**	Y	Y	Y	Y	Y	Y
8 **Kustoff**	Y	Y	N	Y	Y	Y
9 Cohen	N	Y	Y	Y	Y	Y
TEXAS						
1 **Gohmert**	Y	N	N	Y	Y	Y
2 **Poe**	Y	Y	Y	N	?	Y
3 **Johnson, S.**	?	?	?	?	?	?
4 **Ratcliffe**	?	?	?	?	?	?
5 **Hensarling**	Y	Y	Y	Y	Y	Y
6 **Barton**	?	?	Y	Y	Y	Y
7 **Culberson**	Y	Y	Y	Y	Y	Y
8 **Brady**	Y	Y	Y	Y	Y	Y
9 Green, A.	N	Y	Y	Y	Y	Y
10 **McCaul**	Y	Y	Y	Y	Y	Y
11 **Conaway**	Y	Y	Y	Y	Y	Y
12 **Granger**	Y	Y	Y	Y	Y	Y
13 **Thornberry**	Y	Y	Y	Y	Y	Y
14 **Weber**	Y	Y	N	Y	Y	Y
15 Gonzalez	N	Y	Y	Y	Y	Y
16 O'Rourke	N	Y	Y	Y	Y	Y
17 **Flores**	Y	Y	Y	Y	Y	Y
18 Jackson Lee	N	Y	Y	Y	Y	Y
19 **Arrington**	Y	Y	Y	Y	Y	Y
20 Castro	N	Y	Y	Y	Y	Y
21 **Smith**	Y	Y	Y	Y	Y	Y
22 **Olson**	?	?	Y	Y	Y	Y
23 **Hurd**	Y	Y	Y	Y	Y	Y
24 Marchant	Y	Y	N	Y	Y	Y
25 **Williams**	Y	Y	Y	Y	Y	Y
26 **Burgess**	Y	Y	Y	Y	Y	Y
27 Cloud	Y	N	N	Y	Y	Y
28 Cuellar	N	Y	Y	Y	Y	Y
29 Green, G.	?	?	Y	Y	Y	Y
30 Johnson, E.B.	N	Y	Y	Y	Y	Y
31 **Carter**	Y	Y	N	Y	Y	Y
32 **Sessions**	Y	Y	Y	?	Y	Y
33 Veasey	N	Y	Y	Y	Y	Y
34 Vela	?	?	?	?	?	?
35 Doggett	N	Y	Y	Y	Y	Y
36	Y	Y	N	Y	Y	Y
UTAH						
1 **Bishop**	?	?	Y	Y	Y	Y
2 **Stewart**	Y	Y	Y	Y	Y	Y
3 **Curtis**	Y	Y	Y	Y	Y	Y
4 **Love**	?	?	?	?	?	?
VERMONT						
AL Welch	N	Y	Y	Y	Y	Y
VIRGINIA						
1 **Wittman**	Y	Y	Y	Y	Y	Y
2 **Taylor**	Y	N	Y	Y	Y	Y
3 Scott	N	Y	Y	Y	Y	Y
4 McEachin	N	Y	Y	Y	Y	Y
5 **Garrett**	Y	N	Y	Y	Y	Y
6 **Goodlatte**	Y	Y	Y	?	?	?
7 **Brat**	Y	N	Y	Y	Y	Y
8 Beyer	N	Y	Y	Y	Y	N
9 **Griffith**	Y	?	Y	Y	Y	Y
10 **Comstock**	?	?	?	?	?	?
11 Connolly	N	Y	Y	Y	Y	Y
WASHINGTON						
1 DelBene	N	Y	Y	Y	Y	Y
2 Larsen	N	Y	Y	Y	Y	Y
3 **Herrera Beutler**	?	?	Y	Y	Y	Y
4 **Newhouse**	Y	Y	Y	Y	Y	Y
5 **McMorris Rodgers**	Y	Y	Y	Y	Y	Y
6 Kilmer	N	Y	Y	Y	Y	Y
7 Jayapal	N	Y	Y	Y	Y	Y
8 **Reichert**	Y	Y	Y	Y	Y	Y
9 Smith	N	Y	Y	Y	Y	Y
10 Heck	N	Y	Y	Y	Y	Y
WEST VIRGINIA						
1 **McKinley**	Y	Y	Y	Y	Y	Y
2 **Mooney**	Y	N	Y	Y	Y	Y
3 **Vacant**						
WISCONSIN						
1 **Ryan**						
2 Pocan	N	Y	Y	Y	Y	Y
3 Kind	?	?	?	?	?	?
4 Moore	N	Y	Y	Y	Y	Y
5 **Sensenbrenner**	Y	Y	Y	N	Y	Y
6 **Grothman**	Y	Y	Y	Y	Y	Y
7 **Duffy**	Y	Y	N	Y	Y	Y
8 **Gallagher**	Y	N	Y	Y	Y	Y
WYOMING						
AL **Cheney**	Y	Y	Y	Y	Y	Y

VOTE NUMBER

452. S2896. LOBBYIST DISCLOSURES/PASSAGE. Collins, R-Ga., motion to suspend the rules and pass the bill that would require federal lobbyists to disclose certain state and federal convictions, including those for bribery, when registering under the Lobbying Disclosure Act. Motion agreed to 391-0: R 216-0; D 175-0. Dec. 20, 2018.

453. S2961. CHILD ABUSE PREVENTION/PASSAGE. Collins, R-Ga., motion to suspend the rules and pass the bill that would reauthorize Justice Department programs that seek to prevent and assist victims of child abuse. Annually through fiscal 2023, it would authorize $25 million for these programs. Motion agreed to 388-2: R 213-2; D 175-0. Dec. 20, 2018.

454. S2679. SURPLUS PROPERTY FOR VETERAN OWNER BUSINESSES/ PASSAGE. Marshall, R-Kan., motion to suspend the rules and pass the bill that would provide veteran-owned small businesses access to surplus or excess property. Motion agreed to 389-1: R 213-1; D 176-0. Dec. 20, 2018.

455. HR7227. IRS OPERATIONS/PASSAGE. Rice, R-S.C., motion to suspend the rules and pass the bill which contains a number of provisions related to Internal Revenue Service operations and modernization. It would establish an independent office of appeals within the agency to resolve taxpayer controversies and make several modifications or clarifications related to IRS operations, services, and authorities. It also includes provisions to update IRS information technology systems, other electronic systems, and cybersecurity measures. Motion agreed to 378-11: R 203-11; D 175-0. Dec. 20, 2018.

456. HR4227. VEHICULAR TERRORISM/PASSAGE. Estes, R-Kan., motion to suspend the rules and concur in the Senate amendment to the bill that would direct the secretary of the Department of Homeland Security to examine how the department is managing the threat of vehicular terrorism and to develop a strategy to work with first responders and the private sector to improve the prevention, mitigation and response to such threats. Motion agreed to 388-2: R 211-2; D 177-0. Dec. 20, 2018.

457. S2652. STEPHEN GLEASON CONGRESSIONAL MEDAL/PASSAGE. Huizenga, R-Mich., motion to suspend the rules and pass the bill that would authorize the presentation of a Congressional Gold Medal to Stephen Michael Gleason, for his work advocating for individuals affected by amyotrophic lateral sclerosis and research on the disease. Motion agreed to 390-2: R 212-2; D 178-0. Dec. 20, 2018.

	452	453	454	455	456	457
ALABAMA						
1 **Byrne**	Y	Y	Y	Y	Y	Y
2 **Roby**	Y	Y	Y	Y	Y	Y
3 **Rogers**	Y	Y	Y	Y	Y	Y
4 **Aderholt**	Y	Y	Y	Y	Y	Y
5 **Brooks**	Y	Y	Y	Y	Y	Y
6 **Palmer**	Y	Y	Y	Y	Y	Y
7 Sewell	Y	Y	Y	Y	Y	Y
ALASKA						
AL **Young**	Y	Y	Y	Y	Y	Y
ARIZONA						
1 O'Halleran	Y	Y	Y	Y	Y	Y
2 **McSally**	Y	Y	Y	Y	Y	Y
3 Grijalva	Y	Y	Y	Y	Y	Y
4 **Gosar**	Y	Y	Y	N	Y	Y
5 **Biggs**	Y	Y	Y	N	Y	Y
6 **Schweikert**	Y	Y	Y	Y	Y	Y
7 Gallego	Y	Y	Y	Y	Y	Y
8 **Lesko**	Y	Y	Y	Y	Y	Y
9 Sinema	?	?	?	?	?	?
ARKANSAS						
1 **Crawford**	Y	Y	Y	Y	Y	Y
2 **Hill**	Y	Y	Y	Y	Y	Y
3 **Womack**	Y	Y	Y	Y	Y	Y
4 **Westerman**	Y	Y	Y	Y	Y	Y
CALIFORNIA						
1 **LaMalfa**	Y	Y	Y	Y	Y	Y
2 Huffman	Y	Y	Y	Y	Y	Y
3 Garamendi	Y	Y	Y	Y	Y	Y
4 **McClintock**	Y	Y	Y	Y	Y	Y
5 Thompson	Y	Y	Y	Y	Y	Y
6 Matsui	Y	Y	Y	Y	Y	Y
7 Bera	Y	Y	Y	Y	Y	Y
8 **Cook**	Y	Y	Y	Y	Y	Y
9 McNerney	Y	Y	Y	Y	Y	Y
10 **Denham**	Y	Y	Y	Y	Y	?
11 DeSaulnier	Y	Y	Y	Y	Y	Y
12 Pelosi	Y	Y	Y	Y	Y	Y
13 Lee	Y	Y	Y	Y	Y	Y
14 Speier	Y	Y	Y	Y	Y	Y
15 Swalwell	?	?	?	?	?	?
16 Costa	?	?	?	?	?	?
17 Khanna	Y	Y	Y	Y	Y	Y
18 Eshoo	Y	Y	Y	Y	Y	Y
19 Lofgren	Y	Y	Y	Y	Y	Y
20 Panetta	Y	Y	Y	Y	Y	Y
21 **Valadao**	Y	Y	Y	Y	Y	Y
22 **Nunes**	Y	Y	Y	Y	Y	Y
23 **McCarthy**	Y	Y	Y	Y	Y	Y
24 Carbajal	Y	Y	Y	Y	Y	Y
25 **Knight**	Y	Y	Y	Y	Y	Y
26 Brownley	Y	Y	Y	Y	Y	Y
27 Chu	Y	Y	Y	Y	Y	Y
28 Schiff	Y	Y	Y	Y	Y	Y
29 Cardenas	Y	Y	Y	Y	Y	Y
30 Sherman	Y	Y	Y	Y	Y	Y
31 Aguilar	Y	Y	Y	Y	Y	Y
32 Napolitano	Y	Y	Y	Y	Y	Y
33 Lieu	Y	Y	Y	Y	Y	Y
34 Gomez	Y	Y	Y	Y	Y	Y
35 Torres	Y	Y	Y	Y	Y	Y
36 Ruiz	Y	Y	Y	Y	Y	Y
37 Bass	Y	Y	Y	Y	Y	Y
38 Sánchez, Linda	Y	Y	Y	Y	Y	Y
39 **Royce**	Y	Y	Y	Y	Y	Y
40 Roybal-Allard	Y	Y	Y	Y	Y	Y
41 Takano	Y	Y	Y	Y	Y	Y
42 **Calvert**	Y	Y	Y	Y	Y	Y
43 Waters	Y	Y	Y	Y	Y	Y
44 Barragan	Y	?	Y	Y	Y	Y
45 **Walters**	?	?	?	?	?	?
46 Correa	Y	Y	Y	Y	Y	Y
47 Lowenthal	?	?	?	?	?	?
48 **Rohrabacher**	Y	Y	Y	Y	Y	Y
49 **Issa**	?	?	?	?	?	?
50 **Hunter**	Y	Y	Y	Y	Y	Y
51 Vargas	Y	Y	Y	Y	Y	Y
52 Peters	Y	Y	Y	Y	Y	Y
53 Davis	Y	Y	Y	Y	Y	Y

	452	453	454	455	456	457
COLORADO						
1 DeGette	Y	Y	Y	Y	Y	Y
2 Polis	?	?	?	?	?	?
3 **Tipton**	Y	Y	Y	Y	Y	Y
4 **Buck**	Y	Y	Y	N	Y	Y
5 **Lamborn**	Y	Y	Y	Y	Y	Y
6 **Coffman**	Y	Y	Y	Y	Y	Y
7 Perlmutter	Y	Y	Y	Y	Y	Y
CONNECTICUT						
1 Larson	Y	Y	Y	Y	Y	Y
2 Courtney	Y	Y	Y	Y	Y	Y
3 DeLauro	Y	Y	Y	Y	Y	Y
4 Himes	Y	Y	Y	Y	Y	Y
5 Esty	Y	Y	Y	Y	Y	Y
DELAWARE						
AL Blunt Rochester	Y	Y	Y	Y	Y	Y
FLORIDA						
1 **Gaetz**	Y	Y	Y	N	?	Y
2 **Dunn**	Y	Y	Y	Y	Y	Y
3 **Yoho**	Y	Y	Y	Y	Y	Y
4 **Rutherford**	Y	Y	Y	Y	?	Y
5 Lawson	Y	Y	Y	Y	Y	Y
6 Vacant						
7 Murphy	Y	Y	Y	Y	Y	Y
8 **Posey**	Y	Y	Y	Y	Y	Y
9 Soto	Y	Y	Y	Y	Y	Y
10 Demings	Y	Y	Y	Y	Y	Y
11 **Webster**	Y	Y	Y	Y	Y	Y
12 **Bilirakis**	Y	Y	Y	Y	Y	Y
13 Crist	Y	Y	Y	Y	Y	Y
14 Castor	Y	Y	Y	Y	Y	Y
15 **Ross**	?	?	?	?	?	?
16 **Buchanan**	Y	Y	Y	Y	Y	Y
17 **Rooney, T.**	Y	Y	Y	Y	Y	Y
18 **Mast**	Y	Y	Y	Y	Y	Y
19 **Rooney, F.**	Y	Y	Y	Y	Y	Y
20 Hastings	?	?	?	?	?	?
21 Frankel	Y	Y	Y	Y	Y	Y
22 Deutch	Y	Y	Y	Y	Y	Y
23 Wasserman Schultz	Y	Y	Y	Y	Y	Y
24 Wilson	?	Y	Y	Y	Y	Y
25 **Diaz-Balart**	Y	Y	Y	Y	Y	Y
26 **Curbelo**	Y	Y	Y	Y	Y	Y
27 **Ros-Lehtinen**	Y	Y	Y	Y	Y	Y
GEORGIA						
1 **Carter**	Y	Y	Y	Y	Y	Y
2 Bishop	Y	Y	Y	Y	Y	Y
3 **Ferguson**	Y	Y	Y	Y	Y	Y
4 Johnson	Y	Y	Y	Y	Y	Y
5 Lewis	Y	Y	Y	Y	Y	Y
6 **Handel**	Y	Y	Y	Y	Y	Y
7 **Woodall**	Y	Y	Y	Y	Y	Y
8 **Scott, A.**	Y	?	?	?	?	?
9 **Collins**	Y	Y	Y	Y	Y	Y
10 **Hice**	Y	Y	Y	N	Y	Y
11 **Loudermilk**	Y	Y	Y	Y	Y	Y
12 **Allen**	Y	Y	Y	Y	Y	Y
13 Scott, D.	?	?	?	?	?	?
14 **Graves**	Y	Y	Y	Y	Y	Y
HAWAII						
1 Hanabusa	?	?	?	?	?	?
2 Gabbard	Y	Y	Y	Y	Y	Y
IDAHO						
1 **Labrador**	Y	Y	Y	Y	Y	Y
2 **Simpson**	Y	Y	Y	?	?	Y
ILLINOIS						
1 Rush	Y	Y	Y	Y	Y	Y
2 Kelly	Y	Y	Y	Y	Y	Y
3 Lipinski	Y	Y	Y	Y	Y	Y
4 Gutierrez	Y	Y	Y	?	Y	Y
5 Quigley	Y	Y	Y	Y	Y	Y
6 **Roskam**	Y	Y	Y	Y	Y	Y
7 Davis, D.	?	?	?	?	?	?
8 Krishnamoorthi	Y	Y	Y	Y	Y	Y
9 Schakowsky	Y	Y	Y	Y	Y	Y
10 Schneider	Y	Y	Y	Y	Y	Y
11 Foster	Y	Y	Y	Y	Y	Y
12 **Bost**	Y	Y	Y	Y	Y	Y
13 **Davis, R.**	Y	Y	Y	Y	Y	Y

KEY	**Republicans**	Democrats	*Independents*
Y Voted for (yea)		X Paired against	C Voted "present" to avoid possible conflict of interest
# Paired for		– Announced against	
+ Announced for		P Voted "present"	? Did not vote or otherwise make a position known
N Voted against (nay)			

ILLINOIS (cont.)

		452	453	454	455	456	457
14	**Hultgren**	?	?	?	?	?	?
15	**Shimkus**	Y	Y	Y	Y	Y	Y
16	**Kinzinger**	Y	Y	Y	Y	Y	Y
17	Bustos	Y	Y	Y	Y	Y	Y
18	**LaHood**	Y	Y	Y	Y	Y	Y

INDIANA

		452	453	454	455	456	457
1	Visclosky	Y	Y	Y	Y	Y	Y
2	**Walorski**	Y	Y	Y	Y	Y	Y
3	**Banks**	Y	Y	Y	Y	Y	Y
4	**Rokita**	Y	Y	Y	Y	Y	Y
5	**Brooks**	Y	Y	Y	Y	Y	Y
6	**Messer**	?	?	?	?	?	?
7	Carson	Y	Y	Y	Y	Y	Y
8	**Bucshon**	Y	Y	Y	Y	Y	Y
9	**Hollingsworth**	Y	Y	Y	Y	Y	Y

IOWA

		452	453	454	455	456	457
1	**Blum**	Y	Y	Y	N	Y	Y
2	Loebsack	Y	Y	Y	Y	Y	Y
3	**Young**	Y	Y	Y	Y	Y	Y
4	**King**	Y	Y	Y	Y	Y	Y

KANSAS

		452	453	454	455	456	457
1	**Marshall**	Y	Y	Y	Y	Y	Y
2	**Jenkins**	?	?	?	?	?	?
3	**Yoder**	Y	Y	Y	Y	Y	Y
4	**Estes**	Y	Y	Y	Y	Y	Y

KENTUCKY

		452	453	454	455	456	457
1	**Comer**	Y	Y	Y	Y	Y	Y
2	**Guthrie**	Y	Y	Y	Y	Y	Y
3	Yarmuth	Y	Y	Y	Y	Y	Y
4	**Massie**	Y	N	Y	Y	N	N
5	**Rogers**	Y	Y	Y	Y	Y	Y
6	**Barr**	Y	Y	Y	Y	Y	Y

LOUISIANA

		452	453	454	455	456	457
1	**Scalise**	Y	Y	Y	Y	Y	Y
2	Richmond	Y	Y	Y	Y	Y	Y
3	**Higgins**	Y	Y	Y	Y	Y	Y
4	**Johnson**	Y	Y	Y	Y	Y	Y
5	**Abraham**	Y	Y	Y	Y	Y	Y
6	**Graves**	Y	Y	Y	Y	Y	Y

MAINE

		452	453	454	455	456	457
1	Pingree	Y	Y	Y	Y	Y	Y
2	**Poliquin**	Y	Y	Y	Y	Y	Y

MARYLAND

		452	453	454	455	456	457
1	**Harris**	Y	Y	Y	Y	Y	Y
2	Ruppersberger	Y	Y	Y	Y	Y	Y
3	Sarbanes	Y	Y	?	Y	Y	Y
4	Brown	Y	Y	Y	Y	Y	Y
5	Hoyer	Y	Y	Y	Y	Y	Y
6	Delaney	Y	Y	Y	Y	Y	Y
7	Cummings	Y	Y	Y	Y	Y	Y
8	Raskin	Y	Y	Y	Y	Y	Y

MASSACHUSETTS

		452	453	454	455	456	457
1	Neal	Y	Y	Y	Y	Y	Y
2	McGovern	Y	Y	Y	Y	Y	Y
3	Tsongas	Y	Y	Y	Y	Y	Y
4	Kennedy	Y	Y	Y	Y	Y	Y
5	Clark	Y	Y	Y	Y	Y	Y
6	Moulton	Y	Y	Y	Y	Y	Y
7	Capuano	Y	Y	Y	Y	Y	Y
8	Lynch	Y	Y	Y	Y	Y	Y
9	Keating	?	?	?	?	?	?

MICHIGAN

		452	453	454	455	456	457
1	**Bergman**	Y	Y	Y	Y	Y	Y
2	**Huizenga**	Y	Y	Y	Y	Y	Y
3	*Amash*	Y	N	N	N	N	N
4	**Moolenaar**	Y	Y	Y	Y	Y	Y
5	Kildee	Y	Y	Y	Y	Y	Y
6	**Upton**	Y	Y	Y	Y	Y	Y
7	**Walberg**	Y	Y	Y	Y	Y	Y
8	**Bishop**	?	?	?	?	?	?
9	Levin	Y	Y	Y	Y	Y	Y
10	**Mitchell**	Y	Y	Y	Y	Y	Y
11	**Trott**	?	?	?	?	?	?
12	Dingell	Y	Y	Y	Y	Y	Y
13	Jones	Y	Y	Y	Y	Y	Y
14	Lawrence	Y	Y	Y	Y	Y	Y

MINNESOTA

		452	453	454	455	456	457
1	Walz	?	?	?	?	?	?
2	**Lewis**	Y	Y	Y	Y	Y	Y
3	**Paulsen**	Y	Y	Y	Y	Y	Y
4	McCollum	Y	Y	Y	?	Y	Y
5	Ellison	Y	Y	Y	?	Y	Y
6	**Emmer**	Y	Y	Y	Y	Y	Y
7	Peterson	?	?	?	?	?	?
8	Nolan	Y	Y	Y	Y	Y	Y

MISSISSIPPI

		452	453	454	455	456	457
1	**Kelly**	Y	Y	Y	Y	Y	Y
2	Thompson	?	?	?	?	?	?
3	**Harper**	Y	Y	Y	Y	Y	?
4	**Palazzo**	Y	Y	Y	Y	Y	Y

MISSOURI

		452	453	454	455	456	457
1	Clay	Y	Y	Y	Y	Y	Y
2	**Wagner**	Y	Y	Y	Y	Y	Y
3	**Luetkemeyer**	Y	Y	Y	Y	Y	Y
4	**Hartzler**	Y	Y	Y	Y	Y	Y
5	Cleaver	Y	Y	Y	Y	Y	Y
6	**Graves**	Y	Y	Y	Y	Y	Y
7	**Long**	Y	Y	Y	Y	Y	Y
8	**Smith**	Y	Y	Y	Y	Y	Y

MONTANA

		452	453	454	455	456	457
AL	**Gianforte**	Y	Y	Y	Y	Y	Y

NEBRASKA

		452	453	454	455	456	457
1	**Fortenberry**	Y	Y	Y	Y	Y	Y
2	**Bacon**	Y	Y	Y	Y	Y	Y
3	**Smith**	Y	Y	Y	Y	Y	Y

NEVADA

		452	453	454	455	456	457
1	Titus	Y	Y	Y	Y	Y	Y
2	**Amodei**	Y	Y	?	Y	Y	Y
3	Rosen	?	?	?	?	?	?
4	Kihuen	Y	Y	Y	Y	Y	Y

NEW HAMPSHIRE

		452	453	454	455	456	457
1	Shea-Porter	+	+	+	+	+	+
2	Kuster	Y	Y	Y	Y	Y	Y

NEW JERSEY

		452	453	454	455	456	457
1	Norcross	Y	Y	Y	Y	Y	Y
2	**LoBiondo**	Y	Y	Y	Y	Y	Y
3	**MacArthur**	Y	Y	Y	Y	Y	Y
4	**Smith**	Y	Y	Y	Y	Y	Y
5	Gottheimer	Y	Y	Y	Y	Y	Y
6	Pallone	Y	Y	Y	Y	Y	Y
7	**Lance**	Y	Y	Y	Y	Y	Y
8	Sires	Y	Y	Y	Y	Y	Y
9	Pascrell	Y	Y	Y	Y	Y	Y
10	Payne	Y	Y	Y	Y	Y	Y
11	**Frelinghuysen**	Y	Y	Y	Y	Y	Y
12	Watson Coleman	Y	Y	Y	Y	Y	Y

NEW MEXICO

		452	453	454	455	456	457
1	Lujan Grisham	?	?	?	?	?	?
2	**Pearce**	Y	Y	Y	Y	Y	Y
3	Luján	Y	Y	Y	Y	Y	Y

NEW YORK

		452	453	454	455	456	457
1	**Zeldin**	Y	Y	Y	Y	Y	Y
2	**King**	Y	Y	Y	Y	Y	Y
3	Suozzi	Y	Y	Y	Y	Y	Y
4	Rice	Y	Y	Y	Y	Y	Y
5	Meeks	Y	Y	Y	Y	Y	Y
6	Meng	Y	Y	Y	Y	Y	Y
7	Velázquez	Y	Y	Y	Y	Y	Y
8	Jeffries	Y	Y	Y	Y	Y	Y
9	Clarke	Y	Y	Y	Y	Y	Y
10	Nadler	Y	Y	Y	Y	Y	Y
11	**Donovan**	Y	Y	Y	Y	Y	Y
12	Maloney, C.	Y	Y	Y	Y	Y	Y
13	Espaillat	Y	Y	Y	Y	Y	Y
14	Crowley	?	?	?	?	?	?
15	Serrano	Y	Y	Y	Y	Y	Y
16	Engel	Y	Y	Y	Y	Y	Y
17	Lowey	Y	Y	Y	Y	Y	Y
18	Maloney, S.P.	Y	Y	Y	Y	Y	Y
19	**Faso**	Y	Y	Y	Y	Y	Y
20	Tonko	Y	Y	Y	Y	Y	Y
21	**Stefanik**	Y	Y	Y	Y	Y	Y
22	**Tenney**	Y	Y	Y	Y	Y	Y
23	**Reed**	Y	Y	Y	Y	Y	Y
24	**Katko**	Y	Y	Y	Y	Y	Y
25	Morelle	Y	Y	Y	Y	Y	Y
26	Higgins	?	Y	Y	Y	?	Y
27	**Collins**	Y	Y	Y	Y	Y	Y

NORTH CAROLINA

		452	453	454	455	456	457
1	Butterfield	Y	Y	Y	Y	Y	Y
2	**Holding**	Y	Y	Y	Y	Y	Y
3	**Jones**	?	?	?	?	?	?
4	Price	Y	Y	Y	Y	Y	Y
5	**Foxx**	Y	Y	Y	Y	Y	Y
6	**Walker**	Y	Y	?	Y	Y	Y
7	**Rouzer**	Y	Y	Y	Y	Y	Y
8	**Hudson**	Y	Y	Y	Y	Y	Y
9	**Pittenger**	?	Y	Y	Y	Y	Y
9	Vacant						
10	**McHenry**	Y	Y	Y	Y	Y	Y
11	**Meadows**	Y	Y	Y	Y	Y	Y
12	Adams	Y	Y	Y	Y	Y	Y
13	**Budd**	Y	Y	Y	Y	Y	Y

NORTH DAKOTA

		452	453	454	455	456	457
AL	**Cramer**	?	?	?	?	?	?

OHIO

		452	453	454	455	456	457
1	**Chabot**	Y	Y	Y	Y	Y	Y
2	**Wenstrup**	Y	Y	Y	Y	Y	Y
3	Beatty	Y	Y	Y	Y	Y	Y
4	**Jordan**	Y	Y	Y	Y	Y	Y
5	**Latta**	Y	Y	Y	Y	Y	Y
6	**Johnson**	Y	Y	Y	Y	Y	Y
7	**Gibbs**	Y	Y	Y	Y	Y	Y
8	**Davidson**	Y	Y	Y	Y	Y	Y
9	Kaptur	Y	Y	Y	Y	Y	Y
10	**Turner**	Y	Y	Y	Y	Y	Y
11	Fudge	Y	Y	Y	Y	Y	Y
12	Balderson	Y	Y	Y	Y	Y	Y
13	Ryan	Y	Y	Y	Y	Y	Y
14	Joyce	Y	Y	Y	Y	Y	Y
15	Stivers	Y	Y	Y	Y	Y	Y
16	Renacci	Y	Y	Y	Y	Y	Y

OKLAHOMA

		452	453	454	455	456	457
1	**Hern**	Y	Y	Y	Y	Y	Y
2	**Mullin**	Y	Y	Y	Y	Y	Y
3	**Lucas**	Y	Y	Y	Y	Y	Y
4	**Cole**	Y	Y	Y	Y	Y	Y
5	**Russell**	?	?	?	?	?	?

OREGON

		452	453	454	455	456	457
1	Bonamici	Y	Y	Y	Y	Y	Y
2	**Walden**	Y	Y	Y	Y	Y	Y
3	Blumenauer	Y	?	Y	Y	Y	Y
4	DeFazio	Y	Y	Y	Y	Y	Y
5	Schrader	?	Y	Y	Y	Y	Y

PENNSYLVANIA

		452	453	454	455	456	457
1	Brady	Y	Y	Y	Y	Y	Y
2	Evans	Y	Y	Y	Y	Y	Y
3	**Kelly**	Y	Y	Y	Y	Y	Y
4	**Perry**	Y	Y	Y	N	Y	Y
5	**Thompson**	Y	Y	Y	Y	Y	Y
6	**Costello**	Y	Y	Y	Y	Y	Y
7	Scanlon	Y	Y	Y	Y	Y	Y
8	**Fitzpatrick**	Y	Y	Y	Y	Y	Y
9	**Shuster**	Y	Y	Y	Y	Y	Y
10	**Marino**	Y	Y	Y	Y	Y	Y
11	**Barletta**	Y	Y	Y	Y	Y	Y
12	**Rothfus**	Y	Y	Y	Y	Y	Y
13	Boyle	Y	Y	Y	Y	Y	Y
14	Doyle	Y	Y	Y	Y	Y	Y
15	Wild	Y	Y	Y	Y	Y	Y
16	**Smucker**	Y	Y	Y	Y	Y	Y
17	Cartwright	Y	Y	Y	Y	Y	Y
18	Lamb	Y	Y	Y	Y	Y	Y

RHODE ISLAND

		452	453	454	455	456	457
1	Cicilline	Y	Y	Y	Y	Y	Y
2	Langevin	Y	Y	Y	Y	Y	Y

SOUTH CAROLINA

		452	453	454	455	456	457
1	**Sanford**	Y	Y	Y	N	Y	Y
2	**Wilson**	Y	Y	Y	Y	Y	Y
3	**Duncan**	?	?	?	?	?	?
4	**Gowdy**	Y	Y	Y	Y	Y	Y
5	**Norman**	Y	Y	Y	Y	Y	Y
6	Clyburn	Y	Y	Y	Y	Y	Y
7	**Rice**	Y	Y	Y	Y	Y	Y

SOUTH DAKOTA

		452	453	454	455	456	457
AL	**Noem**	?	?	?	?	?	?

TENNESSEE

		452	453	454	455	456	457
1	**Roe**	Y	Y	Y	Y	Y	Y
2	**Duncan**	Y	Y	Y	N	Y	Y
3	**Fleischmann**	Y	Y	Y	Y	Y	Y
4	**DesJarlais**	Y	Y	Y	Y	Y	Y
5	Cooper	Y	Y	Y	Y	Y	Y
6	**Black**	?	?	?	?	?	?
7	**Blackburn**	Y	Y	Y	Y	Y	Y
8	**Kustoff**	Y	Y	Y	Y	Y	Y
9	Cohen	Y	Y	Y	Y	Y	Y

TEXAS

		452	453	454	455	456	457
1	**Gohmert**	Y	Y	Y	Y	Y	Y
2	**Poe**	Y	Y	Y	Y	Y	Y
3	**Johnson, S.**	?	?	?	?	?	?
4	**Ratcliffe**	?	?	?	?	?	?
5	**Hensarling**	Y	Y	Y	Y	Y	Y
6	**Barton**	Y	Y	Y	Y	Y	Y
7	**Culberson**	Y	Y	Y	Y	Y	Y
8	**Brady**	Y	Y	Y	Y	Y	Y
9	Green, A.	Y	Y	Y	Y	Y	Y
10	**McCaul**	Y	Y	Y	Y	Y	Y
11	**Conaway**	Y	Y	Y	Y	Y	Y
12	**Granger**	Y	Y	Y	Y	Y	Y
13	**Thornberry**	Y	Y	Y	Y	Y	Y
14	**Weber**	Y	Y	Y	Y	Y	Y
15	Gonzalez	Y	Y	?	Y	Y	Y
16	O'Rourke	Y	Y	Y	Y	Y	Y
17	**Flores**	Y	Y	Y	Y	Y	Y
18	Jackson Lee	Y	Y	Y	Y	Y	Y
19	**Arrington**	Y	Y	Y	Y	Y	Y
20	Castro	Y	Y	Y	Y	Y	Y
21	**Smith**	Y	Y	Y	Y	Y	Y
22	**Olson**	Y	Y	Y	Y	Y	Y
23	**Hurd**	Y	Y	Y	Y	Y	Y
24	**Marchant**	Y	Y	Y	Y	Y	Y
25	**Williams**	Y	Y	Y	Y	Y	Y
26	**Burgess**	Y	Y	Y	Y	Y	Y
27	Cloud	Y	Y	Y	Y	Y	Y
28	Cuellar	Y	?	Y	Y	Y	Y
29	Green, G.	Y	Y	Y	Y	Y	Y
30	Johnson, E.B.	Y	Y	Y	Y	Y	Y
31	**Carter**	Y	Y	Y	Y	Y	Y
32	**Sessions**	Y	Y	Y	Y	Y	Y
33	Veasey	Y	Y	Y	Y	Y	Y
34	Vela	?	?	?	?	?	?
35	Doggett	Y	Y	Y	Y	Y	Y
36	**Babin**	Y	Y	Y	Y	Y	Y

UTAH

		452	453	454	455	456	457
1	**Bishop**	Y	Y	Y	Y	Y	Y
2	**Stewart**	Y	Y	Y	Y	Y	Y
3	**Curtis**	Y	Y	Y	Y	Y	Y
4	**Love**	?	?	?	?	?	?

VERMONT

		452	453	454	455	456	457
AL	Welch	Y	Y	Y	Y	Y	Y

VIRGINIA

		452	453	454	455	456	457
1	**Wittman**	Y	Y	Y	Y	Y	Y
2	**Taylor**	Y	Y	Y	Y	Y	Y
3	Scott	Y	Y	Y	Y	Y	Y
4	McEachin	Y	Y	Y	Y	Y	Y
5	**Garrett**	Y	?	Y	Y	Y	Y
6	**Goodlatte**	Y	Y	Y	Y	Y	Y
7	**Brat**	Y	Y	Y	N	Y	Y
8	Beyer	Y	Y	Y	Y	Y	Y
9	**Griffith**	Y	Y	Y	Y	Y	Y
10	**Comstock**	?	?	?	?	?	?
11	Connolly	Y	Y	Y	Y	Y	Y

WASHINGTON

		452	453	454	455	456	457
1	DelBene	Y	Y	Y	Y	Y	Y
2	Larsen	Y	Y	Y	Y	Y	Y
3	**Herrera Beutler**	Y	Y	Y	Y	Y	Y
4	**Newhouse**	Y	Y	Y	Y	Y	Y
5	**McMorris Rodgers**	Y	Y	Y	Y	Y	Y
6	Kilmer	Y	Y	Y	Y	Y	Y
7	Jayapal	Y	Y	Y	Y	Y	Y
8	**Reichert**	Y	Y	Y	Y	Y	Y
9	Smith	Y	Y	Y	Y	Y	Y
10	Heck	Y	Y	Y	Y	Y	Y

WEST VIRGINIA

		452	453	454	455	456	457
1	**McKinley**	Y	Y	Y	Y	Y	Y
2	**Mooney**	Y	Y	Y	Y	Y	Y
3	Vacant						

WISCONSIN

		452	453	454	455	456	457
1	**Ryan**						
2	Pocan	Y	Y	Y	Y	Y	Y
3	Kind	?	?	?	?	?	?
4	Moore	Y	Y	Y	Y	Y	Y
5	**Sensenbrenner**	Y	Y	Y	Y	Y	Y
6	**Grothman**	Y	Y	Y	Y	Y	Y
7	**Duffy**	Y	Y	Y	Y	Y	Y
8	**Gallagher**	Y	Y	Y	Y	Y	Y

WYOMING

		452	453	454	455	456	457
AL	**Cheney**	Y	Y	Y	Y	Y	Y

VOTE NUMBER

458. S2765. RURAL INVESTMENT ADVISORS/PASSAGE. Huizenga, R-Mich., motion to suspend the rules and pass the bill that would exempt investment advisors working only with licensed rural business investment companies from a requirement that they register with the Securities and Exchange Commission. Motion agreed to 389-0: R 213-0; D 176-0. Dec. 20, 2018.

459. HR5509. STEM EDUCATION GRANTS/PASSAGE. Smith, R-Texas, motion to suspend the rules and concur in the Senate amendment to the bill that would direct the National Science Foundation director to provide grants for STEM education and research. It would require the NSF to devote at least $5 million annually through fiscal 2021 for grants to community colleges and certificate programs in STEM fields; at least $2.5 million annually through fiscal 2021 for grants to higher education institutions to provide STEM research and internship opportunities; and at least $2.5 million annually through fiscal 2021 for grants to higher education institutions and non-profits for research on STEM education best practices. It would also require an NSF report on the national technical workforce. Motion agreed to 378-13: R 200-13; D 178-0. Dec. 20, 2018.

460. S7. NASA LEASING/PASSAGE. Smith, R-Texas, motion to suspend the rules and pass the bill that would extend, through Dec. 31, 2019, the authority for NASA to lease the agency's non-excess property. Motion agreed to 390-0: R 212-0; D 178-0. Dec. 20, 2018.

461. S2200. DROUGHT INFORMATION SYSTEM/PASSAGE. Smith, R-Texas, motion to suspend the rules and pass the bill that would reauthorize through fiscal 2023 the National Oceanic and Atmospheric Administration's national drought information system. It would authorize $13.5 million for the program in fiscal 2019, with the amount increasing by $250,000 annually through fiscal 2023. Motion agreed to 379-9: R 204-9; D 175-0. Dec. 20, 2018.

462. HR767. ADDRESSING HUMAN TRAFFICKING/PASSAGE. Guthrie, R-Ky., motion to suspend the rules and concur in the Senate amendment to the bill that would establish in statute a Health and Human Services Department program training health care professionals to identify and serve victims of human trafficking. Annually through fiscal 2024, it would authorize $4 million for the program. Motion agreed to 386-6: R 208-6; D 178-0. Dec. 20, 2018.

463. S2322. CHEESE LABELLING/PASSAGE. Guthrie, R-Ky., motion to suspend the rules and pass the bill as amended, that would define "natural cheese" and other types of cheese, primarily for labeling purposes. Motion rejected 230-162: R 194-20; D 36-142. Dec. 20, 2018.

	458	459	460	461	462	463
ALABAMA						
1 Byrne	Y	Y	Y	Y	Y	Y
2 Roby	Y	Y	Y	Y	Y	Y
3 Rogers	Y	Y	Y	Y	Y	Y
4 Aderholt	Y	Y	Y	Y	Y	Y
5 Brooks	Y	Y	Y	Y	Y	Y
6 Palmer	Y	Y	Y	Y	Y	Y
7 Sewell	Y	Y	Y	Y	Y	N
ALASKA						
AL Young	Y	Y	Y	Y	Y	Y
ARIZONA						
1 O'Halleran	Y	Y	Y	Y	Y	N
2 McSally	Y	Y	Y	Y	Y	Y
3 Grijalva	Y	Y	Y	Y	Y	N
4 Gosar	Y	N	Y	Y	Y	N
5 Biggs	Y	N	Y	N	N	N
6 Schweikert	Y	Y	Y	Y	Y	Y
7 Gallego	Y	Y	Y	Y	Y	Y
8 Lesko	Y	Y	Y	Y	Y	Y
9 Sinema	?	?	?	?	?	?
ARKANSAS						
1 Crawford	?	?	?	?	?	?
2 Hill	Y	Y	Y	Y	Y	Y
3 Womack	Y	Y	Y	Y	Y	Y
4 Westerman	Y	Y	Y	Y	Y	Y
CALIFORNIA						
1 LaMalfa	Y	Y	Y	Y	Y	Y
2 Huffman	Y	Y	Y	Y	Y	N
3 Garamendi	Y	Y	Y	Y	Y	Y
4 McClintock	Y	N	Y	Y	Y	N
5 Thompson	Y	Y	Y	Y	Y	N
6 Matsui	Y	Y	Y	Y	Y	N
7 Bera	Y	Y	Y	Y	Y	Y
8 Cook	Y	Y	Y	Y	Y	Y
9 McNerney	Y	Y	Y	Y	Y	N
10 Denham	?	?	?	Y	Y	Y
11 DeSaulnier	Y	Y	Y	Y	Y	N
12 Pelosi	Y	Y	Y	Y	Y	N
13 Lee	Y	Y	Y	Y	Y	N
14 Speier	Y	Y	Y	Y	Y	N
15 Swalwell	?	?	?	?	?	?
16 Costa	?	?	?	?	?	?
17 Khanna	Y	Y	Y	Y	Y	N
18 Eshoo	Y	Y	Y	Y	Y	N
19 Lofgren	Y	Y	Y	Y	Y	N
20 Panetta	Y	Y	Y	Y	Y	Y
21 Valadao	Y	Y	Y	Y	Y	Y
22 Nunes	Y	Y	Y	Y	Y	Y
23 McCarthy	Y	Y	Y	Y	Y	Y
24 Carbajal	Y	Y	Y	Y	Y	N
25 Knight	Y	Y	Y	Y	Y	Y
26 Brownley	Y	Y	Y	Y	Y	N
27 Chu	Y	Y	Y	Y	Y	N
28 Schiff	Y	Y	Y	Y	Y	N
29 Cardenas	Y	Y	Y	Y	Y	N
30 Sherman	Y	Y	Y	Y	Y	N
31 Aguilar	Y	Y	Y	Y	Y	N
32 Napolitano	Y	Y	Y	?	Y	N
33 Lieu	Y	Y	Y	Y	Y	N
34 Gomez	Y	Y	Y	Y	Y	N
35 Torres	Y	Y	Y	Y	Y	N
36 Ruiz	Y	Y	Y	Y	Y	N
37 Bass	Y	Y	Y	Y	Y	N
38 Sánchez, Linda	Y	Y	Y	Y	Y	N
39 Royce	Y	Y	Y	Y	Y	Y
40 Roybal-Allard	Y	Y	Y	Y	Y	N
41 Takano	Y	Y	Y	Y	Y	N
42 Calvert	Y	Y	Y	Y	Y	Y
43 Waters	Y	Y	Y	Y	Y	N
44 Barragan	Y	Y	Y	Y	Y	N
45 Walters	?	?	?	?	?	?
46 Correa	Y	Y	Y	Y	Y	N
47 Lowenthal	?	?	?	?	?	?
48 Rohrabacher	Y	Y	Y	Y	Y	Y
49 Issa	?	?	?	?	?	?
50 Hunter	Y	Y	Y	Y	Y	Y
51 Vargas	Y	Y	Y	Y	Y	N
52 Peters	Y	Y	Y	Y	Y	N
53 Davis	Y	Y	Y	Y	Y	N
COLORADO						
1 DeGette	Y	Y	Y	Y	Y	N
2 Polis	?	?	?	?	?	?
3 Tipton	Y	Y	Y	Y	Y	Y
4 Buck	Y	N	Y	Y	Y	N
5 Lamborn	Y	Y	Y	Y	Y	Y
6 Coffman	Y	Y	Y	Y	Y	Y
7 Perlmutter	Y	Y	Y	Y	Y	Y
CONNECTICUT						
1 Larson	Y	Y	Y	Y	Y	Y
2 Courtney	Y	Y	Y	Y	Y	Y
3 DeLauro	Y	Y	Y	Y	Y	N
4 Himes	Y	Y	Y	Y	Y	Y
5 Esty	Y	Y	Y	Y	Y	N
DELAWARE						
AL Blunt Rochester	Y	Y	Y	Y	Y	N
FLORIDA						
1 Gaetz	?	N	Y	Y	Y	N
2 Dunn	Y	Y	Y	Y	Y	Y
3 Yoho	Y	Y	Y	Y	Y	Y
4 Rutherford	Y	Y	Y	Y	Y	Y
5 Lawson	Y	Y	Y	Y	Y	Y
6 Vacant						
7 Murphy	Y	Y	Y	Y	Y	Y
8 Posey	Y	Y	Y	Y	Y	Y
9 Soto	Y	Y	Y	Y	Y	N
10 Demings	Y	Y	Y	Y	Y	N
11 Webster	Y	Y	Y	Y	Y	Y
12 Bilirakis	Y	Y	Y	Y	Y	Y
13 Crist	Y	Y	Y	Y	Y	N
14 Castor	Y	Y	Y	Y	Y	N
15 Ross	?	?	?	?	?	?
16 Buchanan	Y	Y	Y	Y	Y	Y
17 Rooney, T.	Y	Y	Y	Y	Y	Y
18 Mast	Y	Y	Y	Y	Y	Y
19 Rooney, F.	Y	Y	Y	Y	Y	Y
20 Hastings	?	?	?	?	?	?
21 Frankel	Y	Y	Y	Y	Y	N
22 Deutch	Y	Y	Y	Y	Y	N
23 Wasserman Schultz	Y	Y	Y	Y	Y	N
24 Wilson	Y	Y	Y	Y	Y	N
25 Diaz-Balart	Y	Y	Y	Y	Y	Y
26 Curbelo	Y	Y	Y	Y	Y	Y
27 Ros-Lehtinen	Y	Y	Y	Y	Y	Y
GEORGIA						
1 Carter	Y	Y	Y	Y	Y	Y
2 Bishop	Y	Y	Y	Y	Y	Y
3 Ferguson	Y	Y	Y	?	Y	Y
4 Johnson	Y	Y	Y	Y	Y	N
5 Lewis	Y	Y	Y	Y	Y	N
6 Handel	Y	Y	Y	Y	Y	Y
7 Woodall	Y	Y	Y	Y	Y	Y
8 Scott, A.	?	?	?	?	?	?
9 Collins	Y	Y	Y	Y	Y	Y
10 Hice	Y	Y	Y	Y	Y	Y
11 Loudermilk	Y	Y	Y	Y	Y	Y
12 Allen	Y	Y	Y	Y	Y	Y
13 Scott, D.	?	?	?	?	?	?
14 Graves	Y	Y	Y	Y	Y	Y
HAWAII						
1 Hanabusa	?	?	?	?	?	?
2 Gabbard	Y	Y	Y	Y	Y	N
IDAHO						
1 Labrador	Y	Y	Y	Y	Y	Y
2 Simpson	Y	Y	Y	Y	Y	Y
ILLINOIS						
1 Rush	Y	Y	Y	Y	Y	N
2 Kelly	Y	Y	Y	Y	Y	N
3 Lipinski	Y	Y	Y	Y	Y	N
4 Gutierrez	Y	Y	Y	?	Y	N
5 Quigley	Y	Y	Y	Y	Y	N
6 Roskam	Y	Y	Y	Y	Y	Y
7 Davis, D.	?	?	?	?	?	?
8 Krishnamoorthi	Y	Y	Y	Y	Y	N
9 Schakowsky	Y	Y	Y	Y	Y	N
10 Schneider	Y	Y	Y	Y	Y	N
11 Foster	Y	Y	Y	Y	Y	N
12 Bost	Y	Y	Y	Y	Y	Y
13 Davis, R.	Y	Y	Y	Y	Y	Y

	458	459	460	461	462	463
14 **Hultgren**	?	?	?	?	?	?
15 **Shimkus**	Y	Y	Y	Y	Y	Y
16 **Kinzinger**	Y	Y	Y	Y	Y	Y
17 Bustos	Y	Y	Y	Y	Y	Y
18 **LaHood**	Y	?	Y	Y	Y	Y
INDIANA						
1 Visclosky	Y	Y	Y	Y	Y	N
2 **Walorski**	Y	Y	Y	Y	Y	Y
3 **Banks**	Y	Y	Y	Y	Y	Y
4 Rokita	Y	Y	Y	Y	Y	Y
5 **Brooks**	Y	Y	Y	Y	Y	Y
6 **Messer**	?	?	?	?	?	?
7 Carson	Y	Y	Y	Y	Y	N
8 **Bucshon**	Y	Y	Y	Y	Y	Y
9 **Hollingsworth**	Y	Y	Y	Y	Y	Y
IOWA						
1 **Blum**	Y	Y	Y	Y	Y	Y
2 Loebsack	Y	Y	Y	Y	Y	Y
3 **Young**	Y	Y	Y	Y	Y	Y
4 **King**	Y	Y	Y	Y	Y	Y
KANSAS						
1 **Marshall**	Y	Y	Y	Y	Y	Y
2 **Jenkins**	?	?	?	?	?	?
3 **Yoder**	Y	Y	Y	Y	Y	Y
4 **Estes**	Y	Y	Y	Y	Y	Y
KENTUCKY						
1 **Comer**	Y	Y	Y	Y	Y	Y
2 **Guthrie**	Y	Y	Y	Y	Y	Y
3 Yarmuth	Y	Y	Y	Y	Y	Y
4 **Massie**	Y	N	Y	N	N	N
5 **Rogers**	Y	Y	Y	Y	Y	Y
6 **Barr**	Y	Y	Y	Y	Y	Y
LOUISIANA						
1 **Scalise**	Y	Y	Y	Y	Y	Y
2 Richmond	Y	Y	Y	Y	Y	N
3 **Higgins**	Y	Y	Y	Y	Y	Y
4 **Johnson**	Y	Y	Y	Y	Y	N
5 **Abraham**	Y	Y	Y	Y	Y	Y
6 **Graves**	Y	Y	Y	Y	Y	Y
MAINE						
1 Pingree	Y	Y	Y	Y	Y	N
2 **Poliquin**	Y	Y	Y	Y	Y	Y
MARYLAND						
1 **Harris**	Y	N	Y	N	Y	N
2 Ruppersberger	Y	Y	Y	Y	Y	N
3 Sarbanes	Y	Y	Y	Y	Y	N
4 Brown	Y	Y	Y	Y	Y	N
5 Hoyer	Y	Y	Y	Y	Y	N
6 Delaney	Y	Y	Y	Y	Y	Y
7 Cummings	Y	Y	Y	Y	Y	N
8 Raskin	Y	Y	Y	Y	Y	N
MASSACHUSETTS						
1 Neal	Y	Y	Y	Y	Y	N
2 McGovern	Y	Y	Y	Y	Y	N
3 Tsongas	Y	Y	Y	Y	Y	N
4 Kennedy	Y	Y	Y	Y	Y	N
5 Clark	Y	Y	Y	Y	Y	N
6 Moulton	Y	Y	Y	Y	Y	N
7 Capuano	Y	Y	Y	?	Y	N
8 Lynch	Y	Y	Y	Y	Y	N
9 Keating	?	?	?	?	?	?
MICHIGAN						
1 **Bergman**	Y	Y	Y	Y	Y	Y
2 **Huizenga**	Y	Y	Y	Y	Y	Y
3 *Amash*	Y	N	Y	N	N	N
4 **Moolenaar**	Y	Y	Y	Y	Y	Y
5 Kildee	Y	Y	Y	Y	Y	Y
6 **Upton**	Y	Y	Y	Y	Y	Y
7 **Walberg**	Y	Y	Y	Y	Y	Y
8 **Bishop**	?	?	?	?	?	?
9 Levin	Y	Y	Y	Y	Y	N
10 **Mitchell**	Y	Y	Y	Y	Y	Y
11 **Trott**	?	?	?	?	?	?
12 Dingell	Y	Y	Y	Y	Y	N
13 Jones	Y	Y	Y	Y	Y	N
14 Lawrence	Y	Y	Y	Y	Y	N
MINNESOTA						
1 Walz	?	?	?	?	?	?
2 **Lewis**	Y	Y	Y	Y	Y	Y
3 **Paulsen**	Y	Y	Y	Y	Y	Y
4 McCollum	Y	Y	Y	Y	Y	N

	458	459	460	461	462	463
5 Ellison	?	Y	Y	Y	Y	N
6 **Emmer**	Y	Y	Y	Y	Y	Y
7 Peterson	?	?	?	?	?	?
8 Nolan	Y	Y	Y	Y	Y	Y
MISSISSIPPI						
1 **Kelly**	Y	Y	Y	Y	Y	Y
2 Thompson	?	?	?	?	?	?
3 **Harper**	Y	Y	Y	Y	Y	Y
4 **Palazzo**	Y	Y	Y	Y	Y	Y
MISSOURI						
1 Clay	Y	Y	Y	Y	Y	N
2 **Wagner**	Y	Y	Y	Y	Y	Y
3 **Luetkemeyer**	Y	Y	Y	Y	Y	Y
4 **Hartzler**	Y	Y	Y	Y	Y	Y
5 Cleaver	Y	Y	Y	Y	Y	Y
6 **Graves**	Y	Y	Y	Y	Y	Y
7 **Long**	Y	Y	Y	Y	Y	Y
8 **Smith**	Y	Y	Y	Y	Y	Y
MONTANA						
AL **Gianforte**	Y	Y	Y	Y	Y	Y
NEBRASKA						
1 **Fortenberry**	Y	Y	Y	Y	Y	Y
2 **Bacon**	Y	Y	Y	Y	Y	Y
3 **Smith**	Y	Y	?	?	?	?
NEVADA						
1 Titus	Y	Y	Y	Y	Y	N
2 **Amodei**	Y	Y	Y	Y	Y	Y
3 Rosen	?	?	?	?	?	?
4 Kihuen	Y	Y	Y	Y	Y	N
NEW HAMPSHIRE						
1 Shea-Porter	+	+	+	+	+	–
2 Kuster	Y	Y	Y	Y	Y	N
NEW JERSEY						
1 Norcross	Y	Y	Y	Y	Y	N
2 **LoBiondo**	Y	Y	Y	Y	Y	Y
3 **MacArthur**	Y	Y	Y	Y	Y	Y
4 **Smith**	Y	Y	Y	Y	Y	N
5 Gottheimer	Y	Y	Y	Y	Y	N
6 Pallone	Y	Y	Y	Y	Y	N
7 **Lance**	Y	Y	Y	Y	Y	Y
8 Sires	Y	Y	Y	Y	Y	N
9 Pascrell	?	Y	Y	Y	Y	N
10 Payne	Y	Y	Y	Y	Y	Y
11 **Frelinghuysen**	Y	Y	Y	Y	Y	Y
12 Watson Coleman	Y	Y	Y	Y	Y	N
NEW MEXICO						
1 Lujan Grisham	?	?	?	?	?	?
2 **Pearce**	Y	Y	Y	Y	Y	Y
3 Luján	Y	Y	Y	Y	Y	Y
NEW YORK						
1 **Zeldin**	Y	Y	Y	Y	Y	Y
2 **King**	Y	Y	Y	Y	Y	Y
3 Suozzi	Y	Y	Y	Y	Y	N
4 Rice	Y	Y	Y	Y	Y	Y
5 Meeks	Y	Y	Y	Y	Y	N
6 Meng	Y	Y	Y	Y	Y	N
7 Velázquez	Y	Y	Y	Y	Y	N
8 Jeffries	Y	Y	Y	Y	Y	N
9 Clarke	Y	Y	Y	Y	Y	N
10 Nadler	Y	Y	Y	Y	Y	N
11 **Donovan**	Y	Y	Y	Y	Y	Y
12 Maloney, C.	Y	Y	Y	Y	Y	N
13 Espaillat	Y	Y	Y	Y	Y	N
14 Crowley	?	?	?	?	?	?
15 Serrano	Y	Y	Y	Y	Y	N
16 Engel	Y	Y	Y	Y	Y	N
17 Lowey	Y	Y	Y	Y	Y	N
18 Maloney, S.P.	Y	Y	Y	Y	Y	Y
19 **Faso**	Y	Y	Y	Y	Y	Y
20 Tonko	Y	Y	Y	Y	Y	N
21 **Stefanik**	Y	Y	Y	Y	Y	Y
22 **Tenney**	Y	Y	Y	Y	Y	Y
23 **Reed**	Y	Y	Y	Y	Y	Y
24 **Katko**	Y	Y	Y	Y	Y	Y
25 Morelle	Y	Y	Y	Y	Y	N
26 Higgins	Y	Y	Y	Y	Y	N
27 **Collins**	Y	Y	Y	Y	Y	Y
NORTH CAROLINA						
1 Butterfield	Y	Y	Y	Y	Y	N
2 **Holding**	Y	Y	Y	Y	Y	Y
3 **Jones**	?	?	?	?	?	?
4 Price	Y	Y	Y	Y	Y	N

	458	459	460	461	462	463
5 **Foxx**	Y	Y	Y	Y	Y	Y
6 **Walker**	Y	Y	?	Y	Y	Y
7 **Rouzer**	Y	Y	Y	Y	Y	Y
8 **Hudson**	Y	Y	Y	Y	Y	Y
9 **Pittenger**	Y	Y	Y	Y	Y	Y
9 **Vacant**						
10 **McHenry**	Y	Y	Y	Y	Y	Y
11 **Meadows**	Y	Y	Y	Y	Y	Y
12 Adams	Y	Y	Y	Y	Y	N
13 **Budd**	Y	Y	Y	Y	Y	Y
NORTH DAKOTA						
AL **Cramer**	?	?	?	?	?	?
OHIO						
1 **Chabot**	Y	Y	Y	Y	Y	Y
2 **Wenstrup**	Y	Y	Y	Y	Y	Y
3 Beatty	Y	Y	Y	Y	Y	N
4 **Jordan**	Y	Y	Y	Y	Y	Y
5 **Latta**	Y	Y	Y	Y	Y	Y
6 **Johnson**	Y	Y	Y	Y	Y	Y
7 **Gibbs**	Y	Y	Y	Y	Y	Y
8 **Davidson**	Y	Y	Y	Y	Y	Y
9 Kaptur	Y	Y	Y	Y	Y	N
10 **Turner**	Y	Y	Y	Y	Y	Y
11 Fudge	Y	Y	Y	Y	Y	N
12 Balderson	Y	Y	Y	Y	Y	Y
13 Ryan	Y	Y	Y	Y	Y	Y
14 **Joyce**	Y	Y	Y	Y	Y	Y
15 **Stivers**	Y	Y	Y	Y	Y	Y
16 **Renacci**	Y	Y	Y	Y	Y	Y
OKLAHOMA						
1 Hern	Y	Y	Y	Y	Y	Y
2 **Mullin**	Y	Y	Y	Y	Y	Y
3 **Lucas**	Y	Y	Y	Y	Y	Y
4 **Cole**	Y	Y	Y	Y	Y	Y
5 **Russell**	?	?	?	?	?	?
OREGON						
1 Bonamici	Y	Y	Y	Y	Y	Y
2 **Walden**	Y	Y	Y	Y	Y	Y
3 Blumenauer	Y	Y	Y	Y	Y	N
4 DeFazio	Y	Y	Y	Y	Y	Y
5 Schrader	Y	Y	Y	Y	Y	Y
PENNSYLVANIA						
1 Brady	Y	Y	Y	Y	Y	N
2 Evans	Y	Y	Y	Y	Y	N
3 **Kelly**	Y	Y	Y	Y	Y	Y
4 **Perry**	Y	Y	Y	N	Y	N
5 **Thompson**	Y	Y	Y	Y	Y	Y
6 **Costello**	Y	Y	Y	Y	Y	Y
7 Scanlon	Y	Y	Y	Y	Y	Y
8 **Fitzpatrick**	Y	Y	Y	Y	Y	Y
9 **Shuster**	Y	Y	Y	Y	Y	Y
10 **Marino**	Y	Y	Y	Y	Y	Y
11 **Barletta**	Y	Y	Y	Y	Y	Y
12 **Rothfus**	Y	Y	Y	Y	Y	Y
13 Boyle	Y	Y	Y	Y	Y	N
14 Doyle	Y	Y	Y	Y	Y	N
15 Wild	Y	Y	Y	Y	Y	N
16 **Smucker**	Y	Y	Y	Y	Y	Y
17 Cartwright	Y	Y	Y	Y	Y	N
18 Lamb	Y	Y	Y	Y	Y	N
RHODE ISLAND						
1 Cicilline	Y	Y	Y	Y	Y	N
2 Langevin	Y	Y	Y	Y	Y	N
SOUTH CAROLINA						
1 **Sanford**	Y	N	Y	Y	Y	N
2 **Wilson**	Y	Y	Y	Y	Y	Y
3 **Duncan**	?	?	?	?	?	?
4 **Gowdy**	Y	Y	Y	Y	Y	Y
5 **Norman**	Y	Y	Y	Y	Y	Y
6 Clyburn	Y	Y	Y	Y	Y	N
7 **Rice**	Y	N	Y	Y	Y	Y
SOUTH DAKOTA						
AL **Noem**	?	?	?	?	?	?
TENNESSEE						
1 **Roe**	Y	Y	Y	Y	Y	Y
2 **Duncan**	Y	N	Y	N	Y	Y
3 **Fleischmann**	Y	Y	Y	Y	Y	Y
4 **DesJarlais**	Y	Y	Y	Y	Y	Y
5 Cooper	Y	Y	Y	Y	Y	Y
6 **Black**	?	?	?	?	?	?
7 **Blackburn**	Y	Y	Y	Y	Y	Y
8 **Kustoff**	Y	Y	Y	Y	Y	Y
9 Cohen	Y	Y	Y	Y	Y	Y

	458	459	460	461	462	463
TEXAS						
1 **Gohmert**	Y	Y	Y	Y	N	Y
2 **Poe**	Y	N	Y	Y	N	N
3 **Johnson, S.**	?	?	?	?	?	?
4 **Ratcliffe**	?	?	?	?	?	?
5 **Hensarling**	Y	Y	Y	Y	Y	Y
6 **Barton**	Y	Y	Y	Y	Y	Y
7 **Culberson**	Y	Y	Y	Y	Y	Y
8 **Brady**	Y	Y	Y	Y	Y	Y
9 Green, A.	Y	Y	Y	Y	Y	N
10 **McCaul**	Y	Y	Y	Y	Y	Y
11 **Conaway**	Y	Y	Y	Y	Y	Y
12 **Granger**	Y	Y	Y	Y	Y	Y
13 **Thornberry**	Y	Y	Y	Y	Y	Y
14 **Weber**	Y	Y	Y	Y	N	Y
15 Gonzalez	Y	Y	Y	Y	Y	N
16 O'Rourke	Y	Y	Y	Y	Y	Y
17 **Flores**	Y	Y	Y	Y	Y	Y
18 Jackson Lee	Y	Y	Y	Y	Y	N
19 **Arrington**	Y	Y	Y	Y	Y	Y
20 Castro	Y	Y	Y	Y	Y	N
21 **Smith**	Y	Y	Y	Y	Y	Y
22 **Olson**	Y	Y	Y	Y	Y	Y
23 **Hurd**	Y	Y	Y	Y	Y	Y
24 Marchant	Y	Y	Y	Y	Y	Y
25 **Williams**	Y	Y	Y	Y	Y	Y
26 **Burgess**	Y	Y	Y	Y	Y	N
27 Cloud	Y	Y	Y	Y	Y	N
28 Cuellar	Y	Y	Y	Y	Y	N
29 Green, G.	Y	Y	Y	Y	Y	N
30 Johnson, E.B.	Y	Y	Y	Y	Y	N
31 **Carter**	Y	Y	Y	Y	Y	Y
32 **Sessions**	Y	Y	Y	Y	Y	Y
33 Veasey	Y	Y	Y	Y	Y	N
34 Vela	?	?	?	?	?	?
35 Doggett	Y	Y	Y	Y	Y	N
36 **Babin**	Y	Y	Y	Y	Y	Y
UTAH						
1 **Bishop**	Y	Y	Y	Y	Y	Y
2 **Stewart**	Y	Y	Y	Y	Y	Y
3 **Curtis**	Y	Y	Y	Y	Y	Y
4 **Love**	?	?	?	?	?	?
VERMONT						
AL Welch	Y	Y	Y	Y	Y	Y
VIRGINIA						
1 **Wittman**	Y	Y	Y	Y	Y	Y
2 **Taylor**	Y	Y	Y	N	Y	Y
3 Scott	Y	Y	Y	Y	Y	N
4 McEachin	Y	Y	Y	Y	Y	N
5 **Garrett**	Y	Y	Y	Y	Y	N
6 **Goodlatte**	Y	Y	Y	Y	Y	Y
7 **Brat**	Y	Y	Y	Y	Y	N
8 Beyer	Y	Y	Y	Y	Y	Y
9 **Griffith**	Y	Y	Y	Y	Y	N
10 **Comstock**	?	?	?	?	?	?
11 Connolly	Y	Y	Y	Y	Y	N
WASHINGTON						
1 DelBene	Y	Y	Y	Y	Y	Y
2 Larsen	Y	Y	Y	Y	Y	N
3 **Herrera Beutler**	Y	Y	Y	Y	Y	Y
4 **Newhouse**	Y	Y	Y	Y	Y	Y
5 **McMorris Rodgers**	Y	Y	Y	Y	Y	Y
6 Kilmer	Y	Y	Y	Y	Y	Y
7 Jayapal	Y	Y	Y	Y	Y	N
8 **Reichert**	Y	Y	Y	Y	Y	Y
9 Smith	Y	Y	Y	Y	Y	N
10 Heck	Y	Y	Y	Y	Y	N
WEST VIRGINIA						
1 **McKinley**	Y	Y	Y	Y	Y	Y
2 **Mooney**	Y	Y	Y	Y	Y	Y
3 **Vacant**						
WISCONSIN						
1 **Ryan**						
2 Pocan	Y	Y	Y	Y	Y	Y
3 Kind	?	?	?	?	?	?
4 Moore	Y	Y	Y	Y	Y	Y
5 **Sensenbrenner**	Y	Y	Y	N	Y	Y
6 **Grothman**	Y	N	Y	N	Y	Y
7 **Duffy**	Y	Y	Y	Y	Y	Y
8 **Gallagher**	Y	Y	Y	Y	Y	Y
WYOMING						
AL **Cheney**	Y	Y	Y	Y	Y	Y

VOTE NUMBER

464. HR6418. VA WEBSITE ACCESSIBILITY/PASSAGE. Roe, R-Tenn., motion to suspend the rules and pass the bill, as amended, that would require the Veterans Affairs Department to examine and ensure that all of its websites are accessible to individuals with disabilities. Motion agreed to 387-0: R 210-0; D 177-0. Dec. 20, 2018.

465. S3444. VA CLINIC DESIGNATION/PASSAGE. Roe, R-Tenn., motion to suspend the rules and pass the bill that would designate the community-based outpatient clinic of the Department of Veterans Affairs in Lake Charles, Louisiana, as the "Douglas Fournet Department of Veterans Affairs Clinic." Motion agreed to 388-0: R 211-0; D 177-0. Dec. 20, 2018.

466. S3777. VA HOUSING STIPENDS/PASSAGE. Roe, R-Tenn., motion to suspend the rules and pass the bill that would direct the Veterans Affairs Department to establish a team of specialists, or "Tiger Team," to address the difficulties encountered by the VA in making proper housing stipend payments to veterans as required in the Forever GI Bill. It would also require the VA to develop and implement a plan to address the difficulties. Motion agreed to 389-0: R 212-0; D 177-0. Dec. 20, 2018.

467. KEEPING THE FEDERAL GOVERNMENT OPEN/MOTION TO TABLE. McCarthy, R-Calif., motion to table the Pelosi, D-Calif., motion to appeal the ruling of the chair that the Pelosi resolution, unofficially titled "a resolution to keep government open," does not qualify as a question of the privileges of the House. Motion agreed to 187-170: R 187-0; D 0-170. Dec. 20, 2018.

468. HRES1183. SHORT-TERM CONTINUING FISCAL 2019 APPROPRIATIONS/ PREVIOUS QUESTION. Cole, R-Okla., motion to order the previous question (thus ending debate and the possibility of amendment) on the rule (H Res 1183) that would provide for House floor consideration of the bill HR 695 which is the legislative vehicle for a short-term continuing resolution that would fund the government through Feb. 8, 2019, and provide funds for the construction of a U.S-Mexico border wall and emergency disaster relief funding. Motion agreed to 223-178: R 223-0; D 0-178. Dec. 20, 2018.

469. HRES1183. SHORT-TERM CONTINUING FISCAL 2019 APPROPRIATIONS/ RULE. Adoption of the rule that would provide for House floor consideration of the bill HR 695 which is the legislative vehicle for a short-term continuing resolution that would fund the government through Feb. 8, 2019, and would provide funds for the construction of a U.S-Mexico border wall and emergency disaster relief funding. Adopted 221-179: R 221-0; D 0-179. Dec. 20, 2018.

	464	465	466	467	468	469
ALABAMA						
1 Byrne	Y	Y	Y	Y	Y	Y
2 Roby	Y	Y	Y	Y	Y	Y
3 Rogers	Y	Y	Y	Y	Y	Y
4 Aderholt	Y	Y	Y	Y	Y	Y
5 Brooks	Y	Y	Y	Y	Y	Y
6 Palmer	Y	Y	Y	Y	Y	Y
7 Sewell	Y	Y	Y	N	N	N
ALASKA						
AL Young	Y	Y	Y	?	Y	Y
ARIZONA						
1 O'Halleran	Y	Y	Y	N	N	N
2 McSally	Y	Y	Y	Y	Y	Y
3 Grijalva	Y	Y	Y	N	N	N
4 Gosar	Y	Y	Y	Y	Y	Y
5 Biggs	Y	Y	Y	Y	Y	Y
6 Schweikert	Y	Y	Y	Y	Y	Y
7 Gallego	Y	Y	Y	N	N	N
8 Lesko	Y	Y	Y	Y	Y	Y
9 Sinema	?	?	?	?	?	?
ARKANSAS						
1 Crawford	?	?	?	?	Y	Y
2 Hill	Y	Y	Y	Y	Y	Y
3 Womack	Y	Y	Y	Y	Y	Y
4 Westerman	Y	Y	Y	?	Y	Y
CALIFORNIA						
1 LaMalfa	Y	Y	Y	?	Y	Y
2 Huffman	Y	Y	Y	N	N	N
3 Garamendi	Y	Y	Y	N	N	N
4 McClintock	Y	Y	Y	Y	Y	Y
5 Thompson	Y	Y	Y	N	N	N
6 Matsui	Y	Y	Y	N	N	N
7 Bera	Y	Y	Y	N	N	N
8 Cook	Y	Y	Y	Y	Y	Y
9 McNerney	Y	Y	Y	N	N	N
10 Denham	Y	Y	Y	?	Y	Y
11 DeSaulnier	Y	Y	Y	N	N	N
12 Pelosi	Y	Y	Y	N	N	N
13 Lee	Y	Y	Y	?	N	N
14 Speier	Y	Y	Y	N	N	N
15 Swalwell	?	?	?	?	?	?
16 Costa	?	?	?	?	?	N
17 Khanna	Y	Y	Y	N	N	N
18 Eshoo	Y	Y	Y	N	N	N
19 Lofgren	Y	Y	Y	N	N	N
20 Panetta	Y	Y	Y	N	N	N
21 Valadao	Y	Y	Y	Y	Y	Y
22 Nunes	Y	Y	Y	Y	Y	Y
23 McCarthy	Y	Y	Y	Y	Y	Y
24 Carbajal	Y	Y	Y	N	N	N
25 Knight	Y	Y	Y	Y	Y	Y
26 Brownley	Y	Y	Y	N	N	N
27 Chu	Y	Y	Y	N	N	N
28 Schiff	Y	Y	Y	N	N	N
29 Cardenas	Y	Y	Y	N	N	N
30 Sherman	Y	Y	Y	N	N	N
31 Aguilar	Y	Y	Y	N	N	N
32 Napolitano	Y	Y	Y	N	N	N
33 Lieu	Y	Y	Y	N	N	N
34 Gomez	Y	Y	Y	N	N	N
35 Torres	Y	Y	Y	N	N	N
36 Ruiz	Y	Y	Y	N	N	N
37 Bass	Y	Y	Y	N	N	N
38 Sánchez, Linda	Y	Y	Y	N	N	N
39 Royce	Y	Y	Y	Y	Y	Y
40 Roybal-Allard	Y	Y	Y	N	N	N
41 Takano	Y	Y	Y	?	N	N
42 Calvert	Y	Y	Y	Y	Y	Y
43 Waters	Y	Y	Y	N	N	N
44 Barragan	Y	Y	Y	N	N	N
45 Walters	?	?	?	?	Y	Y
46 Correa	Y	Y	Y	N	N	N
47 Lowenthal	?	?	?	?	?	?
48 Rohrabacher	Y	Y	Y	Y	Y	Y
49 Issa	?	?	?	?	?	?
50 Hunter	Y	Y	Y	Y	Y	Y
51 Vargas	Y	Y	Y	N	N	N
52 Peters	Y	Y	Y	N	N	N
53 Davis	Y	Y	Y	N	N	N

	464	465	466	467	468	469
COLORADO						
1 DeGette	Y	Y	Y	N	N	N
2 Polis	?	?	?	?	?	?
3 Tipton	Y	Y	Y	Y	Y	Y
4 Buck	Y	Y	Y	?	Y	Y
5 Lamborn	Y	Y	Y	Y	Y	Y
6 Coffman	Y	Y	Y	Y	Y	Y
7 Perlmutter	Y	Y	Y	N	N	N
CONNECTICUT						
1 Larson	Y	Y	Y	N	N	N
2 Courtney	Y	Y	Y	N	N	N
3 DeLauro	Y	Y	Y	N	N	N
4 Himes	Y	Y	Y	N	N	N
5 Esty	Y	Y	Y	N	N	N
DELAWARE						
AL Blunt Rochester	Y	Y	Y	N	N	N
FLORIDA						
1 Gaetz	Y	Y	Y	?	Y	Y
2 Dunn	?	?	?	?	Y	Y
3 Yoho	Y	Y	Y	?	Y	Y
4 Rutherford	Y	Y	Y	Y	Y	Y
5 Lawson	Y	Y	Y	N	N	N
6 Vacant						
7 Murphy	Y	Y	Y	N	N	N
8 Posey	Y	Y	Y	Y	Y	Y
9 Soto	Y	Y	Y	N	N	N
10 Demings	Y	Y	Y	N	N	N
11 Webster	Y	Y	Y	Y	Y	Y
12 Bilirakis	Y	Y	Y	Y	Y	Y
13 Crist	Y	Y	Y	N	N	N
14 Castor	Y	Y	Y	N	N	N
15 Ross	?	?	?	Y	Y	Y
16 Buchanan	Y	Y	Y	Y	Y	Y
17 Rooney, T.	Y	Y	Y	Y	Y	Y
18 Mast	Y	Y	Y	Y	Y	Y
19 Rooney, F.	Y	Y	Y	Y	Y	Y
20 Hastings	?	?	?	?	?	?
21 Frankel	Y	Y	Y	N	N	N
22 Deutch	Y	Y	Y	N	N	N
23 Wasserman Schultz	Y	Y	Y	N	N	N
24 Wilson	Y	Y	Y	N	N	N
25 Diaz-Balart	Y	Y	Y	Y	Y	Y
26 Curbelo	Y	Y	Y	Y	Y	Y
27 Ros-Lehtinen	Y	Y	Y	Y	Y	Y
GEORGIA						
1 Carter	Y	Y	Y	Y	Y	Y
2 Bishop	Y	Y	Y	N	N	N
3 Ferguson	Y	Y	Y	Y	Y	Y
4 Johnson	Y	Y	Y	N	N	N
5 Lewis	Y	Y	Y	N	N	N
6 Handel	Y	Y	Y	Y	Y	Y
7 Woodall	Y	Y	Y	Y	Y	Y
8 Scott, A.	?	?	?	?	Y	Y
9 Collins	Y	Y	Y	Y	Y	Y
10 Hice	Y	Y	Y	Y	Y	Y
11 Loudermilk	Y	Y	Y	Y	Y	Y
12 Allen	?	?	?	?	Y	Y
13 Scott, D.	?	?	?	?	?	?
14 Graves	Y	Y	Y	Y	Y	Y
HAWAII						
1 Hanabusa	?	?	?	?	?	?
2 Gabbard	Y	Y	Y	N	N	N
IDAHO						
1 Labrador	Y	Y	Y	Y	Y	Y
2 Simpson	Y	Y	Y	Y	Y	Y
ILLINOIS						
1 Rush	Y	Y	Y	N	?	N
2 Kelly	Y	Y	Y	N	N	N
3 Lipinski	Y	Y	Y	N	N	N
4 Gutierrez	Y	Y	?	?	N	N
5 Quigley	Y	Y	Y	N	N	N
6 Roskam	Y	Y	Y	?	?	?
7 Davis, D.	?	?	?	?	?	?
8 Krishnamoorthi	Y	Y	Y	N	N	N
9 Schakowsky	Y	Y	Y	N	N	N
10 Schneider	Y	Y	Y	N	N	N
11 Foster	Y	Y	Y	N	N	N
12 Bost	Y	Y	Y	Y	Y	Y
13 Davis, R.	Y	Y	Y	?	Y	Y
14 Hultgren	?	?	?	?	?	?

KEY	**Republicans**	Democrats	*Independents*
Y Voted for (yea)		X Paired against	C Voted "present" to avoid possible conflict of interest
# Paired for		– Announced against	
+ Announced for		P Voted "present"	? Did not vote or otherwise make a position known
N Voted against (nay)			

	464	465	466	467	468	469
16 **Kinzinger**	Y	Y	Y	Y	Y	Y
17 Bustos	Y	Y	Y	N	N	N
18 **LaHood**	Y	Y	Y	Y	Y	Y
INDIANA						
1 Visclosky	Y	Y	Y	N	N	N
2 **Walorski**	Y	Y	Y	Y	Y	Y
3 **Banks**	Y	Y	Y	Y	Y	Y
4 Rokita	Y	Y	Y	Y	Y	Y
5 **Brooks**	Y	Y	Y	Y	Y	Y
6 **Messer**	?	?	?	?	?	?
7 Carson	Y	Y	Y	N	N	N
8 **Bucshon**	Y	Y	Y	Y	Y	Y
9 **Hollingsworth**	Y	Y	Y	Y	Y	Y
IOWA						
1 **Blum**	Y	Y	Y	Y	Y	Y
2 Loebsack	Y	Y	Y	N	N	N
3 **Young**	Y	Y	Y	Y	Y	Y
4 **King**	Y	Y	Y	Y	Y	Y
KANSAS						
1 **Marshall**	Y	Y	Y	?	Y	Y
2 **Jenkins**	?	?	?	?	?	?
3 **Yoder**	Y	Y	Y	Y	Y	Y
4 **Estes**	Y	Y	Y	?	Y	Y
KENTUCKY						
1 **Comer**	Y	Y	Y	?	Y	Y
2 **Guthrie**	Y	Y	Y	Y	Y	Y
3 Yarmuth	Y	Y	Y	N	N	N
4 **Massie**	Y	Y	Y	Y	Y	Y
5 **Rogers**	Y	Y	Y	Y	Y	Y
6 **Barr**	Y	Y	Y	?	Y	Y
LOUISIANA						
1 **Scalise**	Y	Y	Y	Y	Y	Y
2 Richmond	Y	Y	Y	N	N	N
3 **Higgins**	Y	Y	Y	Y	Y	Y
4 **Johnson**	Y	Y	Y	Y	Y	Y
5 **Abraham**	Y	Y	Y	Y	Y	Y
6 **Graves**	Y	Y	Y	Y	Y	Y
MAINE						
1 Pingree	Y	Y	Y	N	N	N
2 **Poliquin**	Y	Y	Y	Y	Y	Y
MARYLAND						
1 **Harris**	Y	Y	Y	Y	Y	Y
2 Ruppersberger	Y	Y	Y	N	N	N
3 Sarbanes	Y	Y	Y	N	N	N
4 Brown	Y	Y	Y	N	N	N
5 Hoyer	Y	Y	Y	N	N	N
6 Delaney	Y	Y	Y	N	N	N
7 Cummings	Y	Y	Y	N	N	N
8 Raskin	Y	Y	Y	N	N	N
MASSACHUSETTS						
1 Neal	Y	Y	Y	N	N	N
2 McGovern	Y	Y	Y	N	N	N
3 Tsongas	Y	Y	Y	?	N	N
4 Kennedy	Y	Y	Y	N	N	N
5 Clark	Y	Y	Y	N	N	N
6 Moulton	Y	Y	Y	N	N	N
7 Capuano	Y	Y	Y	?	?	?
8 Lynch	Y	Y	Y	?	N	N
9 Keating	?	?	?	?	?	?
MICHIGAN						
1 **Bergman**	Y	Y	Y	Y	Y	Y
2 **Huizenga**	Y	Y	Y	Y	Y	Y
3 *Amash*	Y	Y	Y	Y	Y	Y
4 **Moolenaar**	Y	Y	Y	Y	Y	Y
5 Kildee	Y	Y	Y	N	N	N
6 **Upton**	Y	Y	Y	Y	Y	Y
7 **Walberg**	Y	Y	Y	Y	Y	Y
8 **Bishop**	?	?	?	Y	Y	Y
9 Levin	Y	Y	Y	N	N	N
10 **Mitchell**	Y	Y	Y	Y	Y	Y
11 **Trott**	?	?	?	?	?	?
12 Dingell	Y	Y	Y	N	N	N
13 Jones	Y	Y	Y	N	N	N
14 Lawrence	Y	Y	Y	N	N	N
MINNESOTA						
1 Walz	?	?	?	?	?	?
2 **Lewis**	Y	Y	Y	?	Y	Y
3 **Paulsen**	Y	Y	Y	Y	Y	Y
4 McCollum	Y	Y	Y	N	N	N

	464	465	466	467	468	469
5 Ellison	Y	Y	Y	N	N	N
6 **Emmer**	Y	Y	Y	Y	Y	Y
7 Peterson	?	?	?	?	N	N
8 Nolan	Y	Y	Y	N	N	N
MISSISSIPPI						
1 **Kelly**	Y	Y	Y	Y	Y	Y
2 Thompson	?	?	?	?	?	?
3 **Harper**	Y	Y	Y	Y	Y	Y
4 **Palazzo**	Y	Y	Y	Y	Y	Y
MISSOURI						
1 Clay	Y	Y	Y	N	N	N
2 **Wagner**	Y	Y	Y	Y	Y	Y
3 **Luetkemeyer**	Y	Y	Y	Y	Y	Y
4 **Hartzler**	Y	Y	Y	Y	Y	Y
5 Cleaver	Y	Y	Y	N	N	N
6 **Graves**	Y	Y	Y	Y	Y	Y
7 **Long**	Y	Y	Y	Y	Y	Y
8 **Smith**	Y	Y	Y	Y	Y	Y
MONTANA						
AL **Gianforte**	Y	Y	Y	?	Y	Y
NEBRASKA						
1 **Fortenberry**	Y	Y	Y	Y	Y	Y
2 **Bacon**	Y	Y	Y	Y	Y	Y
3 **Smith**	?	?	?	?	Y	Y
NEVADA						
1 Titus	Y	Y	Y	N	N	N
2 **Amodei**	Y	Y	Y	Y	Y	Y
3 Rosen	?	?	?	?	?	?
4 Kihuen	Y	Y	Y	N	N	N
NEW HAMPSHIRE						
1 Shea-Porter	+	+	+	-	-	-
2 Kuster	Y	Y	Y	N	N	N
NEW JERSEY						
1 Norcross	Y	Y	Y	N	N	N
2 **LoBiondo**	Y	Y	Y	Y	Y	Y
3 **MacArthur**	Y	Y	Y	Y	Y	?
4 **Smith**	Y	Y	Y	Y	Y	Y
5 Gottheimer	Y	Y	Y	N	N	N
6 Pallone	Y	Y	Y	N	N	N
7 **Lance**	Y	Y	Y	Y	Y	Y
8 Sires	Y	Y	Y	N	N	N
9 Pascrell	Y	Y	Y	N	N	N
10 Payne	Y	Y	Y	N	N	N
11 **Frelinghuysen**	Y	Y	Y	Y	Y	Y
12 Watson Coleman	Y	Y	Y	N	N	N
NEW MEXICO						
1 Lujan Grisham	?	?	?	?	?	?
2 **Pearce**	Y	Y	Y	?	Y	Y
3 Luján	Y	Y	Y	N	N	N
NEW YORK						
1 **Zeldin**	Y	Y	Y	Y	Y	Y
2 **King**	Y	Y	Y	Y	Y	Y
3 Suozzi	Y	Y	Y	N	N	N
4 Rice	Y	Y	Y	N	N	N
5 Meeks	Y	Y	Y	N	N	N
6 Meng	Y	Y	Y	N	N	N
7 Velázquez	Y	Y	Y	N	N	N
8 Jeffries	Y	Y	Y	N	N	N
9 Clarke	Y	Y	Y	N	N	N
10 Nadler	Y	Y	Y	N	N	N
11 **Donovan**	Y	Y	Y	Y	Y	Y
12 Maloney, C.	Y	Y	Y	N	N	N
13 Espaillat	Y	Y	Y	N	N	N
14 Crowley	?	?	?	?	?	?
15 Serrano	Y	Y	Y	N	N	N
16 Engel	Y	Y	Y	N	N	N
17 Lowey	?	Y	Y	N	N	N
18 Maloney, S.P.	Y	Y	Y	N	N	N
19 **Faso**	Y	Y	Y	Y	Y	Y
20 Tonko	Y	Y	Y	N	N	N
21 **Stefanik**	Y	Y	Y	Y	Y	Y
22 **Tenney**	Y	Y	Y	Y	Y	Y
23 **Reed**	Y	Y	Y	?	Y	Y
24 **Katko**	Y	Y	Y	?	Y	Y
25 Morelle	Y	Y	Y	N	N	N
26 Higgins	Y	Y	Y	N	N	N
27 **Collins**	Y	Y	Y	Y	Y	Y
NORTH CAROLINA						
1 Butterfield	Y	Y	Y	N	N	N
2 **Holding**	Y	Y	Y	Y	Y	Y
3 **Jones**	?	?	?	?	?	?
4 Price	Y	Y	Y	N	N	N

	464	465	466	467	468	469
5 **Foxx**	Y	Y	Y	Y	Y	Y
6 **Walker**	Y	Y	Y	Y	Y	Y
7 **Rouzer**	?	?	?	?	Y	Y
8 **Hudson**	Y	Y	Y	Y	Y	Y
9 **Pittenger**	Y	Y	Y	Y	Y	Y
9 **Vacant**						
10 **McHenry**	Y	Y	Y	Y	Y	Y
11 **Meadows**	Y	Y	Y	Y	Y	Y
12 Adams	Y	Y	Y	N	N	N
13 **Budd**	Y	Y	Y	Y	Y	Y
NORTH DAKOTA						
AL **Cramer**	?	?	?	?	Y	Y
OHIO						
1 **Chabot**	Y	Y	Y	Y	Y	Y
2 **Wenstrup**	Y	Y	Y	Y	Y	Y
3 Beatty	Y	Y	Y	N	N	N
4 **Jordan**	Y	Y	Y	Y	Y	Y
5 **Latta**	Y	Y	Y	Y	Y	Y
6 **Johnson**	Y	Y	Y	Y	Y	Y
7 **Gibbs**	Y	Y	Y	Y	Y	Y
8 **Davidson**	Y	Y	Y	Y	Y	Y
9 Kaptur	Y	Y	Y	N	N	N
10 **Turner**	Y	Y	Y	Y	Y	Y
11 Fudge	Y	Y	Y	N	N	N
12 Balderson	Y	Y	Y	Y	Y	Y
13 Ryan	Y	Y	Y	N	N	N
14 **Joyce**	Y	Y	Y	Y	Y	Y
15 **Stivers**	Y	Y	Y	Y	Y	Y
16 **Renacci**	Y	Y	Y	Y	Y	Y
OKLAHOMA						
1 Hern	Y	Y	Y	Y	Y	Y
2 **Mullin**	Y	Y	Y	Y	Y	Y
3 **Lucas**	Y	Y	Y	Y	Y	Y
4 **Cole**	Y	Y	Y	Y	Y	Y
5 **Russell**	?	?	?	?	Y	Y
OREGON						
1 Bonamici	Y	Y	Y	N	N	N
2 **Walden**	Y	Y	Y	Y	Y	Y
3 Blumenauer	Y	Y	Y	N	N	N
4 DeFazio	Y	?	Y	N	N	N
5 Schrader	Y	Y	Y	N	N	?
PENNSYLVANIA						
1 Brady	Y	Y	Y	N	N	N
2 Evans	Y	Y	Y	N	N	N
3 **Kelly**	Y	Y	Y	Y	Y	Y
4 **Perry**	Y	Y	Y	Y	Y	Y
5 **Thompson**	Y	Y	Y	?	Y	Y
6 **Costello**	Y	Y	Y	Y	Y	Y
7 Scanlon	Y	Y	Y	N	N	N
8 **Fitzpatrick**	Y	Y	Y	Y	Y	Y
9 **Shuster**	Y	Y	Y	Y	Y	Y
10 **Marino**	Y	Y	Y	Y	Y	Y
11 **Barletta**	Y	Y	Y	Y	Y	Y
12 **Rothfus**	Y	Y	Y	Y	Y	Y
13 Boyle	Y	Y	Y	N	N	N
14 Doyle	Y	Y	Y	N	N	N
15 Wild	Y	Y	Y	N	N	N
16 **Smucker**	Y	Y	Y	Y	Y	Y
17 Cartwright	Y	Y	Y	N	N	N
18 Lamb	Y	Y	Y	N	N	N
RHODE ISLAND						
1 Cicilline	Y	Y	Y	N	N	N
2 Langevin	Y	Y	Y	N	N	N
SOUTH CAROLINA						
1 **Sanford**	Y	Y	Y	Y	Y	Y
2 **Wilson**	Y	Y	Y	Y	Y	Y
3 **Duncan**	?	?	?	?	?	?
4 **Gowdy**	Y	Y	Y	Y	Y	Y
5 **Norman**	Y	Y	Y	Y	Y	Y
6 Clyburn	Y	Y	Y	N	N	N
7 **Rice**	Y	Y	Y	Y	Y	Y
SOUTH DAKOTA						
AL **Noem**	?	?	?	?	?	?
TENNESSEE						
1 **Roe**	Y	Y	Y	Y	Y	Y
2 **Duncan**	Y	Y	Y	Y	Y	Y
3 **Fleischmann**	Y	Y	Y	Y	Y	Y
4 **DesJarlais**	Y	Y	Y	Y	Y	Y
5 Cooper	Y	Y	Y	N	N	N
6 **Black**	?	?	?	?	?	?
7 **Blackburn**	Y	Y	Y	Y	Y	Y
8 **Kustoff**	Y	Y	Y	Y	Y	Y
9 Cohen	Y	Y	Y	N	N	N

	464	465	466	467	468	469
TEXAS						
1 **Gohmert**	Y	Y	Y	Y	Y	Y
2 **Poe**	Y	Y	Y	?	Y	Y
3 **Johnson, S.**	?	Y	Y	Y	Y	Y
4 **Ratcliffe**	?	?	?	?	?	?
5 **Hensarling**	Y	Y	Y	?	Y	Y
6 **Barton**	Y	Y	Y	Y	Y	Y
7 **Culberson**	Y	Y	Y	Y	Y	Y
8 **Brady**	Y	Y	Y	Y	Y	Y
9 Green, A.	Y	Y	Y	N	N	N
10 **McCaul**	Y	Y	Y	Y	Y	?
11 **Conaway**	Y	Y	Y	?	Y	Y
12 **Granger**	Y	Y	Y	Y	Y	Y
13 **Thornberry**	Y	Y	Y	Y	Y	Y
14 **Weber**	Y	Y	Y	Y	Y	Y
15 Gonzalez	Y	Y	Y	N	N	N
16 O'Rourke	Y	Y	Y	?	N	N
17 **Flores**	Y	Y	Y	Y	Y	Y
18 Jackson Lee	Y	Y	Y	N	N	N
19 **Arrington**	Y	Y	Y	?	Y	Y
20 Castro	Y	Y	Y	N	N	N
21 **Smith**	Y	Y	Y	?	Y	Y
22 **Olson**	Y	Y	Y	Y	Y	Y
23 **Hurd**	?	Y	Y	Y	Y	Y
24 Marchant	Y	Y	Y	Y	Y	Y
25 **Williams**	Y	Y	Y	Y	Y	Y
26 **Burgess**	Y	Y	Y	?	Y	Y
27 Cloud	Y	Y	Y	Y	Y	Y
28 Cuellar	Y	Y	Y	N	N	N
29 Green, G.	Y	Y	Y	N	N	N
30 Johnson, E.B.	Y	Y	Y	N	N	N
31 **Carter**	Y	Y	Y	Y	Y	Y
32 **Sessions**	Y	Y	Y	Y	Y	Y
33 Veasey	Y	Y	Y	N	N	N
34 Vela	?	?	?	?	N	N
35 Doggett	Y	Y	Y	N	N	N
36 **Babin**	Y	Y	Y	Y	Y	Y
UTAH						
1 **Bishop**	Y	Y	Y	Y	Y	Y
2 **Stewart**	Y	Y	Y	Y	Y	Y
3 **Curtis**	Y	Y	Y	Y	Y	Y
4 **Love**	?	?	?	?	?	?
VERMONT						
AL Welch	Y	Y	Y	N	N	N
VIRGINIA						
1 **Wittman**	Y	Y	Y	Y	Y	Y
2 **Taylor**	Y	Y	Y	?	Y	Y
3 Scott	Y	Y	Y	N	N	N
4 McEachin	Y	Y	Y	N	N	N
5 **Garrett**	Y	Y	Y	Y	Y	Y
6 **Goodlatte**	Y	Y	Y	Y	Y	Y
7 **Brat**	Y	Y	Y	Y	Y	Y
8 Beyer	Y	Y	Y	N	N	N
9 **Griffith**	Y	Y	Y	Y	Y	Y
10 **Comstock**	?	?	?	?	?	?
11 Connolly	Y	Y	Y	N	N	N
WASHINGTON						
1 DelBene	Y	Y	Y	N	N	N
2 Larsen	Y	Y	Y	N	N	N
3 **Herrera Beutler**	Y	Y	Y	Y	Y	Y
4 **Newhouse**	Y	Y	Y	?	Y	Y
5 **McMorris Rodgers**	Y	Y	Y	Y	Y	Y
6 Kilmer	Y	Y	Y	N	N	N
7 Jayapal	Y	Y	Y	N	N	N
8 **Reichert**	Y	Y	Y	Y	Y	Y
9 Smith	Y	Y	Y	?	N	N
10 Heck	Y	Y	Y	N	N	N
WEST VIRGINIA						
1 **McKinley**	Y	Y	Y	Y	Y	Y
2 **Mooney**	Y	Y	Y	Y	Y	Y
3 **Vacant**						
WISCONSIN						
1 **Ryan**						
2 Pocan	Y	Y	Y	N	N	N
3 Kind	?	?	?	?	?	?
4 Moore	Y	Y	Y	N	N	N
5 **Sensenbrenner**	Y	Y	Y	Y	Y	Y
6 **Grothman**	Y	Y	Y	Y	Y	Y
7 **Duffy**	Y	Y	Y	Y	Y	Y
8 **Gallagher**	Y	Y	Y	Y	Y	Y
WYOMING						
AL **Cheney**	Y	?	Y	Y	Y	Y

VOTE NUMBER

470. HR88. TAX PROVISION PACKAGE/MOTION TO CONCUR. Brady, R-Texas, motion to concur in the Senate amendment to a bill (HR 88), with a further House amendment, comprised of a package of tax-related bills. The bill would extend and gradually phase out through 2024 a biodiesel tax credit, make permanent a railroad track maintenance credit at a reduced rate, and provide temporary tax relief for victims of hurricanes and wildfires. It would delay or repeal certain health-related taxes enacted as part of the 2010 healthcare overhaul. The bill also contains a number of provisions related to tax-favored retirement savings plans and operations of the Internal Revenue Service. Motion agreed to 220-183: R 220-3; D 0-180. Dec. 20, 2018.

471. HR2606. NATIVE AMERICAN LAND INHERITANCE/PASSAGE. McClintock, R-Calif., motion to suspend the rules and concur in the Senate amendment to the bill that would remove the Native American blood percentage requirement for individuals who inherit restricted-fee land originally allotted to certain Native American tribes in Oklahoma. Motion agreed to 399-0: R 220-0; D 179-0. Dec. 20, 2018.

472. HR695. SHORT-TERM CONTINUING FISCAL 2019 APPROPRIATIONS/ MOTION TO CONCUR. Frelinghuysen, R-N.J., motion to concur in the Senate amendment to the House amendment to the Senate amendment to the bill, with a further House amendment. The bill is the legislative vehicle for a short-term continuing resolution that would fund the government through Feb. 8, 2019. It would also authorize $5.7 billion for construction of a border wall on the U.S.-Mexico border, as well as an estimated $7.8 billion in emergency disaster relief funding. Passed 217-185: R 217-8; D 0-177. Dec. 20, 2018.

473. HR6602. NEW JERSEY COASTAL TRAIL/PASSAGE. McClintock, R-Calif., motion to suspend the rules and pass the bill that would reauthorize through fiscal 2025 National Park Service co-management of the New Jersey Coastal Heritage Trail Route along the state's eastern and southern coast. It would also direct the NPS to prepare a strategic plan for local engagement and sustainability of the route. Motion agreed to 382-9: R 211-9; D 171-0. Dec. 20, 2018.

474. HRES1063. LINCOLN ROOM DESIGNATION/PASSAGE. Mast, R-Fla., motion to suspend the rules and agree to the resolution that would designate room H-226 of the United States Capitol as the "Lincoln Room." Motion agreed to 366-0: R 203-0; D 163-0. Dec. 21, 2018.

475. HR7318. PUBLIC BUILDINGS REFORM BOARD/PASSAGE. Mast, R-Fla., motion to suspend the rules and pass the bill that would modify the selection process for the Public Buildings Reform Board and would change the termination date of the board to six years after the board has been appointed. Motion agreed to 372-2: R 203-1; D 169-1. Dec. 21, 2018.

	470	471	472	473	474	475
ALABAMA						
1 **Byrne**	Y	Y	Y	Y	Y	Y
2 **Roby**	Y	Y	Y	Y	?	?
3 **Rogers**	Y	Y	Y	Y	?	?
4 **Aderholt**	Y	Y	Y	Y	Y	Y
5 **Brooks**	Y	Y	Y	N	Y	Y
6 **Palmer**	Y	Y	Y	Y	Y	Y
7 Sewell	N	Y	N	Y	?	Y
ALASKA						
AL **Young**	Y	Y	Y	Y	Y	Y
ARIZONA						
1 O'Halleran	N	Y	N	Y	Y	Y
2 **McSally**	Y	Y	Y	Y	Y	Y
3 Grijalva	N	Y	N	Y	Y	Y
4 **Gosar**	Y	Y	Y	Y	Y	Y
5 **Biggs**	Y	Y	Y	N	Y	Y
6 **Schweikert**	Y	Y	Y	Y	Y	Y
7 Gallego	N	Y	N	Y	Y	Y
8 **Lesko**	Y	Y	Y	Y	Y	Y
9 Sinema	?	?	?	?	?	?
ARKANSAS						
1 **Crawford**	Y	Y	Y	Y	Y	Y
2 **Hill**	Y	Y	Y	Y	Y	Y
3 **Womack**	Y	Y	Y	Y	Y	Y
4 **Westerman**	Y	Y	Y	Y	Y	Y
CALIFORNIA						
1 **LaMalfa**	Y	Y	Y	Y	Y	Y
2 Huffman	N	Y	N	Y	Y	?
3 Garamendi	N	Y	N	Y	Y	Y
4 **McClintock**	Y	Y	Y	Y	Y	Y
5 Thompson	N	Y	N	Y	Y	Y
6 Matsui	N	Y	N	Y	Y	Y
7 Bera	N	Y	N	Y	Y	Y
8 **Cook**	Y	Y	Y	Y	Y	Y
9 McNerney	N	Y	N	Y	Y	Y
10 **Denham**	Y	Y	Y	Y	?	?
11 DeSaulnier	N	Y	N	Y	Y	Y
12 Pelosi	N	Y	N	Y	?	Y
13 Lee	N	Y	N	Y	Y	Y
14 Speier	N	Y	N	Y	Y	Y
15 Swalwell	?	?	?	?	?	?
16 Costa	N	Y	N	Y	Y	Y
17 Khanna	N	Y	N	Y	Y	Y
18 Eshoo	N	Y	N	Y	Y	Y
19 Lofgren	N	Y	N	Y	Y	Y
20 Panetta	N	Y	N	?	Y	Y
21 **Valadao**	Y	Y	N	Y	Y	Y
22 **Nunes**	Y	Y	Y	Y	Y	Y
23 **McCarthy**	Y	Y	Y	Y	Y	Y
24 Carbajal	N	Y	N	Y	Y	Y
25 **Knight**	Y	Y	Y	Y	Y	Y
26 Brownley	N	Y	N	Y	Y	Y
27 Chu	N	Y	N	Y	Y	Y
28 Schiff	N	Y	N	Y	Y	Y
29 Cardenas	N	Y	N	Y	Y	Y
30 Sherman	N	Y	N	Y	Y	Y
31 Aguilar	N	Y	N	Y	Y	Y
32 Napolitano	N	Y	N	Y	Y	Y
33 Lieu	N	Y	N	Y	Y	Y
34 Gomez	N	Y	N	Y	Y	Y
35 Torres	N	Y	N	Y	Y	Y
36 Ruiz	N	Y	N	Y	Y	Y
37 Bass	N	Y	N	Y	Y	Y
38 Sánchez, Linda	N	Y	N	Y	Y	Y
39 **Royce**	Y	Y	Y	Y	Y	Y
40 Roybal-Allard	N	Y	N	Y	Y	Y
41 Takano	N	Y	N	Y	Y	Y
42 **Calvert**	Y	Y	Y	Y	Y	Y
43 Waters	N	Y	N	?	Y	Y
44 Barragan	N	Y	N	Y	Y	Y
45 **Walters**	Y	Y	Y	Y	Y	Y
46 Correa	N	Y	N	Y	Y	Y
47 Lowenthal	–	?	–	?	?	?
48 **Rohrabacher**	Y	Y	Y	Y	?	?
49 **Issa**	Y	Y	?	Y	Y	Y
50 **Hunter**	Y	Y	Y	Y	Y	Y
51 Vargas	N	Y	N	Y	Y	Y
52 Peters	N	Y	N	Y	Y	Y
53 Davis	N	Y	N	Y	Y	Y

	470	471	472	473	474	475
COLORADO						
1 DeGette	N	Y	N	Y	Y	Y
2 Polis	?	?	?	?	?	?
3 **Tipton**	Y	Y	Y	Y	Y	Y
4 **Buck**	Y	Y	N	Y	Y	Y
5 **Lamborn**	Y	Y	Y	Y	Y	Y
6 **Coffman**	Y	Y	Y	Y	?	Y
7 Perlmutter	N	Y	N	Y	Y	Y
CONNECTICUT						
1 Larson	N	Y	N	?	Y	Y
2 Courtney	N	Y	N	Y	Y	Y
3 DeLauro	N	Y	N	Y	Y	Y
4 Himes	N	Y	N	Y	Y	Y
5 Esty	N	Y	N	Y	Y	Y
DELAWARE						
AL Blunt Rochester	N	Y	N	Y	Y	Y
FLORIDA						
1 **Gaetz**	Y	Y	Y	Y	Y	Y
2 **Dunn**	Y	Y	Y	Y	Y	Y
3 **Yoho**	Y	Y	Y	N	Y	Y
4 **Rutherford**	Y	Y	Y	Y	Y	Y
5 Lawson	N	Y	N	Y	Y	Y
6 Vacant						
7 Murphy	N	Y	N	Y	Y	Y
8 **Posey**	Y	Y	Y	Y	Y	Y
9 Soto	N	Y	N	Y	Y	Y
10 Demings	N	Y	N	Y	Y	Y
11 **Webster**	Y	Y	Y	Y	Y	Y
12 **Bilirakis**	Y	Y	Y	Y	Y	Y
13 Crist	N	Y	N	Y	Y	Y
14 Castor	N	Y	N	?	Y	Y
15 **Ross**	Y	Y	Y	Y	?	?
16 **Buchanan**	Y	Y	Y	Y	Y	Y
17 **Rooney, T.**	Y	Y	Y	?	?	?
18 **Mast**	Y	Y	Y	Y	Y	Y
19 **Rooney, F.**	Y	Y	Y	Y	Y	Y
20 Hastings	?	?	?	?	?	?
21 Frankel	N	Y	N	Y	Y	Y
22 Deutch	N	Y	N	Y	Y	Y
23 Wasserman Schultz	N	Y	N	Y	Y	Y
24 Wilson	N	Y	N	Y	Y	Y
25 **Diaz-Balart**	Y	Y	Y	Y	Y	Y
26 **Curbelo**	Y	Y	Y	Y	Y	Y
27 **Ros-Lehtinen**	Y	Y	N	Y	Y	Y
GEORGIA						
1 **Carter**	Y	Y	Y	Y	Y	Y
2 Bishop	N	Y	N	Y	Y	Y
3 **Ferguson**	Y	Y	Y	Y	Y	Y
4 Johnson	N	Y	N	Y	Y	Y
5 Lewis	N	Y	N	Y	Y	Y
6 **Handel**	Y	?	Y	Y	Y	Y
7 **Woodall**	Y	Y	Y	Y	Y	Y
8 **Scott, A.**	Y	Y	Y	Y	Y	Y
9 **Collins**	Y	Y	Y	Y	Y	?
10 **Hice**	Y	Y	Y	Y	Y	Y
11 **Loudermilk**	Y	Y	Y	?	Y	Y
12 **Allen**	Y	Y	Y	Y	Y	Y
13 **Scott, D.**	?	?	?	?	?	?
14 **Graves**	Y	Y	Y	?	Y	?
HAWAII						
1 Hanabusa	?	?	?	?	?	?
2 Gabbard	N	Y	N	Y	Y	Y
IDAHO						
1 **Labrador**	Y	Y	Y	Y	Y	Y
2 **Simpson**	Y	Y	Y	Y	Y	Y
ILLINOIS						
1 Rush	N	Y	N	Y	Y	Y
2 Kelly	N	Y	N	Y	Y	Y
3 Lipinski	N	Y	N	Y	?	?
4 Gutierrez	N	Y	N	Y	?	?
5 Quigley	N	Y	N	Y	Y	Y
6 **Roskam**	?	?	?	?	?	?
7 Davis, D.	?	?	?	?	?	?
8 Krishnamoorthi	N	Y	N	Y	Y	Y
9 Schakowsky	N	Y	N	Y	Y	Y
10 Schneider	N	Y	N	Y	Y	Y
11 Foster	N	Y	N	Y	Y	Y
12 **Bost**	Y	Y	Y	Y	Y	Y
13 **Davis, R.**	Y	Y	Y	Y	Y	Y

KEY	**Republicans**	Democrats	*Independents*	
Y Voted for (yea)		X Paired against	C Voted "present" to avoid possible conflict of interest	
# Paired for		– Announced against		
+ Announced for		P Voted "present"	? Did not vote or otherwise make a position known	
N Voted against (nay)				

	470	471	472	473	474	475
14 **Hultgren**	?	?	?	?	?	?
15 **Shimkus**	Y	Y	Y	Y	Y	Y
16 **Kinzinger**	Y	Y	Y	Y	Y	Y
17 Bustos	N	Y	N	Y	Y	Y
18 **LaHood**	Y	Y	Y	Y	Y	Y
INDIANA						
1 Visclosky	N	Y	N	Y	?	?
2 **Walorski**	Y	Y	Y	Y	Y	Y
3 **Banks**	Y	Y	Y	Y	Y	Y
4 Rokita	N	Y	Y	Y	Y	Y
5 **Brooks**	Y	Y	Y	Y	Y	Y
6 **Messer**	?	?	Y	Y	?	Y
7 Carson	N	Y	N	Y	Y	Y
8 **Bucshon**	Y	Y	Y	Y	Y	Y
9 **Hollingsworth**	Y	Y	Y	Y	Y	Y
IOWA						
1 **Blum**	Y	Y	Y	Y	?	?
2 Loebsack	N	Y	N	Y	Y	Y
3 **Young**	Y	Y	Y	Y	Y	Y
4 **King**	Y	Y	Y	Y	Y	Y
KANSAS						
1 **Marshall**	Y	Y	Y	Y	Y	Y
2 **Jenkins**	?	?	?	?	?	?
3 **Yoder**	Y	Y	Y	Y	Y	Y
4 **Estes**	Y	Y	Y	Y	Y	Y
KENTUCKY						
1 **Comer**	Y	Y	Y	Y	Y	Y
2 **Guthrie**	Y	Y	Y	Y	Y	Y
3 Yarmuth	N	Y	?	Y	Y	Y
4 **Massie**	Y	Y	Y	N	Y	N
5 **Rogers**	Y	Y	Y	Y	Y	Y
6 **Barr**	Y	Y	Y	Y	Y	?
LOUISIANA						
1 **Scalise**	Y	Y	Y	Y	Y	Y
2 Richmond	N	Y	?	Y	Y	Y
3 **Higgins**	Y	Y	Y	Y	Y	Y
4 **Johnson**	Y	Y	Y	Y	Y	Y
5 **Abraham**	Y	Y	Y	Y	Y	Y
6 **Graves**	Y	Y	Y	Y	Y	Y
MAINE						
1 Pingree	N	Y	N	Y	Y	Y
2 **Poliquin**	Y	Y	Y	Y	Y	Y
MARYLAND						
1 **Harris**	Y	Y	Y	?	Y	Y
2 Ruppersberger	N	Y	N	Y	Y	Y
3 Sarbanes	N	Y	N	Y	Y	Y
4 Brown	N	Y	N	Y	Y	Y
5 Hoyer	N	Y	N	Y	Y	Y
6 Delaney	N	Y	N	?	Y	Y
7 Cummings	N	Y	N	Y	Y	Y
8 Raskin	N	Y	N	Y	Y	Y
MASSACHUSETTS						
1 Neal	N	Y	N	Y	Y	Y
2 McGovern	N	Y	N	Y	Y	Y
3 Tsongas	N	Y	N	?	Y	Y
4 Kennedy	N	Y	N	Y	Y	Y
5 Clark	N	Y	N	Y	Y	Y
6 Moulton	N	Y	N	Y	Y	Y
7 Capuano	?	?	?	?	?	?
8 Lynch	N	Y	N	Y	Y	Y
9 Keating	?	?	?	?	?	?
MICHIGAN						
1 **Bergman**	Y	Y	Y	Y	Y	Y
2 **Huizenga**	Y	Y	Y	Y	Y	Y
3 *Amash*	N	Y	N	N	Y	Y
4 **Moolenaar**	Y	Y	Y	Y	Y	Y
5 Kildee	N	Y	N	Y	Y	Y
6 **Upton**	Y	Y	N	Y	Y	Y
7 **Walberg**	Y	Y	Y	Y	Y	Y
8 **Bishop**	Y	Y	Y	Y	Y	Y
9 Levin	N	Y	N	Y	Y	Y
10 **Mitchell**	Y	Y	Y	Y	Y	Y
11 **Trott**	?	?	?	?	?	?
12 Dingell	N	Y	N	Y	Y	Y
13 Jones	N	Y	N	Y	Y	Y
14 Lawrence	N	Y	N	Y	Y	Y
MINNESOTA						
1 Walz	?	?	?	?	?	?
2 **Lewis**	Y	Y	Y	Y	?	?
3 **Paulsen**	Y	Y	N	Y	Y	Y
4 McCollum	N	Y	N	Y	Y	Y

	470	471	472	473	474	475
5 Ellison	N	?	?	?	?	?
6 **Emmer**	Y	Y	Y	Y	Y	Y
7 Peterson	N	Y	N	Y	Y	Y
8 Nolan	N	Y	N	?	?	Y
MISSISSIPPI						
1 **Kelly**	Y	Y	Y	Y	Y	Y
2 Thompson	?	?	?	?	?	?
3 **Harper**	Y	Y	Y	Y	Y	Y
4 **Palazzo**	Y	Y	Y	Y	Y	Y
MISSOURI						
1 Clay	N	Y	N	Y	?	?
2 **Wagner**	Y	Y	Y	Y	Y	Y
3 **Luetkemeyer**	Y	Y	Y	Y	Y	Y
4 **Hartzler**	Y	Y	Y	Y	Y	Y
5 Cleaver	N	Y	N	Y	Y	Y
6 **Graves**	Y	Y	Y	Y	Y	Y
7 **Long**	Y	Y	Y	Y	Y	Y
8 **Smith**	Y	Y	Y	Y	Y	Y
MONTANA						
AL **Gianforte**	Y	Y	Y	Y	Y	Y
NEBRASKA						
1 **Fortenberry**	Y	Y	Y	Y	Y	Y
2 **Bacon**	Y	Y	Y	Y	Y	Y
3 **Smith**	Y	Y	Y	Y	Y	Y
NEVADA						
1 Titus	N	Y	N	Y	Y	Y
2 **Amodei**	Y	Y	Y	Y	Y	Y
3 Rosen	?	?	?	?	+	+
4 Kihuen	N	Y	N	Y	Y	Y
NEW HAMPSHIRE						
1 Shea-Porter	–	+	–	+	+	+
2 Kuster	N	Y	N	Y	Y	Y
NEW JERSEY						
1 Norcross	N	Y	N	Y	Y	Y
2 **LoBiondo**	Y	Y	Y	Y	Y	Y
3 **MacArthur**	Y	Y	Y	Y	Y	Y
4 **Smith**	Y	Y	Y	Y	Y	Y
5 Gottheimer	N	Y	N	Y	Y	Y
6 Pallone	N	Y	N	Y	Y	Y
7 **Lance**	Y	Y	Y	Y	Y	Y
8 Sires	N	Y	N	Y	Y	Y
9 Pascrell	N	Y	N	Y	Y	Y
10 Payne	N	Y	N	Y	Y	Y
11 **Frelinghuysen**	Y	Y	Y	Y	Y	Y
12 Watson Coleman	N	Y	N	Y	Y	Y
NEW MEXICO						
1 Lujan Grisham	?	?	?	?	?	?
2 **Pearce**	Y	Y	Y	Y	Y	Y
3 Luján	N	Y	N	Y	Y	Y
NEW YORK						
1 **Zeldin**	Y	Y	Y	Y	Y	Y
2 **King**	Y	Y	Y	Y	Y	Y
3 Suozzi	N	Y	N	Y	Y	Y
4 Rice	N	Y	N	Y	?	?
5 Meeks	N	Y	N	Y	Y	Y
6 Meng	N	Y	N	Y	Y	Y
7 Velázquez	N	Y	N	Y	Y	Y
8 Jeffries	N	Y	N	Y	Y	Y
9 Clarke	N	Y	N	Y	?	?
10 Nadler	N	Y	N	Y	?	Y
11 **Donovan**	Y	Y	Y	Y	Y	Y
12 Maloney, C.	N	Y	N	Y	Y	Y
13 Espaillat	N	Y	N	Y	Y	Y
14 Crowley	?	?	?	?	?	?
15 Serrano	N	Y	N	Y	Y	Y
16 Engel	N	Y	N	Y	?	?
17 Lowey	N	Y	N	Y	Y	Y
18 Maloney, S.P.	N	Y	N	Y	Y	Y
19 **Faso**	Y	Y	Y	Y	Y	Y
20 Tonko	N	Y	N	Y	Y	Y
21 **Stefanik**	Y	Y	Y	Y	Y	Y
22 **Tenney**	Y	Y	Y	Y	Y	Y
23 **Reed**	Y	Y	Y	Y	Y	?
24 **Katko**	Y	Y	Y	Y	Y	Y
25 Morelle	N	Y	N	Y	Y	Y
26 Higgins	N	Y	N	Y	Y	Y
27 **Collins**	Y	Y	Y	Y	Y	Y
NORTH CAROLINA						
1 Butterfield	N	Y	N	Y	?	Y
2 **Holding**	Y	Y	Y	Y	?	?
3 **Jones**	?	?	?	?	?	?
4 Price	N	Y	N	Y	Y	Y

	470	471	472	473	474	475
5 **Foxx**	Y	Y	Y	Y	Y	Y
6 **Walker**	Y	Y	Y	Y	Y	Y
7 **Rouzer**	Y	Y	Y	Y	Y	Y
8 **Hudson**	Y	Y	Y	Y	Y	Y
9 **Pittenger**	Y	Y	Y	Y	?	?
9 **Vacant**						
10 **McHenry**	Y	?	Y	Y	Y	Y
11 **Meadows**	Y	Y	Y	Y	Y	Y
12 Adams	N	Y	N	Y	Y	Y
13 **Budd**	Y	Y	Y	Y	Y	Y
NORTH DAKOTA						
AL **Cramer**	Y	Y	Y	?	Y	Y
OHIO						
1 **Chabot**	Y	Y	Y	Y	Y	Y
2 **Wenstrup**	Y	Y	Y	Y	Y	Y
3 Beatty	N	Y	N	Y	Y	Y
4 **Jordan**	Y	Y	Y	Y	Y	Y
5 **Latta**	Y	Y	Y	Y	Y	Y
6 **Johnson**	Y	Y	Y	Y	Y	Y
7 **Gibbs**	Y	Y	Y	Y	Y	Y
8 **Davidson**	Y	Y	Y	Y	Y	Y
9 Kaptur	N	Y	N	Y	Y	Y
10 **Turner**	Y	Y	Y	Y	Y	Y
11 Fudge	N	Y	N	Y	Y	Y
12 Balderson	Y	Y	Y	Y	Y	Y
13 Ryan	N	Y	N	Y	Y	Y
14 **Joyce**	Y	Y	Y	Y	?	Y
15 **Stivers**	Y	Y	Y	Y	Y	Y
16 **Renacci**	Y	Y	Y	Y	Y	Y
OKLAHOMA						
1 Hern	Y	Y	Y	Y	Y	Y
2 **Mullin**	Y	Y	Y	Y	Y	Y
3 **Lucas**	Y	Y	Y	Y	Y	Y
4 **Cole**	Y	Y	Y	Y	Y	Y
5 **Russell**	Y	Y	Y	Y	Y	Y
OREGON						
1 Bonamici	N	Y	N	Y	Y	Y
2 **Walden**	Y	Y	Y	Y	Y	Y
3 Blumenauer	N	Y	N	Y	Y	Y
4 DeFazio	N	Y	N	?	Y	Y
5 Schrader	N	Y	N	Y	Y	Y
PENNSYLVANIA						
1 Brady	N	Y	N	Y	?	?
2 Evans	N	Y	N	Y	Y	Y
3 **Kelly**	Y	Y	Y	Y	Y	Y
4 **Perry**	Y	Y	Y	Y	Y	Y
5 **Thompson**	Y	Y	Y	Y	Y	Y
6 **Costello**	Y	Y	Y	Y	Y	Y
7 Scanlon	N	Y	N	Y	Y	Y
8 **Fitzpatrick**	Y	Y	Y	Y	Y	Y
9 **Shuster**	Y	Y	Y	Y	?	?
10 **Marino**	Y	Y	Y	Y	Y	Y
11 **Barletta**	Y	Y	Y	Y	Y	Y
12 **Rothfus**	Y	Y	Y	Y	Y	Y
13 Boyle	N	Y	N	Y	Y	Y
14 Doyle	N	Y	N	?	Y	Y
15 Wild	N	Y	N	Y	Y	Y
16 **Smucker**	Y	Y	Y	Y	Y	Y
17 Cartwright	N	Y	N	Y	Y	Y
18 Lamb	N	Y	N	Y	Y	Y
RHODE ISLAND						
1 Cicilline	N	Y	N	Y	Y	Y
2 Langevin	N	Y	N	Y	Y	Y
SOUTH CAROLINA						
1 **Sanford**	N	Y	Y	Y	Y	Y
2 **Wilson**	Y	Y	Y	Y	Y	Y
3 **Duncan**	?	?	?	?	Y	Y
4 **Gowdy**	Y	Y	Y	Y	?	?
5 **Norman**	Y	Y	Y	Y	Y	Y
6 Clyburn	N	Y	N	Y	Y	Y
7 **Rice**	Y	Y	Y	N	Y	Y
SOUTH DAKOTA						
AL **Noem**	?	?	?	?	?	?
TENNESSEE						
1 **Roe**	Y	Y	Y	Y	Y	Y
2 **Duncan**	Y	Y	Y	Y	Y	Y
3 **Fleischmann**	Y	Y	Y	Y	Y	Y
4 **DesJarlais**	Y	Y	Y	Y	Y	Y
5 Cooper	N	Y	N	Y	Y	Y
6 **Black**	?	?	?	?	?	?
7 **Blackburn**	Y	Y	Y	Y	?	?
8 **Kustoff**	Y	Y	Y	Y	Y	Y
9 Cohen	N	Y	N	Y	Y	N

	470	471	472	473	474	475
TEXAS						
1 **Gohmert**	Y	Y	Y	Y	Y	Y
2 **Poe**	Y	Y	Y	?	?	?
3 **Johnson, S.**	Y	Y	Y	Y	Y	Y
4 **Ratcliffe**	?	?	Y	Y	Y	Y
5 **Hensarling**	Y	Y	Y	Y	Y	Y
6 **Barton**	Y	Y	Y	Y	Y	Y
7 **Culberson**	Y	?	?	Y	?	?
8 **Brady**	Y	Y	Y	Y	Y	Y
9 Green, A.	N	Y	N	Y	Y	Y
10 **McCaul**	Y	Y	Y	Y	Y	Y
11 **Conaway**	Y	Y	Y	Y	Y	Y
12 **Granger**	Y	Y	Y	Y	Y	Y
13 **Thornberry**	Y	Y	Y	Y	Y	Y
14 **Weber**	Y	Y	Y	Y	Y	Y
15 Gonzalez	N	Y	N	Y	?	Y
16 O'Rourke	N	Y	N	Y	Y	Y
17 **Flores**	Y	Y	Y	Y	Y	Y
18 Jackson Lee	N	Y	N	Y	Y	Y
19 **Arrington**	Y	Y	Y	Y	Y	Y
20 Castro	N	Y	N	Y	Y	Y
21 **Smith**	Y	Y	Y	Y	Y	Y
22 **Olson**	Y	Y	Y	Y	Y	Y
23 **Hurd**	Y	Y	N	Y	Y	Y
24 Marchant	Y	Y	Y	Y	Y	Y
25 **Williams**	Y	Y	Y	Y	Y	Y
26 **Burgess**	Y	Y	Y	Y	Y	Y
27 Cloud	Y	Y	Y	Y	Y	Y
28 Cuellar	N	Y	N	Y	Y	Y
29 Green, G.	N	Y	N	Y	Y	Y
30 Johnson, E.B.	N	Y	N	Y	Y	Y
31 **Carter**	Y	Y	Y	Y	Y	Y
32 **Sessions**	Y	Y	Y	Y	Y	Y
33 Veasey	N	Y	N	Y	Y	Y
34 Vela	N	Y	N	Y	Y	Y
35 Doggett	N	Y	N	Y	Y	Y
36 **Babin**	Y	Y	Y	Y	?	Y
UTAH						
1 **Bishop**	Y	Y	Y	Y	Y	Y
2 **Stewart**	Y	Y	Y	Y	Y	Y
3 **Curtis**	Y	Y	Y	Y	Y	Y
4 **Love**	?	?	?	?	?	?
VERMONT						
AL Welch	N	Y	N	Y	Y	Y
VIRGINIA						
1 **Wittman**	Y	Y	Y	Y	Y	Y
2 **Taylor**	Y	Y	Y	Y	?	?
3 Scott	N	Y	N	Y	Y	Y
4 McEachin	N	Y	N	Y	Y	Y
5 **Garrett**	Y	Y	Y	N	Y	Y
6 **Goodlatte**	Y	Y	Y	Y	Y	?
7 **Brat**	Y	Y	Y	Y	Y	Y
8 Beyer	N	Y	N	Y	Y	Y
9 **Griffith**	Y	Y	Y	N	Y	Y
10 **Comstock**	?	?	?	?	?	?
11 Connolly	N	Y	N	Y	Y	Y
WASHINGTON						
1 DelBene	N	Y	N	Y	Y	Y
2 Larsen	N	Y	N	Y	Y	Y
3 **Herrera Beutler**	Y	Y	Y	Y	Y	Y
4 **Newhouse**	Y	Y	Y	Y	?	?
5 **McMorris Rodgers**	Y	Y	Y	Y	Y	Y
6 Kilmer	N	Y	N	Y	Y	Y
7 Jayapal	N	Y	N	Y	Y	Y
8 **Reichert**	Y	Y	Y	Y	Y	Y
9 Smith	N	Y	N	Y	?	Y
10 Heck	N	Y	N	Y	Y	Y
WEST VIRGINIA						
1 **McKinley**	Y	Y	Y	Y	Y	Y
2 **Mooney**	Y	Y	Y	N	Y	Y
3 **Vacant**						
WISCONSIN						
1 **Ryan**			Y			
2 Pocan	N	Y	N	Y	Y	Y
3 Kind	?	?	?	?	?	?
4 Moore	N	Y	N	Y	Y	Y
5 **Sensenbrenner**	Y	Y	Y	Y	?	?
6 **Grothman**	Y	Y	Y	Y	Y	Y
7 **Duffy**	Y	Y	Y	Y	Y	Y
8 **Gallagher**	Y	Y	Y	Y	Y	Y
WYOMING						
AL **Cheney**	Y	Y	Y	Y	Y	Y

VOTE NUMBER

476. HR7319. FEDERAL PROPERTY LEASING/PASSAGE. Mast, R-Fla., motion to suspend the rules and pass the bill that would modify the process for the Public Buildings Reform Board to identify and sell high-value property by allowing property sold through this process to be leased back to the government, however the property can be leased back to the government only for a period of three years and only for the purpose of facilitating the sale of the property. Motion agreed to 372-1: R 204-0; D 168-1. Dec. 21, 2018.

477. HR7329. COAST GUARD AUTHORIZATION CORRECTIONS/PASSAGE. Mast, R-Fla., motion to suspend the rules and pass the bill that would make technical corrections to the fiscal 2018 Coast Guard reauthorization bill. Motion agreed to 378-2: R 205-1; D 173-1. Dec. 21, 2018.

478. S3367. TRANSPORTATION DEPARTMENT REPORTS/PASSAGE. Mast, R-Fla., motion to suspend the rules and pass the bill that would modify a number of Transportation Department reporting requirements. Motion agreed to 381-2: R 207-1; D 174-1. Dec. 21, 2018.

479. HR7293. SLAUGHTER POST OFFICE/PASSAGE. Walker, R-N.C., motion to suspend the rules and pass the bill that would designate the postal facility located at 770 Ayrault Road in Fairport, N.Y., as the "Louise and Bob Slaughter Post Office." Motion agreed to 375-6: R 200-6; D 175-0. Dec. 21, 2018.

480. S2276. AGENCY BUDGET JUSTIFICATION/PASSAGE. Walker, R-N.C., motion to suspend the rules and pass the bill that would require all federal agencies to report on the status of any recommendations made to their agencies by the Government Accountability Office and Office of Inspector General related to annual budget justification documents. Motion agreed to 382-2: R 208-2; D 174-0. Dec. 21, 2018.

481. S3031. FEDERAL PERSONAL PROPERTY/PASSAGE. Walker, R-N.C., motion to suspend the rules and pass the bill that would direct the General Services Administration to modify regulations surrounding federal personal property, and would require an annual assessment and inventory of capitalized personal property. Motion agreed to 383-1: R 208-1; D 175-0. Dec. 21, 2018.

	476	477	478	479	480	481
ALABAMA						
1 Byrne	Y	Y	Y	Y	Y	Y
2 Roby	?	Y	Y	Y	Y	Y
3 Rogers	?	Y	Y	Y	Y	Y
4 Aderholt	Y	Y	Y	Y	Y	Y
5 Brooks	Y	N	N	Y	N	N
6 Palmer	Y	Y	Y	Y	Y	Y
7 Sewell	Y	Y	Y	Y	Y	Y
ALASKA						
AL Young	Y	Y	Y	?	Y	Y
ARIZONA						
1 O'Halleran	Y	Y	Y	Y	Y	Y
2 McSally	Y	Y	Y	Y	Y	Y
3 Grijalva	Y	Y	Y	Y	Y	Y
4 Gosar	Y	Y	Y	Y	Y	Y
5 Biggs	Y	Y	Y	Y	N	Y
6 Schweikert	Y	Y	Y	Y	Y	Y
7 Gallego	Y	Y	Y	Y	Y	Y
8 Lesko	Y	Y	Y	Y	Y	Y
9 Sinema	?	?	?	?	?	?
ARKANSAS						
1 Crawford	Y	Y	Y	Y	Y	Y
2 Hill	Y	Y	Y	Y	Y	Y
3 Womack	Y	Y	Y	Y	Y	Y
4 Westerman	Y	Y	Y	Y	Y	Y
CALIFORNIA						
1 LaMalfa	Y	Y	Y	Y	Y	Y
2 Huffman	Y	Y	Y	Y	Y	Y
3 Garamendi	Y	Y	Y	Y	Y	Y
4 McClintock	Y	Y	Y	Y	Y	Y
5 Thompson	Y	Y	Y	Y	Y	Y
6 Matsui	Y	Y	Y	Y	Y	Y
7 Bera	Y	Y	Y	Y	Y	Y
8 Cook	Y	Y	Y	Y	Y	Y
9 McNerney	Y	Y	Y	Y	Y	Y
10 Denham	?	?	?	?	?	?
11 DeSaulnier	Y	Y	Y	Y	Y	Y
12 Pelosi	Y	Y	Y	Y	Y	Y
13 Lee	Y	Y	Y	Y	Y	Y
14 Speier	Y	Y	Y	Y	Y	Y
15 Swalwell	?	?	?	?	?	?
16 Costa	Y	Y	Y	Y	Y	Y
17 Khanna	Y	Y	Y	Y	Y	Y
18 Eshoo	Y	Y	Y	Y	Y	Y
19 Lofgren	Y	Y	Y	Y	Y	Y
20 Panetta	Y	Y	Y	Y	Y	Y
21 Valadao	Y	Y	Y	Y	Y	Y
22 Nunes	Y	Y	Y	Y	Y	Y
23 McCarthy	Y	Y	Y	Y	Y	Y
24 Carbajal	Y	Y	Y	Y	Y	Y
25 Knight	Y	Y	Y	Y	Y	Y
26 Brownley	Y	Y	Y	Y	Y	Y
27 Chu	Y	Y	Y	Y	Y	Y
28 Schiff	Y	Y	Y	Y	Y	Y
29 Cardenas	Y	Y	Y	Y	Y	Y
30 Sherman	Y	Y	Y	Y	?	Y
31 Aguilar	Y	Y	Y	Y	Y	Y
32 Napolitano	?	Y	Y	Y	Y	Y
33 Lieu	Y	Y	Y	Y	Y	Y
34 Gomez	Y	Y	Y	Y	Y	Y
35 Torres	Y	Y	Y	Y	Y	Y
36 Ruiz	Y	Y	Y	Y	Y	Y
37 Bass	Y	Y	Y	Y	Y	Y
38 Sánchez, Linda	Y	Y	Y	Y	Y	Y
39 Royce	Y	?	Y	Y	Y	Y
40 Roybal-Allard	Y	Y	Y	Y	Y	Y
41 Takano	Y	Y	Y	Y	Y	Y
42 Calvert	Y	Y	Y	Y	Y	Y
43 Waters	Y	Y	Y	Y	Y	Y
44 Barragan	Y	Y	Y	Y	Y	Y
45 Walters	Y	Y	Y	Y	Y	Y
46 Correa	Y	Y	Y	Y	Y	Y
47 Lowenthal	?	?	?	?	?	?
48 Rohrabacher	?	?	?	Y	Y	Y
49 Issa	Y	Y	Y	Y	Y	Y
50 Hunter	Y	Y	Y	Y	Y	Y
51 Vargas	Y	Y	Y	Y	Y	Y
52 Peters	Y	Y	Y	Y	Y	Y
53 Davis	Y	Y	Y	Y	Y	Y

	476	477	478	479	480	481
COLORADO						
1 DeGette	Y	Y	Y	Y	Y	Y
2 Polis	?	?	?	?	?	?
3 Tipton	Y	Y	Y	Y	Y	Y
4 Buck	Y	Y	Y	Y	Y	Y
5 Lamborn	Y	Y	Y	Y	Y	Y
6 Coffman	?	Y	Y	Y	Y	Y
7 Perlmutter	Y	Y	Y	Y	Y	Y
CONNECTICUT						
1 Larson	Y	Y	Y	Y	Y	Y
2 Courtney	Y	Y	Y	Y	Y	Y
3 DeLauro	Y	Y	Y	Y	Y	Y
4 Himes	Y	Y	Y	Y	Y	Y
5 Esty	Y	Y	Y	Y	Y	Y
DELAWARE						
AL Blunt Rochester	Y	Y	Y	Y	Y	Y
FLORIDA						
1 Gaetz	Y	Y	Y	Y	Y	Y
2 Dunn	Y	Y	Y	Y	Y	Y
3 Yoho	Y	Y	Y	N	Y	Y
4 Rutherford	Y	Y	Y	Y	Y	Y
5 Lawson	Y	Y	Y	Y	Y	Y
6 Vacant						
7 Murphy	Y	Y	Y	Y	Y	Y
8 Posey	Y	Y	Y	Y	Y	Y
9 Soto	Y	Y	Y	Y	Y	Y
10 Demings	Y	Y	Y	Y	Y	Y
11 Webster	Y	Y	Y	?	?	?
12 Bilirakis	Y	Y	Y	Y	Y	Y
13 Crist	Y	Y	Y	Y	Y	Y
14 Castor	Y	Y	Y	Y	Y	Y
15 Ross	?	?	?	?	?	?
16 Buchanan	Y	Y	Y	Y	Y	Y
17 Rooney, T.	?	?	?	?	?	?
18 Mast	Y	Y	Y	Y	Y	Y
19 Rooney, F.	Y	Y	?	Y	Y	Y
20 Hastings	?	?	?	?	?	?
21 Frankel	Y	Y	Y	Y	Y	Y
22 Deutch	Y	Y	Y	Y	Y	Y
23 Wasserman Schultz	Y	Y	Y	Y	Y	Y
24 Wilson	Y	Y	Y	Y	Y	Y
25 Diaz-Balart	Y	Y	Y	Y	Y	Y
26 Curbelo	Y	Y	Y	Y	Y	Y
27 Ros-Lehtinen	Y	Y	Y	Y	Y	Y
GEORGIA						
1 Carter	Y	Y	Y	Y	Y	Y
2 Bishop	Y	Y	Y	Y	Y	Y
3 Ferguson	Y	Y	Y	Y	Y	Y
4 Johnson	Y	Y	Y	Y	Y	Y
5 Lewis	Y	Y	Y	Y	Y	Y
6 Handel	Y	Y	Y	Y	Y	Y
7 Woodall	Y	Y	Y	Y	Y	Y
8 Scott, A.	Y	Y	Y	Y	Y	Y
9 Collins	?	?	?	?	?	?
10 Hice	Y	Y	Y	N	Y	Y
11 Loudermilk	Y	Y	Y	Y	Y	Y
12 Allen	Y	Y	Y	Y	Y	Y
13 Scott, D.	?	?	?	?	?	?
14 Graves	?	?	Y	Y	Y	Y
HAWAII						
1 Hanabusa	?	?	?	?	?	?
2 Gabbard	Y	Y	Y	Y	Y	Y
IDAHO						
1 Labrador	Y	Y	Y	Y	Y	Y
2 Simpson	Y	Y	Y	Y	Y	Y
ILLINOIS						
1 Rush	Y	Y	Y	Y	Y	Y
2 Kelly	Y	Y	Y	Y	Y	Y
3 Lipinski	?	?	Y	Y	Y	Y
4 Gutierrez	?	?	?	?	?	?
5 Quigley	Y	Y	Y	Y	Y	Y
6 Roskam	?	?	?	?	?	?
7 Davis, D.	?	?	?	?	?	?
8 Krishnamoorthi	Y	Y	Y	Y	Y	Y
9 Schakowsky	Y	Y	Y	Y	Y	Y
10 Schneider	Y	Y	Y	Y	Y	Y
11 Foster	?	Y	Y	Y	Y	Y
12 Bost	Y	Y	Y	Y	Y	Y
13 Davis, R.	Y	Y	Y	Y	Y	Y

KEY	**Republicans**	*Democrats*	*Independents*
Y Voted for (yea)		**X** Paired against	**C** Voted "present" to avoid possible conflict of interest
# Paired for		**–** Announced against	
+ Announced for		**P** Voted "present"	**?** Did not vote or otherwise make a position known
N Voted against (nay)			

	476	477	478	479	480	481
14 Hultgren	?	?	?	?	?	?
15 Shimkus	Y	Y	Y	Y	Y	Y
16 Kinzinger	Y	Y	Y	Y	Y	
17 Bustos	Y	Y	Y	Y	Y	
18 LaHood	Y	Y	Y	Y	Y	
INDIANA						
1 Visclosky	?	Y	Y	Y	Y	Y
2 **Walorski**	Y	Y	Y	Y	Y	
3 **Banks**	Y	Y	Y	Y	Y	
4 **Rokita**	Y	Y	Y	Y	Y	
5 **Brooks**	Y	Y	Y	Y	Y	
6 **Messer**	Y	Y	Y	Y	Y	
7 Carson	Y	Y	Y	Y	Y	
8 **Bucshon**	Y	Y	Y	Y	Y	
9 **Hollingsworth**	Y	Y	Y	Y	Y	
IOWA						
1 **Blum**	?	?	?	?	?	?
2 Loebsack	Y	Y	Y	Y	Y	Y
3 **Young**	Y	Y	Y	Y	Y	Y
4 **King**	Y	Y	Y	Y	Y	Y
KANSAS						
1 **Marshall**	Y	Y	Y	Y	Y	
2 **Jenkins**	?	?	?	?	?	?
3 **Yoder**	Y	Y	Y	Y	Y	
4 **Estes**	Y	Y	Y	Y	Y	
KENTUCKY						
1 **Comer**	Y	Y	Y	Y	Y	
2 **Guthrie**	Y	Y	Y	Y	Y	
3 Yarmuth	Y	Y	Y	Y	Y	
4 **Massie**	Y	Y	Y	N	Y	Y
5 **Rogers**	Y	Y	Y	Y	Y	
6 **Barr**	Y	Y	Y	Y	Y	
LOUISIANA						
1 **Scalise**	Y	Y	Y	Y	Y	
2 Richmond	Y	Y	Y	Y	Y	
3 **Higgins**	Y	Y	Y	Y	Y	
4 **Johnson**	Y	Y	Y	N	Y	Y
5 **Abraham**	Y	Y	Y	Y	Y	
6 **Graves**	Y	Y	Y	Y	Y	
MAINE						
1 Pingree	Y	Y	Y	Y	Y	
2 **Poliquin**	Y	Y	Y	Y	Y	
MARYLAND						
1 **Harris**	Y	Y	Y	N	Y	Y
2 Ruppersberger	Y	Y	Y	Y	Y	
3 Sarbanes	Y	Y	Y	Y	Y	
4 Brown	Y	Y	Y	Y	Y	
5 Hoyer	Y	Y	Y	Y	Y	
6 Delaney	Y	Y	Y	Y	Y	
7 Cummings	Y	Y	Y	Y	Y	
8 Raskin	Y	Y	Y	Y	Y	
MASSACHUSETTS						
1 Neal	Y	Y	Y	Y	Y	Y
2 McGovern	Y	Y	Y	Y	Y	Y
3 Tsongas	Y	Y	Y	Y	Y	Y
4 Kennedy	Y	Y	Y	Y	Y	Y
5 Clark	Y	Y	Y	Y	Y	Y
6 Moulton	Y	Y	Y	Y	Y	Y
7 Capuano	?	?	?	?	?	?
8 Lynch	Y	Y	Y	Y	Y	Y
9 Keating	?	?	?	?	?	?
MICHIGAN						
1 **Bergman**	Y	Y	Y	Y	Y	Y
2 **Huizenga**	Y	Y	Y	Y	Y	Y
3 *Amash*	Y	Y	Y	Y	Y	Y
4 **Moolenaar**	Y	Y	Y	Y	Y	Y
5 Kildee	Y	Y	Y	Y	Y	Y
6 Upton	Y	Y	Y	Y	Y	Y
7 **Walberg**	Y	Y	Y	Y	Y	Y
8 **Bishop**	Y	Y	Y	Y	Y	Y
9 Levin	Y	Y	Y	Y	Y	Y
10 **Mitchell**	Y	Y	Y	Y	Y	Y
11 **Trott**	?	?	?	?	?	?
12 Dingell	Y	Y	Y	Y	Y	Y
13 Jones	Y	Y	Y	Y	Y	Y
14 Lawrence	Y	Y	Y	Y	Y	Y
MINNESOTA						
1 Walz	?	?	?	?	?	?
2 **Lewis**	?	?	?	?	?	?
3 **Paulsen**	?	?	?	?	?	?
4 McCollum	Y	Y	Y	Y	Y	Y

	476	477	478	479	480	481
5 Ellison	?	?	?	?	?	?
6 **Emmer**	Y	Y	Y	Y	Y	Y
7 Peterson	Y	Y	Y	Y	Y	Y
8 Nolan	Y	Y	Y	Y	Y	Y
MISSISSIPPI						
1 **Kelly**	Y	Y	Y	Y	Y	Y
2 Thompson	?	?	?	?	?	?
3 **Harper**	Y	Y	Y	Y	Y	Y
4 **Palazzo**	Y	Y	Y	Y	Y	Y
MISSOURI						
1 Clay	?	?	?	?	?	?
2 **Wagner**	Y	Y	Y	Y	Y	Y
3 **Luetkemeyer**	Y	Y	Y	Y	Y	Y
4 **Hartzler**	Y	Y	Y	Y	Y	Y
5 Cleaver	Y	Y	Y	Y	Y	Y
6 **Graves**	Y	Y	Y	Y	Y	Y
7 **Long**	Y	Y	Y	Y	Y	Y
8 **Smith**	Y	Y	Y	Y	Y	Y
MONTANA						
AL **Gianforte**	Y	Y	Y	Y	Y	Y
NEBRASKA						
1 **Fortenberry**	Y	Y	Y	Y	Y	?
2 **Bacon**	Y	Y	Y	Y	Y	Y
3 **Smith**	Y	Y	Y	Y	Y	Y
NEVADA						
1 Titus	Y	Y	Y	Y	Y	Y
2 **Amodei**	Y	Y	Y	Y	Y	Y
3 Rosen	+	+	+	+	+	+
4 Kihuen	Y	Y	Y	Y	Y	Y
NEW HAMPSHIRE						
1 Shea-Porter	+	+	+	+	+	+
2 Kuster	Y	Y	Y	Y	Y	Y
NEW JERSEY						
1 Norcross	Y	Y	Y	Y	Y	Y
2 **LoBiondo**	Y	Y	Y	Y	Y	Y
3 **MacArthur**	Y	Y	Y	Y	Y	Y
4 **Smith**	Y	Y	Y	Y	Y	Y
5 Gottheimer	Y	Y	Y	Y	Y	Y
6 Pallone	Y	Y	Y	Y	Y	Y
7 **Lance**	Y	Y	Y	Y	Y	Y
8 Sires	Y	Y	Y	Y	Y	Y
9 Pascrell	Y	Y	Y	Y	Y	Y
10 Payne	Y	Y	Y	Y	Y	Y
11 **Frelinghuysen**	Y	Y	Y	Y	Y	Y
12 Watson Coleman	Y	Y	Y	Y	Y	Y
NEW MEXICO						
1 Lujan Grisham	?	?	?	?	?	?
2 **Pearce**	Y	Y	Y	Y	Y	Y
3 Luján	Y	Y	Y	Y	Y	Y
NEW YORK						
1 **Zeldin**	Y	Y	Y	Y	Y	Y
2 **King**	Y	Y	Y	Y	Y	Y
3 Suozzi	Y	Y	Y	Y	Y	Y
4 Rice	?	?	?	?	?	?
5 Meeks	Y	Y	Y	Y	Y	Y
6 Meng	Y	Y	Y	Y	Y	Y
7 Velázquez	Y	Y	Y	Y	Y	Y
8 Jeffries	Y	Y	Y	Y	Y	Y
9 Clarke	?	Y	Y	Y	Y	Y
10 Nadler	Y	Y	Y	Y	Y	Y
11 **Donovan**	Y	Y	Y	Y	Y	Y
12 Maloney, C.	Y	Y	Y	Y	Y	Y
13 Espaillat	Y	Y	Y	Y	Y	Y
14 Crowley	?	?	?	?	?	?
15 Serrano	Y	Y	Y	Y	Y	Y
16 Engel	Y	Y	Y	Y	Y	Y
17 Lowey	Y	Y	Y	Y	Y	Y
18 Maloney, S.P.	Y	Y	Y	Y	Y	Y
19 **Faso**	Y	Y	Y	Y	Y	Y
20 Tonko	Y	Y	Y	Y	Y	Y
21 **Stefanik**	Y	Y	Y	Y	Y	Y
22 **Tenney**	Y	Y	Y	Y	Y	Y
23 **Reed**	Y	Y	Y	Y	Y	Y
24 **Katko**	Y	Y	Y	Y	Y	Y
25 Morelle	Y	Y	Y	Y	Y	Y
26 Higgins	Y	Y	Y	Y	Y	Y
27 **Collins**	Y	Y	Y	?	Y	Y
NORTH CAROLINA						
1 Butterfield	Y	Y	Y	Y	Y	Y
2 **Holding**	?	?	?	?	?	?
3 **Jones**	?	?	?	?	?	?
4 Price	Y	Y	Y	Y	Y	Y

	476	477	478	479	480	481
5 **Foxx**	Y	Y	Y	Y	Y	Y
6 **Walker**	Y	Y	Y	Y	Y	Y
7 **Rouzer**	Y	Y	Y	Y	Y	Y
8 **Hudson**	Y	Y	Y	Y	Y	Y
9 **Pittenger**	?	?	?	?	?	?
9 Vacant						
10 **McHenry**	Y	Y	Y	Y	Y	Y
11 **Meadows**	Y	Y	Y	Y	Y	Y
12 Adams	Y	Y	Y	Y	Y	Y
13 **Budd**	Y	?	Y	Y	Y	Y
NORTH DAKOTA						
AL **Cramer**	Y	Y	Y	Y	Y	Y
OHIO						
1 **Chabot**	Y	Y	Y	Y	Y	Y
2 **Wenstrup**	Y	Y	Y	Y	Y	Y
3 Beatty	Y	Y	Y	Y	Y	Y
4 **Jordan**	Y	Y	Y	Y	Y	Y
5 **Latta**	Y	Y	Y	Y	Y	Y
6 **Johnson**	Y	Y	Y	Y	Y	Y
7 **Gibbs**	Y	Y	Y	Y	Y	Y
8 **Davidson**	Y	Y	Y	Y	Y	Y
9 Kaptur	Y	Y	Y	Y	Y	Y
10 **Turner**	Y	Y	Y	Y	Y	Y
11 Fudge	Y	Y	Y	Y	Y	Y
12 Balderson	Y	Y	Y	Y	Y	Y
13 Ryan	Y	Y	Y	Y	Y	Y
14 Joyce	Y	Y	Y	Y	Y	Y
15 **Stivers**	Y	Y	Y	Y	Y	Y
16 **Renacci**	Y	Y	Y	Y	Y	Y
OKLAHOMA						
1 **Hern**	Y	Y	Y	Y	Y	Y
2 **Mullin**	Y	Y	Y	Y	Y	Y
3 **Lucas**	Y	Y	Y	Y	Y	Y
4 **Cole**	Y	Y	Y	Y	Y	Y
5 **Russell**	Y	Y	Y	Y	Y	Y
OREGON						
1 Bonamici	Y	Y	Y	Y	Y	Y
2 **Walden**	Y	Y	Y	Y	Y	Y
3 Blumenauer	Y	Y	Y	Y	Y	Y
4 DeFazio	Y	Y	Y	Y	Y	Y
5 Schrader	Y	Y	Y	Y	Y	Y
PENNSYLVANIA						
1 Brady	?	?	?	?	?	?
2 Evans	Y	Y	Y	Y	Y	Y
3 **Kelly**	Y	Y	Y	Y	Y	Y
4 **Perry**	Y	Y	Y	Y	Y	Y
5 **Thompson**	Y	Y	Y	Y	Y	Y
6 **Costello**	Y	Y	Y	Y	Y	Y
7 Scanlon	Y	Y	Y	Y	Y	Y
8 **Fitzpatrick**	Y	Y	Y	Y	Y	Y
9 **Shuster**	?	?	?	?	?	?
10 **Marino**	Y	Y	Y	Y	Y	Y
11 **Barletta**	Y	Y	Y	Y	Y	Y
12 **Rothfus**	Y	Y	Y	N	Y	Y
13 Boyle	Y	Y	Y	Y	Y	Y
14 Doyle	Y	Y	Y	Y	Y	Y
15 Wild	Y	Y	Y	Y	Y	Y
16 **Smucker**	Y	Y	Y	Y	Y	Y
17 Cartwright	Y	Y	Y	Y	Y	Y
18 Lamb	Y	Y	Y	Y	Y	Y
RHODE ISLAND						
1 Cicilline	Y	Y	Y	Y	Y	Y
2 Langevin	Y	Y	Y	Y	Y	Y
SOUTH CAROLINA						
1 **Sanford**	Y	Y	Y	P	Y	Y
2 **Wilson**	Y	Y	Y	Y	Y	Y
3 **Duncan**	Y	Y	Y	Y	Y	Y
4 **Gowdy**	?	?	?	?	?	?
5 **Norman**	Y	Y	Y	Y	Y	Y
6 Clyburn	Y	Y	Y	Y	Y	Y
7 **Rice**	Y	Y	Y	Y	Y	Y
SOUTH DAKOTA						
AL **Noem**	?	?	?	?	?	?
TENNESSEE						
1 **Roe**	Y	Y	Y	Y	Y	Y
2 **Duncan**	Y	Y	Y	Y	Y	Y
3 **Fleischmann**	Y	Y	Y	Y	Y	Y
4 **DesJarlais**	Y	Y	Y	Y	Y	Y
5 Cooper	Y	Y	Y	Y	Y	Y
6 **Black**	?	?	?	?	?	?
7 **Blackburn**	?	?	?	?	?	?
8 **Kustoff**	?	?	?	?	?	?
9 Cohen	N	N	N	Y	Y	Y

	476	477	478	479	480	481
TEXAS						
1 **Gohmert**	Y	Y	Y	Y	Y	Y
2 Poe	?	?	?	?	?	?
3 **Johnson, S.**	Y	Y	Y	Y	Y	Y
4 **Ratcliffe**	Y	Y	Y	Y	Y	Y
5 **Hensarling**	Y	Y	Y	Y	Y	Y
6 **Barton**	Y	Y	Y	Y	Y	Y
7 **Culberson**	?	?	?	?	?	?
8 **Brady**	?	Y	Y	Y	Y	Y
9 Green, A.	Y	Y	Y	Y	Y	Y
10 **McCaul**	Y	Y	Y	Y	Y	Y
11 **Conaway**	Y	Y	Y	Y	Y	Y
12 **Granger**	Y	Y	Y	Y	Y	Y
13 **Thornberry**	Y	Y	Y	Y	Y	Y
14 **Weber**	Y	Y	Y	Y	Y	Y
15 Gonzalez	Y	Y	Y	Y	Y	Y
16 O'Rourke	Y	Y	Y	Y	Y	Y
17 **Flores**	Y	Y	Y	Y	Y	Y
18 Jackson Lee	Y	Y	Y	Y	Y	Y
19 **Arrington**	Y	Y	Y	Y	Y	Y
20 Castro	Y	Y	Y	Y	Y	Y
21 **Smith**	Y	Y	Y	Y	Y	Y
22 **Olson**	Y	Y	Y	Y	Y	Y
23 **Hurd**	Y	Y	?	Y	Y	Y
24 **Marchant**	Y	Y	Y	Y	Y	Y
25 **Williams**	Y	Y	Y	Y	Y	Y
26 **Burgess**	Y	Y	Y	Y	Y	Y
27 **Cloud**	Y	Y	Y	Y	Y	Y
28 **Cuellar**	Y	Y	Y	Y	Y	Y
29 Green, G.	Y	Y	Y	Y	Y	Y
30 Johnson, E.B.	Y	Y	Y	Y	Y	Y
31 **Carter**	Y	Y	Y	Y	Y	Y
32 **Sessions**	Y	Y	Y	Y	Y	Y
33 Veasey	?	Y	Y	Y	Y	Y
34 Vela	Y	Y	Y	Y	Y	Y
35 Doggett	Y	Y	Y	Y	Y	Y
36 **Babin**	Y	Y	Y	Y	Y	Y
UTAH						
1 **Bishop**	Y	Y	Y	Y	Y	Y
2 **Stewart**	Y	Y	Y	Y	Y	Y
3 **Curtis**	Y	Y	Y	Y	Y	Y
4 **Love**	?	?	?	?	?	?
VERMONT						
AL Welch	Y	Y	Y	Y	Y	Y
VIRGINIA						
1 **Wittman**	Y	Y	Y	Y	Y	Y
2 **Taylor**	?	?	?	?	?	?
3 Scott	Y	Y	Y	Y	Y	Y
4 McEachin	Y	Y	Y	Y	Y	Y
5 **Garrett**	Y	Y	Y	Y	Y	Y
6 **Goodlatte**	?	?	?	?	?	?
7 **Brat**	Y	Y	Y	Y	Y	Y
8 Beyer	Y	Y	Y	Y	Y	Y
9 **Griffith**	Y	Y	Y	Y	Y	Y
10 **Comstock**	Y	Y	Y	Y	Y	Y
11 Connolly	Y	Y	Y	Y	Y	Y
WASHINGTON						
1 DelBene	Y	Y	Y	Y	Y	Y
2 Larsen	Y	Y	Y	Y	Y	Y
3 **Herrera Beutler**	Y	Y	Y	Y	Y	Y
4 **Newhouse**	?	?	Y	Y	Y	Y
5 **McMorris Rodgers**	Y	Y	Y	Y	Y	Y
6 Kilmer	Y	Y	Y	Y	Y	Y
7 Jayapal	Y	Y	Y	Y	Y	Y
8 **Reichert**	Y	Y	Y	Y	Y	Y
9 Smith	Y	Y	Y	Y	Y	Y
10 Heck	Y	Y	Y	Y	Y	Y
WEST VIRGINIA						
1 **McKinley**	Y	Y	Y	Y	Y	Y
2 **Mooney**	Y	Y	Y	Y	Y	Y
3 Vacant						
WISCONSIN						
1 **Ryan**						
2 Pocan	Y	Y	Y	Y	Y	Y
3 Kind	?	?	?	?	?	?
4 Moore	Y	Y	Y	Y	Y	Y
5 **Sensenbrenner**	?	?	?	?	?	?
6 **Grothman**	Y	Y	Y	P	Y	Y
7 **Duffy**	Y	Y	Y	Y	Y	Y
8 **Gallagher**	Y	Y	Y	Y	Y	Y
WYOMING						
AL **Cheney**	Y	Y	Y	Y	Y	Y

VOTE NUMBER

482. S3191. CIVIL RIGHTS COLD CASES/PASSAGE. Walker, R-N.C., motion to suspend the rules and pass the bill that would direct the National Archives and Records Administration to create a collection of civil rights cold case records and establish a review board to facilitate the review and public release of the records. It would require all cold case records to be collected and made public within 25 years of enactment. Motion agreed to 376-6: R 203-6; D 173-0. Dec. 21, 2018.

483. HCONRES149. EVIDENCE-BASED POLICYMAKING CORRECTIONS/ PASSAGE. Mitchell, R-Mich., motion to suspend the rules and agree to the concurrent resolution that would make certain corrections in the enrollment of the Foundations for Evidence-Based Policymaking Act. Motion agreed to 362-12: R 188-12; D 174-0. Dec. 21, 2018.

484. HR4174. AGENCY DATA USE/PASSAGE. Walker, R-N.C., motion to suspend the rules and concur in the Senate amendment to the bill that would require each federal agency to develop and make public a comprehensive inventory of its data assets, and would direct the Government Accountability Office to establish a public online catalogue of this data. It would require each agency to submit an annual policy plan to the Office of Management and Budget, including the agency's plans to develop evidence supporting its policymaking, and would create an interagency advisory committee on agency data use for evidence-building. Motion agreed to 356-17: R 182-17; D 174-0. Dec. 21, 2018.

485. S3277. COMMERCIAL SPACE ACTIVITY/PASSAGE. Smith, R-Texas, motion to suspend the rules and pass the bill that would establish the Commerce Department's Office of Space Commerce as the primary office responsible for authorizing and supervising the operation of nongovernmental activities in space. It would direct the Transportation secretary to establish standards for this authorization of certain nongovernmental space activities related to data collection and imagery. Motion rejected 239-137: R 194-7; D 45-130. Dec. 21, 2018.

486. S3661. WORLD WAR II COMMEMORATION/PASSAGE. Graves, R-Mo., motion to suspend the rules and pass the bill that would authorize a Department of Defense program commemorating the 75th anniversary of World War II and direct the Defense secretary to coordinate commemorative activities with non-profit organizations and federal, state, and local governments. It would authorize expenditures of up to $5 million annually through fiscal 2021 for related activities. Motion agreed to 370-0: R 201-0; D 169-0. Dec. 21, 2018.

487. HR2200. HUMAN TRAFFICKING PREVENTION/PASSAGE. Royce, R-Calif., motion to suspend the rules and concur in the Senate amendment to the bill that would authorize $65 million annually through fiscal 2021 to the State Department for activities and programs to prevent human trafficking, protect victims of trafficking, assist foreign countries in meeting standards for the elimination of trafficking and train law enforcement officials and prosecutors to combat human trafficking. It would authorize additional funds for programs that report and monitor trafficking, as well as programs that assist trafficking victims in the United States. Motion agreed to 368-7: R 194-7; D 174-0. Dec. 21, 2018.

Member	482	483	484	485	486	487
ALABAMA						
1 Byrne	Y	Y	Y	Y	Y	Y
2 Roby	Y	Y	Y	Y	Y	Y
3 Rogers	Y	Y	Y	Y	Y	Y
4 Aderholt	Y	?	?	Y	Y	Y
5 Brooks	Y	N	N	Y	Y	N
6 Palmer	Y	Y	Y	Y	Y	Y
7 Sewell	Y	Y	Y	Y	Y	Y
ALASKA						
AL Young	Y	Y	Y	N	Y	Y
ARIZONA						
1 O'Halleran	Y	Y	Y	N	Y	Y
2 McSally	Y	Y	Y	Y	Y	Y
3 Grijalva	Y	Y	Y	N	Y	Y
4 Gosar	N	N	N	Y	Y	N
5 Biggs	Y	N	N	Y	Y	N
6 Schweikert	Y	Y	Y	Y	Y	Y
7 Gallego	Y	Y	Y	N	Y	Y
8 Lesko	Y	Y	Y	Y	Y	Y
9 Sinema	?	?	?	?	?	?
ARKANSAS						
1 Crawford	Y	Y	Y	Y	Y	Y
2 Hill	Y	Y	Y	Y	Y	Y
3 Womack	Y	Y	Y	Y	Y	Y
4 Westerman	Y	Y	Y	Y	Y	Y
CALIFORNIA						
1 LaMalfa	Y	Y	Y	Y	Y	Y
2 Huffman	Y	Y	Y	N	Y	Y
3 Garamendi	Y	?	?	?	?	?
4 McClintock	Y	Y	Y	Y	Y	Y
5 Thompson	Y	Y	Y	N	Y	Y
6 Matsui	Y	Y	Y	N	Y	Y
7 Bera	Y	Y	Y	Y	Y	Y
8 Cook	Y	Y	Y	Y	Y	Y
9 McNerney	Y	Y	Y	N	Y	Y
10 Denham	?	?	?	?	?	?
11 DeSaulnier	Y	Y	Y	N	Y	Y
12 Pelosi	Y	Y	Y	N	Y	Y
13 Lee	Y	Y	Y	N	Y	Y
14 Speier	Y	Y	Y	N	Y	Y
15 Swalwell	?	Y	Y	N	Y	Y
16 Costa	Y	Y	Y	Y	Y	Y
17 Khanna	Y	Y	Y	N	Y	Y
18 Eshoo	Y	?	?	?	?	?
19 Lofgren	Y	Y	Y	N	Y	Y
20 Panetta	Y	Y	Y	Y	Y	Y
21 Valadao	Y	Y	Y	Y	Y	Y
22 Nunes	Y	Y	Y	Y	Y	Y
23 McCarthy	Y	Y	Y	Y	Y	Y
24 Carbajal	Y	Y	Y	N	Y	Y
25 Knight	Y	Y	Y	Y	Y	Y
26 Brownley	Y	Y	Y	N	Y	Y
27 Chu	Y	Y	Y	N	Y	Y
28 Schiff	Y	Y	Y	Y	Y	Y
29 Cardenas	Y	Y	Y	N	Y	Y
30 Sherman	Y	Y	Y	N	Y	Y
31 Aguilar	Y	Y	Y	N	Y	Y
32 Napolitano	Y	Y	Y	N	Y	Y
33 Lieu	Y	Y	Y	N	Y	Y
34 Gomez	Y	Y	Y	N	Y	Y
35 Torres	Y	Y	Y	N	Y	Y
36 Ruiz	Y	Y	Y	N	Y	Y
37 Bass	Y	Y	Y	N	Y	Y
38 Sánchez, Linda	Y	Y	Y	N	Y	Y
39 Royce	Y	Y	Y	Y	Y	Y
40 Roybal-Allard	Y	Y	Y	N	Y	Y
41 Takano	Y	Y	Y	N	Y	Y
42 Calvert	Y	Y	Y	Y	Y	Y
43 Waters	Y	Y	Y	N	Y	Y
44 Barragan	Y	Y	Y	N	Y	Y
45 Walters	Y	?	?	?	?	?
46 Correa	Y	Y	Y	N	Y	Y
47 Lowenthal	?	?	?	?	?	?
48 Rohrabacher	Y	Y	Y	Y	Y	Y
49 Issa	Y	Y	Y	Y	Y	Y
50 Hunter	Y	Y	Y	Y	Y	Y
51 Vargas	Y	Y	Y	N	Y	Y
52 Peters	Y	Y	Y	N	Y	Y
53 Davis	Y	Y	Y	N	Y	Y
COLORADO						
1 DeGette	Y	Y	Y	Y	Y	Y
2 Polis	?	?	?	?	?	?
3 Tipton	Y	Y	Y	Y	Y	Y
4 Buck	Y	N	N	Y	Y	Y
5 Lamborn	Y	Y	Y	Y	Y	Y
6 Coffman	Y	Y	Y	Y	Y	Y
7 Perlmutter	Y	Y	Y	Y	Y	Y
CONNECTICUT						
1 Larson	Y	Y	Y	N	?	Y
2 Courtney	Y	Y	Y	N	?	Y
3 DeLauro	Y	Y	Y	N	Y	Y
4 Himes	Y	Y	Y	N	Y	Y
5 Esty	Y	Y	Y	N	Y	Y
DELAWARE						
AL Rochester	Y	Y	Y	Y	Y	Y
FLORIDA						
1 Gaetz	Y	Y	N	Y	Y	N
2 Dunn	Y	Y	Y	Y	Y	Y
3 Yoho	Y	Y	Y	Y	Y	Y
4 Rutherford	Y	Y	Y	Y	Y	Y
5 Lawson	Y	Y	Y	Y	Y	Y
6 Vacant						
7 Murphy	Y	Y	Y	Y	Y	Y
8 Posey	Y	Y	Y	Y	Y	Y
9 Soto	Y	Y	Y	Y	Y	Y
10 Demings	Y	Y	Y	Y	Y	Y
11 Webster	?	?	?	?	?	?
12 Bilirakis	Y	Y	Y	Y	Y	Y
13 Crist	Y	Y	Y	Y	Y	Y
14 Castor	Y	Y	Y	Y	Y	Y
15 Ross	?	?	?	?	?	?
16 Buchanan	Y	Y	Y	Y	Y	Y
17 Rooney, T.	?	?	?	?	?	?
18 Mast	Y	Y	Y	Y	Y	Y
19 Rooney, F.	Y	?	?	?	?	?
20 Hastings	?	?	?	?	?	?
21 Frankel	Y	Y	Y	Y	Y	Y
22 Deutch	Y	Y	Y	Y	Y	Y
23 Wasserman Schultz	Y	Y	Y	Y	Y	Y
24 Wilson	Y	Y	Y	N	Y	Y
25 Diaz-Balart	Y	Y	Y	Y	Y	Y
26 Curbelo	Y	Y	Y	Y	Y	Y
27 Ros-Lehtinen	Y	Y	Y	Y	Y	Y
GEORGIA						
1 Carter	Y	Y	Y	Y	Y	Y
2 Bishop	Y	Y	Y	Y	Y	Y
3 Ferguson	Y	Y	Y	Y	Y	Y
4 Johnson	Y	Y	Y	N	Y	Y
5 Lewis	Y	Y	Y	N	Y	Y
6 Handel	Y	Y	Y	Y	Y	Y
7 Woodall	Y	Y	Y	Y	Y	Y
8 Scott, A.	Y	Y	Y	Y	Y	Y
9 Collins	?	Y	Y	Y	Y	Y
10 Hice	Y	Y	N	Y	Y	Y
11 Loudermilk	Y	Y	Y	Y	Y	Y
12 Allen	Y	Y	Y	Y	Y	Y
13 Scott, D.	?	Y	Y	Y	Y	Y
14 Graves	Y	Y	Y	Y	Y	Y
HAWAII						
1 Hanabusa	?	?	?	?	?	?
2 Gabbard	Y	Y	Y	N	Y	Y
IDAHO						
1 Labrador	Y	Y	Y	Y	Y	Y
2 Simpson	Y	Y	Y	Y	Y	Y
ILLINOIS						
1 Rush	Y	Y	Y	N	Y	Y
2 Kelly	Y	Y	Y	N	Y	Y
3 Lipinski	Y	Y	Y	N	Y	Y
4 Gutierrez	?	?	?	?	?	?
5 Quigley	Y	Y	Y	N	Y	Y
6 Roskam	?	?	?	?	?	?
7 Davis, D.	Y	Y	Y	N	Y	Y
8 Krishnamoorthi	Y	Y	Y	N	Y	Y
9 Schakowsky	Y	Y	Y	N	Y	Y
10 Schneider	Y	Y	Y	Y	Y	Y
11 Foster	Y	Y	Y	Y	Y	Y
12 Bost	Y	Y	Y	N	Y	Y
13 Davis, R.	Y	Y	Y	Y	Y	Y

KEY   **Republicans**   Democrats   *Independents*

Y Voted for (yea)	X Paired against	C Voted "present" to avoid possible conflict of interest
# Paired for	– Announced against	
+ Announced for	P Voted "present"	? Did not vote or otherwise make a position known
N Voted against (nay)		

	482	483	484	485	486	487
14 **Hultgren**	?	?	?	?	?	?
15 **Shimkus**	Y	Y	Y	Y	Y	Y
16 **Kinzinger**	Y	?	?	?	?	?
17 Bustos	Y	Y	Y	N	Y	Y
18 **LaHood**	Y	Y	Y	Y	Y	Y
INDIANA						
1 Visclosky	Y	Y	Y	N	Y	Y
2 **Walorski**	Y	Y	Y	Y	Y	Y
3 **Banks**	Y	Y	Y	Y	Y	Y
4 Rokita	Y	N	Y	Y	Y	Y
5 **Brooks**	Y	Y	Y	Y	Y	Y
6 **Messer**	Y	Y	Y	Y	Y	Y
7 Carson	Y	Y	Y	N	Y	Y
8 **Bucshon**	Y	Y	Y	Y	Y	Y
9 **Hollingsworth**	Y	Y	Y	Y	Y	Y
IOWA						
1 **Blum**	?	?	?	?	?	?
2 Loebsack	Y	Y	Y	N	Y	Y
3 **Young**	Y	Y	Y	N	Y	Y
4 **King**	Y	Y	Y	Y	Y	Y
KANSAS						
1 **Marshall**	Y	Y	Y	Y	Y	Y
2 **Jenkins**	?	?	?	?	?	?
3 **Yoder**	Y	Y	Y	Y	Y	Y
4 **Estes**	Y	Y	Y	Y	Y	Y
KENTUCKY						
1 **Comer**	Y	Y	Y	Y	Y	Y
2 **Guthrie**	Y	Y	Y	Y	Y	Y
3 Yarmuth	Y	Y	Y	N	Y	Y
4 **Massie**	N	N	N	N	Y	N
5 **Rogers**	Y	Y	Y	Y	Y	Y
6 **Barr**	Y	Y	Y	Y	Y	Y
LOUISIANA						
1 **Scalise**	Y	Y	Y	Y	Y	Y
2 Richmond	Y	Y	Y	N	Y	Y
3 **Higgins**	Y	Y	Y	Y	Y	Y
4 **Johnson**	Y	Y	N	Y	Y	Y
5 **Abraham**	Y	Y	Y	Y	Y	Y
6 **Graves**	Y	Y	Y	Y	Y	Y
MAINE						
1 Pingree	Y	Y	Y	N	Y	Y
2 **Poliquin**	Y	Y	Y	Y	Y	Y
MARYLAND						
1 **Harris**	N	Y	N	Y	Y	Y
2 Ruppersberger	Y	Y	Y	Y	Y	Y
3 Sarbanes	?	Y	Y	N	Y	Y
4 Brown	Y	Y	Y	N	Y	Y
5 Hoyer	Y	Y	Y	Y	Y	Y
6 Delaney	Y	Y	Y	N	Y	Y
7 Cummings	Y	Y	Y	N	Y	Y
8 Raskin	Y	Y	Y	N	Y	Y
MASSACHUSETTS						
1 Neal	Y	Y	Y	N	Y	Y
2 McGovern	Y	Y	Y	N	Y	Y
3 Tsongas	Y	Y	Y	N	Y	Y
4 Kennedy	Y	Y	Y	N	Y	Y
5 Clark	Y	Y	Y	N	Y	Y
6 Moulton	Y	Y	Y	Y	Y	Y
7 Capuano	?	?	?	?	?	?
8 Lynch	Y	Y	Y	N	?	Y
9 Keating	?	?	?	?	?	?
MICHIGAN						
1 **Bergman**	Y	Y	Y	Y	Y	Y
2 **Huizenga**	Y	Y	Y	Y	Y	Y
3 *Amash*	N	N	N	N	Y	N
4 **Moolenaar**	Y	Y	Y	Y	Y	Y
5 Kildee	Y	Y	Y	N	Y	Y
6 **Upton**	Y	?	?	?	?	?
7 **Walberg**	Y	Y	Y	Y	Y	Y
8 **Bishop**	Y	Y	Y	Y	Y	Y
9 Levin	Y	Y	Y	N	Y	Y
10 **Mitchell**	Y	Y	Y	Y	Y	Y
11 **Trott**	?	?	?	?	?	?
12 Dingell	Y	Y	Y	N	Y	Y
13 Jones	Y	Y	Y	N	Y	Y
14 Lawrence	Y	Y	Y	N	Y	Y
MINNESOTA						
1 Walz	?	?	?	?	?	?
2 **Lewis**	?	?	?	?	?	?
3 **Paulsen**	Y	Y	Y	Y	Y	Y
4 McCollum	Y	Y	Y	Y	Y	Y

	482	483	484	485	486	487
5 Ellison	?	?	?	?	?	?
6 **Emmer**	Y	Y	Y	Y	Y	Y
7 Peterson	Y	Y	Y	N	Y	Y
8 Nolan	Y	?	?	?	?	?
MISSISSIPPI						
1 **Kelly**	Y	Y	Y	Y	Y	Y
2 Thompson	?	Y	Y	N	Y	Y
3 **Harper**	Y	Y	Y	Y	Y	Y
4 **Palazzo**	Y	Y	Y	Y	Y	Y
MISSOURI						
1 Clay	Y	Y	Y	Y	Y	Y
2 **Wagner**	Y	Y	Y	Y	Y	Y
3 **Luetkemeyer**	Y	Y	Y	Y	Y	Y
4 **Hartzler**	Y	Y	Y	Y	Y	Y
5 Cleaver	Y	Y	Y	Y	?	Y
6 **Graves**	Y	Y	Y	N	Y	Y
7 **Long**	Y	Y	Y	Y	Y	Y
8 **Smith**	Y	Y	Y	Y	Y	Y
MONTANA						
AL **Gianforte**	Y	Y	Y	Y	Y	Y
NEBRASKA						
1 **Fortenberry**	Y	Y	Y	Y	Y	Y
2 **Bacon**	Y	Y	Y	Y	Y	Y
3 **Smith**	Y	Y	Y	Y	Y	Y
NEVADA						
1 Titus	Y	Y	Y	N	Y	Y
2 **Amodei**	Y	Y	Y	Y	Y	Y
3 Rosen	+	+	+	–	+	+
4 Kihuen	Y	Y	Y	N	Y	Y
NEW HAMPSHIRE						
1 Shea-Porter	+	+	+	+	+	+
2 Kuster	Y	Y	Y	N	Y	Y
NEW JERSEY						
1 Norcross	Y	Y	Y	N	Y	Y
2 **LoBiondo**	Y	Y	Y	Y	Y	Y
3 **MacArthur**	Y	Y	Y	Y	Y	Y
4 **Smith**	Y	Y	Y	Y	Y	Y
5 Gottheimer	Y	Y	Y	Y	Y	Y
6 Pallone	Y	Y	Y	N	Y	Y
7 **Lance**	Y	Y	Y	Y	Y	Y
8 Sires	Y	Y	Y	N	Y	Y
9 Pascrell	Y	Y	Y	N	Y	Y
10 Payne	Y	Y	Y	N	Y	Y
11 **Frelinghuysen**	Y	Y	Y	Y	Y	Y
12 Watson Coleman	Y	Y	Y	N	Y	Y
NEW MEXICO						
1 Lujan Grisham	?	?	?	?	?	?
2 **Pearce**	Y	Y	Y	Y	Y	Y
3 Luján	Y	Y	Y	N	Y	Y
NEW YORK						
1 **Zeldin**	Y	?	?	?	?	?
2 **King**	Y	Y	Y	Y	Y	Y
3 Suozzi	Y	Y	Y	Y	Y	Y
4 Rice	?	Y	Y	N	Y	Y
5 Meeks	Y	Y	Y	N	Y	Y
6 Meng	Y	Y	Y	N	Y	Y
7 Velázquez	Y	Y	?	N	Y	Y
8 Jeffries	Y	Y	Y	N	Y	Y
9 Clarke	Y	Y	Y	N	Y	Y
10 Nadler	Y	Y	Y	N	Y	Y
11 **Donovan**	Y	Y	Y	Y	Y	Y
12 Maloney, C.	Y	Y	Y	N	Y	Y
13 Espaillat	Y	Y	Y	N	Y	Y
14 Crowley	?	?	?	?	?	?
15 Serrano	Y	Y	Y	N	Y	Y
16 Engel	Y	Y	Y	N	Y	?
17 Lowey	Y	Y	Y	N	Y	Y
18 Maloney, S.P.	Y	Y	Y	N	Y	Y
19 **Faso**	Y	Y	Y	Y	Y	Y
20 Tonko	Y	Y	Y	N	Y	Y
21 **Stefanik**	Y	Y	Y	Y	Y	Y
22 **Tenney**	Y	Y	Y	Y	Y	Y
23 **Reed**	Y	Y	Y	Y	Y	Y
24 **Katko**	Y	Y	Y	Y	Y	Y
25 Morelle	?	Y	Y	N	Y	Y
26 Higgins	Y	Y	Y	Y	Y	Y
27 **Collins**	Y	Y	Y	Y	Y	Y
NORTH CAROLINA						
1 Butterfield	Y	Y	Y	N	Y	Y
2 **Holding**	?	Y	Y	Y	Y	Y
3 **Jones**	?	?	?	?	?	?
4 Price	Y	Y	Y	N	Y	Y

	482	483	484	485	486	487
5 **Foxx**	?	Y	Y	N	Y	Y
6 **Walker**	Y	Y	Y	Y	Y	Y
7 **Rouzer**	Y	Y	Y	Y	Y	Y
8 **Hudson**	Y	?	?	?	?	?
9 **Pittenger**	?	?	?	?	?	?
9 **Vacant**						
10 **McHenry**	Y	Y	Y	Y	Y	Y
11 **Meadows**	Y	Y	Y	Y	Y	Y
12 Adams	Y	Y	Y	N	Y	Y
13 **Budd**	Y	Y	Y	Y	Y	Y
NORTH DAKOTA						
AL **Cramer**	Y	Y	Y	Y	Y	Y
OHIO						
1 **Chabot**	Y	Y	Y	Y	Y	Y
2 **Wenstrup**	Y	+	+	+	+	+
3 Beatty	Y	Y	Y	N	Y	Y
4 **Jordan**	Y	Y	N	Y	Y	Y
5 **Latta**	Y	Y	Y	Y	Y	Y
6 **Johnson**	Y	Y	Y	Y	Y	Y
7 **Gibbs**	Y	Y	Y	Y	Y	Y
8 **Davidson**	N	Y	Y	Y	Y	Y
9 Kaptur	Y	Y	Y	Y	Y	Y
10 **Turner**	Y	Y	Y	Y	Y	Y
11 Fudge	Y	?	?	?	?	?
12 Balderson	Y	Y	Y	Y	Y	Y
13 Ryan	Y	Y	Y	Y	Y	Y
14 **Joyce**	Y	Y	Y	Y	Y	Y
15 **Stivers**	Y	Y	Y	Y	Y	Y
16 **Renacci**	Y	?	?	?	?	?
OKLAHOMA						
1 Hern	Y	Y	Y	Y	Y	Y
2 **Mullin**	Y	Y	Y	Y	Y	Y
3 **Lucas**	Y	Y	Y	Y	Y	Y
4 **Cole**	Y	Y	Y	Y	Y	Y
5 **Russell**	Y	?	?	?	?	?
OREGON						
1 Bonamici	Y	Y	Y	Y	Y	Y
2 **Walden**	Y	Y	Y	Y	Y	Y
3 Blumenauer	Y	?	?	?	?	?
4 DeFazio	Y	Y	Y	N	Y	Y
5 Schrader	Y	Y	Y	N	Y	Y
PENNSYLVANIA						
1 Brady	?	Y	Y	N	Y	Y
2 Evans	Y	Y	Y	N	Y	Y
3 **Kelly**	Y	Y	Y	Y	Y	Y
4 **Perry**	Y	N	N	Y	Y	Y
5 **Thompson**	Y	Y	Y	Y	Y	Y
6 **Costello**	Y	Y	Y	Y	Y	Y
7 Scanlon	Y	Y	Y	N	?	Y
8 **Fitzpatrick**	Y	Y	Y	Y	Y	Y
9 **Shuster**	?	?	?	?	?	?
10 **Marino**	Y	Y	Y	Y	Y	Y
11 **Barletta**	Y	?	?	?	?	?
12 **Rothfus**	Y	Y	Y	Y	Y	Y
13 Boyle	Y	Y	Y	N	Y	Y
14 Doyle	Y	Y	Y	N	Y	Y
15 Wild	Y	Y	Y	N	Y	Y
16 **Smucker**	Y	Y	Y	Y	Y	Y
17 Cartwright	Y	Y	Y	N	Y	Y
18 Lamb	Y	Y	Y	Y	Y	Y
RHODE ISLAND						
1 Cicilline	Y	Y	Y	N	Y	Y
2 Langevin	Y	Y	Y	N	?	Y
SOUTH CAROLINA						
1 **Sanford**	Y	Y	Y	Y	Y	N
2 **Wilson**	Y	Y	Y	Y	Y	Y
3 **Duncan**	Y	Y	Y	Y	Y	Y
4 **Gowdy**	?	?	?	?	?	?
5 **Norman**	Y	Y	Y	Y	Y	Y
6 Clyburn	Y	Y	Y	N	Y	Y
7 **Rice**	Y	Y	Y	Y	Y	Y
SOUTH DAKOTA						
AL **Noem**	?	?	?	?	?	?
TENNESSEE						
1 **Roe**	Y	Y	Y	Y	Y	Y
2 **Duncan**	Y	Y	Y	Y	Y	Y
3 **Fleischmann**	Y	Y	Y	Y	Y	Y
4 **DesJarlais**	Y	Y	Y	Y	Y	Y
5 Cooper	Y	Y	Y	N	Y	Y
6 **Black**	?	?	?	?	?	?
7 **Blackburn**	?	?	?	?	?	?
8 **Kustoff**	Y	Y	Y	Y	Y	Y
9 Cohen	Y	Y	Y	N	Y	Y

	482	483	484	485	486	487
TEXAS						
1 **Gohmert**	N	N	N	N	Y	Y
2 **Poe**	?	?	?	?	?	?
3 **Johnson, S.**	Y	Y	Y	Y	Y	Y
4 **Ratcliffe**	Y	?	?	?	?	?
5 **Hensarling**	Y	Y	Y	Y	Y	Y
6 **Barton**	Y	Y	Y	Y	Y	Y
7 **Culberson**	?	Y	Y	Y	Y	Y
8 **Brady**	Y	Y	Y	Y	Y	Y
9 Green, A.	Y	Y	Y	N	Y	Y
10 **McCaul**	Y	Y	Y	Y	Y	Y
11 **Conaway**	Y	Y	Y	Y	Y	Y
12 **Granger**	Y	Y	Y	Y	Y	Y
13 **Thornberry**	Y	Y	Y	Y	Y	Y
14 **Weber**	Y	Y	Y	Y	Y	Y
15 Gonzalez	Y	Y	Y	Y	Y	Y
16 O'Rourke	Y	?	Y	Y	Y	Y
17 **Flores**	Y	Y	Y	Y	Y	Y
18 Jackson Lee	Y	Y	Y	N	Y	Y
19 **Arrington**	Y	?	?	?	?	?
20 Castro	Y	Y	Y	N	Y	Y
21 **Smith**	Y	?	?	?	?	?
22 **Olson**	Y	Y	Y	Y	Y	Y
23 **Hurd**	Y	Y	Y	Y	Y	Y
24 Marchant	Y	Y	Y	Y	Y	Y
25 **Williams**	Y	Y	Y	Y	Y	Y
26 **Burgess**	Y	N	N	Y	Y	Y
27 Cloud	Y	Y	Y	Y	Y	Y
28 Cuellar	Y	Y	Y	Y	Y	Y
29 Green, G.	Y	?	?	?	?	?
30 Johnson, E.B.	Y	?	?	?	?	?
31 **Carter**	Y	Y	Y	Y	Y	Y
32 **Sessions**	Y	Y	Y	Y	Y	Y
33 Veasey	Y	Y	Y	N	Y	Y
34 Vela	Y	Y	Y	Y	Y	Y
35 Doggett	Y	Y	Y	N	Y	Y
36 **Babin**	Y	Y	Y	Y	Y	Y
UTAH						
1 **Bishop**	Y	Y	Y	Y	Y	Y
2 **Stewart**	Y	Y	Y	Y	Y	Y
3 **Curtis**	Y	Y	Y	Y	Y	Y
4 **Love**	?	?	?	?	?	?
VERMONT						
AL Welch	Y	Y	Y	N	Y	Y
VIRGINIA						
1 **Wittman**	Y	Y	Y	Y	Y	Y
2 **Taylor**	?	?	?	?	?	?
3 Scott	?	Y	Y	N	Y	Y
4 McEachin	Y	Y	Y	Y	Y	Y
5 **Garrett**	Y	Y	N	Y	Y	Y
6 **Goodlatte**	?	Y	Y	Y	Y	Y
7 **Brat**	Y	N	N	Y	Y	Y
8 Beyer	Y	Y	Y	Y	Y	Y
9 **Griffith**	Y	N	N	Y	Y	Y
10 **Comstock**	Y	Y	Y	Y	Y	Y
11 Connolly	Y	Y	Y	Y	Y	Y
WASHINGTON						
1 DelBene	Y	Y	Y	Y	Y	Y
2 Larsen	Y	Y	Y	N	Y	Y
3 **Herrera Beutler**	Y	Y	Y	Y	Y	Y
4 **Newhouse**	Y	Y	Y	Y	Y	Y
5 **McMorris Rodgers**	Y	Y	Y	Y	Y	Y
6 Kilmer	Y	Y	Y	N	Y	Y
7 Jayapal	Y	Y	Y	N	Y	Y
8 **Reichert**	Y	Y	Y	Y	Y	Y
9 Smith	Y	Y	Y	Y	Y	Y
10 Heck	Y	Y	Y	Y	Y	Y
WEST VIRGINIA						
1 **McKinley**	Y	Y	Y	Y	Y	Y
2 **Mooney**	Y	Y	Y	Y	Y	Y
3 **Vacant**						
WISCONSIN						
1 **Ryan**						
2 Pocan	Y	Y	Y	N	Y	Y
3 Kind	?	?	?	?	?	?
4 Moore	Y	Y	Y	N	Y	Y
5 **Sensenbrenner**	?	Y	?	Y	Y	Y
6 **Grothman**	Y	Y	Y	Y	Y	Y
7 **Duffy**	Y	Y	Y	Y	Y	Y
8 **Gallagher**	Y	Y	Y	Y	Y	Y
WYOMING						
AL **Cheney**	Y	?	?	?	?	?

III HOUSE VOTES

VOTE NUMBER

488. S1023. FOREST AND REEF CONSERVATION/PASSAGE. Royce, R-Calif., motion to suspend the rules and pass the bill that would reauthorize a 1998 act to conserve tropical forests internationally, and expand its scope to also focus on coral reef conservation. It would authorize $20 million annually through fiscal 2020 for conservation programs, including grants to other countries for maintaining coral reef ecosystems. Motion agreed to 332-43: R 157-43; D 175-0. Dec. 21, 2018.

489. S1158. GENOCIDE PREVENTION/PASSAGE. Royce, R-Calif., motion to suspend the rules and pass the bill that would train foreign service officers assigned to countries at risk or experiencing mass atrocities in how to recognize warning signs or potential atrocities as well as prevention and response activities. Motion agreed to 367-4: R 194-4; D 173-0. Dec. 21, 2018.

490. S1580. INTERNATIONAL EDUCATION ACCESS/PASSAGE. Royce, R-Calif., motion to suspend the rules and pass the bill that would authorize the State Department and the U.S. Agency for International Development, in coordination with multilateral organizations, the private sector, and civil society, to prioritize and advance ongoing efforts to support programs that provide safe primary and secondary education for displaced children, especially girls. Motion agreed to 362-5: R 188-5; D 174-0. Dec. 21, 2018.

491. S1862. HUMAN TRAFFICKING STANDARDS/PASSAGE. Royce, R-Calif., motion to suspend the rules and pass the bill, as amended, that would amend the Trafficking Victims Protection Act to modify criteria for determining whether countries are meeting the minimum standards for the elimination of human trafficking, and actions to be taken against countries that fail to meet such standards, as well as changing other provisions relating to compliance standards and developments banks when dealing with human trafficking. Motion agreed to 370-0: R 197-0; D 173-0. Dec. 21, 2018.

492. S3247. INTERNATIONAL WOMEN'S ENTREPRENEURSHIP/PASSAGE. Royce, R-Calif., motion to suspend the rules and pass the bill that would modify programs managed by the U.S. Agency for International Development aimed at women's entrepreneurship and economic empowerment. Motion agreed to 352-18: R 178-18; D 174-0. Dec. 21, 2018.

493. S512. NUCLEAR REGULATORY LICENSING/PASSAGE. Kinzinger, R-Ill., motion to suspend the rules and pass the bill that would modify Nuclear Regulatory Commission licensing and fee processes, including several provisions related to the development of advanced nuclear reactor designs. It would also require the Commission to report on uranium recovery licensing. Motion agreed to 361-10: R 192-6; D 169-4. Dec. 21, 2018.

	488	489	490	491	492	493
ALABAMA						
1 **Byrne**	Y	Y	Y	Y	Y	Y
2 **Roby**	Y	Y	Y	Y	Y	Y
3 **Rogers**	Y	Y	Y	Y	Y	Y
4 **Aderholt**	Y	Y	Y	Y	Y	Y
5 **Brooks**	N	Y	Y	Y	N	N
6 **Palmer**	N	Y	Y	Y	Y	Y
7 Sewell	Y	Y	Y	Y	Y	Y
ALASKA						
AL **Young**	Y	Y	Y	Y	Y	Y
ARIZONA						
1 O'Halleran	Y	Y	Y	Y	Y	Y
2 **McSally**	Y	Y	Y	Y	Y	Y
3 Grijalva	Y	Y	Y	Y	Y	N
4 **Gosar**	N	N	Y	Y	N	Y
5 **Biggs**	N	N	N	Y	N	N
6 **Schweikert**	Y	Y	Y	Y	Y	Y
7 Gallego	Y	Y	Y	Y	Y	Y
8 **Lesko**	Y	Y	Y	Y	Y	Y
9 Sinema	?	?	?	?	?	?
ARKANSAS						
1 **Crawford**	Y	Y	Y	Y	Y	Y
2 **Hill**	Y	Y	Y	Y	Y	Y
3 **Womack**	Y	Y	Y	Y	Y	Y
4 **Westerman**	Y	Y	Y	Y	Y	Y
CALIFORNIA						
1 **LaMalfa**	Y	Y	?	Y	N	Y
2 Huffman	Y	Y	Y	Y	Y	N
3 Garamendi	?	?	?	?	?	?
4 **McClintock**	N	Y	Y	Y	N	N
5 Thompson	Y	Y	Y	Y	Y	Y
6 Matsui	Y	Y	Y	Y	Y	Y
7 Bera	Y	Y	Y	Y	Y	Y
8 **Cook**	Y	Y	Y	Y	Y	Y
9 McNerney	Y	Y	Y	Y	Y	Y
10 **Denham**	?	?	?	?	?	?
11 DeSaulnier	Y	Y	Y	Y	Y	Y
12 Pelosi	Y	Y	Y	Y	Y	Y
13 Lee	Y	Y	Y	Y	Y	Y
14 Speier	Y	Y	Y	Y	Y	Y
15 Swalwell	Y	Y	Y	Y	Y	Y
16 Costa	Y	Y	Y	Y	Y	Y
17 Khanna	Y	Y	Y	Y	Y	Y
18 Eshoo	?	?	?	?	?	?
19 Lofgren	Y	Y	Y	Y	Y	Y
20 Panetta	Y	Y	Y	Y	Y	Y
21 **Valadao**	Y	Y	Y	Y	Y	Y
22 **Nunes**	Y	Y	Y	Y	Y	Y
23 **McCarthy**	Y	Y	Y	Y	Y	Y
24 Carbajal	Y	Y	Y	Y	Y	Y
25 **Knight**	Y	Y	Y	Y	Y	Y
26 Brownley	Y	Y	Y	Y	Y	Y
27 Chu	Y	Y	Y	Y	Y	Y
28 Schiff	Y	Y	Y	Y	Y	Y
29 Cardenas	Y	Y	Y	Y	Y	Y
30 Sherman	Y	Y	Y	Y	Y	Y
31 Aguilar	Y	Y	Y	Y	Y	Y
32 Napolitano	Y	Y	Y	Y	Y	Y
33 Lieu	Y	Y	Y	Y	Y	Y
34 Gomez	Y	Y	Y	Y	Y	Y
35 Torres	Y	Y	Y	Y	Y	Y
36 Ruiz	Y	Y	Y	Y	Y	Y
37 Bass	Y	Y	Y	Y	Y	Y
38 Sánchez, Linda	Y	Y	Y	Y	Y	Y
39 **Royce**	Y	Y	Y	Y	Y	Y
40 Roybal-Allard	Y	Y	Y	Y	Y	Y
41 Takano	Y	Y	Y	Y	Y	Y
42 **Calvert**	Y	Y	Y	Y	Y	Y
43 Waters	Y	Y	Y	Y	Y	Y
44 Barragan	Y	Y	Y	Y	Y	Y
45 **Walters**	?	?	?	?	?	?
46 Correa	Y	Y	Y	Y	Y	Y
47 Lowenthal	+	?	?	?	?	?
48 **Rohrabacher**	Y	Y	Y	Y	N	Y
49 **Issa**	Y	Y	?	?	?	?
50 **Hunter**	N	Y	Y	Y	N	Y
51 Vargas	Y	Y	Y	Y	Y	Y
52 Peters	Y	Y	Y	Y	Y	Y
53 Davis	Y	Y	Y	Y	Y	Y

	488	489	490	491	492	493
COLORADO						
1 DeGette	Y	Y	Y	Y	Y	Y
2 Polis	?	?	?	?	?	?
3 **Tipton**	Y	Y	Y	Y	Y	Y
4 **Buck**	N	Y	Y	Y	Y	Y
5 **Lamborn**	Y	Y	Y	Y	Y	Y
6 **Coffman**	Y	Y	Y	Y	Y	Y
7 Perlmutter	Y	Y	Y	Y	Y	Y
CONNECTICUT						
1 Larson	Y	?	Y	Y	Y	Y
2 Courtney	Y	Y	Y	Y	Y	Y
3 DeLauro	Y	Y	Y	Y	Y	Y
4 Himes	Y	Y	Y	Y	Y	Y
5 Esty	Y	Y	Y	Y	Y	Y
DELAWARE						
AL Blunt Rochester	Y	Y	Y	Y	Y	Y
FLORIDA						
1 **Gaetz**	N	Y	Y	Y	N	Y
2 **Dunn**	Y	Y	Y	Y	Y	Y
3 **Yoho**	N	Y	Y	Y	Y	Y
4 **Rutherford**	Y	Y	Y	Y	Y	Y
5 Lawson	Y	Y	Y	Y	Y	Y
6 Vacant						
7 Murphy	Y	Y	Y	Y	Y	Y
8 **Posey**	N	Y	Y	Y	N	Y
9 Soto	Y	Y	Y	Y	Y	Y
10 Demings	Y	Y	Y	Y	Y	Y
11 **Webster**	?	?	?	?	?	?
12 **Bilirakis**	Y	Y	Y	Y	?	Y
13 Crist	Y	Y	Y	Y	Y	Y
14 Castor	Y	Y	Y	Y	Y	Y
15 **Ross**	?	?	?	?	?	?
16 **Buchanan**	Y	Y	Y	Y	Y	Y
17 **Rooney, T.**	?	?	?	?	?	?
18 **Mast**	Y	Y	Y	Y	Y	Y
19 **Rooney, F.**	?	?	?	?	?	?
20 Hastings	?	?	?	?	?	?
21 Frankel	Y	Y	Y	Y	Y	Y
22 Deutch	Y	Y	Y	Y	Y	Y
23 Wasserman Schultz	Y	Y	Y	Y	Y	Y
24 Wilson	Y	Y	Y	Y	Y	Y
25 **Diaz-Balart**	Y	Y	Y	Y	Y	Y
26 **Curbelo**	Y	Y	Y	Y	Y	Y
27 **Ros-Lehtinen**	Y	Y	Y	Y	Y	Y
GEORGIA						
1 **Carter**	Y	Y	Y	Y	Y	Y
2 Bishop	Y	Y	Y	Y	Y	Y
3 **Ferguson**	Y	Y	Y	Y	Y	Y
4 Johnson	Y	Y	Y	Y	Y	N
5 Lewis	Y	Y	Y	Y	Y	Y
6 **Handel**	Y	Y	?	Y	Y	Y
7 **Woodall**	Y	Y	Y	Y	Y	Y
8 **Scott, A.**	N	Y	Y	Y	Y	Y
9 **Collins**	Y	Y	Y	Y	Y	Y
10 **Hice**	N	Y	Y	Y	Y	Y
11 **Loudermilk**	N	Y	Y	Y	Y	Y
12 **Allen**	Y	Y	Y	Y	Y	Y
13 Scott, D.	Y	Y	Y	Y	Y	Y
14 **Graves**	Y	?	Y	Y	Y	Y
HAWAII						
1 Hanabusa	?	?	?	?	?	?
2 Gabbard	Y	Y	Y	Y	Y	Y
IDAHO						
1 **Labrador**	Y	Y	Y	Y	N	Y
2 **Simpson**	Y	Y	Y	Y	Y	Y
ILLINOIS						
1 Rush	Y	Y	Y	Y	Y	Y
2 Kelly	Y	Y	Y	Y	Y	Y
3 Lipinski	Y	Y	Y	Y	Y	Y
4 Gutierrez	?	?	?	?	?	?
5 Quigley	Y	Y	Y	Y	Y	Y
6 **Roskam**	?	?	?	?	?	?
7 Davis, D.	Y	Y	Y	Y	Y	Y
8 Krishnamoorthi	Y	Y	Y	Y	Y	Y
9 Schakowsky	Y	Y	Y	Y	Y	N
10 Schneider	Y	Y	Y	Y	Y	Y
11 Foster	Y	Y	Y	Y	Y	Y
12 **Bost**	Y	Y	Y	Y	Y	Y
13 **Davis, R.**	Y	Y	Y	Y	Y	Y

	488	489	490	491	492	493
14 **Hultgren**	?	?	?	?	?	?
15 **Shimkus**	Y	Y	Y	Y	Y	Y
16 **Kinzinger**	?	?	?	?	?	?
17 Bustos	Y	Y	Y	Y	Y	Y
18 **LaHood**	Y	Y	Y	Y	Y	Y
INDIANA						
1 Visclosky	Y	Y	Y	Y	Y	Y
2 **Walorski**	Y	Y	Y	Y	Y	Y
3 **Banks**	Y	Y	Y	Y	Y	Y
4 Rokita	Y	Y	Y	Y	N	Y
5 **Brooks**	Y	Y	Y	Y	Y	Y
6 **Messer**	Y	Y	Y	Y	Y	Y
7 Carson	Y	Y	Y	Y	Y	Y
8 **Bucshon**	Y	Y	Y	Y	Y	Y
9 **Hollingsworth**	Y	Y	Y	Y	Y	Y
IOWA						
1 **Blum**	?	?	?	?	?	?
2 Loebsack	Y	Y	Y	Y	Y	Y
3 **Young**	Y	Y	Y	Y	Y	Y
4 **King**	Y	Y	Y	?	N	Y
KANSAS						
1 **Marshall**	N	Y	Y	Y	Y	Y
2 **Jenkins**	?	?	?	?	?	?
3 **Yoder**	Y	Y	Y	Y	Y	Y
4 **Estes**	Y	Y	Y	Y	Y	Y
KENTUCKY						
1 **Comer**	N	Y	Y	Y	Y	Y
2 **Guthrie**	Y	Y	Y	Y	Y	Y
3 Yarmuth	Y	Y	Y	Y	Y	Y
4 **Massie**	N	N	N	Y	N	N
5 **Rogers**	Y	Y	Y	Y	Y	Y
6 **Barr**	Y	Y	Y	Y	Y	Y
LOUISIANA						
1 **Scalise**	Y	Y	Y	Y	?	?
2 Richmond	Y	Y	Y	Y	Y	Y
3 **Higgins**	N	Y	Y	Y	Y	Y
4 **Johnson**	N	Y	Y	Y	Y	Y
5 **Abraham**	Y	Y	Y	Y	Y	Y
6 **Graves**	?	Y	Y	Y	?	Y
MAINE						
1 Pingree	Y	Y	Y	Y	Y	Y
2 **Poliquin**	Y	Y	Y	Y	Y	Y
MARYLAND						
1 **Harris**	N	Y	Y	Y	N	N
2 Ruppersberger	Y	Y	Y	Y	Y	Y
3 Sarbanes	Y	Y	Y	Y	Y	?
4 Brown	Y	Y	Y	Y	Y	Y
5 Hoyer	Y	Y	Y	Y	Y	Y
6 Delaney	Y	Y	Y	Y	Y	Y
7 Cummings	Y	Y	Y	Y	Y	Y
8 Raskin	Y	Y	Y	Y	Y	Y
MASSACHUSETTS						
1 Neal	Y	Y	Y	Y	Y	Y
2 McGovern	Y	Y	Y	Y	Y	Y
3 Tsongas	Y	Y	Y	Y	Y	Y
4 Kennedy	Y	Y	Y	Y	Y	Y
5 Clark	Y	Y	Y	Y	Y	Y
6 Moulton	Y	Y	Y	Y	Y	Y
7 Capuano	?	?	?	?	?	?
8 Lynch	Y	Y	Y	Y	Y	Y
9 Keating	?	?	?	?	?	?
MICHIGAN						
1 **Bergman**	Y	Y	Y	Y	Y	Y
2 **Huizenga**	Y	Y	Y	Y	Y	Y
3 *Amash*	N	N	N	Y	N	N
4 **Moolenaar**	Y	Y	Y	Y	Y	Y
5 Kildee	Y	Y	Y	Y	Y	Y
6 **Upton**	?	?	?	?	?	?
7 **Walberg**	Y	Y	Y	Y	Y	Y
8 **Bishop**	N	Y	Y	Y	Y	Y
9 Levin	Y	Y	Y	Y	Y	Y
10 **Mitchell**	Y	Y	Y	Y	Y	Y
11 **Trott**	?	?	?	?	?	?
12 Dingell	Y	Y	Y	Y	Y	Y
13 Jones	Y	Y	Y	Y	Y	Y
14 Lawrence	Y	Y	Y	Y	Y	Y
MINNESOTA						
1 Walz	?	?	?	?	?	?
2 **Lewis**	?	?	?	?	?	?
3 **Paulsen**	Y	Y	Y	Y	Y	Y
4 McCollum	Y	Y	Y	Y	Y	Y
5 Ellison	?	?	?	?	?	?
6 **Emmer**	Y	Y	Y	Y	Y	Y
7 Peterson	Y	Y	Y	Y	Y	Y
8 Nolan	?	?	?	?	?	?
MISSISSIPPI						
1 **Kelly**	Y	Y	Y	Y	Y	Y
2 Thompson	Y	Y	Y	Y	Y	Y
3 **Harper**	Y	Y	Y	Y	Y	Y
4 **Palazzo**	Y	Y	Y	Y	Y	Y
MISSOURI						
1 Clay	Y	Y	Y	Y	Y	Y
2 **Wagner**	Y	Y	Y	Y	Y	Y
3 **Luetkemeyer**	Y	Y	Y	Y	Y	Y
4 **Hartzler**	Y	Y	?	Y	Y	Y
5 Cleaver	Y	Y	Y	Y	Y	Y
6 **Graves**	Y	Y	Y	Y	Y	Y
7 **Long**	Y	Y	Y	Y	Y	Y
8 **Smith**	Y	Y	Y	Y	Y	Y
MONTANA						
AL **Gianforte**	Y	Y	Y	Y	Y	Y
NEBRASKA						
1 **Fortenberry**	Y	Y	Y	Y	Y	Y
2 **Bacon**	Y	Y	Y	Y	Y	Y
3 **Smith**	Y	Y	Y	Y	Y	Y
NEVADA						
1 Titus	Y	Y	Y	Y	Y	Y
2 **Amodei**	Y	Y	Y	Y	Y	Y
3 Rosen	+	+	+	+	+	+
4 Kihuen	Y	Y	Y	Y	Y	Y
NEW HAMPSHIRE						
1 Shea-Porter	+	+	+	+	+	+
2 Kuster	Y	Y	Y	Y	Y	Y
NEW JERSEY						
1 Norcross	Y	Y	Y	Y	Y	Y
2 **LoBiondo**	Y	Y	Y	Y	Y	Y
3 **MacArthur**	Y	Y	Y	Y	Y	Y
4 **Smith**	Y	Y	Y	Y	Y	Y
5 Gottheimer	Y	Y	Y	Y	Y	Y
6 Pallone	Y	Y	Y	Y	Y	Y
7 **Lance**	Y	Y	Y	Y	Y	Y
8 Sires	Y	Y	Y	Y	Y	Y
9 Pascrell	Y	Y	Y	Y	Y	Y
10 Payne	Y	Y	Y	Y	Y	Y
11 **Frelinghuysen**	Y	Y	Y	Y	Y	Y
12 Watson Coleman	Y	Y	Y	Y	Y	Y
NEW MEXICO						
1 Lujan Grisham	?	?	?	?	?	?
2 **Pearce**	N	Y	Y	Y	Y	Y
3 Luján	Y	Y	Y	Y	Y	Y
NEW YORK						
1 **Zeldin**	?	?	?	?	?	?
2 **King**	Y	Y	Y	Y	Y	Y
3 Suozzi	Y	Y	Y	Y	Y	Y
4 Rice	Y	Y	Y	Y	Y	Y
5 Meeks	Y	Y	Y	Y	Y	Y
6 Meng	Y	Y	Y	Y	Y	Y
7 Velázquez	Y	?	?	?	?	?
8 Jeffries	Y	Y	Y	Y	Y	Y
9 Clarke	Y	Y	Y	Y	Y	Y
10 Nadler	Y	Y	Y	Y	Y	Y
11 **Donovan**	Y	Y	Y	Y	Y	Y
12 Maloney, C.	Y	Y	Y	Y	Y	Y
13 Espaillat	Y	Y	Y	Y	Y	Y
14 Crowley	?	?	?	?	?	?
15 Serrano	Y	Y	Y	Y	Y	Y
16 Engel	Y	Y	Y	Y	Y	Y
17 Lowey	Y	Y	Y	?	Y	Y
18 Maloney, S.P.	Y	Y	Y	Y	Y	Y
19 **Faso**	Y	Y	Y	Y	Y	Y
20 Tonko	Y	Y	Y	Y	Y	Y
21 **Stefanik**	Y	Y	Y	Y	Y	Y
22 **Tenney**	Y	Y	Y	Y	Y	Y
23 **Reed**	Y	Y	Y	Y	Y	Y
24 **Katko**	Y	Y	Y	Y	Y	Y
25 Morelle	Y	Y	Y	Y	Y	Y
26 Higgins	Y	Y	Y	Y	Y	Y
27 **Collins**	Y	Y	Y	Y	Y	Y
NORTH CAROLINA						
1 Butterfield	Y	Y	Y	Y	Y	Y
2 **Holding**	Y	Y	Y	Y	Y	Y
3 **Jones**	?	?	?	?	?	?
4 Price	Y	Y	Y	Y	Y	Y
5 **Foxx**	Y	Y	Y	Y	Y	Y
6 **Walker**	Y	?	?	?	?	?
7 **Rouzer**	Y	Y	Y	Y	Y	Y
8 **Hudson**	?	?	?	?	?	?
9 **Pittenger**	?	?	?	?	?	?
9 **Vacant**						
10 **McHenry**	Y	Y	Y	?	Y	Y
11 **Meadows**	N	Y	Y	Y	Y	Y
12 Adams	Y	Y	Y	Y	Y	Y
13 **Budd**	N	Y	Y	Y	Y	Y
NORTH DAKOTA						
AL **Cramer**	Y	Y	?	Y	Y	Y
OHIO						
1 **Chabot**	Y	Y	Y	Y	Y	Y
2 **Wenstrup**	+	+	+	+	+	+
3 Beatty	Y	Y	Y	Y	Y	Y
4 **Jordan**	N	Y	Y	Y	Y	Y
5 **Latta**	Y	Y	Y	Y	Y	Y
6 **Johnson**	Y	Y	Y	Y	Y	Y
7 **Gibbs**	Y	Y	Y	Y	Y	Y
8 **Davidson**	N	Y	Y	Y	Y	Y
9 Kaptur	Y	Y	Y	Y	Y	Y
10 **Turner**	Y	Y	Y	Y	Y	Y
11 Fudge	?	?	?	?	?	?
12 Balderson	Y	Y	Y	Y	Y	Y
13 Ryan	Y	Y	Y	Y	Y	Y
14 **Joyce**	Y	Y	Y	Y	Y	Y
15 **Stivers**	Y	Y	Y	Y	Y	Y
16 **Renacci**	?	?	?	?	?	?
OKLAHOMA						
1 Hern	N	Y	Y	Y	Y	Y
2 **Mullin**	Y	Y	Y	Y	Y	Y
3 **Lucas**	Y	Y	Y	Y	Y	Y
4 **Cole**	Y	Y	Y	Y	Y	Y
5 **Russell**	?	?	?	?	?	?
OREGON						
1 Bonamici	Y	Y	Y	Y	Y	Y
2 **Walden**	Y	Y	Y	Y	Y	Y
3 Blumenauer	?	?	?	?	?	?
4 DeFazio	Y	Y	Y	Y	Y	Y
5 Schrader	Y	Y	Y	Y	Y	Y
PENNSYLVANIA						
1 Brady	Y	Y	Y	Y	Y	Y
2 Evans	Y	Y	Y	Y	Y	Y
3 **Kelly**	Y	Y	Y	Y	Y	Y
4 **Perry**	N	Y	Y	Y	Y	Y
5 **Thompson**	Y	Y	Y	Y	Y	Y
6 **Costello**	Y	Y	Y	Y	Y	Y
7 Scanlon	Y	Y	Y	Y	Y	Y
8 **Fitzpatrick**	Y	Y	Y	Y	Y	Y
9 **Shuster**	?	?	?	?	?	?
10 **Marino**	Y	Y	Y	Y	Y	Y
11 **Barletta**	?	?	?	?	?	?
12 **Rothfus**	Y	Y	Y	Y	Y	Y
13 Boyle	Y	Y	Y	Y	Y	Y
14 Doyle	Y	Y	Y	Y	Y	Y
15 Wild	Y	Y	Y	Y	Y	Y
16 **Smucker**	Y	Y	Y	Y	Y	Y
17 Cartwright	Y	Y	Y	Y	Y	Y
18 Lamb	Y	Y	Y	Y	Y	Y
RHODE ISLAND						
1 Cicilline	Y	Y	Y	Y	Y	Y
2 Langevin	Y	Y	Y	Y	Y	Y
SOUTH CAROLINA						
1 **Sanford**	N	Y	Y	Y	Y	Y
2 **Wilson**	Y	Y	Y	Y	Y	Y
3 **Duncan**	N	Y	Y	Y	Y	Y
4 **Gowdy**	?	?	?	?	?	?
5 **Norman**	N	Y	Y	Y	Y	Y
6 Clyburn	Y	Y	Y	Y	Y	Y
7 **Rice**	Y	Y	Y	Y	Y	Y
SOUTH DAKOTA						
AL **Noem**	?	?	?	?	?	?
TENNESSEE						
1 **Roe**	Y	Y	Y	Y	Y	Y
2 **Duncan**	N	Y	Y	Y	N	Y
3 **Fleischmann**	Y	Y	Y	Y	Y	Y
4 **DesJarlais**	N	Y	Y	Y	Y	Y
5 Cooper	Y	Y	Y	Y	Y	Y
6 **Black**	?	?	?	?	?	?
7 **Blackburn**	?	?	?	?	?	?
8 **Kustoff**	Y	Y	Y	Y	Y	Y
9 Cohen	Y	Y	Y	Y	Y	Y
TEXAS						
1 **Gohmert**	N	Y	N	Y	N	Y
2 **Poe**	?	?	?	?	?	?
3 **Johnson, S.**	Y	Y	Y	Y	Y	Y
4 **Ratcliffe**	?	?	?	?	?	?
5 **Hensarling**	Y	Y	Y	Y	Y	Y
6 **Barton**	Y	Y	?	Y	Y	Y
7 **Culberson**	Y	Y	Y	Y	Y	Y
8 **Brady**	Y	Y	Y	Y	Y	Y
9 Green, A.	Y	Y	Y	Y	Y	Y
10 **McCaul**	Y	Y	Y	Y	Y	Y
11 **Conaway**	N	Y	Y	Y	Y	Y
12 **Granger**	N	Y	Y	Y	Y	Y
13 **Thornberry**	N	Y	Y	Y	Y	Y
14 **Weber**	Y	Y	Y	Y	Y	Y
15 Gonzalez	Y	Y	Y	Y	Y	Y
16 O'Rourke	Y	Y	Y	Y	Y	Y
17 **Flores**	Y	Y	Y	Y	Y	Y
18 Jackson Lee	Y	Y	Y	Y	Y	Y
19 **Arrington**	?	?	?	?	?	?
20 Castro	Y	Y	Y	Y	Y	Y
21 **Smith**	?	?	?	?	?	?
22 **Olson**	Y	Y	Y	Y	Y	Y
23 **Hurd**	Y	Y	Y	Y	Y	Y
24 Marchant	Y	Y	Y	Y	Y	Y
25 **Williams**	Y	Y	Y	Y	Y	Y
26 **Burgess**	Y	Y	Y	Y	Y	Y
27 Cloud	N	Y	Y	Y	Y	Y
28 Cuellar	Y	Y	Y	Y	Y	Y
29 Green, G.	?	?	?	?	?	?
30 Johnson, E.B.	?	?	?	?	?	?
31 **Carter**	Y	Y	Y	Y	Y	Y
32 **Sessions**	Y	Y	Y	Y	Y	Y
33 Veasey	Y	Y	Y	Y	Y	Y
34 Vela	Y	Y	Y	Y	Y	Y
35 Doggett	Y	Y	Y	Y	Y	Y
36 **Babin**	Y	Y	Y	Y	Y	Y
UTAH						
1 **Bishop**	Y	Y	Y	Y	Y	Y
2 **Stewart**	Y	Y	Y	Y	Y	Y
3 **Curtis**	Y	Y	Y	Y	Y	Y
4 **Love**	?	?	?	?	?	?
VERMONT						
AL Welch	Y	Y	Y	Y	Y	Y
VIRGINIA						
1 **Wittman**	Y	Y	Y	Y	Y	Y
2 **Taylor**	?	?	?	?	?	?
3 Scott	Y	Y	Y	Y	Y	Y
4 McEachin	Y	Y	Y	Y	Y	Y
5 **Garrett**	N	Y	Y	Y	N	Y
6 **Goodlatte**	Y	Y	Y	Y	Y	Y
7 **Brat**	N	Y	Y	Y	N	Y
8 Beyer	Y	Y	Y	Y	Y	Y
9 **Griffith**	N	Y	Y	Y	Y	Y
10 **Comstock**	Y	Y	Y	Y	Y	Y
11 Connolly	Y	Y	Y	Y	Y	Y
WASHINGTON						
1 DelBene	Y	Y	Y	Y	Y	Y
2 Larsen	Y	Y	Y	Y	Y	Y
3 **Herrera Beutler**	Y	Y	Y	Y	Y	Y
4 **Newhouse**						
Rodgers	Y	Y	Y	Y	Y	Y
6 Kilmer	Y	Y	Y	Y	Y	Y
7 Jayapal	Y	Y	Y	Y	Y	Y
8 **Reichert**	Y	?	Y	Y	Y	Y
9 Smith	Y	Y	Y	Y	Y	Y
10 Heck	Y	Y	Y	Y	Y	Y
WEST VIRGINIA						
1 **McKinley**	Y	Y	Y	Y	Y	Y
2 **Mooney**	N	Y	Y	Y	Y	Y
3 **Vacant**						
WISCONSIN						
1 **Ryan**						
2 Pocan	Y	Y	Y	Y	Y	Y
3 Kind	?	?	?	?	?	?
4 Moore	Y	Y	Y	Y	Y	Y
5 **Sensenbrenner**	Y	Y	N	Y	Y	Y
6 **Grothman**	Y	Y	Y	Y	Y	Y
7 **Duffy**	Y	Y	Y	Y	Y	Y
8 **Gallagher**	N	Y	Y	Y	Y	Y
WYOMING						
AL **Cheney**	?	?	?	?	?	?

VOTE NUMBER

494. S1934. ALASKA GENERATOR REGULATION/PASSAGE. Shimkus, R-Ill., motion to suspend the rules and pass the bill that would require the Environmental Protection Agency administrator to revise clean air standards with respect to the manufacture and use of certain compression-ignition engines used to provide power in remote areas of Alaska. Motion rejected 202-171: R 195-5; D 7-166. Dec. 21, 2018.

495. HR6287. 9/11 MEMORIALS/PASSAGE. McClintock, R-Calif., motion to suspend the rules and concur in the Senate amendment to the bill that would authorize Interior Department grants for the operation of specific memorials related to the terrorist attacks that took place Sept. 11, 2001, and would set specific requirements for grant recipients. The grant amounts would be determined by the secretary. Motion agreed to 371-3: R 198-3; D 173-0. Dec. 21, 2018.

496. S3456. NATHANIEL REED WILDLIFE REFUGE/PASSAGE. McClintock, R-Calif., motion to suspend the rules and pass the bill that would redesignate the Hobe Sound National Wildlife Refuge in Florida as the Nathaniel P. Reed Hobe Sound National Wildlife Refuge. Motion agreed to 365-5: R 192-5; D 173-0. Dec. 21, 2018.

497. HR7388. FLOOD INSURANCE EXTENSION/PASSAGE. Walker, R-N.C., motion to suspend the rules and pass the bill that would extend the authorization and authorities under the National Flood Insurance Program through through May 31, 2019. The program is administered by the Federal Emergency Management Agency and offers federally-backed flood insurance to individuals and entities in communities that adopt certain flood plain management standards. It would also state that FEMA may not restrict organizations from selling private flood insurance as a condition of participating in program activities. Motion rejected 148-226: R 146-55; D 2-171. Dec. 21, 2018.

498. PROCEDURAL MOTION/CHANGE CONVENING TIME. Collins, R-Ga., motion that when the House adjourns on Friday, Dec. 21, it next convene for legislative business at noon on Saturday, Dec. 22, 2018. Motion agreed to 187-184: R 186-12; D 1-172. Dec. 21, 2018.

499. HCONRES148. FLOOD INSURANCE EXTENSION CORRECTION/ PASSAGE. MacArthur, R-N.J., motion to suspend the rules and agree to the concurrent resolution (H Con Res 148), that would make a correction in the enrollment of the National Flood Insurance Program Extension Act. Motion agreed to 344-25: R 175-25; D 169-0. Dec. 21, 2018.

	494	495	496	497	498	499
ALABAMA						
1 Byrne	Y	Y	Y	Y	Y	Y
2 Roby	Y	Y	Y	Y	Y	Y
3 Rogers	Y	Y	Y	Y	Y	Y
4 Aderholt	Y	Y	Y	Y	Y	Y
5 Brooks	N	Y	Y	N	N	N
6 Palmer	Y	Y	Y	N	Y	Y
7 Sewell	N	Y	Y	N	N	Y
ALASKA						
AL Young	Y	Y	Y	N	Y	Y
ARIZONA						
1 O'Halleran	Y	Y	Y	N	N	Y
2 McSally	Y	Y	Y	Y	Y	Y
3 Grijalva	N	Y	Y	N	N	Y
4 Gosar	Y	Y	Y	N	N	N
5 Biggs	Y	Y	N	N	N	N
6 Schweikert	Y	Y	Y	Y	Y	N
7 Gallego	N	Y	Y	N	N	Y
8 Lesko	Y	Y	Y	N	Y	Y
9 Sinema	?	?	?	?	?	?
ARKANSAS						
1 Crawford	Y	Y	Y	N	Y	Y
2 Hill	Y	Y	Y	Y	Y	Y
3 Womack	Y	Y	Y	Y	Y	Y
4 Westerman	Y	Y	Y	N	Y	Y
CALIFORNIA						
1 LaMalfa	Y	Y	Y	Y	Y	Y
2 Huffman	N	Y	Y	N	N	Y
3 Garamendi	?	?	?	?	?	?
4 McClintock	Y	Y	Y	Y	Y	N
5 Thompson	N	Y	Y	N	N	Y
6 Matsui	N	Y	Y	N	N	Y
7 Bera	N	Y	Y	N	N	Y
8 Cook	Y	Y	Y	Y	Y	Y
9 McNerney	N	Y	Y	N	N	Y
10 Denham	?	?	?	?	?	?
11 DeSaulnier	N	Y	Y	N	N	Y
12 Pelosi	?	?	Y	N	N	Y
13 Lee	N	Y	Y	N	N	Y
14 Speier	N	Y	Y	N	N	Y
15 Swalwell	N	Y	Y	N	N	Y
16 Costa	Y	Y	Y	N	N	Y
17 Khanna	N	Y	Y	N	N	Y
18 Eshoo	?	?	?	?	?	?
19 Lofgren	N	Y	Y	N	N	Y
20 Panetta	N	Y	Y	N	N	Y
21 Valadao	Y	Y	Y	Y	Y	Y
22 Nunes	Y	Y	Y	Y	Y	Y
23 McCarthy	Y	Y	Y	Y	Y	Y
24 Carbajal	N	Y	Y	N	N	Y
25 Knight	Y	Y	Y	Y	Y	Y
26 Brownley	N	Y	Y	N	N	Y
27 Chu	N	Y	Y	N	N	Y
28 Schiff	N	Y	Y	N	N	Y
29 Cardenas	N	Y	Y	N	N	Y
30 Sherman	N	Y	Y	N	N	Y
31 Aguilar	N	Y	Y	N	N	Y
32 Napolitano	N	Y	Y	N	N	Y
33 Lieu	N	Y	Y	N	N	Y
34 Gomez	N	Y	Y	N	N	Y
35 Torres	N	Y	Y	N	N	Y
36 Ruiz	Y	Y	Y	N	N	?
37 Bass	N	Y	Y	N	N	?
38 Sánchez, Linda	N	Y	Y	N	N	Y
39 Royce	Y	Y	Y	Y	Y	Y
40 Roybal-Allard	N	Y	Y	N	N	Y
41 Takano	N	Y	Y	N	N	Y
42 Calvert	Y	Y	Y	Y	Y	Y
43 Waters	N	Y	Y	Y	N	Y
44 Barragan	N	Y	Y	N	N	Y
45 Walters	?	?	?	?	?	?
46 Correa	N	Y	Y	N	N	Y
47 Lowenthal	?	?	?	?	?	?
48 Rohrabacher	Y	Y	Y	N	Y	Y
49 Issa	?	?	?	?	?	?
50 Hunter	Y	Y	Y	Y	Y	Y
51 Vargas	N	Y	Y	N	N	Y
52 Peters	N	Y	Y	N	N	Y
53 Davis	N	Y	Y	N	N	Y

	494	495	496	497	498	499
COLORADO						
1 DeGette	N	Y	Y	N	N	Y
2 Polis	?	?	?	?	?	?
3 Tipton	Y	Y	Y	Y	Y	Y
4 Buck	Y	Y	Y	N	N	?
5 Lamborn	Y	Y	Y	Y	Y	Y
6 Coffman	Y	Y	Y	Y	Y	Y
7 Perlmutter	N	Y	Y	N	N	Y
CONNECTICUT						
1 Larson	N	Y	Y	N	N	?
2 Courtney	N	Y	Y	N	N	Y
3 DeLauro	N	Y	Y	N	N	Y
4 Himes	N	Y	Y	N	N	Y
5 Esty	N	Y	Y	N	N	Y
DELAWARE						
AL Blunt Rochester	N	Y	Y	N	N	Y
FLORIDA						
1 Gaetz	N	Y	Y	N	Y	Y
2 Dunn	Y	Y	Y	Y	Y	Y
3 Yoho	Y	Y	Y	N	N	Y
4 Rutherford	Y	Y	Y	N	Y	Y
5 Lawson	N	Y	Y	N	N	Y
6 Vacant						
7 Murphy	N	Y	Y	N	N	Y
8 Posey	Y	Y	Y	Y	Y	Y
9 Soto	N	Y	Y	N	N	Y
10 Demings	N	Y	Y	N	N	Y
11 Webster	?	?	?	?	?	?
12 Bilirakis	Y	Y	Y	N	Y	Y
13 Crist	N	Y	Y	N	N	Y
14 Castor	N	Y	Y	N	N	Y
15 Ross	?	?	?	?	?	?
16 Buchanan	Y	Y	Y	Y	Y	Y
17 Rooney, T.	?	?	?	?	?	?
18 Mast	Y	Y	Y	Y	Y	Y
19 Rooney, F.	?	?	?	?	?	?
20 Hastings	?	?	?	?	?	?
21 Frankel	N	Y	Y	N	N	Y
22 Deutch	N	Y	Y	N	N	Y
23 Wasserman Schultz	N	Y	Y	N	N	Y
24 Wilson	N	Y	Y	N	N	Y
25 Diaz-Balart	Y	Y	Y	N	Y	Y
26 Curbelo	Y	Y	Y	N	Y	Y
27 Ros-Lehtinen	Y	Y	Y	N	Y	Y
GEORGIA						
1 Carter	Y	Y	Y	Y	Y	Y
2 Bishop	N	Y	Y	N	N	Y
3 Ferguson	Y	Y	Y	Y	?	Y
4 Johnson	N	Y	Y	N	N	Y
5 Lewis	N	Y	Y	N	N	Y
6 Handel	Y	Y	Y	Y	Y	Y
7 Woodall	Y	Y	Y	Y	Y	Y
8 Scott, A.	Y	Y	Y	Y	Y	Y
9 Collins	Y	Y	Y	Y	Y	Y
10 Hice	Y	Y	Y	Y	Y	Y
11 Loudermilk	Y	Y	?	Y	Y	Y
12 Allen	Y	Y	Y	Y	Y	Y
13 Scott, D.	N	Y	Y	N	N	Y
14 Graves	Y	Y	Y	Y	Y	Y
HAWAII						
1 Hanabusa	?	?	?	?	?	?
2 Gabbard	Y	Y	Y	N	N	Y
IDAHO						
1 Labrador	Y	Y	Y	Y	Y	N
2 Simpson	Y	Y	Y	N	Y	Y
ILLINOIS						
1 Rush	N	Y	Y	N	N	Y
2 Kelly	N	Y	Y	N	N	Y
3 Lipinski	N	Y	Y	N	N	Y
4 Gutierrez	?	?	?	?	?	?
5 Quigley	N	Y	Y	N	N	Y
6 Roskam	?	?	?	?	?	?
7 Davis, D.	N	Y	Y	N	N	Y
8 Krishnamoorthi	N	Y	Y	N	N	Y
9 Schakowsky	N	Y	Y	N	N	Y
10 Schneider	N	Y	Y	N	N	Y
11 Foster	N	Y	Y	N	N	Y
12 Bost	Y	Y	Y	Y	Y	Y
13 Davis, R.	Y	Y	Y	Y	Y	Y

	494	495	496	497	498	499
14 **Hultgren**	?	?	?	?	?	?
15 **Shimkus**	Y	Y	Y	Y	Y	Y
16 **Kinzinger**	?	?	?	?	?	Y
17 Bustos	N	Y	Y	N	N	Y
18 **LaHood**	Y	Y	Y	Y	Y	Y
INDIANA						
1 Visclosky	N	Y	Y	N	N	Y
2 **Walorski**	Y	Y	Y	Y	Y	Y
3 **Banks**	Y	Y	Y	Y	Y	Y
4 Rokita	Y	Y	Y	Y	Y	Y
5 **Brooks**	Y	Y	Y	Y	Y	Y
6 **Messer**	Y	Y	Y	Y	Y	?
7 Carson	N	Y	Y	N	N	Y
8 **Bucshon**	Y	Y	Y	Y	Y	Y
9 **Hollingsworth**	Y	Y	Y	N	Y	Y
IOWA						
1 **Blum**	?	?	?	?	?	?
2 Loebsack	N	Y	Y	N	N	Y
3 **Young**	Y	Y	Y	N	Y	Y
4 **King**	Y	Y	Y	N	Y	Y
KANSAS						
1 **Marshall**	Y	Y	Y	N	Y	Y
2 **Jenkins**	?	?	?	?	?	?
3 **Yoder**	Y	Y	Y	Y	Y	Y
4 **Estes**	Y	Y	Y	Y	Y	Y
KENTUCKY						
1 **Comer**	Y	Y	Y	N	Y	Y
2 **Guthrie**	Y	Y	Y	Y	Y	Y
3 Yarmuth	N	Y	Y	N	N	Y
4 **Massie**	Y	N	N	Y	N	N
5 **Rogers**	Y	Y	Y	Y	Y	Y
6 **Barr**	Y	Y	Y	Y	Y	N
LOUISIANA						
1 **Scalise**	?	Y	Y	Y	Y	Y
2 Richmond	N	Y	Y	N	N	Y
3 **Higgins**	Y	Y	Y	Y	Y	Y
4 **Johnson**	Y	Y	Y	N	Y	Y
5 **Abraham**	Y	Y	Y	Y	Y	Y
6 **Graves**	Y	Y	Y	N	Y	Y
MAINE						
1 Pingree	N	Y	Y	N	N	Y
2 **Poliquin**	Y	Y	Y	Y	Y	Y
MARYLAND						
1 **Harris**	N	Y	Y	Y	N	Y
2 Ruppersberger	N	Y	Y	N	N	Y
3 Sarbanes	N	Y	Y	N	N	Y
4 Brown	N	Y	Y	N	N	Y
5 Hoyer	N	Y	Y	N	N	Y
6 Delaney	N	Y	Y	N	N	Y
7 Cummings	N	Y	Y	N	N	Y
8 Raskin	N	Y	Y	N	N	Y
MASSACHUSETTS						
1 Neal	N	Y	Y	N	N	Y
2 McGovern	N	Y	Y	N	N	Y
3 Tsongas	N	Y	?	?	?	?
4 Kennedy	N	Y	Y	N	N	Y
5 Clark	N	Y	Y	N	N	Y
6 Moulton	N	Y	Y	N	N	Y
7 Capuano	?	?	?	?	?	?
8 Lynch	N	Y	Y	N	N	Y
9 Keating	?	?	?	?	?	?
MICHIGAN						
1 **Bergman**	Y	Y	Y	Y	Y	Y
2 **Huizenga**	Y	Y	Y	Y	Y	N
3 *Amash*	N	N	N	N	N	N
4 **Moolenaar**	Y	Y	Y	Y	Y	Y
5 Kildee	N	Y	Y	N	N	Y
6 **Upton**	?	?	?	?	?	Y
7 **Walberg**	Y	Y	Y	Y	Y	Y
8 **Bishop**	Y	Y	Y	N	Y	Y
9 Levin	N	Y	Y	N	N	Y
10 **Mitchell**	Y	Y	Y	N	Y	Y
11 **Trott**	Y	Y	Y	Y	Y	Y
12 Dingell	N	Y	Y	N	N	Y
13 Jones	N	Y	Y	N	N	Y
14 Lawrence	N	Y	Y	N	N	Y
MINNESOTA						
1 Walz	?	?	?	?	?	?
2 **Lewis**	?	?	?	?	?	?
3 **Paulsen**	Y	Y	Y	Y	Y	?
4 McCollum	N	Y	Y	N	N	Y

	494	495	496	497	498	499
5 Ellison	?	?	?	?	?	?
6 **Emmer**	Y	Y	Y	Y	Y	Y
7 Peterson	Y	Y	Y	Y	N	Y
8 Nolan	?	?	?	?	?	?
MISSISSIPPI						
1 **Kelly**	Y	Y	Y	Y	Y	Y
2 Thompson	N	Y	Y	N	N	Y
3 **Harper**	Y	Y	Y	N	Y	Y
4 **Palazzo**	Y	Y	Y	N	Y	Y
MISSOURI						
1 Clay	N	Y	Y	N	N	Y
2 **Wagner**	Y	Y	Y	Y	Y	Y
3 **Luetkemeyer**	Y	Y	Y	Y	Y	Y
4 **Hartzler**	Y	Y	Y	Y	?	Y
5 Cleaver	N	Y	Y	N	N	Y
6 **Graves**	Y	Y	Y	N	Y	Y
7 **Long**	Y	Y	Y	Y	Y	Y
8 **Smith**	Y	Y	Y	Y	Y	Y
MONTANA						
AL **Gianforte**	Y	Y	Y	Y	Y	Y
NEBRASKA						
1 **Fortenberry**	Y	Y	Y	Y	Y	Y
2 **Bacon**	Y	Y	Y	Y	Y	Y
3 **Smith**	Y	Y	Y	Y	N	Y
NEVADA						
1 Titus	N	Y	Y	N	N	Y
2 **Amodei**	Y	Y	Y	Y	Y	Y
3 Rosen	–	+	+	–	–	+
4 Kihuen	N	Y	Y	N	N	Y
NEW HAMPSHIRE						
1 Shea-Porter	–	+	+	–	–	+
2 Kuster	N	Y	Y	N	N	Y
NEW JERSEY						
1 Norcross	N	Y	Y	N	N	Y
2 **LoBiondo**	Y	Y	Y	N	Y	Y
3 **MacArthur**	Y	Y	Y	Y	Y	Y
4 **Smith**	Y	Y	Y	N	Y	Y
5 Gottheimer	N	Y	Y	N	N	Y
6 Pallone	N	Y	Y	N	N	Y
7 **Lance**	Y	Y	Y	N	Y	Y
8 Sires	N	Y	Y	N	N	Y
9 Pascrell	N	Y	Y	N	N	Y
10 Payne	N	Y	Y	N	N	Y
11 **Frelinghuysen**	Y	Y	Y	N	Y	Y
12 Watson Coleman	N	Y	Y	N	N	Y
NEW MEXICO						
1 Lujan Grisham	?	?	?	?	?	?
2 **Pearce**	Y	Y	Y	Y	Y	N
3 Luján	N	Y	Y	N	N	Y
NEW YORK						
1 **Zeldin**	?	?	?	?	?	Y
2 **King**	Y	Y	Y	N	Y	Y
3 Suozzi	N	Y	Y	N	N	Y
4 Rice	N	Y	Y	N	N	Y
5 Meeks	N	Y	Y	N	N	Y
6 Meng	N	Y	Y	N	N	Y
7 Velázquez	?	?	?	?	?	?
8 Jeffries	N	Y	Y	N	N	Y
9 Clarke	N	Y	Y	N	N	Y
10 Nadler	N	Y	Y	N	N	Y
11 **Donovan**	Y	Y	Y	N	Y	Y
12 Maloney, C.	N	Y	Y	N	N	Y
13 Espaillat	N	Y	Y	N	N	Y
14 Crowley	?	?	?	?	?	?
15 Serrano	N	Y	Y	N	N	Y
16 Engel	N	Y	Y	N	N	Y
17 Lowey	N	Y	Y	N	N	Y
18 Maloney, S.P.	N	Y	Y	N	N	Y
19 **Faso**	Y	Y	Y	Y	Y	Y
20 Tonko	N	Y	Y	N	N	Y
21 **Stefanik**	Y	Y	Y	N	Y	Y
22 **Tenney**	Y	Y	Y	Y	Y	Y
23 **Reed**	Y	Y	Y	Y	Y	Y
24 **Katko**	Y	Y	Y	Y	Y	Y
25 Morelle	N	Y	Y	N	N	Y
26 Higgins	N	Y	Y	N	N	Y
27 **Collins**	Y	Y	Y	Y	Y	Y
NORTH CAROLINA						
1 Butterfield	N	Y	Y	N	N	Y
2 **Holding**	Y	Y	Y	Y	Y	Y
3 **Jones**	?	?	?	?	?	?
4 Price	N	Y	Y	N	N	Y

	494	495	496	497	498	499
5 **Foxx**	Y	Y	Y	N	Y	N
6 **Walker**	Y	Y	Y	N	Y	Y
7 **Rouzer**	Y	Y	Y	Y	Y	Y
8 **Hudson**	?	?	?	?	?	Y
9 **Pittenger**	?	?	?	?	?	?
9 **Vacant**						
10 **McHenry**	Y	Y	Y	Y	Y	Y
11 **Meadows**	Y	Y	Y	Y	Y	?
12 Adams	N	Y	Y	N	N	Y
13 **Budd**	Y	Y	Y	Y	Y	Y
NORTH DAKOTA						
AL **Cramer**	Y	Y	Y	Y	Y	Y
OHIO						
1 **Chabot**	Y	Y	Y	Y	Y	Y
2 **Wenstrup**	+	+	+	+	+	Y
3 Beatty	N	Y	Y	N	N	?
4 **Jordan**	Y	Y	Y	Y	Y	?
5 **Latta**	Y	Y	Y	Y	Y	Y
6 **Johnson**	Y	Y	Y	Y	Y	Y
7 **Gibbs**	Y	Y	Y	Y	Y	Y
8 **Davidson**	Y	Y	Y	Y	Y	N
9 Kaptur	N	Y	Y	N	N	Y
10 **Turner**	Y	Y	Y	Y	Y	Y
11 Fudge	?	?	?	?	?	?
12 Balderson	Y	Y	Y	Y	Y	Y
13 Ryan	N	Y	Y	N	N	Y
14 **Joyce**	Y	Y	Y	N	Y	Y
15 **Stivers**	Y	Y	Y	Y	Y	Y
16 **Renacci**	?	?	?	?	?	?
OKLAHOMA						
1 Hern	Y	Y	Y	N	Y	Y
2 **Mullin**	Y	Y	Y	N	Y	Y
3 **Lucas**	Y	Y	Y	N	Y	Y
4 **Cole**	Y	Y	Y	Y	Y	Y
5 **Russell**	?	?	?	?	?	Y
OREGON						
1 Bonamici	N	Y	Y	N	N	Y
2 **Walden**	Y	Y	Y	N	Y	Y
3 Blumenauer	?	?	?	?	?	?
4 DeFazio	N	Y	Y	N	N	Y
5 Schrader	Y	Y	Y	N	Y	Y
PENNSYLVANIA						
1 Brady	N	Y	Y	N	N	?
2 Evans	N	Y	Y	N	N	Y
3 **Kelly**	Y	Y	Y	Y	Y	Y
4 **Perry**	Y	Y	Y	Y	Y	N
5 **Thompson**	Y	Y	Y	Y	Y	Y
6 **Costello**	Y	Y	Y	N	Y	Y
7 Scanlon	N	Y	Y	N	N	Y
8 **Fitzpatrick**	Y	Y	Y	N	Y	Y
9 **Shuster**	?	?	?	?	?	?
10 **Marino**	Y	Y	Y	Y	Y	Y
11 **Barletta**	?	?	?	?	?	?
12 **Rothfus**	Y	Y	Y	Y	Y	Y
13 Boyle	N	Y	Y	N	N	Y
14 Doyle	N	Y	Y	N	N	Y
15 Wild	N	Y	Y	N	N	Y
16 **Smucker**	Y	Y	Y	Y	Y	Y
17 Cartwright	N	Y	Y	N	N	Y
18 Lamb	N	Y	Y	N	N	Y
RHODE ISLAND						
1 Cicilline	N	Y	Y	N	N	Y
2 Langevin	N	Y	Y	N	N	Y
SOUTH CAROLINA						
1 **Sanford**	N	N	P	Y	Y	Y
2 **Wilson**	Y	Y	Y	Y	Y	Y
3 **Duncan**	Y	Y	Y	Y	N	N
4 **Gowdy**	?	?	?	?	?	?
5 **Norman**	Y	Y	Y	N	Y	N
6 Clyburn	N	Y	Y	N	N	Y
7 **Rice**	Y	Y	P	Y	Y	Y
SOUTH DAKOTA						
AL **Noem**	?	?	?	?	?	?
TENNESSEE						
1 **Roe**	Y	Y	Y	Y	Y	Y
2 **Duncan**	Y	Y	Y	N	Y	?
3 **Fleischmann**	Y	Y	Y	N	Y	Y
4 **DesJarlais**	Y	Y	Y	Y	Y	N
5 Cooper	N	Y	Y	N	N	Y
6 **Black**	?	?	?	?	?	?
7 **Blackburn**	?	?	?	?	?	?
8 **Kustoff**	Y	Y	Y	Y	Y	Y
9 Cohen	N	Y	Y	N	N	Y

	494	495	496	497	498	499
TEXAS						
1 **Gohmert**	Y	Y	Y	Y	Y	Y
2 **Poe**	?	?	?	?	?	?
3 **Johnson, S.**	Y	Y	Y	Y	Y	?
4 **Ratcliffe**	?	?	?	?	?	?
5 **Hensarling**	Y	Y	Y	Y	Y	N
6 **Barton**	Y	Y	Y	Y	Y	?
7 **Culberson**	Y	Y	Y	Y	Y	Y
8 **Brady**	Y	Y	Y	Y	Y	Y
9 Green, A.	N	Y	Y	N	N	Y
10 **McCaul**	Y	Y	Y	Y	Y	Y
11 **Conaway**	Y	Y	Y	N	Y	Y
12 **Granger**	Y	Y	Y	Y	Y	Y
13 **Thornberry**	Y	Y	Y	Y	Y	Y
14 **Weber**	Y	Y	Y	Y	Y	Y
15 Gonzalez	N	Y	Y	N	N	Y
16 O'Rourke	N	Y	Y	N	N	Y
17 **Flores**	Y	Y	Y	Y	Y	Y
18 Jackson Lee	N	Y	Y	N	N	Y
19 **Arrington**	?	?	?	?	?	?
20 Castro	N	Y	Y	N	N	Y
21 **Smith**	?	?	?	?	?	?
22 **Olson**	Y	Y	Y	Y	Y	Y
23 **Hurd**	Y	Y	Y	Y	Y	Y
24 Marchant	Y	Y	Y	Y	Y	Y
25 **Williams**	Y	Y	Y	Y	Y	N
26 **Burgess**	Y	Y	Y	Y	Y	N
27 Cloud	Y	Y	Y	Y	Y	Y
28 Cuellar	N	Y	Y	N	N	Y
29 Green, G.	?	?	?	?	?	?
30 Johnson, E.B.	?	?	?	?	?	?
31 **Carter**	Y	Y	Y	Y	Y	Y
32 **Sessions**	Y	Y	Y	Y	Y	Y
33 Veasey	N	Y	Y	N	N	Y
34 Vela	N	Y	Y	N	N	Y
35 Doggett	N	Y	Y	N	N	Y
36 **Babin**	Y	Y	Y	Y	Y	Y
UTAH						
1 **Bishop**	Y	Y	Y	Y	Y	Y
2 **Stewart**	Y	Y	Y	N	Y	N
3 **Curtis**	Y	Y	Y	Y	Y	Y
4 **Love**	?	?	?	?	?	?
VERMONT						
AL Welch	N	Y	Y	N	N	Y
VIRGINIA						
1 **Wittman**	Y	Y	Y	Y	Y	Y
2 **Taylor**	?	?	?	?	?	?
3 Scott	N	Y	Y	N	N	Y
4 McEachin	N	Y	Y	N	N	Y
5 **Garrett**	Y	Y	?	N	Y	Y
6 **Goodlatte**	Y	Y	Y	Y	Y	Y
7 **Brat**	Y	Y	Y	Y	Y	Y
8 Beyer	Y	Y	Y	N	N	Y
9 **Griffith**	Y	Y	Y	Y	N	Y
10 **Comstock**	Y	Y	Y	Y	Y	Y
11 Connolly	N	Y	Y	N	N	Y
WASHINGTON						
1 DelBene	N	Y	Y	N	N	Y
2 Larsen	N	Y	Y	N	N	Y
3 **Herrera Beutler**	Y	Y	Y	Y	N	Y
4 **Newhouse**	Y	Y	Y	Y	Y	Y
5 **McMorris Rodgers**	Y	Y	Y	Y	Y	Y
6 Kilmer	N	Y	Y	N	N	Y
7 Jayapal	N	Y	Y	N	N	Y
8 **Reichert**	Y	Y	Y	Y	?	?
9 Smith	N	Y	Y	N	N	Y
10 Heck	N	Y	Y	N	N	Y
WEST VIRGINIA						
1 **McKinley**	Y	Y	Y	Y	Y	Y
2 **Mooney**	Y	Y	N	Y	Y	N
3 **Vacant**						
WISCONSIN						
1 **Ryan**						
2 Pocan	N	Y	Y	N	N	Y
3 Kind	?	?	?	?	?	?
4 Moore	N	Y	Y	N	N	Y
5 **Sensenbrenner**	Y	Y	Y	N	Y	N
6 **Grothman**	Y	Y	N	Y	Y	Y
7 **Duffy**	Y	Y	Y	Y	Y	N
8 **Gallagher**	Y	Y	Y	N	Y	N
WYOMING						
AL **Cheney**	?	?	?	?	?	Y

VOTE NUMBER

500. S3628. FLOOD INSURANCE EXTENSION/PASSAGE. MacArthur, R-N.J., motion to suspend the rules and pass the bill that would extend the authorization and authorities under the National Flood Insurance Program through through May 31, 2019. The program is administered by the Federal Emergency Management Agency and offers federally-backed flood insurance to individuals and entities in communities that adopt certain flood plain management standards. Motion agreed to 315-48: R 152-47; D 163-1. Dec. 21, 2018.

	500
ALABAMA	
1 **Byrne**	Y
2 **Roby**	Y
3 **Rogers**	Y
4 **Aderholt**	Y
5 **Brooks**	N
6 **Palmer**	N
7 Sewell	Y
ALASKA	
AL **Young**	Y
ARIZONA	
1 O'Halleran	Y
2 **McSally**	Y
3 Grijalva	Y
4 **Gosar**	N
5 **Biggs**	N
6 **Schweikert**	N
7 Gallego	Y
8 **Lesko**	N
9 Sinema	?
ARKANSAS	
1 **Crawford**	Y
2 **Hill**	N
3 **Womack**	Y
4 **Westerman**	N
CALIFORNIA	
1 **LaMalfa**	Y
2 Huffman	Y
3 Garamendi	?
4 **McClintock**	N
5 Thompson	Y
6 Matsui	Y
7 Bera	Y
8 **Cook**	Y
9 McNerney	Y
10 **Denham**	?
11 DeSaulnier	Y
12 Pelosi	Y
13 Lee	Y
14 Speier	Y
15 Swalwell	Y
16 Costa	?
17 Khanna	Y
18 Eshoo	?
19 Lofgren	Y
20 Panetta	Y
21 **Valadao**	Y
22 **Nunes**	Y
23 **McCarthy**	Y
24 Carbajal	?
25 **Knight**	Y
26 Brownley	Y
27 Chu	Y
28 Schiff	Y
29 Cardenas	Y
30 Sherman	Y
31 Aguilar	Y
32 Napolitano	Y
33 Lieu	Y
34 Gomez	Y
35 Torres	Y
36 Ruiz	Y
37 Bass	?
38 Sánchez, Linda	Y
39 **Royce**	Y
40 Roybal-Allard	Y
41 Takano	Y
42 **Calvert**	Y
43 Waters	Y
44 Barragan	Y
45 **Walters**	?
46 Correa	?
47 Lowenthal	?
48 **Rohrabacher**	Y
49 **Issa**	Y
50 **Hunter**	Y
51 Vargas	Y
52 Peters	Y
53 Davis	Y

	500
COLORADO	
1 DeGette	Y
2 Polis	?
3 **Tipton**	Y
4 **Buck**	?
5 **Lamborn**	Y
6 **Coffman**	Y
7 Perlmutter	Y
CONNECTICUT	
1 Larson	?
2 Courtney	Y
3 DeLauro	?
4 Himes	Y
5 Esty	Y
DELAWARE	
AL Blunt Rochester	Y
FLORIDA	
1 **Gaetz**	Y
2 **Dunn**	Y
3 **Yoho**	N
4 **Rutherford**	Y
5 Lawson	Y
6 **Vacant**	
7 Murphy	Y
8 **Posey**	+
9 Soto	Y
10 Demings	Y
11 **Webster**	?
12 **Bilirakis**	Y
13 Crist	Y
14 Castor	Y
15 **Ross**	?
16 **Buchanan**	Y
17 **Rooney, T.**	?
18 **Mast**	Y
19 **Rooney, F.**	?
20 Hastings	?
21 Frankel	Y
22 Deutch	Y
23 Wasserman Schultz	
24 Wilson	Y
25 **Diaz-Balart**	Y
26 **Curbelo**	Y
27 **Ros-Lehtinen**	Y
GEORGIA	
1 **Carter**	Y
2 Bishop	Y
3 **Ferguson**	Y
4 Johnson	Y
5 Lewis	Y
6 **Handel**	Y
7 **Woodall**	Y
8 **Scott, A.**	Y
9 **Collins**	Y
10 **Hice**	N
11 **Loudermilk**	Y
12 **Allen**	Y
13 Scott, D.	Y
14 **Graves**	Y
HAWAII	
1 Hanabusa	?
2 Gabbard	Y
IDAHO	
1 **Labrador**	?
2 **Simpson**	Y
ILLINOIS	
1 Rush	Y
2 Kelly	Y
3 Lipinski	Y
4 Gutierrez	?
5 Quigley	Y
6 **Roskam**	?
7 Davis, D.	Y
8 Krishnamoorthi	Y
9 Schakowsky	Y
10 Schneider	Y
11 Foster	Y
12 **Bost**	Y
13 **Davis, R.**	Y

District	Member	500
14	**Hultgren**	?
15	**Shimkus**	Y
16	**Kinzinger**	Y
17	Bustos	Y
18	**LaHood**	Y
INDIANA		
1	Visclosky	Y
2	**Walorski**	Y
3	**Banks**	Y
4	Rokita	N
5	**Brooks**	Y
6	**Messer**	?
7	Carson	Y
8	**Bucshon**	Y
9	**Hollingsworth**	N
IOWA		
1	**Blum**	?
2	Loebsack	Y
3	**Young**	Y
4	**King**	Y
KANSAS		
1	**Marshall**	Y
2	**Jenkins**	?
3	**Yoder**	Y
4	**Estes**	Y
KENTUCKY		
1	**Comer**	Y
2	**Guthrie**	Y
3	Yarmuth	Y
4	**Massie**	N
5	**Rogers**	Y
6	**Barr**	N
LOUISIANA		
1	**Scalise**	Y
2	Richmond	Y
3	**Higgins**	Y
4	**Johnson**	Y
5	**Abraham**	Y
6	**Graves**	Y
MAINE		
1	Pingree	Y
2	**Poliquin**	Y
MARYLAND		
1	**Harris**	Y
2	Ruppersberger	Y
3	Sarbanes	Y
4	Brown	Y
5	Hoyer	Y
6	Delaney	Y
7	Cummings	Y
8	Raskin	Y
MASSACHUSETTS		
1	Neal	Y
2	McGovern	Y
3	Tsongas	Y
4	Kennedy	Y
5	Clark	Y
6	Moulton	Y
7	Capuano	?
8	Lynch	Y
9	Keating	?
MICHIGAN		
1	**Bergman**	Y
2	**Huizenga**	N
3	*Amash*	N
4	**Moolenaar**	Y
5	Kildee	Y
6	**Upton**	Y
7	**Walberg**	N
8	**Bishop**	Y
9	Levin	Y
10	**Mitchell**	Y
11	**Trott**	Y
12	Dingell	Y
13	Jones	Y
14	Lawrence	Y
MINNESOTA		
1	Walz	?
2	**Lewis**	?
3	**Paulsen**	Y
4	McCollum	Y
5	Ellison	?
6	**Emmer**	Y
7	Peterson	Y
8	Nolan	?
MISSISSIPPI		
1	**Kelly**	Y
2	Thompson	Y
3	**Harper**	Y
4	**Palazzo**	Y
MISSOURI		
1	Clay	Y
2	**Wagner**	?
3	**Luetkemeyer**	N
4	**Hartzler**	Y
5	Cleaver	Y
6	**Graves**	Y
7	**Long**	Y
8	**Smith**	N
MONTANA		
AL	**Gianforte**	Y
NEBRASKA		
1	**Fortenberry**	Y
2	**Bacon**	Y
3	**Smith**	Y
NEVADA		
1	Titus	Y
2	**Amodei**	Y
3	Rosen	+
4	Kihuen	Y
NEW HAMPSHIRE		
1	Shea-Porter	+
2	Kuster	Y
NEW JERSEY		
1	Norcross	Y
2	**LoBiondo**	Y
3	**MacArthur**	Y
4	**Smith**	Y
5	Gottheimer	Y
6	Pallone	Y
7	**Lance**	Y
8	Sires	Y
9	Pascrell	Y
10	Payne	Y
11	**Frelinghuysen**	Y
12	Watson Coleman	Y
NEW MEXICO		
1	Lujan Grisham	?
2	**Pearce**	N
3	Luján	Y
NEW YORK		
1	**Zeldin**	Y
2	**King**	Y
3	Suozzi	Y
4	Rice	Y
5	Meeks	Y
6	Meng	Y
7	Velázquez	?
8	Jeffries	Y
9	Clarke	Y
10	Nadler	Y
11	**Donovan**	Y
12	Maloney, C.	Y
13	Espaillat	Y
14	Crowley	?
15	Serrano	?
16	Engel	Y
17	Lowey	Y
18	Maloney, S.P.	Y
19	**Faso**	Y
20	Tonko	Y
21	**Stefanik**	Y
22	**Tenney**	Y
23	**Reed**	Y
24	**Katko**	Y
25	Morelle	Y
26	Higgins	Y
27	**Collins**	Y
NORTH CAROLINA		
1	**Butterfield**	Y
2	**Holding**	Y
3	**Jones**	?
4	Price	Y
5	**Foxx**	N
6	**Walker**	N
7	**Rouzer**	Y
8	**Hudson**	N
9	**Pittenger**	?
9	Vacant	
10	**McHenry**	Y
11	**Meadows**	N
12	**Adams**	Y
13	**Budd**	N
NORTH DAKOTA		
AL	**Cramer**	Y
OHIO		
1	**Chabot**	N
2	**Wenstrup**	N
3	Beatty	?
4	**Jordan**	N
5	**Latta**	N
6	**Johnson**	Y
7	**Gibbs**	Y
8	**Davidson**	N
9	Kaptur	Y
10	**Turner**	Y
11	Fudge	?
12	Balderson	Y
13	Ryan	Y
14	**Joyce**	Y
15	**Stivers**	Y
16	**Renacci**	?
OKLAHOMA		
1	**Hern**	Y
2	**Mullin**	Y
3	**Lucas**	Y
4	**Cole**	Y
5	**Russell**	Y
OREGON		
1	**Bonamici**	Y
2	**Walden**	Y
3	Blumenauer	?
4	DeFazio	Y
5	Schrader	Y
PENNSYLVANIA		
1	Brady	?
2	Evans	Y
3	**Kelly**	Y
4	**Perry**	Y
5	**Thompson**	Y
6	**Costello**	Y
7	Scanlon	Y
8	**Fitzpatrick**	Y
9	**Shuster**	?
10	**Marino**	Y
11	**Barletta**	?
12	**Rothfus**	N
13	**Boyle**	Y
14	**Doyle**	Y
15	**Wild**	Y
16	**Smucker**	Y
17	**Cartwright**	Y
18	**Lamb**	Y
RHODE ISLAND		
1	**Cicilline**	Y
2	**Langevin**	Y
South Carolina		
1	**Sanford**	Y
2	**Wilson**	Y
3	**Duncan**	N
4	**Gowdy**	?
5	**Norman**	N
6	Clyburn	Y
7	**Rice**	Y
SOUTH DAKOTA		
AL	**Noem**	?
TENNESSEE		
1	**Roe**	Y
2	**Duncan**	?
3	**Fleischmann**	Y
4	**DesJarlais**	N
5	Cooper	Y
6	**Black**	?
7	**Blackburn**	?
8	**Kustoff**	Y
9	Cohen	Y
TEXAS		
1	**Gohmert**	N
2	**Poe**	?
3	**Johnson, S.**	?
4	**Ratcliffe**	?
5	**Hensarling**	N
6	**Barton**	?
7	**Culberson**	Y
8	**Brady**	?
9	Green, A.	Y
10	**McCaul**	Y
11	**Conaway**	N
12	**Granger**	Y
13	**Thornberry**	Y
14	**Weber**	Y
15	Gonzalez	Y
16	O'Rourke	Y
17	**Flores**	Y
18	Jackson Lee	Y
19	**Arrington**	?
20	Castro	Y
21	**Smith**	Y
22	**Olson**	Y
23	**Hurd**	Y
24	Marchant	Y
25	**Williams**	N
26	**Burgess**	Y
27	Cloud	N
28	Cuellar	Y
29	Green, G.	?
30	Johnson, E.B.	?
31	**Carter**	Y
32	**Sessions**	Y
33	Veasey	Y
34	Vela	Y
35	Doggett	Y
36	**Babin**	Y
UTAH		
1	**Bishop**	Y
2	**Stewart**	N
3	**Curtis**	Y
4	**Love**	?
VERMONT		
AL	Welch	Y
VIRGINIA		
1	**Wittman**	Y
2	**Taylor**	?
3	Scott	Y
4	McEachin	Y
5	**Garrett**	N
6	**Goodlatte**	Y
7	**Brat**	N
8	Beyer	Y
9	**Griffith**	Y
10	**Comstock**	Y
11	Connolly	N
WASHINGTON		
1	DelBene	Y
2	Larsen	Y
3	**Herrera Beutler**	Y
4	**Newhouse**	Y
5	**McMorris Rodgers**	Y
6	Kilmer	Y
7	Jayapal	Y
8	**Reichert**	?
9	Smith	Y
10	Heck	Y
WEST VIRGINIA		
1	**McKinley**	Y
2	**Mooney**	N
3	Vacant	
WISCONSIN		
1	**Ryan**	
2	Pocan	Y
3	Kind	?
4	Moore	Y
5	**Sensenbrenner**	N
6	**Grothman**	Y
7	**Duffy**	N
8	**Gallagher**	N
WYOMING		
AL	**Cheney**	Y

CQ

SENATE ROLL CALL VOTES

Senate Roll Call Index by Subject

Senate Roll Call Index by Bill Number

VOTE NUMBER

1. ROOD NOMINATION/CONFIRMATION. Confirmation of President Donald Trump's nomination of John C. Rood of Arizona to be undersecretary of Defense for policy. Confirmed 81-7: R 40-0; D 40-6. Jan. 03, 2018.

2. CAMPBELL NOMINATION/CLOTURE. Motion to invoke cloture (thus limiting debate) on the nomination of William L. Campbell Jr. of Tennessee to be U.S. district judge for the Middle District of Tennessee. Motion agreed to 89-1: R 43-0; D 44-1. Jan. 8, 2018.

3. CAMPBELL NOMINATION/CONFIRMATION. Confirmation of President Donald Trump's nomination of William L. Campbell Jr. of Tennessee to be U.S. district judge for the Middle District of Tennessee. Confirmed 97-0: R 48-0; D 47-0. Jan. 9, 2018.

4. PARKER NOMINATION/CLOTURE. Motion to invoke cloture (thus limiting debate) on the nomination of Thomas Lee Robinson Parker of Tennessee to be U.S. district judge for the Western District of Tennessee. Motion agreed to 96-1: R 48-0; D 46-1. Jan. 9, 2018.

5. PARKER NOMINATION/CONFIRMATION. Confirmation of President Donald Trump's nomination of Thomas Lee Robinson Parker of Tennessee to be U.S. district judge for the Western District of Tennessee. Confirmed 98-0: R 50-0; D 46-0. Jan. 10, 2018.

6. BROWN NOMINATION/CLOTURE. Motion to invoke cloture (thus limiting debate) on the nomination of Michael L. Brown of Georgia to be U.S. district judge for the Northern District of Georgia. Motion agreed to 97-1: R 50-0; D 45-1. Jan. 10, 2018.

	1	2	3	4	5	6
ALABAMA						
Shelby	Y	Y	Y	Y	Y	Y
Jones	Y	Y	Y	Y	Y	Y
ALASKA						
Murkowski	?	Y	Y	Y	Y	Y
Sullivan	Y	Y	Y	Y	Y	Y
ARIZONA						
McCain	?	?	?	?	?	?
Flake	Y	Y	Y	Y	Y	Y
ARKANSAS						
Boozman	Y	Y	Y	Y	Y	Y
Cotton	Y	Y	Y	Y	Y	Y
CALIFORNIA						
Feinstein	Y	Y	Y	Y	Y	Y
Harris	N	Y	Y	Y	Y	Y
COLORADO						
Bennet	Y	Y	Y	Y	Y	Y
Gardner	Y	Y	Y	Y	Y	Y
CONNECTICUT						
Blumenthal	Y	Y	Y	Y	Y	Y
Murphy	Y	Y	Y	Y	Y	Y
DELAWARE						
Carper	Y	Y	Y	Y	Y	Y
Coons	Y	Y	Y	Y	Y	Y
FLORIDA						
Nelson	Y	Y	Y	Y	Y	Y
Rubio	+	Y	Y	Y	Y	Y
GEORGIA						
Isakson	Y	?	?	?	Y	Y
Perdue	?	?	Y	Y	Y	Y
HAWAII						
Schatz	Y	Y	Y	Y	Y	Y
Hirono	Y	N	Y	N	Y	N
IDAHO						
Crapo	Y	Y	Y	Y	Y	Y
Risch	+	Y	Y	Y	Y	Y
ILLINOIS						
Durbin	Y	Y	Y	Y	Y	Y
Duckworth	Y	Y	Y	Y	Y	Y
INDIANA						
Donnelly	Y	?	Y	Y	Y	Y
Young	Y	Y	Y	Y	Y	Y
IOWA						
Grassley	Y	Y	Y	Y	Y	Y
Ernst	Y	Y	Y	Y	Y	Y
KANSAS						
Roberts	Y	?	Y	Y	Y	Y
Moran	?	Y	Y	Y	Y	Y
KENTUCKY						
McConnell	Y	Y	Y	Y	Y	Y
Paul	Y	Y	Y	Y	Y	Y
LOUISIANA						
Cassidy	Y	Y	Y	Y	Y	Y
Kennedy	Y	Y	Y	Y	Y	Y
MAINE						
Collins	Y	Y	Y	Y	Y	Y
King	Y	Y	Y	Y	Y	Y
MARYLAND						
Cardin	Y	Y	Y	Y	Y	Y
Van Hollen	Y	Y	Y	Y	Y	Y
MASSACHUSETTS						
Warren	N	Y	Y	Y	Y	Y
Markey	N	Y	Y	Y	Y	Y
MICHIGAN						
Stabenow	Y	Y	Y	Y	Y	Y
Peters	Y	Y	Y	Y	Y	Y
MINNESOTA						
Klobuchar	Y	Y	Y	Y	Y	Y
Smith	Y	Y	Y	Y	Y	Y
MISSISSIPPI						
Cochran	Y	Y	Y	Y	Y	Y
Wicker	Y	Y	Y	Y	Y	Y
MISSOURI						
McCaskill	Y	Y	Y	Y	Y	Y
Blunt	Y	Y	Y	Y	Y	Y

	1	2	3	4	5	6
MONTANA						
Tester	Y	+	Y	Y	Y	Y
Daines	Y	Y	Y	Y	Y	Y
NEBRASKA						
Fischer	Y	Y	Y	Y	Y	Y
Sasse	Y	Y	Y	Y	Y	Y
NEVADA						
Heller	?	Y	Y	Y	Y	Y
Cortez Masto	Y	Y	Y	Y	Y	Y
NEW HAMPSHIRE						
Shaheen	Y	Y	Y	Y	Y	Y
Hassan	Y	Y	Y	Y	Y	Y
NEW JERSEY						
Menendez	Y	Y	Y	Y	Y	Y
Booker	N	Y	Y	Y	+	+
NEW MEXICO						
Udall	Y	Y	Y	Y	Y	Y
Heinrich	Y	Y	Y	Y	Y	Y
NEW YORK						
Schumer	Y	Y	Y	Y	Y	Y
Gillibrand	N	Y	Y	Y	Y	Y
NORTH CAROLINA						
Burr	?	Y	Y	Y	Y	Y
Tillis	Y	Y	Y	Y	Y	Y
NORTH DAKOTA						
Hoeven	Y	Y	Y	Y	Y	Y
Heitkamp	Y	Y	Y	Y	Y	Y
OHIO						
Brown	Y	Y	Y	Y	Y	Y
Portman	Y	Y	Y	Y	Y	Y
OKLAHOMA						
Inhofe	Y	Y	Y	Y	Y	Y
Lankford	Y	Y	Y	Y	Y	Y
OREGON						
Wyden	N	Y	Y	Y	Y	Y
Merkley	?	Y	Y	Y	Y	Y
PENNSYLVANIA						
Casey	Y	Y	Y	Y	Y	Y
Toomey	Y	?	Y	Y	Y	Y
RHODE ISLAND						
Reed	Y	Y	Y	Y	Y	Y
Whitehouse	Y	Y	Y	Y	Y	Y
SOUTH CAROLINA						
Graham	Y	Y	Y	Y	Y	Y
Scott	?	Y	Y	Y	Y	Y
SOUTH DAKOTA						
Thune	Y	Y	Y	Y	Y	Y
Rounds	Y	Y	Y	Y	Y	Y
TENNESSEE						
Alexander	+	+	Y	Y	Y	Y
Corker	Y	?	Y	Y	Y	Y
TEXAS						
Cornyn	Y	Y	Y	Y	Y	Y
Cruz	Y	?	?	?	Y	Y
UTAH						
Hatch	?	Y	Y	Y	Y	Y
Lee	Y	Y	Y	Y	Y	Y
VERMONT						
Leahy	Y	Y	Y	Y	Y	Y
Sanders	N	Y	Y	Y	Y	Y
VIRGINIA						
Warner	Y	Y	Y	Y	Y	Y
Kaine	Y	Y	Y	Y	Y	Y
WASHINGTON						
Murray	Y	Y	Y	Y	Y	Y
Cantwell	Y	Y	Y	Y	Y	Y
WEST VIRGINIA						
Manchin	Y	Y	Y	Y	Y	Y
Capito	Y	Y	Y	Y	Y	Y
WISCONSIN						
Johnson	Y	Y	Y	Y	Y	Y
Baldwin	Y	Y	Y	Y	Y	Y
WYOMING						
Enzi	Y	Y	Y	Y	Y	Y
Barrasso	Y	Y	Y	Y	Y	Y

KEY   **Republicans**   Democrats   *Independents*

Y	Voted for (yea)	X	Paired against
#	Paired for	–	Announced against
+	Announced for	P	Voted "present"
N	Voted against (nay)		

C   Voted "present" to avoid possible conflict of interest

?   Did not vote or otherwise make a position known

VOTE NUMBER

7. BROWN NOMINATION/CONFIRMATION. Confirmation of President Donald Trump's nomination of Michael L. Brown of Georgia to be U.S. district judge for the Northern District of Georgia. Confirmed 92-0: R 45-0; D 45-0. Jan. 11, 2018.

8. COUNTS NOMINATION/CLOTURE. Motion to invoke cloture (thus limiting debate) on the nomination of Walter D. Counts III of Texas to be U.S. district judge for the Western District of Texas. Motion agreed to 90-1: R 45-0; D 44-1. Jan. 11, 2018.

9. COUNTS NOMINATION/CONFIRMATION. Confirmation of President Donald Trump's nomination of Walter D. Counts III of Texas to be U.S. district judge for the Western District of Texas. Confirmed 96-0: R 48-0; D 46-0. Jan. 11, 2018.

10. S139. FISA AMENDMENTS REAUTHORIZATION/MOTION TO PROCEED. McConnell, R-Ky., motion to proceed to the House message to accompany the bill that would reauthorize for six years, through 2023, the Foreign Intelligence Surveillance Act, which governs electronic surveillance of foreign terrorism suspects. Motion agreed to 68-27: R 42-5; D 25-21. Jan. 11, 2018.

11. S139. FISA AMENDMENTS REAUTHORIZATION/CLOTURE. McConnell, R-Ky., motion to invoke cloture (thus limiting debate) in the McConnell motion to concur in the House amendment to the bill that would reauthorize for six years, through 2023, the Foreign Intelligence Surveillance Act, which governs electronic surveillance of foreign terrorism suspects. Motion agreed to 60-38: R 41-8; D 18-29. Jan. 16, 2018.

12. S139. FISA AMENDMENTS REAUTHORIZATION/MOTION TO CONCUR. McConnell, R-Ky., motion to concur in the House amendment to the bill that would reauthorize for six years, through 2023, the Foreign Intelligence Surveillance Act, which governs electronic surveillance of foreign terrorism suspects.The bill would reauthorize Section 702 surveillance authorities on foreign targets, and would require the development of procedures for searching the Section 702 database that would protect the Fourth Amendment rights of U.S. citizens. The bill would prohibit the FBI from accessing information without an order from the secret FISA court in certain cases. The measure would increase penalties for the unauthorized removal of classified documents or information. Motion agreed to 65-34: R 43-7; D 21-26. Jan. 18, 2018.

	7	8	9	10	11	12
ALABAMA						
Shelby	Y	Y	Y	Y	Y	Y
Jones	Y	Y	Y	Y	Y	Y
ALASKA						
Murkowski	Y	Y	Y	Y	N	N
Sullivan	Y	Y	Y	?	N	N
ARIZONA						
McCain	?	?	?	?	?	?
Flake	Y	Y	Y	Y	Y	Y
ARKANSAS						
Boozman	Y	Y	Y	Y	Y	Y
Cotton	?	?	Y	Y	Y	Y
CALIFORNIA						
Feinstein	Y	Y	Y	Y	Y	Y
Harris	Y	Y	Y	N	N	N
COLORADO						
Bennet	Y	Y	Y	Y	N	N
Gardner	Y	Y	Y	N	N	N
CONNECTICUT						
Blumenthal	Y	Y	Y	Y	N	N
Murphy	Y	Y	Y	N	N	N
DELAWARE						
Carper	Y	Y	Y	Y	Y	Y
Coons	Y	Y	Y	N	N	N
FLORIDA						
Nelson	Y	Y	Y	Y	Y	Y
Rubio	Y	Y	Y	Y	Y	Y
GEORGIA						
Isakson	Y	Y	Y	Y	Y	Y
Perdue	?	?	Y	Y	Y	Y
HAWAII						
Schatz	Y	Y	Y	N	N	N
Hirono	Y	N	Y	N	N	N
IDAHO						
Crapo	Y	Y	Y	Y	Y	Y
Risch	Y	Y	Y	Y	Y	Y
ILLINOIS						
Durbin	+	+	Y	N	N	N
Duckworth	Y	Y	Y	Y	Y	Y
INDIANA						
Donnelly	Y	Y	Y	Y	Y	Y
Young	Y	Y	Y	Y	Y	Y
IOWA						
Grassley	Y	Y	Y	Y	Y	Y
Ernst	Y	Y	Y	Y	Y	Y
KANSAS						
Roberts	Y	Y	Y	Y	Y	Y
Moran	Y	Y	Y	N	N	Y
KENTUCKY						
McConnell	Y	Y	Y	Y	Y	Y
Paul	Y	Y	Y	N	N	N
LOUISIANA						
Cassidy	Y	Y	Y	Y	Y	Y
Kennedy	Y	Y	Y	Y	Y	Y
MAINE						
Collins	Y	Y	Y	Y	Y	Y
King	Y	Y	Y	Y	Y	Y
MARYLAND						
Cardin	Y	Y	Y	Y	N	N
Van Hollen	Y	Y	Y	N	N	N
MASSACHUSETTS						
Warren	Y	Y	Y	N	N	N
Markey	Y	Y	Y	N	N	N
MICHIGAN						
Stabenow	Y	Y	Y	Y	N	Y
Peters	Y	Y	Y	Y	Y	Y
MINNESOTA						
Klobuchar	Y	Y	Y	Y	Y	Y
Smith	Y	Y	Y	N	N	N
MISSISSIPPI						
Cochran	Y	Y	Y	Y	Y	Y
Wicker	Y	Y	Y	Y	Y	Y
MISSOURI						
McCaskill	Y	Y	Y	Y	Y	Y
Blunt	Y	Y	Y	Y	Y	Y
MONTANA						
Tester	Y	Y	Y	N	N	N
Daines	Y	Y	Y	N	N	N
NEBRASKA						
Fischer	Y	Y	Y	Y	Y	Y
Sasse	Y	Y	Y	Y	Y	Y
NEVADA						
Heller	?	?	?	?	N	N
Cortez Masto	Y	Y	Y	Y	Y	Y
NEW HAMPSHIRE						
Shaheen	Y	Y	Y	Y	Y	Y
Hassan	Y	Y	Y	Y	Y	Y
NEW JERSEY						
Menendez	Y	Y	Y	N	N	N
Booker	+	+	+	-	N	N
NEW MEXICO						
Udall	Y	Y	Y	N	N	N
Heinrich	Y	Y	Y	N	N	N
NEW YORK						
Schumer	Y	Y	Y	Y	N	Y
Gillibrand	Y	Y	Y	N	N	N
NORTH CAROLINA						
Burr	Y	Y	Y	Y	Y	Y
Tillis	Y	Y	Y	Y	Y	Y
NORTH DAKOTA						
Hoeven	Y	Y	Y	Y	Y	Y
Heitkamp	Y	Y	Y	Y	Y	Y
OHIO						
Brown	Y	Y	Y	N	N	N
Portman	Y	Y	Y	Y	Y	Y
OKLAHOMA						
Inhofe	Y	Y	Y	Y	Y	Y
Lankford	Y	Y	Y	Y	Y	Y
OREGON						
Wyden	Y	Y	Y	N	N	N
Merkley	Y	Y	Y	N	N	N
PENNSYLVANIA						
Casey	Y	Y	Y	Y	Y	Y
Toomey	Y	Y	Y	?	Y	Y
RHODE ISLAND						
Reed	Y	Y	Y	Y	Y	Y
Whitehouse	Y	Y	Y	Y	Y	Y
SOUTH CAROLINA						
Graham	?	?	Y	Y	Y	Y
Scott	Y	Y	Y	Y	Y	Y
SOUTH DAKOTA						
Thune	Y	Y	Y	Y	Y	Y
Rounds	Y	Y	Y	Y	Y	Y
TENNESSEE						
Alexander	+	+	+	+	Y	Y
Corker	Y	Y	Y	Y	Y	Y
TEXAS						
Cornyn	Y	Y	Y	Y	Y	Y
Cruz	Y	Y	Y	Y	N	Y
UTAH						
Hatch	Y	Y	Y	Y	Y	Y
Lee	Y	Y	Y	N	N	N
VERMONT						
Leahy	Y	Y	Y	N	N	N
Sanders	Y	?	Y	N	N	N
VIRGINIA						
Warner	Y	Y	Y	Y	Y	Y
Kaine	Y	Y	Y	Y	N	Y
WASHINGTON						
Murray	Y	Y	Y	N	N	N
Cantwell	Y	Y	Y	N	N	N
WEST VIRGINIA						
Manchin	Y	Y	Y	Y	Y	Y
Capito	Y	Y	Y	Y	Y	Y
WISCONSIN						
Johnson	Y	Y	Y	Y	Y	Y
Baldwin	Y	Y	Y	N	N	N
WYOMING						
Enzi	Y	Y	Y	Y	Y	Y
Barrasso	Y	Y	Y	Y	Y	Y

KEY   **Republicans**   Democrats   *Independents*

Y	Voted for (yea)
#	Paired for
+	Announced for
N	Voted against (nay)
X	Paired against
-	Announced against
P	Voted "present"
C	Voted "present" to avoid possible conflict of interest
?	Did not vote or otherwise make a position known

VOTE NUMBER

13. HR195. SHORT-TERM FISCAL 2018 CONTINUING APPROPRIATIONS AND CHIP FUNDING/MOTION TO PROCEED. McConnell, R-Ky., motion to proceed to the House amendment to the Senate amendment to the bill that would provide funding for federal government operations and services at current levels through Feb. 16, 2018 and would fund the state Children's Health and Insurance Programs at $21.5 billion annually through fiscal 2023. Motion agreed to 97-2: R 48-2; D 47-0. Jan. 18, 2018.

14. HR195. SHORT-TERM FISCAL 2018 CONTINUING APPROPRIATIONS AND CHIP FUNDING/CLOTURE. McConnell, R-Ky., motion to invoke cloture (thus limiting debate) on the motion to concur in the House amendment to the Senate amendment to the bill that would provide funding for federal government operations and services at current levels through Feb. 16, 2018 and would fund the state Children's Health and Insurance Programs at $21.5 billion annually through fiscal 2023. Motion rejected 50-49: R 45-5; D 5-42. Jan. 20, 2018.

15. HR195. SHORT-TERM FISCAL 2018 CONTINUING APPROPRIATIONS AND CHIP FUNDING/MOTION TO TABLE. McConnell, R-Ky., motion to table (kill) the motion to refer the House message to accompany the bill to the Senate Appropriations Committee with instructions. Motion agreed to 55-44: R 50-0; D 5-42. Jan. 20, 2018.

16. HR195. SHORT-TERM FISCAL 2018 CONTINUING APPROPRIATIONS AND CHIP FUNDING/CLOTURE. McConnell, R-Ky., motion to invoke cloture (thus limiting debate) on the McConnell motion to concur in the House amendment to the Senate amendment to the bill with McConnell amendment no. 1917 that would provide funding for federal government operations and services at current levels through Feb. 8, 2018, and fund the state Children's Health and Insurance Programs at $21.5 billion annually starting in fiscal 2018 and would gradually increase the funding annually through fiscal 2023. Motion agreed to 81-18: R 48-2; D 32-15. Jan. 22, 2018.

17. HR195. SHORT-TERM FISCAL 2018 CONTINUING APPROPRIATIONS AND CHIP FUNDING/MOTION TO CONCUR. McConnell, R-Ky., motion to concur in the House amendment to the Senate amendment to the bill with a further McConnell amendment no. 1917 that would provide funding for federal government operations and services at current levels through Feb. 8, 2018. The measure would fund the state Children's Health and Insurance Programs at $21.5 billion annually starting in fiscal 2018, and would gradually increase the funding annually through fiscal 2023. It would suspend or delay three health-related taxes enacted as part of the 2010 health care overhaul. It would allow the ballistic missile defense funding included in the last short-term funding bill to be used for certain related intelligence activities. Additionally, it would prohibit the Government Publishing Office from providing a free printed copy of the Federal Register to any member of Congress or other U.S. government office unless a specific issue or a subscription was requested by the member or office. Motion agreed to 81-18: R 48-2; D 32-15. Jan. 22, 2018.

18. POWELL NOMINATION/CLOTURE. Motion to invoke cloture (thus limiting debate) on the nomination of Jerome H. Powell of Maryland to be chairman of the Federal Reserve System Board of Governors. Motion agreed to 84-12: R 44-3; D 39-8. Jan. 23, 2018.

	13	14	15	16	17	18
ALABAMA						
Shelby	Y	Y	Y	Y	Y	Y
Jones	Y	Y	Y	Y	Y	Y
ALASKA						
Murkowski	Y	Y	Y	Y	Y	Y
Sullivan	Y	Y	Y	Y	Y	Y
ARIZONA						
McCain	?	?	?	?	?	?
Flake	Y	N	Y	Y	Y	Y
ARKANSAS						
Boozman	Y	Y	Y	Y	Y	Y
Cotton	Y	Y	Y	Y	Y	Y
CALIFORNIA						
Feinstein	Y	N	N	N	N	N
Harris	Y	N	N	N	N	N
COLORADO						
Bennet	Y	N	N	Y	Y	Y
Gardner	Y	Y	Y	Y	Y	Y
CONNECTICUT						
Blumenthal	Y	N	N	N	N	N
Murphy	Y	N	N	N	N	N
DELAWARE						
Carper	Y	N	N	Y	Y	Y
Coons	Y	N	N	Y	Y	Y
FLORIDA						
Nelson	Y	N	N	Y	Y	Y
Rubio	Y	Y	Y	Y	Y	Y
GEORGIA						
Isakson	Y	Y	Y	Y	Y	Y
Perdue	Y	Y	Y	Y	Y	Y
HAWAII						
Schatz	Y	N	N	Y	Y	Y
Hirono	Y	N	N	N	N	Y
IDAHO						
Crapo	Y	Y	Y	Y	Y	Y
Risch	Y	Y	Y	Y	Y	Y
ILLINOIS						
Durbin	Y	N	N	Y	Y	Y
Duckworth	Y	N	N	Y	Y	Y
INDIANA						
Donnelly	Y	Y	Y	Y	Y	Y
Young	Y	Y	Y	Y	Y	Y
IOWA						
Grassley	Y	Y	Y	Y	Y	Y
Ernst	Y	Y	Y	Y	Y	Y
KANSAS						
Roberts	Y	Y	Y	Y	Y	Y
Moran	Y	Y	Y	Y	Y	Y
KENTUCKY						
McConnell	Y	N	Y	Y	Y	Y
Paul	N	N	Y	N	N	N
LOUISIANA						
Cassidy	Y	Y	Y	Y	Y	Y
Kennedy	Y	Y	Y	Y	Y	Y
MAINE						
Collins	Y	Y	Y	Y	Y	Y
King	Y	N	N	Y	Y	Y
MARYLAND						
Cardin	Y	N	N	Y	Y	Y
Van Hollen	Y	N	N	Y	Y	Y
MASSACHUSETTS						
Warren	Y	N	N	N	N	N
Markey	Y	N	N	N	N	N
MICHIGAN						
Stabenow	Y	N	N	Y	Y	Y
Peters	Y	N	N	Y	Y	Y
MINNESOTA						
Klobuchar	Y	N	N	Y	Y	Y
Smith	Y	N	N	Y	Y	Y
MISSISSIPPI						
Cochran	Y	Y	Y	Y	Y	Y
Wicker	Y	Y	Y	Y	Y	Y
MISSOURI						
McCaskill	Y	Y	Y	Y	Y	Y
Blunt	Y	Y	Y	Y	Y	Y
MONTANA						
Tester	Y	N	N	N	N	Y
Daines	Y	Y	Y	Y	Y	Y
NEBRASKA						
Fischer	Y	Y	Y	Y	Y	Y
Sasse	Y	Y	Y	Y	Y	Y
NEVADA						
Heller	Y	Y	Y	Y	Y	Y
Cortez Masto	Y	N	N	N	N	Y
NEW HAMPSHIRE						
Shaheen	Y	N	N	Y	Y	Y
Hassan	Y	N	N	Y	Y	Y
NEW JERSEY						
Menendez	Y	N	N	N	N	Y
Booker	Y	N	N	N	N	N
NEW MEXICO						
Udall	Y	N	N	Y	Y	Y
Heinrich	Y	N	N	Y	Y	Y
NEW YORK						
Schumer	Y	N	N	Y	Y	Y
Gillibrand	Y	N	N	N	N	N
NORTH CAROLINA						
Burr	Y	Y	Y	Y	Y	Y
Tillis	Y	Y	Y	Y	Y	?
NORTH DAKOTA						
Hoeven	Y	Y	Y	Y	Y	Y
Heitkamp	Y	Y	Y	Y	Y	Y
OHIO						
Brown	Y	N	N	Y	Y	Y
Portman	Y	Y	Y	Y	Y	Y
OKLAHOMA						
Inhofe	Y	Y	Y	Y	Y	Y
Lankford	Y	Y	Y	Y	Y	Y
OREGON						
Wyden	Y	N	N	N	N	N
Merkley	Y	N	N	N	N	N
PENNSYLVANIA						
Casey	Y	N	N	Y	Y	Y
Toomey	Y	Y	Y	Y	Y	Y
RHODE ISLAND						
Reed	Y	N	N	Y	Y	Y
Whitehouse	Y	N	N	Y	Y	Y
SOUTH CAROLINA						
Graham	Y	N	N	Y	Y	Y
Scott	Y	Y	Y	Y	Y	?
SOUTH DAKOTA						
Thune	Y	Y	Y	Y	Y	Y
Rounds	Y	Y	Y	Y	Y	Y
TENNESSEE						
Alexander	Y	Y	Y	Y	Y	Y
Corker	Y	Y	Y	Y	Y	?
TEXAS						
Cornyn	Y	Y	Y	Y	Y	Y
Cruz	Y	Y	Y	Y	N	N
UTAH						
Hatch	Y	Y	Y	Y	Y	Y
Lee	N	N	Y	N	N	N
VERMONT						
Leahy	Y	N	N	N	N	Y
Sanders	Y	N	N	N	N	N
VIRGINIA						
Warner	Y	N	N	Y	Y	Y
Kaine	Y	N	N	Y	Y	Y
WASHINGTON						
Murray	Y	N	N	Y	Y	Y
Cantwell	Y	N	N	Y	Y	Y
WEST VIRGINIA						
Manchin	Y	Y	Y	Y	Y	Y
Capito	Y	Y	Y	Y	Y	Y
WISCONSIN						
Johnson	Y	Y	Y	Y	Y	Y
Baldwin	Y	N	N	Y	Y	Y
WYOMING						
Enzi	Y	Y	Y	Y	Y	Y
Barrasso	Y	Y	Y	Y	Y	Y

KEY Republicans Democrats *Independents*

Y	Voted for (yea)	X	Paired against	C	Voted "present" to avoid possible conflict of interest
#	Paired for	-	Announced against	?	Did not vote or otherwise make a position known
+	Announced for	P	Voted "present"		
N	Voted against (nay)				

VOTE NUMBER

19. POWELL NOMINATION/CONFIRMATION. Confirmation of President Donald Trump's nomination of Jerome H. Powell of Maryland to be chairman of the Board of Governors of the Federal Reserve System. Confirmed 84-13: R 44-4; D 39-8. Jan. 23, 2018.

20. AZAR NOMINATION/CLOTURE. Motion to invoke cloture (thus limiting debate) on the nomination of Alex M. Azar II of Indiana to be secretary of Health and Human Services. Motion agreed to 54-43: R 47-1; D 6-41. Jan. 23, 2018.

21. AZAR NOMINATION/CONFIRMATION. Confirmation of President Donald Trump's nomination of Alex M. Azar II of Indiana to be secretary of Health and Human Services. Confirmed 55-43: R 48-1; D 6-41. Jan. 24, 2018.

22. BROWNBACK NOMINATION/CLOTURE. Motion to invoke cloture (thus limiting debate) on the nomination of Samuel D. Brownback of Kansas to be ambassador at large for International Religious Freedom. Motion agreed to 49-49: R 49-0; D 0-47. Jan. 24, 2018.

23. BROWNBACK NOMINATION/CONFIRMATION. Confirmation of President Donald Trump's nomination of Samuel D. Brownback of Kansas to be ambassador at large for International Religious Freedom. Confirmed 49-49: R 49-0; D 0-47. Jan. 24, 2018.

24. JAMES NOMINATION/CONFIRMATION. Confirmation of President Donald Trump's nomination of R. D. James of Missouri to be an assistant secretary of the Army. Confirmed 89-1: R 45-0; D 43-0. Jan. 25, 2018.

State / Senator	19	20	21	22	23	24
ALABAMA						
Shelby	Y	Y	Y	Y	Y	Y
Jones	Y	Y	Y	N	N	Y
ALASKA						
Murkowski	Y	Y	Y	Y	Y	Y
Sullivan	Y	Y	Y	Y	Y	Y
ARIZONA						
McCain	?	?	?	?	?	?
Flake	Y	Y	Y	Y	Y	Y
ARKANSAS						
Boozman	Y	Y	Y	Y	Y	Y
Cotton	Y	Y	Y	Y	Y	Y
CALIFORNIA						
Feinstein	N	N	N	N	N	Y
Harris	N	N	N	N	N	Y
COLORADO						
Bennet	Y	N	N	N	N	Y
Gardner	Y	Y	Y	Y	Y	Y
CONNECTICUT						
Blumenthal	N	N	N	N	N	?
Murphy	Y	N	N	N	N	Y
DELAWARE						
Carper	Y	Y	Y	N	N	Y
Coons	Y	Y	Y	N	N	Y
FLORIDA						
Nelson	Y	N	N	N	N	Y
Rubio	N	Y	Y	Y	Y	Y
GEORGIA						
Isakson	Y	Y	Y	Y	Y	Y
Perdue	Y	Y	Y	Y	Y	Y
HAWAII						
Schatz	Y	N	N	N	N	Y
Hirono	Y	N	N	N	N	Y
IDAHO						
Crapo	Y	Y	Y	Y	Y	Y
Risch	Y	Y	Y	Y	Y	?
ILLINOIS						
Durbin	Y	N	N	N	N	+
Duckworth	Y	N	N	N	N	Y
INDIANA						
Donnelly	Y	Y	Y	N	N	Y
Young	Y	Y	Y	Y	Y	Y
IOWA						
Grassley	Y	Y	Y	Y	Y	Y
Ernst	Y	Y	Y	Y	Y	Y
KANSAS						
Roberts	Y	Y	Y	Y	Y	Y
Moran	Y	Y	Y	Y	Y	?
KENTUCKY						
McConnell	Y	Y	Y	Y	Y	Y
Paul	N	N	N	Y	Y	Y
LOUISIANA						
Cassidy	Y	Y	Y	Y	Y	Y
Kennedy	Y	Y	Y	Y	Y	Y
MAINE						
Collins	Y	Y	Y	Y	Y	Y
King	Y	Y	Y	N	N	Y
MARYLAND						
Cardin	Y	N	N	N	N	Y
Van Hollen	Y	N	N	N	N	Y
MASSACHUSETTS						
Warren	N	N	N	N	N	Y
Markey	N	N	N	N	N	Y
MICHIGAN						
Stabenow	Y	N	N	N	N	Y
Peters	Y	N	N	N	N	Y
MINNESOTA						
Klobuchar	Y	N	N	N	N	Y
Smith	Y	N	N	N	N	Y
MISSISSIPPI						
Cochran	Y	Y	Y	Y	Y	Y
Wicker	Y	Y	Y	Y	Y	Y
MISSOURI						
McCaskill	Y	N	N	N	N	+
Blunt	Y	Y	Y	Y	Y	Y
MONTANA						
Tester	Y	N	N	N	N	Y
Daines	Y	Y	Y	Y	Y	Y
NEBRASKA						
Fischer	Y	Y	Y	Y	Y	Y
Sasse	Y	Y	Y	Y	Y	Y
NEVADA						
Heller	Y	Y	Y	Y	Y	Y
Cortez Masto	Y	N	N	N	N	Y
NEW HAMPSHIRE						
Shaheen	Y	N	N	N	N	Y
Hassan	Y	N	N	N	N	Y
NEW JERSEY						
Menendez	Y	N	N	N	N	Y
Booker	N	N	N	N	N	Y
NEW MEXICO						
Udall	Y	N	N	N	N	Y
Heinrich	Y	N	N	N	N	Y
NEW YORK						
Schumer	Y	N	N	N	N	Y
Gillibrand	N	N	N	N	N	Y
NORTH CAROLINA						
Burr	Y	Y	Y	Y	Y	?
Tillis	Y	Y	Y	Y	Y	Y
NORTH DAKOTA						
Hoeven	Y	Y	Y	Y	Y	Y
Heitkamp	Y	Y	Y	N	N	Y
OHIO						
Brown	Y	N	N	N	N	Y
Portman	Y	Y	Y	Y	Y	Y
OKLAHOMA						
Inhofe	Y	Y	Y	Y	Y	Y
Lankford	Y	Y	Y	Y	Y	Y
OREGON						
Wyden	Y	N	N	N	N	Y
Merkley	N	N	N	N	N	Y
PENNSYLVANIA						
Casey	Y	N	N	N	N	?
Toomey	Y	Y	Y	Y	Y	?
RHODE ISLAND						
Reed	Y	N	N	N	N	Y
Whitehouse	Y	N	N	N	N	Y
SOUTH CAROLINA						
Graham	Y	Y	Y	Y	Y	Y
Scott	?	?	Y	Y	Y	Y
SOUTH DAKOTA						
Thune	Y	Y	Y	Y	Y	Y
Rounds	Y	Y	Y	Y	Y	Y
TENNESSEE						
Alexander	Y	Y	Y	Y	Y	Y
Corker	?	?	?	?	?	?
TEXAS						
Cornyn	Y	Y	Y	Y	Y	Y
Cruz	N	Y	Y	Y	Y	Y
UTAH						
Hatch	Y	Y	Y	Y	Y	Y
Lee	N	Y	Y	Y	Y	Y
VERMONT						
Leahy	Y	N	N	N	N	Y
Sanders	N	N	N	N	N	N
VIRGINIA						
Warner	Y	N	N	N	N	Y
Kaine	Y	N	N	N	N	Y
WASHINGTON						
Murray	Y	N	N	N	N	Y
Cantwell	Y	N	N	N	N	Y
WEST VIRGINIA						
Manchin	Y	Y	Y	N	N	Y
Capito	Y	Y	Y	Y	Y	Y
WISCONSIN						
Johnson	Y	Y	Y	Y	Y	Y
Baldwin	Y	N	N	N	N	Y
WYOMING						
Enzi	Y	Y	Y	Y	Y	Y
Barrasso	Y	Y	Y	Y	Y	Y

KEY   **Republicans**   Democrats   *Independents*

Y Voted for (yea)	**X** Paired against	**C** Voted "present" to avoid possible conflict of interest
# Paired for	**–** Announced against	**?** Did not vote or otherwise make a position known
+ Announced for	**P** Voted "present"	
N Voted against (nay)		

VOTE NUMBER

25. S2311. TWENTY-WEEK ABORTION BAN/CLOTURE. Motion to invoke cloture (thus limiting debate) on the motion to proceed to the bill that would prohibit abortions in cases where the probable age of the fetus is 20 weeks or later and would impose criminal penalties on doctors who violate the ban, with certain exceptions. The bill would require a second doctor trained in neonatal resuscitation to be present for abortions where the fetus has the "potential" to survive outside the womb. Motion rejected 51-46: R 48-2; D 3-42. Jan. 29, 2018.

26. STRAS NOMINATION/CLOTURE. Motion to invoke cloture (thus limiting debate) on the nomination of David R. Stras of Minnesota to be a U.S circuit judge for the Eighth Circuit. Motion agreed to 57-41: R 50-0; D 7-39. Jan. 29, 2018.

27. STRAS NOMINATION/CONFIRMATION. Confirmation of President Donald Trump's nomination of David R. Stras of Minnesota to be a U.S circuit judge for the Eighth Circuit. Confirmed 56-42: R 49-0; D 7-40. Jan. 30, 2018.

28. IANCU NOMINATION/CONFIRMATION. Confirmation of President Donald Trump's nomination of Andrei Iancu of California to be under secretary of Commerce for Intellectual Property and director of the U.S. Patent and Trademark Office. Confirmed 94-0: R 47-0; D 45-0. Feb. 5, 2018.

29. HR695. FISCAL 2018 DEFENSE APPROPRIATIONS/CLOTURE. Motion to invoke cloture (thus limiting debate) on the motion to concur in the House amendment to the Senate amendment to the bill that would provide $659.2 billion in discretionary funding for the Defense Department in fiscal 2018. The total would include $584 billion in base Defense Department funding subject to spending caps. It also would include $75.1 billion in overseas contingency operations funding, $1.2 billion of which would be for additional U.S. troops in Afghanistan. The bill would provide approximately $191.7 billion for operations and maintenance and $138.2 billion for military personnel, including a 2.4 percent pay raise. It also would provide $34.3 billion for defense health programs. The measure would prohibit use of funds to construct or modify potential facilities in the United States to house Guantanamo Bay detainees. It would also make permanent a pilot program that allows volunteer groups to obtain criminal history background checks on prospective employees through a fingerprint check using state and federal records, which are the original provisions of the bill. Motion rejected 55-44: R 49-1; D 6-41. Feb. 8, 2018.

30. HR1892. FISCAL 2018 ONGOING APPROPRIATIONS PACKAGE/ CLOTURE. Motion to invoke cloture (thus limiting debate) on the motion to concur in the House amendment to the Senate amendment to the bill with McConnell amendment no. 1930 that would provide funding for federal government operations and services at current levels through March 23, 2018. Motion agreed to 73-26: R 35-15; D 37-10. Feb. 9, 2018.

	25	26	27	28	29	30			25	26	27	28	29	30
ALABAMA								**MONTANA**						
Shelby	Y	Y	Y	Y	Y	Y		Tester	N	N	N	Y	N	Y
Jones	N	Y	Y	Y	N	Y		**Daines**	Y	Y	Y	Y	Y	N
ALASKA								**NEBRASKA**						
Murkowski	N	Y	Y	Y	Y	Y		**Fischer**	Y	Y	Y	Y	Y	Y
Sullivan	Y	Y	Y	Y	Y	Y		**Sasse**	Y	Y	Y	Y	Y	Y
ARIZONA								**NEVADA**						
McCain	?	?	?	?	?	?		**Heller**	Y	Y	Y	Y	Y	Y
Flake	Y	Y	Y	Y	Y	N		Cortez Masto	N	N	N	Y	Y	Y
ARKANSAS								**NEW HAMPSHIRE**						
Boozman	Y	Y	Y	Y	Y	Y		Shaheen	N	N	N	Y	N	Y
Cotton	Y	Y	Y	Y	Y	Y		Hassan	N	N	N	Y	N	Y
CALIFORNIA								**NEW JERSEY**						
Feinstein	N	N	N	Y	N	N		Menendez	N	N	N	Y	N	N
Harris	N	N	N	Y	N	N		Booker	N	N	N	Y	N	N
COLORADO								**NEW MEXICO**						
Bennet	N	N	N	Y	N	N		Udall	N	N	N	Y	N	Y
Gardner	Y	Y	Y	Y	Y	Y		Heinrich	N	N	N	+	N	Y
CONNECTICUT								**NEW YORK**						
Blumenthal	N	N	N	Y	N	Y		Schumer	N	N	N	Y	N	Y
Murphy	N	N	N	Y	N	Y		Gillibrand	N	N	N	Y	N	Y
DELAWARE								**NORTH CAROLINA**						
Carper	N	N	N	Y	N	Y		**Burr**	Y	Y	Y	Y	N	N
Coons	N	N	N	Y	N	Y		**Tillis**	Y	Y	Y	Y	Y	Y
FLORIDA								**NORTH DAKOTA**						
Nelson	?	?	N	Y	Y	Y		**Hoeven**	Y	Y	Y	Y	Y	Y
Rubio	Y	Y	Y	Y	Y	Y		Heitkamp	N	Y	Y	Y	Y	Y
GEORGIA								**OHIO**						
Isakson	Y	Y	Y	Y	Y	Y		Brown	N	N	N	Y	N	Y
Perdue	Y	Y	Y	Y	Y	Y		Portman	Y	Y	Y	Y	Y	Y
HAWAII								**OKLAHOMA**						
Schatz	N	N	N	Y	N	Y		**Inhofe**	Y	Y	Y	Y	Y	Y
Hirono	N	N	N	Y	N	N		**Lankford**	Y	Y	Y	Y	Y	N
IDAHO								**OREGON**						
Crapo	Y	Y	Y	Y	Y	N		Wyden	N	N	N	Y	N	Y
Risch	Y	Y	Y	Y	Y	N		Merkley	N	N	N	Y	N	Y
ILLINOIS								**PENNSYLVANIA**						
Durbin	N	N	N	Y	N	Y		Casey	Y	N	N	Y	N	Y
Duckworth	N	N	N	Y	N	Y		**Toomey**	Y	Y	Y	?	Y	N
INDIANA								**RHODE ISLAND**						
Donnelly	Y	Y	Y	Y	Y	Y		Reed	N	N	N	Y	N	Y
Young	Y	Y	Y	Y	Y	Y		Whitehouse	N	N	N	Y	N	Y
IOWA								**SOUTH CAROLINA**						
Grassley	Y	Y	Y	Y	Y	N		**Graham**	Y	Y	Y	Y	N	Y
Ernst	Y	Y	Y	Y	Y	N		**Scott**	Y	Y	Y	Y	Y	Y
KANSAS								**SOUTH DAKOTA**						
Roberts	Y	Y	Y	Y	Y	Y		**Thune**	Y	Y	Y	Y	Y	Y
Moran	Y	Y	Y	Y	Y	Y		**Rounds**	Y	Y	Y	Y	Y	Y
KENTUCKY								**TENNESSEE**						
McConnell	Y	Y	Y	Y	Y	Y		**Alexander**	Y	Y	Y	+	Y	Y
Paul	Y	Y	Y	Y	N	N		**Corker**	Y	Y	Y	Y	Y	N
LOUISIANA								**TEXAS**						
Cassidy	Y	Y	Y	Y	Y	Y		**Cornyn**	Y	Y	Y	Y	Y	Y
Kennedy	Y	Y	Y	Y	Y	Y		**Cruz**	Y	Y	Y	Y	Y	Y
MAINE								**UTAH**						
Collins	N	Y	Y	Y	Y	Y		**Hatch**	Y	Y	Y	Y	Y	Y
King	N	N	N	Y	N	Y		**Lee**	Y	Y	Y	Y	Y	N
MARYLAND								**VERMONT**						
Cardin	N	N	N	Y	N	Y		Leahy	N	N	N	Y	N	Y
Van Hollen	N	N	N	Y	N	Y		*Sanders*	N	N	N	Y	N	N
MASSACHUSETTS								**VIRGINIA**						
Warren	N	N	N	Y	N	N		Warner	N	Y	Y	Y	N	Y
Markey	N	N	N	Y	N	N		Kaine	N	N	N	Y	N	Y
MICHIGAN								**WASHINGTON**						
Stabenow	N	N	N	Y	N	Y		Murray	N	N	N	Y	N	Y
Peters	N	N	N	?	N	Y		Cantwell	N	N	N	Y	N	N
MINNESOTA								**WEST VIRGINIA**						
Klobuchar	N	Y	Y	Y	N	Y		Manchin	Y	Y	Y	Y	Y	Y
Smith	N	N	N	Y	N	Y		**Capito**	Y	Y	?	Y	Y	Y
MISSISSIPPI								**WISCONSIN**						
Cochran	Y	Y	Y	?	Y	Y		**Johnson**	Y	Y	Y	Y	Y	N
Wicker	Y	Y	Y	Y	Y	Y		Baldwin	?	N	N	Y	N	Y
MISSOURI								**WYOMING**						
McCaskill	N	Y	Y	Y	Y	Y		**Enzi**	Y	Y	Y	Y	Y	N
Blunt	Y	Y	Y	Y	Y	Y		**Barrasso**	Y	Y	Y	Y	Y	Y

KEY   **Republicans**   Democrats   *Independents*

Y	Voted for (yea)	X	Paired against	C	Voted "present" to avoid possible conflict of interest
#	Paired for	–	Announced against		
+	Announced for	P	Voted "present"	?	Did not vote or otherwise make a position known
N	Voted against (nay)				

VOTE NUMBER

31. HR1892. FISCAL 2018 ONGOING APPROPRIATIONS PACKAGE/ MOTION TO CONCUR. McConnell, R-Ky., motion to concur in the House amendment to the Senate amendment to the bill with McConnell amendment no. 1930 that would provide funding for federal government operations and services at current levels through March 23, 2018. The bill, as amended, would increase defense spending caps to $629 billion for fiscal 2018 and $647 billion for fiscal 2019, and would increase non-defense spending caps by $63 billion in fiscal 2018 and $68 billion in fiscal 2019. It would suspend the debt ceiling through March 1, 2019, and would provide $89.3 billion in emergency supplemental funding including $23.5 billion in funding for the Federal Emergency Management Agency Disaster Relief Fund, $28 billion in funding to the Department of Housing and Urban Development Community Development Fund, and $4.9 billion in additional Medicaid funding for Puerto Rico and the U.S. Virgin Islands. It would authorize funding for community health centers through fiscal 2019, and would provide for an additional authorization of the Children's Health Insurance Program from fiscal 2023 to fiscal 2027. The underlying bill would allow the governor of a state, territory, possession or the mayor of the District of Columbia to order that the United States flag be flown at half-staff to honor the death of a first responder who dies while serving in the line of duty. Motion agreed to 71-28: R 34-16; D 36-11. Feb. 9, 2018.

32. HR2579. LEGISLATIVE VEHICLE FOR IMMIGRATION OVERHAUL MEASURES/CLOTURE. Motion to invoke cloture (thus limiting debate) on the McConnell, R-Ky., motion to proceed to the bill that would modify the definition of a "qualified health plan" to allow, beginning in 2020, for new tax credits proposed by the American Health Care Act (HR 1628) to be used by individuals or families to pay for continued group health coverage under CO-BRA, provided that the AHCA is enacted into law. The bill is intended to serve as the legislative vehicle for immigration overhaul measures. Motion agreed to 97-1: R 49-1; D 46-0. Feb. 12, 2018.

33. HR2579. LEGISLATIVE VEHICLE FOR IMMIGRATION OVERHAUL MEASURES/CLOTURE. Motion to invoke cloture (thus limiting debate) on the Durbin, D-Ill., for Coons, D-Del., amendment no. 1955 to Schumer, D-N.Y., amendment no. 1958, to the bill that would provide conditional permanent residence to recipients of the Deferred Action for Childhood Arrivals immigration program if they meet certain qualifications, and would authorize $110 million annually, for fiscal 2018 through fiscal 2022, for grants for border security activities in states with international or maritime borders. It would also authorize the construction of additional ports of entry along U.S. borders and would create temporary immigration judge and Board of Immigration Appeals staff attorney positions, to exist through fiscal 2020. Motion rejected 52-47: R 4-46; D 46-1. Feb. 15, 2018.

34. HR2579. LEGISLATIVE VEHICLE FOR IMMIGRATION OVERHAUL MEASURES/CLOTURE. Motion to invoke cloture (thus limiting debate) on the McConnell, R-Ky., for Toomey, R-Pa., amendment no. 1948 to Grassley, R-Iowa, amendment no. 1959 to the bill, that would prohibit certain economic development grant funding from being provided to a ""sanctuary jurisdiction." which would be defined as a state, or political subdivision of a state, that has a statute, policy or practice which prohibits or restricts any government entity or official from sharing information related to an individual's immigration status with a federal, state or local entity. Motion rejected 54-45: R 50-0; D 4-43. Feb. 15, 2018.

35. HR2579. LEGISLATIVE VEHICLE FOR IMMIGRATION OVERHAUL MEASURES/CLOTURE. Motion to invoke cloture (thus limiting debate) on the Schumer, D-N.Y., amendment no. 1958, as modified, to the language proposed to be stricken by Grassley, R-Iowa, amendment no. 1959, to the bill that would appropriate $25 billion, to be available from fiscal 2019 through 2027, for various border security purposes, such as physical barriers, technology and facilities. It would prohibit the deportation of recipients of the Deferred Action for Childhood Arrivals immigration program if they meet certain qualifications, and would reduce the cap on family-sponsored immigrant visas. It would require the Homeland Security Department to prioritize the enforcement of immigration activities for aliens that have committed felonies or misdemeanors, and those who are unlawfully present in the United States and arrived after June 30, 2018. Motion rejected 54-45: R 8-42; D 44-3. Feb. 15, 2018.

	31	32	33	34	35	36
ALABAMA						
Shelby	Y	Y	N	Y	N	Y
Jones	Y	Y	Y	N	Y	N
ALASKA						
Murkowski	Y	Y	Y	Y	Y	Y
Sullivan	Y	Y	N	Y	N	Y
ARIZONA						
McCain	?	?	?	?	?	?
Flake	N	Y	Y	Y	Y	Y
ARKANSAS						
Boozman	Y	Y	N	Y	N	Y
Cotton	Y	Y	N	Y	N	Y
CALIFORNIA						
Feinstein	N	Y	Y	N	Y	N
Harris	N	Y	Y	N	N	N
COLORADO						
Bennet	N	Y	Y	N	Y	N
Gardner	Y	Y	Y	Y	Y	Y
CONNECTICUT						
Blumenthal	Y	Y	Y	N	Y	N
Murphy	Y	Y	Y	N	Y	N
DELAWARE						
Carper	Y	Y	Y	N	Y	N
Coons	Y	Y	Y	N	Y	N
FLORIDA						
Nelson	Y	Y	Y	N	Y	N
Rubio	Y	Y	N	Y	N	Y
GEORGIA						
Isakson	Y	Y	N	Y	Y	Y
Perdue	Y	Y	N	Y	N	Y
HAWAII						
Schatz	Y	Y	Y	N	Y	N
Hirono	N	Y	Y	N	Y	N
IDAHO						
Crapo	N	Y	N	Y	N	Y
Risch	N	Y	N	Y	N	Y
ILLINOIS						
Durbin	Y	Y	Y	N	Y	N
Duckworth	Y	Y	Y	N	Y	N
INDIANA						
Donnelly	Y	Y	Y	Y	Y	Y
Young	Y	Y	N	Y	N	Y
IOWA						
Grassley	N	Y	N	Y	N	Y
Ernst	Y	Y	N	Y	N	Y
KANSAS						
Roberts	Y	Y	N	Y	N	Y
Moran	Y	Y	N	Y	N	N
KENTUCKY						
McConnell	Y	Y	N	Y	N	Y
Paul	N	Y	N	Y	N	N
LOUISIANA						
Cassidy	N	Y	N	Y	N	Y
Kennedy	N	Y	N	Y	N	N
MAINE						
Collins	Y	Y	Y	N	Y	N
King	Y	Y	Y	N	Y	N
MARYLAND						
Cardin	Y	Y	Y	N	Y	N
Van Hollen	Y	Y	Y	N	Y	N
MASSACHUSETTS						
Warren	N	Y	Y	N	Y	N
Markey	N	Y	Y	N	Y	N
MICHIGAN						
Stabenow	Y	Y	Y	Y	Y	N
Peters	Y	Y	Y	N	Y	N
MINNESOTA						
Klobuchar	Y	Y	Y	N	Y	N
Smith	Y	Y	Y	N	Y	N
MISSISSIPPI						
Cochran	Y	Y	N	Y	N	Y
Wicker	Y	Y	N	Y	N	Y
MISSOURI						
McCaskill	Y	Y	Y	Y	Y	N
Blunt	Y	Y	N	Y	N	Y

	31	32	33	34	35	36
MONTANA						
Tester	Y	Y	Y	N	Y	N
Daines	N	Y	N	Y	N	N
NEBRASKA						
Fischer	Y	Y	N	Y	N	Y
Sasse	N	Y	N	Y	N	N
NEVADA						
Heller	Y	Y	N	Y	N	Y
Cortez Masto	Y	Y	Y	N	Y	N
NEW HAMPSHIRE						
Shaheen	Y	Y	Y	N	Y	N
Hassan	Y	Y	Y	N	Y	N
NEW JERSEY						
Menendez	Y	Y	Y	N	Y	N
Booker	N	Y	Y	N	Y	N
NEW MEXICO						
Udall	Y	Y	Y	N	Y	N
Heinrich	Y	Y	Y	N	N	N
NEW YORK						
Schumer	Y	Y	Y	N	Y	N
Gillibrand	N	Y	Y	N	Y	N
NORTH CAROLINA						
Burr	N	Y	N	Y	N	Y
Tillis	Y	Y	N	Y	N	Y
NORTH DAKOTA						
Hoeven	Y	Y	N	Y	N	Y
Heitkamp	Y	Y	Y	N	Y	N
OHIO						
Brown	Y	Y	Y	N	Y	N
Portman	Y	Y	N	Y	N	Y
OKLAHOMA						
Inhofe	Y	Y	N	Y	N	N
Lankford	N	Y	N	Y	N	Y
OREGON						
Wyden	N	Y	Y	N	Y	N
Merkley	N	Y	Y	N	Y	N
PENNSYLVANIA						
Casey	Y	Y	Y	N	Y	N
Toomey	N	Y	N	Y	N	Y
RHODE ISLAND						
Reed	Y	Y	Y	N	Y	N
Whitehouse	Y	Y	Y	N	Y	N
SOUTH CAROLINA						
Graham	Y	Y	Y	Y	Y	Y
Scott	Y	Y	N	Y	N	Y
SOUTH DAKOTA						
Thune	Y	Y	N	Y	Y	Y
Rounds	Y	Y	Y	Y	Y	Y
TENNESSEE						
Alexander	Y	Y	N	Y	Y	Y
Corker	N	Y	N	Y	N	Y
TEXAS						
Cornyn	Y	Y	N	Y	N	Y
Cruz	Y	N	N	Y	N	N
UTAH						
Hatch	Y	Y	N	Y	N	Y
Lee	N	Y	N	Y	N	N
VERMONT						
Leahy	Y	?	Y	N	Y	N
Sanders	N	Y	Y	N	Y	N
VIRGINIA						
Warner	Y	Y	Y	N	Y	N
Kaine	Y	Y	Y	N	Y	N
WASHINGTON						
Murray	Y	Y	Y	N	Y	N
Cantwell	N	Y	Y	N	Y	N
WEST VIRGINIA						
Manchin	Y	Y	N	Y	Y	Y
Capito	Y	Y	N	Y	N	Y
WISCONSIN						
Johnson	N	Y	N	Y	N	Y
Baldwin	Y	Y	Y	N	Y	N
WYOMING						
Enzi	N	Y	N	Y	N	N
Barrasso	Y	Y	N	Y	N	N

KEY	**Republicans**	Democrats	*Independents*
Y Voted for (yea)		**X** Paired against	**C** Voted "present" to avoid possible conflict of interest
# Paired for		**–** Announced against	
+ Announced for		**P** Voted "present"	**?** Did not vote or otherwise make a position known
N Voted against (nay)			

VOTE NUMBER

36. HR2579. LEGISLATIVE VEHICLE FOR IMMIGRATION OVERHAUL MEASURES/CLOTURE. Motion to invoke cloture (thus limiting debate) on the Grassley, R-Iowa, substitute amendment no. 1959 to the bill, that would overhaul various aspects of the U.S. immigration system, including border security policies and infrastructure and the Deferred Action for Childhood Arrivals program. It would cancel the removal of, and provide temporary resident status to certain DACA recipients. It would appropriate $25 billion, to be available through fiscal 2031, for border security enforcement. It would eliminate the diversity visa lottery program, would modify which individuals can receive visas and would reallocate the number of allowable visas between visa categories. It would place additional limits on which individuals can become naturalized citizens. Motion rejected 39-60: R 36-14; D 3-44. Feb. 15, 2018.

37. BRANCH NOMINATION/CLOTURE. Motion to invoke cloture (thus limiting debate) on the nomination of Elizabeth L. Branch of Georgia to be the U.S. circuit judge for the Eleventh Circuit. Motion agreed to 72-22: R 46-0; D 25-21. Feb. 26, 2018.

38. BRANCH NOMINATION/CONFIRMATION. Confirmation of President Donald Trump's nomination of Elizabeth L. Branch of Georgia to be U.S. circuit judge for the Eleventh Circuit. Confirmed 73-23: R 48-0; D 24-22. Feb. 27, 2018.

39. VOUGHT NOMINATION/CLOTURE. Motion to invoke cloture (thus limiting debate) on the nomination of Russell Vought of Virginia to be deputy director of the Office of Management and Budget. Motion agreed to 49-48: R 49-0; D 0-46. Feb. 27, 2018.

40. VOUGHT NOMINATION/CONFIRMATION. Confirmation of President Donald Trump's nomination of Russell Vought of Virginia to be deputy director of the Office of Management and Budget. Confirmed 49-49: R 49-0; D 0-47. Feb. 28, 2018.

41. QUATTLEBAUM NOMINATION/CLOTURE. Motion to invoke cloture on the nomination of A. Marvin Quattlebaum Jr. of South Carolina to be U.S. district judge for the District of South Carolina. Motion agreed to 69-29: R 49-0; D 19-28. Feb. 28, 2018.

42. QUATTLEBAUM NOMINATION/CONFIRMATION. Confirmation of President Donald Trump's nomination of A. Marvin Quattlebaum Jr. of South Carolina to be U.S. district judge for the District of South Carolina. Confirmed 69-28: R 48-0; D 20-27. March 01, 2018.

	37	38	39	40	41	42
ALABAMA						
Shelby	Y	Y	Y	Y	Y	Y
Jones	?	?	?	N	Y	Y
ALASKA						
Murkowski	Y	Y	Y	Y	Y	Y
Sullivan	?	?	Y	Y	Y	Y
ARIZONA						
McCain	?	?	?	?	?	?
Flake	Y	Y	Y	Y	Y	?
ARKANSAS						
Boozman	Y	Y	Y	Y	Y	Y
Cotton	Y	Y	Y	Y	Y	Y
CALIFORNIA						
Feinstein	Y	Y	N	N	N	N
Harris	N	N	N	N	N	N
COLORADO						
Bennet	Y	Y	N	N	Y	Y
Gardner	Y	Y	Y	Y	Y	Y
CONNECTICUT						
Blumenthal	N	N	N	N	N	N
Murphy	Y	N	N	N	N	N
DELAWARE						
Carper	Y	Y	N	N	Y	Y
Coons	Y	Y	N	N	Y	Y
FLORIDA						
Nelson	Y	Y	N	N	Y	Y
Rubio	Y	Y	Y	Y	Y	Y
GEORGIA						
Isakson	Y	Y	Y	Y	Y	Y
Perdue	Y	Y	Y	Y	Y	Y
HAWAII						
Schatz	Y	N	N	N	N	N
Hirono	N	Y	N	N	N	Y
IDAHO						
Crapo	Y	Y	Y	Y	Y	Y
Risch	Y	Y	Y	Y	Y	Y
ILLINOIS						
Durbin	Y	Y	N	N	N	N
Duckworth	N	N	N	N	N	N
INDIANA						
Donnelly	Y	Y	N	N	Y	Y
Young	Y	Y	Y	Y	Y	Y
IOWA						
Grassley	Y	Y	Y	Y	Y	Y
Ernst	Y	Y	Y	Y	Y	Y
KANSAS						
Roberts	Y	Y	Y	Y	Y	Y
Moran	Y	Y	Y	Y	Y	Y
KENTUCKY						
McConnell	Y	Y	Y	Y	Y	Y
Paul	Y	Y	Y	Y	Y	Y
LOUISIANA						
Cassidy	Y	Y	Y	Y	Y	Y
Kennedy	Y	Y	Y	Y	Y	Y
MAINE						
Collins	Y	Y	Y	Y	Y	Y
King	Y	Y	N	N	Y	Y
MARYLAND						
Cardin	Y	Y	N	N	N	N
Van Hollen	Y	Y	N	N	N	N
MASSACHUSETTS						
Warren	N	N	N	N	N	N
Markey	N	N	N	N	N	N
MICHIGAN						
Stabenow	N	N	N	N	N	N
Peters	N	N	N	N	N	N
MINNESOTA						
Klobuchar	Y	Y	N	N	N	N
Smith	Y	Y	N	N	N	N
MISSISSIPPI						
Cochran	Y	Y	Y	Y	Y	Y
Wicker	Y	Y	Y	Y	Y	Y
MISSOURI						
McCaskill	Y	Y	N	N	Y	Y
Blunt	Y	Y	Y	Y	Y	Y
MONTANA						
Tester	Y	Y	N	N	Y	Y
Daines	Y	Y	Y	Y	Y	Y
NEBRASKA						
Fischer	Y	Y	Y	Y	Y	Y
Sasse	Y	Y	Y	Y	Y	Y
NEVADA						
Heller	?	Y	Y	Y	Y	Y
Cortez Masto	N	N	N	N	Y	Y
NEW HAMPSHIRE						
Shaheen	Y	Y	N	N	Y	Y
Hassan	Y	Y	N	N	Y	Y
NEW JERSEY						
Menendez	N	N	N	N	N	N
Booker	N	N	N	N	N	N
NEW MEXICO						
Udall	N	N	N	N	N	N
Heinrich	N	N	N	N	N	N
NEW YORK						
Schumer	N	N	N	N	N	N
Gillibrand	N	N	N	N	N	N
NORTH CAROLINA						
Burr	Y	Y	Y	Y	Y	Y
Tillis	Y	Y	Y	Y	Y	Y
NORTH DAKOTA						
Hoeven	Y	Y	Y	Y	Y	Y
Heitkamp	Y	Y	N	N	Y	Y
OHIO						
Brown	N	N	N	N	N	N
Portman	Y	Y	Y	Y	Y	Y
OKLAHOMA						
Inhofe	Y	Y	Y	Y	Y	Y
Lankford	Y	Y	Y	Y	Y	Y
OREGON						
Wyden	N	N	N	N	N	N
Merkley	N	N	N	N	N	N
PENNSYLVANIA						
Casey	Y	Y	N	N	N	N
Toomey	Y	Y	Y	Y	Y	Y
RHODE ISLAND						
Reed	N	N	N	N	Y	Y
Whitehouse	Y	Y	N	N	Y	Y
SOUTH CAROLINA						
Graham	Y	Y	Y	Y	Y	Y
Scott	Y	Y	Y	Y	Y	Y
SOUTH DAKOTA						
Thune	Y	Y	Y	Y	Y	Y
Rounds	+	?	?	?	?	?
TENNESSEE						
Alexander	Y	Y	Y	Y	Y	Y
Corker	?	Y	Y	Y	Y	Y
TEXAS						
Cornyn	Y	Y	Y	Y	Y	Y
Cruz	Y	Y	Y	Y	Y	Y
UTAH						
Hatch	Y	Y	Y	Y	Y	Y
Lee	Y	Y	Y	Y	Y	Y
VERMONT						
Leahy	Y	Y	N	N	Y	Y
Sanders	N	N	N	N	N	N
VIRGINIA						
Warner	Y	Y	N	N	Y	Y
Kaine	Y	Y	N	N	Y	Y
WASHINGTON						
Murray	N	N	N	N	N	N
Cantwell	N	N	N	N	N	N
WEST VIRGINIA						
Manchin	Y	Y	N	N	Y	Y
Capito	Y	Y	Y	Y	Y	Y
WISCONSIN						
Johnson	Y	Y	Y	Y	Y	Y
Baldwin	Y	Y	N	N	Y	Y
WYOMING						
Enzi	Y	Y	Y	Y	Y	Y
Barrasso	Y	Y	Y	Y	Y	Y

KEY	**Republicans**	Democrats	*Independents*

Y Voted for (yea)	X Paired against	C Voted "present" to avoid possible conflict of interest
# Paired for	– Announced against	? Did not vote or otherwise make a position known
+ Announced for	P Voted "present"	
N Voted against (nay)		

VOTE NUMBER

43. SCHOLER NOMINATION/CLOTURE. Motion to invoke cloture (thus limiting debate) on the nomination of Karen G. Scholer of Texas to be U.S. district judge for the Northern District of Texas Motion agreed to 96-1: R 48-0; D 46-1. March 01, 2018.

44. SELF NOMINATION/CLOTURE. Motion to invoke cloture (thus limiting debate) on the nomination of Tilman E. Self III of Georgia to be U.S. district judge for the Middle District of Georgia. Motion agreed to 85-12: R 48-0; D 36-11. March 01, 2018.

45. DOUGHTY NOMINATION/CLOTURE. Motion to invoke cloture (thus limiting debate) on the nomination of Terry A. Doughty of Louisiana to be U.S. district judge for the Western District of Louisiana. Motion agreed to 94-2: R 48-0; D 44-2. March 01, 2018.

46. SCHOLER NOMINATION/CONFIRMATION. Confirmation of President Donald Trump's nomination of Karen Gren Scholer of Texas to be U.S. district judge for the Northern District of Texas Confirmed 95-0: R 47-0; D 46-0. March 5, 2018.

47. SELF NOMINATION/CONFIRMATION. Confirmation of President Donald Trump's nomination of Tilman Eugene Self III of Georgia to be U.S. district judge for the Middle District of Georgia. Confirmed 85-11: R 47-0; D 37-10. March 5, 2018.

48. S2155. BANK REGULATION THRESHOLDS/CLOTURE. Motion to invoke cloture (thus limiting debate) on the McConnell, R-Ky., motion to proceed to the bill that would apply the more stringent bank regulation provisions of the 2010 financial overhaul to banks with $250 billion in assets, instead of those with $50 billion in assets. Motion agreed to 67-32: R 50-0; D 16-31. March 6, 2018.

	43	44	45	46	47	48
ALABAMA						
Shelby	Y	Y	Y	Y	Y	Y
Jones	Y	Y	Y	Y	Y	Y
ALASKA						
Murkowski	Y	Y	Y	?	?	Y
Sullivan	Y	Y	Y	?	?	Y
ARIZONA						
McCain	?	?	?	?	?	?
Flake	?	?	?	Y	Y	Y
ARKANSAS						
Boozman	Y	Y	Y	Y	Y	Y
Cotton	Y	Y	Y	Y	Y	Y
CALIFORNIA						
Feinstein	Y	Y	Y	Y	Y	N
Harris	Y	N	Y	Y	N	N
COLORADO						
Bennet	Y	Y	Y	Y	Y	Y
Gardner	Y	Y	Y	Y	Y	Y
CONNECTICUT						
Blumenthal	Y	Y	Y	Y	N	N
Murphy	Y	Y	Y	Y	Y	N
DELAWARE						
Carper	Y	Y	Y	Y	Y	Y
Coons	Y	Y	Y	Y	Y	Y
FLORIDA						
Nelson	Y	Y	Y	Y	Y	Y
Rubio	Y	Y	Y	Y	Y	Y
GEORGIA						
Isakson	Y	Y	Y	Y	Y	Y
Perdue	Y	Y	Y	Y	Y	Y
HAWAII						
Schatz	Y	N	Y	Y	Y	N
Hirono	N	N	N	Y	Y	N
IDAHO						
Crapo	Y	Y	Y	Y	Y	Y
Risch	Y	Y	Y	Y	Y	Y
ILLINOIS						
Durbin	Y	Y	Y	Y	Y	N
Duckworth	Y	Y	Y	Y	Y	N
INDIANA						
Donnelly	Y	Y	Y	Y	Y	Y
Young	Y	Y	Y	Y	Y	Y
IOWA						
Grassley	Y	Y	Y	Y	Y	Y
Ernst	Y	Y	Y	Y	Y	Y
KANSAS						
Roberts	Y	Y	Y	Y	Y	Y
Moran	Y	Y	Y	Y	Y	Y
KENTUCKY						
McConnell	Y	Y	Y	Y	Y	Y
Paul	Y	Y	Y	Y	Y	Y
LOUISIANA						
Cassidy	Y	Y	Y	Y	Y	Y
Kennedy	Y	Y	Y	Y	Y	Y
MAINE						
Collins	Y	Y	Y	Y	Y	Y
King	Y	Y	Y	Y	Y	Y
MARYLAND						
Cardin	Y	Y	?	Y	Y	N
Van Hollen	Y	Y	Y	Y	Y	N
MASSACHUSETTS						
Warren	Y	N	Y	Y	N	N
Markey	Y	N	Y	Y	N	N
MICHIGAN						
Stabenow	Y	N	Y	Y	N	Y
Peters	Y	N	Y	Y	N	Y
MINNESOTA						
Klobuchar	Y	Y	Y	Y	Y	N
Smith	Y	Y	Y	Y	Y	N
MISSISSIPPI						
Cochran	Y	Y	Y	Y	Y	Y
Wicker	Y	Y	Y	Y	Y	Y
MISSOURI						
McCaskill	Y	Y	Y	Y	Y	Y
Blunt	Y	Y	Y	Y	Y	Y
MONTANA						
Tester	Y	Y	Y	Y	Y	Y
Daines	Y	Y	Y	Y	Y	Y
NEBRASKA						
Fischer	Y	Y	Y	Y	Y	Y
Sasse	Y	Y	Y	Y	Y	Y
NEVADA						
Heller	Y	Y	Y	Y	Y	Y
Cortez Masto	Y	Y	Y	Y	Y	N
NEW HAMPSHIRE						
Shaheen	Y	Y	Y	Y	Y	Y
Hassan	Y	Y	Y	Y	Y	Y
NEW JERSEY						
Menendez	Y	N	Y	Y	N	N
Booker	Y	N	Y	Y	N	N
NEW MEXICO						
Udall	Y	Y	Y	Y	Y	N
Heinrich	Y	Y	Y	Y	Y	N
NEW YORK						
Schumer	Y	Y	Y	Y	Y	N
Gillibrand	Y	N	Y	Y	N	N
NORTH CAROLINA						
Burr	Y	Y	Y	Y	Y	Y
Tillis	Y	Y	Y	Y	Y	Y
NORTH DAKOTA						
Hoeven	Y	Y	Y	Y	Y	Y
Heitkamp	Y	Y	Y	?	Y	Y
OHIO						
Brown	Y	Y	Y	Y	Y	N
Portman	Y	Y	Y	Y	Y	Y
OKLAHOMA						
Inhofe	Y	Y	Y	Y	Y	Y
Lankford	Y	Y	Y	Y	Y	Y
OREGON						
Wyden	Y	Y	Y	Y	Y	N
Merkley	Y	N	N	Y	N	N
PENNSYLVANIA						
Casey	Y	Y	Y	Y	Y	N
Toomey	Y	Y	Y	Y	Y	Y
RHODE ISLAND						
Reed	Y	Y	Y	Y	Y	N
Whitehouse	Y	Y	Y	Y	Y	N
SOUTH CAROLINA						
Graham	Y	Y	Y	Y	Y	Y
Scott	Y	Y	Y	Y	Y	Y
SOUTH DAKOTA						
Thune	Y	Y	Y	Y	Y	Y
Rounds	?	?	?	Y	Y	Y
TENNESSEE						
Alexander	Y	Y	Y	Y	Y	Y
Corker	Y	Y	Y	Y	Y	Y
TEXAS						
Cornyn	Y	Y	Y	Y	Y	Y
Cruz	Y	Y	Y	+	+	Y
UTAH						
Hatch	Y	Y	Y	Y	Y	Y
Lee	Y	Y	Y	Y	Y	Y
VERMONT						
Leahy	Y	Y	Y	Y	Y	N
Sanders	Y	N	Y	Y	N	N
VIRGINIA						
Warner	Y	Y	Y	Y	Y	Y
Kaine	Y	Y	Y	Y	Y	Y
WASHINGTON						
Murray	Y	Y	Y	Y	Y	N
Cantwell	Y	Y	Y	Y	Y	N
WEST VIRGINIA						
Manchin	Y	Y	Y	Y	Y	Y
Capito	Y	Y	Y	Y	Y	Y
WISCONSIN						
Johnson	Y	Y	Y	Y	Y	Y
Baldwin	Y	Y	Y	Y	Y	N
WYOMING						
Enzi	Y	Y	Y	Y	Y	Y
Barrasso	Y	Y	Y	Y	Y	Y

KEY   Republicans   Democrats   *Independents*

Y Voted for (yea)	**X** Paired against	**C** Voted "present" to avoid possible conflict of interest
# Paired for	**–** Announced against	
+ Announced for	**P** Voted "present"	**?** Did not vote or otherwise make a position known
N Voted against (nay)		

VOTE NUMBER

49. DOUGHTY NOMINATION/CONFIRMATION. Confirmation of President Donald Trump's nomination of Terry A. Doughty of Louisiana to be U.S. district judge for the Western District of Louisiana. Confirmed 98-0: R 50-0; D 46-0. March 6, 2018.

50. S2155. BANK REGULATION THRESHOLDS/CLOTURE. Motion to invoke cloture (thus limiting debate) on the McConnell, R-Ky., for Crapo, R-Idaho, substitute amendment no. 2151, as modified, that would apply the more stringent bank regulation provisions of the 2010 financial overhaul to fewer banks. The substitute amendment would lift the threshold for disclosure requirements to $10 million for employee-owned securities and would allow venture capital funds to have up to 250 investors and still be exempt from certain registering requirements. It would prevent certain high interest rate loans to veterans from being guaranteed or insured. It would prohibit automatic default on student loans in the case of death or bankruptcy of a cosigner. It would require a Government Accountability Office report to Congress on the rate of foreclosures in Puerto Rico before and after Hurricane Maria. Motion agreed to 66-30: R 49-0; D 16-29. March 12, 2018.

51. S2155. BANK REGULATION THRESHOLDS/SECURITIES, VENTURE CAPITAL AND LOAN REGULATIONS. McConnell, R-Ky., for Crapo, R-Idaho, substitute amendment no. 2151, as modified, that would apply the more stringent bank regulation provisions of the 2010 financial overhaul to fewer banks. The substitute amendment would lift the threshold for disclosure requirements to $10 million for employee-owned securities and would allow venture capital funds to have up to 250 investors and still be exempt from certain registering requirements. It would prevent certain high interest rate loans to veterans from being guaranteed or insured. It would prohibit automatic default on student loans in the case of death or bankruptcy of a cosigner. It would require a Government Accountability Office report to Congress on the rate of foreclosures in Puerto Rico before and after Hurricane Maria. Adopted 67-31: R 50-0; D 16-30. March 14, 2018.

52. S2155. BANK REGULATION THRESHOLDS/CLOTURE. Motion to invoke cloture on the bill that would apply the more stringent bank regulation provisions of the 2010 financial overhaul to banks with $250 billion in assets, instead of those with at least $50 billion in assets. It would also allow banks with less than $10 billion in assets to trade with depositors' money. The bill would lift the threshold for disclosure requirements to $10 million for employee-owned securities and would allow venture capital funds to have up to 250 investors and be exempt from certain registering requirements. Motion agreed to 67-31: R 50-0; D 16-30. March 14, 2018.

53. S2155. BANK REGULATION THRESHOLDS/MOTION TO WAIVE. Crapo, R-Idaho, motion to waive all applicable sections of the Congressional Budget Act and any applicable budget resolutions with respect to a Sanders, I-Vt., point of order that the bill violates section 4106 of the fiscal 2018 budget resolution. Motion agreed to 67-31: R 50-0; D 16-30. March 14, 2018.

54. S2155. BANK REGULATION THRESHOLDS/PASSAGE. Passage of the bill that would apply the more stringent bank regulation provisions of the 2010 financial overhaul to banks with $250 billion in assets, instead of those with at least $50 billion in assets. It would also allow banks with less than $10 billion in assets to trade with depositors' money. The bill would lift the threshold for disclosure requirements to $10 million for employee-owned securities and would allow venture capital funds to have up to 250 investors and be exempt from certain registering requirements. It would provide consumers with the right to request a "security freeze" on their credit reports, which would prohibit a consumer reporting agency from releasing information from the consumer's credit report without express authorization. It would define a "qualified mortgage" as any residential mortgage loan held by a bank, removing the requirement that for a "qualified mortgage" a bank must determine that a mortgage recipient has the ability to repay. Passed 67-31: R 50-0; D 16-30. March 14, 2018.

	49	50	51	52	53	54
ALABAMA						
Shelby	Y	Y	Y	Y	Y	Y
Jones	Y	Y	Y	Y	Y	Y
ALASKA						
Murkowski	Y	Y	Y	Y	Y	Y
Sullivan	Y	Y	Y	Y	Y	Y
ARIZONA						
McCain	?	?	?	?	?	?
Flake	Y	Y	Y	Y	Y	Y
ARKANSAS						
Boozman	Y	Y	Y	Y	Y	Y
Cotton	Y	Y	Y	Y	Y	Y
CALIFORNIA						
Feinstein	?	N	N	N	N	N
Harris	Y	N	N	N	N	N
COLORADO						
Bennet	Y	Y	Y	Y	Y	Y
Gardner	Y	Y	Y	Y	Y	Y
CONNECTICUT						
Blumenthal	Y	N	N	N	N	N
Murphy	Y	N	N	N	N	N
DELAWARE						
Carper	Y	Y	Y	Y	Y	Y
Coons	Y	Y	Y	Y	Y	Y
FLORIDA						
Nelson	Y	Y	Y	Y	Y	Y
Rubio	Y	Y	Y	Y	Y	Y
GEORGIA						
Isakson	Y	Y	Y	Y	Y	Y
Perdue	Y	Y	Y	Y	Y	Y
HAWAII						
Schatz	Y	N	N	N	N	N
Hirono	Y	N	N	N	N	N
IDAHO						
Crapo	Y	Y	Y	Y	Y	Y
Risch	Y	Y	Y	Y	Y	Y
ILLINOIS						
Durbin	Y	N	N	N	N	N
Duckworth	Y	?	N	N	N	N
INDIANA						
Donnelly	Y	Y	Y	Y	Y	Y
Young	Y	Y	Y	Y	Y	Y
IOWA						
Grassley	Y	Y	Y	Y	Y	Y
Ernst	Y	Y	Y	Y	Y	Y
KANSAS						
Roberts	Y	Y	Y	Y	Y	Y
Moran	Y	Y	Y	Y	Y	Y
KENTUCKY						
McConnell	Y	Y	Y	Y	Y	Y
Paul	Y	?	Y	Y	Y	Y
LOUISIANA						
Cassidy	Y	Y	Y	Y	Y	Y
Kennedy	Y	Y	Y	Y	Y	Y
MAINE						
Collins	Y	Y	Y	Y	Y	Y
King	Y	Y	Y	Y	Y	Y
MARYLAND						
Cardin	Y	N	N	N	N	N
Van Hollen	Y	N	N	N	N	N
MASSACHUSETTS						
Warren	Y	N	N	N	N	N
Markey	Y	N	N	N	N	N
MICHIGAN						
Stabenow	Y	Y	Y	Y	Y	Y
Peters	Y	Y	Y	Y	Y	Y
MINNESOTA						
Klobuchar	Y	N	N	N	N	N
Smith	Y	N	N	N	N	N
MISSISSIPPI						
Cochran	Y	Y	Y	Y	Y	Y
Wicker	Y	Y	Y	Y	Y	Y
MISSOURI						
McCaskill	Y	Y	Y	Y	Y	Y
Blunt	Y	Y	Y	Y	Y	Y
MONTANA						
Tester	Y	Y	Y	Y	Y	Y
Daines	Y	Y	Y	Y	Y	Y
NEBRASKA						
Fischer	Y	Y	Y	Y	Y	Y
Sasse	Y	Y	Y	Y	Y	Y
NEVADA						
Heller	Y	Y	Y	Y	Y	Y
Cortez Masto	Y	N	N	N	N	N
NEW HAMPSHIRE						
Shaheen	Y	Y	Y	Y	Y	Y
Hassan	Y	Y	Y	Y	Y	Y
NEW JERSEY						
Menendez	Y	N	N	N	N	N
Booker	Y	N	N	N	N	N
NEW MEXICO						
Udall	Y	N	N	N	N	N
Heinrich	Y	–	–	–	–	–
NEW YORK						
Schumer	Y	N	N	N	N	N
Gillibrand	Y	N	N	N	N	N
NORTH CAROLINA						
Burr	Y	Y	Y	Y	Y	Y
Tillis	Y	Y	Y	Y	Y	Y
NORTH DAKOTA						
Hoeven	Y	Y	Y	Y	Y	Y
Heitkamp	Y	Y	Y	Y	Y	Y
OHIO						
Brown	Y	N	N	N	N	N
Portman	Y	Y	Y	Y	Y	Y
OKLAHOMA						
Inhofe	Y	Y	Y	Y	Y	Y
Lankford	Y	Y	Y	Y	Y	Y
OREGON						
Wyden	Y	N	N	N	N	N
Merkley	Y	N	N	N	N	N
PENNSYLVANIA						
Casey	Y	N	N	N	N	N
Toomey	Y	Y	Y	Y	Y	Y
RHODE ISLAND						
Reed	Y	N	N	N	N	N
Whitehouse	Y	N	N	N	N	N
SOUTH CAROLINA						
Graham	Y	Y	Y	Y	Y	Y
Scott	Y	Y	Y	Y	Y	Y
SOUTH DAKOTA						
Thune	Y	Y	Y	Y	Y	Y
Rounds	Y	Y	Y	Y	Y	Y
TENNESSEE						
Alexander	Y	Y	Y	Y	Y	Y
Corker	Y	Y	Y	Y	Y	Y
TEXAS						
Cornyn	Y	Y	Y	Y	Y	Y
Cruz	Y	Y	Y	Y	Y	Y
UTAH						
Hatch	Y	Y	Y	Y	Y	Y
Lee	Y	Y	Y	Y	Y	Y
VERMONT						
Leahy	Y	N	N	N	N	N
Sanders	Y	N	N	N	N	N
VIRGINIA						
Warner	Y	Y	Y	Y	Y	Y
Kaine	Y	Y	Y	Y	Y	Y
WASHINGTON						
Murray	Y	N	N	N	N	N
Cantwell	Y	N	N	N	N	N
WEST VIRGINIA						
Manchin	Y	Y	Y	Y	Y	Y
Capito	Y	Y	Y	Y	Y	Y
WISCONSIN						
Johnson	Y	Y	Y	Y	Y	Y
Baldwin	Y	N	N	N	N	N
WYOMING						
Enzi	Y	Y	Y	Y	Y	Y
Barrasso	Y	Y	Y	Y	Y	Y

KEY	**Republicans**	Democrats	*Independents*	
Y	Voted for (yea)	X Paired against	C	Voted "present" to avoid possible conflict of interest
#	Paired for	– Announced against		
+	Announced for	P Voted "present"	?	Did not vote or otherwise make a position known
N	Voted against (nay)			

VOTE NUMBER

55. MCALEENAN NOMINATION/CLOTURE. Motion to invoke cloture (thus limiting debate) on the nomination of Kevin K. McAleenan of Hawaii to be commissioner of U.S. Customs and Border Protection. Motion agreed to 79-19: R 50-0; D 28-18. March 14, 2018.

56. MCALEENAN NOMINATION/CONFIRMATION. Confirmation of President Donald Trump's nomination of Kevin K. McAleenan of Hawaii to be commissioner of U.S. Customs and Border Protection. Confirmed 77-19: R 47-0; D 29-18. March 19, 2018.

57. HR1865. WEBSITES FACILITATING SEX TRAFFICKING/CLOTURE. Motion to invoke cloture (thus limiting debate) on the motion to proceed to the bill that would make it a federal crime to use or operate a website to promote or facilitate prostitution. Motion agreed to 94-2: R 46-1; D 46-1. March 19, 2018.

58. SJRES54. U.S. MILITARY FORCES IN YEMEN/MOTION TO TABLE. Corker, R-Tenn., motion to table (kill) the Sanders, I-Vt., motion to discharge from the Senate Foreign Relations Committee the joint resolution that would require the removal of most of the U.S. military forces in Yemen. Motion agreed to 55-44: R 45-5; D 10-37. March 20, 2018.

59. HR1865. WEBSITES FACILITATING SEX TRAFFICKING/MOTION TO WAIVE. Wyden, D-Ore., motion to waive all applicable sections of the Congressional Budget Act and any applicable budget resolutions with respect to the Wyden, D-Ore., amendment no. 2213. Motion rejected 21-78: R 0-50; D 20-27. March 21, 2018.

60. HR1865. WEBSITES FACILITATING SEX TRAFFICKING/PASSAGE. Passage of the bill that would make it a federal crime to use or operate a website to promote or facilitate prostitution. The bill would permit a state to prosecute promotion of online prostitution or trafficking under state law as long as the state's laws mirror federal prohibitions. The bill would also allow the victims of online sex trafficking or prostitution to recover civil damages from the website operator and from those who developed or posted the material. Passed (thus cleared for the president) 97-2: R 49-1; D 46-1. March 21, 2018.

	55	56	57	58	59	60		55	56	57	58	59	60
ALABAMA							**MONTANA**						
Shelby	Y	Y	Y	Y	N	Y	Tester	Y	Y	Y	N	N	Y
Jones	Y	Y	Y	Y	Y	Y	**Daines**	Y	Y	Y	N	N	Y
ALASKA							**NEBRASKA**						
Murkowski	Y	Y	Y	Y	N	Y	**Fischer**	Y	Y	Y	Y	N	Y
Sullivan	Y	Y	Y	Y	N	Y	**Sasse**	Y	Y	Y	Y	N	Y
ARIZONA							**NEVADA**						
McCain	?	?	?	?	?	?	**Heller**	Y	Y	Y	Y	N	Y
Flake	Y	Y	Y	Y	N	Y	Cortez Masto	Y	Y	Y	Y	N	Y
ARKANSAS							**NEW HAMPSHIRE**						
Boozman	Y	Y	Y	Y	N	Y	Shaheen	Y	Y	Y	N	N	Y
Cotton	Y	Y	Y	Y	N	Y	Hassan	Y	Y	Y	N	N	Y
CALIFORNIA							**NEW JERSEY**						
Feinstein	N	N	Y	N	N	Y	Menendez	N	N	Y	Y	N	Y
Harris	N	N	Y	N	N	Y	Booker	N	N	Y	N	Y	Y
COLORADO							**NEW MEXICO**						
Bennet	Y	Y	Y	N	N	Y	Udall	N	N	Y	N	Y	Y
Gardner	Y	Y	Y	Y	N	Y	Heinrich	–	N	Y	N	Y	Y
CONNECTICUT							**NEW YORK**						
Blumenthal	N	N	Y	N	N	Y	Schumer	N	N	Y	N	N	Y
Murphy	Y	Y	Y	N	N	Y	Gillibrand	N	N	Y	N	Y	Y
DELAWARE							**NORTH CAROLINA**						
Carper	Y	Y	Y	N	N	Y	**Burr**	Y	?	?	Y	N	Y
Coons	Y	Y	Y	Y	Y	Y	**Tillis**	Y	Y	Y	Y	N	Y
FLORIDA							**NORTH DAKOTA**						
Nelson	Y	Y	Y	Y	N	Y	**Hoeven**	Y	Y	Y	Y	N	Y
Rubio	Y	Y	Y	Y	N	Y	Heitkamp	Y	Y	Y	Y	N	Y
GEORGIA							**OHIO**						
Isakson	Y	Y	Y	Y	N	Y	Brown	Y	Y	Y	Y	N	Y
Perdue	Y	Y	Y	Y	N	Y	**Portman**	Y	Y	Y	Y	N	Y
HAWAII							**OKLAHOMA**						
Schatz	N	N	Y	N	N	Y	**Inhofe**	Y	Y	Y	Y	N	Y
Hirono	Y	Y	Y	N	Y	Y	**Lankford**	Y	Y	Y	Y	N	Y
IDAHO							**OREGON**						
Crapo	Y	Y	Y	Y	N	Y	Wyden	Y	Y	N	N	Y	N
Risch	Y	Y	Y	Y	N	Y	Merkley	N	N	Y	N	Y	Y
ILLINOIS							**PENNSYLVANIA**						
Durbin	N	N	Y	N	N	Y	Casey	Y	Y	Y	N	Y	Y
Duckworth	N	N	Y	N	N	Y	**Toomey**	Y	?	?	Y	N	Y
INDIANA							**RHODE ISLAND**						
Donnelly	Y	Y	Y	Y	Y	Y	Reed	Y	Y	Y	Y	N	Y
Young	Y	Y	Y	Y	N	Y	Whitehouse	Y	Y	Y	Y	N	Y
IOWA							**SOUTH CAROLINA**						
Grassley	Y	Y	Y	Y	N	Y	**Graham**	Y	Y	Y	Y	N	Y
Ernst	Y	Y	Y	Y	N	Y	**Scott**	Y	Y	Y	Y	N	Y
KANSAS							**SOUTH DAKOTA**						
Roberts	Y	?	?	Y	N	Y	**Thune**	Y	Y	Y	Y	N	Y
Moran	Y	Y	Y	N	N	Y	**Rounds**	Y	Y	Y	Y	N	Y
KENTUCKY							**TENNESSEE**						
McConnell	Y	Y	Y	Y	N	Y	**Alexander**	Y	Y	Y	Y	N	Y
Paul	Y	N	N	N	N	N	**Corker**	Y	Y	Y	Y	N	Y
LOUISIANA							**TEXAS**						
Cassidy	Y	Y	Y	Y	N	Y	**Cornyn**	Y	Y	Y	Y	N	Y
Kennedy	Y	Y	Y	Y	N	Y	**Cruz**	Y	Y	Y	Y	N	Y
MAINE							**UTAH**						
Collins	Y	Y	Y	N	N	Y	**Hatch**	Y	Y	Y	Y	N	Y
King	Y	Y	Y	N	N	Y	**Lee**	Y	Y	Y	N	N	Y
MARYLAND							**VERMONT**						
Cardin	N	N	Y	N	N	Y	Leahy	Y	Y	Y	N	Y	Y
Van Hollen	N	N	Y	N	Y	Y	*Sanders*	N	N	Y	N	Y	Y
MASSACHUSETTS							**VIRGINIA**						
Warren	N	N	Y	N	N	Y	Warner	Y	Y	Y	N	N	Y
Markey	N	N	Y	N	Y	Y	Kaine	N	N	Y	N	N	Y
MICHIGAN							**WASHINGTON**						
Stabenow	Y	Y	Y	N	Y	Y	Murray	N	Y	Y	N	Y	Y
Peters	Y	Y	Y	N	Y	Y	Cantwell	Y	Y	Y	N	Y	Y
MINNESOTA							**WEST VIRGINIA**						
Klobuchar	Y	Y	Y	N	N	Y	Manchin	Y	Y	Y	Y	N	Y
Smith	Y	Y	Y	N	N	Y	**Capito**	Y	Y	Y	Y	N	Y
MISSISSIPPI							**WISCONSIN**						
Cochran	Y	Y	Y	Y	N	Y	**Johnson**	Y	Y	Y	N	N	Y
Wicker	Y	Y	Y	Y	N	Y	Baldwin	Y	Y	Y	N	N	Y
MISSOURI							**WYOMING**						
McCaskill	Y	Y	Y	N	Y	Y	**Enzi**	Y	Y	Y	Y	N	Y
Blunt	Y	Y	Y	Y	N	Y	**Barrasso**	Y	Y	Y	Y	N	Y

KEY	**Republicans**	Democrats	*Independents*

Y	Voted for (yea)	X	Paired against	C	Voted "present" to avoid possible conflict of interest
#	Paired for	–	Announced against		
+	Announced for	P	Voted "present"	?	Did not vote or otherwise make a position known
N	Voted against (nay)				

VOTE NUMBER

61. PROCEDURAL MOTION/REQUIRE ATTENDANCE. McConnell, R-Ky., motion to instruct the Senate sergeant of arms to request the attendance of absent senators. Motion agreed to 91-6: R 42-6; D 47-0. March 22, 2018.

62. HR1625. FISCAL 2018 OMNIBUS APPROPRIATIONS/CLOTURE. Motion to invoke cloture on the motion to concur in the House amendment to the Senate amendment to the bill that would provide roughly $1.3 trillion in funding for federal government operations and services through Sept. 30, 2018. Motion agreed to 67-30: R 27-21; D 39-8. March 23, 2018.

63. HR1625. FISCAL 2018 OMNIBUS APPROPRIATIONS/MOTION TO CONCUR. McConnell, R-Ky., motion to concur in the House amendment to the Senate amendment to the bill that would provide roughly $1.3 trillion in funding for federal government operations and services through Sept. 30, 2018. The measure would provide a total of $654.6 billion in additional funding to the Defense Department, including $589.5 billion in discretionary funding and $65.2 billion in funding for the Overseas Contingency Operations account. It would provide $98.7 billion to the Health and Human Services Department, including $5.1 billion to the Food and Drug Administration and $5.5 billion to the Indian Health Service. It would provide $3.4 billion to the Substance Abuse and Mental Health Services Administration for substance abuse block grants, and would provide roughly $3.7 billion to the National Institutes of Health, including an additional $500 million for research into opioid addiction. It would provide $47.7 billion to the Homeland Security Department, including $1.6 billion for the purpose of bolstering security measures on the U.S.-Mexico border, including the construction of new fencing along sections of the border, and would provide $7.1 billion for Immigration and Customs Enforcement operations and enforcement. The measure includes provisions from multiple bills related to school safety and firearms regulations, including a bill (S 2135) that would require the Department of Justice to certify that appropriate records have been submitted to the National Instant Criminal Background Check System by federal agencies and state governments with respect to individuals who are not eligible to purchase firearms. The measure includes language from the bill (S 2495) that would authorize $75 million a year through fiscal 2028 for the Secure Our Schools grant program and would revise it to more explicitly focus the program on preventing student violence. Motion agreed to 65-32: R 25-23; D 39-8. March 23, 2018.

64. BOOM NOMINATION/CLOTURE. Motion to invoke cloture (thus limiting debate) on the nomination of Claria Horn Boom of Kentucky to be U.S. district judge for the Eastern and Western Districts of Kentucky. Motion agreed to 96-2: R 50-0; D 45-1. April 9, 2018.

65. BOOM NOMINATION/CONFIRMATION. Confirmation of President Donald Trump's nomination of Claria Horn Boom of Kentucky to be U.S. district judge for the Eastern and Western Districts of Kentucky. Confirmed 96-1: R 50-0; D 45-0. April 10, 2018.

66. RING NOMINATION/CLOTURE. Motion to invoke cloture (thus limiting debate) on the nomination of John F. Ring of the District of Columbia to be a member of the National Labor Relations Board. Motion agreed to 50-47: R 50-0; D 0-45. April 10, 2018.

	61	62	63	64	65	66			61	62	63	64	65	66
ALABAMA								**MONTANA**						
Shelby	Y	Y	Y	Y	Y	Y		Tester	Y	Y	Y	Y	Y	N
Jones	Y	Y	Y	Y	Y	N		**Daines**	Y	N	N	Y	Y	Y
ALASKA								**NEBRASKA**						
Murkowski	Y	Y	Y	Y	Y	Y		**Fischer**	Y	N	N	Y	Y	Y
Sullivan	Y	N	N	Y	Y	Y		**Sasse**	Y	N	N	Y	Y	Y
ARIZONA								**NEVADA**						
McCain	?	?	?	?	?	?		**Heller**	Y	Y	Y	Y	Y	Y
Flake	Y	N	N	Y	Y	Y		Cortez Masto	Y	Y	Y	Y	Y	N
ARKANSAS								**NEW HAMPSHIRE**						
Boozman	Y	Y	Y	Y	Y	Y		Shaheen	Y	Y	Y	Y	Y	N
Cotton	N	N	N	Y	Y	Y		Hassan	Y	Y	Y	Y	Y	N
CALIFORNIA								**NEW JERSEY**						
Feinstein	Y	N	N	Y	Y	N		Menendez	Y	Y	Y	Y	Y	N
Harris	Y	N	N	Y	Y	N		Booker	Y	N	N	Y	+	–
COLORADO								**NEW MEXICO**						
Bennet	Y	Y	Y	Y	Y	N		Udall	Y	Y	Y	Y	Y	N
Gardner	Y	N	N	Y	Y	Y		Heinrich	Y	Y	Y	Y	Y	N
CONNECTICUT								**NEW YORK**						
Blumenthal	Y	Y	Y	Y	Y	N		Schumer	Y	Y	Y	Y	Y	N
Murphy	Y	Y	Y	Y	Y	N		Gillibrand	Y	N	N	Y	Y	N
DELAWARE								**NORTH CAROLINA**						
Carper	Y	Y	Y	Y	Y	N		**Burr**	?	?	?	Y	Y	Y
Coons	Y	Y	Y	Y	Y	N		**Tillis**	Y	Y	N	Y	Y	Y
FLORIDA								**NORTH DAKOTA**						
Nelson	Y	Y	Y	Y	Y	N		**Hoeven**	Y	Y	Y	Y	Y	Y
Rubio	N	Y	Y	Y	Y	Y		Heitkamp	Y	Y	Y	Y	Y	N
GEORGIA								**OHIO**						
Isakson	Y	Y	Y	Y	Y	Y		Brown	Y	Y	Y	Y	Y	N
Perdue	Y	N	N	Y	Y	Y		Portman	Y	Y	Y	Y	Y	Y
HAWAII								**OKLAHOMA**						
Schatz	Y	Y	Y	Y	Y	N		**Inhofe**	Y	Y	Y	Y	Y	Y
Hirono	Y	Y	Y	N	Y	N		**Lankford**	Y	N	N	Y	Y	Y
IDAHO								**OREGON**						
Crapo	Y	N	N	Y	Y	Y		Wyden	Y	Y	Y	Y	Y	N
Risch	Y	N	N	Y	Y	Y		Merkley	Y	N	N	Y	Y	N
ILLINOIS								**PENNSYLVANIA**						
Durbin	Y	N	Y	Y	Y	N		Casey	Y	Y	Y	Y	Y	N
Duckworth	Y	Y	Y	?	?	?		**Toomey**	?	?	–	Y	Y	Y
INDIANA								**RHODE ISLAND**						
Donnelly	Y	Y	Y	Y	Y	N		Reed	Y	Y	Y	Y	Y	N
Young	Y	Y	Y	Y	Y	Y		Whitehouse	Y	Y	Y	Y	Y	N
IOWA								**SOUTH CAROLINA**						
Grassley	Y	N	N	Y	Y	Y		**Graham**	Y	Y	Y	Y	Y	Y
Ernst	Y	Y	N	Y	Y	Y		**Scott**	Y	Y	Y	Y	Y	Y
KANSAS								**SOUTH DAKOTA**						
Roberts	Y	Y	Y	Y	Y	Y		**Thune**	Y	Y	Y	Y	Y	Y
Moran	Y	Y	Y	Y	Y	Y		**Rounds**	Y	Y	Y	Y	Y	Y
KENTUCKY								**TENNESSEE**						
McConnell	Y	Y	Y	Y	Y	Y		**Alexander**	N	Y	Y	Y	Y	Y
Paul	Y	N	N	Y	Y	Y		**Corker**	N	N	N	Y	Y	Y
LOUISIANA								**TEXAS**						
Cassidy	N	N	N	Y	Y	Y		**Cornyn**	Y	Y	Y	Y	Y	Y
Kennedy	Y	N	N	Y	Y	Y		**Cruz**	Y	N	N	Y	Y	Y
MAINE								**UTAH**						
Collins	Y	Y	Y	Y	Y	Y		**Hatch**	Y	Y	Y	Y	Y	Y
King	Y	Y	Y	Y	Y	N		**Lee**	N	N	N	Y	Y	Y
MARYLAND								**VERMONT**						
Cardin	Y	Y	Y	Y	Y	N		Leahy	Y	Y	Y	Y	Y	N
Van Hollen	Y	Y	Y	Y	Y	N		*Sanders*	Y	N	N	N	N	N
MASSACHUSETTS								**VIRGINIA**						
Warren	Y	N	N	Y	Y	N		Warner	Y	Y	Y	Y	Y	N
Markey	Y	Y	N	Y	Y	N		Kaine	Y	Y	Y	Y	Y	N
MICHIGAN								**WASHINGTON**						
Stabenow	Y	Y	Y	Y	Y	N		Murray	Y	Y	Y	Y	Y	N
Peters	Y	Y	Y	Y	Y	N		Cantwell	Y	Y	Y	Y	Y	N
MINNESOTA								**WEST VIRGINIA**						
Klobuchar	Y	Y	Y	Y	Y	N		Manchin	Y	Y	Y	Y	Y	N
Smith	Y	Y	Y	Y	Y	N		**Capito**	Y	Y	Y	Y	Y	Y
MISSISSIPPI								**WISCONSIN**						
Wicker	Y	N	Y	Y	Y	Y		**Johnson**	Y	N	N	Y	Y	Y
MISSOURI								Baldwin	Y	Y	Y	Y	Y	N
McCaskill	Y	N	N	Y	Y	Y		**WYOMING**						
Blunt	Y	Y	Y	Y	Y	Y		**Enzi**	Y	N	N	Y	Y	Y
								Barrasso	Y	N	N	Y	Y	Y

VOTE NUMBER

67. RING NOMINATION/CONFIRMATION. Confirmation of President Donald Trump's nomination of John F. Ring of the District of Columbia to be a member of the National Labor Relations Board. Confirmed 50-48: R 50-0; D 0-46. April 11, 2018.

68. PIZZELLA NOMINATION/CLOTURE. Motion to invoke cloture (thus limiting debate) on the nomination of Patrick Pizzella of Virginia to be deputy secretary of Labor. Motion agreed to 50-48: R 50-0; D 0-46. April 11, 2018.

69. PIZZELLA NOMINATION/CONFIRMATION. Confirmation of President Donald Trump's nomination of Patrick Pizzella of Virginia to be deputy secretary of Labor. Confirmed 50-48: R 50-0; D 0-46. April 12, 2018.

70. WHEELER NOMINATION/CLOTURE. Motion to invoke cloture (thus limiting debate) on the nomination of Andrew Wheeler of Virginia to be deputy administrator of the Environmental Protection Agency. Motion agreed to 53-45: R 50-0; D 3-43. April 12, 2018.

71. WHEELER NOMINATION/CONFIRMATION. Confirmation of President Donald Trump's nomination of Andrew Wheeler of Virginia to be deputy administrator of the Environmental Protection Agency. Confirmed 53-45: R 50-0; D 3-43. April 12, 2018.

72. BROOMES NOMINATION/CLOTURE. Motion to invoke cloture (thus limiting debate) on the nomination John W. Broomes of Kansas to be U.S. district judge for the District of Kansas. Motion agreed to 74-24: R 50-0; D 23-23. April 12, 2018.

	67	68	69	70	71	72
ALABAMA						
Shelby	Y	Y	Y	Y	Y	Y
Jones	N	N	N	N	N	Y
ALASKA						
Murkowski	Y	Y	Y	Y	Y	Y
Sullivan	Y	Y	Y	Y	Y	Y
ARIZONA						
McCain	?	?	?	?	?	?
Flake	Y	Y	Y	Y	Y	Y
ARKANSAS						
Boozman	Y	Y	Y	Y	Y	Y
Cotton	Y	Y	Y	Y	Y	Y
CALIFORNIA						
Feinstein	N	N	N	N	N	N
Harris	N	N	N	N	N	N
COLORADO						
Bennet	N	N	N	N	N	Y
Gardner	Y	Y	Y	Y	Y	Y
CONNECTICUT						
Blumenthal	N	N	N	N	N	Y
Murphy	N	N	N	N	N	Y
DELAWARE						
Carper	N	N	N	N	N	Y
Coons	N	N	N	N	N	N
FLORIDA						
Nelson	N	N	N	N	N	Y
Rubio	Y	Y	Y	Y	Y	Y
GEORGIA						
Isakson	Y	Y	Y	Y	Y	Y
Perdue	Y	Y	Y	Y	Y	Y
HAWAII						
Schatz	N	N	N	N	N	Y
Hirono	N	N	N	N	N	N
IDAHO						
Crapo	Y	Y	Y	Y	Y	Y
Risch	Y	Y	Y	Y	Y	Y
ILLINOIS						
Durbin	N	N	N	N	N	Y
Duckworth	?	?	?	–	–	?
INDIANA						
Donnelly	N	N	N	Y	Y	Y
Young	Y	Y	Y	Y	Y	Y
IOWA						
Grassley	Y	Y	Y	Y	Y	Y
Ernst	Y	Y	Y	Y	Y	Y
KANSAS						
Roberts	Y	Y	Y	Y	Y	Y
Moran	Y	Y	Y	Y	Y	Y
KENTUCKY						
McConnell	Y	Y	Y	Y	Y	Y
Paul	Y	Y	Y	Y	Y	Y
LOUISIANA						
Cassidy	Y	Y	Y	Y	Y	Y
Kennedy	Y	Y	Y	Y	Y	Y
MAINE						
Collins	Y	Y	Y	Y	Y	Y
King	N	N	N	N	N	Y
MARYLAND						
Cardin	N	N	N	N	N	Y
Van Hollen	N	N	N	N	N	N
MASSACHUSETTS						
Warren	N	N	N	N	N	N
Markey	N	N	N	N	N	N
MICHIGAN						
Stabenow	N	N	N	N	N	N
Peters	N	N	N	N	N	N
MINNESOTA						
Klobuchar	N	N	N	N	N	Y
Smith	N	N	N	N	N	N
MISSISSIPPI						
Wicker	Y	Y	Y	Y	Y	Y
Hyde-Smith	Y	Y	Y	Y	Y	Y
MISSOURI						
McCaskill	N	N	N	N	N	Y
Blunt	Y	Y	Y	Y	Y	Y

	67	68	69	70	71	72
MONTANA						
Tester	N	N	N	N	N	Y
Daines	Y	Y	Y	Y	Y	Y
NEBRASKA						
Fischer	Y	Y	Y	Y	Y	Y
Sasse	Y	Y	Y	Y	Y	Y
NEVADA						
Heller	Y	Y	Y	Y	Y	Y
Cortez Masto	N	N	N	N	N	N
NEW HAMPSHIRE						
Shaheen	N	N	N	N	N	N
Hassan	N	N	N	N	N	N
NEW JERSEY						
Menendez	N	N	N	N	N	Y
Booker	N	N	N	N	N	N
NEW MEXICO						
Udall	N	N	N	N	N	N
Heinrich	N	N	N	N	N	N
NEW YORK						
Schumer	N	N	N	N	N	Y
Gillibrand	N	N	N	N	N	N
NORTH CAROLINA						
Burr	Y	Y	Y	Y	Y	Y
Tillis	Y	Y	Y	Y	Y	Y
NORTH DAKOTA						
Hoeven	Y	Y	Y	Y	Y	Y
Heitkamp	N	N	N	Y	Y	Y
OHIO						
Brown	N	N	N	N	N	N
Portman	Y	Y	Y	Y	Y	Y
OKLAHOMA						
Inhofe	Y	Y	Y	Y	Y	Y
Lankford	Y	Y	Y	Y	Y	Y
OREGON						
Wyden	N	N	N	N	N	N
Merkley	N	N	N	N	N	N
PENNSYLVANIA						
Casey	N	N	N	N	N	Y
Toomey	Y	Y	Y	Y	Y	Y
RHODE ISLAND						
Reed	N	N	N	N	N	Y
Whitehouse	N	N	N	N	N	N
SOUTH CAROLINA						
Graham	Y	Y	Y	Y	Y	Y
Scott	Y	Y	Y	Y	Y	Y
SOUTH DAKOTA						
Thune	Y	Y	Y	Y	Y	Y
Rounds	Y	Y	Y	Y	Y	Y
TENNESSEE						
Alexander	Y	Y	Y	Y	Y	Y
Corker	Y	Y	Y	Y	Y	Y
TEXAS						
Cornyn	Y	Y	Y	Y	Y	Y
Cruz	Y	Y	Y	Y	Y	Y
UTAH						
Hatch	Y	Y	Y	Y	Y	Y
Lee	Y	Y	Y	Y	Y	Y
VERMONT						
Leahy	N	N	N	N	N	Y
Sanders	N	N	N	N	N	N
VIRGINIA						
Warner	N	N	N	N	N	N
Kaine	N	N	N	N	N	Y
WASHINGTON						
Murray	N	N	N	N	N	N
Cantwell	N	N	N	N	N	N
WEST VIRGINIA						
Manchin	N	N	N	Y	Y	Y
Capito	Y	Y	Y	Y	Y	Y
WISCONSIN						
Johnson	Y	Y	Y	Y	Y	Y
Baldwin	N	N	N	N	N	Y
WYOMING						
Enzi	Y	Y	Y	Y	Y	Y
Barrasso	Y	Y	Y	Y	Y	Y

KEY	**Republicans**	Democrats	*Independents*

Y Voted for (yea)	X Paired against	C Voted "present" to avoid possible conflict of interest
# Paired for	– Announced against	? Did not vote or otherwise make a position known
+ Announced for	P Voted "present"	
N Voted against (nay)		

VOTE NUMBER

73. JENNINGS NOMINATION/CLOTURE. Motion to invoke cloture (thus limiting debate) on the nomination Rebecca Grady Jennings of Kentucky to be U.S. district judge for the Western District of Kentucky. Motion agreed to 94-2: R 49-0; D 44-1. April 12, 2018.

74. S140. TRIBAL WATER SYSTEMS AND LABOR RELATIONS/CLOTURE. Motion to invoke cloture (thus limiting debate) on the motion to concur in the House amendment to the bill that would amend the White Mountain Apache Tribe Water Rights Quantification Act of 2010 to specify that settlement funds may be used for the planning, design and construction of the tribe's rural water system. In addition, the bill would also amend the National Labor Relations Act to exclude Native American tribes and any institutions or enterprises owned or operated by a Native American tribe from being defined as employers under the NLRA. Motion rejected 55-41: R 47-1; D 7-39. April 16, 2018.

75. SJRES57. INDIRECT AUTOMOBILE LOAN DISAPPROVAL/MOTION TO PROCEED. McConnell, R-Ky., motion to proceed to the joint resolution that would nullify and disapprove of a Consumer Financial Protection Bureau rule that provides guidance to third parties that offer indirect financing for automobile loans. The rule states that such third party lenders are treated as creditors under the Equal Credit Opportunity Act and the lenders may not mark up the rate of an indirect loan in relation to a borrower's race, color, religion, national origin, sex, marital status, age or receipt of income from any public assistance program. Motion agreed to 50-47: R 49-0; D 1-45. April 17, 2018.

76. SJRES57. INDIRECT AUTOMOBILE LOAN DISAPPROVAL/PASSAGE. Passage of a bill that would nullify and disapprove of a Consumer Financial Protection Bureau rule that provides guidance to third parties that offer indirect financing for automobile loans. The rule states that such third party lenders are treated as creditors under the Equal Credit Opportunity Act and the lenders may not mark up the rate of an indirect loan in relation to a borrower's race, color, religion, national origin, sex, marital status, age or receipt of income from any public assistance program. Passed 51-47: R 50-0; D 1-45. April 18, 2018.

77. S140. TRIBAL WATER SYSTEMS, LABOR RELATIONS AND COAST GUARD REAUTHORIZATION/CLOTURE. Motion to invoke cloture (thus limiting debate) on the motion to concur in the House amendment to the bill with further amendment no. 2232 that would reauthorize the Coast Guard and Federal Maritime Commission for fiscal 2018 and fiscal 2019. The amendment would also allow the Coast Guard to establish standards for ballast water discharges within U.S. inland navigable waterways. Motion rejected 56-42: R 49-1; D 7-39. April 18, 2018.

78. BRIDENSTINE NOMINATION/CLOTURE. Motion to invoke cloture (thus limiting debate) on the nomination of James Bridenstine of Oklahoma to be administrator of the National Aeronautics and Space Administration. Motion agreed to 50-48: R 50-0; D 0-46. April 18, 2018.

	73	74	75	76	77	78
ALABAMA						
Shelby	Y	Y	Y	Y	Y	Y
Jones	Y	N	N	N	Y	N
ALASKA						
Murkowski	Y	Y	Y	Y	Y	Y
Sullivan	Y	Y	Y	Y	Y	Y
ARIZONA						
McCain	?	?	?	?	?	?
Flake	Y	Y	Y	Y	Y	Y
ARKANSAS						
Boozman	Y	Y	Y	Y	Y	Y
Cotton	Y	Y	Y	Y	Y	Y
CALIFORNIA						
Feinstein	Y	N	N	N	N	N
Harris	Y	N	N	N	N	N
COLORADO						
Bennet	Y	N	N	N	N	N
Gardner	Y	Y	Y	Y	Y	Y
CONNECTICUT						
Blumenthal	Y	N	N	N	N	N
Murphy	Y	N	N	N	N	N
DELAWARE						
Carper	Y	N	N	N	N	N
Coons	?	N	N	N	N	N
FLORIDA						
Nelson	Y	N	N	Y	N	N
Rubio	Y	+	Y	Y	Y	Y
GEORGIA						
Isakson	Y	Y	Y	Y	Y	Y
Perdue	Y	Y	Y	Y	Y	Y
HAWAII						
Schatz	Y	N	N	N	N	N
Hirono	N	N	N	N	N	N
IDAHO						
Crapo	Y	Y	Y	Y	Y	Y
Risch	Y	Y	Y	Y	Y	Y
ILLINOIS						
Durbin	Y	N	N	N	N	N
Duckworth	?	+	?	?	?	?
INDIANA						
Donnelly	Y	N	N	Y	N	N
Young	Y	Y	Y	Y	Y	Y
IOWA						
Grassley	Y	Y	Y	Y	Y	Y
Ernst	Y	Y	Y	Y	Y	Y
KANSAS						
Roberts	Y	Y	Y	Y	Y	Y
Moran	Y	Y	Y	Y	Y	Y
KENTUCKY						
McConnell	Y	Y	Y	Y	N	Y
Paul	Y	Y	Y	Y	Y	Y
LOUISIANA						
Cassidy	Y	Y	Y	Y	Y	Y
Kennedy	Y	Y	Y	Y	Y	Y
MAINE						
Collins	Y	Y	Y	Y	Y	Y
King	Y	Y	N	N	N	N
MARYLAND						
Cardin	Y	N	N	N	N	N
Van Hollen	Y	N	N	N	N	N
MASSACHUSETTS						
Warren	Y	N	N	N	N	N
Markey	Y	N	N	N	N	N
MICHIGAN						
Stabenow	Y	N	N	N	N	N
Peters	Y	N	N	N	N	N
MINNESOTA						
Klobuchar	Y	N	N	N	N	N
Smith	Y	N	N	N	N	N
MISSISSIPPI						
Wicker	Y	Y	Y	Y	Y	Y
Hyde-Smith	Y	Y	Y	Y	Y	Y
MISSOURI						
McCaskill	Y	N	N	N	Y	N
Blunt	Y	Y	Y	Y	Y	Y

	73	74	75	76	77	78
MONTANA						
Tester	Y	Y	N	N	N	N
Daines	Y	Y	Y	Y	Y	Y
NEBRASKA						
Fischer	Y	Y	Y	Y	Y	Y
Sasse	Y	Y	Y	Y	Y	Y
NEVADA						
Heller	Y	Y	Y	Y	Y	Y
Cortez Masto	Y	N	N	N	N	N
NEW HAMPSHIRE						
Shaheen	Y	N	N	N	N	N
Hassan	Y	N	N	N	N	N
NEW JERSEY						
Menendez	Y	N	N	N	N	N
Booker	Y	N	N	N	N	N
NEW MEXICO						
Udall	Y	N	N	N	N	N
Heinrich	Y	Y	N	N	N	N
NEW YORK						
Schumer	Y	N	N	N	N	N
Gillibrand	Y	N	N	N	N	N
NORTH CAROLINA						
Burr	Y	Y	Y	Y	Y	Y
Tillis	Y	?	?	Y	Y	Y
NORTH DAKOTA						
Hoeven	Y	Y	Y	Y	Y	Y
Heitkamp	Y	Y	N	N	Y	N
OHIO						
Brown	Y	N	N	N	N	N
Portman	Y	N	Y	Y	Y	Y
OKLAHOMA						
Inhofe	Y	Y	Y	Y	Y	Y
Lankford	Y	Y	Y	Y	Y	Y
OREGON						
Wyden	Y	N	N	N	N	N
Merkley	Y	N	N	N	N	N
PENNSYLVANIA						
Casey	Y	N	N	Y	N	N
Toomey	?	Y	Y	Y	Y	Y
RHODE ISLAND						
Reed	Y	N	N	N	N	N
Whitehouse	Y	N	N	N	N	N
SOUTH CAROLINA						
Graham	Y	Y	Y	Y	Y	Y
Scott	Y	Y	Y	Y	Y	Y
SOUTH DAKOTA						
Thune	Y	Y	Y	Y	Y	Y
Rounds	Y	Y	Y	Y	Y	Y
TENNESSEE						
Alexander	Y	Y	Y	Y	Y	Y
Corker	Y	Y	Y	Y	Y	Y
TEXAS						
Cornyn	Y	Y	Y	Y	Y	Y
Cruz	Y	Y	Y	Y	Y	Y
UTAH						
Hatch	Y	Y	Y	Y	Y	Y
Lee	Y	Y	Y	Y	Y	Y
VERMONT						
Leahy	Y	N	N	N	N	N
Sanders	N	N	N	N	N	N
VIRGINIA						
Warner	Y	Y	N	N	N	N
Kaine	Y	Y	N	N	N	N
WASHINGTON						
Murray	Y	N	N	N	N	N
Cantwell	Y	N	N	N	N	N
WEST VIRGINIA						
Manchin	Y	N	Y	Y	Y	N
Capito	Y	Y	Y	Y	Y	Y
WISCONSIN						
Johnson	Y	Y	Y	Y	Y	Y
Baldwin	Y	N	N	N	N	N
WYOMING						
Enzi	Y	Y	Y	Y	Y	Y
Barrasso	Y	Y	Y	Y	Y	Y

KEY	**Republicans**	Democrats	*Independents*	
Y Voted for (yea)		X Paired against		C Voted "present" to avoid possible conflict of interest
# Paired for		– Announced against		
+ Announced for		P Voted "present"		? Did not vote or otherwise make a position known
N Voted against (nay)				

VOTE NUMBER

79. MUNIZ NOMINATION/CONFIRMATION. Confirmation of President Donald Trump's nomination of Carlos G. Muniz of Florida to be general counsel for the Department of Education. Confirmed 55-43: R 50-0; D 5-41. April 18, 2018.

80. BRIDENSTINE NOMINATION/CONFIRMATION. Confirmation of President Donald Trump's nomination of James Bridenstine of Oklahoma to be administrator of the National Aeronautics and Space Administration. Confirmed 50-49: R 50-0; D 0-47. April 19, 2018.

81. DUNCAN NOMINATION/CLOTURE. Motion to invoke cloture (thus limiting debate) on the nomination of Stuart Kyle Duncan of Louisiana to be a U.S. circuit judge for the Fifth Circuit. Motion agreed to 50-44: R 49-0; D 1-42. April 23, 2018.

82. DUNCAN NOMINATION/CONFIRMATION. Confirmation of President Donald Trump's nomination of Stuart Kyle Duncan of Louisiana to be a U.S. circuit judge for the Fifth Circuit. Confirmed 50-47: R 49-0; D 1-45. April 24, 2018.

83. POMPEO NOMINATION/CLOTURE. Motion to invoke cloture (thus limiting debate) on the nomination of Mike Pompeo of Kansas to be secretary of State. Motion agreed to 57-42: R 50-0; D 6-41. April 26, 2018.

84. POMPEO NOMINATION/CONFIRMATION. Confirmation of President Donald Trump's nomination of Mike Pompeo of Kansas to be secretary of State. Confirmed 57-42: R 50-0; D 6-41. April 26, 2018.

	79	80	81	82	83	84
ALABAMA						
Shelby	Y	Y	Y	Y	Y	Y
Jones	Y	N	N	N	Y	Y
ALASKA						
Murkowski	Y	Y	Y	Y	Y	Y
Sullivan	Y	Y	Y	Y	Y	Y
ARIZONA						
McCain	?	?	?	?	?	?
Flake	Y	Y	Y	Y	Y	Y
ARKANSAS						
Boozman	Y	Y	Y	Y	Y	Y
Cotton	Y	Y	Y	Y	Y	Y
CALIFORNIA						
Feinstein	N	N	?	N	N	N
Harris	N	N	N	N	N	N
COLORADO						
Bennet	N	N	N	N	N	N
Gardner	Y	Y	Y	Y	Y	Y
CONNECTICUT						
Blumenthal	N	N	N	N	N	N
Murphy	N	N	N	N	N	N
DELAWARE						
Carper	N	N	N	N	N	N
Coons	N	N	N	N	N	N
FLORIDA						
Nelson	Y	N	–	N	Y	Y
Rubio	Y	Y	Y	Y	Y	Y
GEORGIA						
Isakson	Y	Y	?	Y	Y	Y
Perdue	Y	Y	Y	Y	Y	Y
HAWAII						
Schatz	N	N	N	N	N	N
Hirono	N	N	?	N	N	N
IDAHO						
Crapo	Y	Y	Y	Y	Y	Y
Risch	Y	Y	Y	Y	Y	Y
ILLINOIS						
Durbin	N	N	N	N	N	N
Duckworth	?	N	?	?	N	N
INDIANA						
Donnelly	Y	N	N	N	Y	Y
Young	Y	Y	Y	Y	Y	Y
IOWA						
Grassley	Y	Y	Y	Y	Y	Y
Ernst	Y	Y	Y	Y	Y	Y
KANSAS						
Roberts	Y	Y	Y	Y	Y	Y
Moran	Y	Y	Y	Y	Y	Y
KENTUCKY						
McConnell	Y	Y	Y	Y	Y	Y
Paul	Y	Y	Y	?	Y	Y
LOUISIANA						
Cassidy	Y	Y	Y	Y	Y	Y
Kennedy	Y	Y	Y	Y	Y	Y
MAINE						
Collins	Y	Y	Y	Y	Y	Y
King	N	N	N	N	Y	Y
MARYLAND						
Cardin	N	N	N	N	N	N
Van Hollen	N	N	N	N	N	N
MASSACHUSETTS						
Warren	N	N	N	N	N	N
Markey	N	N	N	N	N	N
MICHIGAN						
Stabenow	N	N	N	N	N	N
Peters	N	N	N	N	N	N
MINNESOTA						
Klobuchar	N	N	N	N	N	N
Smith	N	N	N	N	N	N
MISSISSIPPI						
Wicker	Y	Y	Y	Y	Y	Y
Hyde-Smith	Y	Y	Y	Y	Y	Y
MISSOURI						
McCaskill	N	N	N	N	Y	Y
Blunt	Y	Y	Y	Y	Y	Y

	79	80	81	82	83	84
MONTANA						
Tester	N	N	N	N	N	N
Daines	Y	Y	Y	Y	Y	Y
NEBRASKA						
Fischer	Y	Y	Y	Y	Y	Y
Sasse	Y	Y	Y	Y	Y	Y
NEVADA						
Heller	Y	Y	Y	Y	Y	Y
Cortez Masto	N	N	N	N	N	N
NEW HAMPSHIRE						
Shaheen	N	N	N	N	N	N
Hassan	N	N	N	N	N	N
NEW JERSEY						
Menendez	N	N	N	N	N	N
Booker	N	N	N	N	N	N
NEW MEXICO						
Udall	N	N	N	N	N	N
Heinrich	N	N	N	N	N	N
NEW YORK						
Schumer	N	N	N	N	N	N
Gillibrand	N	N	N	N	N	N
NORTH CAROLINA						
Burr	Y	Y	Y	Y	Y	Y
Tillis	Y	Y	Y	Y	Y	Y
NORTH DAKOTA						
Hoeven	Y	Y	Y	Y	Y	Y
Heitkamp	Y	N	N	N	Y	Y
OHIO						
Brown	N	N	N	N	N	N
Portman	Y	Y	Y	Y	Y	Y
OKLAHOMA						
Inhofe	Y	Y	Y	Y	Y	Y
Lankford	Y	Y	Y	Y	Y	Y
OREGON						
Wyden	N	N	N	N	N	N
Merkley	N	N	N	N	N	N
PENNSYLVANIA						
Casey	N	N	N	N	N	N
Toomey	Y	Y	Y	Y	Y	Y
RHODE ISLAND						
Reed	N	N	N	N	N	N
Whitehouse	N	N	N	N	N	N
SOUTH CAROLINA						
Graham	Y	Y	Y	Y	Y	Y
Scott	Y	Y	Y	Y	Y	Y
SOUTH DAKOTA						
Thune	Y	Y	Y	Y	Y	Y
Rounds	Y	Y	Y	Y	Y	Y
TENNESSEE						
Alexander	Y	Y	Y	Y	Y	Y
Corker	Y	Y	Y	Y	Y	Y
TEXAS						
Cornyn	Y	Y	Y	Y	Y	Y
Cruz	Y	Y	Y	Y	Y	Y
UTAH						
Hatch	Y	Y	Y	Y	Y	Y
Lee	Y	Y	Y	Y	Y	Y
VERMONT						
Leahy	N	N	N	N	N	N
Sanders	N	N	N	N	N	N
VIRGINIA						
Warner	N	N	N	N	N	N
Kaine	N	N	N	N	N	N
WASHINGTON						
Murray	N	N	N	N	N	N
Cantwell	N	N	N	N	N	N
WEST VIRGINIA						
Manchin	Y	N	Y	Y	Y	Y
Capito	Y	Y	Y	Y	Y	Y
WISCONSIN						
Johnson	Y	Y	Y	Y	Y	Y
Baldwin	N	N	N	N	N	N
WYOMING						
Enzi	Y	Y	Y	Y	Y	Y
Barrasso	Y	Y	Y	Y	Y	Y

KEY	**Republicans**	Democrats	*Independents*	
Y Voted for (yea)		X Paired against		C Voted "present" to avoid possible conflict of interest
# Paired for		– Announced against		
+ Announced for		P Voted "present"		? Did not vote or otherwise make a position known
N Voted against (nay)				

VOTE NUMBER

85. GRENELL NOMINATION/CONFIRMATION. Confirmation of President Donald Trump's nomination of Richard Grenell of California to be U.S. ambassador to the Republic of Germany. Confirmed 56-42: R 50-0; D 6-40. April 26, 2018.

86. ENGELHARDT NOMINATION/CLOTURE. Motion to invoke cloture (thus limiting debate) on the nomination of Kurt D. Engelhardt of Louisiana to be a U.S. circuit judge for the Fifth Circuit. Motion agreed to 64-31: R 48-0; D 15-30. May 7, 2018.

87. ENGELHARDT NOMINATION/CONFIRMATION. Confirmation of President Donald Trump's nomination of Kurt D. Engelhardt of Louisiana to be a U.S. circuit judge for the Fifth Circuit. Confirmed 62-34: R 49-0; D 12-33. May 9, 2018.

88. BRENNAN NOMINATION/CLOTURE. Motion to invoke cloture (thus limiting debate) on the nomination of Michael B. Brennan of Wisconsin to be a U.S. circuit judge for the Seventh Circuit. Motion agreed to 49-47: R 49-0; D 0-45. May 9, 2018.

89. BRENNAN NOMINATION/CONFIRMATION. Confirmation of President Donald Trump's nomination of Michael B. Brennan of Wisconsin to be a U.S. circuit judge for the Seventh Circuit. Confirmed 49-46: R 49-0; D 0-44. May 10, 2018.

90. CARSON NOMINATION/CLOTURE. Motion to invoke cloture (thus limiting debate) on the nomination of Joel M. Carson III of New Mexico to be a U.S. circuit judge for the Tenth Circuit. Motion agreed to 71-24: R 49-0; D 21-23. May 10, 2018.

	85	86	87	88	89	90
ALABAMA						
Shelby	Y	Y	Y	Y	Y	Y
Jones	Y	Y	Y	N	N	Y
ALASKA						
Murkowski	Y	Y	Y	Y	Y	Y
Sullivan	Y	Y	Y	Y	Y	Y
ARIZONA						
McCain	?	?	?	?	?	?
Flake	Y	Y	Y	Y	Y	Y
ARKANSAS						
Boozman	Y	Y	Y	Y	Y	Y
Cotton	Y	Y	Y	Y	Y	Y
CALIFORNIA						
Feinstein	N	Y	N	N	N	Y
Harris	N	N	N	N	N	N
COLORADO						
Bennet	N	Y	Y	N	N	Y
Gardner	Y	Y	Y	Y	Y	Y
CONNECTICUT						
Blumenthal	N	N	N	N	N	N
Murphy	N	Y	Y	N	N	Y
DELAWARE						
Carper	N	Y	N	N	N	Y
Coons	N	Y	Y	N	?	?
FLORIDA						
Nelson	N	Y	Y	N	N	Y
Rubio	Y	Y	Y	Y	Y	Y
GEORGIA						
Isakson	Y	?	Y	Y	Y	Y
Perdue	Y	Y	Y	Y	Y	Y
HAWAII						
Schatz	N	N	N	N	N	Y
Hirono	N	N	N	N	N	N
IDAHO						
Crapo	Y	Y	Y	Y	Y	Y
Risch	Y	Y	Y	Y	Y	Y
ILLINOIS						
Durbin	N	N	N	N	N	Y
Duckworth	?	?	?	?	?	?
INDIANA						
Donnelly	Y	Y	+	–	N	Y
Young	Y	Y	Y	Y	Y	Y
IOWA						
Grassley	Y	Y	Y	Y	Y	Y
Ernst	Y	Y	Y	Y	Y	Y
KANSAS						
Roberts	Y	Y	Y	Y	Y	Y
Moran	Y	Y	Y	Y	Y	Y
KENTUCKY						
McConnell	Y	Y	Y	Y	Y	Y
Paul	Y	Y	Y	Y	Y	Y
LOUISIANA						
Cassidy	Y	Y	Y	Y	Y	Y
Kennedy	Y	Y	Y	Y	Y	Y
MAINE						
Collins	Y	Y	Y	Y	Y	Y
King	N	Y	Y	N	N	Y
MARYLAND						
Cardin	N	N	N	N	N	N
Van Hollen	N	N	N	N	N	N
MASSACHUSETTS						
Warren	N	N	N	N	N	N
Markey	N	N	N	N	N	N
MICHIGAN						
Stabenow	N	N	N	N	N	N
Peters	N	N	N	N	N	N
MINNESOTA						
Klobuchar	N	Y	Y	N	N	N
Smith	N	N	N	N	N	N
MISSISSIPPI						
Wicker	Y	Y	Y	Y	Y	Y
Hyde-Smith	Y	Y	Y	Y	Y	Y
MISSOURI						
McCaskill	Y	Y	Y	N	N	Y
Blunt	Y	Y	Y	Y	Y	Y
MONTANA						
Tester	Y	Y	Y	N	N	Y
Daines	Y	Y	Y	Y	Y	Y
NEBRASKA						
Fischer	Y	Y	Y	Y	Y	Y
Sasse	Y	Y	Y	Y	Y	Y
NEVADA						
Heller	Y	Y	Y	Y	Y	Y
Cortez Masto	N	N	N	N	N	N
NEW HAMPSHIRE						
Shaheen	N	N	N	N	N	Y
Hassan	N	N	N	N	N	Y
NEW JERSEY						
Menendez	N	N	N	N	N	Y
Booker	N	N	N	N	–	–
NEW MEXICO						
Udall	N	N	N	N	N	N
Heinrich	N	N	N	N	N	N
NEW YORK						
Schumer	N	N	N	N	N	N
Gillibrand	N	N	N	N	N	N
NORTH CAROLINA						
Burr	Y	Y	Y	Y	Y	Y
Tillis	Y	Y	Y	Y	Y	Y
NORTH DAKOTA						
Hoeven	Y	Y	Y	Y	Y	Y
Heitkamp	Y	Y	Y	N	N	Y
OHIO						
Brown	N	N	N	N	N	N
Portman	Y	Y	Y	Y	Y	Y
OKLAHOMA						
Inhofe	Y	Y	Y	Y	Y	Y
Lankford	Y	Y	Y	Y	Y	Y
OREGON						
Wyden	N	N	N	N	N	N
Merkley	N	–	N	N	N	N
PENNSYLVANIA						
Casey	N	N	N	N	N	N
Toomey	Y	Y	Y	Y	Y	Y
RHODE ISLAND						
Reed	N	N	N	N	N	N
Whitehouse	N	N	N	N	N	N
SOUTH CAROLINA						
Graham	Y	?	?	?	?	?
Scott	Y	Y	Y	Y	Y	Y
SOUTH DAKOTA						
Thune	Y	Y	Y	Y	Y	Y
Rounds	Y	Y	Y	Y	Y	Y
TENNESSEE						
Alexander	Y	Y	Y	Y	Y	Y
Corker	Y	Y	Y	Y	Y	Y
TEXAS						
Cornyn	Y	Y	Y	Y	Y	Y
Cruz	Y	Y	Y	Y	Y	Y
UTAH						
Hatch	Y	Y	Y	Y	Y	Y
Lee	Y	Y	Y	Y	Y	Y
VERMONT						
Leahy	N	Y	Y	N	N	Y
Sanders	N	N	N	N	N	N
VIRGINIA						
Warner	N	Y	N	N	N	Y
Kaine	N	N	N	N	N	N
WASHINGTON						
Murray	N	N	N	N	N	N
Cantwell	N	N	N	N	N	N
WEST VIRGINIA						
Manchin	Y	Y	Y	N	N	Y
Capito	Y	Y	Y	Y	Y	Y
WISCONSIN						
Johnson	Y	Y	Y	Y	Y	Y
Baldwin	N	N	N	N	N	N
WYOMING						
Enzi	Y	Y	Y	Y	Y	Y
Barrasso	Y	Y	Y	Y	Y	Y

KEY	**Republicans**	Democrats	*Independents*

Y Voted for (yea)	X Paired against	C Voted "present" to avoid possible conflict of interest
# Paired for	– Announced against	
+ Announced for	P Voted "present"	? Did not vote or otherwise make a position known
N Voted against (nay)		

VOTE NUMBER

91. NALBANDIAN NOMINATION/CLOTURE. Motion to invoke cloture (thus limiting debate) on the nomination of John B. Nalbandian of Kentucky to be a U.S. circuit judge for the Sixth Circuit. Motion agreed to 52-43: R 49-0; D 3-41. May 10, 2018.

92. SCUDDER NOMINATION/CONFIRMATION. Confirmation of President Donald Trump's nomination of Michael Y. Scudder of Illinois to be a U.S. circuit judge for the Seventh Circuit. Confirmed 90-0: R 44-0; D 44-0. May 14, 2018.

93. ST. EVE NOMINATION/CONFIRMATION. Confirmation of President Donald Trump's nomination of Amy J. St. Eve of Illinois to be a U.S. circuit judge for the Seventh Circuit. Confirmed 91-0: R 44-0; D 45-0. May 14, 2018.

94. CARSON NOMINATION/CONFIRMATION. Confirmation of President Donald Trump's nomination of Joel M. Carson III of New Mexico to be a U.S. circuit judge for the Tenth Circuit. Confirmed 77-21: R 50-0; D 26-20. May 15, 2018.

95. NALBANDIAN NOMINATION/CONFIRMATION. Confirmation of President Donald Trump's nomination of John B. Nalbandian of Kentucky to be a U.S. circuit judge for the Sixth Circuit. Confirmed 53-45: R 50-0; D 3-43. May 15, 2018.

96. SJRES52. "NET NEUTRALITY" DISAPPROVAL/MOTION TO PROCEED. Markey, D-Mass., motion to proceed to the joint resolution that would nullify and disapprove of a Federal Communication Commission rule that classifies broadband internet access service as an information service and mobile broadband internet access service as a private mobile radio service. Motion agreed to 52-47: R 3-47; D 47-0. May 16, 2018.

	91	92	93	94	95	96
ALABAMA						
Shelby	Y	Y	Y	Y	Y	N
Jones	N	Y	Y	Y	N	Y
ALASKA						
Murkowski	Y	Y	Y	Y	Y	Y
Sullivan	Y	Y	Y	Y	Y	N
ARIZONA						
McCain	?	?	?	?	?	?
Flake	Y	Y	Y	Y	Y	N
ARKANSAS						
Boozman	Y	Y	Y	Y	Y	N
Cotton	Y	Y	Y	Y	Y	N
CALIFORNIA						
Feinstein	N	Y	Y	Y	N	Y
Harris	N	Y	Y	N	N	Y
COLORADO						
Bennet	N	Y	Y	Y	N	Y
Gardner	Y	Y	Y	Y	Y	N
CONNECTICUT						
Blumenthal	N	Y	Y	Y	N	Y
Murphy	N	Y	Y	Y	N	Y
DELAWARE						
Carper	N	Y	Y	Y	N	Y
Coons	?	Y	Y	Y	N	Y
FLORIDA						
Nelson	N	+	Y	Y	N	Y
Rubio	Y	Y	Y	Y	Y	N
GEORGIA						
Isakson	Y	Y	Y	Y	Y	N
Perdue	Y	Y	Y	Y	Y	N
HAWAII						
Schatz	N	Y	Y	Y	N	Y
Hirono	N	Y	Y	N	N	Y
IDAHO						
Crapo	Y	Y	Y	Y	Y	N
Risch	Y	Y	Y	Y	Y	N
ILLINOIS						
Durbin	N	Y	Y	Y	N	Y
Duckworth	?	+	+	?	?	Y
INDIANA						
Donnelly	Y	Y	Y	Y	Y	Y
Young	Y	Y	Y	Y	Y	N
IOWA						
Grassley	Y	Y	Y	Y	Y	N
Ernst	Y	Y	Y	Y	Y	N
KANSAS						
Roberts	Y	Y	Y	Y	Y	N
Moran	?	Y	Y	Y	Y	N
KENTUCKY						
McConnell	Y	Y	Y	Y	Y	N
Paul	Y	Y	Y	Y	Y	N
LOUISIANA						
Cassidy	Y	Y	Y	Y	Y	N
Kennedy	Y	Y	Y	Y	Y	Y
MAINE						
Collins	Y	Y	Y	Y	Y	Y
King	N	Y	Y	Y	N	Y
MARYLAND						
Cardin	N	Y	Y	Y	N	Y
Van Hollen	N	Y	Y	Y	N	Y
MASSACHUSETTS						
Warren	N	Y	Y	N	N	Y
Markey	N	Y	Y	N	N	Y
MICHIGAN						
Stabenow	N	Y	Y	N	N	Y
Peters	N	Y	Y	N	N	Y
MINNESOTA						
Klobuchar	N	Y	Y	Y	N	Y
Smith	N	Y	Y	N	N	Y
MISSISSIPPI						
Wicker	Y	Y	Y	Y	Y	N
Hyde-Smith	Y	Y	Y	Y	Y	N
MISSOURI						
McCaskill	N	Y	Y	Y	N	Y
Blunt	Y	?	?	Y	Y	N

	91	92	93	94	95	96
MONTANA						
Tester	N	Y	Y	Y	Y	N
Daines	Y	Y	Y	Y	Y	N
NEBRASKA						
Fischer	Y	Y	Y	Y	Y	N
Sasse	Y	Y	Y	Y	Y	N
NEVADA						
Heller	Y	?	?	Y	Y	N
Cortez Masto	N	Y	Y	N	N	Y
NEW HAMPSHIRE						
Shaheen	N	Y	Y	Y	N	Y
Hassan	N	Y	Y	Y	N	Y
NEW JERSEY						
Menendez	N	Y	Y	N	N	Y
Booker	–	Y	Y	N	N	Y
NEW MEXICO						
Udall	N	Y	Y	Y	N	Y
Heinrich	N	Y	Y	Y	N	Y
NEW YORK						
Schumer	N	Y	Y	Y	N	Y
Gillibrand	N	Y	Y	N	N	Y
NORTH CAROLINA						
Burr	Y	Y	Y	Y	Y	N
Tillis	Y	Y	Y	Y	Y	N
NORTH DAKOTA						
Hoeven	Y	Y	Y	Y	Y	N
Heitkamp	Y	Y	Y	Y	Y	Y
OHIO						
Brown	N	Y	Y	N	N	Y
Portman	Y	Y	Y	Y	Y	N
OKLAHOMA						
Inhofe	Y	Y	Y	Y	Y	N
Lankford	Y	?	?	Y	Y	N
OREGON						
Wyden	N	Y	Y	N	N	Y
Merkley	N	Y	Y	N	N	Y
PENNSYLVANIA						
Casey	N	Y	Y	N	N	Y
Toomey	Y	Y	Y	Y	Y	N
RHODE ISLAND						
Reed	N	Y	Y	N	N	Y
Whitehouse	N	Y	Y	N	N	Y
SOUTH CAROLINA						
Graham	Y	?	?	Y	Y	N
Scott	Y	Y	Y	Y	Y	N
SOUTH DAKOTA						
Thune	Y	Y	Y	Y	Y	N
Rounds	Y	Y	Y	Y	Y	N
TENNESSEE						
Alexander	Y	Y	Y	Y	Y	N
Corker	Y	Y	Y	Y	Y	N
TEXAS						
Cornyn	Y	Y	Y	Y	Y	N
Cruz	Y	?	?	Y	Y	N
UTAH						
Hatch	Y	Y	Y	Y	Y	N
Lee	Y	?	?	Y	Y	N
VERMONT						
Leahy	N	Y	Y	Y	N	Y
Sanders	N	Y	Y	N	N	Y
VIRGINIA						
Warner	N	Y	Y	Y	N	Y
Kaine	N	Y	Y	Y	N	Y
WASHINGTON						
Murray	N	Y	Y	N	N	Y
Cantwell	N	Y	Y	N	N	Y
WEST VIRGINIA						
Manchin	Y	?	?	Y	Y	Y
Capito	Y	Y	Y	Y	Y	N
WISCONSIN						
Johnson	Y	Y	Y	Y	Y	N
Baldwin	N	Y	Y	N	N	Y
WYOMING						
Enzi	Y	Y	Y	Y	Y	N
Barrasso	Y	Y	Y	Y	Y	N

KEY	**Republicans**	Democrats	*Independents*	
Y Voted for (yea)		**X** Paired against		**C** Voted "present" to avoid possible conflict of interest
# Paired for		**–** Announced against		**?** Did not vote or otherwise make a position known
+ Announced for		**P** Voted "present"		
N Voted against (nay)				

VOTE NUMBER

97. SJRES52. "NET NEUTRALITY" DISAPPROVAL/PASSAGE. Passage of the joint resolution that would nullify and disapprove of a Federal Communication Commission rule that classifies broadband internet access service as an information service and mobile broadband internet access service as a private mobile radio service. The rule overturns a 2015 order from the FCC that imposed common-carrier mandates that prevented internet providers from blocking certain websites or tying certain content to higher fees. Passed 52-47: R 3-47; D 47-0. May 16, 2018.

98. ZAIS NOMINATION/CONFIRMATION. Confirmation of President Donald Trump's nomination of Mitchell Zais of South Carolina to be deputy secretary of Education. Confirmed 50-48: R 50-0; D 0-46. May 16, 2018.

99. SCONRES36. ALTERNATE FISCAL 2019 BUDGET RESOLUTION/MOTION TO PROCEED. Paul, R-Ky., motion to proceed to the resolution that would repeal the current two-year budget agreement, set a new budget for fiscal 2019 and would set new broad spending and revenue targets for the next 10 years. Motion rejected 21-76: R 21-29; D 0-45. May 17, 2018.

100. HASPEL NOMINATION/CLOTURE. Motion to invoke cloture (thus limiting debate) on the nomination of Gina Haspel of Kentucky to be director of the Central Intelligence Agency. Motion agreed to 54-44: R 48-1; D 6-41. May 17, 2018.

101. HASPEL NOMINATION/CONFIRMATION. Confirmation of President Donald Trump's nomination of Gina Haspel of Kentucky to be director of the Central Intelligence Agency. Confirmed 54-45: R 48-2; D 6-41. May 17, 2018.

102. BAIOCCO NOMINATION/CLOTURE. Motion to invoke cloture (thus limiting debate) on the nomination of Dana Baiocco of Ohio to be a commissioner of the Consumer Product Safety Commission. Motion agreed to 49-45: R 48-0; D 1-43. May 21, 2018.

	97	98	99	100	101	102
ALABAMA						
Shelby	N	Y	N	Y	Y	Y
Jones	Y	N	N	N	N	N
ALASKA						
Murkowski	Y	Y	N	Y	Y	Y
Sullivan	N	Y	N	Y	Y	Y
ARIZONA						
McCain	?	?	?	?	?	?
Flake	N	Y	Y	Y	N	Y
ARKANSAS						
Boozman	N	Y	N	Y	Y	Y
Cotton	N	Y	N	Y	Y	Y
CALIFORNIA						
Feinstein	Y	N	N	N	N	N
Harris	Y	N	N	N	N	N
COLORADO						
Bennet	Y	N	N	N	N	N
Gardner	N	Y	N	Y	Y	Y
CONNECTICUT						
Blumenthal	Y	N	N	N	N	N
Murphy	Y	N	N	N	N	N
DELAWARE						
Carper	Y	N	N	N	N	N
Coons	Y	N	N	N	N	N
FLORIDA						
Nelson	Y	N	N	Y	N	Y
Rubio	N	Y	Y	Y	Y	Y
GEORGIA						
Isakson	N	Y	N	Y	Y	Y
Perdue	N	Y	N	Y	Y	Y
HAWAII						
Schatz	Y	N	N	N	N	N
Hirono	Y	N	N	N	N	N
IDAHO						
Crapo	N	Y	Y	Y	Y	Y
Risch	N	Y	Y	Y	Y	Y
ILLINOIS						
Durbin	Y	N	N	N	N	N
Duckworth	Y	?	?	N	N	-
INDIANA						
Donnelly	Y	N	N	Y	N	N
Young	N	Y	N	+	Y	Y
IOWA						
Grassley	N	Y	Y	Y	Y	Y
Ernst	N	Y	Y	Y	Y	Y
KANSAS						
Roberts	N	Y	N	Y	Y	Y
Moran	N	Y	Y	Y	Y	Y
KENTUCKY						
McConnell	N	Y	N	Y	Y	Y
Paul	N	Y	Y	N	N	Y
LOUISIANA						
Cassidy	N	Y	N	Y	Y	Y
Kennedy	Y	Y	Y	Y	Y	Y
MAINE						
Collins	Y	Y	Y	Y	Y	Y
King	Y	N	N	N	N	N
MARYLAND						
Cardin	Y	N	N	N	N	N
Van Hollen	Y	N	N	N	N	N
MASSACHUSETTS						
Warren	Y	N	N	N	N	N
Markey	Y	N	N	N	N	N
MICHIGAN						
Stabenow	Y	N	N	N	N	N
Peters	Y	N	N	N	N	N
MINNESOTA						
Klobuchar	Y	N	N	N	N	N
Smith	Y	N	N	N	N	N
MISSISSIPPI						
Wicker	N	Y	N	Y	Y	Y
Hyde-Smith	N	Y	N	Y	Y	Y
MISSOURI						
McCaskill	Y	N	N	N	N	N
Blunt	N	Y	N	Y	Y	Y

	97	98	99	100	101	102
MONTANA						
Tester	Y	N	N	N	N	-
Daines	N	Y	Y	Y	Y	Y
NEBRASKA						
Fischer	N	Y	Y	Y	Y	Y
Sasse	N	Y	Y	Y	Y	Y
NEVADA						
Heller	N	Y	N	Y	Y	Y
Cortez Masto	Y	N	N	N	N	N
NEW HAMPSHIRE						
Shaheen	Y	N	N	Y	Y	?
Hassan	Y	N	N	N	N	N
NEW JERSEY						
Menendez	Y	N	N	N	N	N
Booker	Y	N	-	N	N	N
NEW MEXICO						
Udall	Y	N	N	N	N	N
Heinrich	Y	N	N	N	N	N
NEW YORK						
Schumer	Y	N	N	N	N	N
Gillibrand	Y	N	N	N	N	N
NORTH CAROLINA						
Burr	N	Y	N	Y	Y	Y
Tillis	N	Y	N	Y	Y	Y
NORTH DAKOTA						
Hoeven	N	Y	N	Y	Y	?
Heitkamp	Y	N	N	Y	N	N
OHIO						
Brown	Y	N	N	N	N	N
Portman	N	Y	N	Y	Y	Y
OKLAHOMA						
Inhofe	N	Y	N	Y	Y	Y
Lankford	N	Y	Y	Y	Y	Y
OREGON						
Wyden	Y	N	N	N	N	N
Merkley	Y	N	N	N	N	N
PENNSYLVANIA						
Casey	Y	N	N	N	N	N
Toomey	N	Y	Y	Y	Y	Y
RHODE ISLAND						
Reed	Y	N	N	N	N	N
Whitehouse	Y	N	N	N	N	N
SOUTH CAROLINA						
Graham	N	Y	N	Y	Y	Y
Scott	N	Y	N	Y	Y	Y
SOUTH DAKOTA						
Thune	N	Y	N	Y	Y	Y
Rounds	N	Y	N	Y	Y	Y
TENNESSEE						
Alexander	N	Y	N	Y	Y	Y
Corker	N	Y	N	Y	Y	Y
TEXAS						
Cornyn	N	Y	Y	Y	Y	Y
Cruz	N	Y	Y	Y	Y	Y
UTAH						
Hatch	N	Y	N	Y	Y	Y
Lee	N	Y	Y	Y	Y	Y
VERMONT						
Leahy	Y	N	N	N	N	N
Sanders	Y	N	N	N	N	N
VIRGINIA						
Warner	Y	N	N	Y	Y	N
Kaine	Y	N	N	N	N	N
WASHINGTON						
Murray	Y	N	N	N	N	N
Cantwell	Y	N	N	N	N	N
WEST VIRGINIA						
Manchin	Y	N	N	Y	Y	Y
Capito	N	Y	N	Y	Y	?
WISCONSIN						
Johnson	N	Y	Y	Y	Y	Y
Baldwin	Y	N	N	N	N	N
WYOMING						
Enzi	N	Y	Y	Y	Y	Y
Barrasso	N	Y	Y	Y	Y	Y

KEY	**Republicans**	Democrats	*Independents*

Y	Voted for (yea)	X Paired against	C Voted "present" to avoid possible conflict of interest
#	Paired for	– Announced against	
+	Announced for	P Voted "present"	? Did not vote or otherwise make a position known
N	Voted against (nay)		

VOTE NUMBER

103. BAIOCCO NOMINATION/CONFIRMATION. Confirmation of President Donald Trump's nomination of Dana Baiocco of Ohio to be a commissioner of the Consumer Product Safety Commission. Confirmed 50-45: R 49-0; D 1-43. May 22, 2018.

104. S2372. VETERANS' HEALTH CARE/CLOTURE. Motion to invoke cloture (thus limiting debate) on the McConnell motion to concur in the House amendment to the bill. Motion agreed to 91-4: R 47-2; D 43-1. May 22, 2018.

105. MONTGOMERY NOMINATION/CONFIRMATION. Confirmation of President Donald Trump's nomination of Brian D. Montgomery, of Texas, to be an assistant secretary of the Housing and Urban Development Department. Confirmed 74-23: R 49-0; D 24-22. May 23, 2018.

106. S2372. VETERANS' HEALTH CARE/MOTION TO CONCUR. McConnell, R-Ky., motion to concur in the House amendment to the bill that would consolidate programs that allow veterans to seek medical care outside of the VA into a new singular entity, the Veterans Community Care Program. The bill would continue the current VA Choice Program for one year, and would authorize an additional $5.2 billion for the costs of providing non-VA medical care through the old program and for transitioning to the new program. It would also authorize the VA to enter into Veterans Care Agreements that would include care standards for providers and private facilities, and would allow veterans to access care at federally-qualified health centers walk-in clinics. The bill would also create a commission to review VA modernization proposals and includes other provisions related to the recruitment of health care professionals. The bill would also require the Interior Department to provide an outer burial receptacle for new graves in open cemeteries that are controlled by the National Park Service, and would require the Department to reimburse veterans' survivors who had purchased one on their own. Motion agreed to 92-5: R 47-2; D 44-2. May 23, 2018.

107. MCWILLIAMS NOMINATION/CLOTURE. Motion to invoke cloture (thus limiting debate) on the nomination of Jelena McWilliams of Ohio to be a chairperson of the Board of Directors of the Federal Deposit Insurance Corporation. Motion agreed to 72-25: R 49-0; D 22-24. May 23, 2018.

108. MCWILLIAMS NOMINATION/CLOTURE. Motion to invoke cloture (thus limiting debate) on the nomination of Jelena McWilliams of Ohio to be a member of the Board of Directors of the Federal Deposit Insurance Corporation. Motion agreed to 73-23: R 49-0; D 23-23. May 23, 2018.

	103	104	105	106	107	108
ALABAMA						
Shelby	Y	Y	Y	Y	Y	Y
Jones	N	Y	Y	Y	Y	Y
ALASKA						
Murkowski	Y	Y	Y	Y	Y	Y
Sullivan	Y	Y	Y	Y	Y	Y
ARIZONA						
McCain	?	?	?	?	?	?
Flake	Y	Y	?	?	?	?
ARKANSAS						
Boozman	Y	Y	Y	Y	Y	Y
Cotton	Y	Y	Y	Y	Y	Y
CALIFORNIA						
Feinstein	N	Y	N	Y	N	N
Harris	N	Y	N	Y	N	N
COLORADO						
Bennet	?	?	Y	Y	Y	Y
Gardner	+	+	Y	Y	Y	Y
CONNECTICUT						
Blumenthal	N	Y	N	N	N	N
Murphy	N	Y	Y	Y	Y	Y
DELAWARE						
Carper	N	Y	Y	Y	Y	Y
Coons	N	Y	Y	Y	Y	Y
FLORIDA						
Nelson	N	Y	Y	Y	Y	Y
Rubio	Y	Y	Y	Y	Y	Y
GEORGIA						
Isakson	Y	Y	Y	Y	Y	Y
Perdue	Y	Y	Y	Y	Y	Y
HAWAII						
Schatz	N	Y	N	N	N	N
Hirono	N	Y	N	Y	N	N
IDAHO						
Crapo	Y	Y	Y	Y	Y	Y
Risch	Y	Y	Y	Y	Y	Y
ILLINOIS						
Durbin	N	Y	N	Y	N	N
Duckworth	-	+	?	?	?	?
INDIANA						
Donnelly	N	Y	Y	Y	Y	Y
Young	Y	Y	Y	Y	Y	Y
IOWA						
Grassley	Y	Y	Y	Y	Y	Y
Ernst	Y	Y	Y	Y	Y	Y
KANSAS						
Roberts	Y	Y	Y	Y	Y	Y
Moran	Y	Y	Y	Y	Y	Y
KENTUCKY						
McConnell	Y	Y	Y	Y	Y	Y
Paul	Y	Y	Y	Y	Y	Y
LOUISIANA						
Cassidy	Y	Y	Y	Y	Y	Y
Kennedy	Y	Y	Y	Y	Y	Y
MAINE						
Collins	Y	Y	Y	Y	Y	Y
King	N	Y	Y	Y	Y	Y
MARYLAND						
Cardin	?	?	Y	Y	Y	Y
Van Hollen	N	Y	Y	Y	Y	Y
MASSACHUSETTS						
Warren	N	Y	N	Y	N	N
Markey	N	Y	N	Y	N	N
MICHIGAN						
Stabenow	N	Y	N	Y	N	N
Peters	N	Y	Y	Y	Y	Y
MINNESOTA						
Klobuchar	N	Y	Y	Y	Y	Y
Smith	N	Y	Y	Y	N	N
MISSISSIPPI						
Wicker	Y	Y	Y	Y	Y	Y
Hyde-Smith	Y	Y	Y	Y	Y	Y
MISSOURI						
McCaskill	N	Y	Y	Y	Y	Y
Blunt	Y	Y	Y	Y	Y	Y

	103	104	105	106	107	108
MONTANA						
Tester	N	Y	Y	Y	Y	Y
Daines	Y	Y	Y	Y	Y	Y
NEBRASKA						
Fischer	Y	Y	Y	Y	Y	Y
Sasse	Y	Y	Y	Y	Y	Y
NEVADA						
Heller	Y	Y	Y	Y	Y	Y
Cortez Masto	N	Y	N	Y	N	N
NEW HAMPSHIRE						
Shaheen	N	Y	N	Y	N	Y
Hassan	N	Y	Y	Y	Y	Y
NEW JERSEY						
Menendez	N	Y	Y	Y	Y	Y
Booker	N	Y	Y	Y	N	N
NEW MEXICO						
Udall	N	Y	N	Y	N	N
Heinrich	N	Y	N	Y	N	N
NEW YORK						
Schumer	N	Y	N	Y	N	N
Gillibrand	N	Y	N	Y	N	N
NORTH CAROLINA						
Burr	Y	Y	Y	Y	Y	Y
Tillis	Y	Y	Y	Y	Y	Y
NORTH DAKOTA						
Hoeven	Y	Y	Y	Y	Y	Y
Heitkamp	N	Y	Y	Y	Y	Y
OHIO						
Brown	N	Y	N	Y	N	N
Portman	Y	Y	Y	Y	Y	Y
OKLAHOMA						
Inhofe	Y	Y	Y	Y	Y	Y
Lankford	Y	Y	Y	Y	Y	Y
OREGON						
Wyden	N	Y	N	Y	N	N
Merkley	N	N	N	N	N	N
PENNSYLVANIA						
Casey	N	Y	N	Y	Y	Y
Toomey	Y	Y	Y	Y	Y	Y
RHODE ISLAND						
Reed	N	Y	N	Y	Y	Y
Whitehouse	N	Y	N	Y	N	N
SOUTH CAROLINA						
Graham	Y	Y	Y	Y	Y	Y
Scott	Y	Y	Y	Y	Y	Y
SOUTH DAKOTA						
Thune	Y	Y	Y	Y	Y	Y
Rounds	Y	N	Y	N	Y	Y
TENNESSEE						
Alexander	Y	Y	Y	Y	Y	Y
Corker	Y	Y	Y	N	Y	Y
TEXAS						
Cornyn	Y	Y	Y	Y	Y	Y
Cruz	Y	Y	Y	Y	Y	Y
UTAH						
Hatch	Y	Y	Y	Y	Y	Y
Lee	Y	N	Y	Y	Y	Y
VERMONT						
Leahy	N	Y	Y	Y	Y	Y
Sanders	N	N	N	N	N	?
VIRGINIA						
Warner	N	Y	Y	Y	Y	Y
Kaine	N	Y	Y	Y	Y	Y
WASHINGTON						
Murray	N	Y	N	Y	N	N
Cantwell	N	Y	N	Y	N	N
WEST VIRGINIA						
Manchin	Y	Y	Y	Y	Y	Y
Capito	Y	Y	Y	Y	Y	Y
WISCONSIN						
Johnson	Y	Y	Y	Y	Y	Y
Baldwin	N	Y	Y	Y	N	N
WYOMING						
Enzi	Y	Y	Y	Y	Y	Y
Barrasso	Y	Y	Y	Y	Y	Y

KEY **Republicans**   Democrats   *Independents*

Y Voted for (yea)	X Paired against	C Voted "present" to avoid possible conflict of interest
# Paired for	- Announced against	
+ Announced for	P Voted "present"	? Did not vote or otherwise make a position known
N Voted against (nay)		

VOTE NUMBER

109. MCWILLIAMS NOMINATION/CONFIRMATION. Confirmation of President Donald Trump's nomination of Jelena McWilliams of Ohio to be chairperson of the Board of Directors of the Federal Deposit Insurance Corporation. Confirmed 69-24: R 46-0; D 22-23. May 24, 2018.

110. EVANS NOMINATION/CLOTURE. Motion to invoke cloture (thus limiting debate) on the nomination of James R. Evans of Georgia to be U.S. ambassador to Luxembourg. Motion agreed to 49-44: R 46-0; D 3-42. May 24, 2018.

111. EVANS NOMINATION/CONFIRMATION. Confirmation of President Donald Trump's nomination of James R. Evans of Georgia to be U.S. ambassador to Luxembourg. Confirmed 48-43: R 45-0; D 3-42. May 24, 2018.

112. WIER NOMINATION/CLOTURE. Motion to invoke cloture (thus limiting debate) on the nomination of Robert E. Wier of Kentucky to be a U.S. district judge or the Eastern District of Kentucky. Motion agreed to 90-1: R 48-0; D 40-1. June 4, 2018.

113. WIER NOMINATION/CONFIRMATION. Confirmation of President Donald Trump's nomination of Robert E. Wier of Kentucky to be a U.S. district judge or the Eastern District of Kentucky. Confirmed 95-0: R 50-0; D 43-0. June 5, 2018.

114. RODRIGUEZ NOMINATION/CLOTURE. Motion to invoke cloture (thus limiting debate) on the nomination of Fernando Rodriguez Jr. of Texas to be a U.S. district judge for the Southern District of Texas. Motion agreed to 94-1: R 50-0; D 42-1. June 5, 2018.

	109	110	111	112	113	114
ALABAMA						
Shelby	Y	Y	Y	Y	Y	Y
Jones	Y	N	N	Y	Y	Y
ALASKA						
Murkowski	Y	Y	Y	Y	Y	Y
Sullivan	Y	Y	Y	Y	Y	Y
ARIZONA						
McCain	?	?	?	?	?	?
Flake	?	?	?	?	Y	Y
ARKANSAS						
Boozman	Y	Y	Y	Y	Y	Y
Cotton	Y	Y	Y	Y	Y	Y
CALIFORNIA						
Feinstein	N	N	N	Y	Y	Y
Harris	N	N	N	Y	Y	Y
COLORADO						
Bennet	Y	N	N	Y	Y	Y
Gardner	Y	Y	Y	Y	Y	Y
CONNECTICUT						
Blumenthal	N	N	N	Y	Y	Y
Murphy	Y	N	N	Y	Y	Y
DELAWARE						
Carper	Y	N	N	Y	Y	Y
Coons	Y	N	N	?	?	?
FLORIDA						
Nelson	Y	N	N	+	Y	Y
Rubio	+	+	+	Y	Y	Y
GEORGIA						
Isakson	Y	Y	Y	Y	Y	Y
Perdue	Y	Y	Y	Y	Y	Y
HAWAII						
Schatz	N	N	N	Y	Y	Y
Hirono	N	N	N	N	Y	N
IDAHO						
Crapo	Y	Y	Y	Y	Y	Y
Risch	Y	Y	Y	Y	Y	Y
ILLINOIS						
Durbin	N	N	N	Y	Y	Y
Duckworth	?	?	?	?	?	?
INDIANA						
Donnelly	Y	Y	Y	Y	Y	Y
Young	Y	Y	Y	?	Y	Y
IOWA						
Grassley	Y	Y	Y	Y	Y	Y
Ernst	Y	Y	Y	Y	Y	Y
KANSAS						
Roberts	Y	Y	Y	Y	Y	Y
Moran	Y	Y	?	Y	Y	Y
KENTUCKY						
McConnell	Y	Y	Y	Y	Y	Y
Paul	Y	Y	Y	Y	Y	Y
LOUISIANA						
Cassidy	Y	Y	Y	Y	Y	Y
Kennedy	Y	Y	Y	Y	Y	Y
MAINE						
Collins	Y	Y	Y	Y	Y	Y
King	Y	N	N	Y	Y	Y
MARYLAND						
Cardin	Y	N	N	Y	Y	Y
Van Hollen	Y	N	N	Y	Y	Y
MASSACHUSETTS						
Warren	N	N	N	Y	Y	Y
Markey	N	N	N	Y	Y	Y
MICHIGAN						
Stabenow	N	N	N	Y	Y	Y
Peters	Y	N	N	Y	Y	Y
MINNESOTA						
Klobuchar	Y	N	N	Y	Y	Y
Smith	N	N	N	Y	Y	Y
MISSISSIPPI						
Wicker	Y	Y	Y	Y	Y	Y
Hyde-Smith	Y	Y	Y	Y	Y	Y
MISSOURI						
McCaskill	Y	N	N	Y	Y	Y
Blunt	Y	Y	Y	Y	Y	Y
MONTANA						
Tester	Y	Y	Y	Y	Y	Y
Daines	Y	Y	Y	Y	Y	Y
NEBRASKA						
Fischer	Y	Y	Y	Y	Y	Y
Sasse	Y	Y	Y	Y	Y	Y
NEVADA						
Heller	?	?	?	Y	Y	Y
Cortez Masto	N	N	N	Y	Y	Y
NEW HAMPSHIRE						
Shaheen	Y	N	N	?	Y	Y
Hassan	?	?	?	Y	Y	Y
NEW JERSEY						
Menendez	Y	N	N	+	+	+
Booker	N	N	N	Y	Y	Y
NEW MEXICO						
Udall	N	N	N	Y	Y	Y
Heinrich	N	N	N	+	+	+
NEW YORK						
Schumer	N	N	N	Y	Y	Y
Gillibrand	N	N	N	Y	Y	Y
NORTH CAROLINA						
Burr	Y	Y	Y	Y	Y	Y
Tillis	Y	Y	Y	Y	Y	Y
NORTH DAKOTA						
Hoeven	Y	Y	Y	Y	Y	Y
Heitkamp	Y	Y	Y	Y	Y	Y
OHIO						
Brown	N	N	N	Y	Y	Y
Portman	Y	Y	Y	Y	Y	Y
OKLAHOMA						
Inhofe	Y	Y	Y	Y	Y	Y
Lankford	Y	Y	Y	Y	Y	
OREGON						
Wyden	N	N	N	Y	Y	Y
Merkley	N	N	N	Y	Y	Y
PENNSYLVANIA						
Casey	Y	N	N	Y	Y	Y
Toomey	Y	Y	Y	Y	Y	Y
RHODE ISLAND						
Reed	Y	N	N	Y	Y	Y
Whitehouse	N	N	N	Y	Y	Y
SOUTH CAROLINA						
Graham	Y	Y	Y	Y	Y	Y
Scott	Y	Y	Y	Y	Y	Y
SOUTH DAKOTA						
Thune	Y	Y	Y	Y	Y	Y
Rounds	Y	Y	Y	Y	Y	Y
TENNESSEE						
Alexander	Y	Y	Y	Y	Y	Y
Corker	Y	Y	Y	Y	Y	Y
TEXAS						
Cornyn	Y	Y	Y	Y	Y	Y
Cruz	?	?	?	Y	Y	Y
UTAH						
Hatch	Y	Y	Y	Y	Y	Y
Lee	Y	Y	Y	Y	Y	Y
VERMONT						
Leahy	Y	N	N	Y	Y	Y
Sanders	N	N	?	Y	Y	Y
VIRGINIA						
Warner	Y	N	N	Y	Y	Y
Kaine	Y	N	N	Y	Y	Y
WASHINGTON						
Murray	N	N	N	Y	Y	Y
Cantwell	N	N	N	Y	Y	Y
WEST VIRGINIA						
Manchin	Y	N	N	Y	Y	Y
Capito	Y	Y	Y	Y	Y	Y
WISCONSIN						
Johnson	Y	Y	Y	Y	Y	Y
Baldwin	N	N	N	Y	Y	Y
WYOMING						
Enzi	Y	Y	Y	Y	Y	Y
Barrasso	Y	Y	Y	Y	Y	Y

KEY   **Republicans** (bold)   Democrats (roman)   *Independents* (italic)

Y Voted for (yea)	X Paired against	C Voted "present" to avoid possible conflict of interest
# Paired for	– Announced against	
+ Announced for	P Voted "present"	? Did not vote or otherwise make a position known
N Voted against (nay)		

VOTE NUMBER

115. RODRIGUEZ NOMINATION/CONFIRMATION. Confirmation of President Donald Trump's nomination of Fernando Rodriguez, Jr. of Texas to be a U.S. district judge for the Southern District of Texas. Confirmed 96-0: R 50-0; D 44-0. June 5, 2018.

116. AXON NOMINATION/CLOTURE. Motion to invoke cloture (thus limiting debate) on the nomination of Annemarie C. Axon of Alabama to be a U.S. district judge for the Northern District of Alabama. Motion agreed to 84-11: R 49-0; D 34-10. June 5, 2018.

117. AXON NOMINATION/CONFIRMATION. Confirmation of President Donald Trump's nomination of Annemarie C. Axon of Alabama to be a U.S. district judge for the Northern District of Alabama. Confirmed 83-11: R 50-0; D 32-10. June 6, 2018.

118. MARCUS NOMINATION/CONFIRMATION. Confirmation of President Donald Trump's nomination of Kenneth L. Marcus of Virginia to be assistant secretary for civil rights of the Education Department. Confirmed 50-46: R 50-0; D 0-44. June 7, 2018.

119. HR5515. FISCAL 2019 DEFENSE AUTHORIZATION/CLOTURE. Motion to invoke cloture (thus limiting debate) on the McConnell motion to proceed to the bill that would authorize $708.1 billion in discretionary funding for defense programs in fiscal 2019. It would include $69 billion for overseas contingency operations; $241.2 billion for operations and maintenance; $11.3 billion for military construction; $185.8 billion for military personnel; and $33.6 billion for defense health care programs. Motion agreed to 92-4: R 48-1; D 43-2. June 7, 2018.

120. HR5515. FISCAL 2019 DEFENSE AUTHORIZATION/MOTION TO PROCEED. McConnell, R-Ky., motion to proceed to the bill that would authorize $708.1 billion in discretionary funding for defense programs in fiscal 2019. Motion agreed to 91-4: R 48-1; D 42-2. June 11, 2018.

	115	116	117	118	119	120
ALABAMA						
Shelby	Y	Y	Y	Y	Y	Y
Jones	Y	Y	Y	N	Y	Y
ALASKA						
Murkowski	Y	Y	Y	Y	Y	Y
Sullivan	Y	Y	Y	Y	Y	Y
ARIZONA						
McCain	?	?	?	+	?	?
Flake	Y	Y	Y	Y	Y	Y
ARKANSAS						
Boozman	Y	Y	Y	Y	Y	Y
Cotton	Y	Y	Y	Y	Y	Y
CALIFORNIA						
Feinstein	Y	Y	Y	N	Y	Y
Harris	Y	N	N	N	Y	Y
COLORADO						
Bennet	Y	Y	Y	N	Y	Y
Gardner	Y	Y	Y	Y	Y	Y
CONNECTICUT						
Blumenthal	Y	Y	Y	–	Y	Y
Murphy	Y	Y	Y	N	Y	Y
DELAWARE						
Carper	Y	Y	Y	N	Y	Y
Coons	?	?	?	?	?	Y
FLORIDA						
Nelson	Y	Y	Y	N	Y	Y
Rubio	Y	Y	Y	Y	Y	Y
GEORGIA						
Isakson	Y	?	Y	Y	Y	Y
Perdue	Y	Y	Y	Y	Y	Y
HAWAII						
Schatz	Y	Y	Y	N	Y	Y
Hirono	Y	N	N	N	Y	Y
IDAHO						
Crapo	Y	Y	Y	Y	Y	Y
Risch	Y	Y	Y	Y	Y	Y
ILLINOIS						
Durbin	Y	Y	Y	N	Y	Y
Duckworth	?	?	?	–	?	+
INDIANA						
Donnelly	Y	Y	Y	N	Y	Y
Young	Y	Y	Y	Y	Y	Y
IOWA						
Grassley	Y	Y	Y	Y	Y	Y
Ernst	Y	Y	Y	Y	Y	Y
KANSAS						
Roberts	Y	Y	Y	Y	Y	Y
Moran	Y	Y	Y	?	Y	Y
KENTUCKY						
McConnell	Y	Y	Y	Y	Y	Y
Paul	Y	Y	Y	Y	N	N
LOUISIANA						
Cassidy	Y	Y	Y	Y	Y	Y
Kennedy	Y	Y	Y	Y	Y	Y
MAINE						
Collins	Y	Y	Y	Y	Y	Y
King	Y	Y	Y	N	Y	Y
MARYLAND						
Cardin	Y	Y	Y	N	Y	?
Van Hollen	Y	Y	Y	N	Y	Y
MASSACHUSETTS						
Warren	Y	N	N	N	Y	Y
Markey	Y	N	?	N	Y	Y
MICHIGAN						
Stabenow	Y	N	N	N	Y	Y
Peters	Y	N	N	N	Y	Y
MINNESOTA						
Klobuchar	Y	Y	Y	N	Y	Y
Smith	Y	Y	Y	N	Y	Y
MISSISSIPPI						
Wicker	Y	Y	Y	Y	Y	Y
Hyde-Smith	Y	Y	Y	Y	Y	Y
MISSOURI						
McCaskill	Y	Y	Y	N	Y	Y
Blunt	Y	Y	Y	Y	Y	?

	115	116	117	118	119	120
MONTANA						
Tester	Y	Y	Y	N	Y	Y
Daines	Y	Y	Y	Y	Y	Y
NEBRASKA						
Fischer	Y	Y	Y	Y	Y	Y
Sasse	Y	Y	Y	Y	Y	Y
NEVADA						
Heller	Y	Y	Y	Y	Y	Y
Cortez Masto	Y	Y	Y	N	Y	Y
NEW HAMPSHIRE						
Shaheen	Y	Y	Y	N	Y	Y
Hassan	Y	Y	Y	N	Y	Y
NEW JERSEY						
Menendez	Y	N	N	N	Y	Y
Booker	Y	Y	N	N	Y	Y
NEW MEXICO						
Udall	Y	Y	Y	N	Y	Y
Heinrich	+	+	+	N	Y	Y
NEW YORK						
Schumer	Y	Y	Y	N	Y	Y
Gillibrand	Y	N	N	N	Y	?
NORTH CAROLINA						
Burr	Y	Y	Y	Y	Y	Y
Tillis	Y	Y	Y	Y	Y	Y
NORTH DAKOTA						
Hoeven	Y	Y	Y	Y	Y	Y
Heitkamp	Y	Y	Y	N	Y	Y
OHIO						
Brown	Y	Y	Y	N	Y	Y
Portman	Y	Y	Y	Y	Y	Y
OKLAHOMA						
Inhofe	Y	Y	Y	Y	Y	Y
Lankford	Y	Y	Y	Y	Y	Y
OREGON						
Wyden	Y	N	N	N	N	N
Merkley	Y	N	N	N	N	N
PENNSYLVANIA						
Casey	Y	Y	Y	N	Y	Y
Toomey	Y	Y	Y	Y	Y	Y
RHODE ISLAND						
Reed	Y	Y	Y	N	Y	Y
Whitehouse	Y	Y	Y	N	Y	Y
SOUTH CAROLINA						
Graham	Y	Y	Y	Y	Y	Y
Scott	Y	Y	Y	Y	Y	Y
SOUTH DAKOTA						
Thune	Y	Y	Y	Y	Y	Y
Rounds	Y	Y	Y	Y	Y	Y
TENNESSEE						
Alexander	Y	Y	Y	Y	Y	Y
Corker	Y	Y	Y	Y	Y	Y
TEXAS						
Cornyn	Y	Y	Y	Y	Y	Y
Cruz	Y	Y	Y	Y	Y	Y
UTAH						
Hatch	Y	Y	Y	Y	Y	Y
Lee	Y	Y	Y	Y	Y	Y
VERMONT						
Leahy	Y	Y	?	N	Y	Y
Sanders	Y	N	N	N	N	N
VIRGINIA						
Warner	Y	Y	Y	N	Y	Y
Kaine	Y	Y	Y	N	Y	Y
WASHINGTON						
Murray	Y	Y	Y	N	Y	Y
Cantwell	Y	Y	Y	N	Y	Y
WEST VIRGINIA						
Manchin	Y	Y	Y	N	Y	Y
Capito	Y	Y	Y	Y	Y	Y
WISCONSIN						
Johnson	Y	Y	Y	Y	Y	Y
Baldwin	Y	Y	Y	N	Y	Y
WYOMING						
Enzi	Y	Y	Y	Y	Y	Y
Barrasso	Y	Y	Y	Y	Y	Y

KEY	**Republicans**	Democrats	*Independents*
Y Voted for (yea)		X Paired against	C Voted "present" to avoid possible conflict of interest
# Paired for		– Announced against	
+ Announced for		P Voted "present"	? Did not vote or otherwise make a position known
N Voted against (nay)			

VOTE NUMBER

121. HR5515. FISCAL 2019 DEFENSE AUTHORIZATION/MOTION TO TABLE. Inhofe, R-Okla., motion to table (kill) the Reed, D-R.I., amendment no. 2842 to the Lee, R-Utah, amendment no. 2366 that would prohibit the secretary of Energy from developing or modifying nuclear weapons unless authorized by Congress. Motion rejected 47-51: R 47-3; D 0-46. June 13, 2018.

122. HR5515. FISCAL 2019 DEFENSE AUTHORIZATION/MOTION TO TABLE. Inhofe, R-Okla., motion to table (kill) the Lee, R-Utah, amendment no. 2366 that would prohibit imprisonment or detention of any citizen or lawful permanent resident of the United States unless such imprisonment is consistent with the Constitution, and would specify that an authorization of military force, a declaration of war, or any similar authority, would not authorize the indefinite military detention of U.S. citizens without charge or trial. Motion rejected 30-68: R 27-23; D 3-43. June 13, 2018.

123. HR5515. FISCAL 2019 DEFENSE AUTHORIZATION/CLOTURE. Motion to invoke cloture (thus limiting debate) on the Toomey, R-Pa., amendment no. 2700 to the Inhofe, R-Okla., substitute amendment no. 2282, as modified, that would require congressional approval for any new regulation from the Committee on Foreign Investment in the United States. Motion rejected 35-62: R 35-14; D 0-46. June 14, 2018.

124. HR5515. FISCAL 2019 DEFENSE AUTHORIZATION/CLOTURE. Motion to invoke cloture (thus limiting debate) on the Inhofe, R-Okla., substitute amendment no. 2282, as modified, that would authorize $617.6 billion for the Defense Department's base budget, $21.6 billion for national security programs within the Energy Department and $68 billion to support overseas contingency operations. As modified, it would reinstate penalties and prohibitions regarding Chinese technology companies Huawei or ZTE; it would prohibit the transfer of F-35 aircraft or intellectual property or data regarding the aircraft to Turkey until the government of Turkey is determined to not be endangering North Atlantic Treaty Organization members; it would authorize approximately $800.6 million for fiscal 2019 to the Transportation Department for maritime operations, including approximately 60.4 million for operations and programs within the Maritime Administration. The amendment as modified would also require reports to Congress on a range of topics including genocide in Syria, ship repair contract cost estimates, and the phasing out of open burn pits. Motion agreed to 83-14: R 45-4; D 37-9. June 14, 2018.

125. HR5515. FISCAL 2019 DEFENSE AUTHORIZATION/MCCAIN STRATEGIC DEFENSE FELLOWSHIP. Reed, D-R.I., amendment no. 2885 that would establish and authorize $10 million annually for the John S. McCain Strategic Defense Fellows Program within the Defense Department to provide civilians with leadership development and career tracks for senior leadership in the department. Adopted 97-0: R 49-0; D 46-0. June 14, 2018"

126. HR5515. FISCAL 2019 DEFENSE AUTHORIZATION/CLOTURE. Motion to invoke cloture (thus limiting debate) on the bill that would $617.6 billion for the Defense Department's base budget, $21.6 billion for national security programs within the Energy Department and $68 billion to support overseas contingency operations. Motion agreed to 81-15: R 43-6; D 37-8. June 14, 2018.

	121	122	123	124	125	126
ALABAMA						
Shelby	Y	Y	N	Y	Y	Y
Jones	N	N	N	Y	Y	Y
ALASKA						
Murkowski	N	N	N	Y	Y	Y
Sullivan	Y	Y	Y	Y	Y	Y
ARIZONA						
McCain	?	?	?	?	?	?
Flake	Y	N	Y	Y	Y	N
ARKANSAS						
Boozman	Y	Y	N	Y	Y	Y
Cotton	Y	Y	N	Y	Y	Y
CALIFORNIA						
Feinstein	N	N	N	N	Y	N
Harris	N	N	N	N	Y	N
COLORADO						
Bennet	N	N	N	Y	Y	Y
Gardner	Y	N	Y	Y	Y	Y
CONNECTICUT						
Blumenthal	N	N	N	Y	Y	Y
Murphy	N	N	N	Y	Y	Y
DELAWARE						
Carper	N	N	N	Y	Y	Y
Coons	N	N	N	Y	Y	Y
FLORIDA						
Nelson	N	N	N	Y	Y	Y
Rubio	Y	Y	N	Y	Y	Y
GEORGIA						
Isakson	Y	Y	Y	Y	Y	Y
Perdue	Y	Y	Y	Y	Y	Y
HAWAII						
Schatz	N	N	N	Y	Y	Y
Hirono	N	N	N	Y	Y	Y
IDAHO						
Crapo	Y	N	Y	?	Y	Y
Risch	Y	N	N	Y	Y	Y
ILLINOIS						
Durbin	N	N	N	N	Y	N
Duckworth	?	?	?	+	+	+
INDIANA						
Donnelly	N	Y	N	Y	Y	Y
Young	Y	Y	Y	Y	Y	Y
IOWA						
Grassley	Y	Y	Y	Y	Y	Y
Ernst	Y	N	Y	Y	Y	Y
KANSAS						
Roberts	Y	Y	N	Y	Y	Y
Moran	Y	N	Y	Y	?	?
KENTUCKY						
McConnell	Y	Y	Y	Y	Y	Y
Paul	N	N	Y	N	Y	N
LOUISIANA						
Cassidy	Y	N	Y	Y	Y	Y
Kennedy	Y	N	Y	Y	Y	N
MAINE						
Collins	N	N	N	Y	Y	Y
King	N	N	N	Y	Y	Y
MARYLAND						
Cardin	N	N	N	Y	Y	Y
Van Hollen	N	N	N	Y	Y	Y
MASSACHUSETTS						
Warren	N	N	N	N	Y	N
Markey	N	N	N	N	Y	N
MICHIGAN						
Stabenow	N	N	N	Y	Y	Y
Peters	N	N	N	Y	Y	Y
MINNESOTA						
Klobuchar	N	N	N	Y	Y	Y
Smith	N	N	N	Y	Y	Y
MISSISSIPPI						
Wicker	Y	Y	Y	Y	Y	Y
Hyde-Smith	Y	Y	Y	Y	Y	Y
MISSOURI						
McCaskill	N	N	N	Y	Y	Y
Blunt	Y	Y	Y	Y	Y	Y
MONTANA						
Tester	N	N	N	Y	Y	Y
Daines	Y	N	N	Y	Y	Y
NEBRASKA						
Fischer	Y	N	N	Y	Y	Y
Sasse	Y	Y	Y	Y	Y	Y
NEVADA						
Heller	Y	N	Y	Y	Y	Y
Cortez Masto	N	Y	N	Y	Y	Y
NEW HAMPSHIRE						
Shaheen	N	N	N	Y	Y	Y
Hassan	N	N	N	Y	Y	Y
NEW JERSEY						
Menendez	N	N	N	Y	Y	Y
Booker	N	N	N	Y	Y	Y
NEW MEXICO						
Udall	N	N	N	Y	Y	Y
Heinrich	N	N	N	Y	Y	Y
NEW YORK						
Schumer	N	N	N	Y	Y	Y
Gillibrand	N	N	N	N	Y	N
NORTH CAROLINA						
Burr	Y	Y	N	Y	Y	Y
Tillis	Y	Y	Y	Y	Y	Y
NORTH DAKOTA						
Hoeven	Y	N	N	Y	Y	Y
Heitkamp	N	N	N	Y	Y	Y
OHIO						
Brown	N	N	N	Y	Y	Y
Portman	Y	Y	+	Y	Y	Y
OKLAHOMA						
Inhofe	Y	Y	Y	Y	Y	Y
Lankford	Y	N	Y	Y	Y	Y
OREGON						
Wyden	N	N	N	N	Y	N
Merkley	N	N	N	N	Y	N
PENNSYLVANIA						
Casey	N	N	N	Y	Y	Y
Toomey	Y	Y	Y	Y	Y	Y
RHODE ISLAND						
Reed	N	N	N	Y	Y	Y
Whitehouse	N	N	N	Y	Y	Y
SOUTH CAROLINA						
Graham	Y	Y	N	Y	Y	Y
Scott	Y	N	Y	Y	Y	Y
SOUTH DAKOTA						
Thune	Y	Y	Y	Y	Y	Y
Rounds	Y	Y	Y	Y	Y	Y
TENNESSEE						
Alexander	Y	N	Y	Y	Y	Y
Corker	Y	Y	N	Y	N	Y
TEXAS						
Cornyn	Y	Y	N	Y	Y	Y
Cruz	Y	N	Y	Y	Y	Y
UTAH						
Hatch	Y	N	Y	Y	Y	Y
Lee	Y	N	Y	N	Y	N
VERMONT						
Leahy	N	N	N	Y	Y	Y
Sanders	N	N	N	N	Y	N
VIRGINIA						
Warner	N	N	N	Y	Y	Y
Kaine	N	N	N	Y	Y	Y
WASHINGTON						
Murray	N	N	N	Y	Y	Y
Cantwell	N	N	N	Y	Y	Y
WEST VIRGINIA						
Manchin	N	Y	N	Y	Y	?
Capito	Y	Y	Y	Y	Y	Y
WISCONSIN						
Johnson	Y	Y	Y	N	Y	N
Baldwin	N	N	N	Y	Y	Y
WYOMING						
Enzi	Y	N	Y	Y	Y	Y
Barrasso	Y	N	Y	Y	Y	Y

KEY — Republicans — Democrats — *Independents*

- **Y** Voted for (yea)
- **#** Paired for
- **+** Announced for
- **N** Voted against (nay)
- **X** Paired against
- **–** Announced against
- **P** Voted "present"
- **C** Voted "present" to avoid possible conflict of interest
- **?** Did not vote or otherwise make a position known

VOTE NUMBER

127. HR5515. FISCAL 2019 DEFENSE AUTHORIZATION/MOTION TO WAIVE. McConnell, R-Ky., motion to waive all applicable sections of the Congressional Budget Act with respect to a Sanders, I-Vt., point of order that the bill violates Sec. 4106 of the concurrent budget resolution for fiscal 2018. Motion agreed to 81-14: R 41-7; D 39-6. June 18, 2018.

128. HR5515. FISCAL 2019 DEFENSE AUTHORIZATION/PASSAGE. Passage of the bill that would authorize $617.6 billion for the Defense Department's base budget, $21.6 billion for national security programs within the Energy Department and $68 billion to support overseas contingency operations. As modified, it would reinstate penalties and prohibitions regarding Chinese technology companies Huawei or ZTE; it would prohibit the transfer of F-35 aircraft or intellectual property or data regarding the aircraft to Turkey until the government of Turkey is determined to not be endangering North Atlantic Treaty Organization members; it would authorize approximately $800.6 million for fiscal 2019 to the Transportation Department for maritime operations, including approximately 60.4 million for operations and programs within the Maritime Administration. The amendment as modified would also require reports to Congress on a range of topics including genocide in Syria, ship repair contract cost estimates, and the phasing out of open burn pits. Passed 85-10: R 46-2; D 38-7. June 18, 2018.

129. HR5895. FISCAL 2019 ENERGY-WATER, LEGISLATIVE BRANCH, MILITARY CONSTRUCTION-VA APPROPRIATIONS/CLOTURE. Motion to invoke cloture (thus limiting debate) on the McConnell motion to proceed to the House-passed fiscal 2019 three-bill spending package. Motion agreed to 92-3: R 48-0; D 42-3. June 18, 2018.

130. HR5895. FISCAL 2019 ENERGY-WATER, LEGISLATIVE BRANCH, MILITARY CONSTRUCTION-VA APPROPRIATIONS/SENSE OF CONGRESS REGARDING INNOVATION. Gardner, R-Colo., amendment no. 2914, to the Shelby, R-Ala., substitute amendment no. 2910, that would state that it is the sense of Congress that both Congress and the Energy Department should continue to support innovative science research and development at the National Laboratories and other research institutions through funding for a variety of research areas. Adopted 93-3: R 47-3; D 44-0. June 19, 2018.

131. HR5895. FISCAL 2019 ENERGY-WATER, LEGISLATIVE BRANCH, MILITARY CONSTRUCTION-VA APPROPRIATIONS/COST-SHARE PROJECT REPORT. Carper, D-Del., amendment no. 2920, to the Shelby, R-Ala., substitute amendment no. 2910, that would require the secretary of the Army to submit a report to Congress that includes a list of certain cost-share Army Corps of Engineers projects. Adopted 96-0: R 50-0; D 44-0. June 19, 2018.

132. HR5895. FISCAL 2019 ENERGY-WATER, LEGISLATIVE BRANCH, MILITARY CONSTRUCTION-VA APPROPRIATIONS/NUCLEAR MATERIAL RECOVERY PROGRAM. Crapo, R-Idaho, amendment no. 2943, as modified, to the Shelby, R-Ala., substitute amendment no. 2910, that would designate $15 million for a material recovery demonstration project to provide high-assay low-enriched uranium to support advanced reactors. Adopted 87-9: R 49-1; D 37-7. June 20, 2018.

	127	128	129	130	131	132
ALABAMA						
Shelby	Y	Y	Y	Y	Y	Y
Jones	Y	Y	Y	Y	Y	Y
ALASKA						
Murkowski	Y	Y	Y	Y	Y	Y
Sullivan	Y	Y	Y	Y	Y	Y
ARIZONA						
McCain	?	?	?	?	?	?
Flake	Y	Y	Y	Y	Y	N
ARKANSAS						
Boozman	+	+	+	Y	Y	Y
Cotton	Y	Y	Y	Y	Y	Y
CALIFORNIA						
Feinstein	Y	N	Y	Y	Y	N
Harris	N	N	Y	Y	Y	N
COLORADO						
Bennet	Y	Y	Y	Y	Y	Y
Gardner	Y	Y	Y	Y	Y	Y
CONNECTICUT						
Blumenthal	Y	Y	Y	Y	Y	Y
Murphy	Y	Y	Y	Y	Y	Y
DELAWARE						
Carper	Y	Y	Y	Y	Y	Y
Coons	Y	Y	Y	Y	Y	Y
FLORIDA						
Nelson	Y	Y	Y	+	+	Y
Rubio	Y	Y	Y	Y	Y	Y
GEORGIA						
Isakson	Y	Y	Y	Y	Y	Y
Perdue	N	Y	Y	Y	Y	Y
HAWAII						
Schatz	Y	Y	Y	Y	Y	Y
Hirono	Y	Y	Y	Y	Y	Y
IDAHO						
Crapo	Y	Y	Y	Y	Y	Y
Risch	Y	Y	Y	Y	Y	Y
ILLINOIS						
Durbin	Y	Y	Y	Y	Y	Y
Duckworth	+	+	+	?	?	?
INDIANA						
Donnelly	Y	Y	Y	Y	Y	Y
Young	Y	Y	Y	Y	Y	Y
IOWA						
Grassley	Y	Y	Y	Y	Y	Y
Ernst	Y	Y	Y	Y	Y	Y
KANSAS						
Roberts	Y	Y	Y	Y	Y	Y
Moran	Y	Y	Y	Y	Y	Y
KENTUCKY						
McConnell	Y	Y	Y	Y	Y	Y
Paul	N	N	Y	N	Y	Y
LOUISIANA						
Cassidy	?	?	?	Y	Y	Y
Kennedy	N	Y	Y	Y	Y	Y
MAINE						
Collins	Y	Y	Y	Y	Y	Y
King	Y	Y	Y	Y	Y	Y
MARYLAND						
Cardin	Y	Y	Y	Y	Y	?
Van Hollen	Y	Y	Y	Y	Y	Y
MASSACHUSETTS						
Warren	N	N	N	Y	Y	N
Markey	N	N	N	Y	Y	N
MICHIGAN						
Stabenow	Y	Y	Y	Y	Y	Y
Peters	Y	Y	Y	Y	Y	Y
MINNESOTA						
Klobuchar	Y	Y	Y	Y	Y	Y
Smith	Y	Y	Y	Y	Y	Y
MISSISSIPPI						
Wicker	Y	Y	Y	Y	Y	Y
Hyde-Smith	Y	Y	Y	Y	Y	Y
MISSOURI						
McCaskill	Y	Y	Y	Y	Y	Y
Blunt	Y	Y	Y	Y	Y	Y

	127	128	129	130	131	132
MONTANA						
Tester	Y	Y	Y	Y	Y	Y
Daines	Y	Y	Y	Y	Y	Y
NEBRASKA						
Fischer	Y	Y	Y	Y	Y	Y
Sasse	Y	Y	Y	Y	Y	Y
NEVADA						
Heller	Y	Y	Y	Y	Y	Y
Cortez Masto	Y	Y	Y	Y	Y	Y
NEW HAMPSHIRE						
Shaheen	?	?	?	?	?	?
Hassan	Y	Y	Y	Y	Y	Y
NEW JERSEY						
Menendez	Y	Y	Y	Y	Y	Y
Booker	Y	Y	Y	Y	Y	Y
NEW MEXICO						
Udall	Y	Y	Y	Y	Y	Y
Heinrich	Y	Y	Y	Y	Y	Y
NEW YORK						
Schumer	Y	Y	Y	Y	Y	Y
Gillibrand	N	N	N	Y	Y	N
NORTH CAROLINA						
Burr	Y	Y	Y	Y	Y	Y
Tillis	Y	Y	Y	Y	Y	Y
NORTH DAKOTA						
Hoeven	Y	Y	Y	Y	Y	Y
Heitkamp	Y	Y	Y	Y	Y	Y
OHIO						
Brown	Y	Y	Y	Y	Y	Y
Portman	Y	Y	Y	Y	Y	Y
OKLAHOMA						
Inhofe	Y	Y	Y	Y	Y	Y
Lankford	Y	Y	Y	Y	Y	Y
OREGON						
Wyden	N	N	Y	Y	N	N
Merkley	N	N	Y	Y	N	N
PENNSYLVANIA						
Casey	Y	Y	Y	Y	Y	Y
Toomey	Y	Y	Y	N	Y	Y
RHODE ISLAND						
Reed	Y	Y	Y	Y	Y	Y
Whitehouse	Y	Y	Y	Y	Y	Y
SOUTH CAROLINA						
Graham	Y	Y	Y	Y	Y	Y
Scott	Y	Y	Y	Y	Y	Y
SOUTH DAKOTA						
Thune	Y	Y	Y	Y	Y	Y
Rounds	Y	Y	Y	Y	Y	Y
TENNESSEE						
Alexander	Y	Y	Y	Y	Y	Y
Corker	N	Y	Y	Y	Y	Y
TEXAS						
Cornyn	Y	Y	Y	Y	Y	Y
Cruz	Y	Y	Y	Y	Y	Y
UTAH						
Hatch	Y	Y	Y	Y	Y	Y
Lee	N	N	Y	N	Y	Y
VERMONT						
Leahy	Y	Y	Y	Y	Y	Y
Sanders	N	N	Y	Y	Y	N
VIRGINIA						
Warner	Y	Y	Y	Y	Y	Y
Kaine	Y	Y	Y	Y	Y	Y
WASHINGTON						
Murray	Y	Y	Y	Y	Y	Y
Cantwell	Y	Y	Y	Y	Y	Y
WEST VIRGINIA						
Manchin	Y	Y	Y	Y	Y	Y
Capito	Y	Y	Y	Y	Y	Y
WISCONSIN						
Johnson	Y	Y	Y	Y	Y	Y
Baldwin	Y	Y	Y	Y	Y	Y
WYOMING						
Enzi	N	Y	Y	Y	Y	Y
Barrasso	N	Y	Y	Y	Y	Y

KEY	Republicans	Democrats	*Independents*
Y Voted for (yea)		**X** Paired against	**C** Voted "present" to avoid possible conflict of interest
# Paired for		**−** Announced against	
+ Announced for		**P** Voted "present"	**?** Did not vote or otherwise make a position known
N Voted against (nay)			

VOTE NUMBER

133. HR5895. FISCAL 2019 ENERGY-WATER, LEGISLATIVE BRANCH, MILITARY CONSTRUCTION-VA APPROPRIATIONS/DOMESTIC PRODUCTION OF MOLYBDENUM-99. Baldwin, D-Wis., amendment no. 2985, to the Shelby, R-Ala., substitute amendment no. 2910, that would designate $20 million for acceleration of the domestic production of Molybdenum-99. Adopted 95-2: R 48-2; D 45-0. June 20, 2018.

134. HR3. RESCISSION OF APPROPRIATIONS/MOTION TO DISCHARGE. Lee, R-Utah., motion to discharge the Senate Appropriations and Senate Budget Committees from further consideration of the bill that would cut approximately $14.7 billion in previously approved spending. Motion rejected 48-50: R 48-2; D 0-46. June 20, 2018.

135. HR5895. FISCAL 2019 ENERGY-WATER, LEGISLATIVE BRANCH, MILITARY CONSTRUCTION-VA APPROPRIATIONS/VETERANS CRISIS LINE STUDY. Young, R-Ind., amendment no. 2926, to the Shelby, R-Ala., substitute amendment no. 2910, that would require the secretary of Veterans Affairs to study the effectiveness of the Veterans Crisis Line. Adopted 96-0: R 49-0; D 45-0. June 20, 2018.

136. HR5895. FISCAL 2019 ENERGY-WATER, LEGISLATIVE BRANCH, MILITARY CONSTRUCTION-VA APPROPRIATIONS/INSPECTOR GENERAL DOCUMENT ACCESS. Tester, D-Mont., amendment no. 2971, to the Shelby, R-Ala., substitute amendment no. 2910, that would prohibit funds designated in the bill from being used to deny Inspectors General timely access to records and documents of a department or agency. Adopted 96-0: R 49-0; D 45-0. June 20, 2018.

137. HR5895. FISCAL 2019 ENERGY-WATER, LEGISLATIVE BRANCH, MILITARY CONSTRUCTION-VA APPROPRIATIONS/MILITARY PERSONNEL TRANSITION TO CIVILIAN WORKFORCE. Bennet, D-Colo., amendment no. 2983, to the Shelby, R-Ala., substitute amendment no. 2910, that would require a report to Congress that would evaluate the establishment of partnerships between military installations, institutions of higher learning, and the private sector, to train veterans and members of the armed forces to transition into the civilian workforce in the fields of cybersecurity, energy, and artificial intelligence. Adopted 96-0: R 49-0; D 45-0. June 21, 2018.

138. HR5895. FISCAL 2019 ENERGY-WATER, LEGISLATIVE BRANCH, MILITARY CONSTRUCTION-VA APPROPRIATIONS/MOTION TO TABLE. Alexander, R-Tenn., motion to table the Lee, R-Utah, amendment no. 3021, as modified, that would void the EPA's rule regarding the definition of the ""Waters of the United States"" under the Clean Water Act. Motion agreed to 62-34: R 20-29; D 40-5. June 21, 2018.

	133	134	135	136	137	138
ALABAMA						
Shelby	Y	Y	Y	Y	Y	Y
Jones	Y	N	Y	Y	Y	N
ALASKA						
Murkowski	Y	Y	Y	Y	Y	Y
Sullivan	Y	Y	Y	Y	Y	N
ARIZONA						
McCain	?	?	?	?	?	?
Flake	N	Y	Y	Y	Y	N
ARKANSAS						
Boozman	Y	Y	Y	Y	Y	Y
Cotton	Y	Y	Y	Y	Y	N
CALIFORNIA						
Feinstein	Y	N	Y	Y	Y	Y
Harris	Y	N	Y	Y	Y	Y
COLORADO						
Bennet	Y	N	Y	Y	Y	Y
Gardner	Y	Y	Y	Y	Y	N
CONNECTICUT						
Blumenthal	Y	N	Y	Y	Y	Y
Murphy	Y	N	Y	Y	Y	Y
DELAWARE						
Carper	Y	N	Y	Y	Y	Y
Coons	Y	N	Y	Y	Y	Y
FLORIDA						
Nelson	Y	N	Y	Y	Y	Y
Rubio	Y	Y	Y	Y	Y	N
GEORGIA						
Isakson	Y	Y	Y	Y	Y	Y
Perdue	Y	Y	Y	Y	Y	N
HAWAII						
Schatz	Y	N	Y	Y	Y	Y
Hirono	Y	N	Y	Y	Y	Y
IDAHO						
Crapo	Y	Y	Y	Y	Y	N
Risch	Y	Y	Y	Y	Y	N
ILLINOIS						
Durbin	Y	N	Y	Y	Y	Y
Duckworth	?	N	+	+	+	+
INDIANA						
Donnelly	Y	N	Y	Y	Y	N
Young	Y	Y	Y	Y	Y	Y
IOWA						
Grassley	Y	Y	Y	Y	Y	Y
Ernst	Y	Y	Y	Y	Y	N
KANSAS						
Roberts	Y	Y	Y	Y	Y	Y
Moran	Y	Y	Y	Y	Y	Y
KENTUCKY						
McConnell	Y	Y	Y	Y	Y	Y
Paul	N	Y	Y	Y	Y	N
LOUISIANA						
Cassidy	Y	Y	Y	Y	Y	N
Kennedy	Y	Y	Y	Y	Y	N
MAINE						
Collins	Y	N	Y	Y	Y	Y
King	Y	N	Y	Y	Y	Y
MARYLAND						
Cardin	Y	N	Y	Y	Y	Y
Van Hollen	Y	N	Y	Y	Y	Y
MASSACHUSETTS						
Warren	Y	N	Y	Y	Y	Y
Markey	Y	N	Y	Y	Y	Y
MICHIGAN						
Stabenow	Y	N	Y	Y	Y	Y
Peters	Y	N	Y	Y	Y	Y
MINNESOTA						
Klobuchar	Y	N	Y	Y	Y	Y
Smith	Y	N	Y	Y	Y	Y
MISSISSIPPI						
Wicker	Y	Y	Y	Y	Y	Y
Hyde-Smith	Y	Y	Y	Y	Y	N
MISSOURI						
McCaskill	Y	N	Y	Y	Y	N
Blunt	Y	Y	Y	Y	Y	N
MONTANA						
Tester	Y	N	Y	Y	Y	Y
Daines	Y	Y	Y	Y	Y	N
NEBRASKA						
Fischer	Y	Y	Y	Y	Y	N
Sasse	Y	Y	Y	Y	Y	Y
NEVADA						
Heller	Y	Y	Y	Y	Y	N
Cortez Masto	Y	N	Y	Y	Y	Y
NEW HAMPSHIRE						
Shaheen	?	?	?	?	?	?
Hassan	Y	N	Y	Y	Y	Y
NEW JERSEY						
Menendez	Y	N	Y	Y	Y	Y
Booker	Y	N	Y	Y	Y	Y
NEW MEXICO						
Udall	Y	N	Y	Y	Y	Y
Heinrich	Y	N	Y	Y	Y	Y
NEW YORK						
Schumer	Y	N	Y	Y	Y	Y
Gillibrand	Y	N	Y	Y	Y	Y
NORTH CAROLINA						
Burr	Y	N	Y	Y	Y	Y
Tillis	Y	Y	Y	Y	Y	Y
NORTH DAKOTA						
Hoeven	Y	Y	Y	Y	Y	Y
Heitkamp	Y	N	Y	Y	Y	N
OHIO						
Brown	Y	N	Y	Y	Y	Y
Portman	Y	Y	Y	Y	Y	Y
OKLAHOMA						
Inhofe	Y	Y	Y	Y	Y	N
Lankford	Y	Y	Y	Y	Y	N
OREGON						
Wyden	Y	N	Y	Y	Y	Y
Merkley	Y	N	Y	Y	Y	Y
PENNSYLVANIA						
Casey	Y	N	Y	Y	Y	Y
Toomey	Y	Y	Y	Y	Y	N
RHODE ISLAND						
Reed	Y	N	Y	Y	Y	Y
Whitehouse	Y	N	Y	Y	Y	Y
SOUTH CAROLINA						
Graham	Y	Y	Y	Y	Y	Y
Scott	Y	Y	Y	Y	Y	Y
SOUTH DAKOTA						
Thune	Y	Y	Y	Y	Y	Y
Rounds	Y	Y	Y	Y	Y	Y
TENNESSEE						
Alexander	Y	Y	Y	Y	Y	Y
Corker	Y	Y	?	?	?	?
TEXAS						
Cornyn	Y	Y	Y	Y	Y	Y
Cruz	Y	Y	Y	Y	Y	N
UTAH						
Hatch	Y	Y	Y	Y	Y	Y
Lee	Y	Y	Y	Y	Y	N
VERMONT						
Leahy	Y	N	Y	Y	Y	Y
Sanders	Y	N	Y	Y	Y	Y
VIRGINIA						
Warner	Y	N	Y	Y	Y	Y
Kaine	Y	N	Y	Y	Y	Y
WASHINGTON						
Murray	Y	N	Y	Y	Y	Y
Cantwell	Y	N	Y	Y	Y	Y
WEST VIRGINIA						
Manchin	Y	N	Y	Y	Y	N
Capito	Y	Y	Y	Y	Y	N
WISCONSIN						
Johnson	Y	Y	Y	Y	Y	N
Baldwin	Y	N	Y	Y	Y	Y
WYOMING						
Enzi	Y	Y	Y	Y	Y	N
Barrasso	Y	Y	Y	Y	Y	N

KEY   **Republicans**   Democrats   *Independents*

Y	Voted for (yea)	X	Paired against
#	Paired for	–	Announced against
+	Announced for	P	Voted "present"
N	Voted against (nay)		

C   Voted "present" to avoid possible conflict of interest

?   Did not vote or otherwise make a position known

VOTE NUMBER

139. HR5895. FISCAL 2019 ENERGY-WATER, LEGISLATIVE BRANCH, MILITARY CONSTRUCTION-VA APPROPRIATIONS/PASSAGE. Passage of the bill, as amended, that would provide $146.6 billion in discretionary funding for fiscal 2019 to various departments, agencies and legislative operations, including $43.8 billion for the Energy Department, the Army Corps of Engineers, the Interior Department's Bureau of Reclamation; $98 billion for military construction activities and for VA programs and activities; and $4.8 billion for operations of the Senate, joint House-Senate items and legislative branch entities such as the Library of Congress, the Capitol Police, and the Government Accountability Office. Passed 86-5: R 44-2; D 40-3. June 25, 2018.

140. HR2. FARM PROGRAMS/CLOTURE. Motion to invoke cloture (thus limiting debate) on the McConnell, R-Ky., motion to proceed to the bill that would reauthorize many federal farm, nutrition assistance, rural development and other Agriculture Department programs through fiscal 2023. Motion agreed to 89-3: R 45-2; D 42-1. June 25, 2018.

141. HR2. FARM PROGRAMS/MOTION TO TABLE. Roberts, R-Kan., motion to table (kill) the Kennedy, R-La., amendment no. 3383 that would modify work requirements for certain beneficiaries of the Supplemental Nutrition Assistance Program and would require SNAP electronic benefit cards to list all adult beneficiaries on the card, and would require such individuals to show photographic identification when using the card. It would exempt an individual designated as the head of a household from the ID requirement if the EBT card displays a photo of the individual. Motion agreed to 68-30: R 20-30; D 46-0. June 28, 2018.

142. HR2. FARM PROGRAMS/CHECKOFF PROGRAM REGULATION. Roberts, R-Kan., for Lee, R-Utah, amendment no. 3074, that would prohibit the boards that manage checkoff programs from entering into contracts with any entities that engage in activities for the purpose of influencing government policy. Rejected 38-57: R 13-36; D 24-20. June 28, 2018.

143. HR2. FARM PROGRAMS/PASSAGE. Passage of the bill that would reauthorize and extend federal farm and nutrition programs through fiscal 2023, including crop subsidies, conservation, rural development and agricultural trade programs and the Supplemental Nutritional Assistance Program. It would reauthorize and extend supplemental agricultural disaster assistance programs, the current sugar policies and loan rates, several international food aid programs, nonrecourse marketing assistance loans for loan commodities, and several dairy programs, including the dairy risk management program (previously the margin protection program). As amended, it would create new pilot programs that would test strategies for improving the accuracy of the SNAP income verification process. It would allow industrial hemp to be grown in the United States, subject to close regulation at the state level. It would reauthorize the national flood insurance program through Jan. 31, 2019. It would modify the activities permitted on land contracted under the conservation reserve program. Passed 86-11: R 38-11; D 46-0. June 28, 2018.

144. BENNETT NOMINATION/CLOTURE. Motion to invoke cloture (thus limiting debate) on the nomination of Mark Jeremy Bennett of Hawaii to be U.S. circuit judge for the Ninth Circuit. Motion agreed to 72-25: R 25-23; D 45-2. July 9, 2018.

	139	140	141	142	143	144
ALABAMA						
Shelby	Y	Y	Y	N	Y	Y
Jones	Y	Y	Y	N	Y	Y
ALASKA						
Murkowski	Y	Y	Y	N	Y	Y
Sullivan	?	?	Y	Y	Y	?
ARIZONA						
McCain	?	?	?	?	?	?
Flake	?	?	N	Y	N	N
ARKANSAS						
Boozman	Y	Y	Y	N	Y	N
Cotton	Y	Y	N	N	N	N
CALIFORNIA						
Feinstein	Y	Y	Y	N	Y	Y
Harris	Y	Y	Y	Y	Y	Y
COLORADO						
Bennet	Y	Y	Y	Y	Y	Y
Gardner	Y	Y	N	N	Y	N
CONNECTICUT						
Blumenthal	Y	Y	Y	Y	Y	Y
Murphy	Y	Y	Y	Y	Y	Y
DELAWARE						
Carper	Y	Y	Y	N	Y	Y
Coons	Y	Y	Y	N	Y	Y
FLORIDA						
Nelson	Y	Y	Y	N	Y	Y
Rubio	Y	Y	N	Y	Y	Y
GEORGIA						
Isakson	+	Y	Y	N	Y	Y
Perdue	Y	Y	Y	N	Y	Y
HAWAII						
Schatz	Y	Y	Y	Y	Y	Y
Hirono	Y	Y	Y	Y	Y	N
IDAHO						
Crapo	Y	Y	Y	N	Y	N
Risch	Y	Y	N	N	Y	N
ILLINOIS						
Durbin	Y	Y	Y	Y	Y	Y
Duckworth	+	+	?	?	Y	Y
INDIANA						
Donnelly	Y	Y	Y	N	Y	Y
Young	Y	Y	N	N	Y	Y
IOWA						
Grassley	Y	Y	Y	Y	Y	Y
Ernst	Y	Y	N	N	Y	N
KANSAS						
Roberts	Y	Y	Y	N	Y	Y
Moran	Y	Y	Y	N	Y	N
KENTUCKY						
McConnell	Y	Y	N	N	Y	Y
Paul	N	Y	N	Y	N	N
LOUISIANA						
Cassidy	Y	Y	N	N	Y	Y
Kennedy	Y	Y	N	Y	Y	Y
MAINE						
Collins	Y	Y	Y	N	Y	Y
King	Y	Y	Y	N	Y	Y
MARYLAND						
Cardin	Y	Y	Y	Y	Y	Y
Van Hollen	Y	Y	Y	Y	Y	Y
MASSACHUSETTS						
Warren	N	Y	Y	Y	Y	Y
Markey	N	Y	Y	?	Y	Y
MICHIGAN						
Stabenow	Y	Y	Y	N	Y	Y
Peters	Y	Y	Y	N	Y	Y
MINNESOTA						
Klobuchar	?	?	Y	N	Y	Y
Smith	Y	Y	Y	N	Y	Y
MISSISSIPPI						
Wicker	Y	Y	N	N	Y	Y
Hyde-Smith	Y	Y	N	N	Y	Y
MISSOURI						
McCaskill	Y	Y	Y	Y	Y	Y
Blunt	Y	Y	Y	N	Y	N

	139	140	141	142	143	144
MONTANA						
Tester	Y	Y	Y	Y	Y	Y
Daines	Y	Y	N	N	Y	N
NEBRASKA						
Fischer	Y	Y	N	N	Y	?
Sasse	Y	Y	N	N	Y	N
NEVADA						
Heller	Y	N	N	Y	N	N
Cortez Masto	?	?	Y	Y	Y	Y
NEW HAMPSHIRE						
Shaheen	Y	Y	Y	N	Y	Y
Hassan	Y	Y	Y	Y	Y	Y
NEW JERSEY						
Menendez	Y	N	Y	Y	Y	Y
Booker	?	?	Y	Y	Y	N
NEW MEXICO						
Udall	Y	Y	Y	Y	Y	Y
Heinrich	Y	Y	Y	Y	Y	Y
NEW YORK						
Schumer	Y	Y	Y	Y	Y	Y
Gillibrand	N	Y	Y	Y	Y	Y
NORTH CAROLINA						
Burr	Y	Y	N	N	N	N
Tillis	Y	Y	N	N	Y	N
NORTH DAKOTA						
Hoeven	Y	Y	Y	N	Y	N
Heitkamp	Y	Y	Y	N	Y	Y
OHIO						
Brown	Y	Y	Y	Y	Y	Y
Portman	Y	Y	Y	N	Y	Y
OKLAHOMA						
Inhofe	Y	Y	N	N	N	N
Lankford	Y	Y	N	N	N	N
OREGON						
Wyden	Y	Y	Y	N	Y	Y
Merkley	Y	Y	Y	Y	Y	Y
PENNSYLVANIA						
Casey	Y	Y	Y	N	Y	Y
Toomey	Y	Y	N	Y	N	Y
RHODE ISLAND						
Reed	Y	Y	Y	Y	Y	Y
Whitehouse	Y	Y	Y	Y	Y	Y
SOUTH CAROLINA						
Graham	?	?	Y	N	Y	Y
Scott	Y	Y	N	Y	N	Y
SOUTH DAKOTA						
Thune	Y	Y	N	Y	Y	Y
Rounds	Y	Y	Y	N	Y	N
TENNESSEE						
Alexander	Y	Y	Y	-	+	Y
Corker	Y	Y	Y	N	N	Y
TEXAS						
Cornyn	Y	Y	N	N	Y	Y
Cruz	Y	Y	N	N	Y	N
UTAH						
Hatch	Y	Y	Y	N	Y	Y
Lee	N	N	N	Y	N	Y
VERMONT						
Leahy	Y	Y	Y	?	?	Y
Sanders	Y	Y	Y	Y	Y	Y
VIRGINIA						
Warner	Y	Y	Y	N	Y	Y
Kaine	Y	Y	Y	N	Y	Y
WASHINGTON						
Murray	Y	Y	Y	N	Y	Y
Cantwell	Y	Y	Y	N	Y	Y
WEST VIRGINIA						
Manchin	Y	Y	Y	N	Y	Y
Capito	Y	Y	Y	Y	Y	Y
WISCONSIN						
Johnson	Y	Y	N	Y	N	Y
Baldwin	Y	Y	Y	N	Y	Y
WYOMING						
Enzi	Y	Y	N	N	Y	N
Barrasso	Y	Y	N	N	Y	N

KEY	**Republicans**	Democrats	*Independents*

Y Voted for (yea)	X Paired against	C Voted "present" to avoid possible conflict of interest
# Paired for	- Announced against	
+ Announced for	P Voted "present"	? Did not vote or otherwise make a position known
N Voted against (nay)		

VOTE NUMBER

145. BENNETT NOMINATION/CONFIRMATION. Confirmation of President Donald Trump's nomination of Mark Jeremy Bennett of Hawaii to be U.S. circuit judge for the Ninth Circuit. Confirmed 72-27: R 23-27; D 47-0. July 10, 2018.

146. BENCZKOWSKI NOMINATION/CLOTURE. Motion to invoke cloture (thus limiting debate) on the nomination of Brian Allen Benczkowski of Virginia to be an assistant attorney general. Motion agreed to 51-48: R 50-0; D 1-46. July 10, 2018.

147. HR5515. FISCAL 2019 DEFENSE AUTHORIZATION/MOTION TO REQUEST CONFERENCE. McConnell, R-Ky., motion that the Senate insist on its amendments to the bill, agree to the House's request for a conference, and allow the chair to appoint conferees on the bill that would authorize funding for defense programs in fiscal 2019. Motion agreed to 91-8: R 49-1; D 41-6. July 10, 2018.

148. HR5515. FISCAL 2019 DEFENSE AUTHORIZATION/MOTION TO INSTRUCT. Cornyn, R-Texas, motion to instruct Senate conferees on the bill to insist that the final conference report include provisions that would modernize of Committee on Foreign Investment in the United States. Motion agreed to 97-2: R 48-2; D 47-0. July 10, 2018.

149. HR5515. FISCAL 2019 DEFENSE AUTHORIZATION/MOTION TO INSTRUCT. Reed, D-R.I., motion to instruct Senate conferees on the bill to insist that the final conference report include provisions that would reaffirm the commitment of the United States to NATO. Motion agreed to 97-2: R 48-2; D 47-0. July 10, 2018.

150. HR5895. FISCAL 2019 ENERGY-WATER, LEGISLATIVE BRANCH, MILITARY CONSTRUCTION-VA APPROPRIATIONS/MOTION TO INSTRUCT. Cassidy, R-La., motion to instruct Senate conferees on the bill to insist that the final conference report include provisions that would extend the National Flood Insurance Program through Jan. 31, 2019. Motion agreed to 95-4: R 46-4; D 47-0. July 11, 2018.

State / Senator	145	146	147	148	149	150
ALABAMA						
Shelby	Y	Y	Y	Y	Y	Y
Jones	Y	N	Y	Y	Y	Y
ALASKA						
Murkowski	Y	Y	Y	Y	Y	Y
Sullivan	N	Y	Y	Y	Y	Y
ARIZONA						
McCain	?	?	?	?	?	?
Flake	N	Y	Y	Y	Y	N
ARKANSAS						
Boozman	N	Y	Y	Y	Y	Y
Cotton	N	Y	Y	Y	Y	Y
CALIFORNIA						
Feinstein	Y	N	Y	Y	Y	Y
Harris	Y	N	N	Y	Y	Y
COLORADO						
Bennet	Y	N	Y	Y	Y	Y
Gardner	N	Y	Y	Y	Y	Y
CONNECTICUT						
Blumenthal	Y	N	Y	Y	Y	Y
Murphy	Y	N	Y	Y	Y	Y
DELAWARE						
Carper	Y	N	Y	Y	Y	Y
Coons	Y	N	Y	Y	Y	Y
FLORIDA						
Nelson	Y	N	Y	Y	Y	Y
Rubio	Y	Y	Y	Y	Y	Y
GEORGIA						
Isakson	N	Y	Y	Y	Y	Y
Perdue	Y	Y	Y	Y	Y	Y
HAWAII						
Schatz	Y	N	Y	Y	Y	Y
Hirono	Y	N	Y	Y	Y	Y
IDAHO						
Crapo	N	Y	Y	Y	Y	Y
Risch	N	Y	Y	Y	Y	Y
ILLINOIS						
Durbin	Y	N	Y	Y	Y	Y
Duckworth	Y	N	Y	Y	Y	Y
INDIANA						
Donnelly	Y	N	Y	Y	Y	Y
Young	Y	Y	Y	Y	Y	Y
IOWA						
Grassley	Y	Y	Y	Y	Y	Y
Ernst	N	Y	Y	Y	Y	Y
KANSAS						
Roberts	Y	Y	Y	Y	Y	Y
Moran	N	Y	Y	Y	Y	Y
KENTUCKY						
McConnell	Y	Y	Y	Y	Y	Y
Paul	N	Y	N	N	N	Y
LOUISIANA						
Cassidy	Y	Y	Y	Y	Y	Y
Kennedy	Y	Y	Y	Y	Y	Y
MAINE						
Collins	Y	Y	Y	Y	Y	Y
King	Y	N	Y	Y	Y	Y
MARYLAND						
Cardin	Y	N	Y	Y	Y	Y
Van Hollen	Y	N	Y	Y	Y	Y
MASSACHUSETTS						
Warren	Y	N	N	Y	Y	Y
Markey	Y	N	N	Y	Y	Y
MICHIGAN						
Stabenow	Y	N	Y	Y	Y	Y
Peters	Y	N	Y	Y	Y	Y
MINNESOTA						
Klobuchar	Y	N	Y	Y	Y	Y
Smith	Y	N	Y	Y	Y	Y
MISSISSIPPI						
Wicker	Y	Y	Y	Y	Y	Y
Hyde-Smith	Y	Y	Y	Y	Y	Y
MISSOURI						
McCaskill	Y	N	Y	Y	Y	Y
Blunt	N	Y	Y	Y	Y	Y

State / Senator	145	146	147	148	149	150
MONTANA						
Tester	Y	N	Y	Y	Y	Y
Daines	N	Y	Y	Y	Y	Y
NEBRASKA						
Fischer	N	Y	Y	Y	Y	Y
Sasse	N	Y	Y	Y	Y	Y
NEVADA						
Heller	N	Y	Y	Y	Y	Y
Cortez Masto	Y	N	Y	Y	Y	Y
NEW HAMPSHIRE						
Shaheen	Y	N	Y	Y	Y	Y
Hassan	Y	N	Y	Y	Y	Y
NEW JERSEY						
Menendez	Y	N	Y	Y	Y	Y
Booker	Y	N	Y	Y	Y	Y
NEW MEXICO						
Udall	Y	N	Y	Y	Y	Y
Heinrich	Y	N	Y	Y	Y	Y
NEW YORK						
Schumer	Y	N	Y	Y	Y	Y
Gillibrand	Y	N	N	Y	Y	Y
NORTH CAROLINA						
Burr	N	Y	Y	Y	Y	Y
Tillis	Y	Y	Y	Y	Y	Y
NORTH DAKOTA						
Hoeven	N	Y	Y	Y	Y	Y
Heitkamp	Y	N	Y	Y	Y	Y
OHIO						
Brown	Y	N	Y	Y	Y	Y
Portman	N	Y	Y	Y	Y	Y
OKLAHOMA						
Inhofe	N	Y	Y	Y	Y	Y
Lankford	N	Y	Y	Y	Y	N
OREGON						
Wyden	Y	N	N	Y	Y	Y
Merkley	Y	N	N	Y	Y	Y
PENNSYLVANIA						
Casey	Y	N	Y	Y	Y	Y
Toomey	Y	Y	Y	Y	Y	Y
RHODE ISLAND						
Reed	Y	N	Y	Y	Y	Y
Whitehouse	Y	N	Y	Y	Y	Y
SOUTH CAROLINA						
Graham	Y	Y	Y	Y	Y	Y
Scott	N	Y	Y	Y	Y	Y
SOUTH DAKOTA						
Thune	N	Y	Y	Y	Y	Y
Rounds	N	Y	Y	Y	Y	Y
TENNESSEE						
Alexander	Y	Y	Y	Y	Y	Y
Corker	Y	Y	Y	Y	Y	Y
TEXAS						
Cornyn	Y	Y	Y	Y	Y	Y
Cruz	N	Y	Y	Y	Y	Y
UTAH						
Hatch	Y	Y	Y	Y	Y	Y
Lee	Y	Y	N	N	N	Y
VERMONT						
Leahy	Y	N	Y	Y	Y	Y
Sanders	Y	N	N	Y	Y	Y
VIRGINIA						
Warner	Y	N	Y	Y	Y	Y
Kaine	Y	N	Y	Y	Y	Y
WASHINGTON						
Murray	Y	N	Y	Y	Y	Y
Cantwell	Y	N	Y	Y	Y	Y
WEST VIRGINIA						
Manchin	Y	Y	Y	Y	Y	Y
Capito	Y	Y	Y	Y	Y	Y
WISCONSIN						
Johnson	Y	Y	Y	Y	Y	Y
Baldwin	Y	N	Y	Y	Y	Y
WYOMING						
Enzi	N	Y	Y	Y	Y	N
Barrasso	N	Y	Y	Y	Y	N

KEY   **Republicans**   Democrats   *Independents*

Y Voted for (yea)	X Paired against	C Voted "present" to avoid possible conflict of interest
# Paired for	– Announced against	
+ Announced for	P Voted "present"	? Did not vote or otherwise make a position known
N Voted against (nay)		

VOTE NUMBER

151. HR5895. FISCAL 2019 ENERGY-WATER, LEGISLATIVE BRANCH, MILITARY CONSTRUCTION-VA APPROPRIATIONS/MOTION TO INSTRUCT. Corker, R-Tenn., motion to instruct Senate conferees on the bill to insist that the final conference report include provisions that would provide a role for Congress in making a determination on tariffs related to national security concerns. Motion agreed to 88-11: R 39-11; D 47-0. July 11, 2018.

152. BENCZKOWSKI NOMINATION/CONFIRMATION. Confirmation of President Donald Trump's nomination of Brian Allen Benczkowski of Virginia to be an assistant attorney general. Confirmed 51-48: R 50-0; D 1-46. July 11, 2018.

153. NEY NOMINATION/CLOTURE. Motion to invoke cloture (thus limiting debate) on the nomination of Paul C. Ney Jr., of Tennessee to be general counsel of the Department of Defense. Motion agreed to 74-25: R 47-3; D 26-21. July 11, 2018.

154. NEY NOMINATION/CONFIRMATION. Confirmation of President Donald Trump's nomination of Paul C. Ney Jr., of Tennessee to be general counsel of the Department of Defense. Confirmed 70-23: R 44-2; D 25-20. July 12, 2018.

155. STUMP NOMINATION/CONFIRMATION. Confirmation of President Donald Trump's nomination of Scott Stump of Colorado to be assistant secretary for Career, Technical, and Adult Education, Department of Education. Confirmed 85-0: R 42-0; D 41-0. July 16, 2018.

156. BLEW NOMINATION/CONFIRMATION. Confirmation of President Donald Trump's nomination of James Blew of California to be assistant secretary for Planning, Evaluation, and Policy Development, Department of Education. Confirmed 50-49: R 50-0; D 0-47. July 17, 2018.

	151	152	153	154	155	156
ALABAMA						
Shelby	Y	Y	Y	Y	?	Y
Jones	Y	N	Y	Y	?	N
ALASKA						
Murkowski	Y	Y	Y	Y	Y	Y
Sullivan	Y	Y	N	N	Y	Y
ARIZONA						
McCain	?	?	?	?	?	?
Flake	Y	Y	Y	Y	Y	Y
ARKANSAS						
Boozman	Y	Y	Y	Y	+	Y
Cotton	Y	Y	Y	Y	Y	Y
CALIFORNIA						
Feinstein	Y	N	N	N	Y	N
Harris	Y	N	N	N	Y	N
COLORADO						
Bennet	Y	N	Y	Y	Y	N
Gardner	Y	Y	Y	Y	Y	Y
CONNECTICUT						
Blumenthal	Y	N	N	N	Y	N
Murphy	Y	N	Y	Y	Y	N
DELAWARE						
Carper	Y	N	Y	Y	Y	N
Coons	Y	N	Y	Y	Y	N
FLORIDA						
Nelson	Y	N	Y	Y	Y	N
Rubio	Y	Y	Y	Y	Y	Y
GEORGIA						
Isakson	Y	Y	Y	Y	?	Y
Perdue	N	Y	Y	Y	Y	Y
HAWAII						
Schatz	Y	N	N	N	Y	N
Hirono	Y	N	N	N	Y	N
IDAHO						
Crapo	N	Y	Y	Y	Y	Y
Risch	N	Y	Y	Y	Y	Y
ILLINOIS						
Durbin	Y	N	Y	Y	Y	N
Duckworth	Y	N	N	N	Y	N
INDIANA						
Donnelly	Y	N	Y	Y	Y	N
Young	Y	Y	Y	Y	Y	Y
IOWA						
Grassley	Y	Y	Y	Y	Y	Y
Ernst	Y	Y	Y	Y	Y	Y
KANSAS						
Roberts	Y	Y	Y	Y	Y	Y
Moran	Y	Y	Y	?	?	Y
KENTUCKY						
McConnell	Y	Y	Y	Y	Y	Y
Paul	Y	Y	N	?	Y	Y
LOUISIANA						
Cassidy	Y	Y	Y	Y	Y	Y
Kennedy	Y	Y	Y	Y	?	Y
MAINE						
Collins	Y	Y	Y	Y	Y	Y
King	Y	N	Y	Y	Y	N
MARYLAND						
Cardin	Y	N	Y	Y	Y	N
Van Hollen	Y	N	Y	Y	Y	N
MASSACHUSETTS						
Warren	Y	N	N	N	Y	N
Markey	Y	N	N	N	Y	N
MICHIGAN						
Stabenow	Y	N	N	N	+	N
Peters	Y	N	N	N	+	N
MINNESOTA						
Klobuchar	Y	N	Y	Y	Y	N
Smith	Y	N	Y	Y	Y	N
MISSISSIPPI						
Wicker	Y	Y	Y	Y	Y	Y
Hyde-Smith	N	Y	Y	?	Y	Y
MISSOURI						
McCaskill	Y	N	Y	Y	Y	N
Blunt	Y	Y	Y	Y	Y	Y
MONTANA						
Tester	Y	N	Y	Y	Y	N
Daines	Y	Y	Y	Y	Y	Y
NEBRASKA						
Fischer	Y	Y	Y	Y	Y	Y
Sasse	Y	Y	Y	Y	Y	Y
NEVADA						
Heller	N	Y	Y	Y	?	Y
Cortez Masto	Y	N	N	N	Y	N
NEW HAMPSHIRE						
Shaheen	Y	N	Y	?	?	N
Hassan	Y	N	Y	Y	Y	N
NEW JERSEY						
Menendez	Y	N	N	N	Y	N
Booker	Y	N	N	N	Y	N
NEW MEXICO						
Udall	Y	N	Y	Y	Y	N
Heinrich	Y	N	Y	Y	Y	N
NEW YORK						
Schumer	Y	N	N	?	Y	N
Gillibrand	Y	N	N	N	?	N
NORTH CAROLINA						
Burr	Y	Y	Y	Y	Y	Y
Tillis	Y	Y	Y	?	Y	Y
NORTH DAKOTA						
Hoeven	Y	Y	Y	Y	Y	Y
Heitkamp	Y	N	Y	Y	Y	N
OHIO						
Brown	Y	N	N	N	Y	N
Portman	Y	Y	Y	Y	Y	Y
OKLAHOMA						
Inhofe	N	Y	Y	Y	?	Y
Lankford	Y	Y	Y	Y	Y	Y
OREGON						
Wyden	Y	N	N	N	Y	N
Merkley	Y	N	N	N	Y	N
PENNSYLVANIA						
Casey	Y	N	N	N	Y	N
Toomey	Y	Y	Y	Y	Y	Y
RHODE ISLAND						
Reed	Y	N	Y	Y	Y	N
Whitehouse	Y	N	Y	Y	Y	N
SOUTH CAROLINA						
Graham	N	Y	Y	Y	?	Y
Scott	N	Y	Y	Y	Y	Y
SOUTH DAKOTA						
Thune	Y	Y	Y	Y	Y	Y
Rounds	Y	Y	Y	Y	Y	Y
TENNESSEE						
Alexander	Y	Y	Y	Y	Y	Y
Corker	Y	Y	Y	Y	Y	Y
TEXAS						
Cornyn	Y	Y	Y	Y	Y	Y
Cruz	Y	Y	Y	Y	Y	Y
UTAH						
Hatch	Y	Y	Y	Y	Y	Y
Lee	Y	Y	N	N	Y	Y
VERMONT						
Leahy	Y	N	N	N	?	N
Sanders	Y	N	N	N	Y	N
VIRGINIA						
Warner	Y	N	Y	Y	Y	N
Kaine	Y	N	Y	Y	Y	N
WASHINGTON						
Murray	Y	N	Y	Y	Y	N
Cantwell	Y	N	Y	Y	Y	N
WEST VIRGINIA						
Manchin	Y	Y	Y	Y	Y	N
Capito	N	Y	Y	Y	Y	Y
WISCONSIN						
Johnson	Y	Y	Y	Y	Y	Y
Baldwin	Y	N	N	N	Y	N
WYOMING						
Enzi	N	Y	Y	Y	Y	Y
Barrasso	N	Y	Y	Y	Y	Y

KEY   Republicans   Democrats   *Independents*

Y Voted for (yea)	**X** Paired against	**C** Voted "present" to avoid possible conflict of interest
# Paired for	**–** Announced against	
+ Announced for	**P** Voted "present"	**?** Did not vote or otherwise make a position known
N Voted against (nay)		

VOTE NUMBER

157. QUARLES NOMINATION/CLOTURE. Motion to invoke cloture (thus limiting debate) on the nomination of Randal Quarles of Colorado to be a member of the Board of Governors of the Federal Reserve System. Motion agreed to 66-33: R 50-0; D 15-32. July 17, 2018.

158. QUARLES NOMINATION/CONFIRMATION. Confirmation of President Donald Trump's nomination of Randal Quarles of Colorado to be a member of the Board of Governors of the Federal Reserve System. Confirmed 66-33: R 50-0; D 15-32. July 17, 2018.

159. OLDHAM NOMINATION/CLOTURE. Motion to invoke cloture (thus limiting debate) on the nomination of Andrew S. Oldham of Texas to be U.S. circuit judge for the Fifth Circuit. Motion agreed to 50-49: R 50-0; D 0-47. July 17, 2018.

160. OLDHAM NOMINATION/CONFIRMATION. Confirmation of President Donald Trump's nomination of Andrew S. Oldham of Texas to be U.S. circuit judge for the Fifth Circuit. Confirmed 50-49: R 50-0; D 0-47. July 18, 2018.

161. BOUNDS NOMINATION/CLOTURE. Motion to invoke cloture (thus limiting debate) on the nomination of Ryan Wesley Bounds of Oregon to be a U.S. circuit judge for the Ninth Circuit. Motion agreed to 50-49: R 50-0; D 0-47. July 18, 2018.

162. SRES584. RUSSIAN INTERROGATION OF U.S. OFFICIALS/ADOPTION. Adoption of the resolution that would state that it is the sense of Congress that United States should refuse to make available any current or former diplomat, civil servant, political appointee, law enforcement official or member of the armed forces of United States for questioning by the government of Russian President Vladimir Putin. Adopted 98-0: R 49-0; D 47-0. July 19, 2018.

	157	158	159	160	161	162
ALABAMA						
Shelby	Y	Y	Y	Y	Y	?
Jones	Y	Y	N	N	N	Y
ALASKA						
Murkowski	Y	Y	Y	Y	Y	Y
Sullivan	Y	Y	Y	Y	Y	Y
ARIZONA						
McCain	?	?	?	?	?	?
Flake	Y	Y	Y	Y	Y	Y
ARKANSAS						
Boozman	Y	Y	Y	Y	Y	Y
Cotton	Y	Y	Y	Y	Y	Y
CALIFORNIA						
Feinstein	N	N	N	N	N	Y
Harris	N	N	N	N	N	Y
COLORADO						
Bennet	Y	Y	N	N	N	Y
Gardner	Y	Y	Y	Y	Y	Y
CONNECTICUT						
Blumenthal	N	N	N	N	N	Y
Murphy	N	N	N	N	N	Y
DELAWARE						
Carper	Y	Y	N	N	N	Y
Coons	Y	Y	N	N	N	Y
FLORIDA						
Nelson	Y	Y	N	N	N	Y
Rubio	Y	Y	Y	Y	Y	Y
GEORGIA						
Isakson	Y	Y	Y	Y	Y	Y
Perdue	Y	Y	Y	Y	Y	Y
HAWAII						
Schatz	N	N	N	N	N	Y
Hirono	N	N	N	N	N	Y
IDAHO						
Crapo	Y	Y	Y	Y	Y	Y
Risch	Y	Y	Y	Y	Y	Y
ILLINOIS						
Durbin	N	N	N	N	N	Y
Duckworth	N	N	N	N	N	Y
INDIANA						
Donnelly	Y	Y	N	N	N	Y
Young	Y	Y	Y	Y	Y	Y
IOWA						
Grassley	Y	Y	Y	Y	Y	Y
Ernst	Y	Y	Y	Y	Y	Y
KANSAS						
Roberts	Y	Y	Y	Y	Y	Y
Moran	Y	Y	Y	Y	Y	Y
KENTUCKY						
McConnell	Y	Y	Y	Y	Y	Y
Paul	Y	Y	Y	Y	Y	Y
LOUISIANA						
Cassidy	Y	Y	Y	Y	Y	Y
Kennedy	Y	Y	Y	Y	Y	Y
MAINE						
Collins	Y	Y	Y	Y	Y	Y
King	Y	Y	N	N	N	Y
MARYLAND						
Cardin	Y	Y	N	N	N	Y
Van Hollen	Y	Y	N	N	N	Y
MASSACHUSETTS						
Warren	N	N	N	N	N	Y
Markey	N	N	N	N	N	Y
MICHIGAN						
Stabenow	N	N	N	N	N	Y
Peters	Y	Y	N	N	N	Y
MINNESOTA						
Klobuchar	N	N	N	N	N	Y
Smith	N	N	N	N	N	Y
MISSISSIPPI						
Wicker	Y	Y	Y	Y	Y	Y
Hyde-Smith	Y	Y	Y	Y	Y	Y
MISSOURI						
McCaskill	Y	Y	N	N	N	Y
Blunt	Y	Y	Y	Y	Y	Y
MONTANA						
Tester	Y	Y	N	N	N	Y
Daines	Y	Y	Y	Y	Y	Y
NEBRASKA						
Fischer	Y	Y	Y	Y	Y	Y
Sasse	Y	Y	Y	Y	Y	Y
NEVADA						
Heller	Y	Y	Y	Y	Y	Y
Cortez Masto	N	N	N	N	N	Y
NEW HAMPSHIRE						
Shaheen	Y	Y	N	N	N	Y
Hassan	N	N	N	N	N	Y
NEW JERSEY						
Menendez	N	N	N	N	N	Y
Booker	N	N	N	N	N	Y
NEW MEXICO						
Udall	N	N	N	N	N	Y
Heinrich	N	N	N	N	N	Y
NEW YORK						
Schumer	N	N	N	N	N	Y
Gillibrand	N	N	N	N	N	Y
NORTH CAROLINA						
Burr	Y	Y	Y	Y	Y	Y
Tillis	Y	Y	Y	Y	Y	Y
NORTH DAKOTA						
Hoeven	Y	Y	Y	Y	Y	Y
Heitkamp	Y	Y	N	N	N	Y
OHIO						
Brown	N	N	N	N	N	Y
Portman	Y	Y	Y	Y	Y	Y
OKLAHOMA						
Inhofe	Y	Y	Y	Y	Y	Y
Lankford	Y	Y	Y	Y	Y	Y
OREGON						
Wyden	N	N	N	N	N	Y
Merkley	N	N	N	N	N	Y
PENNSYLVANIA						
Casey	N	N	N	N	N	Y
Toomey	Y	Y	Y	Y	Y	Y
RHODE ISLAND						
Reed	N	N	N	N	N	Y
Whitehouse	N	N	N	N	N	Y
SOUTH CAROLINA						
Graham	Y	Y	Y	Y	Y	Y
Scott	Y	Y	Y	Y	Y	Y
SOUTH DAKOTA						
Thune	Y	Y	Y	Y	Y	Y
Rounds	Y	Y	Y	Y	Y	Y
TENNESSEE						
Alexander	Y	Y	Y	Y	Y	Y
Corker	Y	Y	Y	Y	Y	Y
TEXAS						
Cornyn	Y	Y	Y	Y	Y	Y
Cruz	Y	Y	Y	Y	Y	Y
UTAH						
Hatch	Y	Y	Y	Y	Y	Y
Lee	Y	Y	Y	Y	Y	Y
VERMONT						
Leahy	N	N	N	N	N	Y
Sanders	N	N	N	N	N	Y
VIRGINIA						
Warner	Y	Y	N	N	N	Y
Kaine	N	N	N	N	N	Y
WASHINGTON						
Murray	N	N	N	N	N	Y
Cantwell	N	N	N	N	N	Y
WEST VIRGINIA						
Manchin	Y	Y	N	N	N	Y
Capito	Y	Y	Y	Y	Y	Y
WISCONSIN						
Johnson	Y	Y	Y	Y	Y	Y
Baldwin	N	N	N	N	N	Y
WYOMING						
Enzi	Y	Y	Y	Y	Y	Y
Barrasso	Y	Y	Y	Y	Y	Y

KEY	**Republicans**	Democrats	*Independents*

Y Voted for (yea)	X Paired against	C Voted "present" to avoid possible conflict of interest
# Paired for	– Announced against	
+ Announced for	P Voted "present"	? Did not vote or otherwise make a position known
N Voted against (nay)		

VOTE NUMBER

163. WILKIE NOMINATION/CONFIRMATION. Confirmation of President Donald Trump's nomination of Robert L. Wilkie of North Carolina to be secretary of Veterans Affairs. Confirmed 86-9: R 47-0; D 38-8. July 23, 2018.

164. HR6147. ANTICIPATED LEGISLATIVE VEHICLE FOR FISCAL 2019 INTERIOR-ENVIRONMENT, FIN SERV, AGRICULTURE, TRANSPORTATION-HUD APPROPRIATIONS/TAX PREPARATION ASSISTANCE PROGRAMS. Collins, R-Maine, for Heller, R-Nev., amendment no. 3405, to the Shelby, R-Ala., substitute amendment no. 3399, that would increase funding for grants for tax return preparation assistance programs by $5 million. Adopted 98-1: R 49-1; D 47-0. July 24, 2018.

165. HR6147. ANTICIPATED LEGISLATIVE VEHICLE FOR FISCAL 2019 INTERIOR-ENVIRONMENT, FIN SERV, AGRICULTURE, TRANSPORTATION-HUD APPROPRIATIONS/AMTRAK ON-TIME PERFORMANCE. Collins, R-Maine, for Durbin, D-Ill., amendment no. 3422, to the Shelby, R-Ala., substitute amendment no. 3399, that would require the Amtrak's inspector general to update the report entitled, "Effects of Amtrak's Poor On-Time Performance." and make the updated report publicly available. Adopted 99-0: R 50-0; D 47-0. July 24, 2018.

166. HR6147. ANTICIPATED LEGISLATIVE VEHICLE FOR FISCAL 2019 INTERIOR-ENVIRONMENT, FIN SERV, AGRICULTURE, TRANSPORTATION-HUD APPROPRIATIONS/VOLCANO-DAMAGED INFRASTRUCTURE REPORT. Murkowski, R-Alaska, for Schatz, D-Hawaii, amendment no. 3407, to the Shelby, R-Ala., substitute amendment no. 3399, that would require the Interior Department to report to Congress on department infrastructure damaged by a volcanic eruption covered by a major disaster declaration in calendar year 2018. Adopted 97-1: R 48-1; D 47-0. July 24, 2018.

167. HR6147. ANTICIPATED LEGISLATIVE VEHICLE FOR FISCAL 2019 INTERIOR-ENVIRONMENT, FIN SERV, AGRICULTURE, TRANSPORTATION-HUD APPROPRIATIONS/SEAFOOD INSPECTIONS. Murkowski, R-Alaska, for Kennedy, R-La., amendment no. 3430, to the Shelby, R-Ala., substitute amendment no. 3399, that would require that at least $15 million of the funds appropriated by the bill be used for inspections of foreign seafood manufacturers. Adopted 87-11: R 40-9; D 45-2. July 24, 2018.

168. HR6147. ANTICIPATED LEGISLATIVE VEHICLE FOR FISCAL 2019 INTERIOR-ENVIRONMENT, FIN SERV, AGRICULTURE, TRANSPORTATION-HUD APPROPRIATIONS/EXCEPTIONS FOR GRAIN INSPECTION. Daines, R-Mont., for Moran, R-Kan., amendment no. 3433, to the Shelby, R-Ala., substitute amendment no. 3399, that would prohibit funds appropriated by the bill from being used to revoke exceptions to the requirement that certain government officials inspecting or weighing grain not operate outside of their designated areas of responsibility. Adopted 98-0: R 50-0; D 46-0. July 25, 2018.

	163	164	165	166	167	168
ALABAMA						
Shelby	Y	Y	Y	Y	Y	Y
Jones	Y	Y	Y	Y	Y	Y
ALASKA						
Murkowski	Y	Y	Y	Y	Y	Y
Sullivan	Y	Y	Y	Y	Y	Y
ARIZONA						
McCain	?	?	?	?	?	?
Flake	Y	Y	Y	Y	N	Y
ARKANSAS						
Boozman	Y	Y	Y	Y	Y	Y
Cotton	Y	Y	Y	Y	Y	Y
CALIFORNIA						
Feinstein	N	Y	Y	Y	Y	Y
Harris	N	Y	Y	Y	Y	Y
COLORADO						
Bennet	Y	Y	Y	Y	Y	Y
Gardner	Y	Y	Y	Y	Y	Y
CONNECTICUT						
Blumenthal	Y	Y	Y	Y	Y	Y
Murphy	Y	Y	Y	Y	Y	Y
DELAWARE						
Carper	Y	Y	Y	Y	Y	Y
Coons	Y	Y	Y	Y	Y	Y
FLORIDA						
Nelson	Y	Y	Y	Y	Y	Y
Rubio	Y	Y	Y	Y	Y	Y
GEORGIA						
Isakson	Y	Y	Y	Y	N	Y
Perdue	Y	Y	Y	Y	Y	Y
HAWAII						
Schatz	Y	Y	Y	Y	Y	Y
Hirono	Y	Y	Y	Y	Y	Y
IDAHO						
Crapo	Y	Y	Y	Y	N	Y
Risch	Y	Y	Y	Y	N	Y
ILLINOIS						
Durbin	Y	Y	Y	Y	Y	Y
Duckworth	Y	Y	Y	Y	Y	?
INDIANA						
Donnelly	Y	Y	Y	Y	Y	Y
Young	Y	Y	Y	Y	Y	Y
IOWA						
Grassley	Y	Y	Y	Y	Y	Y
Ernst	Y	Y	Y	Y	Y	Y
KANSAS						
Roberts	Y	Y	Y	Y	Y	Y
Moran	Y	Y	Y	Y	Y	Y
KENTUCKY						
McConnell	Y	Y	Y	Y	Y	Y
Paul	Y	N	Y	N	N	Y
LOUISIANA						
Cassidy	Y	Y	Y	Y	Y	Y
Kennedy	?	Y	Y	Y	Y	Y
MAINE						
Collins	Y	Y	Y	Y	Y	Y
King	Y	Y	Y	Y	Y	Y
MARYLAND						
Cardin	Y	Y	Y	Y	Y	Y
Van Hollen	Y	Y	Y	Y	Y	Y
MASSACHUSETTS						
Warren	N	Y	Y	Y	Y	Y
Markey	N	Y	Y	Y	Y	Y
MICHIGAN						
Stabenow	Y	Y	Y	Y	Y	Y
Peters	Y	Y	Y	Y	Y	Y
MINNESOTA						
Klobuchar	Y	Y	Y	Y	Y	Y
Smith	Y	Y	Y	Y	Y	Y
MISSISSIPPI						
Wicker	Y	Y	Y	Y	Y	Y
Hyde-Smith	Y	Y	Y	Y	Y	Y
MISSOURI						
McCaskill	Y	Y	Y	Y	Y	Y
Blunt	Y	Y	Y	?	?	Y

	163	164	165	166	167	168
MONTANA						
Tester	Y	Y	Y	Y	Y	Y
Daines	Y	Y	Y	Y	Y	Y
NEBRASKA						
Fischer	Y	Y	Y	Y	Y	Y
Sasse	Y	Y	Y	N	N	Y
NEVADA						
Heller	Y	Y	Y	Y	Y	Y
Cortez Masto	Y	Y	Y	Y	Y	Y
NEW HAMPSHIRE						
Shaheen	Y	Y	Y	Y	N	Y
Hassan	Y	Y	Y	Y	N	Y
NEW JERSEY						
Menendez	Y	Y	Y	Y	Y	Y
Booker	N	Y	Y	Y	Y	Y
NEW MEXICO						
Udall	Y	Y	Y	Y	Y	Y
Heinrich	Y	Y	Y	Y	Y	Y
NEW YORK						
Schumer	Y	Y	Y	Y	Y	Y
Gillibrand	N	Y	Y	Y	Y	Y
NORTH CAROLINA						
Burr	?	Y	Y	Y	Y	Y
Tillis	Y	Y	Y	Y	Y	Y
NORTH DAKOTA						
Hoeven	Y	Y	Y	Y	Y	Y
Heitkamp	Y	Y	Y	Y	Y	Y
OHIO						
Brown	?	Y	Y	Y	Y	Y
Portman	Y	Y	Y	Y	Y	Y
OKLAHOMA						
Inhofe	Y	Y	Y	Y	Y	Y
Lankford	Y	Y	Y	Y	N	Y
OREGON						
Wyden	N	Y	Y	Y	Y	Y
Merkley	N	Y	Y	Y	Y	Y
PENNSYLVANIA						
Casey	Y	Y	Y	Y	Y	Y
Toomey	Y	Y	Y	Y	N	Y
RHODE ISLAND						
Reed	Y	Y	Y	Y	Y	Y
Whitehouse	Y	Y	Y	Y	Y	Y
SOUTH CAROLINA						
Graham	Y	Y	Y	Y	Y	Y
Scott	Y	Y	Y	Y	Y	Y
SOUTH DAKOTA						
Thune	Y	Y	Y	Y	Y	Y
Rounds	Y	Y	Y	Y	Y	Y
TENNESSEE						
Alexander	Y	Y	Y	Y	Y	Y
Corker	?	Y	Y	Y	Y	Y
TEXAS						
Cornyn	Y	Y	Y	Y	Y	Y
Cruz	Y	Y	Y	Y	Y	Y
UTAH						
Hatch	Y	Y	Y	Y	Y	Y
Lee	Y	Y	Y	N	N	Y
VERMONT						
Leahy	Y	Y	Y	Y	Y	Y
Sanders	N	Y	Y	Y	Y	Y
VIRGINIA						
Warner	Y	Y	Y	Y	Y	Y
Kaine	Y	Y	Y	Y	Y	Y
WASHINGTON						
Murray	Y	Y	Y	Y	Y	Y
Cantwell	Y	Y	Y	Y	Y	Y
WEST VIRGINIA						
Manchin	Y	Y	Y	Y	Y	Y
Capito	Y	Y	Y	Y	Y	Y
WISCONSIN						
Johnson	Y	Y	Y	Y	Y	Y
Baldwin	Y	Y	Y	Y	Y	Y
WYOMING						
Enzi	Y	Y	Y	Y	Y	Y
Barrasso	Y	Y	Y	Y	Y	Y

KEY	Republicans	Democrats	*Independents*
Y Voted for (yea)		**X** Paired against	**C** Voted "present" to avoid possible conflict of interest
# Paired for		**–** Announced against	
+ Announced for		**P** Voted "present"	**?** Did not vote or otherwise make a position known
N Voted against (nay)			

VOTE NUMBER

169. HR6147. ANTICIPATED LEGISLATIVE VEHICLE FOR FISCAL 2019 INTERIOR-ENVIRONMENT, FIN SERV, AGRICULTURE, TRANSPORTATION-HUD APPROPRIATIONS/LONG-DISTANCE PASSENGER RAIL. Daines, R-Mont., for Udall, D-N.M., amendment no. 3414, as modified, to the Shelby, R-Ala., substitute amendment no. 3399, that would express the sense of Congress that long-distance rail passenger rail is important to rural communities and such services should be sustained. Adopted 95-4: R 46-4; D 47-0. July 25, 2018.

170. HR6147. ANTICIPATED LEGISLATIVE VEHICLE FOR FISCAL 2019 INTERIOR-ENVIRONMENT, FIN SERV, AGRICULTURE, TRANSPORTATION-HUD APPROPRIATIONS/SYNTHETIC OPIOID INVESTIGATIONS. Collins, R-Maine, for Manchin, D-W.Va., amendment no. 3553, to the Shelby, R-Ala., substitute amendment no. 3399, that would require that at least $1 million of the funds appropriated by the bill be used to investigate the synthetic opioid trade, specifically the trade of fentanyl with Chinese origins, and would require the Treasury Department to report to Congress on the effects of the efforts of individuals in China to subvert U.S. laws and supply persons in the United States with synthetic opioids. Adopted 99-0: R 50-0; D 47-0. July 25, 2018.

171. HR6147. ANTICIPATED LEGISLATIVE VEHICLE FOR FISCAL 2019 INTERIOR-ENVIRONMENT, FIN SERV, AGRICULTURE, TRANSPORTATION-HUD APPROPRIATIONS/OVERALL FUNDING REDUCTION. Collins, R-Maine, for Paul, R-Ky., amendment no. 3543, to the Shelby, R-Ala., substitute amendment no. 3399, that would reduce the funds appropriated in each division of the bill by 11.39 percent. Rejected 25-74: R 25-25; D 0-47. July 25, 2018.

172. GRANT NOMINATION/CLOTURE. Motion to invoke cloture (thus limiting debate) on the nomination of Britt Cagle Grant of Georgia to be a U.S. a circuit judge for the Eleventh Circuit. Motion agreed to 52-44: R 49-0; D 3-42. July 30, 2018.

173. S1182. FLOOD INSURANCE EXTENSION/MOTION TO CONCUR. McConnell, R-Ky., motion to concur in the House amendment to the bill that would extend the authorization of the National Flood Insurance Program through Nov. 30, 2018. Motion agreed to 86-12: R 37-12; D 47-0. July 31, 2018.

174. GRANT NOMINATION/CONFIRMATION. Confirmation of President Donald Trump's nomination of Britt Cagle Grant of Georgia to be U.S. circuit judge for the Eleventh Circuit. Confirmed 52-46: R 49-0; D 3-44. July 31, 2018.

	169	170	171	172	173	174
ALABAMA						
Shelby	Y	Y	N	Y	N	Y
Jones	Y	Y	N	N	Y	N
ALASKA						
Murkowski	Y	Y	N	Y	Y	Y
Sullivan	Y	Y	N	Y	Y	Y
ARIZONA						
McCain	?	?	?	?	?	?
Flake	Y	Y	Y	?	?	?
ARKANSAS						
Boozman	Y	Y	N	Y	Y	Y
Cotton	Y	Y	Y	Y	N	Y
CALIFORNIA						
Feinstein	Y	Y	N	N	Y	N
Harris	Y	Y	N	N	Y	N
COLORADO						
Bennet	Y	Y	N	N	Y	N
Gardner	Y	Y	N	Y	Y	Y
CONNECTICUT						
Blumenthal	Y	Y	N	N	Y	N
Murphy	Y	Y	N	N	Y	N
DELAWARE						
Carper	Y	Y	N	N	Y	N
Coons	Y	Y	N	N	Y	N
FLORIDA						
Nelson	Y	Y	N	–	Y	N
Rubio	Y	Y	N	Y	Y	Y
GEORGIA						
Isakson	Y	Y	N	Y	Y	Y
Perdue	Y	Y	Y	Y	Y	Y
HAWAII						
Schatz	Y	Y	N	N	Y	N
Hirono	Y	Y	N	N	Y	N
IDAHO						
Crapo	Y	Y	Y	Y	Y	Y
Risch	Y	Y	Y	Y	N	Y
ILLINOIS						
Durbin	Y	Y	N	N	Y	N
Duckworth	Y	Y	N	N	Y	N
INDIANA						
Donnelly	Y	Y	N	N	Y	N
Young	Y	Y	N	Y	Y	Y
IOWA						
Grassley	Y	Y	Y	Y	Y	Y
Ernst	Y	Y	Y	Y	Y	Y
KANSAS						
Roberts	Y	Y	N	Y	Y	Y
Moran	Y	Y	N	Y	Y	Y
KENTUCKY						
McConnell	Y	Y	N	Y	Y	Y
Paul	N	Y	Y	Y	N	Y
LOUISIANA						
Cassidy	Y	Y	Y	Y	Y	Y
Kennedy	Y	Y	Y	Y	Y	Y
MAINE						
Collins	Y	Y	N	Y	Y	Y
King	Y	Y	N	N	Y	N
MARYLAND						
Cardin	Y	Y	N	N	Y	N
Van Hollen	Y	Y	N	N	Y	N
MASSACHUSETTS						
Warren	Y	Y	N	N	Y	N
Markey	Y	Y	N	N	Y	N
MICHIGAN						
Stabenow	Y	Y	N	N	Y	N
Peters	Y	Y	N	N	Y	N
MINNESOTA						
Klobuchar	Y	Y	N	N	Y	N
Smith	Y	Y	N	N	Y	N
MISSISSIPPI						
Wicker	Y	Y	N	Y	Y	Y
Hyde-Smith	Y	Y	N	Y	Y	Y
MISSOURI						
McCaskill	Y	Y	N	N	Y	N
Blunt	Y	Y	N	Y	Y	Y
MONTANA						
Tester	Y	Y	N	Y	Y	Y
Daines	Y	Y	Y	Y	Y	Y
NEBRASKA						
Fischer	Y	Y	N	Y	Y	Y
Sasse	N	Y	Y	Y	N	Y
NEVADA						
Heller	Y	Y	N	Y	Y	Y
Cortez Masto	Y	Y	N	N	Y	N
NEW HAMPSHIRE						
Shaheen	Y	Y	N	N	Y	N
Hassan	Y	Y	N	N	Y	N
NEW JERSEY						
Menendez	Y	Y	N	N	Y	N
Booker	Y	Y	N	N	Y	N
NEW MEXICO						
Udall	Y	Y	N	N	Y	N
Heinrich	Y	Y	N	N	Y	N
NEW YORK						
Schumer	Y	Y	N	N	Y	N
Gillibrand	Y	Y	N	N	Y	N
NORTH CAROLINA						
Burr	Y	Y	Y	Y	Y	Y
Tillis	Y	Y	N	Y	Y	Y
NORTH DAKOTA						
Hoeven	Y	Y	N	Y	Y	Y
Heitkamp	Y	Y	N	Y	Y	Y
OHIO						
Brown	Y	Y	N	Y	Y	N
Portman	Y	Y	N	Y	Y	Y
OKLAHOMA						
Inhofe	Y	Y	Y	Y	N	Y
Lankford	Y	Y	Y	Y	N	Y
OREGON						
Wyden	Y	Y	N	N	Y	N
Merkley	Y	Y	N	N	Y	N
PENNSYLVANIA						
Casey	Y	Y	N	N	Y	N
Toomey	N	Y	Y	Y	N	Y
RHODE ISLAND						
Reed	Y	Y	N	N	Y	N
Whitehouse	Y	Y	N	N	Y	N
SOUTH CAROLINA						
Graham	Y	Y	N	Y	Y	Y
Scott	Y	Y	Y	Y	Y	Y
SOUTH DAKOTA						
Thune	Y	Y	Y	Y	Y	Y
Rounds	Y	Y	N	Y	Y	Y
TENNESSEE						
Alexander	Y	Y	N	Y	Y	Y
Corker	Y	Y	Y	Y	Y	Y
TEXAS						
Cornyn	Y	Y	Y	Y	Y	Y
Cruz	Y	Y	Y	Y	Y	Y
UTAH						
Hatch	Y	Y	N	Y	Y	Y
Lee	N	Y	Y	Y	N	Y
VERMONT						
Leahy	Y	Y	N	N	Y	N
Sanders	Y	Y	N	N	Y	N
VIRGINIA						
Warner	Y	Y	N	–	Y	N
Kaine	Y	Y	N	N	Y	N
WASHINGTON						
Murray	Y	Y	N	N	Y	N
Cantwell	Y	Y	N	N	Y	N
WEST VIRGINIA						
Manchin	Y	Y	N	Y	Y	Y
Capito	Y	Y	N	Y	Y	Y
WISCONSIN						
Johnson	Y	Y	Y	Y	N	Y
Baldwin	Y	Y	N	N	Y	N
WYOMING						
Enzi	Y	Y	Y	Y	N	Y
Barrasso	Y	Y	Y	Y	N	Y

KEY   **Republicans**   Democrats   *Independents*

Y	Voted for (yea)	X	Paired against
#	Paired for	–	Announced against
+	Announced for	P	Voted "present"
N	Voted against (nay)		
C	Voted "present" to avoid possible conflict of interest		
?	Did not vote or otherwise make a position known		

VOTE NUMBER

175. HR6147. ANTICIPATED LEGISLATIVE VEHICLE FOR FISCAL 2019 INTERIOR-ENVIRONMENT, FIN SERV, AGRICULTURE, TRANSPORTATION-HUD APPROPRIATIONS/CLOTURE. Motion to invoke cloture (thus limiting debate) on the Shelby, R-Ala., substitute amendment no. 3399 that would provide $154.2 billion in discretionary funding for fiscal 2019 to various departments and agencies. Motion agreed to 94-4: R 46-3; D 46-1. July 31, 2018.

176. HR6147. ANTICIPATED LEGISLATIVE VEHICLE FOR FISCAL 2019 INTERIOR-ENVIRONMENT, FIN SERV, AGRICULTURE, TRANSPORTATION-HUD APPROPRIATIONS/ELECTION SECURITY GRANTS. Collins, R-Maine, for Leahy, D-Vt., amendment no. 3464, to the Shelby, R-Ala., substitute amendment no. 3399, that would appropriate $250 million for election security grants. Rejected 50-47: R 1-47; D 47-0. 08 01, 2018.

177. HR6147. ANTICIPATED LEGISLATIVE VEHICLE FOR FISCAL 2019 INTERIOR-ENVIRONMENT, FIN SERV, AGRICULTURE, TRANSPORTATION-HUD APPROPRIATIONS/FOOD LABELING. Collins, R-Maine, for Lee, R-Utah, amendment no. 3522, to the Shelby, R-Ala., substitute amendment no. 3399, that would prohibit any of the funds appropriated by the bill to the Food and Drug Administration from being used to enforce standards that would consider a food product misbranded if the food product's name contains the name of a common food, preceded by a word that identifies an alternative or the absence of the characterizing ingredient, e.g., nut milk. Rejected 14-84: R 10-39; D 4-43. 08 01, 2018.

178. HR6147. ANTICIPATED LEGISLATIVE VEHICLE FOR FISCAL 2019 INTERIOR-ENVIRONMENT, FIN SERV, AGRICULTURE, TRANSPORTATION-HUD APPROPRIATIONS/DAIRY GRANTS. Collins, R-Maine, for Baldwin, D-Wis., amendment no. 3524, to the Shelby, R-Ala., substitute amendment no. 3399, that would appropriate $7 million for grants for the provision of technical assistance, process improvement and marketing for dairy products. Adopted 83-15: R 34-15; D 47-0. 08 01, 2018.

179. HR6147. DISTRICT OF COLUMBIA HEALTH INSURANCE/MOTION TO TABLE. Leahy, D-Vt., motion to table (kill) the Collins, R-Maine, for Cruz, R-Texas, amendment no. 3402 that would prohibit the District of Columbia from using funds appropriated by the bill to enforce certain health insurance requirements. Motion agreed to 54-44: R 5-44; D 47-0. 08 01, 2018.

180. HR6147. FISCAL 2019 INTERIOR-ENVIRONMENT, FINANCIAL SERVICES, AGRICULTURE, TRANSPORTATION-HUD APPROPRIATIONS/PASSAGE. Passage of the bill, as amended, that would provide $154.2 billion in discretionary funding for fiscal 2019 to various departments and agencies, including $35.9 billion for the Interior Department, the EPA and related agencies; $23.7 for the Treasury Department, the Office of Personnel Management and other agencies and the District of Columbia; $23.2 for the Agriculture Department and related agencies; and $71.4 for the departments of Transportation and Housing and Urban Development and related agencies. It would require that $5.2 million of EPA funding be used to study algal blooms, would prohibit the Federal Transit Administration from buying buses and rail cars from certain state-owned companies, and would require that up to $6 million of the bill's funds be used for grants for the integration of drone technology into businesses. Passed 92-6: R 43-6; D 47-0. 08 01, 2018.

	175	176	177	178	179	180
ALABAMA						
Shelby	Y	N	N	Y	Y	Y
Jones	Y	Y	N	Y	Y	Y
ALASKA						
Murkowski	Y	N	N	Y	Y	Y
Sullivan	Y	N	Y	Y	N	Y
ARIZONA						
McCain	?	?	?	?	?	?
Flake	?	?	?	?	?	?
ARKANSAS						
Boozman	Y	N	N	Y	N	Y
Cotton	Y	N	N	N	N	Y
CALIFORNIA						
Feinstein	Y	Y	N	Y	Y	Y
Harris	Y	Y	N	Y	Y	Y
COLORADO						
Bennet	Y	Y	N	Y	Y	Y
Gardner	Y	N	N	Y	N	Y
CONNECTICUT						
Blumenthal	Y	Y	N	Y	Y	Y
Murphy	Y	Y	N	Y	Y	Y
DELAWARE						
Carper	Y	Y	N	Y	Y	Y
Coons	Y	Y	N	Y	Y	Y
FLORIDA						
Nelson	Y	Y	N	Y	Y	Y
Rubio	Y	N	Y	N	N	Y
GEORGIA						
Isakson	Y	N	N	Y	N	Y
Perdue	Y	N	N	Y	N	Y
HAWAII						
Schatz	Y	Y	Y	Y	Y	Y
Hirono	Y	Y	N	Y	Y	Y
IDAHO						
Crapo	Y	N	N	Y	N	Y
Risch	Y	N	N	Y	N	Y
ILLINOIS						
Durbin	Y	Y	N	Y	Y	Y
Duckworth	Y	Y	N	Y	Y	Y
INDIANA						
Donnelly	Y	Y	N	Y	Y	Y
Young	Y	N	Y	Y	N	Y
IOWA						
Grassley	Y	N	N	Y	N	Y
Ernst	Y	N	N	Y	N	Y
KANSAS						
Roberts	Y	N	N	Y	N	Y
Moran	Y	N	N	Y	N	Y
KENTUCKY						
McConnell	Y	N	N	Y	N	Y
Paul	N	N	Y	N	N	N
LOUISIANA						
Cassidy	Y	N	Y	N	Y	Y
Kennedy	Y	N	N	N	N	Y
MAINE						
Collins	Y	N	N	Y	N	Y
King	Y	Y	N	Y	Y	Y
MARYLAND						
Cardin	Y	Y	N	Y	Y	Y
Van Hollen	Y	Y	N	Y	Y	Y
MASSACHUSETTS						
Warren	Y	Y	N	Y	Y	Y
Markey	Y	Y	N	Y	Y	Y
MICHIGAN						
Stabenow	Y	Y	N	Y	Y	Y
Peters	Y	Y	N	Y	Y	Y
MINNESOTA						
Klobuchar	Y	Y	N	Y	Y	Y
Smith	Y	Y	N	Y	Y	Y
MISSISSIPPI						
Wicker	Y	N	N	Y	N	Y
Hyde-Smith	Y	N	N	Y	N	Y
MISSOURI						
McCaskill	Y	Y	N	Y	Y	Y
Blunt	Y	N	N	Y	N	Y

	175	176	177	178	179	180
MONTANA						
Tester	Y	Y	N	Y	Y	Y
Daines	Y	N	N	N	N	Y
NEBRASKA						
Fischer	Y	N	N	Y	N	Y
Sasse	Y	N	N	N	N	N
NEVADA						
Heller	Y	N	N	Y	N	Y
Cortez Masto	Y	Y	N	Y	Y	Y
NEW HAMPSHIRE						
Shaheen	Y	Y	N	Y	Y	Y
Hassan	Y	Y	N	Y	Y	Y
NEW JERSEY						
Menendez	Y	Y	Y	Y	Y	Y
Booker	Y	Y	Y	Y	Y	Y
NEW MEXICO						
Udall	Y	Y	Y	Y	Y	Y
Heinrich	Y	Y	Y	Y	Y	Y
NEW YORK						
Schumer	Y	Y	N	Y	Y	Y
Gillibrand	N	Y	N	Y	Y	Y
NORTH CAROLINA						
Burr	Y	?	N	Y	N	Y
Tillis	Y	N	N	N	N	Y
NORTH DAKOTA						
Hoeven	Y	N	N	Y	N	Y
Heitkamp	Y	Y	N	Y	Y	Y
OHIO						
Brown	Y	Y	N	Y	Y	Y
Portman	Y	N	N	Y	N	Y
OKLAHOMA						
Inhofe	Y	N	N	Y	N	Y
Lankford	Y	N	N	N	N	Y
OREGON						
Wyden	Y	Y	N	Y	Y	Y
Merkley	Y	Y	N	Y	Y	Y
PENNSYLVANIA						
Casey	Y	Y	N	Y	Y	Y
Toomey	N	N	Y	N	N	N
RHODE ISLAND						
Reed	Y	Y	N	Y	Y	Y
Whitehouse	Y	Y	N	Y	Y	Y
SOUTH CAROLINA						
Graham	Y	N	N	Y	N	Y
Scott	Y	N	N	N	N	Y
SOUTH DAKOTA						
Thune	Y	N	N	Y	N	Y
Rounds	Y	N	N	Y	N	Y
TENNESSEE						
Alexander	Y	N	N	Y	N	Y
Corker	Y	Y	N	N	N	Y
TEXAS						
Cornyn	Y	N	N	Y	N	Y
Cruz	Y	N	Y	N	N	Y
UTAH						
Hatch	Y	N	N	Y	N	Y
Lee	N	N	Y	N	N	N
VERMONT						
Leahy	Y	Y	N	Y	Y	Y
Sanders	Y	Y	N	Y	Y	Y
VIRGINIA						
Warner	Y	Y	N	Y	Y	Y
Kaine	Y	Y	N	Y	Y	Y
WASHINGTON						
Murray	Y	Y	N	Y	Y	Y
Cantwell	Y	Y	N	Y	Y	Y
WEST VIRGINIA						
Manchin	Y	Y	N	Y	Y	Y
Capito	Y	N	Y	N	N	Y
WISCONSIN						
Johnson	Y	N	N	Y	N	N
Baldwin	Y	Y	N	Y	Y	Y
WYOMING						
Enzi	Y	N	N	Y	N	Y
Barrasso	Y	N	N	Y	N	Y

KEY	**Republicans**	Democrats	*Independents*	
Y	Voted for (yea)	X	Paired against	C	Voted "present" to avoid possible conflict of interest
#	Paired for	-	Announced against		
+	Announced for	P	Voted "present"	?	Did not vote or otherwise make a position known
N	Voted against (nay)				

VOTE NUMBER

181. HR5515. FISCAL 2019 DEFENSE AUTHORIZATION/CONFERENCE REPORT. Adoption of the conference report to accompany the bill that would authorize $708.1 billion for defense-related programs, with $639.1 billion for the Defense Department's base budget, and $69 billion for overseas contingency operations. Specifically, it would authorize $65 million for the development of low-yield nuclear weapons. It would also authorize $18.8 billion for Navy aircraft procurement, $16.5 billion for Air Force aircraft, and $24.1 billion for Navy shipbuilding. It would not reimpose a ban on U.S. exports to the Chinese company ZTE. Adopted (thus cleared for the president) 87-10: R 46-2; D 40-7. 08 01, 2018.

182. QUATTLEBAUM NOMINATION/CLOTURE. Motion to invoke cloture (thus limiting debate) on the nomination of A. Marvin Quattlebaum Jr. of South Carolina to be a U.S. circuit judge for the Fourth Circuit. Motion **AGREED TO 61-28: R 42-0; D 18-27. 08 15, 2018.**

183. QUATTLEBAUM NOMINATION/CONFIRMATION. Confirmation of President Donald Trump's nomination of A. Marvin Quattlebaum Jr. of South Carolina to be a U.S. circuit judge for the Fourth Circuit. Confirmed 62-28: R 43-0; D 18-27. 08 16, 2018.

184. RICHARDSON NOMINATION/CLOTURE. Motion to invoke cloture (thus limiting debate) on the nomination of Julius Ness Richardson of South Carolina to be a U.S. circuit judge for the Fourth Circuit Motion agreed to 80-10: R 43-0; D 36-9. 08 16, 2018.

185. RICHARDSON NOMINATION/CONFIRMATION. Confirmation of President Donald Trump's nomination of Julius Ness Richardson of South Carolina to be a U.S. circuit judge for the Fourth Circuit. Confirmed 81-8: R 42-0; D 38-7. 08 16, 2018.

186. HR6157. ANTICIPATED LEGISLATIVE VEHICLE FOR FISCAL 2019 DEFENSE, LABOR-HHS-EDUCATION APPROPRIATIONS/FIREFIGHTER CANCER REGISTRY. McConnell, R-Ky., for Menendez, D-N.J., amendment no. 3705 to Shelby, R-Ala., substitute amendment no. 3695, that would appropriate $1 million for the establishment of a voluntary registry of firefighters to collect relevant history and occupational information and link it to available cancer registry data collected by existing state cancer registries, and would decrease funding for general management of the Department of Health and Human Services by the same amount. Adopted 85-0: R 41-0; D 42-0. 08 20, 2018.

	181	182	183	184	185	186
ALABAMA						
Shelby	Y	Y	Y	Y	Y	Y
Jones	Y	Y	Y	Y	Y	Y
ALASKA						
Murkowski	Y	Y	Y	Y	Y	Y
Sullivan	Y	Y	Y	Y	Y	Y
ARIZONA						
McCain	?	?	?	?	?	?
Flake	?	?	?	?	?	Y
ARKANSAS						
Boozman	Y	Y	Y	Y	Y	Y
Cotton	Y	Y	Y	Y	Y	Y
CALIFORNIA						
Feinstein	Y	N	N	Y	Y	Y
Harris	N	N	N	Y	Y	Y
COLORADO						
Bennet	Y	Y	Y	Y	Y	Y
Gardner	Y	Y	Y	Y	Y	Y
CONNECTICUT						
Blumenthal	Y	N	N	N	N	Y
Murphy	Y	N	N	Y	Y	Y
DELAWARE						
Carper	Y	Y	Y	Y	Y	Y
Coons	Y	Y	Y	Y	Y	Y
FLORIDA						
Nelson	Y	Y	Y	Y	Y	Y
Rubio	N	+	+	+	+	Y
GEORGIA						
Isakson	Y	Y	Y	Y	Y	Y
Perdue	Y	Y	Y	Y	Y	Y
HAWAII						
Schatz	Y	N	N	N	N	?
Hirono	Y	N	N	N	N	Y
IDAHO						
Crapo	Y	Y	Y	Y	Y	Y
Risch	Y	Y	Y	Y	Y	?
ILLINOIS						
Durbin	N	+	+	+	+	Y
Duckworth	Y	N	N	Y	Y	Y
INDIANA						
Donnelly	Y	Y	Y	Y	Y	Y
Young	Y	Y	Y	Y	Y	Y
IOWA						
Grassley	Y	Y	Y	Y	Y	Y
Ernst	Y	Y	Y	Y	Y	Y
KANSAS						
Roberts	Y	Y	Y	Y	Y	Y
Moran	Y	Y	Y	Y	?	?
KENTUCKY						
McConnell	Y	Y	Y	Y	Y	Y
Paul	?	Y	Y	Y	Y	Y
LOUISIANA						
Cassidy	Y	Y	Y	Y	Y	Y
Kennedy	Y	Y	Y	Y	Y	Y
MAINE						
Collins	Y	Y	Y	Y	Y	Y
King	Y	Y	Y	Y	Y	Y
MARYLAND						
Cardin	Y	N	N	Y	Y	Y
Van Hollen	Y	N	N	N	Y	Y
MASSACHUSETTS						
Warren	N	N	N	N	N	Y
Markey	N	N	N	N	N	Y
MICHIGAN						
Stabenow	Y	N	N	Y	Y	Y
Peters	Y	N	N	Y	Y	Y
MINNESOTA						
Klobuchar	Y	N	N	Y	Y	Y
Smith	Y	N	N	Y	Y	Y
MISSISSIPPI						
Wicker	Y	Y	Y	Y	Y	Y
Hyde-Smith	Y	Y	Y	Y	Y	?
MISSOURI						
McCaskill	Y	Y	Y	Y	Y	Y
Blunt	Y	Y	Y	Y	Y	Y
MONTANA						
Tester	Y	Y	Y	Y	Y	Y
Daines	Y	Y	Y	Y	Y	Y
NEBRASKA						
Fischer	Y	Y	Y	Y	Y	Y
Sasse	Y	Y	Y	Y	Y	Y
NEVADA						
Heller	Y	Y	Y	Y	Y	?
Cortez Masto	Y	N	N	Y	Y	Y
NEW HAMPSHIRE						
Shaheen	Y	Y	Y	Y	Y	Y
Hassan	Y	Y	Y	Y	Y	Y
NEW JERSEY						
Menendez	Y	N	N	Y	Y	Y
Booker	Y	N	N	Y	Y	Y
NEW MEXICO						
Udall	Y	N	N	Y	Y	Y
Heinrich	Y	N	N	Y	Y	Y
NEW YORK						
Schumer	Y	N	N	Y	Y	Y
Gillibrand	N	N	N	N	N	Y
NORTH CAROLINA						
Burr	Y	?	Y	Y	Y	Y
Tillis	Y	?	?	?	?	Y
NORTH DAKOTA						
Hoeven	Y	Y	Y	Y	Y	+
Heitkamp	Y	Y	Y	Y	Y	+
OHIO						
Brown	Y	N	N	Y	Y	Y
Portman	Y	Y	Y	Y	Y	Y
OKLAHOMA						
Inhofe	Y	?	?	?	?	?
Lankford	Y	Y	Y	Y	Y	Y
OREGON						
Wyden	N	N	N	N	Y	Y
Merkley	N	N	N	N	N	?
PENNSYLVANIA						
Casey	Y	N	N	Y	Y	Y
Toomey	Y	?	?	?	?	?
RHODE ISLAND						
Reed	Y	Y	Y	Y	Y	Y
Whitehouse	Y	Y	Y	Y	Y	Y
SOUTH CAROLINA						
Graham	Y	Y	Y	Y	Y	Y
Scott	Y	Y	Y	Y	Y	Y
SOUTH DAKOTA						
Thune	Y	Y	Y	Y	Y	Y
Rounds	Y	Y	Y	Y	Y	Y
TENNESSEE						
Alexander	Y	+	+	+	+	Y
Corker	Y	Y	Y	Y	Y	Y
TEXAS						
Cornyn	Y	Y	Y	Y	Y	Y
Cruz	Y	Y	Y	Y	Y	?
UTAH						
Hatch	Y	Y	Y	Y	Y	Y
Lee	N	?	?	?	?	?
VERMONT						
Leahy	Y	Y	Y	Y	Y	Y
Sanders	N	N	N	N	N	Y
VIRGINIA						
Warner	Y	Y	Y	Y	Y	Y
Kaine	Y	Y	Y	Y	Y	Y
WASHINGTON						
Murray	Y	?	?	?	?	?
Cantwell	Y	N	N	Y	Y	Y
WEST VIRGINIA						
Manchin	Y	Y	Y	Y	Y	Y
Capito	Y	Y	Y	Y	Y	Y
WISCONSIN						
Johnson	Y	Y	Y	Y	Y	Y
Baldwin	Y	Y	Y	Y	Y	Y
WYOMING						
Enzi	Y	Y	Y	Y	Y	Y
Barrasso	Y	Y	Y	Y	Y	Y

KEY	**Republicans**	Democrats	*Independents*
Y	Voted for (yea)	X Paired against	C Voted "present" to avoid possible conflict of interest
#	Paired for	- Announced against	
+	Announced for	P Voted "present"	? Did not vote or otherwise make a position known
N	Voted against (nay)		

VOTE NUMBER

187. HR6157. ANTICIPATED LEGISLATIVE VEHICLE FOR FISCAL 2019 DEFENSE, LABOR-HHS-EDUCATION APPROPRIATIONS/POW/MIA IDENTIFICATION. McConnell, R-Ky., for Fischer, R-Neb., amendment no. 3706 to Shelby, R-Ala., substitute amendment no. 3695, that would increase, then decrease, funding for POW/MIA identification at the Department of Defense by $10 million. Adopted 85-0: R 41-0; D 42-0. 08 20, 2018.

188. HR6157. ANTICIPATED LEGISLATIVE VEHICLE FOR FISCAL 2019 DEFENSE, LABOR-HHS-EDUCATION APPROPRIATIONS/MILITARY ELECTRONIC HEALTH RECORD SYSTEM. McConnell, R-Ky., for Nelson, D-Fla., amendment no. 3773 to Shelby, R-Ala., substitute amendment no. 3695, that would require the Government Accountability Office to report to Congress on the implementation of the Military Health System Genesis electronic health record system. Adopted 95-0: R 49-0; D 44-0. 08 21, 2018.

189. HR6157. ANTICIPATED LEGISLATIVE VEHICLE FOR FISCAL 2019 DEFENSE, LABOR-HHS-EDUCATION APPROPRIATIONS/NATIONAL SUICIDE PREVENTION LIFELINE. McConnell, R-Ky., for Kennedy, R-La., amendment no. 3703 to Shelby, R-Ala., substitute amendment no. 3695, that would increase, then decrease, funding for the National Suicide Prevention Lifeline by $2.8 million. Adopted 95-0: R 49-0; D 44-0. 08 21, 2018.

190. HR6157. ANTICIPATED LEGISLATIVE VEHICLE FOR FISCAL 2019 DEFENSE, LABOR-HHS-EDUCATION APPROPRIATIONS/CLOTURE. Motion to invoke cloture (thus limiting debate) on the Shelby, R-Ala., substitute amendment no. 3695, as amended, that would provide $856.9 billion in discretionary funding for fiscal 2019 to Departments of Defense, Labor, Health and Human Services, and Education. Motion agreed to 90-6: R 45-5; D 44-0. 08 23, 2018.

191. HR6157. ANTICIPATED LEGISLATIVE VEHICLE FOR FISCAL 2019 DEFENSE, LABOR-HHS-EDUCATION APPROPRIATIONS/PLANED PARENTHOOD FUNDING. Paul, R-Ky., amendment no. 3967 to the Shelby, R-Ala. substitute amendment no. no. 3695 to the bill that would prohibit federal funds from going to Planned Parenthood. Rejected 45-48: R 45-2; D 0-44. 08 23, 2018.

192. HR6157. ANTICIPATED LEGISLATIVE VEHICLE FOR FISCAL 2019 DEFENSE, LABOR-HHS-EDUCATION APPROPRIATIONS/MOTION TO WAIVE. Leahy, D-Vt., motion to waive all applicable sections of the Congressional Budget Act with respect to an Enzi, R-Wyo., point of order that the fiscal 2019 Defense and Labor-HHS-Education appropriations package violates Sec. 314(a) of the concurrent budget resolution for fiscal 2018. Motion agreed to 68-24: R 22-24; D 44-0. 08 23, 2018.

	187	188	189	190	191	192
ALABAMA						
Shelby	Y	Y	Y	Y	Y	Y
Jones	Y	Y	Y	Y	N	Y
ALASKA						
Murkowski	Y	Y	Y	Y	N	Y
Sullivan	Y	Y	Y	Y	Y	Y
ARIZONA						
McCain	?	?	?	?	?	?
Flake	Y	Y	Y	N	Y	N
ARKANSAS						
Boozman	Y	Y	Y	Y	Y	N
Cotton	Y	Y	Y	Y	Y	N
CALIFORNIA						
Feinstein	Y	Y	Y	Y	N	Y
Harris	Y	Y	Y	Y	N	Y
COLORADO						
Bennet	?	Y	Y	Y	N	Y
Gardner	Y	Y	Y	Y	Y	Y
CONNECTICUT						
Blumenthal	Y	Y	Y	Y	N	Y
Murphy	Y	Y	Y	Y	N	Y
DELAWARE						
Carper	Y	Y	Y	Y	N	Y
Coons	Y	Y	Y	Y	N	Y
FLORIDA						
Nelson	Y	Y	Y	Y	N	Y
Rubio	Y	Y	Y	Y	Y	Y
GEORGIA						
Isakson	Y	Y	Y	Y	Y	N
Perdue	Y	Y	Y	Y	Y	N
HAWAII						
Schatz	?	?	?	?	?	?
Hirono	Y	Y	Y	+	–	+
IDAHO						
Crapo	Y	Y	Y	Y	Y	N
Risch	?	Y	Y	Y	Y	N
ILLINOIS						
Durbin	Y	Y	Y	Y	N	Y
Duckworth	Y	Y	Y	Y	N	Y
INDIANA						
Donnelly	Y	Y	Y	Y	N	Y
Young	Y	Y	Y	Y	Y	Y
IOWA						
Grassley	Y	Y	Y	N	Y	N
Ernst	Y	Y	Y	Y	Y	N
KANSAS						
Roberts	Y	Y	Y	Y	Y	Y
Moran	?	Y	Y	Y	Y	Y
KENTUCKY						
McConnell	Y	Y	Y	Y	Y	Y
Paul	Y	Y	N	N	Y	N
LOUISIANA						
Cassidy	Y	Y	Y	Y	Y	N
Kennedy	Y	Y	Y	Y	Y	N
MAINE						
Collins	Y	Y	Y	Y	N	Y
King	Y	Y	Y	Y	N	Y
MARYLAND						
Cardin	Y	Y	Y	Y	N	Y
Van Hollen	Y	Y	Y	Y	N	Y
MASSACHUSETTS						
Warren	Y	Y	Y	Y	N	Y
Markey	Y	Y	Y	Y	N	Y
MICHIGAN						
Stabenow	Y	Y	Y	Y	N	Y
Peters	Y	Y	Y	Y	N	Y
MINNESOTA						
Klobuchar	Y	Y	Y	Y	N	Y
Smith	Y	Y	Y	Y	N	Y
MISSISSIPPI						
Wicker	Y	Y	Y	Y	Y	Y
Hyde-Smith	?	Y	Y	Y	Y	Y
MISSOURI						
McCaskill	Y	Y	Y	Y	N	Y
Blunt	Y	Y	Y	Y	Y	Y

	187	188	189	190	191	192
MONTANA						
Tester	Y	Y	Y	Y	N	Y
Daines	Y	Y	Y	Y	Y	Y
NEBRASKA						
Fischer	Y	Y	Y	Y	?	?
Sasse	Y	Y	Y	Y	Y	N
NEVADA						
Heller	?	Y	Y	Y	Y	Y
Cortez Masto	Y	Y	Y	Y	N	Y
NEW HAMPSHIRE						
Shaheen	Y	Y	Y	Y	N	Y
Hassan	Y	Y	Y	Y	N	Y
NEW JERSEY						
Menendez	Y	Y	Y	Y	N	Y
Booker	Y	Y	Y	Y	N	Y
NEW MEXICO						
Udall	Y	?	?	Y	N	Y
Heinrich	Y	Y	Y	Y	N	Y
NEW YORK						
Schumer	Y	Y	Y	Y	N	Y
Gillibrand	Y	Y	Y	Y	N	Y
NORTH CAROLINA						
Burr	Y	Y	Y	Y	Y	Y
Tillis	Y	Y	Y	Y	Y	Y
NORTH DAKOTA						
Hoeven	+	Y	Y	Y	Y	Y
Heitkamp	+	Y	Y	Y	N	Y
OHIO						
Brown	Y	Y	Y	Y	N	Y
Portman	Y	Y	Y	Y	Y	Y
OKLAHOMA						
Inhofe	?	Y	Y	Y	Y	N
Lankford	Y	Y	Y	Y	Y	N
OREGON						
Wyden	Y	Y	Y	Y	N	Y
Merkley	?	Y	Y	Y	N	Y
PENNSYLVANIA						
Casey	Y	Y	Y	Y	N	Y
Toomey	?	?	?	N	Y	N
RHODE ISLAND						
Reed	Y	Y	Y	Y	N	Y
Whitehouse	Y	Y	Y	Y	N	Y
SOUTH CAROLINA						
Graham	Y	Y	Y	Y	Y	Y
Scott	Y	Y	Y	Y	Y	N
SOUTH DAKOTA						
Thune	Y	Y	Y	Y	Y	N
Rounds	Y	Y	Y	Y	Y	N
TENNESSEE						
Alexander	Y	Y	Y	Y	Y	Y
Corker	Y	Y	Y	?	?	?
TEXAS						
Cornyn	Y	Y	Y	Y	Y	?
Cruz	?	Y	Y	Y	+	?
UTAH						
Hatch	Y	Y	Y	Y	Y	N
Lee	?	Y	N	N	Y	N
VERMONT						
Leahy	Y	Y	Y	Y	N	Y
Sanders	Y	Y	Y	N	N	Y
VIRGINIA						
Warner	Y	Y	Y	Y	N	Y
Kaine	Y	Y	Y	Y	N	Y
WASHINGTON						
Murray	?	?	?	?	?	?
Cantwell	Y	Y	Y	Y	N	Y
WEST VIRGINIA						
Manchin	Y	Y	Y	Y	N	Y
Capito	Y	Y	Y	Y	Y	Y
WISCONSIN						
Johnson	Y	Y	Y	Y	Y	N
Baldwin	Y	Y	Y	Y	N	Y
WYOMING						
Enzi	Y	Y	Y	Y	Y	N
Barrasso	Y	Y	Y	Y	Y	N

KEY	**Republicans**	Democrats	*Independents*	
Y	Voted for (yea)	X Paired against	C Voted "present" to avoid possible conflict of interest	
#	Paired for	– Announced against		
+	Announced for	P Voted "present"	? Did not vote or otherwise make a position known	
N	Voted against (nay)			

VOTE NUMBER

193. HR6157. FISCAL 2019 DEFENSE, LABOR-HHS-EDUCATION APPROPRIATIONS/PASSAGE. Passage of the bill that would provide $856.9 billion in discretionary funding for fiscal 2019 to various departments and agencies, including $675 billion for the Defense Department and the $179.3 billion for the Labor, Health and Human Services and Education departments. The bill would provide $90.1 billion in discretionary spending for the Health and Human Services Department, $71.4 billion for the Education Department and $12.1 billion for the Labor Department. The bill would decease funding for military assistance to foreign military units in Afghanistan, militias fighting the Islamic State terrorist group and other areas conflicts. It would eliminate funding for a proposed evolved expendable launch vehicle rocket. It would also appropriate funding for the Firefighter Cancer Registry and prioritize funding for the National Suicide Prevention Lifeline. Passed 85-7: R 40-6; D 44-0. 08 23, 2018.

194. JOHNSON NOMINATION/CLOTURE. Motion to invoke cloture (thus limiting debate) on the nomination of Lynn A. Johnson of Colorado to be assistant secretary for Family Support, Department of Health and Human Services. Motion agreed to 60-28: R 45-0; D 14-27. 08 27, 2018.

195. JOHNSON NOMINATION/CONFIRMATION. Confirmation of President Donald Trump's nomination of Lynn A. Johnson of Colorado to be assistant secretary for Family Support, Department of Health and Human Services. Confirmed 67-28: R 47-0; D 19-27. 08 28, 2018.

196. CLARIDA NOMINATION/CLOTURE. Motion to invoke cloture (thus limiting debate) on the nomination of Richard Clarida of Connecticut to be vice chairman of the Board of Governors of the Federal Reserve System. Motion agreed to 69-26: R 46-1; D 23-23. 08 28, 2018.

197. CLARIDA NOMINATION/CONFIRMATION. Confirmation of President Donald Trump's nomination of Richard Clarida of Connecticut to be vice chairman of the Board of Governors of the Federal Reserve System. Confirmed 69-26: R 46-1; D 23-23. 08 28, 2018.

198. HUNT NOMINATION/CONFIRMATION. Confirmation of President Donald Trump's nomination of Joseph H. Hunt of Maryland to be an assistant attorney general. Confirmed 72-23: R 47-0; D 24-22. 08 28, 2018.

	193	194	195	196	197	198
ALABAMA						
Shelby	Y	Y	Y	Y	Y	Y
Jones	Y	?	Y	Y	Y	Y
ALASKA						
Murkowski	Y	?	?	?	?	?
Sullivan	Y	Y	Y	Y	Y	Y
ARIZONA						
Flake	N	Y	Y	Y	?	?
ARKANSAS						
Boozman	Y	Y	Y	Y	Y	Y
Cotton	Y	Y	Y	Y	Y	Y
CALIFORNIA						
Feinstein	Y	N	N	N	N	N
Harris	Y	N	N	N	N	N
COLORADO						
Bennet	Y	Y	Y	Y	Y	Y
Gardner	Y	Y	Y	Y	Y	Y
CONNECTICUT						
Blumenthal	Y	N	N	Y	Y	N
Murphy	Y	Y	Y	Y	Y	Y
DELAWARE						
Carper	Y	?	N	Y	Y	N
Coons	Y	N	N	Y	Y	Y
FLORIDA						
Nelson	Y	Y	Y	Y	Y	Y
Rubio	Y	Y	Y	Y	Y	Y
GEORGIA						
Isakson	Y	Y	Y	Y	Y	Y
Perdue	Y	Y	Y	Y	Y	Y
HAWAII						
Schatz	?	N	N	N	N	N
Hirono	+	+	Y	N	N	Y
IDAHO						
Crapo	N	?	Y	Y	Y	Y
Risch	N	Y	Y	Y	Y	Y
ILLINOIS						
Durbin	Y	N	N	N	N	N
Duckworth	Y	N	N	N	N	N
INDIANA						
Donnelly	Y	Y	Y	Y	Y	Y
Young	Y	Y	Y	Y	Y	Y
IOWA						
Grassley	Y	Y	Y	Y	Y	Y
Ernst	Y	Y	Y	Y	Y	Y
KANSAS						
Roberts	Y	Y	Y	Y	Y	Y
Moran	Y	Y	Y	Y	Y	Y
KENTUCKY						
McConnell	Y	Y	Y	Y	Y	Y
Paul	N	Y	N	N	Y	Y
LOUISIANA						
Cassidy	Y	?	Y	Y	Y	Y
Kennedy	Y	Y	Y	Y	Y	Y
MAINE						
Collins	Y	Y	Y	Y	Y	Y
King	Y	Y	Y	N	N	Y
MARYLAND						
Cardin	Y	N	N	Y	Y	Y
Van Hollen	Y	N	N	Y	Y	N
MASSACHUSETTS						
Warren	Y	N	N	N	N	N
Markey	Y	N	N	N	N	N
MICHIGAN						
Stabenow	Y	N	N	N	N	N
Peters	Y	N	N	Y	Y	Y
MINNESOTA						
Klobuchar	Y	N	N	Y	Y	Y
Smith	Y	N	N	Y	Y	Y
MISSISSIPPI						
Wicker	Y	Y	Y	Y	Y	Y
Hyde-Smith	Y	Y	Y	Y	Y	Y
MISSOURI						
McCaskill	Y	Y	Y	Y	Y	Y
Blunt	Y	Y	Y	Y	Y	Y
MONTANA						
Tester	Y	Y	Y	Y	Y	Y
Daines	Y	Y	Y	Y	Y	Y
NEBRASKA						
Fischer	?	Y	Y	Y	Y	Y
Sasse	Y	Y	Y	Y	Y	Y
NEVADA						
Heller	Y	Y	Y	Y	Y	Y
Cortez Masto	Y	N	N	N	N	N
NEW HAMPSHIRE						
Shaheen	Y	Y	Y	Y	Y	Y
Hassan	Y	Y	Y	Y	Y	Y
NEW JERSEY						
Menendez	Y	N	N	N	N	N
Booker	Y	N	N	N	N	N
NEW MEXICO						
Udall	Y	N	N	N	N	N
Heinrich	Y	N	N	N	N	N
NEW YORK						
Schumer	Y	N	Y	N	N	N
Gillibrand	Y	N	N	N	N	N
NORTH CAROLINA						
Burr	Y	Y	Y	Y	Y	Y
Tillis	Y	Y	Y	Y	Y	Y
NORTH DAKOTA						
Hoeven	Y	Y	Y	Y	Y	Y
Heitkamp	Y	Y	Y	Y	Y	Y
OHIO						
Brown	Y	N	N	N	N	N
Portman	Y	Y	Y	Y	Y	Y
OKLAHOMA						
Inhofe	Y	Y	Y	Y	Y	Y
Lankford	Y	Y	Y	Y	Y	Y
OREGON						
Wyden	Y	Y	N	N	N	N
Merkley	Y	N	N	N	N	N
PENNSYLVANIA						
Casey	Y	Y	Y	Y	N	Y
Toomey	N	Y	Y	Y	Y	Y
RHODE ISLAND						
Reed	Y	N	N	Y	Y	N
Whitehouse	Y	N	N	N	N	Y
SOUTH CAROLINA						
Graham	Y	?	?	?	Y	Y
Scott	Y	Y	Y	Y	Y	Y
SOUTH DAKOTA						
Thune	Y	Y	Y	Y	Y	Y
Rounds	Y	Y	Y	Y	Y	Y
TENNESSEE						
Alexander	Y	Y	Y	Y	Y	Y
Corker	?	Y	Y	Y	Y	Y
TEXAS						
Cornyn	?	Y	Y	Y	Y	Y
Cruz	+	?	?	?	?	?
UTAH						
Hatch	Y	Y	Y	Y	Y	Y
Lee	N	Y	Y	Y	Y	Y
VERMONT						
Leahy	Y	?	?	?	?	?
Sanders	N	N	N	N	N	N
VIRGINIA						
Warner	Y	N	N	Y	Y	Y
Kaine	Y	Y	Y	Y	Y	Y
WASHINGTON						
Murray	?	?	Y	N	N	Y
Cantwell	Y	Y	N	N	N	Y
WEST VIRGINIA						
Manchin	Y	?	Y	Y	Y	Y
Capito	Y	Y	Y	Y	Y	Y
WISCONSIN						
Johnson	Y	Y	Y	Y	Y	Y
Baldwin	Y	Y	N	N	N	Y
WYOMING						
Enzi	Y	Y	Y	Y	Y	Y
Barrasso	Y	Y	Y	Y	Y	Y

KEY	**Republicans**	Democrats	*Independents*

Y Voted for (yea)	X Paired against	C Voted "present" to avoid possible conflict of interest
# Paired for	– Announced against	
+ Announced for	P Voted "present"	? Did not vote or otherwise make a position known
N Voted against (nay)		

VOTE NUMBER

199. PATELUNAS NOMINATION/CONFIRMATION. Confirmation of President Donald Trump's nomination of Isabel Marie Keenan Patelunas of Pennsylvania to be assistant secretary for Intelligence and Analysis, Department of the Treasury. Confirmed 75-20: R 47-0; D 27-19. 08 28, 2018.

200. GOODWIN NOMINATION/CONFIRMATION. Confirmation of President Donald Trump's nomination of Charles Barnes Goodwin of Oklahoma to be U.S. district judge for the Western District of Oklahoma. Confirmed 52-42: R 46-0; D 6-40. 08 28, 2018.

201. ROISMAN NOMINATION/CLOTURE. Motion to invoke cloture (thus limiting debate) on the nomination of Elad Roisman of Maine to be a member of the Securities and Exchange Commission. Motion agreed to 83-14: R 50-0; D 32-14. Oct. 4, 2018.

202. ROISMAN NOMINATION/CONFIRMATION. Confirmation of President Donald Trump's nomination of Elad Roisman of Maine to be a member of the Securities and Exchange Commission. Confirmed 85-14: R 50-0; D 34-13. Oct. 5, 2018.

203. LANZA NOMINATION/CONFRIMATION. Confirmation of President Donald Trump's nomination of Dominic W. Lanza of Arizona to be U.S. district judge for the District of Arizona. Confirmed 60-35: R 48-0; D 11-34. Oct. 6, 2018.

204. WILLIAMS NOMINATION/CONFIRMATION. Confirmation of President Donald Trump's nomination of Charles J. Williams of Iowa to be a U.S. district judge for the Northern District of Iowa. Confirmed 79-12: R 44-0; D 34-11. Oct. 6, 2018.

	199	200	201	202	203	204
ALABAMA						
Shelby	Y	Y	Y	Y	Y	Y
Jones	Y	N	Y	Y	Y	Y
ALASKA						
Murkowski	?	?	Y	Y	Y	Y
Sullivan	Y	Y	Y	Y	Y	Y
ARIZONA						
Flake	?	?	Y	Y	Y	Y
ARKANSAS						
Boozman	Y	Y	Y	Y	Y	Y
Cotton	Y	Y	Y	Y	Y	Y
CALIFORNIA						
Feinstein	Y	N	N	N	N	Y
Harris	Y	N	N	N	?	N
COLORADO						
Bennet	N	N	Y	Y	N	Y
Gardner	Y	Y	Y	Y	Y	Y
CONNECTICUT						
Blumenthal	N	N	N	N	N	Y
Murphy	N	N	Y	N	N	Y
DELAWARE						
Carper	N	N	Y	Y	N	Y
Coons	N	N	Y	Y	Y	Y
FLORIDA						
Nelson	Y	N	Y	Y	–	+
Rubio	Y	Y	Y	Y	Y	Y
GEORGIA						
Isakson	Y	Y	Y	Y	Y	Y
Perdue	Y	Y	Y	Y	?	?
HAWAII						
Schatz	N	N	N	Y	N	N
Hirono	N	N	Y	N	Y	N
IDAHO						
Crapo	Y	Y	Y	Y	Y	Y
Risch	Y	Y	Y	Y	Y	Y
ILLINOIS						
Durbin	N	N	Y	N	Y	Y
Duckworth	Y	N	Y	Y	Y	Y
INDIANA						
Donnelly	Y	Y	Y	Y	Y	Y
Young	Y	Y	Y	Y	Y	Y
IOWA						
Grassley	Y	Y	Y	Y	Y	Y
Ernst	Y	Y	Y	Y	Y	Y
KANSAS						
Roberts	Y	Y	Y	Y	Y	Y
Moran	Y	Y	Y	Y	?	?
KENTUCKY						
McConnell	Y	Y	Y	Y	Y	Y
Paul	Y	?	Y	Y	Y	Y
LOUISIANA						
Cassidy	Y	Y	Y	Y	Y	Y
Kennedy	Y	Y	Y	Y	Y	Y
MAINE						
Collins	Y	Y	Y	Y	Y	Y
King	Y	N	Y	Y	Y	Y
MARYLAND						
Cardin	N	N	Y	N	Y	Y
Van Hollen	Y	N	Y	Y	N	Y
MASSACHUSETTS						
Warren	N	N	N	N	N	N
Markey	N	N	N	N	N	N
MICHIGAN						
Stabenow	Y	N	Y	Y	N	N
Peters	Y	N	Y	N	N	N
MINNESOTA						
Klobuchar	Y	Y	Y	Y	N	Y
Smith	Y	Y	Y	Y	N	Y
MISSISSIPPI						
Wicker	Y	Y	Y	Y	Y	Y
Hyde-Smith	Y	Y	Y	Y	Y	Y
MISSOURI						
McCaskill	Y	Y	Y	Y	Y	Y
Blunt	Y	Y	Y	Y	Y	Y

	199	200	201	202	203	204
MONTANA						
Tester	Y	Y	Y	Y	Y	Y
Daines	Y	Y	Y	Y	Y	?
NEBRASKA						
Fischer	Y	Y	Y	Y	Y	Y
Sasse	Y	Y	Y	Y	Y	Y
NEVADA						
Heller	Y	Y	Y	Y	Y	Y
Cortez Masto	Y	N	Y	N	N	Y
NEW HAMPSHIRE						
Shaheen	Y	N	Y	N	N	?
Hassan	Y	Y	Y	N	N	Y
NEW JERSEY						
Menendez	N	N	N	N	N	N
Booker	N	N	N	N	N	N
NEW MEXICO						
Udall	N	N	Y	N	N	Y
Heinrich	Y	N	Y	N	N	Y
NEW YORK						
Schumer	Y	N	N	N	N	Y
Gillibrand	N	N	N	N	N	N
NORTH CAROLINA						
Burr	Y	Y	Y	Y	?	?
Tillis	Y	Y	Y	Y	Y	Y
NORTH DAKOTA						
Hoeven	Y	Y	Y	Y	Y	Y
Heitkamp	Y	N	Y	Y	Y	Y
OHIO						
Brown	N	N	?	Y	N	Y
Portman	Y	Y	Y	Y	Y	Y
OKLAHOMA						
Inhofe	Y	Y	Y	Y	Y	?
Lankford	Y	Y	Y	Y	Y	Y
OREGON						
Wyden	N	N	Y	Y	N	N
Merkley	N	N	N	N	N	N
PENNSYLVANIA						
Casey	Y	N	Y	Y	N	Y
Toomey	Y	Y	Y	Y	Y	Y
RHODE ISLAND						
Reed	Y	N	Y	Y	Y	Y
Whitehouse	Y	N	N	N	N	Y
SOUTH CAROLINA						
Graham	Y	Y	Y	Y	Y	Y
Scott	Y	Y	Y	Y	Y	Y
SOUTH DAKOTA						
Thune	Y	Y	Y	Y	Y	Y
Rounds	Y	Y	Y	Y	Y	Y
TENNESSEE						
Alexander	Y	Y	Y	Y	Y	Y
Corker	Y	Y	Y	Y	Y	?
TEXAS						
Cornyn	Y	Y	Y	Y	Y	Y
Cruz	?	?	Y	Y	Y	?
UTAH						
Hatch	Y	Y	Y	Y	Y	Y
Lee	Y	Y	Y	Y	Y	Y
VERMONT						
Leahy	?	?	Y	Y	Y	Y
Sanders	N	N	?	N	N	N
VIRGINIA						
Warner	Y	N	Y	Y	N	Y
Kaine	Y	N	Y	Y	N	Y
WASHINGTON						
Murray	Y	N	Y	Y	N	Y
Cantwell	N	N	Y	Y	N	Y
WEST VIRGINIA						
Manchin	Y	N	Y	Y	Y	Y
Capito	Y	Y	Y	Y	Y	Y
WISCONSIN						
Johnson	Y	Y	Y	Y	Y	Y
Baldwin	Y	N	N	N	N	Y
WYOMING						
Enzi	Y	Y	Y	Y	Y	Y
Barrasso	Y	Y	Y	Y	Y	Y

KEY   Republicans   Democrats   *Independents*

Y Voted for (yea)	X Paired against
# Paired for	– Announced against
+ Announced for	P Voted "present"
N Voted against (nay)	

C Voted "present" to avoid possible conflict of interest

? Did not vote or otherwise make a position known

VOTE NUMBER

205. RETTIG NOMINATION/CLOTURE. Motion to invoke cloture (thus limiting debate) on the nomination of Charles P. Rettig of California to be commissioner of the Internal Revenue Service. Motion agreed to 63-34: R 49-0; D 14-32. Oct. 12, 2018.

206. RETTIG NOMINATION/CONFIRMATION. Confirmation of President Donald Trump's nomination of Charles P. Rettig of California to be commissioner of the Internal Revenue Service. Confirmed 64-33: R 49-0; D 15-31. Oct. 12, 2018.

207. HR5895. FISCAL 2019 ENERGY-WATER, LEGISLATIVE BRANCH, MILITARY CONSTRUCTION-VA APPROPRIATIONS/CONFERENCE REPORT. Adoption of the conference report to accompany the fiscal 2019 three-bill spending package: Energy-Water, Legislative Branch, Military Construction-VA that would provide $147.5 billion in discretionary funding for fiscal 2019 to various departments, agencies and legislative operations, including $35.7 billion for the Energy Department, $7 billion for the Army Corps of Engineers, and $1.6 billion for the Interior Department's Bureau of Reclamation. It would provide $98.1 billion for military construction activities and for VA programs and activities, and $4.8 billion for operations of the House, Senate, joint House-Senate items and legislative branch entities such as the Library of Congress, the Capitol Police, and the Government Accountability Office. Adopted 92-5: R 47-2; D 43-3. Oct. 12, 2018.

208. S2554. DRUG PRICE DISCLOSURE/FEDERALLY-REGULATED PLAN LIMITATION. Alexander, R-Tenn., for Lee, R-Utah, amendment no. 4011 that would limit the application of the bill's prohibition of pharmacy drug price disclosure restrictions to federally-regulated, self-insured plans. Rejected 11-89: R 11-40; D 0-47. Oct. 17, 2018.

209. S2554. DRUG PRICE DISCLOSURE/PASSAGE. Passage of the bill that would prohibit insurers from restricting pharmacies from informing insurance enrollees about any difference in the price of a drug when the enrollee uses insurance compared to paying for the drug without using insurance. Passed 98-2: R 49-2; D 47-0. Oct. 17, 2018.

210. HR6. OPIOID ABUSE PREVENTION AND HEALTH PROGRAMS/ PASSAGE. Passage of the bill that would modify Medicare and Medicaid and a variety of other health programs in relation to opioid abuse. It would authorize $500 million annually, for fiscal 2019 through fiscal 2021, for opioid-response grants to states and tribes. It would authorize 10 million annually, for fiscal 2019 through fiscal 2023, for the establishment and operation of opioid recovery centers. It would also authorize the Office of National Drug Control Policy. It would require a study on Medicaid drug review and utilization requirements. The Senate amendment to the bill would remove provisions in the House bill that would allow for Medicaid reimbursements for residential substance abuse facilities and would also not require offsets. Passed 99-1: R 50-1; D 47-0. Oct. 17, 2018.

	205	206	207	208	209	210
ALABAMA						
Shelby	Y	Y	Y	N	Y	Y
Jones	Y	Y	Y	N	Y	Y
ALASKA						
Murkowski	Y	Y	Y	N	Y	Y
Sullivan	Y	Y	Y	N	Y	Y
ARIZONA						
Flake	Y	Y	N	Y	Y	Y
Kyl	Y	Y	Y	N	Y	Y
ARKANSAS						
Boozman	Y	Y	Y	N	Y	Y
Cotton	Y	Y	Y	N	Y	Y
CALIFORNIA						
Feinstein	N	N	Y	N	Y	Y
Harris	N	N	Y	N	Y	Y
COLORADO						
Bennet	Y	Y	Y	N	Y	Y
Gardner	Y	Y	Y	N	Y	Y
CONNECTICUT						
Blumenthal	N	N	Y	N	Y	Y
Murphy	Y	Y	Y	N	Y	Y
DELAWARE						
Carper	N	N	Y	N	Y	Y
Coons	N	N	Y	N	Y	Y
FLORIDA						
Nelson	–	–	+	N	Y	Y
Rubio	Y	Y	Y	N	Y	Y
GEORGIA						
Isakson	?	?	+	N	Y	Y
Perdue	Y	Y	Y	N	Y	Y
HAWAII						
Schatz	Y	Y	Y	N	Y	Y
Hirono	N	N	Y	N	Y	Y
IDAHO						
Crapo	Y	Y	Y	Y	Y	Y
Risch	Y	Y	Y	Y	Y	Y
ILLINOIS						
Durbin	N	N	Y	N	Y	Y
Duckworth	N	N	Y	N	Y	Y
INDIANA						
Donnelly	Y	Y	Y	N	Y	Y
Young	Y	Y	Y	N	Y	Y
IOWA						
Grassley	Y	Y	Y	N	Y	Y
Ernst	Y	Y	Y	N	Y	Y
KANSAS						
Roberts	Y	Y	Y	N	Y	Y
Moran	Y	Y	Y	N	Y	Y
KENTUCKY						
McConnell	Y	Y	Y	N	Y	Y
Paul	Y	Y	N	N	N	N
LOUISIANA						
Cassidy	Y	Y	Y	N	Y	Y
Kennedy	Y	Y	Y	N	Y	Y
MAINE						
Collins	Y	Y	Y	N	Y	Y
King	N	N	Y	N	Y	Y
MARYLAND						
Cardin	N	Y	Y	N	Y	Y
Van Hollen	N	N	Y	N	Y	Y
MASSACHUSETTS						
Warren	N	N	N	N	Y	Y
Markey	N	N	N	N	Y	Y
MICHIGAN						
Stabenow	N	N	Y	N	Y	Y
Peters	N	N	Y	N	Y	Y
MINNESOTA						
Klobuchar	N	N	Y	N	Y	Y
Smith	N	N	Y	N	Y	Y
MISSISSIPPI						
Wicker	Y	Y	Y	N	Y	Y
Hyde-Smith	Y	Y	Y	Y	Y	Y
MISSOURI						
McCaskill	Y	Y	Y	N	Y	Y
Blunt	Y	Y	Y	N	Y	Y
MONTANA						
Tester	N	N	Y	N	Y	Y
Daines	Y	Y	Y	Y	Y	Y
NEBRASKA						
Fischer	Y	Y	Y	N	Y	Y
Sasse	Y	Y	Y	Y	Y	Y
NEVADA						
Heller	Y	Y	Y	N	Y	Y
Cortez Masto	Y	Y	Y	N	Y	Y
NEW HAMPSHIRE						
Shaheen	Y	Y	Y	N	Y	Y
Hassan	Y	Y	Y	N	Y	Y
NEW JERSEY						
Menendez	N	N	Y	N	Y	Y
Booker	N	N	Y	N	Y	Y
NEW MEXICO						
Udall	N	N	Y	N	Y	Y
Heinrich	N	N	Y	N	Y	Y
NEW YORK						
Schumer	N	N	Y	N	Y	Y
Gillibrand	N	N	N	N	Y	Y
NORTH CAROLINA						
Burr	Y	?	?	N	Y	Y
Tillis	Y	Y	Y	N	Y	Y
NORTH DAKOTA						
Hoeven	Y	Y	Y	N	Y	Y
Heitkamp	Y	Y	Y	N	Y	Y
OHIO						
Brown	Y	Y	Y	N	Y	Y
Portman	Y	Y	Y	N	Y	Y
OKLAHOMA						
Inhofe	Y	Y	Y	N	Y	Y
Lankford	Y	Y	Y	N	Y	Y
OREGON						
Wyden	N	N	Y	N	Y	Y
Merkley	N	N	Y	N	Y	Y
PENNSYLVANIA						
Casey	Y	Y	Y	N	Y	Y
Toomey	+	Y	Y	Y	Y	Y
RHODE ISLAND						
Reed	N	N	Y	N	Y	Y
Whitehouse	N	N	Y	N	Y	Y
SOUTH CAROLINA						
Graham	Y	Y	Y	N	Y	Y
Scott	Y	Y	Y	Y	Y	Y
SOUTH DAKOTA						
Thune	Y	Y	Y	N	Y	Y
Rounds	Y	Y	Y	N	Y	Y
TENNESSEE						
Alexander	Y	Y	Y	N	Y	Y
Corker	Y	Y	Y	N	Y	Y
TEXAS						
Cornyn	Y	Y	Y	N	Y	Y
Cruz	Y	Y	Y	N	Y	Y
UTAH						
Hatch	Y	Y	Y	Y	Y	Y
Lee	Y	Y	Y	Y	N	N
VERMONT						
Leahy	Y	Y	Y	N	Y	Y
Sanders	N	N	Y	N	Y	Y
VIRGINIA						
Warner	N	N	Y	N	Y	Y
Kaine	N	N	Y	N	Y	Y
WASHINGTON						
Murray	N	N	Y	N	Y	Y
Cantwell	N	N	Y	N	Y	Y
WEST VIRGINIA						
Manchin	Y	Y	Y	N	Y	Y
Capito	Y	Y	Y	N	Y	Y
WISCONSIN						
Johnson	Y	Y	Y	Y	Y	Y
Baldwin	N	N	Y	N	Y	Y
WYOMING						
Enzi	Y	Y	Y	N	Y	Y
Barrasso	Y	Y	Y	N	Y	Y

KEY	Republicans	Democrats	*Independents*

Y Voted for (yea)	**X** Paired against	**C** Voted "present" to avoid possible conflict of interest
# Paired for	**–** Announced against	
+ Announced for	**P** Voted "present"	**?** Did not vote or otherwise make a position known
N Voted against (nay)		

III SENATE VOTES

VOTE NUMBER

211. HR6157. FISCAL 2019 DEFENSE, LABOR-HHS-EDUCATION APPROPRIATIONS/CLOTURE. Motion to invoke cloture (thus limiting debate) on the conference report to accompany the bill that would provide $855.1 billion in discretionary funding for fiscal 2019 to the Departments of Defense, Labor, Health and Human Services, and Education. Motion agreed to 92-8: R 44-7; D 47-0. Oct. 18, 2018.

212. HR6157. FISCAL 2019 DEFENSE, LABOR-HHS-EDUCATION APPROPRIATIONS/CONFERENCE REPORT. Adoption of the conference report on the bill that would provide $855.1 billion in discretionary funding for fiscal 2019 to various departments and agencies, including $674.4 billion for the Defense Department and $178.1 billion for the Labor, Health and Human Services and Education departments. The Defense Department total would include $606.5 billion in base Defense Department funding subject to spending caps, and would include $67.9 billion in overseas contingency operations funding. The bill would provide $90.3 billion in discretionary spending for the Health and Human Services Department, $71.4 billion for the Education Department and $12.1 billion for the Labor Department. The measure would also provide funding for federal government operations until Dec. 7, 2018, at an annualized rate of approximately $1.3 trillion. Adopted 93-7: R 45-6; D 47-0. Oct. 18, 2018.

213. WOLCOTT NOMINATION/CONFIRMATION. Confirmation of President Donald Trump's nomination of Jackie Wolcott of Virginia to be a representative of the United States of America to the International Atomic Energy Agency; and to be a representative of the United States of America to the Vienna Office of the United Nations, en bloc. Confirmed 75-19: R 45-1; D 29-17. Oct. 24, 2018.

214. FELDMAN NOMINATION/CLOTURE. Motion to invoke cloture (thus limiting debate) on the nomination of Peter A. Feldman of the District of Columbia to be a commissioner of the Consumer Product Safety Commission. Motion agreed to 76-18: R 46-0; D 29-17. Oct. 24, 2018.

215. FELDMAN NOMINATION/CONFRIMATION. Confirmation of President Donald Trump's nomination of Peter A. Feldman of the District of Columbia to be a commissioner of the Consumer Product Safety Commission. Confirmed 80-19: R 50-0; D 29-18. Oct. 25, 2018.

216. FELDMAN NOMINATION/CLOTURE. Motion to invoke cloture (thus limiting debate) on the nomination of Peter A. Feldman of the District of Columbia to be a commissioner of the Consumer Product Safety Commission for a seven-year term that would begin in 2019. Motion agreed to 50-49: R 50-0; D 0-47. Oct. 25, 2018.

	211	212	213	214	215	216
ALABAMA						
Shelby	Y	Y	Y	Y	Y	Y
Jones	Y	Y	Y	Y	Y	N
ALASKA						
Murkowski	Y	Y	Y	Y	Y	Y
Sullivan	Y	Y	Y	Y	Y	Y
ARIZONA						
Flake	Y	N	?	?	?	?
Kyl	Y	Y	Y	Y	Y	Y
ARKANSAS						
Boozman	Y	Y	Y	Y	Y	Y
Cotton	Y	Y	Y	Y	Y	Y
CALIFORNIA						
Feinstein	Y	Y	N	Y	Y	N
Harris	Y	Y	N	N	N	N
COLORADO						
Bennet	Y	Y	Y	Y	Y	Y
Gardner	Y	Y	Y	Y	Y	Y
CONNECTICUT						
Blumenthal	Y	Y	Y	N	N	N
Murphy	Y	Y	Y	Y	Y	N
DELAWARE						
Carper	Y	Y	Y	Y	Y	N
Coons	Y	Y	Y	Y	Y	N
FLORIDA						
Nelson	Y	Y	Y	Y	Y	N
Rubio	Y	Y	Y	Y	Y	Y
GEORGIA						
Isakson	Y	Y	Y	Y	Y	Y
Perdue	N	N	Y	Y	Y	Y
HAWAII						
Schatz	Y	Y	N	N	N	N
Hirono	Y	Y	Y	N	N	N
IDAHO						
Crapo	Y	Y	Y	Y	Y	Y
Risch	Y	Y	Y	Y	Y	Y
ILLINOIS						
Durbin	Y	Y	N	N	N	N
Duckworth	Y	Y	Y	Y	Y	N
INDIANA						
Donnelly	Y	Y	Y	Y	Y	N
Young	Y	Y	Y	Y	Y	Y
IOWA						
Grassley	Y	Y	Y	Y	Y	Y
Ernst	N	Y	Y	Y	Y	Y
KANSAS						
Roberts	Y	Y	Y	Y	Y	Y
Moran	Y	Y	Y	Y	Y	Y
KENTUCKY						
McConnell	Y	Y	Y	Y	Y	Y
Paul	N	N	-	?	Y	Y
LOUISIANA						
Cassidy	Y	Y	Y	Y	Y	Y
Kennedy	Y	Y	Y	Y	Y	Y
MAINE						
Collins	Y	Y	Y	Y	Y	Y
King	Y	Y	Y	Y	Y	N
MARYLAND						
Cardin	Y	Y	N	N	Y	N
Van Hollen	Y	Y	N	Y	Y	N
MASSACHUSETTS						
Warren	Y	Y	N	N	N	N
Markey	Y	Y	N	Y	N	N
MICHIGAN						
Stabenow	Y	Y	N	N	N	N
Peters	Y	Y	Y	Y	N	N
MINNESOTA						
Klobuchar	Y	Y	Y	Y	Y	N
Smith	Y	Y	Y	Y	Y	N
MISSISSIPPI						
Wicker	Y	Y	Y	Y	Y	Y
Hyde-Smith	Y	Y	Y	Y	Y	Y
MISSOURI						
McCaskill	Y	Y	Y	Y	Y	N
Blunt	Y	Y	Y	Y	Y	Y
MONTANA						
Tester	Y	Y	Y	Y	Y	N
Daines	N	Y	Y	Y	Y	Y
NEBRASKA						
Fischer	Y	Y	Y	Y	Y	Y
Sasse	Y	N	?	?	Y	Y
NEVADA						
Heller	Y	Y	N	Y	Y	Y
Cortez Masto	Y	Y	Y	Y	Y	N
NEW HAMPSHIRE						
Shaheen	Y	Y	Y	Y	Y	N
Hassan	Y	Y	Y	Y	Y	N
NEW JERSEY						
Menendez	Y	Y	Y	N	N	N
Booker	Y	Y	N	N	N	N
NEW MEXICO						
Udall	Y	Y	N	N	Y	N
Heinrich	Y	Y	N	N	N	N
NEW YORK						
Schumer	Y	Y	Y	N	N	N
Gillibrand	Y	Y	N	N	N	N
NORTH CAROLINA						
Burr	Y	Y	Y	Y	Y	Y
Tillis	Y	Y	Y	Y	Y	Y
NORTH DAKOTA						
Hoeven	Y	Y	Y	Y	Y	Y
Heitkamp	Y	Y	Y	Y	Y	N
OHIO						
Brown	Y	Y	Y	N	N	N
Portman	Y	Y	Y	Y	Y	Y
OKLAHOMA						
Inhofe	Y	Y	Y	Y	Y	Y
Lankford	N	Y	Y	Y	Y	Y
OREGON						
Wyden	Y	Y	N	N	N	N
Merkley	Y	Y	?	?	N	N
PENNSYLVANIA						
Casey	Y	Y	Y	Y	Y	N
Toomey	N	N	Y	Y	Y	Y
RHODE ISLAND						
Reed	Y	Y	N	N	N	N
Whitehouse	Y	Y	N	N	N	N
SOUTH CAROLINA						
Graham	Y	Y	Y	Y	Y	Y
Scott	Y	Y	Y	Y	Y	Y
SOUTH DAKOTA						
Thune	Y	Y	Y	Y	Y	Y
Rounds	Y	Y	Y	Y	Y	Y
TENNESSEE						
Alexander	Y	Y	Y	Y	Y	Y
Corker	Y	Y	?	?	Y	Y
TEXAS						
Cornyn	Y	Y	Y	Y	Y	Y
Cruz	Y	Y	Y	Y	Y	Y
UTAH						
Hatch	Y	Y	Y	Y	Y	Y
Lee	N	N	Y	Y	Y	Y
VERMONT						
Leahy	Y	Y	N	Y	Y	N
Sanders	N	N	N	N	N	N
VIRGINIA						
Warner	Y	Y	Y	Y	Y	N
Kaine	Y	Y	Y	Y	Y	N
WASHINGTON						
Murray	Y	Y	Y	Y	Y	N
Cantwell	Y	Y	Y	Y	Y	N
WEST VIRGINIA						
Manchin	Y	Y	Y	Y	Y	N
Capito	Y	Y	Y	Y	Y	Y
WISCONSIN						
Johnson	Y	Y	?	?	Y	Y
Baldwin	Y	Y	Y	Y	Y	N
WYOMING						
Enzi	Y	Y	Y	Y	Y	Y
Barrasso	Y	Y	Y	Y	Y	Y

KEY	**Republicans**	Democrats	*Independents*	
Y	Voted for (yea)	X Paired against	C Voted "present" to avoid possible conflict of interest	
#	Paired for	– Announced against		
+	Announced for	P Voted "present"	? Did not vote or otherwise make a position known	
N	Voted against (nay)			

VOTE NUMBER

217. FELDMAN NOMINATION/CONFIRMATION. Confirmation of President Donald Trump's nomination of Peter A. Feldman of the District of Columbia to be a commissioner of the Consumer Product Safety Commission for a seven-year term that would begin in 2019. Confirmed 51-49: R 51-0; D 0-47. Oct. 26, 2018.

218. PORTER NOMINATION/CONFIRMATION. Confirmation of President Donald Trump's nomination of Lisa Porter of Virginia to be a deputy under secretary of Defense. Confirmed 98-1: R 49-1; D 47-0. Oct. 27, 2018.

219. HR302. FAA REAUTHORIZATION AND SUPPLEMENTAL DISASTER APPROPRIATIONS/CLOTURE. Motion to invoke cloture on the McConnell, R-Ky., motion to concur in the House amendment to the Senate amendment to the bill that would reauthorize federal aviation programs through fiscal 2023, and would appropriate $1.7 billion in emergency supplemental disaster funding. Motion agreed to 90-7: R 45-4; D 43-3. 10 01, 2018.

220. HR302. FAA REAUTHORIZATION AND SUPPLEMENTAL DISASTER APPROPRIATIONS/MOTION TO CONCUR. McConnell, R-Ky., motion to concur in the House amendment to the Senate amendment to the bill that would reauthorize federal aviation programs through fiscal 2023. The measure would authorize $10.2 billion in fiscal 2018, which would gradually increase to $11.6 billion in fiscal 2023, for Federal Aviation Administration operations; $3.4 billion annually for the Aviation Trust Fund for the Airport Improvement Program; $3.3 billion in fiscal 2018, which would gradually increase to $3.7 billion in fiscal 2023, for facilities and equipment; and $189 million in fiscal 2018, which would gradually increase to $214 million in fiscal 2023, for research and development. It would also ban e-cigarettes and talking on a cell phone during a passenger flight. It would prohibit airlines from involuntarily removing passengers from a plane after they have checked in and taken their seats, and would require the FAA to establish minimum seat dimensions on passenger airlines. The bill would also appropriate $1.7 billion in emergency supplemental funding for activities by HUD's Community Development Fund to aid disaster relief and recovery efforts in areas hit by natural disasters. It would also extend medical professional liability insurance coverage to sports medicine professionals who provide certain medical services to athletes outside their home state. Motion agreed to 93-6: R 47-3; D 44-3. 10 03, 2018.

221. HR6. OPIOID ABUSE PREVENTION AND HEALTH PROGRAMS/MOTION TO CONCUR. Thune, R-S.D., motion to concur in the House amendment to the Senate amendment to the bill that would modify Medicare and Medicaid and a variety of other health programs in relation to opioid abuse. It would expand both Medicare and Medicaid to cover medication-assisted treatment for substance use disorder and would place new requirements on states regarding Medicaid drug review and utilization requirements. It would appropriate $15 million annually, from fiscal 2019 through 2023, to support the establishment or operation of public health laboratories to detect synthetic opioids. It would allow Medicaid patients with opioid use or cocaine use disorders to stay up to 30 days per year in certain treatment facilities with more than 16 beds. Motion agreed to 98-1: R 49-1; D 47-0. 10 03, 2018.

222. KAVANAUGH NOMINATION/CLOTURE. Motion to invoke cloture (thus limiting debate) on the nomination of Brett M. Kavanaugh of Maryland to be an associate justice of the Supreme Court of the United States. Motion agreed to 51-49: R 50-1; D 1-46. 10 5, 2018.

	217	218	219	220	221	222
ALABAMA						
Shelby	Y	Y	Y	Y	Y	Y
Jones	N	Y	Y	Y	Y	N
ALASKA						
Murkowski	Y	Y	Y	Y	Y	N
Sullivan	Y	?	Y	Y	Y	Y
ARIZONA						
Flake	Y	Y	?	Y	Y	Y
Kyl	Y	Y	Y	Y	Y	Y
ARKANSAS						
Boozman	Y	Y	Y	Y	Y	Y
Cotton	Y	Y	Y	Y	Y	Y
CALIFORNIA						
Feinstein	N	Y	Y	Y	Y	N
Harris	N	Y	Y	Y	Y	N
COLORADO						
Bennet	N	Y	Y	Y	Y	N
Gardner	Y	Y	Y	Y	Y	Y
CONNECTICUT						
Blumenthal	N	Y	Y	Y	Y	N
Murphy	N	Y	Y	Y	Y	N
DELAWARE						
Carper	N	Y	Y	Y	Y	N
Coons	N	Y	Y	Y	Y	N
FLORIDA						
Nelson	N	Y	?	Y	Y	N
Rubio	Y	Y	Y	Y	Y	Y
GEORGIA						
Isakson	Y	Y	Y	Y	Y	Y
Perdue	Y	Y	Y	Y	Y	Y
HAWAII						
Schatz	N	Y	Y	Y	Y	N
Hirono	N	Y	Y	Y	Y	N
IDAHO						
Crapo	Y	Y	Y	Y	Y	Y
Risch	Y	Y	Y	Y	Y	Y
ILLINOIS						
Durbin	N	Y	Y	Y	Y	N
Duckworth	N	Y	Y	Y	Y	N
INDIANA						
Donnelly	N	Y	Y	Y	Y	N
Young	Y	Y	Y	Y	Y	Y
IOWA						
Grassley	Y	Y	Y	Y	Y	Y
Ernst	Y	Y	Y	Y	Y	Y
KANSAS						
Roberts	Y	Y	Y	Y	Y	Y
Moran	Y	Y	Y	Y	Y	Y
KENTUCKY						
McConnell	Y	Y	Y	Y	Y	Y
Paul	Y	N	N	N	Y	Y
LOUISIANA						
Cassidy	Y	Y	Y	Y	Y	Y
Kennedy	Y	Y	Y	Y	Y	Y
MAINE						
Collins	Y	Y	Y	Y	Y	Y
King	N	Y	Y	Y	Y	N
MARYLAND						
Cardin	N	Y	Y	Y	Y	N
Van Hollen	N	Y	Y	Y	Y	N
MASSACHUSETTS						
Warren	N	Y	Y	Y	Y	N
Markey	N	Y	N	N	Y	N
MICHIGAN						
Stabenow	N	Y	Y	Y	Y	N
Peters	N	Y	Y	Y	Y	N
MINNESOTA						
Klobuchar	N	Y	Y	Y	Y	N
Smith	N	Y	Y	Y	Y	N
MISSISSIPPI						
Wicker	Y	Y	Y	Y	Y	Y
Hyde-Smith	Y	Y	Y	Y	Y	Y
MISSOURI						
McCaskill	N	Y	Y	Y	Y	N
Blunt	Y	Y	Y	Y	Y	Y
MONTANA						
Tester	N	Y	Y	Y	Y	N
Daines	Y	Y	Y	Y	Y	Y
NEBRASKA						
Fischer	Y	Y	Y	Y	Y	Y
Sasse	Y	Y	Y	Y	Y	Y
NEVADA						
Heller	Y	Y	?	Y	Y	Y
Cortez Masto	N	Y	Y	Y	Y	N
NEW HAMPSHIRE						
Shaheen	N	Y	Y	Y	Y	N
Hassan	N	Y	Y	Y	Y	N
NEW JERSEY						
Menendez	N	Y	Y	Y	Y	N
Booker	N	Y	Y	Y	Y	N
NEW MEXICO						
Udall	N	Y	Y	Y	Y	N
Heinrich	N	Y	Y	Y	Y	N
NEW YORK						
Schumer	N	Y	Y	Y	Y	N
Gillibrand	N	Y	Y	Y	Y	N
NORTH CAROLINA						
Burr	Y	Y	Y	Y	Y	Y
Tillis	Y	Y	Y	Y	Y	Y
NORTH DAKOTA						
Hoeven	Y	Y	Y	Y	Y	Y
Heitkamp	N	Y	Y	Y	Y	N
OHIO						
Brown	N	Y	Y	Y	Y	N
Portman	Y	Y	Y	Y	Y	Y
OKLAHOMA						
Inhofe	Y	Y	Y	Y	Y	Y
Lankford	Y	Y	Y	Y	Y	Y
OREGON						
Wyden	N	Y	N	N	Y	N
Merkley	N	Y	N	N	Y	N
PENNSYLVANIA						
Casey	N	Y	Y	Y	Y	N
Toomey	Y	Y	N	Y	Y	Y
RHODE ISLAND						
Reed	N	Y	Y	Y	Y	N
Whitehouse	N	Y	Y	Y	Y	N
SOUTH CAROLINA						
Graham	Y	Y	Y	Y	Y	Y
Scott	Y	Y	Y	Y	Y	Y
SOUTH DAKOTA						
Thune	Y	Y	Y	Y	Y	Y
Rounds	Y	Y	Y	Y	Y	Y
TENNESSEE						
Alexander	Y	Y	Y	Y	Y	Y
Corker	Y	Y	Y	Y	Y	Y
TEXAS						
Cornyn	Y	Y	Y	Y	Y	Y
Cruz	Y	Y	Y	?	?	Y
UTAH						
Hatch	Y	Y	Y	Y	Y	Y
Lee	Y	Y	N	N	N	Y
VERMONT						
Leahy	N	Y	Y	Y	Y	N
Sanders	N	Y	Y	Y	Y	N
VIRGINIA						
Warner	N	Y	Y	Y	Y	N
Kaine	N	Y	Y	Y	Y	N
WASHINGTON						
Murray	N	Y	Y	Y	Y	N
Cantwell	N	Y	Y	Y	Y	N
WEST VIRGINIA						
Manchin	N	Y	Y	Y	Y	Y
Capito	Y	Y	Y	Y	Y	Y
WISCONSIN						
Johnson	Y	Y	Y	Y	Y	Y
Baldwin	N	Y	Y	Y	Y	N
WYOMING						
Enzi	Y	Y	Y	Y	Y	Y
Barrasso	Y	Y	N	N	Y	Y

KEY	**Republicans**	Democrats	*Independents*	
Y Voted for (yea)		**X** Paired against		**C** Voted "present" to avoid possible conflict of interest
# Paired for		**–** Announced against		
+ Announced for		**P** Voted "present"		**?** Did not vote or otherwise make a position known
N Voted against (nay)				

VOTE NUMBER

223. KAVANAUGH NOMINATION/CONFIRMATION. Confirmation of President Donald Trump's nomination of Brett M. Kavanaugh of Maryland to be an associate justice of the Supreme Court of the United States. Confirmed 50-48: R 49-0; D 1-46. 10 6, 2018.

224. S3021. WATER INFRASTRUCTURE PROJECTS AUTHORIZATION/ CLOTURE. McConnell, R-Ky., motion to invoke cloture on the motion to concur in the House amendment to the bill that that would authorize 12 new Army Corps of Engineers water resources projects, including navigation, flood control, harbor expansion and natural disaster damage projects. It would also deauthorize nine projects, would authorize the corps to conduct feasibility studies for more than 35 possible projects, and would require the corps to expedite feasibility studies for 30 projects. It would require that most watershed assessments that take place after a major disaster be conducted at federal expense. It would require the corps to conduct a study on the ability of the corps to carry out its missions and the potential effects of transferring the corps from the Defense Department to another federal agency. It would also authorize $4.4 billion for a loan fund program for states to finance drinking water infrastructure for fiscal years 2019 through 2021. Motion agreed to 96-3: R 49-2; D 45-1. 10 9, 2018.

225. S3021. WATER INFRASTRUCTURE PROJECTS AUTHORIZATION/ MOTION TO CONCUR. McConnell, R-Ky., motion to concur in the House amendment to the bill that would authorize 12 new Army Corps of Engineers water resources projects, including navigation, flood control, harbor expansion and natural disaster damage projects. It would also deauthorize nine projects, would authorize the corps to conduct feasibility studies for more than 35 possible projects, and would require the corps to expedite feasibility studies for 30 projects. It would require that most watershed assessments that take place after a major disaster be conducted at federal expense. It would require the corps to conduct a study on the ability of the corps to carry out its missions and the potential effects of transferring the corps from the Defense Department to another federal agency. It would also authorize $4.4 billion for a loan fund program for states to finance drinking water infrastructure for fiscal years 2019 through 2021. Motion agreed to 99-1: R 50-1; D 47-0. 10 10, 2018.

226. SJRES63. SHORT-TERM HEALTH INSURANCE PLANS/PASSAGE. Passage of the resolution that would nullify and disapprove of the rule from the Departments of Treasury, Labor, and Health and Human Services that would expand the duration of short-term health insurance plans. Rejected 50-50: R 1-50; D 47-0. 10 10, 2018.

227. CLARK NOMINATION/CLOTURE. Motion to invoke cloture (thus limiting debate) on the nomination of Jeffrey Bossert Clark of Virginia to be an assistant attorney general. Motion agreed to 53-44: R 51-0; D 2-42. 10 10, 2018.

228. CLARK NOMINATION/CONFIRMATION. Confirmation of President Donald Trump's nomination of Jeffrey Bossert Clark of Virginia to be an assistant attorney general. Confirmed 52-45: R 50-0; D 2-43. 10 11, 2018.

	223	224	225	226	227	228
ALABAMA						
Shelby	Y	Y	Y	N	Y	Y
Jones	N	Y	Y	Y	N	N
ALASKA						
Murkowski	P	Y	Y	N	Y	Y
Sullivan	Y	Y	Y	N	Y	Y
ARIZONA						
Flake	Y	Y	Y	N	Y	Y
Kyl	Y	Y	Y	N	Y	Y
ARKANSAS						
Boozman	Y	Y	Y	N	Y	Y
Cotton	Y	Y	Y	N	Y	Y
CALIFORNIA						
Feinstein	N	Y	Y	Y	N	N
Harris	N	Y	Y	Y	N	N
COLORADO						
Bennet	N	Y	Y	Y	N	N
Gardner	Y	Y	Y	N	Y	Y
CONNECTICUT						
Blumenthal	N	Y	Y	Y	N	N
Murphy	N	Y	Y	Y	N	N
DELAWARE						
Carper	N	Y	Y	Y	N	N
Coons	N	Y	Y	Y	N	N
FLORIDA						
Nelson	N	Y	Y	Y	-	-
Rubio	Y	Y	Y	N	Y	+
GEORGIA						
Isakson	Y	Y	Y	N	Y	Y
Perdue	Y	Y	Y	N	Y	Y
HAWAII						
Schatz	N	N	Y	Y	N	N
Hirono	N	Y	Y	Y	N	N
IDAHO						
Crapo	Y	Y	Y	N	Y	Y
Risch	Y	Y	Y	N	Y	Y
ILLINOIS						
Durbin	N	Y	Y	Y	N	N
Duckworth	N	Y	Y	Y	N	N
INDIANA						
Donnelly	N	Y	Y	Y	N	N
Young	Y	Y	Y	N	Y	Y
IOWA						
Grassley	Y	Y	Y	N	Y	Y
Ernst	Y	Y	Y	N	Y	Y
KANSAS						
Roberts	Y	Y	Y	N	Y	Y
Moran	Y	Y	Y	N	Y	Y
KENTUCKY						
McConnell	Y	Y	Y	N	Y	Y
Paul	Y	Y	Y	N	Y	Y
LOUISIANA						
Cassidy	Y	Y	Y	N	Y	Y
Kennedy	Y	Y	Y	N	Y	Y
MAINE						
Collins	Y	Y	Y	Y	Y	Y
King	N	Y	Y	Y	N	N
MARYLAND						
Cardin	N	Y	Y	Y	N	N
Van Hollen	N	Y	Y	Y	N	N
MASSACHUSETTS						
Warren	N	Y	Y	Y	N	N
Markey	N	Y	Y	Y	N	N
MICHIGAN						
Stabenow	N	Y	Y	Y	N	N
Peters	N	Y	Y	Y	N	N
MINNESOTA						
Klobuchar	N	Y	Y	Y	N	N
Smith	N	Y	Y	Y	N	N
MISSISSIPPI						
Wicker	Y	Y	Y	N	Y	Y
Hyde-Smith	Y	Y	Y	N	Y	Y
MISSOURI						
McCaskill	N	Y	Y	Y	Y	Y
Blunt	Y	Y	Y	N	Y	Y

	223	224	225	226	227	228
MONTANA						
Tester	N	Y	Y	Y	N	N
Daines	?	Y	Y	N	Y	Y
NEBRASKA						
Fischer	Y	Y	Y	N	Y	Y
Sasse	Y	Y	Y	N	Y	Y
NEVADA						
Heller	Y	Y	Y	N	Y	Y
Cortez Masto	N	Y	Y	Y	N	N
NEW HAMPSHIRE						
Shaheen	N	Y	Y	Y	N	N
Hassan	N	Y	Y	Y	N	N
NEW JERSEY						
Menendez	N	Y	Y	Y	N	N
Booker	N	+	Y	Y	N	N
NEW MEXICO						
Udall	N	Y	Y	Y	N	N
Heinrich	N	Y	Y	Y	N	N
NEW YORK						
Schumer	N	Y	Y	Y	N	N
Gillibrand	N	Y	Y	Y	N	N
NORTH CAROLINA						
Burr	Y	N	Y	N	Y	Y
Tillis	Y	Y	Y	N	Y	Y
NORTH DAKOTA						
Hoeven	Y	Y	Y	N	Y	Y
Heitkamp	N	Y	Y	Y	?	?
OHIO						
Brown	N	Y	Y	Y	N	N
Portman	Y	Y	Y	N	Y	Y
OKLAHOMA						
Inhofe	Y	Y	Y	N	Y	Y
Lankford	Y	Y	Y	N	Y	Y
OREGON						
Wyden	N	Y	Y	Y	?	N
Merkley	N	Y	Y	Y	N	N
PENNSYLVANIA						
Casey	N	Y	Y	Y	N	N
Toomey	Y	Y	Y	N	Y	Y
RHODE ISLAND						
Reed	N	Y	Y	Y	N	N
Whitehouse	N	Y	Y	Y	N	N
SOUTH CAROLINA						
Graham	Y	Y	Y	N	Y	Y
Scott	Y	Y	Y	N	Y	Y
SOUTH DAKOTA						
Thune	Y	Y	Y	N	Y	Y
Rounds	Y	Y	Y	N	Y	Y
TENNESSEE						
Alexander	Y	Y	Y	N	Y	Y
Corker	Y	Y	Y	N	Y	Y
TEXAS						
Cornyn	Y	Y	Y	N	Y	Y
Cruz	Y	Y	Y	N	Y	Y
UTAH						
Hatch	Y	Y	Y	N	Y	Y
Lee	Y	N	N	N	Y	Y
VERMONT						
Leahy	N	Y	Y	Y	N	N
Sanders	N	Y	Y	Y	N	N
VIRGINIA						
Warner	N	Y	Y	Y	N	N
Kaine	N	Y	Y	Y	N	N
WASHINGTON						
Murray	N	Y	Y	Y	N	N
Cantwell	N	Y	Y	Y	N	N
WEST VIRGINIA						
Manchin	Y	Y	Y	Y	Y	Y
Capito	Y	Y	Y	N	Y	Y
WISCONSIN						
Johnson	Y	Y	Y	N	Y	Y
Baldwin	N	Y	Y	Y	N	N
WYOMING						
Enzi	Y	Y	Y	N	Y	Y
Barrasso	Y	Y	Y	N	Y	Y

KEY	**Republicans**	Democrats	*Independents*
Y Voted for (yea)		X Paired against	C Voted "present" to avoid possible conflict of interest
# Paired for		- Announced against	
+ Announced for		P Voted "present"	? Did not vote or otherwise make a position known
N Voted against (nay)			

VOTE NUMBER

229. DREIBAND NOMINATION/CLOTURE. Motion to invoke cloture (thus limiting debate) on the nomination of Eric S. Dreiband of Maryland to be an assistant attorney general. Motion agreed to 50-47: R 50-0; D 0-45. 10 11, 2018.

230. DREIBAND NOMINATION/CONFIRMATION. Confirmation of President Donald Trump's nomination of Eric S. Dreiband of Maryland to be an assistant attorney general. Confirmed 50-47: R 50-0; D 0-45. 10 11, 2018.

231. PORTER NOMINATION/CONFIRMATION. Confirmation of President Donald Trump's nomination of David James Porter of Pennsylvania to be a U.S. circuit judge from the Third Circuit. Confirmed 50-45: R 50-0; D 0-43. 10 11, 2018.

232. NELSON NOMINATION/CONFIRMATION. Confirmation of President Donald Trump's nomination of Ryan Douglas Nelson of Idaho to be a U.S. circuit judge for the Ninth Circuit. Confirmed 51-44: R 50-0; D 1-42. 10 11, 2018.

233. SULLIVAN NOMINATION/CONFIRMATION. Confirmation of President Donald Trump's nomination of Richard J. Sullivan of New York to be a U.S. circuit judge for the Second Circuit. Confirmed 79-16: R 50-0; D 28-15. 10 11, 2018.

234. RAY NOMINATION/CONFIRMATION. Confirmation of President Donald Trump's nomination of William M. Ray II of Georgia to be a U.S. district judge for the Northern District of Georgia. Confirmed 54-41: R 50-0; D 4-39. 10 11, 2018.

	229	230	231	232	233	234
ALABAMA						
Shelby	Y	Y	Y	Y	Y	Y
Jones	N	N	N	Y	Y	Y
ALASKA						
Murkowski	Y	Y	Y	Y	Y	Y
Sullivan	Y	Y	Y	Y	Y	Y
ARIZONA						
Flake	Y	Y	Y	Y	Y	Y
Kyl	Y	Y	Y	Y	Y	Y
ARKANSAS						
Boozman	Y	Y	Y	Y	Y	Y
Cotton	Y	Y	Y	Y	Y	Y
CALIFORNIA						
Feinstein	N	N	?	?	?	?
Harris	N	N	N	N	N	N
COLORADO						
Bennet	N	N	N	N	Y	N
Gardner	Y	Y	Y	Y	Y	Y
CONNECTICUT						
Blumenthal	N	N	N	N	Y	N
Murphy	N	N	N	N	Y	N
DELAWARE						
Carper	N	N	N	N	Y	N
Coons	N	N	N	N	Y	N
FLORIDA						
Nelson	–	–	–	–	+	–
Rubio	+	+	?	?	?	?
GEORGIA						
Isakson	Y	Y	Y	Y	Y	Y
Perdue	Y	Y	Y	Y	Y	Y
HAWAII						
Schatz	N	N	N	N	Y	N
Hirono	N	N	N	N	N	N
IDAHO						
Crapo	Y	Y	Y	Y	Y	Y
Risch	Y	Y	Y	Y	Y	Y
ILLINOIS						
Durbin	N	N	N	N	Y	N
Duckworth	N	N	N	N	Y	N
INDIANA						
Donnelly	N	N	N	N	Y	Y
Young	Y	Y	Y	Y	Y	Y
IOWA						
Grassley	Y	Y	Y	Y	Y	Y
Ernst	Y	Y	Y	Y	Y	Y
KANSAS						
Roberts	Y	Y	Y	Y	Y	Y
Moran	Y	Y	Y	Y	Y	Y
KENTUCKY						
McConnell	Y	Y	Y	Y	Y	Y
Paul	Y	Y	Y	Y	Y	Y
LOUISIANA						
Cassidy	Y	Y	Y	Y	Y	Y
Kennedy	Y	Y	Y	Y	Y	Y
MAINE						
Collins	Y	Y	Y	Y	Y	Y
King	N	N	N	N	Y	N
MARYLAND						
Cardin	N	N	N	N	Y	N
Van Hollen	N	N	N	N	Y	N
MASSACHUSETTS						
Warren	N	N	N	N	N	N
Markey	N	N	N	N	N	N
MICHIGAN						
Stabenow	N	N	N	N	N	N
Peters	N	N	N	N	Y	N
MINNESOTA						
Klobuchar	N	N	N	N	N	N
Smith	N	N	N	N	N	N
MISSISSIPPI						
Wicker	Y	Y	Y	Y	Y	Y
Hyde-Smith	Y	Y	Y	Y	Y	Y
MISSOURI						
McCaskill	N	N	N	N	Y	N
Blunt	Y	Y	Y	Y	Y	Y

	229	230	231	232	233	234
MONTANA						
Tester	N	N	N	N	Y	Y
Daines	Y	Y	Y	Y	Y	Y
NEBRASKA						
Fischer	Y	Y	Y	Y	Y	Y
Sasse	Y	Y	Y	Y	Y	Y
NEVADA						
Heller	Y	Y	Y	Y	Y	Y
Cortez Masto	N	N	N	N	N	N
NEW HAMPSHIRE						
Shaheen	N	N	N	N	Y	N
Hassan	N	N	N	N	Y	N
NEW JERSEY						
Menendez	N	N	N	N	Y	N
Booker	N	N	N	N	N	N
NEW MEXICO						
Udall	N	N	N	N	N	N
Heinrich	N	N	+	+	+	+
NEW YORK						
Schumer	N	N	N	N	Y	N
Gillibrand	N	N	N	N	N	N
NORTH CAROLINA						
Burr	Y	Y	Y	Y	Y	Y
Tillis	Y	Y	Y	Y	Y	Y
NORTH DAKOTA						
Hoeven	Y	Y	Y	Y	Y	Y
Heitkamp	?	?	?	?	?	?
OHIO						
Brown	N	N	N	N	Y	N
Portman	Y	Y	Y	Y	Y	Y
OKLAHOMA						
Inhofe	Y	Y	Y	Y	Y	Y
Lankford	Y	Y	Y	Y	Y	Y
OREGON						
Wyden	N	N	N	N	Y	N
Merkley	N	N	N	N	N	N
PENNSYLVANIA						
Casey	N	N	N	N	Y	N
Toomey	Y	Y	Y	Y	Y	Y
RHODE ISLAND						
Reed	N	N	N	N	Y	N
Whitehouse	N	N	N	N	Y	N
SOUTH CAROLINA						
Graham	Y	Y	Y	Y	Y	Y
Scott	Y	Y	Y	Y	Y	Y
SOUTH DAKOTA						
Thune	Y	Y	Y	Y	Y	Y
Rounds	Y	Y	Y	Y	Y	Y
TENNESSEE						
Alexander	Y	Y	Y	Y	Y	Y
Corker	Y	Y	Y	Y	Y	Y
TEXAS						
Cornyn	Y	Y	Y	Y	Y	Y
Cruz	Y	Y	Y	Y	Y	Y
UTAH						
Hatch	Y	Y	Y	Y	Y	Y
Lee	Y	Y	Y	Y	Y	Y
VERMONT						
Leahy	N	N	N	N	Y	N
Sanders	N	N	N	N	N	N
VIRGINIA						
Warner	N	N	N	N	Y	N
Kaine	N	N	N	N	Y	N
WASHINGTON						
Murray	N	N	N	N	N	N
Cantwell	N	N	N	N	N	N
WEST VIRGINIA						
Manchin	N	N	N	N	Y	Y
Capito	Y	Y	Y	Y	Y	Y
WISCONSIN						
Johnson	Y	Y	Y	Y	Y	Y
Baldwin	N	N	N	N	Y	N
WYOMING						
Enzi	Y	Y	Y	Y	Y	Y
Barrasso	Y	Y	Y	Y	Y	Y

KEY   **Republicans**   Democrats   *Independents*

Y Voted for (yea)	X Paired against	C Voted "present" to avoid possible conflict of interest
# Paired for	– Announced against	
+ Announced for	P Voted "present"	? Did not vote or otherwise make a position known
N Voted against (nay)		

||| SENATE VOTES

VOTE NUMBER

235. BURKE NOMINATION/CONFIRMATION. Confirmation of President Donald Trump's nomination of Liles Clifton Burke of Alabama to be a U.S. district judge for the Northern District of Alabama. Confirmed 55-40: R 50-0; D 5-38. 10 11, 2018.

236. JUNEAU NOMINATION/CONFIRMATION. Confirmation of President Donald Trump's nomination of Michael Joseph Juneau of Louisiana to be a U.S. district judge for the Western District of Louisiana. Confirmed 54-41: R 50-0; D 4-39. 10 11, 2018.

237. NORRIS NOMINATION/CONFIRMATION. Confirmation of President Donald Trump's nomination of Mark Saalfield Norris Sr. of Tennessee to be a U.S. district judge for the Western District of Tennessee. Confirmed 51-44: R 50-0; D 1-42. 10 11, 2018.

238. RICHARDSON NOMINATION/CONFIRMATION. Confirmation of President Donald Trump's nomination of Eli Jeremy Richardson of Tennessee to be a U.S. district judge for the Middle District of Tennessee. Confirmed 52-43: R 50-0; D 2-41. 10 11, 2018.

239. KLEEH NOMINATION/CONFIRMATION. Confirmation of President Donald Trump's nomination of Thomas S. Kleeh of West Virginia to be a U.S. district judge for the Northern District of West Virginia. Confirmed 65-30: R 50-0; D 14-29. 10 11, 2018.

240. S140. COAST GUARD REAUTHORIZATION/CLOTURE. McConnell, R-Ky., motion to invoke cloture (thus limiting debate) on the McConnell motion to concur in the House amendment to the bill with a further amendment that would reauthorize the Coast Guard at $9.8 billion for fiscal 2018 and $10.5 billion for fiscal 2019. It would also task the Coast Guard with enforcing EPA regulations regarding ballast water discharge. Motion agreed to 93-5: R 50-0; D 42-4. Sept. 13, 2018.

	235	236	237	238	239	240
ALABAMA						
Shelby	Y	Y	Y	Y	Y	Y
Jones	Y	Y	Y	N	Y	Y
ALASKA						
Murkowski	Y	Y	Y	Y	Y	Y
Sullivan	Y	Y	Y	Y	Y	Y
ARIZONA						
Flake	Y	Y	Y	Y	Y	Y
Kyl	Y	Y	Y	Y	Y	Y
ARKANSAS						
Boozman	Y	Y	Y	Y	Y	Y
Cotton	Y	Y	Y	Y	Y	Y
CALIFORNIA						
Feinstein	?	?	?	?	?	N
Harris	N	N	N	N	N	N
COLORADO						
Bennet	N	N	N	N	N	Y
Gardner	Y	Y	Y	Y	Y	Y
CONNECTICUT						
Blumenthal	N	N	N	N	N	Y
Murphy	N	N	N	N	N	Y
DELAWARE						
Carper	N	N	N	N	N	Y
Coons	N	N	N	N	Y	Y
FLORIDA						
Nelson	-	-	-	-	+	Y
Rubio	?	?	?	?	?	Y
GEORGIA						
Isakson	Y	Y	Y	Y	Y	?
Perdue	Y	Y	Y	Y	Y	Y
HAWAII						
Schatz	N	N	N	N	N	Y
Hirono	N	N	N	N	N	Y
IDAHO						
Crapo	Y	Y	Y	Y	Y	Y
Risch	Y	Y	Y	Y	Y	Y
ILLINOIS						
Durbin	N	N	N	N	N	Y
Duckworth	N	N	N	N	N	Y
INDIANA						
Donnelly	Y	Y	Y	Y	Y	Y
Young	Y	Y	Y	Y	Y	Y
IOWA						
Grassley	Y	Y	Y	Y	Y	Y
Ernst	Y	Y	Y	Y	Y	Y
KANSAS						
Roberts	Y	Y	Y	Y	Y	Y
Moran	Y	Y	Y	Y	Y	Y
KENTUCKY						
McConnell	Y	Y	Y	Y	Y	Y
Paul	Y	Y	Y	Y	Y	Y
LOUISIANA						
Cassidy	Y	Y	Y	Y	Y	Y
Kennedy	Y	Y	Y	Y	Y	Y
MAINE						
Collins	Y	Y	Y	Y	Y	Y
King	N	N	N	N	Y	Y
MARYLAND						
Cardin	N	N	N	N	N	N
Van Hollen	N	N	N	N	N	Y
MASSACHUSETTS						
Warren	N	N	N	N	N	Y
Markey	N	N	N	N	N	Y
MICHIGAN						
Stabenow	N	N	N	N	N	Y
Peters	N	N	N	N	N	Y
MINNESOTA						
Klobuchar	N	N	N	N	N	Y
Smith	N	N	N	N	N	Y
MISSISSIPPI						
Wicker	Y	Y	Y	Y	Y	Y
Hyde-Smith	Y	Y	Y	Y	Y	Y
MISSOURI						
McCaskill	Y	Y	N	Y	Y	?
Blunt	Y	Y	Y	Y	Y	Y
MONTANA						
Tester	Y	N	N	N	Y	Y
Daines	Y	Y	Y	Y	Y	Y
NEBRASKA						
Fischer	Y	Y	Y	Y	Y	Y
Sasse	Y	Y	Y	Y	Y	Y
NEVADA						
Heller	Y	Y	Y	Y	Y	Y
Cortez Masto	N	N	N	N	N	Y
NEW HAMPSHIRE						
Shaheen	N	N	N	N	Y	Y
Hassan	N	N	N	N	Y	Y
NEW JERSEY						
Menendez	N	N	N	N	N	Y
Booker	N	N	N	N	N	Y
NEW MEXICO						
Udall	N	N	N	N	N	Y
Heinrich	+	+	+	-	+	Y
NEW YORK						
Schumer	N	N	N	N	N	N
Gillibrand	N	N	N	N	N	N
NORTH CAROLINA						
Burr	Y	Y	Y	Y	Y	Y
Tillis	Y	Y	Y	Y	Y	Y
NORTH DAKOTA						
Hoeven	Y	Y	Y	Y	Y	Y
Heitkamp	?	?	?	?	?	Y
OHIO						
Brown	N	N	N	N	N	Y
Portman	Y	Y	Y	Y	Y	Y
OKLAHOMA						
Inhofe	Y	Y	Y	Y	Y	Y
Lankford	Y	Y	Y	Y	Y	Y
OREGON						
Wyden	N	N	N	N	N	Y
Merkley	N	N	N	N	N	Y
PENNSYLVANIA						
Casey	N	N	N	N	N	Y
Toomey	Y	Y	Y	Y	Y	Y
RHODE ISLAND						
Reed	N	N	N	N	Y	Y
Whitehouse	N	N	N	N	Y	Y
SOUTH CAROLINA						
Graham	Y	Y	Y	Y	Y	Y
Scott	Y	Y	Y	Y	Y	Y
SOUTH DAKOTA						
Thune	Y	Y	Y	Y	Y	Y
Rounds	Y	Y	Y	Y	Y	Y
TENNESSEE						
Alexander	Y	Y	Y	Y	Y	Y
Corker	Y	Y	Y	Y	Y	Y
TEXAS						
Cornyn	Y	Y	Y	Y	Y	Y
Cruz	Y	Y	Y	Y	Y	Y
UTAH						
Hatch	Y	Y	Y	Y	Y	Y
Lee	Y	Y	Y	Y	Y	Y
VERMONT						
Leahy	N	N	N	N	Y	Y
Sanders	N	N	N	N	N	N
VIRGINIA						
Warner	N	N	N	N	N	Y
Kaine	N	N	N	N	N	Y
WASHINGTON						
Murray	N	N	N	N	N	Y
Cantwell	N	N	N	N	N	Y
WEST VIRGINIA						
Manchin	Y	Y	N	Y	Y	Y
Capito	Y	Y	Y	Y	Y	Y
WISCONSIN						
Johnson	Y	Y	Y	Y	Y	Y
Baldwin	N	N	N	N	N	Y
WYOMING						
Enzi	Y	Y	Y	Y	Y	Y
Barrasso	Y	Y	Y	Y	Y	Y

KEY   Republicans   Democrats   *Independents*

Y Voted for (yea)	X Paired against
# Paired for	- Announced against
+ Announced for	P Voted "present"
N Voted against (nay)	C Voted "present" to avoid possible conflict of interest
	? Did not vote or otherwise make a position known

VOTE NUMBER

241. S140. COAST GUARD REAUTHORIZATION/MOTION TO CONCUR. McConnell, R-Ky., motion to concur in the House amendment to the bill with a further Senate amendment, as modified, that would reauthorize the Coast Guard at $9.8 billion for fiscal 2018 and $10.5 billion for fiscal 2019 and would direct the service to enforce EPA's ballast water discharging rules aimed at reducing the introduction of invasive species into new waters. It would also exempt the Delta Queen paddle wheel boat from laws and regulations that require vessels with overnight accommodations for 50 or more passengers be made of fireproof materials. Motion agreed to 94-6: R 51-0; D 42-5. Sept. 14, 2018.

242. BOWAN NOMINATION/CLOTURE. Motion to invoke cloture (thus limiting debate) on the nomination of Michelle Bowman of Kansas to be a member of the Board of Governors of the Federal Reserve System. Motion agreed to 63-36: R 50-1; D 13-33. Sept. 14, 2018.

243. SJRES65. BAHRAIN ARMS SALES/MOTION TO TABLE. Corker, R-Tenn., motion to table (kill) the Paul, R-Ky., motion to discharge the Senate Foreign Relations Committee from further consideration of a joint resolution (S J Res 65) that would disapprove of the proposed export to the government of the Kingdom of Bahrain of certain defense articles and services. Motion agreed to 77-21: R 48-3; D 28-17. Sept. 15, 2018.

244. BOWMAN NOMINATION/CONFIRMATION. Confirmation of President Donald Trump's nomination of Michelle Bowman of Kansas to be a member of the board of governors for the Federal Reserve. Confirmed 64-34: R 50-1; D 14-31. Sept. 15, 2018.

245. VADEN NOMINATION/CLOTURE. Motion to invoke cloture (thus limiting debate) on the nomination of Stephen Vaden of Tennessee to be general counsel of the Department of Agriculture. Motion agreed to 49-45: R 46-0; D 3-44. Sept. 26, 2018.

246. VADEN NOMINATION/CONFIRMATION. Confirmation of President Donald Trump's nomination of Stephen Vaden of Tennessee to be general counsel of the Department of Agriculture. Confirmed 53-46: R 50-0; D 3-44. Sept. 27, 2018.

	241	242	243	244	245	246
ALABAMA						
Shelby	Y	Y	Y	Y	Y	Y
Jones	Y	Y	Y	Y	N	N
ALASKA						
Murkowski	Y	Y	Y	Y	Y	Y
Sullivan	Y	Y	Y	Y	Y	Y
ARIZONA						
Flake	Y	Y	Y	Y	Y	Y
Kyl	Y	Y	Y	Y	Y	Y
ARKANSAS						
Boozman	Y	Y	Y	Y	Y	Y
Cotton	Y	Y	Y	Y	Y	Y
CALIFORNIA						
Feinstein	Y	N	N	N	N	N
Harris	N	N	N	N	N	N
COLORADO						
Bennet	Y	Y	Y	Y	N	N
Gardner	Y	Y	Y	Y	Y	Y
CONNECTICUT						
Blumenthal	Y	N	Y	N	N	N
Murphy	Y	N	Y	?	N	N
DELAWARE						
Carper	Y	Y	Y	Y	N	N
Coons	Y	Y	?	Y	N	N
FLORIDA						
Nelson	Y	?	+	?	N	N
Rubio	Y	Y	Y	Y	Y	Y
GEORGIA						
Isakson	Y	Y	Y	Y	Y	Y
Perdue	Y	Y	Y	Y	Y	Y
HAWAII						
Schatz	Y	N	Y	N	N	N
Hirono	Y	N	N	N	N	N
IDAHO						
Crapo	Y	Y	Y	Y	?	Y
Risch	Y	Y	Y	Y	Y	Y
ILLINOIS						
Durbin	Y	N	N	N	N	N
Duckworth	Y	N	Y	N	N	N
INDIANA						
Donnelly	Y	Y	Y	Y	Y	Y
Young	Y	Y	Y	Y	Y	Y
IOWA						
Grassley	Y	Y	Y	Y	Y	Y
Ernst	Y	Y	Y	Y	Y	Y
KANSAS						
Roberts	Y	Y	Y	Y	Y	Y
Moran	Y	Y	N	Y	?	Y
KENTUCKY						
McConnell	Y	Y	Y	Y	Y	Y
Paul	Y	N	N	N	Y	Y
LOUISIANA						
Cassidy	Y	Y	Y	Y	Y	Y
Kennedy	Y	Y	Y	Y	Y	Y
MAINE						
Collins	Y	Y	Y	Y	Y	Y
King	Y	N	Y	N	N	N
MARYLAND						
Cardin	N	N	Y	N	N	N
Van Hollen	N	N	N	N	N	N
MASSACHUSETTS						
Warren	Y	N	N	N	N	N
Markey	Y	N	N	N	N	N
MICHIGAN						
Stabenow	Y	N	Y	N	Y	N
Peters	Y	Y	N	Y	N	N
MINNESOTA						
Klobuchar	Y	N	Y	N	N	N
Smith	Y	N	Y	N	N	N
MISSISSIPPI						
Wicker	Y	Y	Y	Y	?	Y
Hyde-Smith	Y	Y	Y	Y	?	?
MISSOURI						
McCaskill	Y	N	Y	Y	N	N
Blunt	Y	Y	Y	Y	Y	Y
MONTANA						
Tester	Y	Y	Y	Y	N	N
Daines	Y	Y	Y	Y	Y	Y
NEBRASKA						
Fischer	Y	Y	Y	Y	Y	Y
Sasse	Y	Y	Y	Y	Y	Y
NEVADA						
Heller	Y	Y	Y	Y	Y	Y
Cortez Masto	Y	N	Y	N	N	N
NEW HAMPSHIRE						
Shaheen	Y	Y	Y	Y	N	N
Hassan	Y	Y	Y	Y	N	N
NEW JERSEY						
Menendez	Y	N	Y	N	N	N
Booker	Y	N	N	N	N	N
NEW MEXICO						
Udall	Y	N	Y	N	N	N
Heinrich	Y	N	Y	N	N	N
NEW YORK						
Schumer	N	N	Y	N	N	N
Gillibrand	N	N	N	N	N	N
NORTH CAROLINA						
Burr	Y	Y	Y	Y	Y	Y
Tillis	Y	Y	Y	Y	Y	Y
NORTH DAKOTA						
Hoeven	Y	Y	Y	Y	Y	Y
Heitkamp	Y	Y	Y	Y	Y	Y
OHIO						
Brown	Y	N	Y	N	N	N
Portman	Y	Y	Y	Y	Y	Y
OKLAHOMA						
Inhofe	Y	Y	Y	Y	Y	Y
Lankford	Y	Y	Y	Y	Y	Y
OREGON						
Wyden	Y	N	N	N	N	N
Merkley	Y	N	N	N	N	N
PENNSYLVANIA						
Casey	Y	N	N	N	N	N
Toomey	Y	Y	Y	Y	Y	Y
RHODE ISLAND						
Reed	Y	N	N	N	N	N
Whitehouse	Y	N	Y	N	N	N
SOUTH CAROLINA						
Graham	Y	Y	Y	Y	?	Y
Scott	Y	Y	Y	Y	Y	Y
SOUTH DAKOTA						
Thune	Y	Y	Y	Y	Y	Y
Rounds	Y	Y	Y	Y	Y	Y
TENNESSEE						
Alexander	Y	Y	Y	Y	Y	Y
Corker	Y	Y	Y	Y	Y	Y
TEXAS						
Cornyn	Y	Y	Y	Y	Y	Y
Cruz	Y	Y	Y	Y	Y	Y
UTAH						
Hatch	Y	Y	Y	Y	Y	Y
Lee	Y	Y	N	Y	Y	Y
VERMONT						
Leahy	Y	N	N	N	N	N
Sanders	N	N	N	N	?	N
VIRGINIA						
Warner	Y	Y	Y	Y	N	N
Kaine	Y	Y	Y	Y	N	N
WASHINGTON						
Murray	Y	N	N	N	N	N
Cantwell	Y	N	N	N	N	N
WEST VIRGINIA						
Manchin	Y	Y	Y	Y	N	N
Capito	Y	Y	Y	Y	Y	Y
WISCONSIN						
Johnson	Y	Y	Y	Y	Y	Y
Baldwin	Y	N	N	N	N	N
WYOMING						
Enzi	Y	Y	Y	Y	Y	Y
Barrasso	Y	Y	Y	Y	Y	Y

KEY   **Republicans**   Democrats   *Independents*

Y Voted for (yea)	X Paired against	C Voted "present" to avoid possible conflict of interest
# Paired for	– Announced against	? Did not vote or otherwise make a position known
+ Announced for	P Voted "present"	
N Voted against (nay)		

VOTE NUMBER

247. KELLEY NOMINATION/CLOTURE. Motion to invoke cloture (thus limiting debate) on the nomination of Karen Kelley of Pennsylvania to be deputy secretary of Commerce. Motion agreed to 62-37: R 50-0; D 11-36. Sept. 27, 2018.

248. KELLEY NOMINATION/CONFIRMATION. Confirmation of President Donald Trump's nomination of Karen Kelley of Pennsylvania to be deputy secretary of Commerce. Confirmed 62-38: R 51-0; D 10-37. Sept. 28, 2018.

249. FARR NOMINATION/CLOTURE. Motion to invoke cloture (thus limiting debate) on the nomination of Thomas Farr of North Carolina to be U.S. District judge for the Eastern District of North Carolina. Motion agreed to 50-50: R 50-1; D 0-47. Sept. 28, 2018.

250. SJRES54. U.S. MILITARY FORCES IN YEMEN/MOTION TO DISCHARGE. Sanders, I-Vt., motion to discharge the Senate Foreign Relations Committee from further consideration of a joint resolution that would require the removal of most of the U.S. military forces in Yemen. Motion agreed to 63-37: R 14-37; D 47-0. Sept. 28, 2018.

251. KOBES NOMINATION/CLOTURE. Motion to invoke cloture (thus limiting debate) on the nomination of Jonathan Kobes of South Dakota to be U.S. Circuit judge for the Eighth Circuit. Motion agreed to 49-49: R 49-0; D 0-47. Sept. 29, 2018.

252. KRANINGER NOMINATION/CLOTURE. Motion to invoke cloture (thus limiting debate) on the nomination of Kathleen Kraninger of Ohio to be director of the Bureau of Consumer Financial Protection. Motion agreed to 50-49: R 50-0; D 0-47. Sept. 29, 2018.

	247	248	249	250	251	252
ALABAMA						
Shelby	Y	Y	Y	N	Y	Y
Jones	Y	Y	N	Y	N	N
ALASKA						
Murkowski	Y	Y	Y	Y	Y	Y
Sullivan	Y	Y	Y	N	Y	Y
ARIZONA						
Flake	Y	Y	N	Y	+	Y
Kyl	Y	Y	N	N	Y	Y
ARKANSAS						
Boozman	Y	Y	Y	N	Y	Y
Cotton	Y	Y	Y	N	Y	Y
CALIFORNIA						
Feinstein	N	N	N	Y	N	N
Harris	N	N	N	Y	N	N
COLORADO						
Bennet	N	N	N	Y	N	N
Gardner	Y	Y	Y	N	Y	Y
CONNECTICUT						
Blumenthal	N	N	N	Y	N	N
Murphy	Y	N	N	Y	N	N
DELAWARE						
Carper	N	N	N	Y	N	N
Coons	N	N	N	Y	N	N
FLORIDA						
Nelson	Y	Y	N	Y	N	N
Rubio	Y	Y	N	N	Y	Y
GEORGIA						
Isakson	Y	Y	Y	N	Y	Y
Perdue	Y	Y	Y	N	Y	Y
HAWAII						
Schatz	Y	Y	N	Y	N	N
Hirono	N	N	N	Y	N	N
IDAHO						
Crapo	Y	Y	Y	N	Y	Y
Risch	Y	Y	Y	N	Y	Y
ILLINOIS						
Durbin	N	N	N	Y	N	N
Duckworth	N	N	N	Y	N	N
INDIANA						
Donnelly	Y	Y	N	Y	N	N
Young	Y	Y	Y	Y	Y	Y
IOWA						
Grassley	Y	Y	Y	N	Y	Y
Ernst	Y	Y	Y	N	Y	Y
KANSAS						
Roberts	Y	Y	Y	N	Y	Y
Moran	Y	Y	Y	Y	Y	Y
KENTUCKY						
McConnell	Y	Y	Y	N	Y	Y
Paul	Y	Y	Y	Y	Y	Y
LOUISIANA						
Cassidy	Y	Y	Y	Y	Y	Y
Kennedy	Y	Y	Y	N	Y	Y
MAINE						
Collins	Y	Y	Y	Y	Y	Y
King	Y	Y	N	Y	N	N
MARYLAND						
Cardin	N	N	N	Y	N	N
Van Hollen	N	N	N	Y	N	N
MASSACHUSETTS						
Warren	N	N	N	Y	N	N
Markey	N	N	N	Y	N	N
MICHIGAN						
Stabenow	N	N	N	Y	N	N
Peters	N	N	N	Y	N	N
MINNESOTA						
Klobuchar	N	N	N	Y	N	N
Smith	N	N	N	Y	N	N
MISSISSIPPI						
Wicker	Y	Y	Y	N	Y	Y
Hyde-Smith	?	Y	Y	N	Y	Y
MISSOURI						
McCaskill	Y	Y	N	Y	N	N
Blunt	Y	Y	Y	N	Y	Y

	247	248	249	250	251	252
MONTANA						
Tester	Y	Y	N	Y	N	N
Daines	Y	Y	Y	Y	Y	Y
NEBRASKA						
Fischer	Y	Y	Y	N	Y	Y
Sasse	Y	Y	Y	N	Y	Y
NEVADA						
Heller	Y	Y	Y	N	Y	Y
Cortez Masto	N	N	N	Y	N	N
NEW HAMPSHIRE						
Shaheen	Y	Y	N	Y	N	N
Hassan	N	N	N	Y	N	N
NEW JERSEY						
Menendez	N	N	N	Y	N	N
Booker	N	N	N	Y	N	N
NEW MEXICO						
Udall	N	N	N	Y	N	N
Heinrich	N	N	N	Y	N	N
NEW YORK						
Schumer	N	N	N	Y	N	N
Gillibrand	N	N	N	Y	N	N
NORTH CAROLINA						
Burr	Y	Y	Y	N	Y	Y
Tillis	Y	Y	Y	N	Y	Y
NORTH DAKOTA						
Hoeven	Y	Y	Y	N	Y	Y
Heitkamp	Y	Y	N	Y	N	N
OHIO						
Brown	N	N	N	Y	N	N
Portman	Y	Y	Y	Y	Y	Y
OKLAHOMA						
Inhofe	Y	Y	Y	N	+	?
Lankford	Y	Y	Y	N	Y	Y
OREGON						
Wyden	N	N	N	Y	N	N
Merkley	N	N	N	Y	N	N
PENNSYLVANIA						
Casey	Y	Y	N	Y	N	N
Toomey	Y	Y	Y	Y	Y	Y
RHODE ISLAND						
Reed	N	N	N	Y	N	N
Whitehouse	N	N	N	Y	N	N
SOUTH CAROLINA						
Graham	Y	Y	Y	Y	Y	Y
Scott	Y	Y	Y	N	Y	Y
SOUTH DAKOTA						
Thune	Y	Y	Y	N	Y	Y
Rounds	Y	Y	Y	N	Y	Y
TENNESSEE						
Alexander	Y	Y	Y	Y	Y	Y
Corker	Y	Y	Y	Y	Y	Y
TEXAS						
Cornyn	Y	Y	Y	N	Y	Y
Cruz	Y	Y	Y	N	Y	Y
UTAH						
Hatch	Y	Y	Y	Y	Y	Y
Lee	Y	Y	Y	Y	Y	Y
VERMONT						
Leahy	N	N	N	Y	N	N
Sanders	N	N	N	Y	N	N
VIRGINIA						
Warner	N	N	N	Y	N	N
Kaine	N	N	N	Y	N	N
WASHINGTON						
Murray	N	N	N	Y	N	N
Cantwell	N	N	N	Y	N	N
WEST VIRGINIA						
Manchin	Y	Y	N	Y	N	N
Capito	Y	Y	Y	N	Y	Y
WISCONSIN						
Johnson	Y	Y	Y	N	Y	Y
Baldwin	N	N	N	Y	N	N
WYOMING						
Enzi	Y	Y	Y	N	Y	Y
Barrasso	Y	Y	Y	N	Y	Y

KEY	**Republicans**	Democrats	*Independents*
Y Voted for (yea)		X Paired against	C Voted "present" to avoid possible conflict of interest
# Paired for		- Announced against	? Did not vote or otherwise make a position known
+ Announced for		P Voted "present"	
N Voted against (nay)			

VOTE NUMBER

253. MCNAMEE NOMINATION/CLOTURE. Motion to invoke cloture (thus limiting debate) on the nomination of Bernard McNamee or Virginia to be a member of the Federal Energy Regulatory Commission for the remainder of the term expiring June 30, 2020. Motion agreed to 50-49: R 50-0; D 0-47. Dec. 5, 2018.

254. MCNAMEE NOMINATION/CONFIRMATION. Confirmation of President Donald Trump's nomination of Bernard McNamee of Virginia to be a member of the Federal Energy Regulatory Commission for the remainder of the term expiring June 30, 2020. Confirmed 50-49: R 50-0; D 0-47. Dec. 6, 2018.

255. KRANINGER NOMINATION/CONFIRMATION. Confirmation of President Donald Trump's nomination of Kathleen Kraninger of Ohio to be director of the Bureau of Consumer Financial Protection. Confirmed 50-49: R 50-0; D 0-47. Dec. 6, 2018.

256. MUZINICH NOMINATION/CLOTURE. Motion to invoke cloture (thus limiting debate) on the nomination of Justin Muzinich of New York to be deputy secretary of the Treasury. Motion agreed to 55-43: R 50-0; D 4-42. Dec. 10, 2018.

257. MUZINICH NOMINATION/CONFIRMATION. Confirmation of President Donald Trump's nomination of Justin Muzinich of New York to be deputy secretary of the Treasury. Confirmed 55-44: R 50-0; D 4-43. Dec. 11, 2018.

258. KOBES NOMINATION/CONFIRMATION. Confirmation of President Donald Trump's nomination of Jonathan A. Kobes of South Dakota to be a United States Circuit judge for the Eighth Circuit. Confirmed 50-50: R 50-1; D 0-47. Dec. 11, 2018.

	253	254	255	256	257	258
ALABAMA						
Shelby	Y	Y	Y	Y	Y	Y
Jones	N	N	N	Y	Y	N
ALASKA						
Murkowski	Y	Y	Y	Y	Y	Y
Sullivan	Y	Y	Y	Y	Y	Y
ARIZONA						
Flake	Y	Y	Y	Y	Y	N
Kyl	Y	Y	Y	Y	Y	Y
ARKANSAS						
Boozman	Y	Y	Y	Y	Y	Y
Cotton	Y	Y	Y	Y	Y	Y
CALIFORNIA						
Feinstein	N	N	N	N	N	N
Harris	N	N	N	N	N	N
COLORADO						
Bennet	N	N	N	N	N	N
Gardner	Y	Y	Y	Y	Y	Y
CONNECTICUT						
Blumenthal	N	N	N	N	Y	N
Murphy	N	N	N	N	N	N
DELAWARE						
Carper	N	N	N	N	N	N
Coons	N	N	N	Y	Y	N
FLORIDA						
Nelson	N	N	N	Y	Y	N
Rubio	Y	Y	Y	Y	Y	Y
GEORGIA						
Isakson	Y	Y	Y	Y	Y	Y
Perdue	Y	Y	Y	Y	Y	Y
HAWAII						
Schatz	N	N	N	N	N	N
Hirono	N	N	N	N	N	N
IDAHO						
Crapo	Y	Y	Y	Y	Y	Y
Risch	Y	Y	Y	Y	Y	Y
ILLINOIS						
Durbin	N	N	N	N	N	N
Duckworth	N	N	N	N	N	N
INDIANA						
Donnelly	N	N	N	N	N	N
Young	Y	Y	Y	Y	Y	Y
IOWA						
Grassley	Y	Y	Y	Y	Y	Y
Ernst	Y	Y	Y	Y	Y	Y
KANSAS						
Roberts	Y	Y	Y	Y	Y	Y
Moran	Y	Y	Y	Y	Y	Y
KENTUCKY						
McConnell	Y	Y	Y	Y	Y	Y
Paul	Y	Y	Y	Y	Y	Y
LOUISIANA						
Cassidy	Y	Y	Y	Y	Y	Y
Kennedy	Y	Y	Y	Y	Y	Y
MAINE						
Collins	Y	Y	Y	Y	Y	Y
King	N	N	N	Y	Y	N
MARYLAND						
Cardin	N	N	N	N	N	N
Van Hollen	N	N	N	N	N	N
MASSACHUSETTS						
Warren	N	N	N	N	N	N
Markey	N	N	N	N	N	N
MICHIGAN						
Stabenow	N	N	N	N	N	N
Peters	N	N	N	N	N	N
MINNESOTA						
Klobuchar	N	N	N	N	N	N
Smith	N	N	N	N	N	N
MISSISSIPPI						
Wicker	Y	Y	Y	Y	Y	Y
Hyde-Smith	Y	Y	Y	Y	Y	Y
MISSOURI						
McCaskill	N	N	N	?	N	N
Blunt	Y	Y	Y	Y	Y	Y
MONTANA						
Tester	N	N	N	N	N	N
Daines	Y	Y	Y	Y	Y	Y
NEBRASKA						
Fischer	Y	Y	Y	Y	Y	Y
Sasse	Y	Y	Y	Y	Y	Y
NEVADA						
Heller	Y	Y	Y	Y	Y	Y
Cortez Masto	N	N	N	N	N	N
NEW HAMPSHIRE						
Shaheen	N	N	N	N	N	N
Hassan	N	N	N	N	N	N
NEW JERSEY						
Menendez	N	N	N	N	N	N
Booker	N	N	N	N	N	N
NEW MEXICO						
Udall	N	N	N	N	N	N
Heinrich	N	N	N	N	N	N
NEW YORK						
Schumer	N	N	N	N	N	N
Gillibrand	N	N	N	N	N	N
NORTH CAROLINA						
Burr	Y	Y	Y	Y	Y	Y
Tillis	?	?	?	?	?	Y
NORTH DAKOTA						
Hoeven	Y	Y	Y	Y	Y	Y
Heitkamp	N	N	N	N	N	N
OHIO						
Brown	N	N	N	N	N	N
Portman	Y	Y	Y	Y	Y	Y
OKLAHOMA						
Inhofe	Y	Y	Y	Y	Y	Y
Lankford	Y	Y	Y	Y	Y	Y
OREGON						
Wyden	N	N	N	N	N	N
Merkley	N	N	N	N	N	N
PENNSYLVANIA						
Casey	N	N	N	N	N	N
Toomey	Y	Y	Y	Y	Y	Y
RHODE ISLAND						
Reed	N	N	N	N	N	N
Whitehouse	N	N	N	N	N	N
SOUTH CAROLINA						
Graham	Y	Y	Y	Y	Y	Y
Scott	Y	Y	Y	Y	Y	Y
SOUTH DAKOTA						
Thune	Y	Y	Y	Y	Y	Y
Rounds	Y	Y	Y	Y	Y	Y
TENNESSEE						
Alexander	Y	Y	Y	Y	Y	Y
Corker	Y	Y	Y	Y	Y	Y
TEXAS						
Cornyn	Y	Y	Y	Y	Y	Y
Cruz	Y	Y	Y	Y	Y	Y
UTAH						
Hatch	Y	Y	Y	Y	Y	Y
Lee	Y	Y	Y	Y	Y	Y
VERMONT						
Leahy	N	N	N	N	N	N
Sanders	N	N	N	N	N	N
VIRGINIA						
Warner	N	N	N	N	N	N
Kaine	N	N	N	N	N	N
WASHINGTON						
Murray	N	N	N	N	N	N
Cantwell	N	N	N	N	N	N
WEST VIRGINIA						
Manchin	N	N	N	N	N	N
Capito	Y	Y	Y	Y	Y	Y
WISCONSIN						
Johnson	Y	Y	Y	Y	Y	Y
Baldwin	N	N	N	N	N	N
WYOMING						
Enzi	Y	Y	Y	Y	Y	Y
Barrasso	Y	Y	Y	Y	Y	Y

KEY	**Republicans**	Democrats	*Independents*
Y Voted for (yea)	**X** Paired against	**C** Voted "present" to avoid possible conflict of interest
# Paired for	**–** Announced against	
+ Announced for	**P** Voted "present"	**?** Did not vote or otherwise make a position known
N Voted against (nay)		

VOTE NUMBER

259. HR2. FARM PROGRAMS/CONFERENCE REPORT. Adoption of the conference report on the bill that would reauthorize and extend federal farm and nutrition programs through fiscal 2023, including crop subsidies, conservation, rural development and agricultural trade programs and the Supplemental Nutritional Assistance Program. It would reauthorize and extend supplemental agricultural disaster assistance programs, sugar policies and loan rates, several international food aid programs, nonrecourse marketing assistance loans for loan commodities, and several dairy programs, including the dairy risk management program (previously the margin protection program). It would create new pilot programs that would test strategies for improving the accuracy of the SNAP income verification process. It would allow industrial hemp to be grown in the United States, subject to close regulation at the state level. It would modify the activities permitted on land contracted under the conservation reserve program. Adopted (thus sent to the Senate) 87-13: R 38-13; D 47-0. Dec. 11, 2018.

260. SJRES64. CHARITABLE CONTRIBUTORS REPORTING/PASSAGE. Passage of the joint resolution that would disapprove of the Treasury Department's rule on reporting to the IRS contributors to some tax-exempt entities that are not 501(c)(3) organizations. Passed 50-49: R 1-49; D 47-0. Dec. 12, 2018.

261. SJRES54. U.S. MILITARY FORCES IN YEMEN/MOTION TO PROCEED. Sanders, I-Vt., motion to proceed to the joint resolution that would require the removal of most of the U.S. military forces in Yemen. Motion agreed to 60-39: R 11-39; D 47-0. Dec. 12, 2018.

262. SJRES54. U.S. MILITARY FORCES IN YEMEN/GERMANENESS STANDARD. Agreeing to a point of order that would establish that amendments offered under 50 USC 1546a be germane to the underlying joint resolution to which they are offered. Adopted 96-3: R 47-3; D 47-0. Dec. 12, 2018.

263. SJRES54. U.S. MILITARY FORCES IN YEMEN/IN-FLIGHT REFUELING. Young, R-Ind., amendment no. 4080 that would modify the bill's definition of ""hostilities"" to include in-flight refueling of non-U.S. aircraft conducting missions as part of the ongoing civil war in Yemen. Adopted 58-41: R 9-41; D 47-0. Dec. 13, 2018.

264. SJRES54. U.S. MILITARY FORCES IN YEMEN/MILITARY COOPERATION WITH ISRAEL. Cornyn, R-Texas amendment no. 4096, as modified, that would clarify that nothing in the joint resolution shall be construed to disrupt any military operations and cooperation with Israel. Adopted 99-0: R 50-0; D 47-0. Dec. 13, 2018.

	259	260	261	262	263	264
ALABAMA						
Shelby	Y	N	N	Y	N	Y
Jones	Y	Y	Y	Y	Y	Y
ALASKA						
Murkowski	N	N	Y	Y	Y	Y
Sullivan	Y	N	N	Y	N	Y
ARIZONA						
Flake	N	N	Y	Y	N	Y
Kyl	N	N	N	Y	N	Y
ARKANSAS						
Boozman	Y	N	N	Y	N	Y
Cotton	N	N	N	Y	N	Y
CALIFORNIA						
Feinstein	Y	Y	Y	Y	Y	Y
Harris	Y	Y	Y	Y	Y	Y
COLORADO						
Bennet	Y	Y	Y	Y	Y	Y
Gardner	Y	N	N	Y	N	Y
CONNECTICUT						
Blumenthal	Y	Y	Y	Y	Y	Y
Murphy	Y	Y	Y	Y	Y	Y
DELAWARE						
Carper	Y	Y	Y	Y	Y	Y
Coons	Y	Y	Y	Y	Y	Y
FLORIDA						
Nelson	Y	Y	Y	Y	Y	Y
Rubio	N	N	N	Y	N	Y
GEORGIA						
Isakson	Y	N	N	Y	N	Y
Perdue	Y	N	N	Y	N	Y
HAWAII						
Schatz	Y	Y	Y	Y	Y	Y
Hirono	Y	Y	Y	Y	Y	Y
IDAHO						
Crapo	Y	N	N	Y	N	Y
Risch	Y	N	Y	Y	N	Y
ILLINOIS						
Durbin	Y	Y	Y	Y	Y	Y
Duckworth	Y	Y	Y	Y	Y	Y
INDIANA						
Donnelly	Y	Y	Y	Y	Y	Y
Young	Y	N	Y	Y	Y	Y
IOWA						
Grassley	N	N	N	Y	N	Y
Ernst	Y	N	N	Y	N	Y
KANSAS						
Roberts	Y	N	N	Y	N	Y
Moran	Y	N	Y	Y	Y	Y
KENTUCKY						
McConnell	Y	N	N	Y	N	Y
Paul	N	N	Y	N	Y	Y
LOUISIANA						
Cassidy	Y	N	Y	Y	Y	Y
Kennedy	N	N	N	Y	N	Y
MAINE						
Collins	Y	Y	Y	Y	Y	Y
King	Y	Y	Y	Y	Y	Y
MARYLAND						
Cardin	Y	Y	Y	Y	Y	Y
Van Hollen	Y	Y	Y	Y	Y	Y
MASSACHUSETTS						
Warren	Y	Y	Y	Y	Y	Y
Markey	Y	Y	Y	Y	Y	Y
MICHIGAN						
Stabenow	Y	Y	Y	Y	Y	Y
Peters	Y	Y	Y	Y	Y	Y
MINNESOTA						
Klobuchar	Y	Y	Y	Y	Y	Y
Smith	Y	Y	Y	Y	Y	Y
MISSISSIPPI						
Wicker	Y	N	N	Y	N	Y
Hyde-Smith	Y	N	N	Y	N	Y
MISSOURI						
McCaskill	Y	Y	Y	Y	Y	Y
Blunt	Y	N	N	Y	N	Y

	259	260	261	262	263	264
MONTANA						
Tester	Y	Y	Y	Y	Y	Y
Daines	Y	N	Y	Y	N	Y
NEBRASKA						
Fischer	Y	N	N	Y	N	Y
Sasse	Y	N	N	Y	N	Y
NEVADA						
Heller	Y	N	N	Y	N	Y
Cortez Masto	Y	Y	Y	Y	Y	Y
NEW HAMPSHIRE						
Shaheen	Y	Y	Y	Y	Y	Y
Hassan	Y	Y	Y	Y	Y	Y
NEW JERSEY						
Menendez	Y	Y	Y	Y	Y	Y
Booker	Y	Y	Y	Y	Y	Y
NEW MEXICO						
Udall	Y	Y	Y	Y	Y	Y
Heinrich	Y	Y	Y	Y	Y	Y
NEW YORK						
Schumer	Y	Y	Y	Y	Y	Y
Gillibrand	Y	Y	Y	Y	Y	Y
NORTH CAROLINA						
Burr	Y	N	N	Y	N	Y
Tillis	Y	?	?	?	?	?
NORTH DAKOTA						
Hoeven	Y	N	N	Y	N	Y
Heitkamp	Y	Y	Y	Y	Y	Y
OHIO						
Brown	Y	Y	Y	Y	Y	Y
Portman	Y	N	N	Y	N	Y
OKLAHOMA						
Inhofe	Y	N	N	Y	N	Y
Lankford	Y	N	N	Y	N	Y
OREGON						
Wyden	Y	Y	Y	Y	Y	Y
Merkley	Y	Y	Y	Y	Y	Y
PENNSYLVANIA						
Casey	Y	Y	Y	Y	Y	Y
Toomey	N	N	N	Y	N	Y
RHODE ISLAND						
Reed	Y	Y	Y	Y	Y	Y
Whitehouse	Y	Y	Y	Y	Y	Y
SOUTH CAROLINA						
Graham	Y	N	N	Y	N	Y
Scott	Y	N	N	Y	N	Y
SOUTH DAKOTA						
Thune	Y	N	N	Y	N	Y
Rounds	Y	N	N	Y	N	Y
TENNESSEE						
Alexander	Y	N	N	Y	Y	Y
Corker	Y	N	N	Y	Y	Y
TEXAS						
Cornyn	Y	N	N	Y	N	Y
Cruz	Y	N	N	N	N	Y
UTAH						
Hatch	Y	N	N	Y	N	Y
Lee	N	N	Y	N	Y	Y
VERMONT						
Leahy	Y	Y	Y	Y	Y	Y
Sanders	Y	Y	Y	Y	Y	Y
VIRGINIA						
Warner	Y	Y	Y	Y	Y	Y
Kaine	Y	Y	Y	Y	Y	Y
WASHINGTON						
Murray	Y	Y	Y	Y	Y	Y
Cantwell	Y	Y	Y	Y	Y	Y
WEST VIRGINIA						
Manchin	Y	Y	Y	Y	Y	Y
Capito	Y	N	N	Y	N	Y
WISCONSIN						
Johnson	N	N	N	Y	N	Y
Baldwin	Y	Y	Y	Y	Y	Y
WYOMING						
Enzi	N	N	N	Y	N	Y
Barrasso	N	N	N	Y	N	Y

KEY	**Republicans**	Democrats	*Independents*	
Y	Voted for (yea)	X	Paired against	C	Voted "present" to avoid possible conflict of interest
#	Paired for	-	Announced against		
+	Announced for	P	Voted "present"	?	Did not vote or otherwise make a position known
N	Voted against (nay)				

VOTE NUMBER

265. SJRES54. U.S. MILITARY FORCES IN YEMEN/CONTINUATION OF OPERATIONS IN YEMEN. Cotton, R-Ark., amendment no. 4098 that would allow U.S. Forces to continue operation to support efforts to disrupt Houthi attacks against locations outside of Yemen. Rejected 45-54: R 45-5; D 0-47. Dec. 13, 2018.

266. SJRES54. U.S. MILITARY FORCES IN YEMEN/PASSAGE. Passage of the joint resolution that would direct the president to remove U.S. armed forces from hostilities in or affecting the Republic of Yemen, except forces engaged in operations directed at Al Qaeda or associated forces, by not later than the 30 days after the date of the adoption of the joint resolution unless and until a declaration of war or specific authorization for such use of armed forces has been enacted. Passed 56-41: R 7-41; D 47-0. Dec. 13, 2018.

267. S756. CRIMINAL RECIDIVISM PROGRAMS, JUDICIAL AND PRISON SYSTEM MODIFICATIONS/CLOTURE. McConnell, R-Ky., motion to invoke cloture (thus limiting debate) on the McConnell motion to concur in the House amendment to the bill with a further amendment that would change sentencing laws and provide for programs to support prisoners returning to society. Motion agreed to 82-12: R 33-12; D 47-0. Dec. 17, 2018.

268. S756. CRIMINAL RECIDIVISM PROGRAMS, JUDICIAL AND PRISON SYSTEM MODIFICATIONS/NOTIFICATION OF VICTIMS. Kennedy, R-La., amendment no. 4109, Pt. 1, that would require the Bureau of Prisons to notify victims, or victims' next-of-kin, of the date on which an offender is set to be released, and would require the bureau to make publicly available the offender's rearrest data. Rejected 32-67: R 32-18; D 0-47. Dec. 18, 2018.

269. S756. CRIMINAL RECIDIVISM PROGRAMS, JUDICIAL AND PRISON SYSTEM MODIFICATIONS/WARDEN INVOLVENT IN EARLY RELEASE. Kennedy, R-La., amendment no. 4109, Pt. 2, that would require a warden of a given federal correctional facility to approve of the release of a prisoner under their direction after having notified the victim of the offender being released, and after having reviewed any statement made by the victim or the victim's next-of-kin. Rejected 33-66: R 33-17; D 0-47. Dec. 18, 2018.

270. S756. CRIMINAL RECIDIVISM PROGRAMS, JUDICIAL AND PRISON SYSTEM MODIFICATIONS/EXCLUSION OF ADDITIONAL OFFENSES. Kennedy, R-La., amendment no. 4109, Pt. 3, that would add nine offenses to a list of those that would prevent inmates from qualifying for a program that would allow them to serve a latter part of their sentence in a halfway house or home confinement. Rejected 37-62: R 36-14; D 1-46. Dec. 18, 2018.

	265	266	267	268	269	270
ALABAMA						
Shelby	Y	N	Y	Y	Y	Y
Jones	N	Y	Y	N	N	N
ALASKA						
Murkowski	Y	N	N	Y	Y	Y
Sullivan	Y	N	N	Y	Y	Y
ARIZONA						
Flake	Y	Y	Y	N	N	N
Kyl	Y	N	N	Y	Y	Y
ARKANSAS						
Boozman	Y	N	Y	Y	Y	Y
Cotton	Y	N	N	Y	Y	Y
CALIFORNIA						
Feinstein	N	Y	Y	N	N	N
Harris	N	Y	Y	N	N	N
COLORADO						
Bennet	N	Y	Y	N	N	N
Gardner	Y	N	Y	Y	Y	Y
CONNECTICUT						
Blumenthal	N	Y	Y	N	N	N
Murphy	N	Y	Y	N	N	N
DELAWARE						
Carper	N	Y	Y	N	N	N
Coons	N	Y	Y	N	N	N
FLORIDA						
Nelson	N	Y	Y	N	N	N
Rubio	Y	N	Y	Y	Y	Y
GEORGIA						
Isakson	Y	N	Y	N	Y	N
Perdue	Y	N	Y	Y	Y	Y
HAWAII						
Schatz	N	Y	Y	N	N	N
Hirono	N	Y	Y	N	N	N
IDAHO						
Crapo	Y	N	Y	Y	Y	Y
Risch	Y	N	N	Y	Y	Y
ILLINOIS						
Durbin	N	Y	Y	N	N	N
Duckworth	N	Y	Y	N	N	N
INDIANA						
Donnelly	N	Y	Y	N	N	N
Young	N	Y	Y	N	N	Y
IOWA						
Grassley	Y	N	Y	N	N	N
Ernst	Y	N	Y	N	N	N
KANSAS						
Roberts	Y	N	Y	N	N	N
Moran	N	Y	Y	N	N	N
KENTUCKY						
McConnell	Y	N	Y	Y	Y	Y
Paul	N	Y	Y	N	N	N
LOUISIANA						
Cassidy	Y	N	?	N	N	Y
Kennedy	Y	N	N	Y	Y	Y
MAINE						
Collins	Y	Y	Y	Y	N	Y
King	N	Y	Y	N	N	N
MARYLAND						
Cardin	N	Y	Y	N	N	N
Van Hollen	N	Y	Y	N	N	N
MASSACHUSETTS						
Warren	N	Y	Y	N	N	N
Markey	N	Y	Y	N	N	N
MICHIGAN						
Stabenow	N	Y	Y	N	N	N
Peters	N	Y	Y	N	N	Y
MINNESOTA						
Klobuchar	N	Y	Y	N	N	N
Smith	N	Y	Y	N	N	N
MISSISSIPPI						
Wicker	Y	N	Y	N	N	N
Hyde-Smith	Y	N	Y	N	N	N
MISSOURI						
McCaskill	N	Y	Y	N	N	N
Blunt	Y	N	Y	Y	Y	Y
MONTANA						
Tester	N	Y	Y	N	N	N
Daines	N	Y	Y	Y	Y	Y
NEBRASKA						
Fischer	Y	N	Y	Y	Y	Y
Sasse	Y	N	N	Y	Y	Y
NEVADA						
Heller	Y	?	?	N	Y	Y
Cortez Masto	N	Y	Y	N	N	N
NEW HAMPSHIRE						
Shaheen	N	Y	Y	N	N	N
Hassan	N	Y	Y	N	N	N
NEW JERSEY						
Menendez	N	Y	Y	N	N	N
Booker	N	Y	Y	N	N	N
NEW MEXICO						
Udall	N	Y	Y	N	N	N
Heinrich	N	Y	Y	N	N	N
NEW YORK						
Schumer	N	Y	Y	N	N	N
Gillibrand	N	Y	Y	N	N	N
NORTH CAROLINA						
Burr	Y	N	N	Y	Y	Y
Tillis	?	?	?	Y	Y	N
NORTH DAKOTA						
Hoeven	Y	N	Y	Y	Y	Y
Heitkamp	N	Y	Y	N	N	N
OHIO						
Brown	N	Y	Y	N	N	N
Portman	Y	N	Y	Y	Y	Y
OKLAHOMA						
Inhofe	Y	N	Y	Y	Y	Y
Lankford	Y	N	Y	N	N	N
OREGON						
Wyden	N	Y	Y	N	N	N
Merkley	N	Y	Y	N	N	N
PENNSYLVANIA						
Casey	N	Y	Y	N	N	N
Toomey	Y	N	Y	Y	Y	Y
RHODE ISLAND						
Reed	N	Y	Y	N	N	N
Whitehouse	N	Y	Y	N	N	N
SOUTH CAROLINA						
Graham	Y	?	?	?	?	?
Scott	Y	N	Y	Y	Y	Y
SOUTH DAKOTA						
Thune	Y	N	Y	Y	Y	Y
Rounds	Y	N	N	Y	Y	Y
TENNESSEE						
Alexander	Y	N	#	N	N	N
Corker	Y	N	Y	N	N	Y
TEXAS						
Cornyn	Y	N	Y	Y	Y	Y
Cruz	Y	N	Y	Y	Y	Y
UTAH						
Hatch	Y	N	Y	N	N	N
Lee	N	Y	Y	N	N	N
VERMONT						
Leahy	N	Y	Y	N	N	N
Sanders	N	Y	Y	N	N	N
VIRGINIA						
Warner	N	Y	Y	N	N	N
Kaine	N	Y	Y	N	N	N
WASHINGTON						
Murray	N	Y	Y	N	N	N
Cantwell	N	Y	Y	N	N	N
WEST VIRGINIA						
Manchin	N	Y	Y	N	N	N
Capito	Y	N	Y	Y	Y	Y
WISCONSIN						
Johnson	Y	N	?	N	N	Y
Baldwin	N	Y	Y	N	N	N
WYOMING						
Enzi	Y	N	N	Y	Y	Y
Barrasso	Y	N	N	Y	Y	Y

KEY   Republicans   Democrats   *Independents*

Y Voted for (yea)	**X** Paired against	**C** Voted "present" to avoid possible conflict of interest
# Paired for	**–** Announced against	
+ Announced for	**P** Voted "present"	**?** Did not vote or otherwise make a position known
N Voted against (nay)		

VOTE NUMBER

271. S756. CRIMINAL RECIDIVISM PROGRAMS, JUDICIAL AND PRISON SYSTEM MODIFICATIONS/MOTION TO CONCUR. McConnell, R-Ky., motion to concur in the House amendment to the bill with a further Senate amendment, as modified, that would seek to reduce numbers of federally incarcerated individuals through changes in sentencing laws. The bill would seek to do so, in part, by allowing judges more flexibility when handing down sentences below the mandatory minimum for nonviolent drug offenders. It would also establish programs to provide support for prisoners returning to society in an attempt to reduce rates of recidivation. Motion agreed to 87-12: R 38-12; D 47-0. Dec. 18, 2018.

272. MAGUIRE NOMINATION/CLOTURE. Motion to invoke cloture (thus limiting debate) on the nomination of Joseph Maguire of Florida to be director of the National Counterterrorism Center, Office of the Director of National Intelligence. Motion agreed to 95-1: R 48-1; D 45-0. Dec. 19, 2018.

273. PROCEDURAL MOTION/REQUIRE ATTENDANCE. McConnell, R-Ky., motion to instruct the sergeant at arms to request the attendance of absent senators. Motion agreed to 71-21: R 27-17; D 43-3. Dec. 19, 2018.

274. HR695. SHORT-TERM CONTINUING FISCAL 2019 APPROPRIATIONS/MOTION TO PROCEED. McConnell, R-Ky., motion to proceed to the House message to accompany the bill that would provide short-term continuing fiscal 2019 appropriations and funding for the president's proposed border wall project. Motion agreed to 47-47: R 46-0; D 1-45. Dec. 21, 2018.

	271	272	273	274
ALABAMA				
Shelby	N	Y	Y	Y
Jones	Y	Y	Y	Y
ALASKA				
Murkowski	N	Y	Y	Y
Sullivan	N	Y	Y	Y
ARIZONA				
Flake	Y	Y	Y	Y
Kyl	N	Y	Y	?
ARKANSAS				
Boozman	Y	Y	Y	Y
Cotton	N	Y	N	Y
CALIFORNIA				
Feinstein	Y	Y	Y	?
Harris	Y	Y	Y	N
COLORADO				
Bennet	Y	Y	Y	N
Gardner	Y	Y	Y	Y
CONNECTICUT				
Blumenthal	Y	Y	Y	N
Murphy	Y	Y	Y	N
DELAWARE				
Carper	Y	Y	Y	N
Coons	Y	Y	Y	N
FLORIDA				
Nelson	Y	Y	Y	N
Rubio	N	Y	N	Y
GEORGIA				
Isakson	Y	Y	?	?
Perdue	Y	Y	Y	Y
HAWAII				
Schatz	Y	Y	N	N
Hirono	Y	Y	N	N
IDAHO				
Crapo	Y	Y	?	Y
Risch	N	Y	Y	Y
ILLINOIS				
Durbin	Y	Y	Y	N
Duckworth	Y	Y	Y	N
INDIANA				
Donnelly	Y	Y	Y	N
Young	Y	Y	N	Y
IOWA				
Grassley	Y	Y	Y	Y
Ernst	Y	Y	Y	Y
KANSAS				
Roberts	Y	Y	Y	Y
Moran	Y	Y	N	Y
KENTUCKY				
McConnell	Y	Y	Y	Y
Paul	Y	N	N	?
LOUISIANA				
Cassidy	Y	Y	Y	Y
Kennedy	N	Y	N	Y
MAINE				
Collins	Y	Y	N	Y
King	Y	Y	Y	N
MARYLAND				
Cardin	Y	Y	Y	N
Van Hollen	Y	Y	Y	N
MASSACHUSETTS				
Warren	Y	Y	Y	N
Markey	Y	Y	Y	N
MICHIGAN				
Stabenow	Y	Y	Y	N
Peters	Y	Y	Y	N
MINNESOTA				
Klobuchar	Y	Y	Y	N
Smith	Y	Y	Y	N
MISSISSIPPI				
Wicker	Y	Y	N	Y
Hyde-Smith	Y	Y	Y	Y
MISSOURI				
McCaskill	Y	Y	?	N
Blunt	Y	?	Y	Y
MONTANA				
Tester	Y	Y	Y	N
Daines	Y	Y	N	Y
NEBRASKA				
Fischer	Y	Y	Y	Y
Sasse	N	Y	N	Y
NEVADA				
Heller	Y	Y	?	?
Cortez Masto	Y	Y	Y	N
NEW HAMPSHIRE				
Shaheen	Y	Y	Y	N
Hassan	Y	Y	Y	N
NEW JERSEY				
Menendez	Y	Y	Y	N
Booker	Y	Y	Y	N
NEW MEXICO				
Udall	Y	Y	Y	N
Heinrich	Y	Y	Y	N
NEW YORK				
Schumer	Y	Y	Y	N
Gillibrand	Y	Y	N	N
NORTH CAROLINA				
Burr	Y	Y	?	Y
Tillis	Y	Y	?	Y
NORTH DAKOTA				
Hoeven	Y	Y	Y	Y
Heitkamp	Y	Y	Y	N
OHIO				
Brown	Y	Y	Y	N
Portman	Y	Y	Y	Y
OKLAHOMA				
Inhofe	Y	Y	?	Y
Lankford	Y	Y	N	Y
OREGON				
Wyden	Y	Y	Y	N
Merkley	Y	Y	Y	N
PENNSYLVANIA				
Casey	Y	Y	Y	N
Toomey	Y	Y	N	Y
RHODE ISLAND				
Reed	Y	Y	Y	N
Whitehouse	Y	?	N	N
SOUTH CAROLINA				
Graham	?	Y	N	Y
Scott	Y	Y	Y	Y
SOUTH DAKOTA				
Thune	Y	Y	Y	Y
Rounds	N	Y	Y	Y
TENNESSEE				
Alexander	Y	Y	N	Y
Corker	Y	Y	?	Y
TEXAS				
Cornyn	Y	Y	Y	Y
Cruz	Y	N	Y	Y
UTAH				
Hatch	Y	Y	Y	?
Lee	Y	Y	N	Y
VERMONT				
Leahy	Y	Y	Y	N
Sanders	Y	Y	N	N
VIRGINIA				
Warner	Y	?	Y	N
Kaine	Y	Y	Y	N
WASHINGTON				
Murray	Y	Y	Y	N
Cantwell	Y	Y	Y	N
WEST VIRGINIA				
Manchin	Y	Y	Y	N
Capito	Y	Y	Y	Y
WISCONSIN				
Johnson	Y	?	Y	Y
Baldwin	Y	Y	Y	N
WYOMING				
Enzi	N	Y	N	Y
Barrasso	N	Y	Y	Y

KEY	Republicans	Democrats	Independents

Y	Voted for (yea)	X Paired against	C Voted "present" to avoid possible conflict of interest
#	Paired for	− Announced against	
+	Announced for	P Voted "present"	? Did not vote or otherwise make a position known
N	Voted against (nay)		